CCTV Surveillance

CCTV Surveillance

Analog and Digital Video Practices and Technology

Second Edition

by Herman Kruegle

AMSTERDAM • BOSTON • HEIDELBERG • LONDON • NEW YORK • OXFORD
PARIS • SAN DIEGO • SAN FRANCISCO • SINGAPORE • SYDNEY • TOKYO

Butterworth–Heinemann is an imprint of Elsevier

Senior Acquisitions Editor: Mark Listewnik
Assistant Editor: Kelly Weaver
Marketing Manager: Christian Nolin
Project Manager: Jeff Freeland
Cover Designer: Eric DeCicco
Compositor: Integra Software Services Pvt. Ltd.
Cover Printer: Phoenix Color Corp.
Text Printer/Binder: The Maple-Vail Book Manufacturing Group

Elsevier Butterworth–Heinemann
30 Corporate Drive, Suite 400, Burlington, MA 01803, USA
Linacre House, Jordan Hill, Oxford OX2 8DP, UK

♾ Recognizing the importance of preserving what has been written, Elsevier prints its books on
acid-free paper whenever possible.

Library of Congress Cataloging-in-Publication Data
Kruegle, Herman.
  CCTV surveillance : analog and digital video practices and technology / Herman Kruegle—2nd ed.
    p.   cm.
  ISBN-13: 978-0-7506-7768-4 (casebound : alk. paper)
  ISBN-10: 0-7506-7768-6 (casebound : alk. paper) 1. Closed-circuit television—Design and construction.
    2. Television in security systems.   I. Title.
TK6680.K78 2005
621.389'28—dc22

                              2005022280

British Library Cataloguing-in-Publication Data
A catalogue record for this book is available from the British Library.

ISBN-13: 978-0-7506-7768-4
ISBN-10: 0-7506-7768-6

For information on all Butterworth–Heinemann publications
visit our Web site at www.books.elsevier.com

Printed in the United States of America
06 07 08 09 10 11   10 9 8 7 6 5 4 3 2 1

Photo Credits

The publisher and author would like to thank the listed manufacturers for the photographs used in the figures.

Accele Electronics	8-9A, 8-9B
Allan Broadband	25-14A
American Dynamics	12-1, 17-1E
Avida	2-7C, 2-7E, 2-7G, 2-7H, 2-16A, 2-16B, 2-17A, 2-17B, 2-17C, 2-17D, 2-17E, 2-17F, 4-18A, 4-27C, 4-27D, 4-27E, 4-30, 4-33A, 4-33B, 4-36, 4-37, 4-38, 4-40, 15-2A, 15-2C, 15-8A, 15-8C, 15-10B, 15-12, 15-15A, 15-15B, 16-7, 18-5A, 18-6A, 18-6B, 18-7, 18-10, 18-11A, 18-11B, 18-14A, 18-14B, 18-20A, 18-23D, 18-24, 19-22A, 19-22B, 21-2A, 21-2B, 21-4A, 21-4B, 21-4C, 22-4A, 22-4C, 22-5, 22-10B, 22-10C, 22-23A, 22-23B, 22-25, 22-26, 22-27
Axis Communications	5-14B, 7-28A, 7-34A, 7-34B, 7-35A, 7-35B
CBC America	15-9A
Canon USA	4-14A
Casio USA	7-36A
Cohu, Inc.	2-10A, 2-10F
Controp USA	17-24
COP-USA	18-19B
Dell Star	6-35A
D-Link	7-36B
Digispec	13-8A
FM Systems	25-13B
Global Solar	23-11A, 23-11C
Gossen	25-15A
Greenlee	25-21A, 25-21B
Gyrozoom	4-14B
Hitachi	2-26D, 17-22A
Honeywell Security	9-12C, 15-2D, 15-7D, 15-10D, 15-13, 22-10B
ICU	13-8C, 13-8D
IFS/GE Security	6-28, 6-30
Ikegami Electronics (U.S.A. Inc.)	2-10C, 4-38, 8-5A
Integral Tech	7-36C
Intellicom	25-22A, 25-22B
International Fiber Systems	6-28, 6-30
Ipix	2-15B
Instrumentation Tech Systems	16-6A, 16-6B
Keithley	25-14B
Leader Instruments	25-1A, 25-2A, 25-2B, 25-2C, 25-6A, 25-10, 25-11
Lowering Systems	14-8C, 14-8D
Mace	15-10C
Mannix	25-15B
Marshall	8-16A
Mitsubishi	2-28A, 10-1

NVT	6-9A, 6-9B
Omniscope	2-15A
Panasonic Security Systems	Cover image (bottom), 2-10B, 2-26A, 2-26C, 2-27B, 2-27C, 5-14A, 8-9D, 14-4B, 14-5B, 14-6A, 15-2B, 17-2, 18-20B, 20-4A, 20-4B, 20-5B
Parkut	22-26, 22-27
Pelco	14-5C, 15-7C, 15-14B, 15-17, 17-1A, 17-1C, 17-11B
Pentax	2-7A, 2-14, 4-12A
Radiant	13-8B
Rainbow	4-12B, 4-19, 4-22A, 4-22B
RF-Links	18-25B
Remote Video Surveillance	9-12B
Sanyo Security Products	Cover image (middle right), 2-27A, 5-14C, 8-5B, 8-9C, 9-12A, 14-1A, 15-6C, 15-6D, 15-10A, 17-1D
Sagebrush Technology	17-14
Selectronic	8-10A
Semco	6-38C
SOHOware	7-10
Sony Electronics	4-26, 4-31, 5-22, 7-28B, 14-1B, 14-4A, 17-22B
Smarter Systems	23-13
Tektronix	25-1B, 25-1C, 25-6B, 25-13A
Thorlabs	25-17
Trango	6-35B, 6-35C
Uni-Solar Ovonic	23-11B
Vicon	2-26B, 2-30A, 2-30C, 14-3, 14-5A, 14-5D, 14-6B, 15-1A, 15-1B, 15-5, 15-6A, 15-6B, 15-9B, 15-11, 15-14A, 15-14C, 15-19B, 17-1B, 17-10A, 17-11A
Videolarm	2-29E, 14-7A, 14-7B, 14-7C, 14-8A, 14-8B, 15-7A, 15-8B, 15-8D, 15-9C, 15-14D, 15-19A, 17-13, 17-15A, 17-15B, 22-4B
Watec	18-19A, 18-19C
Winsted	20-2A, 20-2B, 20-3A, 20-3B

For Carol

Contents

Foreword			xi
Preface			xiii
Acknowledgments			xv
Part 1	Chapter 1	Video's Critical Role in the Security Plan	1
	Chapter 2	Video Technology Overview	13
Part 2	Chapter 3	Natural and Artificial Lighting	47
	Chapter 4	Lenses and Optics	71
	Chapter 5	Cameras—Analog, Digital, and Internet	109
	Chapter 6	Analog Video, Voice, and Control Signal Transmission	145
	Chapter 7	Digital Transmission—Video, Communications, Control	199
	Chapter 8	Analog Monitors and Digital Displays	251
	Chapter 9	Analog, Digital Video Recorders	275
	Chapter 10	Hard Copy Video Printers	305
	Chapter 11	Video Switchers	321
	Chapter 12	Quads and Multiplexers	341
	Chapter 13	Video Motion Detectors	353
	Chapter 14	Dome Cameras	373
	Chapter 15	Integrated Cameras, Camera Housings, and Accessories	387
	Chapter 16	Electronic Video Image Splitting, Reversal, and Annotation	405
	Chapter 17	Camera Pan/Tilt Mechanisms	415
	Chapter 18	Covert Video Surveillance	445
	Chapter 19	Low-Light-Level Cameras, Thermal Infrared Imagers	469
	Chapter 20	Control Room/Console Design	497
	Chapter 21	Rapid Deployment Video Systems	507
	Chapter 22	Applications and Solutions—Sample Scenarios	513
	Chapter 23	System Power Sources	553
	Chapter 24	Video-Security Systems Integration	577
	Chapter 25	Video System Test Equipment	583
	Chapter 26	Video Check List	601
	Chapter 27	Education, Standards, Certification	605
	Chapter 28	New Video Technology	609
Glossary			615
Bibliography			639
Index			643

Foreword

A few years ago I had the privilege of addressing a Congressional Subcommittee on Technology and Procurement Policy, chaired by Congressman Tom Davis. In addition to examining GSA's efforts to secure federal buildings, the Subcommittee was interested in hearing and learning about new physical security technology. When I leaf through the pages of this book, I again realize the enormity of the task undertaken by the Subcommittee, the necessity for doing so, and the importance of this type of information to not only security professionals, but now to IT professionals as well.

Closed circuit television (CCTV) and other related video security and surveillance technology has advanced further and faster in the period from 2001 to 2005 than in any prior comparable time period. IP cameras, mapping, servers, platforms, LANs, WANs, and VPNs, wireless, digital migration, algorithms, etc. are all converging along with other related security system technologies such as access control, life safety, intrusion alarms, etc. with the intent to configure fully integrated systems. This is the new direction for the security industry as digital technology has become pervasive across all product lines, opening the door to more software-oriented control platforms on the enterprise level.

So who is the better person to chronicle, explain, and put these terms and technology into perspective than Herman Kruegle, one of the industry's foremost experts on video surveillance and related technologies. I have had the privilege of knowing and working with Herman for many years. He is a consummate professional who has the innate ability to explain the technical aspects of this emerging technology in a manner we can all understand and put into practice. Herman's first book, *CCTV Surveillance – Video Practices and Technology*, is considered, by most of us in the industry, to be the bible of CCTV, and I fully expect this revised edition will rise to even greater popularity.

In the pages following, readers will find concise and intelligent descriptions of the analog and digital video practices and technology we have all grown up with. But more important, Herman has included, in this revised edition, his explanation of the newest audio/video information technology (AV/IT) developments, products utilizing the technology and applications for same. Security professionals, system integrators, architects and engineers, IT managers, or end users who are looking for a resource to help them navigate this complex field of IP Video Security will not be disappointed. The material is well researched and thoughtfully laid out to help insure the reader's understanding and to hopefully allow them to go on to designing, installing, and using digital video surveillance to its fullest capacity.

Frank Abram

Preface

Following the same philosophy contained in the first edition, the second edition is written for and contains information valuable to the end-user as well as the technical practitioner. Each chapter begins with an overview and then presents equipment available with their characteristics, features, and application.

The first edition of CCTV Surveillance in 1995 asked the question "why write a CCTV surveillance book?". At that time, analog CCTV had progressed from a vacuum tube to a solid state technology that provided reliable, longlife small cameras produced at prices affordable for most security applications.

A decade later, significant advances have been made in camera sensors, computers, and digital transmission technology to warrant a complete review of CCTV's role in the security industry. The migration from legacy analog components to digital technology and the emergence of the Internet have accelerated the utilization of Internet protocol (IP) video and remote monitoring in security. The internet has permitted the widespread interconnection of other technologies including intrusion and fire and intrusion alarm systems, access control, and other communications and control.

The ease of interconnection afforded by digital transmission of video and other pertinent security data anywhere in a facility, local environment or globally, engenders a new meaning to video transmission and remote viewing.

The explosion of high-capacity magnetic disk, solid state, and optical data storage memories has permitted the generation of new products including digital video recorders (DVR) and data compression algorithms to compress and store video images and replace the time-honored magnetic video cassette recorder (VCR).

In this second edition of CCTV Surveillance, I have attempted to add these new technologies to the "non-changing" basic technologies covered in the first edition. Physics does not change—only the technology and products do.

This new revised edition of CCTV Surveillance includes the new digital video technology and contains eight new chapters:

Chapter 7	Digital Transmission, Video, Communications and Control
Chapter 10	Hard Copy Video Printers
Chapter 12	Quads and Multiplexers
Chapter 14	Dome Cameras
Chapter 20	Control Room/Console Design
Chapter 21	Rapid Deployment Video Systems
Chapter 24	Video-Security Systems Integration
Chapter 25	Video System Test Equipment

Chapter 7   Wired and wireless digital transmission represents possibly the most significant technology advancement in the video security industry. It makes use of the Internet and intranets for remote video, data, and audio communication over existing hard wire communication links. Chapter 7 includes an analysis of digital wireless video transmission using the family of 802.11x protocol spread spectrum technology (SST). Prior to 1995–98 the Internet was not available for commercial use and remote video monitoring and control was accomplished primarily over existing telephone lines or expensive satellite links with limited functionality. Ease of installation, camera addressing, and identification using IP cameras has opened a new vista in video transmission and remote monitoring.

Chapter 10—This chapter describes the new technological advances made in hard-copy printers that improve the quality and reduce the cost of monochrome and color video printouts. The advances in ink-jet and laser printer technologies using inexpensive, large solid state memories and high resolution linear CCD imagers have been driven by the consumer and business markets, and have given the security industry access to low-cost, color, hard copy prints rivaling photographic resolution and quality.

Chapter 12—While available in 1995, multiplexers have taken on new importance because of the significant increase in the number of cameras used in a typical security installation and their ability to be integrated into DVRs that were not available five years ago.

Chapter 14—Dome cameras are now everywhere in security systems. In 1995 they were used primarily in selected locations: casinos, department stores, supermarkets, malls, and in outdoor parking lot applications. The public at large has accepted their presence almost everywhere. Domes are easy to install and can be small and aesthetic. Dome cameras are adjustable in pointing direction (manual or motorized, pan and tilt), and many have motorized zoom lenses to change the camera field of view (FOV). The use of small dome cameras has exploded because of significant cost reduction and sophistication of pointing and zooming capabilities. Fast pan/tilt camera modules with remote control via analog or digital communications over two-wire or wireless communication links are reasons for their popularity.

Chapter 20—Consoles and Control Rooms have become more complex and require more design attention for their successful implementation. This chapter analyzes the console and security control room with regard to lighting, monitor locations, operator control placement, and the other human factors required for guard efficiency and comfort.

Chapter 21—There has always been a requirement for a transportable Rapid Deployment Security (RDS) systems having video and alarm intrusion equipment for protecting personnel and assets. The Post-911 era with real terror threats has initiated the need for RDS equipment to protect military, government, business, and other personnel on travel. The majority of these systems consist of alarm intrusion and analog or digital video viewing system. These RDS systems are carried from one location to another and deployed quickly to set up an alarm perimeter and real-time video monitoring and recording. Analog or digital transmission allows local or remote monitoring. After use, the RDS equipment is disassembled and stored in its carrying case, ready for another deployment. The much smaller size of the video and alarm equipment has accelerated its use and acceptance.

Chapter 22—The Video Applications chapter has been updated and expanded to include digital video applications including the combination of legacy analog and IP cameras. One video monitoring application uses on-site local networks and a second application uses the Internet and IP cameras, signal routers, and servers for remote site video monitoring. Security applications require complete integration of communication, video, alarm, access control, and fire to provide monitoring by the local security force, and corporate executives at a local or remote site(s). The integration of these security functions provides the safety and security necessary to protect personnel and assets at any facility.

Chapter 25—Installation and maintenance of video equipment requires the use of video and computer test equipment. Prior to the widespread use of digital technology in security systems, a limited range of test equipment was used. Now with the many computer interfaces and Internet protocols and connection to the Internet, more sophisticated test equipment and some knowledge of software and computer programming is necessary. Parameters to be tested and monitored include: (a) video signal level and quality; (b) control data signals for pan, tilt, zoom, focus; and (c) digital signal protocols for multiplexers, IP cameras, signal routers and servers, DVRs, etc.

Acknowledgments

Over the years I have had opportunities to speak with many individuals who provided technical insight in video technology and electro-optics. I particularly appreciate the discussions with Stanley Dolin and Lee Gallagher, on the subjects of optics, the physics of lighting, lenses, and optical sensors. I found very helpful the technical discussions on cameras with Frank Abram, Sanyo Security Products, and Victor Houk. I thank Dr. Gerald Herskowitz, Stevens Institute of Technology for contributing to the fiber-optic section in Chapter 6 and reviewing other sections on video transmission. I thank Robert Wimmer and Fredrick Nilsson for their excellent technical articles in security journals, company publications, as well as technical seminars on many aspects of video security. Thanks to Charlie Pierce for his interest in my book over the years and enthusiasm and excellence in presenting stimulating educational video seminars. Eric Kruegle, Avida Inc., contributed his expertise on various aspects of digital video. In particular I appreciate his help in wired and wireless video transmission, compression, and encryption in Chapter 7. Eric was also instrumental in keeping my computer alive, and I thank him for rescuing me late at night from missing files and software surprises.

I acknowledge the initial encouragement of Kevin Kopp and editorial advice of Greg Franklin at Butterworth (now Elsevier) during the formative stages of the first edition of CCTV Surveillance in 1995. I thank all staff at Elsevier for bringing out this second edition successfully: Pam Chester for her assistance in the formulation of this edition, Mark Listewnik for his constant encouragement, professional suggestions, and diligence in bringing this large project to a successful conclusion, Jeff Freeland for providing the meticulous final editing and effort in completing this large endeavor.

I gratefully acknowledge the dedication, patience, and skill of my wife, Carol, in assisting in the preparation of this book.

I would like to thank the manufacturers for the use of the many photographs that illustrate the components used in video security applications. Each of them contribute to the education of the security professional and assist the consultant, systems integrator, and end user in designing and implementing the best security system possible.

PART I

Chapter 1
Video's Critical Role in the Security Plan

CONTENTS

1.1 Protection of Assets
    1.1.1 Overview
    1.1.2 Background
1.2 The Role of Video in Asset Protection
    1.2.1 Video as Part of the Emergency and
        Disaster Plan
        1.2.1.1 Protecting Life and Minimizing
                Injury
        1.2.1.2 Reducing Exposure of Physical Assets
                and Optimizing Loss Control
        1.2.1.3 Restoring Normal Operations
                Quickly
        1.2.1.4 Documenting an Emergency
        1.2.1.5 Emergency Shutdown and
                Restoration
        1.2.1.6 Testing the Plan
        1.2.1.7 Standby Power and Communications
    1.2.2 Security Investigations
    1.2.3 Safety
    1.2.4 The Role of the Guard
    1.2.5 Employee Training and Education
1.3 Synergy through Integration
    1.3.1 Integrated Functions
    1.3.2 System Hardware
1.4 Video's Role and Its Applications
    1.4.1 Video System Solutions
    1.4.2 Overt vs. Covert Video
    1.4.3 Security Surveillance Applications
    1.4.4 Safety Applications
    1.4.5 Video Access Control
1.5 The Bottom Line

1.1 PROTECTION OF ASSETS

The protection of personnel and assets is a management function. Three key factors governing the planning of an assets protection program are: (1) an adequate plan designed to prevent losses from occurring, (2) adequate countermeasures to limit unpreventable losses, and (3) support of the protection plan by top management.

1.1.1 Overview

Most situations today require a complete safety/security plan. The plan should contain requirements for intrusion detection, video assessment, fire detection, access control, and full two-way communication. Critical functions and locations must be monitored using wired and wireless backup communications.

The most significant driving force behind the explosion in the use of closed-circuit television (CCTV) has been the worldwide increase in theft and terrorism and the commensurate concern and need to protect personnel and assets. The terrorist attack on September 11, 2001, brought about a quantum jump and a complete reevaluation of the personnel and asset security requirements to safe-guard a facility. To meet this new threat, video security has taken on the lead role in protecting personnel and assets. Today every state-of-the-art security system must include video as a key component to provide the "remote eyes" for security, fire, and safety.

The fateful day of September 11, 2001, has dramatized the importance of reliable communications and remote visualization of images via remote video cameras. Many lives were saved (and lost) as a consequence of the voice, video, alarm, and fire equipment in place and in use at the time of the fateful attack on the World Trade Center in New York. The availability of *operational* wired and wireless two-way communication between command and control headquarters and responders (police, fire, emergency) played a crucial role in life and death. The availability (or absence) at command posts of real-time video images at crucial locations in the Twin Towers during the attack and evacuation contributed to the action taken by command personnel during the tragedy. The use (or absence) of wireless transmission from the remote video cameras in the Twin Towers clearly had an impact on the number of survivors and casualties.

During the 1990s, video components (cameras, recorders, monitors, etc.) technology matured from the legacy analog to a digital imaging technology and became compatible with computers and now forms an essential part of the security solution. In the late 1990s, digital cameras were introduced into the consumer market, thereby significantly reducing price and as a result found widespread use in the security industry. Simultaneously, powerful microprocessors, large hard disk computer memory storage, and random access memory (RAM) became available from the personal computer/laptop industry, thereby providing the computing power necessary to control, view, record, and play back digital CCTV cameras in the security system.

The home run came with the availability and explosive acceptance and use of the Internet (and intranet) as a new means of long distance two-way communication of voice, data, and most importantly *video*. For over a decade the long distance transmission of video was limited to slow telephone transmission of video images—snap-shots (slow-scan video). The use of dedicated high speed (expensive) land lines or expensive satellite communications was limited to government and large-clientele users. Now the Internet provides near-live (near real-time) video transmission communications over an inexpensive, easily accessible worldwide transmission network.

The application and integration of video into safety and security systems has come of age as a reliable, cost-effective means for assessing and responding to terrorist attacks and other life-threatening situations. Video is an effective means for deterring crimes and protecting assets and for apprehending and prosecuting offenders.

Security personnel today have the responsibility for multifaceted security and safety systems in which video often plays the key role. With today's increasing labor costs and the need for each security officer to provide more functionality, video more than ever before is earning its place as a cost-effective means for improving security and safety while reducing security budgets.

Loss of assets and time due to theft is a growing cancer on our society that eats away at the profits of every organization or business, be it government, retail, service, or manufacturing. The size of the organization makes no difference to the thief. The larger the organization, the more the theft occurs and the greater the opportunity for losses. The more valuable the product, the greater the temptation for a thief to steal it. A properly designed and applied video system can be an extremely profitable investment for an institution to cut losses. The prime objective of the video system should not be the apprehension of

thieves but rather the deterrence of crime through security. A successful thief needs privacy—a video system can deny that privacy.

As a security by-product, video has emerged as an effective training tool for managers and security personnel. Every installation/establishment should have a security plan in place *prior* to an incident. Video-based training is easy to implement using the abundance of inexpensive camcorders and playback equipment available and the commercial video production training video services available. The use of training videos results in standardized procedures and improved employee efficiency and productivity.

The public at large has accepted the use of video systems in most public facilities. Video is being applied to reduce asset losses and increase corporate profits and bottom line. Many case histories show that after the installation of video, shoplifting and employee thefts drop sharply. The number of thefts cannot be counted exactly but shrinkage can be measured. It has been shown that video is an effective psychological deterrent to crime and an effective tool for criminal prosecution.

Theft is not only the unauthorized removal of valuable property but also the removal of information, such as computer software, CDs, magnetic tape and disks, optical disks, microfilm, and hard copy. Video surveillance systems provide a means for successfully deterring such thievery and/or detecting or apprehending offenders. The use of video prevents the destruction of property, vandalizing buildings, defacing elevator interiors, painting graffiti on art objects and facilities, stealing computers, and demolishing furniture or other valuable equipment. Video offers the greatest potential benefit when integrated with other sensing systems and used to view remote areas. Video provides the "eyes" for many security devices and functions such as: (1) fire sensors: smoke detector alarms, (2) watching for presence (or absence) of personnel in an area, (3) evacuation of personnel—determining route for evacuation, access (emergency or intruder) to determine response, respond, and monitor response. When combined with fire and smoke detectors, CCTV cameras in inaccessible areas can be used to give advance warning of a fire.

Video is the critical link in the overall security of a facility but organizations must develop a complete security plan rather than adopt piecemeal protection measures. To optimize use of video technology, the practitioner and end user must understand all of its aspects—from light sources to video monitors and recorders. The capabilities and limitations of video during daytime and nighttime operation must also be understood.

1.1.2 Background

Throughout history, humans have valued their own life and the lives of their loved ones above all else. Next in value has been their property. Over the centuries many techniques have been developed to protect property against invaders or aggressors threatening to take or destroy it.

In the past as in the present, manufacturing, industrial, and government organizations have hired "watchmen" to protect their facilities. These private security personnel wearing uniforms and using equipment much like the police do are hired to prevent crime and bodily harm, and deter or prevent theft on the premises. The very early guard companies were Pinkerton's and Burns. Contract protection organizations were hired to safeguard their employees and assets in emergency and personal threat situations.

A significant increase in guard use came with the start of World War II. Many guards were employed to secure industrial work sites manufacturing military equipment and doing classified work, and to guard government facilities. Private corporations obtained such protection through contract agencies to guard classified facilities and work.

In the early 1960s, as electronic technology advanced, alarm systems and video were introduced. Radio Corporation of America (RCA), Motorola, and General Electric were the pioneering companies that began manufacturing vacuum-tube television cameras for the security industry. The use of video cameras during the 1960s and 1970s grew rapidly because of increased reliability, lower cost, and technological improvements in the tube-type camera technology. In the 1980s growth continued at a more modest level with further improvements in functions and availability of other accessories for video security systems.

The most significant advance in video technology during the 1980s was the invention and introduction of the solid-state video camera. By the early 1990s the solid-state camera using the charged coupled device (CCD) image sensor was the choice for new security installations and was rapidly replacing the tube cameras. In the past, the camera—in particular, the vidicon tube sensor—was the critical component in the video system. The camera determined the overall performance and quality of visual intelligence obtainable from the security system. The vidicon tube was the weakest link in the system and was subject to degradation with age and usage. The complexity and variability of the image tube and its analog electrical nature made it less reliable than the other solid-state components. Performance varied considerably between different camera models and camera manufacturers, and as a function of temperature and age. By contrast, the solid-state CCD sensor and newer metal oxide semiconductor (MOS) and complimentary MOS (CMOS) sensor cameras have long life and are stable over all operating conditions. Another factor in the explosive use of video in security systems has been the rapid improvement in equipment capability at affordable prices. This has been the result of the widespread use of solid-state camcorders

by consumers (lower manufacturing costs), and the availability of low-cost video cassette recorders (VCRs), digital video recorders (DVRs), and personal computer (PC)-based equipment.

The 1990s saw the integration of computer technology with video security technology. All components were solid state. Digital video technology needed large-scale digital memories to manipulate and store video images and the computer industry had them. To achieve satisfactory video image transmission and storage, the video signal had to be "compressed" to transmit it over the existing narrowband phone line networks. The video-computer industry already had compression for broadcast, industrial, and government requirements. The video industry needed a fast and low-cost means to transmit the video images to remote locations and the US government's Defense Advanced Research Projects Agency (DARPA) had already developed the Internet, the predecessor of the World Wide Web (WWW). The Internet (and intranet) communications channels and the WWW now provide this extraordinary worldwide ability to transmit and receive video and audio, and communicate and control data anywhere.

1.2   THE ROLE OF VIDEO IN ASSET PROTECTION

Video provides multiple functions in the overall security plan. It provides the function of asset protection by monitoring location of assets and activity in their location. It is used to detect unwanted entry into a facility beginning at a perimeter location and following an unauthorized person throughout a facility. Figure 1-1 shows a typical single site video system using either legacy analog or digital, or a combination of both technologies.

In a perimeter protection role, video is used with intrusion-detection alarm devices as well as video motion detection to alert the guard at the security console that an intrusion has occurred. If an intrusion occurs, multiple CCTV cameras located throughout the facility follow the intruder so that there is a proper response by guard personnel or designated employees. Management must determine whether specific guard reaction is required and what the response will be.

Video monitoring allows the guard to be more effective, but it also improves security by permitting the camera scene to be transmitted to other control centers or personnel. The video image can be documented with a VCR, DVR, and/or printed out on a hard copy video printer.

The video system for the multiple site application is best implemented using a combination of analog/digital or an all-digital solution (Figure 1-2).

Local site installations already using analog video cameras, monitors, etc. can be retained and integrated with new digital Internet Protocol (IP) cameras, local area networks (LANs), intranets, and the Internet to facilitate remote site video monitoring. The digital transmission

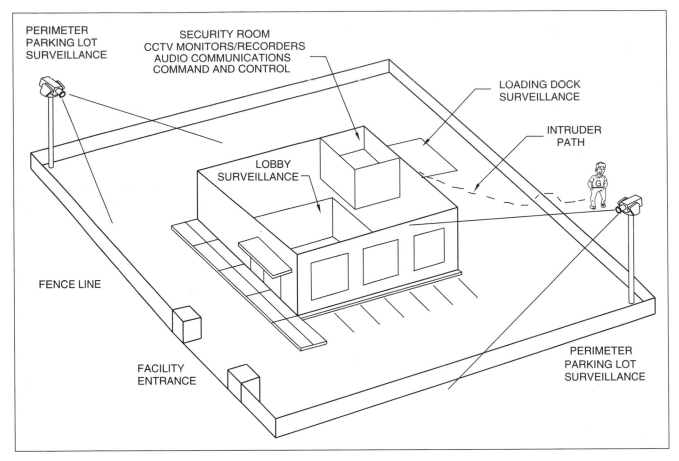

FIGURE 1-1   Single site video security system

network provides two-way communications of audio and controls and excellent video image transmission to remote sites. The digital signals can be encrypted to prevent eavesdropping by unauthorized outside personnel. Using a digital signal backbone allows adding additional cameras to the network or changing their configuration in the system.

In the relatively short history of CCTV and video there have been great innovations in the permanent recording of video images. These new technologies have been brought about by the consumer demand for video camcorders, the television broadcast industry, and government requirements for military and aerospace hardware and software. One result of these requirements was the development of the VCR and DVR. The ability to record video images provided the video security industry with a new dimension, i.e. going beyond real-time camera surveillance. The availability of VCR and DVR technology resulting from the consumer market has made possible the excellent time-lapse VCRs and large storage PC-based DVR systems. These technologies provide permanent documentation of the video images in analog (magnetic tape) and digital (solid state and hard disk drive) storage media. The use of time-lapse recorders, computer hard disks and video printers give management the tools to present hard

evidence for criminal prosecution. This ability to provide a permanent record of evidence is of prime importance to personnel responsible for providing security.

Prior to the mid-1990s the CCTV security industry primarily used monochrome solid-state cameras. In the 1990s the widespread use of color camcorders in the video consumer market accelerated the availability of these reliable, stable, long-life cameras for the security industry. While monochrome cameras are still specified in low light level (LLL) and nighttime security applications, color is now the norm in most security applications. The increased sensitivity and resolution of color cameras and the significant decrease in cost of color cameras have resulted in their widespread use. Many monochrome cameras being used for LLL applications are being augmented with *active* infrared (IR) illuminators. Also coming into use is a new generation of *passive* monochrome thermal IR imaging cameras that detect the differences in *temperature* of objects in the scene, compared to the scene background. These cameras operate in total darkness. There has also been an explosion in the use of covert video surveillance through the use of small, inexpensive color cameras.

The development of smaller solid-state cameras has resulted in a decrease in the size of ancillary video equipment. Camera lenses, dome cameras, housings, pan/tilt

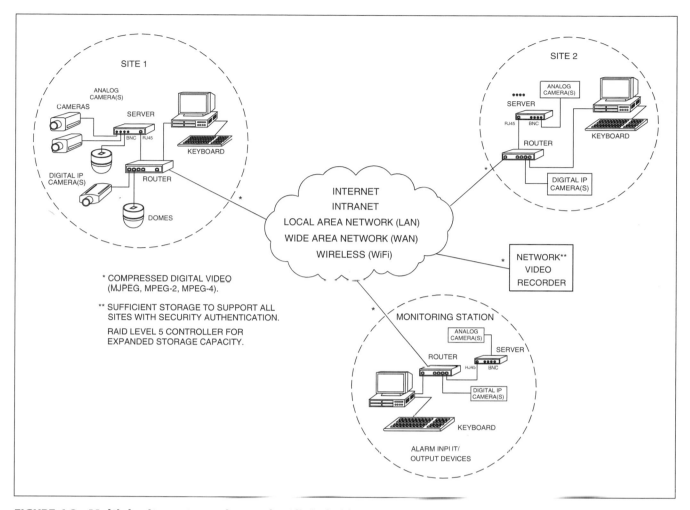

FIGURE 1-2   Multiple site system using analog/digital video

mechanisms, and brackets are smaller in size and weight resulting in lower costs and providing more aesthetic installations. The small cameras and lenses satisfy covert video applications and are easy to conceal.

The potential importance of color in surveillance applications can be illustrated very clearly: turn off the color on a television monitor to make it a monochrome scene. It is obvious how much information is lost when the colors in the scene change to shades of gray. Objects that were easily identified in the color scene become difficult to identify in the monochrome scene. It is much easier to pick out a person with a red shirt in the color image than in a monochrome image.

The security industry has long recognized the value of color to enhance personnel and article identification in video surveillance and access control. One reason why we can identify subjects more easily in color is that we are used to seeing color, both in the real world and on our TV at home. When we see a monochrome scene we have to make an additional effort to recognize certain information (besides the actual missing colors) thereby decreasing the intelligence available. Color provides more accurate identification of personnel and objects and leads

to a higher degree of apprehension and conviction of criminals.

1.2.1 Video as Part of the Emergency and Disaster Plan

Every organization regardless of size should have an emergency and disaster control plan that includes video as a critical component. Depending on the organization an anti-terrorist plan should take highest priority. Part of the plan should be a procedure for succession of personnel in the event one or more members of top management are unavailable when disaster strikes. In large organizations the plan should include the designation of alternate headquarters if possible, a safe document-storage facility, and remote (off-site if possible) video operations capability. The plan must provide for medical aid and assure the welfare of all employees in the organization. Using video as a source of information, there should be a method to alert employees in the event of a dangerous condition and a plan to provide for quick police and emergency response. There should be an emergency shutdown plan and restoration procedures with designated employees acting as leaders. There should be CCTV cameras stationed along evacuation routes and instructions for practice tests. The evacuation plan should be prepared *in advance and tested.*

A logical and effective disaster control plan should do the following:

- Define emergencies and disasters that could occur as they relate to the particular organization.
- Establish an organization and specific tasks with personnel designated to carry out the plan immediately before, during, and immediately following a disaster.
- Establish a method for utilizing the organization's resources, in particular video, to analyze the disaster situation and bring to bear all available resources.
- Recognize a plan to change from normal operations into and out of the disaster emergency mode as soon as possible.

Video plays a very important role in any emergency, disaster and anti-terrorist plan:

- Video helps protect human life by enabling security or safety officials to see remote locations and view first hand what is happening, where it is happening, what is most critical, and what areas must be attended to first.
- Aids in minimizing personal injury by permitting "remote eyes" to get to those people who require immediate attention, or to send personnel to the area being hit hardest to remove them from the area, or to bring in equipment to protect them.
- Video reduces the exposure of physical assets to oncoming disaster, such as fire or flood, and prevents or at least assesses document removal (of assets) by intruders or any unauthorized personnel.
- Video documents the equipment and assets that were in place prior to the disaster, recording them on VCR, DVR or storage on an enterprise network to be compared to the remaining assets after the disaster has occurred. It also documents personnel and their activities before, during, and after an incident.
- Probably more so than any other part of a security system, video will aid management and the security force in minimizing any disaster or emergency. It is useful in restoring an organization to normal operation by determining that no additional emergencies are in progress and that procedures and traffic flow are normal in those restored areas.

1.2.1.1 Protecting Life and Minimizing Injury

Through the intelligence gathered from the video system, security and disaster control personnel should move all personnel to places of safety and shelter. Personnel assigned to disaster control and remaining in a threatened area should be protected by using video to monitor their safety, and the access and egress at these locations. By such monitoring, advance notice is available to provide a means of support and assistance for those persons if injured, and personnel that must be rescued or relieved.

1.2.1.2 Reducing Exposure of Physical Assets and Optimizing Loss Control

Assets should be stored or secured properly before an emergency so that they will be less vulnerable to theft or loss. Video is an important tool for continually monitoring safe areas during and after a disaster to ensure that the material is not removed. In an emergency or disaster, the well-documented plan will call for specific personnel to locate highly valued assets, secure them, and evacuate personnel.

1.2.1.3 Restoring Normal Operations Quickly

After an emergency situation has been brought under control, security personnel can monitor and maintain the security of assets and help determine that employees are safe and have returned to their normal work routine.

1.2.1.4 Documenting an Emergency

For purposes of: (1) future planning, (2) liability and insurance, and (3) evaluation by management and security personnel, video coverage of critical areas and operations during an emergency is an excellent tool and can reduce financial losses significantly. Video recordings of assets lost or stolen or personnel injured or killed can support a company's claim that it was not negligent and that it initiated a prudent emergency and disaster plan *prior* to the event. Although video can provide crucial documentation of an event, it should be supplemented with high-resolution photographs of specific instances or events.

If perimeter fences or walls were destroyed or damaged in a disaster, video can help prevent and document intrusion or looting by employees, spectators, or other outsiders.

1.2.1.5 Emergency Shutdown and Restoration

In the overall disaster plan, shutting down equipment such as machinery, utilities, processes, and so on, must be considered. If furnaces, gas generators, electrical power equipment, boilers, high-pressure air or oil systems, chemical equipment, or rapidly rotating machinery could cause damage if left unattended they should be shut down as soon as possible. Again, video surveillance can be crucial to determine if the equipment has been shut down properly, if personnel must enter the area to do so, or if it must be shut down by other means.

1.2.1.6   Testing the Plan

While a good emergency plan is essential, it should not be tested for the first time in an actual disaster situation. Deficiencies are always discovered during testing. Also, a test serves to train the personnel who will carry out the plan if necessary. Video can help evaluate the plan to identify shortcomings and show personnel what they did right and wrong. Through such peer review a practical and efficient plan can be put in place to minimize losses to the organization.

1.2.1.7   Standby Power and Communications

During any emergency or disaster, primary power and communications between locations will probably be disrupted. Therefore, a standby power-generation system should be provided for emergency monitoring and response. This standby power comprised of a backup gas-powered generator or an uninterruptible power supply with DC batteries to extend backup operation time will keep emergency lighting, communications, and strategic video equipment online as needed. Most installations use a power sensing device that monitors the normal supply of power at various locations. When the device senses that power has been lost, the various backup equipments automatically switch to the emergency power source.

A prudent security plan anticipating an emergency will include a means to power vital, audio, video, and other sensor equipment to ensure its operation during the event. Since emergency video and audio communications must be maintained over remote distances, alternative communication pathways should be supplied in the form of either auxiliary hard-wired cable (copper wire or fiber optics) or a wireless (RF, microwave, infrared) transmission system. It is usually practical to provide a backup path to only the critical cameras, not all of them. The standby generator supplying power to the video, safety, and emergency equipment must be sized properly. For equipment that normally operates on 120 volt AC, inverters are used to convert the low voltage from the backup DC batteries (typically 12 or 24 volts DC) to the required 120 volts AC (or 230 volts AC).

1.2.2   Security Investigations

Security investigators have used video very successfully with respect to safeguarding company assets and preventing theft, negligence, outside intrusion, and so on. By using small, low-cost, covert CCTV (hidden camera and lens), it is easy to positively identify a person or to document an event without being noticed. Better video image quality, smaller lenses and cameras, wireless video transmission, and easier installation and removal of such equipment have led to this high success. Many lenses and cameras that can be hidden in rooms, hallways, or stationary objects are available today. Equipment to provide such surveillance is available for indoor or outdoor locations in bright sunlight or in no light (IR-illuminated or thermal cameras).

1.2.3   Safety

Closed circuit television equipment is installed not always for security reasons alone but also for safety purposes as well. Security personnel can be alerted to unsafe practices or accidents that require immediate attention. An attentive guard can use CCTV cameras distributed throughout a facility in stairwells, loading docks, around machinery, etc. to observe and immediately document any safety violations or incidents.

1.2.4   The Role of the Guard

Security guards are employed to protect plant assets and personnel. Security and corporate management are aware that guards are only one element of an organization's complete security plan. As such, the cost to implement the guard force and its ability to protect assets and personnel are analyzed in relation to the costs and roles of other technological security solutions. In this respect video has much to contribute: increased security for relatively low capital investment and low operating cost, as compared with a guard. Guards using video can increase the security coverage or protection of a facility. Alternatively, installing new CCTV equipment enables guards to monitor remote sites, allowing guard count and security costs to be reduced significantly.

1.2.5   Employee Training and Education

Video can be used as a powerful training tool. It is used widely in education and the training of security personnel because it can demonstrate lessons and examples vividly to the trainee. In this post-9/11 era, security personnel should receive professional training by all means including real video footage. Video is an important tool for the security trainer. Example procedures of all types can be shown conveniently in a short time period, and with instructions given during the presentation. Videotaped real-life situations (not simulations or performances) can demonstrate the consequences of mis-applied procedures and the benefits of proper planning and execution by trained and knowledgeable personnel.

Every organization can supplement live training with either professional training videos or actual scenes from their own video system, demonstrating good and poor practices as well as proper guard reaction in real cases of intrusion, unacceptable employee behavior, and so on. Such internal video systems can also be used in training exercises: trainees may take part in videotaped simulations, which are later critiqued by their supervisor. Trainees can then observe their own actions to find ways to improve and become more effective. Finally, such internal video systems are very important tools during rehearsals or tests of an emergency or disaster plan. After the run-through, all team members can monitor their own reactions, and managers or other professionals can critique them.

1.3 SYNERGY THROUGH INTEGRATION

Video equipment is most effective when integrated with other security hardware and procedures to form a coherent security system. When video is combined with the other security sensors the total security system is more than the individual subsystems. Synergy obtains when video assessment is combined with intrusion and motion alarm sensors, electronic access control, fire alarms, communications, and security guard personnel (Figure 1-3).

1.3.1 Integrated Functions

Functionally the integrated security system is designed as a coordinated combination of equipment, personnel, and procedures that: (a) uses each component in a way that enhances the use of every other component and (b) optimally achieves the system's stated objective.

In designing a security system, each element's potential contribution to loss prevention, asset protection, or personnel safety must be considered. The security plan must specify as a minimum: (a) where and when unusual behavior should be detected, (b) what the response should be, and (c) how it should be reported and recorded. If the intruder has violated a barrier or fence the intrusion-detection system should be able to determine that a person—not an animal, bird, insect, leaf, or other object—passed through the barrier. Video provides the most positive means for establishing this information. This breech in security must then be communicated by some means to security personnel so that a reaction force has sufficient information to permit an appropriate response.

In another scenario, if material is being removed by an unauthorized person in an interior location, a video surveillance system activated by a video motion detector (VMD) alarm should alert a guard and transmit the video information to security personnel for appropriate action. In both cases a guard force would be dispatched and the event recorded on a VCR, DVR or network storage and/or printed as hard copy for guard response, documentation, and prosecution.

In summary, it is the combination of sensors, communication channels, monitoring displays, documentation equipment and a guard force that provides the synergy to maximize the security function. The integration of video, intrusion-detection alarms, access control, and security guards increases the overall security asset protection and employee safety at a facility.

1.3.2 System Hardware

Since a complete video security system may be assembled from components manufactured by different companies,

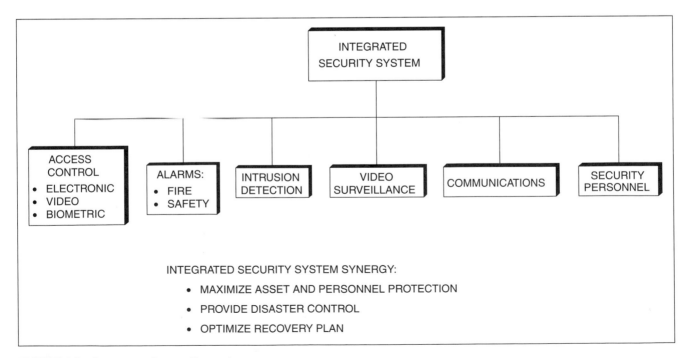

FIGURE 1-3   Integrated security system

all equipment must be compatible. The video equipment should be specified by one consulting or architecture/engineering firm, and the system and service should be purchased, installed, and maintained through a single system integrator, dealer/installer, or general contractor. If a major supplier provides a turnkey system, including all equipment, training, and maintenance, the responsibility of system operation resides with *one* vendor, which is easier to control. Buying from one source also permits management to go back to one installer or general contractor if there are any problems instead of having to point fingers or negotiate for service among several vendors.

Choosing a single supplier obviously requires thorough analysis to determine that the supplier: (1) will provide a system that meets the requirements of the facility, (2) will be available for maintenance when required, and (3) will still be in business in 5 or 10 years. There are many companies that can supply complete video systems including cameras and housings, lenses, pan/tilt mechanisms, multiplexers, time-lapse VCRs or DVRs, analog and digital networks, and other security equipment required for an integrated video system. If the end user chooses components from various manufacturers, care must be taken by the system designer and installer to be aware of the differences and interface the equipment properly.

If the security plan calls for a simple system with potential for later expansion the equipment should be modular and ready to accept new technology as it becomes available. Many larger manufacturers of security equipment anticipate this integration and expansion requirement and design their products accordingly.

Service is a key ingredient for successful system operation. If one component fails, repair or replacement must be done quickly, so that the system is not shut down. Near-continuous operation is accomplished by the direct replacement method, immediate maintenance by an in-house service organization, or quick-response service calls from the installer/contractor. Service consideration should be addressed during the planning and initial design stages, as they affect choice of manufacturer and service provider. Most vendors use the replacement technique to maintain and service equipment. If part of the system fails, the vendor replaces the defective equipment and sends it to the factory for repair. This service policy decreases security system downtime.

The key to a successful security plan is to choose the right equipment and service company, one that is customer oriented and knowledgeable about reliable, technologically superior products that satisfy the customer needs.

1.4 VIDEO'S ROLE AND ITS APPLICATIONS

In its broadest sense, the purpose of CCTV in any security plan is to provide remote eyes for a security operator: to create live-action displays from a distance. The video system should have recording means—either a VCR or a DVR, or other storage media—to maintain permanent records for training or evidence. Following are some applications for which video provides an effective solution:

- When overt visual observation of a scene or activity is required from a remote location.
- An area to be observed contains hazardous material or some action that may kill or injure personnel. Such areas may have toxic chemicals, biological or radioactive material, substances with high potential for fire or explosion, or items that may emit X-ray radiation or other nuclear radiation.
- Visual observation of a scene must be covert. It is much easier to hide a small camera and lens in a target location than to station a person in the area.
- There is little activity to watch in an area, as in an intrusion-detection location or a storage room, but significant events must be recorded in the area when they occur. Integration of video with alarm sensors and a time-lapse/real-time VCR or DVR provides an extremely powerful solution.
- Many locations must be observed simultaneously by one person from a central security location.
- Tracing a person or vehicle from an entrance into a facility to a final destination. The security force can predict where the person or vehicle can be interdicted.
- Often a guard or security officer must only review a scene for activity periodically. The use of video eliminates the need for a guard to make rounds to remote locations, which is wasteful of the guard's time.
- When a crime has been committed, capturing the scene using the video camera and recorder to have a permanent record and hard copy printout of the activity and event. The proliferation of high-quality printed images from VCR/DVR equipment has clearly made the case for using video for creating permanent records.

1.4.1 Video System Solutions

The most effective way to determine that a theft has occurred, when, where, and by whom, is to use video for detection and recording. The particular event can be identified, stored, and later reproduced for display or hard copy. Personnel can be identified on monochrome or color CCTV monitors. Most security installations use color CCTV cameras that provide sufficient information to document the activity and event or identify personnel or articles. The color camera permits easier identification of personnel and objects.

If there is an emergency or disaster and security personnel must see if personnel are in a particular area, video can provide an instantaneous assessment of personnel location and availability.

In many cases during normal operations, security personnel can help ensure the safety of personnel in a facility, determine that employees or visitors have not entered the facility, or confirm that personnel have exited the facility. Such functions are used for example where dangerous jobs are performed or hazardous material is handled.

The synergistic combination of audio and video information from a remote site provides for effective security. Several camera manufacturers and installers combine video and audio (one-way or duplex) using an external microphone or one installed directly in the camera. The video and audio signals are transmitted over the same coaxial, unshielded-twisted-pair (UTP), or fiber-optic cable, to the security monitoring location where the scene is viewed live and/or recorded. When there is activity in the camera area the video and audio signals are switched to the monitor and the guard sees and hears the activity in the scene and initiates a response.

1.4.2 Overt vs. Covert Video

Most video installations use both overt and covert (hidden) CCTV cameras, with more cameras overt than covert. Overt installations are designed to deter crime and provide general surveillance of remote areas such as parking lots, perimeter fence lines, warehouses, entrance lobbies, hallways, or production areas. When CCTV cameras and lenses are exposed, all managers, employees, and visitors realize that the premises are under constant video surveillance. When the need arises, covert installations are used to detect and observe clandestine activity. While overt video equipment is often large and not meant to be concealed, covert equipment is usually small and designed to be hidden in objects in the environment or behind a ceiling or wall. Overt cameras are usually installed permanently whereas covert cameras are usually designed to be installed quickly, left in place for a few hours, days, or weeks, and then removed. Since minimizing installation time is desirable when installing covert cameras, video signal transmission often is wireless rather than wired.

1.4.3 Security Surveillance Applications

Many video applications fall broadly into two types, indoor and outdoor. This division sets a natural boundary between equipment types: those suitable for controlled indoor environments and those suitable for harsher outdoor environments. The two primary parameters are environmental factors and lighting factors. The indoor system requires artificial lighting that may or may not be augmented by daylight. The indoor system is subject to only mild indoor temperature and humidity variations, dirt, dust, and smoke. The outdoor system must withstand extreme temperatures, precipitation (fog, rain, and snow), wind, dirt, dust, sand, salt, and smoke. The outdoor systems use natural daylight and artificial lighting at night supplied either by parking lights or by a co-located infrared (IR) source. Some cameras can automatically switch from color operation during daylight, to monochrome when the lighting decreases below some specified level for nighttime operation.

Most video security applications use fixed, permanently installed video equipment. These systems are installed for months and years and left in place until they are superseded by new equipment or they are no longer required. There are many cases, however, where there is a requirement for a *rapid deployment* of video equipment to be used for a *short* period of time: days, weeks, or sometimes months, and then removed to be used again in another application. Chapter 21 describes some of these transportable rapid deployment video systems.

1.4.4 Safety Applications

In public, government, industrial, and other facilities, a safety, security, and personnel protection plan must guard personnel from harm caused by accident, human error, sabotage, or terrorism. Security forces are expected to monitor the conditions and activities at all locations in the facility through the use of CCTV cameras.

In a hospital room or hallway the video cameras may serve a dual function: monitoring patients while also determining the status and location of employees, visitors, and others. A guard can watch entrance and exit doors, hallways, operating rooms, drug dispensaries, and other vital areas.

Safety personnel can use video for evacuation and to determine if all personnel have left the area and are safe. Security personnel can use video for remote traffic monitoring and control and to ascertain high-traffic locations and how best to control them. Video plays a critical role in public safety, as a tool for monitoring vehicular traffic on highways and city streets, in truck and bus depots, at public rail and subway facilities, airports, power plants, just to name a few.

1.4.5 Video Access Control

As security requirements become more complex and demanding, video access control and electronic access control equipments should work synergistically with each other. For medium- to low-level access control security requirements, electronic card-reading systems are adequate after a person has first been identified at some exterior perimeter location. For higher security, personal biometric descriptors (iris scanning, fingerprint, etc.) and/or video identification are necessary.

Video surveillance is often used with electronic or video access control equipment. Video access control uses video to identify a person requesting access at a remote location, on foot or in a vehicle. A guard can compare the live image and the photo ID carried by the person on a video monitor and then either allow or deny entry. For the highest level of access control security the guard uses a system to compare the live image of the person to an image of the person retrieved from a video image database or one stored in a smart card. The two images are displayed side by side on a split-screen monitor along with other pertinent information. The video access control system can be combined with an electronic access control system to increase security and provide a means to track all attempted entries.

There are several biometric video access control systems which can positively identify a person enrolled in the system using iris, facial, or retina identification.

1.5   THE BOTTOM LINE

The synergy of a CCTV security system implies the following functional scenario:

- An intrusion alarm sensor or VMD will detect an unauthorized intrusion or entry or attempt to remove equipment from an area.
- A video camera located somewhere in the alarm area is viewing the area at the location or may be pointed manually or automatically (from the guard site) to view the alarm area.
- The information from the alarm sensor and/or camera is transmitted immediately to the security console, monitored by personnel, and/or recorded for permanent documentation.
- The security operator receiving the alarm information has a plan to dispatch personnel to the location or to take some other appropriate action.
- After dispatching a security person to the alarm area the guard resumes normal security duties to view the response, give additional instruction, and monitor any future event.
- After a reasonable amount of time the person dispatched should neutralize the intrusion or other event. The security guard resumes monitoring that situation to bring it to a successful conclusion and continues monitoring the facility.

The use of video plays a crucial role in the overall security system plan. During an intrusion, disaster or theft, the video system provides information to the guard, who must make some identification of the perpetrator, assess the problem, and respond appropriately. An installation containing suitable and sufficient alarm sensors and video

cameras permits the guard to follow the progress of the event and assist the response team in countering the attack.

The use of video and the VMD capability to track an intruder is most effective. With an intrusion alarm and visual video information, all the elements are in place for a timely, reliable transfer of information to the security officer. For maximum effectiveness, all parts of the security system must work together synergistically. If an intrusion alarm fails, the command post may not see the intruder with sufficient advance notice. If the video fails, the guard cannot identify the perpetrator or evaluate the extent of the security breach even though he may know that an intrusion has occurred. It is important that the security officer be alert and that proper audio and visual cues are provided to alert the guard when an alarm has occurred. If inadequate alarm annunciation is provided and the guard misses or misinterprets the alarm and video input, the data from either or both are not acted upon and the system fails.

In an emergency such as a terrorist attack, fire, flood, malfunctioning machinery, burst utility pipeline, etc. the operation of video, safety sensors, and human response at the console are all required. Video is an inexpensive investment for preventing accidents and minimizing damage when an accident occurs. Since the *reaction time* to a terrorist attack, fire or other disaster is critical, having various cameras at the critical locations before personnel arrive is very important. Closed circuit television cameras act as real-time eyes at the emergency location, permitting security and safety personnel to send the appropriate reaction force with adequate equipment to provide optimum response. In the case of a fire, while a sprinkler may activate or a fire sensor may produce an alarm, a CCTV camera can quickly ascertain whether the event is a false alarm, a minor alarm, or a major event. The automatic sprinkler and fire alarm system might alert the guard to the event but the video "eyes" viewing the actual scene prior to the emergency team's dispatch often save lives and reduce asset losses.

In the case of a security violation, if a sensor detects an intrusion the guard monitoring the video cameras can determine if the intrusion requires the dispatch of personnel or some other response. In the event of a major, well-planned attack on a facility by a terrorist organization or other intrusion, a diversionary tactic such as a false alarm can quickly be discovered through the use of video thereby preventing an inappropriate response.

To justify expenditures on security and safety equipment an organization must expect a positive return on investment. The value of assets protected must be greater than the amount spent on security, and the security system must adequately protect personnel and visitors. An effective security system reduces theft, saves money, and saves lives.

Chapter 2
Video Technology Overview

CONTENTS

2.1 Overview
2.2 The Video System
    2.2.1 The Role of Light and Reflection
    2.2.2 The Lens Function
    2.2.3 The Camera Function
    2.2.4 The Transmission Function
    2.2.5 The Monitor Function
    2.2.6 The Recording Function
2.3 Scene Illumination
    2.3.1 Natural Light
    2.3.2 Artificial Light
2.4 Scene Characteristics
    2.4.1 Target Size
    2.4.2 Reflectivity
    2.4.3 Effects of Motion
    2.4.4 Scene Temperature
2.5 Lenses
    2.5.1 Fixed-Focal-Length Lens
    2.5.2 Zoom Lens
    2.5.3 Vari-Focal Lens
    2.5.4 Panoramic—360° Lens
    2.5.5 Covert Pinhole Lens
    2.5.6 Special Lenses
2.6 Cameras
    2.6.1 The Scanning Process
        2.6.1.1 Raster Scanning
        2.6.1.2 Digital and Progressive Scan
    2.6.2 Solid-State Cameras
        2.6.2.1 Analog
        2.6.2.2 Digital
        2.6.2.3 Internet
    2.6.3 Low-Light-Level Intensified Camera
    2.6.4 Thermal Imaging Camera
    2.6.5 Panoramic 360° Camera

2.7 Transmission
    2.7.1 Hard-Wired
        2.7.1.1 Coaxial Cable
        2.7.1.2 Unshielded Twisted Pair
        2.7.1.3 LAN, WAN, Intranet and Internet
    2.7.2 Wireless
    2.7.3 Fiber Optics
2.8 Switchers
    2.8.1 Standard
    2.8.2 Microprocessor-Controlled
2.9 Quads and Multiplexers
2.10 Monitors
    2.10.1 Monochrome
    2.10.2 Color
    2.10.3 CRT, LCD, Plasma Displays
    2.10.4 Audio/Video
2.11 Recorders
    2.11.1 Video Cassette Recorder (VCR)
    2.11.2 Digital Video Recorder (DVR)
    2.11.3 Optical Disk
2.12 Hard-copy Video Printers
2.13 Ancillary Equipment
    2.13.1 Camera Housings
        2.13.1.1 Standard-rectangular
        2.13.1.2 Dome
        2.13.1.3 Specialty
        2.13.1.4 Plug and Play
    2.13.2 Pan/Tilt Mounts
    2.13.3 Video Motion Detector (VMD)
    2.13.4 Screen Splitter
    2.13.5 Camera Video Annotation
        2.13.5.1 Camera ID
        2.13.5.2 Time and Date
    2.13.6 Image Reversal
2.14 Summary

2.1 OVERVIEW

The second half of the 1990s has witnessed a quantum jump in video security technology. This technology has manifest with a new generation of video components, i.e. digital cameras, multiplexers, DVRs, etc. A second significant activity has been the integration of security systems with computer-based LANs, wide area networks (WANs), wireless networks (WiFi), intranets and, Internet and the World Wide Web (WWW) communications systems.

Although today's video security system hardware is based on new technology which takes advantage of the great advances in microprocessor computing power, solid-state and magnetic memory, digital processing, and wired and wireless video signal transmission (analog, digital over the Internet, etc.), the basic video system still requires the lens, camera, transmission medium (wired cable, wireless), monitor, recorder, etc. This chapter describes current video security system components and is an introduction to their operation.

The primary function of any video security or safety system is to provide remote eyes for the security force located at a central control console or remote site. The video system includes the illumination source, the scene to be viewed, the camera lens, the camera, and the means of transmission to the remote monitoring and recording equipment. Other equipment often necessary to complete the system include video switchers, multiplexers, VMDs, housings, scene combiners and splitters, and character generators.

This chapter describes the technology used to: (1) capture the visual image, (2) convert it to a video signal, (3) transmit the signal to a receiver at a remote location, (4) display the image on a video monitor, and (5) record and print it for permanent record. Figure 2-1 shows the simplest video application requiring only one video camera and monitor.

The printer and video recorder are optional. The camera may be used to monitor employees, visitors, or people entering or leaving a building. The camera could be located in the lobby ceiling and pointed at the reception area, the front door, or an internal access door. The monitor might be located hundreds or thousands of feet away, in another building or another city or country with the security personnel viewing that same lobby, front door, or reception area. The video camera/monitor system effectively extends the eyes, reaching from observer location to the observed location. The basic one-camera system shown in Figure 2-1 includes the following hardware components.

- **Lens.** Light from the illumination source reflects off the scene. The lens collects the light from the scene

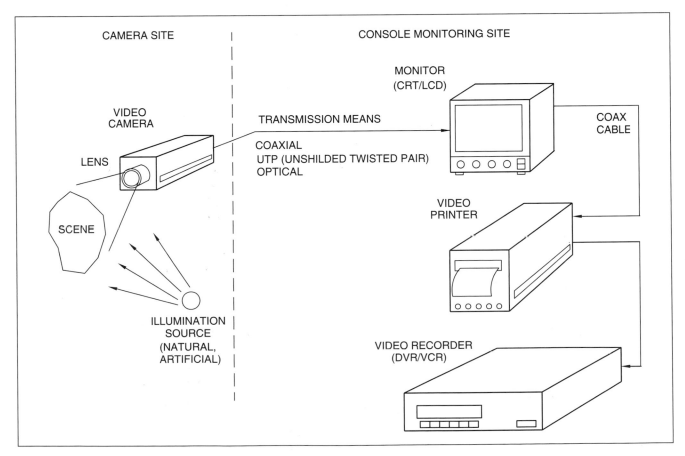

FIGURE 2-1   Single camera video system

and forms an image of the scene on the light-sensitive camera sensor.

- **Camera.** The camera sensor converts the visible scene formed by the lens into an electrical signal suitable for transmission to the remote monitor, recorder, and printer.
- **Transmission Link.** The transmission media carries the electrical video signal from the camera to the remote monitor. Hard-wired media choices include: (a) coaxial, (b) two-wire unshielded twisted-pair (UTP), (c) fiber-optic cable, (d) LAN, (e) WAN, (f) intranet, and (g) Internet network. Wireless choices include: (a) radio frequency (RF), (b) microwave, or (c) optical infrared (IR). Signals can be analog or digital.
- **Monitor.** The video monitor or computer screens display (CRT, LCD or plasma) the camera image by converting the electrical video signal back into a visible image on the monitor screen.
- **Recorder.** The camera scene is permanently recorded by a real-time or TL VCR onto a magnetic tape cassette or by a DVR using a magnetic disk hard drive.
- **Hard-copy Printer.** The video printer produces a hard-copy paper printout of any live or recorded video

image, using thermal, inkjet, laser, or other printing technology.

The first four components are required to make a simple video system work. The recorder and/or printer is required if a permanent record is required.

Figure 2-2 shows a block diagram of a multi-camera analog video security system using these components plus additional hardware and options to expand the capability of the single-camera system to multiple cameras, monitors, recorders, etc. providing a more complex video security system.

Additional ancillary supporting equipment for more complex systems includes: camera switchers, quads, multiplexers, environmental camera housings, camera pan/tilt mechanisms, image combiners and splitters, and scene annotators.

- **Camera Switcher, Quad, Multiplexer.** When a CCTV security system has multiple cameras, an electronic switcher, quad, or multiplexer is used to select different cameras automatically or manually to display the images on a single or multiple monitors, as individual or multiple scenes. The quad can digitally combine four

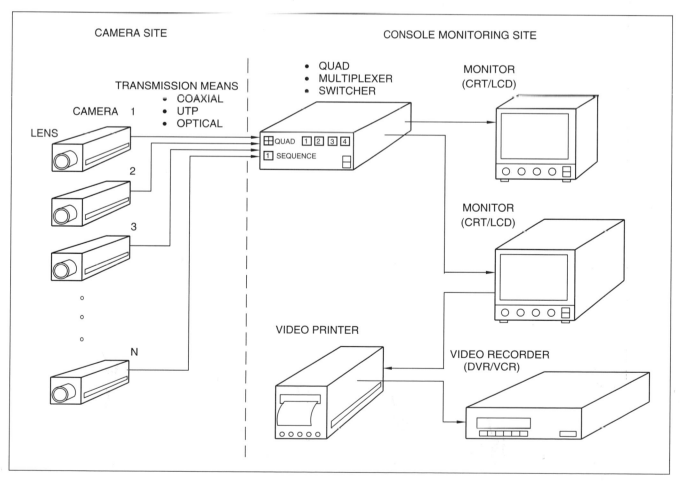

FIGURE 2-2 Comprehensive video security system

cameras. The multiplexer can digitally combine 4, 9, 16, and even 32 separate cameras.

- **Housings.** The many varieties of camera/lens housings fall into three categories: indoor, outdoor and integral camera/housing assemblies. Indoor housings protect the camera and lens from tampering and are usually constructed from lightweight materials. Outdoor housings protect the camera and lens from the environment: from precipitation, extremes of heat and cold, dust, dirt, and vandalism.

  - *Dome Housing.* The dome camera housing uses a hemispherical clear or tinted plastic dome enclosing a fixed camera or a camera with pan/tilt and zoom lens capability.
  - *Plug and Play Camera/Housing Combination.* To simplify surveillance camera installations many manufacturers are now packaging the camera-lens-housing as a complete assembly. These plug-and-play cameras are ready to mount in a wall or ceiling and to connect the power in and the video out.

- *Pan/Tilt Mechanism.* When a camera must view a large area, a pan and tilt mount is used to rotate it horizontally (panning) and to tilt it, providing a large angular coverage.
- *Splitter/Combiner/Inserter.* An optical or electronic image combiner or splitter is used to display more than one camera scene on a single monitor.
- *Annotator.* A time and date generator annotates the video scene with chronological information. A camera identifier puts a camera number (or name—FRONT DOOR, etc.) on the monitor screen to identify the scene displayed by the camera.

The digital video surveillance system includes most of the devices in the analog video system. The primary differences manifest in using digital electronics and digital processing within the video devices. Digital video components use digital signal processing (DSP), digital video signal compression, digital transmission, recording and viewing. Figure 2-3 illustrates these devices and signal paths and the overall system block diagram for the digital video system.

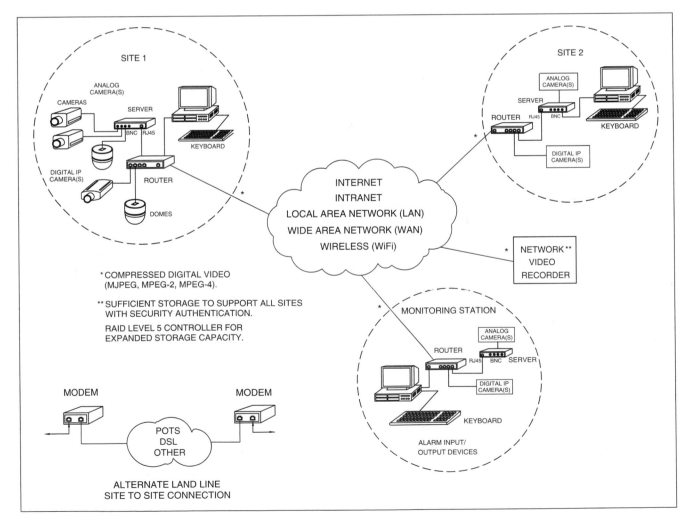

FIGURE 2-3 Networked digital video system block diagram

2.2 THE VIDEO SYSTEM

Figure 2-4 shows the essentials of the CCTV camera environment: illumination source, camera, lens, and the camera–lens combined field of view (FOV), that is the scene the camera–lens combination sees.

2.2.1 The Role of Light and Reflection

A scene or target area to be viewed is illuminated by natural or artificial light sources. Natural sources include the sun, the moon (reflected sunlight), and starlight. Artificial sources include incandescent, sodium, metal arc, mercury, fluorescent, infrared, and other man-made lights. Chapter 3 describes all of these light sources in detail.

The camera lens receives the light reflected from the scene. Depending on the scene to be viewed the amount of light reflected from objects in the scene can vary from 5 or 10% to 80 or 90% of the light incident on the scene. Typical values of reflected light for normal scenes such as foliage, automobiles, personnel, and streets fall in the range from about 25–65%. Snow-covered scenes may reach 90%.

The amount of light received by the lens is a function of the brightness of the light source, the reflectivity of the scene, and the transmission characteristics of the intervening atmosphere. In outdoor applications there is usually a considerable optical path from the source to the scene and back to the camera; therefore the transmission through the atmosphere must be considered. When atmospheric conditions are clear, there is generally little or no attenuation of the reflected light from the scene. However, when there is precipitation (rain, snow, or sleet, or when fog intervenes) or in dusty, smoky, or sand-blown environments, this attenuation might be substantial and must be considered. Likewise in hot climates thermal effects (heat waves) and humidity can cause severe attenuation and/or distortion of the scene. Complete attenuation of the reflected light from the scene (zero visibility) can occur, in which case no scene image is formed.

Since most solid-state cameras operate in the visible and near-infrared wavelength region the general rule of thumb with respect to visibility is that if the human eye cannot see the scene neither can the camera. Under this situation, no amount of increased lighting will help; however, if the visible light can be filtered out of the scene and only the IR portion used, scene visibility might be increased

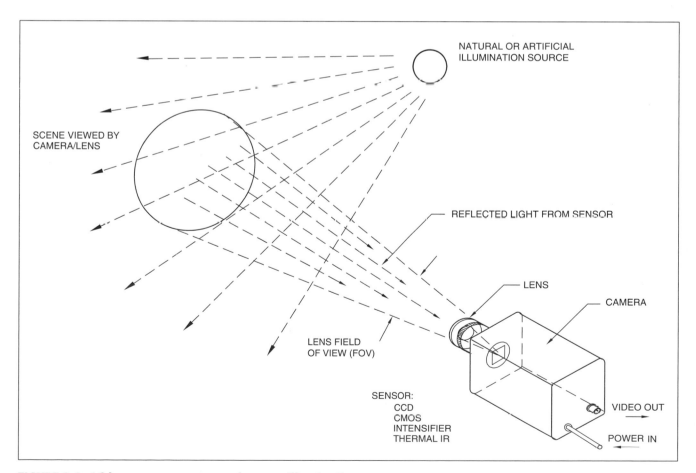

FIGURE 2-4 Video camera, scene, and source illumination

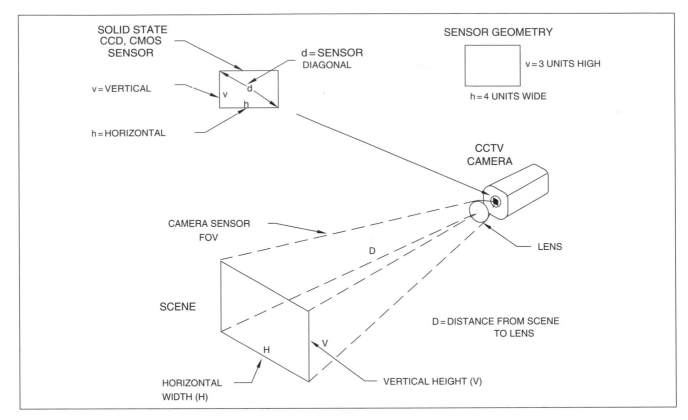

FIGURE 2-5   Video scene and sensor geometry

somewhat. This problem can often be overcome by using a thermal infrared (IR) imaging camera that works outside of the visible wavelength range. These thermal IR cameras produce a monochrome display with reduced image quality and are much more expensive than the charge coupled device (CCD) or complimentary metal oxide semiconductor (CMOS) cameras (see Section 2.6.4). Figure 2-5 illustrates the relationship between the viewed scene and the scene image on the camera sensor.

The lens located on the camera forms an image of the scene and focuses it onto the sensor. Almost all video systems used in security systems have a 4-by-3 aspect ratio (4 units wide by 3 units high) for both the image sensor and the field of view. The width parameter is designated as h, and H, and the vertical as v, and V. Some cameras have a 16 units wide by 9 units high definition television (HDTV) format.

2.2.2   The Lens Function

The camera lens is analogous to the lens of the human eye (Figure 2-6) and collects the reflected radiation from the scene much like the lens of your eye or a film camera. The function of the lens is to collect reflected light from the scene and focus it into an image onto the CCTV camera sensor. A fraction of the light reaching the scene from the natural or artificial illumination source is reflected

toward the camera and intercepted and collected by the camera lens. As a general rule, the larger the lens diameter, the more light will be gathered, the brighter the image on the sensor, and the better the final image on the monitor. This is why larger-aperture (diameter) lenses, having a higher optical throughput, are better (and more expensive) than smaller-diameter lenses that collect less light. Under good lighting conditions—bright indoor lighting, outdoors under sunlight—the large-aperture lenses are not required and there is sufficient light to form a bright image on the sensor by using small-diameter lenses.

Most video applications use a fixed-focal-length (FFL) lens. The FFL lens like the human eye lens covers a constant angular field of view (FOV). The FFL lens images a scene with constant *fixed* magnification. A large variety of CCTV camera lenses are available with different focal lengths (FLs) that provide different FOVs. Wide-angle, medium-angle, and narrow-angle (telephoto) lenses produce different magnifications and FOVs. Zoom and varifocal lenses can be adjusted to have variable FLs and FOVs.

Most CCTV lenses have an iris diaphragm (as does the human eye) to adjust the open area of the lens and change the amount of light passing through it and reaching the sensor. Depending on the application, manual or automatic-iris lenses are used. In an automatic-iris CCTV lens, as in a human eye lens, the iris closes automatically when the illumination is too high and opens automatically

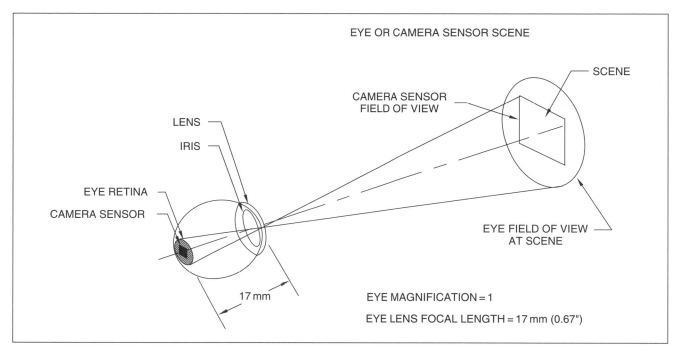

EYE OR CAMERA SENSOR SCENE

SCENE

CAMERA SENSOR
FIELD OF VIEW

CAMERA SENSOR
FIELD OF VIEW

LENS

IRIS

EYE RETINA
CAMERA SENSOR

EYE FIELD OF VIEW
AT SCENE

17 mm

EYE MAGNIFICATION = 1

EYE LENS FOCAL LENGTH = 17 mm (0.67")

FIGURE 2-6   Comparing the human eye to the video camera lens

when it is too low, thereby maintaining the optimum illumination on the sensor at all times. Figure 2-7 shows representative samples of CCTV lenses, including FFL, varifocal, zoom, pinhole, and a large catadioptric lens for long range outdoor use (which combines both mirror and glass optical elements). Chapter 4 describes CCTV lens characteristics in detail.

2.2.3 The Camera Function

The lens focuses the scene onto the camera image sensor which acts like the retina of the eye or the film in a photographic camera. The video camera sensor and electronics convert the visible image into an equivalent electrical signal suitable for transmission to a remote monitor. Figure 2-8 is a block diagram of a typical analog CCTV camera.

The camera converts the optical image produced by the lens into a time-varying electric signal that changes (modulates) in accordance with the light-intensity distribution throughout the scene. Other camera electronic circuits produce synchronizing pulses so that the time-varying video signal can later be displayed on a monitor or recorder, or printed out as hard copy on a video printer. While cameras may differ in size and shape depending on specific type and capability, the scanning process used by most cameras is essentially the same. Almost all cameras must scan the scene, point by point, as a function of time. (An exception is the image intensifier.) Solid-state CCD or CMOS color and monochrome cameras are used in

most applications. In scenes with low illumination, sensitive CCD cameras with infrared (IR) illuminators are used. In scenes with very low illumination and where no active illumination is permitted (i.e. covert) low-light-level (LLL) intensified CCD (ICCD) cameras are used. These cameras are complex and expensive (Chapter 19).

Figure 2-9 shows a block diagram of a the analog camera with (a) digital signal processing (DSP) and (b) the all digital internet protocol (IP) video camera.

In the early 1990s the non-broadcast, tube-type color cameras available for security applications lacked long-term stability, sensitivity, and high resolution. Color cameras did not find much use in security applications until solid-state color CCTV cameras became available through the development of solid state color sensor technology and widespread use of consumer color CCD cameras used in camcorders. Color cameras have now become standard in security systems and most CCTV security cameras in use today are color. Figure 2-10 shows representative CCTV cameras including monochrome and color solid-state CCD and CMOS cameras, a small single board camera, and a miniature remote head camera. Chapters 5, 14, 15 and 19 describe standard and LLL security CCTV cameras in detail.

2.2.4 The Transmission Function

Once the camera has generated an electrical video signal representing the scene image, the signal is transmitted to a remote security monitoring site via some transmission

(A) MOTORIZED ZOOM   (B) CATADIOPTRIC LONG FFL   (C) FLEXIBLE FIBER OPTIC

(D) WIDE FOV FFL   (E) RIGID FIBER OPTIC

(F) NARROW FOV (TELEPHOTO) FFL   (G) MINI-LENS   (H) STRAIGHT AND RIGHT-ANGLE PINHOLE LENSES

FIGURE 2-7   Representative video lenses

means: coaxial cable, two-wire twisted-pair, LAN, WAN, intranet, Internet, fiber optic, or wireless techniques. The choice of transmission medium depends on factors such as distance, environment, and facility layout.

If the distance between the camera and the monitor is short (10–500 feet), coaxial cable, UTP, and fiber optic or wireless is used. For longer distances (500 to several thousand feet) or where there are electrical disturbances, fiber-optic cable and UTP are preferred. For very long distances and in harsh environments (frequent lightning storms) or between separated buildings where no electrical grounding between buildings is in place, fiber optics is the choice. In applications where the camera and monitor are separated by roadways or where there is no right-of-

way, wireless systems using RF, microwave or optical transmission is used. For transmission over many miles or from city to city the only choice is the digital or Internet IP camera using compression techniques and transmitting over the Internet and WWW. Images from these Internet systems are not real-time but sometimes come close to real-time. Chapters 6 and 7 describe all of these video transmission media.

2.2.5 The Monitor Function

At the monitoring site a cathode ray tube (CRT), LCD or plasma monitor converts the video signal back into a

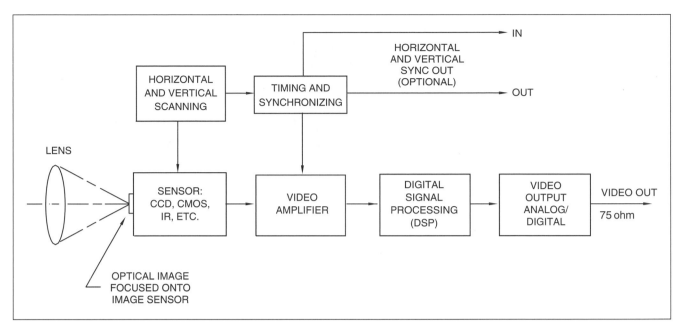

FIGURE 2-8   Analog CCTV camera block diagram

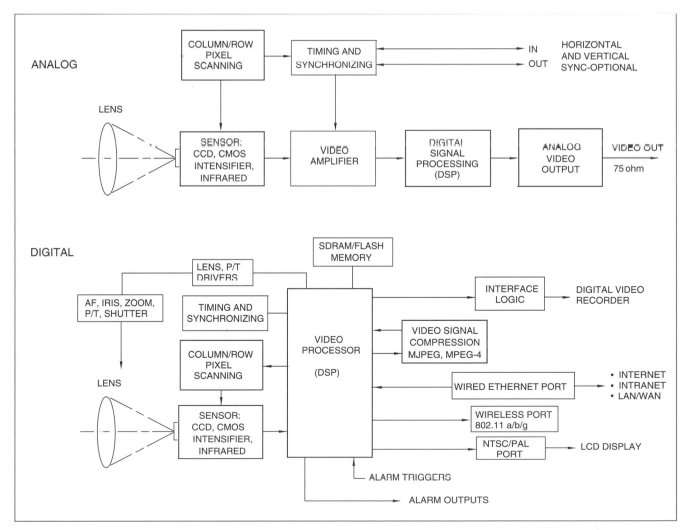

FIGURE 2-9   Analog camera with DSP and all digital camera block diagram

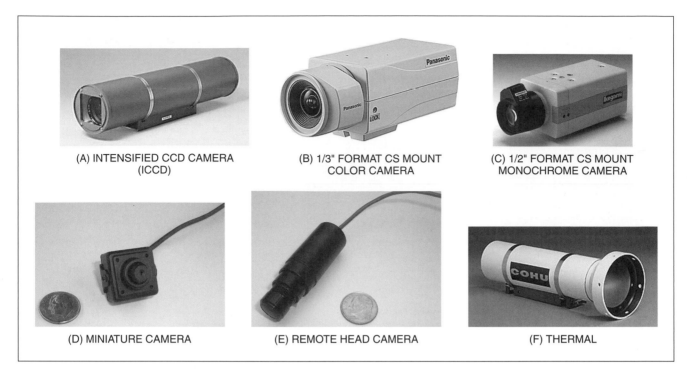

| (A) INTENSIFIED CCD CAMERA (ICCD) | (B) 1/3" FORMAT CS MOUNT COLOR CAMERA | (C) 1/2" FORMAT CS MOUNT MONOCHROME CAMERA |
| (D) MINIATURE CAMERA | (E) REMOTE HEAD CAMERA | (F) THERMAL |

FIGURE 2-10   Representative video cameras

visual image on the monitor face via electronic circuitry similar but inverse to that in the camera. The final scene is produced by a scanning electron beam in the CRT in the video monitor. This beam activates the phosphor on the cathode-ray tube, thereby producing a representation of the original image onto the faceplate of the monitor. Alternatively the video image is displayed point by point on an LCD or plasma screen. Chapter 8 describes monitor and display technology and hardware. A permanent record of the monitor video image is made using a VCR tape or DVR hard disk magnetic recorder and a permanent hard copy is printed with a video printer.

2.2.6   The Recording Function

For decades the VCR has been used to record monochrome and color video images. The real-time and TL VCR magnetic tape systems have been a reliable and efficient means for recording security scenes.

Beginning in the mid-1990s the DVR was developed using a computer hard disk drive and digital electronics to provide video image recording. The availability of large memory disks (hundreds of megabytes) made these machines available for long duration security recording. Significant advantages of the DVR over the VCR are the high reliability of the disk as compared with the cassette tape, its ability to perform high speed searches (retrieval of images) anywhere on the disk, absence of image deterioration after many copies are made.

2.3   SCENE ILLUMINATION

A scene is illuminated by either natural or artificial illumination. Monochrome cameras can operate with any type of light source. Color cameras need light that contains all the colors in the visible spectrum and light with a reasonable balance of all the colors to produce a satisfactory color image.

2.3.1   Natural Light

During daytime the amount of illumination and spectral distribution of light (color) reaching a scene depends on the time of day and atmospheric conditions. The color spectrum of the light reaching the scene is important if color CCTV is being used. Direct sunlight produces the highest-contrast scene, allowing maximum identification of objects. On a cloudy or overcast day, less light is received by the objects in the scene resulting in less contrast. To produce an optimum camera picture under the wide variation in light levels (daytime to nighttime), an automatic-iris camera system is required. Table 2-1 shows the light levels for outdoor illumination under bright sun, partial clouds, and overcast day down to overcast night.

Scene illumination is measured in foot candles (Fc) and can vary over a range of 10,000 to 1 (or more). This exceeds the dynamic operating range of most camera sensors for producing a good-quality video image. After the sun has gone below the horizon and if the moon is overhead, reflected sunlight from the moon illuminates the

CONDITION	ILLUMINATION		COMMENTS
	(FtCd)	(lux)	
DIRECT SUNLIGHT	10,000	107,500	DAYLIGHT RANGE
FULL DAYLIGHT	1,000	10,750	
OVERCAST DAY	100	1,075	
VERY DARK DAY	10	107.5	
TWILIGHT	1	10.75	
DEEP TWILIGHT	.1	1.075	
FULL MOON	.01	.1075	LOW LIGHT LEVEL RANGE
QUARTER MOON	.001	.01075	
STARLIGHT	.0001	.001075	
OVERCAST NIGHT	.00001	.0001075	

NOTE: 1 lux = .093 FtCd

Table 2-1 Light Levels under Daytime and Nighttime Conditions

scene and may be detected by a sensitive monochrome camera. Detection of information in a scene under this condition requires a very sensitive camera since there is very little light reflected into the camera lens from the scene. As an extreme, when the moon is not overhead or is obscured by cloud cover, the only light received is ambient light from: (1) local man-made lighting sources, (2) night-glow caused by distant ground lighting reflecting off particulate (pollution), clouds, and aerosols in the lower atmosphere, and (3) direct light caused by starlight. This is the most severe lighting condition and requires either: (1) ICCD, (2) monochrome camera with IR LED illumination, or (3) thermal IR camera. Table 2-2 summarizes the light levels occurring under daylight and these LLL conditions and the operating ranges of typical cameras. The equivalent metric measure of light level (lux) compared with the foot candle (Fc) is given. One Fc is equivalent to approximately 9.3 lux.

2.3.2 Artificial Light

Artificial illumination is often used to augment outdoor lighting to obtain adequate video surveillance at night. The light sources used are: tungsten, tungsten-halogen, metal-arc, mercury, sodium, xenon, IR lamps, and light emitting diode (LED) IR arrays. Figure 2-11 illustrates several examples of these lamps.

The type of lighting chosen depends on architectural requirements and the specific application. Often a particular lighting design is used for safety reasons so that personnel at the scene can see better, as well as for improving the video picture. Tungsten and tungsten halogen lamps have by far the most balanced color and are best for color cameras. The most efficient visual outdoor light types are

the low- and high-pressure sodium-vapor lamps to which the human eye is most sensitive. These lamps, however, do not produce all colors (missing blue and green) and therefore are not good light sources for color cameras. Metal-arc lamps have excellent color rendition. Mercury arc lamps provide good security illumination but are missing the color red and therefore are not as good as the metal-arc lamps at producing excellent-quality color video images. Long-arc xenon lamps having excellent color rendition are often used in outdoor sports arenas and large parking areas.

Light emitting diode IR illumination arrays either mounted in monochrome video cameras or located near the camera are used to illuminate scenes when sufficient lighting is not available. Since they only emit energy in the IR spectrum they can only be used with monochrome cameras. They are used at short ranges (10–25 feet) with wide angle lenses (50–75° FOV) or at medium long ranges (25–200 feet) with medium to narrow FOV lenses (5–20°).

Artificial indoor illumination is similar to outdoor illumination, with fluorescent lighting used extensively in addition to the high-pressure sodium, metal-arc and mercury lamps. Since indoor lighting has a relatively constant light level, automatic-iris lenses are often unnecessary. However, if the CCTV camera views a scene near an outside window or a door where additional light comes in during the day, or if the indoor lighting changes between daytime and nighttime operation, then an automatic-iris lens or electronically shuttered camera is required. The illumination level from most indoor lighting is significantly lower by 100–1000 times than that of sunlight. Chapter 3 describes outdoor natural and artificial lighting and indoor man-made lighting systems available for video surveillance use.

CAMERA REQUIREMENT PER LIGHTING CONDITIONS

ILLUMINATION CONDITION	ILLUMINATION (FtCd)	(lux)	VIDICON *	CCD	CMOS	ICCD	ISIT *
OVERCAST NIGHT	.00001	.0001075					
STARLIGHT	.0001	.001075					
QUARTER MOON	.001	.01075					
FULL MOON	.01	.1075					
DEEP TWILIGHT	.1	1.075					
TWILIGHT	1	10.075					
VERY DARK DAY	10	107.5		OPERATING RANGE OF TYPICAL CAMERAS			
OVERCAST DAY	100	1,075					
FULL DAYLIGHT	1,000	10,750					
DIRECT SUNLIGHT	10,000	107,500					

* FOR REFERENCE ONLY

Table 2-2   Camera Capability under Natural Lighting Conditions

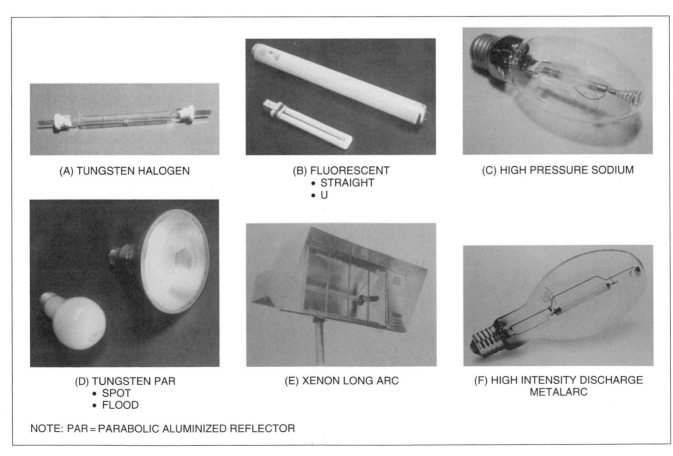

(A) TUNGSTEN HALOGEN

(B) FLUORESCENT
• STRAIGHT
• U

(C) HIGH PRESSURE SODIUM

(D) TUNGSTEN PAR
• SPOT
• FLOOD

(E) XENON LONG ARC

(F) HIGH INTENSITY DISCHARGE METALARC

NOTE: PAR = PARABOLIC ALUMINIZED REFLECTOR

FIGURE 2-11   Representative artificial light sources

2.4 SCENE CHARACTERISTICS

The quality of the video image depends on various scene characteristics that include: (1) the scene lighting level, (2) the sharpness and contrast of objects relative to the scene background, (3) whether objects are in a simple, uncluttered background or in a complicated scene, and (4) whether objects are stationary or in motion. These scene factors will determine whether the system will be able to detect, determine orientation, recognize, or identify objects and personnel. As will be seen later the scene illumination—via sunlight, moonlight, or artificial sources—and the actual scene contrast play important roles in the type of lens and camera necessary to produce a quality image on the monitor.

2.4.1 Target Size

In addition to the scene's illumination level and the object's contrast with respect to the scene background, the object's apparent size—that is, its angular FOV as seen by the camera—influences a person's ability to detect it. (Try to find a football referee with a striped shirt in a field of zebras.)

The requirements of a video system are a function of the application. These include: (1) detection of the object or movement in the scene; (2) determination of the object's orientation; (3) recognition of the type of object in the scene, that is, adult or child, car or truck; or (4) identification of the object (Who is the person? Exactly what kind of truck is it?). Making these distinctions depends on the system's resolution, contrast, and signal-to-noise ratio (S/N). In a typical scene the average observer can detect a target about one-tenth of a degree in angle. This can be related to a standard video picture that has 525 horizontal lines (NTSC) and about 350 TV line vertical and 500 TV line horizontal resolution. Figure 2-12 and Table 2-3 summarize the number of lines required to detect, orient, recognize, or identify an object in a television picture. The number of TV lines required will increase for conditions of poor lighting, highly complex backgrounds, reduced contrast, or fast movement of the camera or target.

2.4.2 Reflectivity

The reflectivity of different materials varies greatly depending on its composition and surface texture. Table 2-4 gives

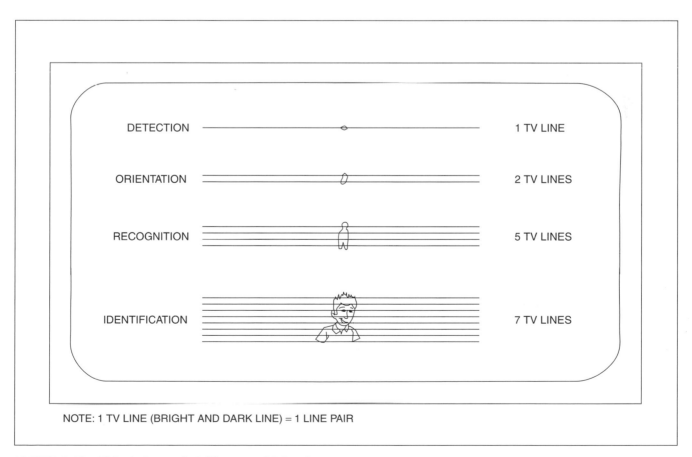

FIGURE 2-12 Object size vs. intelligence obtained

INTELLIGENCE	MINIMUM* TV LINES
DETECTION	1 ± 0.25
ORIENTATION	1.4 ± 0.35
RECOGNITION	4 ± 0.8
IDENTIFICATION	6.4 ± 1.5

* ONE TV LINE CORRESPONDS TO A LIGHT AND DARK LINE (ONE TV LINE PAIR)

Table 2-3   TV Lines vs. Intelligence Obtained

some examples of materials and objects viewed by video cameras and their respective reflectivities.

Since the camera responds to the amount of light reflected from the scene it is important to recognize that objects have a large range of reflectivities. The objects with the highest reflectivities produce the brightest images. To detect one object located within the area of another the objects must differ in reflectivity, color, or texture. Therefore, if a red box is in front of a green wall and both have the same reflectivity and texture, the box will not be seen on a monochrome video system. In this case, the total reflectivity in the visible spectrum is the same for the green wall and the red box. This is where the color camera shows its advantage over the monochrome camera.

The case of a color scene is more complex. While the reflectivity of the red box and the green wall may be the same as averaged over the entire visible spectrum from blue to red, the color camera can distinguish between green and red.

It is easier to identify a scene characteristic by a difference in color in a color scene than it is to identify it by a difference in gray scale (intensity) in a monochrome scene. For this reason the target size required to make an identification in a color scene is generally less than it is to make the same identification in a monochrome scene.

2.4.3   Effects of Motion

A moving object in a video image is easier to detect, but more difficult to recognize than a stationary one provided that the camera can respond to it. Low light level cameras produce sharp images for stationary scenes but smeared images for moving targets. This is caused by a phenomenon called "lag" or "smear." Solid-state sensors (CCD, CMOS, and ICCD) do not exhibit smear or lag at normal light levels and can therefore produce sharp images of both stationary and moving scenes. Some image intensifiers exhibit smear when the scene moves fast or when there is a bright light in the FOV of the lens.

When the target in the scene moves very fast the inherent camera scan rate (30 frames per second) causes a blurred image of this moving target in the camera. This is analogous to the blurred image in a still photograph when the shutter speed is too slow for the action. There is no cure for this as long as the standard NTSC (National Television System Committee) television scan rate (30 frames per second) is used. However, CCTV snapshots can be

MATERIAL	REFLECTIVITY (%)*
SNOW	85–95
ASPHALT	5
PLASTER (WHITE)	90
SAND	40–60
TREES	20
GRASS	40
CLOTHES	15–30
CONCRETE-NEW	40
CONCRETE-OLD	25
CLEAR WINDOWS	70
HUMAN FACE	15–25
WOOD	10–20
PAINTED WALL (WHITE)	75–90
RED BRICK	25–35
PARKING LOT AND AUTOMOBILES	40
ALUMINUM BUILDING (DIFFUSE)	65–70

* VISIBLE SPECTRUM: 400–700 NANOMETERS

Table 2-4   Reflectivity of Common Materials

taken without any blurring using fast-shuttered CCD cameras. For special applications in which fast-moving targets must be imaged and tracked, higher scan rate cameras are available.

2.4.4 Scene Temperature

Scene temperature has no effect on the video image in a CCD, CMOS, or ICCD sensor. These sensors do not respond to temperature changes or temperature differences in the scene. On the other hand, IR thermal imaging cameras do respond to temperature differences and changes in temperature in the scene. Thermal imagers do not respond to visible light or the very near-IR radiation like that produced by IR LEDs. The sensitivity of IR thermal imagers is defined as the smallest change in temperature in the scene that can be detected by the thermal camera.

2.5 LENSES

A lens collects reflected light from the scene and focuses it onto the camera image sensor. This is analogous to the lens of the human eye focusing a scene onto the retina at the back of the eye (Figure 2-6). As in the human eye, the camera lens inverts the scene image on the image sensor, but the eye and the camera electronics compensate (invert the image) to perceive an upright scene. The retina of the human eye differs from any CCTV lens in that it focuses a sharp image only in the central 10% of its total 160° FOV. All vision outside the central focused scene is out of focus. This central imaging part of the human eye can be characterized as a medium FL lens: 16–25 mm. In principle, Figure 2-6 represents the function of any lens in a video system.

Many different lens types are used for video surveillance and safety applications. They range from the simplest FFL manual-iris lenses to the more complex variable-focal-length (vari-focal) and zoom lenses, with an automatic iris being an option for all types.

In addition, pinhole lenses are available for covert applications, split-image lenses for viewing multiple scenes on one camera, right-angle lenses for viewing a scene perpendicular to the camera axis, and rigid or flexible fiber-optic lenses for viewing through thick walls, under doors, etc.

2.5.1 Fixed-Focal-Length Lens

Figure 2-13 illustrates three fixed focal length (FFL) or fixed FOV lenses with narrow (telephoto), medium, and wide FOVs and the corresponding FOV obtained when used with a 1/3-inch camera sensor format.

Wide-FOV (short FL) lenses permit viewing a very large scene (wide angle) with low magnification and therefore provide low resolution and low identification capabilities. Narrow-FOV or telephoto lenses have high magnification, with high resolution and high identification capabilities.

2.5.2 Zoom Lens

The zoom lens is more versatile and complex than the FFL lens. Its FL is variable from wide-angle to narrow-angle (telephoto) FOV (Figure 2-14).

The overall camera/lens FOV depends on the lens FL and the camera sensor size as shown in Figure 2-14. Zoom lenses consist of multiple lens groups that are moved within the lens barrel by means of an external zooming ring (manual or motorized), thereby changing the lens FL and angular FOV without having to switch lenses or refocusing. Zoom focal length ratios can range from 6 to 1 up to 50 to 1. Zoom lenses are usually large and used on pan/tilt mounts viewing over large areas and distances (25–500 feet).

2.5.3 Vari-Focal Lens

The vari-focal lens is a variable focal length lens used in applications where a FFL lens would be used. In general they are smaller and cost much less than zoom lenses. Like the zoom lens, the vari-focal lens is used because its focal length (angular FOV) can be changed manually or automatically, using a motor, by rotating the barrel on the lens. This feature makes it convenient to adjust the FOV to a precise angle when installed on the camera. Typical vari-focal lenses have focal lengths of 3–8 mm, 5–12 mm, 8–50 mm. With just these three lenses focal lengths of from 3 to 50 mm (91–5° horizontal FOV) can be covered on a 1/3-inch format sensor. Unlike zoom lenses, vari-focal lenses must be refocused each time the FL and the FOV are changed. They are not suitable for zoom or pan/tilt applications.

2.5.4 Panoramic—360° Lens

There has always been a need to see "all around," i.e. an entire room or other location, seeing 360° with *one* panoramic camera and lens. In the past, 360° FOV camera viewing systems have only been achieved by using multiple cameras and lenses and combining the scenes on a split-screen monitor.

Panoramic lenses have been available for many years but have only recently been combined with digital electronics and sophisticated mathematical transformations to take advantage of their capabilities. Figure 2-15 shows two lenses having a 360° horizontal FOV and a 90° vertical FOV.

The panoramic lens collects light from the 360° panoramic scene and focuses it onto the camera sensor as

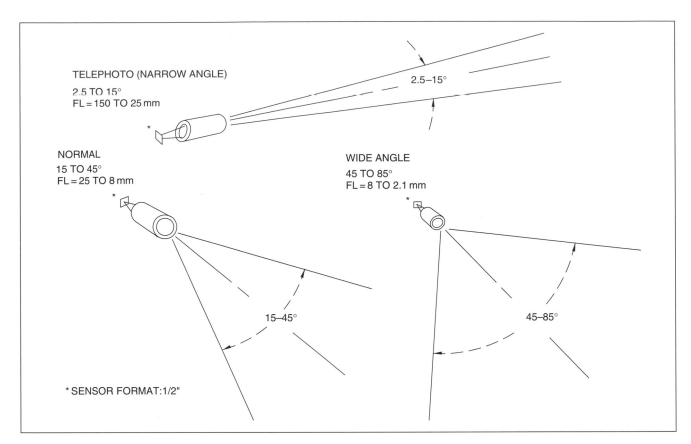

FIGURE 2-13   Representative FFL lenses and their fields of view (FOV)

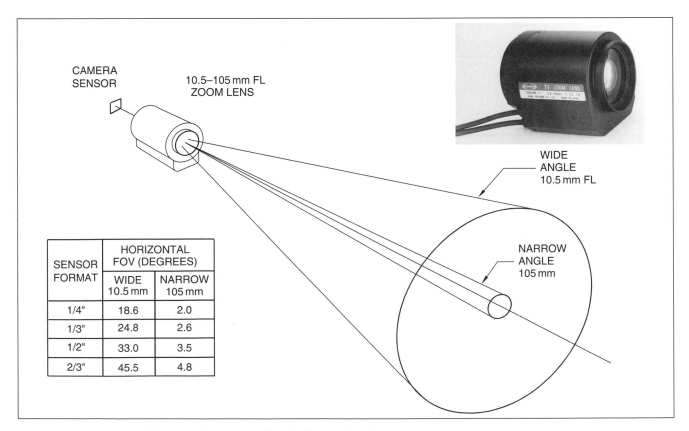

SENSOR FORMAT	HORIZONTAL FOV (DEGREES)	
	WIDE 10.5 mm	NARROW 105 mm
1/4"	18.6	2.0
1/3"	24.8	2.6
1/2"	33.0	3.5
2/3"	45.5	4.8

FIGURE 2-14   Zoom video lens horizontal field of view (FOV)

(A)   (B)

FIGURE 2-15   Panoramic 360° lens

a donut-shaped image. The electronics and mathematical algorithm converts this donut-shaped panoramic image into the rectangular (horizontal and vertical) format for normal monitor viewing (Section 2.6.5).

2.5.5   Covert Pinhole Lens

This special security lens is used when the lens and CCTV camera must be hidden. The front lens element or aperture is small (from 1/16 to 5/16 of an inch in diameter). While this is not the size of a pinhead it nevertheless

has been labeled a pinhole lens. Figure 2-16 shows examples of straight and right-angle pinhole lenses used with C or CS mount cameras. The very small mini-pinhole lenses are used on the low-cost, small board cameras.

2.5.6   Special Lenses

Some special lenses useful in security applications include split-image, right-angle, relay, and fiber optic (Figure 2-17).

(A) PINHOLE LENSES   (B) MINI-LENSES

FIGURE 2-16   Pinhole and mini-pinhole lenses

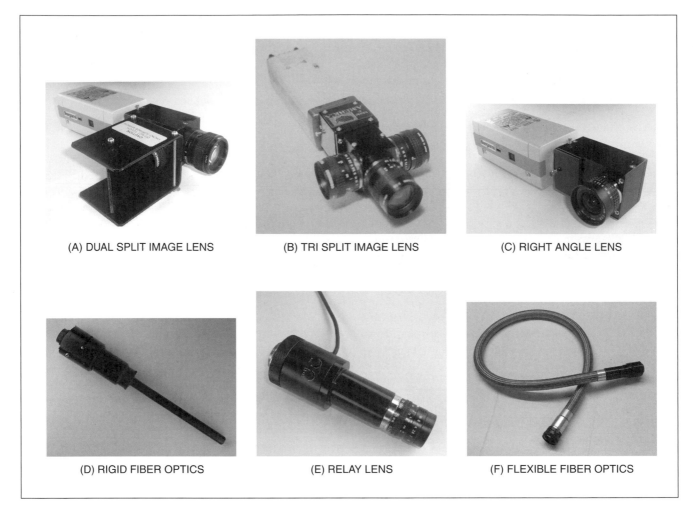

(A) DUAL SPLIT IMAGE LENS   (B) TRI SPLIT IMAGE LENS   (C) RIGHT ANGLE LENS

(D) RIGID FIBER OPTICS   (E) RELAY LENS   (F) FLEXIBLE FIBER OPTICS

FIGURE 2-17   Special video lenses

The dual-split and tri-split lenses use only one camera to produce multiple scenes. These are useful for viewing the same scene with different magnifications or different scenes with the same or different magnifications. Using only one camera can reduce cost and increases reliability. These lenses are useful when two or three views are required and only one camera was installed.

The right-angle lens permits a camera using a wide-angle lens installed to view a scene that is perpendicular to the camera's optical axis. There are no restrictions on the focal lengths so they can be used in wide- or narrow-angle applications.

The flexible and rigid coherent fiber-optic lenses are used to mount a camera several inches to several feet away from the front lens as might be required to view from the opposite side of a wall or in a hazardous environment. The function of the fiber-optic bundle is to transfer the focused visual image from one location to another. This may be useful for: (1) protecting the camera, and (2) locating the lens in one environment (outdoors) and the camera in another (indoors).

2.6 CAMERAS

The camera lens focuses the visual scene image onto the camera sensor area point-by-point and the camera electronics transforms the visible image into an electrical signal. The camera video signal (containing all picture information) is made up of frequencies from 30 cycles per second, or 30 hertz (Hz), to 4.2 million cycles per second, or 4.2 megahertz (MHz). The video signal is transmitted via a cable (or wireless) to the monitor display.

Almost all security cameras in use today are color or monochrome CCD with the rapid emergence of CMOS types. These cameras are available as low-cost single printed circuit board (PCB) cameras with small lenses already built in, with or without a housing used for covert and overt surveillance applications. More expensive cameras in a housing are larger and more rugged and have a C or CS mechanical mount for accepting any type of lens. These cameras have higher resolution and light sensitivity and other electrical input/output features suitable for multiple camera CCTV systems. The CCD and CMOS cameras with LED IR illumination arrays can extend the use of these cameras to nighttime use. For LLL applications, the ICCD and IR cameras provide the highest sensitivity and detection capability.

Significant advancements in camera technology have been made in the last few years particularly in the use of digital signal processing (DSP) in the camera, and development of the IP camera. All security cameras manufactured between the 1950s and 1980s were the vacuum tube type, either vidicon, silicon, or LLL types using silicon intensified target (SIT) and intensified SIT (ISIT). In the 1980s the CCD and CMOS solid-state video image sensors were developed and remain the mainstay in the security industry. Increased consumer demand for video recorders using CCD sensors in camcorders and the CMOS sensor in digital still frame cameras caused a technology explosion and made these small, high resolution, high sensitivity, monochrome and color solid-state cameras available for security systems.

The security industry now has at its disposal both analog and digital surveillance cameras. Up until the mid-1990s analog cameras dominated, with only rare use of DSP electronics, and the digital Internet camera was only being introduced to the security market. Advances in solid-state circuitry, the demand from the consumer market and the availability of the Internet were responsible for the rapid use of digital cameras for security applications.

2.6.1 The Scanning Process

Two methods used in the camera and monitor video scanning process are *raster* scanning and *progressive* scanning. In the past, analog video systems have all used the raster scanning technique, however, newer digital systems are now using progressive scanning. All cameras use some form of scanning to generate the video picture. A block diagram of the CCTV camera and a brief description of the analog raster scanning process and video signal are shown in Figures 2-8, 2-9, 2-18, and 2-19.

The camera sensor converts the optical image from the lens into an electrical signal. The camera electronics process the video signal and generate a composite video signal containing the picture information (luminance and color) and horizontal and vertical synchronizing pulses. Signals are transmitted in what is called a *frame* of picture

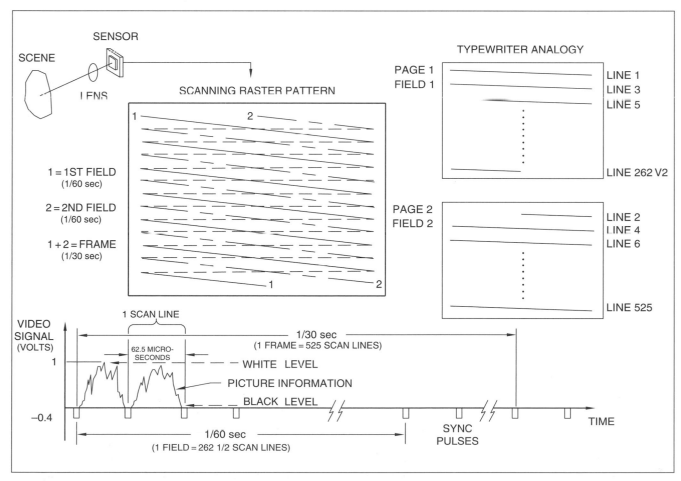

FIGURE 2-18   Analog video scanning process and video display signal

video, made up of two *fields* of information. Each field is transmitted in 1/60 of a second and the entire frame in 1/30 of a second, for a repetition rate of 30 frames per second (fps). In the United States, this format is the Electronic Industries Association (EIA) standard called the NTSC (National Television System Committee) system. The European standard uses 625 horizontal lines with a field taking 1/50 of a second and a frame 1/25 of a second and a repetition rate of 25 fps.

2.6.1.1   Raster Scanning

In the NTSC system the first picture field is created by scanning $262\frac{1}{2}$ horizontal lines. The second field of the frame contains the second $262\frac{1}{2}$ lines, which are synchronized so that they fall between the gaps of the first field lines thus producing one completely interlaced picture frame containing 525 lines. The scan lines of the second field fall *exactly* halfway between the lines of the first field resulting in a 2-to-1 *interlace* system. As shown in Figure 2-18 the first field starts at the upper-left corner (of the camera sensor or the CRT monitor) and progresses down the sensor (or screen), line by line, until it ends at the bottom center of the scan.

Likewise the second field starts at the top center of the screen and ends at the lower-right corner. Each time one line in the field traverses from the left side of the scan to the right it corresponds to one horizontal line as shown in the video waveform at the bottom of Figure 2-18. The video waveform consists of negative synchronization pulses and positive picture information. The horizontal and vertical synchronization pulses are used by the video monitor (and VCR, DVR, or video printer) to synchronize the video picture and paint an exact replica in time and intensity of the camera scanning function onto the monitor face. Black picture information is indicated on the waveform at the bottom (approximately 0 volts) and the white picture information at the top (1 volt). The amplitude of a standard NTSC signal is 1.4 volts peak to peak. In the 525-line system the *picture* information consists of approximately 512 lines. The lines with no picture information are necessary for vertical blanking, which is the time when the camera electronics or the beam in the monitor CRT moves from the bottom to the top to start a new field.

Random-interlace cameras do not provide complete synchronization between the first and the second fields. The horizontal and the vertical scan frequencies are not locked together and therefore fields do not interlace exactly. This condition, however, results in an acceptable picture, and the asynchronous condition is difficult to detect. The 2-to-1 interlace system has an advantage when multiple cameras are used with multiple monitors and/or recorders in that they prevent jump or jitter when switching from one camera to the next.

The scanning process for solid-state cameras is different. The solid-state sensor consists of an array of very small picture elements (pixels) that are read out serially (sequentially) by the camera electronics to produce the same NTSC format—525 TV lines in 1/30 of a second (30 fps)—as shown in Figure 2-19.

The use of digital cameras and digital monitors has changed the way the camera and monitor signals are processed, transmitted, and displayed. The final presentation on the monitor looks similar to the analog method but instead of seeing 525 horizontal lines (NTSC system), individual pixels are seen in a *row* and *column* format. In the digital system the camera scene is divided into rows and columns of individual pixels (small points in the scene) each representing the light intensity and color for each point in the scene. The digitized scene signal is transmitted to the digital display be it LCD, plasma, or other, and reproduced on the monitor screen pixel-by-pixel providing a faithful representation of the original scene.

2.6.1.2   Digital and Progressive Scan

The digital scanning is accomplished in either the 2-to-1 interlace mode as in the analog system, or in a *progressive* mode. In the progressive mode each line is scanned in linear sequence: line 1, then line 2, line 3, etc. Solid-state camera sensors and monitor displays can be manufactured with a variety of horizontal and vertical pixels formats. The standard aspect ratio is 4:3 as in the analog system, the wide-screen 16:9, and others are used. Likewise there are many different combinations of the number of pixels in the sensor and display available. Some standard formats for color CCD cameras are $512\,h \times 492\,v$ for 330 TV line resolution and $768\,h \times 494\,v$ for 480 TV line resolution, and for color LCD monitors is $1280\,h \times 1024\,v$.

2.6.2   Solid-State Cameras

Video security cameras have gone through rapid technological change during the last half of the 1980s to the present. For decades the vidicon tube camera was the only security camera available. In the 1980s the more sensitive and rugged silicon-diode tube camera was the best available. In the late 1980s the invention and development of the digital CCD and later the CMOS cameras replaced the tube camera. This technology coincided with rapid advancement in DSP in cameras, the IP camera, and use of digital transmission of the video signal over local and wide area networks and the Internet.

The two generic solid-state cameras accounting for most security applications are the CCD and the CMOS.

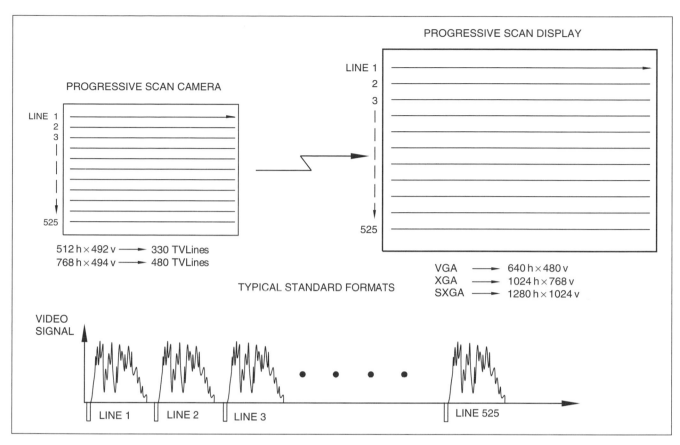

FIGURE 2-19 Digital and progressive scanning process and video display signal

The first generation of solid-state cameras available from most manufacturers had 2/3 inch (sensor diagonal) and 1/2-inch sensor formats. As the technology improved, smaller formats evolved. Most solid-state cameras in use today are available in three image sensor formats: 1/2-, 1/3-, and 1/4-inch. The 1/2-inch format produces higher resolution and sensitivity at a higher cost. The 1/2-inch and smaller formats permitted the use of smaller, less expensive lenses as compared with the larger formats. Many manufacturers now produce 1/3-inch and 1/4-inch format cameras with excellent resolution and light sensitivity. Solid-state sensor cameras are superior to their predecessors because of their: (1) precise, repeatable pixel geometry, (2) low power requirements, (3) small size, (4) excellent color rendition and stability, and (5) ruggedness and long life expectancy. At present, solid-state cameras have settled into three main categories: (1) analog, (2) digital, and (3) Internet.

2.6.2.1 Analog

Analog cameras have been with the industry since CCTV has been used in security. Their electronics are straightforward and the technology is still used in many applications.

2.6.2.2 Digital

Since the second half of 1990s there has been an increased use of DSP in cameras. It significantly improves the performance of the camera by: (1) automatically adjusting to large light level changes (eliminating the automatic-iris), (2) integrating the VMD into the camera, and (3) automatically switching the camera from color operation to higher sensitivity monochrome operation, as well as other features and enhancements.

2.6.2.3 Internet

The most recent camera technology advancement is manifest in the IP camera. This camera is configured with electronics that connects to the Internet, WWW network through an Internet service provider (ISP). Each camera is provided with a registered Internet address and can transmit the video image anywhere on the network. This is really remote video monitoring at its best! The camera site is viewed from anywhere by entering the camera Internet address (ID number) and proper password. Password security is used so that only authorized users can enter the website and view the camera image. Two-way communication is used so that the user can control camera parameters and direct the camera operation (pan, tilt, zoom, etc.) from the monitoring site.

2.6.3   Low-Light-Level Intensified Camera

When a security application requires viewing during nighttime conditions where the available light is moonlight, starlight, or other residual reflected light, and the surveillance must be covert (no active illumination like IR LEDs), LLL intensified CCD cameras are used. The ICCD cameras have sensitivities between 100 and 1000 times higher than the best solid-state cameras. The increased sensitivity is obtained through the use of a *light amplifier* mounted in between the lens and the CCD sensor. LLL cameras cost between 10 and 20 times more than CCD cameras. Chapter 19 describes the characteristics of these cameras.

2.6.4   Thermal Imaging Camera

An alternative to the ICCD camera is the thermal IR camera. Visual cameras see only visible light energy from the blue end of the visible spectrum to the red end (approximately 400–700 nanometers). Some monochrome cameras see beyond the visible region into the near-IR region of the spectrum up to 1000 nanometers (nm). This IR energy, however, is not thermal IR energy. Thermal IR cameras using thermal sensors respond to thermal energy in the 3–5 micrometer (μm) and 8–14 μm

range. The IR sensors respond to the changes in *heat* (thermal) energy emitted by the targets in the scene. Thermal imaging cameras can operate in complete darkness. They require no visible or IR illumination whatever. They are truly passive nighttime monochrome imaging sensors. They can detect humans and any other warm objects (animals, vehicle engines, ships, aircraft, warm/hot spots in buildings) or other objects against a scene background.

2.6.5   Panoramic 360° Camera

Powerful mathematical techniques combined with the unique 360° panoramic lens (see Section 2.5.4) have made possible a 360° panoramic camera. In operation the lens collects and focuses the 360° horizontal by up to 90° vertical scene (one-half of a sphere, a hemisphere) onto the camera sensor. The image takes the form of a "donut" on the sensor (Figure 2-20).

The camera/lens is located at the origin (0). The scene is represented by the surface of the hemisphere. As shown, a small part (slice) of the scene area (A,B,C,D) is "mapped" onto the sensor as a,b,c,d. In this way the full scene is mapped onto the sensor. Direct presentation of the donut-ring video image onto the monitor does not result in a useful picture to work with. That is where the use of a

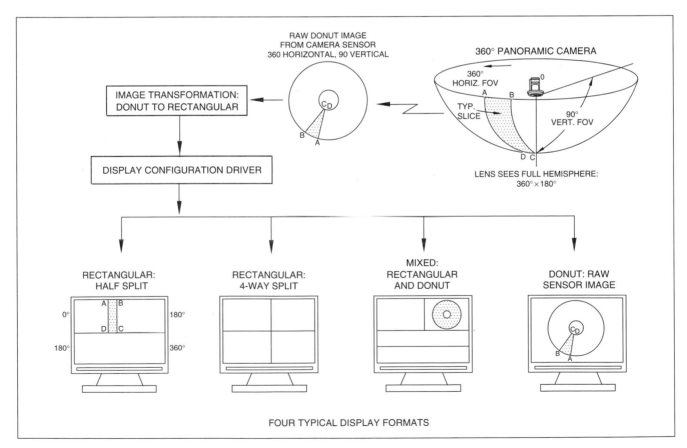

FIGURE 2-20   Panoramic 360° camera

powerful mathematical algorithm comes in. Digital processing in the computer using the algorithm transforms the donut-shaped image into the normal format seen on a monitor, i.e. horizontal and vertical.

All of the 0 to 360° horizontal by 90° vertical images cannot be presented on a monitor in a useful way – there is just too much picture "squeezed" into the small screen area. This condition is solved by computer software by looking at only a section of the entire scene at any particular time.

The main attributes of the panoramic system are: (1) captures a full 360° FOV, (2) can digitally pan/tilt to anywhere in the scene and digitally zoom any scene area, (3) has no moving parts (no motors, etc. that can wear out), and (4) multiple operators can view any part of the scene in real-time or at a later time.

The panoramic camera requires a high resolution camera since so much scene information is contained in the image. Camera technology has progressed so that these digital cameras are available and can present a good image of a zoomed-in portion of the panoramic scene.

2.7 TRANSMISSION

By definition, the camera must be remotely located from the monitor and therefore the video signal must be transmitted by some means from one location to another. In security applications, the distance between the camera and the monitor may be from tens of feet to many miles or perhaps completely around the globe. The transmission path may be inside buildings, outside buildings, above ground, under ground, through the atmosphere, or in almost any environment imaginable. For this reason the transmission means must be carefully assessed and an optimum choice of hardware made to satisfactorily transmit the video signal from the camera to the monitoring site. There are many ways to transmit the video signal from the camera to the monitoring site. Figure 2-21 shows some examples of transmission cables.

The signal can be analog or digital. The signal can be transmitted via electrical conductors using coaxial cable or UTP, by fiber optic, by LAN or WAN, intranet or Internet.

Particular attention should be paid to transmission means when transmitting color video signals since the color signal is significantly more complex and susceptible to distortion than monochrome. Chapters 6 and 7 describe and analyze the characteristics, advantages, and disadvantages of all of the transmission means and the hardware available to transmit the video signal.

2.7.1 Hard-Wired

There are several hard-wired means for transmitting a video signal, including coaxial cable, UTP, LAN, WAN, intranet, Internet, and fiber-optic cable. Fiber-optic cable

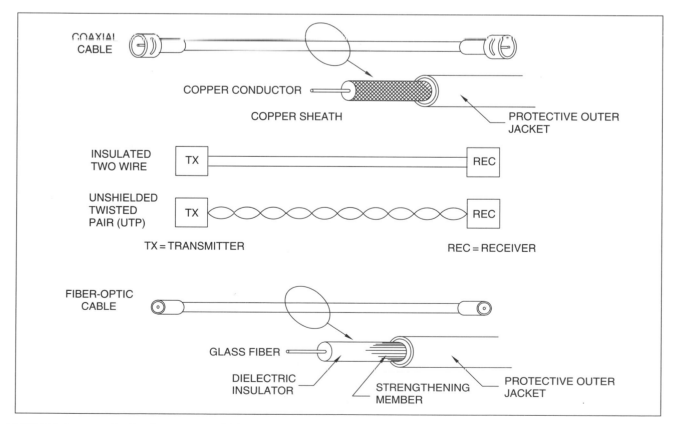

FIGURE 2-21 Hard wired copper and fiber-optic transmission means

is used for long distances and when there is interfering electrical noise. Local area networks and Internet connections are digital transmission techniques used in larger security systems and where the signal must be transmitted over existing computer networks or over long distances.

2.7.1.1   Coaxial Cable

The most common video signal transmission method is the coaxial cable. This cable has been used since the inception of CCTV and continues to be used to this day. The cable is inexpensive, easy to terminate at the camera and monitor ends, and transmits a faithful video signal with little or no distortion or loss. This cable has a 75 ohm electrical impedance which matches the impedance of the camera and monitor insuring a distortion-free video image. This coaxial cable has a copper electrical shield and center conductor works well over distances up to 1000 feet.

2.7.1.2   Unshielded Twisted Pair

In the 1990s unshielded twisted pair (UTP) video transmission came into vogue. The technique uses a transmitter at the camera and a receiver at the monitor with two twisted copper wires connecting them. Several reasons for its increased popularity are: (1) can be used over longer distances than coaxial cable, (2) uses inexpensive wire, (3) many locations already have two-wire twisted-pair installed, (4) low-cost transmitter and receiver, and (5) higher electrical noise immunity as compared to coaxial cable. The UTP using a sophisticated electronic transmitter and receiver can transmit the video signal up to 2000–3000 feet.

2.7.1.3   LAN, WAN, Intranet and Internet

The evolution of the LAN, WAN, intranet and Internet revolutionized the transmission of video signals in a new form—digital—which significantly expanded the scope and effectiveness of video for security systems. The widespread use of business computers and consequent use of these networks provided an existing digital network protocol and communications suitable for video transmission. The Internet and WWW attained widespread use in the late 1990s and truly revolutionized digital video transmission. This global computer network provided the digital backbone path to transmit digital video, audio, and command signals from anywhere on the globe.

The video signal transmission techniques described so far provide a means for real-time transmission of a video signal, requiring a full 4.2 MHz bandwidth to reproduce real-time motion. When these techniques cannot be used for real-time video, alternative digital techniques are used. In these systems, a non-real-time video transmission takes place, so that some scene action is lost. Depending on the action in the scene, the resolution, from near real-time

(15 fps.) to slow-scan (a few frames/sec) of the video image are transmitted. The digitized and compressed video signal is transmitted over a LAN or Internet network and decompressed and reconstructed at the receiver/monitoring site.

2.7.2   Wireless

In legacy analog video surveillance systems, it is often more economical or beneficial to transmit the real-time video signal without cable—wireless—from the camera to the monitor using a radio frequency (RF) or IR atmospheric link. In digital video systems using digital transmission, the use of wireless networks (WiFi) permits routing the video and control signals to *any* remote location. In both the analog and the digital systems some form of video scrambling or encryption is often used to remove the possibility of eavesdropping by unauthorized personnel outside the system. Three important applications for wireless transmission are: (1) covert and portable rapid deployment video installations, (2) building-to-building transmission over a roadway, and (3) parking lot light poles to building. The Federal Communications Commission (FCC) restricts some wireless transmitting devices using microwave frequencies or RF to government and law enforcement use but has given approval for many RF and microwave transmitters for general security use. These FCC approved devices operate above the normal television frequency bands at approximately 920 MHz, 2.4 GHz, and 5.8 GHz. The atmospheric IR link is used when a high security link is required. This link does not require an FCC approval and transmits a video image over a narrow beam of visible light or near-IR energy. The beam is very difficult to intercept (tap). Figure 2-22 illustrates some of the wireless transmission techniques available today.

2.7.3   Fiber Optics

Fiber-optic transmission technology has advanced significantly in the last 5–10 years and represents a highly reliable, secure means of transmission. Fiber-optic transmission holds several significant advantages over other hard-wired systems: (1) very long transmission paths up to many miles without any significant degradation in the video signal with monochrome or color, (2) immunity to external electrical disturbances from weather or electrical equipment, (3) very wide bandwidth, permitting one or more video, control, and audio signals to be multiplexed on a single fiber, and (4) resistance to tapping (eavesdropping) and therefore a very secure transmission means.

While the installation and termination of fiber-optic cable requires a more skilled technician, it is well within the capability of qualified security installers. Many hard-wired installations requiring the optimum color and resolution rendition use fiber-optic cable.

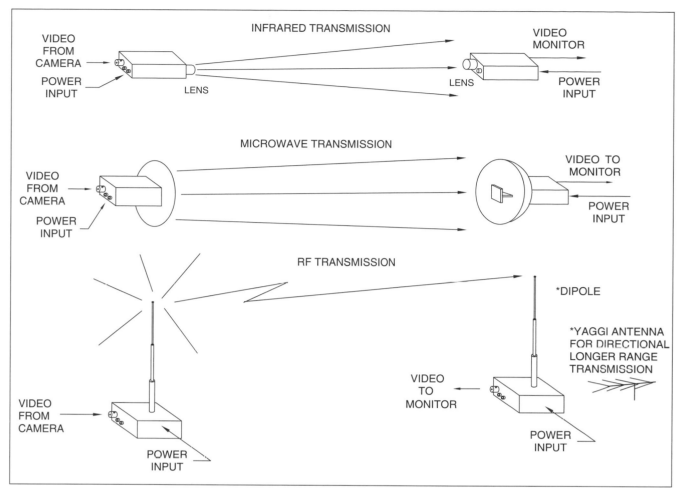

FIGURE 2-22   RF, microwave and IR video transmission links

2.8   SWITCHERS

The video switcher accepts video signals from many different video cameras and connects them to one or more monitors or recorders. Using manual or automatic activation or an alarming signal input, the switcher selects one or more of the cameras and directs its video signal to a specified monitor, recorder, or some other device or location.

2.8.1   Standard

There are four basic switcher types: manual, sequential, homing, and alarming. Figure 2-23 shows how these are connected into the video security system.

The manual switcher connects one camera at a time to the monitor, recorder, or printer. The sequential switcher automatically switches the cameras in sequence to the output device. The operator can override the automatic sequence with the homing sequential switcher. The alarming switcher connects the alarmed camera to the output device automatically, when an alarm is received.

2.8.2   Microprocessor-Controlled

When the security system requires many cameras in various locations with multiple monitors and other alarm input functions, a microprocessor-controlled switcher and keyboard is used to manage these additional requirements (Figure 2-24).

In large security systems the switcher is microprocessor controlled and can switch hundreds of cameras to dozens of monitors, recorders, or video printers via an RS-232 or other communication control link. Numerous manufacturers make comprehensive keyboard-operated, computer-controlled consoles that integrate the functions of the switcher, pan/tilt pointing, automatic scanning, automatic preset pointing for pan/tilt systems, and many other functions. The power of the software-programmable console resides in its flexibility, expandability, and ability to accommodate a large variety of applications and changes in facility design. In place of a dedicated hardware system built for each specific application this computer-controlled system can be configured via software for the application. Chapter 11 describes types of switchers and their functions and applications.

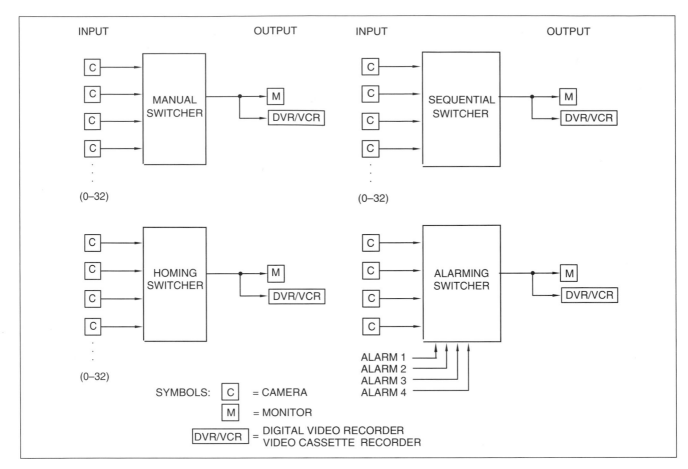

FIGURE 2-23   Basic video switcher types

2.9   QUADS AND MULTIPLEXERS

A quad or a multiplexer is used when multiple camera scenes need to be displayed on one video monitor. It is interposed between the cameras and the monitor, accepts multiple camera inputs, memorizes the scenes from each camera, compresses them, and then displays multiple scenes on a single video monitor. Equipment is available to provide 2, 4, 9, 16, and up to 32 separate video scenes on one single monitor. Figure 2-25 shows a block diagram of quad and multiplexer systems.

The most popular presentation is the quad screen showing four pictures. This presentation significantly improves camera viewing ability in multi-camera systems, decreases security guard fatigue, and requires three fewer monitors in a four-camera system. There is a loss of resolution when more than one scene is presented on the monitor with resolution decreasing as the number of scenes increases. One-quarter of the resolution of a full screen is obtained on a quad display (half in horizontal and half in vertical). Quads and multiplexers have front panel controls so that: (1) a full screen image of a camera can be selected, (2) multiple cameras can be displayed (quad, 9, etc.), or

(3) the full screen images of all cameras can be sequentially switched with dwell times for each camera, set by the operator. Chapter 12 describes video quads and multiplexers in detail.

2.10   MONITORS

Video monitors can be divided into several categories: (1) monochrome, (2) color, (3) CRT, (4) LCD, (5) plasma, and (6) computer display. Contrary to a popular misconception, larger video monitors do not necessarily have better picture resolution or the ability to increase the amount of intelligence available in the picture. All US NTSC security monitors have 525 horizontal lines—regardless of their size or whether they are monochrome or color; therefore the vertical resolution is about the same regardless of the CRT monitor size. The horizontal resolution is determined by the system bandwidth. With the NTSC limitation the best picture quality is obtained by choosing a monitor having resolution equal to or better than the camera or transmission link bandwidth. With the use of a higher resolution computer monitor and corresponding higher resolution camera and commensurate bandwidth to match, higher resolution video images are

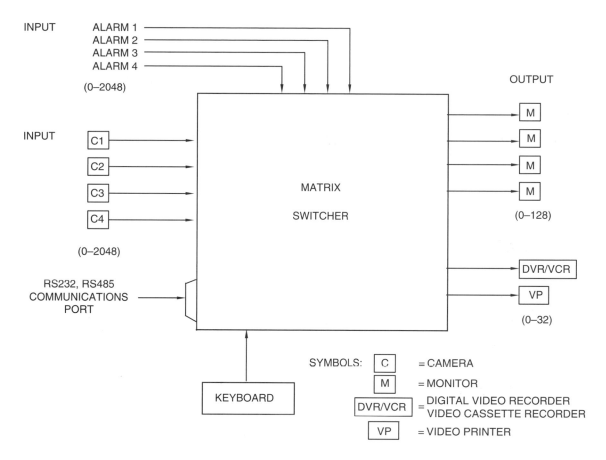

FIGURE 2-24   Microprocessor controlled switcher and keyboard

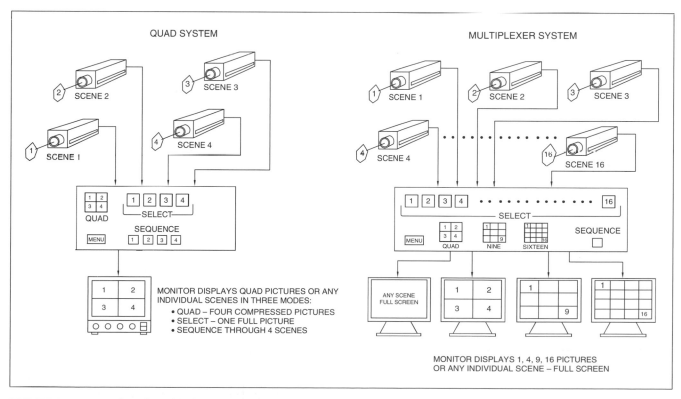

FIGURE 2-25   Quad and multiplexer block diagrams

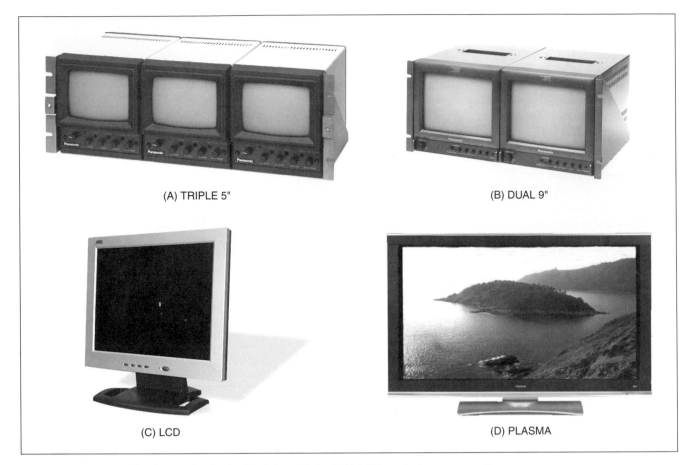

(A) TRIPLE 5"

(B) DUAL 9"

(C) LCD

(D) PLASMA

FIGURE 2-26   Standard 5- and 9-inch single/multiple CRT, LCD and plasma monitors

obtained. Chapter 8 gives more detailed characteristics of monochrome and color monitors used in the security industry. Figure 2-26 shows representative examples of video monitors.

2.10.1   Monochrome

Until the late 1990s the most popular monitor used in CCTV systems was the monochrome CRT monitor. It is still used and is available in sizes ranging from a 1-inch-diagonal viewfinder to a large 27-inch-diagonal CRT. By far the most popular monochrome monitor size is the 9-inch-diagonal that optimizes video viewing for a person seated about 3 feet away. A second reason for its popularity is that two of these monitors fit into the standard EIA 19-inch-wide rack-mount panel. Figure 2-26b shows two 9-inch monitors in a dual rack-mounted version. A triple rack-mount version of a 5-inch-diagonal monitor is used when space is at a premium. The triple rack-mounted monitor is popular, since three fit conveniently into the 19-inch EIA rack. The optimum viewing distance for the triple 5-inch-diagonal monitor is about 1.5 feet.

2.10.2   Color

Color monitors are now in widespread use and range in size from 3 to 27 inch diagonal and have required viewing distances and capabilities similar to those of monochrome monitors. Since color monitors require three different-colored dots to produce one pixel of information on the monitor, they have lower horizontal resolution than monochrome monitors. Popular color monitor sizes are 13, 15, and 17 inch diagonal.

2.10.3   CRT, LCD, Plasma Displays

The video security picture is displayed on three basic types of monitor screens: (1) cathode ray tube (CRT), (2) liquid crystal display (LCD), and most recently (3) the plasma display (Figure 2-26d). The analog CRT has seen excellent service from the inception of video and continues as a strong contender providing a low-cost, reliable security monitor. The digital LCD monitor is growing in popularity because of its smaller size (smaller depth), 2–3 inches vs. 12–20 inches for the CRT. The LCD is an all solid-state display accepts the VGA computer signal. Most small (3–10 inch diagonal) and many large (10–17 inch diagonal)

LCD monitors also accept an analog video input. The most recent monitor entry into the security market is the digital plasma display. This premium display excels in resolution and brightness and viewing angle and produces the highest quality image in the industry. It is also the most expensive. Screen sizes range from 20 to 42 inches diagonal. Overall depths are small and range in size from 3 to 4 inches. They are available in 4:3 and HDTV 16 : 9 format.

2.10.4 Audio/Video

Many monitors have built-in audio channel with speakers, to produce audio and video simultaneously.

2.11 RECORDERS

The video camera, transmission means, and monitor provide the remote eyes for the security guard but as soon as the action or event is over the image disappears from the monitor screen forever. When a permanent record of the live video scene is required a VCR, DVR, network recorder, or optical disk recorder is used (Figure 2-27).

The video image can be recorded in real-time, near real-time, or TL. The VCRs record the video signal on a magnetic tape cassette with a maximum real-time recording time of 6 hours and near real-time of 24 hours. When extended periods of recording are required (longer than the 6 hour real-time cassette), a TL recorder is used. In the TL process the video picture is not recorded continuously (real-time), but rather "snap-shots" are recorded. These snap shots are spread apart in time by a fraction of a second or even seconds so that the total elapsed time for the recording can extend for hundreds of hours. Some present TL systems record over an elapsed time of 1280 hours.

The DVR records the video image on a computer magnetic HD(hard drive) and the optical disk storage on an optical disk media. The DVR and optical disk systems have a significant advantage over the VCR with respect to retrieval time of a particular video frame. VCRs take many minutes to fast-forward or fast-rewind the magnetic tape to locate a particular frame on the tape. Retrieval times on DVRs and optical disks are typically a fraction of

a second. The VCR cassette tape is transportable and the DVR and optical disk systems are available with or without removable disks. This means that the video images (digital data) can be transported to remote locations or stored in a vault for safekeeping. The removable DVR and optical disks are about the same size as Victor Home System (VHS) cassettes. Chapter 9 describes analog and digital video recording equipment in detail. The digital DVR technology has all but replaced the analog VCR.

2.11.1 Video Cassette Recorder (VCR)

Magnetic storage media have been used universally to record the video image. The VCR uses the standard VHS cassette format. The 8 mm Sony format is used in portable surveillance equipment because of its smaller size. Super VHS and Hi-8 formats are used to obtain higher resolution. VCRs can be subdivided into two classes: real-time and TL. The TL recorder has significantly different mechanical and electrical features permitting it to take snapshots of a scene at predetermined (user-selectable) intervals. It can also record in real-time when activated by an alarm or other input command. Real-time recorders can record up to 6 hours in monochrome or color. Time-lapse VCRs are available for recording time-lapse sequences up to 720 hours.

2.11.2 Digital Video Recorder (DVR)

The DVR has emerged as the new generation of magnetic recorder of choice. A magnetic HD like those used in a microcomputer can store many thousands of images and many hours of video in digital form. The rapid implementation and success of the DVR has resulted from the availability of inexpensive digital magnetic memory storage devices and the advancements made in digital signal compression techniques. Present DVRs are available in single channel, 4 and 16 channels and may be cascaded to provide many more channels.

A significant feature of the DVR is the ability to access (retrieve) a particular frame or recorded time period anywhere on the disk in a fraction of a second. The digital

| (A) SINGLE CHANNEL DVR | (B) 16 CHANNEL DVR | (C) 32 CHANNEL NVR |

FIGURE 2-27   DVR and NVR video disk storage equipment

technology also allows making many generations (copies) of the stored video images without any errors or degradation of the image.

2.11.3 Optical Disk

When very large volumes of video images need to be recorded, an optical disk system is used. Optical disks have a much larger video image database capacity than magnetic disks given the same physical space they occupy. These disks can record hundreds of times longer than their magnetic counterparts.

2.12 HARD-COPY VIDEO PRINTERS

A hard-copy printout of a video image is often required as evidence in court, as a tool for apprehending a vandal or thief, or as a duplicate record of some document or person. The printout is produced by a hard-copy video printer, a thermal printer that "burns" the video image onto coated paper or an ink-jet or laser printer. The thermal technique used by many hard-copy printer manufacturers produces excellent-quality images in monochrome or color. Figure 2-28 shows a monochrome thermal printer and a sample of the hard-copy image quality it produces.

In operation, the image displayed on the monitor or played back from the recorder is immediately memorized by the printer and printed out in less than 10 seconds. This is particularly useful if an intrusion or unauthorized act has occurred and been observed by a security guard. An automatic alarm or a security guard can initiate printing the image of the alarm area or of the suspect and the

printout can then be given to another guard to take action. For courtroom uses, time, date, and any other information can be annotated on the printed image. Chapter 10 describes hard-copy video printer systems in detail.

2.13 ANCILLARY EQUIPMENT

Most video security systems require additional accessories and equipment, including: (1) camera housings, (2) camera pan/tilt mechanisms and mounts, (3) camera identifiers, (4) VMDs, (5) image splitters/inserters, and (6) image combiners. These are described in more detail in Chapters 13, 15, 16, and 17. The two accessories most often used with the basic camera, monitor and transmission link, described previously are camera housings and pan/tilt mounts. Outdoor housings are used to protect the camera and lens from vandalism and the environment. Indoor housings are used primarily to prevent vandalism and for aesthetic reasons. The motorized pan/tilt mechanisms rotate and point the system camera and lens via commands from a remote control console.

2.13.1 Camera Housings

Indoor and outdoor camera housings protect cameras and lenses from dirt, dust, harmful chemicals, the environment, and vandalism. The most common housings are rectangular metal or plastic products, formed from high impact indoor or outdoor plastic, painted steel, or stainless steel (Figure 2-29). Other shapes and types include cylindrical (tube), corner-mount, ceiling- mount, and dome housings.

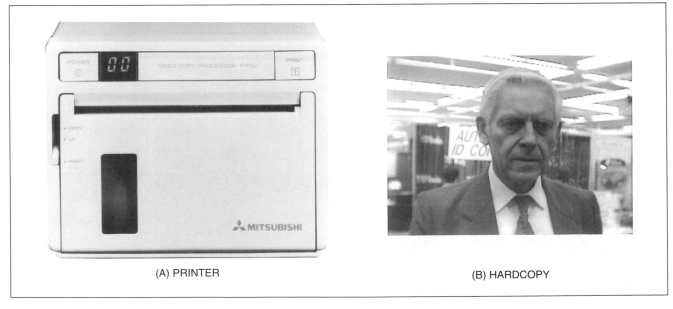

(A) PRINTER   (B) HARDCOPY

FIGURE 2-28   Thermal monochrome video printer and hard copy

FIGURE 2-29 Standard indoor/outdoor video housings: (a) corner, (b) elevator corner, (c) ceiling, (d) outdoor environmental rectangular, (e) dome, (f) plug and play

2.13.1.1 Standard-rectangular

The rectangular type housing is the most popular. It protects the camera from the environment and provides a window for the lens to view the scene. The housings are available for indoor or outdoor use with a weatherproof and tamper resistant design. Options include: heaters, fans, and window washers.

2.13.1.2 Dome

A significant part of video surveillance is accomplished using cameras housed in the dome housing configuration. The dome camera housing can range from a simple fixed monochrome or color camera in a hemispherical dome to a "speed-dome" housing having a high resolution color camera with remote controlled pan/tilt/zoom/focus. Other options include presets and image stabilization. The dome-type housing consists of a plastic hemispherical dome on the bottom half. The housing can be clear, tinted, or treated with a partially transmitting optical coating that allows the camera to see in any direction. In a freestanding application (e.g. on a pole, pedestal, or overhang), the top half of the housing consists of a protective cover and a means for attaching the dome to the structure. When the dome housing is mounted in a ceiling, a simpler housing cover is provided and mounted above the ceiling level to support the dome.

2.13.1.3 Specialty

There are many other specialty housings for mounting in or on elevators, ceilings, walls, tunnels, pedestals, hallways, etc. These special types include: explosion proof, bullet proof and extreme environmental construction for artic and desert use.

2.13.1.4 Plug and Play

In an effort to reduce installation time for video surveillance cameras, manufacturers have combined the camera, lens, and housing in one assembly ready to be mounted on a ceiling, wall or pole and plugged into the power source and video transmission cable. These assemblies are available in the form of domes, corner mounts, ceiling mounts, etc. making for easy installation in indoor or outdoor applications. Chapter 15 describes these camera housing assemblies and their specific applications in detail.

2.13.2 Pan/Tilt Mounts

To extend the angle of coverage of a CCTV lens/camera system a motorized pan/tilt mechanism is often used. Figure 2-30 shows three generic outdoor pan/tilt types: top-mounted, side-mounted, and dome camera.

The pan/tilt motorized mounting platform permits the camera and lens to rotate horizontally (pan) or vertically (tilt) when it receives an electrical command from the central monitoring site. Thus the camera lens is not limited by its inherent FOV and can view a much larger area of a scene. A camera mounted on a pan/tilt platform is usually provided with a zoom lens. The zoom lens varies the FOV in the pointing direction of the camera/lens from a command from the central security console. The combination of the pan/tilt and zoom lens provides the widest angular coverage for video surveillance. There is one disadvantage with the pan/tilt/zoom configuration compared with the fixed camera installation. When the camera and lens are

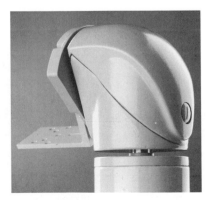

| (A) TOP-MOUNTED | (B) SIDE-MOUNTED | (C) INDOOR DOME |

FIGURE 2-30   Video pan/tilt mechanisms: top-mounted, side-mounted, indoor dome

pointing in a particular direction via the pan/tilt platform, most of the other scene area the camera is designed to cover is not being viewed. This dead area or dead time is unacceptable in many security applications and therefore a careful consideration should be given to the adequacy of their wide-FOV pan/tilt design. Pan/tilt platforms range from small, indoor, lightweight units that only pan, up to large, outdoor, environmental designs carrying large cameras, zoom lenses, and large housings. Choosing the correct pan/tilt mechanism is important since it generally requires more service and maintenance than any other part of the video system. Chapter 17 describes several generic pan/tilt designs and their features.

2.13.3 Video Motion Detector (VMD)

Another important component in a video surveillance system is a VMD that produces an alarm signal based on a change in the video scene. The VMD can be built into the camera or be a separate component inserted between the camera and the monitor software in a computer. The VMD electronics, either analog or digital, store the video frames, compare subsequent frames to the stored frames, and then determine whether the scene has changed. In operation the VMD digital electronics decides whether the change is significant and whether to call it an alarm to alert the guard or some equipment, or declare it a false alarm. Chapter 13 describes various VMD electronics, their capabilities and their limitations.

2.13.4 Screen Splitter

The electronic or optical screen splitter takes a part of several camera scenes (two, three, or more), combines the scenes and displays them on one monitor. The splitters do not compress the image. In an *optical* splitter the image combining is implemented optically at the camera lens and requires no electronics. The *electronic* splitter/combiner is located between the camera output and the monitor input. Chapter 16 describes these devices in detail.

2.13.5 Camera Video Annotation

2.13.5.1 Camera ID

When multiple cameras are used in a video system some means must be provided to identify the camera. The system uses a camera identifier component that electronically assigns an alphanumeric code and/or name to each camera displayed on a monitor, recorded on a recorder, or printed on a printer. Alphanumeric and symbol character generators are available to annotate the video signal with the names of cameras, locations in a building, etc.

2.13.5.2 Time and Date

When time and date is required on the video image a time/date generator is used to annotate the video picture. This information is mandatory for any prosecution or courtroom procedure.

2.13.6 Image Reversal

Occasionally video surveillance systems use a single mirror to view the scene. This mirror reverses the video image from the normal left-to-right to a right-to-left (reversed image). The image reversal unit corrects the reversal. Chapter 16 describes this device.

2.14 SUMMARY

Video surveillance serves as the remote eyes for management and the security force. It provides security personnel with advance notice of breeches in security, hostile, and terrorist acts, and is a part of the plan to protect personnel and assets. It is a critical subsystem for any comprehensive security plan. In this chapter an introduction to most of the current video technology and equipment has been described.

Lighting plays an important role in determining whether a satisfactory video picture will be obtained with monochrome and color cameras and LLL ICCD cameras. Thermal IR cameras are insensitive to light and only require temperature differences between the target and the background.

There are many types of lenses available for video systems: FFL, vari-focal, zoom, pinhole, panoramic, etc. The vari-focal and zoom lenses extend the FOV of the FFL lens. The panoramic 360° lens provides entire viewing of the scene. The proper choice of lens is necessary to maximize the intelligence obtained from the scene.

Many types of video cameras are available: color, monochrome (with or without IR illumination), LLL intensified, and thermal IR, analog and digital, simple and full featured, daytime and nighttime. There are cameras with built-in VMD to alert security guards and improve their ability to detect and locate personnel and be alerted to activity in the scene.

An important component of the video system is the analog or digital video signal transmission means from the camera to the remote site, to the monitoring and recording site. Hard wire or fiber optics is best if the situation permits. Analog works for short distances and digital for long distances. The Internet works globally.

In multiple camera systems the quad and multiplexers permit multi-camera displays on one monitor. Fewer monitors in the security room can improve guard performance.

The CRT monitor is still a good choice for many video applications. The LCD is the solid-state digital replacement for the CRT. The plasma displays provides an all solid state design that has the highest resolution, brightness, and largest viewing angle, but at the highest cost.

Until about the year 2000 the only practical means for recording a permanent image of the scene was the VCR real-time or TL recorder. Now, new and upgraded systems replace the VCR with the DVR recorder with its increased reliability and fast search and retrieve capabilities, to distribute the recorded video over a LAN, WAN, intranet or Internet or wirelessly-WiFi using one of the 802.11 protocols.

Thermal, ink-jet and laser hard copy printers produce monochrome and color prints for immediate picture dissemination and permanent records for archiving.

All types of camera/lens housings are available for indoor and outdoor applications. Specialty cameras/ housings are available for elevators, stairwells, dome housings for public facilities: casinos, shopping malls, extreme outdoor environments, etc.

Pan/tilt assemblies for indoor and outdoor scenarios significantly increase the overall FOV of the camera system. Small, compact speed domes have found widespread use in many indoor and outdoor video surveillance environments.

Plug and play surveillance cameras permit quick installation and turn-on and are available in almost every housing configuration and camera type.

The video components summarized above are used in most video security applications including: (1) retail stores, (2) manufacturing plants, (3) shopping malls, (4) offices (5) airports, (6) seaports, (7) bus and rail terminals, (8) government facilities etc. There is widespread use of small video cameras and accessories for temporary covert applications. The small size and ease of deployment of many video components and the flexibility in transmission means over short and long distances has made rapid deployment equipment for portable personnel protection systems practical and important. Chapters 21 and 22 describe video surveillance systems designed for some of these applications.

It is clear that the direction the video security industry is taking is the integration of the video security function with digital computing technology and the other parts of the security system: access control, intrusion alarms, fire and two-way communications. Video security is rapidly moving from the legacy analog technology to the digital automatic video surveillance (AVS) technology.

PART II

Chapter 3
Natural and Artificial Lighting

CONTENTS

3.1 Overview
3.2 Video Lighting Characteristics
    3.2.1 Scene Illumination
        3.2.1.1 Daytime/Nighttime
        3.2.1.2 Indoor/Outdoor
    3.2.2 Light Output
    3.2.3 Spectral Output
    3.2.4 Beam Angle
3.3 Natural Light
    3.3.1 Sunlight
    3.3.2 Moonlight and Starlight
3.4 Artificial Light
    3.4.1 Tungsten Lamps
    3.4.2 Tungsten-Halogen Lamps
    3.4.3 High-Intensity-Discharge Lamps
    3.4.4 Low-Pressure Arc Lamps
    3.4.5 Compact Short-Arc Lamps
    3.4.6 Infrared Lighting
        3.4.6.1 Filtered Lamp Infrared Source
        3.4.6.2 Infrared-Emitting Diodes
        3.4.6.3 Thermal (Heat) IR Source
3.5 Lighting Design Considerations
    3.5.1 Lighting Costs
        3.5.1.1 Operating Costs
        3.5.1.2 Lamp Life
    3.5.2 Security Lighting Levels
    3.5.3 High-Security Lighting
3.6 Summary

3.1 OVERVIEW

Scene lighting affects the performance of any monochrome or color video security system. Whether the application is indoor or outdoor, daytime or nighttime, the amount of available light and its color (wavelength) energy spectrum must be considered, evaluated, and compared with the sensitivity of the cameras to be used. In bright sunlight daytime applications some cameras require the use of an automatic-iris lens or electronic shutter. In nighttime applications the light level and characteristics of available and artificial light sources must be analyzed and matched to the camera's spectral and illumination sensitivities to ensure a good video picture. In applications where additional lighting can be installed the available types of lamps—tungsten, tungsten-halogen, metal-arc, sodium, mercury, and others—must be compared to optimize video performance. In applications where no additional lighting is permissible, the existing illumination level, color spectrum, and beam angle must be evaluated and matched to the video camera/lens combination.

An axiom in video security applications is: the more light the better the picture. The quality of the monitor picture is affected by how much light is available and how well the sensor responds to the colors in the light source. This is particularly true when color cameras are used since they need more light and the correct colors of light, than monochrome cameras. The energy from light radiation is composed of a spectrum of colors, including "invisible light" produced by long-wavelength IR and short-wavelength ultraviolet (UV) energy. Most monochrome CCTV cameras respond to visible and near-IR energy but color cameras are made to respond to visible light only.

Although many consider lighting to be only a decorator's or an architect's responsibility, the type and intensity is of paramount importance in any video security system and therefore the security professional must be knowledgeable.

This chapter analyzes the available natural and artificial light sources and provides information to help in choosing an optimum light source or in determining whether existing light levels are adequate.

3.2 VIDEO LIGHTING CHARACTERISTICS

The illumination present in the scene determines the amount of light ultimately reaching the CCTV camera lens. It is therefore an important factor in the quality of the video image. The illumination can be from natural sources such as the sun, moon, starlight or thermal (heat), or from artificial sources such as tungsten, mercury, fluorescent, sodium, metal-arc, LEDs or other lamps. Considerations about the source illuminating a scene include: (1) source spectral characteristics, (2) beam angle over which the source radiates, (3) intensity of the source, (4) variations in that intensity, and (5) location of the CCTV camera relative to the source. Factors to be considered in the scene include: (1) reflectance of objects in the scene, (2) complexity of the scene, (3) motion in the scene, and (4) degree of contrast in the scene.

3.2.1 Scene Illumination

In planning a video system it is necessary to know the kind of illumination, the intensity of light falling on a surface, and how the illumination varies as a function of distance from the light source.

The video camera image sensor responds to reflected light from the scene. To obtain a better understanding of scene and camera illumination, consider Figure 3-1, which shows the illumination source, the scene to be viewed, and the CCTV camera and lens. The radiation from the illuminating source reaches the video camera by first reflecting off the objects in the scene.

3.2.1.1 Daytime/Nighttime

Before any camera system is chosen the site should be surveyed to determine whether the area under surveillance will receive direct sunlight and whether the camera will be pointed toward the sun (to the south or the west). Whenever possible, cameras should be pointed away from the sun to reduce glare and potential damage to the camera. Also, when the camera views a bright background or bright source, persons or objects near the camera may be hard to identify since not much light illuminates them from the direction of the camera. The light level from different sources varies from a maximum of 10,000 FtCd for natural bright sunlight to a minimum of 1 FtCd (from artificial lamplight at night), giving a ratio of 10,000 to 1.

During nighttime, dawn or dusk operation, the camera system may see moonlight and/or starlight, and reflected

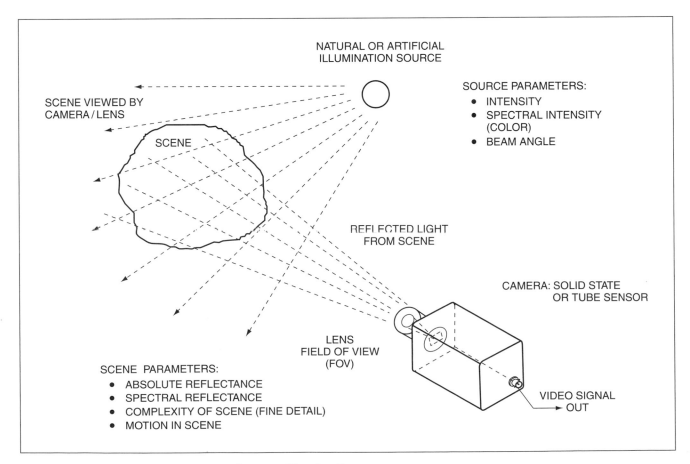

FIGURE 3-1   CCTV camera, scene, and source illumination

light from artificial illumination. For nighttime operation the most widely used lamps are tungsten, tungsten-halogen, sodium, mercury, and high-intensity-discharge (HID) metal-arc and xenon types.

3.2.1.2 Indoor/Outdoor

For indoor applications, the solid-state CCD and CMOS cameras usually have sufficient sensitivity and dynamic range to produce a good image and can operate with manual-iris lenses. When video surveillance cameras view an outdoor scene, the light source is natural or artificial, depending on the time of day. During the daytime, operating conditions will vary, depending on whether there is bright sun, clouds, overcast sky, or precipitation; the light's color or spectral energy, as well as its intensity, will vary.

The CCTV camera for outdoor applications, where the light level and scene contrast range widely, requires automatic light-level adjustment, usually an automatic-iris lens or an electronic shutter in the camera. Most outdoor cameras must have automatic-iris-control lenses or shuttered CCDs to adjust over the large light-level range encountered. Very often an expensive CCTV camera may cost less

than having to increase the lighting in a parking lot or exterior perimeter in order to obtain a satisfactory picture with a less expensive camera.

3.2.2 Light Output

The amount of light produced by any light source is defined by a parameter called the "candela"—related to the light from one candle (Figure 3-2).

One FtCd of illumination is defined as the amount of light received from a 1-candela source at a distance of 1 foot. A light meter calibrated in FtCd will measure 1 FtCd at a distance of 1 foot from that source. As shown in Figure 3-2, the light falling on a 1-square-foot area at a distance of 2 feet is one-quarter FtCd. This indicates that the light level varies inversely as the *square* of the distance between the source and observer. Doubling the distance from the source reduces the light level to *one-quarter* of its original level. Note that exactly four times the area is illuminated by the same amount of light—which explains why each quarter of the area receives only a quarter of the light.

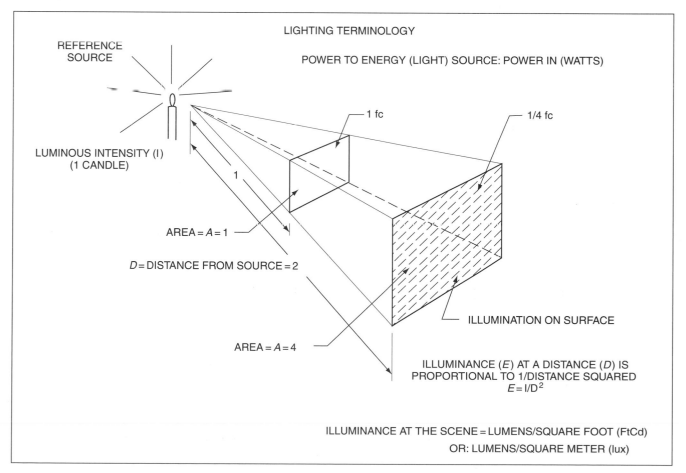

FIGURE 3-2 Illumination defined—the inverse square law

3.2.3 Spectral Output

Since different CCTV camera types respond to different colors it is important to know what type of light source is illuminating the surveillance area as well as what type might have to be added to get the required video picture. Figure 3-3 shows the spectral light–output characteristics from standard tungsten, tungsten-halogen, and sodium artificial sources, as well as that from natural sunlight.

Superimposed on the figure is the spectral sensitivity of the human eye. Each source produces light at different wavelengths or colors. To obtain the maximum utility from any video camera it must be sensitive to the light produced by the natural or artificial source. Sunlight, moonlight, and tungsten lamps produce energy in a range in which all video cameras are sensitive. Solid-state CCD sensors are sensitive to visible and near-IR sources but many CCD cameras have IR cut filters which reduce this IR sensitivity.

3.2.4 Beam Angle

Another characteristic important in determining the amount of light reaching a scene is the beam angle over which the source radiates.

One parameter used to classify light sources is their light-beam pattern: Do they emit a wide, medium, or narrow beam of light? The requirement for this parameter is determined by the FOV of the camera lens used and the total scene to be viewed. It is best to match the camera lens FOV (including any pan and tilt motion) to the light-beam radiation pattern to obtain the best uniformity of illumination over the scene, and the best picture quality and light efficiency. Most lighting manufacturers have the coefficient of utilization (CU) for specific fixture luminaires. The CU expresses how much light the fixture luminaire (lens) directs to the desired location (example: CU = 75%). Figure 3-4 shows the beam patterns of natural and artificial light sources. The natural sources are inherently wide while artificial sources are available in narrow-beam (a few degrees) to wide-beam (30–90°) patterns.

The sun and moon, as well as some artificial light sources operating without a reflector, radiate over an entire scene. Artificial light sources and lamps almost always use lenses and reflectors and are designed or can sometimes be adjusted to produce narrow- or wide-angle beams. If a large area is to be viewed, either a single wide-beam source or multiple sources must be located within the scene to illuminate it fully and uniformly. If a small scene at a long

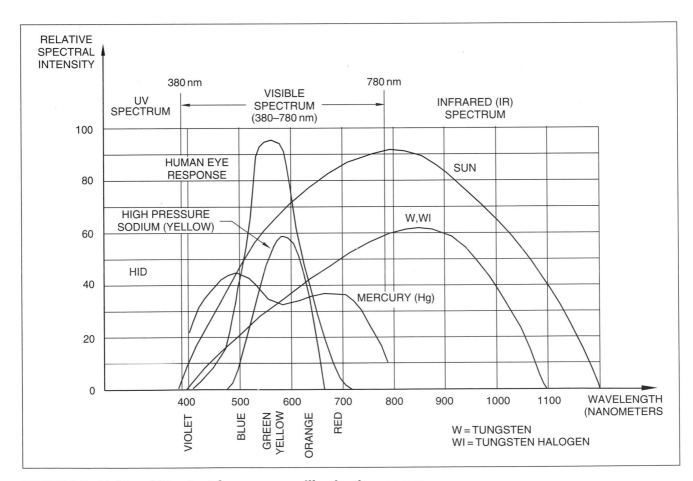

FIGURE 3-3   Light and IR output from common illumination sources

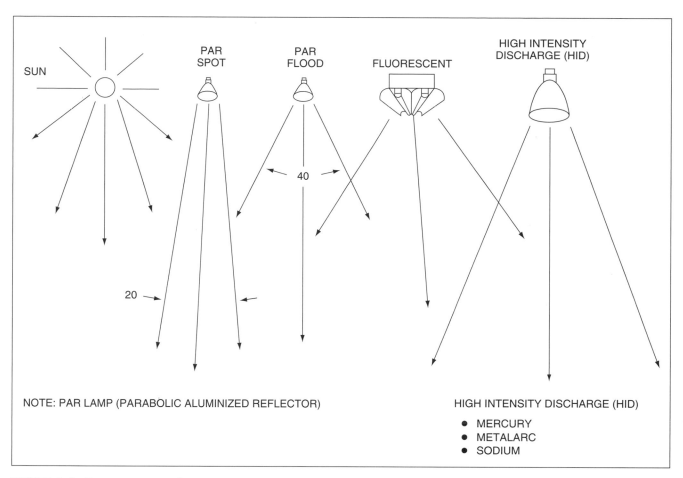

FIGURE 3-4   Beam patterns from common sources

range is to be viewed, it is necessary to illuminate only that part of the scene to be viewed, resulting in a reduction in the total power needed from the source.

3.3   NATURAL LIGHT

There are two broad categories of light and heat sources: natural and artificial. Natural light sources include the sun, moon (reflected sunlight), stars, and thermal (heat). The visible natural sources contain the colors of the visible spectrum (blue to red) as shown in Figure 3-3. Sunlight and moonlight contain IR radiation in addition to visible light spectra and are classified as broadband light sources, that is, they contain all colors and wavelengths. Far-IR radiation in the 3–5 micrometer (μm) and 8–11 μm spectrum produces heat energy. Only thermal IR imaging cameras are sensitive to this far-IR energy.

Artificial light sources can be broadband or narrowband, i.e. containing only a limited number of colors or all of them. Monochrome video systems cannot perceive the color distribution or spectrum of colors from different light sources. The picture quality of monochrome cameras depends solely on the *total* amount of energy emitted

from the lamp that the camera is sensitive to. When the lamp output spectrum falls within the range of the camera sensor spectral sensitivity then the camera produces the best picture.

For color video systems the situation is more complex and critical. Broadband light sources containing most of the visible colors are necessary for a color camera. To get a good color balance the illumination source should match the sensor sensitivity. For the camera to be able to respond to all the colors in the visible spectrum the light source must contain all the colors of the spectrum. Color cameras have an automatic white-balance control that automatically adjusts the camera electronics to produce the correct color balance. The light source must contain the colors in order for them to be seen on the monitor. Broadband light sources such as the sun, tungsten or tungsten-halogen, and xenon produce the best color pictures because they contain *all* the colors in the spectrum.

If the scene in Figure 3-1 is illuminated by sunlight, moonlight, or starlight, it will receive uniform illumination. If it is illuminated by several artificial sources, the lighting may vary considerably over the FOV of the camera and lens. For outdoor applications the camera system must operate over the full range from direct sunlight

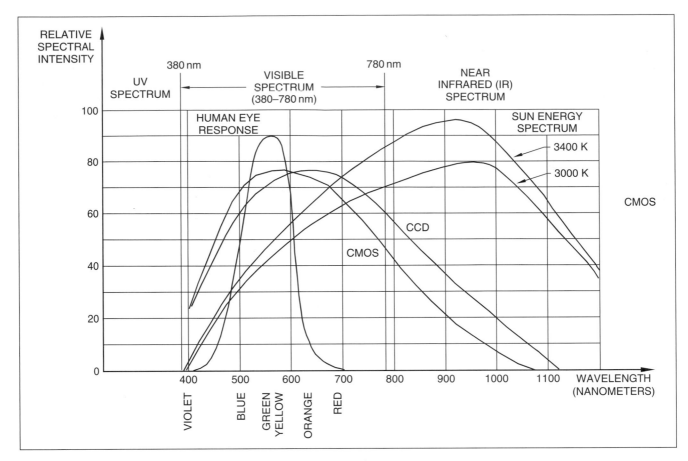

FIGURE 3-5   Spectral characteristics of natural sources and camera sensors

to nighttime conditions, and must have an automatic light control means to compensate for this light-level change. Figure 3-5 summarizes the characteristics of natural sources, i.e. the sun, moon, and starlight, and how different camera types respond to them.

Table 3-1 summarizes the overall light-level ranges, from direct sunlight to overcast starlight.

3.3.1 Sunlight

The sun is the energy source illuminating an outdoor scene during the daylight hours. The sun emits a continuum of all wavelengths and colors to which monochrome and color television cameras are sensitive. This continuum includes visible radiation in the blue, green, yellow, orange, red, and also in the IR range of the spectrum. The sun also produces long wavelength thermal IR heat energy that is used by thermal (heat) imaging IR cameras. All monochrome and color solid-state cameras are sensitive to the visible spectrum, and some monochrome cameras to the visible and near-IR spectrum. Color cameras are sensitive to all the color wavelengths in the visible spectrum (as is the human eye), but color cameras are purposely designed to be insensitive to near-IR wavelengths.

During the first few hours in the morning and the last few hours in the evening, the sunlight's spectrum is shifted toward the orange–red region, so things look predominantly orange and red. During the midday hours, when the sun is brightest and most intense, blues and greens are

LIGHTING CONDITION	LIGHT LEVEL	
	fc*	lux**
UNOBSTRUCTED SUN	10,000	100,000
SUN WITH LIGHT CLOUD	7,000	70,000
SUN WITH HEAVY CLOUD	2,000	20,000
SUNRISE, SUNSET	50	500
TWILIGHT	.4	4
FULL MOON	.02	.2
QUARTER MOON	.002	.02
OVERCAST MOON	.0007	.007
CLEAR NIGHT SKY	.0001	.001
AVERAGE STARLIGHT	.00007	.0007
OVERCAST NIGHT SKY	.000005	.00005

*LUMENS PER SQUARE FOOT (fc)
**LUMENS PER SQUARE METER (lux)
NOTE: 1 fc EQUALS APPROXIMATELY 10 lux

Table 3-1   Light-Level Range from Natural Sources

brightest and reflect the most balanced white light. For this reason a color camera must have an automatic white-balance control that adjusts for color shift during the day, so that the resulting video picture is color corrected.

3.3.2 Moonlight and Starlight

After the sun sets in an environment with no artificial lighting, the scene may be illuminated by the moon, the stars, or both. Since moonlight is the reflected light from the sun it contains most of the colors emitted from the sun. However, the low level of illumination reaching the earth from the moon (or stars) prevents color cameras (and the human eye) from providing good color rendition.

3.4 ARTIFICIAL LIGHT

The following sections describe some of the artificial light sources in use today and how their characteristics affect their use in video security applications. Artificial light sources consist of the several types of lamps used in outdoor parking lots, storage facilities, fence lines, or in indoor environments for lighting rooms, hallways, work areas, elevators, etc. Two types of lamps are common: tungsten or tungsten-halogen lamps having solid filaments, and gaseous or arc lamps containing low- or high-pressure gas in an enclosed envelope. Arc lamps can be further classified into HID, low-pressure, and high-pressure short-arc types. High-intensity-discharge-lamps are used most extensively because of their high efficacy (efficiency in converting electrical energy into light energy) and long life. Low-pressure arc lamps include fluorescent and low-pressure sodium types used in many indoor and outdoor installations. Long-arc xenon lamps are used in large outdoor sports arenas. High-pressure short-arc lamps find use in applications that require a high-efficiency, well-directed narrow beam to illuminate a target at long distances (hundreds or thousands of feet). Such lamps include xenon, metal-halide, high-pressure sodium, and mercury. For covert security applications some lamps are fitted with a visible-light-blocking filter so that only invisible IR radiation illuminates the scene.

Narrow-band light sources such as mercury-arc or sodium-vapor lamps do not produce a continuous spectrum of colors, so color is rendered poorly. A mercury lamp has little red light output and therefore red objects appear nearly black when illuminated by a mercury arc. Likewise a high-pressure sodium lamp contains large quantities of yellow, orange, and red light and therefore a blue or blue–green object will look dark or gray or brown in its light. A low-pressure sodium lamp produces only yellow light and consequently is unsuitable for color video applications.

A significant advance in tungsten lamp development came with the use of a halogen element (iodine or bromine) in the lamp's quartz envelope, with the lamp operating in what is called the "tungsten-halogen cycle." This operation increases a lamp's rated life significantly even though it operates at a high temperature and light output. Incandescent filament lamps are available with power ratings from a fraction of a watt to 10 kilowatts.

High intensity discharge arc lamps comprise a broad class of lamps in which the arc discharge takes place between electrodes contained in a transparent or translucent bulb. The spectral radiation output and intensity are determined principally by the chemical compounds and gaseous elements that fill the bulb. The lamp is started using a high-voltage ignition circuit with some form of electrical ballasting used to stabilize the arc. In contrast, tungsten lamps operate directly from the power source.

Compact short-arc lamps are only a few inches in size but emit high-intensity, high-lumen output radiation with a variety of spectral characteristics.

Long-arc lamps, such as fluorescent, low-pressure sodium vapor, and xenon have output spectral characteristics determined by the gas in the arc or the tube-wall emitting material. The fluorescent lamp has a particular phosphor coating on the inside of the glass and bulb that determines its spectral output. Power outputs available from arc-discharge lamps range from a few watts up to many tens of kilowatts.

An important aspect of artificial lighting is the consideration of the light-beam pattern from the lamp and the camera lens FOV. A wide-beam flood lamp will illuminate a large area with a fairly uniform intensity of light and therefore produce a well-balanced picture. A narrow-beam light or spotlight will illuminate a small area and consequently areas at the edge of the scene and beyond will be darker. A scene that is illuminated non-uniformly (i.e. with high contrast) and having "hotspots" will result in a non-uniform picture. For maximum efficiency the camera–lens combination FOV should match the lamp beam angle. If a lamp illuminates only a particular area of the scene the camera–lens combination FOV should only be viewing that area illuminated by the lamp. This source beam angle problem does not exist for areas lighted by natural illumination such as the sun, which usually uniformly illuminates the entire scene except for shadows.

3.4.1 Tungsten Lamps

The first practical artificial lighting introduced in 1907 took the form of an incandescent filament tungsten lamp. These lamps used a tungsten mixture formed into a filament and produced an efficacy (ratio of light out to power in) of approximately 7 lumens per watt of visible light. This represented a great increase over anything existing at the time, but represents a low efficiency compared to most other present lamp types. In 1913 ductile tungsten wire fabricated into coiled filaments increased efficacy to 20 lumens per watt.

Today the incandescent lamp is commonplace and is still used in most homes, businesses, factories, and public facilities. While its efficacy does not measure up to that of the arc lamp, the tungsten and tungsten-halogen incandescent lamps nevertheless offer a low-cost installation for many applications. Since it is an incandescent source, it radiates all the colors in the visible spectrum as well as the near-IR spectrum providing an excellent light source for monochrome and color cameras. Its two disadvantages when compared with arc lamps are: (1) relatively low efficacy, which makes it more expensive to operate, and (2) relatively short operating life of several thousand hours.

Incandescent filament lamp efficacy increases with filament operating temperature; however, lamp life expectancy decreases rapidly as lamp filament temperature increases. Maximum practical efficacy is about 35 lumens per watt in high-wattage lamps operated at approximately 3500 K color temperature. A tungsten lamp cannot operate at this high temperature since it will last only a few hours. At lower temperatures, life expectancy increases to several thousand hours, which is typical of incandescent lamps used in general lighting.

An incandescent lamp consists of a tungsten filament surrounded by an inert gas sealed inside a transparent or frosted-glass envelope. The purpose of the frosted glass is to increase the apparent size of the lamp, thereby

decreasing its peak intensity and reducing glare and hotspots in the illuminated scene.

Incandescent lamp filaments are usually coiled to increase their efficiency. The coils are sometimes coiled again (coiled-coiled) to further increase the filament area and increase the luminance. Filament configurations are designed to optimize the radiation patterns for specific applications. Sometimes long and narrow filaments are used and mounted into cylindrical reflectors to produce a rectangular beam pattern. Others have small filaments so as to be incorporated into parabolic reflectors to produce a narrow collimated beam (spotlight). Others have larger filament areas and are used to produce a wide-angle beam (such as a floodlight). Figure 3-6 shows several lamp configurations.

Figure 3-7 shows some standard lamp luminaires used in industrial, residential, and security applications. The luminaire fixtures house the tungsten, HID, and low-pressure lamps.

The tungsten-halogen lamp design is a significant improvement over the incandescent lamp. In conventional gas-filled, tungsten-filament incandescent lamps, tungsten molecules evaporate from the incandescent filament, flow to the relatively cool inner surface of the bulb wall (glass). The tungsten adheres to the glass and forms a thin film that gradually thickens during the life of the lamp and causes the bulb to darken. This molecular action reduces the lumen light output and efficacy in two ways. First, evaporation of tungsten from the filament reduces the filament wire's diameter and increases its resistance, so

(A) TUNGSTEN HALOGEN IN QUARTZ ENVELOPE   (B) TUNGSTEN FILAMENT   (C) TUNGSTEN HALOGEN IN PARABOLIC ALUMINIZED REFLECTOR (PAR)

FIGURE 3-6   Generic tungsten, tungsten–Halogen lamp configurations

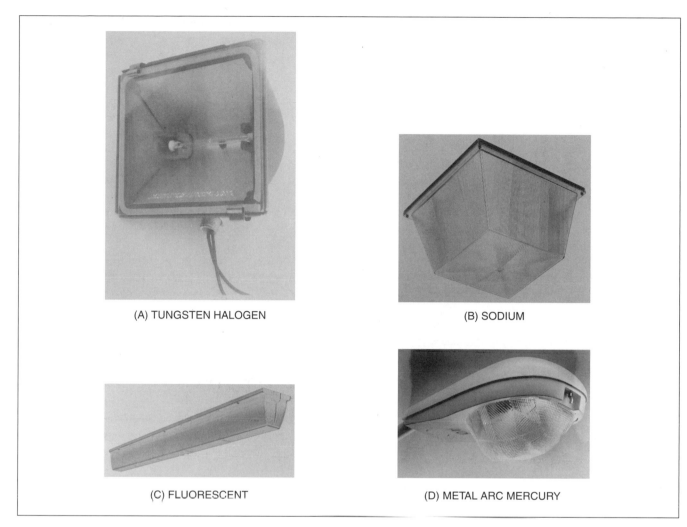

(A) TUNGSTEN HALOGEN

(B) SODIUM

(C) FLUORESCENT

(D) METAL ARC MERCURY

FIGURE 3-7   Standard lamp luminaires

that light output and color temperature increase. Second, the tungsten deposited on the bulb wall increases the opacity (reduces transmission of light through the glass) as it thickens. Figure 3-8 illustrates the relative amount of energy produced by tungsten-filament and halogen-quartz-tungsten lamps as compared with other arc-lamp types, including fluorescent, metal-arc, and sodium, in the visible and near-IR spectral range.

On an absolute basis, the energy produced by the tungsten lamp in the visible spectral region is significantly lower than that provided by HID lamps. However, the total amount of energy produced by the tungsten lamp over the entire spectrum is comparable to that of the other lamps. Figure 3-8 shows the human eye response and spectral sensitivity of standard CCTV camera sensors.

3.4.2 Tungsten-Halogen Lamps

The discovery of the tungsten-halogen cycle significantly increased the operating life of the tungsten lamp. Tungsten-halogen lamps, like conventional incandescent

lamps, use a tungsten filament in a gas-filled light-transmitting envelope and emit light with a spectral distribution similar to that of a tungsten lamp. Unlike the standard incandescent lamp, the tungsten-halogen lamp contains a trace vapor of one of the halogen elements (iodine or bromine) along with the usual inert fill gas. Also, tungsten-halogen lamps operate at much higher gas pressure and bulb temperature than non-halogen incandescent lamps. The higher gas pressure retards the tungsten evaporation, allowing the filament to operate at a higher temperature, resulting in higher efficiencies than conventional incandescent lamps. To withstand these higher temperatures and pressures, the lamps use quartz bulbs or high-temperature "hard" glass. The earliest version of these lamps used fused quartz bulbs and iodine vapor and were called "quartz iodine lamps." After it was found that other halogens could be used, the more generic tungsten-halogen lamp is now used.

The important result achieved with the addition of halogen was caused by the "halogen regenerative cycle," which maintains a nearly constant light output and color temperature throughout the life of the lamp and significantly

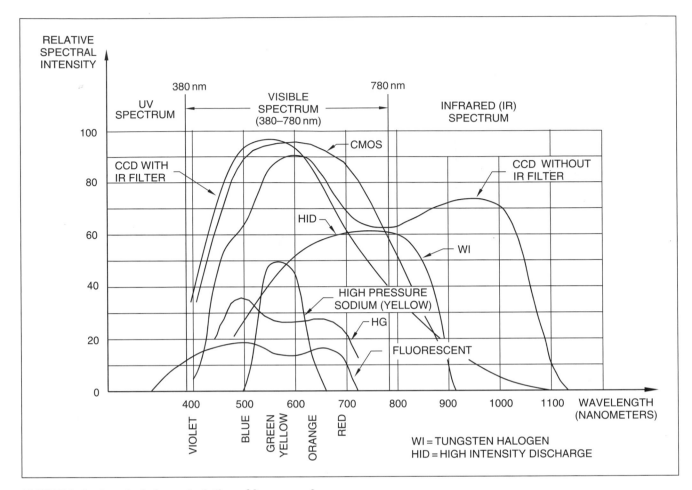

FIGURE 3-8 Spectral characteristics of lamps and camera sensors

extends the life of the lamp. The halogen chemical cycle permits the use of more compact bulbs compared to those of tungsten filament lamps of comparable ratings and permits increasing either lamp life or lumen output and color temperature to values significantly above those of conventional tungsten filament lamps.

Incandescent and xenon lamps are good illumination sources for IR video applications when the light output is filtered with a covert filter (one that blocks or absorbs the transmission of visible radiation) and they transmit only the near-IR radiation. Figure 3-9 shows a significant portion of the emitted spectrum of the lamp radiation falling in the near-IR region that is invisible to the human eye but to which solid-state silicon sensor cameras are sensitive. The reason for this is shown in Figure 3-9, which details the spectral characteristics of these lamps.

When an IR-transmitting/visible-blocking filter is placed in front of a tungsten-halogen lamp, only the IR energy illuminates the scene and reflects back to the CCTV camera lens. This combination produces an image on the video monitor from an illumination source that is invisible to the eye. This technology is commonly referred to as "seeing in the dark" i.e. there is no visible radiation

and yet a video image is discernible. Some monochrome solid-state CCD and CMOS sensors are responsive to this near-IR radiation. Since the IR region has no "color," color cameras are designed to be insensitive to the filtered IR energy. Approximately 90% of the energy emitted by the tungsten-halogen lamp occurs in the IR region. However, only a fraction of this IR light can be used by silicon sensors, since they are responsive only up to approximately 1100 nanometers (nm). The remaining IR energy above 1100 nm manifests as heat, which does not contribute to the image. While the IR source is not visible to the human eye it is detectable by silicon camera devices and other night vision devices (Chapter 19).

3.4.3 High-Intensity-Discharge Lamps

An enclosed arc high-intensity-discharge (HID) lamp is in widespread use for general lighting and security applications. There are three major types of HID lamps, each one having a relatively small arc tube mounted inside a heat-conserving outer jacket and filled with an inert gas to prevent oxidation of the hot arc tube seals (Figure 3-10).

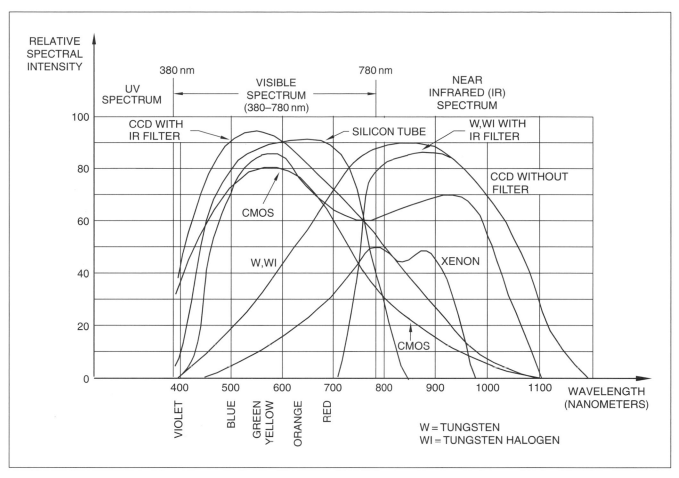

FIGURE 3-9   Filtered tungsten and xenon lamps vs. camera spectral sensitivity

The principle in all vapor-arc lighting systems is the same: (1) an inert gas is contained within the tube to spark ignition, (2) the inert gas carries current from one electrode to the other, (3) the current develops heat and vaporizes the solid metal or metallic-oxide inside the tube, and (4) light is discharged from the vaporized substance through the surface of the discharge tube and into the area to be lighted.

The three most popular HID lamps are: (1) mercury in a quartz tube, (2) metal halide in a quartz tube, and (3) high-pressure sodium in a translucent aluminum-oxide tube. Each type differs in electrical input, light output, shape, and size. While incandescent lamps require no auxiliary equipment and operate directly from a suitable voltage, discharge sources in HID lamps require a high-voltage starting device and electrical ballast while in operation. The high-voltage ignition provides the voltage necessary to start the lamp; once the lamp is started, the ballast operates the lamp at the rated power (wattage) or current level. The ballast consumes power, which must be factored into calculations of system efficiency. HID lamps, unlike incandescent or fluorescent lamps, require several minutes to warm up before reaching full brightness. If turned

off momentarily they take several minutes before they can be turned on again (reignited).

The primary overriding advantages of HID lamps are high efficacy and their long life, provided they are operated at a minimum of several hours per start. Lamp lifetime is typically 16,000 to 24,000 hours and light efficacy ranges from 60 to 140 lumens per watt. These lamps cannot be electrically dimmed without drastically affecting the starting warm-up luminous efficiency, color, and life.

These lamps are the most widely used lamps for lighting industrial and commercial buildings, streets, sports fields, etc. One disadvantage of short-arc lamps just mentioned is their significant warm-up time—usually several minutes to ten minutes. If accidentally or intentionally turned off, these lamps cannot be restarted until they have cooled down sufficiently to reignite the arc. This may be 2–5 minutes and then take an additional 5 minutes to return to full brightness. Dual-HID bulbs are now available, which include two identical HID lamp units, only one of which operates at a time. If the first lamp is extinguished momentarily, the cold lamp may be ignited immediately, eliminating the waiting time to allow the first lamp to cool down.

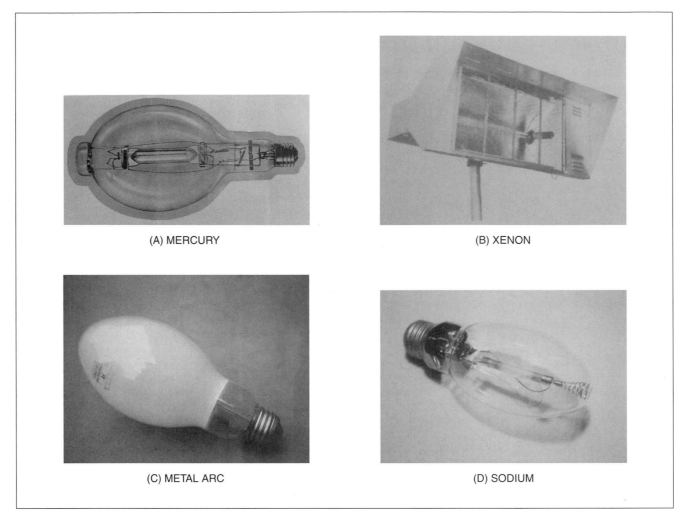

(A) MERCURY

(B) XENON

(C) METAL ARC

(D) SODIUM

FIGURE 3-10   High-intensity-discharge lamps

Mercury HID lamps are available in sizes from 40 to 1500 watts. Spectral output is high in the blue region but extremely deficient in the red region. Therefore they should be used in monochrome but not color video applications (Figure 3-11).

A second class of HID lamp is the metal-halide that is filled with mercury-metallic iodides. These lamps are available with power ratings from 175 to 1500 watts. The addition of metallic salts to the mercury arc improves the efficacy and color by adding emission lines in the red end of the spectrum. With different metallic additives or different phosphor coatings on the outside of the lamp, the lamp color varies from an incandescent spectrum to a daylight spectrum. The color spectrum from the metal-halide lamp is significantly improved over the mercury lamp and can be used for monochrome or color video applications.

The third class of HID lamp is the high-pressure sodium lamp. This lamp contains a special ceramic-arc tube material that withstands the chemical attack of sodium at high temperatures, thereby permitting high luminous efficiency and yielding a broader spectrum, compared with low-pressure sodium arcs. However, because the gas is only sodium, the spectral output distribution from the high-pressure sodium HID lamp is yellow–orange and has only a small amount of blue and green. For this reason the lamp is not suitable for good color video security applications. The primary and significant advantage of the high-pressure sodium lamp over virtually all other lamps is its high efficacy, approximately 60–140 lumens per watt. It also enjoys a long life, approximately 24,000 hours. The sodium lamp is an extremely good choice for monochrome surveillance applications. High-intensity-discharge lamps are filled to atmospheric pressure (when not operating) and rise to several atmospheres when operating. This makes them significantly safer than short-arc lamps that are under much higher pressure at all times.

The choice of lamp is often determined by architectural criteria, but the video designer should be aware of the color characteristics of each lamp to ensure their suitability for monochrome or color video.

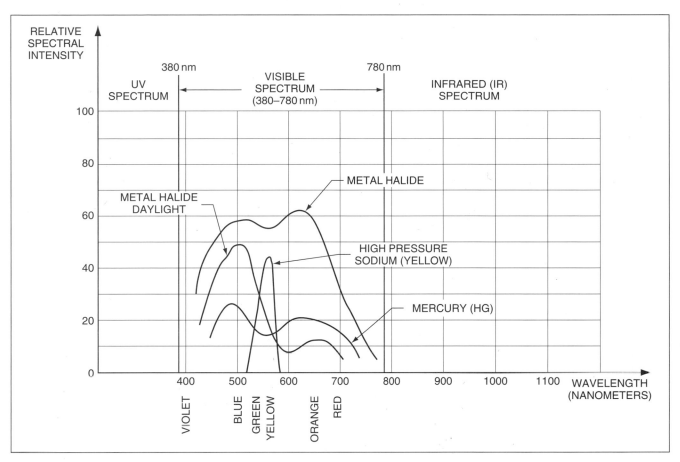

FIGURE 3-11   Spectral output from HID lamps

3.4.4 Low-Pressure Arc Lamps

Fluorescent and low-pressure sodium lamps are examples of low-pressure arc lamp illumination sources. These lamps have tubular bulb shapes and long arc lengths (several inches to several feet). A ballast is necessary for proper operation, and a high-voltage pulse is required to ignite the arc and start the lamp.

The most common type is the fluorescent lamp with a relatively high efficacy of approximately 60 lumens per watt. The large size of the arc tube (diameter as well as length) requires that it be placed in a large luminaire (reflector) to achieve a defined beam shape. For this reason, fluorescent lamps are used for large-area illumination and produce a fairly uniform pattern. The fluorescent lamp system is sensitive to the surrounding air temperature and therefore is used indoors or in moderate temperatures. When installed outdoors in cold weather a special low-temperature ballast must be used to ensure that the starting pulse is high enough to start the lamp.

The fluorescent lamp combines a low-pressure mercury arc with a phosphor coating on the interior of the bulb. The lamp arc produces UV radiation from the low-pressure mercury arc, which is converted into visible radiation by the phosphor coating on the inside wall of the outside tube. A variety of phosphor coatings is available to produce almost any color quality (Figure 3-12).

Colors range from "cool white," which is the most popular variety, to daylight, blue white, and so on. Lamps are available with input powers from 4 watts to approximately 200 watts. Tube lengths vary from 6 to 56 inches (15–144 cm). Fluorescent lamps can be straight, circular, or U-shaped. Fluorescent lamps can emit a continuous spectrum like an incandescent lamp simulating a daylight spectrum and suitable for color cameras.

A second class of low-pressure lamp is the sodium lamp which emits a single yellow color (nearly monochromatic). These lamps have ratings from 18 to 180 watts. The low-pressure sodium lamp has the highest efficacy output of any lamp type built to date, approximately 180 lumens per watt. While the efficacy is high, the lamp's pure yellow light limits it to some monochrome video surveillance applications and to roadway lighting applications. If used with color cameras, only yellow objects will appear yellow; all other objects will appear brown or black.

The low-pressure sodium light utilizes pure metal sodium with an inert-gas combination of neon–argon enclosed in a discharge tube about 28 inches long. The pressure in the tube is actually below atmospheric

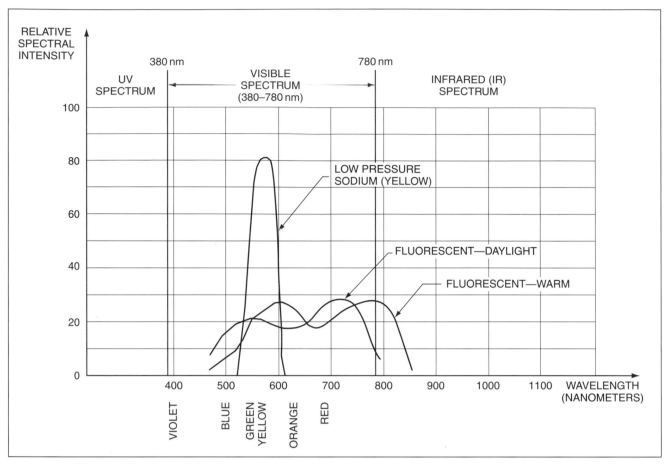

FIGURE 3-12   Light output from low pressure arc lamps

pressure, which causes the glass to collapse inward if it is ruptured—a good safety feature.

A unique advantage of the low-pressure sodium amber light is its better "modeling" (showing of texture and shape) of any illuminated surface, for both the human eye and the CCTV camera. It provides more contrast, and since the monochrome CCTV camera responds to contrast, images under this light are clearer, according to some reports. The yellow output from the sodium lamp is close to the wavelength region at which the human eye has its peak visual response (560 nanometers).

Some security personnel and the police have identified low-pressure sodium as a uniquely advantageous off-hour lighting system for security because the amber yellow color clearly tells people to keep out. This yellow security lighting also sends the psychological message that the premises are well guarded.

3.4.5 Compact Short-Arc Lamps

Enclosed short-arc lamps comprise a broad class of lamps in which the arc discharge takes place between two closely spaced electrodes, usually tungsten, and is contained in a rugged transparent or frosted bulb. The spectrum radiated by these lamps is usually determined by the elements and chemical compounds inside.

They are called short-arc because the arc is short compared with its electrode size, spacing, and bulb size and operates at relatively high currents and low voltages. Such lamps are available with power ratings ranging from less than 50 watts to more than 25 kilowatts. These lamps usually operate at less than 100 volts, although they need a high-voltage pulse (several thousand volts) to start. Most short-arc lamps operate on AC or DC power and require some form of current-regulating device (ballast) to maintain a uniform output radiation.

Several factors limit the useful life of compact lamps compared with HID lamps, especially the high current density required which reduces electrode lifetime. Compact short-arc lamps generally have a life in the low thousands of hours and operate at internal pressures up to hundreds of atmospheres. Therefore they must be operated in protected enclosures and handled with care. The most common short-arc lamps are mercury, mercury-xenon, and xenon. Figure 3-13 shows the spectral output of mercury-xenon lamps.

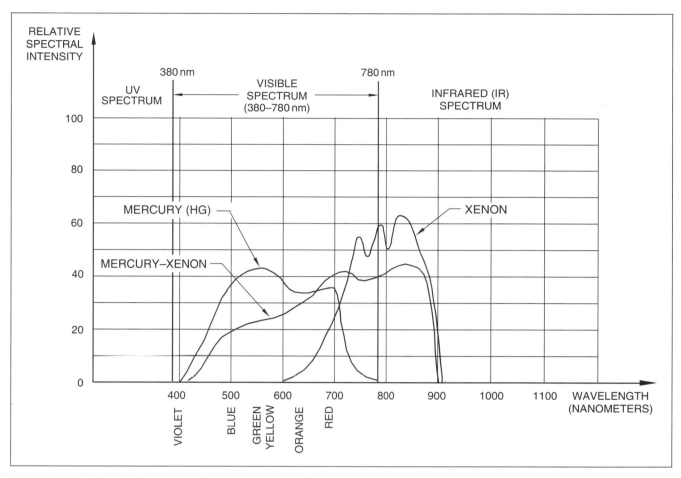

FIGURE 3-13 Spectral outputs of mercury–xenon lamps

Short-arc xenon lamps are not common in security applications because of their high cost and short lifetime. However, they play an important role for IR sources used in covert surveillance. The light output from the mercury arc lamp is primarily in the blue region of the visible spectrum and therefore only fair results are obtained with monochrome CCD or CMOS solid-state cameras. Despite mercury lighting's good appearance to the human eye, typical solid-state cameras respond poorly to it.

The mercury-xenon lamp, containing a small amount of mercury in addition to xenon gas, offers fair color rendition. Immediately after lamp ignition the output is essentially the same as the spectrum of a xenon lamp. The xenon gas produces a background continuum that improves the color rendition. As the mercury vaporizes over several minutes, the spectral output becomes that of mercury vapor, with light output in the blue, green, yellow, and orange portions of the spectrum. The xenon short-arc's luminous efficiency ranges from 20 to 53 lumens per watt over lamp wattage ranges of 200–7000 watts.

The color temperature of the arc is approximately 6000 K, which is almost identical to that of sunlight. The xenon lamp output consists of specific colors as well as a continuum and some IR radiation, and produces similar color lighting to that of the sun (Figure 3-13). The greater percentage of the continuum radiation at all wavelengths closely matches the spectral radiation characteristics of sunlight. Compared with all other short-arc lamps, the xenon lamp is the ideal artificial light choice for accurate color rendition. The lamp spectral output does not change with lamp life, so color rendition is good over the useful life of the lamp. Color output is virtually independent of operating temperature and pressure, thereby ensuring good color rendition under adverse operating conditions.

Xenon lamps are turned on with starting voltage pulses of 10–50 kilovolts (kV). Typical lamps reach full output intensity within a few seconds after ignition. The luminous efficiency of the xenon lamp ranges from 15 to 50 lumens per watt over a wattage range of approximately 75 to 10,000 watts.

A characteristic unique to the compact short-arc lamp is the small size of the radiating source, usually a fraction of a millimeter to a few millimeters in diameter. Due to optical characteristics, one lamp in a suitable reflector can produce a very concentrated beam of light. Parabolic and spherical reflectors, among others, are used to provide optical control of the lamp output: the parabolic for search- or spotlights and the spherical for floodlights. Compact short-arc lamps are often mounted in a parabolic reflector to produce a highly collimated beam used to illuminate distant objects. This configuration also produces an excellent IR spotlight when an IR transmitting filter is mounted in front of the lamp. Even when not used for spotlighting, the small arc size of compact short-arc lamps allows the luminaire reflector to be significantly smaller than other lamp reflectors.

Mounting orientation can affect the performance of short-arc lamps. Most xenon lamps are designed for vertical or horizontal operation but many mercury-xenon and mercury lamps must be operated vertically to prevent premature burnout.

3.4.6 Infrared Lighting

A covert IR lighting system is a solution when conventional security lighting is not appropriate, for example when the presence of a security system (1) would attract unwanted attention, (2) would alert intruders to a video surveillance system, or (3) would disturb neighbors.

There are two generic techniques for producing IR lighting. One method uses the IR energy from a thermal incandescent or xenon lamp. These IR sources are fitted with optical filters that block the visible radiation so that only IR radiation is transmitted from the lamp

housing to illuminate the scene. The second technique uses a non-thermal IR LED or LED array to generate IR radiation through electronic recombination in a semiconductor device. Both techniques produce narrow or wide beams, resulting in excellent images when the scene is viewed with an IR-sensitive camera, such as a solid-state CCD, CMOS, or ICCD camera.

3.4.6.1 Filtered Lamp Infrared Source

Xenon and incandescent lamps can illuminate a scene many hundreds of feet from the camera and produce sufficient IR radiation to be practical for a covert video system (Figure 3-9). Since thermal IR sources (tungsten, xenon lamps) consume significant amounts of power and become hot, they may require a special heat sink or air cooling to operate continuously. Figure 3-14 shows the configuration of several tungsten and xenon lamp IR sources that produce IR beams and that have built-in reflectors and IR transmitting (visual blocking) filters.

These lamp systems use thin-film dichroic optical coatings (a light-beam splitter) and absorbing filters that direct the very-near-IR rays toward the front of the lamp and out into the beam, while reflecting visible and long-IR radiation to the back of the lamp, where it is absorbed

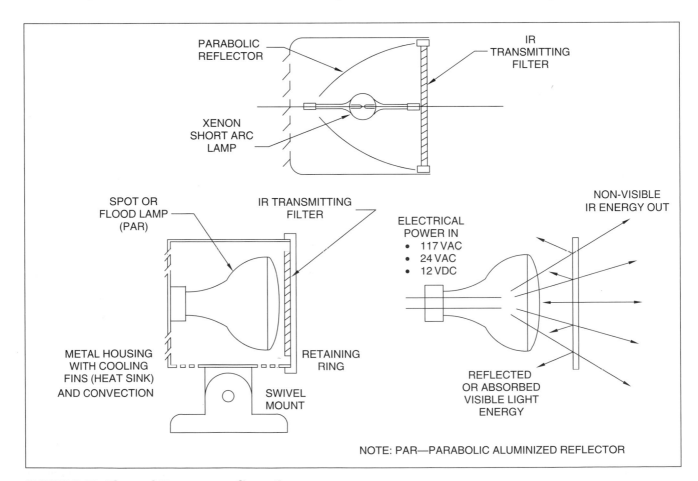

FIGURE 3-14   Thermal IR source configurations

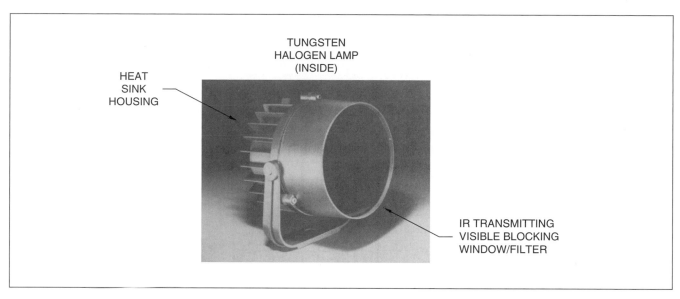

FIGURE 3-15 High-efficiency thermal (IR) lamp

by the housing material. The housing acts as an efficient heat sink that effectively dissipates the heat. The system can operate continuously in hot environments without a cooling fan.

An especially efficient configuration using a tungsten-halogen lamp as the radiating source and a unique filtering and cooling technique is shown in Figure 3-15.

The figure shows the functioning parts of a 500-watt IR illuminating source using a type PAR 56 encapsulated tungsten-halogen lamp. The PAR 56 lamp filament operates at a temperature of approximately 3000 K and has an average rated life of 2000–4000 hours. The lamp's optical dichroic mirror coatings on the internal surfaces of the reflector and front cover lens are made of multiple layers of silicon dioxide and titanium dioxide. In addition to this interference filter, there is a "cold" mirror—a quartz-substrate shield—between the tungsten-halogen lamp and the coated cover lens to control direct visible-light output from the filament. The lamp optics have a visible absorbing filter between the lamp and the front lens that transmits less than 0.1% of all wavelengths shorter than 730 nanometers. This includes the entire visible spectrum. The compound effect of this filtering ensures that only IR radiation leaves the front of the lamp and that visible and long-IR radiation (longer than is useful to the silicon camera sensor) cannot leave the front of the lamp. The lamp output is consequently totally invisible to the human eye. The IR lamp system is available with different front lenses to produce beam patterns for a wide range of applications, covering wide scene illumination to long-range spotlighting.

Table 3-2 summarizes the types of lamp lenses available and the horizontal and vertical beam angles they produce. These beam angles vary from 12° for a narrow beam (spotlight) to 68° for a very wide beam (flood lamp).

3.4.6.2 Infrared-Emitting Diodes

Video security systems for covert and nighttime illumination are using IR LEDs consisting of an array of gallium arsenide (GaAs) semiconductor diodes. These LEDs emit a narrow band of deep red 880 nm or IR 950 nm radiation and no other discernible visible light. These efficient devices typically convert 50% of electrical energy to optical IR radiation. They operate just slightly above room temperature, dissipate little heat and therefore usually require minimum cooling. The light is generated in the diode at the PN-junction and emits IR radiation when electrically biased in a forward direction. The 800–900 nm IR energy is directed toward the magnifying dome lens built into each LED emitter and directed toward the scene. To adequately illuminate an entire scene requires an array of ten, hundred to several hundred diodes that are connected in series with the power source. The array is powered from a conventional 12 VDC or 117 VAC source. The IR light output from each diode adds up to produce enough radiation to illuminate the scene and target with sufficient IR energy to produce a good video picture with a solid-state CCD or CMOS camera. Figure 3-16 shows an IR LED GaAs array that produces a high-efficiency IR beam for covert and nighttime applications.

3.4.6.3 Thermal (Heat) IR Source

All objects emit light when sufficiently hot. Changing the temperature of an object changes the intensity and color of the light emitted from it. For instance, iron glows dull red when first heated, then red-orange when it becomes hotter and eventually white hot. In a steel mill, molten iron appears yellow–white because it is hotter than the red-orange of the lower-temperature iron. The tungsten filament of an incandescent lamp is hotter yet and emits

SOURCE	TYPE	INPUT POWER (WATTS) (VOLTAGE)	BEAM ANGLE (DEGREES)	MAXIMUM RANGE (ft)
WIDE FLOOD	FILTERED WI INCANDESCENT	100	60 HORIZ 60 VERT	30
SPOT	FILTERED WI INCANDESCENT	100	10 HORIZ 10 VERT	200
WIDE FLOOD	FILTERED WI INCANDESCENT	500	40 HORIZ 16 VERT	90
SPOT	FILTERED WI INCANDESCENT	500	12 HORIZ 8 VERT	450
FLOOD	FILTERED XENON ARC	400 (AC)	40	500
SPOT	FILTERED XENON ARC	400 (AC)	12	1500
FLOOD	LED	50 (12 VDC)	30	200
FLOOD	LED	8 (12 VDC)	40	70

WI = TUNGSTEN HALOGEN
LED = LIGHT EMITTING DIODE (880 nm-DEEP RED GLOW, 950 nm-INVISIBLE IR)
WI AND XENON THERMAL LAMPS USE VISUAL BLOCKING FILTERS

Table 3-2   Beam angles for IR Lamps

nearly white light. Any object that is hot enough to glow is said to be incandescent: hence the term for heated-filament bulbs. A meaningful parameter for describing color is the *color temperature* or *apparent color temperature* of an object when heated to various temperatures.

In the laboratory a special radiating source that emits radiation with 100% efficiency at all wavelengths when heated is called a *blackbody* radiator. The blackbody radiator emits energy in the ultraviolet, visible, and infrared spectrums following specific physical laws.

Tungsten lamps and the sun radiate energy like a blackbody because they radiate with a *continuous* spectrum, that is, they emit at all wavelengths and colors. Other sources such as mercury, fluorescent, sodium, and metal-arc lamps do not emit a continuous spectrum but only produce narrow bands of colors: mercury produces a green–blue band; sodium produces a yellow–orange band. Thermal IR cameras are used to view temperature differences in objects in a scene (Chapter 19).

3.5 LIGHTING DESIGN CONSIDERATIONS

The design of the lighting system for video security systems requires consideration of: (1) initial installation cost, (2) efficiency of lamp type chosen, (3) cost of operation,

(4) maintenance costs, (5) spectral intensity, and (6) beam angle of the lamp and luminaire.

3.5.1 Lighting Costs

The cost of lighting an indoor or an outdoor area depends on factors including: (1) initial installation, (2) maintenance, and (3) operating costs (energy usage). The initial installation costs are lowest for incandescent lighting, followed by fluorescent lighting, and then by HID lamps. All incandescent lamps can be connected directly to a voltage supply. They are available for alternating current electrical supply voltages of: 240, 120, and 24 VAC and direct current 12 VDC with no need for electrical ballasting or high-voltage starting circuits. All that is required is a suitably designed luminaire that directs the lamp illumination into the desired beam pattern. Some incandescent lamps are pre-focused with built-in luminaires to produce spot or flood beam coverage. Fluorescent lamps are installed in diffuse light reflectors and require only an igniter and simple ballast for starting and running. HID lamps require more complex ballast networks, which are more expensive, larger and bulkier, consume electrical power, and add to installation and operating costs.

All lamps and lamp fixtures are designed for easy lamp replacement. Fluorescent and HID lamps that have

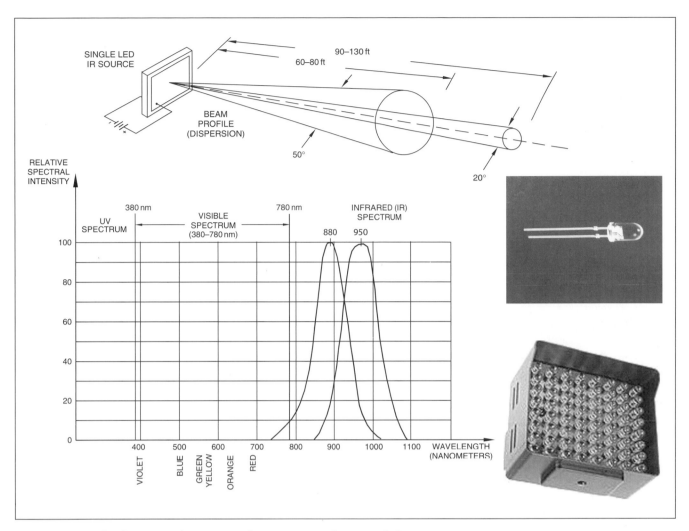

FIGURE 3-16   Single LED and LED array beam output characteristics

ballast modules and high-voltage starting circuits require additional maintenance since they will fail sometime during the lifetime of the installation. Table 3-3 compares the common lamp types including the deep red and IR LEDs.

3.5.1.1   Operating Costs

Energy efficiency of the illumination system must be considered in a video security system. Translated into dollars and cents, this relates to the number of lumens or light output per kilowatt of energy input that additional lighting might cost or that could be saved if an LLL ICCD video camera or thermal IR camera was installed.

The amount of light available directly affects the quality and quantity of intelligence on the video monitor. If the lighting already exists on the premises, the security professional must determine quantitatively whether the lamp type is suitable and the amount of lighting is sufficient. The result of a site survey will determine whether more

lighting must be added. Computer design programs are available to calculate the location and size of the lamps necessary to illuminate an area with a specified number of FtCds. If adding lighting is an option, the analysis will compare that cost with the cost of installing more sensitive and expensive video cameras.

If the video security system includes color cameras, the choice of lighting becomes even more critical. All color cameras require a higher level of lighting than their monochrome counterparts. To produce a color image having a signal-to-noise ratio or noise-free picture as good as a monochrome system, as much as ten times more lighting is required. To obtain faithful color reproduction of facial tones, objects, and other articles in the scene, the light sources chosen or already installed must produce enough of these colors for the camera to detect and balance them. Since a large number of different generic lighting types are currently installed in industrial and public sites, the security professional must be knowledgeable in the spectral output of such lights.

TYPE	SPECTRAL OUTPUT	EFFICIENCY * LUMENS/WATT		LIFETIME (HOURS)	POWER RANGE (WATTS)	WARM–UP/ RESTRIKE (MINUTES)
		INITIAL	MEAN			
MERCURY	BLUE–GREEN	32–63	25–43	16,000–24,000	50–1,000	5–7/3–6
HIGH PRESSURE SODIUM	YELLOW–WHITE	64–140	58–126	20,000–24,000	35–1,000	3–4/1
METAL ARC: METAL HALIDE MULTI-VAPOR	GREEN–YELLOW	80–115	57–92	10,000–20,000	175–1,000	2–4/10–15
FLUORESCENT	WHITE	74–100	49–92	12,000–20,000	28–215	IMMEDIATE
INCANDESCENT: TUNGSTEN TUNGSTEN HALOGEN	YELLOW–WHITE YELLOW–WHITE	17–24	15–23	750–1,000 2,000	100–1,500	IMMEDIATE IMMEDIATE

*REFERRED TO AS EFFICACY IN LIGHTING (LUMENS/WATT)

Table 3-3   Comparison of Lamp Characteristics

TYPE	LIFETIME (HOURS)	INITIAL COST	OPERATING COST	TOTAL OWNING AND OPERATING COST
MERCURY	16,000–24,000	HIGH	MEDIUM	MEDIUM
HIGH PRESSURE SODIUM	20,000–24,000	HIGH	LOW	LOW
METAL ARC: METAL HALIDE MULTI-VAPOR	10,000–20,000	HIGH	LOW	LOW
FLUORESCENT	12,000–20,000	MEDIUM	MEDIUM	MEDIUM
INCANDESCENT: TUNGSTEN HALOGEN TUNGSTEN	750–1,000 2,000	LOW	HIGH	HIGH

Table 3-4   Light Output vs. Lamp Type over Rated Life

Since the lamp operating costs often exceeds the initial installation and maintenance costs put together, it is important to know the efficacy of each lamp type. To appreciate the significant differences in operating costs for the different lamp types, Table 3-4 compares the average light output over the life of each lamp.

For the various models of incandescent, mercury vapor (HID), fluorescent, and high-pressure sodium lamps, lamp life in hours is compared with input power and operating cost, kilowatt-hours (kWh) used, based on 4000 hours of annual operation. The comparisons are made for lamps used in different applications, including dusk-to-dawn lighting, wall-mounted aerial lighting, and floodlighting. In each application, there is a significant saving in operational costs (energy costs) between the high-pressure sodium and fluorescent lamps as compared with the mercury vapor and standard incandescent lamps. Choosing the more efficient lamp over the less efficient one can result in savings of double or triple the operational costs, depending on the cost of electricity in a particular location.

3.5.1.2   Lamp Life

Lamp life plays a significant role in determining the cost efficiency of different light sources. Actual lamp replacement costs and labor costs must be considered, as well as the additional risk of interrupted security due to unavailable lighting. Table 3-5 summarizes the average lamp life in hours for most lamp types in use today.

At the top of the list are the high- and low-pressure sodium lamps and the HID mercury vapor lamp, each providing approximately 24,000 hours of average lamp life. Next, some fluorescent lamp types have a life of 10,000 hours. At the bottom of the list are the incandescent and quartz-halogen lamps, having rated lives of

TYPE	LIFETIME (HOURS)	POWER IN (WATTS)	LUMENS OUT (fc)
MERCURY	24,000	100 250 1,000	4,100 12,100 57,500
HIGH PRESSURE SODIUM	24,000	50 150 1,000	4,000 16,000 1,40,000
METAL ARC: METAL HALIDE MULTI-VAPOR	7,500 20,000 3,000	175 400 1,500	14,000 34,000 1,55,000
FLUORESCENT	18,000 12,000 10,000	30 60 215	1,950 5,850 15,000
INCANDESCENT: TUNGSTEN TUNGSTEN HALOGEN	2,000	250	4,000

Table 3-5   Lamp Life vs. Lamp Type

approximately 1000–2000 hours. If changing lamps is inconvenient or costly, high-pressure sodium lamps should be used in place of incandescent types. Using high-pressure sodium rather than tungsten will save 12 trips to the site to replace a defective lamp, and having 12 fewer burned-out lamps will reduce the amount of time the video surveillance system will be down. High pressure sodium lamps, however, will not produce good color rendering.

Lamp designs require specifications of wattage, voltage, bulb type, base type, efficacy, lumen output, color temperature, life, operating cost, and other special features. Color temperature, power input, and life ratings of a lamp are closely related and cannot be varied independently. For a given wattage, the lumen output and the color temperature decrease as the life expectancy increases.

In incandescent lamps, filament power (watts) is roughly proportional to the fourth power of filament temperature. So a lamp operated *below* its rated voltage has a longer life. A rule of thumb: Filament life is doubled for each 5% reduction in voltage; conversely, filament life is halved for each 5% increase in voltage.

3.5.2 Security Lighting Levels

In addition to the lamp parameters and energy requirements, the size and shape of the luminaire, spacing between lamps, and height of the lamp above the surface illuminated must be considered. Although each video application has special illumination requirements, primary responsibility for lighting is usually left to architects or illumination engineers. To provide adequate lighting in an industrial security or safety environment in building hall-ways, stairwells, outdoor perimeters, or parking lot facilities, different lighting designs are needed.

Table 3-6 tabulates recommended light-level requirements for locations including parking lots, passenger platforms, building exteriors, and pedestrian walkways.

The video system designer or security director often has no option to increase or change installed lighting and must first determine whether the lighting is sufficient for the CCTV application and then make a judicious choice of CCTV camera to obtain a satisfactory picture. If lighting is not sufficient, the existing lighting can sometimes be augmented by "fill-in" lighting at selected locations to provide the extra illumination needed by the camera. Chapters 4, 5, and 19 cover video lenses, cameras, and LLL cameras respectively, and offer some options for video equipment when sufficient lighting is not available.

3.5.3 High-Security Lighting

Lighting plays a key role in maintaining high security in correctional facilities. Lighting hardware requires special fixtures to ensure survival under adverse conditions. High-security lamps and luminaires are designed specifically to prevent vandalism and are often manufactured using high-impact molded polycarbonate enclosures to withstand vandalism and punishing weather conditions without breakage or loss of lighting efficiency (Figure 3-17).

These luminaires are designed to house incandescent, HID, and other lamp types to provide the necessary light intensity and the full spectrum of color rendition required for monochrome and color video security systems. Most fixtures feature tamper-proof screws that prevent the luminaire from being opened by unauthorized personnel. For indoor applications, high-impact polycarbonate fluorescent lamp luminaires offer a good solution. The molded polycarbonate lenses have molded tabs that

TYPE	LOCATION	LIGHT LEVEL	
		FtCd	lux
PARKING AREA	INDOOR	5–50	50–500
LOADING DOCKS	INDOOR	20	200
GARAGES—REPAIR	INDOOR	50–100	500–1000
GARAGES—ACTIVE TRAFFIC	INDOOR	10–20	100–200
PRODUCTION/ASSEMBLY AREA			
ROUGH MACHINE SHOP/SIMPLE ASSY.	INDOOR	20–50	200–500
MEDIUM MACHINE SHOP/MODERATE DIFFICULT ASSY.	INDOOR	50–100	500–1000
DIFFICULT MACHINE WORK/ASSY.	INDOOR	200–500	2000–5000
FINE BENCH/MACHINE WORK, ASSY.	INDOOR	200–500	2000–5000
STORAGE ROOMS/WAREHOUSES ACTIVE—LARGE/SMALL	INDOOR	15–30	150–300
INACTIVE	INDOOR	5	50
STORAGE YARDS	OUTDOOR	1–20	10–200
PARKING-OPEN (HIGH–MEDIUM ACTIVITY)			
PARKING-COVERED	OUTDOOR	1–2	10–20
(PARKING, PEDESTRIAL AREA)			
PARKING ENTRANCES DAY	OUTDOOR	5	50
NIGHT	OUTDOOR	5–50	50–500

NOTE: 1 FtCd EQUALS APPROXIMATELY 10 lux

Table 3-6   Recommended Light Levels for Typical Security Applications

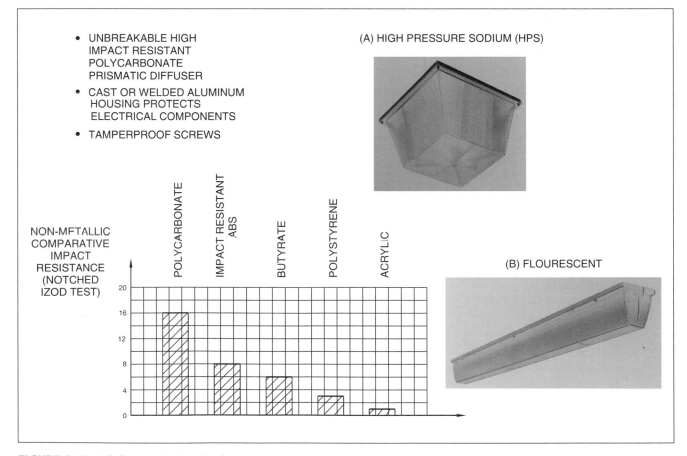

- UNBREAKABLE HIGH IMPACT RESISTANT POLYCARBONATE PRISMATIC DIFFUSER
- CAST OR WELDED ALUMINUM HOUSING PROTECTS ELECTRICAL COMPONENTS
- TAMPERPROOF SCREWS

(A) HIGH PRESSURE SODIUM (HPS)

(B) FLOURESCENT

NON-METALLIC COMPARATIVE IMPACT RESISTANCE (NOTCHED IZOD TEST)

POLYCARBONATE
IMPACT RESISTANT ABS
BUTYRATE
POLYSTYRENE
ACRYLIC

FIGURE 3-17   High security luminaires

engage special slots in the steel-backed plate and prevent the luminaire from being opened, thereby minimizing exposure of the fluorescent lamps to vandalism. Applications include prison cells, juvenile-detention facilities, high-security hospital wards, parking garages, public housing hallways, stairwells, and underground tunnels.

3.6 SUMMARY

The quality of the final video picture and the intelligence it conveys depend heavily on the natural and/or artificial light sources illuminating the scene. For optimum results, an analysis of the lamp parameters (spectrum, illumination level, beam pattern) must be made and matched to the spectral and sensitivity characteristics of the camera. Color systems require careful analysis when they are used with natural illumination during daylight hours and with broad-spectrum color-balanced artificial illumination sources. Using multiple light sources having different color balances in the same scene can produce poor color rendition in the video image. If the illumination level is marginal, measure it with a light meter (Chapter 25) to quantify the actual light reaching the camera from the scene. If there is insufficient light for the standard solid-state video camera, augment the lighting with additional fill-in sources or choose a more sensitive ICCD camera (Chapter 19). As with the human eye, lighting holds the key to clear sight.

Chapter 4
Lenses and Optics

CONTENTS

4.1 Overview
4.2 Lens Functions and Properties
    4.2.1 Focal Length and Field of View
        4.2.1.1 Field-of-View Calculations
            4.2.1.1.1 Tables for Scene Sizes vs. FL for 1/4-, 1/3-, and 1/2-Inch Sensors
            4.2.1.1.2 Tables for Angular FOV vs. FL for 1/4-, 1/3-, and 1/2-Inch Sensor Sizes
        4.2.1.2 Lens and Sensor Formats
    4.2.2 Magnification
        4.2.2.1 Lens–Camera Sensor Magnification
        4.2.2.2 Monitor Magnification
        4.2.2.3 Combined Camera and Monitor Magnification
    4.2.3 Calculating the Scene Size
        4.2.3.1 Converting One Format to Another
    4.2.4 Calculating Angular FOV
    4.2.5 Lens Finder Kit
    4.2.6 Optical Speed: f-number
    4.2.7 Depth of Field
    4.2.8 Manual and Automatic Iris
        4.2.8.1 Manual Iris
        4.2.8.2 Automatic-Iris Operation
    4.2.9 Auto-Focus Lens
    4.2.10 Stabilized Lens
4.3 Fixed Focal Length Lens
    4.3.1 Wide-Angle Viewing
    4.3.2 Narrow-Angle Telephoto Viewing
4.4 Vari-Focal Lens
4.5 Zoom Lens
    4.5.1 Zooming
    4.5.2 Lens Operation
    4.5.3 Optical Speed
    4.5.4 Configurations
    4.5.5 Manual or Motorized

4.5.6 Adding a Pan/Tilt Mechanism
4.5.7 Preset Zoom and Focus
4.5.8 Electrical Connections
4.5.9 Initial Lens Focusing
4.5.10 Zoom Pinhole Lens
4.5.11 Zoom Lens–Camera Module
4.5.12 Zoom Lens Checklist
4.6 Pinhole Lens
    4.6.1 Generic Pinhole Types
    4.6.2 Sprinkler Head Pinhole
    4.6.3 Mini-Pinhole
4.7 Special Lenses
    4.7.1 Panoramic Lens—360°
    4.7.2 Fiber-Optic and Bore Scope Optics
    4.7.3 Bi-Focal, Tri-Focal Image Splitting Optics
    4.7.4 Right-Angle Lens
    4.7.5 Relay Lens
4.8 Comments, Checklist and Questions
4.9 Summary

4.1 OVERVIEW

The function of the camera lens is to collect the reflected light from a scene and focus it onto a camera sensor. Choosing the proper lens is very important, since its choice determines the amount of light received by the camera sensor, the FOV on the monitor, and the quality of the image displayed. Understanding the characteristics of the lenses available and following a step-by-step design procedure simplifies the task and ensures an optimum design.

A CCTV lens functions like the human eye. Both collect light reflected from a scene or emitted by a luminous light source and focus the object scene onto some receptor—the retina or the camera sensor. The human eye has a fixed-focal-length (FFL) lens and variable iris diaphragm, which compares to an FFL, automatic-iris video lens. The eye has an iris that opens and closes just like an automatic-iris camera lens and automatically adapts to changes in light level. The iris—whether in the eye or in the camera—optimizes the light level reaching the receptor, thereby providing the best possible image. The iris in the eye is a muscle-controlled membrane; the automatic iris in a video lens is a motorized device.

Of the many different kinds of lenses used in video security applications the most common is the FFL lens, which is available in wide-angle (90°), medium-angle (40°), and narrow-angle (5°) FOVs. To cover a wide scene and also obtain a close-up (telephoto) view with the same camera, a variable-FOV vari-focal or zoom lens is used. The vari-focal lens is used to "fine tune" the focal length (FL) to a specific FL for the application. To further increase the camera's FOV a zoom lens mounted on a pan/tilt platform is used.

The pinhole lens is used for covert video surveillance applications since it has a small front diameter and can easily be hidden. There are many other specialty lenses, including split-image, fiber optic, right-angle, and automatic focus.

A relatively new lens—the panoramic 360° lens—is used to obtain a 360° horizontal by up to 90° vertical FOV. This lens must be used with a digital computer and software algorithm to make use of the donut-shaped image it produces on the camera sensor. The software converts the image to a 360° panoramic display.

4.2 LENS FUNCTIONS AND PROPERTIES

A lens focuses an image of the scene onto the CCTV camera sensor (Figure 4-1). The sensor can be a CCD, CMOS, ICCD, or thermal IR imager.

The lens in a human and a camera have some similarities: they both collect light and focus it onto a receptor (Figure 4-2).

They have one important difference: the human lens has one FFL and the retina is one size, but the camera lens may have many different FLs and the sensor may have different sizes. The unaided human eye is limited to seeing a fixed and constant FOV, whereas the video system can be modified to obtain a range of FOVs. The eye has an automatic-iris diaphragm to optimize the light level reaching the retina. The camera lens has an iris (either manual or automatic) to control the light level reaching the sensor (Figure 4-3).

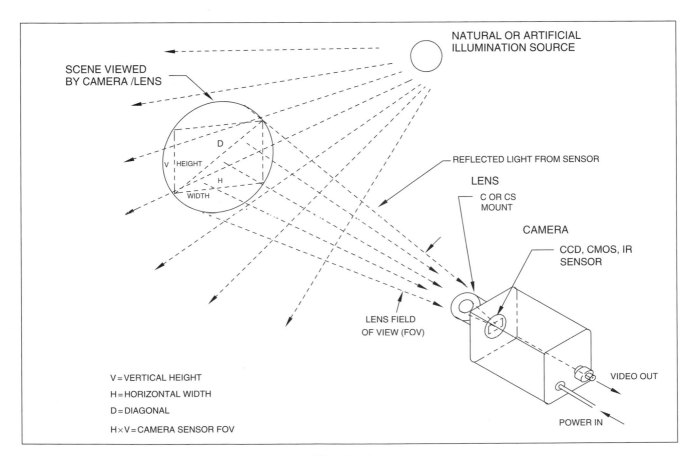

V = VERTICAL HEIGHT

H = HORIZONTAL WIDTH

D = DIAGONAL

H × V = CAMERA SENSOR FOV

FIGURE 4-1   CCTV camera/lens, scene, and source illumination

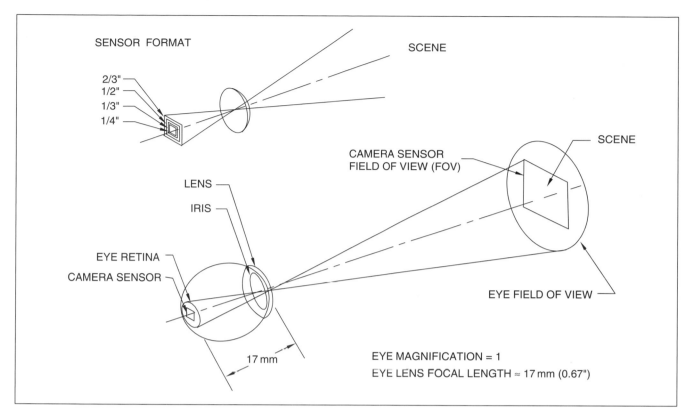

FIGURE 4-2 Comparing the human eye to a CCTV lens and camera sensor

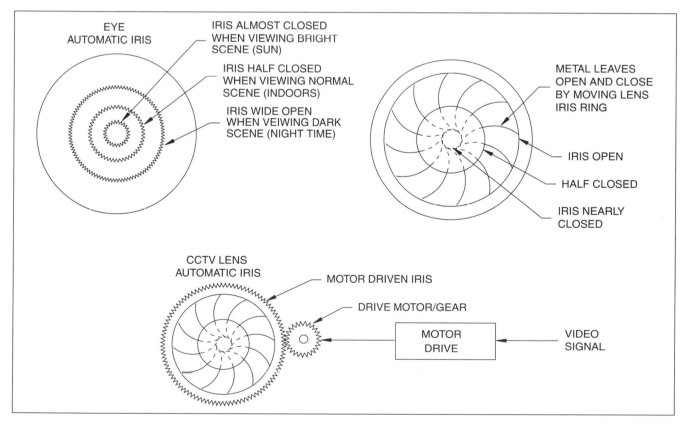

FIGURE 4-3 Comparing the human eye and CCTV camera lens iris

4.2.1 Focal Length and Field of View

In the human eye, magnification and FOV are set by the lens FL and retina size. When the human eye and the video camera lens and sensor see the same basic picture, they are said to have the same FOV and magnification. In practice, a lens that has an FL and FOV similar to that of the human eye is referred to as a *normal* lens with a magnification $M = 1$. The human eye's focal length—the distance from the center of the lens at the front of the eye to the retina in the back of the eye—is about 17 mm (0.67 inch) (Figure 4-2).

Most people see approximately the same FOV and magnification ($M = 1$). Specifically, the video lens and camera format corresponding to the $M = 1$ condition is a 25 mm FL lens on a 1-inch (diagonal) format camera, a 16 mm lens on a 2/3-inch format camera, a 12.5 mm lens on a 1/2-inch camera, an 8 mm lens on a 1/3-inch camera, and a 6 mm lens on a 1/4-inch sensor. The 1-inch format designation was derived from the development of the original vidicon television tube, which had a nominal tube diameter of 1 inch (25.4 mm) and an actual scanned area (active sensor size) of approximately 16 mm in diameter. Figure 4-4 shows the FOV as seen with a lens having magnifications of 1, 3, and 1/3 respectively.

Lenses with much shorter FL used with these sensors are referred to as wide-angle lenses and lenses with much longer FL are referred to as narrow-angle (telephoto) lens. Between these two are medium FL lenses. Telephoto lenses used with video cameras act like a telescope: they magnify the image viewed, narrow the FOV, and effectively bring the object of interest closer to the eye. While there is no device similar to the telescope for the wide-angle example, if there were, the device would broaden the FOV, allowing the eye to see a wider scene than is normal and at the same time causing objects to appear farther away from the eye. One can see this condition when looking through a telescope backwards. This also occurs with the automobile passenger side-view mirror, a concave mirror that causes the scene image to appear farther away, and therefore smaller than it actually is (de-magnified).

Just as your own eyes have a specific FOV—the scene you can see—so does the video camera. The camera FOV is determined by the simple geometry shown in Figure 4-5.

The scene has a width (W) and a height (H) and is at a distance (D) away from the camera lens. Once the scene has been chosen, three factors determine the correct FL lens to use: (1) the size of the scene (H, W), (2) the distance between the scene and camera lens (D), and (3) the camera image sensor size (1/4-, 1/3-, or 1/2-inch format).

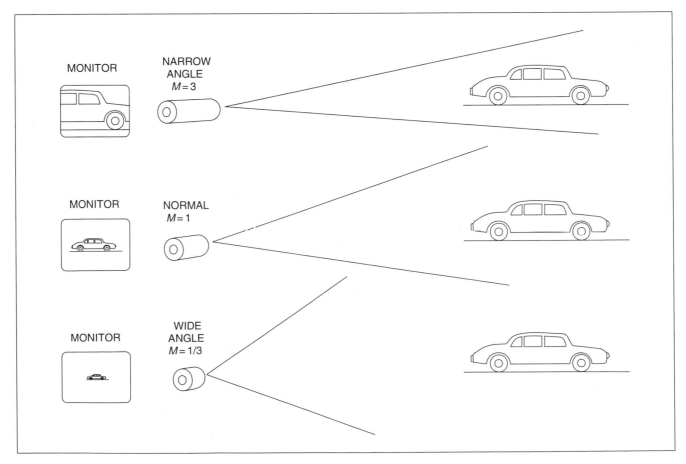

FIGURE 4-4   Lens FOV for magnifications of 3, 1, and 1/3

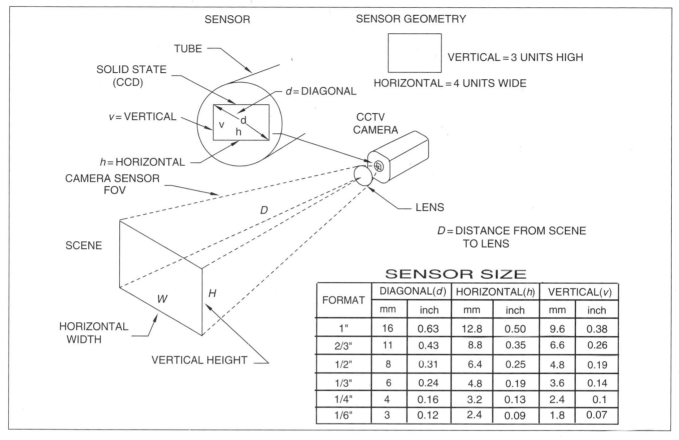

FIGURE 4-5   Camera/lens sensor geometry and formats

4.2.1.1 Field-of-View Calculations

There are many tables, graphs, monographs, and linear and circular slide rules for determining the angles and sizes of a scene viewed at varying distances by a video camera with a given sensor format and FL lens. One convenient aid in the form of transparent circular scales, called a "Lens Finder Kit," eliminates the calculations required to choose a video camera lens (Section 4.2.5). Such kits are based on the simple geometry shown in Figure 4-6.

Since light travels in straight lines, the action of a lens can be drawn on paper and easily understood. Bear in mind that while commercial video lenses are constructed from multiple lens elements, the single lens shown in Figure 4-6 for the purpose of calculation has the same effective FL as the video lens. By simple geometry, the scene size viewed by the sensor is inversely proportional to the lens FL. Shown in Figure 4-6 is a camera sensor of horizontal width (h) and vertical height (v). For a 1/2-inch CCD sensor, this would correspond to $h = 6.4$ mm and $v = 4.8$ mm. The lens FL is the distance behind the lens at which the image of a distant object (scene) would focus. The figure shows the projected area of the sensor on the scene at some distance D from the lens. Using the eye analogy, the sensor and lens project a scene W wide × H high (the eye sees a circle as did the original vidicon). As with the human eye, the video lens inverts the image, but

the human brain and the electronics re-inverts the image in the camera to provide an upright image. Figure 4-6 shows how to measure or calculate the scene size ($W \times H$) as detected by a rectangular video sensor format and lens with horizontal and vertical angular FOVs θ_H and θ_V, respectively.

4.2.1.1.1 Tables for Scene Sizes vs. FL for 1/4-, 1/3-, and 1/2-Inch Sensors

Tables 4-1, 4-2, and 4-3 give scene-size values for the 1/4-, 1/3-, and 1/2-inch sensors, respectively, as a function of the distance from the camera to the object and the lens FL. The tables include scene sizes for most available lenses ranging from 2.1 to 150 mm FL.

To find the horizontal FOV θ_H, we use the geometry of similar triangles:

$$\frac{h}{W} = \frac{FL}{D}, \quad W = \frac{h}{FL} \times D \qquad (4\text{-}1)$$

The horizontal angular FOV θ_H is then derived as follows:

$$\tan \frac{\theta_H}{2} = \frac{h/2}{FL}$$

$$\frac{\theta_H}{2} = \tan^{-1} \frac{h}{2\,FL}$$

$$\theta_H = 2 \tan^{-1} \frac{h}{2\,FL} \qquad (4\text{-}2)$$

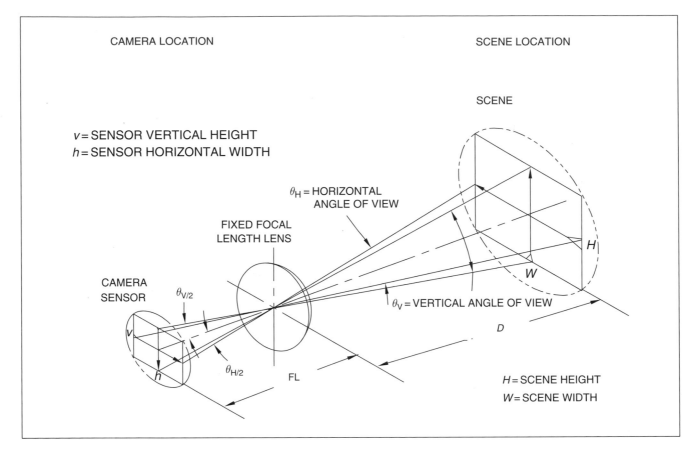

FIGURE 4-6   Sensor, lens and scene geometry

LENS FOCAL LENGTH (mm)	ANGULAR FIELD OF VIEW: $H \times V$ (DEG.)	1/4-INCH SENSOR FORMAT LENS GUIDE							
		CAMERA TO SCENE DISTANCE (D) IN FEET WIDTH AND HEIGHT OF AREA ($W \times H$) IN FEET							
		5	10	20	30	40	50	75	100
		$W \times H$	$W \times H$	$W \times H$	$W \times H$	$W \times H$	$W \times H$	$W \times H$	$W \times H$
2.1	81.2×60.9	8.6×6.4	17×12.9	34×26	51×39	69×51	86×64	129×96	171×129
2.2	78.6×59.0	8.2×6.1	16.4×12.2	33×25	49×37	65×49	82×63	123×92	164×123
2.3	76.1×57.1	7.8×5.9	15.6×11.8	31×23	47×35	62×47	78×59	117×86	157×117
2.6	69.4×52	6.9×5.2	13.9×10.4	28×21	42×31	55×42	69×52	104×78	138×104
3.0	61.9×46.4	6.0×4.5	12×9	24×18	36×27	48×36	60×45	90×68	120×90
3.6	53.1×39.8	5.0×3.8	10×7.5	20×15	30×23	40×30	50×38	75×57	100×76
3.8	50.7×38.0	4.7×3.6	9.5×7.1	19×14	28×21	38×28	47×36	71×54	94×72
4.0	48.5×36.4	4.5×3.4	9×6.8	18×14	27×20	36×27	45×34	68×51	90×68
4.3	45.4×34.1	4.2×3.1	8.4×6.3	16.7×12.5	25×19	33×25	42×31	63×47	84×62
6.0	33.4×25.0	3×2.3	6×4.5	12×9	18×13.5	24×18	30×23	45×35	60×46
8.0	25.4×19.0	2.3×1.7	4.5×3.4	9×6.8	13.5×10.1	18×13.5	23×17	35×26	46×34
12.0	17.1×12.8	1.5×1.1	3×2.2	6×4.4	9.0×6.8	12×9	15×11	23×17	30×23
16.0	12.8×9.6	1.1×.8	2.3×1.7	4.5×3.4	6.8×5.1	9×6.8	11.2×8.4	17×13	22×17
25.0	8.2×6.2	.72×.54	1.4×1.1	2.9×2.1	4.3×3.2	5.8×4.3	7.2×5.4	10.8×8.1	14.4×10.8

NOTE: 1/4-INCH LENSES ARE DESIGNED FOR 1/4-INCH SENSOR FORMATS ONLY AND WILLNOT WORK ON 1/3-INCH OR 1/2-INCH SENSORS. LENS FOCAL LENGTHS ARE NOMINAL PER MANUFACTURERS' LITERATURE.
ANGULAR FOV AND $W \times H$ ARE DERIVED FROM EQUATIONS 4-1 TO 4-4 AND VERTICAL FOV FROM STANDARD 4:3 MONITOR RATIO: $V = 0.75H$.

Table 4-1   1/4-Inch Sensor FOV and Scene Sizes vs. FL and Camera-to-Scene Distance

LENS FOCAL LENGTH (mm)	ANGULAR FIELD OF VIEW: $H \times V$ (DEG.)	1/3-INCH SENSOR FORMAT LENS GUIDE CAMERA TO SCENE DISTANCE (D) IN FEET WIDTH AND HEIGHT OF AREA ($W \times H$) IN FEET							
		5	10	20	30	40	50	75	100
		$W \times H$	$W \times H$	$W \times H$	$W \times H$	$W \times H$	$W \times H$	$W \times H$	$W \times H$
2.3	92.4×69.3	10.4×7.8	20.8×15.6	41.6×31.2	63×47	83×62	104×78	156×117	208×156
2.6	85.4×64.1	9.2×6.9	18.5×13.8	36.8×27.6	55×41	77×58	92×69	138×104	184×138
2.8	81.2×60.9	8.6×6.5	17.2×13	34.4×26	51×39	69×52	86×65	129×98	172×130
3.6	67.4×50.5	6.7×5.0	13.3×10	26.7×20	40×30	53×40	67×50	101×75	134×100
3.8	64.6×48.4	6.3×4.7	12.6×9.5	25×18.9	37.9×28.4	50.5×37.9	63×47	95×71	123×92
4.0	61.9×46.4	6.0×4.5	12×9	24×18	36×27	48×36	60×45	90×68	120×90
4.5	56.1×42.1	5.3×4.0	10.6×8	21.2×15.9	31.8×23.9	42.4×31.8	53×40	80×60	106×80
6.0	43.6×32.7	4.0×3.0	8.0×6	16×12	24×18	32×24	40×30	60×45	80×60
8.0	33.4×25.0	3.0×2.3	6×4.5	12×9	18×13.5	24×18	30×22.5	45×34	60×45
12.0	26.6×20.0	2.0×1.5	4.0×3.0	8.0×6.0	12.0×9.0	16×12	20×15	30×23	40×30
16.0	17.1×12.8	1.5×1.2	3.0×2.3	6.0×4.5	9.0×6.8	12.0×9.0	15.0×11.3	23×17	30×22.5
25.0	11.0×8.2	.96×.72	1.9×1.4	3.8×2.9	5.8×4.4	7.7×5.8	9.6×7.2	14.4×10.8	19.2×14.4
50.0	5.5×4.1	.48×.36	.96×.72	1.9×1.4	2.9×2.2	3.8×2.8	4.8×3.6	7.2×5.4	9.6×7.2
75.0	3.7×2.8	.32×.24	.64×.50	1.3×.96	1.9×1.4	2.6×1.9	3.2×2.4	4.8×3.6	6.4×4.8

NOTE: MOST 1/3-INCH LENSES WILL NOT WORK ON 1/2-INCH SENSORS BUT ALL WILL WORK ON ALL 1/4-INCH SENSORS.
LENS FOCAL LENGTHS ARE NOMINAL PER MANUFACTURERS' LITERATURE.
ANGULAR FOV AND $W \times H$ ARE DERIVED FROM EQUATIONS 4-1 TO 4-4 AND VERTICAL FOV FROM STANDARD 4:3 MONITOR RATIO: $V = 0.75H$.

Table 4-2   1/3-Inch Sensor FOV and Scene Sizes vs. FL and Camera-to-Scene Distance

LENS FOCAL LENGTH (mm)	ANGULAR FIELD OF VIEW: $H \times V$ (DEG.)	1/2-INCH SENSOR FORMAT LENS GUIDE CAMERA TO SCENE DISTANCE (D) IN FEET WIDTH AND HEIGHT OF AREA ($W \times H$) IN FEET							
		5	10	20	30	40	50	75	100
		$W \times H$	$W \times H$	$W \times H$	$W \times H$	$W \times H$	$W \times H$	$W \times H$	$W \times H$
1.4	133×100	23×17	46×34	91×69	137×103	183×137	228×171	342×257	457×348
2.6	101.8×76.4	12.3×9.2	24.6×18	49×37	74×55	98×74	123×92	185×138	246×184
3.5	84.9×63.7	9.1×6.9	18.2×13.8	37×28	55×41	73×55	91×69	137×104	182×138
3.6	83.3×62.5	8.9×6.7	17.8×13.4	36×27	53×40	71×53	89×67	134×101	178×134
3.7	81.7×61.3	8.6×6.5	17.2×13.0	35×26	52×39	69×52	86×65	129×98	172×130
4.0	77.3×58.0	8.0×6.0	16.0×12.0	32×24	48×36	64×24	80×60	120×90	160×120
4.2	74.6×56.0	7.6×5.7	15.2×11.4	30×23	48×34	61×46	76×57	114×86	156×114
4.5	70.8×53.1	7.1×5.3	14.2×10.6	28×21	43×32	57×43	71×53	107×80	142×107
4.8	67.4×50.5	6.7×5.0	13.4×10.0	27×20	40×30	53×40	67×50	101×75	134×100
6.0	56.1×42.1	5.3×4.0	10.6×8.0	21×16	32×24	43×32	53×40	80×60	106×80
7.5	46.2×34.7	4.3×3.2	8.6×6.4	17.1×12.8	26×19	34×26	43×32	65×48	86×64
8.0	43.6×32.7	4.0×3.0	8.0×6.0	16×12	24×18	32×24	40×30	60×45	80×60
12.0	29.9×22.4	2.7×2.0	5.3×4.0	10.7×8	16×12	21.3×16	27×20	41×30	53×40
16.0	22.6×17.0	2.0×1.5	4.0×1.5	8×6	12×9	16×12	20×15	30×23	40×30
25.0	14.6×10.9	1.3×1.0	2.6×2.0	5.1×3.8	7.7×5.8	10.2×7.7	12.8×9.6	19×14	25.6×19.2
50.0	7.3×5.5	.64×.48	1.3×1.0	2.6×1.9	3.8×2.9	5.1×3.8	6.4×4.8	6.5×4.8	12.8×9.6
75.0	4.9×3.7	.43×.32	.85×.64	1.7×1.3	2.6×1.9	3.4×2.6	4.3×3.2	3.2×2.4	8.6×6.4
150.0	2.4×1.8	.21×.16	.43×.32	.85×.64	1.3×.96	1.7×1.3	2.1×1.6	9.6×7.2	4.3×3.2

NOTE: ALL 1/2-INCH FORMAT LENSES WILL WORK ON 1/3- AND 1/4-INCH SENSORS.
LENS FOCAL LENGTHS ARE NOMINAL PER MANUFACTURERS' LITERATURE.
ANGULAR FOV AND $W \times H$ ARE DERIVED FROM EQUATIONS 4-1 TO 4-4.

Table 4-3   1/2-Inch Sensor FOV and Scene Sizes vs. FL and Camera-to-Scene Distance

For the vertical FOV, similar triangles give:

$$\frac{v}{H} = \frac{FL}{D}, \quad H = \frac{v}{FL} \times D \qquad (4\text{-}3)$$

The vertical angular FOV θ_V is then derived from the geometry:

$$\tan\frac{\theta_v}{2} = \frac{v/2}{FL}$$

$$\frac{\theta_v}{2} = \tan^{-1}\frac{v}{2\,FL}$$

$$\theta_v = 2\tan^{-1}\frac{v}{2\,FL} \qquad (4\text{-}4)$$

4.2.1.1.2 Tables for Angular FOV vs. FL for 1/4-, 1/3-, and 1/2-Inch Sensor Sizes

Table 4-4 shows the angular FOV obtainable with 1/4-, 1/3-, 1/2-, and 2/3-inch sensors with some standard lenses from 1.4 to 150 mm FL. The values of angular FOV in Table 4-4 can be calculated from Equations 4-2 and 4-4.

4.2.1.2 Lens and Sensor Formats

Fixed focal length lenses must be used with either the image sensor size (format) for which they were designed or with a smaller sensor size. They cannot be used with larger sensor sizes because unacceptable image distortion and image darkening (vignetting) at the edges of the image occurs. When a lens manufacturer lists a lens for a 1/3-inch sensor format, it can be used on a 1/4-inch sensor but not on a 1/2-inch sensor without producing image vignetting. This problem of incorrect lens choice for a given format size occurs most often when a C or CS mount 1/3-inch format lens is incorrectly used on a 1/2-inch format camera. Since the lens manufacturer does not "over design" the lens, that is, make glass lens element diameters larger than necessary, check the manufacturer's specifications for proper choice.

4.2.2 Magnification

The overall magnification from a specific camera, lens, and monitor depends on three factors: (1) lens FL, (2) camera sensor format, and (3) the monitor size (diagonal). Video magnification is analogous to film magnification: the sensor is equivalent to the film negative, and the monitor is equivalent to the photo print.

4.2.2.1 Lens–Camera Sensor Magnification

The combination of the lens FL and the camera sensor size defines the magnification M_s at the camera location. For a specific camera, the sensor size is fixed. Therefore, no matter how large the image from the lens is at the sensor, the camera will see only as much of the image as will fit onto the sensor. Lens magnification is measured relative to the eye which is defined as a *normal* lens. The eye has approximately a 17-mm FL and is equivalent to a 25-mm FL lens on a 1-inch format camera sensor.

Therefore, the magnification of a 1-inch (16-mm format) sensor is

$$M_s = \frac{\text{Lens focal length (mm)}}{\text{Sensor diagonal (mm)}}$$

$$M_{s\ (1\ \text{inch})} = \frac{FL}{16\,\text{mm}} \qquad (4\text{-}5)$$

For 2/3 inch (11-mm format) the magnification is

$$M_{s\ (2/3\ \text{inch})} = \frac{FL}{11\,\text{mm}} \qquad (4\text{-}6)$$

For 1/2 inch (8-mm format) the magnification is

$$M_{s\ (1/2\ \text{inch})} = \frac{FL}{8\,\text{mm}} \qquad (4\text{-}7)$$

For 1/3 inch (5.5-mm format) the magnification is

$$M_{s\ (1/3\ \text{inch})} = \frac{FL}{5.5\,\text{mm}} \qquad (4\text{-}8)$$

For 1/4 inch (4-mm format) the magnification is

$$M_{s\ (1/4\ \text{inch})} = \frac{FL}{4\,\text{mm}} \qquad (4\text{-}9)$$

Example: From Equation 4-7, a 16-mm FL lens on a $\frac{1}{2}$-inch format camera would have a magnification of

$$M_{s\ (1/2\ \text{inch})} = \frac{FL}{8\,\text{mm}} = \frac{16\,\text{mm}}{8\,\text{mm}} = 2$$

4.2.2.2 Monitor Magnification

When the camera image is displayed on the CCTV monitor, a further magnification of the object scene takes place. The monitor magnification M_m is equivalent to the ratio of the monitor diagonal (d_m) to the sensor diagonal (d_s) or

$$M_{(\text{monitor})} = M_m = \frac{d_m}{d_s} \qquad (4\text{-}10)$$

Example: From Equation 4-10, for a 9-inch diagonal monitor ($d_m = 9$ inches) and a 1/2 sensor format ($d_s = 8\,\text{mm} = 0.315$ inch)

$$M_m = \frac{9}{0.315} = 28.57$$

LENS FOCAL LENGTH (mm)	MAXIMUM IMAGE FORMAT	OPTICAL SPEED: $f/\#$	LENS MOUNT TYPE	1/4 INCH SENSOR HORIZONTAL	1/4 INCH SENSOR VERTICAL	1/3 INCH SENSOR HORIZONTAL	1/3 INCH SENSOR VERTICAL	1/2 INCH SENSOR HORIZONTAL	1/2 INCH SENSOR VERTICAL	2/3 INCH SENSOR HORIZONTAL	2/3 INCH SENSOR VERTICAL
1.4	1/2	1.4	CS	101	76	135	101	180	135		
2.1	1/4	1.0	CS	91	70						
2.2	1/3	1.2	CS	93	69						
2.3	1/3	1.4	CS	89	67	113	85				
2.6	1/2	1.6	CS	72	54	100	75	128	96		
2.8	1/3	1.2	CS	71	53	96	72				
3.0	1/4	1.0	CS	65	49						
3.5	1/2	1.4	CS, C	59	44	78	59	104	78		
3.6	1/2	1/6	CS, C	54	41	72	54	93	71		
3.7	1/2	1.6	CS	53	40	71	53	94	70		
3.8	1/3	1.4	CS	51	39	68	51				
4.0	1/2	1.2	CS	50	37	65	50	89	67		
4.2	1/2	1.6	CS	49	36	64	49	87	65		
4.3	1/4	1.4	CS	42	35						
4.5	1/2	1.4	CS, C	44	34	59	45	79	59		
4.8	1/2	1.4	CS, C	39	29	52	39	69	52	96	74
6.0	1/2	1.0	CS	33	25	57	43	57	43		
7.5	2/3	1.4	CS, C	26	20	35	26	46	35		
8.0	2/3	1.2	CS	25	19	33	25	45	34	58	45
12.0	2/3	1.2	CS, C	18	13	24	18	30	23	39	29
16.0	2/3	1.4	CS, C	13	10	17	13	22	17	31	23
25.0	2/3	1.4	CS, C	8	6	12	9	15	11	20	15
50.0	2/3	1.4	CS, C	4.1	3.1	5.5	4.1	7.3	5.5	10	7.5
75.0	2/3	1.4	CS, C	2.8	2.1	3.7	2.8	4.8	3.6	6.8	5
150.0	1/2	1.6	CS, C	1.4	1.1	1.8	1.4	2.4	1.8	3.3	2.5

(Overall column group heading: CAMERA ANGULAR FIELD OF VIEW (FOV) (DEGREES))

NOTE: ALL FOCAL LENGTHS AND ANGULAR FOVs BASED ON MANUFACTURER'S LITERATURE.
ALL THE LARGER FORMAT LENSES CAN BE USED ON SMALLER FORMAT SENSORS.
LENSES ARE ALSO AVAILABLE HAVING SMALLER FORMATS AND LOWER $f/\#$s THAN THOSE LISTED.

Table 4-4 Representative Fixed Lenses Angular FOV vs. Sensor Format and Lens Focal Length

4.2.2.3 Combined Camera and Monitor

The combined lens, sensor, and monitor magnification is

$$M = M_s \times M_m$$

For the example above and Equation 4-11, the overall magnification of the 8-mm FL lens, 1/2-inch format camera, and a 9-inch monitor is

$$M = M_s \times M_m = 2 \times 28.57 = 57.14$$

Table 4-5 summarizes the magnification for the entire video system, for a 9- and 17-inch monitor and various lenses and camera formats. It should be noted that increasing the magnification by using a larger monitor does not increase the information in the scene; it only increases the size of the displayed picture and permits viewing the monitor from a greater distance.

4.2.3 Calculating the Scene Size

Equations 4-1 and 4-3 are used to calculate scene size. For example, calculate the horizontal and vertical scene size as seen by a 1/2-inch CCD sensor using a 12.5 mm FL lens at a distance $D = 25$ ft. A 1/2-inch sensor is 6.4 mm wide and 4.8 mm high. From Equation 4-1 for horizontal scene width:

$$\text{Scene width} = W = \frac{h}{\text{FL}} \times D$$

$$W = \frac{6.4\,\text{mm}}{12.5\,\text{mm}} \times 25\,\text{ft} = 12.8\,\text{ft}$$

For vertical scene height, using Equation 4-1:

$$\text{Scene height} = H = \frac{v}{\text{FL}} \times D$$

$$H = \frac{4.8\,\text{mm}}{12.5\,\text{mm}} \times 25\,\text{ft} = 9.6\,\text{ft}$$

4.2.3.1 Converting One Format to Another

To obtain scene sizes (width and height) for a 1/6-inch sensor, divide all the scene sizes in the 1/3-inch table (Table 4-2) by 2. For a 2/3-inch sensor, multiple all the scene sizes in the 1/3-inch table (Table 4-2) by 2.

Understanding Tables 4-1, 4-2, and 4-3 makes it easy to choose the right lens for the required FOV coverage. As an example, choose a lens for viewing all of a building 15 feet high by 20 feet long from a distance of 40 feet with a 1/2-inch format video camera (Figure 4-7). From Table 4-3, a 12-mm FL lens will just do the job.

If a 1/4-inch format video camera were used, a lens with an FL of 16 mm would be needed (from Table 4-4, a scene 16.7 feet high by 22.5 feet wide would be viewed).

If a 1/3-inch format video camera were used, a lens with an FL of 9 mm would be used (from Table 4-2, a scene 15.2 feet high by 20 feet wide would be viewed).

4.2.4 Calculating Angular FOV

Equations 4-2 and 4-4 are used to calculate the horizontal and vertical angular FOV of the lens–camera combination. Table 4-4 shows the angular FOV obtainable with some

CAMERA FORMAT (inch/mm)	MONITOR SIZE (inch)	LENS FOCAL LENGTH mm	TOTAL MAGNIFICATION
1/6 (0.11/2.75)	9	2.4	72.7
		30	909.1
	17	2.4	137.4
		30	1717.2
1/4 (0.15/4.0)	9	2.6	37.3
		25.0	358.3
	17	2.6	70.4
		25.0	676.8
1/3 (0.22/5.5)	9	3.8	28.7
		50.0	377.0
	17	3.8	54.0
		50.0	712.2
1/2 (0.31/8.0)	9	4.8	17.1
		75.0	267.8
	17	4.8	32.4
		75.0	506.0

ALL VALUES BASED ON SENSOR AND MONITOR DIAGONAL

$\text{MAGNIFICATION} = M_s \times M_m, \text{ WHERE } M_s = \dfrac{\text{LENS FL}}{\text{SENSOR DIAGONAL}} \text{ and, } M_m = \dfrac{\text{MONITOR DIAGONAL}}{\text{SENSOR DIAGONAL}}$

EXAMPLE: 1/3-inch FORMAT SENSOR, 3.8 mm FL LENS (0.15 inch), AND 17-inch MONITOR

$$M = \frac{3.8\,\text{mm}}{5.5\,\text{mm}} \times \frac{17\,\text{inch}}{0.22\,\text{inch}} = 54$$

Table 4-5   Monitor Magnification vs. Camera/Monitor Size and Lens Focal Length

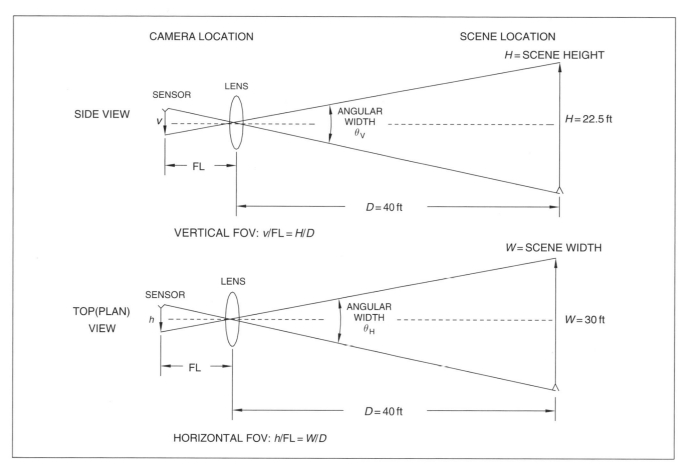

FIGURE 4-7   Calculating the focal length for viewing a building

standard lenses from 2.6 to 75 mm focal length. For the previous example, calculate the horizontal and vertical angular FOVs θ_H and θ_V for a 1/2-inch CCD sensor using a 12.5 mm FL lens. The distance need not be supplied, since an angular measure is independent of distance.

From Equation 4-2, for horizontal angular FOV:

$$\tan\frac{\theta_H}{2} = \frac{h/2}{\text{FL}} = \frac{6.6\,\text{mm}/2}{12.5\,\text{mm}} = 0.264$$

$$\frac{\theta_H}{2} = 14.8°$$

$$\theta_H = 29.6°$$

From Equation 4-4 for vertical angular FOV:

$$\tan\frac{\theta_v}{2} = \frac{v/2}{\text{FL}} = \frac{4.8\,\text{mm}/2}{12.5\,\text{mm}} = 0.192$$

$$\frac{\theta_v}{2} = 10.9°$$

$$\theta_v = 21.8°$$

Table 4-4 summarizes angular FOV values for some standard lenses from 1.4 to 150 mm FL lenses used on the 1/4-, 1/3-, 1/2- and 2/3-inch sensors. To obtain the angular FOV for sensor sizes, *multiply* or *divide* the angles by the ratio of the sensor size. Rule of thumb: for a given lens, angular FOV increases for larger sensor size, decreases for smaller sensor size.

4.2.5   Lens Finder Kit

Tables and slide rules for finding lens angular FOVs abound. Over the years many charts and devices have been available to simplify the task of choosing the best lens for a particular security application. Figure 4-8 shows how to quickly determine the correct lens for an application using the Lens Finder Kit (copyright H. Kruegle).

There is a separate scale for each of the three camera-sensor sizes: 1/4-, 1/3-, 1/2-inch (the 1/4- and 1/3-inch are shown). The scale for each camera format shows the FL of standard lenses and the corresponding angular horizontal and vertical FOVs that the camera will see.

To use the kit, the plastic disk is placed on the facility plan drawing and the lens FL giving the desired camera FOV coverage is chosen. For example, a 1/4-inch format camera is to view a horizontal FOV (θ_H) in a front lobby 30 feet wide at a distance of 30 feet from the camera (Figure 4-9). What FL lens should be used?

THE LENS FINDER KIT USES THREE TRANSPARENT PROTRACTOR DISKS TO HELP
CHOOSE THE BEST LENS WHEN USING THE 1/4-, 1/3- AND 1/2-INCH CCTV CAMERA
FORMATS WITH C OR CS MOUNTS. THE DISKS ARE UNIVERSAL AND CAN BE USED
ON ANY SCALE DRAWING. HOW TO USE:

1. SELECT THE DISK TO MATCH THE CAMERA FORMAT: 1/4-, 1/3- OR 1/2-INCH.
2. USING A SCALE DRAWING OF THE FLOOR PLAN (ANY SCALE), PLACE THE CENTER HOLE OF
   THE DISK AT THE PROPOSED CAMERA LOCATION ON THE FLOOR PLAN.
3. ROTATE THE DISK UNTIL ONE SEGMENT (PIE SECTION) TOTALLY INCLUDES THE HORIZONTAL
   FIELD OF VIEW REQUIRED.
4. USE THE FOCAL LENGTH LENS DESIGNATED IN THE SEGMENT ON THE DISK.
5. IF THE SCALE DRAWING INCLUDES AN ELEVATION VIEW, FOLLOW STEPS 1 THROUGH 4 AND
   USE THE VERTICAL ANGLE DESIGNATED IN EACH PIE SEGMENT FOR THE VERTICAL FIELD
   OF VIEW OF THE LENS.

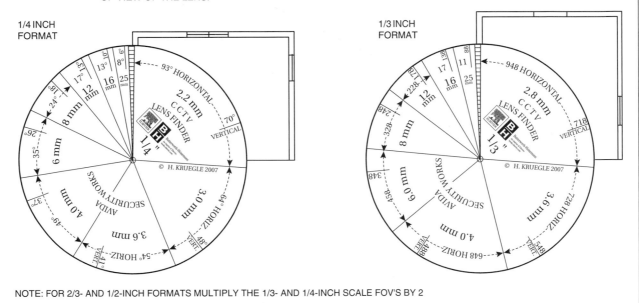

NOTE: FOR 2/3- AND 1/2-INCH FORMATS MULTIPLY THE 1/3- AND 1/4-INCH SCALE FOV'S BY 2

FIGURE 4-8   Choosing a lens with the Lens Finder Kit

To find the horizontal angular FOV θ_H, draw the following lines to scale on the plan: one line to a distance 30 feet from the camera to the center of the scene to be viewed, a line 30 feet long and perpendicular to the first line, and two lines from the camera location to the endpoints of the second 30-foot line. Place the 1/4-inch Lens Finder Kit on the top view (plan) drawing with its center at the camera location and choose the FL closest to the horizontal angle required. A 3.6 mm FL lens is closest. This lens will see a horizontal scene width of 30 feet. Likewise for scene height: using the side-view (elevation) drawing, the horizontal scene height is 22.5 feet.

4.2.6   Optical Speed: f-number

The optical speed or f-number (f/#) of a lens defines its light-gathering ability. The optical speed of a lens—how much light it collects and transmits to the camera sensor—is defined by a parameter called the f-number (f/#).

As the FL of a lens becomes longer, its optical aperture or diameter (d) must increase proportionally to keep the f-number the same. The f-number is related to the FL and the lens diameter (clear aperture) d by the following equation:

$$f/\# = \frac{FL}{d} \qquad (4\text{-}11)$$

For example, an f/2.0 lens transmits four times as much light as an f/4.0 lens. The f-number relationship is analogous to water flowing through a pipe. If the pipe diameter is doubled, four times as much water flows through it. Likewise, if the f-number is halved (i.e. if the lens diameter is doubled), four times as much light will be transmitted through the lens.

In practice the f-number obtained is worse than this because of various losses caused by imperfect lens transmission, reflection, absorption, and other lens imaging properties. The amount of light (I) collected and transmitted

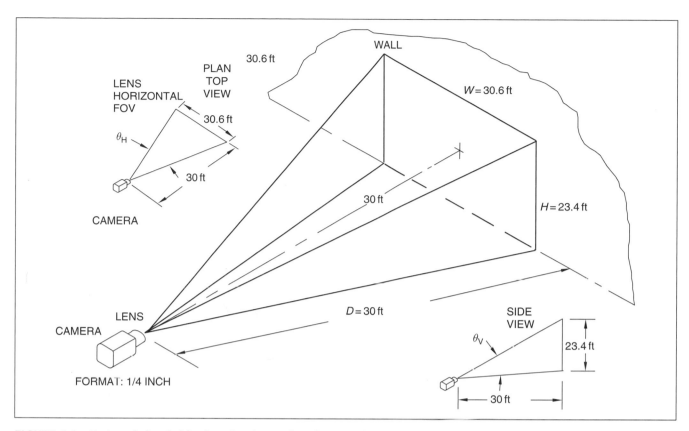

FIGURE 4-9 Determining lobby lens horizontal and vertical FOVs

through the lens system varies inversely as the square of the lens f-number (K = constant):

$$I = \frac{K}{(\text{f}/\#)^2}$$

Long-FL lenses are larger (and costlier) than short-FL lenses, due to the cost of the larger optical elements. It can be seen from Equation 4-11 that the larger the d is made, the smaller the f/# is, i.e. more light gets to the camera sensor. The more light the lens can collect and transfer to the camera image sensor the better the picture quality: a larger lens permits the camera to operate at lower light levels. This light-gathering ability depends on the size (diameter) of the optics: the larger the optics the more the light that can be collected.

Most human eyes have the same size lens (approximately 7 mm lens diameter). In video systems, however, the lens size (the diameter of the front lens) varies over a wide range. The optical speed of video lenses varies significantly: it varies as the square of the diameter of the lens. This means a lens having a diameter twice that of another will pass four times as much light through it. Like a garden hose, when the diameter is doubled, the flow is quadrupled (Figure 4-10).

The more the light passing through a lens and reaching the video sensor the better the contrast and picture image

quality. Lenses with low f-numbers, such as f/1.4 or f/1.6, pass more light than lenses with high f-numbers. The lens optical speed is related to the FL and diameter by the equation f/# = focal length/diameter. So the larger the FL given the same lens diameter, the "slower" the lens (less light reaches the sensor). A slow lens might have an f-number of f/4 or f/8.

Most lenses have an iris ring usually marked with numbers such as 1.4, 2.0, 2.8, 4.0, 5.6, 8.0, 11, 16, 22, C, representing optical speed, f-numbers, or f-stops. The difference between each of the iris settings represents a difference of a factor of 2 in the light transmitted by the lens. Opening the lens from, say, f/2.0 to f/1.4 doubles the light transmitted. Only half the light is transmitted when the iris opening is reduced from, say, f/5.6 to f/8. Changing the iris setting two f-numbers changes the light by a factor of 4 (or 1/4), and so on. Covering the f/# range from f/1.4 to f/22 spans a light-attenuation range of 256 to 1. The C designation on the lens indicates when the lens iris is closed and no light is transmitted.

In general, faster lenses collect more light energy from the scene, are larger, and are more expensive. In calculating the overall cost of a video camera lens system, a more expensive, fast lens often overrides the higher cost incurred if a more sensitive camera is needed or additional lighting must be installed.

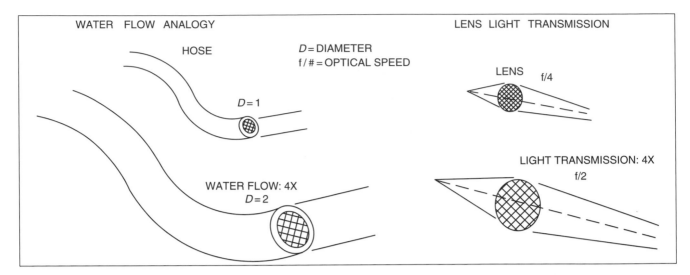

FIGURE 4-10 Light transmission through a lens

4.2.7 Depth of Field

The depth of field in an optical system is the distance that an object in the scene can be moved toward or away from the lens and still be in good focus. In other words, it is the *range* of distance toward and away from the camera lens in which objects in the scene remain in focus. Ideally this range would be very large: say, from a few feet from the lens to hundreds of feet, so that essentially *all* objects of interest in the scene would be in sharp focus. In practice this is not achieved because the depth of field is: (1) *inversely* proportional to the focal length, and (2) *directly* proportional to the f-number. Medium to long FFL lenses operating at low f-numbers—say, f/1.2 to f/4.0—do not focus sharp images over their useful range of from 2 or 3 feet to hundreds of feet. Long focal length lenses—say, 50–300 mm—have a short depth of field and can produce sharp images only over short distances and must be refocused manually or automatically (auto-focus) when viewing objects at different scene distances.

When these lenses are used with their iris closed down to, say, f/8 to f/16, the depth of field increases significantly and objects are in sharp focus at almost all distances in the scene. Short focal length lenses (2.7–5 mm) have a long depth of field. They can produce sharp images from a few feet to 50–100 feet even when operating at low f-numbers

4.2.8 Manual and Automatic Iris

The lens iris is either manually or automatically adjusted to optimize the light level reaching the sensor (Figure 4-3). The manual iris is adjusted with a ring on the lens. The auto-iris uses an internal mechanism and motor (or galvanometer) to adjust the iris.

4.2.8.1 Manual Iris

The manual-iris video lens has movable metal "leaves" forming the iris. The amount of light entering the camera is determined by rotating an external iris ring, which opens and closes these internal leaves. Figure 4-11 shows a manual iris FFL lens and the change in light transmitted through it at different settings of the iris.

Solid-state CCD and CMOS camera sensors can operate over wide light-level changes with manual-iris lenses but require automatic-iris lenses when used over their full light-level range, that is, from bright sunlight to low-level nighttime lighting. Some solid-state cameras use electronic shuttering (Section 5.5.3) and do not require an automatic-iris lens.

4.2.8.2 Automatic-Iris Operation

Automatic-iris lenses have an electro-optical mechanism whereby the amount of light passing through the lens is adjusted depending on the amount of light available from the scene and the sensitivity of the camera.

The camera video signal provides the information used for adjusting the light passing through the lens. The system works something like this: if a scene is too bright for the camera, the video signal will be strong (large in amplitude). This large signal will activate a motor or galvanometer that causes the lens iris circular opening to become smaller in diameter, thereby reducing the amount of light reaching the camera. When the amount of light reaching the camera produces a predetermined signal level, the motor or galvanometer in the lens stops and maintains that light level through the lens. Likewise if too little light reaches the camera, the video camera signal level is small and the automatic-iris motor or galvanometer opens up the iris diaphragm, allowing more light to reach the camera. In both the high and the low light level conditions the automatic-iris mechanism produces the best

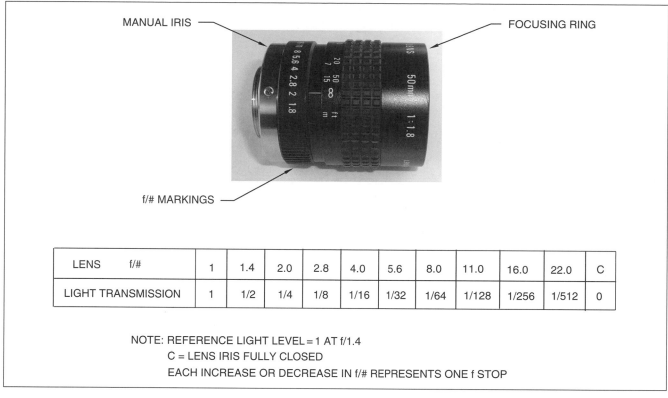

MANUAL IRIS

FOCUSING RING

f/# MARKINGS

LENS f/#	1	1.4	2.0	2.8	4.0	5.6	8.0	11.0	16.0	22.0	C
LIGHT TRANSMISSION	1	1/2	1/4	1/8	1/16	1/32	1/64	1/128	1/256	1/512	0

NOTE: REFERENCE LIGHT LEVEL = 1 AT f/1.4
C = LENS IRIS FULLY CLOSED
EACH INCREASE OR DECREASE IN f/# REPRESENTS ONE f STOP

FIGURE 4-11   Lens f/# vs. light transmission

contrast picture. Automatic-iris lenses are available to compensate the full range of light, from bright sunlight to darkness.

There are two types of automatic-iris lenses: direct drive and video drive. The two methods used to control these two lens types are: DC motor (or galvanometer) drive or video signal drive. With the DC drive method the camera has all the electronics and directly drives the DC motor in the lens with a positive or a negative signal to open and close the iris depending on the light level. With the video method the camera video signal drives the electronics in the lens which then drives the DC motor (or galvanometer) in the lens. Figure 4-12 shows some common automatic-iris lenses.

A feature available on some automatic-iris lenses is called *average-peak* response weighting which permits optimizing the picture still further based on the variation in lighting conditions within the scene. Scenes with high-contrast objects (bright headlight, etc.) are better compensated for by setting the automatic-iris control to *peak*, so that the lens ignores (compensates for) the bright spots and highlights in the scene (see Section 5.5.5). Low-contrast scenes are better compensated by setting the control to *average*. Figure 4-13 illustrates some actual scenes obtained when these adjustments are made. Automatic-iris lenses should only be used with cameras having a fixed video gain in their system.

Automatic-iris lenses are more expensive than their manual counterparts, with the price ratio varying by about two or three to one.

4.2.9 Auto-Focus Lens

Auto-focus lenses were originally developed for the consumer camcorder market and are now available to the security market (similar to the solid-state sensor evolution). There are two types of auto-focus techniques in use. One auto-focus system uses a ranging (distance measuring) means to automatically focus the scene image onto the sensor. A second type analyzes the video signal in by means of DSP electronics, and forces the lens to focus on the target in the scene. The function of both these types of systems is to keep objects of interest in focus on the camera sensor even though they move toward or away from the lens. These lenses are particularly useful when a person (or vehicle) enters a camera FOV and moves toward or away from the camera. The auto-focus lens changes focus from the surrounding scene and focuses on the moving object (automatically) to keep the moving object in focus. Various types of automatic-focusing techniques are used, including: (1) active IR ranging, (2) ultrasonic wave, (3) solid-state triangulation, and (4) video signal DSP.

(A) DC MOTOR IN LENS, ELECTRONICS IN CAMERA   (B) VIDEO ELECTRONICS IN CAMERA

FIGURE 4-12   Automatic-iris fixed focal length (FFL) lenses

(A) HIGH CONTRAST SCENES OPTIMIZED USING MEDIUM RESPONSE WEIGHTING

(B) NORMAL CONTRAST SCENES OPTIMIZED USING PEAK RESPONSE WEIGHTING

(C) LOW CONTRAST SCENES OPTIMIZED USING AVERAGE RESPONSE WEIGHTING

FIGURE 4-13   Automatic-iris enhanced video scenes

4.2.10   Stabilized Lens

A stabilized lens is used when it is necessary to remove unwanted motion of the lens and camera with respect to the scene being viewed. Applications for stabilized lenses include handheld cameras, cameras on moving ground vehicles, airborne platforms, ships, and cameras on towers and buildings. Stabilized lenses can remove significant image vibration (blurring) in pan/tilt mounted cameras that are buffeted by wind or the motion caused by the moving vehicle. The stabilized lens system has movable optical components and/or active electronics that compensate for (move in the opposite direction to) the relative motion between the camera and the scene. An extreme example of a stabilized video camera system is the video image from a helicopter. The motion compensation results in a steady, vibration free scene image on the monitor. Figure 4-14 shows a stabilized security lens and samples of pictures taken with and without the stabilization on.

4.3   FIXED FOCAL LENGTH LENS

Video lenses come in many varieties, from the simple, small, and inexpensive mini pinhole and "bottle cap" lenses to complex, large, expensive, motorized, automatic-iris zoom lenses. Each camera application requires a specific scene to be viewed and a specific intelligence to be extracted from the scene if it is to be useful in a security application. Monitoring a small front lobby or room to see if a person is present may require only a simple lens. It is difficult, however, to determine the activity of a person 100–200 feet away in a large showroom. Apprehending a thief or thwarting a terrorist may require a high-quality, long FL zoom lens and a high resolution camera mounted on a pan/tilt platform. Covert cameras using pinhole lenses are often used to uncover internal theft, shoplifting, or other inappropriate or criminal activity. They can be concealed in inconspicuous locations, installed quickly, and moved on short notice. The following sections describe common and special lens types used in video surveillance applications.

The majority of lenses used in video applications are FFL lenses. Most of these lenses are available with a manual focusing ring to adjust the amount of light passing through the lens and reaching the image sensor. The very short FL lenses (less than 6 mm) often have no manual iris. FFL lenses are the workhorses of the industry. Their attributes include low cost, ease of operation, and long life. Most FFL lenses are optically fast and range in speed from $f/1.2$ to $f/1.8$, providing sufficient light for most cameras to produce an excellent quality picture. The manual-iris lenses are suitable for medium light-level when used with most solid-state cameras.

Most FFL lenses have a mount which in the industry for attaching the lens to the camera is called a C or CS mount (Figure 4-15).

The C mount has been a standard in the CCTV industry for many years while the CS mount was introduced in the mid-1990s to match the trend toward smaller camera sensor formats and their correspondingly smaller lens requirements. The C and CS mount has a 1 inch 32 threads per inch thread. Most security surveillance cameras are now manufactured with a CS mount and supplied with a 5 mm thick spacer adapter ring which allows a C mount lens to be attached to the CS mount camera. The C mount focuses the scene image 0.69 inches (17.5 mm) behind the lens onto the camera sensor. The CS mount focuses the scene image 0.394 inches (10 mm) behind the lens onto the sensor. Commonly used CS mount FLs vary from 2.5 mm

(A) LENS

(C) UNSTABILIZED IMAGE

(B) LENS

(D) STABILIZED IMAGE

FIGURE 4-14   Stabilized lenses and results

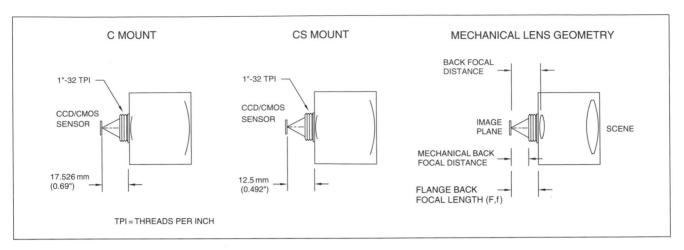

FIGURE 4-15   C and CS mount lens mounting dimensions

(wide-angle) to 200 mm (telephoto). The C mount is also used for long FL lenses having large physical dimensions. Large optics are designed to be used with almost any sensor format size from 1/4 to 1 inch. Lenses with FLs longer than approximately 300 mm are large and expensive. As the FL becomes longer the diameter of the lens increases and costs escalate accordingly. Most FFL lenses are available in a motorized or automatic-iris version. These are necessary when they are used with LLL ICCD cameras in daytime and nighttime applications where light level must be controlled via an automatic iris or neutral density filters depending on the scene illumination.

With the widespread use of smaller cameras and lenses a new set of lens–camera mounts developed. They were not given any special name but are referred to as 11 mm, 12 mm (the most common), and 13 mm mounts. The dimensions refer to the diameter of the thread on the lens and the camera mount. Figure 4-16 shows these lens mounts. Note that the threads are not all the same (the 13 mm mount is different from the 11 mm and 12 mm).

4.3.1   Wide-Angle Viewing

While the human eye has peripheral vision and can detect the presence and movement of objects over a wide angle

(160°), the eye sees a focused image in only about the central 10° of its FOV. No video camera has this unique eye characteristic, but a video system's FOV can be increased (or decreased) by replacing the lens with one having a shorter (or longer) FL. The eye cannot change its FOV without the use of external optics.

Choosing different FL lenses brings trade-offs: reducing the FL increases the FOV but reduces the magnification, thereby making objects in the scene smaller and less discernible (i.e. decreasing resolution). Increasing the FL has the opposite effect.

To increase the FOV of a CCTV camera, a short-FL lens is used. The FOV obtained with wide-angle lenses can be calculated from Equations 4-1, 4-2, 4-3, and 4-4, or by using Table 4-4, or the Lens Finder Kit. For example, substituting an 8 mm FL, wide-angle lens for a 16 mm lens on any camera doubles the FOV. The magnification is reduced to one-half, and the camera sees "twice as much but half as well." By substituting a 4 mm FL lens for the 16 mm lens, the FOV quadruples. We see sixteen times as much scene area but one-fourth as well.

A 2.8 mm FL lens is an example of a wide-angle lens; it has an 82° horizontal by 67° vertical FOV on a 1/3-inch sensor. A super wide FOV lens for a 1/2-inch sensor is the 3.5 mm FL lens, with an FOV approximately 90° horizontal by 75° vertical. Using a wide-angle lens reduces

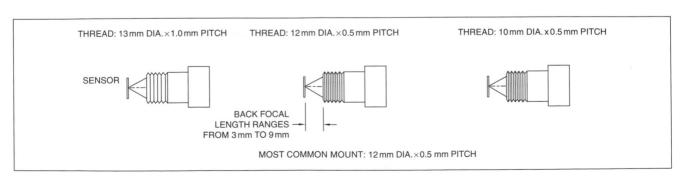

FIGURE 4-16   Mini-lens mounting dimensions

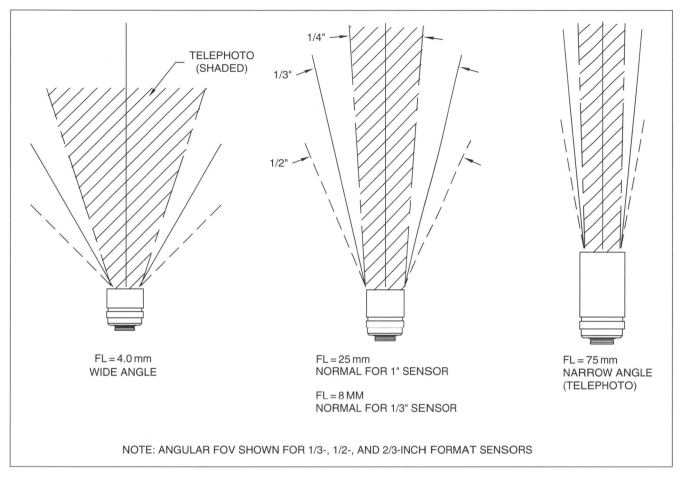

TELEPHOTO
(SHADED)

1/4"

1/3"

1/2"

FL = 4.0 mm
WIDE ANGLE

FL = 25 mm
NORMAL FOR 1" SENSOR

FL = 8 MM
NORMAL FOR 1/3" SENSOR

FL = 75 mm
NARROW ANGLE
(TELEPHOTO)

NOTE: ANGULAR FOV SHOWN FOR 1/3-, 1/2-, AND 2/3-INCH FORMAT SENSORS

FIGURE 4-17   Wide-angle, normal, and narrow-angle (Telephoto) FFL lenses vs. format

the resolution or ability to discern objects in a scene. Figure 4-17 shows a comparison of the FOV seen on 1/4-, 1/3-, and 1/2-inch format cameras with wide-angle, normal, and telephoto lenses.

4.3.2   Narrow-Angle Telephoto Viewing

When the lens FL increases above the standard M = 1 magnification condition the FOV decreases and the magnification increases. Such a lens is called a medium- or narrow-angle (telephoto) lens. The lens magnification is determined by Equations 4-5, 4-10, 4-8, and 4-9 for the reference (1 inch) and three commonly used sensor sizes (see also Table 4-4 and the Lens Finder Kit).

Outdoor security applications often require viewing scenes hundreds and sometimes thousands of feet away from the camera. To detect and/or identify objects, persons, or activity at these ranges requires very long-FL lenses. Long-FL lenses between 150 and 1200 mm are usually used outdoors to view these parking lots or other remote areas. These large lenses require very stable mounts and rugged pan-tilt drives to obtain good picture quality. The lenses must be large (3–8 inches in diameter)

to collect enough light from the distant scene and have usable f-numbers (f/2.5 to f/8) for the video camera to produce a good picture on the monitor.

Fixed focal length lenses having FLs from 2.6 mm up to several hundred millimeters are refractive- or glass-type. Above approximately 300 mm FL, refractive glass lenses become too large and expensive, and reflective mirror optics or mirror and glass optics are used to achieve optically fast (low f-number) lenses with lower weight and size. These long FL telephoto lenses, called "Cassegrain" or "catadioptric lenses," cost hundreds to thousands of dollars. Figure 4-18 shows a schematic of these lenses, a 700 mm f/8.0 and a 300 mm f/5.6 lens used for long-range outdoor surveillance applications.

4.4   VARI-FOCAL LENS

The vari-focal lens is a variable focal length lens developed to be used in place of an FFL lens (Figure 4-19).

In general it is smaller and costs much less than a zoom lens. The advantage of the vari-focal lens over an FFL lens is that its focal length and FOV can be changed manually

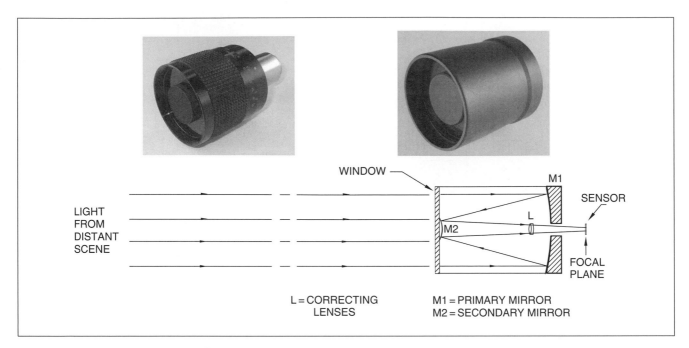

FIGURE 4-18   Long-range, long-focal length catadioptric lenses

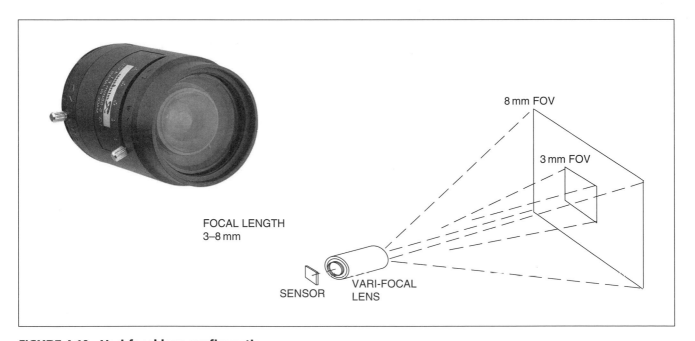

FIGURE 4-19   Vari-focal lens configuration

by rotating the barrel on the lens. This feature makes it convenient to adjust the lens FOV to a precise angle while installed on the camera. The lenses were developed to be used in place of FFL lenses to "fine tune" the FL for a particular application. Having the ability to adjust the FL "on the job" makes it easier for the installer and at the same time permits the customer to select the *exact* FOV necessary to observe the desired scene area. One minor inconvenience of the vari-focal lens is that it must be refocused each time the FL is changed. Typical vari-focal lenses are available with focal lengths of: 3–8 mm, 5–12 mm, 8–50 mm, 10–120 mm (Table 4-6). With just these few lenses focal lengths of from 1.8–120 mm and 144–1.6° FOVs can be covered continuously (i.e.—any focal length in the range). The vari-focal lenses are a subset and simplified version of zoom lenses but they are not a suitable replacement for the zoom lens in a variable FOV pan/tilt application.

FOCAL LENGTH (mm)	ZOOM RATIO	FORMAT (INCH)	OPTICAL SPEED f/#	HORIZONTAL ANGULAR FOV (DEG.)							
				1/4 INCH		1/3 INCH		1/2 INCH		2/3 INCH	
				WIDE	TELE	WIDE	TELE	WIDE	TELE	WIDE	TELE
1.4–3.1	2.2:1	1/3	1.4	121	69.5	185	94.5				
1.6–3.4	2.1:1	1/3	1.4	135	101	180	84.3				
1.8–3.6	2:1	1/3	1.6	144	79.0						
2.2–6	2.7:1	1/4	1.2	90.0	34.7						
2.7–12	4.4:1	1/3	1.2	75	56	97.4	23.8				
2.8–12	4.3:1	1/3	1.4	73	54.7	97.4	24.1				
3.0–8	2.7:1	1/3	1.4	67.0	26.0	89.5	34.0				
3.0–8	2.7:1	1/3	1.0	67.0	27	91	36				
3.5–8	2.3:1	1/3	1.4	58.7	26.5	79.8	35.4				
3.6–18	5:1	1/2	1.8	54.4	11.5	72.3	54.3	95.9	20.0		
4.5–12.5	2.8:1	1/2	1.2	45.9	34.4	61.2	45.9	81.6	30.0		
5.0–50	10:1	1/3	1.3	39.0	4.2	52	5.6				
5.5–82.5	15:1	1/3	1.8	35.3	2.5	47.1	3.3				
6–12	2:1	1/2	1.4	31.6	16.8	42.1	22.4	56.1	29.9		
6–15	2.5:1	1/2	1.4	33.1	14.4	44.1	19.2	59.1	25.7		
6–60	10:1	1/3	1.6	32.7	3.5	43.6	4.7				
7–70	10:1	1/2	1.8	29.0	3.0	38.2	4.0	50.0	5.1		
8–16	2:1	1/2	1.6	24.5	12.6	33.6	16.8	43.5	22.4	59.8	30.8
8–80	10:1	1/2	1.6	25	26	33.0	3.5	42.9	4.6		
10–30	3:1	1/2	1.4	20	7.1	27	9.4	36	12.5		
10–40	4:1	1/3	1.4	20.6	5.3	27.5	7.0				
20–100	5:1	1/3	1.6	10.2	2.1	13.6	2.8				

NOTE: HORIZONTAL ANGULAR FOV FROM MANUFACTURERS' SPECIFICATIONS

Table 4-6 Representative Vari-Focal Lenses—Focal Length, Vari-Focal Zoom Ratio vs. Sensor Format, Horizontal FOV

4.5 ZOOM LENS

Zoom and vari-focal lenses are variable FL lenses. The lens components in these assemblies are moved to change their relative physical positions, thereby varying the FL and angle of view through a specified range of magnifications. Prior to the invention of zoom optics, quick conversion to different FLs was achieved by mounting three or four different FFL lenses on a turret with a common lens mount in front of the CCTV camera sensor and rotating each lens into position, one at a time, in front of the sensor. The lenses usually had wide, medium, and short FLs to achieve different angular coverage. This turret lens was obviously not a variable-FL lens and had limited use.

4.5.1 Zooming

Zooming is a lens feature that permits seeing detailed close-up views (high magnification) of a subject (scene target) or a broad (low magnification), overall view of an area. Zoom lenses allow a smooth, continuous change in the angular FOV. The angle of view can be made narrower or wider depending on the zoom setting. As a result, a scene can be made to appear close-up (high magnification) or far away (low magnification), giving the impression of camera movement toward or away from the scene, even though the camera remains in a fixed position. Figure 4-20 shows the continuously variable nature of the zoom lens and how the FOV of the video camera can be changed without replacing the lens.

To implement zooming, several elements in the lens are physically moved to vary the FL and thereby vary the angular FOV and magnification. Tables 4-1, 4-2, 4-3, and 4-4, and the Lens Finder Kit can be used to determine the FOV for any zoom lens. By adjusting the zoom ring setting, one can view narrow-, medium-, or wide-angle scenes. This allows a person to view a scene with a wide-angle perspective and then close in on one portion of the scene that is of specific interest. The zoom lens can be made significantly more useful and providing the camera a still wider FOV by mounting it on a pan/tilt platform controlled from a remote console. The pan/tilt positioning and the zoom lens variable FOV from wide to narrow angle and anywhere in between provide a large dynamic FOV capability.

4.5.2 Lens Operation

The zoom lens is a cleverly designed assembly of lens elements that can be moved to change the FL from a wide angle to a narrow angle (telephoto) while the image on the sensor *remains in focus* (Figure 4-21). This is a significant difference from the vari-focal lens

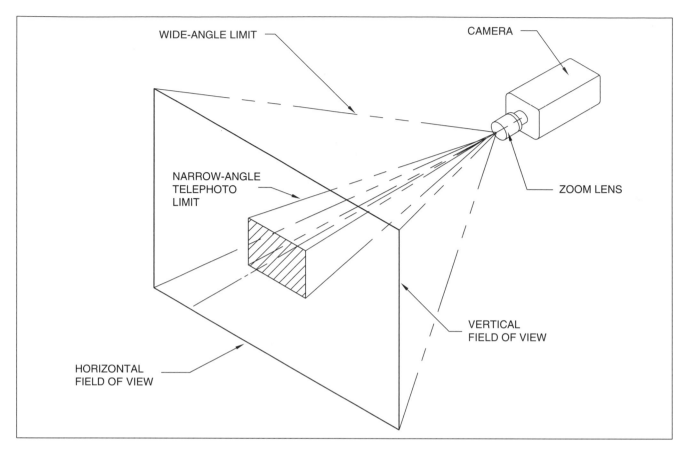

FIGURE 4-20   Zoom lens variable focal length function

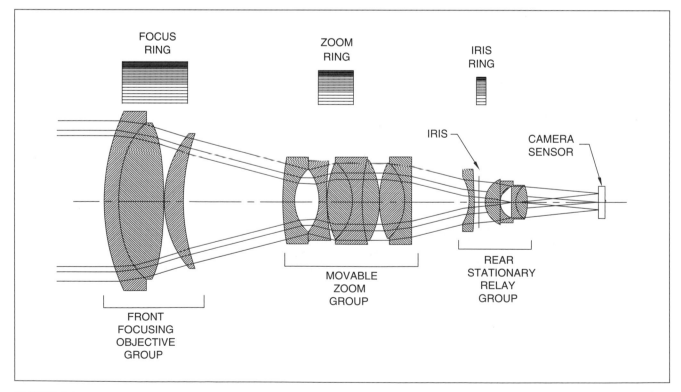

FIGURE 4-21   Zoom lens configuration

which must be re-focused each time its FL is changed (Section 4.4).

A zoom FL lens combines at least three moveable groups of elements:

1. The front focusing objective group that can be adjusted over a limited distance with an external focus ring to initially fine-focus the image onto the camera sensor.
2. A movable zoom group located between the front and the rear group that moves appreciably (front to back) using a separate external zoom ring. The zoom group also contains corrective elements to optimize the image over the full zoom range. Other lenses are also moved a small amount to automatically adjust and keep the image on the sensor in sharp focus, thereby eliminating subsequent external adjustment of the front focusing group.
3. The rear stationary relay group at the camera end of the zoom lens that determines the final image size when it is focused on the camera sensor.

Each lens group normally consists of several elements. When the zoom group is positioned correctly, it sees the image produced by the objective group and creates a new image from it. The rear relay group picks up the image from the zoom group and relays it to the camera sensor. In a well-designed zoom lens a scene in focus at the wide-angle (short-FL) setting remains in focus at the narrow-angle (telephoto) setting and everywhere in between.

4.5.3 Optical Speed

Since the FL of a zoom lens is variable and its entrance aperture is fixed, its f-number is not fixed (see Equation 4-11). For this reason, zoom lens manufacturers often list the f-number for the zoom lens at the wide and narrow FLs, with the f-number at the wide-angle setting being

faster (more light throughput, lower f-number) than at the telephoto setting. For example, a 11–110 mm zoom lens may be listed as f/1.8 when set at 11 mm FL and f/4 when set at 110 mm FL. The f-number for any other FL in between the two settings lies in between these two values.

4.5.4 Configurations

Many manufacturers produce a large variety of manual and motorized zoom lenses suitable for a wide variety of applications. Figure 4-22 shows two very different zoom lenses used for surveillance applications.

The manual zoom lens shown has a 8.5–51 mm FL (6:1 zoom ratio) and has an optical speed of f/1.6. The long range lens shown has a large zoom ratio of 21:1. This lens has an FL range of 30–750 mm and speed of f/4.6.

Figure 4-23 shows the FOVs obtained from a 11–110 mm FL zoom lens on a 1/2-inch sensor camera at three zoom FL settings.

Table 4-7 is a representative list of manual and motorized zoom lenses, from a small, lightweight, inexpensive 8–48 mm FL zoom lens to a large, expensive, 13.5–600 mm zoom lens used in high-risk security areas by industry, military, and government agencies.

Zoom lenses are available with magnification ratios from 6:1 to 50:1. Many have special features, including remotely controlled preset zoom and focus positions, auto-focus and stabilization.

4.5.5 Manual or Motorized

The FL of a zoom lens is changed by moving an external zoom ring either manually or with an electric motor. When the zoom lens iris, focus, or zoom setting must be adjusted remotely, a motorized lens with a remote controller is used. The operator can control and change these

(A) MANUAL   (B) MOTORIZED

FIGURE 4-22   Manual and motorized zoom lenses

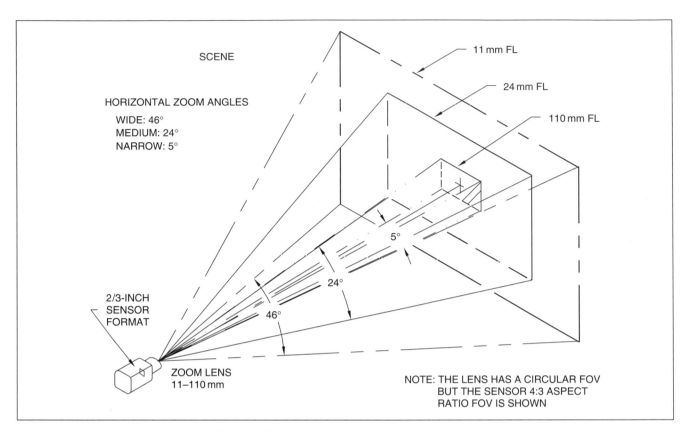

FIGURE 4-23   Zoom lens FOV at different focal length settings

FOCAL LENGTH (mm)	ZOOM RATIO	FORMAT (INCH)	OPTICAL SPEED: f/#	HORIZONTAL ANGULAR FOV (DEG.)							
				1/4 INCH		1/3 INCH		1/2 INCH		2/3 INCH	
				WIDE	T ELE	WIDE	TELE	WIDE	TELE	WIDE	TELE
4.5–54	12:1	1/4	1.1	43.5	3.7						
4.6–28	6:1	1/4	1.0	41.6	7.5						
5.5–77	14:1	1/3	1.4	36.2	2.6	47.1	3.5				
5.5–187	34:1	1/3	1.8	35.0	1.1	46.6	1.5				
5.7–34.2	6:1	1/3	1.0	34.5	6.1	46	8.1				
5.8–121.8	21:1	1/3	1.6	33.8	1.7	45	2.3				
6–72	12:1	1/3	1.5	33.4	2.8	43.6	3.8				
6–90	15:1	1/3	1.2	33.0	2.3	43.8	3.1				
7.5–105	14:1	1/2	1.4	27.0	2.0	35.5	2.6	46.2	3.5		
8–48	6:1	1/2	1.0	24.9	4.4	33.0	5.9	43.2	7.7		
8–96	12:1	1/2	2.0	25.3	2.2	33.4	2.8	43.5	3.7		
8–160	20:1	1/2	2.0	25.1	1.3	33.4	1.7	43.6	2.3		
9–180	20:1	1/3	1.2	22.6	1.2	30.3	1.5				
10.5–105	10:1	2/3	1.4	18.6	2.0	24.8	2.6	33.0	3.5	45.5	4.8
10–140	14:1	2/3	1.9	19.9	1.5	26.4	2.0	35.0	2.7	47.5	3.6
10–200	20:1	1/2	2.5	20.3	1.1	27.0	1.4	35.5	1.8		
10–300	30:1	1/2	1.5	20.0	0.7	26.6	0.9	35.5	1.25		
12.5–75	6:1	2/3	1.6	16.1	2.8	21.4	3.7	28.4	4.9	38.8	6.7
12–120	10:1	1/2	1.8	16.6	1.7	22.1	2.3	29.4	3.1		
12–240	20:1	1/2	1.6	17.2	0.9	23.0	1.2	30.8	1.6		
16–160	10:1	1	1.8	16.8	1.8	22.4	2.4	30.8	3.2	44.9	4.6
10–500	50:1	1/2	4.0	13.7	0.3	18.2	0.4	35.5	0.7		

NOTE: NOMINAL HORIZONTAL ANGULAR FOV FROM MANUFACTURERS' SPECIFICATION

Table 4-7   Representative Motorized Zoom Lenses—Focal Length, Zoom Ratio vs. Sensor Formats, Horizontal FOV

settings remotely using toggle switch controls on the console or automatically through preprogrammed software. The motor and gear mechanisms effecting these changes are mounted within the zoom lens. Manual zoom lenses are not very practical for surveillance since an operator is not located at the camera location and cannot manually adjust the zoom lens.

4.5.6 Adding a Pan/Tilt Mechanism

A zoom lens and camera pointed in a fixed direction provides limited viewing. When the zoom lens is viewing wide angle it sees a large FOV, but when it is zoomed to a narrow angle it will zoom in and magnify only in one pointing direction—straight ahead of the camera. This is of limited use unless it is pointing at a area of importance such as an entrance door, entry/exit gate, receptionist, i.e. *one* single location.

To fully utilize a zoom lens it is mounted on a pan-tilt mechanism so that the lens can be pointed in almost any direction (Figure 4-24).

By varying the lens zoom control and moving the pan/tilt platform, a wide dynamic FOV is achieved. The pan-tilt and lens controller remotely adjusts pan, tilt, zoom, and focus. The lens usually has an automatic iris, but in some cases the operator can choose a manual- or automatic-iris setting on the lens or the controller. In surveillance applications, one shortcoming of a pan-tilt mounted zoom lens is the existence of "dead zone" viewing areas since the lens cannot point and see in all directions at once.

4.5.7 Preset Zoom and Focus

In a computer-controlled surveillance system a motorized zoom lens with electronic preset functions is used. In this mode of operation as a preset zoom lens, the zoom and focus ring positions are monitored electrically and memorized by the computer during system setup. These settings (presets) are then automatically repeated on command by the computer software at a later time. In this surveillance application, this feature allows the computer to point the camera–lens combination according to a set of predetermined conditions and adjust pointing and the zoom lens FL and focus: i.e. (1) azimuth and elevation angle, (2) focused at a specific distance and (3) iris set to a specific f-number opening. When a camera needs to turn to another preset set of conditions in response to an alarm sensor or other input, the preset feature eliminates the need for human response and significantly reduces the time to acquire a new target.

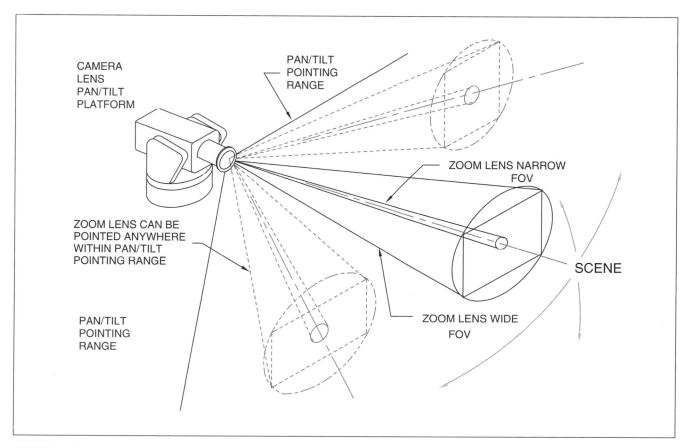

FIGURE 4-24 Dynamic FOV of pan/tilt-mounted zoom lens

4.5.8　Electrical Connections

The motorized zoom lens contains electronics, motors, and clutches to control the movement of the zoom, focus, and iris adjustment rings, and end-of-travel limit switches to protect the gear mechanism.

Since the electrical connections have not been standardized among manufacturers, the manufacturer's lens wiring diagram must be consulted for proper wiring. Figure 4-25 shows a typical wiring schematic for zoom, focus, and iris mechanisms. The zoom, focus, and iris motors are controlled with positive and negative DC voltages from the lens controller, using the polarity specified by the manufacturer.

4.5.9　Initial Lens Focusing

To achieve the performance characteristics designed into a zoom lens, the lens must be properly focused onto the camera sensor during the initial installation. Since the lens operates over a wide range of focal lengths it must be tested and checked to ensure that it is in focus at the wide-angle and telephoto settings. To perform a critical focusing of the zoom lens the aperture (iris) must be wide open (set to the lowest f-number) for all back-focus adjustments of the camera sensor. This provides the conditions for a *minimum* depth of field, and the conditions to perform the most critical focusing. Therefore, adjustments must be performed in subdued lighting, or with optical filters in front of the lens, to reduce the light and allow the lens iris to open fully to get minimum depth of field. The following steps should be followed to focus the lens:

1. With the camera operating, view an object at least 50 feet away.
2. Make sure the lens iris is wide open so that focusing is most critical.
3. Set the lens focus control to the extreme *far* position.
4. Adjust the lens zoom control to the extreme wide-angle position (shortest FL).
5. Adjust the camera sensor position adjustment control to obtain the best focus on the monitor.
6. Move the lens zoom to the extreme telephoto (longest FL) setting.
7. Adjust the lens focus control (on the controller) for the best picture.
8. Re-check the focus at the wide-angle (position of shortest FL).

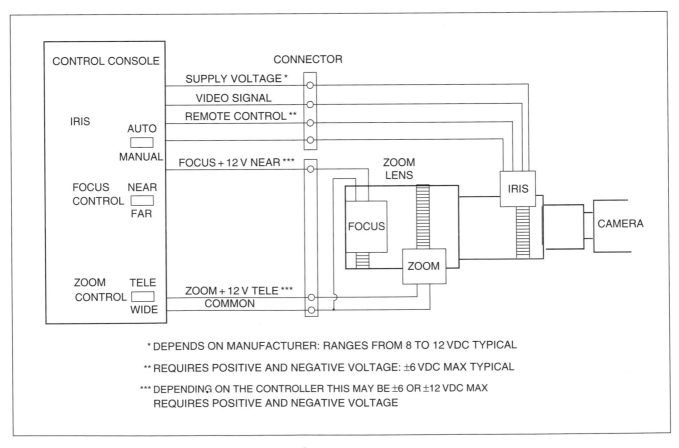

FIGURE 4-25　Motorized zoom lens electrical configuration

4.5.10 Zoom Pinhole Lens

Pinhole lenses with a small front lens element are common place in covert video surveillance applications. Zoom pinhole lenses while not as common as FFL pinhole lenses are available in straight and right-angle configuration. One lens has an FL range of 4−12 mm and an optical speed of f/4.0.

4.5.11 Zoom Lens–Camera Module

The requirement for a compact zoom lens and camera combination has been satisfied with the zoom lens–camera module. This module evolved out of a requirement for a lightweight, low-inertia camera lens for use in high-speed pan-tilt dome installations in casinos and retail stores. The camera–lens module has a mechanical cube configuration (Figure 4-26) so that it can easily be incorporated into small pan-tilt dome housings and be pointed in any direction at *high speeds.*

The module assembly includes the following components and features: (1) rugged, compact mechanical structure suitable for high-speed pan-tilt platforms, (2) large optical zoom ratio, typically 20:1, and (3) sensitive 1/4- or 1/3-inch solid-state color camera with excellent sensitivity and resolution. Options include: (1) automatic-focus capability, (2) image stabilization, and (3) electronic zoom.

4.5.12 Zoom Lens Checklist

The following should be considered when applying a zoom lens:

FIGURE 4-26 Compact zoom lens–camera cube

- What FOV is required? See Tables 4-1, 4-2, 4-3, 4-4, and the Lens Finder Kit.
- Can a zoom lens cover the FOV or must a pan-tilt platform be used?
- Is the scene lighting constant or widely varying? Is a manual or automatic iris required?
- What is the camera format: 1/4-, 1/3-, 1/2-inch?
- What is the camera lens mount type: C, or CS?
- Is auto-focus or stabilization needed?
- Is electronic zoom required to extend the FL range?

Zoom lenses on pan-tilt platforms significantly increase the viewing capability of a video system by providing a large range of FLs all in one lens. The increased complexity and precision required in the manufacture of zoom lenses makes them cost three to ten times as much as an FFL lens.

4.6 PINHOLE LENS

A pinhole lens is a special security lens with a relatively small front diameter so that it can be hidden in a wall, ceiling, or some object. Covert pinhole lens–camera assemblies have been installed in emergency lights, exit signs, ceiling-mounted lights, table lamps, and even disguised as a building sprinkler head fixture. Any object that can house the camera and pinhole lens and can disguise or hide the front lens element is a candidate for a covert installation. In practice the front lens is considerably larger than a pinhole, usually 0.06−0.38 inch in diameter, but nevertheless it can be successfully hidden from view. Variations of the pinhole lens include straight or right-angle, manual or automatic iris, narrow-taper or stubby-front shape (Figure 4-27). The lenses shown are for use with C or CS mount cameras. Whether to use the straight or right-angle pinhole lens depends on the application. A detailed description and review of covert camera and pinhole lenses are presented in Chapter 18.

4.6.1 Generic Pinhole Types

A feature that distinguishes two generic pinhole lens designs from each other is the shape and size of the front taper (Figure 4-28). The slow tapering design permits easier installation than the fast taper and also has a faster optical speed, since the larger front lens collects more light.

The optical speed (f-number) of the pinhole lens is important for the successful implementation of a covert camera system. The lower the f-number of the lens, the more the light reaching the camera and the better the video picture. An f/2.2 lens transmits 2.5 times more light than an f/3.5. The best theoretical f-number is equal to

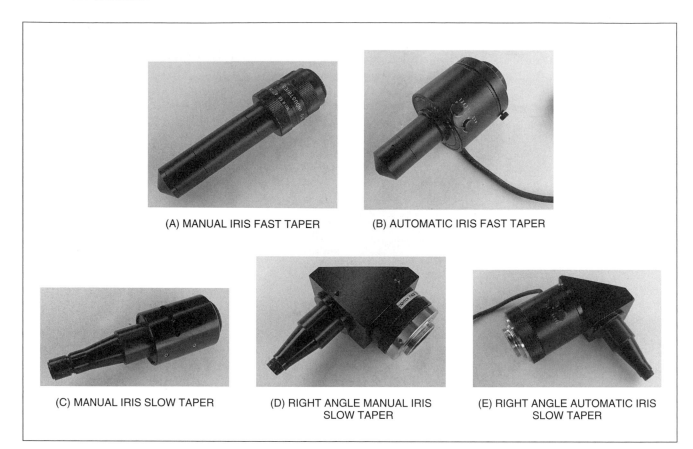

(A) MANUAL IRIS FAST TAPER

(B) AUTOMATIC IRIS FAST TAPER

(C) MANUAL IRIS SLOW TAPER

(D) RIGHT ANGLE MANUAL IRIS
SLOW TAPER

(E) RIGHT ANGLE AUTOMATIC IRIS
SLOW TAPER

FIGURE 4-27   Straight and right-angle pinhole lenses

the FL divided by the entrance lens diameter (d). From Equation 4-11:

$$f/\# = \frac{FL}{d}$$

For a pinhole lens, the light getting through the lens to the camera sensor is limited primarily by the diameter of the front lens or the mechanical opening through which it views. For this reason, the larger the lens entrance diameter, the more light gets through to the image sensor, resulting in a better picture quality, if all other conditions remain the same.

4.6.2   Sprinkler Head Pinhole

There are many types of covert lenses available for the security industry: pinhole, mini, fiber optic, camera-lenses covertly concealed in objects. The sprinkler head camera is a unique pinhole lens hidden in a ceiling sprinkler fixture which makes it extremely difficult for an observer standing at floor level to detect or identify. This unique device provides an extremely useful covert surveillance system. Figure 4-29 shows the configuration and two versions of the sprinkler head lens, the straight and right-angle.

This pinhole lens and camera combination is concealed in and above a ceiling using a modified sprinkler head to view the room below the ceiling. For investigative purposes, fixed pinhole lenses pointing in one specific direction are usually suitable. To look in different directions there is a panning sprinkler head version. An integral camera-lens-sprinkler head design is shown in Section 18.3.5.

4.6.3   Mini-Pinhole

Another generic family of covert lenses is the mini-lens group (Figure 4-30). They are available in conventional on-axis and special off-axis versions. Their front mechanical shape can be flat or cone shaped.

These lenses are very small, some with a cone-shaped front, typically less than 1/2 inch diameter by 1/2 inch long and mount directly onto a small video camera. The front lens in these mini-lenses ranges from 1/16 inch to 3/8 inch diameter. The cone-shaped mini-lens is easier to install in many applications. These mini-lenses are optically fast having speeds of f/1.4 to f/1.8 and can be used in places unsuitable for larger pinhole lenses. An f/1.4 mini-pinhole lens transmits five times more light than an f/3.5 pinhole lens. Mini-pinhole lenses are available in FLs from 2.1 to 11 mm and when combined with a good camera

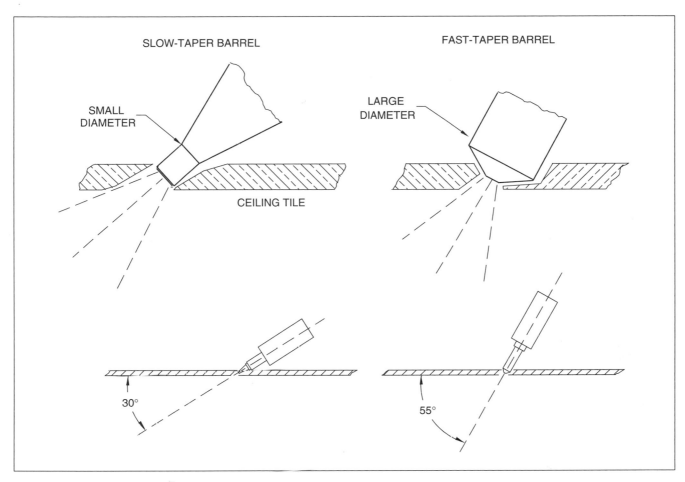

FIGURE 4-28   Short vs. long tapered pinhole lenses

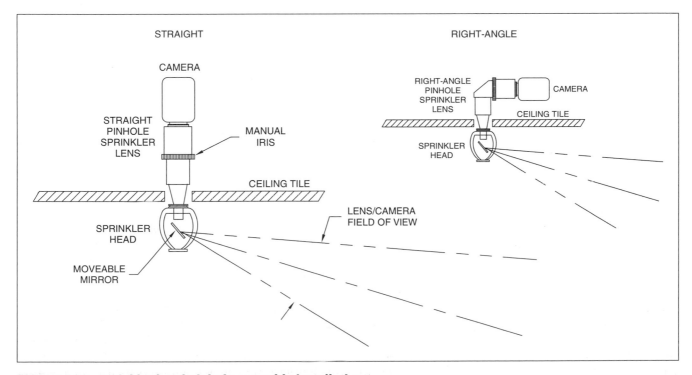

FIGURE 4-29   Sprinkler head pinhole assembly installation

FIGURE 4-30 Mini-pinhole lenses

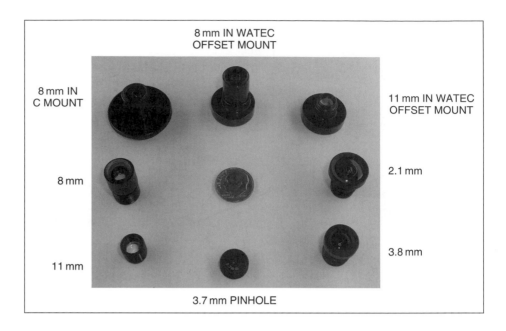

result in the fastest covert cameras available. A useful variation of the standard mini-lens is the off-axis mini-lens. This lens is mounted offset from the camera axis, which causes the camera to look off to one side, up, or down, depending on the offset direction chosen. Chapter 18 describes pinhole and mini-lenses in detail.

4.7   SPECIAL LENSES

There are several special video security lenses and lens functions that deserve consideration. These include: (1) a new panoramic 360° lens, (2) fiber-optic and bore scope, (3) split-image, (4) right-angle, (5) relay, (6) automatic-focus, (7) stabilized, and (8) long-range. The new panoramic lens must be integral with a camera and used with computer hardware and software (Section 5.10). The other special lenses are used in applications when standard FFL, vari-focal or zoom lenses are not suitable. The auto-focus and stabilizing functions are used to enhance the performance of zoom lenses, vari-focal, fixed focus lenses, etc.

4.7.1   Panoramic Lens—360°

There has always been a need to see "all around" i.e. an entire room or other location, seeing 360° with one panoramic camera and lens. To date, a 360° FOV camera system has only been achieved with multiple cameras and lenses and combining the images on a split-screen monitor. This lens is usually mounted in the ceiling of a room or on a tower. Panoramic *lenses* have been available for many years but have only recently been combined with powerful digital electronics, sophisticated mathematical transformations and compression algorithms to take

advantage of their capabilities. The availability of high resolution solid-state cameras has made it possible to map a 360° by 90° hemispherical FOV into a standard rectangular monitor format with good resolution. Figure 4-31 shows two panoramic lens having a 360° horizontal FOV and a 90° vertical FOV.

In operation the lens collects light from the 360° panoramic scene and focuses it onto the camera sensor as a donut-shaped image (Figure 4-32). The electronics and mathematical algorithm convert this donut-shaped panoramic image into the rectangular (horizontal and vertical) format for normal monitor viewing. (Section 2.6.5 describes the panoramic camera in detail.)

4.7.2   Fiber-Optic and Bore Scope Optics

Coherent fiber-optic bundle lenses can sometimes solve difficult video security applications. Not to be confused with the single or multiple strands of fiber commonly used to transmit the video signal over long distances, the coherent fiber-optic lens has many thousands of individual glass fibers positioned adjacent to each other. These thousands of fibers transmit a coherent image from an objective lens, over a distance of several inches to several feet, where the image is then transferred again by means of a relay lens to the camera sensor. A high-resolution 450 TV lines coherent fiber bundle consists of several hundred thousand glass fibers that transfer a focused image from one end of the fiber bundle to the other. Coherent optics means that each point in the image on the front end of the fiber bundle corresponds to a point at the rear end. Since the picture quality obtained with fiber-optic lenses is not as good as that obtained with all glass lenses, such lenses should only

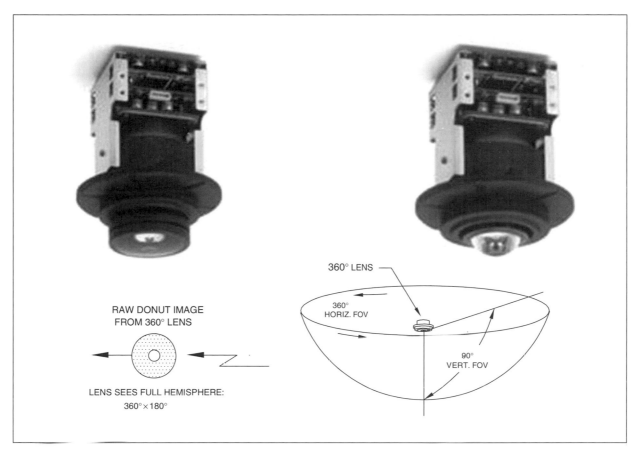

FIGURE 4-31 Panoramic 360° lens camera module

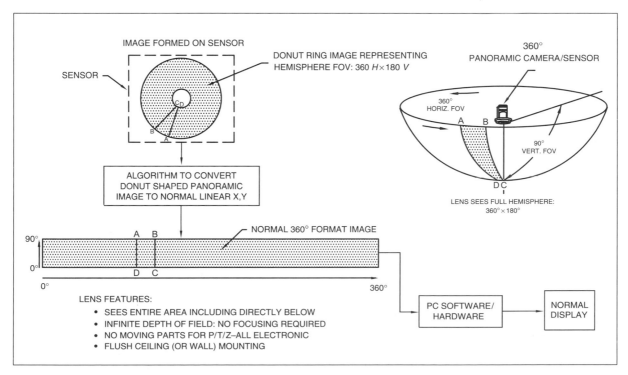

FIGURE 4-32 Panoramic lens layout and description

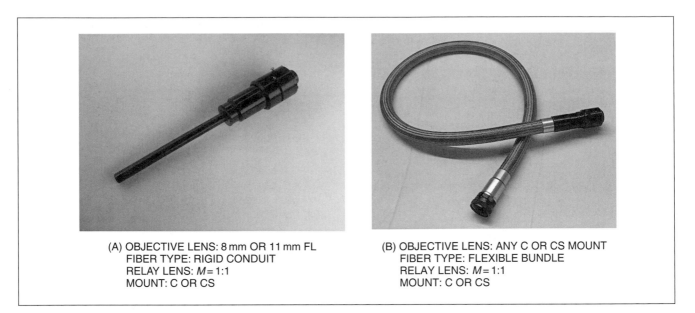

(A) OBJECTIVE LENS: 8 mm OR 11 mm FL
    FIBER TYPE: RIGID CONDUIT
    RELAY LENS: $M = 1{:}1$
    MOUNT: C OR CS

(B) OBJECTIVE LENS: ANY C OR CS MOUNT
    FIBER TYPE: FLEXIBLE BUNDLE
    RELAY LENS: $M = 1{:}1$
    MOUNT: C OR CS

FIGURE 4-33   Rigid and flexible fiber optic lenses

be used when no other lens–camera system will solve the problem. Fiber-optic lenses are expensive and available in rigid or flexible configurations (Figure 4-33).

In the complete fiber-optic lens, the fiber bundle is to be preceded by an objective lens, FFL or other, which focuses the scene onto the front end of the bundle and followed by a relay lens that focuses the image at the rear end of the bundle onto the sensor (Figure 4-34).

Fiber-optic lenses are used in security applications for viewing through thick walls (or ceilings), or any installation where the camera must be a few inches to several feet away from the front lens, for example the camera

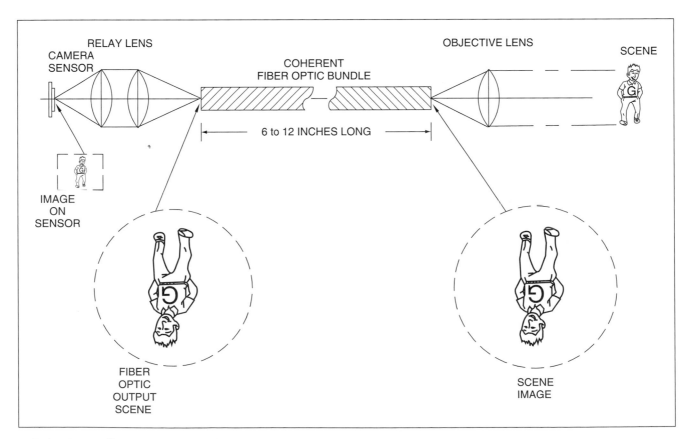

FIGURE 4-34   Fiber-optic lens configuration

on an accessible side of a wall and the front of the lens on the inaccessible scene side. In this situation the lens is a foot away from the camera sensor. Chapter 18 shows how coherent fiber-optic lenses are used in covert security applications.

The bore scope lens is another class of viewing optics for video cameras (Figure 4-35). This lens has a rigid tube of 6–30 inches long and a diameter of 0.04–0.5 inches. The two generic designs, single rod lens and multiple small lenses, transmit the image from the front objective lens to the rear lens and onto a camera sensor. The single rod lens uses a unique graded index (GRIN) glass rod, to refocus the image along its length.

Bore scope lenses can only transmit a small amount of light because of the small rod or lens diameters. This results in high f-numbers, typically f/11 to f/30. The slow speed limits the bore scope application to well-illuminated environments and sensitive cameras. The image quality of the bore scope lens is better than that of the fiber-optic lens, since it uses all glass lenses. Figure 4-35 shows the diagram of a GRIN bore scope lens 0.125 inches in diameter and 12 inches long, and an all-lens bore scope with a diameter of 0.187 inches and a length of 18 inches. The latter has a mirror at the tip to allow viewing at right-angles to the lens axis.

4.7.3 Bi-Focal, Tri-Focal Image Splitting Optics

A lens for imaging two independent scenes onto a single video camera is called an image-splitting or bi-focal lens. The split-image lens has two female C or CS lens ports for two objective lenses. The lens views two different scenes with two separate lenses, and combines the scenes onto one camera sensor (Figure 4-36).

Each of the two objective lenses can have the same or different FLs and will correspondingly produce the same or different magnifications. The split-image lens accomplishes this with only *one* camera. Depending on the orientation of the bifocal lens system on the camera, the image is split either vertically or horizontally. Any fixed-focus, pinhole, vari-focal, zoom, or other lens that mechanically fits onto the C or CS mount can be used. The adjustable mirror mounted on the side lens allows the camera to look in almost any direction. This external mirror can point at the same scene as the front lens. In this case, if the front lens is a wide-angle lens (4 mm FL) and the side lens is a narrow-angle lens (50 mm FL), a bifocal lens system results: *one* camera views a wide-field and narrow-field *simultaneously* (Figure 4-36). Note that the horizontal scene FOV covered by each lens is *one-half* of the total lens FOV. For example, with the 4 mm and 50 mm FL lenses on a 1/3-inch camera and a vertical split (as shown), the

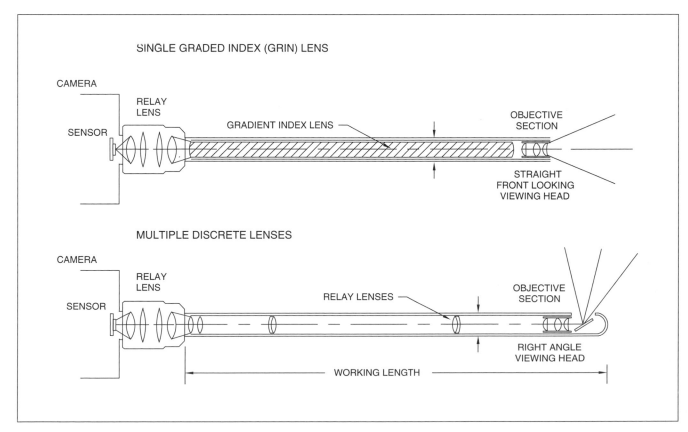

FIGURE 4-35 Bore scope lens system

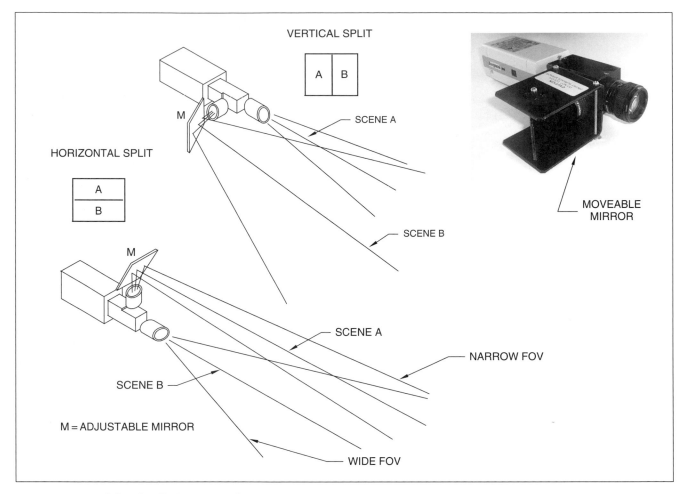

FIGURE 4-36   Bi-focal split-image optics

4 mm lens displays a 30 × 45 feet scene, and the 50-mm lens displays a 2.4 × 3.6 feet scene at a distance of 50 feet. The horizontal FOV of each lens has been reduced by *one-half* of what each lens would see if the lens were mounted directly onto the camera (60 × 45 feet for the 4 mm lens and 4.8 × 3.6 feet for the 50 mm lens). By rotating the split-image lens 90° about the camera optical axis a horizontal split is obtained. In this case the vertical FOV is halved. It should be noted that the bifocal lens *inverts* the picture on the monitor, a condition that is simply corrected by inverting the camera.

A three-way or tri-split optical image-splitting lens views three scenes (Figure 4-37). The tri-split lens provides the ability to view three different scenes with the same or different magnifications with *one* camera. Each scene occupies *one-third* of the monitor screen. Adjustable optics on the lens permit changing the pointing elevation angle of the three front lenses so that they can look close-in for short hallway applications and all the way out (near horizontal) for long hallways. Like the bi-split lens, this lens inverts the monitor image, which is corrected by inverting the camera. Both the bi-split and the tri-split lenses work on 1/4-, 1/3-, or 1/2-inch camera formats.

The image splitting is accomplished without electronic splitters and is useful when only one camera is installed but two or three scenes need to be monitored.

4.7.4   Right-Angle Lens

The right-angle lens permits mounting a camera parallel to a wall or ceiling while the lens views a scene at 90° to the camera axis and wall or ceiling (Figure 4-38).

When space is limited behind a wall, a ceiling, in an automatic teller machine (ATM) or an elevator cab, the right-angle lens is a solution. The right-angle optical system permits use of wide-angle lenses (2.6 mm, 110° FOV) looking at right angles to the camera axis. This cannot be accomplished by using a mirror and a wide-angle lens directly on the camera since the entire scene will not be reflected by the mirror to the lens on the camera. The edges of the scene will not appear on the monitor because of picture *vignetting* (Figure 4-39).

The right-angle adapter permits the use of any FL lens that will mechanically fit into its C or CS mount and works with 1/4-, 1/3-, or 1/2-inch camera formats.

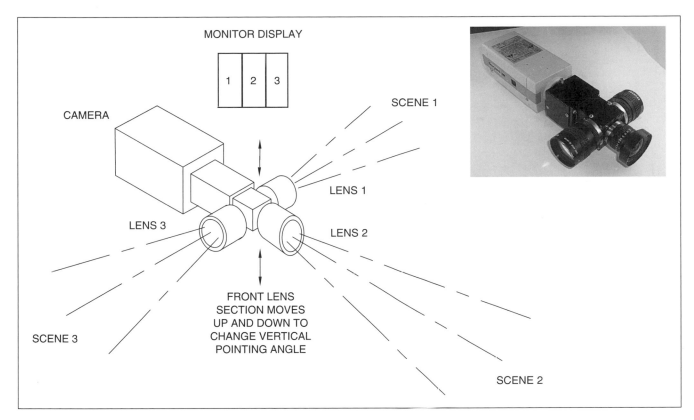

FIGURE 4-37   Tri-split lens views three scenes

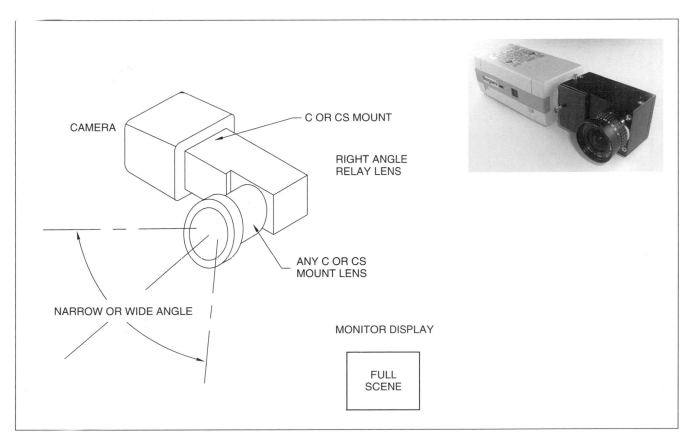

FIGURE 4-38   Right angle lens

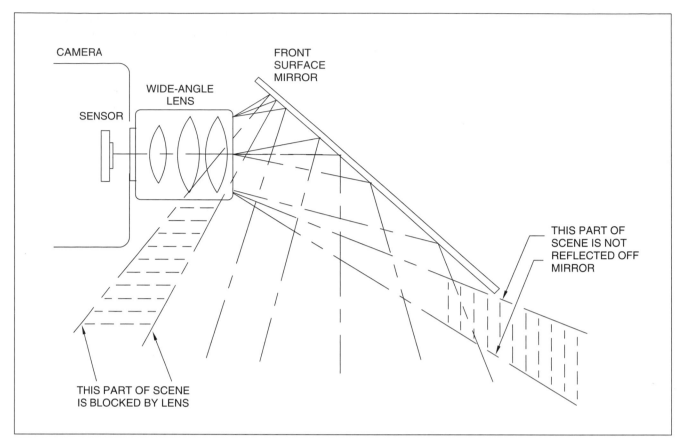

FIGURE 4-39   Picture vignetting from wide-angle lens and mirror

4.7.5 Relay Lens

The relay lens is used to transfer a scene image focused by any standard lens, fiber-optic or bore scope lens onto the camera sensor (Figure 4-40).

The relay lens must always be used with some other objective lens and does not produce an image in and of itself. When used at the fiber bundle output end, a fiber-optic lens re-images the scene onto the sensor. When incorporated into split-image or right-angle optics,

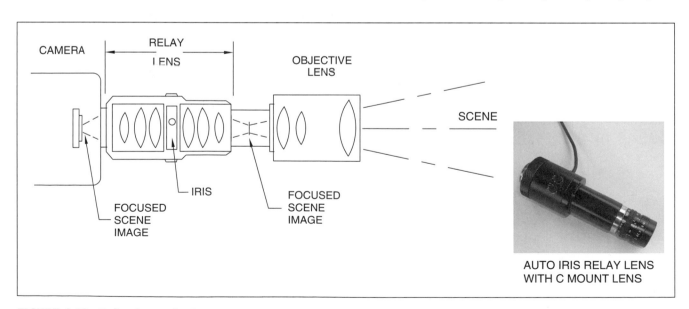

FIGURE 4-40   Relay lens adapter

it re-images the "split" scene or right-angle scene onto the sensor. The relay lens can be used with a standard FFL, pinhole, zoom, or other lens as a lens extender with unit magnification ($M = 1$), for the purpose of optically "moving" the sensor out in front of the camera.

4.8 COMMENTS, CHECKLIST AND QUESTIONS

- A standard objective lens inverts the picture image, and the video camera electronics re-invert the picture so that it is displayed right-side-up on the monitor.
- The 25 mm FL lens is considered the standard or reference lens for the 1-inch (actually 16 mm diagonal) format sensor. This lens–camera combination is defined to have a magnification of $M = 1$ and is similar to the normal FOV of the human eye. The standard lens for a 2/3-inch format sensor is 16 mm; for a 1/2-inch sensor is 12.5 mm; for a 1/3-inch sensor is 8 mm; and for a 1/4-inch sensor is 6 mm. All these combinations produce a magnification $M = 1$. They all have the same angular FOV and therefore view the same size scene.
- A short-FL lens has a wide FOV (Table 4-3; 4.8 mm, 1/2-inch sensor sees a 13.4 feet wide × 10.0 feet high scene at 10 feet).
- A long-FL lens has a narrow FOV (Table 4-3; 75 mm, 1/2-inch sensor sees a 4.3 feet wide × 3.2 feet high scene at 50 feet).
- To determine what FOV is required for an application, consult Tables 4-1, 4-2, 4-3, 4-4 and the Lens Finder Kit.
- If the exact FOV desired cannot be obtained with an FFL, use a vari-focal lens.
- Does the application require a manual or motorized zoom lens, a pan-tilt mount?
- Is the scene lighting constant or widely varying? Is a manual or automatic iris required?
- What is the camera format (1/4-, 1/3-, 1/2-inch)?
- What type of camera lens mount: C, CS, mini 11 mm, 12 mm, 13 mm, bayonet, or other?

4.9 SUMMARY

The task of choosing the right lens for a security application is an important aspect in designing a video security system. The large variety of focal lengths and lens types make the proper lens choice a challenging one. The lens tables and Lens Finder Kit provide convenient tools for choosing the optimum FL lens to be used and the resulting angular FOV obtained with the chosen sensor size.

The common FFL lenses used in most video systems have FLs in the range of 2.8–75 mm. Super wide-angle applications may use a 2.1 mm FL. Super telephoto applications may use FLs from 100 to 300 mm. Most in the range of 2.8–75 mm are available with a manual or automatic iris.

Vari-focal lenses are often chosen when the exact FL desired cannot be obtained with the FFL. The vari-focal lens can "fine tune" the focal length exactly to obtain the angular FOV required. Vari-focal lenses are available in manual and auto-iris configurations. Vari-focal lenses must be re-focused when their FL is changed.

Zoom lenses are used when the camera and lens must be scanned over a large scene area and the magnification of the scene must be changed. This is accomplished by mounting the camera-lens on a pan-tilt platform capable of remotely panning and tilting the camera-lens assembly and zooming the zoom lens. Zoom lenses are available with FLs from 8 to 200 mm with zoom ratios from 6 to 50 to 1. The zoom lens is available with a manual or automatic iris.

When the video security application requires that the camera and lens be hidden, covert pinhole lenses and mini-pinhole lenses are used. The pinhole lenses are mounted to cameras having a C or CS mounts. The mini-pinhole lenses are mounted directly onto a small single board camera (with or without housing) and hidden behind walls or ceilings or mounted into common objects: PIR motion sensor, clock, emergency light, sprinkler head, etc.). Chapter 18 describes covert video lenses and systems in more detail.

Special lenses like the bi- and tri-split, fiber-optic or bore scope lenses are only used when other simpler techniques can not be used.

The newly implemented 360° panoramic lens is used with a computer system and can view a 360° horizontal FOV and up to a 90° vertical FOV. This lens has taken an important place in digital video surveillance systems. The computer transforms the complex donut-shaped image into a useful rectangular image on the monitor.

Chapter 5
Cameras—Analog, Digital, and Internet

CONTENTS

5.1   Overview
5.2   Camera Function
    5.2.1   The Scanning Process
    5.2.2   The Video Signal
        5.2.2.1   Monochrome Signal
        5.2.2.2   Color Signal
5.3   Camera Types
    5.3.1   Analog Camera
        5.3.1.1   Monochrome
        5.3.1.2   Color—Single Sensor
        5.3.1.3   Color—Monochrome
                Switchover
        5.3.1.4   Color—Three Sensor
    5.3.2   Digital Camera
        5.3.2.1   Digital Signal Processing (DSP)
        5.3.2.2   Smart Camera
        5.3.2.3   Legal Considerations
    5.3.3   Internet Camera
        5.3.3.1   The IP Camera ID
        5.3.3.2   Remote Viewing
        5.3.3.3   Compression for Transmission
    5.3.4   Low Light Level ICCD
    5.3.5   Thermal IR
    5.3.6   Universal System Bus (USB)
5.4   Basic Sensor Types
    5.4.1   Solid State—Visible
        5.4.1.1   Charge Coupled Device (CCD)
        5.4.1.2   Complementary Metal Oxide
                Semiconductor (CMOS)
    5.4.2   ICCD, SIT, ISIT—Visible/Near IR
    5.4.3   Thermal IR
    5.4.4   Sensor Fusion—Visible/IR
5.5   Camera Features—Analog/Digital
    5.5.1   Video Motion Detection (VMD)
    5.5.2   Electronic Zooming
    5.5.3   Electronic Shuttering
    5.5.4   White Balance
    5.5.5   Video Bright Light Compression
    5.5.6   Geometric Accuracy
5.6   Camera Resolution/Sensitivity
    5.6.1   Vertical Resolution
    5.6.2   Horizontal Resolution
    5.6.3   Static vs. Dynamic Resolution
    5.6.4   Sensitivity
5.7   Sensor Formats
    5.7.1   Solid-State
    5.7.2   Image Intensifier
    5.7.3   Thermal IR
5.8   Camera Lens Mounts
    5.8.1   C and CS Mounts
    5.8.2   Mini-Lens Mounts
    5.8.3   Bayonet Mount
    5.8.4   Lens–Mount Interferences
5.9   Zoom Lens–camera Module
5.10 Panoramic 360° Camera
5.11 High Definition Television (HDTV)
5.12 Summary

5.1   OVERVIEW

The function of a video camera is to convert the focused visual (or IR) light image from the camera lens into a time-varying electrical video signal for later presentation on a monitor display or permanent recording on a video recorder. The lens collects the reflected light from the scene and focuses it onto the camera image sensor. The sensor converts the light image into a time-varying electronic signal. The camera electronics process the information from the sensor and via the video signal sends it to a viewing monitor by way of coaxial cable, fiber optics, two-wire unshielded twisted-pair (UTP), wireless, or other transmission means. Figure 5-1 shows a simple video camera/lens and monitor system.

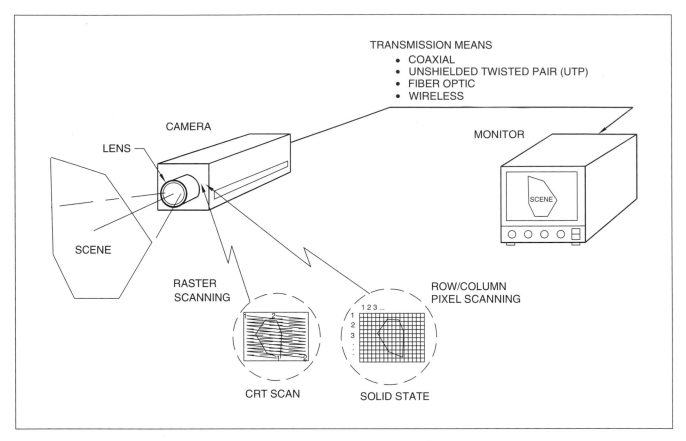

FIGURE 5-1   Video system with lens, camera, transmission means, and monitor

The monochrome or color, solid-state or thermal IR cameras analyze the scene by scanning an array of horizontal and vertical pixels in the camera sensor. This process generates an electrical signal representing the light and color information in the scene as a function of time, so that the scene can be reconstructed on the monitor or recorded for later use.

Unlike film cameras, human eyes, and LLL image intensifiers that see a *complete* picture continuously, a video camera scans an image—*point by point*—until it has scanned the entire scene, i.e. one frame. In this respect the camera scan is similar to the action of a typewriter: the type element starts at the left corner of the page and moves across to the right corner, completing a single line of type. The typewriter carriage then returns to the left side of the paper, moves down to the next line, and starts again.

In most video cameras, interlaced scanning is like a typewriter that adds a *second* carriage return after each line, repeating the lines until it reaches the bottom of the page. This is how it completes one *field*, or half the video image. The scanner/typewriter then moves back up the page and begins typing on the second line at the left or in the middle of the line just below the first line. It continues this way, moving down and filling in the lines between the original lines, until the entire page is complete. In this way the scanning completes the second field

and produces one full video *frame*. This electronic process repeats (like putting in a new sheet of paper) for each frame. Some cameras produce the video signal using progressive scanning in which every line is scanned one after the other rather than skipping a line. Computer monitors use progressive scanning.

In the mid-1980s the solid-state CCD video sensor became a commercial reality. This new device replaced the vidicon tube and silicon tube image sensors and represented a significant advance in camera technology. The use of the solid-state "chip" sensor made the camera 100% solid-state offering significant advantages over any and all tube cameras: long life, no aging, no image burn-in, geometric accuracy, excellent sensitivity and resolution, low power consumption, and small size.

Several different sensor types are available for video security applications with the most prominent and widely used being the CCD, CMOS, ICCD, and thermal IR. The CCD and CMOS are used in daylight and some nighttime applications and respond to visible and near-IR energy. The ICCD is used in low-light-level nighttime applications. The thermal IR camera is used in nighttime applications when there is no visible or near-IR radiation and/or there is a smoke, dust, or fog environment.

Solid-state cameras use a silicon array of photo-sensor sites (pixels) to convert the input light image into an electronic video signal that is then amplified and passed on to a monitor for display. Most solid-state sensors are charge-transfer devices (CTD) that are available in three types depending on the manufacturing technology: (1) the CCD, (2) the charge-priming device (CPD), and (3) the charge-injection device (CID). A fourth sensor type introduced more recently to the security market is the CMOS. By far the most popular devices used in security camera applications are the CCD and CMOS. The CID is reserved primarily for military and industrial applications. Solid-state and thermal cameras are significantly smaller weigh less, and consume less power than the prior tube cameras. A packaged solid-state image sensor is typically 3/4 inch × 3/4 inch × 1/4 inch or smaller while its prior, tube predecessor was 3/4 inch in diameter and 5 inches long or larger. Solid-state cameras consume from a fraction of a watt to several watts compared to 8–20 watts for the tube camera.

The security field began using color cameras after the technology for solid-state color cameras developed in the consumer camcorder market. These color cameras have a single solid-state sensor with an integral three-color filter and an automatic white-balancing circuit to provide a reliable and sensitive device.

To produce a noise-free monochrome or color picture with sufficient resolution to identify objects of interest, the sensor must have sufficient sensitivity to respond to available natural daytime or artificial lighting. As mentioned, security video cameras sensitive to visible and/or near-IR lighting can be represented by two general categories: (1) CCD and CMOS solid-state, and (2) LLL ICCD. Separate from these visible and near-IR cameras is a third category operating in the thermal (heat energy) IR region which is responsive to the *difference in temperature* in the scene rather than *reflected light* from the scene. The LLL and thermal cameras are described in Chapter 19.

In subsequent sections each parameter contributing to the function and operation of these security cameras is described.

All security cameras have a lens mount in front of the sensor to mechanically couple an objective lens or optical system to the camera. The original C mount was designed for the larger 1/2-, 2/3-, and 1-inch tube and solid-state sensor formats and still accounts for many camera installations. Currently the most popular mount is the CS mount. It is designed for the 1/4-, 1/3-, and 1/2-inch format sensor cameras and their correspondingly smaller objective lenses. The CS mount configuration evolved from the original C mount as cameras sensors became smaller. Small printed circuit board cameras used for covert surveillance use a mini-mount with 10, 12, and 13 mm thread diameters (see Section 5.8).

5.2 CAMERA FUNCTION

This section describes the functioning of the major parts of a solid-state analog and digital video camera and the video signal. Figure 5-2 is a generalized block diagram for the analog and digital video camera electronics.

The camera sensor function is to convert a visual or IR light image into a temporary sensor image which the camera scanning mechanism successively reads, point by point or line by line, to produce a time-varying electrical signal representing the scene light intensity. In a color camera this function is accomplished threefold to convert the three primary colors—red, green, and blue—representing the scene, into an electrical signal.

The analog video camera consists of: (1) image sensor, (2) electronic scanning system with synchronization, (3) timing electronics, (4) video amplifying and processing electronics, and (5) video signal synchronizing and

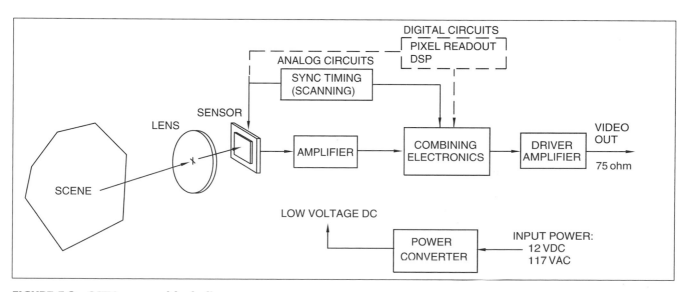

FIGURE 5-2 CCTV camera block diagram

combining electronics. The synchronizing and combining electronics produce a composite video output signal. To provide meaningful images when the scene varies in real-time, scanning must be sufficiently fast—at least 30 fps—to capture and replay moving target scenes. The video camera must have suitable synchronizing signals so that a monitor, recorder or printer at the receiving location can be synchronized to produce a stable, flicker-free display or recording.

The digital video camera (see dotted block) consists of: (1) image sensor, (2) row and column pixel read-out circuitry, (3) DSP circuits, and (4) video synchronizing and combining electronics. The synchronizing and combining electronics produce a composite video output signal.

The following description of the video process applies to all solid-state, LLL and thermal cameras. The lens forms a focused image on the sensor. The sensor image readout is performed in a process called "linear" (or raster) scanning. The video picture is formed by interrogating and extracting the light level on each pixel in the rows and columns. The brightness and color at each pixel varies as a function of the focused scene image so that the signal obtained is a representation of the scene intensity and color profile.

5.2.1 The Scanning Process

One video *frame* is composed of two *fields*. In the US the NTSC system is based on the 60 Hz power line frequency and 1/30 second per frame (30 fps), each frame containing 525 horizontal lines. In the European system, based on a 50 Hz power line frequency and 1/25 second per frame, each frame has 625 horizontal lines.

This solid-state analog video output signal has the same format as that from its tube camera predecessor. Two methods of scanning have been used: *2:1 interlace* and *random interlace*. Present cameras use the 2:1 interlace scanning technique to reduce the amount of flicker in the picture and improve motion display while maintaining the same video signal bandwidth. In both scanning methods, every other line of pixels is scanned. In the NTSC system, each field contains 262½ television lines. This scanning mode is called two-field, odd-line scanning (Figure 5-3).

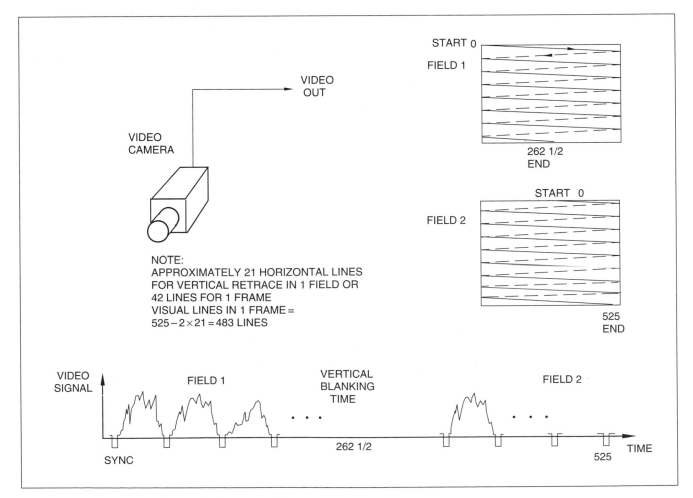

FIGURE 5-3   NTSC two-field/odd-line scanning process

In the NTSC standard, 60 fields and 30 frames are completed per second. With 525 TV lines per frame and 30 fps, there are 15,750 TV lines per second. In the standard NTSC system, the vertical blanking interval uses 21 lines per field, or a total of 42 lines per frame. Subtracting these 42 lines from the 525-line frame leaves 483 *active* picture lines per frame representing the scene. By convention, the scanning function of every camera and every receiver monitor starts from the upper left corner of the image and proceeds horizontally across to the right of the sensor. Each time it reaches the right side of the image it quickly returns to a point just below its starting point on the left side. This occurs during what is called the "horizontal blanking interval" of the video signal. This process is continued and repeated until the sensor is completely read out and eventually reaches the bottom of the image, thereby completing one field. At this point the sensor readout stops (or in the case of the CRT monitor the beam turns off again) and returns to the top of the image: this time is called the "vertical blanking interval." For the second field (a full frame consists of two fields), the scan lines fall in between those of the first field. By this method the scan lines of the two fields are *interlaced*, which

reduces image flicker and allows the signal to occupy the same transmission bandwidth it would occupy if it were performing progressive scanning. When the second field is completed and the scanning spot arrives at the lower right corner, it quickly returns to the upper left corner to repeat the entire process.

For the solid-state camera, the light-induced charge in the individual pixels in the sensor must be clocked out of the sensor into the camera electronics (Figure 5-4).

The time-varying video signal from the individual pixels clocked out in the horizontal rows and vertical columns likewise generates the two interlaced fields. In the case of the tube camera, a moving electron beam in the tube does the scanning similar to the CRT in the tube monitor.

By scanning the target twice (remember the typewriter analogy), the sensor is scanned, starting at the top left side of the picture, and a signal representing the scene image is produced. First the odd lines are scanned, until one field of 262½ lines is completed. Then the beam returns to the top left of the sensor and scans the 262½ even-numbered lines, until a total picture frame of 525 lines is completed. Two separate fields of alternate lines are combined to make the complete picture frame every 1/30th of a

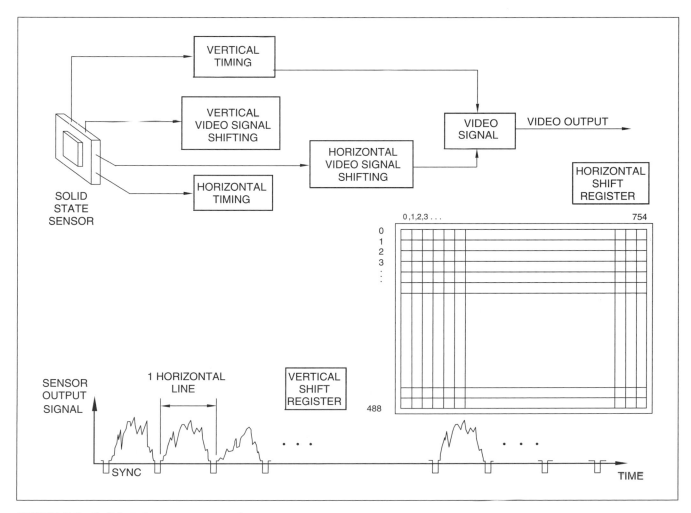

FIGURE 5-4 Solid-state camera scanning process

second. This TV camera signal is then transmitted to the monitor, where it re-creates the picture in an inverse fashion. This base-band video signal has a voltage level from 0 to 1 volt (1 volt peak to peak) and is contained in a 4–10 MHz electrical bandwidth, depending on the system resolution. The synchronizing signals are contained in the 0.5 volt timing pulses.

5.2.2 The Video Signal

The video signal can be better understood by looking at the single horizontal line of the composite signal shown in Figure 5-5.

The signal is divided into two basic parts: (1) the scene illumination intensity information and (2) the synchronizing pulses. Synchronization pulses with 0.1-microsecond rise and fall times contain frequency components of up to 2.5 MHz. Other high frequencies are generated in the video signal when the image scene detail contains rapidly changing light-to-dark picture levels of small size and are represented by about 4.2 MHz, and for good fidelity must be reproduced by the electronic circuits. These high-frequency video signal components represent rapid

changes in the scene—either moving targets or very small objects. To produce a stable image on the monitor, the synchronizing pulses must be very sharp and the electronic bandwidth wide enough to accurately reproduce them. The color signal in addition to a luminance (Y) intensity component includes an additional chrominance (C) color component in the form of a "color burst" signal. The color signal can also be represented by three primary color components: red, green, and blue (RGB), each having waveforms similar to the monochrome signal (without the color burst signal).

5.2.2.1 Monochrome Signal

The monochrome camera signal contains intensity information representing the illumination on the sensor. For the monochrome camera, all color information from the scene is combined and represented in one video signal. The monochrome signal contains four components:

1. horizontal line synchronization pulses
2. setup (black) level
3. luminance (gray-scale) level
4. field synchronizing pulses.

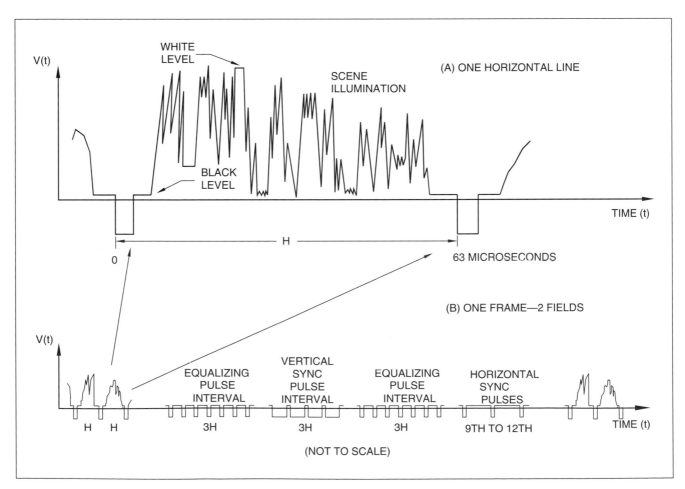

FIGURE 5-5 Monochrome NTSC CCTV video signal

5.2.2.2 Color Signal

Any video color signal is made up of three component parts:

1. Luminance—over all (Black and White)
2. Hue—tint or color
3. Saturation—color intensity of the hue.

A black and white video signal describes only the luminance. The luminance, hue, and saturation of picture information can be approximated by the unique combination of primary color information. The primary colors in this additive color process consist of red, green, and blue (RGB) color signals. These primary colors can be combined to give the colors frequently seen in a color bar test pattern. These colors are described by turning on the primary color component parts, either full "on" to full "off." To produce the other colors needed, the intensity of the individual primary colors must be *continuously variable* from full on to full off (like the light dimmer on a light switch).

The color camera signal contains light intensity and color information. It must separate the spectral distribution of the scene illumination into the RGB color components (Figure 5-6). The color video signal is far more complex than its monochrome counterpart, and the timing accuracy, linearity, and frequency response of the electronic circuits are more critical in order to achieve high-quality color pictures. The color video signal contains seven components necessary to extract the color and intensity information from the picture scene and later reproduce it on a color monitor:

1. horizontal line synchronization pulses
2. color synchronization (color burst signal)
3. setup (black) level
4. luminance (gray-scale) level
5. color hue (tint)
6. color saturation (vividness)
7. field synchronizing pulses.

Figure 5-7 shows the video waveform with some of these components.

Horizontal Line Synchronization Pulses. The first component the *horizontal line synchronization pulses* of the composite video signal has three parts: (1) *the front porch*, which isolates the synchronization pulses from the active picture information of the previous line, (2) the *back porch*, which isolates the synchronization pulses from the active picture information of the next scanned line, and (3) *the horizontal line sync pulse*, which synchronizes the receiver, monitor, or recorder to the camera.

Color Synchronization (Burst Signal). The second component, the *color synchronization*, is a short burst of color information used as phase synchronization for the color information in the color portion of each horizontal line. The front porch, synchronization pulse, color burst, and back porch make up the horizontal blanking interval. This color burst signal, occurring during the back-porch interval of the video signal, serves as a color synchronization signal for the chrominance signal.

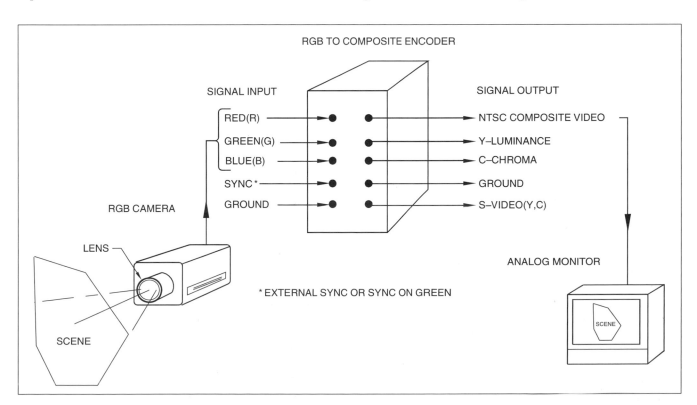

FIGURE 5-6   RGB to composite video encoding block diagram

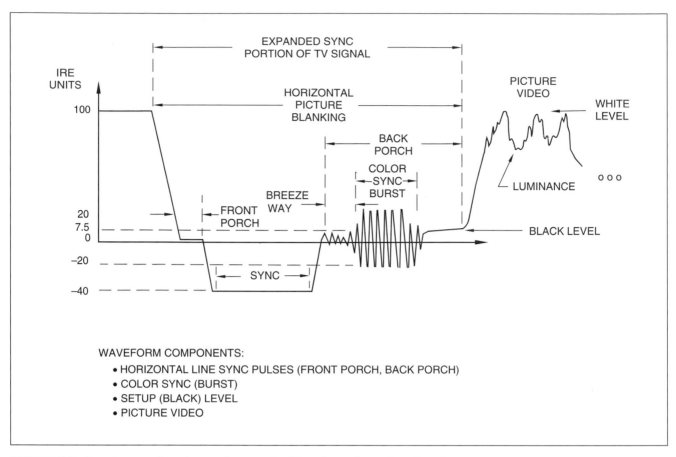

FIGURE 5-7 Luminance signal superimposed with sub-carrier color signal

Setup. The third component of the color television waveform is the *setup* or black level, representing the video signal amplitude under zero light conditions.

Luminance. The fourth component is the *luminance* black-and-white picture detail information. Changes and shifts of light as well as the average light level are part of this information.

Color Hue, and Saturation. The fifth and sixth components are the *color hue*, and *color saturation* information. This information is combined with the black-and-white picture detail portion of the waveform to produce the color image.

Field Synchronization Pulse. This component maintains the vertical synchronization and proper interlace.

These seven components form the composite waveform for a color video signal.

The chrominance and the luminance make up the analog component parts of any video color signal. By keeping these component parts separated, the interaction between chrominance and luminance that could produce picture distortion in the NTSC encoded signal is minimized. By keeping the chrominance and luminance components separated, picture quality can be improved dramatically.

The output of high-end video security systems is in a form of three RGB signals. In most cases for video security, these RGB signals are combined (or encoded) into a single video signal that is a composite of the primary color information, or dual video signals: (1) luminance (Y) and (2) chrominance (C), representing the intensity and color information, respectively. For the composite signal the RGB signals go into an encoder and a single encoded color signal comes out: the composite video signal. In the USA, the color encoding standards were established by the national television systems committee (NTSC). European and other countries use a color encoding standard called phase alternation line (PAL) or sequential with memory (SECAM). Figure 5-6 shows the block diagram for the RGB to composite video encoding.

In the NTSC system the luminance (Y) or black-and-white component of the video signal is used as a base upon which the color signal is built. The color signal rides on the base signal as a "sub-carrier" signal. Figure 5-7 shows this sub-carrier signal superimposed on the base luminance signal which then completely describes the color and monochrome video signals.

After much experimentation it was found that by combining the three RGB video signals in specific proportions an accurate rendition of the original color signal was obtained. These ratios were: 30% of the red video signal, 59% of the green video signal, and 11% of the blue video signal. To this signal was added the saturation and hue information. This involved the generation of two additional combinations of the RGB video signals. In the NTSC color system the hue and saturation of a color system are described as a result of combining the proper proportions of an *I* modulating level and a *Q* modulating level, consisting of specific ratios of RGB signals. To obtain accurate color rendition, the proper ratio and phase relationships of the signals (expressed in degrees) are required. This analysis is explored in detail in Chapter 25 with the use of vector scopes.

5.3 CAMERA TYPES

Video security cameras are represented by several generic forms including: (1) analog, (2) digital, (3) Internet, (4) LLL, and (5) thermal IR. For daytime applications, monochrome, color, analog, digital, and IP cameras are used. When remote surveillance is required an IP camera is used. For low light and nighttime applications the LLL ICCD image intensified camera is used. For very low light level or no light level applications, thermal IR cameras are used.

5.3.1 Analog Camera

Until about the year 2000, all security cameras were CCD and CMOS analog types. With the development of higher density integrated circuits, digital signal processing (DSP) was added and the use of digital cameras is now common place. This section describes the monochrome and color analog cameras.

5.3.1.1 Monochrome

Most CCD and CMOS image sensors have wide spectral ranges covering the entire visible range of 400–700 nanometers (nm) and the near-IR spectral region of 800–900 nm. Figure 5-8 shows the spectral response of a visible and near-IR CCD sensor with and without filters.

Some monochrome cameras are responsive to near-IR energy from natural light or IR LED illuminators. These cameras are operated without IR cutoff filters.

When the CCD or CMOS camera is pointed toward a strong light source or bright object, the sensor is often overloaded due to the high sensitivity of the imager in

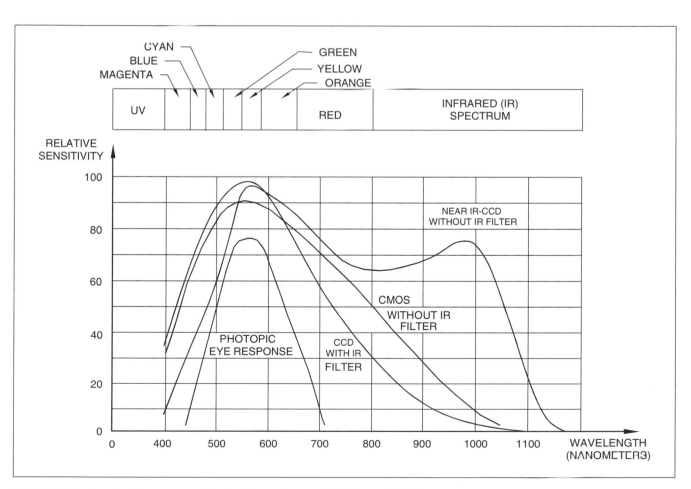

FIGURE 5-8   Spectral response of a visible and near-IR CCD, and CMOS sensor

the near-IR region. This overload produces a bright-light band above and below the object on the monitor display. If the illuminating source contains a bright spot of IR radiation, such as from sunlight or a car headlight, the IR cutoff filter should be used to prevent sensor overload.

Monochrome cameras generally operate in most types of scene lighting providing the light level is sufficient. Light sources such as mercury vapor, metal arc, tungsten, and low- and high-pressure sodium are widely used for monochrome camera applications.

5.3.1.2 Color—Single Sensor

There are two generic color video camera types: single-sensor and three-sensor with prism. The single color sensor is the by far the most common type used in security applications (Figure 5-9).

This camera has a complex color-imaging sensor that contains an overlay of three integral optical filters to produce signals responding to the three primary colors: red (R), green (G), and blue (B), which are sufficient to reproduce all the colors in the visible spectrum. The three color filters divide the total number of pixels on the sensor by three, so that each filter type covers one third of the pixels. The sensor is followed by video electronics and clocking signals to synchronize the composite video color signal. A higher quality alternative to the composite signal is found in some color cameras having a 3-wire RGB, or a 2-wire Y and C output signal.

Since the single sensor camera has only one sensor, the light from the lens must be split into thirds, thereby decreasing the overall camera sensitivity by three. Since each resolution element on the display monitor is composed of three colors, the resolution likewise is reduced by this factor of 3. However, because of its relatively low cost the single-sensor camera is still much more widely used than the more expensive three-sensor prism type.

Color cameras are supplied with IR blocking filters since the IR energy does not supply any color information and would only overload the sensor and/or distort the color rendition. The IR filter alters the spectral response of the CCD imager to match the visible color spectrum (Figure 5-10). The two curves represent the sensor with and without the IR filter in place.

In order to obtain good color rendition when using color cameras, the light source must have sufficient energy between 400 nm (0.4 micron) and 790 nm (0.79 micron) corresponding to the visible light spectrum. The IR blocking filters restrict the optical bandwidth reaching the color sensor to within this range so that color cameras cannot be used with IR light sources having radiation to the range of 800–1200 nm.

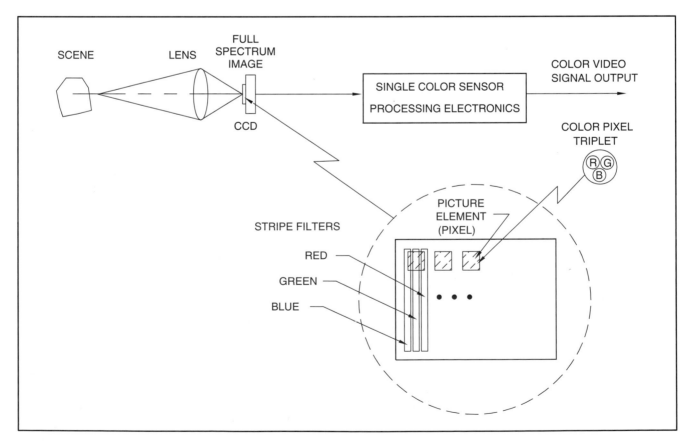

FIGURE 5-9   Single-sensor color video camera block diagram

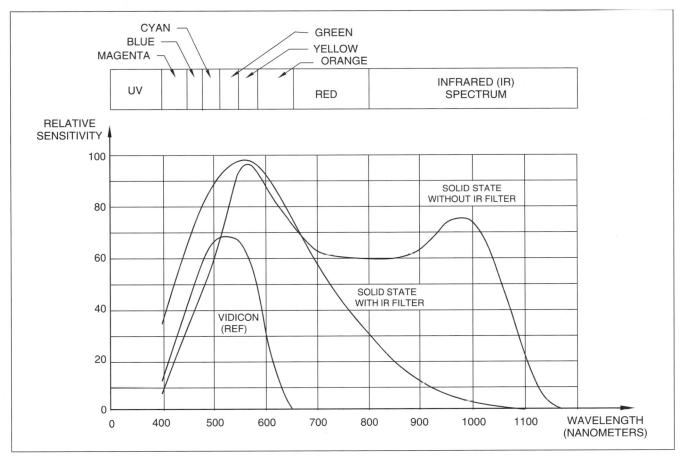

FIGURE 5-10 Spectral response of CCD imagers with and without IR filters

The color tube camera and early versions of the color CCD camera had external white-balance sensors and circuits to compensate for color changes. Present solid-state color cameras incorporate automatic white-balance compensation as an integral part of the camera (see Section 5.5.4).

5.3.1.3 Color—Monochrome Switchover

Many applications (particularly outdoor) require cameras that operate in daytime and nighttime. To accomplish this, some cameras incorporate automatic conversion from color to monochrome operation. This automatic switchover significantly increases effectiveness of the camera in daytime and nighttime operation and reduces the number of cameras required and the overall cost. The conversion (switchover) is accomplished electronically and/or optically. Using the optical technique to switch from the daytime mode to the nighttime mode, an IR blocking filter is mechanically moved out of the optical path so that visible *and* near-IR radiation falls onto the color sensor. Simultaneously the three-component color signal is combined into one monochrome signal resulting in a typical tenfold increase in camera sensitivity (Figure 5-11).

5.3.1.4 Color—Three Sensor

The three-sensor color camera uses a beam-splitting prism interposed between the lens and three solid-state sensors to produce the color video signal (Figure 5-12).

The function of the prism is to split the full visible spectrum into the three primary colors, R, G, and B. Each individual sensor has its own video electronics and clocking signals synchronized together to eventually produce three separate signals proportional to the RGB color content in the original scene. The display from this camera when compared with the single-sensor camera has three times the number of pixels and shows a picture having almost three times higher resolution and sensitivity, and a picture with a rendition closer to the true colors in the scene. This camera is well suited for the higher resolution analog S-VHS, Hi-8 VCRs, and digital DVRs and digital versatile disks (DVDs) now available for higher resolution security applications (Chapter 9). S-VHS, Hi-8 and DVR recorders can use the higher resolution Y (luminance) and C (chrominance) signals, or RGB signals representing the color scene. The camera output signals (Y, C or RGB) can be combined to produce a standard composite video output signal. This optical light combining prism and three-sensor technique is significantly more costly than a single-sensor camera, but results in a signal having

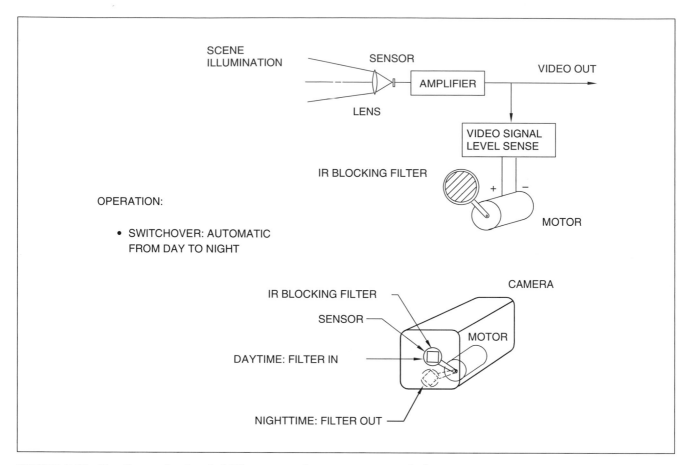

FIGURE 5-11 Daytime color to nighttime monochrome camera switchover

significantly superior color fidelity and higher resolution and sensitivity.

5.3.2 Digital Camera

Although most electronics have moved into a digital computer world, until recently video security was still operating in analog terms. For the camera an analog output signals is typically recorded downstream as an analog signal. There is presently a strong migration toward a digital video world using digital electronics in all the components of the video system. Digital signal processing (DSP) has been the driving force behind this migration. The initial first step occurred with the introduction of DSP cameras and has continued with the development of advanced PC-driven switching devices, digital ID cameras, and DVRs. Today's DSP cameras are less expensive than the analog cameras they are replacing and have more features. Likewise DVRs replacing analog VCRs have increased resolution, improved reliability, and provide easy access to and routing of the stored video records.

The advancements in digital technology have made color video more practical, effective, and economical. Presently color cameras now account for 70–80% of all video camera sales. This is directly attributable to

higher performance and lower cost provided by digital technology.

Most *average* resolution digital video cameras used in security applications have about 512 by 576 active pixels. High resolution cameras typically have 752 by 582 active pixels. The latter is equivalent to SVHS-quality analog video recording and has a bandwidth of approximately 6–7 MHz. Since VHS quality is sufficient for many applications, the standard full screen image format or fractional screen common intermediate format (CIF)—with 352 by 240 (NTSC) pixels for the luminance signal Y and 176 by 144 pixels for the chrominance signals U and V—was defined. The use of CIF resolution considerably reduces the amount of data being recorded or transmitted while providing adequate image quality.

Presently the CCD camera is the camera of choice in digital systems. However, the CCD is being challenged by CMOS technology because of their lower prices, smaller size, and lower power requirements. While many customers want to make use of their existing analog components in a digital system upgrade, replacement of analog components to digital components makes most sense. This is particularly true if the system will be used to send the video signal over the Internet or other digital networks since analog video signals sent over the Internet require a high bandwidth than when digital components

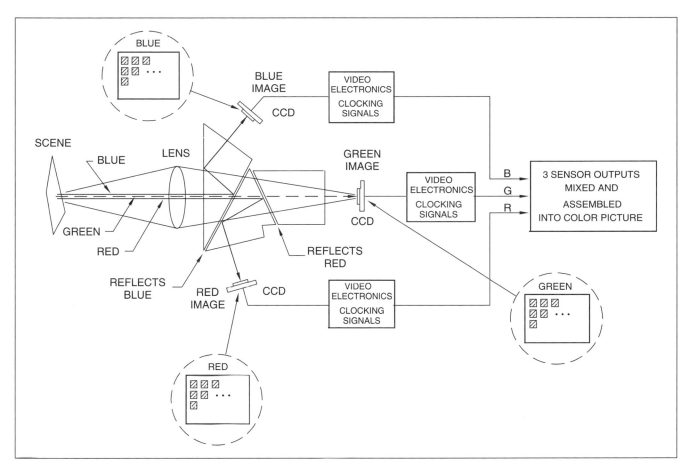

FIGURE 5-12   Three sensor color camera using prism

are used. Analog signals can be converted to digital signals before sending the signal across the network but this requires special converters. It is more cost-effective to buy a digital camera and put it directly on the network.

5.3.2.1 Digital Signal Processing (DSP)

The introduction of DSP cameras and advanced digital technology has thrown the entire video security industry into a major tailspin—digital video security is here to stay. The word "digital," when referring to CCTV cameras, only means that the camera incorporates digital enhancement or processing of the video signal and not that the output signal is a digital signal. These cameras offer improved image quality and features such as back-light compensation, iris control, shuttering, electronic zoom, and electronic sensitivity control to improve picture intelligence and overcome large lighting variations and other problems.

The output signal from most surveillance cameras is still an analog signal. This is because the required maximum operating distance needed in most systems is longer than most digital signals can be transmitted. A camera with true digital output would have a very limited operating distance (a few hundred feet) which would not be very

useful in most video security applications. The solution for this is the use of network cameras and system networking equipment leading to the use of Internet cameras transmitting over: (1) local area network (LAN), (2) wide area network (WAN) or WLAN, (3) wireless networks (WiFi), (4) intranets, and (5) the Internet, as a means for long-distance monitoring. As mentioned earlier, most DSP camera outputs are analog and use the communication channels listed above.

Since the signal-to-noise ratio (SNR) in DSP cameras is better than in analog cameras, manufacturers can increase the amplification using automatic gain control (AGC) resulting in a higher quality video image under poor lighting conditions. The typical SNR for a non-DSP camera is between 46 and 48 dB. Cameras with DSP have an SNR of between 50 and 54 dB. Note that every 3 dB change in signal strength equals a 50% improvement in the signal level.

One new DSP signal processing technology employs circuitry that expands the dynamic range of an image sensor up to 64 times over that of a conventional CCD camera and brings camera performance closer to the capabilities of the human eye. The camera simultaneously views bright and dark light levels and digitally processes the bright and dim images independently. In this new technique a long exposure is used in the dark portions of the scene, and a short exposure in the bright portions. The signals are later combined using DSP into an enhanced image incorporating the best portions of each exposure, and the composite image is sent as a standard analog signal to the monitor or recorder.

In the analog video world, if a video signal is weak or noisy it can be amplified or filtered but the digital video world is different. The digital video signal is immune to many external signal disturbances but it can tolerate only so many errors and then the signal is *gone*. A sudden signal drop-off is referred to as the *cliff effect* in which the video signal is momentarily lost—a complete video picture break-up or drop-out (see Figure 5-13).

5.3.2.2 Smart Camera

The introduction of smart digital cameras has changed the architecture of video surveillance systems so that they can now perform automated video security (AVS). Most analog video systems allow the security officer to make decisions based on the information seen on the video monitor. With the availability of smart digital video cameras and DSP electronics, decisions are made by the *camera* rather than the security personnel.

The evolution from analog to digital cameras has provided the ability to incorporate *intelligence* into the camera and make the video camera a *smart* camera. In the past if a guard saw a person walking the wrong way in a restricted area, the guard would sound an alarm or alert someone in the area to investigate the activity. Smart cameras now have VMD algorithms to distinguish different types of objects and direction of movement. It is a small task to have software sound an alarm or alert someone automatically and free the guard for other tasks.

As another example, software algorithms have been developed that can perform menial tasks. If a store manager wants to know how many people entered the front door and went to a particular aisle or location, today's smart cameras have software that can analyze the video and provide this information automatically. The camera's DSP takes all the incoming video and converts it to a format that it can use to perform the analysis and make decisions. The resulting output then interfaces to other devices to carry out the decisions.

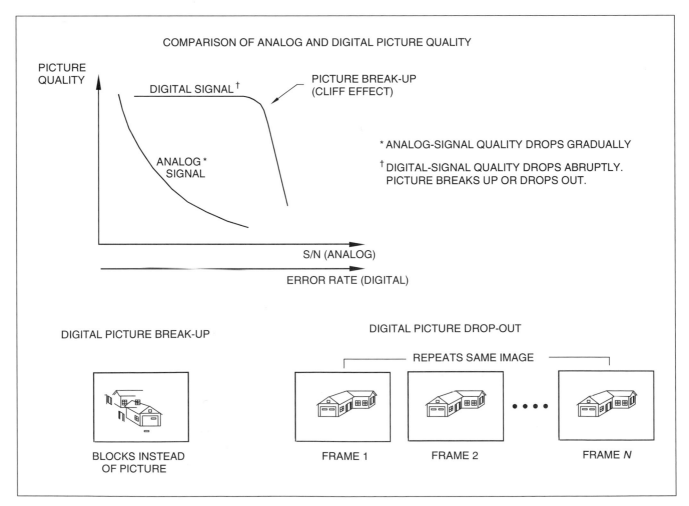

FIGURE 5-13   Digital video signal picture break-up or drop-out

To effectively implement AVS and video intelligence across multiple cameras requires moving the image analysis into the camera. By running all or part of the video analysis software in the camera, reliability is improved in the overall system by eliminating a *single point of failure.* There is also improved scalability in the system since additional cameras do not impact the central AVS system. By performing the video analysis in the camera, the analysis software takes advantage of the uncorrupted video, and has the ability to instantly adjust to changes in the scene to optimize it for the algorithm. Since transmission bandwidth is limited, the smart camera decides what if any video should be sent from the camera and how much compression should be applied to the video signal before transmitting it. This technique reduces signal degradation since the information has already been acted upon in the camera.

Cameras can be made smarter through the use of DSP. Not only can a camera make a record of an event, but it can now evaluate the importance and relevance of that event. By processing images at the camera level, the camera electronics can make decisions as to how to capture an image. When an event occurs, such as movement in the image, the camera electronics determine if the movement is in a field of interest. Likewise it can recognize a person as the main object vs. a dog or piece of paper blowing in the wind. The camera can determine whether a person needs to know about the event and alert security personnel automatically. This feature allows a single person to manage a much greater number of cameras than would otherwise be possible with an analog system and can *significantly* reduce employee expenses. If there is no activity the camera can capture the scene at a lower resolution or frame rate, thereby reducing the bandwidth required, minimizing the impact a digital camera will have on a network, and conserving storage capacity in the recorder.

5.3.2.3 *Legal Considerations*

There are legal factors to consider when using a digital camera or digital video system for court and prosecution purposes. In the digital process the camera image can be manipulated pixel-by-pixel, with text or other modifications made in the image after the original image has been recorded. There is a bias in the courts that points out that compressed video can be manipulated. Therefore, it is suggested that the scene be captured using an uncompressed, full JPEG image at a high frame rate with a smart camera when an event is potentially important. However, without a smart camera, in the time it takes to alert a person and await a response to capture the event in JPEG, the important moment could already have taken place. A smart camera could make this determination itself and thus be more responsive by increasing the resolution and frame rate automatically. The camera could also intelligently zoom in on the target to get more detail and information, something analog cameras cannot do without human intervention.

5.3.3 **Internet Camera**

The Internet camera using the IP and the Internet has become a critical component in the use of AVS. Prior to the Internet, video security was focused on the use of video to bring the visual scene to the security officer. Using the power of the Internet and digital IP cameras, the camera scenes can now be transmitted directly to a security officer located anywhere on the network (Figure 5-14).

To uniquely identify any specific camera on the network, an ID address and a password are assigned to the camera. The camera when connected to the network can be interrogated from any Internet port, anywhere in the

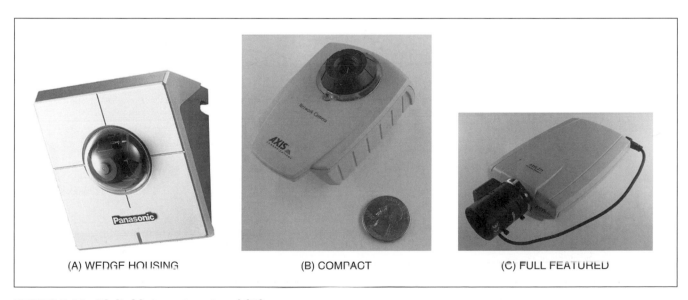

(A) WEDGE HOUSING   (B) COMPACT   (C) FULL FEATURED

FIGURE 5-14   Digital internet protocol (IP) cameras

world. During installation the camera is assigned an Internet address so that the user can view the camera scene using the appropriate password and camera ID number and commanding it to send the picture over the network to the monitoring port. Likewise the security operator can transmit command signals to the camera and platform to perform pan, tilt, zoom, etc.

5.3.3.1 The IP Camera ID

The IP camera is assigned a digital address so that it can be accessed from anywhere on the network—locally or remotely. The network permits direct two-way communications for commanding the camera in pan, tilt, and zoom while simultaneously receiving the image from the remote Internet camera. The IP camera is given an Internet protocol (IP) address having the form shown in Table 5-1.

5.3.3.2 Remote Viewing

Remote viewing or AVS is the direction that the video security industry is taking. This powerful new tool allows viewing anywhere in the world using the Internet camera and the Internet as its transmission means. This AVS function means that all security personnel can gain access to camera control, etc. depending on password authorization, thereby significantly increasing the effectiveness of the video security system.

The ability to view a scene remotely via the Internet, intranet, or other long-distance communications path reliably and economically has resulted in the implementation of AVS. The ability to receive a video picture from the camera and command the camera to pan, tilt, zoom, etc. all from the security control room at any remote distance

has significantly increased the functionality and value of video security systems.

5.3.3.3 Compression for Transmission

Long before digital video transmission was envisioned, engineers realized the need to compress the color video signal. The color systems were designed to be compatible with monochrome video signals already in use. The color video signal had to fit in the same bandwidth space as the monochrome signal. This color compatibility was not an easy engineering task and created many trade-offs that can only be solved with digital video transmission. In an ideal system the color signal would be transmitted as three, high-resolution primary channels red, green, and blue (RGB), each with its own luminance and color information. Even before the analog color video signal is converted to digital data and compressed using data compression algorithms, the video signal has been compressed using analog matrix coding. It has not been possible to send a high-quality, high-resolution computer digital video signal through a standard real-time video transmission system. It is the same as trying to pass high-quality stereo sound through a telephone: even with extensive coding it is not possible. In the analog system video noise manifests itself as grain in the color picture, or smearing, or contrast and brightness problems that cause tint (hue) changes and picture rolling or breakup. None of these analog problems should occur in a well-designed digital video system. However, digital video has a whole new set of problems such as aliasing, compression artifacts, jagged edges, jumpy motion, and just plain poor quality due to low data bit rate or compression. There is no digital video system benchmark at present to accurately compare different video systems.

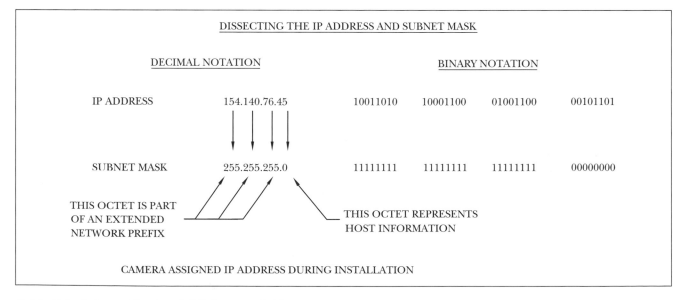

Table 5-1 Internet Protocol (IP) Camera Address

To transmit the wide bandwidth video signal over a narrow bandwidth communication channel requires that the video signal be compressed at the camera location and decompressed at the monitoring location. The compression algorithms used for video removes redundant signal and picture information both within each video frame (intra-frame) and or redundant information from frame to frame (inter-frame). The techniques (algorithms) used to remove this redundant information have been developed by several technical groups and manufacturers. Several of the most common algorithms are M-JPEG, MPEG-4, and H.264 developed by the Joint Motion Picture Engineers Group. These compression formats use frame-by-frame compression. A wavelet compression algorithm called JPEG 2000 was created as the successor to the original JPEG format developed in the late 1980s for still digital video (single frame) and photography. This algorithm is based on state-of-the-art wavelet techniques, but is designed for static imaging applications, on the Internet for e-commerce, digital photography, image databases, cell phones, and PDAs, rather than for real-time video transmission.

There are basically two different types of video compression: (1) lossy, and (2) lossless (Chapter 7). Lossy compression as its name implies means that the final displayed picture is not an exact replica of the original camera signal. The amount of compression determines how much the final signal departs from the original. As a rule of thumb, the more the compression the more the departure from the original. The compression range for a lossy system can vary from 10 to 1, to 400 to 1 reduction in signal bandwidth.

Digital video compression is simply a system for reducing the redundancy in the data words that describe every pixel on the screen. Compression is used to reduce the data size for a given video frame and de-compression is used to convert the compressed signal back into a form like the original video signal. How closely this compressed signal matches the original input video depends on the quality and the power of the compression algorithm. There are several generic types of compression techniques available to the digital video engineer. Two basic types are: *inter-frame* compression, which occurs in between frames, and *intra-frame* which occurs within a frame. Inter-frame compression is based on the fact that for most scenes there is not a great change in data from one frame to the next. It takes advantage of the condition that only a part of the scene changes or has motion and therefore only those portions which are *different* are compressed.

5.3.4 Low Light Level ICCD

The most sensitive LLL camera (Chapter 19) is the intensified CCD (ICCD). In special applications the silicon intensified target (SIT), and intensified SIT (ISIT) are used, but these prior generation tube cameras have all but been replaced by the ICCD camera. These LLL cameras share many of the characteristics of the monochrome CCD and CMOS described earlier but include a *light intensification* means to *amplify* the light thereby responding to much lower light levels. The most sensitive solid-state video camera is the ICCD and is used to view scenes illuminated under very low-light-level artificial lighting, moonlight, and starlight conditions. These LLL cameras have an image intensifier coupled to an imaging tube or solid-state sensor and can view scenes hundreds to thousands of feet from the camera under nighttime conditions.

5.3.5 Thermal IR

Thermal IR imaging systems are different from LLL night-vision systems based on ICCD image-intensifying sensors. The ICCD responds to *reflected* sunlight, artificial lighting, moonlight, and starlight to form a visual image. It also responds to the reflected light from near-IR emitting LEDs and filtered IR thermal lamp sources. In contrast, thermal imaging systems respond *exclusively* to the *heat* from warm or hot emitting objects. The availability of non-cooled (room temperature) thermal IR detector technology is now driving the IR imaging security market. The primary reasons are significant cost reduction, room temperature operation, and improved camera operating characteristics.

5.3.6 Universal System Bus (USB)

The Universal system bus (USB) is a transmission protocol developed to permit disparate electronic equipment, cameras, etc. to communicate with a computer. The original narrower bandwidth USB-1 protocol has been surpassed by the new wideband USB-2 which interfaces the real-time video signal with the computer USB port.

5.4 BASIC SENSOR TYPES

Background. Solid-state CCD sensors are a family of image-sensing silicon semiconductor components invented at Bell Telephone Laboratories in 1969. The CCD imagers used in security applications are small, rugged, and low in power consumption.

The solid-state CID camera was invented at the General Electric Company in the 1970s. Unlike all other solid-state sensors, this camera can address or scan any pixel in a random sequence, rather than in the row and column sequence used in the others. Although this feature has not been used in the security field in the past, some new digital cameras are taking advantage of this capability. When the CID camera is scanned in the normal NTSC pattern, it has attributes similar to those of other solid-state cameras.

Most video security installations use visible light monochrome or color solid-state cameras. Prior to the use of the solid-state cameras all video cameras used sensors based on vacuum tube technology. The only instance in which this technology is now used in video security practice is in the LLL, SIT, and ISIT camera. Prior to the solid-state sensor camera, video cameras utilized tube technology for the sensor and solid-state transistors and integrated circuits for all signal processing. The tube cameras (mostly monochrome) used a scanning electron beam to convert the optical image into an electronic signal. The camera tube consisted of a transparent window, the light-sensitive target, and a scanning electron beam assembly. In operation, the electron beam scanned across the sensor target area by means of electromagnetic coils positioned around the exterior of the tube that deflected the beam horizontally and vertically. The video signal was extracted from the tube by means of the electron beam with a new picture extracted every 1/30th of a second. Tube cameras were available in sizes of 1/2-, 2/3-, and 1-inch formats. Tube cameras were susceptible to image burn-in when exposed to bright light sources and had a maximum lifetime expectancy of only a few years.

Functionally, the camera lens focuses the scene image onto the target surface after passing through the sensor window. The rear surface of the sensitive target area is scanned by the electronic beam to produce an electrical signal representative of the scene image. Solid-state electronics then amplified this electrical signal to a level of 1 volt and combined it with the synchronizing pulses. These electronics produce the composite video signal consisting of an amplitude-modulated signal representing the instantaneous intensity of the light signal on the sensor and the horizontal and vertical synchronizing pulses.

Tube monochrome cameras provided excellent resolution because the target was a homogeneous continuous surface. With small electron beam spots sizes, high resolutions of 500–600 TV lines for a 2/3-inch camera and 1000 TV lines for a 1 inch diameter vidicon tube were obtained. The workhorse of the industry was the monochrome vidicon tube that was sensitive to visible light. Later the monochrome silicon and Newvicon (Panasonic trademark) types were developed that were sensitive to visible and near-IR energy. These tube cameras operated with light levels from bright sunlight (10,000 FtCd) down to 1 FtCd. The vidicon was the least sensitive type with the silicon or Newvicon tube being a better choice for dawn to dusk applications having sensitivities between 10 and 100 times higher than the vidicon depending on the spectral color and IR content of the illumination. The silicon diode had a high sensitivity in the red region of the visible spectrum and in the near-IR spectrum and could "see in the dark" when the scene was illuminated with an IR source. The silicon camera was the most sensitive tube-type camera and had the highest resistance to bright light damage.

5.4.1 Solid State—Visible

The CCD sensor was a new technology that replaced the tube camera. The CCD solid-state sensor camera reduced cost, power consumption, and product size, and was considerably more stable and reliable than the tube-type.

The CCD and newer CMOS sensor video cameras operate significantly differently than did their predecessor tube cameras. No electron beam scans the sensor. Solid-state sensors have hundreds of pixels in the horizontal and vertical directions equivalent to several hundred thousand *pixels* over the entire sensor area. A pixel is the smallest sensing element on the sensor and converts light energy into an electrical charge, and then to an electrical current signal. Arranged in a checker-board pattern, sensor pixels come with a specific number of rows and columns. The total number determines the resolution of the camera.

Solid-state image sensors are available in several types, but all fall into two basic categories: charge transfer device (CTD) and CMOS. The generic CTD class can further be divided into CCD, CPD, and CID. Of these three types, the CCD and CMOS are by far the most popular.

Charge coupled devices provide quality video performance manifesting low noise, wide dynamic range, good sensitivity, fair anti-blooming and anti-smear reduction capabilities, and operate at real-time (30 fps) video rates.

5.4.1.1 Charge Coupled Device (CCD)

At approximately the same time the CCD was invented in 1969 at the Bell Telephone Laboratories in New Jersey, the Philips research laboratory in the Netherlands was also working on an imaging transfer device. The Philips device was called a "bucket brigade device" (BBD), which was essentially a circuit constructed by wiring discrete MOS transistors and capacitors together. The BBD was never seriously considered for use as an imaging device, but the concept of a "bucket brigade" provides a concise functional mechanism similar to the CCD in which charge is passed from one storage site to the next through a series of MOS capacitors.

By placing pixels in a line and stacking multiple lines, an area array detector is created. As the camera lens focuses the light from a single point in the scene onto each pixel, the incident light on each pixel generates an electron charge "packet" whose intensity is proportional to the incident light. Each charge packet corresponds to a pixel. Each row of pixels represents one line of horizontal video information. If the pattern of incident radiation is a focused light image from the optical lens system, then the charge packets created in the pixel array are a faithful reproduction of that image.

In the process, called "charge coupling," the electrical charges are collectively transferred from each CCD pixel to an adjacent storage element by use of external synchronizing or clocking voltages. In the CCD sensor the image scene is moved out of the silicon sensor via timed clocking pulses that in effect push out the signal, line by line, at a precisely determined clocked time. The amount of charge in any individual pixel depends on the light intensity in the scene, and represents a single point of the intelligence in the picture. To produce the equivalent of scanning, a periodic clock voltage is applied to the CCD sensor causing the discrete charge packets in each pixel to move out for processing and transmission. The image sensor has both vertical and horizontal transfer clocking signals as well as storage registers, to deliver an entire field of video information once, during each integration period, 1/30th of a second in the NTSC system. CCD sensors require other timing circuits, clocks, bias voltages made by standard manufacturing processes, and five or more support chips.

All CCD image sensors consume relatively low power and operate at low voltages. They are not damaged by intense light but suffer some saturation and blooming under intense illumination. Most recent devices contain anti-blooming geometry and exposure control (electronic shuttering) to reduce optical overload. Typical device parameters for a 1/3-inch format CCD available today arc: 771×492 pixels (horizontal by vertical) for monochrome and 768×494 for color cameras. They have horizontal resolutions of 570 TV lines for monochrome and 480 TV lines for color. Sensitivities are 0.05 lux (F/1.2 lens) for monochrome and 0.5 lux (F/1.0 lens) for color. The CCD sensors are available in formats of 1/4-, 1/3-, and 1/2-inch, and in some special cameras in a 1/5-, 1/6-, or 2/3-inch format. All have the standard 4×3 aspect ratio. Typical dynamic ranges for monochrome and color are 100 to 1 without shuttering, and 3000 to 1 with electronic shuttering times range from 1/16–1/10,000 second.

Interline Transfer. There are several different CCD sensor pixel architectures used by different manufacturers. The two most common types are the inter-line transfer (ILT) and frame transfer (FT). Figure 5-15 shows the pixel organization and readout technique for the ILT CCD image sensor.

The pixel organization has precisely aligned photosensors with vertical inter-linearly arrayed shift registers, and a horizontal shift register linked with the vertical shift registers as shown. The photo-sensor sites respond to light variations that generate electronic charges proportional to

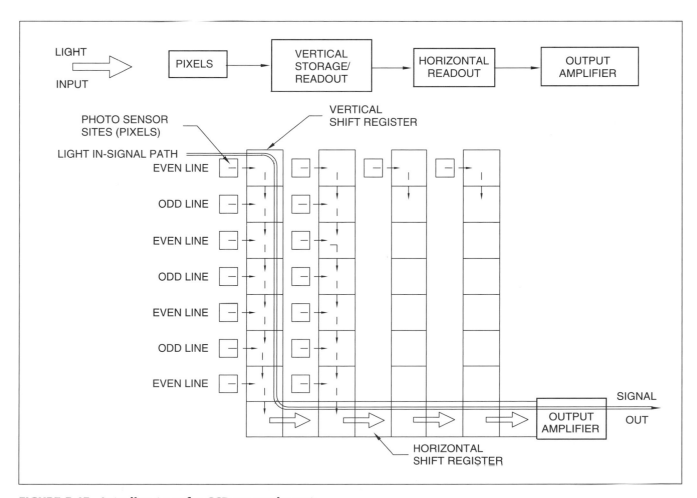

FIGURE 5-15 Interline transfer CCD sensor layout

the light intensity. The charges are passed into the vertical shift registers simultaneously and then transferred to the horizontal shift registers successively until they reach the sensor output amplifier. The camera electronics further amplify and process the signal. Each pixel and line of information in the ILT device is transferred out of the sensor array *line-by-line*, eventually clocking out all 525 lines and thereby scanning the entire sensor to produce a frame of video. This sequence is repeated to produce a continuous video signal.

Frame Transfer.   In the FT CCD, the entire 525 lines are transferred out of the light sensitive array and simultaneously, and stored temporarily in an adjacent nonilluminated silicon buffer array (Figure 5-16).

The basic FT CCD structure is composed of two major elements: a photo-plane and a companion *memory* section. First the photo-plane is exposed to light. After exposure the charge produced is quickly transferred to the companion memory and then read out of memory—one line at a time for the entire frame time. While this memory is being read out, the photo-plane is being exposed for the next image. Although full-pixel storage memory is required for this structure, it has the big advantage of having all the pixels exposed at the same time. CMOS technology on the other hand exposes a line until it is time to read out that line, then that line is transferred to the output register. Consequently the beginning and end of each exposure time of each line is different for every line, i.e. all pixels are not exposed at the same time. The difference between CCD and CMOS is seen when there is motion in the scene. The CCD works better whenever the scene consists of significant motion relative to a line time.

The FT CCD imager has photo-sites (pixels) arranged in an X-Y matrix of rows and columns. Each site has a light-sensitive photodiode and an adjacent charge site which receives no light. The pixel photodiode converts the light photons into charge (electrons). The number of electrons produced is proportional to the number of photoelectrons (light intensity). The light is collected over the entire sensor simultaneously and then transferred to the adjacent site, and then each row is read out to a horizontal transfer register. The charge packets for each row are read out serially and then sensed by a charge-to-voltage converter and amplifier section.

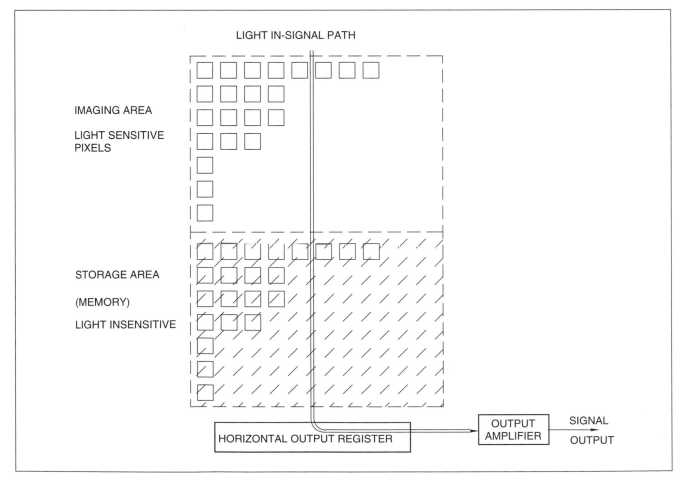

FIGURE 5-16   Frame transfer CCD sensor pixel organization

5.4.1.2 Complementary Metal Oxide Semiconductor (CMOS)

For more than two decades solid-state CCD has been the technology of choice for security cameras. However, they are now being challenged by the CMOS sensor. CMOS research sponsored by NASA and has led to many commercial applications of the CMOS imagers.

In the past CMOS image sensors were relegated to low resolution applications but now they have sufficient pixels for serious security applications. Charge coupled device sensors will still have a place in the high resolution, high sensitivity applications but the CMOS has found increasing application for main-stream video security.

The holy grail in most CMOS imager ventures has been the "camera-on-a-chip" in which a single CMOS chip includes the imaging sensor, timing and control, as well as post-processing circuitry. The CMOS-type sensor exhibits high picture quality but has a lower sensitivity than the CCD. In the CMOS device, the electric signals are read out *directly* through an array of transistor switches rather than line by line as in the CCD sensor.

The CMOS sensor has come into vogue because of the advantage of incorporating on-board analog to digital converters, timing circuits, clocks, and synchronization circuits on the chip. The sensor is manufactured using standard silicon processes, the same as those used in computer chip fabrication, resulting in lower fabrication costs. A CMOS sensor uses about 10–20% as much power as a comparable CCD.

Digital signals from CMOS sensors are always transmitted (not stored as in the CCD sensor) and therefore do not need a DSP. Significant improvements have been made in CMOS cameras for low light level indoor applications. The typical CMOS camera requires a light level of 0.5–1 FtCd. In general, CCD cameras operate in lower light conditions than CMOS cameras.

Using the standard semiconductor production lines it is possible to add a microprocessor or DSP, random access memory (RAM), read only memory (ROM), and a USB controller to the same IC.

Complementary metal oxide semiconductor sensors are lower-priced than CCD and will likely remain so because they are manufactured using the most common silicon processing techniques and are also easier to integrate with other electronic circuitry. CMOS sensors are inherently better than their CCD counterpart in light overload situations and exhibit far less blooming than the CCD. When the CCD is pointed at a bright lamp (100 watt incandescent or other) light source, a white blob is seen around the bulb which obscures the fixture and ceiling scene adjacent to it. With the CMOS the fixture and ceiling detail is seen.

Active Pixel Sensor (APS). The CMOS APS digital camera-on-a-chip technology has progressed rapidly since its invention by the scientists at the NASA Jet Propulsion Laboratory (California).

In the 1990s Stanford University developed a new technology to improve CMOS sensors called the "active pixel sensor" (APS). This digital pixel system (DPS) technology produced higher quality, sharper images, and included an amplifier and analog-to-digital converter (ADC) within each image sensor pixel. The ADCs convert the light signal values into digital values at the point of *light capture*. Figure 5-17a shows how the DPS works, illustrating that

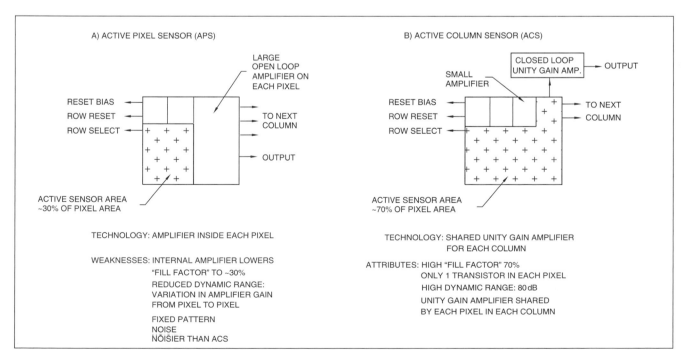

FIGURE 5-17 CMOS active pixel sensor (APS) and active column sensor (ACS)

the charge is removed just before saturation of the pixel occurs, thereby insuring that each pixel is neither under nor over exposed.

Because each pixel has its own ADC, each *pixel in effect acts as its own camera.* These sensors have in effect thousands of "cameras" which are combined to create high-quality video frames and pictures. One disadvantages of the APS technology is that it reduces the "fill factor" (sensitivity, dynamic range) and produces fixed pattern noise. A salient advantage of the technology is that high-lighted areas do not saturate and cause blooming or smearing as when illuminated by a street light or automobile light for applications in nighttime highway surveillance or vehicle license plate identification. The CMOS APS devices are immune to smear and have 30–40% fill factors.

To increase sensor sensitivity, modern on-chip microlenses are formed by an inexpensive process. These lenses act as "funnels" to direct light incident across an entire pixel toward the sensitive portions of the pixel (not an imaging lens). Microlenses increase the responsivity of some low-fill-factor sensors by a factor of two to three. The fill factor is the ratio of optically illuminated area of the sensitive silicon area to the total silicon area in a particular pixel.

Active Column Sensor (ACS).   To overcome some of the disadvantages of the APS CMOS sensor (sensitivity, noise), suppliers have developed active column sensor (ACS) CMOS sensors (Figure 5-17b).

The CMOS sensors have had limitations for the video security industry but the ACS process has the potential of overcoming these limitations.

The ACS CMOS imager technology eliminates non-uniformity of gain by using a unity gain amplifier at each pixel site. Active column sensor also increases the 30% fill factor for APS technology to 70% for ACS. These sensors can also operate at much faster clock speeds and therefore produce no smear for fast motion in the image or fast pan/tilt applications. They offer outstanding anti-blooming capability in both rows and columns which makes them well suited for high- and low-lighted scenes. They rank high in video quality as do CCD imagers.

The ACS technology, CMOS imager could do to the CCD sensor what the CCD did to the vidicon.

The Internet requires the best image quality at very low cost for video graphics array (VGA) and common intermediate format (CIF) display resolution. The ACS CMOS sensor sensitivity has so improved that CMOS sensors are now comparable to the CCD.

Prior to the use of ACS imager technology, most CMOS imagers used the APS technology, the technique of placing an amplifier inside each pixel. This reduced the fill factor and therefore the sensitivity and the dynamic range of the sensor. The ACS process uses a unity gain amplifier which reduces the non-uniformity of the individual pixels and results in a higher fill factor and higher dynamic range.

In the coming years CMOS sensors should exhibit no limitation whatsoever regarding frame speed, resolution, sensitivity, and noise in comparison with CCD sensors. Most available CCD sensors have a signal-to-noise ratio (S/N) of no greater than 58 dB. Some advanced CMOS sensor arrays already have a 66 dB sensitivity and from 1024×1034 to 4096×4096 pixels.

Table 5-2 compares the sensitivity of different types of CCD and CMOS solid-state sensors (see also section 5.6).

5.4.2   ICCD, SIT, ISIT—Visible/Near IR

For dawn and dusk outdoor illumination only the best CCD cameras can produce a usable video picture. ICCD cameras can operate under the light of a quarter-moon with 0.001 FtCd. The ISIT camera can produce an image with only 0.0001 FtCd, which is the light available from stars on a moonless night. These LLL cameras offer a 100–1000 times improvement in sensitivity over the best monochrome CCD or CMOS cameras. They *intensify* light, whereas the CCD and CMOS *detect* light. The ICCD uses a light intensifier tube or micro-channel plate (MCP) intensifier to amplify the available light up to 50,000 times.

The resulting sensitivity approaches that of the SIT camera, is much smaller, requires much less power, and eliminates the blurring characteristics of the SIT under very low light level conditions.

The ICCD camera system has sufficient sensitivity and automatic light compensation to be used in surveillance applications from full sunlight to quarter moonlight conditions. The cameras are provided with automatic light-level compensation mechanisms having a 100 million to 1 light-level range and built-in protection to prevent sensor degradation or overload when viewing bright scenes.

For viewing the lowest light levels, the ISIT camera provides the widest dynamic range from full sunlight to starlight conditions, having a 4 billion to 1 automatic light-level range control. Though large, these cameras have been used in critical LLL security applications. The ISIT camera uses an SIT tube with an additional light amplification stage and is still the lowest (and most expensive) LLL camera available. A description of these LLL cameras is given in Chapter 19.

5.4.3   Thermal IR

The infrared spectrum is generally defined as followings: the near IR or short-wave IR covers from 700 to 3000 nm (0.75–3 microns (μm)), the mid-wave IR from 3 to 5 microns, and the long-wave IR from 8 to 14 microns. Short-wave IR camera systems use the natural *reflection and emission* from targets and are used in applications making use of available LLL radiation from reflected moonlight, sky glow (near cities or other nighttime lighted facilities), or artificially generated radiation from IR LEDs or filtered IR lamp sources. Mid-wave IR systems use the energy

FORMAT TYPE	DESCRIPTION	HORIZONTAL RESOLUTION (TV LINES)	SENSITIVITY* (Lux)		COMMENTS
			COLOR	B/W	
1/6 CCD	COLOR (NTSC), B/W	480	5.0	—	REMOTE HEAD 7 mm DIAMETER
1/6 CCD	COLOR (NTSC), B/W	470	2.5	0.1	ULTRA-FAST IP SPEED DOME
1/6 CCD	COLOR (PAL), B/W	460	2.5	0.1	ULTRA-FAST IP SPEED DOME
1/4 CCD	COLOR (NTSC), B/W	470	0.5	0.01	SPEED DOME, SURVEILLANCE
1/4 CCD	COLOR (PAL), B/W	470	0.5	0.01	SPEED DOME, SURVEILLANCE
1/4 CCD	COLOR (NTSC), B/W	510	1.0	0.06	SURVEILLANCE
1/4 CMOS	COLOR (NTSC)	380	3.0		GENERAL SURVEILLANCE
1/3 CCD	COLOR (NTSC), B/W0	480/570 (B/W)	0.8	0.1	SURVEILLANCE-DAY/NIGHT
1/3 CCD	MONOCHROME (NTSC)	380	—	0.5	SURVEILLANCE
1/3 CCD	COLOR (NTSC), B/W	480	1.0	0.05	SURVEILLANCE
1/3 CMOS	COLOR (NTSC)	380	2.0		COVERT SURVEILLANCE
1/3 CMOS	MONOCHROME (NTSC)	400	—	0.05	SURVEILLANCE
1/3 CMOS	COLOR (NTSC)	380	1.0**	0.05**	COVERT SURVEILLANCE
1/2 CCD	COLOR (NTSC), B/W	480	0.15	0.015	SURVEILLANCE
1/2 CCD	COLOR (PAL), B/W	480	0.15	0.015	SURVEILLANCE
1/2 CCD	MONOCHROME (NTSC)	570	—	0.07	HIGH RESOLUTION B/W

* SENSITIVITY IS A MEASURE OF THE LIGHT LEVEL AT 3200 Degrees KELVIN COLOR TEMPERATURE NECESSARY TO PRODUCE A FULL 1 VOLT PEAK TO PEAK VIDEO SIGNAL.

** MINIMUM ILLUMINATION = THE LIGHT LEVEL TO OBTAIN A RECOGNIZABLE VIDEO SCENE.

B/W = BLACK/WHITE (MONOCHROME)

Table 5-2   Sensitivity of Representative CCD and CMOS Image Sensors

from hot sources (fires, bright lamps, gun barrel emission, explosives and very hot, red hot, white hot objects) that provide good thermal emission. Long-wave IR systems use the *differences* in radiation from room temperature emitters like humans, animals, vehicles, ships and aircraft (engine areas), warm buildings, and other hot objects as compared to their surroundings. The IR thermal camera is the only system that can "see" when the visible or near-IR radiation suitable for visible, near- or mid-IR sensors is too low to detect. These systems see in total darkness and can often "see" through smoke and fog.

The use of IR cameras relies on thermal differences (contrast)—heat emitted by target vs. heat emitted by the background surrounding it—thereby providing images with better contrast than using ICCD image intensification. Thermal sensors require very little temperature difference between the target and background for the sensor to detect the target.

Thermal IR cameras look like video cameras in their mechanical and electrical characteristics but the lenses required are different in that the glass in standard visible light or near-IR cameras is replaced by a lens using an infrared transmitting material such as germanium. Thermal systems are readily available for security application but cost between 10 and 100 times more than standard

video cameras. These lower resolution IR cameras have a comparatively small number of pixels that result in a pixilated picture, but there is often sufficient intelligence to determine the objects or activity in the scene. Electronic smoothing of the picture is often used to improve the displayed scene. The use of pseudocolors, i.e. different colors representing different temperatures, is a significant aid in interpreting the scene. Medium resolution systems typically have 320×256 pixel arrays and high resolution systems have 640×512 arrays (military, very expensive). See Chapter 19 for examples of thermal IR imagers.

The human body glows (radiates energy) like a 100 watt bulb in the IR spectrum but only if it is viewed in the correct spectrum, i.e. the long-wave IR spectrum. The wavelengths of the radiation emitted by most terrestrial objects lie between about 3 and 12 μm in the mid- and far-IR region of the spectrum. The peak of the human body radiation (at 98° Fahrenheit) is at about 9 μm.

Infrared detectors fall into two different categories: photovoltaic and thermal. The photovoltaic detectors generate an electrical current directly proportional to the number of *photons* incident on the detector. Thermal detectors respond to the *change in resistance* or some other temperature-dependent parameter in the material. As the absorbed light *heats* up, the material (pixels) changes in resistance or capacitance producing a change in the electrical circuit.

Pyroelectric and bolometric detectors are the two types of detectors that form the basis of most non-cooled thermal IR camera designs.

5.4.4 Sensor Fusion—Visible/IR

A technique called "multi-spectral imaging" in which an image is displayed from two different detectors operating at different wavelengths is finding increased use in the security field.

Displaying the images from two different wavelength regions (sensor fusion) *on the same monitor* significantly increases intelligence obtained from the combined scene. In the 3–5 micron region some targets and backgrounds "reverse" their energy levels. This change can be detected when the two signals are subtracted. In normal single detector systems this signal reversal is averaged out and not detected, thereby reducing detection capability.

A powerful sensor fusion technique uses the combination of an image-intensified camera and a thermal IR camera to significantly improve seeing under adverse nighttime conditions having smoke, dust, and fog. The fusion of near-IR and far-IR cameras with combined overlay display results in a significantly improved night vision system. The system combines the strengths of image intensification (a clear sharp picture) with the advantages of thermal IR (high detection capability). This provides the ability to see in practically any non-illuminated nighttime environmental condition.

5.5 CAMERA FEATURES—ANALOG/DIGITAL

Analog cameras are limited to a few automatic compensating functions: (1) automatic gain control (AGC), (2) white light balance (WB). Digital cameras with DSP on the other hand can have many automatic functions. Some are described below.

5.5.1 Video Motion Detection (VMD)

The second-most often used intrusion-detection device (first is the pyroelectric infrared (PIR)) in the security industry is the VMD. The digital VMD uses an analog-to-digital device to convert the analog video signal to a digital signal. The DSP circuits then respond to the movement or activity in the image as recognized as a specific type and rate change within a defined area using a preset minimum sensitivity for size and speed. While PIR intrusion sensors detect the change in the *temperature* of a particular part of the viewed area, the VMD senses a change

in the *contrast* within the camera scene from the normal quiescent video image. These digital VMD modules are now small enough to be incorporated directly into a video camera housing or larger, more sophisticated ones connected in between the camera and the video monitor. These digital VMDs are much more immune to RFI and EFI interferences and temperature changes that can cause false alarms in the PIR devices. Prior analog VMD technology exhibited an array of false alarm problems related to changes in scene lighting, shadows, cable or wireless transmission noise, etc. With the advancement of CCD cameras and DSP circuitry, the reliability and false alarm rate have been managed, resulting in reliable VMD detectors with the CCD and CMOS cameras scene contrast analysis replaced by localized pixel analysis. It is now possible to digitally analyze changes in *individual or small groups of pixels*, resulting in increased levels of reliability and reduced false alarm rate. Recent improvements in the digital VMD have addressed problems associated with false alarms due to foreign objects moving through the field of view at rates of speeds too fast or too slow rates to be of interest. The products available have automatic adjustments (algorithms) to process the video signal data to exclude these false alarms. Other false alarms caused by natural weather changes, i.e. clouds coming into the field of view, or small animals and birds or other debris passing through the camera field of view have for the most part been eliminated. These new digital systems have resulted in low false alarm rates and systems that only respond to intruders.

Digital VMDs do not require a computer for operation and are usually provided with an RS232 interface for computer integration and remote programming and reporting. This approach to operation and control provides a user-friendly interface to most users that are familiar with a menu-driven screen and mouse operation. Physically they consist of modular units or are designed in the form of plug-in boards for easy installation into existing camera equipment.

5.5.2 Electronic Zooming

Prior to video cameras incorporating DSP electronics, the only option for zooming the video camera system was through the use of zoom lens optics. Electronic zoom was first perfected in consumer CCD and CMOS camcorders and still cameras and then in the security industry. The electronic zooming technique makes use of magnifying the image electronically by selecting a portion of the sensor area and presenting its magnified video image onto the monitor screen. Zoom ratios of from 5:1 to 20:1 are available depending on the basic resolution of the sensor. Since only a selected portion of the entire sensor is used, electronic zooming can often be combined with electronic pan and tilt by moving the area used in the sensor over different parts of the entire sensor area. This results in electronically panning and tilting while the camera and lens are held stationary.

5.5.3 Electronic Shuttering

It is essential to match the camera sensor sensitivity to the lighting in the scene. In general the more the lighting available the less sensitive the camera has to be. Digital signal processing technology permits the camera to adapt to the scene illumination through the use of electronic shuttering of the camera. The camera electronics adapt so that it is optimally adjusted for the scene light level, which changes the sensitivity of the sensor to compensate for varying light levels. This electronic sensitivity control (ESC) allows for small changes in light levels found in indoor applications such as lobby areas, hallways with external windows, storage areas, or where an outside door is occasionally opened. It is not for use in outdoor applications having large light level changes (due to circuitry limitations), where the use of an automatic-iris lens is usually required. It often permits the use of a manual-iris lens assembly, which reduces the overall cost of the camera–lens combination, rather than an auto-iris.

5.5.4 White Balance

Automatic white balance is required so that when the camera is initially turned on, it properly balances its color circuits to a white background, which in turn is determined by the type of illumination at the scene. The camera constantly checks the white-balance circuitry and makes any minor compensation for variations in the illumination color temperature, i.e. the spectrum of colors in the viewed scene.

Color cameras are sensitive to the *color temperature* of light as defined by the color rendering index (CRI) of light sources. A common problem for many color camera systems is their inability to reproduce the exact color of an object when using different light sources with different CRIs. Color rendering is the term used to describe how well a light source is able to produce the actual color of the viewed object without causing a shift or error in color. The color temperature determines the white component of the light source composed of the totality of all the colors in the light source spectrum. Different types of lamps produce different ranges of "white" light and these differences must be compensated for. This compensation is performed by the WB circuits of the camera. Today's DSP cameras have automatic WB electronics that can adjust between color temperatures from 2800 to 7600 K which encompasses most lighting conditions. Chapter 3 shows the spectral output from common light sources and video camera spectral sensitivities used in security applications.

5.5.5 Video Bright Light Compression

One major improvement resulting from the use of DSP in cameras is back light compensation (BLC). The DSP camera with BLC adjusts to and can simultaneously view dark and bright scene areas thereby increasing the camera dynamic range by more than thirty times over conventional cameras. This technique is ideal for many applications where there are highly contrasted lighting conditions or where contrast conditions change throughout the course of viewing. The camera accomplishes this by digitizing the image signal, at two different rates. Short times (faster speed) register the bright image areas, and long times (slower speed) register dark image areas. The two signals are processed together in the camera and combined into a single signal at the output. Until the use of BLC these conditions did not permit a clear view of the entire image and required the use of high-end cameras with digital back-light masking capabilities.

Back light compensation allows cameras to be pointing at brightly lighted building entrances and exits, ATMs, or underground parking facilities. Other applications include casinos where interior lighting is designed to brighten gaming and cash areas and to soften lounges, seating areas, and aisles. Another application is a loading dock that is illuminated with different light levels and poses a similar problem during the course of any given day. Exterior lighting conditions in these areas vary from dark to blinding sunshine. In another interior application, jewelry counters often feature brightly illuminated display areas with subdued lighting in the surrounding areas. Now cameras with DSP compensation can be used to continuously monitor both interior and exterior areas under virtually any lighting condition, applications that were previously not possible with analog camera designs.

5.5.6 Geometric Accuracy

One of the significant advantages solid-state image sensors have over their tube sensor predecessors is the precise geometric location of the pixels with respect to one another. In a CCD, CMOS, or thermal IR sensor, the locations of the individual photo-sensor pixel sites are known exactly since they are determined during manufacture of the sensor and never move.

5.6 CAMERA RESOLUTION/SENSITIVITY

When classifying a video camera the two specifications that are most important are the resolution and sensitivity. Unfortunately in many data sheets there is confusion surrounding these terms.

Resolution. Resolution is the quality of definition and clarity of the picture, and is defined in discernible TV lines; the more the lines the higher the resolution and the better the picture quality. Resolution is a function of the number of pixels (picture elements) in the CCD chip. In other words, the resolution is directly proportional to the number of pixels in the CCD sensor. In some data sheets, two types of resolution are defined: vertical and horizontal. Vertical resolution is equal to the number of discernible horizontal lines in the picture and is limited by either the 525 or the 625 line resolution as defined in the NTSC or CCIR standards. Horizontal resolution relates to the number of lines reproduced in the picture in the vertical direction, and depends on the bandwidth.

Sensitivity. Sensitivity is a measure of how low a light level a camera can respond to and still produce a usable or minimum quality picture. It is measured in FtCd or lux for CCD, CMOS, and ICCD cameras operating and the visible and near-IR wavelength range, and in delta-temp (Δt) in the mid- and far-IR. One FtCd equals approximately 9.3 lux. The smaller the number (FtCd, lux or Δt) the more sensitive the camera. Typical values for state-of-the-art cameras are: (1) monochrome camera 0.1−0.001 lux, (2) color camera (single sensor) 1 FtCd–5 FtCd, (3) thermal IR 0.1 Δt.

5.6.1 Vertical Resolution

Vertical resolution in the analog scanning system is derived from the 504 effective scanning lines in the 525-line NTSC television system. The camera scanning dissects a vertical line appearing in the scene into 483 separate segments. Since each scanning line on the monitor has a discrete width, some of the scene detail between the lines is lost. As a general rule approximately 30% of any scene is lost (called the "Kell factor"). Therefore, the standard 525-line NTSC television system produces 340 vertical TV lines of resolution (483 effective lines × 0.7). In any standard 525-line CCTV system, the maximum achievable vertical resolution is approximately 350 TV lines. In a 625-line system, the maximum achievable vertical resolution is approximately 408 TV lines.

Vertical resolution in the digital system is just the number of vertical camera pixels. However, if a digital camera is displayed on a 525 (or 625) line analog CRT display, then the resolution is limited to the 350 (or 408) TV lines of the analog system.

5.6.2 Horizontal Resolution

The NTSC standard provides a full video frame composed of 525 lines, with 483 lines for the image and two vertical blanking intervals composed of 21 retrace lines each.

The TV industry adopted a viewing format with a width-to-height ratio of 4:3 and specifies horizontal resolution in *TV lines per picture height*. The horizontal resolution on the monitor tube depends on how fast the video signal changes its intensity as it traces the image on a horizontal line. The traditional method for testing and presenting video resolution test results is to use the Electronic Industries Association (EIA) resolution target (Figure 5-18).

If only one resolution is defined in a camera data sheet, the manufacturer is referring to the horizontal resolution. There are several ways for measuring the horizontal resolution. The most common is to use a video resolution chart which has horizontal and vertical lines as the target scene. The camera resolution is the point where the lines start to merge and cannot be separated. This chart-measuring technique can be subjective since different people perceive, when the lines merge, differently. The resolution of the monitor must be higher than the camera.

The minimum-spaced discernible black-and-white transition boundaries in the two wedge areas are the vertical limiting (horizontal wedge) and horizontal limiting (vertical wedge) resolution values. Various industries using electronic imaging devices have specified resolution criteria dependent on the particular discipline involved. In the analog video security industry the concept of TV lines is defined as the resolution parameter.

A more scientific technique for measuring the horizontal resolution is by measuring the bandwidth of the signal. The bandwidth of the video signal from the camera is measured on an oscilloscope (see Chapter 25). Multiplying the bandwidth by 80 TV lines/MHz gives the resolution of the camera. For example if the bandwidth is 6 MHz the camera resolution will be 6 × 80 or 480 TV lines.

The horizontal resolution is determined by the maximum speed or frequency response (bandwidth) of the video electronics and video signal. While the vertical resolution is determined solely by the number of lines or pixels chosen— and thus not variable under the US standard of 525 lines— the horizontal resolution depends on the electrical performance of the individual camera, transmission system, and monitor. Most standard cameras with a 6 MHz bandwidth produce a horizontal resolution in excess of 450 TV lines. The horizontal resolution of the system is therefore limited to approximately 80 lines/MHz of bandwidth.

The solid-state-imaging industry has adopted pixels as its resolution parameter. To obtain TV-line resolution equivalent when the number of pixels are specified, multiply the number of pixels by 0.75. In photography, line pairs or cycles per millimeter is the resolving power notation. While all these parameters are useful, they tend to be confusing. For the purposes of CCTV security applications, the TV line notation is used. For reference, the other parameters are defined as follows:

- One cycle is equivalent to one line pair.
- One line pair is equivalent to two TV lines.
- One TV line is equivalent to 1.25 pixels.

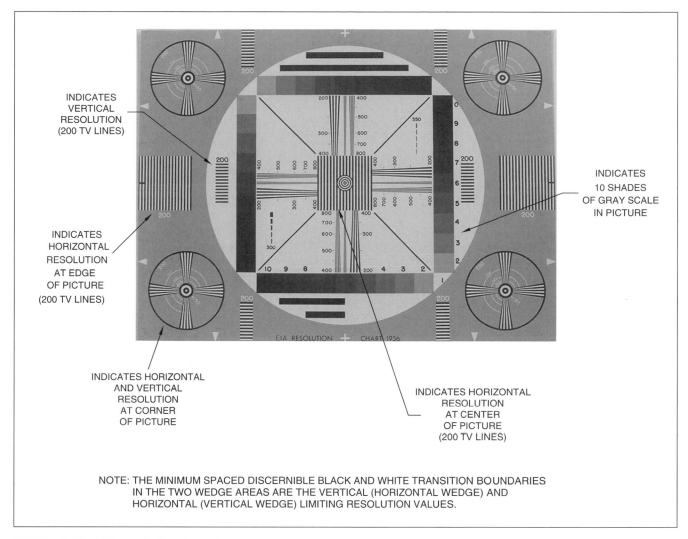

INDICATES
VERTICAL
RESOLUTION
(200 TV LINES)

INDICATES
HORIZONTAL
RESOLUTION
AT EDGE
OF PICTURE
(200 TV LINES)

INDICATES
10 SHADES
OF GRAY SCALE
IN PICTURE

INDICATES HORIZONTAL
AND VERTICAL
RESOLUTION
AT CORNER
OF PICTURE

INDICATES HORIZONTAL
RESOLUTION
AT CENTER
OF PICTURE
(200 TV LINES)

NOTE: THE MINIMUM SPACED DISCERNIBLE BLACK AND WHITE TRANSITION BOUNDARIES
IN THE TWO WEDGE AREAS ARE THE VERTICAL (HORIZONTAL WEDGE) AND
HORIZONTAL (VERTICAL WEDGE) LIMITING RESOLUTION VALUES.

FIGURE 5-18   EIA resolution target

One cycle is equivalent to one black-and-white transition and represents the minimum sampling information needed to resolve the elemental areas of the scene image.

A figure *of merit* for solid-state CCTV cameras is the total number of pixels reproduced in a picture area. A typical value is 380,000 pixels for a good 525-line CCTV system.

A parameter deserving mention that is used in lens, camera, and image-intensifier literature is the modulation transfer function (MTF). This concept was introduced to assist in predicting the overall system performance when cascading several devices such as the lens, camera, transmission medium, and monitor or recorder in one system. The MTF provides a figure of merit for a part of the system (such as the camera or monitor) acting alone or when the parts are combined with other elements of the system. It is used particularly in the evaluation of LLL devices (Chapter 19).

The resolution for a good monochrome security camera is 550–600 TV lines and for a color camera is 450–480 TV lines. The data sheets from manufacturers of solid-state cameras (and monitors) often quote the number of pixels instead of TV line resolution. However, unless the number of pixels is converted into equivalent TV lines, it is hard to compare picture resolution. Table 5-3 summarizes the state of the art in solid-state sensors and gives information on the horizontal and vertical pixels available for representative 1/6, 1/4-, 1/3-, and 1/2-inch format types.

When monochrome solid-state sensor cameras were first introduced, the sensors had a maximum horizontal resolution of approximately 200 TV lines per picture height. These early low-resolution sensors had 288 horizontal by 394 vertical pixels. Present-day sensors have horizontal resolutions of 400–600 TV lines per picture height. Medium-resolution camera sensors have 510(H) × 492(V) pixels, and high-resolution cameras have 739(H) × 484(V) pixels.

Improvements in the resolution of solid-state sensors to match the best tube sensors have resulted from various approaches with the most successful increase coming from increased pixel density. These strides in decreasing the pixel size have resulted from the techniques used to

TYPE	DESCRIPTION	HORIZONTAL	VERTICAL	TOTAL	RESOLUTION (TV LINES)	COMMENTS
1/6 CCD	COLOR (NTSC)	811	508	412,000	480	7 mm DIAMETER SENSOR HEAD
1/6 CCD	COLOR (NTSC)	736	480	340,000	470	ULTRA-FAST IP SPEED DOME
1/6 CCD	COLOR (PAL)	736	544	400,000	460	ULTRA-FAST IP SPEED DOME
1/4 CCD	COLOR (NTSC)	768	494	380,000	480	SURVEILLANCE
1/4 CCD	COLOR (NTSC), B/W	768	494	380,000	470	NETWORK IP SPEED DOME
1/4 CCD	COLOR (PAL), B/W	752	582	438,000	470	NETWORK IP SPEED DOME
1/4 CMOS	COLOR (NTSC)	640	480	307,200	480	NETWORK IP
1/3 CCD	MONOCHROME (NTSC)	510	492	251,000	380	SURVEILLANCE
1/3 CCD	MONOCHROME (CCIR)	512	582	297,000	380	SURVEILLANCE
1/3 CCD	COLOR (NTSC), B/W	771	492	380,000	480/570 (B/W)	DAY/NIGHT SURVEILLANCE
1/3 CCD	COLOR (NTSC)	768	494	380,000	480	SURVEILLANCE
1/3 CCD	COLOR (PAL)	811	508	412,000	480	SURVEILLANCE
1/3 CMOS	COLOR (NTSC)	640	480	307,200	340	COVERT SURVEILLANCE
1/2 CCD	COLOR (NTSC), B/W	768	494	380,000	480	DAY/NIGHT SURVEILLANCE
1/2 CCD	COLOR (PAL), B/W	752	582	440,000	480	DAY/NIGHT SURVEILLANCE
1/2 CCD	MONOCHROME (NTSC)	811	508	412,000	570	HIGH RESOLUTION B/W

*RESOLUTION IS THE ABILITY TO JUST DISCERN TWO ADJACENT BLACK LINES SEPARATED BY A WHITE SPACE. THE SYSTEM SHOULD HAVE A GRAY SCALE WITH A MINIMUM OF 10 LINES FROM BLACK TO WHITE.

FOR DIGITAL VIDEO SYSTEMS THE HORIZONTAL AND VERTICAL RESOLUTIONS ARE APPROXIMATELY 0.75 × NUMBER OF PIXELS.

FOR LEGACY NTSC AND PAL SYSTEMS, VERTICAL RESOLUTION IS LIMITED BY THE 525 AND 625 HORIZONTAL LINE SCAN RATE AND THE HORIZONTAL RESOLUTION BY THE SYSTEM BANDWIDTH.

B/W = BLACK/WHITE (MONOCHROME)

Table 5-3 Resolution of Representative Solid-State CCD and CMOS Cameras

manufacture very large scale integrated (VLSI) devices for computers. Image sensors are VLSI devices. The majority of solid-state sensors in use today have a 1/4-, 1/3- or 1/2-inch image format. There are some available with 1/5- and 1/6-inch image formats, and larger ones with 2/3-inch formats.

Several other techniques are used to improve resolution. In one camera configuration, image-shift enhancement results in a doubling of the ILT CCD imager horizontal resolution by shifting the visual image in front of the CCD sensor by one-half pixel. This technique simultaneously reduces aliasing, which causes a fold-back of the high-frequency signal components, resulting in "herringbone" or jagged edges in the image. This artifact is often seen when viewing plaid patterns on clothing and screens, with medium to low resolution solid-state cameras. Aliasing reduces resolution and causes considerable loss in picture intelligence.

Another technique used to improve the horizontal resolution without increasing the pixel count is offsetting each row of pixels by one-half pixel, generating a zigzag of the pixel rows. This arrangement, in conjunction with corresponding clocking, allows simultaneous readout of two horizontal rows and nearly doubles the horizontal

resolution compared with conventional detectors with identical pixel counts.

5.6.3 Static vs. Dynamic Resolution

The previous section described *static resolution*. This represents resolution achieved when a camera views a stationary scene. When a camera views a moving target—a person walking through the scene, a car passing by—or the camera scans a scene, a new parameter called *dynamic resolution* is defined. Under either the moving-target or scanning condition, extracting intelligence from the scene depends on resolving, detecting, and identifying fine detail. The solid-state camera has the ability to resolve rapid movement without degradation in resolution under almost all suitable lighting conditions.

When high resolution is required while viewing very fast moving targets, solid-state cameras with an electronic shutter are used to capture the action. Many solid-state cameras have a variable-shutter-speed function, with common shutter speeds of 1/60, 1/1000, and 1/2000. This shuttering technique is equivalent to using a fast shutter speed on a film camera. The ability to shutter solid-state cameras results in advantages similar to those obtained in photography: the moving object or fast-scan panning that would normally produce a blurred image can now produce a sharp one. The only disadvantage this technique has is that since a decreased amount of light enters the camera, the scene lighting must be adequate for the system to work successfully.

5.6.4 Sensitivity

Sensitivity of a camera is measured in foot candles (FtCd) or lux (1 FtCd = 9.3 lux) and usually refers to the minimum light level required to get an acceptable video picture. There is a great deal of confusion in the video industry over camera specifications with respect to what an *acceptable* video picture is. Manufacturers use two definitions for camera sensitivity: (1) sensitivity at the camera sensor faceplate and (2) minimum scene illumination.

Sensitivity at the faceplate indicates the minimum light required at the *sensor* chip to get an acceptable video picture. Minimum scene illumination indicates the minimum light required at the *scene* to get an acceptable video picture. When sensitivity is defined as the minimum scene illumination, parameters such as the scene reflectance, the lens optical speed (f/#), usable video, automatic gain control (on, off), and shutter speed should be defined.

With regard to reflectance, most camera manufactures use 89% or 75% (white surface) reflectance surface to define the minimum scene illumination. If the actual scene being viewed has the same reflectance as the data sheet then this is a correct measurement. This is usually not the case. Typical light reflectivities of different materials range from snow 90%, grass 40%, brick 25%, to black-top 5%. It is apparent that if the camera is viewing a black car, only about 5% of the light is reflected back to the camera and therefore at least fifteen times more light is required at the scene to give the same amount of light that would come from a white surface.

One camera technology that significantly increases the sensitivity of the CCD sensor over existing devices by a factor of two uses an on-chip lens (OCL) technique. By manufacturing the sensor with microscopic lenses on each pixel, the incoming light is concentrated on the photo-sensor areas thereby increasing the sensitivity of the camera. An improvement particularly important in CMOS sensors incorporates microscopic lenses that cover the active area of each pixel as well as the inactive area between pixels, thereby eliminating the ineffective areas between the microlenses. This increases sensitivity by over a factor of two and reduces the smear level significantly compared to that of the original technology.

5.7 SENSOR FORMATS

The development of the superior solid-state CCD sensor color camera for the VCR home consumer market accelerated the use of color cameras in the security industry. There are three popular image format sizes for solid-state security cameras: 1/4-, 1/3-, and 1/2-inch. All security sensor formats have a horizontal-by-vertical geometry of 4×3 as defined in the EIA and NTSC standards. For a given lens, the 1/4-inch format sensor sees the smallest scene image and the 1/2-inch sees the largest, with the 1/3-inch format camera seeing proportionally in between.

The ISIT tube cameras using the 1-inch tube to provide LLL capabilities have by all intents and purposes been replaced by their solid-state counterpart, the ICCD. As a basis for comparison with other formats, Figure 5-19 shows the solid state CCD, CMOS, and tube image formats compared to photographic film formats.

For reference the 16 mm semiprofessional film camera, and the 35 mm film camera used for bank holdup and forensic applications is shown. Table 5-4 lists the three popular video image format sizes: 1/4-, 1/3-, and 1/2-inch, and four less used sizes: 1-, 2/3-, 1/6-, and 1/5-inch.

For reference, the physical target area in tube cameras is *circular* and usually corresponds to the diagonal of the lens image circle. The tube active target is the inscribed 4×3 rectangular aspect ratio area scanned by the electron beam in the tube. Since each pixel is used in the solid-state camera image the target area in the solid-state sensor is the full sensor 4×3 format array. The camera sensor format is important since it determines the lens format size with which it must operate and, along with the lens focal length (FL), sets the video system field of view (FOV).

As a general rule, the larger the sensor size, the larger the diameter of the lens glass size required which translates into increased lens size, weight, and cost. Any lens designed for a larger format can be used on a smaller format camera. The opposite is not true, for example a lens designed for a 1/3-inch format will not work properly on a 1/2-inch format camera and will produce vignetting (dark area surrounding the image).

5.7.1 Solid-State

Most solid-state cameras using CCD or CMOS sensor technology have 1/4-, 1/3-, and 1/2-inch formats. The sensor arrays are rectangular in shape and have the active area sizes as listed in Table 5-4 and shown in Figure 5-19. Significant progress has been made in producing exceptionally high-quality 1/4-, 1/3-, and 1/2-inch format sensors that rival the sensitivity of some of earlier larger 2/3- and 1 inch solid-state or tube sensors. Most color cameras used in security applications have single-chip sensors with three-color stripe filters integral with the image sensor. Typical sensitivities for these color cameras

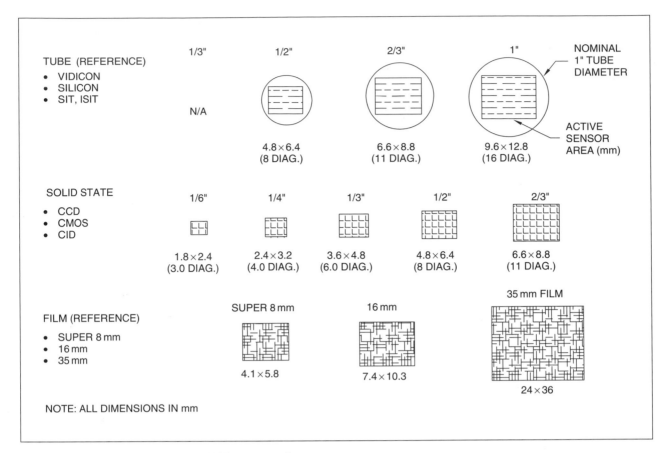

FIGURE 5-19   Tube, solid state and film image formats

IMAGE SENSOR SIZE						
FORMAT	DIAGONAL (d)		HORIZONTAL (h)		VERTICAL (v)	
1" (REFERENCE)	mm	inches	mm	inches	mm	inches
	16	0.63	12.8	0.50	9.6	0.38
2/3"	11	0.43	8.8	0.35	6.6	0.26
*1/2"	8	0.31	6.4	0.25	4.8	0.19
*1/3"	6	0.24	4.8	0.19	3.6	0.14
*1/4"	4	0.16	3.2	0.13	2.4	0.1
1/6"	3	0.12	2.4	0.09	1.8	0.07

* MOST COMMON CCTV SENSOR FORMATS

Table 5-4   CCTV Camera Sensor Formats

range from 0.5 to 2.0 FtCd (4.6 to 18.6 lux) for full video, which is less sensitive than their monochrome counterpart by a factor of about 10. Low resolution color cameras have a horizontal resolution of about 330 TV lines. High-resolution color cameras have a horizontal resolution of about 480 TV lines.

5.7.2   Image Intensifier

The most common image intensifier is the ICCD and uses standard monochrome resolution CCD image formats. Typical values for the format resolution are 500–600 for a 1/2-inch sensor.

5.7.3 Thermal IR

The thermal IR camera uses a long-wave IR array fabricated using completely different manufacturing techniques as compared with CCD or ICCD manufacture. These sensors are far more difficult to manufacture and have far lower yields than do other solid-state sensors. As a result the number of pixels in the sensor is significantly less. Typical sensor arrays have 280–320 horizontal TV line resolution. Future generations of these thermal IR cameras will have near equivalent resolution to those of CCD and CMOS cameras.

5.8 CAMERA LENS MOUNTS

Several lens-to-camera mounts are standard in the CCTV industry. Some are mechanically interchangeable and others are not. Care must be taken so that the lens mount matches the camera mount. The two widely used camera-lens mounts are the C and CS mount. Small surveillance cameras use the 10, 12, and 13 mm thread diameter minilens mounts. The 10 and 12 mm diameter mounts have a 0.5 mm pitch and the 13 mm diameter mount has a 1.0 mm pitch. Large bayonet mounts are used with specialized cameras and lenses on some occasions. These lens-to-camera mounts are described in the following sections.

5.8.1 C and CS Mounts

For many years, all 1-, 2/3-, and 1/2-inch cameras used an industry-standard mount called the C mount to mechanically couple the lens to the camera. Figure 5-20 shows the mechanical details of the C and CS mounts.

The C mount camera has a 1-inch-diameter hole with 32 threads per inch (TPI) and the C mount lens has a matching thread (1–32 TPI) that screws into the camera thread. The distance between the lens rear mounting surface and the image sensor for the C mount is 0.69 inches (17.526 mm).

With the introduction of the smaller 1/4- and 1/3-inch (and 1/2-inch) format cameras and lenses, it became possible and desirable to reduce the size of the lens and the distance between the lens and the sensor. A mount adopted by the industry for 1/4-, 1/3-, and 1/2-inch-sensor-format cameras became the CS mount. The CS mount matches the C mount in diameter and thread but the distance between the lens rear mounting surface and the image sensor for the CS mount is 0.492 inches (12.5 mm). The CS mount is 0.2 inches (5 mm) shorter than the C mount. Since the lens is 5 mm closer to the sensor, the lens can be made smaller in diameter. A C mount lens can be used on a CS mount camera if a 5 mm spacer is interposed between the lens and the camera and if the lens format covers the camera format size. The advantage

of the CS mount system is that the lens can be smaller, lighter, and less expensive than its C mount counterpart. The CS mount camera is completely compatible with the common C mount lens when a 5 mm spacer ring is inserted between the C mount lens and the CS mount camera. The opposite is not true: a CS mount lens *will not* work on a C mount camera. Table 5-5 summarizes the present lens mount parameters.

5.8.2 Mini-Lens Mounts

The proliferation of small minilenses (see Chapter 4) and small CCD and CMOS cameras has led to widespread use of smaller lens/camera mounts. Manufacturers supply these mini-lenses and cameras with mounts having metric thread sizes of 10, 12, or 13 mm diameter and thread pitches of 0.5 and 1.0 mm. The two widely used sizes are the 10 and 12 mm diameter with 0.5 mm pitch.

5.8.3 Bayonet Mount

The large 2.25-inch-diameter bayonet mount is used primarily in custom security, industrial, broadcast, and military applications with three-sensor color cameras, LLL cameras, and long FL large lenses. It is only in limited use in the security field.

5.8.4 Lens–Mount Interferences

Figure 5-21 illustrates a potential problem with some lenses when used with CCD or solid-state cameras. Some of the shorter-FL lenses (2.2, 2.6, 3.5, and 4.8 mm) have a protrusion that extends behind the C or CS mount or mini-mount and can interfere with the filter or window used with the solid-state sensor. This mechanical interference prevents the lens from fully seating in the mount, thereby causing the image to be out of focus. Most lens and camera manufacturers are aware of the problem and for the most part have designed lenses and cameras that are compatible. However, since lenses are often interchanged, the potential problem exists and the security designer should be aware of the condition.

5.9 ZOOM LENS–CAMERA MODULE

The requirement for a compact zoom lens and camera combination has been satisfied with a zoom lens–camera module. This module evolved out of a requirement for a lightweight, low inertia camera-lens for use in high speed pan/tilt dome installations in casinos, airports, malls, retail stores, etc. The camera–lens module has a mechanical *cube* configuration so that it can easily be incorporated into a

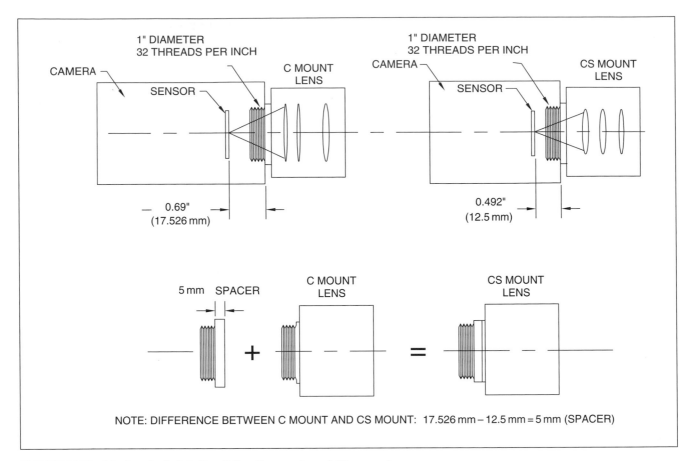

FIGURE 5-20   Mechanical details of the C mount and CS mount

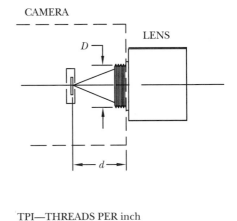

MOUNT TYPE	MOUNTING SURFACE TO SENSOR DISTANCE (*d*)		MOUNT TYPE
	inch	mm	THREAD: DIAMETER (*D*)
C	0.069	17.526	1-inch DIA. 32 TPI
CS	0.492	12.5	1-inch DIA. 32 TPI
MINI: 10 mm	VARIES FROM * 3.5 mm (0.14") TO 9 mm (0.35")		10 mm DIA. 0.50 mm PITCH
MINI: 12 mm			12 mm DIA. 0.50 mm PITCH
MINI: 12 mm			13 mm DIA. 0.50 mm PITCH

*VARIES WITH MANUFACTURER
TO CONVERT A C MOUNT LENS TO A CS MOUNT, ADD A 5 mm SPACER

Table 5-5   Standard Camera/Lens Mount Parameters

pan/tilt dome housing and be pointed in any direction at high speeds (Figure 5-22).

The module assembly includes the following components and features: (1) rugged, compact mechanical structure suitable for high-speed pan/tilt platforms; (2) large optical zoom ratio, typically 16 or 20 to 1; (3) large elec-

tronic zoom ratio, typically 8 or 10 to 1; and (4) a 1/4-inch solid-state color camera with excellent sensitivity and resolution. Options include: (1) automatic focus and (2) image stabilization capability (see Section 4.5.11).

The automatic-focusing option is useful providing the lens is zooming *slowly* and the module is not panning or

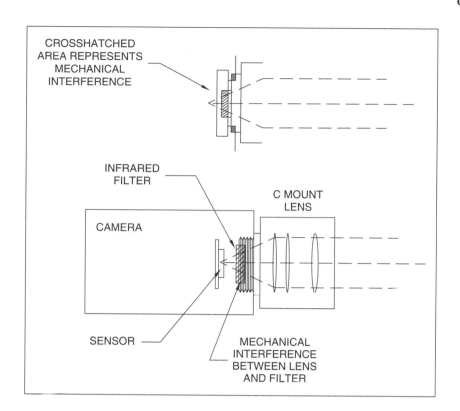

CROSSHATCHED AREA REPRESENTS MECHANICAL INTERFERENCE

INFRARED FILTER

CAMERA

C MOUNT LENS

SENSOR

MECHANICAL INTERFERENCE BETWEEN LENS AND FILTER

FIGURE 5-21 Lens-mount interference

FIGURE 5-22   Zoom lens–camera module

tilting rapidly. When a person walks into the lens FOV the automatic-focus lens changes focus from the surrounding scene to the moving person, keeping the person in focus. The auto-focus system keeps the person in focus even though they move toward or away from the lens. Auto-focus is ineffective while the lens is zooming and should not be used if the module is panning and/or tilting rapidly. In this situation the system becomes "confused" and does not know what object to focus on, causing the person to be out of focus in the picture. The zoom lens in a typical module has an FL range of 3.6–80 mm (f/1.6

at the 3.6 mm FL setting). At the wide-angle setting the lens and camera covers a 54° horizontal angular FOV. At the telephoto setting, it covers a 2.5° horizontal angular FOV. The lens–camera module is also available, packaged for mounting on standard pan/tilt platforms.

5.10 PANORAMIC 360° CAMERA

There has always been a need to see "all around" an entire room or area, seeing 360° horizontally and 90° vertically with one panoramic camera and lens. Early versions of such a 360° FOV camera systems were achieved using multiple cameras and lenses and combining the scenes as a split screen on the monitor. Panoramic lenses have been available for many years but have only recently been combined with high resolution digital cameras and DSP electronics using sophisticated mathematical transforms to take advantage of their very wide-angle capabilities. The availability of high resolution solid-state cameras has made it possible to map a 360° by 90° hemispherical FOV onto a rectangular monitor with good resolution. Figure 4-31 shows a panoramic camera and operational diagram having a 360° horizontal and a 90° vertical FOV.

In operation, the lens collects light from the 360° panoramic scene and focuses it onto the camera sensor as a donut-shaped image (Figures 4-31 and 4-32). The electronics and mathematical algorithm convert this donut-shaped panoramic image into the rectangular (horizontal and vertical) format for normal monitor viewing. In operation, a joystick or computer mouse is used to electronically

FIGURE 5-23 High definition television (HDTV) formats

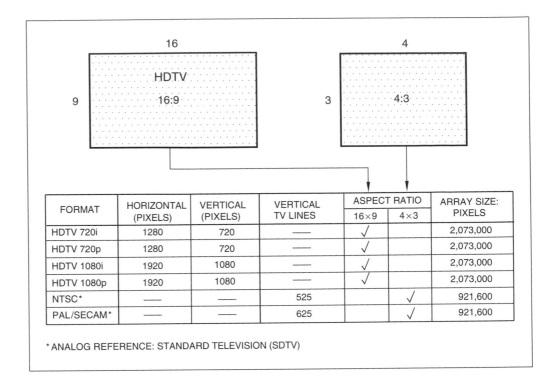

FORMAT	HORIZONTAL (PIXELS)	VERTICAL (PIXELS)	VERTICAL TV LINES	ASPECT RATIO 16×9	ASPECT RATIO 4×3	ARRAY SIZE: PIXELS
HDTV 720i	1280	720	——	√		2,073,000
HDTV 720p	1280	720	——	√		2,073,000
HDTV 1080i	1920	1080	——	√		2,073,000
HDTV 1080p	1920	1080	——	√		2,073,000
NTSC*	——	——	525		√	921,600
PAL/SECAM*	——	——	625		√	921,600

*ANALOG REFERENCE: STANDARD TELEVISION (SDTV)

pan and tilt the camera so that at any given time a *segment* of the 360° horizontal by 90° vertical image is displayed on the monitor.

5.11 HIGH DEFINITION TELEVISION (HDTV)

High definition television (HDTV) provides a new video display format having a 16 × 9 horizontal by vertical format, thereby providing a significantly increased resolution over that of standard NTSC 4 × 3 format (Figure 5-23).

The reason for defining this new format is to provide: (1) a higher resolution or definition video display, (2) one that has a format that better matches the view seen by the human eye (wider horizontal view), and (3) a format more closely matching the many images that the eye sees, i.e. landscapes, parking lots, etc. This new format was originally developed for the consumer market; however, it will find its way into the video security market because of the superior monitor display format and resolution it provides. The new HDTV format and size has many variations and has not yet been standardized in the security industry. Not all HDTV images have the same number of horizontal lines or the same resolutions. The way the different picture formats are painted on the screen is also different. HDTV formats available include: 720p, 1080i, and 1080p/24. The first number in the type designation is the vertical resolution or how many scan lines there are from the top to the bottom of the picture. This first designation is usually followed by a letter. The letter is either an "i" or "p." These are the abbreviations for interlaced (i) or progressive (p) scans respectively. Progressive means that the whole picture is painted from the top of the screen to the bottom and then a new frame is painted over again. Interlaced means only half the image is painted first (odd-numbered lines) and then the other half of the image is painted (even-numbered lines). There seems to be a general consensus that the progressive scan is better than the interlaced. All present NTSC video security video systems using the 4 × 3 format use 2:1 interlaced lines and every computer monitor uses progressive. The last number in the designation 24, 30, or 60 refers to the frame rate.

At present, the best HDTV system is 1080i, and interlaced 30 frame/60 fields per second, system similar to NTSC, but with the 16 × 9 picture format of HDTV. HDTV video improves the intelligence provided in many security displays since it presents a wider horizontal aspect ratio, has higher resolution, and can support a larger screen size. The increased resolution produces crisper, sharper images.

5.12 SUMMARY

There have been many important improvements and innovations in the development of the video camera and its use in the security field. The single most significant advances in CCTV camera technology have been the development of the CCD and CMOS solid-state camera image sensor, IR thermal cameras, IP camera, and the use of DSP. These sensors and camera electronics offer a compelling advantage over original vacuum-tube technology because of solid-state reliability, inherent long life, low cost, low-voltage operation, low power dissipation, geometric reproducibility, absence of image lag, DSP, and visible and/or IR response. These solid-state cameras have provided the increased performance, reliability, and stability needed in monochrome, color, and IR video security systems.

The availability of solid-state color cameras has made a significant impact on the security video industry. Color cameras provide enhanced video surveillance because of their increased ability to display and recognize objects and persons. The choices available for lighting in most security applications is sufficient for most color cameras to have satisfactory sensitivity and resolution. Solid-state color cameras have excellent color rendition, maintain color balance, and need no color rebalancing when light level or lighting color temperature varies.

Intensified charge coupled device cameras coupled to tube or micro-channel plate intensifiers provide the low light sensitivity required in dawn to dusk applications and some nighttime applications. Room temperature, thermal IR cameras have provided the "eyes" when no visible or near-IR light is available and visible sensors are inoperable.

Chapter 6
Analog Video, Voice, and Control Signal Transmission

CONTENTS

6.1 Overview
6.2 Base-band Signal Analysis
    6.2.1 Video Picture Signal
    6.2.2 Video Synchronization Signal
    6.2.3 Voice Signal
    6.2.4 Control Data Signals
    6.2.5 Modulation and Demodulation
    6.2.6 Signal Bandwidth
6.3 Wired Video Transmission
    6.3.1 Coaxial Cable
        6.3.1.1 Unbalanced Single-Conductor Cable
        6.3.1.2 Connectors
        6.3.1.3 Amplifiers
    6.3.2 Balanced Two-Conductor Twin-axial Cable Transmission
        6.3.2.1 Indoor Cable
        6.3.2.2 Outdoor Cable
        6.3.2.3 Electrical Interference
        6.3.2.4 Grounding Problems
        6.3.2.5 Aluminum Cable
        6.3.2.6 Plenum Cable
    6.3.3 Two-Wire Cable Unshielded Twisted Pair (UTP) Transmission
        6.3.3.1 Balanced 2-Wire Attributes
        6.3.3.2 The UTP Technology
        6.3.3.3 UTP Implementation with Video, Audio, and Control Signals
        6.3.3.4 Slow-Scan Transmission
    6.3.4 Fiber-Optic Transmission
        6.3.4.1 Background
        6.3.4.2 Simplified Theory
        6.3.4.3 Cable Types
            6.3.4.3.1 Multimode Step-Index Fiber
            6.3.4.3.2 Multimode Graded-Index Fiber
            6.3.4.3.3 Cable Construction and Sizes
            6.3.4.3.4 Indoor and Outdoor Cables
        6.3.4.4 Connectors and Fiber Termination
            6.3.4.4.1 Coupling Efficiency
            6.3.4.4.2 Cylindrical and Cone Ferrule Connector
            6.3.4.4.3 Fiber Termination Kits
            6.3.4.4.4 Splicing Fibers
        6.3.4.5 Fiber-Optic Transmitter
            6.3.4.5.1 Generic Types
            6.3.4.5.2 Modulation Techniques
            6.3.4.5.3 Operational Wavelengths
        6.3.4.6 Fiber-Optic Receiver
            6.3.4.6.1 Demodulation techniques
        6.3.4.7 Multi-Signal, Single-Fiber Transmission
        6.3.4.8 Fiber Optic—Advantages/ Disadvantages
            6.3.4.8.1 Pro
            6.3.4.8.2 Con
        6.3.4.9 Fiber-Optic Transmission: Checklist
6.4 Wired Control Signal Transmission
    6.4.1 Camera/Lens Functions
    6.4.2 Pan/Tilt Functions
    6.4.3 Control Protocols
6.5 Wireless Video Transmission
    6.5.1 Transmission Types
    6.5.2 Frequency and Transmission Path Considerations

6.5.3   Microwave Transmission
    6.5.3.1   Terrestrial Equipment
    6.5.3.2   Satellite Equipment
    6.5.3.3   Interference Sources
6.5.4   Radio Frequency Transmission
    6.5.4.1   Transmission Path Considerations
    6.5.4.2   Radio Frequency Equipment
6.5.5   Infrared Atmospheric Transmission
    6.5.5.1   Transmission Path Considerations
    6.5.5.2   Infrared Equipment
6.6   Wireless Control Signal Transmission
6.7   Signal Multiplexing/De-multiplexing
    6.7.1   Wideband Video Signal
    6.7.2   Audio and Control Signal
6.8   Secure Video Transmission
    6.8.1   Scrambling
    6.8.2   Encryption
6.9   Cable Television
6.10   Analog Transmission Checklist
    6.10.1   Wired Transmission
        6.10.1.1   Coaxial Cable
        6.10.1.2   Two-Wire UTP
        6.10.1.3   Fiber-Optic Cable
    6.10.2   Wireless Transmission
        6.10.2.1   Radio Frequency (RF)
        6.10.2.2   Microwave
        6.10.2.3   Infrared
6.11   Summary

6.1   OVERVIEW

Closed circuit television (CCTV) and open circuit television (OCTV) video signals are transmitted from the camera to a variety of remote monitors via some form of wired or wireless transmission channel. Control, communications, and audio signals are also transmitted depending on the system. This chapter covers most of the *analog* techniques for transmitting these signals. Chapter 7 describes the techniques for transmission of *digital* signals. Analog transmission is still critically important because of the immense installed base of analog equipment in the security field. These video systems are in operation, and will remain so for many years to come.

In its most common form, the video signal is transmitted at base-band frequencies over a coaxial cable. This chapter identifies techniques and problems associated with transmitting video and other signals from the camera site to the remote monitoring location using wired copper-wire and fiber optics, and through-the-air wireless transmission.

Electrical-wire techniques include coaxial cable and two-wire unshielded twisted-pair (UTP). Coaxial cable is suitable for all video frequencies with minimum distortion or attenuation. Two-wire UTP systems using standard conductors (intercom wire, etc.) use special transmitters and receivers that preferentially boost the high video frequencies to compensate for their loss over the wire length.

Faithful video signal transmission is one of the most important aspects of a video system. Each color video channel requires approximately a 6 MHz bandwidth. Monochrome picture transmission needs only a 4.2 MHz bandwidth. Figure 6-1 shows the single-channel video bandwidth requirements for monochrome and color systems.

Using information from other chapters, it is not difficult to specify a good lens, camera, monitor, and video recorder to produce a high-quality picture. However, if means of transmission does not deliver an adequate signal from the camera to the monitor, recorder, or printer, an unsatisfactory picture will result. The final picture is only as good as the *weakest* link in the system and it is often the transmission means. Good signal transmission requires that the system designer and installer choose the best transmission type, and use high-quality materials, and practices professional installation techniques. A poor transmission system will degrade the specifications for camera, lens, monitoring, and recording equipment.

Fiber optics offers a technology for transmitting high-bandwidth, high-quality, multiplexed video pictures, and audio and control signals over a single fiber. Fiber-optic technology has been an important addition to video signal transmission means. The use of fiber-optic cable has significantly improved the picture quality of the transmitted video signal and provided a more secure, reliable, and cost-effective transmission link. Some advantages of fiber optics over electrical coaxial-cable or two-wire UTP systems include:

- high bandwidth providing higher resolution or simultaneous transmission of multiple video signals;
- no electrical interference to or from other electrical equipments or sources;
- strong resistance to tapping (eavesdropping), thereby providing a secure link; and
- no environmental degradation: unharmed by corrosion, moisture, and electrical storms.

Wireless transmission techniques use radio frequencies (RF) in the very high frequency (VHF) and ultra high frequency (UHF) bands, as well as microwave frequencies at 900 MHz, 1.2 GHz, and 2.4 GHz and 5.8 GHz in the S and X bands (2–50 GHz). Low-power microwave and RF systems can transmit up to several miles with excellent picture quality, but the higher power systems require an FCC (Federal Communications Commission) license for operation. Wireless systems permit independent placement of the CCTV camera in locations that might be inaccessible for coaxial or other cables.

Cable-less video transmission using IR atmospheric propagation is discussed. Infrared laser transmission requires no FCC approval but is limited in range depending on visibility. Transmission ranges from a few hundred

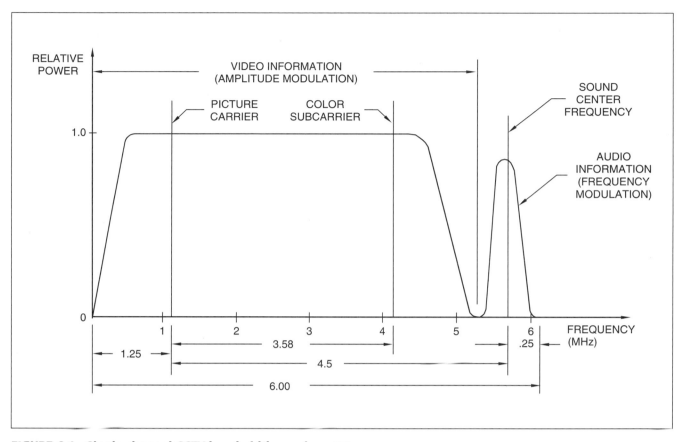

FIGURE 6-1   Single channel CCTV bandwidth requirements

feet in poor visibility to several thousand feet or even many miles in good visibility.

Infrared is capable of bidirectional communication; control signals are sent in the opposite direction to the video signal and audio is sent in both directions.

The wired and wireless transmission techniques outlined above account for the majority of transmission means from the remote camera site to the monitoring site. There are, however, many instances when the video picture must be transmitted over very long distances—tens, hundreds, or thousands of miles, or across continents. These are accomplished using digital techniques (Chapter 7). Two-wire, coaxial, or fiber-optic cables for real-time transmission are often not practical in metropolitan areas where a video picture must be transmitted from one building to another building through congested city streets not in sight of each other.

A technique developed in the 1980s for transmitting a video picture anywhere in the world over telephone lines or any two-wire network is called "slow-scan video transmission." This technique uses a non-real-time two-wire technology that permits the transmission of a video picture from one location to any other location in the world, providing that a two-wire or wireless voice-grade link (telephone line) is available. This system was the forerunner to the present Internet, intranet, and World Wide Web (WWW).

The slow-scan system took a real-time camera video signal and converted into a non-real-time signal and transmitted it at a slower frame rate over any audio communications channel (3000 Hz bandwidth). Unlike conventional video transmission, in which a real-time signal changed every 1/30th of a second, the slow-scan transmission method sent a *single snapshot* of a scene over a time period of 1–72 seconds depending on the resolution specified. This effect is similar to that of opening your eyes once every second or once every minute or somewhere in between. When used with an alarm intrusion or VMD the slow-scan equipment began sending pictures, once every few seconds at low resolution (200 TV lines), or every 32 seconds at high resolution (500 TV lines).

A quantum change and advancement has occurred in the video surveillance industry in the past five years. Computer based systems now use digital techniques and equipments from the camera, transmission means, switching and multiplexing equipment, to the DVRs, solid-state LCD, and plasma monitors. The most dramatic change, however, has been in the use of digital transmission (Chapter 7). Now with the Internet and WWW, and digital signal compression a similar function but much improved transmission is accomplished over any wired or wireless network.

A basic understanding of the capabilities of the aforementioned techniques, as well as the advantages and disadvantages of different transmission means, is essential to optimize the final video picture and avoid costly retrofits. Understanding the transmission requirements when choosing the transmission means and hardware is important because it constitutes the most labor-intensive portion of the video installation. Specifying, installing, and testing the video signal and communication cables for intra-building and inter-building wiring represents the major labor cost in the video installation. If the incorrect cable is specified and installed, and must be removed and replaced with another type, serious cost increases result. In the worst situation, where cables are routed in underground outdoor conduits, it is imperative to use the correct size and type of cable so as to avoid retrenching or replacing cables.

6.2 BASE-BAND SIGNAL ANALYSIS

The video signal generated by the analog camera is called the "base-band video signal." It is called base-band because it contains low frequencies, from 30 Hz for NTSC (25 hertz for CCIR) to 6 MHz. To accomplish fiber-optic transmission and wireless RF, microwave, and IR transmission the base-band signal is modulated with a carrier frequency.

The monochrome or color video signal is a complex analog waveform consisting of the picture information (intensity and color) and synchronizing timing pulses. The waveform was defined in specified by the SMPTE. The full specifications are contained in standards RS-170, RS-170A, and RS-170RGB.

6.2.1 Video Picture Signal

For a monochrome camera the picture information is contained in the single amplitude modulated (AM) intensity waveform. The video signal amplitude for full monochrome and color is 1 volt peak to peak. For a color camera the information is contained in three color waveforms containing the red, green, and blue color contents of the scene. The three colors can faithfully reproduce the color picture. The color signal from the camera sensor can be modified in two different forms: (1) composite video, (2) Y (intensity), C (color), and (3) red (R), green (G), blue (B). The monochrome and color video signals are described in Chapter 5.

6.2.2 Video Synchronization Signal

The video synchronization signals consist of vertical field and frame timing pulses, and horizontal line timing pulses. The NTSC standard field and frame timing pulses occur at 1/60 second. and 1/30 second intervals respectively.

The horizontal line timing pulses occur at 63.5 microsecond intervals. The CCIR/PAL vertical standard timing is 1/50 second, 1/25 second, and 64 microseconds. The magnitude of these timing pulses is shown in Chapter 5.

6.2.3 Voice Signal

In the NTSC standard, the voice and sound information is contained in a sub-carrier centered at 4.5 MHz and at 4.5, 5.5, 6.0 and 6.5 MHz in the CCIR/PAL systems. The signal is frequency modulated (FM) for high fidelity reproduction.

6.2.4 Control Data Signals

While not generating part of the standard NTSC signal, command and control data can be added to the signal. The bits and bytes of digital information are handed during the vertical retrace times between frames and fields. Camera control (on/off, etc.), lens control (focus, zoom, iris control), and camera platform control (pan, tilt, presets, etc.) signals are digitally controlled to perform these functions.

6.2.5 Modulation and Demodulation

To accomplish fiber-optic transmission, the base-band video signal is converted to an FM signal. For RF transmission the base-band video signal is frequency modulated with the RF of the carrier and 928 MHz (also 435, 1200, 1700 MHz and others). For microwave transmission the base-band is modulated with a camera frequency of 2.4 and 5.8 GHz.

6.2.6 Signal Bandwidth

The base-band color video signal for NTSC is 30 Hz–6 MHz (4 MHz for monochrome), and 25 Hz–7 MHz for CCIR/PAL.

6.3 WIRED VIDEO TRANSMISSION

6.3.1 Coaxial Cable

Coaxial cable is used widely for short to medium distances (several hundred to several thousand feet) because its electrical characteristics best match those required to transmit the full-signal bandwidth from the camera to the monitor. The video signal is composed of slowly varying (low-frequency) and rapidly varying (high-frequency) components. Most wires of any type can transmit the low frequencies (20 Hz to a few thousand Hz); practically any wire can carry a telephone conversation. It takes the special coaxial-cable configuration to transmit the full spectrum of frequencies from 20 Hz to 6 MHz without attenuation, as required for high-quality video pictures and audio.

There are basically two types of coaxial and two types of twin-axial cable for use in video transmission systems:

1. 75-ohm unbalanced indoor coaxial cable
2. 75-ohm unbalanced outdoor coaxial cable
3. 124-ohm balanced indoor twin-axial cable
4. 124-ohm balanced outdoor twin-axial cable.

The cable construction for the coaxial and twin-axial types are shown in Figure 6-2. The choice of a particular coaxial cable depends on the environment in which it will be used and the electrical characteristics required. By far the most common coaxial cables are the RG59/U and the RG11/U, having a 75-ohm impedance. For short camera-to-monitor distances (a few hundred feet), preassembled or field-terminated lengths of RG59/U coaxial cable with BNC connectors at each end are used. The BNC connector is a rugged video and RF connector in common use for many decades and the connector of choice for all base-band video connections. Short preassembled lengths of 5, 10, 25, 50, and 100 feet, with BNC-type connectors attached, are available. Long cable runs (several hundred feet and longer) are assembled in the field, made up of a single length of coaxial cable with a connector at each end. For most interior video installations, RG59/U (0.25 inch diameter), or RG11/U (0.5 inch diameter), 75-ohm unbalanced coaxial cable is used. When using the larger diameter RG11/U cable, a larger UHF-type connector is used. When a long cable run of several thousand feet or more is required, particularly between several buildings, or if electrical interference is present, the balanced 124-ohm coaxial cable or fiber-optic cable is used. When the camera and monitoring equipments are in two different buildings, and likely at different ground potentials, an unwanted signal may be impressed on the video signal which shows up as an interference (wide bars on the video screen) and makes the picture unacceptable. A two-wire balanced or fiber-optic cable eliminates this condition.

Television camera manufacturers generally specify the maximum distance between camera and monitor over which their equipment will operate when interconnected with a specific type of cable. Table 6-1 summarizes the transmission properties of coaxial and twin-axial cables when used to transmit the video signal.

In applications with cameras and monitors separated by several thousand feet, video amplifiers are required. Located at the camera output and/or somewhere along the coaxial-cable run, they permit increasing

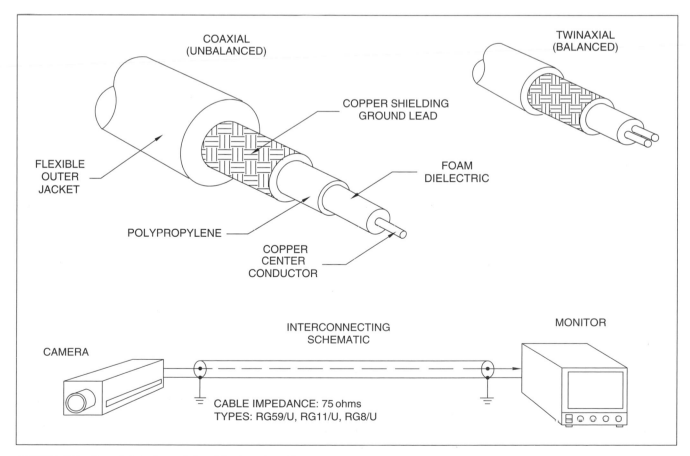

FIGURE 6-2   Coaxial-twin-axial cable construction

COAXIAL TYPE	MAXIMUM RECOMMENDED CABLE LENGTH (D)				CONDUCTOR (GAUGE)	NOMINAL DC RESISTANCE (ohms/1000 ft)
	CABLE ONLY		CABLE WITH AMPLIFIER			
	FEETS	METER	FEETS	METER		
RG59/U	750	230	3,400	1,035	22 SOLID COPPER	10.5
RG59 MINI	200	61	800	250	20 SOLID COPPER	41.0
RG6/U	1,500	455	4,800	1,465	18 SOLID COPPER	6.5
RG11/U	1,800	550	6,500	1,980	14 SOLID COPPER	1.24

CAMERA |←——————— D ———————→| MONITOR

NOTE: IMPEDANCE FOR ALL CABLES = 75 ohms

Table 6-1   Coaxial Cable Run Capabilities

the camera-to-monitor distance to 3400 feet for RG59/U cable and to 6500 feet for RG11/U cable.

The increased use of color television in security applications requires the accurate transmission of the video signal with minimum distortion by the transmitting cable. High-quality coaxial-cable, UTP, and fiber-optic installations satisfy these requirements.

While a coaxial cable is the most suitable hard-wire cable to transmit the video signal, video information transmitted through coaxial cable over long distances is attenuated differently depending on its signal frequencies. Figure 6-3 illustrates the attenuation as a function of distance and frequency as exhibited by standard coaxial cables.

The attenuation of a 10 MHz signal is approximately three times greater than that of a 1 MHz signal when using a high-quality RG11/U cable. In video transmission, a 3000-foot cable run would attenuate the 5 MHz part of the video signal (representing the high-resolution part of the picture) to approximately one-fourth of its original level at the camera; a 1 MHz signal would be attenuated to only half of its original level. At frequencies below 500 kHz, the attenuation is generally negligible for these distances. This variation in attenuation as a function of frequency has an adverse effect on picture resolution and color quality. The signal deterioration appears on monitors in the form of less definition and contrast and poor color rendition. For example, severe high-frequency attenuation of a signal depicting a white picket fence against a dark background

would cause the pickets to merge into a solid, smearing mass, resulting in less intelligence in the picture.

The most commonly used standard coaxial is RG59/U, which also has the highest signal attenuation. For a 6 MHz bandwidth, the attenuation is approximately 1 dB per 100 feet, representing a signal loss of 11%. A 1000-foot run would have a 10 dB loss—that is, only 31.6% of the video signal would reach the monitor end.

In a process called "vidi-plexing," special CCTV cameras transmit both the camera power and the video signal over a single coaxial cable (RG59/U or RG11/U). This single-cable camera reduces installation costs, eliminates power wiring, and is ideal for hard-to-reach locations, temporary installations, or camera sites where power is unavailable.

6.3.1.1 Unbalanced Single-Conductor Cable

The most widely used coaxial cable for video security transmission and distribution systems is the unbalanced coaxial cable, represented by the RG59/U or RG11/U configurations. This cable has a single conductor with a characteristic impedance of 75 ohms, and the video signal is applied between the center conductor and a coaxial braided or foil shield (Figure 6-2).

Single-conductor coaxial cables are manufactured with different impedances, but video transmission uses only the 75-ohm impedance, as specified in EIA standards. Other cables that may look like the 75-ohm cable have a different electrical impedance and will not produce an acceptable

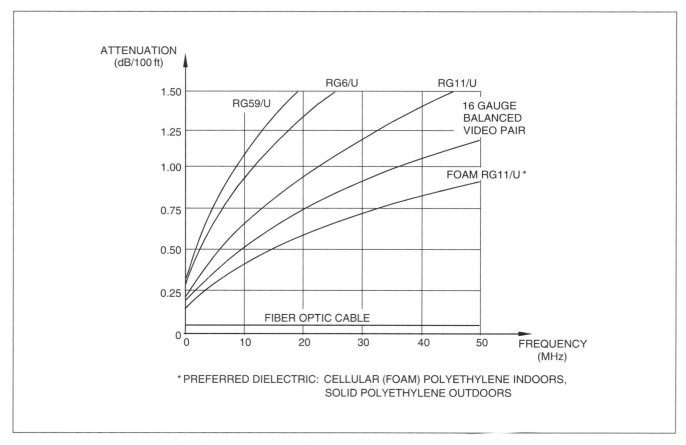

FIGURE 6-3   Coaxial cable signal attenuation vs. frequency

television picture when used at a distance of 25 or 50 feet or more.

The RG59/U and RG11/U cables are available from many manufacturers in a variety of configurations. The primary difference in construction is the amount and type of shielding and the insulator (dielectric) used to isolate the center conductor from the outer shield. The most common shields are standard single copper braid, double braid, or aluminum foil. Aluminum foil–type should not be used for any CCTV application. It is used only for cable television. Common dielectrics are foam, solid plastic, and air, the latter having a spiral insulator to keep the center conductor from touching the outer braid. The cable is called unbalanced, because the signal current path travels in the forward direction from the camera to the monitor on the center conductor and from the monitor back to the camera again on the shield, which produces a voltage difference (potential) across the outer shield. This current (and voltage) has the effect of unbalancing the electrical circuit.

For short cable runs (a few hundred feet), the deleterious effects of the coaxial cable—such as signal attenuation, hum bars on the picture, deterioration of image resolution, and contrast—are not observed. However, as the distance between the camera and monitor increases to 1000–3000 feet, all these effects come into play. In particular, high-frequency attenuation sometimes requires

equalizing equipment in order to restore resolution and contrast.

Video coaxial cables are designed to transmit maximum signal power from the camera output impedance (75 ohms) with a minimum signal loss. If the cable characteristic impedance is not 75 ohms, excessive signal loss and signal reflection from the receiving end will occur and cause a deteriorated picture.

The cable impedance is determined by the conductor and shield resistance of the core dielectric material, shield construction, conductor diameter, and distance between the conductor and the shield. As a guide, resistance of the center conductor for an RG59/U cable should be approximately 15 ohms per 1000 feet, and for an RG11/U cable, approximately 2.6 ohms per 1000 feet. Table 6-2 summarizes some of the characteristics of the RG59/U and RG11/U coaxial cables.

6.3.1.2   Connectors

Coaxial cables are terminated with several types of connectors: the PL-259, used with the RG11/U cable, and the BNC, used with the RG59/U cable. The F-type is an RF connector used in cable television systems. Figure 6-4 illustrates these connectors.

The BNC has become the connector of choice in the video industry because it provides a reliable connection

CABLE TYPE	ATTENUATION (dB) @ 5–10 MHZ							
	100 ft	200 ft	300 ft	400 ft	500 ft	1000 ft	1500 ft	2000 ft
RG59/U	1.0	2.0	3.0	4.0	5.0	10.0	15.0	20.0
RG59 MINI	1.3	2.6	3.9	5.2	6.5	13.0	19.5	26.0
RG6/U	.8	1.6	2.4	3.2	4.0	8.0	12.0	16.0
RG11/U	.51	1.02	1.53	2.04	2.55	5.1	7.66	10.2
2422/UL1384*	3.96	7.9	11.9	18.8	19.8	39.6	59.4	79.2
2546*	1.82	3.6	5.5	7.3	9.1	18.2	27.3	36.4
RG179B/U	2.0	4.0	6.0	8.0	10.0	20.0	30.0	40.0
SIAMESE: RG59 (2) #22AWG	1.0	2.0	3.0	4.0	5.0	10.0	15.0	20.0

* MOGAMI
NOTE: IMPEDANCE FOR ALL CABLES = 75 ohms

dB LOSS	1	2	3	4.5	6	8	10.5	14	20
% SIGNAL REMAINING	90	80	70	60	50	40	30	20	10

Table 6-2   Coaxial Cable Attenuation vs. Length

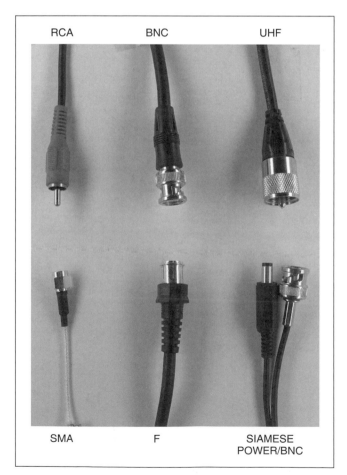

FIGURE 6-4 RCA, BNC, F, SMA, UHF and siamese cable connectors

with minimum signal loss, has a fast and positive twist-on action, and has a small size, so that many connectors can be installed on a chassis when required. There are essentially three types of BNC connectors available: (1) solder, (2) crimp-on, and (3) screw-on.

The most durable and reliable connectors are the solder and crimp-on. They are used when the connector is installed at the point of manufacture or in a suitably equipped electrical shop. The crimp-on and screw-on types are the most commonly used in the field, during installation and repair of a system. Either type can be successfully assembled with few tools in most locations. The crimp-on type uses a sleeve, which is attached to the cable end after the braid and insulation have been properly cut back; it is crimped onto the outer braid and the center conductor with a special crimping plier. When properly installed, this cable termination provides a reliable connection.

To assemble the screw-on type, the braid and insulation are cut back and the connector slid over the end of the cable and then screwed on. This too is a fairly reliable type of connection, but it is not as durable as the crimp-on type, since it can be inadvertently unscrewed from the end of the cable. The screw-on termination is less reliable if the cable must be taken on or off many times.

6.3.1.3 Amplifiers

When the distance between the camera and the monitor exceeds the recommended length for the RG59/U and RG11/U cables, it is necessary to insert a video amplifier to boost the video signal level. The video amplifier is inserted at the camera location or somewhere along the coaxial cable run between the camera and the monitor location (Figure 6-5).

The disadvantage of locating the video amplifier somewhere along the coaxial cable is that since the amplifier requires a source of AC (or DC) power, the power source must be available at its location. Table 6-1 compares the cable-length runs with and without a video amplifier. Note that the distance transmitted can be increased more than fourfold with one of these amplifiers.

When the output from the camera must be distributed to various monitors or separate buildings and locations, a distribution amplifier is used (see Figure 6-5). This amplifier transmits and distributes monochrome and color video signals to multiple locations. In a quad unit, a single video input to the amplifier results in four identical, isolated video outputs capable of driving four 75-ohm RG59/U or RG11/U cables. The distribution amplifier is in effect a power amplifier, boosting the power from the single camera output so that multiple 75-ohm loads can be driven. A potential problem with an unbalanced coaxial cable is that the video signal is applied across the single inner conductor and the outer shield, thereby impressing a small voltage (hum voltage) on the signal. This hum

voltage can be eliminated by using an isolation amplifier, a balanced coaxial cable, or fiber optics.

6.3.2 Balanced Two-Conductor Twin-axial Cable Transmission

Balanced twin-axial cables are less familiar to the CCTV industry than the unbalanced cables. They have a pair of inner conductors surrounded by insulation, a coaxial-type shield, and an outer insulating protective sheath has a characteristic impedance of 124 ohms. They have been used for many years by telephone industry for transmitting video information and other high-frequency data. These cables have an outside diameter (typically 0.5 inch) and their cost, weight, and volume are higher than those of an unbalanced cable. Since the polarity on balanced cables must be maintained, the connector types are usually polarized (keyed). Figure 6-6 shows the construction and configuration of a balanced twin-axial cable system.

The primary purposes for using balanced cable are to increase transmission range and to eliminate the picture degradation found in some unbalanced applications. Unwanted hum bars (dark bars on the television picture)

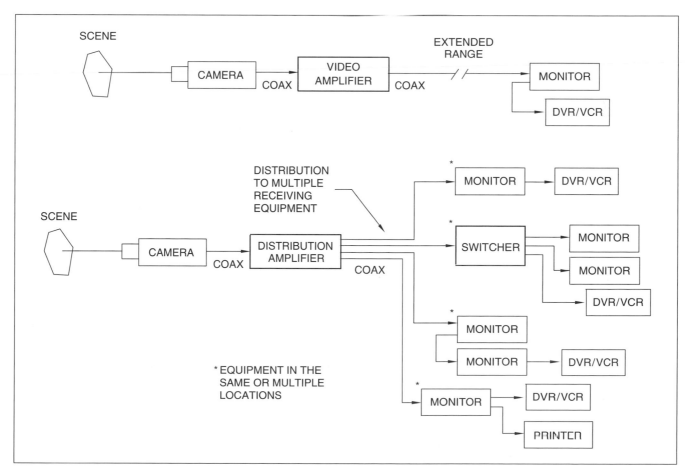

FIGURE 6-5   Video amplifier to extend range and/or distribute signal

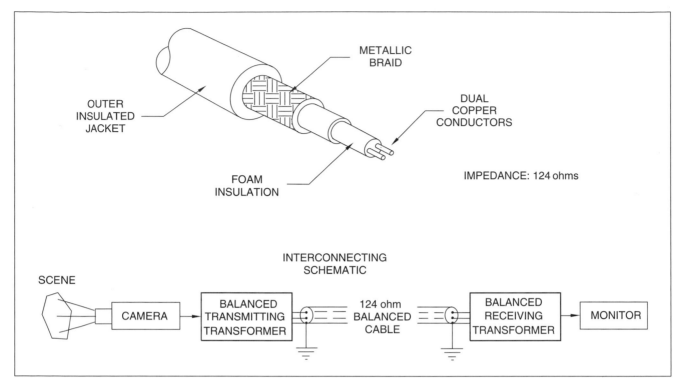

FIGURE 6-6   Balanced twin-axial cable construction and interconnection

are introduced in unbalanced coaxial transmission systems when there is a difference in voltage between the two ends of the coaxial cable (see Section 6.3.1.1). This can often occur when two ends of a long cable run are terminated in different buildings, or when electrical power is derived from different power sources—in different buildings or even within the same building.

Since the signal path and the hum current path through the shield of an unbalanced cable are common and result in the hum problem, a logical solution is to provide a separate path for each. This is accomplished by applying the signal between each center conductor of two parallel unbalanced cables (Figure 6-6). The shields of the two cables carry the ground currents while the two conductors carry the transmitted signal. This technique has been used for many years in the communications industry to reduce or eliminate hum. Since the transmitted video signal travels on the inner conductors, any noise or induced AC hum is applied equally to each conductor. At the termination of the run the disturbances are cancelled while the signal is directed to the load unattenuated. This technique in effect removes the unwanted hum and noise signals.

While the balanced transmission line offers many advantages over the unbalanced line, it has not been in widespread use in the video security industry. The primary reason is the need for transformers at the camera-sending and monitor-receiving ends, as well as the need for two-conductor twin-axial cable. All three hardware items require additional cost as compared with the unbal-

anced single-conductor coaxial cable. The use of UTP transmission has become a popular replacement for the coaxial cable (Section 6.3.3), or fiber optics, described in Section 6.3.4.

6.3.2.1   Indoor Cable

Indoor coaxial cable is small in diameter (0.25 inch), uses a braided shield, and is much more flexible than outdoor cable. To maintain the correct electrical impedance this smaller outside diameter cable requires proportionally smaller inner conductors. This decrease in diameter of the cable conductor causes a corresponding increase in the cable signal attenuation and therefore the RG59/U indoor cable cannot be used over long distances. The impedance of any coaxial cable is directly related to the spacing between the inner conductor and the shield; any change in this spacing caused by tight bends, kinking, indentations, or other factors will change the cable impedance resulting in picture degradation. Since indoor cabling and connectors need no protection from water, solder, crimp-on, or screw-on connectors can be used.

6.3.2.2   Outdoor Cable

Outdoor video transmission applications put additional physical requirements on the coaxial cable. Environmental factors such as precipitation, temperature changes, humidity, and corrosion are present for both above-ground and buried installations. Other above-ground considerations include: wind loading, rodent damage, and electrical storm interference. For direct burial applications, ground shifts, damage due to water, and rodent damage are potential problems. Outdoor coaxial cabling is 1/2 inch in diameter or larger, since the insulation qualities in outside protective sheathing must be superior to those of indoor cables and their electrical qualities are better than indoor RG59/U cables. Outdoor cables have approximately 16 gauge inner-conductor diameters resulting in much less signal loss than the smaller, approximately 18 gauge center conductor indoor RG59/U cables. Outdoor cables are designed and constructed to take much more physical abuse than the indoor RG59/U cable. Outdoor cables are not very flexible and care must be taken with extremely sharp bends. As a rule of thumb, outdoor cabling should always be used for cable runs of more than 1000 feet, regardless of the environment.

Outdoor video cable may be buried, run along the ground, or suspended on utility poles. The exact method should be determined by the length of the cable run, the economics of the installation, and the particular environment. Environment is an important consideration.

In locations with severe weather, electrical storms or high winds, it is prudent to locate the coaxial cable underground, either direct-buried or enclosed in a conduit. This method isolates the cable from the severe environment, improving the life of the cable and reducing signal loss. In locations having rodent or ground-shift problems, enclosing the cable in a separate conduit will protect it. For short cable runs between buildings (less than 600–700 feet) and where the conduit is waterproof, indoor RG59/U cable is suitable.

There are about 25 different types of RG59/U and about 10 different types of RG11/U cable but only a few are suitable for video systems. For optimum performance, choose a cable that has 95% copper shield or more and a copper or copper-clad center conductor. The copper-clad center conductor has a core of steel and copper cladding, has higher tensile strength, and is more suitable for pulling through conduit over long cable runs. While cable with 65% copper shield is available, 95% shielding or more should be used to reduce and prevent outside electromagnetic interference (EMI) signals from penetrating the shield, causing spurious noise on the video signal. A coaxial cable with 95% shield and a copper center conductor will have a loop resistance of approximately 16–57 ohms per 1000 feet.

6.3.2.3 Electrical Interference

For indoor applications, interference and noise can result from the following problems: (1) different ground potentials at the ends of the coaxial cable at different video equipment locations in a building, and (2) coaxial cable near other electrical power distribution equipment or machinery producing high electromagnetic fields.

In outdoor applications, in addition to the above the adverse environmental conditions caused by lightning storms or other high-voltage noise generators, such as transformers on power lines, electrical substations, automobile/truck electrical noise, or other EMI must be considered.

In the case of EMI, a facility site survey should be made of the electromagnetic radiation present in any electrically noisy power distribution equipment. The cables should then be routed away from such equipment so that there is no interference with the television signal.

When a site survey indicates that the coaxial cable must run through an area containing large electrical interfering signals (EMI) caused by large machinery, high-voltage power lines, refrigeration units, microwaves, truck ignition, radio or television stations, fluorescent lamps, two-way radios, motor-generator sets, or other sources, a better shielded cable, such as a twin-axial, tri-axial, UTP, or fiber optic cable may be the answer. The tri-axial cable has a center conductor, an insulator, a shield, a second insulator, a second shield, and the normal outer polyethylene or other covering to protect it from the environment. The double shielding significantly reduces the amount of outside EMI radiation that gets to the center conductor.

The number of horizontal bars on the monitor can indicate where the source of the problem is. If the monitor has six dark bars, multiplying 6 by 60 equals 360, which is close to a 400-cycle frequency. This interference could be caused by an auxiliary motor-generator set often found in large factory machines operating at this frequency. To correct the problem, the cable could be rerouted away from the noise source, replaced with a balanced twin-axial or tri-axial cable, UTP, or for 100% elimination of the problem, upgraded to fiber-optic cable.

If lighting and electrical storms are anticipated and signal loss is unacceptable, outdoor cables must be buried underground and proper high voltage–suppression circuitry must be installed at each end of the cable run and on the input power to the television equipment.

In new installations with long cable runs (several thousand feet to several miles) or where different ground voltages exist, a fiber-optic link is the better solution, although balanced systems and isolation amplifiers can often solve the problem.

6.3.2.4 Grounding Problems

Ground loops are by far the most troublesome and noticeable video cabling problem (Figure 6-7). Ground loops are most easily detected before connecting the cables, by measuring the electrical voltage between the coaxial-cable shield and the chassis to which it is being connected. If the voltage difference is a few volts or more, there is a

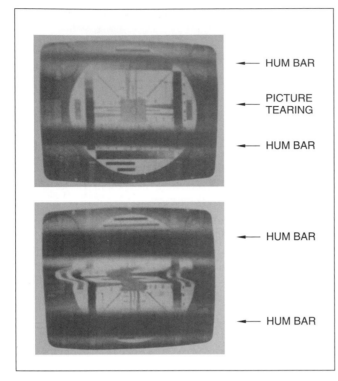

HUM BAR

PICTURE
TEARING

HUM BAR

HUM BAR

HUM BAR

FIGURE 6-7   Hum bars caused by ground loops

potential for a hum problem. As a precaution, it is good practice to measure the voltage difference *before* connecting the cable and chassis for systems with a long run or between any two electrical supplies to prevent any damage to the equipment.

Many large multiple-camera systems have some distortion in the video picture caused by random or periodic noise or if more severe, by hum bars. The hum bar appears as a horizontal distortion across the monitor at two locations: one-third and two-thirds of the way down the picture. If the camera is synchronized or power-line-locked, the bar will be stationary on the screen. If the camera is not line-locked, the distortion or bar will continuously roll slowly through the picture. Sometimes the hum bars are accompanied by sharp tearing regions across the monitor or erratic horizontal pulling at the edge of the screen (Figure 6-7). This is caused by the effect of the high voltages on the horizontal synchronization signal. Other symptoms include uncontrolled vertical rolling of the scene on the screen when there are very high voltages present in the ground loop.

Interference caused by external sources or voltage differences can often be predicted prior to installation. The hum bar and potential difference between two electrical systems usually cannot be determined until the actual installation. The system designer should try to anticipate the problem and, along with the user, be prepared to devote additional equipment and time to solve it. The problem is not related to equipment at the camera or

monitor end or to the cable installed; it is strictly an effect of the particular environment encountered, be it EMI interference or difference in potential between the main power sources at each location. The grounding problem can occur at any remote location, and it can be eliminated inexpensively with the installation of an isolation amplifier. Another solution, described in Section 6.3.4, is the use of fiber-optic transmission means, which eliminates electrical connections entirely.

One totally unacceptable solution is the removal of the third wire on a three-pronged electrical plug, which is used to ground the equipment chassis to earth ground. Not only is such removal a violation of local electrical codes and Underwriters Laboratory (UL) recommendations, it is a hazardous procedure. If the earth ground is removed from the chassis, a voltage can appear on the camera, monitor, or other equipment chassis, producing a "hot" chassis that, if touched, can shock any person with 60–70 volts.

When video cables bridge two power distribution systems, ground loops occur. Consider the situation (Figure 6-8) in which the CCTV camera receives AC power from power source A, while some distance away or in a different building the CCTV monitor receives power from distribution system B.

The camera chassis is at 0 volts (connected to electrical ground) with reference to its AC power input A. The monitor chassis is also at 0 volts with respect to its AC distribution system B. However, the level of the electrical ground in one distribution system may be higher (or lower) than that of the ground in the other system; hence a voltage potential can exist between the two chassis. When a video cable is connected between the two distribution system grounds, the cable shield connects the two chassis and an alternating current flows in the shield between the units. This extraneous voltage (causing a ground-loop current to flow) produces the unwanted hum bars in the video image on the monitor.

The second way in which hum bars can be produced on a television monitor is when two equipment chassis are mechanically connected, such as when a camera is mounted on a pan/tilt unit. If the camera receives power from one distribution system and the chassis of the pan/tilt unit is grounded to another system with a different level, a ground loop and hum bars may result. The size and extent of the horizontal bars depends on the severity of the ground potential difference.

6.3.2.5 Aluminum Cable

Although coaxial cable with aluminum shielding provides 100% shielding, it should only be used for RF cable television (CATV) and master television (MATV) signals used for home video cable reception. This aluminum-shield type should *never* be used for CCTV for two reasons: (1) it

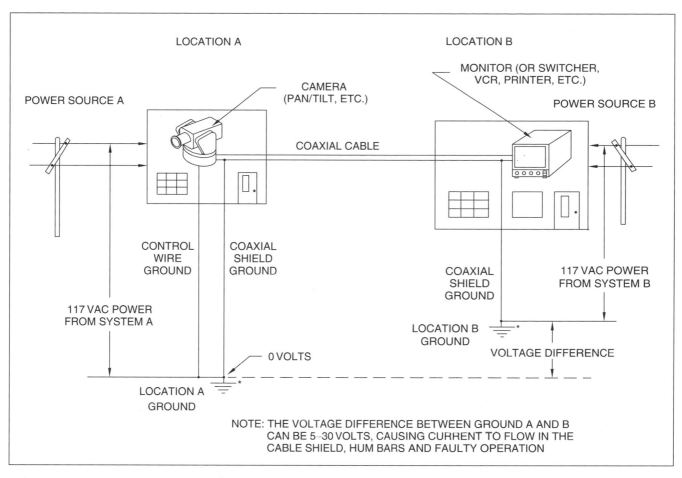

LOCATION A

LOCATION B

POWER SOURCE A

MONITOR (OR SWITCHER, VCR, PRINTER, ETC.)

POWER SOURCE B

CAMERA (PAN/TILT, ETC.)

COAXIAL CABLE

CONTROL WIRE GROUND

COAXIAL SHIELD GROUND

COAXIAL SHIELD GROUND

117 VAC POWER FROM SYSTEM B

117 VAC POWER FROM SYSTEM A

LOCATION B GROUND

VOLTAGE DIFFERENCE

0 VOLTS

LOCATION A GROUND

NOTE: THE VOLTAGE DIFFERENCE BETWEEN GROUND A AND B CAN BE 5–30 VOLTS, CAUSING CURRENT TO FLOW IN THE CABLE SHIELD, HUM BARS AND FAULTY OPERATION

FIGURE 6-8   Two source AC power distribution system

has higher resistance, and (2) it distorts horizontal synchronization pulses.

The added resistance—approximately seven times more than that of a 95% copper or copper-clad shield—increases the video cable loop resistance, causing a reduction in the video signal transmitted along the cable. The higher loop resistance means a smaller video signal reaches the monitoring site, producing less contrast and an inferior picture. Always use a good-grade 95% copper braid RG59/U cable to transmit the video signal up to 1000 feet and an RG11/U to transmit up to 2000 feet. Distortion of the horizontal synchronization pulse causes picture tearing on the monitor, depicting straight-edged objects with ragged edges.

6.3.2.6 Plenum Cable

Another category of coaxial cable is designed to be used in the plenum space in large buildings. This plenum cable has a flame-resistant exterior covering and very low smoke emission. The cable can be used in air-duct air-conditioning returns and does not require a metal conduit for added protection. The cable, designated as "plenum rated," is approved by the National Electrical Code and UL.

6.3.3 Two-Wire Cable Unshielded Twisted Pair (UTP) Transmission

It is convenient, inexpensive, and simple to transmit the video signal over an existing two-wire system. A standard, twisted pair, two-wire telephone, intercom, or other electrical system with an appropriate UTP transmitter and receiver has the capability to transmit all of the high-frequency information required for an excellent resolution monochrome or color picture. The UTP is a CAT-5, CAT-5e, or CAT-3 cable. The higher the level of CAT (5e) cable the greater the distance. Either a passive (no power required) or an active (12VDC, longer distanced) transmitter/receiver pair can be used. The passive system uses a small transmitter and receiver-one at each end of the pair of wires—and transmits the picture at distances of a few hundred feet to 3000 feet. The active powered system (12VDC) can transmit the video image 8000 feet for monochrome and 5000 feet for color. Picture resolution can be equivalent to that obtained with a coaxial cable system. The two-wire pair must have a *continuous* conductive path from the camera to the monitor location. High-frequency emphasis in the transmitter and receiver compensate for any attenuation of the high frequencies. The balanced UTP configuration makes the cable immune to most external electrical interference and in many environments the UTP cable can be located in the same conduit with other data cables.

The UTP system must have a conductive (resistive copper) path for the two wires. The signal path cannot have electrical switching circuits between the camera and the monitor location; however, mechanical splices and connectors are permissible.

The components for the two-wire system can cost more than equivalent coaxial cable since an additional transmitter and receiver are required. However, this cost may be small compared with the cost of installing a new coaxial cable from the camera to the monitor location. Figure 6-9 illustrates the block diagram and connections for the UTP, and active transmitter and receiver pair.

6.3.3.1 Balanced 2-Wire Attributes

The UTP provides a technology that can significantly reduce external electrical radiation from causing noise in the video signal. It also eliminates ground loops present in unbalanced coaxial transmission since isolation designed into the UTP transmitters and receivers.

6.3.3.2 UTP Technology

The UTP technology is based on the concept that any external electrical interference affects each of the two conductors *identically* so that the external disturbance is canceled and has no effect on the video signal. The transmitter unit converts the camera signal 75 ohm impedance to match the UTP 100 ohm CAT-5e impedance and provides the frequency compensation required. The receiver unit amplifies and reconstructs the signal and transmits it over a short distance to the television monitor via 75 ohm coaxial cable. Most active transmitters and receivers have 3 to 5 position dip switches which are set depending on the cable length to optimize the video signal waveform. Both the transmitter and the receiver are powered by either 12VDC or self-powered from the camera or monitor.

The UTP system can be operated with CAT-3, 5, 5e, and 6 as defined in the TIA/EIA 568b.2 standard. CAT-5e is now used for most new video installations and supercedes the extensively installed CAT-5 cable.

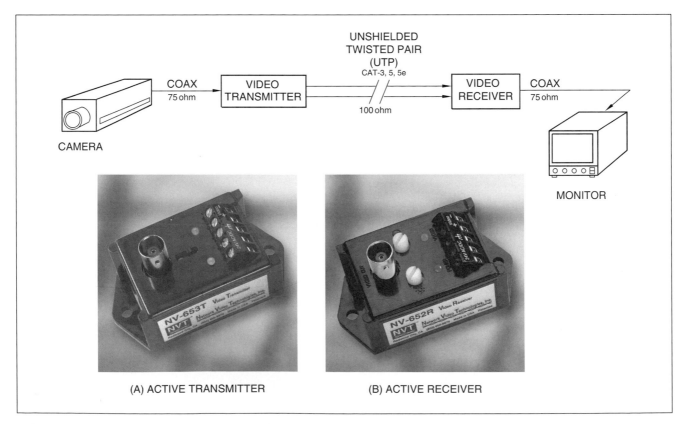

(A) ACTIVE TRANSMITTER   (B) ACTIVE RECEIVER

FIGURE 6-9 Two wire UTP video transmission system

6.3.3.3 UTP Implementation with Video, Audio, and Control Signals

The UTP transmitter is located between the camera and the CAT-5e UTP cable input to transmit video, audio, alarms, and control signals. The receiver is located between the monitor end of the CAT-5e UTP cable and the monitor, recorder, or control console. UTP transmitters are small enough to be part of the camera electronics or can be powered by the camera, audio, and/or control electronics (Figure 6-10).

6.3.3.4 Slow-Scan Transmission

The wireless transmission systems described in the previous sections all result in *real-time* video transmission. A scheme for transmitting the television picture over large distances, even anywhere in the world, uses slow-scan television transmission (Figure 6-11).

This non-real-time technique involves storing one television picture frame (snapshot) and sending it slowly over a telephone or other audio-grade network anywhere within a country or to another country. The received picture is reconstructed at the remote receiver to produce a continuously displayed television snapshot. Each snapshot takes anywhere from several to 72 seconds to transmit, with a resulting picture having from low to high resolution, depending on the speed of transmission. A TL effect is achieved, and every scene frame is transmitted spaced from several to 72 seconds apart.

Through this operation, specific frames are serially captured, sent down the telephone line, and reconstructed by the slow-scan system. Once the receiver has stored the digital picture information, if the transmitter is turned off or the video scene image does not change, the receiver continues to display the last video frame continuously (30 fps) as a still image. The image stored in the receiver or transmitter changes when the system is commanded, manually or automatically, to take a new snapshot. Figure 6-12 illustrates the salient difference between real-time and non-real-time television transmission.

Implementation. Figure 6-12 shows the relationship of non-real-time or slow-scan television transmission. At the camera site the first frame starts at time zero (Figure 6-12a), the second frame at 1/30th of a second, and the third frame at 2/30th of a second (the same as for real-time). Before these frames are transmitted over the audio-grade transmission link, the signal is processed at the camera site in a transmitter processor. The processor captures Frame 1 from the camera, that is, it memorizes (digitizes) the CCTV picture. The processor then slowly (at 2 seconds per frame, as shown in Figure 6-12b) transmits the video frame, element by element, line by line, until the receiver processor located at the monitor site has accepted all 525 lines in that frame.

The significant difference between real-time and slow-scan transmission is the time it takes to transmit the picture. In the real-time case, it is 1/30th of a second, the *real-time* of the frame. In the case of the slow-scan (Figure 6-12b), it may take 2, 4, 8, 32, up to 72 seconds to transmit that single frame to the monitor site. Figure 6-13 is a block diagram of a simplex (one-way) slow-scan system.

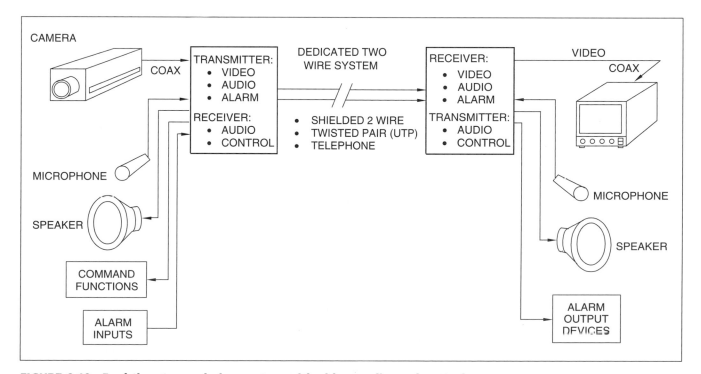

FIGURE 6-10 Real-time transmission system with video, audio, and controls

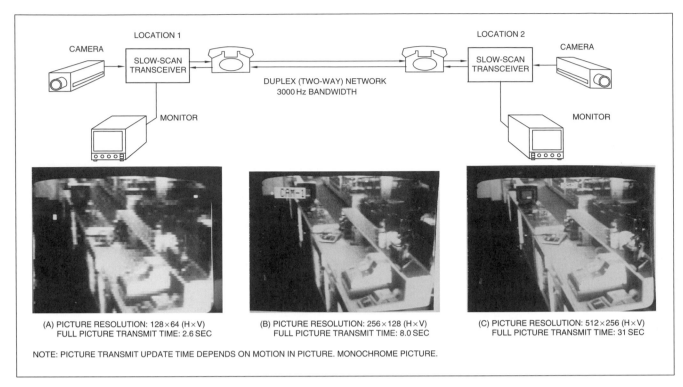

(A) PICTURE RESOLUTION: 128×64 (H×V)
FULL PICTURE TRANSMIT TIME: 2.6 SEC

(B) PICTURE RESOLUTION: 256×128 (H×V)
FULL PICTURE TRANSMIT TIME: 8.0 SEC

(C) PICTURE RESOLUTION: 512×256 (H×V)
FULL PICTURE TRANSMIT TIME: 31 SEC

NOTE: PICTURE TRANSMIT UPDATE TIME DEPENDS ON MOTION IN PICTURE. MONOCHROME PICTURE.

FIGURE 6-11   Slow-scan video transmission and transmitted pictures over telephone lines

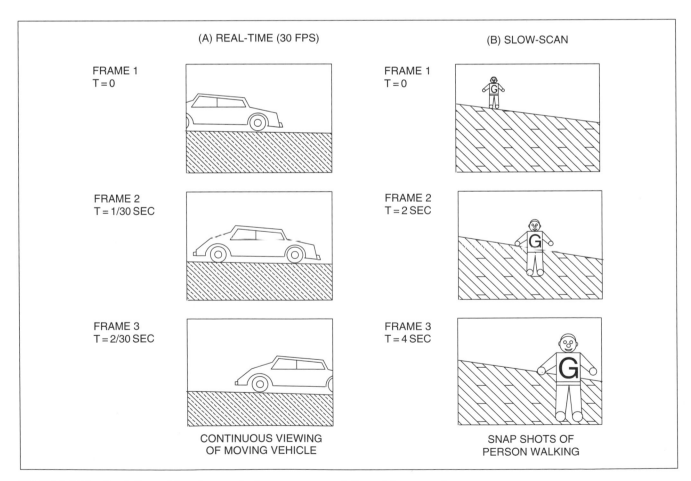

FIGURE 6-12   Real-time video transmission vs. non-real-time (slow-scan)

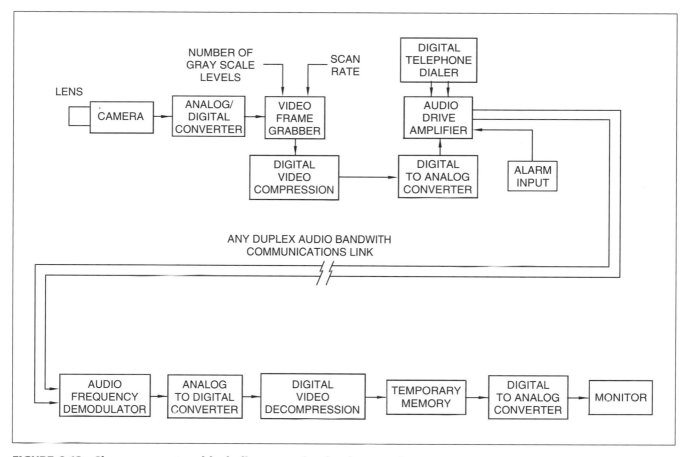

FIGURE 6-13   Slow-scan system block diagram—simplex (one-way)

To increase transmission speed, complex compression and modulation algorithms are used so that only the changing parts of a scene (i.e. the movements) are transmitted. Another technique first transmits areas of high scene activity with high resolution and then areas of lower priority with lower resolution. These techniques increase the transmission of the intelligence in the scene. By increasing transmission time of the frame from 1/30th of a second to several seconds, the choice of cable or transmission path changes significantly. For slow-scan it is possible to send the full video image on a twisted-pair or telephone line or any communications channel having a bandwidth equivalent to audio frequencies, that is, up to only 3000 Hz (instead of a bandwidth up to 4.2 MHz, as needed in real-time transmission). So all existing satellite links, mobile telephones, and other connections can be used. A variation of this equipment for an alarm application can store multiple frames at the transmitting site, so if the information to be transmitted is an alarm, this alarm video image can be stored for a few seconds (every 1/30 second) and then slowly transmitted to the remote monitoring site frame by frame, thereby transmitting all of the alarm frames. Figure 6-14 shows the interconnecting diagram and controls for a typical slow-scan system.

Resolution, Scene Activity vs. Transmit Time.   Transmit time per frame is determined by video picture resolution and activity (motion) in the scene. The larger the number of gray-scale levels and number of colors transmitted, the longer the transmit time per frame of video. If only a few gray-scale levels are transmitted (photocopy quality), or a limited number of colors and a small amount of motion in the scene are present, then there is less picture information to transmit and short (1–8 seconds) transmit times result. High gray-scale levels (256 levels), full color, and motion require more information and longer transmission times. Slow-scan transmission is a compromise between resolution and scene activity and required scene update time.

6.3.4   Fiber-Optic Transmission

6.3.4.1   Background

One of the most significant advances in communications and signal transmission has been the innovation of fiber optics. However, the concept of transmitting video signals over fiber optics is not new. The transmission of optical signals in fibers was investigated in the 1920s and 1930s but it was not until the 1950s that Kapany invented the

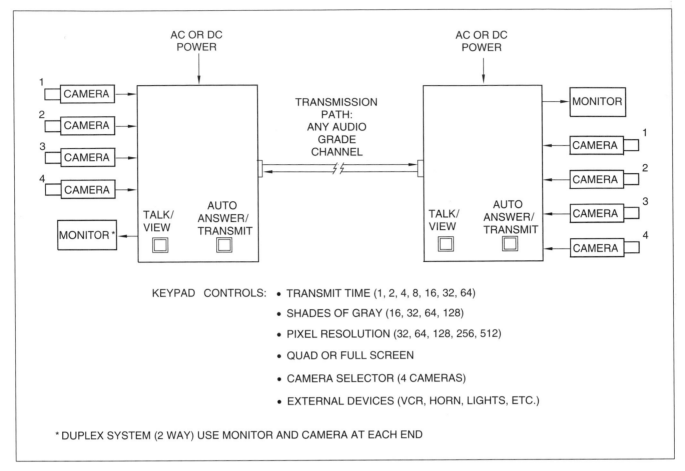

FIGURE 6-14   Slow-scan interconnecting diagram and controls

practical glass-coated (clad) glass fiber and coined the term *fiber optics.*

Clad fiber was actively investigated in the 1960s by K.C. Kao and G.A. Hockham, researchers at Standard Telecommunications Laboratories in England, who proposed that this type of waveguide could form the basis of a new transmission system. In 1967 attenuations through the fiber was more than 1000 dB per kilometer (0.001% transmission/km) which were impractical for transmission purposes, and researchers focused on reducing these losses. Figure 6-16 shows a comparison of fiber-optic transmission vs. other electrical transmission means. In 1970, investigators Kapron, Keck, and Maurer at Corning Glass Works announced a reduction of losses to less than 20 dB per kilometer in fibers hundreds of meters long. In 1972 Corning announced a reduction of 4 dB per one kilometer of cable, and in 1973 Corning broke this record with a 2 dB per kilometer cable. This low-loss achievement made a revolution in transmission of wide-bandwidth, long-distance communications inevitable. In the early 1970s, manufacturers began making glass fibers that were sufficiently low-loss to transmit light signals over practical distances of hundreds or a few thousand feet.

Broadband fiber-optic components are much more expensive than cable. They should be used when there is a definite need for them. Note also that video signals must be digitized to avoid nonlinear transmitter/receiver effects.

Why use fiber-optic transmission when coaxial cables can provide adequate video signal transmission? Today's high-performance video systems require greater reliability and more "throughput," that is, getting more signals from the camera end to the monitor end, over greater distances, and in harsher environments. The fiber-optic transmission system preserves the quality of the video signal and provides a high level of security.

The information-carrying capacity of a transmission line, whether electrical or optical, increases as the carrier frequency increases. The carrier for fiber-optic signals is light, which has frequencies several orders of magnitude (1000 times) greater than radio frequencies, and the higher the carrier frequency the larger the bandwidth that can be modulated onto the cable. Some transmitters and receivers permit multiplexing multiple television signals, control signals, and duplex audio onto the same fiber optic because of its wide bandwidth.

The clarity of the picture transmitted using fiber optics is now limited only by the camera, environment, and

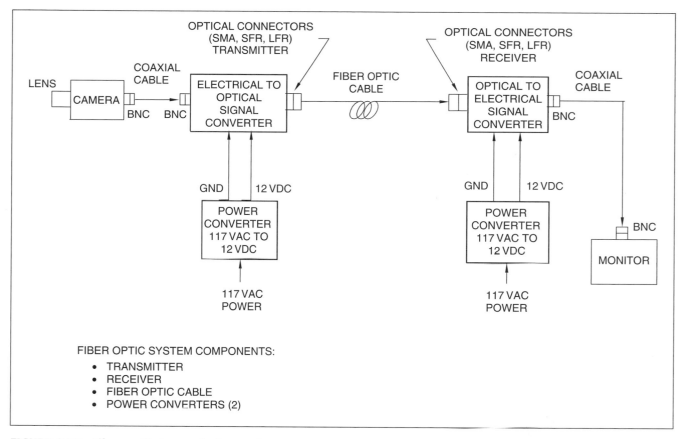

FIGURE 6-15   Fiber optic transmission system

monitoring equipment. Fiber-optic systems can transmit signals from a camera to a monitor over great distances—typically several miles—with virtually no distortion or loss in picture resolution or detail. Figure 6-15 shows the block diagram of the hardware required for a fiber-optic system.

The system uses an electrical-to-optical signal converter/transmitter, a fiber cable for sending the light signal from the camera to the monitor, and a light-to-electrical signal receiver/converter to transform the signal back to a base-band video signal required by the monitor. At both camera and monitor ends standard RG59/U coaxial cable or UTP wire is used to connect the camera and monitor to the system.

A glass fiber optic–based video link offers distinct advantages over copper-wire or coaxial-cable transmission means:

- The system transmits information with greater fidelity and clarity over longer distances.
- The fiber is totally immune to all types of electrical interference—EMI or lightning—and will not conduct electricity. It can touch high-voltage electrical equipment or power lines without a problem.
- The fiber being nonconductive does not create any ground loops.

- The fiber can be serviced while the transmitting or receiving equipment is still energized since no electrical power is involved.
- The fiber can be used where electrical codes and common sense prohibit the use of copper wires.
- The cable will not corrode and the glass fiber is unaffected by salt and most chemicals. The direct-burial type of cable can be laid in most kinds of soil or exposed to most corrosive atmospheres inside chemical plants or outdoors.
- Since there is no electrical connection of any type, the fiber poses no fire hazard to any equipment or facility in even the most flammable atmosphere.
- The fiber is virtually unaffected by atmospheric conditions, so the cable can be mounted aboveground and on telephone poles. When properly applied, the cable is stronger than standard electrical wire or coaxial cable and will therefore withstand far more stress from wind and ice loading.
- Single or multiple fiber-optic cables are much smaller and lighter than a coaxial cable. It is easier to handle and install, and uses less conduit or duct space. A single optical cable weighs 8 pounds per 3300 feet and has an overall diameter of 0.156 inches. A single coaxial cable weighs 330 pounds per 3300 feet and is approximately 0.25 inches in diameter.

- It transmits the video signal more efficiently (i.e. with lower attenuation) and since over distances of less than 50 miles it needs no repeater (amplifier), it is more reliable and easier to maintain.
- It is a more secure transmission medium, since not only is it hard to tap but an attempted tap is easily detected.

The economics of using a fiber-optic system is complex. Users evaluating fiber optics should consider the costs beyond those for the components themselves. The small size, lightweight, and flexibility of fiber optics often present offsetting cost advantages. The prevention of unanticipated problems such as those just listed can easily offset any increased hardware costs of fiber-optic systems.

With such rapid advances, the security system designer should consider fiber optics the optimum means to transmit high-quality television signals from high-resolution monochrome or color cameras to a receiver (monitor, switcher, recorder, printer, and so on) without degradation. This section reviews the attributes of fiber-optic systems, their design requirements, and their applications.

6.3.4.2 Simplified Theory

The fiber-optic system uses a transmitter at the camera and a receiver at the monitor and the fiber cable in between (Figure 6-15). The following sections describe these three components. By far the most critical is the fiber-optic cable, since it must transmit the video light signal over a long distance without attenuation distortion (changing its shape or attenuation at high frequencies). As shown in Figure 6-15, the signal from the camera is sent to the transmitter via standard coaxial cable. At the receiver end, the output from the receiver is likewise sent via standard wire cable to the monitor or recording system.

The optical transmitter at the camera end converts (modulates) the electrical video analog signal into a corresponding optical signal. The output from the transmitter is an optical signal generated by either an LED or an ILD, emitting IR light. When more than one video signal is to be transmitted another option is to transmit multiple signals over one fiber using wavelength multiplexing (Section 6.3.4.7).

The multi-fiber-optic cable consists of multiple glass fibers, each acting as a waveguide or conduit for one video optical signal. The glass fibers are enclosed in a protective outer jacket whose construction depends on the application.

The fiber-optic receiver collects the light from the end of the fiber-optic cable and converts (demodulates) the optical signal back into an electrical signal having the same waveform and characteristics as the original video signal at the camera and then sends it to the monitor or recorder.

The only variation in this block diagram for a single camera is the inclusion of a connection, splice, or repeater that may be required if the cable run is very long (many miles). The connector physically joins the output end of one cable to the input end of another cable. The splice reconnects two fiber ends so as to make them continuous. The repeater amplifies the light signal to provide a good signal at the receiver end.

How does the fiber-optic transmission system differ from the electrical cable systems described in the previous sections? From the block diagram (Figure 6-15) it is apparent that two new hardware components are required: a transmitter and a receiver. The transmitter provides an amplitude- or frequency-modulated representation of the video signal at near-IR wavelengths which the fiber optic transmits, and at a level sufficient to produce a high-quality picture at the receiver end. The receiver collects whatever light energy is available at the output of the fiber-optic cable and converts it efficiently, with all the information from the video signal retained, into an electrical signal that is identical in shape and amplitude to the camera output signal. As with any of the transmission means, the fiber-optic cable attenuates the video signal. Figure 6-16 shows the attenuation frequency for current fiber-optic cable as compared with telephone cable, special high-frequency cable, coaxial cable, and early fiber-optic cable.

The fiber-optic cable efficiently transmits the modulated light signal from the camera end over a long distance to the monitor, while maintaining the signal's shape and amplitude. Characteristics of fiber-optic cable are totally different from those of coaxial cable or two-wire transmission systems.

Before discussing the construction of the fiber-optic cable, we will briefly describe the transmitting light. In any optical material, light travels at a velocity (V_m) characteristic of the material, which is lower than the velocity of light (C) in free space of air (Figure 6-17a).

The ratio (fraction) of the velocity in the material compared with that in free space defines the refractive index (n) of the material:

$$n = \frac{C}{V_m}$$

When light traveling in a medium of a particular refractive index strikes another material of a lower refractive index, the light is bent toward the interface of the two materials (Figure 6-17b). If the angle of incidence is increased, a point is reached where the bent light will travel along the interface of the two materials. This is known as the "critical angle" (θ_C). Light at any angle greater than the critical angle is totally reflected from the interface and follows a zigzag transmission path (Figure 6-17b,c). This zigzag transmission path is exactly what occurs in a fiber-optic cable: the light entering one end of the cable zigzags through the medium and eventually exits at the far end at approximately the same angle. As shown in Figure 6-17c, some incoming light is reflected from the fiber-optic end and never enters the fiber.

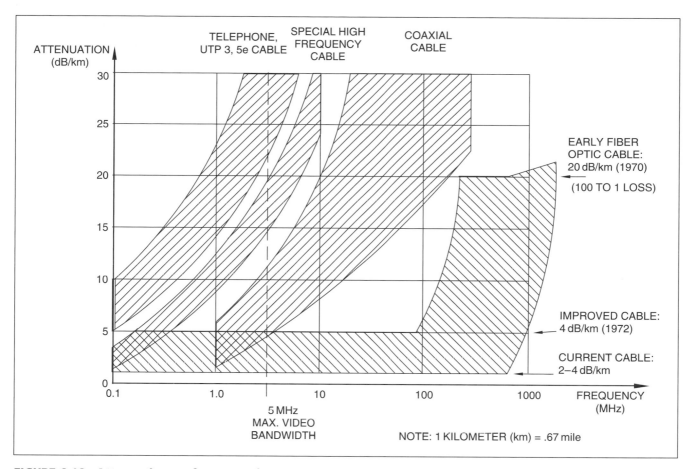

FIGURE 6-16   Attenuation vs. frequency for copper and fiber optic cable

In practice, an optical fiber consists of a core, a cladding, and a protective coating. The core material has a higher index of refraction than the cladding material and therefore the light, as just described, is confined to the core. This core material can be plastic or glass, but glass provides a far superior performance (lower attenuation and greater bandwidth) and therefore is more widespread for long-distance applications.

One parameter often encountered in the literature is the numerical aperture (NA) of a fiber optic, a parameter that indicates the angle of acceptance of light into a fiber—or simply the ease with which the fiber accepts light. The NA is an important fiber parameter that must be considered when determining the signal-loss budget of a fiber-optic system. To visualize the concept, picture a bottle with a funnel (Figure 6-18). The larger the funnel angle, the easier it is to pour liquid into the bottle. The same concept holds for the fiber. The wider the acceptance angle, the higher the NA, the larger the amount of light that can be funneled into the fiber from the transmitter. The larger or higher an optical fiber NA, the easier it is to launch light into the fiber, which correlates to higher coupling efficiency. Since fiber-optic systems are often coupled to LEDs, which are the light generators at the transmitter, and since LEDs have a less-concentrated,

diffuse output beam than ILDs, fiber optics with high NAs allow more collection of the LED output power.

In order for the light from the transmitter to follow the zigzag path of internally reflected rays, the angles of reflection must exceed the critical angle. These reflection angles are associated with "waveguide modes." Depending on the size (diameter) of the fiber-optic core, one or more modes are transmitted down the fiber. The characteristics and properties of these different cables carrying single-mode and multimode fibers are discussed in the next section.

Like radio waves, light is electromagnetic energy. The frequencies of light used in fiber-optic video, voice, and data transmission are approximately 3.6×10^{14}, which is several orders of magnitude higher than the highest radio waves. Wavelength (the reciprocal of frequency) is a more common way of describing light waves. Visible light with wavelengths from about 400 nm for deep violet to 750 nm for deep red covers only a small portion of the electromagnetic spectrum (see Chapter 3). Fiber-optic video transmission uses the near-IR region, extending from approximately 750 to 1500 nm, since glass fibers propagate light at these wavelengths most efficiently, and efficient detectors (silicon and germanium) are available to detect such light.

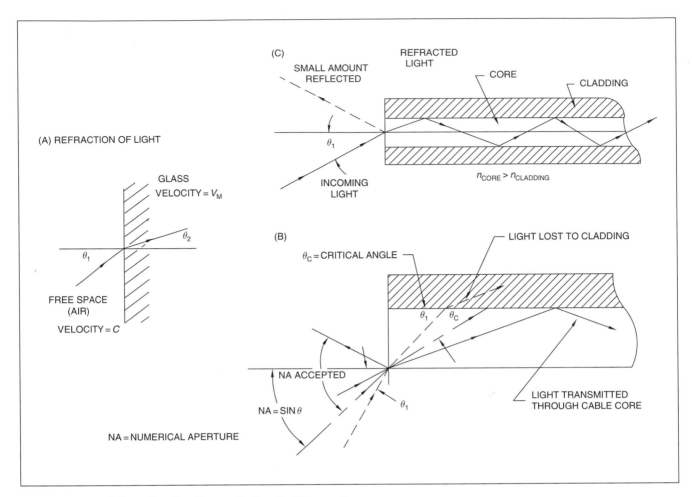

FIGURE 6-17   Light reflection/transmission in fiber optics

6.3.4.3 Cable Types

The most significant part of the fiber-optic signal transmission system is the glass fiber itself, a thin strand of very pure glass approximately the diameter of a human hair. The fiber transmits visible and near-IR frequencies with extremely high efficiency. Most fiber-optic system operate at IR wavelengths of 850, 1300, or 1550 nm. Figure 6-19 shows where these near-IR light frequencies are located with respect to the visible light spectrum.

Most short (several miles long) fiber-optic security systems operate at a wavelength of 850 nm rather than 1300 or 1550 nm because 850 nm LED emitters are more readily available and less expensive than their 1300 nm or 1550 nm counterparts. Likewise, IR detectors are more sensitive at 850 nm. LED and ILD radiation at the 1300 and 1550 nm wavelengths is transmitted along the fiber-optic cables more efficiently than at the 850 nm frequency; they are used for much longer run cables (hundreds of miles).

Two types of fibers are used in security systems: (1) multimode step-index (rarely), and (2) graded-index. These two types are defined by the index of refraction (n) profile of the fiber and the cross section of the fiber core.

The two types have different properties and are used in different applications.

6.3.4.3.1 Multimode Step-Index Fiber
Figure 6-20a illustrates the physical characteristics of the multimode step-index fiber.

The fiber consists of a center core of index $n = 1.47$ and outer cladding of index $n = 2$. Light rays enter the core and are reflected a multiple number of times down the core and exit at the far end. Since this fiber propagates many modes, it is called "multimode step-index." The multimode step-index is usually 50, 100, or even 200 microns (0.002, 0.004, or 0.008 inches) in diameter. The fiber core itself is clad with a thin layer of glass having a sharply different index of refraction. Light travels down the fiber, constantly being reflected back and forth from the interface between the two layers of glass. Light that enters the fiber at a sharp angle is reflected at a sharp angle from the interface and is reflected back and forth many more times, thus traveling more slowly through the fiber than light that enters at a shallow angle. The difference in the arrival time at the end of the fiber limits the bandwidth of the step-index fiber, so that most such fibers provide good signal transmission up to a 20 MHz signal for

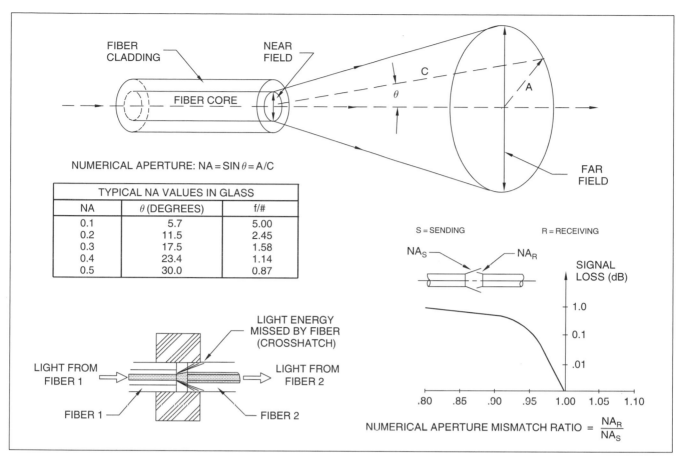

FIGURE 6-18   Fiber optic numerical aperture

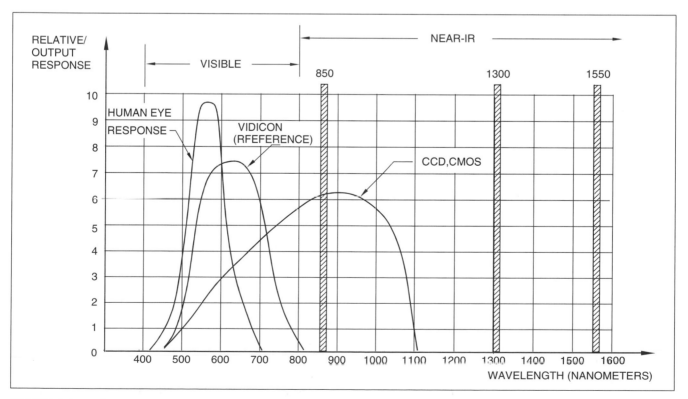

FIGURE 6-19   Fiber optic transmission wavelengths

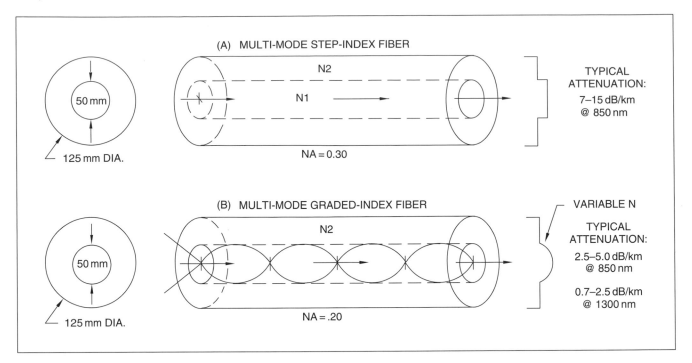

FIGURE 6-20   Multimode fiber optic cable

about 1 kilometer. This limitation is more than adequate for many video applications.

6.3.4.3.2 Multimode Graded-Index Fiber

The multimode graded-index fiber is the workhorse of the video security industry (Figure 6-20b). Its low power attenuation—less than 3 dB (50% loss) per kilometer at 850 nm—makes it well suited for short and long cable runs. Most fibers are available in 50-micron-diameter core with 125-micron total fiber diameter (exclusive of outside protective sheathing). Graded-index fiber sizes are designated by their core/cladding diameter ratio, thus the 50/125 fiber has 50-micron-diameter core and a 125-micron cladding. The typical graded-index fiber has a bandwidth of approximately 1000 MHz and is one of the least expensive fiber types available. The 50/125 fiber provides high efficiency when used with a high-quality LED transmitter or for very long distances or very wide bandwidths, with an ILD source. Table 6-3 lists some of the common cable sizes available.

For the graded-index fiber, the index of refraction (n) of the core is highest at the center and gradually decreases as the distance from the center increases (Figure 6-20b). Light in this type of core travels by refraction: the light rays are continually bent toward the center of the fiber-optic axis. In this manner the light rays traveling in the center of the core have a lower velocity due to the high index of refraction, and the rays at the outer limits travel much

FIBER TYPE	DIAMETER* (MICRONS)			TYPICAL CABLE PARAMETERS					
				SINGLE FIBER		2 FIBER		4 FIBER	
	CORE	CLADDING	BUFFERING	OD (mm)	WEIGHT (kg/km)	OD** (mm)	WEIGHT (kg/km)	OD (mm)	WEIGHT (kg/km)
50/125	50	125	250	2.6	6.5	3.4×6	22	8	55
62.5/125[†]	62.5	125	250	3.0	6.4	3.0×6.1	18	9.4	65.5
100/140	100	140	250	2.6	6.5	3.4	22	7.1	50

* FIBER DIAMETER (1 MICRON = .00004 inch)

** CABLE OUTSIDE DIAMETER OR CROSS SECTION

† MOST WIDELY USED IN SECURITY APPLICATIONS

1 mm = 1000 MICRONS

1 kg/km = 0.671 lb/1000 ft

Table 6-3   Standard Fiber Optic Cable Sizes

faster. This effect causes all the light to traverse the length of the fiber in nearly the same time and greatly reduces the difference in arrival time of light from different modes, thereby increasing the fiber bandwidth–carrying capability. The graded-index fiber satisfies long-haul, wide-bandwidth security system requirements that cannot be met by the multimode step-index fiber.

6.3.4.3.3 Cable Construction and Sizes

A fiber-optic cable consists of a single optical fiber that is surrounded by a tube of plastic substantially larger than the fiber itself. Over this tube is a layer of Kevlar reinforcement material. The entire assembly is then covered with an outer jacket, typically made of polyvinyl chloride (PVC). This construction is generally accepted for use indoors or where the cable is easily pulled through a dry conduit. The two approaches to providing primary protection to a fiber is the tight buffer and loose tube (Figure 6-21).

The tight buffer uses a dielectric (insulator) material such as PVC or polyurethane applied tightly to the fiber. For medium- and high-loss fibers (step-index type), such cable-induced attenuation is small compared with overall attenuation. The tight buffer offers the advantages of smaller bend radii and better crush resistances than loose-

tube cabling. These advantages make tightly buffered fibers useful in applications of short runs where sharp bends are encountered or where cables may be laid under carpeted walking surfaces.

The loose-tube method isolates the fiber from the rest of the cable, allowing the cabling to be twisted, pulled, and otherwise stressed with little effect on the fiber. Microbends caused by tight buffers are eliminated by placing the fiber within a hard plastic tube that has an inside diameter several times larger than the diameter of the fiber. Fibers for long-distance applications typically use a loose tube since decoupling of the fiber from the cable allows the cable to be pulled long lengths during installation. The tubes may be filled with jelly to protect against moisture that could condense and freeze and damage the fiber.

Multimode graded-index fiber is available in several primary core sizes: 50/125, 62.5/125, and 100/140. Table 6-3 summarizes the properties of different fiber-cable types used in security systems, indicating the sizes and weights. The first number, in the fiber designation (50 in 50/125), refers to the core outside diameter size, the second (125) to the glass fiber outside diameter (the sizes exclude reinforcement or sheathing). The fiber size is expressed in microns: 1 micron (μm) equals one one-thousandth of a

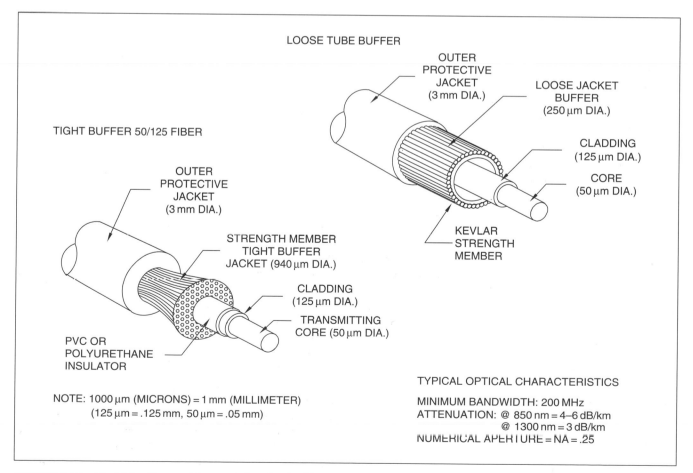

FIGURE 6-21   Tight-buffer and loose-tube single fiber optic cable construction

CABLE LOSS TYPE	TYPICAL LOSS		COMMENTS
	(dB)	(%)	
AXIAL-LATERAL DISPLACEMENT (10%)	0.55	12.0	MOST CRITICAL FACTOR
ANGULAR MISALIGNMENT (2 DEGREES)	0.30	6.7	FUNCTION OF NUMERICAL APERTURE
END SEPARATION (AIR GAP)	0.32	7.0	ESSENTIALLY ELIMINATED USING INDEX MATCHING FLUID
END FINISH: (A) ROUGHNESS (1 MICRON) (B) NON PERPENDICULAR	0.50 0.25	11.0 5.6	INCLUDES FRESNEL LOSS (.35 dB) LOSS NOT COMMONLY FOUND
CORE SIZE MISMATCH: 1% DIAMETER TOLERANCE ±5% DIAMETER TOLERANCE	0.17 0.83	4.0 18.0	LOSS OCCURS ONLY WHEN LARGER CORE COUPLES INTO SMALLER CORE
NUMERICAL APERTURE (NA) DIFFERENCE OF ±0.02 (2%)	1.66	31.6	CRITICAL FACTOR WHEN NA_S IS LARGER THAN NA_R

NOTE: dB = DECIBELS = $10 \text{ LOG} \dfrac{POWER_S}{POWER_R}$ S = SENDING FIBER
R = RECEIVING FIBER

Table 6-4   Fiber Optic Connector Coupling Losses

millimeter (1/1000 mm). By comparison, the diameter of a human hair is about 0.002 inches or 50 microns.

Each size has advantages for particular applications, and all three are EIA standards. The most popular and least expensive multimode fiber is the 50/125, used extensively in video security. It has the lowest NA of any multimode fiber, which allows the highest bandwidth. Because 50/125 has been used for many years, established installers are experienced and comfortable working with it. Many connector types are available for terminating the 50/125 cable, an alternative to the 62.5/125 fiber.

The 50/125 and 62.5/125 were developed for telephone networks and are now used extensively for video. An 85/125 was developed specifically for computer or digital local networks where short distances are required. The slightly larger 85-micron size permits easier connector specifications and LED source requirements.

The 100/140 multimode fiber was developed in response to computer manufacturers, who wanted an LED-compatible, short-wavelength, optical-fiber data link that could handle higher data rates than coaxial cable. While this fiber was developed for the computer market it is excellent for short-haul CCTV security applications. It is least sensitive to fiber-optic geometry variations and connector tolerances which generally means lower losses at joint connections. This is particularly important in industrial environments

where the cable may be disconnected and connected many times. The only disadvantage of 140μ outside-diameter is that it is nonstandard, so available connectors are fewer and more expensive than those for the 125μ size.

6.3.4.3.4   Indoor and Outdoor Cables

Indoor and outdoor fiber-optic cables differ in the jacket surrounding the fiber and the protective sheath that gives it sufficient tensile strength to be pulled through a conduit or overhead duct or strung on poles. Single indoor cables (Figure 6-22) consist of the clad fiber-optic cable surrounded by a Kevlar reinforcement sheath, wrapped in a polyurethane jacket for protection from abrasion and the environment. The outdoor cable has additional protective sheathing for additional environmental protection.

Plenum fiber-optic cables are available for indoor applications that require specific smoke- and flame-retardant characteristics and do not require the use of a metal conduit. When higher tensile strength is needed, additional strands of Kevlar are added outside the polyethylene jacket and another polyethylene jacket provided over these Kevlar reinforcement elements. Some indoor cables utilize a stranded-steel central-strength member or nonmetallic Kevlar. Kevlar is preferred in installations located in explosive areas or areas of high electromagnetic interference, where nonconducting strength members are desirable.

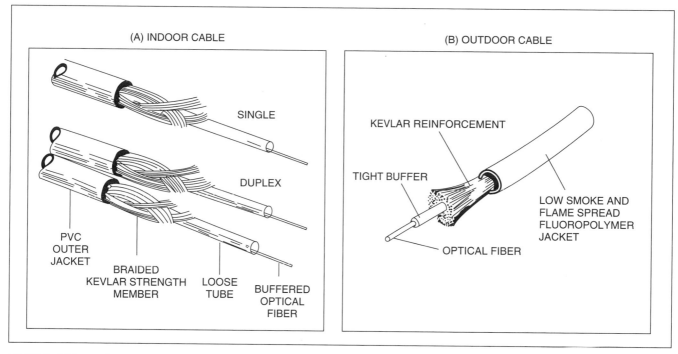

FIGURE 6-22   Indoor and outdoor fiber optic cable construction

The mechanical properties of cables typically found on data sheets include crush resistance, impact resistance, bend radius, and strength.

An outdoor cable or one that will be subjected to heavy stress—in long-cable-run pulls in a conduit or aerial application—uses dual Kevlar/polyethylene layers as just described. The polyethylene coating also retards the deleterious effects of sunlight and weather.

When two fibers are required, two single cable structures may be paired in siamese fashion (side by side) with a jacket surrounding around them.

If additional fiber-optic runs are required, multi-fiber cables (having four, six, eight, or ten fibers) with similar properties are used (Figure 6-23). The fibers are enclosed in a single or multiple buffer tube around a tensile-strength member composed of Kevlar and then surrounded with an outer jacket of Kevlar.

6.3.4.4 Connectors and Fiber Termination

This section describes fiber-optic connectors, techniques for finishing the fiber ends when terminated with connectors, and potential connector problems. For very long cable runs, joining and fusing the actual glass-fiber core and cladding is done by a technique called "splicing." Splicing joins two lengths of cable by fusing the two fibers (locally melting the glass) and physically joining them in a permanent connection (Section 6.3.4.4.4).

Fiber-optic cables require connectors to couple the optical signal from the transmitter at the camera into the fiber-optic cable, and at the monitoring end to couple the light output from the fiber into the receiver. If the fiber-optic cable run is very long or must go through various barriers (e.g. walls), the total run is often fabricated from sections of fiber-optic cable and each end joined with connectors. This is equivalent to an inter-line coaxial connector.

A large variety of optical connectors is available for terminating fiber-optic cables. Most are based on *butt* coupling of cut and polished fibers to allow direct transmission of optical power from one fiber core to the other. Such a connection is made using two mating connectors, precisely centering the two fibers into the connector ferrules and fixing them in place with epoxy. The ferrule and fiber surfaces at the ends of both cables are ground and polished to produce a clean optical surface. The two most common types are the cylindrical and cone ferrule connectors.

6.3.4.4.1 Coupling Efficiency

The efficiency of light transfer from the end of one fiber-optic cable to the following cable or device is a function of six different parameters:

1. Fiber-core lateral or axial misalignment
2. Angular core misalignment
3. Fiber end separation
4. Fiber distortion
5. Fiber end finish
6. Fresnel reflections.

Of these loss mechanisms, distortion loss and the effects of fiber end finish can be minimized by using proper techniques when the fibers are prepared for termination.

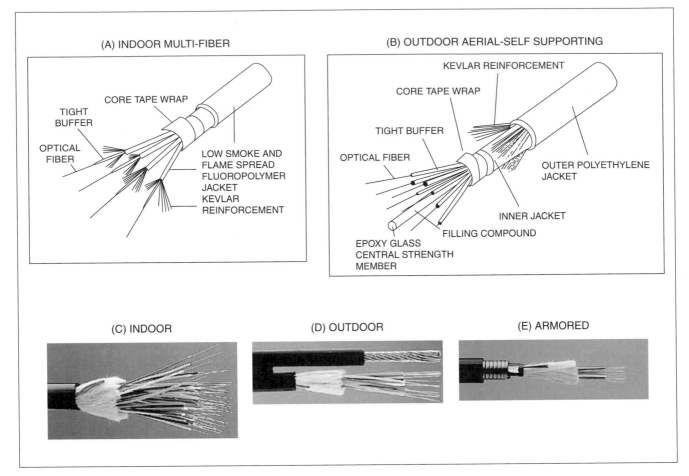

FIGURE 6-23   Multi-conductor fiber optic cable

A chipped or scratched fiber end will scatter much of the light signal power, but proper grinding and polishing minimize these effects in epoxy/polish-type connectors.

Lateral misalignment of fiber cores causes the largest amount of light loss, as shown in Figure 6-24a.

An evaluation of the overlap area of laterally misaligned step-index fibers indicates that a total misalignment of 10% of a core diameter yields a loss of greater than 0.5 dB. This means that a fiber core of 0.002 inches (50 microns) must be placed within 0.0001 inches of the center of its connector for a worst-case lateral misalignment loss of 0.5 dB. While this dimension is small, the connection is readily accomplished in the field.

Present connector designs maintain angular alignment well below one degree (Figure 6-24b), which adds only another 0.1 dB (2.3%) of loss for most fibers.

Fiber end–separation loss depends on the NA of the fiber. Since the optical light power emanating from a transmitting fiber is in the form of a cone, the amount of light coupled into the receiving fiber or device will decrease as the fibers are moved apart from each other (Figure 6-24c). A separation distance of 10% of the core diameter using a fiber with an NA of 0.2 can add another 0.1 dB of loss.

Fresnel losses usually add another 0.3 to 0.4 dB when the connection does not use an index-matching fluid (Figure 6-24d).

The summation of all of these different losses often adds up to 0.5–1.0 dB for ST-type (higher for SMA 1906) terminations and connections (Table 6-4).

6.3.4.4.2 Cylindrical and Cone Ferrule Connector

In the cylindrical ferrule design, the two connectors are joined and the two ferrules are brought into contact inside precisely guiding cylindrical sleeves. Figure 6-25 shows the geometry of this type of connection.

Lateral offset in cylindrical ferrule connectors is usually the largest loss contributor. In a 50-micron graded-index fiber, 0.5 dB (12%) loss results from a 5-micron offset. A loss of 0.5 dB can also result from a 35-micron gap between the ends of the fibers, or from a 2.5° tilted fiber surface. Commercial connectors of this type reach 0.5–1 dB (12–26%) optical loss for ST type and higher for SMA 1906. Optical-index-matching fluids in the gap further reduce the loss.

The cone ferrule termination technique centers the fiber in one connector and insures concentricity with the mating fiber in the other connector using a cone-shaped

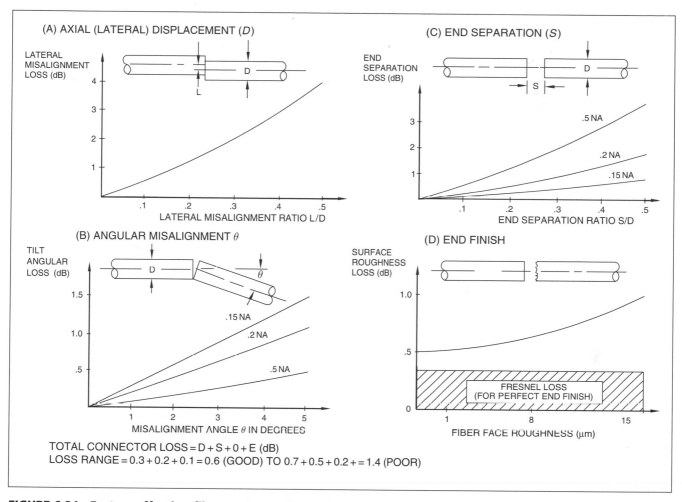

FIGURE 6-24   Factors affecting fiber optic coupling efficiency

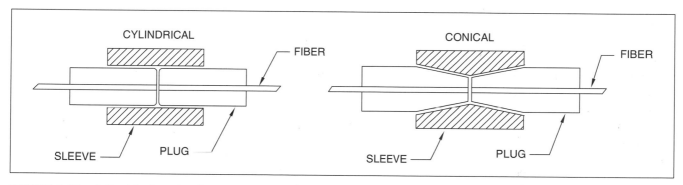

FIGURE 6-25   Cylindrical and conical butt-coupled fiber optic ferrule connectors

plug instead of a cylindrical ferrule. The key to the cone connector design is the placement of the fiber-centering hole (in the cone) in relationship to the true center, which exists when the connector is mated to its other half. A fiber (within acceptable tolerances) is inserted into the ferrule, adhesive is added, and the ferrule is compressed to fit the fiber size while the adhesive sets. The fiber faces and ferrule are polished to an optical finish and the ferrule (with fiber) is placed into the final alignment housing. Most low-loss fiber-optic connections are made utilizing the cone-shaped plug technique. The two most popular cone-shaped designs are the small-fiber resilient (SFR) bonded connector and the SMA, a redesigned coaxial connector style (Figure 6-26).

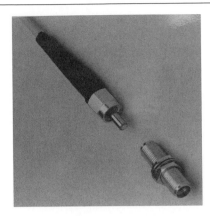

TYPE: SMA
THREADED—SCREW ON

TYPE: ST, SFR (SMALL FIBER
RESILIENT) POLARIZED AND
SPRING LOADED QUARTER
TURN BAYONET LOCK

FIGURE 6-26   SMA and SFR connectors

Both use the cone-shaped ferrule, which provides a reliable, low-cost, easily assembled termination in the field. Both connectors can terminate fibers with diameters of 125-micron cladding.

The technique eliminates almost all fiber and connector error tolerance buildup that normally causes light losses. It makes use of a resilient material for the ferrule, metal for the construction of the retainer assembly, and a rugged metallic connector for termination. The fiber alignment is repeatable after many "connects" and "disconnects" due to the tight interference fit of the cone-shaped ferrule into the cone-shaped mating half. This cone design also forms a sealed interface for a fiber-to-fiber or fiber-to-active-device junction, such as fiber cable to transmitter or fiber cable to receiver. Tolerances in the fiber diameter are absorbed by the resiliency of the plastic ferrule. This connector offers a maximum signal loss of 1.0 dB (26%) and provides repeatable coupling and uncoupling with little increase in light loss.

The popular SMA-style connector is compatible with many other SMA-manufacturer-type connectors and terminates the 125-micron fibers. Internal ferrules insure axial fiber alignment to within 0.1°. The SMA connector has a corrosion-resistant metal body and is available in an environmentally sealed version.

6.3.4.4.3 *Fiber Termination Kits*

An efficient fiber-optic-cable transmission system relies on a high-quality termination of the cable core and cladding. This step requires the use of perhaps unfamiliar but easy techniques with which the installer must be acquainted. Fiber-terminating kits are available from most fiber-cable, connector, and accessory manufacturers. Figure 6-27 shows a complete kit, including all grinding and polishing compounds, alignment jigs, tools, and instructions.

Manufacturers can provide descriptions of the various techniques for terminating the ends of fiber-optic cables, including cable preparation, grinding, polishing, testing, etc.

6.3.4.4.4 *Splicing Fibers*

Splicing of multimode fibers is sometimes necessary in systems having long fiber-optic-cable runs (longer than 2 km). In these applications it is advantageous to splice cable sections together rather than connect them by using connectors. A splice made between two fiber-optic cables can provide a connection with only one-tenth the optical loss of that obtained when a connector is inserted between fibers. Good fusion splices made with an electric arc produce losses as low as 0.05–0.1 dB (1.2–2.3% loss). Making a splice via a fusing technique is more difficult and requires more equipment and skill than terminating the end of a fiber with a connector. It is worth the effort if it eliminates the use of an in-line amplifier. The splice can also be used to repair a damaged cable, eliminating the need to add connector terminations that would decrease the light signal level.

6.3.4.5 *Fiber-Optic Transmitter*

The fiber-optic transmitter is the electro-optic transducer between the camera video electrical signal output and the light signal input to the fiber-optic cable (Figure 6-15). The function of the transmitter is to efficiently and *accurately* convert the electrical video signal into an optical signal and couple it into the fiber optic. The transmitter electronics convert the amplitude-modulated video signal through LED or ILD into an AM or FM light signal, which faithfully represents the video signal. The transmitter consists of an LED for normal security applications or an ILD when a long range transmission is required. The former is used for most CCTV security applications. Figure 6-28 illustrates the block diagram for the transmitter unit.

6.3.4.5.1 *Generic Types*

The LED light source is a semiconductor device made of gallium arsenide (GaAs) or a related semiconductor compound which converts an electrical video signal to an optical signal. The LED is a diode junction that spontaneously emits nearly monochromatic (single wavelength or color) radiation into a narrow light beam when current is passed through it. While the ILD has a very narrow beam

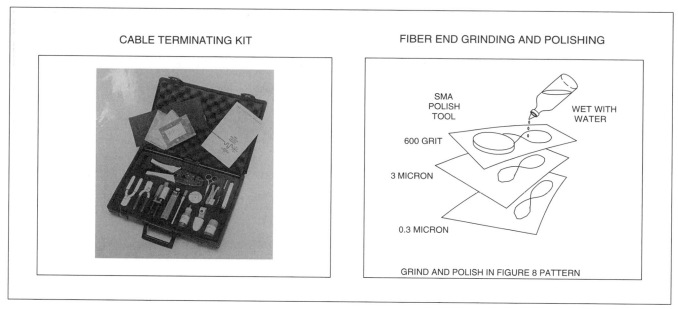

FIGURE 6-27   Fiber optic termination kit

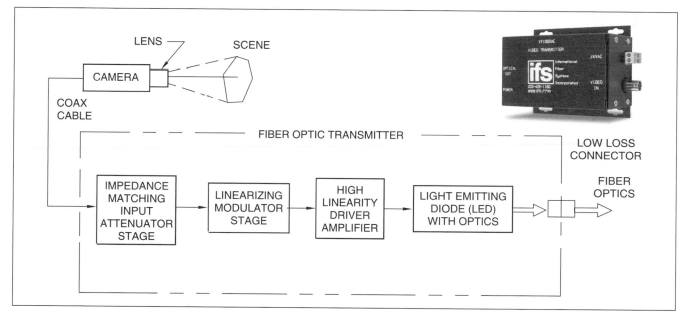

FIGURE 6-28   Block diagram of LED fiber optic transmitter

width and is more powerful, the LED is more reliable, less expensive, and easier to use. The ILD is used in very long distance, wide-bandwidth fiber-optic applications.

The LED's main requirements as a light source are: (1) to have a fast operating speed to meet the bandwidth requirements of the video signal, (2) to provide enough optical power to provide the receiver with a signal-to-noise (S/N) ratio suitable for a good television picture, and (3) to produce a wavelength that takes advantage of the low-loss propagation characteristics of the fiber.

The parameters that constitute a good light source for injecting light into a fiber-optic cable are those that produce as intense a light output into as small a cone diameter as possible. Another factor affecting the light-transmission efficiency is the cone angle of the LED output that can be accepted by and launched down the fiber-optic cable. Figure 6-29 illustrates the LED-coupling problem.

The entire output beam from the LED (illustrated by the cone of light) is not intercepted or collected by the fiber-optic core. This unintercepted illumination loss can be a problem when the light-emitting surface is separated from the end of the fiber core. Most LEDs have a lens at the surface of the LED package to collect the light from the emitting source and concentrate it onto the core of the fiber.

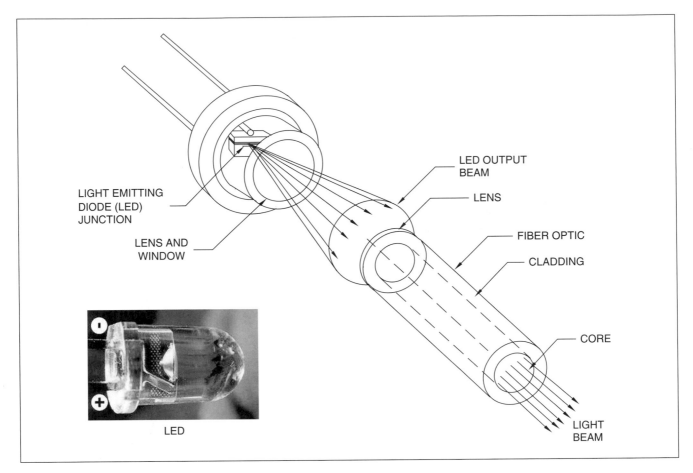

FIGURE 6-29   LED light beam output cone angle

6.3.4.5.2 Modulation Techniques

For video security applications, the electrical signal from the camera is AM or FM and converted to light output variations in the LED or ILD. The optical output power varies directly to the electrical input signal for AM and is constant for FM. LEDs with an 850 nm IR wavelength emission are best suited since they can be amplitude modulated: the electrical video signal can be converted to a light output signal that is a near-linear function of the LED drive current. This produces a very faithful transformation of the electrical video information to the light information that is transmitted along the fiber-optic cable.

6.3.4.5.3 Operational Wavelengths

An important characteristic of the transmitter output is the wavelength of the emitted light. This should be compatible with the fiber's minimum-attenuation wavelength, which is 850 nm (in the IR region) for most CCTV fiber-optic cable. The wavelength of light emitted by an LED depends on the semiconductor material composition. Pure GaAs diodes emit maximum power at a wavelength of 940 nm (near-IR), which is undesirable because most glass fibers have a high attenuation at that wavelength. Adding aluminum to GaAs to produce a GaAlAs diode yields a maximum power output at a wavelength between 800 and 900 nm, with the exact wavelength determined by the percentage

of aluminum. In most transmitters today, the emitting wavelength is 850 nm, which matches the maximum transmission capability of the glass fiber.

Alternative transmitting wavelengths are 1060, 1300, and 1550 nm, which are regions where glass fibers exhibit a lower attenuation and dispersion than at 850 nm. These wavelengths are produced by combining the element indium with gallium arsenide (to get InGaAs) and are used in some long-distance transmission applications.

6.3.4.6 Fiber-Optic Receiver

The term *receiver* at the output end of the fiber-optic cable refers to a light-detecting transducer and its related electronics that provides any necessary signal conditioning to restore the signal to its original shape at the input and additional signal amplification. The most common fiber-optic receiver uses a photodiode to convert the incident light from the fiber into electrical energy. To interface the receiver with the optical fiber, the proper match between light source, fiber-optic cable, and light detector is required. In the AM transmission system, the optical power input at the fiber is modulated so the photodetector operating in the photocurrent mode must provide good linearity, speed, and stability. The photodiode produces

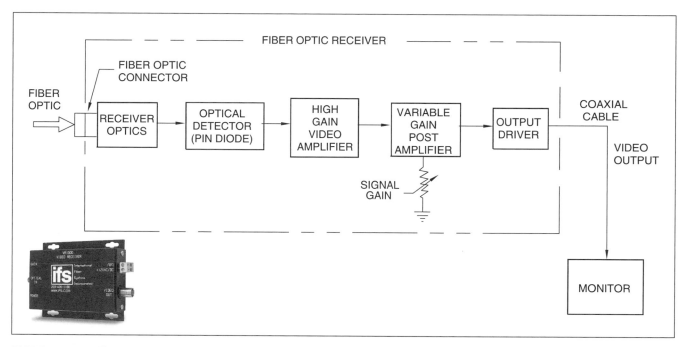

FIGURE 6-30   Fiber optic receiver block diagram

no electrical gain and is therefore followed by circuits that amplify electrical voltage and power to drive the coaxial cable. Figure 6-30 illustrates the block diagram for the receiver unit.

The light exiting from the receiver end of an optical fiber spreads out with a divergence approximately equal to the acceptance cone angle at the transmitter end of the fiber. Photodiodes are packaged with lenses on their housings so that the lens collects this output energy and focuses it down onto the photodiode-sensitive area.

After the light energy is converted into an electrical signal by the photodiode, it is linearly amplified and conditioned to be suitable for transmission over standard coaxial cable or two-wire UTP to a monitor or recorder.

6.3.4.6.1 Demodulation Techniques

The receiver demodulates the video light signal to its original base-band video form. This takes the form of either AM or FM demodulation. Since FM modulation–demodulation is less sensitive to external electrical influences it is the technique of choice in most systems.

6.3.4.7 Multi-Signal, Single-Fiber Transmission

The primary attribute of fiber-optic transmission is the cable's wide signal bandwidth capability. Transmitting a single video signal on a single fiber easily fits within the bandwidth capability of all fiber-optic cables. Modulators and demodulators in transmitters, receivers, and transceivers permit transmission of bidirectional video, audio, and control signals over a single optical-fiber cable. Using the full-duplex capabilities of the system, the transceiver at the camera transmits video and audio signals

from the camera location to the monitor location while simultaneously receiving audio, control, or camera genlock signals from the transceiver at the monitor location. All transmissions occur via the same single optical-fiber cable. The transmitter and receiver contain all circuitry for the bidirectional transmission of pan/tilt, zoom, focus, iris, contact-closure, and video in the opposite direction.

When more than one video signal is to be transmitted by optical fiber between two points, either multiple fibers may be used or the signals may be combined using wavelength division multiplexing (WDM MUX), thus saving the cost of additional fibers and expensive multi-fiber connectors. Using this technique the outputs from each optical transmitter operating at different wavelengths (1060, 1300, and 1550 μm) are modulated by separate video signals and combined on a *single* optical fiber and combined using WDM MUX. These video signals may then be separated at the other end of the fiber by a WDM de-multiplexer (WDM DE-MUX) (Figure 6-31).

Typically two or more wavelengths are provided by two LED transmitters operating at wavelengths between 850 and 1550 nm. The WDM MUX and DE-MUX may be fabricated using an optical coupler and splitter assembly, using lens and grating components. The lens focuses each of the channels onto the grating, which then separates the channels according to wavelength and according to the grating spacing. Data sheets for a typical WDM MUX/DE-MUX devices include the following specifications:

1. *Number of Channels*: The number of video signals that can be multiplexed and de-multiplexed over the optical fiber to which the WDM MUX/DEMUX are connected.

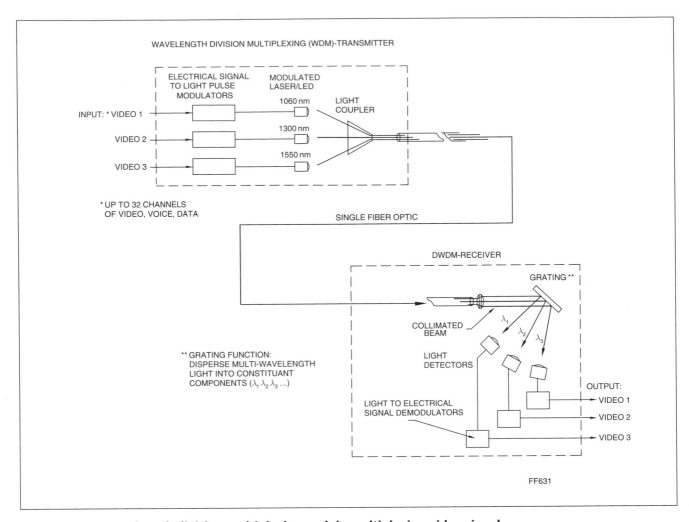

FIGURE 6-31   Wavelength division multiplexing and de-multiplexing video signal

2. *Center Wavelengths*: Center wavelength of the channels over which the video signals are multiplexed.

3. *Channel Spacing*: The minimum distance (wavelength or frequency) between channels in a WDM MUX/DEMUX system. In the illustration the channel spacing is approximately 0.8 nm, approximately 100 GHz.

4. *Bandwidth* (also referred to as *Passband Width*): The line-width of a specific wavelength channel. A manufacturer generally specifies the line-width at 1 dB, 3 dB and 20 dB insertion loss as shown in Figure 6-32.

5. *Maximum Insertion Loss*: Loss sustained by the video signals when the WDM MUX/DE-MUX is applied in a system. Typical values range from 1.5 dB for a 4-channel device to 6 dB for a high number of channels, WDM MUX/DE-MUX.

6. *Isolation*: The loss or attenuation between video signal channels, usually more than 30 dB.

Figure 6-33 illustrates two typical channels over which the video signals 1540.56 μm and 1541.35 μm are multiplexed.

6.3.4.8   *Fiber Optic—Advantages/Disadvantages*

Why go through all the complexity and extra expense of converting the electrical video signal to a light signal and then back again? Fiber optics offers several very important features that no electrical cabling system offers, including:

• ultra-wide bandwidth supporting multiple video, audio, control, and communications signals on one fiber
• complete electrical isolation
• complete noise immunity to RFI, EMI, and electromagnetic pulse (EMP)
• transmission security (fiber-optic cable is hard to tap)
• no spark or fire hazard or short-circuit possibility
• absence of crosstalk
• no RFI/EMI radiation.

Table 6-5 compares the features of coaxial and fiber-optic transmission.

6.3.4.8.1   *Pro*

Widest Bandwidth.   In general the bandwidth capacity is directly proportional to the carrier frequency. Light

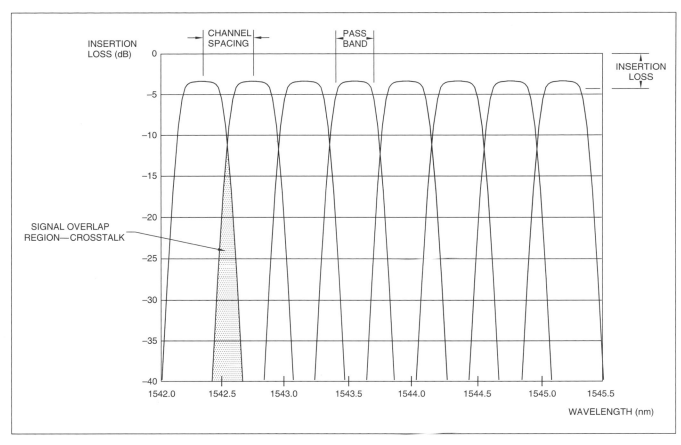

FIGURE 6-32   Line-width vs. insertion loss of a specific wavelength channel

(and near IR) frequencies are approximately 10^{14} Hz. Typical video microwave transmitters operate at 10^{10} GHz or 10^{10} Hz. Fiber optics has a 10^4 or 10,000 times higher bandwidth capability than microwave.

Electrical Isolation.   The complete electrical isolation of the transmitting section (i.e. the camera, lens controller, pan/tilt, and related equipment) from the receiving section (i.e. the monitor, recorder, printer, switching network, and so on) is very important for inter-building and intra-building locations when a different electrical power source is used for each location. Using fiber-optic transmission prevents all possibility of ground loops and ground voltage differences that could require the redesign of a coaxial cable–based system.

RFI, EMI, and EMP Immunity.   When a transmission path runs through a building or outdoors past other electrical equipment, the site survey usually cannot uncover all possible contingencies of existing RFI/EMI noise. This is also true of EMP and lightning strikes. Therefore, using fiber optics in the initial design prevents any problems caused by such noise sources.

Transmission Security.   Since the fiber optic has no electrical noise to leak and no visible light, it exhibits excellent inherent transmission security and it is hard to intercept. Methods for compromising the fiber-optic cable

are difficult, and the intrusion is usually detected. To tap a fiber-optic cable, the bare fiber in the cable must be isolated from its sheath without breaking it. This will probably end the tapping attempt. If the bare fiber is successfully isolated, an optical tap must be made, the simplest of which is achieved by bending the fiber into a small radius and extracting some of the light. If a measurable amount of power is tapped (which is necessary for a useful tap), the tap can be detected by monitoring the power at the system receiver. In contrast, tapping a coaxial cable is easy to do and hard to detect.

No Fire Hazards.   Since no electricity is involved in any part of the fiber-optic cable, there is no chance or opportunity for sparks or electrical short circuits, and hence no fire hazards. Short circuits and other hazards encountered in electrical wiring systems can start fires or cause explosions. When a light-carrying fiber is severed, there is no spark, and a fiber cannot short-circuit in the electrical meaning of the term.

Absence of Crosstalk.   Because the transmission medium is light, there is no crosstalk between any of the fiber-optic cables. Therefore there is no degradation due to the close proximity of cables in the same bundle, as there can be when multiple channels are encased in the same electrical cable.

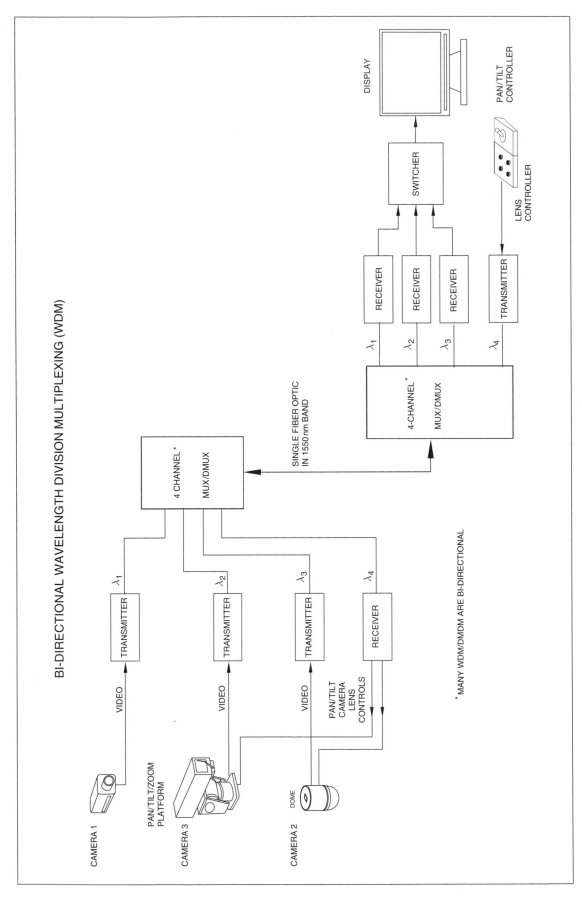

FIGURE 6-33 Video signals and controls multiplexed over four channels

DESIGNATION	CABLE TYPE	ATTENUATION @ 5–10 MHz			OUTSIDE DIAMETER (inches)	WEIGHT (lb) PER 100 ft
		dB/100 ft	dB/1000 ft	dB/km		
RG59	COAXIAL	1.0	10.0	32.8	.242	3.5–4.0
RG59 MINI	COAXIAL	1.3	13.0	42.6	.135	1.5
RG6	COAXIAL	.8	8.0	26.2	.272	7.9
RG11	COAXIAL	.51	5.1	16.7	.405	9–11
2422/UL1384	MINI–COAX	3.96	39.6	129.9	.079	0.9
2546†	MINI–COAX	1.82	18.2	59.7	.13	1.4
2895†	MINI–COAX	2.1	21.0	69.0	.118	1.0
RG179B/U	MINI–COAX	2.0	20.0	65.6	.089	1.0
10/125*	FIBER OPTIC	850 NM** —	—	—	.036	—
		1300 NM .01–.02	.1–.2	.4–.8		
50/125	FIBER OPTIC	850 NM .12–.21	1.2–2.1	4–7.0	.12	.50–1.0
		1300 NM .09–.18	.9–1.8	3–6.0		
140/200	FIBER OPTIC	850 NM .08–.18	.8–1.8	2.5–6.0	.244	—
		1300 NM .02–.14	.2–1.4	.8–4.5		

* USED ONLY IN VERY LONG DISTANCE, WIDE BANDWIDTH APPLICATIONS
** TRANSMISSION WAVELENGTH
    (NANOMETER–NM)
† MOGAMI

1 KILOMETER (km) = 3280 FEET (ft)
1 MILE (Mi) = 1.609 KILOMETERS (km)
1 POUND (lb) = .454 KILOGRAMS (kg)

Table 6-5 Comparison of Fiber Optic and Coaxial Cable Transmission

No RFI or EMI Radiation.   Fibers do not radiate energy. They generate no interference to other systems. Therefore, the fiber-optic cable will not emit any measurable EMI/RFI radiation, and other cabling in the vicinity will suffer no noise degradation. There are no FCC requirements for fiber-optic transmission.

6.3.4.8.2 Con

Higher Cost.   Coaxial cable and connectors are inexpensive and no transmitter/receiver pairs are required. For short distances if new cable must be run, coaxial is the most cost-effective.

Connector Termination More Difficult.   Fiber-optic cable and connectors cost more than coaxial. Terminating fiber cables takes longer than coaxial cables and requires more technical skill.

6.3.4.9 Fiber-Optic Transmission: Checklist

The following are some questions that should be asked when considering the use or design of a new fiber-optic transmission system.

1. What are the lengths of cable runs? If over 500 feet, then fiber optic should be considered. In screen rooms or tempest areas, runs as short as 10 feet sometimes require fiber-optic cable.
2. What size core/clad-diameter fiber should be used? The most common diameter is 50/125 microns.
3. What wavelength should be used—850, 1060, 1300, or 1550 nm? The most common wavelengths are 850 and 1300 nm.
4. How many fibers are necessary for transmitting video, audio, and controls? Should single- or multi-fiber cable be used?
5. Are the cable runs going to be indoors or outdoors? Separate the indoor and outdoor requirements and determine if outdoor fiber cables are required. What will the outdoor environment be (lighting, etc.)?
6. If outdoors, will the fiber be strung on poles, surface-mounted on the ground, undergo direct burial, or pass through a conduit? Choose cable according to manufacturers' recommendations.
7. If indoors, will it be in a conduit, cable tray or trough, plenum, or ceiling? Choose cable according to manufacturers' recommendations.
8. What temperature range will the fiber-optic cable experience? Most cable types will be suitable for most indoor environments. For outdoor use, the cable chosen must operate over the full range of hot and cold temperatures expected and must withstand ice and wind loading if mounted above ground level.
9. Are there any special considerations such as water, ice, chemicals? See manufacturers' specifications for extreme environmental hazards.
10. Are there special safety codes? Fiber-optic cable is available with plenum-grade or special abrasion-resistant construction.

11. Should spare cables be included? Each design is different, but it is prudent to include one or more spare fiber-optic cables to account for cable failure or future system growth. The number of spares also depends on how easy or difficult it is to replace a cable or add to existing cables.

6.4   WIRED CONTROL SIGNAL TRANSMISSION

Fixed cameras do not require any control functions. Moving cameras require pan, tilt, focus and sometimes iris control signals for proper operation.

6.4.1   Camera/Lens Functions

Lenses can require zoom, focus, and iris-control signals.

6.4.2   Pan/Tilt Functions

Moving cameras require pan/tilt functions to scan the camera horizontally, tilt it vertically, and set preset pointing directions to specific locations in the scene.

6.4.3   Control Protocols

The simplest controls can take the form of on/off or proportional voltage control wiring for each function. These direct controls require the largest number of wires. The most standard two- and four-wire control protocol for cameras, lens, and pan/tilt platforms are the RS422 and RS485.

6.5   WIRELESS VIDEO TRANSMISSION

Most video security systems transmit video, audio, and control signals via coaxial cable, two-wire, or fiber-optic transmission means. These techniques are cost-effective and reliable, and provide an excellent solution for transmission. However, there are applications and circumstances that require wireless transmission of video and other signals.

The video signal can be transmitted from the camera to the monitor through the atmosphere, without having to connect the two with hard wire or fiber. The most familiar technique is the transmission of commercial television signals from some distant transmitter tower to consumer television sets, broadcast through the atmosphere on VHF and UHF radio frequency channels.

Commercial broadcasting is of course rigidly controlled by the FCC, whose regulations dictate its precise usage.

Microwave transmission also is controlled by the FCC. Rules are set forth and licenses are required for certain frequencies and applications, which limits usage to specific purposes. The US government currently exercises strict control over transmission of wireless video via RF and microwave. Up until recently, RF and microwave atmospheric video transmission links were limited to governmental agencies (federal, state, and local) that could obtain the necessary licenses. Now some low-power RF and microwave transmitters and receivers suitable for short links (less than a mile) are available for use without an FCC license. High power and RF microwave links are licensable by private users after a frequency check is made with the FCC.

6.5.1   Transmission Types

Some examples of wireless TV transmission described in the following sections include microwave (ground-to-ground station, satellite), RF over VHF or UHF, and light-wave transmission using IR beams. The hardware cost of RF, microwave, and lightwave systems is considerably higher than any of the copper-wire or fiber-optic systems, and such systems should be used only when absolutely necessary as when their use avoids expensive cable installations (such as across roadways), or in temporary or covert applications, wireless transmission becomes cost-effective.

The results obtainable with hard-wired copper-wire or fiber-optic video transmission are usually predictable, with the exception of interference that might occur due to the copper-wire cables running near electromagnetic radiating equipment or electrical storms. The results obtained with wireless transmission are generally not as predictable because of the variable nature of the atmospheric path and materials through which RF, microwave, or light signals must travel, as well as the specific transmitting and propagating characteristics of the particular wavelength or frequency of transmission. Each of the three wireless transmitting regimes acts differently because of the wide diversity in frequencies at which they transmit.

6.5.2   Frequency and Transmission Path Considerations

The RF link constitutes the lowest carrier frequency (Figure 6-34). It penetrates many visually opaque materials, goes around corners, and does not require a line-of-sight path (i.e. a receiver in sight of the transmitter) when transmitting from one location to another. The radio frequencies are, however, susceptible to attenuation and reflection by metallic objects, ground terrain, or large

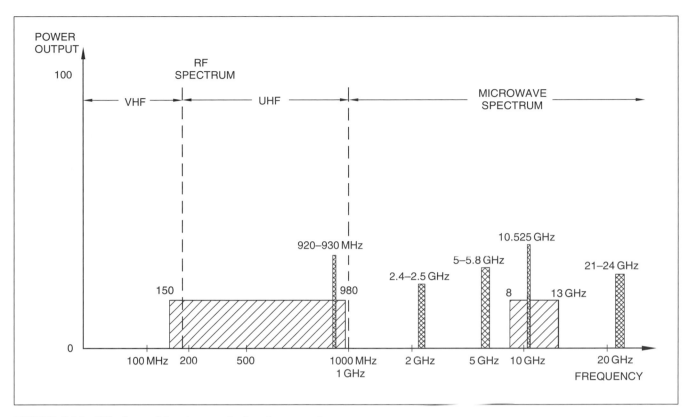

FIGURE 6-34 Wireless video transmission frequencies

buildings or structures, and therefore they sometimes produce unpredictable results.

The microwave link requires an unobstructed line of sight; any metallic or wet objects in the transmission path cause severe attenuation and reflection, often rendering a system useless. However, metallic poles or flat surfaces can sometimes be used to reflect the microwave energy, allowing the beam to turn a corner. Reflection of this type does reduce the energy reaching the receiver and the effective range of the system. Some microwave frequencies penetrate dry nonmetallic structures such as wood or drywall walls and floors, so that non-line-of-sight transmission is possible.

The frequency range most severely attenuated by the atmosphere and blocked completely by any opaque object is a light-wave signal in the near-IR region. The IR beam can be strongly attenuated by heavy fog or precipitation, severely reducing its effective range as compared with clear-line-of-sight, clear-weather conditions. As would be expected, the IR-wavelength system requires a clear line of sight with no opaque obstructions whatsoever between the transmitter and the receiver. The IR beam can be reflected off one or more mirrors to go around corners. The advantages of the IR system over RF and microwave links are: (1) security (since it is hard to tap a narrow light beam), (2) high bandwidth (able to carry multiple channels of information), and (3) bidirectional operation.

6.5.3 Microwave Transmission

Microwave systems applicable in television transmission have been allocated frequencies in bands from 1 to 75 GHz (see Table 6-6).

Microwave frequencies, which approach light-wave frequencies, are usually transmitted and received by parabolically shaped reflector antennas or metallic horns. Even when a line of sight exists, there can be signal fading, caused primarily by changes in atmospheric conditions between the transmitter and the receiver, a problem that must be taken into account in the design. This fading can result at any frequency, but in general is more severe at the higher microwave frequencies.

6.5.3.1 Terrestrial Equipment

For terrestrial use, several manufacturers provide reliable microwave transmission equipment suitable for transmitting video, audio, and control signals over distances of from several hundred feet to 10–20 miles in line-of-sight conditions.

One system transmits a single NTSC video channel and two 20 kHz audio channels over a distance of 1 mile. A high-gain directional antenna is available to extend the system operating range to several miles. Figure 6-35a shows the transmitter and receiver units. This system operates at

BAND/USE*	FREQUENCY BAND (GHz)	SECURITY FREQUENCY RANGE (GHz)	USAGE	RESTRICTIONS
L	1.2–1.7	1.2–1.7	VIDEO TRANSMITTER	GOVERNMENT SECURITY LAW ENFORCEMENT ONLY
S	2.4–2.5	2.4–2.5	VIDEO TRANSMITTER LOW POWER/HIGH POWER FCC PART 15	LOW POWER—NO RESTRICTIONS NO FCC LICENSE REQUIRED HIGH POWER—LICENSE REQURIED
S	2.6–3.95	2.45	CONSUMER MICROWAVE OVEN	
G	3.95–5.85	—		
C	4.9–7.05	—		
C	5–5.8	5–5.8	VIDEO TRANSMITTER LOW POWER/HIGH POWER FCC PART 15	LOW POWER—NO RESTRICTIONS NO FCC LICENSE REQUIRED HIGH POWER—LICENSE REQURIED
J	5.85–8.2	8.4–8.6	VIDEO TRANSMITTER	
H	7.05–10.0	—		
X	8.2–12.4	10.4–10.6		
M	10.0–15.0	10.525	VIDEO, AUDIO, INTRUSION	
P	12.4–18.0	10.35–10.8	VIDEO TRANSMITTER	
N	15.0–22.0	21.2–23.2	VIDEO UP TO 3 Mi RANGE	
K	18.0–26.5	24.125	VIDEO, VOICE, INTRUSION	
R	26.5–40.0	—		
V	40–75	—		

* ALSO SEE TABLE 6-7
FCC PART 15.249 TRANSMITTER, ANY TYPE OF MODULATION
  902–928 MHz–50 mV/M MAXIMUM AT 3 METERS
  2.4–2.F835 GHz–50 mV/M MAXIMUM AT 3 METERS
  5.735–5.875 GHz–250 mV/M MAXIMUM AT 3 METERS

1 GIGAHERTZ (GHz) = 1000 MHz

FCC PART 15.247 TRANSMITTER USING SPREAD SPECTRUM
  902–928 MHz–1 WATT MAXIMUM
  2.4000–2.4835–1 WATT MAXIMUM
  5.725–5.675 GHz–1 WATT MAXIMUM

Table 6-6   Microwave Video Transmission Frequencies

a carrier frequency of 2450–2483.5 MHz with a power output of 1 watt. The transmitter and receiver operate from 11 to 16 volts DC derived from batteries, an AC-to-DC power supply, or 12 volts DC vehicle power. The microwave transmitter utilizes an omnidirectional antenna. A high-gain, low-noise receiver collects the microwave transmitter signal with an omnidirectional or directional antenna. The system has a selectable video bandwidth from 4.2 MHz for enhanced sensitivity or 8 MHz for high resolution and has a single or dual audio sub-carrier channel for audio communications between the two sites. It transmits monochrome or color video with excellent quality.

The 2450–2483.5 MHz band is available for a variety of industrial applications and requires an FCC license for operation. The system operates indoors or outdoors, uses FM, and provides immunity from vehicles, power lines, and other AM-type noise sources. The microwave frequency utilized has the ability to penetrate dry walls and ceilings and reflect off metal surfaces.

Figures 6-35b, c show examples of small short-range microwave transmitters operating at 2.4 GHz and 5.8 GHz designed for outdoor use. These systems use directional patch antennas pointed toward each other to provide the necessary signal at the receiver from the transmitter.

The systems are weatherproof, pedestal mounted, and designed for permanent installation. They transmit excellent full-color or monochrome pictures over an FM carrier in a frequency range of 2.4 GHz and 5.8 GHz with a video bandwidth of 10 MHz. In addition to the video channel, the system is capable of providing up to three voice or data (control) channels. The data channels may be used to control pan/tilt, zoom, focus, and iris at the camera location. Low power systems do not require FCC licensing. FCC licensing is required for high power systems and can be obtained for government and industrial users, providing an authorized interference survey is made to verify that no interference will result in other equipment.

Other variations and functions, the microwave transmitter/receiver systems can perform include:

1. Operation in any frequency band from 8.5 to 12.4 GHz with output powers up to 100 milliwatts.

(A) 2.4 GHz TRANSMITTER/RECEIVER

(B) 2.4 GHz OUTDOOR

(C) LONG RANGE 5.8 GHz

FIGURE 6-35 Monochrome/color microwave video transmission systems

2. Operation as a command-and-control unit providing a multi-channel system for transmitting control signal information. The commands are encoded at the transmitter and decoded at the receiver to control power on/off, lens focus, zoom and iris, and camera motion (pan/tilt).

3. An audio channel to provide simplex (one-way) or duplex (two-way) communications (IR system).

4. The ability to sequence through and transmit the video outputs from multiple surveillance cameras. The receiver and control units are located at the monitor site and the transmitter and sequencer units are located with the CCTV cameras. The camera outputs are fed to the sequencer unit. The operator at the receiver end controls the sequencing of the eight cameras and has the option to: (1) manually advance through the

cameras, (2) have the cameras sequence automatically, or (3) change the camera dwell time.

6.5.3.2 Satellite Equipment

Microwave transmission of video signals can be accomplished via satellite. Such systems are in extensive use for earth-to-satellite-to-earth communications, in which one ground-based antenna transmits to an orbiting synchronous satellite repeater, which relays the microwave signal at a shifted frequency to one or more receivers on earth (Figure 6-36).

While this type of communication and transmission for video security applications was not put into widespread use for analog video systems, it now is enjoying wide special use for digital video Internet (WWW) systems. The satellites used for transmission are in a synchronous orbit at an altitude of 22,300 miles and appear stationary with respect to the earth. Satellites are placed in a synchronous or stationary orbit to permit communications from any two points in the continental USA by a single "up" and a single "down" transmission link. Consequently, a characteristic of domestic satellite video communications is that the trans-mission cost is independent of terrestrial distance. It takes 0.15 seconds for a microwave signal traveling at the speed of light to make a one-way journey to or from the satellite. Therefore, there is a 0.3 second delay between transmission and reception of the video carrier, independent of ground distance. This delay is not usually a problem for transmission of video security signals; however, this must be kept in mind when synchronization of different incoming video signals is required. The signal level reaching the feed horn depends on the size and shape of the antenna (Figure 6-37).

The quality of an antenna is determined by how well it concentrates the radiation intercepted from a target satellite to a single point and by how well it ignores noise and unwanted signals coming from sources other than the target satellite. Three interrelated concepts—gain, beam width, and noise temperature—describe how well an antenna performs. Antenna gain is a measure of how many thousands of times a satellite signal is concentrated by the time it reaches the focus of the antenna. For example, a typical well-built 10-foot-diameter prime-focused antenna dish can have a gain of 40 dB, which is a factor of 10,000 power gain, which means that the signal is

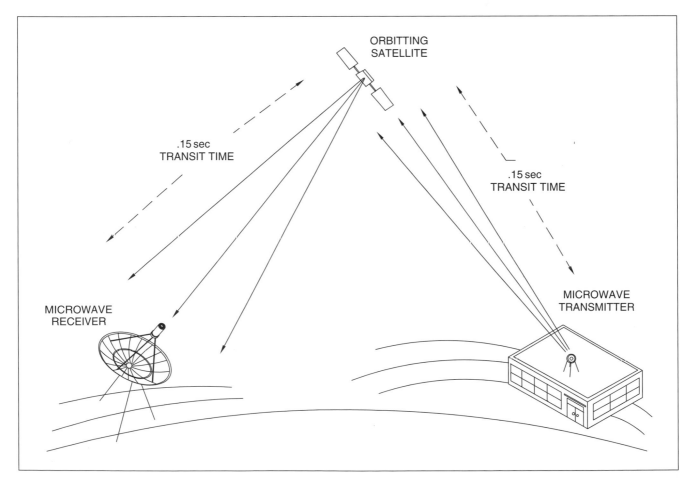

FIGURE 6-36 Satellite video transmission systems

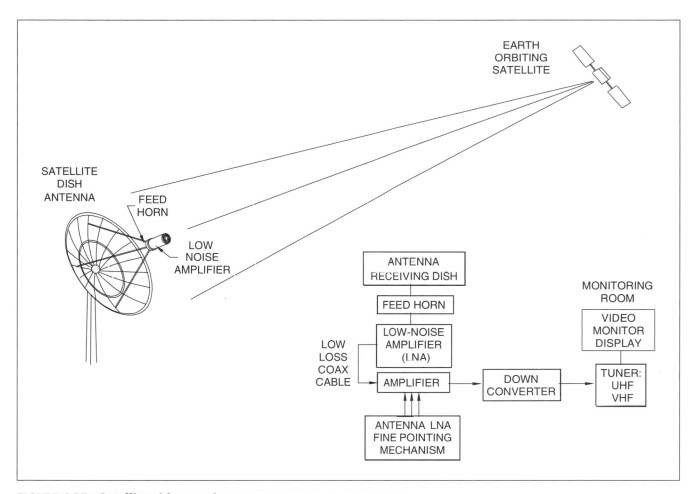

FIGURE 6-37   Satellite video receiver system

concentrated 10,000 times higher at the focal point than anywhere on the antenna. This gain is primarily dependent on the following three factors.

Dish Size.   As the size of a dish increases, more radiation from space is intercepted. Thus if the diameter of an antenna is doubled, the gain is increased fourfold (four times the area).

Frequency.   Gain increases with increasing frequency because higher-frequency microwaves, being closer to the frequency of light, behave a little more like light. Thus they do not spread out like waves in water but can be focused more easily into straight lines like beams of light. Since the gain of a microwave antenna is proportional to the square of the frequency, a signal with twice the frequency is concentrated by an antenna with four times the gain. As an example, if the gain is 10,000 when a signal of 5 GHz is received, then it will have a gain of 40,000 at 10 GHz.

Surface Accuracy.   Gain is further determined by how accurately the surface of an antenna is machined or formed to exactly a parabolic or other selected shape, and how well the shape is maintained under wind loading,

temperature changes, or other environmental conditions. A good antenna will see only a narrow beam width and will be able to pick out a satellite. A poor-quality dish will see too much extraneous noise and will receive less signal energy from the satellite of interest and pick up unwanted energy.

Dish antennas focus on one earth-orbiting satellite at a time and concentrate the faint signals into a feed horn (waveguide) that directs the microwave signal into a low-noise amplifier (LNA). The LNA amplifies the weak signal by 10,000 times and eventually transmits it by cable to the monitoring location.

Figure 6-37 shows a block diagram of a satellite receiver system. The LNA is the first active electronic component in the receiving system that acts on the video signal. The LNA is analogous to the audio preamplifier in that it provides the first critical preamplification. Its noise characteristics generally determine the quality of the final video image seen on the monitor.

The microwave signal from the LNA is fed via coaxial cable to a down converter which converts the satellite microwave signal to a lower frequency. Since the signal level is still very low, a special low-loss coaxial cable must be used and the signal run must be as short as possible. Increasing cable run decreases signal level, thereby decreasing the final S/N. The down-converted microwave signal is eventually converted to VHF or UHF and displayed on a television receiver or converted to base-band and displayed on a monitor.

Today most satellite receivers generate a base-band signal containing the base-band video and audio and synchronizing information that can be fed directly into a video monitor or recorder. The receiver also outputs a channel 3 or 4 modulated signal for the input to a standard television tuner TV set.

6.5.3.3 Interference Sources

Transmission interference occurs when unwanted signals are received along with the desired satellite signal. Of the several types of interference, perhaps the most common and irritating is caused by the reception of nearby microwave signals using the same or adjacent frequency band. Microwaves reflecting off buildings or even passing cars are responsible for the interference. Very often, moving the microwave antenna several feet can significantly reduce the interfering signal levels.

Other interference includes stray signals from adjacent satellites, or uplink or downlink interference. Finally, a predictable form of interference is caused by the sun. Twice a year the sun lines up directly behind each satellite for periods of approximately ten minutes per day for two or three days. Since the sun is a source of massive amounts of radio noise, no transmissions can be received from satellites during these sun outage times. This unavoidable type of interference can be expected during the normal course of operation of an earth satellite station.

6.5.4 Radio Frequency Transmission

Radio frequency (RF) is a wireless video transmission means originally used primarily by government agencies and amateur radio operators. Government frequencies include the 1200 MHz (1.2 GHz) and 1700 MHz (1.7 GHz) bands.

Radio frequency wireless has now found widespread use in commercial security applications in temporary covert and permanent surveillance applications. Video transmitters and receivers transmit monochrome or color video signals over distances of several hundred feet to several miles using small, portable, battery-operated equipment. Operating frequencies cover the 150 to 980 MHz, 2.4 GHz, and 5.8 GHz bands.

While RF transmission provides significant advantages when a wired system is not possible, there are FCC restrictions limiting the use of many such transmitters to government applications. Only low-power transmitters are available for commercial applications. Any RF systems used outside the United States require the approval of the

foreign government. Tables 6-7 and 7-5 summarize the channel frequencies available.

6.5.4.1 Transmission Path Considerations

An RF video signal transmission means can follow either commercial broadcasting standards in which the visual signal are amplitude modulated (AM), or noncommercial standards that use an FM signal. In the commercial standard the audio signal is frequency modulated on the carrier. In both systems the video input signal ranges from a few hertz to 4.5 MHz. For the low-powered transmitter/receiver systems used in security applications, FM modulation has provided far superior performance (increased range and lack of interference) and is the preferred method. The range obtained with an FM RF transmitter is from three to four times that of the AM type.

Transmitting at standard commercial broadcast video standards using AM signals and operating on one of the designated VHF or UHF channels is prohibited by the FCC since any consumer-type receiver could receive and display the video picture. This potential is obviously a disadvantage for covert security surveillance. In the case of FM video transmission, many consumer receivers, though not designed to receive such signals, do display FM signals with some degree of picture quality because of nonlinear and sporadic operation of various receiver circuits. Likewise, the FCC does not permit the commercial use of FM or other modulation techniques in the commercial VHF and UHF channels.

Low-power RF transmission in the 902–928 MHz, 2.4 GHz and 5.8 GHz ranges have been approved for general security applications without an FCC license. The 1.2 and 1.7 GHz bands have not been approved for commercial use.

6.5.4.2 Radio Frequency Equipment

Many manufacturers produce wireless video RF and microwave links operating in the 900 MHz, 2.4 GHz, and 5.8 GHz frequency bands. This equipment operates on FCC-assigned frequencies with specific maximum transmitter output power levels (a few hundred milliwatts). These general-purpose RF links operate at output field strengths 50–250 milliwatts per meter at 3 meters (Part 15 of the FCC specification).

Figure 6-38 illustrates typical RF and microwave video transmission equipments. Figure 6-38a shows two very small, four-channel, low power 1.2 GHz (government use only) and 2.4 GHz transmitters. Any one of four channels can be selected at a time. Figure 6-38b is a small four channel 2.4 GHz transmitter and receiver pair using high-gain Yaggi antennas for increased range and directionality. Figure 6-38c shows a long range 2.4 GHz receiver.

BAND	COMMERCIAL TELEVISION CHANNELS	FREQUENCY RANGE (MHz)	USAGE	RESTRICTIONS
VHF—LOWBAND	2–6	54–88	LOW-MEDIUM POWER SEVERAL MILES RANGE	GOVERNMENT, LAW ENFORCEMENT ONLY
FM RADIO	—	88–108	COMMERCIAL RADIO	FCC REGULATED
VHF—HIGHBAND	7–13	174–216	LOW-MEDIUM POWER, RANGE UP TO SEVERAL MILES	GOVERNMENT, LAW ENFORCEMENT ONLY
SECURITY	—	350–950	SINGLE CHANNEL TRANSMITTER/RECEIVER	GOVERNMENT, LAW ENFORCEMENT ONLY
UHF	14–83	470–890	LOW-MEDIUM POWER, RANGE UP TO SEVERAL MILES	GOVERNMENT, LAW ENFORCEMENT ONLY
SECURITY	—	902–928	LOW POWER, FCC PART 15	NO RESTRICTIONS, NO FCC LICENSE REQUIRED
SECURITY	—	1.2–1.7 GHz	LOW-MEDIUM POWER	GOVERNMENT, LAW ENFORCEMENT ONLY
SECURITY	—	2.4 GHz	LOW POWER, FCC PART 15 [*]	NO RESTRICTIONS, NO FCC LICENSE REQUIRED
SECURITY	—	2.4 GHz	HIGH POWER, FCC PART 90 [**]	GOVERNMENT, LAW ENFORCEMENT ONLY
SECURITY	—	5.8 GHz	LOW POWER SEVERAL MILES RANGE	NO RESTRICTIONS, NO FCC LICENSE REQUIRED

ALL SECURITY FREQUENCY BANDS ARE OUTSIDE THE COMMERCIAL TELEVISION BANDS

[*] INDUSTRIAL, SECURITY, MEDICAL (ISM)

[**] FCC PART 90, 5 WATT MAXIMUM

Table 6-7   RF and Microwave Video Transmission Frequencies

For indoor applications, most RF and microwave transmitter/receiver systems use omnidirectional dipole antennas for ease of operation. For outdoor operation, dipoles or whip antennas are used. High-gain Yaggi antennas are used to increase range and minimize interference from other radiation sources.

The RF and microwave transmitters and receivers have a standard 75-ohm input impedance; however, they require a 50-ohm coaxial cable at the transmitter output and the receiver input. Using a 75-ohm coaxial cable between the antenna and the transmitter output or the receiver input will seriously degrade the performance of the system even if it is short (1–2 ft). Miniature 50-ohm, RG58U, and RG8 coaxial cables terminated in a small SMA or BNC connector are used.

Figure 6-39 shows the approximate distance between transmitter and receiver antennas (range) versus transmitted power, for video transmission. The range values are for smooth and obstacle-free terrain applications using a dipole antenna at the transmitter and receiver. The antennas should be located as high above the ground as possible.

The numbers obtained should be used as a guide only. Actual installation and experience with specific equipment on-site will determine the actual quality of the video image received.

6.5.5 Infrared Atmospheric Transmission

A technique for transmitting a video signal by wireless means uses propagation of an IR beam of light through the atmosphere (Figure 6-40).

The light beam is generated by either an LED or an ILD in the transmitter. The receiver in the optical communication link uses a silicon-diode IR detector, amplifier, and output circuitry to drive the 75-ohm coaxial cable and monitor. The transmitter-to-receiver distance and security requirements of the link determine the type of diode used. Short-range transmissions of up to several hundred feet are accomplished using LED. To obtain good results for longer ranges, up to several miles under clear atmospheric conditions, ILD must be used.

The LED system costs less and has a wider beam, 10–20° wide, making it relatively simple to align the transmitter and receiver. The beam width of a typical ILD transmitter is 0.1° or 0.2°, making it more difficult to align and requiring that the mounting structure for both transmitter and the receiver be very stable in order to maintain alignment. To insure a good, stable signal strength at the receiver, the ILD transmitter and receiver must be securely mounted on the building structure. Additionally, the building structure must not sway, creep, vibrate, or produce appreciable twist due to uneven thermal heating (sun loading).

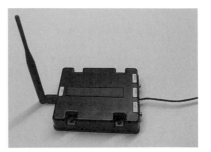

(A) MINIATURE TRANSMITTER
    WITH DIPOLE ANTENNA

    1.2 GHz, 2.4 GHz.

    4 CHANNEL

    POWER OUT: 100 mW

(B) SMALL TRANSMITTER AND
    RECEIVER WITH YAGGI ANTENNA

    2.4 GHz

    4 CHANNEL

    POWER OUT: 0.5 W

(C) RECEIVER WITH
    DIPOLE ANTENNA

    2.4 GHz

FIGURE 6-38   RF and microwave video transmitters

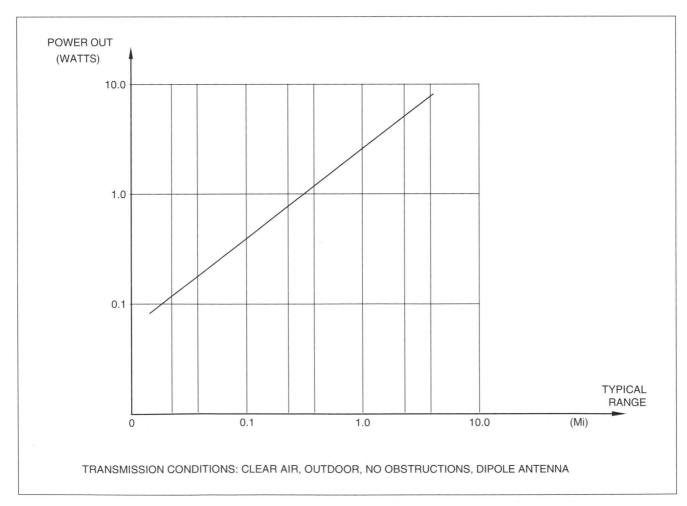

TRANSMISSION CONDITIONS: CLEAR AIR, OUTDOOR, NO OBSTRUCTIONS, DIPOLE ANTENNA

FIGURE 6-39   Transmitter RF power out vs. transmission range

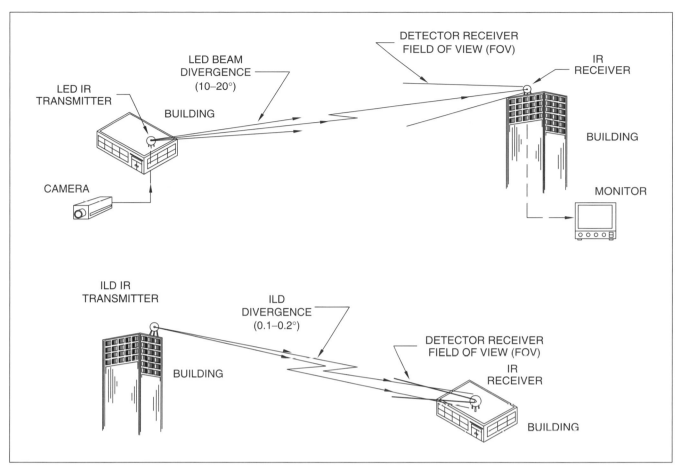

FIGURE 6-40   IR atmospheric video transmission system

Both LED and ILD systems can transmit the IR beam through most transparent window glazing; however, glazing with high tin content severely decreases signal transmission, thereby producing poor video quality. The suitability of the window can be determined only by testing the system. Since many applications require the IR beam to pass through window panes across a city street or between two buildings, window IR transmission tests should be performed prior to designing and installing such a system.

The primary advantages of the ILD system are long-range (under clear atmospheric conditions) and secure video, audio, and control signal transmission. ILD atmospheric links are hard to tap because the tapping device—a laser receiver—must be positioned into the laser beam, which is hard to accomplish undetected.

6.5.5.1 Transmission Path Considerations

Several transmission parameters must be considered in any atmospheric transmission link. Both LED and ILD atmospheric transmission s ystems suffer video signal transmission losses caused by atmosphere path absorption.

Molecular absorption is always present when a light beam travels through a gas (air). At certain wavelengths of light, the absorption in the air is so great as to make that wavelength useless for communications purposes. Wavelength ranges in which the attenuation by absorption is tolerable are called atmospheric windows. These windows have been extensively tabulated in the literature. All LED and ILD systems operate in these atmospheric windows.

Another cause of light signal absorption is particles such as dust and aerosols, which are always present in the atmosphere to some degree. These particles may reach very high concentrations in a geographical area near a body of water. In these locations, improved performance can be achieved by locating the link as high above the ground as possible.

Fog is a third factor causing severe absorption of the IR signal. In fog-prone areas, local weather conditions must be considered when specifying an atmospheric link, since the presence of fog will greatly influence link downtime. Figure 6-41 shows the predicted communication range vs. visibility for a practical LED or ILD atmospheric communications system.

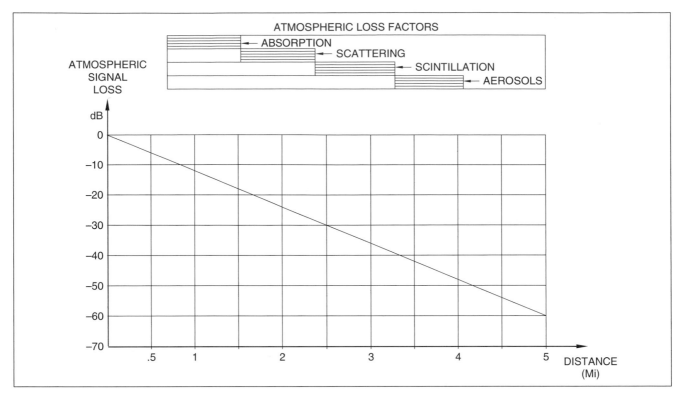

FIGURE 6-41 Atmospheric absorption factors and visibility

In addition to signal loss, the atmosphere contributes signal noise, since it exhibits some degree of turbulence. Turbulence causes a refractive index variation in the signal path (similar to the heat waves seen when there is solar heating in air—the mirage effect) and its subsequent wind-aided turbulent mixing. The net effect of this turbulence is to move or bend the IR beam in an unpredictable direction, so that the transmitter radiation does not reach the remote receiver. To compensate for this turbulence, the transmitter beam is made wide enough so that it is highly unlikely that the beam will miss the receiver. This wider beam, however, results in lower beam intensity, so the received signal on average will be less than from a narrower beam.

6.5.5.2 Infrared Equipment

The transmitter and receiver used in atmospheric IR transmission systems are very similar to those used in the fiber-optic-cable transmission system (Section 6.3.4). The primary differences are in the type of LED (or ILD) in the transmitter and the optics in both the transmitter and the receiver (Figure 6-42).

The optics in the transmitter must couple the maximum amount of light from the emitter into the lens and atmosphere, that is, to produce the specified beam divergence depending on LED or ILD usage. The receiver optics are made as large as practically possible (several inches in diameter) to maximize transmitter beam col-

lection, thereby achieving the highest possible S/N. An example of an atmospheric IR link is shown in Figure 6-43.

The system has a range of approximately 3000 feet and operates at 12 volts DC. For outdoor applications, the transmitter is mounted in an environmental housing with a thermostatically controlled heater and fan, as well as a window washer and wiper.

6.6 WIRELESS CONTROL SIGNAL TRANSMISSION

Signal multiplexing has been used to combine audio and control functions in time-division or frequency-division multiplexing. One system uses the telephone Touch-Tone system, which is standard throughout the world. With this system, an encoder generates a number code corresponding to the given switch (digit) closure. Each switch closure produces a dual Touch-Tone signal which is uniquely defined and recognized by the remote receiver station. All that is needed for transmitting the signal is a twisted-pair or telephone-grade line. With such a system, audio and all of the conceivable camera functions (pan, tilt, zoom focus, on/off, sequencing, and others) can be controlled with a single cable pair or single transmission channel. This concept offers a powerful means for controlling remote equipment with an existing transmission path.

It is sometimes advantageous to combine several video and/or audio and control signals onto one transmission

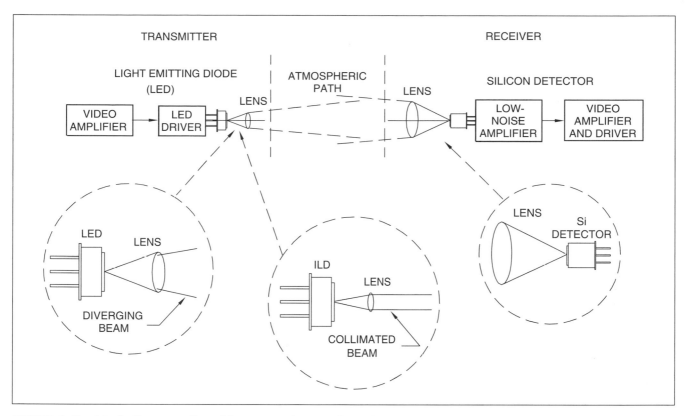

FIGURE 6-42   Block diagram of IR video transmitter and receiver

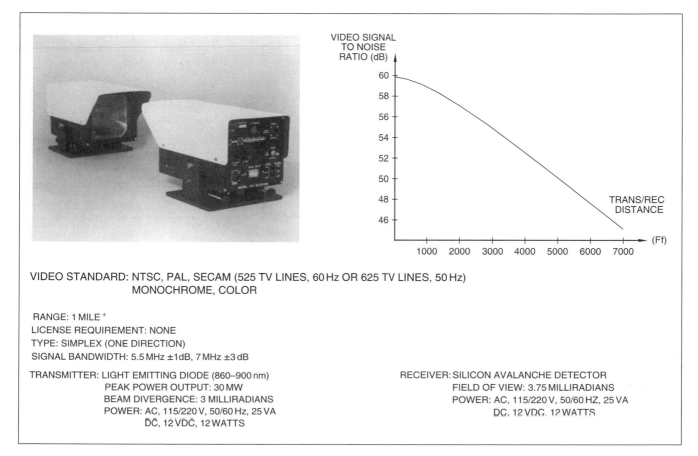

VIDEO STANDARD: NTSC, PAL, SECAM (525 TV LINES, 60 Hz OR 625 TV LINES, 50 Hz)
MONOCHROME, COLOR

RANGE: 1 MILE +
LICENSE REQUIREMENT: NONE
TYPE: SIMPLEX (ONE DIRECTION)
SIGNAL BANDWIDTH: 5.5 MHz ±1dB, 7 MHz ±3 dB

TRANSMITTER: LIGHT EMITTING DIODE (860–900 nm)
PEAK POWER OUTPUT: 30 MW
BEAM DIVERGENCE: 3 MILLIRADIANS
POWER: AC, 115/220 V, 50/60 Hz, 25 VA
DC, 12 VDC, 12 WATTS

RECEIVER: SILICON AVALANCHE DETECTOR
FIELD OF VIEW: 3.75 MILLIRADIANS
POWER: AC, 115/220 V, 50/60 HZ, 25 VA
DC, 12 VDC, 12 WATTS

FIGURE 6-43   IR video transmitter and receiver hardware

channel. This is true when a limited number of cables are available or when transmission is wireless. If cables are already in place or a wireless system is required, the hardware to multiplex the various functions onto one channel is cost-effective. Multiplexing of video signals is used in many CATV installations whereby several VHF and/or UHF video channels are simultaneously transmitted over a single coaxial cable or microwave link. In CCTV systems, modulators and demodulators are available to transmit the video control signals on the same coaxial cable used to transmit the video signal.

6.7   SIGNAL MULTIPLEXING/DE-MULTIPLEXING

It is sometimes desirable or necessary to combine several video signals onto one communications channel and transmit them from the camera location to the monitor location. This technique is called multiplexing. Some systems allow multiplexing video, control, and audio signals onto one channel.

6.7.1   Wideband Video Signal

The camera video signal is an analog base-band signal with frequencies of up to 6 MHz. When more than one video signal must be transmitted over a single wire or wireless channel the signals are multiplexed. This is accomplished by modulating the base-band camera signal with an RF (VHF or HF) or microwave frequency carrier and combining the multiple video signals onto the channel.

6.7.2   Audio and Control Signal

The analog and control signals can be multiplexed with the video signals as sub-carriers on each of the video signals. In the RF band no more than two channels at 928 MHz are practical. In the microwave band at 2.4 GHz up to four channels can be used. At 5.8 GHz up to eight channels can be used.

6.8   SECURE VIDEO TRANSMISSION

When it comes to protecting the integrity of the information on a signal, high-level security applications sometimes require the scrambling of video signals. The video scrambler is a privacy device that alters a television camera output signal to reduce the ability to recognize the transmitted signal when displayed on a standard monitor/receiver. The descrambler device restores the signal to permit retrieval of the original video information.

6.8.1   Scrambling

Video scrambling refers to an *analog* technique to hide, or make covert, the picture intelligence in the picture signal. Basic types include: (1) negative video, (2) moving the horizontal lines, (3) cutting and moving sections of the horizontal lines, and (4) altering or removing the synchronization pulses. All negative video requires that the signal modulator at the camera has some synchronization with the demodulator at the monitoring site.

The key to any analog video scrambling system is to modify one or more basic video signal parameters to prevent an ordinary television receiver or monitor from being able to receive a recognizable picture. The challenges in scrambling-system design are to make the signal secure without degrading the picture quality when it is reconstructed, to minimize the increase in bandwidth or storage requirements for the scrambled signal, and to make the system cost-effective.

There are basically two classes of scrambling techniques. The first modifies the signal with a fixed algorithm, that is, some periodic change in the signal. These systems are comparatively simple and inexpensive to build and are common in CATV pay television, as well as in some security applications. The signals can easily be descrambled once the scrambling code or technique has been discovered. It is relatively straightforward to devise and manufacture a descrambling unit to recover the video signal. One of the earliest techniques for modifying the standard video signal is called video inversion, in which the polarity of the video signal is inverted so that a black-on-white picture appears white-on-black (Figure 6-44).

While this technique destroys some of the intelligence in the picture, the content is still recognizable. Some scrambling systems employ a dynamic video-inversion technique: a parameter such as the polarity is inverted every few lines or fields in a pseudo-random fashion to make the image even more unintelligible. Another early technique was to suppress the vertical and/or horizontal synchronization pulses to cause the picture to roll or tear on the television monitor. Likewise, this technique produced some intelligence loss, but some television receivers could still lock on to the picture, or a descrambler could be built to re-insert the missing pulses and synchronize the picture, making it intelligible again.

A second class of scrambling systems using much more sophisticated techniques modifies the signal with an algorithm that continually changes in some unpredictable or pseudo-random fashion. These more complex dynamic scrambler systems require some communication channel between the transmitter and the receiver in order to provide the descrambling information to the receiver unit, which reconstructs the missing signal. This descrambling information is communicated either by some signal transmitted along with the television image or by some separate

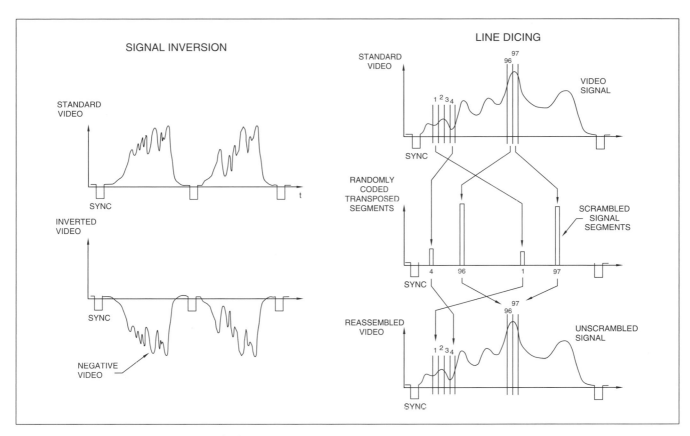

FIGURE 6-44   Video scrambling techniques

means, such as a different channel in the link. The decoding signal can be sent by telephone or other means.

In a much more secure technique known as "line dicing," each horizontal line of the video image is cut into segments that are then transmitted in random order, thereby displacing the different segments horizontally into new locations (Figure 6-44). A picture so constructed on a standard receiver has no intelligence whatsoever. Related to line dicing is a technique known as "line shuffling," in which the scan lines of the video signal are sent not in the normal top-to-bottom image format but in a pseudo-random or unpredictable sequence.

It is often necessary to scramble the audio signal in addition to the video signal, using techniques such as frequency hopping adapted from military technology. Similar to line dicing, this technique breaks up the audio signal into many different bits coming from four or five different audio channels and by jumping from one to another in a pseudo-random fashion scrambles the audio signal. The descrambler is equipped to tune to the different audio channels in synchronism with the transmitting signal, thereby recovering the audio information.

In the most sophisticated dynamic scrambling systems, utilized for direct-broadcast satellites and multi-channel applications, the video and audio signals are scrambled in a way that cannot be decoded even by the equipment manufacturer without the information from the signal

operator. For example, the audio signal can be digitized and then transmitted in the vertical blanking interval, the horizontal blanking interval, or on a separate sub-carrier of the television signal.

6.8.2 Encryption

Video *encryption* refers to digitizing and coding the video signal at the camera using a computer and then decoding the *digitized* signal at the receiver location with the corresponding digital decoder. Digital encryption results in a much higher level of security than analog scrambling. Section 7.7.4 analyzes digital encryption techniques in more detail.

6.9 CABLE TELEVISION

Cable television (CATV) systems distribute multiple channels of video in the VHF or UHF bands using coaxial cable, fiber-optic cable, and RF and microwave links. Consumer-based CATV employs this modulation–demodulation scheme using a coaxial or fiber-optic cable. The multiplexing technique is often used when video information from a large number of cameras must be transmitted to a large number of receivers in a network. Table 6-8 summarizes the VHF and UHF television frequencies used in these CATV RF transmission systems.

In CATV distribution systems, the equipment accepts base-band (composite video) and audio channels and linearly modulates them to any user-selected RF carrier in the UHF (470–770 MHz) spectrum. The modulated signal is then passed through an isolating combiner, where they are multiplexed with the other signals. The combined signal is then transmitted over a communications channel and separated at the receiver end into individual video and audio information channels. At the receiver end the signal is demodulated and the multiple camera signals are separated and presented on multiple monitors or switched one at a time (Figure 6-45).

Cable costs are significantly reduced by modulating multiple channels on a single cable. Since the transmission is done at radio frequencies, design and installation is far more critical as compared with base-band CCTV. High-quality CATV systems are now installed with fiber-optic cable for medium to long distances or distribution within a building.

6.10 ANALOG TRANSMISSION CHECKLIST

Transmitting the video, audio, and control signals faithfully is all important in any security system. This section itemizes some of the factors that should be considered in any design and analysis.

6.10.1 Wired Transmission

The following checklists for coaxial two-wire UTP, and fiber-optic cable transmission systems show some items that should be considered when designing and installing a video security project.

6.10.1.1 Coaxial Cable

1. When using coaxial cable, always terminate all unused inputs and unused outputs in their respective impedances.
2. When calculating coaxial-cable attenuation, always figure the attenuation at the highest frequency to be used; that is, when working with a 6 MHz bandwidth, refer to the cable losses at 6 MHz.
3. In long cable runs do not use an excessive number of connectors since each conductor causes additional attenuation. Avoid splicing coaxial cables without the use of proper connectors, since incorrect splices cause higher attenuation and can cause severe reflection of the signal and thus distortion.

BAND	CHANNEL DESIGNATION		FREQUENCY RANGE PICTURE CARRIER (MHz)	
CATV LOW-BAND	2 → 6 CH2 → CH6		55.25 → 67.25	
CATV MID-BAND	A5 → A1 CH95 → CH99		91.25 → 115.25	
CATV HIGH-BAND	7 → 13 CH23 → CH36		175.25 → 211.25	
CATV MID-BAND	A → I CH14 → CH22		121.25 → 169.25	
CATV SUPER-BAND	J → W CH23 → CH26		217.25 → 295.25	
CATV HYPER-BAND	AA → PPP CH37 → CH78		301.25 → 547.25	

NOTE:

AIRWAVE VHF TV CHANNELS 2–6
OPERATE FROM 55.25–83.25 MHz

AIRWAVE UHF TV CHANNELS 7–13
OPERATE FROM 175.25–211.25 MHz

AIRWAVE FM STATIONS OPERATE
FROM 88.1–107.9 MHz

Table 6-8   Allocated CATV RF Transmission Frequencies

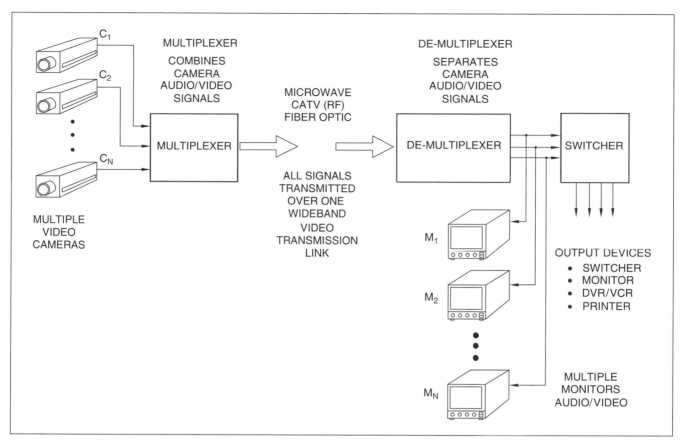

FIGURE 6-45   Multiplexed video transmission system

4. For outdoor applications, be sure that all connectors are waterproof and weatherproof; many are not, so consult the manufacturer.

5. Try to anticipate ground loop problems if unbalanced-coaxial-cable video runs between two power sources are used. Use fiber optics to avoid the problem.

6. Using a balanced coaxial cable (or fiber-optic cable) is usually worth the increased cost in long transmission systems. When connecting long cable runs between several buildings or power sources, measure the voltage before attempting to mate the cable connectors. Be careful, since the voltage between the cable and the connected equipment may be of sufficient potential to harm you.

7. Do not run cable lines adjacent to high-power RF sources such as power lines, heavy electrical equipment, other RFI sources, or electromagnetic sources. Good earth ground is essential when working with long transmission lines. Be sure that there is adequate grounding, and that the ground wire is eventually connected to a water pipe ground.

6.10.1.2 Two-Wire UTP

1. Choose a two-wire twisted-pair having approximately 1 twist for 1–2 inches of wire.

2. Choose a wire gauge between 24 AWG (smallest) and 16 AWG.

3. Choose a reputable UTP transmitter/receiver manufacture. Either have the manufacture supply technical specifications showing performance over the distance required or test the product first.

4. Will the UTP transmitter/receiver be powered from the camera or separate 12 VDC power supply?

6.10.1.3 Fiber-Optic Cable

1. Consider the use of fiber optics when the distance between camera and monitor is more than a few hundred feet (depending on the environment), if it is a color system, and if the camera and monitor are in different buildings or powered by different AC power sources.

2. If the cable is outdoors and above ground, use fiber optics to avoid atmospheric disturbance from lightning.

3. If the cable run is through a hazardous chemical or electrical area, use fiber optics.

4. Use fiber optics when a high-security link is required.

6.10.2 Wireless Transmission

The following checklists for RF, microwave, and IR transmission systems should be considered when designing and installing a video security. The wireless video transmission techniques require more careful scrutiny because of the many variables that can influence the overall performance and success of the system.

6.10.2.1 Radio Frequency (RF)

1. How many channels does the system require? At 928 MHz the maximum number of channels is two to avoid crosstalk between channels.
2. Are all cameras approximately in the same location? If in different locations the crosstalk is minimized.
3. RF transmission is susceptible to external electrical interference. Are there probable interferences in the area?
4. Range is a function of the transmitter power and intervening atmosphere and objects (buildings, trees, etc.). Is there a line of sight between the transmitter and the receiver?
5. Is the transmission path indoors or outdoors?
6. For indoor transmission, reflection and absorption of all objects must be taken into consideration. RF transmission does not penetrate metal objects and is partially absorbed by other materials.
7. For outdoor transmission, obstructions such as trees, buildings, etc. must be considered.

6.10.2.2 Microwave

1. How many channels does the system require? At 2.4 GHz the maximum number of channels is four and for 5.8 GHz is 8 if crosstalk between channels is to be avoided.
2. Are all cameras approximately in the same location? If they are in different locations the crosstalk is minimized.
3. Microwave transmission is susceptible to external interference from other microwave or noise sources. Are there probable interferences in the transmission path?
4. Range is a function of the transmitter power and intervening atmosphere and objects (buildings trees, etc.). Is there a line of sight between the transmitter and receiver? If not metal panels can be used to redirect the microwave transmission.
5. Is the transmission path indoor or outdoor?
6. For indoor transmission, reflection and absorption of metal objects must be taken into consideration, as well

as other building materials. Microwave energy does not transmit through metal objects and only partially through nonmetal.
7. For outdoor transmission, obstructions such as trees, buildings, etc. must be considered.

6.10.2.3 Infrared

1. Infrared transmission is very sensitive to the intervening atmosphere. Dust, fog, and humidity play an important role in the transmission and cause absorption and scattering of the IR signal.
2. Is there a line of sight between the IR transmitter and receiver; no obstructions?
3. Can a mirror be used to "see around a corner"?
4. Are the transmitter (most important) and receiver units mounted on a sturdy nonvibrating mounting. Are the buildings stable and motionless under high wind, and over full sun loading conditions?
5. Is secure transmission needed?

6.11 SUMMARY

Video signal transmission is a key component in any CCTV installation. Success requires a good understanding of transmission systems.

Most systems use coaxial cable, but fiber-optic cable is gaining acceptance because of its better picture quality (particularly with color) and lower risk factor with respect to ground loops and electrical interference. In special situations where coaxial or fiber-optic cable is inappropriate, other wired or wireless means are used, such as RF, microwave, or light-wave transmission. For very long range applications, non-real-time slow-scan systems are appropriate.

Many security system designers consider cabling to be less important than choosing the camera and lens and other monitoring equipment in a CCTV application. Often they attempt to cut costs on cabling equipment and installation time, since they often make up a large fraction of the total system cost. Such equipment is not visible and can seem like an unimportant accessory. However, such cost-cutting can drastically weaken the overall system performance and picture quality.

Chapter 7
Digital Transmission—Video, Communications, Control

CONTENTS

7.1 Overview
    7.1.1 Migration from Analog to Digital
    7.1.2 Local Area Network (LAN), Wide Area Network (WAN), Wireless LAN (WiFi)
    7.1.3 Internet
    7.1.4 Wireless 802.11, Spread Spectrum Modulation (SSM)
    7.1.5 Digital Video Recorder (DVR), Network DVR (NDVR)
    7.1.6 Network Security, Hackers, Viruses, Reliability
7.2 Communication Channels
    7.2.1 Wired Channels
        7.2.1.1 Local Area Network (LAN)
        7.2.1.2 Power over Ethernet (PoE)
        7.2.1.3 Wide Area Network (WAN)
        7.2.1.4 Internet, World Wide Web (WWW)
        7.2.1.5 Leased Land Lines, DSL, Cable
            7.2.1.5.1 PSTN-ISDN Link
            7.2.1.5.2 DSL Link
            7.2.1.5.3 T1 and T3 Links
            7.2.1.5.4 Cable
        7.2.1.6 Fiber Optic
    7.2.2 Wireless Channels
        7.2.2.1 Wireless LAN (WLAN, WiFi)
        7.2.2.2 Mesh Network
        7.2.2.3 Multiple Input/Multiple Output (MIMO)
        7.2.2.4 Environmental Factors: Indoor–Outdoor
        7.2.2.5 Broadband Microwave
        7.2.2.6 Infrared (IR)
7.3 Video Image Quality
    7.3.1 Quality of Service (QoS)
    7.3.2 Resolution vs. Frame Rate
    7.3.3 Picture Integrity, Dropout

7.4 Video Signal Compression
    7.4.1 Lossless Compression
    7.4.2 Lossy Compression
        7.4.2.1 Direct Cosine Transform (DCT)
        7.4.2.2 Discrete Wavelet Transform (DWT)
    7.4.3 Video Compression Algorithms
        7.4.3.1 Joint Picture Experts Group: JPEG
        7.4.3.2 Moving—Joint Picture Experts Group: M-JPEG
        7.4.3.3 Moving Picture Experts Group: MPEG-2, MPEG-4, MPEG-4 Visual
            7.4.3.3.1 MPEG-2 Standard
            7.4.3.3.2 MPEG-4 Standard
            7.4.3.3.3 MPEG-4 Visual Standard
        7.4.3.4 MPEG-4 Advanced Video Coding (AVC)/H.264
        7.4.3.5 JPEG 2000, Wavelet
        7.4.3.6 Other Compression Methods: H.263, SMICT
            7.4.3.6.1 H.263 Standard
            7.4.3.6.2 SMICT Standard
7.5 Internet-Based Remote Video Monitoring—Network Configurations
    7.5.1 Point to Multi-Point
    7.5.2 Point to Point
    7.5.3 Multi-Point to Point
    7.5.4 Video Unicast and Multicast
7.6 Transmission Technology Protocols: WiFi, Spread Spectrum Modulation (SSM)
    7.6.1 Spread Spectrum Modulation (SSM)
        7.6.1.1 Background
        7.6.1.2 Frequency Hopping Spread Spectrum Technology (FHSS)
        7.6.1.3 Slow Hoppers
        7.6.1.4 Fast Hoppers

7.6.1.5   Direct Sequence Spread Spectrum (DSSS)
7.6.2   WiFi Protocol: 802.11 Standards
7.6.2.1   802.11b Standard
7.6.2.2   802.11a Standard
7.6.2.3   802.11g Standard
7.6.2.4   802.11n Standard
7.6.2.5   802.11i Standard
7.6.3   Asynchronous Transfer Mode (ATM)
7.7   Transmission Network Security
7.7.1   Wired Equivalent Privacy (WEP)
7.7.2   Virtual Private Network (VPN)
7.7.3   WiFi Protected Access (WPA)
7.7.4   Advanced Encryption Standard (AES), Digital Encryption Standard (DES)
7.7.5   Firewalls, Viruses, Hackers
7.8   Internet Protocol Network Camera, Address
7.8.1   Internet Protocol Network Camera
7.8.2   Internet Protocol Camera Protocols
7.8.3   Internet Protocol Camera Address
7.9   Video Server, Router, Switch
7.9.1   Video Server
7.9.2   Video Router/Access Point
7.9.3   Video Switch
7.10   Personal Computer, Laptop, PDA, Cell Phone
7.10.1   Personal Computer, Laptop
7.10.2   Personal Digital Assistant (PDA)
7.10.3   Cell Phone
7.11   Internet Protocol Surveillance Systems: Features, Checklist, Pros, Cons
7.11.1   Features
7.11.2   Checklist
7.11.3   Pros
7.11.4   Cons
7.12   Summary

7.1 OVERVIEW

7.1.1 Migration from Analog to Digital

The video security industry is migrating from a technology of CCTV to open circuit television (OCTV) and Automated Video Surveillance (AVS). The OCTV and the AVS technologies make use of networked digital surveillance and digital surveillance systems. There is little doubt that connecting all video cameras directly to a digital video network is becoming commonplace and cost effective in new and existing systems. Classes of video applications using these networking technologies to advantage are: (1) remote video surveillance, (2) remote video alarm verification, (3) rapid deployment video and alarm systems, and (4) remote access to stored digital video images. The OCTV permits multiple security operators to manage many remote facilities, and allows almost instantaneous

monitoring of remote sites via these digital networks. Systems using existing analog video cameras can connect to the Internet via digital servers thereby providing remote site surveillance and camera control. The AVS is achieved through the use of *smart* cameras that can "learn," and the use of other "intelligent" algorithms and electronics that make decisions based on past experience. This "artificial intelligence" significantly reduces the number of decisions the guard must make.

The fastest-growing market segment in the video security field is digital video surveillance. The security industry is rapidly moving toward AVS in which smart cameras and sensors "learn" and make decisions and provide the security officer with enough information to act.

Prior to the year 2001, camera systems were primarily used to catch the bad guys after a crime had been committed. If a large competent well-trained security team was available, the thief or criminal could be caught in the act. The primary video surveillance functions were to:

- Catch perpetrators
- Watch workers
- Protect from litigation
- Watch a perimeter of the facility
- Monitor traffic
- Protect assets.

With more sophisticated analog video systems and the migration to wired and wireless digital local area networks (LAN), intranets, and Internet networks, the security system provided additional functions to:

- Monitor suspicious activities to *prevent* illegal activity
- Identify and apprehend perpetrators of a crime
- All the other activities listed above.

Historically CCTV systems were *closed* and proprietary networks that were controlled by the security manager. Now analog video systems, access control, intrusion detection, fire, safety, environmental sensors, and control and communication systems are often *open* and video images and information are sent over digital networks to multiple managers and multiple sites. From an economic point of view it makes sense to have all these sensors distributed throughout a facility or enterprise and monitored by multiple managers and facilitators. The video security requirements are now often added to the backbone of the information technology (IT) structure. This is in contrast to the analog CCTV methodology that requires individual video feeds connected to a security console with dedicated monitors and recorders and printers that do not operate on a local digital network, an intranet, or the Internet.

The full impact of video surveillance using wireless cameras, monitors, and servers has yet to be realized. Wireless video surveillance is rapidly growing in popularity for monitoring remote locations whether from a personal computer (PC), laptop, personal digital assistant (PDA), or cell phone.

Remote video surveillance systems have three main functions: (1) recording the surveillance camera image, (2) playback of the surveillance image and search of specific event stored video, and (3) remote control of security equipment. The first step in the transmission process for remote video surveillance occurs when the cameras capture visual images from the surveillance area. The cameras (the input terminal) view the target areas, compress the video signals, and transmit them via a transmission means. The monitoring location(s) or control terminal receives the signals and de-compresses them back into visual images, usually achieving near real-time transmission and viewing of them. In an analog system this process involves converting the input signals from analog to digital form and then back to analog form for display on a video monitor, and/or recording on an analog VCR. The video signal is left in digital form when it is recorded on a digital DVR and displayed on an LCD, plasma, or other digital monitor. Networked transmission allows the user to remotely adjust the P/T/Z, focus and aperture (iris diaphragm) settings of the camera at any time from the remote monitoring location. Video monitoring is simplified through the use of digital video motion detectors (DVMDs) and smart cameras. Simultaneous monitoring and control from multiple geographical locations is often required. The video security industry is experiencing revolutionary changes brought upon by digital information technology (IT). This shift in video security from analog to digital began when the analog VCR was replaced by the DVR.

The recent phase of this technology has advanced to the utilization of wired and wireless IT systems and networks. Video systems are expected to be full-time: 24/7/365 video surveillance, voice communications, and control.

7.1.2 Local Area Network (LAN), Wide Area Network (WAN), Wireless LAN (WiFi)

The digital signal transmission channels now available include local area network (LAN), wide area network (WAN), wireless LAN (WLAN, WiFi), intranet, Internet, and World Wide Web (WWW).

7.1.3 Internet

At the core of remote monitoring is a basic network infrastructure exemplified by network cameras, video servers, and computers. All these equipments communicate via a standard called the Internet protocol (IP). The IP is the ideal solution for remote monitoring since it allows users to connect and manage video, audio, data, control PTZ, and other communications over a single network that is accessible to users anywhere in the world. This data is available in most cases by a standard Web browser

and Internet access that can be found on any desktop PC, laptop, and many PDAs and cell phones.

Video servers include an analog camera video input, an image digitizer, an image compressor, a Web server and network connection. The servers digitize the video from the analog cameras and transmit them over the computer network, essentially turning an analog camera into a network camera.

7.1.4 Wireless 802.11, Spread Spectrum Modulation (SSM)

A key component to the digital transmission means is a technology called spread spectrum modulation (SSM). In this type of modulation a transmission code is combined with the information carrying base-band video signal and transmitted over the wireless network. The effect of "spreading" the signal over a wide spectrum of bandwidth provides the ability to transmit many different signals in the same allotted bandwidth with high security. This SSM communication has long been a favorite technology of the military because of its resistance to interception and jamming and was adopted in the Institute of Electrical and Electronic Engineers (IEEE) 802.11 series of transmission standards for digital transmission applications including digital video. The subsets of 802.11 applicable to video transmission are 802.11a, b, c, g, i, and the new n. The SSM technology is used in digital cellular phones, some advanced alarm systems, and radar—just to name a few common applications. The advantages of the technology include cost, bandwidth efficiency, and security. The SSM signals are difficult to detect and are therefore difficult to jam because they produce little or no interference. The products utilizing this technology operate in a license-exempt category. There are no charges to the user from any company or government agency.

7.1.5 Digital Video Recorder (DVR), Network DVR (NDVR)

The digital video recorder (DVR) has been a significant innovation in the video security market. It has rapidly replaced the analog VCR as a means for storing video images. The DVR using lossy or lossless digital compression provides the ability to store video images with little or no degradation. The DVR provides a highly advanced search capability for looking back at recorded images. The DVR also incorporates features such as video motion detection, the ability to have multi-users view the recorded video, and the ability to perform PTZ control functions from the monitoring and recording site. The DVR provides a significant upgrade in image quality and flexibility and serves as an excellent replacement for the analog VCR.

An alternative to the DVR is the network DVR (NDVR). This digital Internet solution takes the streaming (real-time) and non-streaming video from cameras and records them on computers on the network. This makes them available to anyone having access on the network and makes use of the storage capability of the network. Advantages of the NDVR on the IP surveillance system over DVR technology make a strong case for it to be the system of choice for today's enterprise-level surveillance solutions.

The wide bandwidth and high information content of the video signal requires that it be compressed by some means when transmitted over the network. At present there are several compression technologies that operate with wired and wireless digital networks. They each have their own application areas with advantages and disadvantages. Three formats that are very efficient for video transmission are designated by MPEG-2, MPEG-4, and H.264 developed by the Motion Picture Experts Group, an industry standards committee. These compression standards permit near real-time transmission of video images with sufficient resolution and quality for surveillance applications and makes the camera scenes available for remote observation via Internet browsers.

7.1.6 Network Security, Hackers, Viruses, Reliability

An important aspect of the digital revolution is that of security from hackers, viruses, and other adversaries. The digital system must be safeguarded against these intruders via password protection, virtual private networks (VPNs), encryption, and firewalls. Viruses are abundant on the Internet, and must be guarded against when using a remote digital monitoring system. The VPN is a private data network that makes use of the public telecommunication infrastructure, maintaining privacy through the use of firewall protocols and security procedures. Today many companies are using a VPN for both extranets and wide area intranets. Higher levels of security are obtained through the use of WiFi protected access (WPA), digital encryption standard (DES), and advanced encryption standard (AES). A firewall is typically located at the boundary between the Internet and corporate network and controls access into the network. It also defines who has access outside of the network. The firewall is, in physical terms, the access control for the network.

As with any form of video networking, keeping the information safe and error-free is imperative. Errors and contamination are: man-made, due to an equipment failure, external interference, hackers, or viruses. The security industry must put forth all efforts to ensure the information is accurate. State-of-the-art image authentication software has increased the reliability of digital video monitoring by preventing signal tampering. These methods can be incorporated in special compression codes, using date/time stamping or the summation of pixel changes. Demonstrating that the video signal and image has not been tampered with helps ensure the acceptance of this information in a court of law.

7.2 COMMUNICATION CHANNELS

This chapter treats all of the video digital transmission networks including the Internet transmission media with its unique protocols, standards, signal compression, and security requirements. It addresses the specific algorithms required to compress the video frame information image sizes to make them compatible with the existing bandwidths available in wired and wireless transmission channels. It describes the powerful SSM technology used to transmit the digital signal and the industry standard 802.11 SSM protocols relating to video, voice, command, and control transmission.

Digital transmission channels include LAN, WAN, MAN, WiFi, intranet, Internet, and WWW, transmitted via IP and viewed through a Web browser.

The most common form of digital transmission suitable for video transmission is the LAN that is traditionally interconnected via a two-wire unshielded twisted-pair (UTP), coaxial cable, or fiber-optic. When connecting to multiple sites and remote locations the WAN, MAN, and WiFi are the transmission means. When cables are difficult or impossible to install, WiFi is used to transmit to all the different communication devices and locations. The WiFi serves the same purpose as that of a wired or optical LAN: it communicates information among the different devices attached to the LAN but *without* the use of cables. When implementing WiFi transmission there is no physical cabling connecting the different devices together from the monitoring site to the camera locations. These digital channels use 802.11 with all the different variations of the standard using the SSM technology.

The primary factors dictating the choice of a network type for interconnecting different surveillance sites are: (1) the integrity and guaranteed availability of the network connection, (2) the availability of a backup signal path, (3) the data carrying capacity (bandwidth) of the network, and (4) the operating costs for using the network. Wireless can bring a significant reduction for installation labor required when running or moving cabling within a building or from building to building.

7.2.1 Wired Channels

Where video monitoring already exists, wired digital video transmission is accomplished by converting the analog video signal into a digital signal, and then transmitting the digitized camera video signal over a suitable network via modem. At the remote monitoring location a modem converts the digital video signal back into an analog signal. Customers can use their existing telephone service to transmit the video signal. The systems used in the 1980s and early 1990s were generally referred to as *slow-scan* video transmission (Chapter 6). The video equipment often interfaces with alarm intrusion sensors to produce an alarm signal and the video images serve as an assessment of the alarm intrusion.

Wired digital video transmission works especially well in panic alarm situations where a remote location is connected to a central alarm station. If an alarm at a remote location is activated or if a person initiates an alarm with a panic button, a video clip from the camera prior to the alarm, during the alarm, and after the alarm at the remote location is sent to the monitoring station. The operator at the central-station is able to forward the video clip to the police, who now are prepared for what the situation is, how many people were involved, and if there were any weapons. The police can use the video clip to identify and apprehend them.

These systems use the dial-up or public switched telephone network (PSTN) sometimes referred to as the plain old telephone service (POTS) and both are still a common transmitting means. Since the telephone service was designed for the human voice it is not very suitable for high-speed, wide bandwidth video transmission. The wired phone system has a maximum bandwidth of 3000 Hz and a maximum modem bit rate of 56 Kbps. However, only about 40 Kbps is normally realized. A slightly improved version of PSTN is the integrated services data network (ISDN) that gives direct access to digital data transmission at data rates of 64 Kbps.

Since many corporations have already set up LAN/WAN networking systems for IT business applications, the next logical expansion is to these networks for complete integration of video surveillance. A major advantage of IP-addressed, network-capable video devices is the ability to receive a signal *anywhere* using equipment ranging from a simple network Internet browser to special client-based application software products. The high bandwidth requirements for full-frame high-quality video without compression exceed the capability of most WAN network connections. On average, a low-quality image transmitted via networks requires 256 Kbps and can reach 1 Mbps if image quality and refresh rates are increased. Even LANs would be strained as large numbers of cameras attempted to simultaneously pass video signals back to a central video server, DVR, or both.

7.2.1.1 Local Area Network (LAN)

The most common and most extensively installed LAN is the Ethernet. This network is specified in the IEEE 802.3 standard and was originally developed by the Xerox Corporation, and further developed by Xerox, DEC, and Intel corporations. The typical Ethernet LAN uses a coaxial cable or special grade of twisted-pair wires for transmission (Figure 7-1).

For long ranges or transmission through areas having electrical interference, the Ethernet can use fiber-optic transmission technology. The most common lowest bandwidth Ethernet systems is called 10BASE-T and can provide transmission speeds up to 10 Mbps. For fast Ethernet connections a 100BASE-T is used and provides speeds up to 100 Mbps. Gigabit Ethernet systems provide an even higher speed of transmission of 1000 Mbps (1 Gigabit = one billion bits per second). The latter two are used as the backbone for digital transmission systems. Video systems generally use the 10Base-T or 100Base-T networks. WANs connect LANs to form a large structured network sometimes called an *intranet*. These networks can be connected inside buildings and from building to building, and connected to the Internet.

7.2.1.2 Power over Ethernet (PoE)

The PoE, also referred to as power over LAN (PoL) is a technology that integrates data *and* power over standard LAN infrastructure cabled networks (Figure 7-2).

The PoE is a means to supply reliable, uninterrupted power to network cameras, wireless LAN access points, and other Ethernet devices using existing, commonly used category (CAT) cable with four twisted pair conductors and CAT5 cable infrastructure (Figure 7-3).

The PoE is a technology for wired Ethernet LANs that allows the electrical power (current and voltage) necessary for the operation of each device to be carried by the data cables rather than by power cords. This minimizes the number of wires that must be strung in order to install the network. The result is lower cost, less downtime, easier maintenance, and greater installation flexibility than with traditional wiring. Unlike a traditional telephone infrastructure, local power is not always accessible for wireless access points, IP video cameras, phones, or other network devices deployed in ceilings, lobbies, stairwells, or other obscure areas. Adding new wiring for power may be a difficult and costly option. In cases like this, an option is to combine the provision of power with the network connection using PoE technology over any existing or new data communications cabling.

The standard was developed by the IEEE as 802.3af. The standard Ethernet cable uses only two of those pairs for 10BaseT or 100BaseT transmission. Because the Ethernet data pairs are transformer-coupled at each end of the cable, either the spare pairs or the data pairs can be used to power powered-device (PD) equipment. At the power source end of the cable, the power source equipment may apply power to either the spare pairs or the data pair of that cable, but not to both simultaneously. Also the power source equipment may not apply power to non-PoE devices if they are connected to the cable. The PoE uses 48 VDC designated as safety extra low-voltage (SELV) providing

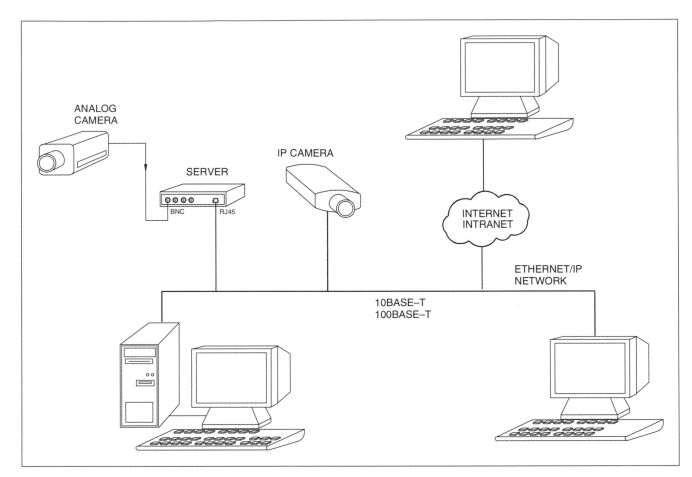

FIGURE 7-1   Ethernet local area network (LAN)

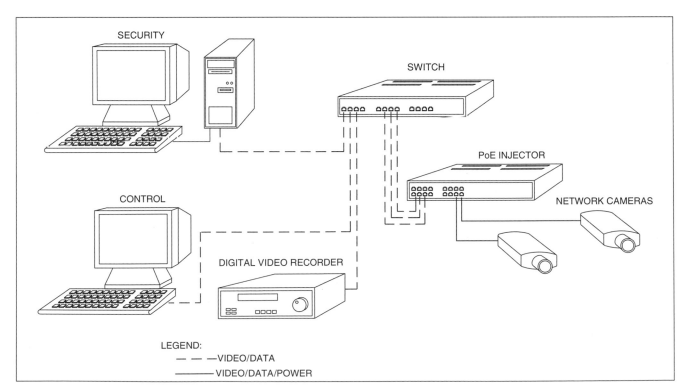

FIGURE 7-2   Digital video network using Power over Ethernet (PoE)

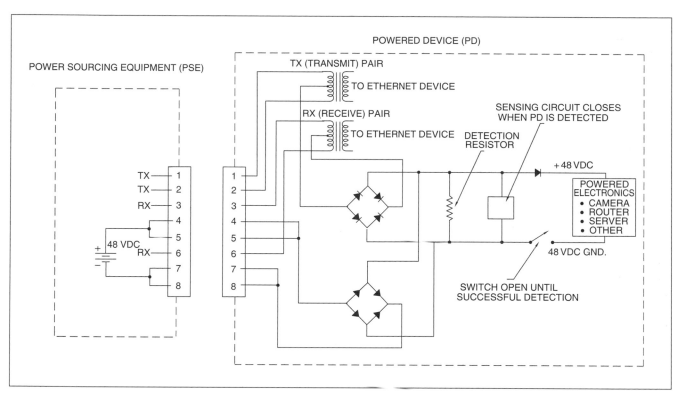

FIGURE 7-3   Power over Ethernet (PoE) connections

an additional safety factor. The PoE has the capability of powering up to a 13 watt load. Table 7-1 summarizes the characteristics of UTP CAT Cables.

The PoE avoids the need for separate power and data cable infrastructure and costly AC outlets near cameras. It reduces installation time, a significant saving in cost. It allows networks cameras to be installed where they are most effective, and not where the AC power outlets reduce the number of cameras and further reduce the surveillance implementation costs. Power delivered over the LAN

CAT CABLE TYPE	BANDWIDTH (MHz)	IMPEDANCE (ohms)	CROSS TALK *NEXT (dB)	APPLICATION
CAT-3	16	100	29	10BaseT LAN STANDARD ETHERNET
CAT-4	20	100	30	10/100BaseT LAN FAST ETHERNET
CAT-5	100	100	32.3	10/100BaseT FAST ETHERNET
CAT-5e	100	100	35.3	1 Mb/s GIGABIT ETHERNET
CAT-6	250	100	44.3	1Mb/s GIGABIT ETHERNET
CAT-7	600	100	62.1	1 Mb/s GIGABIT ETHERNET

* NEAR END CROSS TALK

NOTE: CABLE SPECIFICATIONS TYPICAL FOR UNSHIELDED TWISTED PAIR (UTP)
        AWG (AMERICAN WIRE GUAGE) 22 AND 24
        CAT-3, CAT-5e MOST COMMON FOR VIDEO

Table 7-1   Category (CAT) Cable Specifications

infrastructure is automatically activated when a compatible terminal is identified, and blocked to legacy analog devices that are not compatible. This allows the mixture of analog and power over LAN compatible devices on the same network. Two system types are available: (1) power is supplied directly from the data ports; (2) power is supplied by a device between an ordinary Ethernet switch and the terminals, often referred to as the "power hub." By backing up the power over LAN in the communication room with an uninterrupted power supply (UPS), the entire camera network can continue operation during a power outage. *This is a real must for high-end surveillance systems.*

The inclusion of line detection technology that enables safe equipment installation without concerns of high-voltage damage to laptops, desktops, and other equipment due to a misplaced connection is one of the reasons the power over LAN is much more than an intelligent power source. To take advantage of PoE the power source equipment must be able to detect the presence of a PD at the end of any Ethernet cable connected to it. The PD appliances must assert their PoE compatibility and their maximum power requirements. When the system is powered up the PoE enabled LAN appliances identify themselves by means of a nominal $25\,\text{K}\Omega$ resistance across their power input.

7.2.1.3 Wide Area Network (WAN)

The WANs, in the past, suffered from limited bandwidth. The most common WAN link was a T1 telephone land line supplied by AT&T with a maximum data rate of 1.5 Mbps. Advanced technology WAN systems now incorporate optical OC3 (155 Mbps) and OC12 (622 Mbps) communication links. Figure 7-4 shows a diagram of the WAN as applied to digital video surveillance.

7.2.1.4 Internet, World Wide Web (WWW)

During the 1990s an *open systems* revolution swept through the IT industry, converting thousands of computers connected via proprietary networks to the Internet, a network of networks based on common *standards*. These standards were called transmission control protocol/Internet protocol (TCP/IP) for communications, simple mail transfer protocol (SMTP) for email, hypertext transfer protocol (HTTP, http://) for displaying web pages, and file transfer protocol (FTP) for exchanging files between computers on the Internet. The Internet has made long-range video security monitoring a reality for many security applications (Figure 7-5).

The availability of high-speed computers, large solid state memory, the Internet, and the WWW has brought CCTV surveillance from a legacy analog technology to an OCTV digital technology. The WWW, also known as *The Web*, is a salient contributor to the success of OCTV and AVS. The WWW was developed at the CERN, the European laboratory for Particle Physics in Geneva, Switzerland, by Tim Berners-Lee. The web is a multi-platform operating system that supports multimedia communications on the basis of a Graphical User Interface (GUI). The GUI provides *hypertext* that enables the user to click a highlighted text word in search related files, across web servers, and through hot links: in other words the Web is hyperlinked. In addition to the video, the Web supports graphics and audio with levels of quality and speed depending on the bandwidth available in the network. Since the initial conception of the Web at CERN, its home has moved to the W3 Consortium (W3C), a cooperative venture of CERN, the Massachusetts Institute of Technology (MIT), and INRIA a European organization. Since its organization in 1994 W3C has published numerous technical specifications to improve and expand the use of the WWW.

Security monitoring is no longer limited to local security rooms and security officers, but rather extends out to remote sites and personnel located anywhere around the world. Monitoring equipment includes LCD and plasma display monitors, PCs and laptops, PDAs, and cell phones. The requirement for individual personnel to monitor multiple display monitors has changed to a technology of incorporating smart cameras and VMDs to establish an AVS system.

The Internet is comprised of LANs using a large array of interconnected computers through which video and other communication information is sent over wired and wireless transmission channels. The location of the sender and receiver can be anywhere on the network, viewing scenes from anywhere in the world (Figure 7-6).

The IP is the *method* by which the digital data can be sent from one computer to another over the Internet in the form of *packets*. Any message on the Internet is divided into these sub-messages called packets containing both the senders and receivers address. Because the video message is divided into many packets, each packet may take a different route through a different gateway computer across the Internet. These packets can arrive in a different order than the order in which they were sent. The IP just has the function to deliver them to the receiver's address. It is up to another protocol, the TCP to *put them back together in the right order.*

Each computer on the network is known as a *host* on the Internet and has at least one address that uniquely identifies it from all the other computers on the network. The digital message can consist of an email, a web page, video, or other digital data. When the video or other data stream is sent out over the Internet a *router* (in the form of software or hardware) determines the next network to which a packet in the message should be forwarded toward its final destination. The packet does not go directly from the sender (transmitted location, i.e. camera, etc.) to the receiver but generally goes through a *gateway* computer

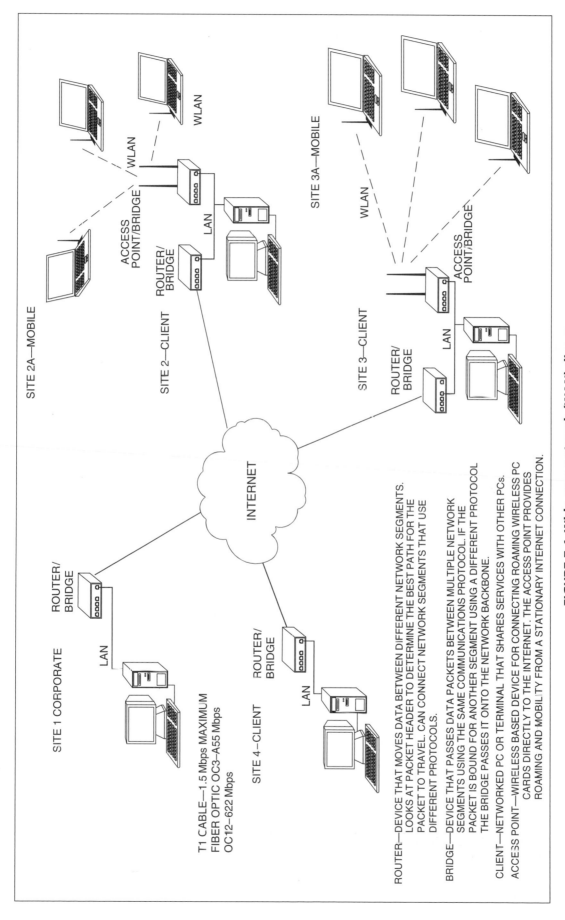

FIGURE 7-4 Wide area network (WAN) diagram

ROUTER—DEVICE THAT MOVES DATA BETWEEN DIFFERENT NETWORK SEGMENTS. LOOKS AT PACKET HEADER TO DETERMINE THE BEST PATH FOR THE PACKET TO TRAVEL. CAN CONNECT NETWORK SEGMENTS THAT USE DIFFERENT PROTOCOLS.

BRIDGE—DEVICE THAT PASSES DATA PACKETS BETWEEN MULTIPLE NETWORK SEGMENTS USING THE SAME COMMUNICATIONS PROTOCOL. IF THE PACKET IS BOUND FOR ANOTHER SEGMENT USING A DIFFERENT PROTOCOL THE BRIDGE PASSES IT ONTO THE NETWORK BACKBONE.

CLIENT—NETWORKED PC OR TERMINAL THAT SHARES SERVICES WITH OTHER PCs.

ACCESS POINT—WIRELESS BASED DEVICE FOR CONNECTING ROAMING WIRELESS PC CARDS DIRECTLY TO THE INTERNET. THE ACCESS POINT PROVIDES ROAMING AND MOBILITY FROM A STATIONARY INTERNET CONNECTION.

T1 CABLE—1.5 Mbps MAXIMUM
FIBER OPTIC OC3–A55 Mbps
OC12–622 Mbps

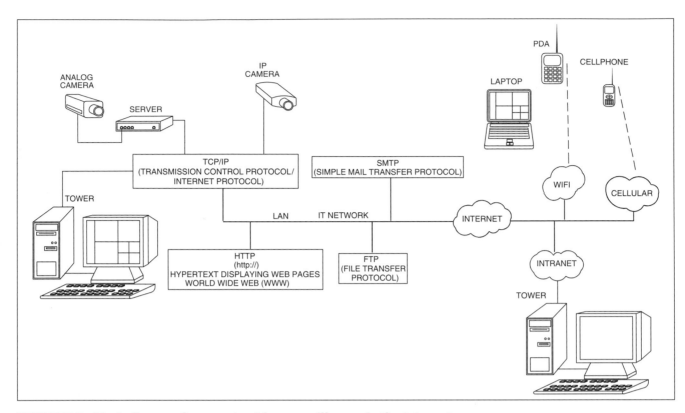

FIGURE 7-5   Block diagram for remote video surveillance via the Internet

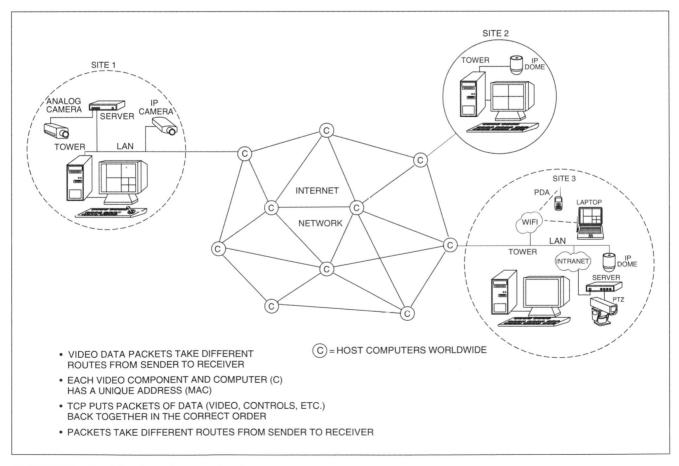

- VIDEO DATA PACKETS TAKE DIFFERENT
  ROUTES FROM SENDER TO RECEIVER
- EACH VIDEO COMPONENT AND COMPUTER (C)
  HAS A UNIQUE ADDRESS (MAC)
- TCP PUTS PACKETS OF DATA (VIDEO, CONTROLS, ETC.)
  BACK TOGETHER IN THE CORRECT ORDER
- PACKETS TAKE DIFFERENT ROUTES FROM SENDER TO RECEIVER

Ⓒ = HOST COMPUTERS WORLDWIDE

FIGURE 7-6   Worldwide video monitoring using Internet system

that forwards the packet onto a next computer toward its final destination.

The Internet allows for complete remote video surveillance, audio communication, and remote control from any one location to any other location on the network.

As soon as a network is connected to the Internet, any authorized computer with a browser can receive security services. For that matter, any security system, even a system that is not networked, can be potentially made Internet based, fully or partially, the moment Internet access is provided.

Traditional central stations are connected to the security systems being monitored by means of a network connection (Ethernet), a telephone dial-up, direct hard wire connection, satellite uplink, or by radio signal. Product literature that sites either "IP addressable" or "TCP/IP" reveals that the product (IP camera, etc.) has some potential for network or Internet-based applications.

An important movement in the Internet industry is the development of application service providers (ASPs). A commercial central station could operate as a security ASP, just as an ASP could monitor security alarms that are reported across the Internet. This could be carried a step further in an example such as connecting police departments, enabling the police not only to view and hear what is happening at a crime scene, but to follow events as they occur before a police response arrives.

7.2.1.5 *Leased Land Lines, DSL, Cable*

There are several wired transmission means for transmitting the digitally encoded video and other data signals. The most common options for gaining connection to the Internet are: (1) leased land lines using PSTN modem, (2) ISDN telephone, (3) asymmetrical digital subscriber line (ADSL), and (4) cable. The PSTN and ISDN do not offer the capacity (bandwidth) to provide multiple channels of high-quality live video, but are a perfectly usable channel for non-real-time video alarm verification or event query searching from DVRs. The ISDN is a logical choice for many video alarm verification applications as it has an excellent reliability specification, is almost universally available, and is competitively priced for the data carrying capacity it provides. Table 7-2 summarizes the bandwidth carrying capacity of these transmission channels.

7.2.1.5.1 *PSTN-ISDN Link*

The dial-up PSTN is the most common of the available transmitting methods for digital video transmission over long distance wired networks. The service was designed for human voice, not high-speed video transmission. The data carrying capacity accessed is at best that of the PSTN modem or ISDN link, and often much less depending on network availability and traffic. On paper, ADSL offers a much faster connection to the Internet. This is based on the assumption that not all users will require all of the bandwidth they have paid for, all of the time. Typically, up

TRANSMISSION TYPE	TYPICAL DOWNLOAD SPEED	TRANSMISSION TIME FOR 25 kb IMAGE (SEC.)	MAX. FRAME RATE FOR 25 kb IMAGE	CONNECTION MODE
PSTN	45 Kbps	6	10 Frames/min	DIAL-UP
ISDN	120 Kbps	2	0.5 Frames/sec	DIAL-UP
IDSL	150 Kbps	2	0.06	DIRECT CONNECTION
ADSL—LOW END	640 Kbps	0.3	3	
ADSL—HIGH END	5 Mbps	0.05	20	
HDSL	1.5 Mbps	0.2	6	
VDSL	20 Mbps	0.01	80	
CABLE MODEM	750 Kbps	0.3	3	
T1	1.5 Mbps	0.2	6	
10BaseT	5 Mbps	0.05	20	
100BaseT	50 Mbps	0.005	200	
1000BaseT	500 Mbps	0.0005	2000 Frames/sec	DIRECT CONNECTION

IDSL: ISDN DSL
ADSL: ASYNCHRONOUS DSL
HDSL: HIGH BIT-RATE DSL
VDSL: VERY HIGH DATA RATE DSL

Table 7-2   PSTN, ISDN, ASDL, Ethernet, and other Cable Speeds

to 20–50 users share the ASDL bandwidth depending on the service selected. For occasional access to stored video, this may be quite acceptable but for multi-channel live surveillance it is unlikely to be satisfactory. If the Internet is used for security applications, it is wise to have a *backup* communications by a more reliable network and to select equipment that can automatically revert to this backup network.

7.2.1.5.2 DSL Link

The DSL technology supplies the necessary bandwidth for numerous applications including high-speed Internet access, dedicated Internet connectivity, and live video monitoring. This digital broadband data line directly connects the client computer to the Internet via existing cables. The speed of DSL varies depending on the connection speed and in some cases the number of people on the network.

7.2.1.5.3 T1 and T3 Links

The T1 and T3 networks have much higher speeds than those previously described. "T1" is a term coined by American Telephone and Telegraph (AT&T) for a system that transfers digital signals at 1.544 Mbps. T3 is the premium transmission method and has almost 30 times the capacity of T1. T3 lines can handle 44.736 Mbps. Fiber optics with its much higher bandwidth and many superior characteristics is replacing T1 and T3 transmission cables.

7.2.1.5.4 Cable

Community Antenna Television (CATV) networks have developed in parallel with DSL, and now compete for Internet access and even voice communication, in addition to the entertainment TV for which they were developed. Cable provides yet another means for transmitting the analog and digital video signal. Access to the Internet is offered by a number of CATV providers. Since the mid-1990s a number of these CATV providers have upgraded much of their traditional coax-based networks with optical fiber, thereby increasing overall network performance considerably. Both the coax and fiber-optic networks can support video and two-way Internet access. With the appropriate electronic upgrades, high-speed Internet access can be provided at end-user costs comparable with DSL networks.

7.2.1.6 Fiber Optic

Fiber optics is used as the transmission media of choice for digital signals transmitted over long distances or where severe electrical disturbances (lightning storms, electrical equipment) are present. The attributes of fiber optics are: (1) long-distance transmission—over many miles without degradation of the signal, (2) ultra-wide bandwidth resulting from the use of optical frequencies, and (3) secure transmission because of the difficulty to *tap* the optical signal.

In analog systems the output signals whether video or audio are analogs of the input signals. Analog signals are susceptible to rapid degradation, electrical noise interference, and distortion along the transmission channel. Analog signals are also degraded when multiple generations or reproductions of signals are required. Digital signals, on the other hand, are immune to such problems. Theoretically any number of signal re-generations is possible with zero loss of quality. However, once the digital signal becomes too small or the interference too large, the signal "breaks up" or totally drops out.

Amplitude modulation (AM), frequency modulation (FM), and pulsed-frequency modulation (PFM) are used in analog video fiber-optic transmission systems. In digitally encoded fiber-optic video transmission the video signals are sampled at very high rates and converted into digital signal formats. In both cases these signals are applied to light emitting diodes (LEDs) or injection laser diodes (ILDs) inside the optical transmitter units. The digital optical signals are transmitted through the fibers and then converted back to analog, base-band electrical video signals inside the optical receiver units. Figure 7-7 compares the AM, FM, and PFM transmission.

The AM video transmission is limited to short distances using multi-mode optical fiber and only available at the 850 nm operating wavelength. The FM transmission, on the other hand, provides very high video transmission performance over long distances and is available for use at 850 and 1300 nm. The 1300 nm wavelength has higher transmission through the atmosphere and is more eye-safe.

The latest generation of fiber-optic video transmission equipment digitizes the analog base-band video signals to provide a digital signal. This is accomplished via analog to digital (A/D) converters or coder-decoders inside the optical transmitters. The digitized signals modulate the LEDs or ILDs and then inject them optically into and through the fibers to the optical receivers where they are converted back into analog base-band signals by internal digital to analog (D/A) converters. Factors affecting the image quality in digitally encoded video transmission and its effect on the electrical dynamic range and signal-to-noise ratio (S/N) of the output video signal is the number of bits employed in the D/A and the compression employed. No video compression is needed in fiber-optic transmission because of the very wide bandwidth capabilities of the fiber optic. This means that the video is transmitted in real-time with zero latency (no delay) and standard 30 fps. A summary of the channels available and speeds of transmission and other parameters are compared in Table 7-3.

7.2.2 Wireless Channels

The WiFi network can be connected to the Internet through the use of a variety of high-speed connections including cable modems, DSL, ISDN, satellite, broadband,

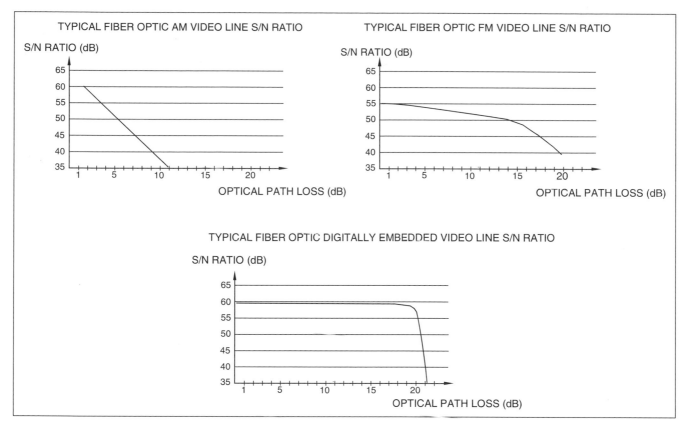

FIGURE 7-7   Comparison of AM, FM and pulse frequency modulation

TRANSMISSION TYPE	THEORETICAL* DOWNLOAD SPEED	TRANSMISSION MEDIA	
PSTN	45 Kbps	UTP	CAT-3
ISDN	120 Kbps	↑	CAT-3
HDSL	1.5 Mbps		CAT-3, 5, 5e
CABLE MODEM	750 Kbps		CAT-3, 5, 5e
10BASE T	5 Mbps		CAT-3, 5, 5e
100BASE T	50 Mbps		CAT-5e
1000BASE T	500 Mbps		CAT-6
T1	1.5 Mbps	↓	CAT-3, 5e
T3	45 Mbps	UTP	CAT-5, 5e
OC3	155 Mbps		FIBER OPTIC
OC12	622 Mbps		FIBER OPTIC

*REALISTIC SPEED APPROXIMATELY 1/2 OF THEORETICAL

Table 7-3   Comparison of Wired UTP and Optical Transmission Channels

etc. The broadband Internet connection connects to a video gateway or access point, and its Internet connection is distributed to all the computers on the network. The access points or gateways function as the "base stations" for the network. They send and receive signals from the WiFi radios to connect the various components of the security system to each other as well as to the Internet. All computers in the WiFi network can then share resources, exchange files, and use a single Internet connection. This is the central connection among all wireless client devices (PC, laptop, printers, etc.) and enables the sharing of the Internet connection with other users on the network.

Access points and gateways have a wide range of features and performance capabilities and provide this basic network connection service.

7.2.2.1 Wireless LAN (WLAN, WiFi)

The WiFi (Wireless Fidelity) devices "connect" to each other by transmitting and receiving signals on a specific frequency of the radio frequency (RF) and microwave bands. The components can connect to each other directly, called *peer to peer* or through a *gateway* or *access point*. The WiFi networks consist of two basic components: (1) WiFi radios and (2) access points or gateways. The WiFi radios are attached to the desktop computer, laptop, or other mobile devices on the network. The access points or gateways act as "base stations," i.e. they send and receive signals from the WiFi radios to connect the various components to each other as well as to the Internet. All the computers in the WiFi network then share resources and exchange files over a single Internet connection.

The IEEE developed a series of 802.11 protocols to meet the requirements of disparate applications, and continues to formulate new ones. The 802.11a, b, g, i, and n standards are most useful for the wireless digital video transmission applications. Table 7-4 summarizes some of the parameters of the standards.

A peer-to-peer network is composed of several WiFi equipped computers talking to each other without using a base station (access point or gateway). All WiFi Certified™ equipment supports this type of wireless setup, which is a good solution for transferring data between computers or when sharing an Internet connection among a few computers.

Many laptop computers and mobile computing devices come with a WiFi radio built into them and are ready to operate wirelessly. For other laptops without such a device, a WiFi radio embedded in a simple Personal Computer Memory Card International Association (PCMCIA) card can be inserted into expansion slot of a laptop computer.

There are other ways to include the desktop PC into the network. Since many PCs do not have card slots for PC cards, the simplest method is to use a universal serial bus (USB) WiFi radio that plugs into an available USB port on the computer.

7.2.2.2 Mesh Network

The mesh network is a topology that provides multiple paths between network nodes. Wired networks have used

IEEE STANDARD	OPERATING FREQUENCY BAND (GHz)	DATA[†] RATES (Mbps)	OPERATING FREQUENCY BANDS (GHz)	MODULATION METHOD	MAX POWER OUTPUT (EIRP)	APPLICATIONS/ COMMENTS
802.11 [*] (LEGACY)	2.4 IR	1, 2	2.4–2.8	DSSS FHSS IR	——	ORIGINAL 802.11 STANDARD FOR WIRELESS LAN
802.11a [**]	5.2, 5.8	6, 12, 24, 9, 18, 36, 48 54 MAXIMUM	300 MHz IN 3 BANDS of 100 MHz each: 5.150 to 5.250 (UNII LOWER BAND) 5.250 to 5.350 (UNII MIDDLE BAND) 5.725 to 5.825 (UNII UPPER BAND)	COFDM	40 mW 200 mW 800 mW	INDOOR INDOOR OUTDOOR
802.11b	2.4	1, 2, 5.5, 11 11 MAXIMUM	83.5 MHz FROM 2.40 GHz to 2.4835 GHz (ISM BAND)	DSSS FDMA	1 WATT TYPICAL: 30 mW	USES FDMA, DSSS
802.11g	2.4	1, 2, 5.5, 11 6, 9, 12, 18, 24, 36, 48, 54	2.4–2.4835	DSSS COFDM		DUAL BAND 2.4 GHz
802.11i	——	——	——	——	——	ADDS HIGH LEVEL AES ENCRYPTION[‡]
802.11n	——	108	20–40 MHz	——	——	VERY HIGH DATA RATE

* IEEE ESTABLISHED STANDARD IN 1997 TO DEFINE MAC (MEDIA ACCESS CONTROL) AND PHY (PHYSICAL) LAYER REQUIREMENTS FOR WIRELESS LAN.

** IEEE ESTABLISHED 802.11a IN 1999

†THEORETICAL MAXIMUM RATES. REALISTIC MAXIMUM APPROXIMATELY ONE–HALF

‡ADVANCED ENCRYPTION STANDARD

ISM—INDUSTRIAL, SCIENTIFIC, MEDICAL
UNII—UNLICENSED NATIONAL INFORMATION INFRASTRUCTURE
COFDM—CODED ORTHONOGONAL FREQUENCY DIVISION MULTIPLEXING
FDMA—FREQUENCY DIVISION MULTIPLE ACCESS
DSSS—DIRECT SEQUENCE SPREAD SPECTRUM
FHSS—FREQUENCY HOPPING SPREAD SPECTRUM
EIRP—EQUIVALENT ISOTROPICALLY RADIATED POWER
IR—INFRARED

Table 7-4   Comparison of IEEE 802.11 Standards

the mesh topology to get redundancy and reliability. Mesh networks make the most sense with wireless transmission because wireless nodes can be set up to form ad hoc networks that connect many nodes. In the wireless application if interference or excess distance between nodes causes a dropped video link the mesh system will find an alternate path through the mesh automatically. The nodes themselves may generate messages to be sent elsewhere or be available to receive data or both. The nodes act as *repeaters* to move the video and other data from point-to-point when they are not transmitting or receiving their own data. What results is a very robust network at low cost. The Mesh network using many closely spaced repeater transceivers (nodes) is shown in Figure 7-8.

Each node can communicate with its nearby neighbors that are within range. The nodes can exchange data between themselves, store it, or forward data meant for a more distant node that is out of range of a nearby node. One of the nodes can also serve as a wired or wireless connection to an Internet node or access point. A particular attribute of the wireless Mesh network using multiple nodes is that it allows the signal to be transmitted over a longer range than would be possible with a normal line-of-sight (LOS) link. In mesh networks *multiple paths*

exist through the network system, increasing the probability that the video signal from the camera will reach the monitoring location. The Mesh configuration is also more reliable since if one of the nodes fails due to a power loss, jamming or other defect, communication is still maintained, i.e. the video, voice, communication, or control signals can be routed through another path. In addition to the reliability aspect, the Mesh configuration offers the benefit of requiring very low transmitted power at any given node because the distance between nodes is usually short. Mesh networks are especially useful in monitoring a large network of image and/or alarm sensors. In portable and rapid deployment applications, low transmit power means low device power consumption and longer battery life. The military has already adopted mesh networks in battlefield systems and many forms of video security are ideal applications for this growing technology.

7.2.2.3 Multiple Input/Multiple Output (MIMO)

Most wideband WiFi networks operate with data rates between 11 and 54 Mbps. There is however a need for greater network bandwidth capacity for wireless LANs. The wireless radio channel for moving video and other

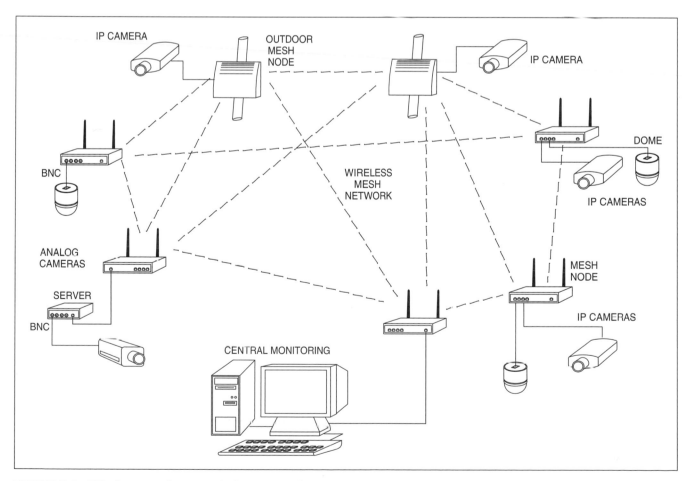

FIGURE 7-8 Wireless mesh transmitting network

digital information over the air waves has a highly variable nature. Unlike the relatively stable environment that exists on wire, cable, or fiber-optic networks, the ability of the air to carry information can and does change over time and often from moment to moment. With this fundamental variability and the overhead inherent in any networking protocol, the actual throughput available from a 54 Mbps connection is often much less than this peak number. As a consequence it is necessary to improve the performance of wireless LANs at the *physical layer* if higher throughputs are to be achieved. One popular approach is to gang together multiple radio channels and to use compression and related techniques to gain some additional advantage in information throughput. The ideal solution is to come up with a technology that simply packs more information per unit of bandwidth and time. This technique applied to wireless transmission is known as *modulation efficiency*—the number of bits per unit of bandwidth and time that can be transmitted through the air at any given time.

Radio signals are subject to serious degradation as they move through space, primarily due to the distance between the transmitter and receiver, interaction with objects in the environment, and interference from other radio signals and reflections of the signal in question itself (known as multi-path). All these artifacts result in a number of forms of fading, the loss in power of the radio signal, as it moves from the transmitter to the receiver.

The technique available today that has been put into practice in a wireless LAN is called *multiple input, multiple output* (MIMO). This technology adds an additional dimension to the radio channel—a *spatial* dimension—allowing a more complex but inherently more reliable radio signal to be communicated (Figure 7-9).

Whereas conventional radio transmission uses a single input, single output, a true MIMO system uses at least two transmit antennas, working simultaneously in a single channel, and at least two receive antennas at the other end of the connection working in the same channel. Generally the number of receive antennas in a MIMO system is usually greater than the number of transmit antennas and the performance of transmission improves with the addition of more receive antennas. Going from a single antenna to two antennas can result in a $10 \times$ (10 dB) improvement in the S/N, a key indicator of reliability and signal quality. Adding a third antenna adds an additional $4 \times$ (5dB) improvement. Figure 7-10 illustrates a six-antenna MIMO receiver.

The MIMO technology relies upon the *interactions* of the signal with the environment in the form of multipath for its benefits—a counterintuitive element in the technology. The phenomenon is attributed to reflections and multi-path transmissions from walls, ceilings, floors, and other objects. By improving the performance of the antennas and the number of them used in the WLAN, the

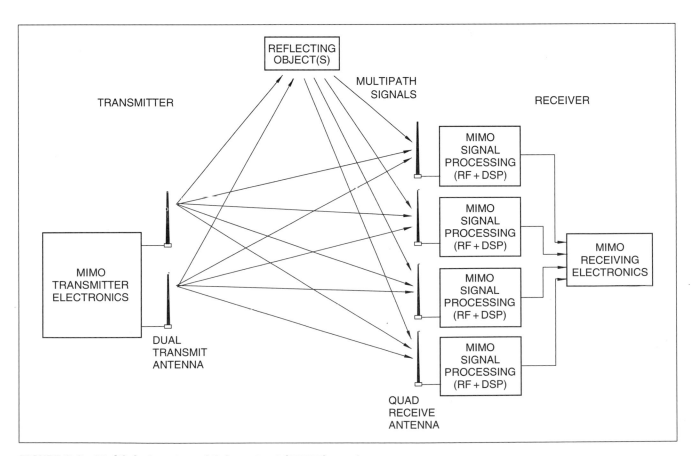

FIGURE 7-9   Multiple input, multiple output (MIMO) receiver

FIGURE 7-10 Six antenna wireless LAN MIMO receiver

overall performance is significantly improved. The MIMO technology introduces a third *spatial* dimension beyond the frequency and time domains, which would otherwise define the radio channel.

The major difference between the MIMO and traditional wireless systems is a utilization of the physical multi-path phenomenon. Unlike traditional modems that are typically impaired by multi-path, MIMO takes advantage of multi-path. The typical radio signal from a point source (single antenna) typically bounces off different objects during transmission, particularly indoors as it interacts with objects in the environment. The result of these interactions is *multi-path fading*, as the signal interferes often destructively with itself. The MIMO takes advantage of multiple paths, using signal processing implemented on digital signal processor (DSP) chips, and using clever algorithms at the transmitter and receiver. Somewhat counter intuitively, MIMO actually *depends* upon multi-path to function correctly and produce improvements, making it even better suited to in-building applications. The MIMO can offer a dramatic improvement in signal throughput over competing WLAN technologies. The new 802.11n standard including MIMO processing in its specification should produce performance of 144–200 Mbps.

7.2.2.4 Environmental Factors: Indoor–Outdoor

Indoor and outdoor environmental effects must always be considered when implementing a wireless analog or digital video system. Atmospheric conditions, objects in the signal's path, incorrect antenna pointing angle can all cause fading and dropouts in the digital video signal. All of these factors affect the quality of service (QoS) in the resulting video image or other communication data. Most analog and digital video transmission takes place using the FCC allocated 902 MHz, 2.4 GHz, and 5.8 GHz bands, each of

which exhibit signal degradation under different conditions. The 902 MHz and 2.4 GHz bands provide the best transmission through most non-metal, dry solid objects, but the 5.8 GHz band exhibits severe attenuation when objects are placed in the path between the transmitter and receiver. The 5.8 GHz band should only be used for short range indoor applications and clear LOS outdoor applications or where specific metal reflectors can be placed to re-direct the microwave beam to the receiver. The 802.11b technology operates at 2.4 GHz and a data rate of 11 Mbps and can handle up to three video data streams at a time. The 802.11g technology operating at 2.4 GHz and a data rate of 54 Mbps, and the 801.11a technology operating at 5.8 GHz and a data rate of 54 Mbps can manage multiple standard video streams. They all require innovative techniques to provide high QoS and quality video images.

One system using a diversity antenna array (not MIMO) provides wireless connections at data rates of up to 54 Mbps over a time domain multi-access (TDMA) proprietary link that uses the 802.11a, 5.8 GHz frequency band. The system permits multiple streams of DVD, cable and satellite digital video, audio, and data to be delivered over the wireless links without degrading quality. The key to the improved QoS is in the front end of the receiver. The RF transceiver employs a spatial wave-front receiver that uses five antennas and two full receiver channels to eliminate multi-path (ghost) signals. It does this by using the five-antenna array to capture the RF signals and then *selects* the best two of five signals. This approach takes *advantage* of the multi-path signals as opposed to other techniques that try to *eliminate* them. After the two signals are selected they are fed into separate independent receive channels that amplify, filter, frequency convert, and eventually feed them to the base-band processor. The base-band chip converts the two analog signals into digital streams and then, using DSP techniques, combines them into one high-quality data stream. When a system is set up it scans the available channels for one that is not in use by any nearby 802.11 WiFi network. The chip then continuously monitors all channels for possible interference and, if a potential interference is detected, the chip looks for another unused channel. The signals that can be processed can come from any source since the chip can process video in any standard format from MPEG-1 to MPEG 4, H 264. It should be pointed out that most systems in use do not use diversity antenna arrays and are therefore limited to transmitting fewer channels of video.

7.2.2.5 Broadband Microwave

Microwave transmission uses ultra-high frequencies to transmit video signals over long distances. There are several frequency ranges assigned to the microwave systems all in the gigahertz ranges. Table 7-5 lists the broadband microwave frequencies bands available for transmission.

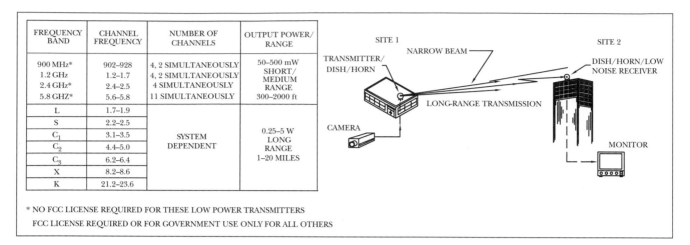

FREQUENCY BAND	CHANNEL FREQUENCY	NUMBER OF CHANNELS	OUTPUT POWER/ RANGE
900 MHz*	902–928	4, 2 SIMULTANEOUSLY	50–500 mW
1.2 GHz	1.2–1.7	4, 2 SIMULTANEOUSLY	SHORT/ MEDIUM RANGE
2.4 GHz*	2.4–2.5	4 SIMULTANEOUSLY	300–2000 ft
5.8 GHZ*	5.6–5.8	11 SIMULTANEOUSLY	
L	1.7–1.9		
S	2.2–2.5		
C_1	3.1–3.5	SYSTEM DEPENDENT	0.25–5 W LONG RANGE 1–20 MILES
C_2	4.4–5.0		
C_3	6.2–6.4		
X	8.2–8.6		
K	21.2–23.6		

* NO FCC LICENSE REQUIRED FOR THESE LOW POWER TRANSMITTERS
FCC LICENSE REQUIRED OR FOR GOVERNMENT USE ONLY FOR ALL OTHERS

Table 7-5 Broadband Microwave Frequencies for Video Transmission

The wavelength of these frequencies is very short and gives rise to the term "microwave." These high-frequency signals are especially susceptible to attenuation and must therefore be amplified frequently if long distances (20–50 miles) separate the transmitter and receiver. Repeaters at intermediate locations between the transmitter and receiver are used when distances exceed 20–30 mi. In order to maximize the strength of the high-frequency signal, focused antennas are used at both ends. Since the microwave frequencies have characteristics similar to light waves, these antennas can take the form of concave metal dishes that collect the maximum amount of incoming signal and reflect it to the receiver detector. The requirement for these tightly focused antennas limits the microwave application, and it is clearly a *point-to-point* rather than a *broadcast* transmission system. These microwave signals will not be passed through buildings, uneven terrain, or any other solid objects. Broadband microwave technology used as a video transmission media is used to interconnect LANs between buildings and over long distances. The microwave dishes must be line-of-sight from transmitter to receiver to collect the microwave signals reliably. Using the microwave technology requires FCC licensing, however once the license is granted for any particular location, that frequency band cannot be licensed to anyone else for any purpose within a 17.5 mi. radius.

7.2.2.6 Infrared (IR)

Infrared (IR) links use IR signals to transmit video, data, and control signals. These IR transmission paths must be set up in a line of sight configuration or the IR signal can be reflected off an infrared reflecting surface (mirror). The major advantage of infrared transmission is its ability to carry a high-bandwidth signal and its immunity to tapping. Its major disadvantage is that the IR beam can be obstructed and it cannot pass through most solid objects. The IR emitter is in the form of an LED or ILD.

7.3 VIDEO IMAGE QUALITY

In both legacy analog and digital video surveillance systems, the criteria for image quality include resolution, frame rate, and color rendition. In digital video monitoring and surveillance applications each camera generates a stream of sequential digital images typically at a rate of 2–20 per second, or 30 per second for real-time. In the video application the data network must be capable of sustaining a throughput required to deliver the packets comprising the video streams being generated by all the cameras. This is one measure of QoS, but QoS also encompasses latency (the delay between transmitting and receiving packets) and jitter (the variations in that delay from packet to packet). The QoS criterion is generally applied to the forward video signal direction since the vast majority of traffic results from these video streams from the camera to the monitor and recorder. The QoS does apply in some cases where the cameras offer centralized in-band control, whether to simply adjust settings from time-to-time or to PTZ the cameras in real-time.

The Internet and other IP-based networks increasingly are being used to support real-time video applications, voice, and audio, all of which are extremely demanding in terms of latency, jitter, and signal loss. The Internet and its original underlying protocols were never intended to support QoS, which is exactly what each of these traffic types requires. The real-time streaming protocol (RTSP) is an application layer (Layer 7, Section 7.8.3) protocol for control over the delivery of data that has real-time properties including both live video data feeds, stored video clips, and audio.

7.3.1 Quality of Service (QoS)

The QoS describes the video image quality and intelligence in the digital video image as determined by the video frame rate and resolution (number of pixels).

The QoS is defined as the control of four network categories: (1) bandwidth, (2) latency, (3) jitter, and (4) traffic loss. Bandwidth is defined as the total network capacity. Latency is the total time it takes for a frame to travel from a sender to a receiver. Latency can be crucial with receivers having QoS requirements. Packets arriving too early require buffering, or worse they may be dropped. Packets arriving to late are not useful and must be discarded. Jitter is the variation in the latency among a group of packets between two nodes. Jitter requires a receiver to perform complex buffering operations so that packets are presented to higher levels with a uniform latency. Traffic loss refers to the packets that never arrive at the receiver.

The video signal requires compression to fit into the bandwidth available in the communication channel, and for the practical compression techniques used, this compression always results in signal degradation (exception lossless transmission). Data transmission is generally considered moving in one direction in a video monitoring or surveillance application: that is the vast majority of traffic results from the video streams flowing from the camera to the monitor or video recorder. There is some traffic that flows in the other direction including controls for the camera functions.

7.3.2 Resolution vs. Frame Rate

Resolution is a measure of how clear and crisp an image appears on the monitor. Each of the individual video components included within a system contributes to the overall image quality, either recorded or displayed on the monitor. The resultant image quality is only as good as the equipment component having the *lowest* resolution. When a high resolution monitor is combined a with a low resolution camera, the result is a low resolution image display. This fact becomes increasingly important when using the system for recording, as the playback image from the recorder is generally less than that obtained when displayed directly on the monitor.

The image quality of the video signal is dependent on: (1) the video frame rate required to reproduce motion in the scene, (2) the resolution required to convey the intelligence required in the scene, and (3) the bandwidth available for the transmission. For a practical transmission with existing communication channels the video signal must first be digitally compressed to fit into the available bandwidth. To achieve the necessary intelligence in the image, the resolution required for the application must be specified and the network must have sufficient bandwidth. When more than one video image (or additional information) is to be displayed on a video monitor, a format called Common Intermediate Format (CIF) is used. Most digital video systems with standard 4×3 formats display three different resolutions: (1) full screen 704×480 pixels (4×3) resulting in the highest resolution, (2) 1/4

screen 352×240 having a proportionally lower but often adequate resolution, and (3) full screen having 704×240 pixels. The 320×240 pixels requires 1/4 the bandwidth and has a $4\times$ faster image transfer rate. The 704×240 has 1/2 the bandwidth of the 704×480 system. The 1/4 CIF format has a resolution of 352×240 pixels with the NTSC system and 352×288 pixels with the PAL system. The three formats described above referred to as CIF are summarized in Table 7-6. Their relative sizes are shown in the inset drawing.

It is often desirable to display the digital video image on only part of the display screen when the screen is being shared with other systems functions (alarms, access control, etc.). In this case the 1/4 CIF is most appropriate. Since the 1/4 CIF requires only 1/4 the bandwidth, it can display the image at $4 \times$ the CIF rate.

7.3.3 Picture Integrity, Dropout

It is very important during digital video signal transmission that the video image have integrity throughout the transmission. The various compression and transmission technologies used for transmitting the video signal have different vulnerabilities to noise and external interference and cause the video image to be degraded in different ways. The temporary loss of the digital signal causes image pixelation or picture breakup which results in the loss of "blocks" of pixels causing parts of the image to be absent and displaying an incomplete picture. In worst case, when the video signal strength (S/N) is sufficiently low and synchronization is lost, video frame "lock-up" occurs and the last full frame transmitted may be displayed as a full frame, partial frame, or none at all. For general surveillance video surveillance applications, degradation or temporary loss of a few frames of video signal can be tolerated. However, in most security applications and especially in strategic surveillance applications this is unacceptable.

7.4 VIDEO SIGNAL COMPRESSION

Video signal compression is the process of converting analog video images into smaller digital files for efficient transfer across a network. Compression provides reduced bandwidth, quicker file transfers, and reduced storage requirements. Compression and decompression are accomplished through the use of special software or hardware or in some cases both.

From the earliest days, video (consumer television) has been a bandwidth hog. Standard broadcast channels require from 4 to 6 MHz of bandwidth to produce a complete picture and sound at full frame rates of 30 fps. In digitized form the signal requires data rates on the order of 2 Mbps.

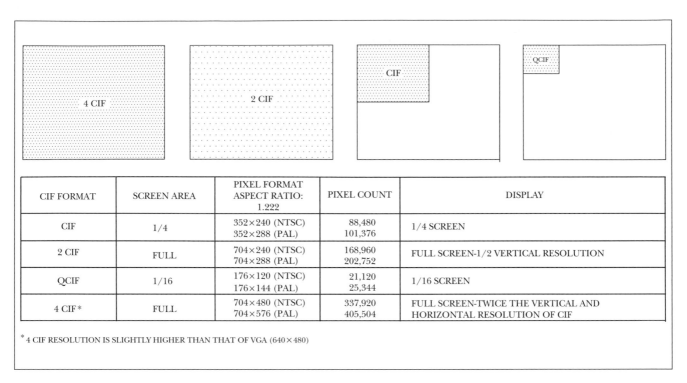

CIF FORMAT	SCREEN AREA	PIXEL FORMAT ASPECT RATIO: 1.222	PIXEL COUNT	DISPLAY
CIF	1/4	352×240 (NTSC) 352×288 (PAL)	88,480 101,376	1/4 SCREEN
2 CIF	FULL	704×240 (NTSC) 704×288 (PAL)	168,960 202,752	FULL SCREEN-1/2 VERTICAL RESOLUTION
QCIF	1/16	176×120 (NTSC) 176×144 (PAL)	21,120 25,344	1/16 SCREEN
4 CIF*	FULL	704×480 (NTSC) 704×576 (PAL)	337,920 405,504	FULL SCREEN-TWICE THE VERTICAL AND HORIZONTAL RESOLUTION OF CIF

* 4 CIF RESOLUTION IS SLIGHTLY HIGHER THAN THAT OF VGA (640×480)

Table 7-6   Common Intermediate Format (CIF) Parameters

In the 1980s this bandwidth limitation for transmitting video signals was addressed by the US government Defense Advanced Research Project Agency (DARPA) to compress NTSC and HDTV type video streams to fit within available bands of the radio frequency spectrum. One result of the initial work done by DARPA and MPEG was the evolution of a family of video compression standards that apply directly to real-time video applications. The MPEG group was founded under the International Organization for Standardization (ISO) and created the first compression standard MPEG-1, in 1992. This standard was directed toward single speed applications like CD-ROM and is still used in today's camcorders and video CD movie rentals. Two years later, MPEG-2 followed, which added frame interlace support and was directed toward applications such as digital TV (DTV) and digital video disk (DVD).

A video stream consists of a series of still images or frames displayed in rapid succession. Each digital image is in the form of a rectangle consisting of an array of picture elements known as *pixels*. Each pixel represents the light intensity that the camera sees in either black and white (monochrome) or color, at that pixel location. The NTSC display contains 720×480 pixels which is known as a 4×3 aspect ratio. High definition television (HDTV) has a higher pixel count of 1920×1024. Table 7-7 summarizes the Advanced Television Systems Committee (ATSC) digital television standards.

In monochrome cameras the intensity is represented by a single pixel. In color cameras the sensors are grouped together in three pixels: one for red, one for green, and one for blue (RGB). The combination of these three colors in different proportions produces every other color. To convert to digital form the output from each pixel in the camera sensor is converted to digital values by use of an A/D converter. For the monochrome camera each pixel is converted into an 8-bit value representing the intensity of the image on the pixel. For the color camera the 8-bit value and an additional 16 bits are used to digitize all three colors (red, green, and blue), resulting in 24 bits (eight bits for each color).

Why is digital video signal compression required? Without video compression an enormous amount of bandwidth is required to efficiently transfer video across a network. A 24-bit color video stream at 640×480 resolution transferring 30 frames in one second creates almost 30 MB (megabyte) of data.

Compression schemes for sending data over a restricted bandwidth have existed for years with the "zip" file of *lossless* compressed data being a popular program. This lossless compression, however, is not sufficient or suitable for video transmission and does not take into account an advantage of unique features of video transmission. In particular, individual frames of video often contain *repetitious* material and often have only small portions of the image or frame that *change* from frame to frame. The zip compression program does not take advantage of this feature.

There are two generic types of digital video compression: lossless and lossy. Lossless as the name implies means that all the information to reproduce every pixel present in the camera output is transmitted to the monitoring

DTV FORMAT INDEX	VERTICAL RESOLUTION (PIXELS)	HORIZONTAL RESOLUTION (PIXELS)	SCREEN FORMAT ASPECT RATIO	SCAN TYPE	REFRESH RATE (Hz)	FORMAT DESCRIPTION H×V, fps i or p *	FORMAT TYPE
1				INTERLACED	30	640×480, 30i	SDTV
2		640	4×3		24	640×480, 24p	
3				PROGRESSIVE	30	640×480, 30p	
4					60	640×480, 60p	
5				INTERLACED	30	704×480, 30p	
6	480	704	4×3		24	704×480, 24p	
7				PROGRESSIVE	30	704×480, 30p	EDTV
8					60	704×480, 60p	
9				INTERLACED	30	704×480, 30i	
10		704	16×9		24	704×480, 34p	
11				PROGRESSIVE	30	704×480, 30p	
12					60	704×480, 60p	
13					24	1280×720, 24p	
14	720	1280	16×9	PROGRESSIVE	30	1280×720, 30p	
15					60	1280×720, 60p	HDTV
16				INTERLACED	30	1920×1080, 30i	
17	1080	1920	16×9	PROGRESSIVE	24	1920×1080, 24p	
18					30	1920×1080, 30p	

DTV—DIGITAL TELEVISION
ATSD—ADVANCED TELEVISION SYSTEMS COMMITTEE
SDTV—STANDARD DEFINITION TELEVISION
EDTV—ENHANCED DIGITAL TELEVISION
HDTV—HIGH DEFINITION TELEVISION

*i—INTERLACED SCAN
p—PROGRESSIVE SCAN
fps —FRAMES PER SECOND

Table 7-7   ATSC Digital Television Standard Scanning Formats

site and reconstructed without any loss in picture quality. This means that the compression algorithms must be able to accurately reconstruct the uncompressed video signal. Lossy compression means that the reconstructed (decompressed) signal can not *exactly* re-create the original video signal.

The following is a calculation of the number of uncompressed RGB signal bits that must be transmitted for a single frame of NTSC video if no compression were to take place:

To transmit 1 frame = 720 pixels × 480 pixels × 24 pixel

= 8,294,400 bits

To transmit 1 second of video = 8,294,400 × 30 fps

= 248,832,000 bits.

From the above it can be seen that it takes over 248 Mb to transmit 1 second of uncompressed full-color video. Clearly few transmission channels can afford to provide this much bandwidth for transmitting any video signals. For this reason some scheme of compression of video signals is required to make a practical remote video security system.

Video compression takes advantage of enormous *spatial* and *temporal* redundancies in natural moving imagery.

Spatial redundancy means that neighboring pixels within a video frame are more likely to be close to the same value (in both brightness and color) than far apart. Temporal redundancy means that neighboring frames in time tend to have a great deal of similar content, such as background information, that is either stationary or moving in predictable ways. Any compression system will perform better if the video signal is preconditioned properly. In practice this means removal of the noise that would otherwise consume precious bits. Figure 7-11 illustrates some examples of spatial and temporal redundancies in a typical video image.

7.4.1   Lossless Compression

Lossless compression is the process of compressing 100% of video data with zero loss. This type of compression does not compress as much as lossy compression since every piece of data is retained. The benefit of this compression is that video data can be compressed and decompressed over and over without any video data degradation. Lossless compression algorithms compress the video data into the smallest package possible without losing any information in the scene. The zip file for standard data (not video) is an example of a lossless compression algorithm since the

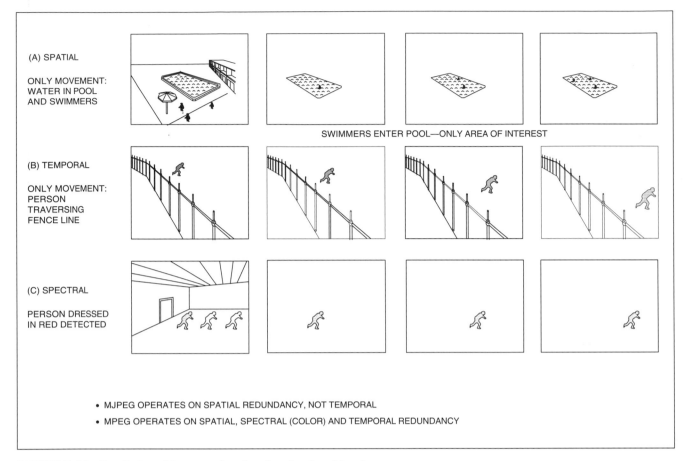

FIGURE 7-11   Spatial and temporal redundancies in video images

data that is compressed can be decompressed and an exact duplicate of the original re-created at the receiver end.

Lossless compression generates an exact duplicate of the input data scene after many compression/decompression cycles: no information is lost. This method, however, can only achieve a modest amount of compression. Typical compression ratios for lossless transmission are from 2:1 to 5:1.

7.4.2 Lossy Compression

In the case of the video signal it is often not necessary that each bit of data be re-created exactly as in the original camera image. Depending on the video quality required at the monitoring location, often much of the video information can be tossed away without noticeably changing the video image that the user sees. The exclusion of this extraneous video results in the ability to achieve high compression rates.

Lossy compression achieves lower bit counts than lossless compression by discarding some of the original video data *before* compression. Video data degradation does occur with lossy compression when it is compressed and decompressed over and over. In other words, every time video data is compressed and decompressed, less of the original video image is retained.

Two common methods for compression are discrete cosine transform (DCT) and discrete wavelet transform (DWT).

7.4.2.1 Direct Cosine Transform (DCT)

The DCT is a lossy compression algorithm that samples the image at regular intervals. This transform divides the video image into 8×8 blocks and analyzes each block individually. It analyzes the components of the image and discards those that do not affect the image as perceived by the human eye. JPEG, MPEG, M-JPEG, H.261, H.263, and H.264 incorporate DCT compression. Lossy compression can eliminate some of the data in the image at a sacrifice to the quality of the image produced. This reduction in bits transmitted, however, provides greater compression ratios than lossless compression and therefore requires less bandwidth. The choice of lossless or lossy compression results in a trade-off of file size vs. image quality. Lossy compression discards redundant information and achieves much higher compression at the sacrifice of not being able to exactly reproduce the original video scene. Typical compression ratios for lossy transmission are from 20:1 to 200:1.

7.4.2.2 Discrete Wavelet Transform (DWT)

Wavelet video compression, rather than operating on pieces of the image, operates on the entire image. The transformation uses a series of filters that determines the content of every pixel in the image. Because the technology works on the entire image there is no mosaic effect when the image is viewed as is sometimes experienced with DCT. While wavelet technology is a lossy compression technique, the lossy effects are not apparent until very high compression ratios of 350:1 are reached. Wavelet compression uses multiple single recorded frames to create a video sequence. It differs from others in that it compresses files more tightly with average file sizes for a wavelet image of about 12 Kb or 360 Kbps at 30 fps. Wavelet compression is based on full frame information and on frequency, not on 8 × 8 pixel blocks as in DCT. Wavelet compression compresses the entire image with multiple filtering at both the high and low frequencies and repeats the procedure several times. This compression method offers compression ratios up to 350:1.

7.4.3 Video Compression Algorithms

Many compression algorithms have evolved over the years to address specific digital data transmission requirements. The International Telecommunications Union (ITU) and the International Organization for Standards (ISO) have developed video compression technology and standards that meet and exceed the requirements for most of today's video security applications as well as anticipated future requirements. The compression standards that are specifically directed toward transmitting single frame and streaming video signals include: (1) MPEG-2, (2) MPEG-4, (3) JPEG, (4) M-JPEG, (5) JPEG-2000, (6) wavelet, (7) H.263, (8) H.264, and (9) super motion image compression technology (SMICT).

The required video frame rates for a security application are primarily determined by the motion in the scene (activity) and the number of pixels required for the specified resolution. When there is little motion in the scene or if the motion is slow, very often less than 30 fps are sufficient to obtain the necessary intelligence in the scene. This reduces the required bandwidth for the transmission of the digital video signal. Frame rates as low as 5 fps can be useful.

7.4.3.1 Joint Picture Experts Group: JPEG

The JPEG is the oldest and most established compression technique and is generally applicable to *still* images or single frames of video. This compression technique divides the image into 8 × 8 blocks of pixels with each block a signed number (plus or minus) and code (Figure 7-12).

The DCT compression software examines the blocks and their size and determines which blocks are redundant and not essential in creating the image. The program transmits the blocks that are essential, which is a reduced number based on the level of compression determined by the system settings. The compression ratio is limited to approximately 10:1. New compression algorithms are evolving that have built upon JPEG and provide higher compression ratios and have higher signal quality with smaller bandwidth requirements. The JPEG uses *still* images to create a video stream and has an average image file size of about 25 Kb per frame or 750 Kbps at 30 fps.

7.4.3.2 Moving—Joint Picture Experts Group: M-JPEG

The M-JPEG compression technology creates a video sequence (stream) from a series of still frame JPEG images. The average file size of an M-JPEG image is about 16 Kb per frame or 480 Kbps at 30 fps. The M-JPEG is a lossy compression method designed to exploit some limitations of the human eye, notably the fact that small color changes are perceived less than small changes in brightness. With a compression ratio of 20:1, compression can be achieved with only a small fraction of image degradation.

7.4.3.3 Moving Picture Experts Group: MPEG-2, MPEG-4, MPEG-4 Visual

7.4.3.3.1 MPEG-2 Standard

The MPEG-2 is the successor to MPEG-1 and has the primary goal of transmitting broadcast video at bit rates between 4 and 9 Kbps. It produces high-quality live camera images using a relatively small amount of bandwidth per camera. It is capable of handling high-definition television (HDTV) and has been adopted as the digital television standard by the FCC and is the compression standard for DVDs. The MPEG-2 NTSC standard has a resolution of 720 × 480 pixels and incorporates both progressive and interlaced scanning although progressive scanning is rarely used in video security applications. Interlaced scanning is the method used in the video security industry to produce images on surveillance monitors.

The MPEG-2 and MPEG-4 are based on the *group of images* (GOI) concept as defined by an I-frame, P-frame, and B-frame (Figure 7-13).

The technology's basic principle is to compare two compressed image groups for transmission over the network. The first frame group is called the I-frame (intra-frame), and uses the first compressed image as a reference frame. This image serves as the reference point for all frames following it that are in the same group. Following the I-frame come the P-frames (predictive), that are coded with reference to the previous frame and can either be an I-frame or another P-frame. The P-frames include the changes, i.e. movement and activity from the leading I-frame. B-frames (bi-directional) are compressed with a low

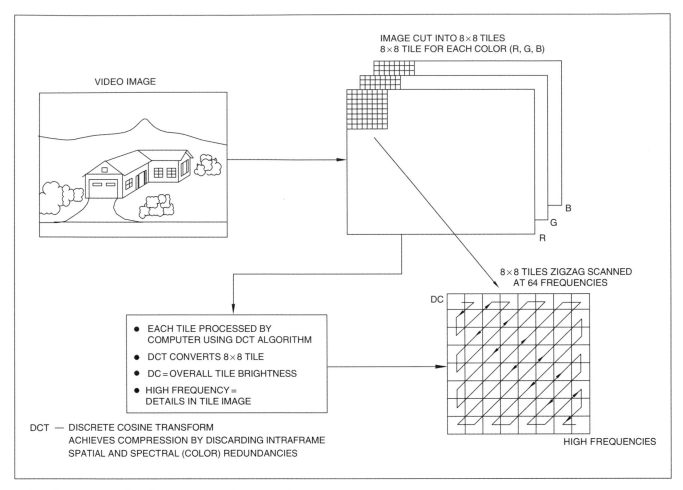

VIDEO IMAGE

IMAGE CUT INTO 8×8 TILES
8×8 TILE FOR EACH COLOR (R, G, B)

B
G
R

- EACH TILE PROCESSED BY
  COMPUTER USING DCT ALGORITHM
- DCT CONVERTS 8×8 TILE
- DC = OVERALL TILE BRIGHTNESS
- HIGH FREQUENCY =
  DETAILS IN TILE IMAGE

DCT — DISCRETE COSINE TRANSFORM
ACHIEVES COMPRESSION BY DISCARDING INTRAFRAME
SPATIAL AND SPECTRAL (COLOR) REDUNDANCIES

8×8 TILES ZIGZAG SCANNED
AT 64 FREQUENCIES

DC

HIGH FREQUENCIES

FIGURE 7-12 JPEG lossless compression technique

bit rate using both the previous and future references (I and P). B-frames are not used as references. Typical GOI lengths are usually 12 or 16 frames. The network viewing stations reconstruct all images based on the reference I images and the difference data in the B- and P-frames. The detail relationship between the three frame types are described in the MPEG standard. The MPEG-2 and MPEG-4 can achieve compression ratios up to approximately 60–100 to 1.

7.4.3.3.2 MPEG-4 Standard

The MPEG-4 standard was introduced in 1998 and has evolved into the first true multimedia and Web compression standard because of its low bit-rate transmission and incorporation of audio and video with point-and-click interaction capabilities. The MPEG-4 uses the GOI concept and I-, P-, B-frames but in addition uses *object*-based compression where individual *objects* within a scene are tracked separately and compressed together. This method offers a very efficient compression ratio that is scalable from 20:1 to 300:1. The primary uses for the MPEG-4 standard are web–streaming media, CD distribution, video-

phone, and broadcast television. The MPEG-4 consists of several standards-termed *layers*:

- Layer 1 describes synchronization and multiplexing of video and audio.
- Layer 2 is a compression codec for video signals.
- Layer 3 is a compression codec for perceptual coding of audio signals.
- Layer 4 describes procedures for testing compliance.
- Layer 5 describes systems for software simulation.
- Layer 6 describes delivery multimedia integration framework.
- Layer 10 is an advanced codec for video signals, also called H.264.

7.4.3.3.3 MPEG-4 Visual Standard

The MPEG-4 *Visual* became an international standard in 1999 with its main feature being the support of object-based compression. Objects in the scene after appropriate identification (segmentation) can be coded as separate bit streams and manipulated independently. This is an important attribute for video security applications. If the target can be automatically recognized, tracked, and segmented from the scene, it can be coded separately from

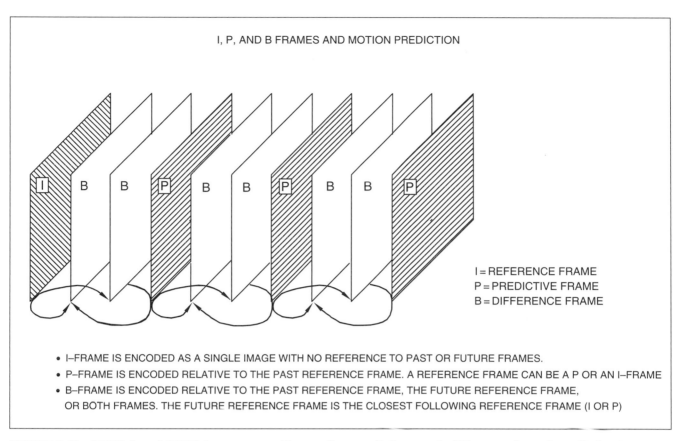

I, P, AND B FRAMES AND MOTION PREDICTION

I = REFERENCE FRAME
P = PREDICTIVE FRAME
B = DIFFERENCE FRAME

- I–FRAME IS ENCODED AS A SINGLE IMAGE WITH NO REFERENCE TO PAST OR FUTURE FRAMES.
- P–FRAME IS ENCODED RELATIVE TO THE PAST REFERENCE FRAME. A REFERENCE FRAME CAN BE A P OR AN I–FRAME
- B–FRAME IS ENCODED RELATIVE TO THE PAST REFERENCE FRAME, THE FUTURE REFERENCE FRAME,
  OR BOTH FRAMES. THE FUTURE REFERENCE FRAME IS THE CLOSEST FOLLOWING REFERENCE FRAME (I OR P)

FIGURE 7-13   MPEG-2 and MPEG-4 compressed image frames: Reference I, difference B, and predictive P

and where appropriate, with higher quality (resolution) than the other areas of the scene.

The MPEG-4 Visual has enhanced functionality compared to MPEG-2. Spatial prediction within I-frames and enhanced error resiliency are two such features. Improved prediction and coding separately improve compression by 15–20% compared to MPEG-2. An advanced feature of MPEG-4 Visual is global motion compensation (GMC). This is especially useful for PTZ applications and mobile applications involving moving ground vehicles, aircraft, and ships, in which camera movement induces most of the image motion. The GMC mode reduces the motion information change to a few parameters per frame as opposed to a separate motion vector for each block of the image. The GMC can lead to significant bit-rate savings in these PTZ motion applications. The MPEG-4 Visual compressors and decompressors (CODECS), having both chips and software, are most often used for the Internet and cell phone applications.

7.4.3.4   MPEG-4 Advanced Video Coding (AVC)/H.264

An improvement over MPEG-4 Visual: MPEG-4 Advanced Video Coding (AVC), also referred to as H.264, offers greater flexibility and greater precision in motion vectors (activity in the scene). The intent of the standard was

also to create one that would be capable of providing good video quality and bit rates that were half or less than previous standards relative to MPEG-2, H.263, or MPEG-4.

The MPEG-4 AVC/H.264 is the most recent video compression standard introduced in 2003. The AVC was jointly developed by MPEG and ITU—a developer of video conferencing standards that calls it H.264. The MPEG-4 AVC achieves better performance than MPEG-2 by about a factor of two, producing similar quality at half the bit rate. The improved performance is mainly due to increased prediction efficiency both within and the between frames. The MPEG-4, MPEG-4 Visual (with or without GMC), and MPEG-4 AVC are superior to MPEG-2 in terms of raw efficiency (quality per bit) and are also more network friendly than MPEG-2.

The H.264 compression system dramatically lowers the bandwidth (by 2 times) required to deliver digital TV (DTV) channels and provides new security business models at a significantly lower cost. Current standard-definition (SD) and the high-definition (HD) digital video are based almost entirely on MPEG-2, the 10-year-old standard that has nearly reached the limit of its video compression efficiency.

The MPEG-4 AVC compression was developed specifically by and for television broadcasting, whether via terrestrial, cable, satellite, or Internet delivery. It uses the same protocol and modulation techniques as MPEG-2 so that MPEG-4 AVC is immediately deployable. By using the same protocol and modulation techniques, MPEG-4 AVC compression reduces the bandwidth by a factor of two, thus requiring 50% less bandwidth or storage capacity compared with MPEG-2 to deliver the same video quality. This means that instead of having to transmit HDTV at 19 Mbps and SD at 4 Mbps, equivalent HD picture quality is obtained at about 8 Mbps, and SP at 2 Mbps, and DVD quality video at less than 1 Mbps. The technology offers greater efficiency and reception with cell phones, PDAs, and specialized pagers. MPEG-4 AVC permits both progressive and interlaced scanning.

The MPEG-4 AVC reaches compression ratios for *low motion* images of 800:1 to 1000:1. With images containing a *high level motion*, MPEG-4 AVC reaches compression ratios of 80:1 to 100:1.

7.4.3.5 JPEG 2000, Wavelet

A newer standard for JPEG compression is JPEG 2000 based on *wavelet* compression algorithms. It has the potential to provide higher resolution at compression ratios of 200:1. The JPEG 2000 was created as the successor to the original JPEG format developed in the late 1980s and is based on state-of-the-art wavelet techniques that provide better compression and advanced system-level functionality. Wavelet video compression operates on the *entire image* at once, rather than on pieces of the image (Figure 7-14).

Wavelet compression in contrast to JPEG and MPEG algorithms is based on full-frame information and on signal *frequency* components. It does not divide the image into 8×8 pixel blocks but analyzes the entire image as a single block.

The JPEG 2000 improves download times of the still image by compressing images to roughly half the size of JPEG. In addition JPEG 2000 permits viewing "something" (a low resolution picture) while waiting for the full high-resolution picture to develop on the screen. JPEG 2000's progressive display initially presents a low-quality image and then updates the display with increasingly higher

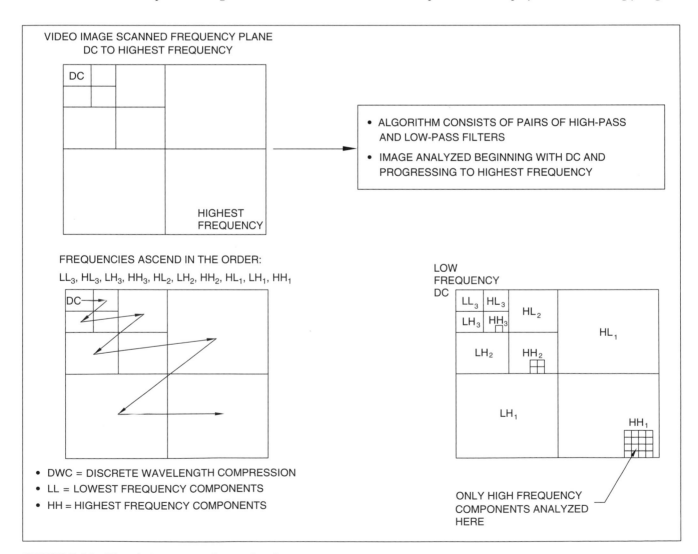

FIGURE 7-14   Wavelet compression technology

quality images. Wavelet compression is similar to JPEG in that it uses multiple single recorded frames to create a video sequence. The average file size for a wavelet image is about 12 Kbps at 30 fps.

Wavelet compression compresses the entire image with multiple filtering, and filters the entire image, both high and low frequencies, and repeats this procedure several times. There is no mosaic effect once the images are viewed because the technology works on the *entire* image at once.

7.4.3.6 Other Compression Methods: H.263, SMICT

7.4.3.6.1 H.263 Standard

The H.263 standard was developed for video conferencing using transmission networks capable of rates below 64 Kbps. It works much the same way MPEG-1 and MPEG-2 work but with reduced functionality to allow very low transmission rates. The H.263 is similar to JPEG except that it only transmits the pixels in each image that have *changed* from the last image, rather than full images. Often the two consecutive images (frames) from a camera are essentially the same and so the H.263 standard takes advantage of this characteristic and uses a frame differencing technique that sends only the *difference* from one frame to the next.

7.4.3.6.2 SMICT Standard

The super motion image compression technology (SMICT) standard has almost the same characteristics of H.264. Based on redundancy in motion, it combines digital signal processing (DSP) hardware compression, with CPU software compression. Utilizing an intelligent non-linear super motion CODEC, SMICT intelligently analyzes the motion changes in the scene that occurred within the frame, eliminates the redundant portion of the image that need not be stored, and compresses the delta (or change) based on motion. Table 7-8 compares the significant parameters of some of the video compression techniques.

The MPEG-7 and the MPEG-21 are new standards being considered.

7.5 INTERNET-BASED REMOTE VIDEO MONITORING—NETWORK CONFIGURATIONS

Wired and wireless digital video networks using LANS, WANS, WiFi, and the Internet have made AVS possible. The digital video signal must be transmitted from the camera location to the monitoring location. For the case of wireless networks there are four basic configurations that are used: (1) point to point—also known as peer to

TYPE	COMPRESSION TRANSFORM	TRANSFORM	BIT RATE	RESOLUTION	FRAME RATE (fps)	LATENCY (TIME LAG)	APPLICATIONS	COMMENTS
JPEG	FRAME-BASED	DCT*	8 Mbps		0–5		STORING STILL VIDEO FRAMES	NOT SUITABLE FOR MOTION VIDEO
MJPEG	FRAME-BASED	DCT	10 Kbps to 3 Mbps	ANY SIZE	0–30	LOW	IP NETWORKS BROADCAST	JPEG PLAYED IN RAPID SUCCESSION
MPEG-1	STREAM-BASED	DCT	1.5 Mbps	352×288 (PAL) 352×240 (NTSC)	UP to 30	MEDIUM	VIDEO CD SOME DVRS	CIF SIZE, VHS TAPE QUALITY
MPEG 2	STREAM-BASED	DCT	2 Mbps to 15 Mbps	720×576 (PAL) 720×480 (NTSC)	24–30	MEDIUM	HDTV	BROADCAST QUALITY
MPEG-4 PART 2	STREAM-BASED	DCT AND WAVLET	10 Kbps to 10 Mbps	640×480 to 4096×2048	1–60	MEDIUM	STREAMING VIDEO INTERNET (WEB)	CCTV WHEN HIGH FRAME RATES REQUIRED OR WHEN SCENE ACTIVITY IS LOW TO MEDIUM
H.263	STREAM-BASED	DCT	30 Kbps to 64 Kbps	128×96 to 704×480	10–15	LOW	TELECONFERENCE	VIDEO STREAMING
H.264/AVC MPEG-4 PART 10	STREAM-BASED	DCT	64 Kbps to 240 Mbps	4096×2048	0–30	LOW	HIGH SPEED VIDEO	NEAR BROADCAST QUALITY. COMPRESSES VIDEO FAR MORE EFFICIENTLY THAN MPEG-4, PART 2
JPEG2000 WAVELET	FRAME-BASED	WAVELET	30 Kbps to 7.5 Mbps	160×120 320×240	8–30	HIGH	SOME CCTV RECORDING	LAG, LIMITED USE IN SECURITY
MPEG-7	———	———	———	———	———	———	BROAD RANGE SMART CARD	MULTI-MEDIA CONTENT NOT YET IN SECURITY

*DIRECT COSINE TRANSFORM. USES INTRA FRAMES (I), PREDICTED FRAMES (P), AND BI-DIRECTIONAL FRAMES (B). I, P, AND B ARE CALLED GROUP OF PICTURES (GOP). AVC—ADVANCED VIDEO CODING

Table 7-8 Comparison of Most Common Compression Standards

peer, (2) multi-point to point, (3) point to multi-point, and (4) mesh. This section describes the four configurations used.

7.5.1 Point to Multi-Point

The point-to-multi-point wireless systems use IP packet radio transmitters and standard Ethernet interfaces to enable high-speed network connections to *multiple* Ethernet switches, routers, or PCs from *one* single location (Figure 7-15).

The network cameras can be connected and conveniently located wherever necessary. Transmission capacities vary from 10 to 60 Mbps and operate at distances up to 10 miles. The point to multi-point (multi-casting) is like a radio or television station in which one signal (station or channel) is broadcast and can be heard (or viewed) by many different users in the same or different locations. With IP multi-cast, the video server needs to transmit only a *single* video stream for each multicast group regardless of the number of clients that will view the information.

7.5.2 Point to Point

Point-to-point wireless video transmission is used in simpler systems to provide connectivity between *two* locations where only a single camera or sensor and a single monitoring location is used and only one to one camera control functions are required (Figure 7-16).

These systems offer higher capacities and greater distances than the point-to-multi-point systems. They are ideal for transmitting video signals from a local central site where a base station is located, to a central command and control center that is located much farther away. Point-to-point systems can connect to remote sites up to 40 miles away from the monitoring site and have transmission bandwidth capacities ranging from ten to several hundred megabits per second.

7.5.3 Multi-Point to Point

The multi-point to point is most commonly used when multiple video cameras are multiplexed into a central control point. Multi-point-to-point systems transmit the video signal from multiple cameras to the remote systems monitoring location (Figure 7-17).

7.5.4 Video Unicast and Multicast

A video broadcast sends out a video data packet intended for transmission to one or multiple nodes on the network. A unicast signal is sent from source to viewer as a standalone stream and required that each viewer have his

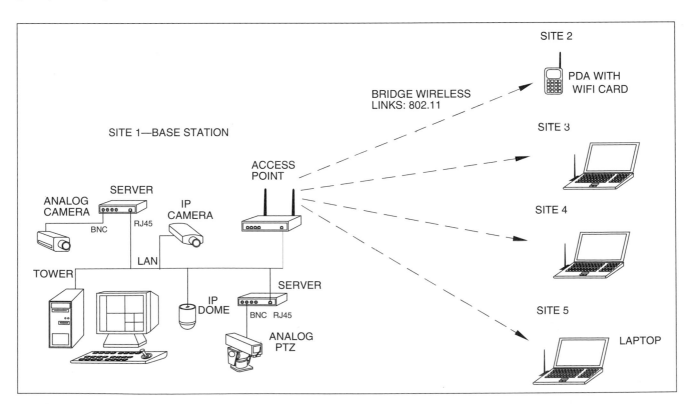

FIGURE 7-15 Point to multi-point wireless network

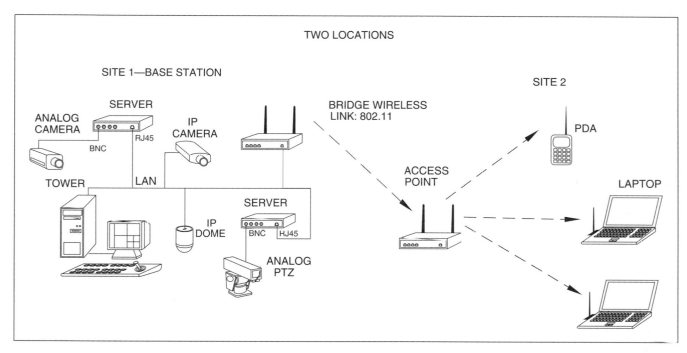

FIGURE 7-16   Point to point wireless network

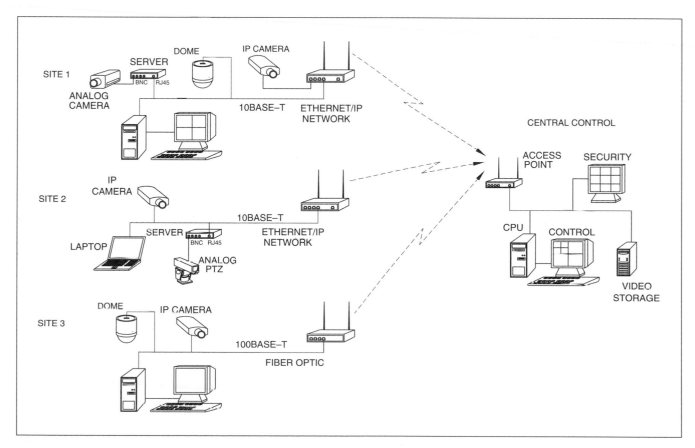

FIGURE 7-17   Multi-point to point wireless network

own video viewer. A multicast stream allows multiple viewers on a network to all share the same feed. The benefit is in bandwidth consumption: for 20 people to view a 1 Mbps video stream as unicast feeds, they would consume a total of 20 Mbps of bandwidth (20 × 1 Mbps). If those same 20 viewers connected to the same feed as a multicast stream, assuming they are all on the same network, they would consume a total of 1 Mbps of bandwidth (Figure 7-18).

7.6 TRANSMISSION TECHNOLOGY PROTOCOLS: WiFi, SPREAD SPECTRUM MODULATION (SSM)

Most wireless LAN systems use spread spectrum technology, a wideband radio frequency technique developed by the military for use in reliable, secure, mission-critical communications systems. Spread spectrum modulation (SSM) is designed to trade off bandwidth efficiency for reliability, integrity, and security. In other words, more bandwidth is consumed than in the case of narrowband transmission, but the trade-off produces a signal that is, in effect, louder and is easier to detect, provided that the receiver knows the parameters of the spread spectrum signal being broadcast. If a receiver is not tuned to the right frequency, a spread spectrum signal looks like background noise (Figure 7-19).

In contrast to SSM, a narrowband radio system transmits and receives information at a specific radio frequency. Narrowband radio keeps the radio signal frequency as narrow as possible, just enough to pass the information. A private telephone line is much like a narrowband radio frequency. When each home in a neighborhood has its own private telephone line, people in one home cannot listen to calls made to other homes. SSM, privacy and non-interference are accomplished by the use of separate radio frequencies, and the radio receiver filters out all radio signals except the one to which it is tuned.

The first publicly available patent on SSM came from the inventors Hedy Lamarr, the Hollywood movie actress, and George Antheil, an avant-garde composer. The patent was granted in 1942 but the engineering details were a closely held military secret for many years. The inventors never profited from their invention, they simply turned the patent over to the US government for use in the World War II effort, and commercial use was delayed

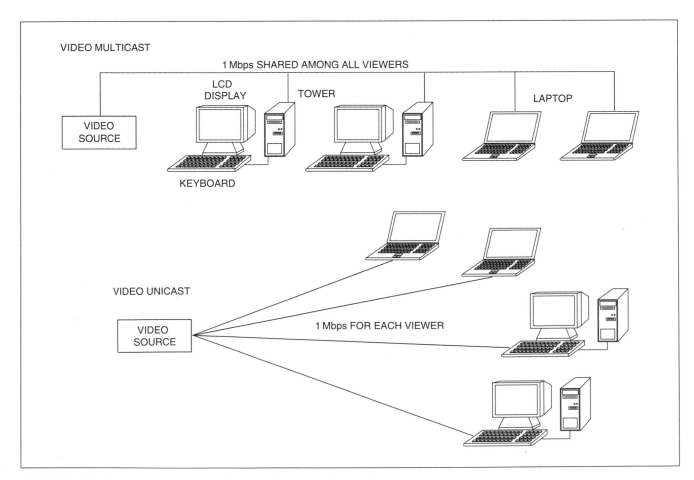

FIGURE 7-18   Video unicast and video multicast configuration

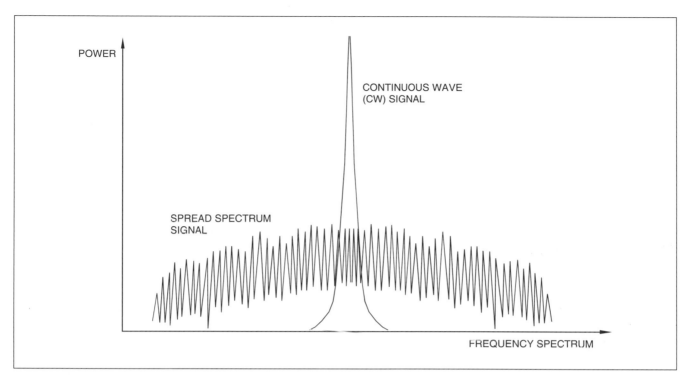

FIGURE 7-19 **Spread spectrum modulation (SSM) compared to narrow band transmission**

until 1985. It was initially developed by the military to avoid jamming and eavesdropping of communication signals. The present global positioning system (GPS), cellular phone, and wireless Internet transmission systems now represent the largest commercial SSM technology applications.

The SSM technology provides reliable and secure communications in environments prone to jamming and/or signals prone to interception by third parties. Most SSM systems operate in the 900 MHz, 2.4 GHz, and 5.8 GHz bands, and require no licensing application and ongoing fees to anyone, providing the strict rules on signal specifications: bandwidth and power output, are adhered to.

The SSM technology is currently the most widely used transmission technique for wireless LANs. The technique spreads the digital signal power over a wide range of frequencies within the band of transmission. The bands for commercial security video transmission range from 902 to 928 MHz, 2.4 to 2.484 GHz, and 5.1 to 5.8 GHz, all of which do not require an FCC license.

There are two types of spread spectrum radio: frequency hopping (FH) and direct sequence (DS). In the 1960s Aerojet General first used the FH concept, the predecessor to SSM for military applications in which the signal frequencies were rapidly switched. The SSM is a similar concept to FH only performed at a much faster rate. The radio signal required very little transmitter power and was immune to noise and interference from other similar systems employing the exact same carrier frequency. The radio signal was secure and completely undetectable by signal spectrum analyzers then available.

7.6.1 Spread Spectrum Modulation (SSM)

7.6.1.1 Background

The purpose of SSM is to improve (reduce) the bit error rate of the signal in the presence of noise or interference. This is achieved by spreading a transmitted signal over a frequency range greater than the minimum bandwidth required for information transmission. By spreading the data transmission over a large bandwidth, the average power level of any one frequency is reduced and less interference is caused to others in the band. Implemented appropriately, others will interfere less with the signal even if others do not employ SSM techniques. While the channel data may be analog or digital, for simplicity a basic digital system is considered.

Frequency hopping the transmitter repeatedly changes the carrier frequency from one to another, referred to as hopping. The hopping pattern is usually controlled by a pseudo noise (PN) code generator. Any narrowband interference can only jam the FH signal for a short period of time in every PN code period.

Direct sequence spread spectrum (DSSS) is the technology in most use today, and spreads the spectrum by modulating the original signal with PN noise. The PN is defined as a wideband sequence of digital bits, called chips that are employed to minimize confusion. The DSSS receiver converts this wideband signal into its original, narrow base-band signal by an operation known as *de-spreading*. While de-spreading its own signal, the receiver spreads any narrowband interfering signals, thereby reducing the interference power in the narrow-band detection system.

A typical spread spectrum radio transmitter transmits a sequence of coding bits, referred to as PN code, and spreads the signal over a radio spectrum 20 MHz wide per channel. At the receiver end both the desired and foreign signals are de-spread to effectively regenerate the desired signal and suppress the foreign signals. In a typical wireless LAN configuration, a transmitter/receiver (transceiver) device, called an *access point*, connects upstream to the wired network from a fixed location using standard cabling.

7.6.1.2 Frequency Hopping Spread Spectrum Technology (FHSS)

Frequency hopping spread spectrum (FHSS) uses a narrowband carrier that changes frequency and a pattern known to both the transmitter and receiver. Properly synchronized, the net effect is to maintain a single logical channel. To an unintended receiver the FHSS appears to be short duration impulse noise. Figure 7-20 illustrates how FHSS works.

The FHSS technique broadcasts the signal over a seemingly random series of radio frequencies and a receiver hops and follows these frequencies in synchronization while receiving the signal message. The message can only be fully received if the series of frequencies is known. Since only the intended receiver knows the transmitter's hopping sequence, only that receiver can successfully receive all the signals.

7.6.1.3 Slow Hoppers

With this technique the data signal is transmitted as a narrowband signal with a bandwidth only wide enough to carry the required data rate. At specific intervals this narrowband signal is moved or *hopped* to a different frequency within the allowed band. The sequence of frequencies follows a pseudo-random sequence known to both the transmitter and the receiver. Once the receiver has acquired the hopping sequence of the transmitter, one or more packets are transmitted before the frequency is hopped to the next channel. Many data bits are transmitted between hops. This technique is useful for narrowband data radios but not for wideband video signals.

7.6.1.4 Fast Hoppers

Similar in manner to slow hoppers, fast hoppers make many hops for each bit of data that is transmitted. In this way each data bit is redundantly transmitted on several different frequencies. At the receiving end, the receiver need only receive a *majority* of the redundant bits correctly in order to recover the data without error. The real benefit of the fast hopper is that true *process gain* is provided by

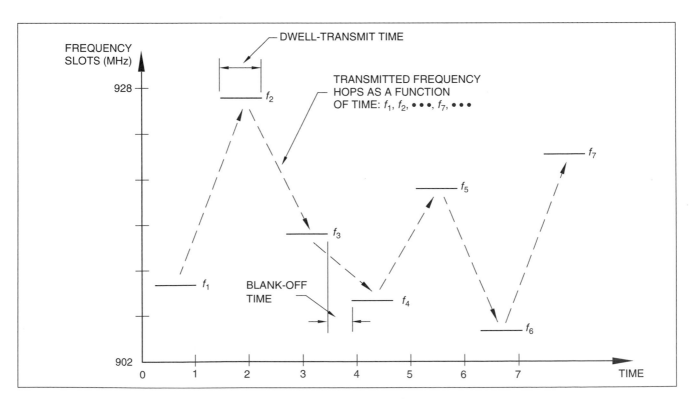

FIGURE 7-20   Frequency hopping spread spectrum (FHSS) technology

the system due to this real-time redundancy of data transmission. This allows interference to exist in the band that would effectively block one or more narrowband channels without causing loss of data.

7.6.1.5 Direct Sequence Spread Spectrum (DSSS)

The DSSS method is the most widely used SSM technique and is currently used in most WiFi systems. The DSSS increases the rate of hopping so that each data bit can be even more redundantly encoded (more process gain) or that a higher bit rate can be transmitted as required in video signals.

The DSSS generates a redundant pattern for each bit to be transmitted. This bit pattern is called a chip (or chipping code). It follows that the longer the chip, the greater the probability that the original data can be recovered and, of course, the more bandwidth required. Even if one or more bits in the chip are damaged during transmission, statistical techniques embedded in the radio can recover the original data without the need for retransmission. To an unintended receiver, DSSS appears as low-power wideband noise and is rejected (ignored) by most narrowband receivers. Figure 7-21 illustrates how this technology works.

The FCC rules on signal specifications limit the practical data throughput for DSSS protocol to 2 Mbps in the 902 MHz band, 8 Mbps in the 2.4 GHz band, and 100 Mbps

in the 5.8 GHz band. The FCC also requires that transmitters must hop through at least 50 channels in the 902 MHz band and 75 channels in the 2.4 GHz band.

The DSSS transmitters spread their transmissions by adding redundant data bits called "chips" to them. The DSSS adds at least 10 chips to each data bit. Once a receiver has received all of the signal and chip bits, it uses a correlator to remove the chips and collapses the signal to its original length. The IEEE 802.11 standard requires 11 chips for DSSS transmission.

The DSSS system can operate when other systems such as microwave radio, two-way communications devices, alarm systems, and/or other DSSS devices are transmitting in close proximity. It also has the ability to select different channels to provide workarounds on the rare occasions that interference occurs.

The magical and non-intuitive element of the DSSS system breakthrough is that by multiplying the PN DDSS spread signal with a copy of the same pseudo noise, the original data signal is recovered. This process is called *correlation* and only occurs if the codes are identical and perfectly aligned in time to within a small fraction of the code clock. By using concurrently different pseudo-random codes, multiple independent communications links can simultaneously operate within the same frequency band. To recover the specific encoded data channel, the inverse function is applied to the received signal. A major breakthrough in DSSS came when it was

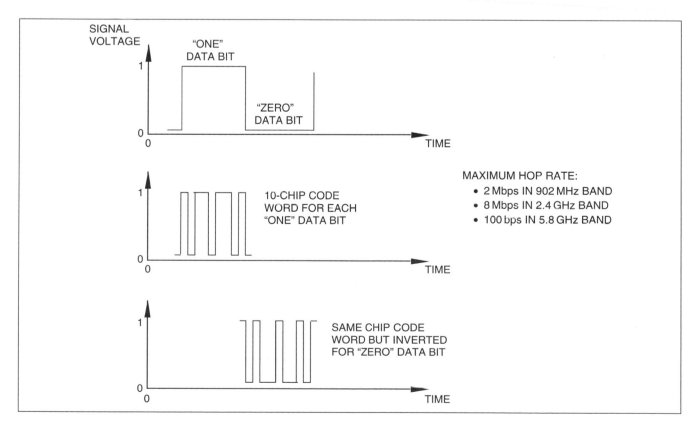

FIGURE 7-21   Direct sequence spread spectrum (DSSS) technology

realized that a pseudo-random digital code or pseudo-random noise contains the frequencies from DC to that of the code clock rate. When the narrowband data signal is multiplied by the pseudo-random code sequence, the spectrum of the signal is spread to a bandwidth twice that of the code (Figure 7-22).

The amount of performance improvement that is achieved against interference is known as the *processing gain* of the system. An ideal estimate for processing gain is the ratio of the spread spectrum bandwidth to the signal information rate:

$$\text{Processing Gain} = \frac{\text{SSM Bandwidth}}{\text{Signal Bandwidth}}$$

It is important to note that data rate (signal bandwidth) and process gain are inversely proportional. In a digital data system, the process gain can be directly determined by the ratio of the pseudo-random code bits, called chips, and data or symbol rate of the desired data. For example, a system that spreads each symbol by 256 chips per symbol has a ratio of 256:1. The process gain is generally expressed in dB, the value of which is determined by the expression:

$$\text{P gain (in dB)} = 10 \, \text{Log Base 10 (Chips/Symbol)}$$

This corresponds to 24 dB for the example of 256 chips/symbol.

In any case, the SSM technique results in a system that is extremely difficult to detect by observers outside the system, does not interfere with other services, and has the capability of carrying a large bandwidth of data, specifically video image transmissions for surveillance applications.

7.6.2 WiFi Protocol: 802.11 Standards

Using a wireless LAN (WLAN, WiFi) dramatically reduces the time and cost of adding PCs and laptops to an established network. For a small or medium company, a complete wireless network can be set up within hours, with minimal disruption to the business. A laptop or PDA with WLAN allows mobile employees to be more productive by working from public "hotspots," at airports, hotels, etc.

Among the most fundamental steps to take when planning a WLAN is to learn about the various IEEE 802.11 standards, decide which one is appropriate for the application requirements, and apply it according to the standard. The WiFi Alliance is responsible for awarding the WiFi certified logo that ensures 802.11 compatibility and multivendor interoperability. The original 802.11 PHY (physical) standard established in June 1997 defined a 2.4 GHz system with a maximum data rate of 2 Mbps. This technology still exists but should not be considered for new deployment. In 1999 the IEEE defined two additions to the 802.11 PHY, namely 802.11b and 802.11a.

There are two basic *categories* of IEEE 802.11 standards.

1. The first are those that specify the fundamental protocols for the complete WiFi system. These are called 802.11a, 802.11b, and 802.11g standards and the new 802.11n standard.

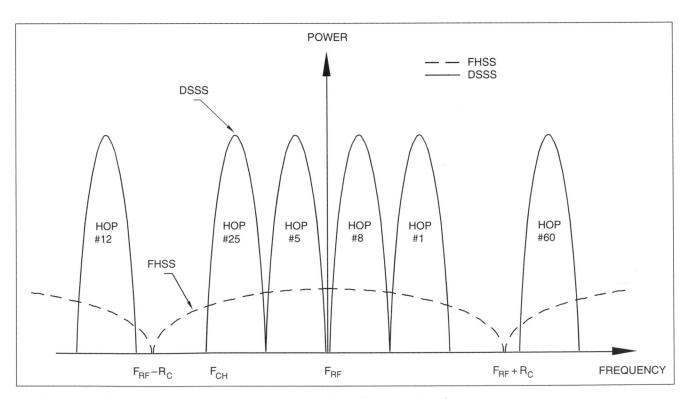

FIGURE 7-22   Direct sequence spread spectrum (DSSS) modulation signal

2. Second, there are extensions that address weaknesses that provide additional functionality to these standards. These are 802.11d, e, f, h, i, and j. Only the 802.11i and 802.11e standards relating to quality of service (QoS) security are considered.

Table 7-9 shows the parameters of these fundamental 802.11 standards.

Each of these standards has unique advantages and disadvantages. Their specific attributes must be considered before choosing one.

7.6.2.1 802.11b Standard

The 802.11b technology uses the 2.4 GHz radio spectrum to deliver data at a rate of 11 Mbps, and allows for three non-overlapping channels to be used simultaneously. The 802.11b standard occupies 83.5 MHz (for North America) from 2.4000 to 2.4835 GHz. The standard 802.11b should be considered if there is no high bandwidth requirement, i.e. near real-time video is not required but there is a need for a wide coverage area. If price is a primary consideration the 802.11b system costs roughly one quarter as much has an 802.11a network covering the same area at the same data rate. Its main disadvantage is its lower maximum link rate. Also since it occupies the 2.4 GHz band used by other technologies this rate may be reduced further due to interference issues.

7.6.2.2 802.11a Standard

The 802.11a technology uses the 5 GHz radio spectrum to deliver data at a rate of 54 Mbps, and allows for 12 channels to be used simultaneously. The 802.11a standard occupies 300 MHz in three different bandwidths of 100 MHz each:

1. 5.150–5.250 GHz, lower band
2. 5.250–5.350 GHz, middle band
3. 5.725–5.825 GHz, upper band.

Table 7-10 lists nine (4 non-overlapping) 20 MHz bandwidth channels available in the 5.8 GHz band.

The 802.11a standard should be considered if the application requires high bandwidth, as required in high frame rate video transmission. It also should be considered when there is a small, densely packed concentration of users. The greater number of non-overlapping channels allows access points to be placed closer together without interference. Two disadvantages of the 802.11a standard is that it is not backward compatible with the older 802.11b standard, and costs roughly four times as much to cover the same area.

IEEE STANDARD	OPERATING FREQUENCY (GHz)	DOWNLOAD SPEED* (Mbps)	BANDWIDTH (MHz)	CHANNELS	APPLICATIONS/COMMENTS
802.11a	5.8	54	TOTAL: 300 EACH CHANNEL: 20	12 12 NON-OVERLAPPING	HIGH BANDWIDTH, HIGH FRAME RATE MANY NON-OVERLAPPING CHANNELS
802.11b	2.4	11	TOTAL: 83.5 EACH CHANNEL: 22	11 3 NON-OVERLAPPING	LOW INTERFERENCE IN AREA REALTIME VIDEO NOT REQUIRED LOW COST
802.11e	—	—	—	—	DEFINES QUALITY of SERVICE (QoC) (a) BANDWIDTH (b) LATENCY (c) JITTER (d) SIGNAL LOSS
802.11g	2.4	11, 54	EACH CHANNEL: 22	3 NON-OVERLAPPING 12 NON-OVERLAPPING	WIDE–AREA COVERAGE HIGH BANDWIDTH DUAL BAND BACKWARD COMPATIBLE WIH 802.11b
802.11i	—	—	—	—	ENHANCED SECURITY– AUTHENTICATION PROTOCOL IMPROVED SECURITY KEY ADDS HIGH LEVEL AES ENCRYPTION
802.11n	—	108 200	—	SUPPORTS MIMO DEPLOYMENT	NEWEST STANDARD: HIGH DATA RATE AND BANDWIDTH. HIGH THROUGHPUT UP TO 600 Mbps. SUPPORTS MIMO DEPLOYMENT.

* THEORETICAL MAXIMUM RATES. REALISTIC MAXIMUM APPROXIMATELY 1/2.

IEEE—INSTITUTE of ELECTRICAL and ELECTRONIC ENGINEERS
MIMO—MULTIPLE–IN MULTIPLE–OUT

Table 7-9   IEEE 802.11 a, b, g, i, and n WiFi Standard Characteristics

CHANNEL	NUMBER FREQUENCY (GHz)	BAND *	MAXIMUM POWER OUT	MODULATION METHOD	CHANNELS
1	5.735				
1A	5.745				
2	5.755				
2A	5.765				9 MAXIMUM
3	5.775	UNII UPPER BAND	800 mW	COFDM	4 NON–OVERLAPPING
3A	5.785				
4	5.795				
4A	5.805				
5	5.815				

* 802.11a OCCUPIES 300 MHz IN THREE DIFFERENT BANDWIDTHS OF 100 MHz EACH
TOTAL OF 9 CHANNELS AVAILABLE: 4 NON-OVERLAPPING.
COFDM—CODED ORTHOGONAL FREQUENCY DIVISION MULTIPLEXING.
UNII—UNLICENSED NATIONAL INFORMATION INFRASTRUCTURE

Table 7-10   Wireless Transmission Channels in 5.8 GHz Band

7.6.2.3 802.11g Standard

The 802.11g technology uses the 2.4 GHz radio spectrum to deliver data at a rate of 54 Mbps, and allows for three channels to be used simultaneously. The 802.11g standard is applicable to high-bandwidth video applications that require wide-area coverage. It should also be considered if backward compatibility with 802.11b is required. The main disadvantage of 802.11g is that maximum data throughput is reduced when 802.11g and 802.11b equipment shares the same network. Since it shares the 2.4 GHz frequency spectrum used by microwave ovens, cordless phones, garage door openers, and other wireless gadgets, it faces the same interference issues as 802.11b.

Manufacturers such as Intel are supplying chipsets that include the IEEE 802.11a, b, and g technologies so that PCs and laptops can continue to connect to corporate wireless LANs without a hardware upgrade requirement even if the enterprise upgrades to a new infrastructure.

7.6.2.4 802.11n Standard

The new 802.11n WiFi standard has high throughput and was created to provide over 100 Mbps *effective* throughput, complementing all broadband access technologies including fiber optic, DSL, cable, and satellite. The goal of the 802.11n protocol standard is to increase the 54 Mbps transmission to over 100 Mbps.

The goal of the newest generation 802.11n standard more than triples the real throughput of WiFi and pushes the 30 Mbps standard to at least 108 Mbps. The new 802.11n standard including MIMO processing in its specification should produce performance of 144–200 Mbps.

Figure 7-23 compares the throughput and distance improvements using the MIMO-based wireless LAN.

7.6.2.5 802.11i Standard

The 802.11i standard provides enhanced security for wireless transmissions. It includes the use of authentication protocol, an improved key distribution framework, and stronger encryption via AES.

7.6.3 Asynchronous Transfer Mode (ATM)

Two common protocols adopted to transmit video, voice, data, and controls over the Internet are the IP and asynchronous transfer mode (ATM). The ATM is a broadband network technology that allows very large amounts of data to be transmitted at a high rate (wide bandwidth). It does this by connecting many links into a single network. This feature has an important implication for transmitting high-quality video with a guaranteed QoS.

The ATM was developed in concept in the early 1980s. Since the early 1990s ATM has been highly touted as the ultimate network switching solution. This is because of its high speed and its ability to serve video and all other information types, and its ability to guarantee each type an appropriate QoS. The ATM is a fast-packet, connection-oriented, cell-switching technology for broadband signals. It has been designed from concept up, to accommodate any form of information: video images, voice, facsimile, and data whether compressed or uncompressed at broadband speeds and on an unbiased basis. Further, all such data can be supported with a very small set of

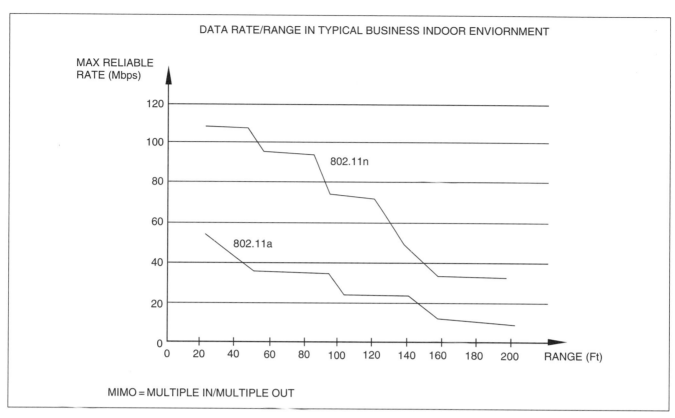

FIGURE 7-23   Rate/range comparison of 802.11a vs. 802.11n MIMO indoors

network protocols, regardless of whether the network is local, metropolitan, or wide area in nature. The ATM generally operates at minimum access speeds of 50 Mbps up to 155 Mbps. The ATM has, however, been slow to be accepted, is clearly on the rise, but it is a long time away before it may ultimately replace all of the circuit-, packet-, and frame-switching technologies currently in place.

7.7   TRANSMISSION NETWORK SECURITY

The WLANs transmit video and data over the air using radio waves. Any WLAN client in the area served by the data transmitter can receive or intercept the information signal. Radio waves travel through ceilings, floors, and walls and can reach unintended recipients on different floors and outside buildings. Given the nature of the technology there is no way to assuredly direct a WLAN transmission to only one recipient.

Users must be conscious of security concerns when planning wireless 802.11 networks. The first step of WLAN security is to perform a network audit to locate rogue access points within the network. The second step involves the basics of configuring and implementing the best security practices at all access points of the WLAN. In 2001, researchers and hackers demonstrated their ability to crack wired equivalency policy (WEP), a standard encryption for 802.11 wireless LANs. Because these encryption

and authentication standards were vulnerable, stronger methods were developed and should be deployed to more completely secure a WLAN. The 802.11i standard has accounted for weaknesses in previous protocols but is still subject to some vulnerability if improperly implemented or by-passed by rogue devices.

Every enterprise network needs a policy to ensure security on the network, and WLANs are no different. While policies will vary based on individual security and management requirements of each WLAN, a thorough policy and enforcement of the policy can protect an enterprise from unnecessary security breaches and performance degradation.

7.7.1   Wired Equivalent Privacy (WEP)

The IEEE 802.11 WLAN standards include a security component called wired equivalent privacy (WEP). The WEP defines how clients and access points identify each other and communicate securely using secret keys and encryption algorithms. Although the algorithms used are well understood and not considered vulnerable, the particular way in which the keys are managed has resulted in a number of easily exploitable weaknesses. The WEP security relies on the user name/password method. Many WLAN access points are shipped with the WEP security *disabled by default*. This allows any WLAN-enabled device to connect to the network *unchallenged*. However, even when WEP is enabled there are still ways to breach the security; it just takes a little longer. As a first basic layer of security it is imperative that network administrators turn WEP "ON" *prior* to deploying access points in the corporate network.

Most enterprises using wireless LANs do not enable the WEP and consequently users should presume that any data sent over such a wireless link can be intercepted. Furthermore with WEP now cracked by malicious hackers, organizations must explore additional measures including virtual private networks (VPNs) and vendor specific authentication schemes to provide more robust protection of the data passed over the wireless link.

Wireless LAN signals do not necessarily stop at the outer walls of a building, a corporate campus border, or a physical plant perimeter. Physical security is ineffective in protecting against wireless LAN intrusions. In some metropolitan areas, hackers armed with portable computers or even PDAs with LAN cards make a game of drive-by invasions of corporate networks. As a first step, existing wireless LANs should be checked to ensure that WEP security protection is enabled.

7.7.2 Virtual Private Network (VPN)

Network architects considering WLAN deployments must look beyond current WEP technology to ensure that security is not compromised. Currently the "best practices" recommendations are to overlay a VPN on top of the WLAN to establish an encrypted tunnel for users and devices to exchange sensitive information securely. Many current out-of-the-box VPN products support alternate methods for authenticating users and devices such as the use of digital IDs. It is extremely important to take advantage of enhanced identification methods for VPN, as a high level of trust is needed to grant users full access to security information. Companies must invest in products that provide secure identification and authentication capabilities with the VPN.

Having a VPN overlay and basic security with a WLAN is comparable to having a security guard in the lobby of a building. The guard calls to let you know that John Doe is there to see you. If you are expecting him you let him through. But, is he who he who really says he is and how would you know until you saw him walk through the door? The security guard alone still leaves the hole in the system. But if the security guard must check John Doe's passport (or a credential he knows to be authentic), there is no way he is coming in without authenticated documentation to prove his identity. Likewise to achieve mutual authentication, the security guard must present his or her own passport to Mr. Doe, so he knows he is at the correct building and not about to meet with an impostor.

To deploy a VPN, the WLAN access point is placed outside the firewall and a VPN gateway is placed between the two. Since the WLAN access point is outside the firewall, it is effectively being treated as an untrustworthy network resource since it blurs the security parameter. Even if WEP security is compromised, no access to corporate resources is possible without a subsequent authenticated VPN.

Most enterprises deploying wireless LANs will be forced to embrace vendor-specific security architecture or use VPNs. A VPN cannot be used everywhere in the wireless LAN architecture due to lack of VPN client support from manufacturers on certain handheld devices and proprietary operating systems.

7.7.3 WiFi Protected Access (WPA)

WiFi protected access (WPA) is an interim standard developed by the WiFi Alliance. It combines several technologies that address known 802.11× security vulnerabilities. It provides an affordable, scalable solution for protecting existing corporate WLANs without the additional expense of the VPN/firewall technology. It includes the uses of the 802.11× standard in the extensible authentication protocol. For encryption it uses the temporal key integrity protocol and WEP 128-bit encryption keys. The WPA is a subset of the 802.11i standard. The WPA interim standard upgrades legacy systems and is an improvement over the WEP system. After upgrading to the WPA standard, firewalls and VPNs are no longer necessary. The national Institute of standards and technology (NIST) will not certify WPA under the FIPS 140-2 security standard. The federal government is mandated to procure a new system that conform to the FIPS 140-2 security standard and will not certify WPA onto this new standard.

7.7.4 Advanced Encryption Standard (AES), Digital Encryption Standard (DES)

The data encryption standard (DES) is probably the most popular secret-key system in use on wired networks today. The much trickier triple DES is a special mode of DES that is used primarily for highly sensitive information. Triple DES uses three software keys. Data is encrypted with the first key, decrypted with the second key, and then encrypted again by the third key. The security chips used in equipment contain a triple-DES encryption/decryption engine that secures the content, avoiding troublesome theft-of-service issues for content providers. Moreover it prevents accidental viewing by another receiver sensor since it locks the data stream to a particular receiver. It provides capability for additional network entry, authentication, and authorization.

The advanced encryption standard (AES) was selected by NIST in October 2000 as an upgrade from the previous DES standard. The AES uses a 128-bit block cipher algorithm and encryption technique for protecting digital digital information. With the ability to use even larger 192-bit and 256-bit keys, if necessary, it offers higher security against brute-force attack than 56-bit DES keys. The 128-bit key size AES standard makes hacking of data nearly impossible.

The AES is replacing both triple DES on wired networks and WEP on wireless LANs. For wireless networks, AES is being built into equipment complying with the new 802.11i protocol.

7.7.5 Firewalls, Viruses, Hackers

A firewall can be a software program, a hardware device, or a combination of both. Basically a firewall is a system or group of systems that enforces an access control policy between two networks. The term "firewall" has become commonplace in discussions of network security. While firewalls certainly play an important role in securing the network, there are certain misconceptions regarding them that lead people to falsely believe that their systems are totally secure once they have a firewall. Firewalls are effective against attacks that attempt to go *through* the firewall, but they cannot protect against attacks that *don't go through* the firewall. Nor can a firewall prevent individual employees with modems from dialing into or out of the network, bypassing the firewall entirely.

The purpose of the firewall is to protect networked computers from intentional hostile intrusion from *outside* the network. Any private network that is connected to a public network needs firewall protection. Any enterprise that connects even a single computer to the Internet via a modem should have personal firewall software.

What can the firewall protect against? Generally firewalls are configured to protect against unauthenticated interactive logins from outside the network. Firewalls help prevent pranksters and vandals from logging into the network computers. A firewall examines all traffic routed between two networks to see if the traffic meets certain criteria. There are two distinct types of firewalls that are commonly used: (1) the packet filtering router and (2) the proxy server. The first type of firewall, the packet filtering router, is a machine that forwards packets between two or more networks. It works on a set of rules and codes and decides whether to forward or block packets based on the rules and codes. The second type of firewall, the proxy server, has had the normal protocols FTP (file transfer protocol) and Telnet replaced with special servers. It relies on special protocols to provide authentication and to forward packets. In some instances the two types of firewalls are combined so that a selected machine is allowed to send packets through a packet filtering router onto an internal network.

7.8 INTERNET PROTOCOL NETWORK CAMERA, ADDRESS

The fastest-growing technology segment in the video security industry is that of networked or IP addressable cameras and associated equipment. As the video industry shifts from traditional legacy analog CCTV monitoring to an OCTV networking system, IP cameras with internal servers are going to completely change the way surveillance is configured (Figure 7-24a,b).

The camera configurations and set up and viewing of video images will be done via a LAN, WAN, MAN, or WLAN backbone, and a standard Web browser. Some security equipment manufacturers are referring to the next generation of video as Internet protocol television (IPTV).

The devices making up a digital video surveillance system are comprised of an IP network camera, a video server, and PC or laptop computer. In portable surveillance applications the laptop, PDA, and cell phone are the monitoring devices. The following sections describe each of these devices and what functional part they play in the overall camera surveillance and control functions.

The industry offers two different methods for networking cameras. The first method is that of incorporating an IP addressable camera into an existing LAN, WAN, or MAN configuration (Figure 7-25).

In this method each camera is assigned a *static* IP address. With proper security codes or passwords this video information can be viewed on a standard Web browser on the network. These IP cameras with their built-in servers generally have capability for four video inputs. At the receiving and monitoring location there are two choices: (1) the system converts the video back into an analog format so that it can be displayed and/or recorded on an analog display and recorder, or (2) the video remains in digital form and is directly displayed on an LCD, PC, or laptop, and recorded on a digital video recorder (DVR). The second method for implementing remote or networked cameras is adapting the existing or standard legacy cameras and configured systems into a local network (Figure 7-26).

The video outputs from the cameras, matrix switchers, and digital recorders are sent via interface adapters onto the input of the LAN, WAN, WLAN, or Internet network. The system starts as a standard security system before the video outputs and system control lines are connected to a standalone or plug-in Ethernet network interface unit.

The security industry is transitioning from an analog to digital system by transporting the digital video images over an IP-based network using IP cameras as the video image source. Networked cameras can connect directly into the existing network via an Ethernet port, and eliminate the coaxial or UTP cabling that is required for analog cameras (Figure 7-27).

When computers are already in place, no additional equipment is needed for viewing the video image from the network camera. The camera output can be viewed

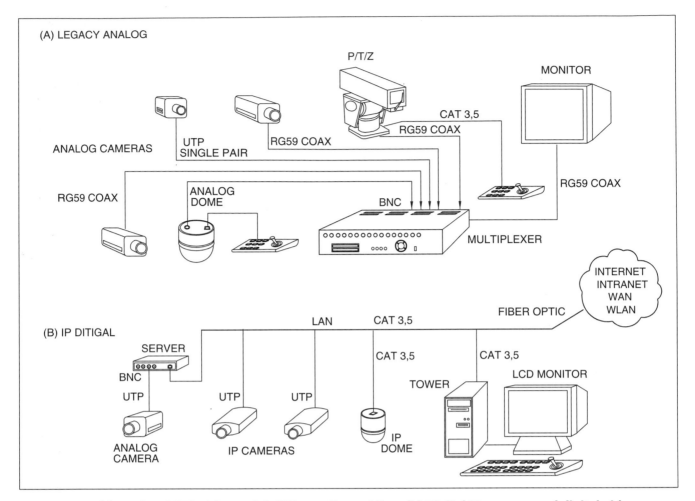

FIGURE 7-24 (a) Analog CCTV with coaxial, UTP, or other cabling, (b) Digital IP cameras and digital video server on wired LAN network

in its simplest form on a Web browser and the computer monitor. If analog cameras are already present at a site the addition of the video server will make those camera images available in any location. To connect to the Internet many different kinds of transmission types are available. These include standard and ISDN modems, DSL modems, cable TV modems, T1 connections, and 10BaseT and 100BaseT Ethernet connections. In addition, cellular-phone modems and various 802.11 wireless network options are also available.

7.8.1 Internet Protocol Network Camera

The network camera has its own IP address and built-in computing functions to handle any network communication (Figure 7-28). Everything needed for viewing images over the network is built into the camera unit. The network camera can be described as a camera and a computer combined. It is connected directly to the network as any other network device and has built-in software for a web server. It can also include alarm input and relay output. More advanced network cameras can be equipped

with functions such as motion detection and analog video output.

An IP compliant network camera contains a lens, a video imaging chip, a compression chip, and a computer. The network camera lens focuses the image onto a CCD or CMOS sensor that captures the image scene and digital electronics transforms the scene into electrical signals. The video signals are then transferred into the computer function, where the images are compressed and sent out over the network (Figure 7-29).

For storing and transmitting images over the network, the video data must be compressed or it will consume too much disk space or bandwidth. If bandwidth is limited the amount of information being sent must be reduced by lowering the frame rate and accepting a lower image quality.

7.8.2 Internet Protocol Camera Protocols

To facilitate communications between devices on a network they must be properly and uniquely addressed. Just as the telephone companies must issue phone numbers that are not duplicated, the computers and devices on the

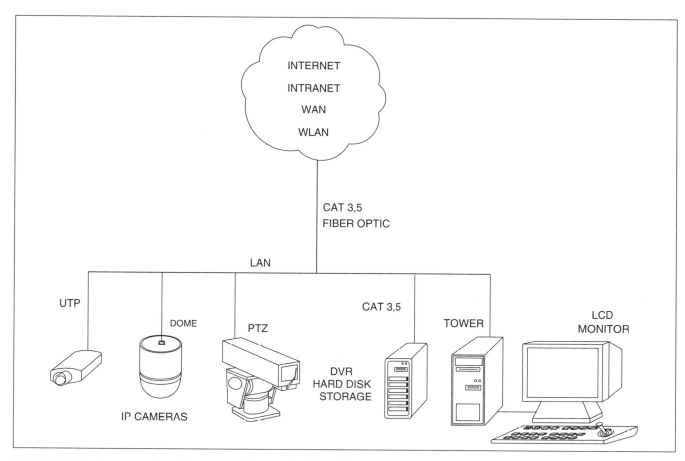

FIGURE 7-25   Incorporating IP cameras in an existing LAN, WAN, or MAN

network must be carefully programmed so that data transmissions can be transmitted and received from one to the other. Each network device has two addresses: (1) media access control (MAC) physical address and (2) IP logical address. The MAC addresses are hard-coded into a device or product at the factory (manufacturer) and typically are never changed. The IP addresses are settable and changeable, allowing networks to be configured and changed. The IP address uniquely identifies a node or device just as a name identifies a particular person. No two devices on the same network should ever have the same address. There are two versions of IP existing in use today. Most networks now use IP version 4 (IPv4) but new systems will begin to use the next-generation IP version 6 (IPv6), a protocol designed to accommodate a much larger number of computer and device address assignments.

The Internet Corporation for Assigned Names and Numbers (ICANN) is a non-profit organization formed in 1999 to assume responsibilities from the federally funded Internet Assigned Numbers Authority (IANA) for assigning parameters for IPs, managing the IP address space, assigning domain names, and managing root server functions. The ICANN assigns IP addresses to organizations desiring to place computers on the Internet. The IP class and the resulting number of available host addresses an organization receives depends on the size of the organization.

The organization assigns the numbers and can reassign them on the basis of either *static* or *dynamic* addressing. Static addressing involves the *permanent* association of an IP address with a specific device or machine. Dynamic addressing assigns an *available* IP address to the machine each time a connection is established. As an example, an Internet Service Provider (ISP) may hold one or more Class C address blocks. Given the limited number of IP addresses available, the ISP assigns an IP address to a user machine each time the dial-up user accesses the ISP to seek connection to the Internet. Once the connection is terminated, that IP address becomes available to other users.

7.8.3   Internet Protocol Camera Address

Unlike traditional analog CCTV systems, network video is based on sets of transmission standards and protocols. These rules are necessary because the video system is no longer a closed system but an open system interconnecting with many clients and users. There are two primary sets of standards that control networking: (1) 802 created by the IEEE and (2) Open Systems Interconnect (OSI) seven-layer model, created by the International Organization for Standardization (IOS). The following sections summarize the standards.

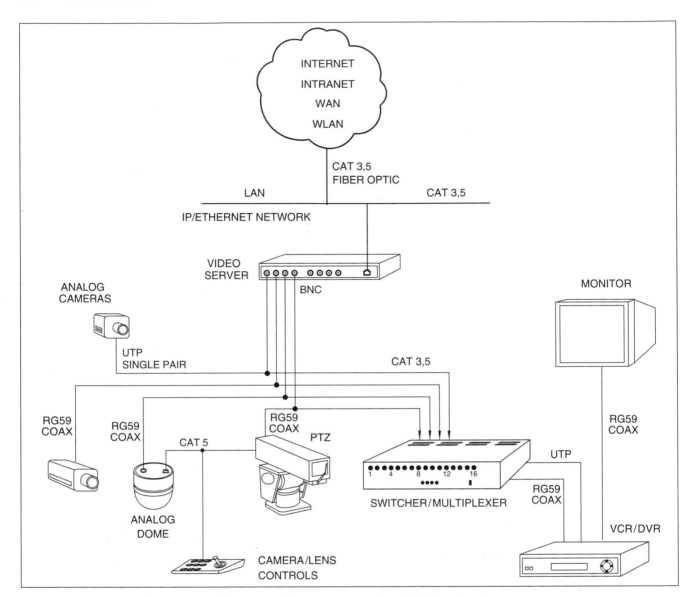

FIGURE 7-26 Diagram to connect legacy analog cameras to the digital network

The OSI seven-layer model is the standard cited in almost all network documents and is the central part of any network foundation. Although all the OSI layers are necessary for communication, the four considered in this analysis are: (1) Physical, (2) Data Link, (3) Network, and (4) Transport. Figure 7.30 summarizes the seven layers of the OSI networking model.

The Physical Layer 1 deals with the hardware of the system. This includes items like servers, routers, hubs, network interface cards, etc. This physical layer has the function of converting digital bits into electronic signals and connecting the devices to the network.

The Data Link Layer 2 provides the interface, or link, between the higher layers in the network hardware. The Data Link Layer has three functions: (1) make sure a connection is available between two network nodes, (2) encapsulate the data into frames for transmission, and (3) ensure that incoming data is received correctly by performing some error checking routines. Layer 2 is divided into two sub layers: *logical ink control* and *media access control.* The media access control layer is better known by MAC which is a hard-coded address assigned to every network interface on any device made to attach to a network. This address is assigned by the manufacture of the device. The MAC addresses are unique throughout the entire world. The address itself is a 48-bit address, consisting of six octets (eight-digit numbers, in binary).

Connections between devices on a network are ultimately made by MAC address, not IP addresses or domain names. Those methods simply assist a device in finding the MAC of another device. The first part of the MAC address, or the first three of octets, is unique to the manufacturer of the device. It is called the *organizational unique identifier.* Every company manufacturing network devices

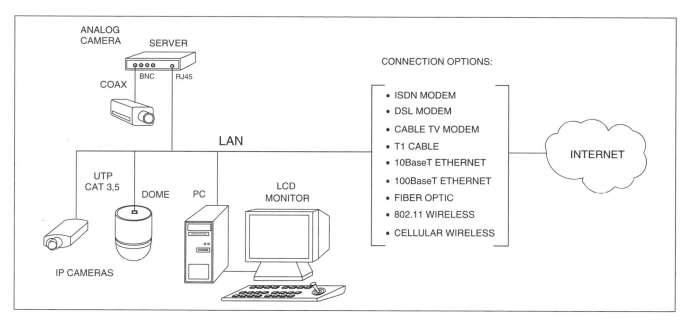

FIGURE 7-27   Diagram to connect networked cameras, Ethernet and Internet

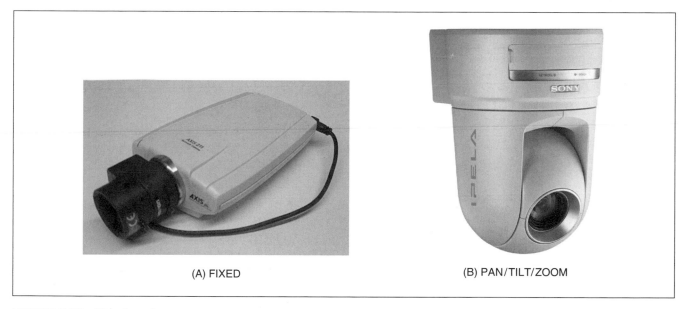

(A) FIXED   (B) PAN/TILT/ZOOM

FIGURE 7-28   IP network camera

has one or several. The second part of the MAC or the last three octets, is unique to each device. No two devices in the world should have the same MAC address.

The second sub-layer in Layer 2 is the logical link control (LLC). The LLC takes the raw data bits from the upper layers and encapsulates them in preparation for transmission. It organizes the data into frames, giving information such as addressing, error checking, etc. After framing and addressing is complete, the frames are then sent to Layer 1 to be converted into electrical pulses and sent across the network.

Layer 3 is the Network layer and is primarily responsible for two functions: addressing and routing. This layer contains the IP protocol, part of the TCP/IP protocol. The "IP address" common to all of us is the Layer 3 responsibility and is unique throughout the entire world. The IP address is a 32-bit address and must be assigned by a user or administrator somewhere and is not set at the factory. Since it is user assignable there is great flexibility in how the address is assigned. The IP address consists of four sets of numbers separated by periods or dots, however, computers actually see the IP address in binary form. The current IP address format is called IP version four, or IPv4, in which there are over 1.3 billion possible addresses.

The last OSI level considered here is the Transport Layer 4. This layer is responsible for reliably getting the packets from point A to point B. This layer supports

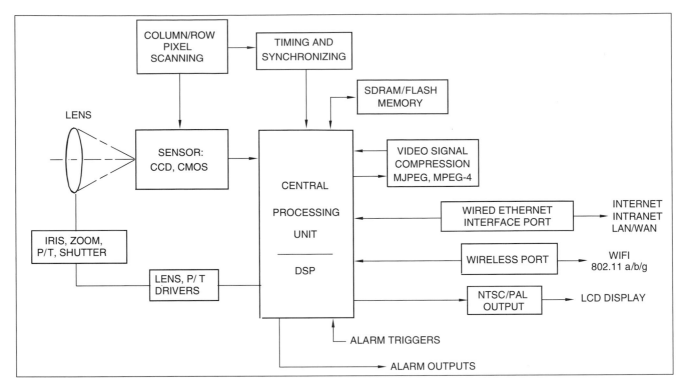

FIGURE 7-29   IP network camera block diagram

FIGURE 7-30 Seven layer open systems interconnect (OSI) model

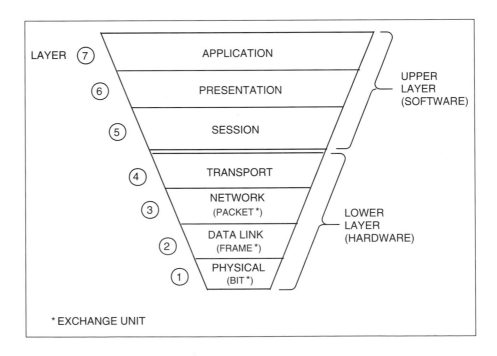

two different transmission methods: *connection-oriented* and *connectionless*. Connection-oriented transmissions are handled by TCP. These are point-to-point connections for guaranteed reception of data. An email message, accessing a Web page or downloading a file are all examples of connection-based exchanges. Error checking is performed on these exchanges because there is a guarantee of data reception. This transmission method *does not* work well for video since video is near real-time requiring large amounts of data to be transmitted and it would fail to produce an acceptable stream of video images for viewing or recording. If an error occurred and the sending device retransmitted parts of the video clip the video stream would not be viewable. For video transmission the connectionless protocol *user datagram protocol* (UDP), which does not guarantee delivery of error-free data, is used. The UDP is the foundation of video multitasking, which is a one-to-many method of video streaming. It is a crucial element of networked video systems.

In spite of the large number of addresses possible in the IPv4 standard, the popularity of TCP/IP protocol, especially the IP-based Internet, has placed a good deal a strain on the IPv4-based numbering scheme. To alleviate this problem, at least partially, in 1993 the concept of supernetting (subnetting) was devised. This technique used the number of 1 bits in the network address to specify the *subnet mask*. This technique reduced the number of routes and therefore the size and complexity of the routing tables that the Internet switches and routers had to support. This subnet technique goes a long way toward easing the pressure on the IPv4 addressing scheme but does not solve the basic problem of the lack of addresses in the future. The new IPv6 protocol resolves this issue through the expansion of the address field to 128 bits, thereby yielding virtually unlimited potential addresses.

A proper IP address consists of four sets of numbers, separated by periods or dots. Each of the four sets of numbers is called an *octet*. The addressing architecture defines five address formats each of which begins with one, two, three, or four bits that identify the *class* of the network. The host portion of an IP address is unique for each device on a network while the network portion is the same on all devices that share a network. The way to distinguish which part of an address is which is called the *subnet mask*. The subnet mask is another 32-bit number that looks similar to an IP address, but does something entirely different. The five address formats are: Class A, B, C, D, and E. Figure 7-31 shows a breakdown of the three classes of network addresses of interest: Class A, B, C.

Each line in each class represents an IP address in binary from bit zero to 32. Under Class A the first eight bits are the network information. This identifies the network itself and is shared by all devices on that network segment. To the right of the vertical divider line, the host information part of the address uniquely identifies each device. A host is any device with an assigned address. When the classes are compared, it is seen by looking at each class the dividing line between network and host *moves*. Class B addresses are divided in the middle with two octets for the network ID and two for the host. Class C addresses have the first three octets for the network and the last one for the host device. Moving the dividing line and changing classes determines how many different networks can be created and how many hosts are on each. When the IP address and subnet mask are compared, anywhere where there is a *one* indicates the network portion of the IP address. Anywhere where there is a *zero* shows the host portion. If two addresses are not on the same subnet they will not be able to talk to each other. Figure 7-32 shows a dissection of an IPv4 IP address with its subnet mask.

The subnet mask is uncovered by comparing the IP address and the subnet mask in binary. Anywhere where a *one* appears in the comparison indicates the network portion of the IP address. Anywhere where there is a *zero* shows the host portion of the address.

The IP addresses are used to identify the camera equipment in a network whether local or on the Internet. These addresses are configured by software: they are not hardware-specific. An IP address can be either *static* or *dynamic*. Static addresses do not change and are usually found on LAN and WAN networks. However, if the network interfaces via dial-up modem, high-speed cable

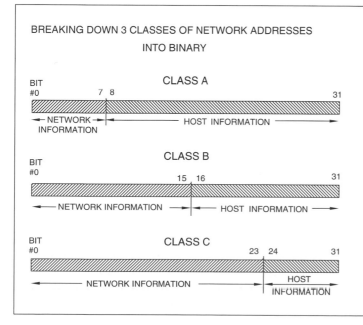

BREAKING DOWN 3 CLASSES OF NETWORK ADDRESSES INTO BINARY

HOW IP VERSION 4 ASSIGNS IP ADDRESSES

NETWORK CLASS	BEGINNING OCTET	NUMBER OF NETWORKS	HOST ADDRESSES PER NETWORK
A	1–126	126	16,777,214
B	128–191	>16,000	65,534
C	192–223	>2,000,000	254

THE GRAY LINES REPRESENT IP ADDRESSES IN BINARY FORM FROM BIT 0 TO 32. UNDER CLASS A, THE FIRST 8 BITS ARE TITLED NETWORK INFORMATION. THESE BITS IDENTIFY THE NETWORK ITSELF AND ARE SHARED BY ALL DEVICES ON THAT NETWORK SEGMENT. AFTER THE VERTICAL DIVIDER LINE THE HOST INFORMATIN PART UNIQUELY IDENTIFIES EACH HARDWARE DEVICE.

FIGURE 7-31   Class A, B, C network addresses

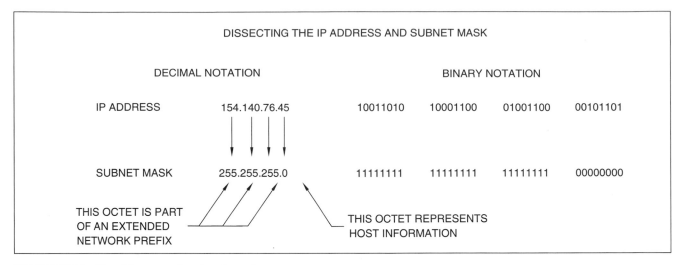

FIGURE 7-32 IP address and subnet mask

modem, or DSL, the IP address is usually dynamic, which means it changes each time the Internet connection is made.

The dynamic host configuration protocol (DHCP) is an IP for automating the configuration of equipment that uses the TCP/IP protocol. It is the IP-addressing method where the network router supplies a temporary IP address to the computer connected to it. If a device is programmed to use DHCP it is likely the device will function on the LAN, but not be accessible from outside the LAN using the Internet.

The DHCP lets network administrators automate and centrally manage the assignment of IP addresses in an organization's network. The DHCP lets the network administrator supervise and distribute IP addresses from a central point and automatically send a new IP address when a computer is plugged into a different location in the network.

The IP address consists of four groups, or quads (octet). The groups are decimal digits separated by periods. An example is: 153.99.12.227. In binary form the IP address is a string of zeros and ones. Part of the IP address represents the network number or address and part represents the local machine address, also known as the host number or address. The most common class used by large organizations is Class B, which allows 16 bits for the network number and 16 for the host number. Therefore, in the example, 153 and 99 represent the network address and 12 and 227 represent the host address. The decimal and binary equivalent IP address would be divided as shown in Figure 7.33

FIGURE 7-33 Converting the decimal IP address to binary

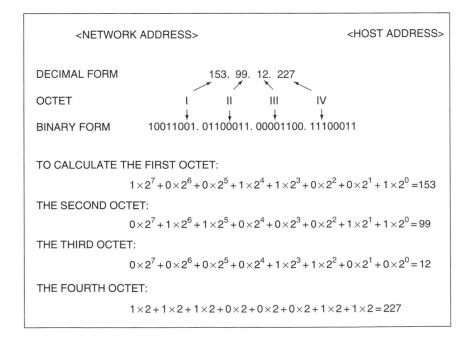

For LAN and WAN systems a special networking board/card must be incorporated into the user's computers. This networking card uses TCP/IP protocol and is capable of interconnecting all of the PCs to the system. By adding a network interface to a camera site which serves as a bridge between analog-based CCTV systems and a digital network, one can view the video image over a computer network as well as control PTZ functions.

Network computers have one IP address for the LAN, and a second one for the LAN connected to the Internet (WAN). The following three methods describe step-by-step procedures to obtain the LAN address of the computer *using* Windows XP.

Method 1

1. *Click* on START in Windows XP.
2. Open the *Control Panel* within the START window and *click* on *Network and Internet Connections.*
3. *Clicking* on *Network Connections* opens a window displaying icons for Network Connections.
4. *Right-click* the Network Connection that is currently "enabled" and *click* Properties.
5. Scroll down the center of the Properties window and *highlight* Internet Protocol.
6. *Click* the Properties button, and a window will display the following information: "Obtain IP Address Automatically." If this button is lit the computer network is using DHCP.

   If the button "Use The Following IP Address" is lit, the network is using "static" IP addresses that do not change periodically. The information boxes below will have values such as:

   - IP—192.168.1.105
   - Subnet Mask—255.255.255.0
   - Default Gateway—192.168.1.4.

   The Subnet Mask indicates the class of network (A, B, or C) being used. The Default Gateway is the LAN IP address of the network router.
8. *Click* OK twice to close the IP address window without changing the settings.

Method 2

Another way to access the LAN IP of a specific computer is to:

1. *Click* START and RUN in Windows XP. *Type* Command and *press* Enter.
2. *Type* IP Config\All in the Command window.

The same LAN IP information detailed above will be displayed on the screen.

Method 3

To obtain the WAN (Internet) IP of the network:

1. *Open* a Web browser such as Internet Explorer.
2. *Type* http://www.whatismyip.com in the address line.
3. *Click* Go.

The IP address of the network will be displayed on the computer screen.

7.9 VIDEO SERVER, ROUTER, SWITCH

A Server is a computer or software program that provides services to clients—such as a file storage (file server), programs (application server), printer sharing (printer server), or modem sharing (modem server).

A Router is a device that moves data between different digital network segments and can look into a packet header to determine the best path for the packet to travel. Routers can connect network segments that use different protocols and allow all users in a network to share a single connection to the Internet or a WAN.

A Switch is a device that improves network performance by segmenting the network and reducing competition for bandwidth.

7.9.1 Video Server

A server is a computer or program that provides services to other computer programs in the same or other computers. A computer running a server program is also frequently referred to as a server. Specific to the Web and a web server is the computer program that serves requested HTML pages of files.

Video servers transform analog video into high-quality digital images for live access over an intranet or the Internet. A video server enables the user to migrate from an existing analog CCTV system into the digital world. Most single video servers can network up to four analog cameras, a cost-effective solution for transmitting high-quality digital video over computer networks. By bridging the analog to digital technology gap, video servers complement previous investments in analog cameras.

A video server digitizes analog video signals and distributes digital images directly over an IP-based computer network, i.e. LAN, intranet, Internet. The video server converts analog cameras into network cameras and enables users to view live images from a Web browser on any network computer, anywhere and at anytime.

The video server can deliver up to 30 fps in NTSC format (25 fps PAL) over a standard Ethernet. It includes one or more analog video inputs, image digitizer, image compressor, a web server, and network/phone modem interface and serial interfaces (Figure 7-34).

The video server receives analog video input from the analog camera which is directed to the image digitizer. The image digitizer converts the analog video into a digital format. The digitized video is transferred to the compression chip, where the video images are compressed to J-MPEG, MPEG-2, MPEG-4, H.264, or other format. The CPU, the Ethernet connection and serial ports, and the

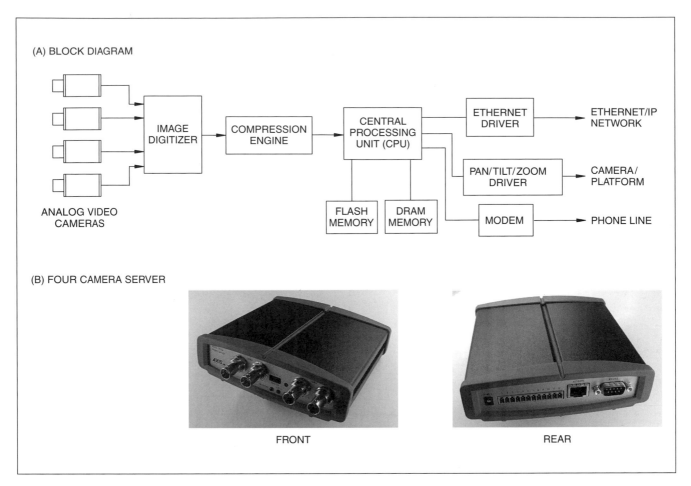

FIGURE 7-34   (a) Video server block diagram, (b) Typical equipment

alarm input and relay output represent the brain or computing functions of the video server. They handle the communication with the network. The CPU processes the actions of the web server and all of the software for drivers for controlling different PTZ cameras. The serial ports (RS-232 and RS-485) enable control of the camera's PTZ functions and other surveillance equipment. There is a modem for connections to telephone or other transmission channels. The alarm input can be used to trigger the video server to start transmitting images. The relay output can start actions such as opening a door. The video server is equipped with image buffers and can send pre-alarm images of an alarm event. The flash memory is the equivalent to the hard disk of the video server and contains all software for the operating system and all applications.

7.9.2   Video Router/Access Point

The video router on the Internet is a device or in some cases software in a computer, that determines the next network to which a packet of digital information should be forwarded, toward its final destination. It connects at least two networks and determines which way to send each information packet. The router can be located at any juncture of a network or gateway including each Internet point-of-presence. The router is often included as part of a network switch (Figure 7.35).

7.9.3   Video Switch

A switch port receives data packets and only forwards those packets to the appropriate port for the intended recipient. This further reduces competition for bandwidth between the clients, servers, or workgroups connected to each switch port.

7.10   PERSONAL COMPUTER, LAPTOP, PDA, CELL PHONE

Personal computers (PC) and laptops are the most widely used appliances for monitoring video surveillance images on the digital network. The Personal digital assistant (PDA) and cell phone are the choice when the absolute minimum in size is required, and image quality is not the primary factor.

FIGURE 7-35   Typical router/access point

7.10.1   Personal Computer, Laptop

Personal computers and laptops have the computing capacity, digital storage, and network interfaces to monitor digital video and other surveillance functions through wired or wireless connections. They contain the displays, operating systems, application software, and communications devices to receive and communicate with all of the cameras and other devices on the security network. Laptops have the added functionality of being mobile, transportable, and battery-operated. This is a very useful attribute for rapid deployment video systems.

7.10.2   Personal Digital Assistant (PDA)

The full impact of video surveillance using wireless cameras, monitors, and servers has yet to be realized. Wireless video surveillance is rapidly growing in popularity for monitoring remote locations, whether from a laptop or a PDA. WiFi video digital transmission provides the ability to deliver near real-time, full-motion video surveillance at 20 fps to PDAs and cell phones at any location having access to the Internet via the WiFi connection. A video server at the surveillance site compresses images and sends them wirelessly to the PDA or cell phone. The systems can provide secure access to validated mobile phones without any eavesdropping. The IP security cameras connected to the network transmit digital video via MPEG-4 video compression wirelessly to PDAs and cell phones. Remote video and alarm surveillance is only a phone call away: anytime of day, anywhere in the world. Software is available that allows PDA users running Microsoft Pocket PC 2002 to receive video, thereby remotely monitoring security areas while mobile. The Axis Camera Explorer (ACE) lets you watch live network video from anywhere, on a PDA (Figure 7-36).

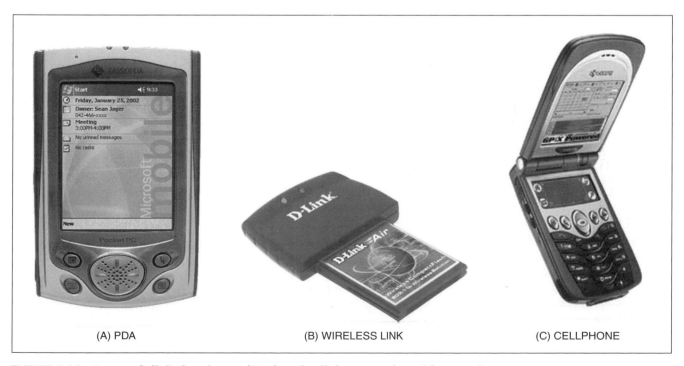

(A) PDA   (B) WIRELESS LINK   (C) CELLPHONE

FIGURE 7-36   Personal digital assistant (PDA) and cellphone used as video receiver

Giving personnel the ability to remotely monitor secure areas greatly increases security functionality. Access to the system via the Internet is accomplished by assigning an IP address to every surveillance device entering an address in a Web browser to connect with the system. Just about any PDA or laptop using Windows CE or Linux with a wireless card and the wireless Web modem can obtain a wireless remote video transmission.

PDAs and Pocket PCs have a slot for a compact flash format WiFi radio. There are also small format WiFi radios for PDAs and mobile data devices offering additional options for wireless connections. A PDA is a very useful monitoring device for a rapid deployment video system.

7.10.3 Cell Phone

The cellular phone network has a sub-carrier that can be used to transmit and receive control data for video cameras and other components. This sub-carrier channel information called the cellular digital packet data (CDPD) transmits the digital data over the cellular telephone network using the *idle* time between cellular voice calls. A mobile data base station (MDBS) resides at each cellular phone cell site that uses a scanning receiver to scan and detect the presence of any voice traffic, based on the signal strength. Providing that there are two channels idle (for transmitting and receiving) the MDBS will establish an air link. The type of sub-carrier available depends on the security service provider.

7.11 INTERNET PROTOCOL SURVEILLANCE SYSTEMS: FEATURES, CHECKLIST, PROS, CONS

The following is a summary of features and key questions that should be considered in selecting a video surveillance transmission technology. Most comments apply to both wired and wireless networks. Some apply to wireless networks only. A list of pros and cons follows the list.

7.11.1 Features

- The IP surveillance provides worldwide remote accessibility. Any video stream, live or recorded, can be accessed and controlled from any location in the world over the wired or wireless network.
- Video images from any number of cameras can be stored in digital format in a host service. This enables the viewing of images from multiple cameras and playback of an entire sequence of events.
- The cost of developing the infrastructure for the Internet and security system services has and will be borne primarily *outside* of the security industry.

- As long as there is access to the Internet, any location in the world that has a PC and a browser can be provided with security system services.
- The IP surveillance uses a more cost-effective infrastructure than analog technologies. Most facilities are already wired with an UTP IT infrastructure. The installation of future directed hybrid systems will be capable of accommodating new analog as well as digital systems and thereby ensure compatibility.
- The IP surveillance technology provides an open, easily integrated platform to connect and manage the enterprise data, video, voice, and control, making management more effective and cost-efficient.
- The IP digital surveillance brings intelligence to the camera level. The VMD, event handling, sensor input, relay output, time and date, and other built-in capabilities allow the camera to make intelligent decisions on when to send alarms, and when and at what frame rate to send video.
- The cost savings for commercial companies and governmental agencies implementing IP technology could be massive. Multinational corporations and government agencies with plants and offices around the world already have worldwide communications networks onto which the security function could be added.

7.11.2 Checklist

- How much bandwidth is available for network transmission?
- How much total storage space is available to store the video images?
- Will video be viewed and recorded remotely?
- Must the video be of high enough quality to be used for personnel identification purposes?
- Does the application require real-time video?
- Are different frame rates needed during certain events or specific times?
- Is a peer-to-peer network or one with a base station (access point) required?
- How many base stations (access points or gateways) are needed?
- How will the WiFi network be connected to the Internet?
- What are the WiFi radio options for PCs, laptop's, PDAs, and cell phones?
- How many users will use a single access point?
- What is the total number of users and computers?
- Will each computer use a WiFi connection?
- Is the video to be interfaced with existing networks?
- What is the available bandwidth that can be reserved for the video signal?
- What image quality and resolution are needed for the application?
- What resolution is needed to identify the person or activity in the scene?

- What frame rate is needed to be activity specific and sufficient to capture motion in the scene?
- Is a wired or wireless network more suitable? Is a wired network preferable to minimize security problems?
- What are the security requirements: standard—strategic?

7.11.3 Pros

There are many advantages to the implementation of IP surveillance technologies using either wired or wireless networks in small or large surveillance applications:

- The IP surveillance scales from one to thousands of cameras in increments of a single camera. There are no 16 channel jumps as in analog systems.
- Automatic transmittal of images over the Internet to a remote location to provide video images of events that just happened.
- Embedding the video images as HTML pages in a web server built right into the camera.
- Transmitting video images over wireless media to PDAs, laptop's, and cell phones at local or remote monitoring locations.
- Remote guard tours to provide increased efficiency of guards and services at a greatly reduced cost.
- Intelligent monitoring and control, including the transmission of images triggered by alarm conditions with pre-alarm images.
- Remote surveillance from anywhere to anywhere, online any time—24/7/365.
- Wireless for convenience and cost considerations.
- Wireless a must when no wired installed network is available.
- Can now integrate video, alarm intrusion, access control, fire, etc. into a seamless security system.

7.11.4 Cons

Security personnel can question the security of Internet-based security systems. Section 7.7 described several important video surveillance security concerns when using digital IP networks. These included: viruses and hackers, and eavesdropping. Another factor of concern is that of reliability of the IP network, i.e. temporary loss of ser-vice. In strategic applications some form of encryption is needed.

- Some locations do not have high-speed Internet access.
- Some Internet service providers (ISPs) may not provide reliable service.

7.12 SUMMARY

Video imaging and storage is going through more technological changes and structural redefinition than any other part of the physical security market. The Internet and WWW has made long-range video security monitoring a reality for many security applications. Likewise the availability of high-speed computers, large solid state memory, and compression technologies have made the sending of real-time video over these networks practical and effective. New methods of wireless transmission including MIMO mesh have improved the range, reliability and QoS of wireless transmission.

This chapter has described the digital video security and Internet transmission media with its unique modulation and demodulation requirements. The specific compression algorithms required to compress the video frame image file sizes to make them compatible with the existing wired and wireless transmission channels available are described. A powerful technology used to transmit the digital signal called SSM has made wireless video transmission a reality. The 802.11 spread spectrum protocols are described as relating to video, voice, and command and control transmission.

Security monitoring is no longer limited to local security rooms and security officers, but rather extends out to remote sites and personnel located anywhere around the world. Monitoring equipment includes flat panel displays, PCs, laptops, PDAs, and cell phones. The requirement for individual personnel to monitor multiple display monitors has changed to a technology of incorporating smart cameras with VMDs to establish an AVS system from local and remote sites.

A key factor to be considered in any wired or wireless digital video network system is protecting the data from unfriendly intruders and viruses. Using WEP, VPN, firewalls, and anti-virus and encryption techniques is paramount.

Chapter 8
Analog Monitors and Digital Displays

CONTENTS

8.1   Overview
8.2   Analog Monitor
    8.2.1   Cathode Ray Tube Technology
        8.2.1.1   Beam Deflection
        8.2.1.2   Spot Size, Resolution
        8.2.1.3   Phosphors
        8.2.1.4   Interlacing and Flicker
        8.2.1.5   Brightness
        8.2.1.6   Audio/Video
        8.2.1.7   Standards
    8.2.2   Monochrome Monitor
    8.2.3   Color Monitor
    8.2.4   Color Model
8.3   Flat-Screen Digital Monitor
    8.3.1   Digital Technology
        8.3.1.1   Pixels, Resolution
    8.3.2   Liquid Crystal Display (LCD)
        8.3.2.1   Brightness
        8.3.2.2   Liquid Crystal Display Modes of Operation
    8.3.3   Plasma
    8.3.4   Organic LED (OLED)
8.4   Monitor Display Formats
    8.4.1   Standard 4:3
    8.4.2   High Definition 16:9
    8.4.3   Split-Screen Presentation
    8.4.4   Screen Size, Resolution
    8.4.5   Multistandard, Multi-Sync
    8.4.6   Monitor Magnification
8.5   Interfacing Analog Signal to Digital Monitor
8.6   Merging Video with PCs
8.7   Special Features
    8.7.1   Interactive Touch-Screen
        8.7.1.1   Infrared
        8.7.1.2   Resistive
        8.7.1.3   Capacitive
        8.7.1.4   Projected Capacitance Technology (PCT)

        8.7.2   Anti-Glare Screen
        8.7.3   Sunlight-Readable Display
8.8   Receiver/Monitor, Viewfinder, Mobile Display
8.9   Projection Display
8.10 Summary

8.1   OVERVIEW

In the late 1990s digital flat-screen devices began to be used in video surveillance systems. Dropping prices, improved performance, and the obvious space advantages of flat-panel displays has caused a rapid shift away from traditional CRT monitors for video security use. Digital video monitors and projectors are reaching new heights of performance and are replacing the longtime workhorse in the industry, the CRT monitor.

This chapter analyzes the monitoring hardware used for video security systems. This hardware consists of a variety of monochrome and color monitors: CRTs, LCDs, plasma screens, and organic LEDs. These monitors vary in size from 5 to 42 inches diagonal. The monitor size depends in part on how many cameras are to be monitored, how many security personnel will be monitoring, and how much room is available in the security room. The question of how many cameras will be viewed sequentially or simultaneously on a single monitor will be analyzed. There is discussion of the consequences of displaying 1, 2, 4, 9, 16, and 32 individual camera pictures on a *single* monitor.

Special features and accessories for these analog and digital displays will be described. These include the *touch screen* that allows an operator to input a command to the security system by touching defined locations on the monitor. Chapter 20 describes the integration of the analog CRT and flat-panel LCD monitor displays into the security console room.

There are several different hardware technologies that exist for displaying the video image, computer data and graphics on video monitors. The technologies include: CRT, LCD, plasma, and OLED. The video projector is used to display images on a large screen for multiple personnel viewing. Monitors can receive an analog video signal and digital information in formats such as SVGA, NTSC, PAL, and SECAM. Color CRT monitors are versatile and often have resolutions from the standard 640×480 pixels to high 2048×1536 pixels with a 32-bit color depth (24-bit common), and a variety of refresh rates from 60 to 75 fps. The sharpness of the analog display is described by the number of TV lines it can display and that of the digital display by the number of pixels. In general the more the pixels the sharper the picture image. Resolution and image quality on analog and digital monitors are described with different parameters: for the analog monitor *TV lines*, for the digital monitor *pixels*.

The horizontal resolution of a 9-inch monochrome analog CRT monitor is approximately 800 TV lines, and for a 9-inch color monitor approximately 500 TV lines. The horizontal resolution of a typical 17-inch monochrome monitor is 800 TV lines and for a 17-inch color monitor approximately 450 TV lines. Vertical resolution is about 350 TV lines on both types as limited by the NTSC standard of 525 horizontal lines.

The horizontal and vertical resolution for a 15-inch digital LCD with a 4×3 format is 1024 pixels by 768 pixels XGA (extended graphics array).

Most monitors are available for 117-volt, 60 Hz (or 230-volt, 50 Hz) AC operation, and many for 12 VDC operation with a 117 VAC to 12 VDC wall converter. Video signal connections are made via RCA plug, BNC, 9 or 25 pin connectors. The two-position switch on the rear of some monitors permits terminating the input video cable in either 75 ohms or high impedance (100,000 ohms). If only one monitor is used, the switch on the rear of the monitor is set to the 75-ohm or low-impedance position matching the cable impedance for best results. If multiple monitors are used, all but the last monitor in the series are set to the high-impedance position. The last monitor is set to the low-impedance 75-ohm position. If a VCR or DVR recorder or a video printer is connected, all the monitors are set to high impedance and the recorder or printer devices set to low impedance. Recorder and printer manufacturers set the impedance to 75 ohms at the factory. Only one 75 ohm terminated device can be used at a time.

Most cameras and monitors have a 4×3 geometric display format, that is, the horizontal-to-vertical size is 4 units by 3 units. The high definition television (HDTV) has a 16 by 9 aspect ratio.

For any application, the security director, security systems provider, and consultant must decide:

• Should each camera be displayed on an individual monitor?

• Should several camera scenes be displayed on one monitor?

• Should the picture from each individual camera be switched to a single monitor via an electronic switcher or multiplexer?

If there is high scene activity, i.e. many people passing into or out of an area, all cameras should be displayed on separate monitors. For installations with infrequent activity or casual surveillance, a manual, automatic, or other switcher or split screen should be used.

Since each installation requires a different number of monitors and has different monitoring criteria depending on the application, each installation becomes a custom design. The final layout and installation of a system should be the collaboration between the security department, management, outside consultants, and security equipment providers (dealer, installer, system integrator).

8.2 ANALOG MONITOR

Up until the late 1990s the CRT monitor has been the technology used in virtually all security applications, including video surveillance, access control, alarm, and fire monitoring. With the widespread use of computer displays in many security departments and the availability of flat-panel technologies for displaying data and video images, the CRT display is still used in most security monitoring applications. The continuing success of the CRT monitor is based on an extremely simple concept, with a relatively simple structure and using electronic solid-state semiconductor circuitry for all other electronic functions in the monitor. While the CRT still utilizes vacuum-tube technology, its combination with semiconductor technology provides the most cost-effective solution to displaying a video image, be it monochrome or color. The CRT monitor has become less expensive while improving in quality and lifetime. These monitors cost less than flat panel digital displays because of their simple construction and long successful history of high-volume production.

While the CRT has enjoyed many years of use, it is likely that plasma displays, LCDs, OLED displays, and other new technologies will eventually make CRT-based displays obsolete in video security applications. These new designs are less bulky, consume less power, and are digitally based. As of mid-2003 some LCDs became directly comparable in price to CRTs.

8.2.1 Cathode Ray Tube Technology

The CRT, invented by Karl Braun, is the most common display device used in video surveillance, computer displays, television sets, and oscilloscopes. The CRT was developed using Philo Farnsworth's work and has been used in all

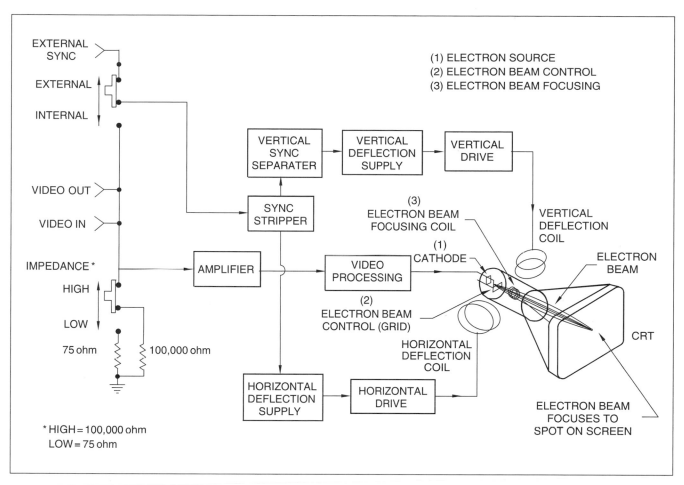

FIGURE 8-1   Block diagram of cathode ray tube (CRT) monitor

television sets until the late-20th century. Components of the monochrome CRT monitor include the video amplifying and deflection circuitry, the video-processing circuits to remove the synchronizing signals from the video signal, and the CRT (Figure 8-1).

The CRT is composed of four basic components: (1) heated cathode (2) electron gun, (3) glass envelope, and (4) phosphor screen. The color CRT requires three electron guns of similar construction to display the three primary colors, red, green, and blue (RGB). The monochrome CRT is relatively easy to manufacture since the screen consists of a uniform coating of a single phosphor material. The yield during manufacture of the CRTs is high (compared to the LCD or plasma displays) since the human eye is far less sensitive to variations in phosphor flaws than it is to the defective pixel or cell failures in flat panel digital displays. The homogeneous and continuous phosphor layer has very high resolution since it is continuous, as contrasted to flat-panel cells (pixels). The resolution of a CRT is limited by the electron beam diameter and the electronic video bandwidth that determines how fast the electron beam can turn on and off.

The lifetime of standard CRTs is legendary, especially under adverse operating conditions with which it is used:

consider the abuse that standard consumer TVs receive but they still continue to operate. The CCTV monitors may be cycled on and off and adjusted over a wide range of brightness and contrast, sometimes beyond their design limits and still operate satisfactorily for many years.

8.2.1.1 Beam Deflection

Cathode rays are streams of high speed electrons emitted from the heated cathode of the vacuum tube. In a CRT the electrons are carefully directed into a beam and this beam is deflected by a magnetic field to scan the surface at the viewing end (anode) which is lined with a phosphorescent material that produces the visible image on the face of the tube for viewing. In the case of the video monitor, and television and computer monitors, the entire front area of the tube is scanned in a fixed pattern called a *raster*. The picture is created by modulating the intensity of the electron beam according to the scene light intensity represented in the video signal. The magnetic field is applied to the neck of the tube via the use of an electromagnetic coil, and the process is referred to as magnetic deflection.

The CRT bends the electron beam at extremely high speed with exact timing and gating to produce a complex picture. Electron beams can be deflected so quickly that pictures on the screen can be refreshed without noticeable flicker. The CRT's electron beam strikes and excites the phosphor screen, which has a high luminous efficiency.

Most CRT monitors use magnetic deflection to deflect the electron beam in the horizontal and vertical directions to produce the scene on the monitor face. Figure 8-1 illustrates the placement of the vertical and horizontal deflection coils at the neck of the CRT. When current flows through the horizontal coils, a horizontal magnetic field is produced across the neck. The amount of horizontal deflection of the electron beam depends on the strength of the magnetic field and therefore the current through the coil. The direction of the beam deflection (left to right) while passing through the horizontal coil depends on the polarity of the field. Likewise for the vertical deflection coil the electron beam is deflected up or down depending on the strength of the magnetic field which in turn depends on the vertical deflection current. The energizing of both the horizontal and the vertical coils causes the raster scan and picture on the CRT monitor. As with the scanning in a tube or solid-state video camera, the video monitor has an aspect ratio of 4:3 with a diagonal of 5 units. The size of the tube is measured from one corner of the screen to the opposite corner and referred to as the diagonal.

A disadvantage of the CRT is its relative size, particularly its depth compared to digital displays that have a short depth. However, if there is sufficient space behind the monitor there is no disadvantage to the CRT monitor size.

8.2.1.2   Spot Size, Resolution

The term "image resolution" describes how much image detail the image can display on an analog or digital monitor. Higher resolution means more image detail. In analog monitors the resolution is generally defined in *TV lines* and defined as the number of black-and-white *line pairs* that are distinguishable in the horizontal and vertical direction. There is sometimes confusion defining the horizontal resolution, since it is sometimes defined as the number of horizontal TV lines in a width equivalent to the vertical height and at other times it is defined as the total number of TV lines along the horizontal axis. The correct definition is the number of TV lines for an equivalent vertical height.

The spot size of the light beam is the diameter of the focused electron beam, which ultimately determines the resolution and quality of the picture. The spot size should be as small as possible to achieve high resolution. Typical spot sizes range from about 0.1 to 1.0 mm. The spot size is smallest at the center of the CRT and largest at the corners (5–10% larger). Deflection along the edges elongates the spot and decreases resolution.

The convention to describe the image resolution in digital raster image displays is with a set of two positive integers where the first number is the number of *pixel* columns (horizontal width) and the second is the number of pixel rows (height). The second most popular convention is to describe the total number of pixels in the image, which is calculated by multiplying the pixel columns by the pixel rows.

8.2.1.3   Phosphors

Cathode ray tube phosphors glow for a time determined by the phosphor material and must be matched to the refresh rate. The use of the white P4 phosphor has been widespread as the standard monochrome television monitor phosphor in the past. It is capable of achieving good focus and small spot size. Its low cost and ready availability contribute to its continued popularity in monitors. P4 is a medium, to medium-short-persistence phosphor. The phosphor "glow" activated by the electron beam fades away fairly rapidly, leaving no cursor trail or temporary "ghost" scene when the monitor is turned off. The P4 phosphor is moderately resistant to phosphor "burn" a term used to describe the permanent dark pattern caused by fixed bright scenes in the video image on the CRT face. The susceptibility to burn is somewhat proportional to persistence, with longer-persistence phosphors more liable to burn-in.

Color tubes use three different phosphorescent materials that emit red, green, and blue light. These colors are emitted from closely packed patterns of clusters or strips (Sony Trinitron) as determined by a *shadow mask*. There are three electron guns (one for each color). The shadow mask ensures that the electrons from each color gun reach only the phosphor dots of its corresponding color, with the shadow mask absorbing electrons that would otherwise hit the wrong phosphor.

8.2.1.4   Interlacing and Flicker

Flicker is the visible fading between image frames displayed on any monitor. In the CRT monitor it occurs when the CRT is driven at too low a *refresh rate* (frame rate) allowing the screen phosphors to lose their excitation between sweeps of the electron gun. On computer monitors using progressive scan (no interlace), if the vertical refresh rate is set at 60 Hz, most monitors will produce a visible flickering effect. Refresh rates of 75–85 Hz and above result in flicker-free viewing on progressively scanned CRTs. Above these rates no noticeable flicker reduction is seen and therefore higher rates are uncommon in video surveillance applications. Although it has become acceptable to call 60 Hz non-interlaced displays flicker-free, a large percentage of the population can see flicker at 60 Hz in peripheral vision when common P4-type phosphors are used. A 19-inch CRT viewed at 27 inches covers more than the central cone vision, and therefore most people see some flicker. While this situation is not ideal, it cannot be overcome because of the inherent 60 Hz power-line frequency. On LCDs, lower refresh rates around 75 Hz are often acceptable.

Interlacing is one of the most common and cost-effective methods used to achieve increased resolution at conventional 60 Hz scan rates. One critical design consideration in interlaced operation is that a long-persistence P39 phosphor must be used; P4 phosphor is not suitable for interlaced operation (the European equivalent of P4 is W). The glow of short- to medium-persistence P4 phosphor begins to fade before it can be refreshed. At the standard US non-interlaced 60 Hz refresh rate this presents no problem: the viewer's eye retains the image long enough to make any fading imperceptible. In an interlaced monitor, the beam skips every other row of phosphor as it moves down the CRT face in successive horizontal scans. Only half the image is refreshed in a vertical sweep cycle, so the frame-refresh rate is effectively 30 Hz (two 1/60 second fields equal 1/30 second frame). The eye cannot retain the image long enough to prevent pronounced flicker in the display if a short- to medium-persistence phosphor is used. The phosphor glow must persist long enough to compensate for the slower refresh rate.

The "flicker threshold" of the human eye is about 50 Hz, with a short- to medium-persistence phosphor. Monitor manufacturers designing for European-standard 50 Hz operation therefore pay particular attention to the phosphor used.

Interlaced scanning is the method used in most video systems to reduce flicker, and since video scene content consists of large white areas, no objectionable flicker is apparent. In computer alphanumeric/graphic displays, most display data consists of small bright or dark elements. Consequently, an annoying flicker results when alphanumeric/graphic data are displayed using interlaced scanning unless a longer-persistence phosphor is used. Therefore the phosphor type used in the video monitor is different from that used for computer terminal monitors.

8.2.1.5 Brightness

The luminance (brightness) of the CRT monitor picture is proportional to the electron beam power, while the resolution depends on the beam diameter. Both of these properties are determined by the electron gun. Very high resolution monitors are available having a resolution of 3000 lines—close to the ergonomic limit of the human eye. Present security systems do not take advantage of this high resolution but some systems display 1000-line horizontal resolution.

8.2.1.6 Audio/Video

As with home television cameras and receivers, some monitors are equipped with audio amplifiers and speakers so that video and audio from the camera location are displayed on and heard from the monitor. The video input impedance is 75 ohms and the audio input impedance is 600 ohms.

8.2.1.7 Standards

The NTSC television format uses 525 lines per frame with about 495 horizontal lines (any number of lines between 482 and 495 may be transmitted at the discretion of the TV station) for the picture content. To produce satisfactory horizontal picture definition—that is, a gray scale and sufficient number of gradations from dark and light per line—a bandwidth of at least 4.2 MHz is required.

CCTV monitors generally conform to EIA specifications EIA-170, RS-330, RS-375, RS-420, and most often to UL specification 1410 for signal specifications and safety. The analog circuitry is usually capable of reproducing a minimum of ten discernible shades of gray, as described in the RS-375 and RS-420 specification.

The outer glass on the front of the CRT allows the light generated by the phosphors to get out of the monitor. However, for color tubes the glass must block dangerous X-rays generated by the impact of the high-energy electron beam. For color monitors the type of glass used is *leaded* glass. Modern CRTs are safe and well within safety limits for humans because of this and other shielding and protective circuits designed to prevent the anode voltage from rising to high levels and producing X-ray emission. CRTs operate at very high voltages that can persist long after the monitor has been switched off. The CRT monitor and especially the tube should not be tampered with unless the technician has had proper engineering training and appropriate precautions have been taken. Since the CRT contains a vacuum, care should be taken to prevent tube implosion caused by improper handling.

8.2.2 Monochrome Monitor

Figure 8-1 shows the block diagram including the video-processing circuits to remove the synchronizing signals from the video signal, the video amplifying and deflection circuitry, and the CRT. In its simplest form, the analog CRT monochrome monitor consists of:

- input video terminating circuit
- video amplifier and driver
- sync stripper
- vertical-deflection circuitry
- horizontal-deflection circuitry
- focusing electronics and
- CRT: cathode electron generator, electron gun, faceplate.

The video input signal to the monitor is a negative sync type, with the scene signal amplitude modulated as the positive portion of the signal (see Figure 5-4), and the synchronizing pulses the negative portion of the signal. Via frequency-selective circuits, the horizontal and vertical synchronization pulses are separated and passed onto the horizontal and vertical drive circuits. The sync-stripper circuit separates the analog video signal from the horizontal and vertical synchronizing pulses. These synchronizing pulses produce the scanning signals for the horizontal and vertical deflection of the electron beam and are similar to those used in the camera to produce scanning of the image sensor. The vertical- and horizontal-deflection electronics drive the vertical and horizontal coils on the neck of the CRT to produce a raster scan.

The CRT consists of: (1) a cathode source that emits electrons to "paint" the picture, (2) a grid (valve) that controls the flow of the electrons as they pass through it, (3) the electron beam that passes a set of electrodes to focus the beam down to a spot, and (4) a phosphor-coated screen that produces the visible picture (Figure 8-2).

When the focused beam passes through the field of the tube's deflection yoke (coils), it is deflected by the yoke to strike the appropriate spot of the tube's phosphor screen. By varying the voltage on the horizontal and vertical coils, the electron beam and spot are made to move across the CRT with the familiar raster pattern. The screen then emits light with intensity proportional to the beam inten-

sity resulting in the video image on the monitor. The CRT monitor accomplishes all this using relatively simple and inexpensive components. In this way the scene received by the camera is reconstructed at the monitor. The block diagram is for any monochrome analog monitor. The color monitor has electronics for the three primary colors: red, green and blue (RGB).

Analog video monitors accept the standard video baseband signal (20 Hz to 6.0 MHz) and display the image on the CRT phosphor. The monitor circuitry is essentially the same as a television receiver but lacks the electronic tuner and associated RF amplifiers and demodulators to receive the VHF or UHF broadcast, cable, and satellite signal. All monochrome and color security monitors accept the standard 525-line NTSC input signals. The video signal enters the monitor via a BNC connector and is terminated by one of two input impedances: 75 ohm to match the coaxial-cable impedance or high impedance: 10,000–100,000 ohms (Figure 8-3).

The high impedance termination does not match the coaxial-cable impedance and is used when the monitor will be terminated by some other equipment such as a looping monitor, a VCR or DVR, or some other device with a 75-ohm impedance. If two or more monitors receive the same video signal from the same source, only one of the monitors—the last one in line—should be set to

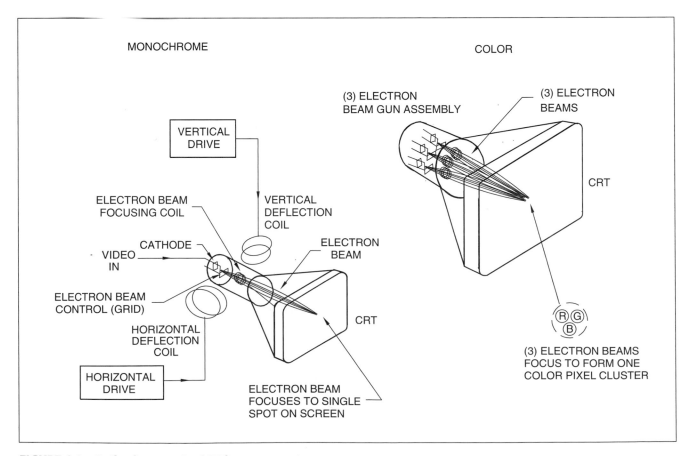

FIGURE 8-2 Cathode ray tube (CRT) components

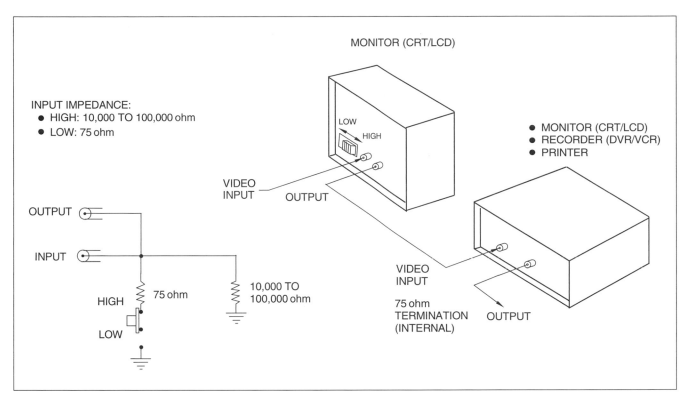

FIGURE 8-3   CCTV monitor terminations and connections

the 75-ohm position. If a recorder rather than a second monitor is used, the recorder automatically terminates the coaxial cable with a 75-ohm resistor.

As shown in the block diagram in Figure 8-3, the monitor has two BNC input connectors in parallel. When only one monitor is used, the impedance switch is moved to the 75-ohm, low-impedance position terminating the coaxial cable. If more than one monitor or auxiliary equipment is used, the terminating switch is left in the high-impedance position, opening the connection to the 75-ohm resistor so that the final termination is determined by a second monitor, recorder, or printer. Some monitors contain an external synchronization input so that the monitor may be synchronized from a central or external source.

The operator controls available on most monochrome monitors are power on/off, contrast, brightness, horizontal hold, and vertical hold. Three other controls sometimes available via screwdriver adjust (front or rear of the monitor) are horizontal size, vertical size, and focus.

8.2.3   Color Monitor

Until recently the major CRT technology used in color monitors employed three electron guns (one for each primary color) arranged in a triangle called the delta-delta system (Figure 8-4a).

A device called a *shadow mask* aligns each electron gun output so that the beam falls on the proper phosphor dot. The shadow mask is a thin steel screen in the CRT containing fine holes that concentrate the electron beam. This technique provides the highest resolution possible but requires the guns to be aligned manually by a technician, as well as expensive convergent-control circuitry.

The composite video input signal in the color monitor contains the information for the correct proportion of R, G, B signals to produce the desired color. It also contains the vertical and horizontal synchronization timing signals needed to steer the three video signals to the correct color guns. Composite video color monitors decode the signal and provide the proper level to generate the desired output from the three electron guns.

Today the most widely used CRT color technique is the precision-in-line (PIL) tube that eliminates most of these difficulties (Figure 8-4b). The PIL tube uses the shadow mask found in its predecessors, but the electron guns are in a single line. The spacing between the holes is termed the *dot pitch* or dot-trio spacing and ultimately determines the tube's resolution. The highest-resolution production PIL tube has approximately a 0.31 mm pitch, and is preconverged by the manufacturer so that no adjustment is necessary in the field. There is a slight decrease in resolution for the PIL as compared with the original delta-delta, but this is a small sacrifice considering that no field adjustment is required. A third CRT color tube called the Trinitron (trademark of Sony Corporation) consists of the phosphor layer consisting of alternate RGB vertical stripes (Figure 8-4c).

Analog CRT monitors are available in many sizes. The 5- and 9- inch diagonal sizes are suitable for side-by-side

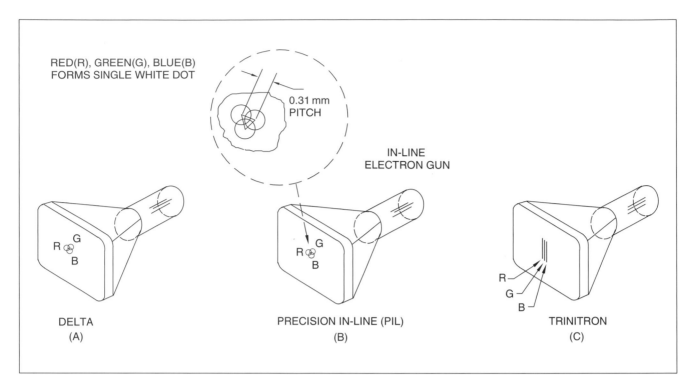

FIGURE 8-4   Color monitor technology

mounting in the standard EIA 19 inch rack. Figure 8-5 shows a few examples of these monitors.

8.2.4   Color Model

Video monitors and computer displays use the RGB color model utilizing the *additive* model in which red, green, and blue light are combined in different proportions to create all the other colors. The idea of the RGB model itself came from the additive light model. Primary colors are related to biological rather than physical concepts, and based on the physiological response of the human eye to light. The human eye contains receptor cells called cones which respond most to yellow, green, and blue lights (wavelengths of 564, 534, and 420 nm, respectively). The color red is perceived when the yellow–green receptor is stimulated significantly more than the green receptor.

FIGURE 8-5   Typical CRT monitors

The RGB model is used to display colors on the CRT, LCD, plasma, and OLED monitors. Each pixel on the screen is represented in the video signal or computer's memory as an independent value for red, green, and blue. These values are then converted into intensities and sent to the CRT or flat-panel display. Using an appropriate combination of red, green, and blue light intensities, the screen can reproduce the colors between its black and white levels. Most computer models use a total of 24 bits of information for each pixel commonly known as *bits per pixel* or *bpp*. This corresponds to eight bits each for red, green, and blue giving a range of 256 possible values or intensities for each color. With this system approximately 16.7 million discrete colors can be reproduced.

In the 24 bpp, RGB values are commonly specified using three integers between 0 and 255, each representing red, green, and blue intensities in that order. For example:

- (0, 0, 0) is black
- (255, 255, 255) is white
- (255, 0, 0) is red
- (0, 255, 0) is green
- (0, 0, 255) is blue
- (255, 255, 0) is yellow
- (0, 255, 255) is cyan
- (255, 0, 255) is magenta.

The colors used in Internet Web design are commonly specified using the RGB model. They are used in the HTML, and related languages with a limited color palette of 216 RGB colors as defined by the Netscape Color Cube. However, with the predominance of 24-bit displays the use of the full 16.7 million colors is used. The RGB color model for HTML was formally adopted as an Internet standard in HTML 3.2.

8.3   FLAT-SCREEN DIGITAL MONITOR

There are several technologies used to manufacture flat-panel digital displays and more are in development. They all have one feature in common: a much better depth profile than the traditional CRT monitor display. Typical flat-panel displays are from 1/2 to 4-inches in depth compared with 10–20 inches for CRT monitors. The most common flat-panel displays are:

- liquid crystal display (LCD)
- plasma
- organic LED (OLED).

The LCD and plasma displays have been in commercial production and in widespread use in the video surveillance industry for several years. The OLED monitors are beginning deployment in small sizes, but are expected to be introduced in large sizes tailored for the security and computer markets. Flat-panel displays offer a small footprint and trendy modern look but have higher costs, and in many cases inferior images compared with traditional CRTs. In some applications, specifically modern portable devices such as laptops, cell phones and PDAs, these negatives are being overcome.

8.3.1   Digital Technology

A *raster graphics* image, *digital image*, or *bitmap* is the display format used by most digital video flat-screen monitors. In general the technology represents a rectangular grid of pixels or points of color on a computer monitor. The color of each pixel is individually defined (RGB) and generally consists of: colored pixels defined by three bytes, one byte for each red, green, and blue pixel. For a monochrome image only black-and-white pictures are required with a single byte for each pixel. This *raster* presentation is distinguished from *vector* graphics in that vector graphics represents an image generated through the use of geometric objects such as lines, curves, arcs, and polygons. The bitmap on the monitor corresponds to the format of the image on the camera, and is stored identically to it in the video displays' computer memory. Each pixel in the map has a specific width and height, and the bitmap representing the image has an overall width and height consisting of a specific number of rows and columns of pixels. The quality of the raster image is determined by the total number of pixels (resolution) and the amount of information in each pixel (often called color depth). The standard for most high-quality displays in 2004 had an image that stored 24 bits (3 bytes) of color information per pixel. Such an image in a typical surveillance application is sampled at 640×480 pixels (total 307,200 pixels). This image will look *good* as compared to an *excellent* image sampled at 1280×1024 (1,310,720 pixels). High-quality, high-resolution pictures such as these generally require compression techniques to reduce the size of the image file stored in the computer's memory and to fit the signal into the limited bandwidth communication transmission channels available. Raster graphics cannot be scaled to a higher resolution i.e. larger screen size without a loss of resolution and image quality (this is in contrast to vector graphics which can easily scale and retain their quality and size on the larger device on which they are displayed).

8.3.1.1   Pixels, Resolution

A *pixel* (contraction of picture elements) represents the smallest *resolution element* made up in the monitor picture, in a computer memory, or in the camera image sensor. Usually the pixels (dots) are so small and so numerous that they cannot be distinguished on the monitor and appear to merge into a smooth image when viewed at a normal distance from the monitor. The pixel dots in the flat-panel display are analogous to the dots used in hard-copy printed matter used to produce a printed image. The color and intensity of each pixel is such that it represents the scene image at that location.

The more the pixels used to represent the image the higher the resolution and the closer the image resembles the original scene. The number of pixels in the image determines the image resolution. The normal VGA display has 640 × 480 pixels. In a monochrome image each pixel has its own brightness between the range of zero and one where zero represents black and one represents white. For example an eight-bit image can display 255 brightness levels. In a color image the number of distinct colors that can be represented by pixels depends on the number of bits per pixel (bpp). Some standard values are:

- 8 bpp provides 256 colors.
- 16 bpp provides 65,536 colors referred to as Highcolor.
- 24 bpp provides 16,777,216 colors referred to as True-color.

In both full color LCD, plasma, OLED flat panels, and CRT monitors, each of the pixels is constructed from three sub-pixels for the three colors, and are spaced closely together. A unique technology is the Sony Trinitron that has three closely spaced stripes of red, green, and blue (Figure 8-4c). Each of the sub-pixels has an intensity determined by its color RGB component values and due to their close proximity they create an illusion of being one specifically tinted pixel.

A recent technique for increasing the apparent resolution of a color display is referred to as "sub-pixel font rendering." This technique uses knowledge of the pixel geometry to manipulate the three colors' sub-pixels separately and works best on LCDs. It also eliminates much of the anti-aliasing in some scenes and is used primarily to improve the appearance of text. Microsoft's ClearType™ that is available in Windows XP is an example using this technology.

The display resolution of a digital video monitor or computer display is represented by the maximum number of pixels that can be displayed on the screen, usually given as a product of the number of columns horizontal (X) and the number of lines vertical (Y). The horizontal number is always stated first.

Common current computer display resolutions are listed in Table 8-1.

The 640 × 480 resolution was introduced by IBM, and has been in use from approximately 1990 to 1997 in their PS/2 VGA multicolor onboard graphics chips. This particular format was chosen partly due to its 4:3 ratio. The 800 × 600 array has been the standard resolution from 1998 to the present, but the 1024 × 768 is fast becoming the standard resolution since it has not only the 4:3 ratio but a higher resolution. Many websites and multimedia products are designed for this resolution. Windows XP is designed to run at 800 × 600 minimum although it is also possible to run applications with the 640 × 480 format.

With 15- and 17-inch digital monitors in use, 1024 × 768 resolution is standard. For 19-inch monitors 1280 × 1024 is the recommended standard. Good 21-inch monitors are capable of 1600 × 1200 resolution. There are also 24-inch wide-screen monitors that can often display 1900+ pixels horizontally.

COMPUTER STANDARD	PIXEL FORMAT	ASPECT RATIO	SCREEN SIZES*	
			LCD	PLASMA
QVGA	320×240	4:3	—	—
VGA	640×480	4:3	15, 17, 20	—
SVGA	800×600	4:3	20	—
XGA	1024×768	4:3	15	42, 43
XGA+	1152×864	4:3	—	—
SXGA+	1400×1050	4:3	—	—
WSXGA	1680×1050	16:10	22	—
WUXGA	1920×1200	16:10	23	—
QXGA	2048×1536	4:3	—	—
HDTV 1080i	1920×1080	16:9	42, 45	42, 50
HDTV 720p	1280×720	16:9	17, 23, 27, 30	42, 50

*DIAGONAL (inch)

Table 8-1   Digital Video Monitor Display Formats

8.3.2 Liquid Crystal Display (LCD)

In 1968 a group at RCA demonstrated the first operational LCD based on the dynamic scattering mode (DSM). In 1969 a former member of the RCA group at Kent State University discovered the twisted nematic field effect in liquid crystals and in 1971 the ILIXCO Company produced the first LCD based on this effect. This technology has now superseded the DSM type and is now used in most LCD displays.

The LCD is a thin lightweight panel consisting of an electrically controlled light polarizing liquid sealed in cells between two transparent polarizing sheets (Figure 8-6). The two polarizing axes of the two sheets are aligned and perpendicular to each other, and each cell is supplied with electrical contacts that allow electric fields to be applied to the liquid inside. In operation, when no electric field is applied, light is polarized by one sheet, rotated through the smooth twisting of the crystal molecules, and then passes through the second sheet. The entire assembly looks nearly transparent with a slight darkening caused by light losses in the original polarizing sheet.

When an electric field is applied to the panel the molecules in the liquid align themselves with the field and inhibit the rotation of the polarized light. Since the light impinges on the polarizing sheet perpendicularly to the direction of polarization, all the light is absorbed in the cell and it appears dark. Most visible wavelengths—all colors—are rotated by LCDs in the same way. In a color LCD each pixel triad is divided into three sections having one red, one green, and one blue filter to project the individual colors. All colors are achieved by varying the relative brightness of the three sections.

8.3.2.1 Brightness

The brightness of a display is defined by a unit of luminance called the "nit" and is often used to quote the brightness of a display. Typical displays have a luminance

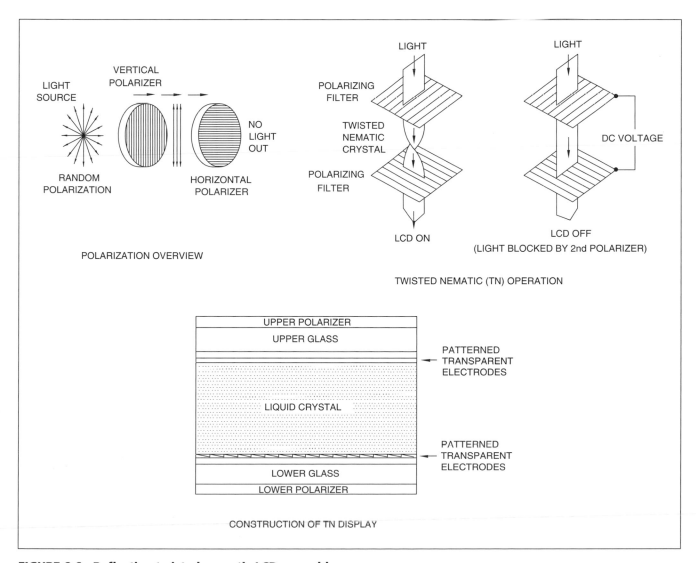

FIGURE 8-6 Reflective twisted nematic LCD assembly

of 200–300 nits. Outdoor high-brightness displays can have luminance in values in the range of 1000–1500 nits.

8.3.2.2 Liquid Crystal Display Modes of Operation

The LCD technology lends itself to several different modes of operation. It can be operated in a transmissive or reflective mode. A transmissive LCD is illuminated from the backside and viewed from the front side. Activated cells therefore appear dark while inactive cells appear bright. The transmissive LCD technology is used in high-brightness indoor applications and for outdoor use. In this mode of operation a lamp assembly is used to illuminate the LCD panel that usually consumes more power than the LCD panel itself (Figure 8-7).

The second LCD technology is the reflective type using ambient light reflected off the display. It has a lower contrast than the transmission type and is not generally useful for video security applications except for battery-operated systems where very low power operation is required. It finds most application where small, handheld monochrome displays are required.

Quality control issues in manufacturing LCD panels are different from CRT monitors. Since the digital panels contain thousands of individual pixels, a defect in the panel is visible whenever one or more of the pixels are not operating. However, the panels still may be useful if only a limited number of pixels are not operating or if the defective pixels are not in the central part of the display. Several criteria are used to grade the individual LCD panels and determine whether they are suitable for security application. One criteria used for passing or failing LCD panels was developed by IBM to quality-check their ThinkPad laptop computers. If the panel had less than a specified number of defective bright dots, or was not dark, it was passed; if more, it was rejected (Figure 8-8).

The first generation LCDs used passive matrix technology. This technology uses a simple conductive grid to deliver current to the liquid crystals in the target area. The second-generation active matrix display uses a grid of transistors with the ability to hold a charge for limited time, much like a capacitor. Because of the switching action of the transistors, only the desired pixel receives a charge, improving the image quality over a passive matrix. The

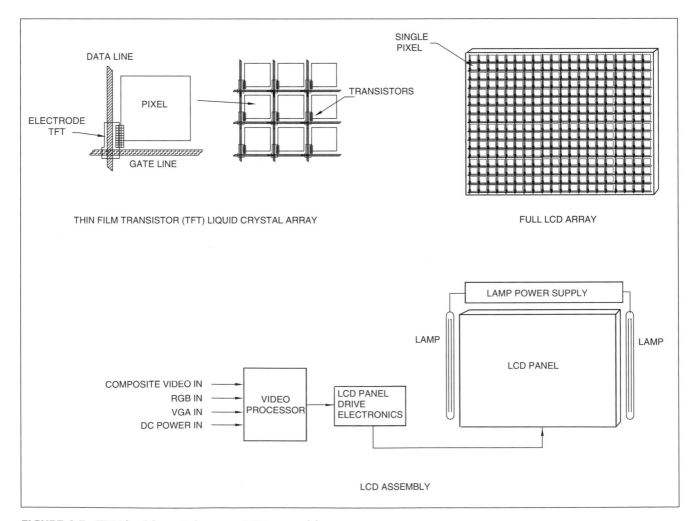

FIGURE 8-7 TFT Liquid crystal array—LCD assembly

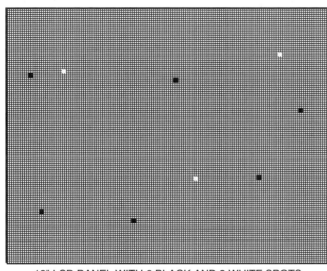

BLEMISH CRITERION USED BY
A MAJOR MANUFACTURER FOR
A 12" DIAGONAL LCD DISPLAY

RESOLUTION	BRIGHT SPOTS	DARK SPOTS	TOTAL SPOTS
QXGA	15	16	16
UXGA	11	16	16
SXGA+	11	13	16
XGA	8	8	9
SVGA	5	5	9

12" LCD PANEL WITH 6 BLACK AND 3 WHITE SPOTS

FIGURE 8-8   Pass/fail quality control criteria for LCD panels

thin-film transistors hold a charge and therefore the pixel remains active until the next refresh occurs.

The AMLED active matrix LCD is in widespread use in the security industry and the only choice of notebook computer manufacturers. They are used due to their lightweight, very good image quality, wide color range, and fast time response. The display contains an active matrix with polarizing sheets and cells of liquid crystal, and a matrix of thin-film transistors (TFTs). These transistors store the electrical state of each pixel in the display while the other pixels are being updated. This method provides a much brighter, sharper display than a passive matrix LCD of the same size. An important specification for these displays is the large viewing angle that they can accommodate. These displays have refresh rates of around 75 Hz.

8.3.3 Plasma

The plasma display is an emissive flat panel where light is created by phosphors that have been excited by a plasma discharge between two flat panels of glass that have a gas discharge containing no mercury (contrary to the back lights of the AMLCD panel). The plasma display uses a mixture of the noble gases neon and xenon. The neon and xenon gases in the plasma display are contained in hundreds of thousands of tiny cells sandwiched between the two plates of glass (Figure 8-9).

The control electrodes are also sandwiched between the glass plates on both sides of cells. Electronics external to the panel behind the cells address each of the pixels cells. To ionize the gas in a particular cell the plasma display's computer charges the electrodes that intersect at that particular cell. When intersecting electrodes are charged with

a voltage difference between them and electric current flows through the gas in the cell, it stimulates the gas and causes it to release ultraviolet photons. The phosphors in the plasma display give off color light when they are excited by these ultraviolet photons. As with other displays every pixel is made up of three separate sub-pixels with different colored phosphor (RGB) to produce the overall color of the pixel by varying the pulses of current flowing through different cells.

Major attributes of the plasma display are that it is very bright (1000 lux or higher), has a wide range of colors, and can be produced in large sizes of up to 80 inches diagonally. Another advantage of the plasma monitor over others is its high contrast ratio, often advertised as high as 4000:1. Since contrast is generally hard to define, an absolute value for the contrast improvement over other technologies is not yet available.

Plasma panels also have very high contrast ratios, creating a near-perfect black image—important when there is a need to discern picture content in LLL scenes. The display panel itself is about one-quarter inch thick while the total thickness including electronics can be less than 4 inches. Plasma displays use approximately the same power as a CRT or AMLCD monitor. Plasma monitors still cost more than all the other digital display technologies.

A main advantage of the plasma display technology over others is that it is very scalable and very large, and wide screens can be produced using extremely thin materials. Plasma displays can have as many as 1024 shades, resulting in a high-quality image. Since each pixel is lit individually, the image is very bright and has a very wide viewing angle. The image quality is nearly as good as the best CRT monitors.

Figure 8-9 shows examples of some standard LCD and plasma monitors.

(A) 6.4" DIAGONAL LCD IN CASE

(B) 6.4" DIAGONAL LCD UNCASED

(C) 17" DIAGONAL LCD

(D) 42" DIAGONAL PLASMA DISPLAY

FIGURE 8-9   Standard LCD and plasma monitors

8.3.4   Organic LED (OLED)

An organic OLED is an LED made of a semiconducting organic polymer (Figure 8-10).

These devices promise to be much cheaper to fabricate than the inorganic LEDs used in other applications. The OLEDs can be fabricated in small or large arrays by using simple screen-printing methods to create the color display. One of the greatest benefits of the OLED display over traditional LCDs is that they do not require a backlight to function. They draw far less power than LCDs and can be used with small portable battery-operated devices which in the past have been using monochrome low resolution LCDs to conserve power. This also means that they will be able to operate for long periods of time with the same amount of battery charge. The first digital camera using an OLED display was shown by the Kodak Company in 2003. This was the first OLED technology and is usually referred to as *small molecule* OLED.

The second technology and improvement over the first was developed by Cambridge Display Technologies and is called "light emitting polymer" (LEP). Although a latecomer, LEP is more promising because it uses a more straightforward production technique (Figure 8-11). The LEP materials can be applied to the substrate by a technique derived from commercial inkjet printing. This means the LEP displays can be made flexible and inexpensively. Organic LEDs operate on the principle of electro-luminescence. An organic dye is the key to the operation of an OLED. To create the electro-luminescence a thin film of the dye is used and a current passed through it in a special way.

The radically different manufacturing process of OLEDs lends itself to many advantages over traditional flat panel displays. Since they can be printed onto a substrate using

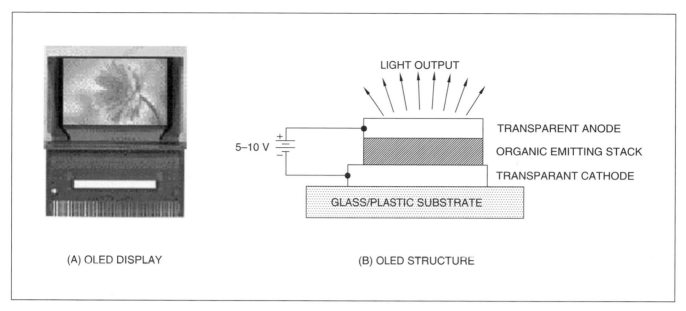

FIGURE 8-10   Organic LED (OLED) panel structure

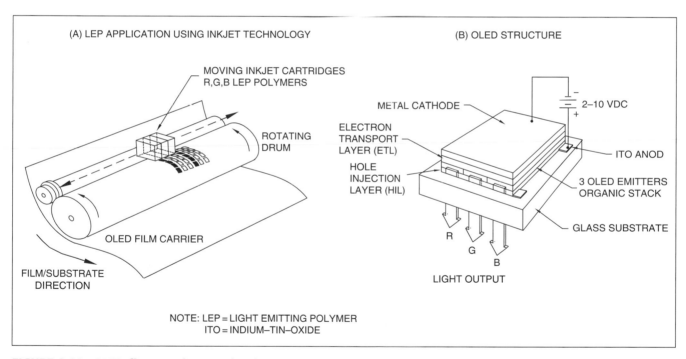

FIGURE 8-11   OLED flat panel LEP technology

traditional ink jet technology they have a significantly lower cost than LCDs or plasma displays. This scalable manufacturing process enables the possibility of much larger displays. Unlike most security LCD monitors employing backlighting, the OLED is capable of showing true black (completely off). In this mode the OLED element produces no light, theoretically allowing for infinite contrast ratio. The range of colors and brightness possible with OLEDs is greater than that of LCDs or plasma displays. Needing no backlight, OLEDs require less than

half the power of LCDs and are well suited for mobile applications where battery operation is necessary.

8.4   MONITOR DISPLAY FORMATS

There are several video formats used in different applications but the most predominant format remains the 4:3, which is used in almost all video security surveillance applications. A new format representing HDTV has not yet made any real impact in the security surveillance field (Figure 8-12).

8.4.1   Standard 4:3

The standard 4 × 3 video format (horizontal × vertical) has been in existence for many years and remains the predominant format at this time for the CRT and LCD. Liquid crystal displays and OLED displays are also manufactured in both the 4 × 3 and 16 × 9 formats.

8.4.2   High Definition 16:9

The 16:9 HDTV format was introduced as a new wide-screen display to satisfy the consumer and presentation markets. This format has not yet found widespread use in the video security sector but could offer advantages in specific applications such as viewing wide-angle outdoor landscape scenes: parking lots, waterfronts, airport runways and aircraft parking area, and public gathering places.

High definition TV has many different pixel formats and screen sizes that provide different resolutions and recommended viewing distances (Table 8-2).

8.4.3   Split-Screen Presentation

Equipment that combines video images can produce a significant reduction in the number of monitors required in a security console room. While the monitors for these displays are the same as those for single-image displays, the image-combining electronics permit displaying multiple camera scenes on one monitor. Chapter 16 describes the hardware to accomplish this function. The hardware takes the form of electronic combining circuits and special

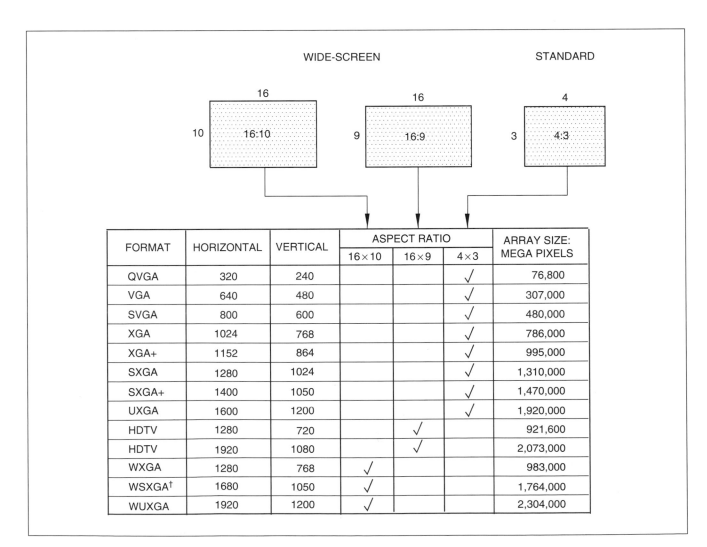

FORMAT	HORIZONTAL	VERTICAL	ASPECT RATIO			ARRAY SIZE: MEGA PIXELS
			16×10	16×9	4×3	
QVGA	320	240			✓	76,800
VGA	640	480			✓	307,000
SVGA	800	600			✓	480,000
XGA	1024	768			✓	786,000
XGA+	1152	864			✓	995,000
SXGA	1280	1024			✓	1,310,000
SXGA+	1400	1050			✓	1,470,000
UXGA	1600	1200			✓	1,920,000
HDTV	1280	720		✓		921,600
HDTV	1920	1080		✓		2,073,000
WXGA	1280	768	✓			983,000
WSXGA†	1680	1050	✓			1,764,000
WUXGA	1920	1200	✓			2,304,000

FIGURE 8-12   Monitor display formats

16:9 DIAGONAL d SCREEN SIZE (INCH)	MINIMUM VIEWING DISTANCE D (ft)	MAXIMUM VIEWING DISTANCE D (ft)
20	2.5	5.0
26	3.3	6.5
30	3.8	7.6
34	4.3	8.5
42	5.3	10.5
47	5.9	11.8
50	6.3	12.5
55	6.9	12.8
60	7.5	15
65	8.1	16.2

THE HDTV DISPLAY ASPECT RATIO IS 16:9 OR ABOUT 1.78:1.
STANDARD ANALOG VGA VIDEO IS 4:3 OR 1.333:1

HDTV IS APPLICABLE TO SURVEILLANCE APPLICATIONS
REQUIRING WIDE HORIZONTAL FIELD OF VIEW, HIGH
RESOLUTION AND LARGE SCREEN SIZE.

Table 8-2 HDTV Screen Sizes vs. Viewing Distance

applications or image-combining optics to produce multiple images—from 2 to 32 images—on one monitor screen.

8.4.4 Screen Size, Resolution

Resolution specifications for monitors refer to a full camera image presented on the monitor. When a split-screen presentation is used the resolution for each of the camera scenes decreases proportionally to the decrease in horizontal width and vertical height. A four-camera (quad) presentation on a monitor decreases the horizontal resolution by two and vertical resolution by two. Likewise, nine camera scenes on a monitor decrease the horizontal resolution by three and vertical resolution by three. When the screens are split to display 16 and 32 images, the horizontal and vertical resolutions decrease proportionately.

8.4.5 Multistandard, Multi-Sync

Multistandard, multisync, and multivoltage television monitor–receiver combinations are available that operate on the US NTSC (525 TV lines) and the European CCIR (625 TV lines) standards. Color systems operate on the NTSC, PAL, and SECAM formats. The multisync monitors are used primarily in computer displays where the computer monitor signal has a scan rate different from

the 60 Hz (or 50 Hz) rate and the monitor must synchronize to that other scan rate. Multivoltage monitors operate from 90 to 270 volts AC, 50–60 Hz for worldwide use.

8.4.6 Monitor Magnification

The overall video system magnification depends on the lens, camera, and monitor parameters. Section 4.2.2 analyzes the magnification as a function of the camera sensor size (1/4", 1/3", etc.), the lens focal length, and the display monitor size (screen diagonal). Table 4-5 summarizes the magnification of the overall video system for various monitor, lens, and sensor sizes.

8.5 INTERFACING ANALOG SIGNAL TO DIGITAL MONITOR

Connecting analog video signals to a digital flat-panel display requires special consideration. All flat-panel products face a common problem. Though all of these displays generate the video image using digital techniques, many of the video sources remain firmly entrenched in the analog world. There are numerous analog sources to contend with. Two pertaining to video security are:

1. Computer video sources with component video and separate digital synchronizing signals (R, G, B, Y, C)
2. Composite video sources including NTSC and PAL signals and the S-video.

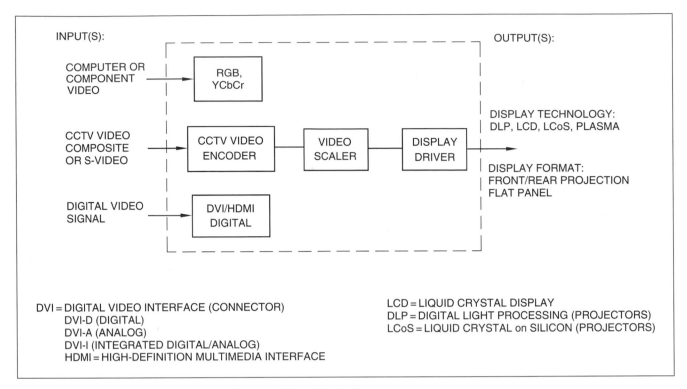

FIGURE 8-13 Analog to digital interface problem-block diagram

There are also numerous digital input signals that must be interfaced to the flat-panel display.

The analog signals need to be converted into a digital form so they can be scaled and optimized for the performance of the targeted digital display device. A typical system block diagram is shown in Figure 8-13.

Ideally a single integrated circuit (IC) would be able to receive all of the different input video signals, perform the required scaling functions, and transmit the resulting data to the digital display subsystem. So far the challenging and often conflicting requirements of such a device have prevented development of a cost-effective single-chip solution to this problem. In operation the device captures RGB computer video at resolutions from VGA to UXGA or YCbCr component video at resolutions from 480i to 1080i, including 720p. It can support resolutions as high as 1600 × 1275 at 75 fps.

Digital video interfacing (DVI) electronics is a form of video connector (interface) made to maximize the display quality of analog video on flat-panel LCD (and other) computer monitors and high-end video cards. It was developed by an industry consortium, the Digital Display Working Group (DDWG).

Existing EIA standards are analog as are the monitors they are connected to. However, multifunctional LCD monitors and plasma screens internally use a digital signal. Using VGA cabling results in the computer signal being converted from the internal digital format to analog on the VGA cable and then back to digital again in the monitor for display. This obviously reduces picture quality, and a better solution is provided by DVI to simply supply the original digital signal to the monitor directly.

The three types of DVI connections are:

1. DVI-D (digital)
2. DVI-A (analog)
3. DVI-I (integrated digital/analog).

One shortcoming of DVI is that it lacks USB pass-throughs. The data format used by DVI is based on the PanelLink™ serial format devised by Silicon Image Inc. A basic DVI-D link consists of four twisted pairs of wire (R,G,B, and clock) to transmit 24 bits per pixel. DVI is the only widespread standard that includes analog and digital transmission options in the same connector.

8.6 MERGING VIDEO WITH PCs

Many CCTV security applications require combining the CCTV image with computer text and/or graphics. To accomplish this, the video and computer display signals must be synchronized, combined, and sent to a monitor. Equipment is available to perform this integration (Chapter 16).

As computer product technologies converge with video products, many theories have been discussed about how PCs and video should mesh, but the optimal blend has yet to be found. Attempts to design a merged PC and video display are complicated by differences in the design of displays used by PC and video applications. Computer monitors have been optimized for reading 10 point–type text and static images from a distance of 2 feet. Accordingly, the physical display size is small and uses a low brightness non-interlaced scan with fast screen refresh to produce a crisp high-definition image that is easy on the eyes at short viewing distances.

Video surveillance imagery on the other hand has been optimized within the constraints of the relatively archaic NTSC system. The system was designed to generate low-resolution high brightness images, using an interlaced scan with low screen refresh rate (30 fps) for viewing moving images on a large display area at distances of 3–6 or even 10 feet. Of particular interest are PC-graphics display technologies that allow the monitor to replace the analog video display without any degradation in picture quality. To produce high fidelity pictures rivaling those of CRT video displays, PCs must incorporate digital video processing technology that adapts the video stream to the characteristics of the PC monitor. This process must preserve the inherent fidelity of the video source while simulating video scan techniques on the PC display. This process requires a combination of techniques to preserve the native resolution of the digital video stream, while simultaneously handling the special de-interlacing and frame-rate conversion tasks necessary to produce high fidelity digital video images.

The nature of the NTSC display format creates enormous challenges. Analog color video produces pictures at a constant rate of 59.94 Hz. With an image size of 640 by 240 pixels, each field contains only half a full 480 line picture vertical resolution. Each field scans only alternate lines of the video display, with adjacent fields scanning 240 lines, each offsetting from the other on the screen by one half-line position. The first, or odd, field which scans the display starts with a half-line scan while the second, or even, field ends with a half-line. A full frame of NTSC video actually contains 525 lines. Approximately 480 of those 525 lines on the monitor are used for the video picture (the active lines), while the remainder makes up the vertical-blanking interval. Therefore there are 262.5 lines in each field. This sequence of field pairs—scanning every other display line with a half-line off-set between fields—creates an interlaced display scan. Each pair combines to form a full 640 by 480 video picture frame.

Complicating matters, each of the fields within a frame are separated in time by 1/60th of a second representing two discrete instances in time, 1/60th of the second apart. To present a true video-like picture, the PC must attempt to copy this display scanning technique as faithfully as possible. To accomplish this, the native resolution of the digital video screen must be preserved from its origin: typically an MPEG-2, or composite video decoder, through to the digital to analog converters (DACs) of the graphics device. Secondly the native video source must

be converted from an interlaced format to a display format that is suitable for the PC's progressive scan display mechanism without introducing any visible image glitches. Finally the PC screen display refresh rate must be locked to the field rate of the original video source to avoid display rate conversion artifacts. The conventional simplistic approach to the interlaced to non-interlaced conversion challenge is to capture both fields of the video frame in local memory and read out both fields simultaneously to the PC display. This interlacing technique ignores the fact that the individual fields within a frame are temporally different. They occur 1/60th of a second apart and visually represent two separate instances in time. A static object such as a circle causes no problems with the simple store and read de-interlacer, but if the object traverses horizontally across the screen a distorted motion occurs between each field within the frame. In the most simplistic de-interlacing PC display, the two fields are displayed at the same instant and feathering or inter-field motion-image artifacts along the edges of horizontally moving objects are easily noticed.

Another major problem that must be addressed is the frame-rate conversion. The field rate of the analog video source is fixed at approximately 60 fields per second whereas PC displays are typically refreshed at a rate of 70 or 75 Hz (frames per second). The PC screen refresh rate should match that of the original video source to truly replicate the analog video behavior. Special digital display frame-locking techniques must be used to ensure that the screen refresh rate precisely tracks the actual field rate of the original digital video source. The most effective frame-locking technique is adaptive, digital frame locking, rather than an analog phase locked loop (PPL) locking technique.

8.7 SPECIAL FEATURES

There are several special features that may be incorporated into analog and digital display monitors. These include:

- Interactive touch-screens allowing the monitor operator to interact actively with the monitor for control and communication functions. Technologies used include resistance, infrared, and capacitance.
- Antiglare screens overlay the monitor display to provide higher contrast of the video image when reflections and glare from the surrounding environment are present.
- Sunlight-readable displays using high brightness flat-panel display technology.

8.7.1 Interactive Touch-Screen

The touch-screen system is particularly useful when guard personnel must quickly and decisively react to an activity. At present the technique is not in widespread use, but as system complexity and knowledge of its availability increase, more security systems will incorporate these touch screens.

There are many ways to input data into the video security system. These range from keyboards to mouse to voice etc. One method that is becoming more popular is going directly to the source, using touch-screen technology. Allowing the user to input information directly eliminates the need for a mouse or other pointing device, thereby simplifying the input process.

Many monitors in security applications display the outputs from video graphics and/or an alphanumeric database generated by a computer. Some advanced systems operate with computer software and hardware that permit interacting with the screen display by touching the screen at specific locations and causing specific actions to occur. The devices are called touch-screen templates and are located at the front of the monitor. The touch screen permits the operator to activate a program or hardware change by touching a specific location on the screen.

Touch-screen interaction between the guard and the hardware and video system has obvious advantages. It frees the guard from a keyboard and provides a faster input command response. Also, the guard does not have to memorize keyboard commands and type the correct keys.

There is also less chance for error with the touch-screen input, since the guard can point to a particular word, symbol, or location on the screen with better accuracy and reliability. Different types of touch screens are available, using different principles of operation.

8.7.1.1 Infrared

Infrared touch screens rely on the interruption of an IR light grid in front of the display screen. This technique uses a row of LEDs and photo-transistor detectors each mounted on two opposite sides to create an invisible grid of IR light in front of the monitor. When the IR beam is interrupted by a finger or other stylus, causing one or more of the photo-transistors to detect the absence of light and transmit a signal with the X,Y coordinates, a signal is returned to the computer electronics to perform a predetermined action. The space within the frame attached to the front of the monitor forms the touch-active area, and a microprocessor calculates where the person has touched the screen. Figure 8-14a shows such a touch screen installed on a monitor. Since there is no film or plastic material placed in front of the monitor, there is no change or reduction in optical clarity of the displayed picture.

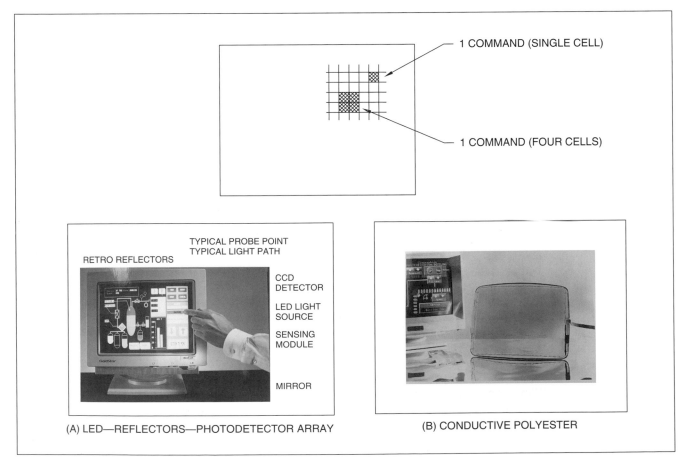

FIGURE 8-14 Monitor touch screens

The IR technology has no limitations in terms of objects that can be used to touch the screen. The one disadvantage is that the screen may react before it is physically touched.

8.7.1.2 Resistive

A second type of touch-screen technology is resistive, which is in common use and inexpensive compared to other methods. One shortcoming of resistive touch-screen is that the indium tin oxide coating typically employed is relatively fragile. The resistive touch panel consists of a transparent, conductive polyester sheet over a rigid acrylic back-plane; both are affixed to the front of the display to form a transparent switch matrix (Figure 8-14b). The switch matrix assembly has 120 separate switch locations that can be labeled with words or symbols on the underlying display, or a scene can be divided into 120 separate locations and interacted with by the operator. Individual touch cells may be grouped together to form larger touch keys via programming commands in the software. Typical light transmission for the resistive touch-screen is 65–75% so that not all the light pass through the screen to the operator and the picture has lower contrast.

Resistive touch screens combine a flexible top layer overlay with a rigid resistive bottom layer that is separated from the top layer by insulated spacer dots. Pressing the flexible top layer creates a contact with the resistive bottom layer and control electronics identify the point at which the contact is made on the screen. This technology provides the benefits of high resolution and the fact that any type of pointing device can be used. One shortcoming of the resistive touch screen is its need for an overlay and spacer dots and therefore it suffers from reduced brightness and optical clarity, and the surface and the flexible top layer can be prone to surface damage, scratches, and chemicals.

If a touch screen is required in an outdoor sunlit application one has to be especially aware that relatively inexpensive analog resistive models can cut light transmission by as much as 20% and reduce the effectiveness of the screen brightness.

8.7.1.3 Capacitive

A third type of interactive touch-screen accessory consists of an optically clear Mylar-polyester membrane that is curved around the monitor's front glass screen and transparent to the user. When the conductive surface of the Mylar is pressed against the conductive surface of the glass by the operator, a capacitance coupling draws the current from each of the four electrodes to the touch point. Current drawn is proportional to the distance of the contact point from each electrode, allowing the X,Y location of the contact point to be determined. This change in voltage is detected by the monitor electronics, which communicate

with the security system to indicate that the person has touched the screen at a particular location.

The conductive coating over the surface of the display screen is connected to electrodes at each of the edges. This technology offers good resolution, fast response time, and the ability to operate with surface contamination on the face of the monitor but it is not suitable for gloved hands. Capacitance touch screens also suffer from some electronic drift, meaning that periodic recalibration is required.

8.7.1.4 Projected Capacitance Technology (PCT)

Projected capacitance technology (PCT) uses embedded micro-fine wires within a glass laminate composite. Each wire has a diameter of approximately one-third of the diameter of a human hair meaning that they become nearly invisible to the human eye when viewed against the powered up display. When a conducting stylus such as finger touches the glass surface of the sensor, a change in capacitance occurs, resulting in a measurable oscillation frequency change in the wires surrounding the contact point. The integrated controller calculates this new capacitance value and these data are transferred to host controller. Software is used to translate the sensor contact point to an absolute screen position. The polyurethane layer incorporating the touch-screen sensor array is sandwiched, and protected between the glass layers and is therefore impervious to accidental and malicious damage, day-to-day wear and tear, and severe scratching. It is able to accept input from bare and gloved hands and needs no additional sealing to prevent the sensor from being affected by moisture, rain, dust, grease, or cleaning fluids.

8.7.2 Anti-Glare Screen

A common problem associated with television monitor viewing is the glare coming from the screen when ambient lighting located above, behind, or to the side of the monitor reflects off the front surface of the monitor. This glare reduces the picture contrast and produces unwanted reflections. In well-designed security console rooms where the designer has taken monitor glare into consideration at the outset, glare will not significantly reduce screen intelligibility or cause viewer fatigue.

For best results, face the monitor in the direction of a darkened area of the room. Keep lights away from the direction in which the monitor is pointing that are either behind the person looking at the monitor or from the ceiling above. If there are windows to the outside of the building where bright sunlight may come through, point the monitors away from the outside windows and toward the inside walls. When this cannot be accomplished and

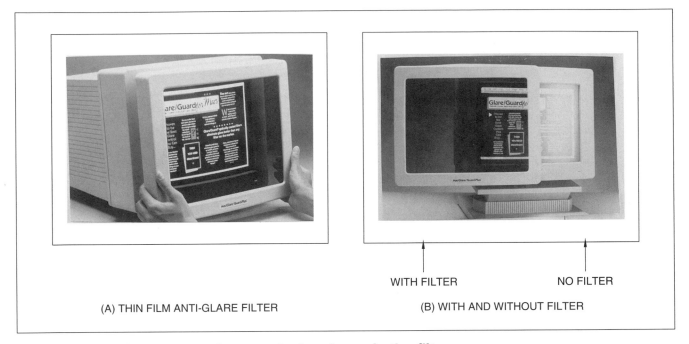

(A) THIN FILM ANTI-GLARE FILTER   (B) WITH AND WITHOUT FILTER

FIGURE 8-15   Monitor contrast enhancement using glare reduction filters

annoying glare would produce fatigue and reduce security, any of the various anti-glare filters available should be applied to the front of a monitor to reduce the glare and increase the contrast of the picture. With a well-designed anti-glare screen and proper installation, glare and reflection levels can be reduced significantly. Figure 8-15 is an un-retouched photograph showing the contrast enhancement (glare reduction) provided by one of these filters.

These anti-glare optical filters are manufactured from polycarbonate or acrylic plastic materials and are suitable for indoor applications. Polycarbonate filters used in outdoor applications can withstand a wider temperature range and are therefore more suitable. The filters come in a range of colors, with the most common being neutral density (gray), green, yellow, or blue. The colored filters are used on graphic and data display computer terminals, whereas the neutral-density types are used for monochrome and color monitors. In the case of color displays, the lighter gray filters should be used for glare reduction.

8.7.3 Sunlight-Readable Display

Display brightness is measured and reported in *nits*. One nit is roughly equal to the brightness of one standard candle. Marketing departments often like to use terminology like ultra-bright and sun-bright, but they do not always make the connection back into engineering units. The following levels of brightness define some of the capabilities of these monitors:

- Bright (150–240 nits). This is the typical brightness of a home or office computer and is suitable for most indoor light conditions.
- High-Bright (250–340 nits). These are brighter than typical panel displays. They can be situated in brightly lit rooms without reducing viewing capacity.
- Ultra-Bright (350–790 nits). These may be suitable for some outdoor applications. They provide good visibility in highly illuminated environments where the light source or bright reflections would not allow Bright or High-Bright units to be easily read or images viewed.
- Sun-Bright (800 nits and up). Displays this bright are suitable for outdoor sunlit applications and can be read in direct sunlight.

Recent advances in LCD monitors have created new outdoor applications for sunlight viewable displays, especially where CRTs are out of the question because of their bulky size. Previously a display that provided 400 nits with a good reflective surface was acceptable. Now the demand has increased to 1500 nits with a minimum display size of about 15 inch diagonal. A 15 inch display can consume as much as 50 W for a brightness of 1500 nits. Displays larger than 10 inch diagonal pose thermal problems when used in a sun-loading environment. Manufacturers have typically used a brute force method, increasing back-light power to increase display brightness. This high power back-light in turn generates tremendous heat that causes an AMLCD to go above its safe operating temperature. Heat is detrimental to AMLCD survivability. To overcome the heating problem massive heat sinks have been employed in addition to expensive antireflective and IR face glass laminated onto the display to block the heat generated by sunlight.

The display parameters required for sunlight readability include:

- Brightness. The display must be bright enough to be legible under full sunlight. The required brightness ranges between 400 and 1500 nits.
- Readability. The display image must be discernible by the naked eye under all viewing conditions from full sunlight to nighttime.

In addition to high brightness monitors, antireflective coatings are often used to minimize reflections caused by sunlight and an infrared coating is used to reject heat caused by sun loading. The rejected heat spectrum covers the near IR spectral region.

8.8 RECEIVER/MONITOR, VIEWFINDER, MOBILE DISPLAY

Various manufacturers produce small lightweight CRT and LCD television monitors or receiver/monitors to accept base-band video signal inputs and/or VHF/UHF commercial RF channels and are powered by 6, 9, or 12 volts DC (Figure 8-16).

These television monitors are particularly useful in portable and mobile surveillance, law enforcement, and for servicing applications. Often a portable surveillance camera will be transmitting the video signal (perhaps also audio) via an RF or UHF video transmitter operating on one of the commercial channels or at 900 MHz or 2.4 GHz. The small receiver-monitors with 1.5- to 5-inch-diagonal CRT or LCD displays can receive and display the transmitted video signal and have an output to provide the

base-band video signal for a VCR, DVR, or video printer at the receiver site. These devices usually have medium resolution (250–400 lines) often sufficient to provide useful security information and for camera installation and testing.

Shock, vibration, and dirt are probably the most common causes of failure for flat-panel displays in harsh environments or used in mobile applications. The typical 15-inch TFT LCD monitor weighs about 13 lbs and so an acceleration of 2 g makes it weigh 26 lbs. Standard office-style LCDs cannot stand up to the kind of shock and vibration found that most mobile environments and to some degree industrial hardening is required. At a minimum they should be shock rated at 1.5 g and have a vibration rating of 1 g. More severe environments call for higher specifications. Aside from shock and vibration, monitors will be subject high levels of grit, grime, water, dust, and oil than would be expected in a normal office environment. This is where the industrial, environmental and structural NEMA ratings are helpful. A few key NEMA ratings for flat-panel displays used in mobile and harsh environments include the following:

- NEMA 3 enclosures are suitable for outdoor applications, and repel falling dirt, rain, sleet, snow, and windblown dust: enclosure contents are undamaged by external ice formation.
- NEMA 4 adds protection from splashing and hose-directed water to NEMA 3 standard.
- NEMA 6 is similar to the NEMA 4 but the enclosure prevents ingress of water during occasional temporary submersion to a limited depth.
- NEMA 6P protects against water ingress after a prolonged submersion.

(A) HIGH RESOULUTION LCD MONITOR

(B) TUNABLE 900 MHz TO 2.4 GHz
2.5" LCD RECEIVER/MONITOR

FIGURE 8-16   Small flat screen receiver/monitor

8.9 PROJECTION DISPLAY

The digital projector is an electro-optical device that converts a video image or computer graphics and data into a bright image that is projected and imaged onto a distant wall or screen using a lens or lens-mirror system.

The projector serves the following purposes:

- Visualization of video and stored computer data for monitoring or presentation.
- Replaces the whiteboard and written documents.
- Provides the ability to view video images and other data by many personnel at the same time.
- Provides the ability to playback images from a VCR, DVR, and digital video disk onto a large screen.

Digital projection technologies include:

- High-intensity CRT
- LCD projectors using LCD light gates
- Texas Instruments DLP technology.

The current dominant technology at the high-end for portable digital projectors is the Texas Instruments DLP technology with LCD projectors dominating the low-end. Digital projectors take the form of a small table-top portable projector using an external screen or a rear projection screen forming a single unified display device. The typical resolution for the portable projector is the SVGA standard (800 × 600 pixels), with more expensive devices supporting the XVGA (1024 × 768 pixels) format. Projectors costs are determined in most part by their resolution and brightness. Higher requirements cost more. For large conference rooms the brightness should be between 1000 and 4000 lumens. CRT devices are only suitable for fixed installations because of their weight.

8.10 SUMMARY

There are several monitor types that can be used in the security room. These include the standard analog CRT monitor and the digital flat-screen LCD, plasma display, and to a lesser extent the new organic light emitting diode (OLED) displays. Where space permits, the standard CRT monitor is a cost-effective solution and can provide a bright, high-resolution monochrome or color image. In more confined spaces or in any completely new installation the flat-panel display should be considered.

The quality of the image displayed is a function of the number of TV lines the analog monitor can display, and the number of horizontal and vertical pixel elements available in the digital flat screen monitor. The standard video format is 4 units wide by 3 units high and is almost exclusively the format used in the video surveillance industry. A new format designed for high definition consumer television monitors has a 16 by 9 format but has limited use in the security industry. Video monitors are available in multistandard, multisync configurations for use with all available voltages and scan rates.

The use of digital flat screen monitors is increasing rapidly, and interfacing digital computer systems with the monitor has brought about problems which need solving. These include interfacing the analog signal provided by most cameras to the new digital monitors. The use of analog cameras and digital Internet cameras in the same surveillance system further complicates the interface of these cameras to the digital displays.

Video monitors are available having special features such as interactive touch screens, anti-glare screens, and sunlight-readable displays. In applications where the guard must make quick, accurate decisions and many cameras and security functions are involved, the touch screen can serve a very important function for making the guard more effective. There are several technologies available for touch screen monitors including: infrared, resistive, capacitive and projected capacitive technology (PCT).

Under difficult indoor and outdoor lighting situations in which reflections are prevalent on the monitor screen, anti-glare filters are available to reduce or eliminate this problem. Under extreme sunlight conditions, new flat-panel displays are available with sunlight-readable displays having very high brightness and high contrast.

There are many new applications in which the use of automated video surveillance from remote sites or mobile monitor stations is required. Using the digital networks LAN, WAN, Wireless LAN (WLAN, WiFi) and Internet cameras, laptop computers, PDAs, and other portable devices using flat-screen display technology are now available.

When video monitoring systems must be portable or transportable or set up rapidly, small mobile, low power flat-panel displays are available with monochrome or color displays. These monitors have low electrical power requirements so that they can operate for days using small rechargeable batteries. Using battery power, these displays are suitable for rapid deployment video surveillance systems and testing and maintenance applications.

When the video scenes must be viewed by many personnel and a large-screen video image is required, video projectors are available for fixed installation or portable use.

Chapter 9
Analog, Digital Video Recorders

CONTENTS

9.1   Overview
    9.1.1   Analog Video Cassette Recorder (VCR)
    9.1.2   Digital Video Recorder (DVR)
        9.1.2.1   DVR in a Box
        9.1.2.2   Basic DVR
        9.1.2.3   Multiplex DVR
        9.1.2.4   Multi-channel DVR
        9.1.2.5   Network Video Recorder (NVR)
9.2   Analog Video Recorder
    9.2.1   Video Cassette Recorder
    9.2.2   VCR Formats
        9.2.2.1   VHS, VHS-C, S-VHS
        9.2.2.2   8 mm, Hi-8 Sony
        9.2.2.3   Magnetic Tape Types
    9.2.3   Time-Lapse(TL) VCR
    9.2.4   VCR Options
        9.2.4.1   Camera Switching/Selecting
        9.2.4.2   RS-232 Communications
        9.2.4.3   Scrambling
        9.2.4.4   On-Screen Annotating and Editing
9.3   Digital Video Recorder (DVR)
    9.3.1   DVR Technology
        9.3.1.1   Digital Hardware Advances
            9.3.1.1.1   Hard Disk Drive storage
            9.3.1.1.2   Video Motion Detection (VMD)
            9.3.1.1.3   Optical-Disk Image Storage
            9.3.1.1.4   Non-Erasable, Write-Once Read-Many (WORM) Disk
            9.3.1.1.5   Erasable Optical Disk
            9.3.1.1.6   Digital Audio Tape (DAT)
        9.3.1.2   Digital Storage Software Advances
        9.3.1.3   Transmission Advances
        9.3.1.4   Communication Control

9.3.2   DVR Generic Types
    9.3.2.1   DVR in a Box
    9.3.2.2   DVR Basic Plug-and-Play VCR Replacement
    9.3.2.3   Multiplex
    9.3.2.4   Multi-Channel
        9.3.2.4.1   Redundant Array of Independent Disks (RAID)
    9.3.2.5   Network Video Recorder (NVR)
    9.3.2.6   Hybrid NVR/DVR System
9.3.3   DVR Operating Systems (OS)
    9.3.3.1   Windows 9X, NT, and 2000 Operating Systems
    9.3.3.2   UNIX
9.3.4   Mobile DVR
9.3.5   Digital Compression, Encryption
    9.3.5.1   JPEG
    9.3.5.2   MPEG-X
    9.3.5.3   Wavelet
    9.3.5.4   SMICT
9.3.6   Image Quality
    9.3.6.1   Resolution
    9.3.6.2   Frame Rate
    9.3.6.3   Bandwidth
9.3.7   Display Format—CIF
9.3.8   Network/DVR Security
    9.3.8.1   Authentication
    9.3.8.2   Watermark
    9.3.8.3   Virtual Private Network (VPN)
        9.3.8.3.1   Trusted VPNs
        9.3.8.3.2   Secure VPNs
        9.3.8.3.3   Hybrid VPNs
    9.3.8.4   Windows Operating System
9.3.9   VCR/DVR Hardware/Software Protection
    9.3.9.1   Uninterrupted Power Supply (UPS)
    9.3.9.2   Grounding

        9.3.9.3   Analog/Digital Hardware
                    Precautions
        9.3.9.4   Maintenance
9.4   Video Recorder Comparison: Pros, Cons
      9.4.1   VCR Pros and Cons
      9.4.2   DVR Pros and Cons
9.5   Checklist and Guidelines
      9.5.1   Checklist
      9.5.2   Guidelines
9.6   Summary

9.1 OVERVIEW

9.1.1 Analog Video Cassette Recorder (VCR)

Prior to 1970s real-time video recording systems used magnetic reel-to-reel tape media and required manually changing of the magnetic tape reels. Operation was cumbersome and unreliable, and the tape was prone to damage or accidental erasing. The recorder required the operator to manually thread the tape from the tape reel through the recorder onto an empty take-up reel, similar to threading 8 mm and 16 mm film projectors. Not very much video security recording was done in this era.

In the 1970s the first analog VCR was introduced to the security industry. The arrival of the VCR permitted easy loading and unloading of the tape cassette without the user contacting the tape. The VCR machines provided real-time 30 fps recording. VCRs found widespread use in security when the VHS tape format became the dominant consumer VCR format. However, most security applications require 24/7/365 day operation without stopping. The consumer VCRs were not designed for continuous use and did not operate in a TL mode, and were not a reliable choice for security applications. The security industry had the manufacturers design industrial versions that have served the security industry for many years. These TL VCRs were especially designed to withstand the additional burden of long-term continuous recording and the start–stop of TL recording.

The VCR was the only viable technology until the late 1990s, and still is a convenient method for recording security video images. During this period specialized functions were added that further enhanced their usefulness which included: (1) alarm activation (2) T-160 24-hour real-time recording, and 40 day extended TL recording (960 hours) on a single cassette.

The recorded video images are used for general surveillance of premises, to apprehend and prosecute thieves and offenders, and to train and correct personnel procedures of security personnel. A played-back camera image from a high-quality recording system can be as valuable as a live observation. The video image on a monitor however is fleeting, but the recorded image can be played back over and over again and a hard copy printed for later use. The original VHS tape can easily be given to the police or other law enforcement agency for investigation or prosecution.

The TL VCR records single pictures at closely spaced time intervals longer than the real-time 1/30-second frame time. This means that the TL mode conserves tape, while permitting the real-time recording of significant security events. When a security event of significance occurs, a VMD or alarm input signal causes the VCR to switch from TL to real-time recording. These real-time events are the ones the security guard would consider important and normally view and act on at a command monitor. TL recording permits the efficient use of a recorder so that changing of VCR tapes is minimized.

Video cassette recorders have some shortcomings however. They can generate grainy and poor quality images during playback because videotapes are frequently reused, and record/playback heads are worn or misaligned, degrading the quality of the video image. VCR tapes are changed manually which leaves room for human error, whereby the tape may not be changed at the required time or a recorded tape is inserted into the machine, erasing previously recorded images. Clean space for storing the videotapes can also become a problem particularly true in high-usage casino applications.

The DVR eliminates all these problems.

9.1.2 Digital Video Recorder (DVR)

The movement from tape-based real-time and TL video recording to today's DVRs has been a vast improvement, and a quantum jump forward in technology. There is a new generation of video cameras, with digital signal processing and IP cameras and other digital devices to interface to the DVRs, CRTs and flat screen LCD and plasma digital monitors. Today's DVRs do not represent the end of the technological advancement, but are rather the beginning of intelligent recording devices that are more user-friendly and economical.

The DVR was first introduced to the video industry in the early 1990s and it recorded the video image on a HD drive in digital form. Why the change to DVR technology? The VCR has been in use for years but has been a weak link in the overall video security system. One important reason is the VCR's requirement for excessive tape maintenance, deterioration of the tapes over time and use, inability to reproduce the high resolution and image quality produced by the digital cameras, and the excessive manpower required to review the tapes. Another disadvantage of the VCR technology is the sheer volume of storage space required to archive the tapes in mid- to large-size systems at casinos, etc. This prompted many a dealers, systems integrators and end users to switch over to DVR equipment.

Another advantage is the significantly better image quality on playback. One reason for this is that the analog VCR only records a *single field* of the video image. The DVR records a *full frame* of information. The VCR reduces the detail of the video image during playback by one half, thereby rendering a poorer image than the original live image. DVRs, on the other hand, record the full video image on the HD and do not introduce picture noise, and provide high stability and higher quality video image. The DVR also eliminates the need for head and tape replacement thereby significantly reducing maintenance over its lifetime.

The DVR converts the incoming video camera signal into a recorded magnetic form on a magnetic HD. The recorder later reconstructs the video signal into a form suitable for display on a video monitor or to be printed on a hard-copy video printer or for transmission to a remote site.

Most DVRs have more than one internal HD drive. The software controlling them automatically moves the recorded images internally, so that if there is a failure, only a portion of the data is lost. The average 80 GByte HD drive can store approximately 100 hours of data, while the VCR can store just 8 hours of data. Images on HD drives do not degrade and can be retrieved, copied, and reused hundreds of times without compromising the picture quality. Important security images can also be stored permanently (archived) on HD drives, recorded on digital audio tape (DAT) recorders, or burned into DVDs for future use.

Digital video recorders provide higher quality images than VCRs particularly during picture pause in which the DVR exhibits no distortion and no picture tearing during pause, single frame advance, or rewind and fast-forward modes. This is true from the first viewing, after many viewings of the same image, regardless of the number of times the digital image is viewed or copied. Switching from VCR to DVR machines eliminates all tape hassles: tapes will not have to be changed, no prying the tape out of the VCR slot, and no cleaning or replacing tape heads again.

Unlike the VCR, the DVR permits programming the picture resolution as required by the application. It can be programmed locally or remotely to permit recording in real-time or TL modes depending on the programming, and can respond to video motion alerts or alarm inputs. The video image quality remains the same regardless of how many times the images are stored or re-recorded.

The DVR hardware is available in several configurations: DVR in a box, DVR Basic (plug-and-play), DVR multiplex, and DVR multi-channel. Large systems networking to remote sites use network video recorders (NVR).

9.1.2.1 DVR in a Box

The DVR in a box is created by adding a printed circuit (PC) card to a PC computer and converting it into a DVR.

This solution might be expedient but it does have some limitations: it has very few user-friendly features. It is used in low-cost, small video systems.

9.1.2.2 Basic DVR

The single channel DVR is the basic replacement for the real-time or TL VCR. The single channel DVR looks, feels, and has the controls similar to a VCR, and can be set by the operator from a local or remote site. It functions like a VCR but has many advantages over the VCR. DVRs produce sharp images over long periods of time and after many copies have been made. The DVR is especially well suited to perform video motion detection and can be activated by external alarms. A primary market for the basic DVR is as a *VCR replacement* in a legacy analog installation. In this application the video cabling infrastructure is already in place for transmission of video images from the cameras to the recorder, and the most cost-effective solution is the basic DVR. A single channel DVR is a cost-effective replacement for a VCR and provides long-term maintenance-free recordings that can be viewed locally, remotely, and transmitted anywhere over wired or wireless networks. Making the switch from the traditional VCR to the DVR is now here at an affordable price and can replace the VCR with no changes to the rest of the system.

9.1.2.3 Multiplex DVR

Midsize DVRs using multiplexer technology provide high-quality recording capabilities for 4–16 cameras. For midsize surveillance systems, DVRs with built-in multiplexers operate like traditional multiplexers connected to VCRs. The equipment offers on-screen menus and require only simple keystrokes to find images or events by alarm input, time, date, camera number, or other identifiers. These recorded images can be stored for days, weeks, or months. DVR multiplexers are available with Ethernet connections to provide high-quality remote transmission to other sites on the network. This makes the video images available at local monitoring sites or at a central monitoring station, thereby providing instant access to critical recordings. The images can be retrieved using standard IP addresses and PCs to make the remote monitoring and recordings available to authorized personnel anywhere on the network.

Multiplexed systems are used in midsize systems to record multiple cameras. While recording multiple cameras, the multiplexed DVR cannot record all cameras in real-time but rather time-share and record the cameras in sequence. DVR time-sharing operates in the same way as a standalone video multiplexer. Multiplexed recorders usually have a maximum storage capacity of 480–600 GByte representing 600–750 hours of real-time recording (depends on resolution). The combination of multiplexer and DVR has the advantage that the interface between the multiplexer and VCR is already accomplished by the manufacturer.

9.1.2.4 Multi-channel DVR

The multi-channel DVR technology requires significantly more HD drives and error correcting codes to reliably store and manipulate the images. The result is a system where all cameras are recorded at all times without any loss of video image information. Large enterprise systems using multi-channel machines can record images from hundreds of cameras for months or more, storing high resolution video image scenes in real-time, near real-time or TL. To store a large number of images the video image files are compressed by removing redundant data in the image file. The number of bytes in each image file is reduced significantly so that the files can be stored efficiently on the HD.

The multi-channel DVR records each camera on individual channels (not multiplexed) and is designed for applications with a large number of cameras as in an Enterprise system. This system can be expanded to nearly an unlimited number of video channels by adding additional HD memory and appropriate software control. The multi-channel DVR permits storing 60 images per second per camera whereas the multiplexed unit divides the 60 images by the number of cameras. The multiplexed scanning often causes a jerky motion of the image during playback and is especially noticeable when the image per second (IPS) for the cameras falls below 15 IPS.

Most DVRs are triplex rather than duplex in design. This means that they can: (1) display and record live video, (2) display the recorded video locally, and (3) display the recorded video remotely all *simultaneously*. In the case of remote viewing, a standard Web browser connected to the Internet via an ISP is all that is needed to view the video images.

Digital video recorders allow fast searching of recorded information based on time, date, video motion detection, alarm input, or other external events. This permits fast retrieval of video images and avoids wading through countless frames of video information as required with standard VCR technology. The operator can view the information of interest in a matter of seconds. This is a primary advantage of DVR technology over VCR.

9.1.2.5 Network Video Recorder (NVR)

The NVR records video and audio data streams received over Ethernet networks using the TCP/IP protocol. The NVR receives compressed video data streams from the transmission channel and transfers the streams to an internal HD for storage in the DVR.

The NVR technique uses the Ethernet networks already in place in most buildings, and features such as motion detection, scene analysis, and alarm notification are employed. These features have added to the growing popularity of network surveillance. All digital video sources or analog cameras connected to video servers feed the digital data streams into the network. A computer with sufficient storage capacity serves as the DVR. The DVR accesses the video data streams of the remote network cameras and video servers and stores them on the HD.

9.2 ANALOG VIDEO RECORDER

9.2.1 Video Cassette Recorder

The innovation of video cassettes and the VCR resulted in wide acceptance of this recording medium for over 25 years. VCRs used the Victor Home System (VHS) video cassette as the recording medium. The newer Sony 8 mm format gained some popularity in the security market because of its small compact size while the VHS-C format found limited use. Present real-time VCR systems record 2, 4, or 6 hours of real-time monochrome or color video with about 300 lines of resolution on one VHS or 8 mm cassette. TL recorders can have total elapsed recording times of up to 960 hours. Most TL recorders have alarm input contacts that switch the recorder to real-time recording when an alarm condition occurs.

The VCR has always been the weakest link in the video security system with respect to image quality and reliability. Both the VHS and 8 mm recorders fall short in that they do not record high resolution camera images. The main reason for this is that both recorders record a *field* rather than a *frame*, thereby losing half the camera resolution. The VHS and 8 mm formats called S-VHS and Hi-8 increased resolution and picture quality but do not meet the resolution capabilities of most monochrome and color cameras. TL recording makes maximum use of the space available on the video cassette by recording individual images at a slow pre-selected rate, thereby slowing the recording rate. Instead of recording at a normal 30 fps the TL VCR records one picture every fraction of a second or every few seconds. Prior to the use of DVRs using computer HD drives, all security installations recorded the video images using VCRs.

The TL tape machine may take about two to three minutes to search from the beginning to the end of the tape since the tape in the TL recorder is advanced and reversed linearly by mechanical devices and motors.

9.2.2 VCR Formats

Almost all security VCRs use the 1/2-inch wide magnetic tape format. A compact cassette called VHS-C and sold by JVC Company found little use in the security industry. In the 1990s Sony developed the compact tape formats using an 8 mm (1/4-inch)-wide tape cartridge. While most security video recorders use the standard VHS cassette format, many portable systems use the more compact Sony 8 mm and Hi-8 cassette.

9.2.2.1 VHS, VHS-C, S-VHS

Standard real-time continuous recording times for VHS tapes are 2, 4, and 6 hours. When these cassettes are used in TL mode, where a single image or a selected sequence of images are recorded, 8, 24, 40, and up to 960 hours can be recorded on a single 2-hour VHS cassette. VCRs record the video scene on magnetic tape using the same laws of physics as used in audiotape recorders (Figure 9-1).

The challenging aspect of recording a video picture on a magnetic tape is that the standard US NTSC video signal has a wide bandwidth and includes frequencies above 4 MHz (4 million cycles per second) and down to 30 Hz, as compared with an audio signal with frequencies between 20 and 20,000 Hz. To record the high video frequencies the tape must slide over the recording head at a speed of approximately 6 meters per second or faster. All VCRs have a helical-scan design, in which the magnetic tape wraps around the revolving drum about half a turn and is pulled slowly around a rapidly rotating drum having magnetic record, playback, and erase heads (Figure 9-2).

This design reduces the cassette tape speed an order of magnitude (one-tenth) slower than the linear recording head tape speed. The audio is recorded conventionally along one edge of the tape as a single (monaural) or a dual (stereo) channel. Along the other tape edge is the control track, normally a 30 Hz square-wave signal (NTSC system) that synchronizes the VCR to the monitor during playback. Some VCR machines have a full-track erase head on the drum to erase any prerecorded material on the tape.

The VHS-C tape format makes use of a small tape cartridge slightly larger than the Sony 8 mm and uses the

VHS electronics and encoding scheme. The VHS-C cartridge is played back on a standard VHS machine with a VHS-C-to-VHS cartridge adapter.

9.2.2.2 8 mm, Hi-8 Sony

Sony developed the smaller 8 mm and Hi-8 format video technology (Figure 9-3).

The format and cassette are significantly smaller than the VHS but maintain image quality and system capability similar to that of the larger format. Cassette running times are 1/2 hour, 1 hour, and 2 hours. The 8 mm configuration is particularly suitable for covert applications requiring a small, light-weight recorder.

The resolution obtained with standard color VHS and 8 mm VCRs, whether operating in real-time or TL mode, is between 230 and 240 TV lines. This is not sufficient for many security applications. Monochrome TL recorders provide 350 TV-line resolution. The new color S-VHS and Hi-8 format real-time and TL recorders increase the horizontal resolution to more than 400 TV lines, suitable for facial identification and other security applications.

As with the standard VHS and 8 mm systems there is no compatibility between the S-VHS and Hi-8 formats. There is some compatibility between VHS and S-VHS, and between 8 mm and Hi-8. Some important differences between and features of the standard VHS and 8 mm, and the S-VHS and Hi-8 formats are as follows:

- S-VHS and Hi-8 recordings cannot be played back on conventional VHS or 8 mm machines.
- S-VHS and Hi-8 video cassettes require high coercivity, fine-grain cobalt-ferric-oxide and metal tapes to record the high-frequency, high-bandwidth signals.
- All S-VHS and Hi-8 recorders can record and playback in standard mode. The cassettes have a special sensing notch that automatically triggers the VCR to switch to the correct mode.

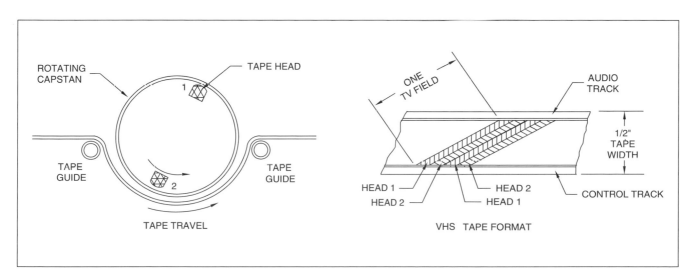

FIGURE 9-1 VHS video cassette recorder geometry and format

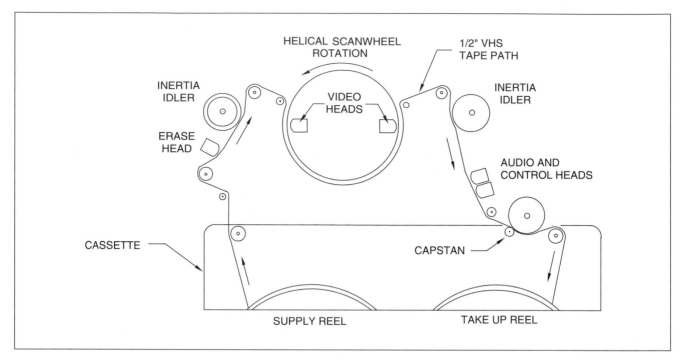

FIGURE 9-2   VHS recorder technology

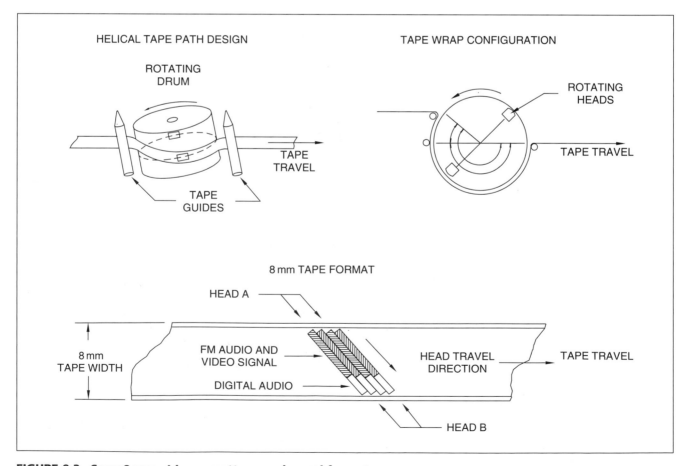

FIGURE 9-3   Sony 8 mm video cassette recorder and format

9.2.2.3 *Magnetic Tape Types*

The magnetic tape *grade* plays a critical role in determining the final quality of the video picture and life of the recorder heads. Manufacturers have improved tape materials resulting in significant improvements in picture quality, and maintaining "clean" pictures (low signal dropout and noise) over long periods of time and after many tape replays. For security applications it is important to choose a high-quality tape with matched characteristics for the VCR equipment and format used.

Most security videotape formats when grouped by size fall into two categories: 8 mm and VHS (Table 9-1).

Video cassette recorders record multiple 2:1 interlaced cameras best by synchronizing them sequentially using a 2:1 sync generator. This technique provides stability, enhances picture quality, and prevents picture roll, jitter, tearing, or other disturbances and artifacts. If random-interlace cameras are used, they should be externally synchronized. Table 9-2 summarizes the physical parameters and record/play times of the VHS and 8 mm tape cassettes.

The real-time or TL VCR provides a means for recording consecutive video images over a period of time ranging from seconds to many hours and recording thousands of individual video pictures on magnetic tape. A 2-hour VHS cassette records 216,000 images of video (2 hr @ 30 frames/sec = 216,000 frames). If camera information (ID) and time and date are coded on the tape, equipment is available for the operator to enter the camera number, time, and date to retrieve the corresponding images on the tape. However, to locate a specific frame, many minutes may be needed to shuttle the tape, playback, and display the image. Locating a specific frame or time on the tape is a lengthy process since the video cassette tape is a *serial* medium and retrieval time is related to the location of the picture on the tape. The random access nature of the DVR or optical HD performs this task easily, resulting in quick retrieval of any image anywhere on the disk (Section 9.3.1).

9.2.3 Time-Lapse (TL) VCR

The TL recorder is a real-time VCR that pauses to record a single video field (or frame) every fraction of a second or number of seconds, based on a predetermined time interval (Figure 9-4).

Standard VCRs record the video scene in real-time: the fields or frames displayed by the camera are sequentially recorded on the tape and then played back in real-time, slow-motion, or a frame at a time. In the TL mode, the VCR records only selected fields (or frames) a fraction of the time. Time-lapse recorders have the ability to record in both real-time and a variety of TL ratios, which are operator-selected either manually or automatically. The automatic switchover from TL mode to real-time mode is triggered by an auxiliary input to the VCR. When the signal from an alarm device or VMD is applied to the VCR input, it records in real-time mode for a predetermined length of time after an alarm is received, and then returns to the TL mode until another alarm is received.

TAPE FORMAT	LUMINANCE (Y) BANDWIDTH (MHz)	CHROMINANCE (C) CENTER FREQUENCY (KHz)	RESOLUTION (TV LINES)
VHS	3.4–4.4 (1.0)	629	240
VHS-C	3.4–4.4 (1.0)	629	240
S-VHS	5.4–7.0 (1.6)	629	400
8 mm	4.2–5.4 (1.2)	743	270
Hi-8	5.7–7.7 (2.0)	743	430
DIGITAL 8	13.5 [*]	3.375 [**]	500
DV	13.5	3.375	500
MINI DV	13.5	3.375	500

[*] SAMPLING RATE

[**] SAMPLING RATE FOR UV CHROMINANCE SIGNALS

Table 9-1   VHS, S-VHS, 8 mm, and Hi-8 Parameter Comparison

TAPE FORMAT		MAXIMUM RESOLUTION (TV LINES)	TAPE WIDTH mm (inches)	CASSETTE SIZE L×W×H (mm) *	PLAYING TIME (HRS)		
					STANDARD (SP)	LONG (LP)	EXTENDED (EP)
VHS-C		240	12.7 (1/2)	188×104×25	0.33	0.66	1.0
VHS:	T-60	240	12.7 (1/2)	188×104×25	1	2	3
	T-120	240	12.7 (1/2)	188×104×25	2	4	6
S-VHS		400	12.7 (1/2)	188×104×25	2	4	6
*8 mm	P6-60	270	8.0 (0.31)	95×62.5×15	1	—	—
	P6-120	270	8.0 (0.31)	95×62.5×15	2	—	—
**Hi-8	P6-60	430	8.0 (0.31)	95×62.5×15	1	2	—
	P6-120	430	8.0 (0.31)	95×62.5×15	2	4	—
DIGITAL 8		500	8.0 (0.31)	95×62.5×15	2	—	—
DV		500	6.35 (0.25)	125×78×14.6	3	—	—
***MINI DV		500	6.35 (0.25)	66×48×12	1	1.5	—

*TAPES AVAILABLE—15, 30, 90, 120 MINUTES

**TAPES AVAILABLE—30, 60, 80 MINUTES (SP MODE)

***TAPES AVAILABLE—45, 90, 120 MINUTES (LP MODE)

Table 9-2   Video Cassette Recorder Tape Physical Parameters and Formats

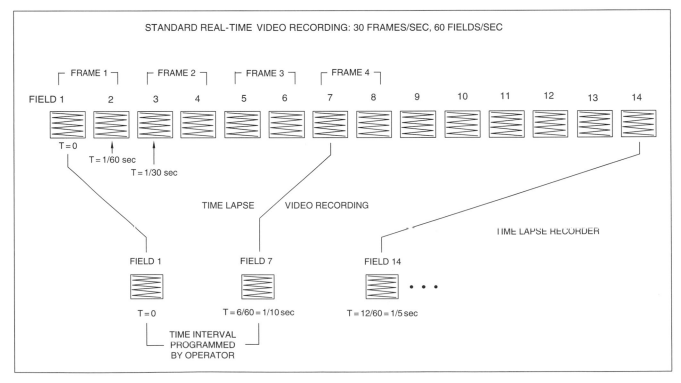

FIGURE 9-4   Time lapse (TL) video cassette recorder (VCR)

Time-lapse video recording consists of selecting specific video images to be recorded at a slower rate than they are being generated by the camera. The video camera generates 30 frames (60 fields) per second. One TV frame consists of the interlaced combination of all the even-numbered lines in one field and all the odd-numbered lines in the second field. Each field is essentially a complete picture of the scene but viewed with only *half* the

TOTAL RECORDING PERIOD *		TIME-LAPSE RATIO	RECORDING/PLAYBACK SPEED (RECORDING INTERVAL)		RECORDING/PLAYBACK (PICTURES/SECOND)	
HOURS	DAYS		1 FIELD PER ___ SEC	1 FRAME PER ___SEC	FIELDS	FRAMES
2**	.083	1:1	0.017	0.034	60	30
12	.50	6:1	0.1	0.2	10	5
24	1	12:1	0.2	0.4	5	2.5
48	2	24:1	0.4	0.8	2.5	1.25
72	3	36:1	0.6	1.2	1.7	0.85
120	5	60:1	1.0	2.0	1.0	0.5
180	7.5	90:1	1.5	3.0	0.66	0.33
240	10	120:1	2.0	4.0	0.50	0.25
360	15	180:1	3.0	6.0	0.33	0.17
480	20	240:1	4.0	8.0	0.25	0.13
600	25	300:1	5.0	10.0	0.20	0.10
720	30	360:1	6.0	12.0	0.16	0.08
960	40	480:1	8.0	16.0	0.2	0.11

*TAPE CASSETTE: T-120

**STANDARD REAL-TIME VIDEO

Table 9-3   Time-Lapse Recording Times vs. Playback Speeds

vertical resolution (262 1/2 horizontal lines). Therefore, by selecting individual fields—as most TL VCRs do—and recording them at a rate slower than 60 per second, the TL VCR records less resolution than available from the camera. When the TL recorded tape is played back and viewed on the monitor at the same speed at which it was recorded, the pictures on the monitor will appear as a series of animated still scenes. Table 9-3 presents a comparison of TL modes as a function of TL ratio, total recording period, recording interval fields, and fields per second recorded.

It is apparent that the larger the TL ratio, the fewer the pictures recorded over any period of time. For example, for a TL ratio of 6:1, the recorder captures 10 images (fields) per second, whereas in real-time (or 1:1) it captures 60. Although the recorder is only recording individual fields spaced out in time, if nothing significant is occurring during these times, no information is lost.

The choice of the particular TL ratio for an application depends on various factors including the following:

- Length of time the VCR will record on a 2-, 4-, or 6-hour video cassette
- Type, number and duration of significant alarm events likely to occur
- Elapsed time period before the cassette can be replaced or reused
- TL ratios available on the VCR.

To minimize tape usage and maximize information recorded, select the lowest TL ratio consistent with the requirement. By carefully analyzing operating conditions

and requirements and using TL, it is possible to record events without sacrificing important information—and at substantially less tape cost than real-time recording.

In the TL recording mode the videotape speed is much slower than in real-time since the video pictures are being recorded intermittently. This maximizes the use of tape storage space and eliminates the inconvenience of having to change the cassette every few hours. To review the tape it is scanned at faster than normal playback speed. When more careful examination of a particular series of images is required, the playback speed is slowed or *paused* (stopped) and a more careful scrutiny of the tape is made.

9.2.4 VCR Options

The following are some VCR options:

- Built-in camera switcher
- Time/date generator
- Sequence or interval recording of multiple cameras on one VCR
- Interface with other devices: cash register, ATM, etc.
- Remote control via RS-232
- 12-volt DC power operation for portable use.

9.2.4.1 Camera Switching/Selecting

Time-lapse VCRs allow recording of multiple cameras and selected playback of numerically coded cameras.

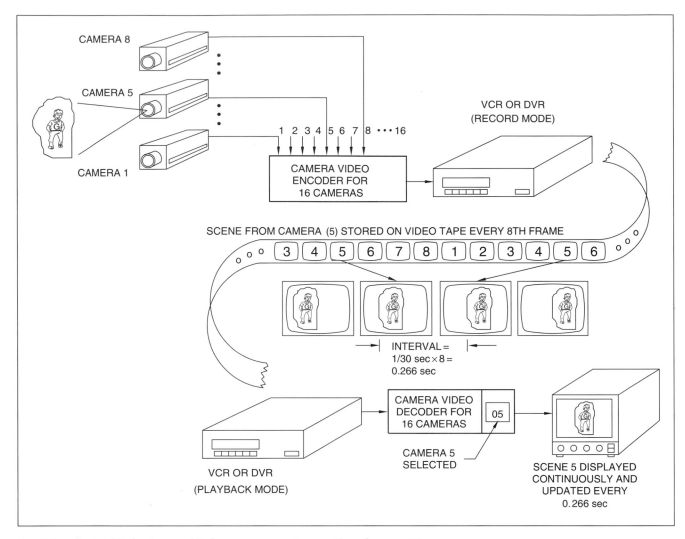

FIGURE 9-5   Multiplexing multiple cameras onto one time-lapse VCR

Figure 9-5 shows the technique for a 16-camera input system using 8 cameras.

The VCR multiplexes up to 16 cameras onto one videotape, reducing equipment cost by eliminating the need for one VCR per camera input. The VCR separates the recordings from each camera and displays the fields from one camera. When many cameras are recorded on one VCR, rather than sorting through scenes from all the cameras when only one is of interest, the operator can select a particular camera for viewing. To locate a specific video image, the operator shuttles the tape, advance or backup, one image at a time. In operation during real-time or TL video recording, the VCR electronics inserts a binary synchronizing code on the video signal for every image with each camera uniquely identified. During real-time playback the scenes from any one of the 16 cameras can be chosen for display. In Figure 9-5 camera scene 5 has been chosen for presentation where the pictures are updated every 0.266 seconds.

9.2.4.2   RS-232 Communications

Video cassette recorders interface and communicate two-way data with computer systems via a RS-232 port enabling the computer to communicate with the VCR and control it. The RS-232 port permits the recorder to communicate via digital networks, telephone lines, dedicated two-wire or wireless channels. The computer becomes a command post for remote control of recorder functions: real-time or TL mode, TL speeds, stop, play, record, fast rewind, fast-forward, scan, reverse-scan, pause, and advance. These remote functions are put at the fingertips of the security operator whether in the console room, at the computer across the street, or at a distant location.

9.2.4.3   Scrambling

Video recordings are often made that contain inherently highly sensitive security information and there is a need for scrambling the video signal on the recording. Equipment

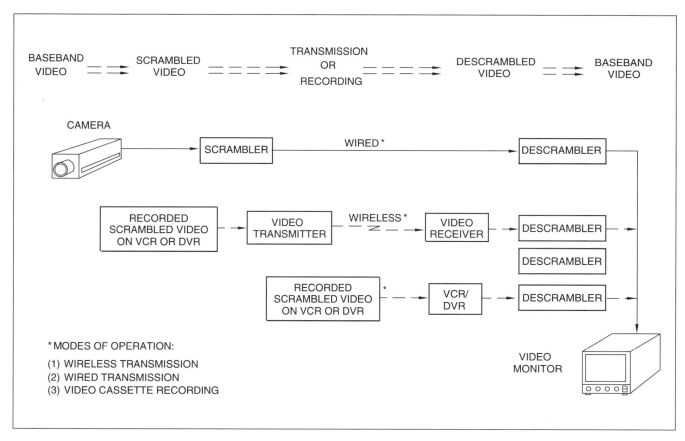

FIGURE 9-6   Video recording scrambling

is available to scramble the videotape signal to prevent unauthorized viewing of video recordings, making it very difficult to reconstruct an intelligible picture (Figure 9-6).

The scrambling technology safeguards the video signal as it is recorded or transmitted, producing a secure signal unusable in its scrambled form. The scrambling code is changed constantly and automatically and renders frame-by-frame decoding fruitless. It is password-protected so that only personnel entitled to view the tape can gain access to it. Time access codes can be programmed to restrict descrambling to a scheduled time interval. The complete system consists of an encoder connected in the camera output and decoder connected at the monitor location.

9.2.4.4 On-Screen Annotating and Editing

Video cassette recorders have built-in alpha-numeric character generators to annotate tape with: time, date, day of week, recording speed, alarm input, camera identifier, and time on/off status information. In retail applications the recorder can annotate the video image with the cash register dollar amount to check a cashier's performance. In a bank ATM application a video image is annotated with the transaction number to identify the person performing the transaction. The RS-232 interface permits the operator to control the on-screen editing of the videotape whenever changes are required.

These are typical text entered by a security operator:

- Superimposed listing of cash register transactions
- Personal identification number (PIN) of an individual using an ID card
- Verification of the authenticity of ID cards used at remote ATMs, gas pumps, retail stores, and cash-dispensing machines
- Record of action taken by security personnel reacting to alarms or video camera activity.

9.3 DIGITAL VIDEO RECORDER (DVR)

There are several key differences between DVRs and VCRs that result in significant advantages for DVR users. The most notable difference between the DVR and VCR is the medium used for recording the video images. VCRs record images on magnetic tapes, while digital systems use HD drives, DATs or DVDs. This differentiation has significant implications in terms of the video image quality, speed of information retrieval, image transmission speed, and remote monitoring capabilities. Digital video systems using DVRs can be accessed over LAN, intranets, and the Internet. This permits security personnel to monitor remote sites across the street, town, or locations hundreds or thousands miles away. Using an Internet browser or other application software on any PC or laptop allows security with personnel or corporate management to view recorded digital video images at a secure IP (Internet protocol) address from anywhere in the world.

Security systems using DVRs can play a major role in alarm verification. Having the ability to perform video assessment from remote locations means the system can be used to prevent false alarm responses by security and police personnel. The ability to remotely and instantly view the alarm site means that if a review of the video images indicates there are *no intruders,* a false alarm can be declared and *no law enforcement* personnel need be notified.

The digital video images are stored on HD drives similar to those used in the PC industry and have storage capacities measured in hundreds of megabytes or gigabytes, providing a low cost storage media for the compressed video files. Small and medium-size systems use several HD drives, while large enterprise systems use a large number of HD drives. These HD drives are synchronized and shared to store images from many video cameras reliably, and available for rapid access by the user. The DVR has high reliability as compared to the VCR recorder. The DVD provides higher image quality as compared to its VCR predecessor.

The DVR video images can be downloaded to an external medium. The Zip file/disk or an email over the Internet is the easiest for the DVR.

9.3.1 DVR Technology

The technology difference between analog and digital recording is that the analog tape recorder incorporates a magnetic field to align the magnetic particles on the surface of the VHS tape to correspond to the video signal image. In contrast, the DVR converts the analog signal into a digital signal of ones and zeros, compresses this digital signal, and then stores it on the magnetic DVR HD drive, DVD, or DAT.

The combination of affordable image compression technologies and large capacity HD drives has made the development of the DVR a reality. Although HD DVR recording like VHS still uses a magnetic recording medium, the digital nature of the data insures that all retrieved footage is an identical copy of the originally recorded signals.

Standard DVRs have some shortcomings when used in mid-range and large size Enterprise systems. Since video inputs are local to the DVR, and a camera source has to be wired at the location of the DVR, this results in a significant investment in cable.

DVRs are rapidly replacing the VCR as the preferred storage/retrieval medium for video security systems. An obvious difference between the two technologies is that

VCRs use standard VHS format magnetic tape, while digital DVRs store images on the DVR HD, DVD, DAT, or any combination of these media.

The operators of DVR can search for recorded information based on time, date, video image, camera input, alarm, or video motion. Operators achieve much faster retrieval times as compared with VCRs. Rather than wading through countless frames of video information, the DVR operator can locate the desired images in a fraction of a second.

The DVR is superior to the VCR in image quality. The VCR records only every other field of the video image, while the DVR records a full frame (two fields per frame) producing twice the resolution. The DVR digital image does not deteriorate on playback or re-recording whereas with the VCR there is deterioration of the image after each new copy is made. The DVR requires far less servicing as compared to the VCR with all its mechanical drives and the VCR magnetic tape is prone to tape failure. DVRs offer additional features such as remote video retrieval, combining the multiplexer with the DVR, pre- and post-image recording, retrieval on alarm, and networking capabilities. The basic block diagram of a DVR is shown in Figure 9-7.

The analog video signal from the camera is converted into a digital signal via the analog-to-digital converter (A/D) at the front end of the DVR. Following the A/D converter is the digital compression electronics with its programmed compression algorithm. The amount of compression (compression ratio) is based on the compression algorithm chosen: JPEG (Joint Photographic Engineers Group), MPEG-4 (Motion Picture Engineers Group), (Wavelet, H.263, H.264, etc.). The compression algorithm chosen is based on the DVR storage capacity and the image rate and quality of the images required. Following the compression electronics is the authentication electronics that imbeds a security code into each image. The digitized video signal is then ready for storage in the HD drive.

The HD drive stores the compressed video image and other data on a magnetic coating on the HD. A magnetic head is held by an actuator alarm and is used to write and read the data. The disk rotates with constant rpm and data is organized on the disk in cylinders and tracks. The tracks are divided into sectors (Figure 9-8).

Hard Disk storage capacity is measured in hundreds of megabytes, gigabytes (1000 MByte), or terabytes (1000 GByte). Video image retrieval is fast but not instantaneous. There is a delay between the time an operator inputs a command to retrieve an image and when the image is displayed on the monitor screen. With DVR systems this time is a small fraction of a second. With VCRs it is seconds to minutes.

Image retention time refers to how long the DVR can record before it begins to write over its oldest images. The amount of recording time required depends on the

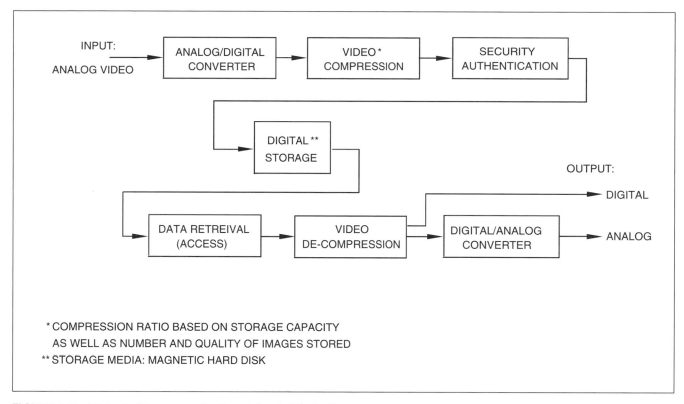

FIGURE 9-7   Digital video recorder (DVR) basic block diagram

application: local codes, regulations, or business classification. Mandated storage times generally range from a week to a month or months. To record for longer periods of time or to archive, a compact disk (CD), additional HD drives, or DAT recorders are used. Since real-time recording and high image resolutions consume significant HD space quickly, the new compression schemes using MPEG-4, H.264, and others are needed to offset these higher image per second (IPS) recording rates and image quality requirements.

In summary, DVRs offer these advantages over analog recorders: (1) better picture quality, (2) less maintenance, (3) random access search, (4) pre- and post-alarm recording, (5) built-in or optional multiplexer, (6) expandable storage for longer recording time, (7) real-time and TL event recording modes, (8) network interface through LAN, WAN, and Internet, (9) motion detection, and (10) password protection.

9.3.1.1   Digital Hardware Advances

9.3.1.1.1   Hard Disk Drive storage
Hard disk drive storage capacity and speed have increased dramatically in the past years and the trend will continue. DVRs can include built-in 40-, 80-, 160-, or 250 GByte HD drives that can provide storage of high-resolution monochrome or color images for days, weeks, or months.

To achieve reliability, the older small computer system interface (SCSI) drives were previously specified as the choice for DVR applications. Now the integrated drive electronics (IDE) drives offer similar performance and reliability at a much lower cost. These IDE HD drives found in mid-range and enterprise recorders provide storage in the terabyte (1000 GByte) range. These enterprise class recorders can have almost unlimited storage using external HD including configurations that can tolerate a failed drive without losing any video recorded video images. The IDE HD drives have narrowed the gap in speed and reliability compared to the relatively expensive SCSI HD drives, making IDE ATA100 thermally compensated drives a popular storage media for DVRs. Figure 9-9 summarizes Digital video storage media.

9.3.1.1.2   Video Motion Detection (VMD)
Every video scene at some time has video motion caused by a person moving, an object moving, or some other motion activity. Many DVRs have VMD built into them. Digital signal processing (DSP) is used to detect the motion in the video image and cause some form of alarm or video representation on the monitor screen. This feature enables the DVR to remain in an inactive or TL operational mode until activity occurs, and increases the recording rate and displays the alarm on-screen in the form of an outlined object of the person moving or other activity in the camera field of view. This technology increases overall video

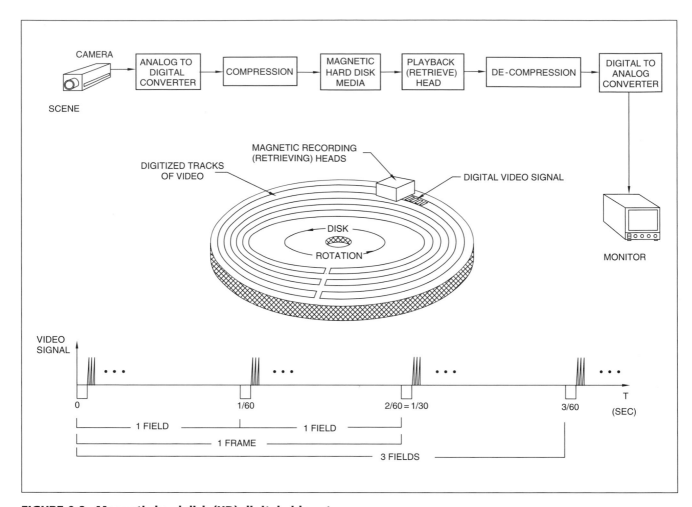

FIGURE 9-8   Magnetic hard disk (HD) digital video storage

image storage time since the DVR does not have to record non-events or records them at a slower rate. When activity occurs it becomes visible on the video screen or causes some other alarm notification. One should be aware that for prosecutorial applications images acquired through a motion detection DVR may be *inadmissible* if there is *no* recording made prior to and after the time of the event.

The ability to respond to alarm inputs—whether individual contact closures or software-generated procedures—are a major feature of DVRs and these important capabilities should be included in the design. The ability to incorporate immediate automatic recording on alarm is one of the features that puts the basic DVR a step above the off-the-shelf PCs equipped with video capture cards and base level software for setting parameters.

Digital video recorders with internal VMD create a searchable audit-trail *by camera* every time there is motion. Unlike when using the VCR, security personnel can quickly find the video images of interest on the DVR by date, time, image motion activation, or alarm input.

9.3.1.1.3 Optical-Disk Image Storage
For very long-term video image recording and archiving, an optical-disk medium is chosen. Optical storage media are durable, removable disks that store video images in digital format. There are two generic systems available: (1) non-erasable write-once read-many (WORM) and (2) erasable. These two electro-optical storage systems are described in the following sections. The optical disk recorder stores the video image on a disk using optical recording media rotating at high speed. The picture is stored and identified by coding the signal to the specific camera and the time and date at which it was put on disk. At a later time the stored picture can be retrieved in random access at high speed. Most optical disks used in security applications are WORM disks since these are admissible in law enforcement investigation and prosecution cases.

9.3.1.1.4 Non-Erasable, Write-Once Read-Many (WORM) Disk
The WORM optical-disk recording system provides a compact means to store large volumes of video images. The drive uses a 800-megabyte, double-sided, removable diskette, which is rugged and reliable. In security applications, a WORM drive has a significant advantage over magnetic recording media because the optical image cannot be overwritten, eliminating the risk of accidental or intentional removal or deletion of video pictures. This is

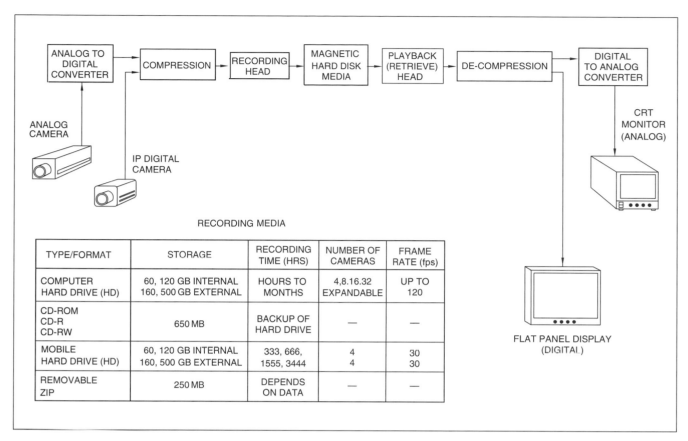

FIGURE 9-9   Digital video storage media

important in law enforcement applications. The WORM disk containing the video images is removable and can therefore be secured under lock and key, stored in a vault when the terminal is shut down or the system is turned off, or sent to another location or person. Reliability is extremely high, with manufacturers quoting indefinite life for the disk and a minimum mean time between failure (MTBF) of greater than 10 years. The reason for this longevity is that nothing touches the disk itself except a light beam used to write onto and read from the disk.

9.3.1.1.5 Erasable Optical Disk

Erasable optical-disk media is now available that can be erased (as on present magnetic media) and overwritten with new images (Figure 9-10). Each image stored on the optical HD is uniquely identified and may be retrieved in random access in less than 1 second. Optical disks store huge amounts of data; approximately 31 reels of data tape are equivalent to one single 5¼-inch-diameter optical disk—the size of an ordinary compact disc. Standard optical disks can store many terabytes of information. While most optical disks used in security are WORM, erasable optical disks are also in use. Erasable disks use the principle of magneto-optics to record the video information onto the disk in digital form. The video image data or other information is erasable, allowing the same disk to be reused many times, just like magnetic HD. Reading,

writing, and erasing the information on the optical disk is done using light energy and not magnetic heads that touch or skim across the recording material. Therefore, magneto-optical disks have a much longer life and a higher reliability than magnetic disks. They are immune to wear and head crashes as occasionally occur in magnetic HD drives. This catastrophic event occurs when a sudden vibration or dust particle cause the mechanical head in the drive to bump into the recording material, thereby damaging it. In the case of the optical disk, the opto-magnetic layer storing the information is imbedded within a layer of plastic or glass, protecting it from dust and wear. The optical disk is an excellent medium when large amounts of high-resolution video images need to be stored and retrieved for later use.

9.3.1.1.6 Digital Audio Tape (DAT)

Digital audio tape is a format for storing or backing up video data (originally for music) on magnetic tape. It was co-developed in the mid-1980s by the Sony and Philips Corporations. DAT uses a rotary-head (or helical scan) format where the read/write head spins diagonally across the tape like a VCR. It uses a small 4 mm-wide tape having a signal quality that can surpass that of a CD and can record data (video images) at a rate of 5 MBytes/minute. The DAT storage capacity is 6 GBytes on a standard 120-minute cartridge. DAT decks have both analog and digital inputs and outputs.

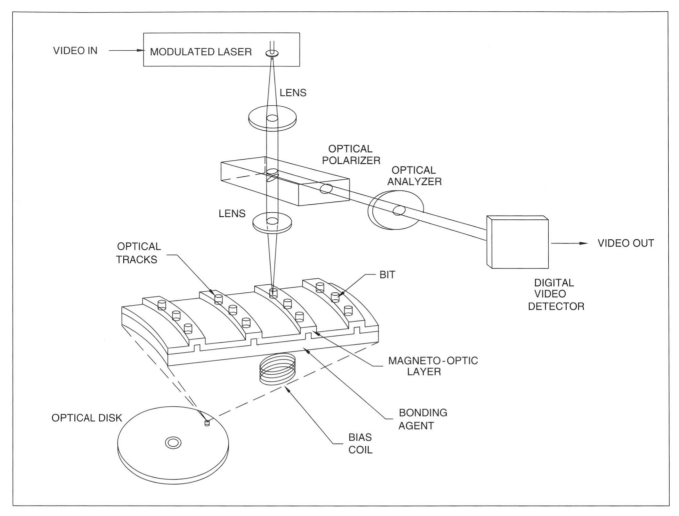

FIGURE 9-10　Erasable optical disk recording

9.3.1.2　Digital Storage Software Advances

Digital technology, faster microprocessors, high density inexpensive solid state memory, and the availability of larger and cheaper HD drives have made DVRs affordable in security video applications. Adding the combination of affordable image compression technologies and large capacity HD drives has made the development of the DVR a reality. Although HD DVR recording like VHS still uses a magnetic recording medium, the *digital* nature of the HD data permits transmitting the video images over networks to remote sites and insures that all retrieved images are identical copies of the original images.

Digital video images can be stored on a HD but several things must be considered since around-the-clock recording of pictures requires a vast amount of storage space. To overcome this, when there is motion in the scene, a start-and-stop recording mode can be implemented. Alternatively only a few frames per second can be stored much as the TL recorder in the analog régime. In Table 9-4 examples of the image sizes and storage requirements for five different image resolutions and image recording rates are given.

The formula for calculating these storage requirements and image rates is:

$$\text{DVR storage capacity} = \frac{\text{HD drive storage capacity}}{\text{image size} \times \text{pictures per day}}$$

$$= \text{storage time in days or hours}$$

Example: Calculate the storage capacity of a 250 GByte DVR to record an image frame rate of 15 images per second with a picture quality set to standard = 18 KByte:

$$\text{DVR storage capacity} = \frac{250\,\text{GByte}}{18\,\text{KByte} \times 15\,\text{ips} \times 86{,}400\,\text{sec}}$$

$$= 10.7\ \text{days}$$

$$= 10\ \text{days and seventeen hours}$$

This calculation is based on the DVR recording continuously at the selected recording speed for a 24-hour period (86,400 sec). This is a worst case scenario, since the DVR can be programmed to record only if motion is present or at selected times of the day. Both of these settings will dramatically increase the unit storage potential and eliminate the storage of unneeded or useless video images.

PICTURE* QUALITY	DVR RECORDING SPEED (IMAGES/SEC)					(250 GByte HARD DRIVE)		
	60	30	15	10	7.5	5	3	1
HIGHEST	1D/3H†	2D/6H	4D/9H	6D/14H	8D/9H	13D/4H	22D/0H	66D/2H
HIGH	1D/17H	3D/3H	6D/14H	9D/21H	13D/4D	19D/19H	33D/0H	99D/4H
STANDARD	2D/16H	5D/1H	10D/17H	15D/9H	20D/12H	30D/19H	51D/9H	154D/7H
BASIC	4D/0H	7D/16H	15D/9H	24D/0H	30D/19H	46D/4H	77D/2H	231D/9H
LOW	8D/0H	15D/10H	30D/19H	46D/4H	61D/16H	92D/12H	154D/7H	462D/20H

*IMAGE SIZES—HIGHEST = 42 KByte
     HIGH = 28 KByte
     STANDARD = 18 KByte
     BASIC = 12 KByte
     LOW = 6 KByte

IMAGES/DAY = 60 pps—5.184 MBytes
     30 ips—2.6 MBytes
     15 ips MODE—1.296 MBytes
     7.5 ips MODE—648 KBytes
     5.0 ips MODE—259.2 KBytes
     3.0 ips MODE—86.4 KBytes
     1.0 ips MODE—86.4 KBytes

**ALL RECORDING TIMES BASED ON 250 GByte HARD DRIVE

†RECORDING TIME: 1D/3H = 1 DAY AND 3 HOURS

FORMULA FOR CALCULATING NUMBER OF IMAGES STORED ON 250 GByte HARD DISK MEMORY

$$\text{RECORDING TIME} = \frac{\text{HARD DISK STORAGE}}{\text{IMAGE SIZE} \times \text{PICTURES/DAY}} = \text{STORAGE TIME IN DAYS AND HOURS}$$

EXAMPLE: HARD DISK STORAGE = 250 GByte
     IMAGE SIZE = 12 KByte
     IMAGES/SEC = 10 ips
     SECONDS IN A DAY = 86,400 Sec
     PICTURES/DAY = 10 ips × 86,400 Sec

$$\text{RECORDING TIME} = \frac{250\,\text{GByte}}{12\,\text{KByte} \times 10\,\text{ips} \times 86,400\,\text{Sec}} = 24.1\,\text{DAYS}$$

Table 9-4   Digital Storage Requirements and Images Per Second (IPS) for Five Different Image Resolutions on a 250 GByte hard drive

9.3.1.3   Transmission Advances

A fast-growing application for DVRs and digital storage systems is for the remote video retrieval via modem or network using LAN, WAN, and wireless (WiFi). Transmission speeds are increasing, compression algorithms are improving, and remote video solutions implementing automated video surveillance (AVS) at remote sites are being installed. New software that allows viewing of multiple IP addressable digital recorders from a central location is increasing and will become a must-have feature. Many companies are implementing digital recording for remote viewing in video systems using LANs, WANs, and Web-based systems. A major advantage of an IP-addressed network is its ability to receive video signals anywhere using equipment ranging from a simple Internet browser to special client-based application software. Using these networks eliminates the need to run new cabling and provides an easy solution for future system expansion.

Cellular transmission is the slowest transmission method for video transmission and is not widely used in the video security market. However, in areas that offer no other service it is the only way to offer remote surveillance. The transmission speed of the cellular system is 9.6 Kbps (bits per second) and is increasing with time. Dial-up or public switched telephone network (PSTN) is the most common method of the available DVR transmission methods, but since it was designed for the human voice and not high-speed video transmission, it does not provide high bandwidth or speed of transmission. This type transmission mode has a maximum speed of 56 Kbps but in spite of the relatively slow service, its cost and availability are the major factors for its continued use.

Integrated systems digital network (ISDN) is a digital phone line with two 64 Kbps channels. Competition from cable and digital subscriber line (DSL) service has reduced the pricing to acceptable levels for the video security market. DSL technology has sufficient bandwidth for high-speed access to the Internet and live video monitoring. This digital broadband link directly connects a premise to the Internet via existing copper telephone lines. The DSL speed is listed as nearly 1.5 Mbps but depends on the routing, the distance from the network hub, and the number of people on the network.

A very high-speed, expensive digital system using dedicated lines is the AT&T T1 network transmitting up to 1.544 Mbps. The T3 lines have almost 30 times the capacity of T1 lines and can handle 44.736 Mbps of data.

The widest transmission network is achieved using a fiber-optic optical carrier (OC) transmission channel. The

TRANSMISSION TYPE	TYPICAL DOWNLOAD SPEED	TRANSMISSION TIME FOR 25 KByte IMAGE (sec)	MAX. FRAME RATE FOR 25 KByte IMAGE	CONNECTION MODE
PSTN	45 Kbps	6	10 Frames/min	DIAL UP
ISDN	120 Kbps	2	0.5 Frames/sec	DIAL UP
IDSL	150 Kbps	2	0.06 ↑	DIRECT CONNECTION
ADSL—LOW END	640 Kbps	0.3	3	↑
ADSL—HIGH END	5 Mbps	0.05	20	
HDSL	1.5 Mbps	0.2	6	
VDSL	20 Mbps	0.01	80	
CABLE MODEM	750 Kbps	0.3	3	
T1	1.5 Mbps	0.2	6	
T3	45 Mbps	0.007	180	
10BaseT	5 Mbps	0.05	20	
100BaseT	50 Mbps	0.005	200	
1000BaseT	500 Mbps	0.0005	2000	
OC3	155 Mbps	0.0019	620	
OC12	622 Mbps	0.0005	2500 ↓	↓
FIREWIRE *	400 Mpbs	0.0008	1600 Frames/sec	DIRECT CONNECTION

*APPLE COMPUTERS VERSION OF IEEE STANDARD 1394

IDSL: ISDN DSL   HDSL: HIGH BIT-RATE DSL
ADSL: ASYNCHRONOUS DSL   VDSL: VERY HIGH DATA RATE DSL

Table 9-5   Parameters of Digital Transmission Channels for DVR Use

OC is used to specify the speed of fiber-optic networks conforming to synchronous optical network with synchronous optical network (SONET) standards. SONET is a physical layer network technology designed to carry large volumes of traffic over relatively long distances on fiber-optic cabling. SONET was originally designed by the American National Standards Institute (ANSI) for the public telephone network in the mid-1980s.

FireWire is an ultra high-speed serial data connection developed by Apple Computer. The technology provides a high-speed serial input/output bus for computer peripherals that can transfer data at speeds of 400 Mbps. It is especially well suited for transferring very large DVR video image files for viewing or archiving. Table 9-5 summarizes the parameters of available digital transmission channels.

9.3.1.4 Communication Control

All the functions available on the VCR and DVR machines can be controlled remotely using communications via the RS232 port(s) on the devices, and transmitted bi-directionally over the network to remote locations. Like-

wise camera functions (zoom, focus, iris, presets, etc.), alarms, pan/tilt, and any internal DVR programming can be done remotely.

9.3.2 DVR Generic Types

The DVDs can be divided into four groups or hardware implementations:

- DVR in a Box-PC Card and a PC
- DVR Basic Plug-and-Play VCR Replacement
- DVR Multiplex
- DVR Multi-channel.

9.3.2.1 DVR in a Box

The DVR in a box is implemented by adding a PC Board card to the standard PC computer that instantly turns the PC into a DVR. The PC card has four video inputs providing a four-channel DVR. It seems simple to do but it does have limitations. The DVR should be a dedicated system operating alone. Mixing and matching the DVR with other software programs can cause the total system to crash. Another shortcoming of many DVR cards is that they do not supply alarm inputs or outputs thus creating a very limited application machine.

9.3.2.2 DVR Basic Plug-and-Play VCR Replacement

The DVR basic Plug-and-Play differs from the DVR in a box in that it is a separate component designed and built specifically to be a DVR. The DVR basic is a self-contained unit having all the front panel controls that the standard industrial real-time/TL VCR has. These DVRs generally have a single- or four-channel video input capability and offer a minimum of setup parameters to permit the user to customize the picture quality, pictures size, or alarming features to meet the particular application. This DVR has been designed as a *drop-in replacement* for an existing analog VCR.

9.3.2.3 Multiplex

The multiplex DVR is the largest of the four groups of DVR types used for video recording. The machine combines an 8- or 16-channel multiplexer with the DVR unit. This multiplex DVR shares the video input in the same way as the standalone video multiplexer. The combined DVR and multiplexer has the advantage that the installer no longer has to worry about the interface wiring and compatibility of setup programs between the two devices. Some of the features that have been included in the multiplex DVR are: (1) motion or activity detection, (2) remote video retrieval by a modem over a digital channel, (3) alarm inputs-contact closures or software generated, and (4) ability to adjust the IPS recorded. Recorders equipped with a multiplexing capability allow users to watch live and recorded images on one monitor while the multiplexing DVR continues to record.

Multiplex DVR technology should be capable of multitasking, duplexing, and triplexing by performing the record and playback and live viewing functions *simultaneously*. VCRs cannot do that but most DVRs can.

The operator using a multiplex DVR with triplex functionality can simultaneously review and archive the video images without interrupting the recording process. Uninterrupted recording ensures that no event will go unrecorded or missed.

One shortcoming of the multiplexed video recorder is that it *does not* record all camera images from each camera connected to the system simultaneously. It incorporates a time-share system to record multiple camera inputs *one at a time*.

The multiplex DVR technology allows a single unit to replace not only the recorder but also all the accessory items needed to run a VCR-based video system. There is no need for separate multiplexers, switchers, or any devices other than the camera, lens, and monitor. Other features

available are the ability to connect and perform remote video retrieval via: modem, wired LAN, WAN, Internet, or wireless WiFi.

9.3.2.4 Multi-Channel

Both the multiplexed and multi-channel DVR systems use a system called redundant array of independent disks (RAID) to control the multiple HD drives and provide management and distribution of the data across the system. Different RAID levels are used depending on the application to optimize fault tolerance, the speed of access, or the size of the files being stored. RAID Levels 1 and 5 are the most commonly used in video security applications.

The multi-channel DVR is designed for high-end applications having many cameras and monitors. Applications using these systems require multiple, month-long storage times, real-time video recording, and a very large number (hundreds) of video inputs. Multi-channel DVRs allow cameras to be recorded at 60 IPS, whereas in the multiplex unit the cameras are time-shared between the images displayed.

The primary difference between a multiplexed DVR and a multi-channel DVR is that the multiplex recorder uses only *one* display while the multi-channel DVR has *multiple* displays, either split screen or multiple monitors. Instead of time-sharing the recorded information, the multi-channel unit records all camera images at 30 IPS *simultaneously*. The system offers the highest performance and playback in a multiple camera system.

The multi-channel DVR units have large HD drives with capability to store an excess of 480 GByte data and expanded storage derived from additional HD external memory and DAT and jukebox storage systems controlled by RAID controllers.

Multi-channel DVRs using many HD drives require coordination and control. In order to store and protect as much information as possible, the RAID must control the HD drive or a DAT jukebox system. The RAID capability controls and protects the HD drive data and provides immediate online access to data despite a single disk failure. Some RAID storage systems can withstand two concurrent disk failures. RAID capability also provides online reconstruction of the contents of the failed disk to a replacement disk.

9.3.2.4.1 Redundant Array of Independent Disks (RAID)

A redundant array of independent disks is a system using multiple HD drives to: (1) share or replace data among the drives and/or (2) improve performance over using a drive singularly. Originally RAID was used to connect inexpensive disks to take advantage of the ability to combine multiple low-cost devices using older technology into an array that together offered greater capacity, reliability, and/or speed than was affordable in a singular device using the newest technology. At its simplest level, RAID is a way of combining multiple hard drives into a single logical unit. In this way the operating system sees only one storage device. For the purposes of video security applications, any system that employs the basic concept of recombining physical disk space for purposes of reliability or performance is a RAID system.

This system was first patented by IBM in 1978. In 1988, RAID Levels 1 through 5 were formally defined in a paper by Patterson, Gibson, and Katz. The original RAID specification suggested a number of prototype RAID levels or combinations of disks. Out of the many combinations and levels only two are in general use in security systems: RAID Level 1 and Level 5. RAID Level 1 array creates an exact copy (or mirror) of all data on two or more disks. This is useful for systems where redundancy is more important than using the maximum storage capacity of the disk. An ideal RAID Level 1 set contains two disks which increases reliability by a factor of two over a single disk. RAID Level 1 implementation can also provide enhanced read performance (playback of the video image), since many implementations can read from one disk while the other is busy.

The RAID Level 5 array uses block-level striping with parity data distributed across all member disks. RAID Level 5 is one of the most popular RAID levels and is frequently used in both hardware and software implementations. Virtually all storage arrays offer RAID Level 5.

Summarizing the two most common RAID formats found in DVR video security systems:

1. RAID Level 1 is the fastest, fault-tolerant RAID configuration and probably the most commonly used. RAID Level 1 is the only choice in a two drive system. In this two drive system the mirrored pair mirror each other and looks like one drive to the operating system. The increased reliability in this configuration is exhibited in that if one drive fails the video image data is available from the other drive.
2. RAID Level 5 provides data striping at the byte level and also uses stripe error correction information. This results in excellent performance and good fault-tolerance. Level 5 provides better storage efficiency than Level 1 but performs a little slower.

9.3.2.5 Network Video Recorder (NVR)

The future of digital video recording will be based on current information technology (IT) infrastructure, namely networking. By employing automatic network replenishment technology, the NVR can cope with network downtimes without sacrificing recording integrity. The concept of a virtual HD eliminates the concern of HD sizes. Figure 9-11 shows a block diagram of the NVR system.

In a new installation where the designer has free reign to design the solution a NVR serving the storage requirements of an entire Enterprise is a choice to consider. One issue to consider if a NVR is used is that video images require large storage data files, and for the NVR installation a separate dedicated network for security may be necessary. Another consideration is that, even to simply receive video, knowledge of setup parameters for the individual camera is necessary, and the NVR would need to be programmed accordingly. Moving to a digital recording solution, whether the DVR, NVR, or a hybrid system combination of DVR, NVR requires careful planning and design.

The NVR solution is a system that uses digital or analog cameras converted to IP cameras using a network server. This digital data is delivered to a network in accordance with the TCP/IP transport protocol and recorded by a NVR.

The HD is usually controlled by a RAID Level 5 controller which can be expanded to other HD drives for increased storage capacity. To overcome storage shortcomings in the midsize and larger systems the NVR is used.

A DVR's capacity is based on the number of HD drives and the storage capacity of each HD. For large numbers of cameras and long archiving times separate DVR units are required. Image retrieval across separate units becomes impractical since most multiplex DVRs are of a one channel design. In order to accommodate 4, 9, 16 or more video inputs, internal or external multiplexers are used. The requirement to time-share the cameras means the IPS usually drops to a few. Dedicated DVRs do not take advantage of common IT principles like RAID storage.

An NVR is basically a standard networked PC with a software application that controls the flow of digital video data. Thanks to the availability of network interface, a concept called *virtual HD* drive can be realized. The virtual memory concept is commonplace in today's computer systems. The central processing unit (CPU) is made to accept the larger virtual size because of a logic unit—the memory management unit (MMU)—which is responsible for loading and unloading just a section of memory that the CPU currently needs. The concept is used for digital video recording. The data that has been successfully copied over the network may then be erased from the local HD which frees capacity on the local HD drive. The net effect is that the local HD will never fill up as long as the network storage device can accept the data. The virtual HD makes the retrieval of recorded video footage especially convenient: instead of searching over several physical disk volumes the user always sees a *single disk* of sufficient capacity.

The most important question that must be considered before attempting remote video surveillance is whether the network available has sufficient bandwidth for video transmission to the remote site. Bandwidth requirements for quality video transmission range from 256 Kbps to 1 Mbps depending on the video compression method used, the image quality required, and image refresh rate (IPS) used

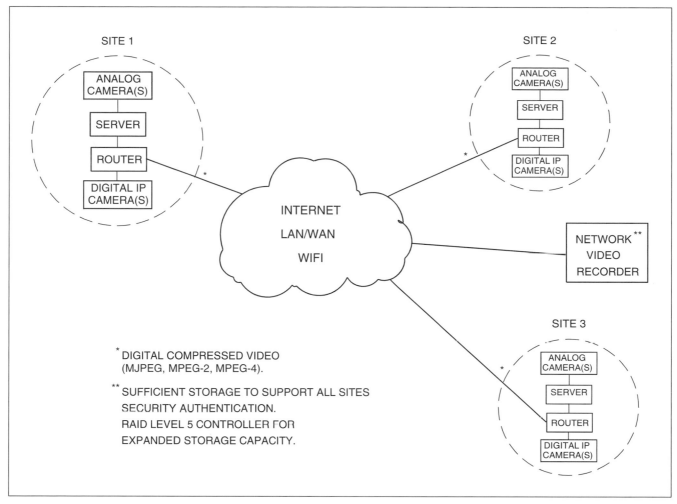

FIGURE 9-11   Network video recorder (NVR) system block diagram

by the application. Most LAN or WAN systems can operate successfully using industry standard 10BaseT or 100BaseT Ethernet supported by standard computer operating systems. If the remote viewing system does not use the Web for its connection it is called an *intranet*. The intranet IP-address assignments and network parameters are controlled by the in-house network manager.

9.3.2.6   Hybrid NVR/DVR System

The hybrid DVR/NVR system incorporates elements of both the DVR and NVR. This type of system uses distributed architecture with analog cameras connected to IP video servers and IP cameras connected directly to the network. The IP video from the IP cameras and the IP video servers are both stored on a server connected to the network. The NVR solution may be the most cost-effective if installed on an existing shared network, but it is highly debatable whether many facilities would allow the increased network traffic created by the video images. Hybrid DVR/NVR solutions open up exciting possibilities in that they can use legacy analog cameras and existing

video cabling as well as IP cameras. The hybrid solution permits the centralization of the system configuration, leading to greater flexibility in locating the equipment to where it is most convenient.

9.3.3   DVR Operating Systems (OS)

The terms *operating system* (OS) and *platform* are familiar terms associated with computer systems. DVRs are computers designed to record video information with other features specifically tailored to the security application. Fundamentally an OS does several things: (1) manages the hardware of the computer system defined as the CPU processor, memory, and disk space, (2) manages software and other housekeeping functions, and (3) provides a consistent way for applications to interface with the hardware without having to know all the details about that hardware. Today's OS take on several forms including the Microsoft Windows family and Linux embedded formats.

Manufacturers of DVR products have built their systems on a variety of proprietary OS platforms. Windows systems include the Windows 9X, XP family, Windows NT, and Windows 2000. Embedded proprietary OS platforms like UNIX are specifically designed to run on a unique DVR product. By nature, this proprietary OS is used by a single manufacturer unless licensed to other competitors. One concern regarding these proprietary platforms is that their distribution is limited and the user should question how extensively the product has been field-tested against a wide variety of software security threats.

9.3.3.1 Windows 9X, NT, XP, and 2000 Operating Systems

The Microsoft Windows 9X, 16 bit families of OS namely Windows 95, 98, and ME have been the primary platforms used by DVR manufacturers. Several reasons why this family of OS has been so popular with the creators of DVR products are that the product is relatively stable, familiar to most users, and less expensive than its client–server counterparts. Since no major changes in the OS have occurred over the lifetime of this family of products, developers of DVR software have been able to avoid making costly software rewrites. There is a downside, however, to the security aspect of the Microsoft 9X family of OS. The Windows 9X family has a fundamental flaw that has been recognized by Microsoft and by the manufacturers of DVR products (see Section 9.3.8).

Significant improvements in Windows 2000 were modifications to the OS core to prevent crashes, to enhance dynamic system configuration, and to increase system uptime, and providing a unique method for self repair. The Windows 2000 has built-in tools that make the OS applications easier to deploy, manage, and support. Centralized management utilities, troubleshooting tools, and support for self-healing applications make the management of an IT infrastructure easier. Windows 2000 also offers use of HD drives and enhanced level of hardware support. These improvements include the largest database of third-party drivers and support for the latest hardware standards. This makes it easier for HD drive users to easily upgrade to the latest versions of software released by the HD drive manufacturer.

9.3.3.2 UNIX

The UNIX OS is designed to be used by many people at the same time. The UNIX is a multi-user and multi-tasking OS developed at the Bell Telephone Laboratories, NJ, by Ken Thompson and Dennis Ritchie in 1969. It is widely used as the master control program in workstations and servers, and as an embedded OS in proprietary DVRs. It has the Internet TCP/IP protocol built-in and is the most common OS for servers on the Internet.

9.3.4 Mobile DVR

Mobile DVRs are embedded systems designed specifically for use in vehicles and rapid deployment systems (RDS) and for short-term security installations (see Chapter 21).

These mobile DVRs are small and rugged, vibration and shock resistant, and the choice for vehicle security, RDS, and surveillance applications are when portability is necessary.

The mobile DVR system can connect from 1 to 4 video cameras and record and display at a full 30 IPS with audio recording as an option. LAN and Internet interface connections are available and vehicle status and speed can be displayed on the recording. The camera images can be displayed individually at full screen or in a quad format. Auto switching from camera to camera is supported and the dwell time per camera can be set by the user. Four input alarm contacts allow each camera to be recorded on receipt of an alarm signal. Video can be recorded continuously, on motion, on alarm or by schedule. The VMD zones can be set in each camera, or the whole field of view of each camera can be used as the motion criterion. Video files can be searched by date, time, and alarm state in a single or quad configuration. ID and password protection are provided at different levels from system manager to system operator. A standard Internet browser for remote connection with user ID protection can monitor the mobile DVR site through the Internet, LAN, WAN, or wireless WiFi.

These mobile DVR systems provide far superior performance over traditional analog VHS VCRs which are prone to hardware failure due to humid and dusty environments and to shock and vibration. These DVRs contain rugged 30 GByte HD drives with input/output RS-232 control ports. DVRs are available having a microcontroller that translates its pushbutton commands into the Sony/Odetics control protocol for full configuration and control through the RS-232 control port. A serial connector allows Windows Control Software to be used for PC-based control and configuration. Figure 9-12 shows examples of fixed mobile DVRs.

9.3.5 Digital Compression, Encryption

Video compression is the science of eliminating as much digital data in the video signal as possible without it being evident to the observer viewing the image. Today's systems have compression ratios ranging from 10:1 to 2400:1 making it possible to transmit or record huge amounts of video data. Basic video compression methods can be classified into two major groups: *lossy and lossless*. Lossy techniques reduce data both through complex mathematical algorithms and through selective removal of visual information that our eyes and brain usually ignore. Lossless

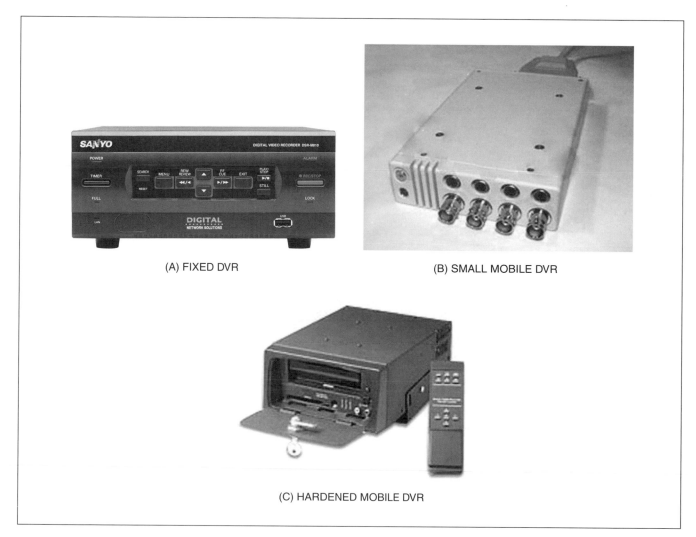

(A) FIXED DVR

(B) SMALL MOBILE DVR

(C) HARDENED MOBILE DVR

FIGURE 9-12   Compact PC-based fixed and mobile DVRs

compression, by contrast, discards only *redundant* information making it possible to reconstruct the *exact* original video image signal.

The need for recording and storing days of video image scenes requires that the signals be compressed to reduce the file size. There are several different compression algorithms utilized in digital VCRs that are mostly derived from the JPEG, MPEG, Wavelet, H.263, and H.264 algorithms. Both JPEG and MPEG are both based on the discrete cosine transform (DCT) in which *blocks* of 8 by 8 pixels are grouped and then transformed into the frequency domain. The Wavelet algorithm transforms the *entire picture* into the frequency domain, resulting in relatively small file sizes as compared to the DCT-based algorithms. Likewise, the H.263 and H.264 are designed for low bit rate systems.

In a typical video signal one image is similar to the next, and it is possible to make a good prediction of what the next frame or field in the sequence will look like. It is also possible to bi-directionally interpolate images based on those that came before and after. The method is to compare the most recent image with the previous image and determine if there was a change, and then decide whether to store or not to store those frames if there has been a change.

There are many techniques used to compress the video image for storage in a DVR. One method is *redundancy reduction* and is accomplished by removing duplication from the signal source before it is compressed and stored.

Three forms of redundant reduction are:

1. Spatial: Correlation is between neighboring pixel values
2. Spectral: Correlation is between different color planes or bands
3. Temporal: Correlation between adjacent frames in the sequence.

A second form of reduction is called *irrelevancy* reduction. This method omits parts of the signal that will not be noticed by the observer. Two areas described by the Human Visual System (HVS) organization are in the low-frequency visual response and color recognition areas.

9.3.5.1 JPEG

The JPEG compression algorithm was introduced in 1974 by the Joint Photographic Expert Group and uses the DCT compression algorithm based on a video stream of 8×8 pixels. This is the algorithm primarily used to download images over the Internet and can achieve compression ratios up to 27:1.

It is designed to exploit known limitations of the human eye, notably the fact that small color changes are perceived less accurately than small changes in brightness. Using all of these compression methods reduces in the file storage size while maintaining a high-quality stored video image.

9.3.5.2 MPEG-X

The MPEG compression algorithm uses the same DCT compression found in JPEG. The difference is that MPEG compression is based on *motion*-compensated block-based transform coding techniques. The primary technique used in this algorithm is conditional refresh where only *changes* in the image scene are compressed and stored which reduces the amount of storage required. This is called inter-frame (I) compression. MPEG uses the same algorithms as JPEG to create one I-frame and then removes the redundancy from successive frames by predicting them from the I-frame, and in coding only the differences from its predictions (P-frames). B-frames are bi-directionally interpolated. MPEG compression allows for three types of frames:

1. I-frame (compress entirely within a frame).
2. P-frame (based on predictions from a previous frame).
3. B-frames (bi-directionally interpolated from previous and succeeding frames).

MPEG-1, MPEG-2, MPEG-4 and the latest MPEG-4 AVC (H.264) are the four basic MPEG forms used in video compression. Each has a different compression ratio:

1. MPEG-1 = 25 to 100:1
2. MPEG-2 = 30 to 100:1
3. MPEG-4 = 50 to 100:1.
4. MPEG-4 AVC = 50 to 200:1 (or more)

MPEG compression forms have large file sizes and therefore many of today's DVR manufacturers have modified this standard to meet the needs of the video security industry. These modified standards called H.263 and H.264 are designed for low bit rate communications. H.263 is better than MPEG-1 or MPEG-2 for low-resolution and low bit rate images. MPEG-4 AVC (H.264) is now considered to be the best video compression standard.

9.3.5.3 Wavelet

Wavelet compression technology is based on *full-frame* information and is based on *frequency* not on 8×8 pixel blocks. It compresses the *entire image*—both the high and low frequencies—and repeats the procedure several times. Wavelet compression can provide compression ratios up to 350:1.

9.3.5.4 SMICT

Super motion image compression technology (SMICT) is a proprietary video compression technology that produces a small file size for high resolution image reproduction. The OS is Windows 2000 or Windows XP. SMICT can provide compression ratios from 40:1 to up to 2400:1. Typical single image file sizes range up to 2500 Bytes. The SMICT compression algorithm includes video authentication. One manufacturers' system can record 16 cameras at the rate of 3 IPS at 220 horizontal TV lines and 320×240 format size onto a single 75 GByte HD for between 30 and 60 days. Recording time is higher if there is less activity in the video image. Using a PSTN connection with a 56 KByte modem, four cameras can be viewed at 2 IPS, each in quad mode.

9.3.6 Image Quality

Video image quality from a DVR is dependent on the resolution in the camera image, the compression algorithm and ratio, and the IPS displayed.

9.3.6.1 Resolution

The term *resolution* is often misused and misunderstood in the security industry. In analog systems the recorded image almost always fills the entire monitor screen. The resolution for analog video cameras and VHS recorders is defined as (1) number of TV lines in a *horizontal width* of the screen equal to the height of the screen or (2) the total number of horizontal TV lines across the width of the monitor. Digital resolution refers to spatial resolution (number of pixels per line) and the number of lines or rows per image, again defined in pixels. Digital resolution is also defined as the total number of pixels on the screen. This definition not only affects the overall resolution of the system but also the overall *size* of the displayed image. The common digital monitor image sizes are defined as 1/4 CIF, CIF, and 4 CIF (see Section 9.3.7).

9.3.6.2 Frame Rate

Most video security applications require that at least 2–5 IPS per camera be recorded to ensure that enough images are captured to clearly identify a person, an object, or activity. A recording rate of 15 IPS is perceived as nearly real-time. This is the minimum rate when all motions and activities are required to be recorded as in locations such as casinos, retail stores, banks, etc. where fast motion and sleight of hand must be detected. When basic DVRs or the multiplex DVRs are used, the number of camera inputs will affect the IPS recording rate for each camera. Today's midsize recorders can record at rates from approximately 60 to 480 IPS. Dividing the IPS rate by the number of cameras in the multiplex systems calculates the average IPS per camera recording speed. In large Enterprise systems a multi-channel DVR or NVR recording system is required. These systems can record a large number of cameras *simultaneously* so that a rate of 5 IPS or higher can be achieved.

The ability to change the number of recorded IPS per video input is important since the main purpose of any DVR and multiplexer is to provide a simple and cost-effective method to monitor live and recorded images via a *multi-screen* display. This form of TL recording eliminates the gaps between video scenes created by conventional sequential switchers.

9.3.6.3 Bandwidth

When video images from DVRs are transmitted to remote locations, the image frame rate and resolution are directly affected by the bandwidth of the transmission network. As a rule of thumb, the wider the network bandwidth, the more the IPS, and the better the resolution (more pixels). Bandwidth requirements for quality video transmission range from 256 Kbps to 1 Mbps depending on the video compression method used, the image quality required, and IPS used by the application.

Cellular phone is the slowest transmission method and not widely used in the video security industry. Its bandwidth is 3000 Hz and has a 9.6 Kbps data rate. Dial-up or PSTN with a modem is the most common transmission method and has a maximum data rate of 56 Kbps. While relatively slow, its low cost and availability contribute to its continued use. ISDN is a digital phone line with two 64 Kbps channels. This costs more than the PSTN but with competition from the cable network and digital subscriber line (DSL), pricing for these are acceptable to the video security industry. Typical speeds for the DSL network is 1.544 Mbps but depends on cable routing, distance, and number of other clients using the same line. Much wider bandwidth choices include the AT&T T1 and T3 lines, and the OC3–OC12 optical fiber networks.

9.3.7 Display Format—CIF

Digital images from DVRs or other sources can be displayed on monitors in full size or a fraction of the monitor screen size. Compression technology is critical and a significant factor in determining the storage required and the final resolution obtained in the digital video image. The CIF image size determines the size (number of pixels) of the captured image. The larger the picture size, the larger the storage required on the hard drive.

The abbreviation CIF has two definitions. The first is Common *Intermediate* Format (CIF), a standard developed by the International Telecommunications Union (ITU) for video teleconferencing, and is the standard in current use throughout the digital video security industry.

Table 9-6 defines this CIF pixel format, aspect ratio, and bit rate for NTSC and PAL systems. The original CIF is also known as Full CIF (FCIF). Quarter CIF is designated as QCIF and Four CIF as 4CIF.

The 4CIF image improves the resolution by a factor of four over the 1CIF image by doubling the number of pixels in both the vertical and horizontal axis. 4CIF uses all the camera pixels and reproduces the best image quality from a high resolution camera.

The ability to identify persons, objects, and activities greatly affects the required stored image format and consequently the resolution of the image. The 1CIF image can be used to identify faces, license plates, and other detail only under favorable conditions. The 4CIF display is the format of choice and uses one of the MPEG-4, H.464, or other high compression standards.

Also shown in Table 9-6, but not to be confused with Common Intermediate Format is the *Common Image Format* also abbreviated CIF, which is the standard frame size for digital video based on Sony's D1 format that defines the two standard SDTV frames.

9.3.8 Network/DVR Security

9.3.8.1 Authentication

An important requirement in any local or remote video monitoring system is the need to keep the video information secure and error-free. DVR image degradation can be caused by equipment failure or produced by man-made activity (hackers, viruses). The security provider must be diligent and make all efforts to ensure that the information is accurate and the system tamperproof. State-of-the-art image authentication software has increased the reliability of digital video monitoring by preventing the tampering of the signal. The safeguards can be incorporated with either special compression methods using date/time stamping or the summation of pixels changes, all of which will insure the acceptance of the digital video record in a court of law.

Some standards of authentication include:

- Images must be from the original VCR tape or DVR hard drive
- Images should be recorded in a WORM drive
- Images should have a *check sum* error checking methodology
- Images should have a date *digital signature*.

COMMON INTERMEDIATE FORMAT* (CIF)	SCREEN AREA	PIXEL FORMAT	ASPECT RATIO	BIT RATE AT 30 FRAMES/SEC (Mbps)
CIF	FULL	352×288 (PAL) 352×240 (NTSC)	1.222	36.5
QCIF (QUARTER CIF)	1/4	176×144 (PAL) 176×120 (NTSC)	1.222	9.1
SQCIF (SUB QUARTER CIF)	—	128×96 (PAL)	1.333 (4×3)	4.4
1/2 CIF	FULL	704×240 (NTSC) 704×288 (PAL)	1.222	18.3
4CIF (4×CIF)	FULL	704×576 (PAL) 704×480 (NTSC)	1.222	146.0
16CIF (16×CIF)	FULL	1408×1152 (PAL) 1408×960 (NTSC)	1.222	583.9

*COMMON INTERMEDIATE FORMAT (CIF) DEVELOPED BY the INTERNATIONAL TELECOMMUNICATIONS UNION (ITU) IN STANDARD H.261 FOR VIDEO TELECONFERENCING. THIS FORMAT IS IN CURRENT USE THROUGHOUT THE DIGITAL VIDEO SECUIRTY INDUSTRY.

MPEG COMPRESSION STANDARDS ARE BASED ON THE CIF FORMATS.

COMMON IMAGE FORMAT**	SCREEN AREA	PIXEL FORMAT
VGA	FULL	640×480
1/4 VGA	1/4	320×240
1/16 VGA	1/16	160×120
D1 (SONY FORMAT)	FULL	720×480 (NTSC) 720×576 (PAL)

**NOT TO BE CONFUSED WITH CIF ABOVE, COMMON IMAGE FORMAT IS A STANDARD FRAME SIZE FOR DIGITAL VIDEO BASED ON SONY'S D1 FORMAT.

Table 9-6   Common Intermediate and Common Image Format (CIF) Parameters

The WORM format allows the operator to review video images as often as required but the images can never be altered. The *check sum* is a method which records the number of levels and pixels per recorded line and stores this information in the recorder's program. On review this sum is checked and if the two are not equal an alarm or visual cue notifies the operator that a change has occurred. Authentication should also include a date/time stamping or digital signature inserted on all recorded video images.

A network authentication protocol called Kerberos is designed to provide strong authentication for client/server applications by using secret-key cryptography. This protocol was developed by the Massachusetts Institute of Technology (MIT) in the mid-1980s, and is free and has been implemented into and available in many commercial products. It was created by MIT as a solution to network security problems. The Kerberos authentication system uses a series of encrypted messages to prove to a verifier that a client is running online on behalf of a particular user. It uses strong cryptography so that a client can prove its identity to a server (and vice versa) across an insecure network connection. Kerberos requires a trusted path through which passwords are entered. If the user enters a password in a program that has already been modified by an attacker (Trojan horse), then an attacker may obtain sufficient information to impersonate the user. After a client and server have used Kerberos to prove their identity, they can also encrypt all of their communications to assure privacy and data integrity as they go about their business. In 1989 Version 5 of the protocol was designed and is in use in many systems today.

9.3.8.2 Watermark

A digital watermark is a digital signal or pattern inserted into a digital image. It is inserted into each unaltered copy of the original image. The digital watermark may also serve as a digital signature for the copies. For law enforcement and prosecution purposes it is critical that digital tapes and disks be watermarked, since digital information may easily be altered and modified through software manipulation. The law in most countries requires that information recorded by DVRs not be altered or modified. An example of such watermarking techniques is used in the Panasonic digital disk recorder utilizing a proprietary algorithm to detect if the image has been altered or modified. If the image has been changed in any way, when it is played back the word altered appears on the monitor indicating that the original image is not being viewed.

9.3.8.3 Virtual Private Network (VPN)

The security of digitally transmitted information has existed in the IT world for many years. With the rapid increase in the use of digital video hardware and transmission networks, the security industry looks to the IT community for additional technologies to make video transmission more secure and safe from external attack. The data security requirements have changed significantly in the past ten years as the Internet has grown, and vastly more companies have come to rely on the Internet for communications and hence the security solutions are necessary.

A VPN is a private data network that makes use of the public telecommunications infrastructure, maintaining privacy and providing security through the use of a tunnel protocol and security procedures.

The VPN provides an encrypted connection between user's distributed sites over a public network such as the Internet. By contrast, a private network uses dedicated circuits and possibly encryption. The VPN is in contrast with the system of home or leased lines that can only be used by one company. The primary purpose of a VPN is to give the company the same capabilities as private leased lines but at a much lower cost. By using the shared public infrastructure, companies today are looking at using VPNs for both extranets and wide area intranets.

There are three basic classifications of VPN technologies: (1) trusted VPN, (2) secure VPN, and (3) Hybrid VPN.

9.3.8.3.1 Trusted VPNs

Before the Internet became nearly universal, a VPN consisted of one or more communication circuits leased from a communications provider where each leased circuit acted like a single wire that was controlled by the customer. The basic idea was that a customer could use these leased circuits in the same way that they use physical cables in their local network. The privacy afforded by these legacy VPNs was only that the communications provider assured the customer that no one else would use the same circuit. The VPN customer trusted the VPN provider to maintain integrity of circuits and to use the best available business practices to avoid snooping of the network traffic. This methodology really offers no real security.

9.3.8.3.2 Secure VPNs

Networks that are constructed using encryption are called secure VPNs. Vendors created protocols that would allow traffic to be encrypted at the edge of one network or at the originating computer, move over the Internet like any other data, and then be decrypted when it reached the corporate network or a receiving computer. This encrypted traffic acted like a tunnel between the two networks. Even if an attacker could see the traffic it could not be read to make a change in the traffic or make use of the data, without the changes being seen by the receiving party who would therefore reject the data. The encrypted tunnel provides a secure path for network applications and requires no changes to the application.

9.3.8.3.3 Hybrid VPNs

The hybrid VPN uses a secure VPN that is run as part of a trusted VPN, creating a third type of VPN. The secure parts of the hybrid VPN can be controlled by the customer or the same provider that provides the trusted part of the hybrid VPN. Sometimes an entire hybrid VPN is secured with the secure VPN, but more commonly only a part of a hybrid VPN is secure.

9.3.8.4 Windows Operating System

Within a year of Windows 95 release, Microsoft identified a major security problem that could not be fixed without a complete software rewrite. Microsoft then embarked on the development of a completely new platform which resulted in Windows NT that was built on the concept of creating a high level network security OS. However, the majority of DVR manufacturers continue to use Windows 95 and Windows 98 rather than take the costly route of rewriting their software with the more secure Windows NT.

The newer Windows 2000, the 32-bit OS that was built on the Windows NT technology provides the users of HD drives many comprehensive security features that protect sensitive video and other security data. These enhanced security features provide local protection in addition to securing information as it is transmitted over a LAN, WAN, WiFi, phone line, or the Internet. With Windows 2000, the system administrator and authorized users can select from multiple levels of security. For advanced users, Windows 2000 also supports standard Internet security features such as IP security, Kerberos authentication, Layer 2 Tunneling Protocol, and VPNs. Many large companies have migrated to Windows 2000 to take advantage of this secure OS.

9.3.9 VCR/DVR Hardware/Software Protection

Both VCRs and DVRs require various types of protection and handling to avoid hardware and software failures. They also require periodic maintenance. In particular, the VCR recorder and the VHS magnetic tape cassettes require special care because of their complex mechanical tape handling mechanism and the vulnerable videotape cassette.

9.3.9.1 Uninterrupted Power Supply (UPS)

Hardware main power protection via power conditioning is a must for VCRs and DVRs. As with computer systems, voltage surge and power line filtration must be included in any recorder installation. Installations in areas prone to lightning or other electrical disturbances require extra precautions. Power protection must not be treated as "just another box" that must be included with the system. Unfortunately, it is usually after a major failure that most people realize that this protection is *critical.* Appropriate protection includes a UPS and surge protector (Chapter 23).

9.3.9.2 Grounding

Like other electronic equipment, DVRs require proper electrical grounding to insure that transient voltages on the power line are safely directed to ground. This ground connection will greatly reduce the possibility of damage to the recorder and its internal HD drive. Such grounding is important in high-risk areas that experience lightning storms and applications where electromagnetic interference (EMI) or radio frequency interference (RFI) may be present. The grounding wire on a three-pronged power cord is sufficient for grounding the recorder, but a check should be made that the AC power socket into which it is plugged is connected to earth ground. This can be tested by using an ohmmeter and measuring the resistance between this location and the earth ground location. It should measure near zero ohms.

9.3.9.3 Analog/Digital Hardware Precautions

Both the analog and digital video recorders contain mechanical moving parts. As such they should be treated with care when installing, moving, or relocating them. Do not rough handle them.

The VCRs and DATs have many mechanical parts which can become misaligned or damaged if the machine is dropped or mishandled, or if tape insertion/removal is performed carelessly. This can render the machine inoperative.

Digital video recorders have one or more HD for storage of the video image. Do not unnecessarily jar or drop the machine as this could damage or reduce the lifetime of the HD. After powering down the DVR, it should not be moved for a few minutes after power shutoff to insure that the HD platter has come to a complete stop and that the HD head that reads and writes information from the disk has come to a parked position.

9.3.9.4 Maintenance

Since the VCR, VCR time lapse, DAT, and DVR recorders are used over a long periods of time, preventative maintenance for these devices is important. To ensure reliable operation this is especially true for the VCR video heads. The video heads rotate at 1800 rpm and the video head gradually wears out and head-to-tape contact is reduced, resulting in a noisy picture. VCRs must be operated in a dust-free, controlled humidity and temperature environment to ensure reliable operation. If the VCR tape fails or the cassette jams, retrieve the cassette and carefully manually remove the broken tape, and then splice the tape to salvage the remaining information recorded.

In the case of the DVR, the PC-based operating system (OS) may crash and therefore it is wise to back up the recorded information onto external backup storage or use a RAID-configured HD drive system. Short of these measures, it is a challenge to retrieve the information from the HD. If DAT recorders are used for backup, head clogging is often difficult to detect because of the powerful error correcting built into these machines. They operate even with only one head operating. To test for head clogging, turnoff the error correction and read the error rate of the unit and see whether it is within the manufacturer's specifications. If not, clean or replace the heads.

9.4 VIDEO RECORDER COMPARISON: PROS, CONS

Although the VCR has served the video surveillance industry well for several decades, the VCR technology has several shortcomings. These have been brought into the limelight with the introduction of the DVR in the late 1990s. The following is a list of many pros and cons for the DVR and VCR.

9.4.1 VCR Pros and Cons

The criteria used to assess the analog VCR and digital DVR cross several boundaries including cost, size of system, hardware already in place, availability of recording media, manpower to administer, and maintenance. The analog VCR has served the security industry well over the last decades but the digital DVR will clearly replace it swiftly.

VCR Pros

- Low cost proven technology with long history of service
- Easy to copy and provide as evidence to law enforcement
- Difficult to alter video images (as compared to digital recorders).

VCR Cons

- Tape heads need regular maintenance and eventually wear out and need replacement
- Tape handling mechanism has many precision mechanical parts that can go out of alignment or fail
- Tape needs to be changed on a regular basis daily depending on application requiring manpower
- Tape is sensitive to humidity, dust, chemicals, and high level magnetic fields.

9.4.2 DVR Pros and Cons

DVR Pros

- Produces a permanently clear and crisp record on a HD drive
- Serves as long-term backup device and requires no additional data management costs
- Reproduces the original picture quality after many copies are made
- Provides multi-channel recording in real-time when required
- Simultaneous recording, viewing, and transmitting to remote site
- Intelligent motion detection acts as alarm sensor
- Multiplexer can be integrated with DVR
- Remote control Pan/tilt, camera zoom/focus/iris
- Nonstop recording limited only by the HD drive storage space available
- Remote access by a LAN, WAN, WiFi, ISBN, DSL, modem, PSTN.

DVR Cons

- Eventual HD failure
- OS and/or application program crash
- Digital data more easily altered unless water-marking or other high level security is built in.

9.5 CHECKLIST AND GUIDELINES

There is a large variety of VCR and DVR hardware to choose from to record the video image. Prior to the late 1990s the VCR was the only technology choice. The DVR is now the major technology choice. This checklist and guideline lists some of the factors to consider when choosing a video recording system.

9.5.1 Checklist

- How many cameras must be recorded?
- How many IPS per camera?
- What quality (resolution) of images is required?
- What is the size of image: 1/4 CIF, CIF, or 4 CIF?
- What length of storage is required?
- What is the location for monitoring?
- How many sites?
- Does the recording system permit limiting the amount of bandwidth required to transmit video across the network?
- Does the remote viewing software allow viewing cameras from multiple systems on the same screen at the same time?
- Does the remote viewing system software allow searching for recorded video and playing back from multiple systems at the same time, on the same screen?
- Can the system be administrated remotely?
- How much training will the staff require to use it efficiently?
- Can the system record at different frame rates, quality settings, and video settings for individual cameras?
- Does the system record video prior to the beginning of the event (pre-alarm recording)?
- Upon alarm condition can the system send an email notification?
- Can different recording schedules be programmed for each hour or day?
- Can the system send video to a remote location for automatic video display upon alarm condition?
- Can multi-camera views be created and then automatically sequenced between them on the video monitor?
- Can the system automatically archive video data to a network storage device?
- Can pan-tilt-zoom cameras be controlled from both the system and the remote software?

9.5.2 Guidelines

- Initially install DVRs in highly sensitive areas to improve image quality, image retrieval, and searching time.
- Enable remote video monitoring for authorized personnel. This can cut travel costs, improve operational efficiency, and make the DVR investment more cost-effective.
- Choose a basic DVR or multiplexed DVR for small- to medium-size installations.
- Choose a multi-channel DVR or NVR for large systems.
- Choose a security level that matches the security requirement.

9.6 SUMMARY

The VCR or DVR records video images to establish an audit trail for the video surveillance activity. It can be viewed at a convenient time by security, law enforcement, or corporate personnel to identify a person, determine the activity that occurred, or assess the responses of security personnel. The video recording provides a permanent medium with which to establish credible evidence for prosecuting a person involved in criminal activity or suspected thereof, and for use in a criminal trial, civil litigation, or dismissal. The video recording provides a basis of comparison with an earlier recording to establish if there was a change in condition at a particular location, such as moved or removed equipment or personnel patterns, including times of arrival and departure.

Video cassette recorders and digital video recorders are excellent tools for training and evaluation of personnel performance. They serve as a source of feedback when evaluating employee performance. By reviewing the recording, management can determine which employees are working efficiently and which employees are not performing up to standards, without on-site supervision.

Magnetic HD DVRs and optical HD recorders have a clear advantage over VCRs when video images must be retrieved quickly from a large database of stored images. Retrieved video images can be printed on thermal, inkjet, or laser printers when: (1) a hard copy audit trail of video images are required for dismissal, court-room, or insurance purposes, (2) a guard needs a hard copy printout when dispatched to apprehend an individual at a suspected crime scene, (3) to produce a permanent hard copy of an activity or accident for insurance purposes, etc. The video record offers the ability to instantly replay a video image and print it. This feature is important in real-time pursuit and apprehension scenarios.

The Internet has and will continue to change how video images will be recorded and distributed locally and to remote sites. The hardware, software, and transmission channels already exist to provide security personnel, corporate management, and government organizations to perform automated video security (AVS).

Chapter 10
Hard Copy Video Printers

CONTENTS

10.1 Overview
10.2 Background
10.3 Printer Technology
    10.3.1 Thermal
            10.3.1.1 Monochrome
            10.3.1.2 Wax Transfer
            10.3.1.3 Color-Dye Diffusion
    10.3.2 Ink Jet, Bubble Jet
    10.3.3 Laser, LED
    10.3.4 Dye-Diffusion, Wax-Transfer
    10.3.5 Film
10.4 Printer Comparison
    10.4.1 Resolution and Speed
    10.4.2 Hardware, Ink Cartridge Cost Factors
    10.4.3 Paper Types
10.5 Summary

10.1 OVERVIEW

Hard-copy printout from a live video monitor and VCR/DVR recorder or other transmitted surveillance images is a necessity to the video security system. Monochrome and color printers permit good to excellent-quality reproduction of the scene image on hard-copy printout. The printed hard-copy image is used by security personnel for apprehending offenders, responding to security violations and for a permanent record of a scene, activity, object, or person.

The video printer is a device that accepts: (1) an analog video signal from a camera or VCR or (2) a digital signal from a computer, a DVR, or an IP camera, and transfers the information to paper (or film). The information can be text, graphics, and video, and can be printed in either color or monochrome depending on the data content. Printers vary greatly in terms of their technology, sophistication, speed, and cost.

10.2 BACKGROUND

The three most popular video printer technologies for video applications are thermal, ink jet, and laser.

Thermal. Early models of thermal hard-copy printers produced crude facsimiles of the monitor picture with low resolution and poor gray-scale rendition. Today's advanced technology enables printers to produce excellent monochrome or color image prints with resolution approaching that of a high-quality camera. Of the several monochrome and color printout technologies available for the security industry, the monochrome thermal printer is the most popular because of its low hardware and paper costs. They need no toner or ink, only a special paper.

Ink Jet, Bubble Jet. The present ink-jet printer was built on the progress made by many earlier versions and has had a long history of development. Among the contributors to the evolution have been the Hewlett Packard (HP) and Canon Companies, claiming a substantial share of credit for the development of the modern ink jet. In 1979 Canon invented and developed the drop-on-demand ink-jet method where ink drops are ejected from a nozzle by the fast growth of an ink vapor bubble on the top surface of a small heater. Canon named this *bubble jet* technology. In 1984 Hewlett-Packard (HP) commercialized the ink-jet printer and it was the first low-cost ink-jet printer based on the bubble jet principle. HP named the technology *thermal inkjet*. Since then, HP and Canon have continuously improved on the technology and currently thermal ink-jet printer dominates the major segment of the *color* printer market. The four major manufacturers now accounting for the majority of ink-jet printer sales are Canon, HP,

Epson, and Lexmark. Ink-jet printers are a common type of computer printer used for video security applications.

Laser, LED. Laser and LED (light emitting diode) printers provide an alternative to the ink-jet and bubble jet printers for producing hard-copy video printouts. Laser and LED printers rely on technology similar to a type of dry process photocopier that was first introduced by Xerox Corp. This process known as electro-photography was invented in 1938 and later developed for their copier machines by Xerox and Canon in the late 1980s.

The first laser printer was created by Xerox researcher Gary Starkweather by modifying a Xerox copier in 1971 and was offered as a product as the Xerox Star 8010 in 1977. The first *successful* laser printer was the HP Laser-Jet, an 8-page per minute (ppm) model, released in 1984. The 8010 used a Canon printing engine controlled by HP-developed software. The laser printer uses a rotating mirror to form the image on the drum. The HP LaserJet printer was quickly followed by laser printers from Brothers Industries, IBM, and others.

The Okidata Company developed and has been producing a printer using LED technology instead of a laser for many years. Okidata and Panasonic now produce LED printers using an array of small LEDs to form the latent image on the drum, and no mirror scanner is required. This LED technology offers some potential advantages over the laser system.

Other. Two other technologies used to produce high-quality color images are: (1) thermal transfer printer (TTP) using thermal plastic wax and (2) thermal sublimation printer (TSP) using dye diffusion. Both techniques produce brilliant colors and excellent resolution. The printer cost is high and the ink cartridges expensive, and therefore these printers are not in high use in security applications. Color laser printers are not used in the video security industry because of their high equipment cost and ink cartridge replacement cost, as compared to other technologies now available.

In addition to the standard monochrome laser printers that use a single toner, there also exist color laser printers that use four toners to print in full color. Color laser printers tend to be about five to ten times as expensive as monochrome.

Polaroid film technology has been used in the video industry for many years and is still used for special applications. It has lost its popularity because of the new thermal, ink-jet, laser, and LED technologies that have become available.

Dot matrix printers are not suitable for monochrome or color video image printing because of their lower resolution and slower speed and high noise levels.

10.3 PRINTER TECHNOLOGY

Most video image printouts are still done with monochrome thermal printers. The reason for this is the significantly lower cost of the printer hardware and the lower cost of the hard-copy printout, since no ink cartridge head or ink is required for the monochrome video printer.

However, the overwhelming use of color video cameras in security monitoring systems has motivated manufacturers to provide cost-effective solutions for printing color images. In a color video system, the lens receives the color picture information and through the color camera converts the light image into three electrical signals corresponding to the red, green, and blue (R, G, B) color components in the scene. These three signals presented to an RGB monitor produce a color image on the monitor. In a color printer, the three primary colors in the video signal, R, G, and B, must be *reversed* to obtain their complementary colors: cyan, magenta, and yellow.

10.3.1 Thermal

Three thermal technologies for producing hard-copy printout are: (1) monochrome, (2) wax transfer, and (3) color-dye diffusion.

10.3.1.1 Monochrome

The monochrome thermal video printer is the most popular type used in security industry. The primary reason is that it can produce resolution comparable to the resolution of the cameras and sufficient printing speed required for video security applications. Another reason for their popularity is that the cost for the hardware, printout paper, and printer head are less than those of other printer technologies. Figure 10-1 shows a monochrome thermal video printer and hard-copy printout.

Thermal monochrome printers create an image by selectively heating coated paper as the paper passes over the thermal printer head (Figure 10-2). The coating turns

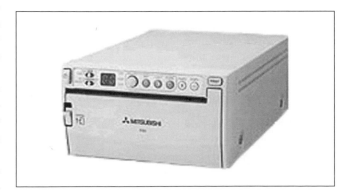

FIGURE 10-1 Thermal video printer

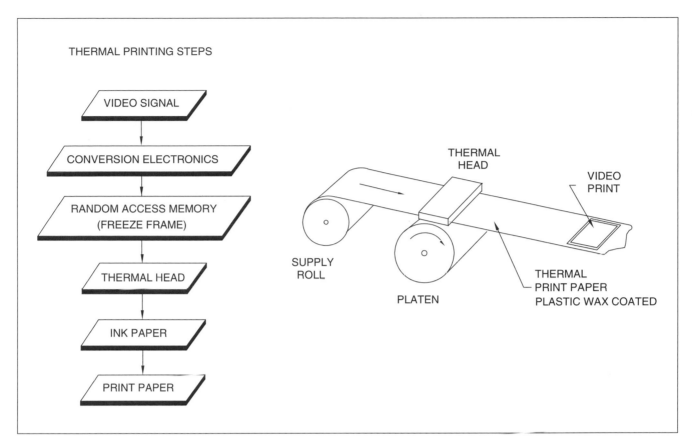

FIGURE 10-2 Thermal printer block diagram

black in the areas where it is heated, creating the image. Care must be taken with the handling and storage of the thermal paper, as it suffers from sensitivity to heat and abrasion which can cause darkening of the paper or fading due to light.

The thermal printer converts the video signal from the camera into a digital signal and stores it in a random access memory (RAM) or other storage device. The video freeze-frame module captures and "freezes" the image as a snapshot of a moving video scene. This temporary storage allows the printer to operate at a much slower speed than the actual real-time video frame rate. After the video image has been captured, it is converted to an electrical drive signal for the thermal head located adjacent to the paper. Depending on the video drive signal level, the paper is locally heated, causing the wax on the paper to melt and turn black (or another color). Depending on the amount of heat applied, a larger or smaller dot is produced providing a gray-scale level to the image. As the video information is scanned across the slowly moving paper, the image is "burned in," thereby creating a facsimile of the video image. Scanning an entire monochrome video image one pixel at a time takes approximately 8 seconds. Since the video image is stored in the printer until a new frame is captured, multiple copies can be made. The printed video image is recorded on a treated paper that resists fading

from sunlight and physical tearing. Figure 10-3 shows a monochrome thermal video printer hard-copy printout.

10.3.1.2 Wax Transfer

In the color TTP, a plastic-wax, single-color-coated ribbon (the width of the paper roll) is inserted between the thermal print head and the paper (Figure 10-4). The ribbon is heated locally from behind causing the wax-based ink coating to melt, and the image to transfer to the paper. The full-color prints are produced in the thermal plastic color printer through the multiple passes of three ribbons having the colors cyan, magenta, and yellow. The inking paper used is divided into three sections with different-colored ink; these three sections pass the thermal printer platen in sequence. As each color passes over the thermal head, an electrical signal proportional to the amount of the respective color in the video signal heats the head so that the ink of the required color is deposited on the paper. Depending on the amount of heat applied, a larger or smaller amount of ink from the paper will be transferred from the base film to the print paper. The first time the paper passes the head, yellow is deposited on it, then magenta, then cyan. By printing these three colors, so that they are superimposed exactly on each other, the printer is able to produce a high-resolution print with excellent

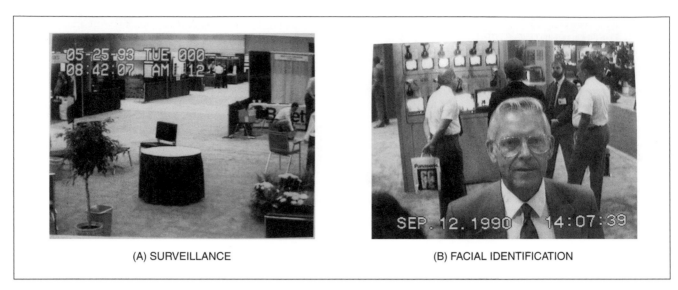

(A) SURVEILLANCE   (B) FACIAL IDENTIFICATION

FIGURE 10-3   Thermal printer quality: surveillance, facial identification

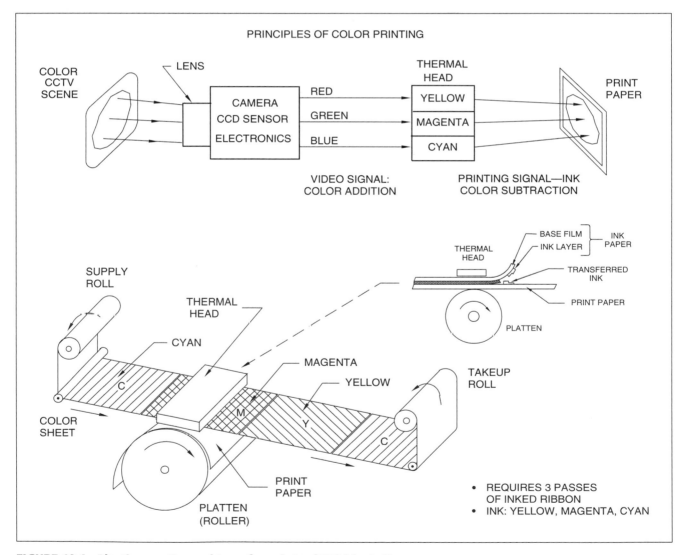

FIGURE 10-4   Plastic wax thermal transfer printer (TTP) block diagram

color rendition. By this principle, each dot on the final print copy is transferred from the base film ink layer to the print paper. Reproducing a satisfactory color image requires precisely engineered mechanical components so that the absolute registration between the three colors is printed. It also requires precise electronic technology to accurately combine the timing, signal, and video fidelity to ensure a faithful video image.

10.3.1.3 Color-Dye Diffusion

The TSP dye-diffusion printing media uses three ink dye papers (Figure 10-5). The TSP printer operates through the use of a polyester-based substrate (donor element) that contains a dye and binder layer, which when heated from the back side of the polyester sublimates (becomes gaseous) and transfers to the paper where the dye then diffuses into the paper itself. The ink paper consists of a cartridge containing three-color sequential printing inks (cyan, magenta, and yellow).

10.3.2 Ink Jet, Bubble Jet

There are two different types of ink-jet printers: the continuous-jet printer and the drop-on-demand printer (Figure 10-6). The continuous-jet printer uses a steady stream of ink droplets emanating from print nozzles under pressure. An electric charge is selectively applied to the droplets, causing some to be deflected toward the print paper and others away from the paper. The printout is the composite of all the individual dots in the image produced in this manner.

The drop-on-demand printer is a simpler and more popular ink-jet printer. This printer forms droplets of ink in the nozzle and ejects them through appropriate timing of electronic signals, thereby producing the desired image on the paper. The majority of ink jet printers produce a single dot size for each dot. Higher resolution types use a technology called *dithering* to increase the resolution and smooth jagged edges in text and lines in graphs and video images. Ink jet printers have found a significant market in the surveillance field and have good resolution, color rendition, and speed per copy.

Most current ink jets work by having a print cartridge with a series of tiny electrically heated chambers constructed using photolithography technology. The printer produces an image by driving a pulse of current through the heating elements. A steam explosion in the chamber forms a bubble which propels the droplets of ink onto the paper. Canon named it the Bubble Jet. When the

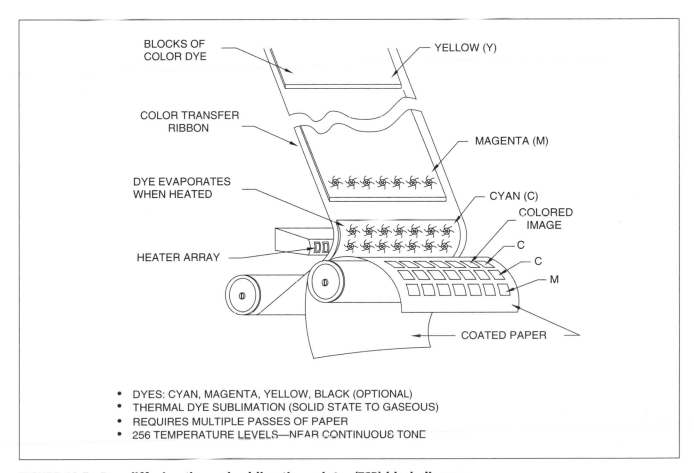

- DYES: CYAN, MAGENTA, YELLOW, BLACK (OPTIONAL)
- THERMAL DYE SUBLIMATION (SOLID STATE TO GASEOUS)
- REQUIRES MULTIPLE PASSES OF PAPER
- 256 TEMPERATURE LEVELS—NEAR CONTINUOUS TONE

FIGURE 10-5 Dye-diffusion thermal sublimation printer (TSP) block diagram

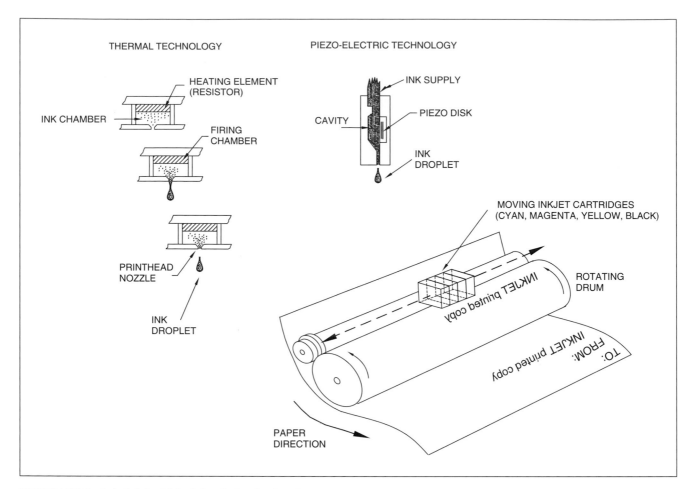

FIGURE 10-6   Ink jet, bubble jet printer technology

bubble condenses, surplus ink is sucked back up from the printing surface. The ink's surface tension pumps another charge of ink into the chamber through a narrow channel attached to an ink reservoir. Epson's micro-piezo technology uses a piezo-crystal in each nozzle instead of a heating element. When current is applied, the crystal bends, forcing a droplet of ink from the nozzle.

The greatest advantages of ink jet printers are quiet operation, capability to produce color images with near photographic quality, and low printer prices. One downside of the ink jet printer is that although they are generally cheaper to buy than the lasers, they are far more expensive to operate when it comes to comparing the cost per page. Ink cartridges used in ink jet printers make them many times more expensive than laser printers to produce the print.

10.3.3 Laser, LED

Laser printers provide an alternative to the ink jet and bubble jet printers for producing hard-copy video printouts. The laser printer can produce high-quality monochrome

images with excellent resolution—300 dots per inch (dpi) and grayscale (halftone) rendition.

Laser and LED printers rely on one and the same technology used in the first photocopying machines. This process is known as electro-photography and was invented in 1938 and later developed by Xerox and Canon in the late 1980s. The electro-photographic process used in laser printers involves six basic steps:

1. A photosensitive surface (photo-conductor) is uniformly charged with static electricity by a corona discharge.
2. Then the charged photo-conductor is exposed to an optical image through light to discharge it selectively and form a latent, invisible image.
3. The latent image development is done by spreading toner, a fine powder, over the surface which adheres only to the charged areas, thereby making the latent image visible.
4. At the next step an electrostatic field transfers the developed image from the photosensitive surface to the sheet of paper.
5. Then the transferred image is fixed permanently to the paper by fusing the toner with pressure and heat.

6. The final step in the process occurs when all excess toner and electrostatic charges are removed from the photoconductor to make it ready for the next printing cycle.

In operation the laser printer uses a laser beam to produce an image on a drum (Figure 10-7). Because an entire page is transmitted to a drum before the toner is applied, laser printers are sometimes called *page printers*. Figure 10-8 shows the schematic diagram of the laser and page printer and Figure 10-9 the rotating mirror scanning mechanism.

Laser printing is accomplished by first projecting an electric charge onto a revolving drum by a primary electrically charged roller. The drum has a surface of a special plastic or garnet. Electronics drives a system that writes light onto the drum. The light causes the electrostatic charge to leak from the exposed parts of the drum. The light from the laser alters the electrical charge on the drum wherever it strikes. The surface of the drum then passes through a bath of very fine particles of dry plastic powder or toner. The charged parts of the drum electrostatically attract the particles of powder. The drum then deposits the powder onto the sheet of paper. The paper passes through a fuser, which with heat and pressure bonds the plastic powder to the paper.

Each of these steps has numerous technical choices. One of the more interesting choices is that some "laser" printers actually use a linear array of LEDs to write the light on the drum instead of using a laser. The toner is essentially ink and also includes either wax or plastic. The chemical composition of the toner is plastic-based or wax-based so that when the paper passes through the fuser assembly the particles of toner will melt. The fuser can be an infrared oven, a heated roller, or in some very fast expensive printers, a xenon strobe light.

The laser printer relies on the laser beam and scanner assembly to form a latent image on the photo conductor bit by bit. The scanning process is similar to electron-beam scanning used in a CRT monitor. The laser beam modulated by electrical signals from the printer's controller is directed through a collimating lens onto the rotating polygon mirror that reflects the laser beam onto the drum. The laser beam then passes through a scanning lens system which makes some corrections to it and scans the beam onto the photo-conductor on the drum. This complex technology is the major key for insuring high precision in the laser spot at the focal plane. Accurate dot generation at a uniform pitch (spacing) ensures the best printer resolution. Figure 10-9 shows the light path through the laser printer from the laser source to the photoconductor on the drum.

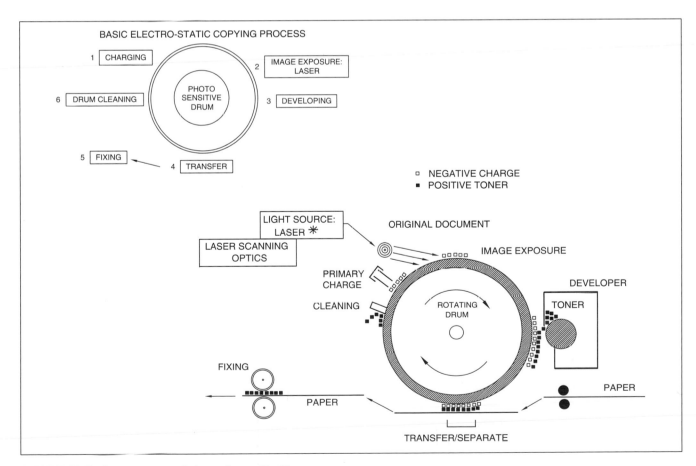

FIGURE 10-7   Laser page printer schematic diagram

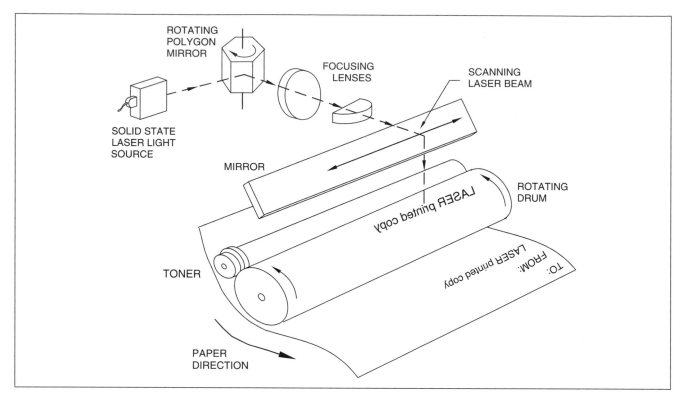

FIGURE 10-8   Laser printer rotating mirror scanning mechanism

A second type of page printer falls under the category of *laser printers* even though it does not use lasers at all. It uses the radiation from a linear array of LEDs to expose the image onto the drum (Figure 10-10). Once the drum is charged, however, the LED printer operates like the laser printer.

The LED printers developed by Okidata and Panasonic use an array of small LEDs instead of using a laser to form the latent image on the drum. In this technology a light source controlled by the printer's CPU illuminates a light-sensitive drum creating an attractive charge on the drum. No mirror scanner is required using this LED technology.

The drum rotates past a toner attracting the toner particles where the drum has been illuminated. The drum rotates the paper to the toner, is transferred, making the image that is fused onto the paper (Figure 10-11).

The LED array consists of thousands of individual digital LED light sources, spanning the width of the image drum directing light through focusing lenses directly onto the drum surface. This methodology can have an advantage over the laser light source system. In the case of the laser, a single light source and a complex system of fixed lenses and mirrors and a rotating mirror deflects the laser beam across the drum as it rotates. Complex timing is used to ensure that the laser produces a linear horizontal track across the drum surface. Careful parallax correction must be employed since the edges of the drum are farther from the laser than the center of the drum. The LED array technology eliminates any possibility of parallax errors or

timing errors since they are arranged across the entire page width and are *fixed*.

The resolution obtained with the laser and solid state LED implementations result in approximately the same resolution although the LED seems to have a slight edge. Laser heads can produce dot sizes of 60 micrometers (μm) whereas LED technology can produce dot sizes as small as 34 μm. Inherently the LED light source should be more reliable than the laser system since it has no moving parts. These LED machines are guaranteed for five full years.

The LED design inherently has a higher speed than the laser design since it has no moving parts. There is a limit to how fast the drum in the laser system can be rotated and still maintain horizontal scanning integrity. In the LED technology there is no scanning or moving parts and therefore it can print faster at higher resolutions than the laser design. As shown in Figure 10-12 the resolution of the LED design at 600 or 1200 dpi remains constant *independent* of the page print speed whereas in the case of the laser design the resolution drops when the print speed is increased. Another advantage of the LED design over the laser is that the LED has a *straight line* paper path that is less susceptible to jams.

One of the chief attributes of these laser printers is resolution. Laser printers can print between 300 and 1200 dpi.

Laser printers produce very high-quality print and are capable of printing an almost unlimited variety of fonts. Most laser printers come with a basic set of fonts called

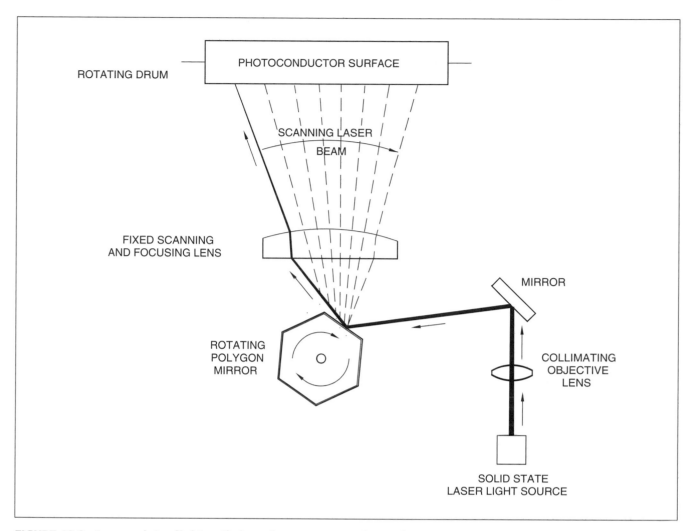

FIGURE 10-9   Laser printer light path from laser source to drum photoconductor

internal or *resident fonts*, but additional fonts can be added in one of two ways:

1. Laser printers have slots to insert font cartridges utilizing read-only memory (ROM). Fonts have been pre-recorded onto these cartridges. The advantage of font cartridges is that none of the printer's memory is used.
2. All laser printers come with a certain amount of RAM that can be expanded upon by using memory boards in the printer's expansion slots. Fonts can then be copied from a disk to the printer's RAM. This is called *down-loading* fonts, and these fonts are often referred to as *soft fonts*, to distinguish them from the *hard fonts* available on font cartridges. The more RAM a printer has, the more fonts that can be downloaded at one time.

Laser printers can print text, graphics, and video images. Significant amounts of memory are required in the printer to print high-resolution graphics and images. For example, to print a full-page graphic/image at 300 dpi requires at least 1 MByte of printer RAM. For a 600 dpi image at least 4 MByte RAM is required.

Laser and LED printers are non-impact type and are therefore very quiet. The speed of laser printers ranges from about 4 to 20 text pages per minute (ppm). If a typical rate of 6 ppm is used, this is equivalent to about 40 characters per second for text printing. Laser printers are controlled through page description languages (PDL) with the two de facto standards for PDLs being:

1. Printer Control Language (PCL) developed by HP
2. PostScript developed by Apple Computer for the Macintosh computer.

PostScript has become the de facto standard for Apple Macintosh printers and for most desktop publishing systems. Most software can print using either of these PDLs. PostScript has some features that PCL lacks. Some printers support both PCL and PostScript.

For video applications, in particular, there is an increased demand for print quality (image resolution, sharpness, and color rendition), and printer manufacturers have devoted considerable amounts of time and money on technology advancements. In particular, they have focused on those that eliminate smear, steps, or

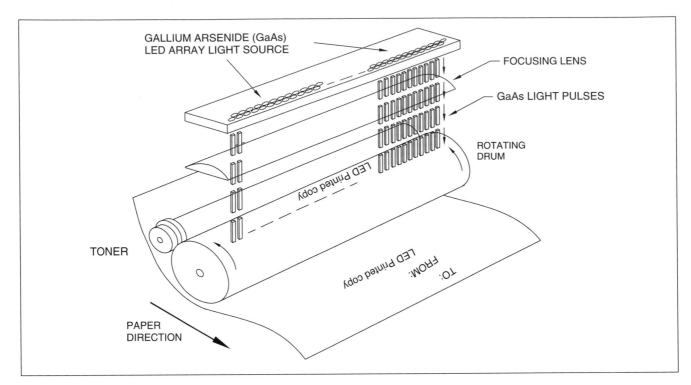

FIGURE 10-10   LED printer schematic diagram with fixed LED page illumination

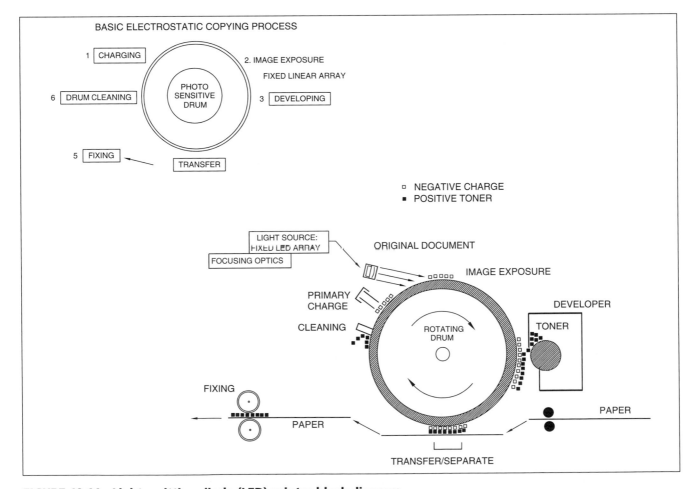

FIGURE 10-11   Light emitting diode (LED) printer block diagram

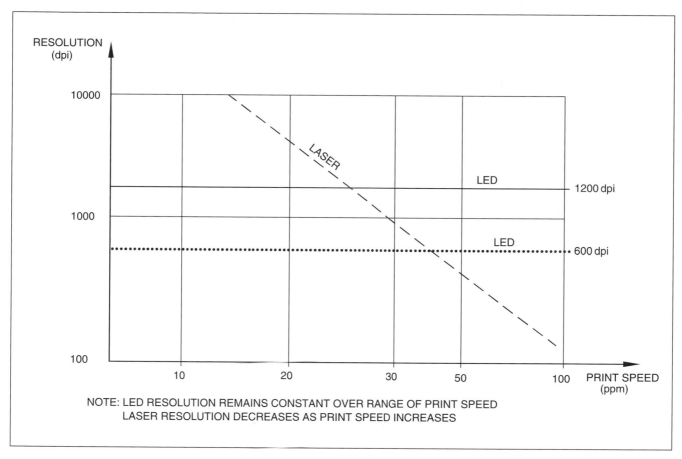

FIGURE 10-12 Resolution vs. printing speed for the LED and laser printers

other jagged edges on straight lines in the video image or graphics. The laser and ink jet technologies both place dots of ink on the paper. In order to smooth out these dots along edges of text, graphics and images, they have implemented technologies to change the *size* and *placement* of the dots to fill in and smooth out the boundaries of letters, and straight lines and curves in the images (Figure 10-13).

In one technology, as many as four different-sized dots are produced and grouped in various combinations along the edges of boundaries to smooth out these images. The result is a crisper better-looking image with sharper edges, smoother curves and none of the jagged edges. The technology changes the size and placement of the dots to fill-in and smooth-out the boundaries.

Both laser and LED printers offer an excellent solution for video image printing to produce high-quality images at high speeds. Table 10.1 compares the laser printer and LED printer specifications.

10.3.4 Dye-Diffusion, Wax-Transfer

The high-resolution thermal laser printer uses an entirely different and more complex principle to produce extremely high resolution continuous-tone laser-printed images. Typical systems have a resolution of 500–600 pixels, have 64 levels of gray scale, and require 60–80 seconds to print out. These printers carry a very high price tag and are normally used for printing still images and therefore have not found their way into the surveillance field.

Thermal wax transfer monochrome and color printers function by adhering a waxed-based ink onto the paper. As the paper and ribbons travel in unison beneath the thermal printer head, the wax-based ink from the transfer ribbon melts onto the paper. When cool, the wax is permanent. This type of thermal printer uses a full size panel of ribbon for each page to be printed regardless of the contents of the page. Monochrome printers have a black panel for each page to be printed, while color printers have three (CMY) or four (CMYK) colored panels for each page. Unlike dye sublimation printers these printers cannot vary the dot intensity, which means that the image must be dithered. These printers are not in widespread use in video security applications.

10.3.5 Film

Hard-copy video images can be printed on black-and-white or color photographic film such as the instant prints developed by Polaroid Corp. The image is first captured

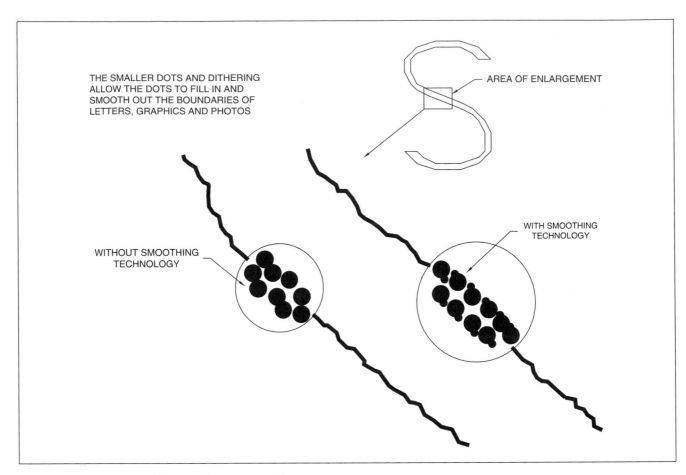

FIGURE 10-13   LED and laser printer smoothing

PRINTER TYPE	LASER PRINTER	LED PRINTER
TECHNOLOGY	(a) ELECTROPHOTOGRAPHY (b) SCANNING LASER BEAM (c) INK TONER IN CARTRIDGE	(a) ELECTROPHOTOGRAPHY (b) LINEAR LED ARRAY (c) INK TONER IN CARTRIDGE
PRINT SPEED— ppm (PAGES/MINUTE)	STANDARD: 4–50 INDUSTRIAL: UP TO 1000	10–26
RESOLUTION— dpi (DOTS/INCH)	300–2400	300–1200, MAINTAINS RESOLUTION AT HIGH SPEEDS
MOVING PARTS	PAPER HANDLING, DRUM, ROTATING MIRROR SCAN WHEEL	PAPER HANDLING, DRUM, (STATIONARY LED ARRAY)
NOISE LEVEL	LOW	VERY QUIET
PRINTER COST	$200–8000	$250–8000
PRINT COST/PAGE	$0.03–0.09 COLOR $0.01–0.03 BLACK/WHITE	$0.03–0.09 COLOR $0.01–0.03 BLACK/WHITE

Table 10-1   Comparison of Laser Printer and LED Printer

in a freeze-frame image storage device. Then the film is exposed and developed with the Polaroid film back. While the resolution and rendition of the image is quite good, Polaroid film is more expensive and more difficult to work with than thermal paper.

10.4 PRINTER COMPARISON

There are several criteria that should be considered by one choosing a video printer. These include resolution, speed, initial cost of equipment, cost of paper, toner or cartridge, and of course the quality of the final printed hard copy.

10.4.1 Resolution and Speed

The thermal printer is in widespread use and can print with a resolution of 250–500 TV lines. This printer is probably the best choice for reproducing monochrome images with reasonable continuous-tone printing.

Monochrome thermal printers provide a fast means— 8 seconds per print—for obtaining a hard-copy printout from any video signal. Operating these printers is relatively inexpensive.

Ink jet printers are capable of producing high-quality print approaching that produced by laser printers. Typically models provide a resolution of 300 dpi but there are models offering higher resolutions.

The laser printer can produce high-quality monochrome images with excellent resolution—300 dpi and halftone (grayscale) rendition. The cost for operating the laser printer depends on a combination of costs: paper usage, toner replacement, drum replacement, and other consumables such as the fuser assembly and transfer assembly. The laser and LED printers can print from a low resolution of 300 dpi to a high resolution of 1200 dpi. By comparison, offset printing usually prints at 1200 or 2400 dpi. Some laser printers achieve higher resolutions using special techniques.

Resolution for thermal dye-diffusion and wax-color video printers is typically 500 dots horizontal, and printout time approximately 80 seconds per print. Since each point (pixel) in a picture or resolution element in the color video image is composed of three separate colors, the actual detail resolution of the image is *one-third* the number of dots, or typically less than 200 TV-line resolution for the printed color image. While this is significantly less than the 500 or 600 TV-line resolution in the monochrome image, the addition of color to the print adds useful information. The print paper roll produces 3- by 4-inch pictures.

10.4.2 Hardware, Ink Cartridge Cost Factors

The thermal printer enjoys popular demand for printing monochrome and color video images because

of its ruggedness, convenience, and reasonable price. Monochrome thermal printers cost from $1100 to $1600. The typical video thermal printer (Figure 10-1) holds a roll of plastic wax-coated thermal paper sufficient to produce one-hundred-and-twenty 3×5-inch video pictures.

There are two main design philosophies in ink jet head design. Each has strengths and weaknesses. Fixed head philosophy uses a built-in print head that is designed to last for the entire life of the printer. Consumable ink cartridge costs are typically lower in this design. If, however, the head is damaged it is usually necessary to replace the entire printer. Epson has traditionally used fixed print heads. In fact, disposable heads have proven to be equally good and are used in the HP and other popular manufacturers' machines.

The disposable head philosophy uses a print head that is part of the replaceable ink head cartridge. Every time the printer runs out of ink the entire cartridge is replaced with a new one. This adds substantially to the cost of consumables but it also means that a damaged or empty print head is only a minor problem and the user can simply buy a new cartridge. HP has traditionally favored the disposable print head as did the Canon in its early models. Canon now uses replaceable print heads in most models that are designed to last the life of the printer, but can be replaced at anytime by the user if they should become clogged or inoperative for some reason. The ink tanks are separate for each ink color. Ink jets print heads can clog, and ink cartridges sometimes cost $30–$40 or more.

To reduce the cost of changing replaceable cartridges, there are companies that sell refilled ink cartridges and also ink kits so that the user can refill the cartridges themselves. These refilled cartridges and kits should be used with caution since the cartridges sometimes tend to get clogged. Some printer manufacturers void their warranties if substitutes to the original cartridges are used.

The HP concept of the disposable ink jet print head was brilliant and original. It resolved the reliability problem by throwing away the print head at the end of its useful life and managed only moderate cost expenditure to fix the printer.

10.4.3 Paper Types

Of the several monochrome and color printout techniques available for the security industry, the monochrome thermal-transfer printers are popular because of the low hardware and paper cost. They need no toner or ink! The printed video image from the monochrome thermal printer is recorded on a Mylar-treated paper, which resists fading from sunlight and physical tearing. Monochrome prints are inexpensive: 5 cents a copy. Color prints cost 60–80 cents a copy, generally less than a photographic film equivalent. Table 10-2 compares some capabilities,

PRINTER TYPE	INK JET–BUBBLE JET	LASER AND LED
TECHNOLOGY	EJECTS INK DROPLETS ONTO PAPER FROM INK CARTRIDGES	ELECTROPHOTOGRAPHY TRANSFERS DRY POWDER (TONER) ONTO PAPER
PRINT SPEED ppm (PAGES/MINUTE)	1–20	4–10
RESOLUTION dpi (DOTS/INCH)	300–1200	300–2400
NOISE LEVEL	LOW	VERY LOW
MOVING PARTS	PAPER HANDLING, MOVING CARTRIDGE	PAPER HANDLING, DRUM, ROTATING SCANNER (LASER)
PRINTER COST	LOW: $100–400	MODERATE: $300–8000 *
PRINT COST/PAGE **	$.02–.05 $.06–.30	$.01–.03 BLACK $.03–.09 COLOR

*HIGH SPEED INDUSTRIAL

**FOR AVERAGE USE, THE INK CARTRIDGE COSTS FOR THE INK JET PRINTER MAY BE MUCH HIGHER THAN FOR THE LASER TONER CARTRIDGE. TOTAL CARTRIDGE COSTS OVER THE LIFE OF THE PRINTER MAY BE SEVERAL TIMES THE PRINTER COST.

Table 10-2   Characteristics and Features of Ink Jet–Bubble Jet and Laser Printers

PRINTER TYPE	TECHNOLOGY	COPYING SPEED PRINTS/SEC.	COMMENTS	RESOLUTION (DOTS/INCH)
THERMAL—MONOCHROME	HEAT BURNS SPECIAL WAXED PAPER TO CAUSE BLACK DOTS TO FORM AN IMAGE. NO TONER OR INK REQUIRED	10–12	MOST POPULAR VIDEO PRINTER CAN FADE WITH AGE	250–600
THERMAL—COLOR	HEAT BURNS SPECIAL 3 COLOR WAXED PAPER TO CAUSE COLORED DOTS TO FORM AN IMAGE. NO TONER OR INK REQUIRED	5–6	POPULAR VIDEO PRINTER	300–350
THERMAL WAX TRANSFER (TWT)	TRANSFERS HEATED DROPLETS OF BLACK AND COLORED WAX ONTO THE PAPER	10–15	BRILLIANT COLORS HIGH RESOLUTION NOT FOR SECURITY (HIGH COST)	500–600
THERMAL DYE SUBLIMATION (TDS)	TRANSFERS INK TO THE PAPER VIA SOLID TO GASEOUS STATE (PHASE CHANGE)	1–2	BRILLIANT COLORS HIGH RESOLUTION NOT FOR SECURITY (HIGH COST)	500–600
INK JET–BUBBLE JET MONOCHROME/COLOR	EJECTS SMALL BLACK, RED, GREEN AND BLUE INK DROPLETS ONTO PAPER FROM AN INK CARTRIDGE	1–20	DOMINATES LOW COST PRINTER MARKET	300–1200
LASER OR LED MONOCHROME	TRANSFERS DRY BLACK POWDER (TONER) TO THE PAPER USING LASER OR LED AND THE ELECTROPHOTOGRAPHY PROCESS	4–10	HIGHEST RESOLUTION MODERATE COST	600–2400
LASER OR LED COLOR	TRANSFERS DRY COLORED POWDERS (TONER) TO THE PAPER USING LASER OR LED AND THE ELECTROPHOTOGRAPHY PROCESS	8–30	COLOR LASER OR LED PRINTERS ARE MOST EXPENSIVE	600–1200

Table 10-3   Characteristics of Video Hard Copy Printers

features, and specifications of the ink jet-bubble jet, laser, and LED printers.

In general, the price of the ink jet printer is significantly lower than that of laser printers. This is primarily because ink jet printers require smaller and simpler mechanical parts than do laser printers. Ink jet printers are especially suitable for portable printers. Color ink jet printers provide an inexpensive solution to print full-color video images and other documents.

Several manufacturers provide models having different resolutions, speeds, and paper sizes. A printer at the low end of the resolution scale has 250 by 250 pixels with 16 shades of gray. This print provides adequate information for many security applications where fine detail is not required. When higher resolution is required, systems having 640 by 640 pixels with 64 levels of gray scale are available. These printers provide a horizontal resolution of 470 TV lines, at a printout speed of 9 seconds per picture. Picture quality from this type system is as good as that which most video camera and lens systems are capable of producing.

Print paper rolls for these systems yield 120–180 pictures per roll with costs per picture ranging from 4 to 10 cents. These pictures represent high-quality monochrome hard copies and are almost equivalent to instant Polaroid photo prints because of the extremely dense pattern of the picture dots and the 64 gray levels. Thermal printers are totally silent, since they are non-impact type and require no ribbons or toners. Large-format printers are also available that produce 8½ by 6-inch monochrome prints.

A high resolution and high speed monochrome video thermal printer with excellent gray-scale rendition is available. The printer uses a direct thermal printing process and has a resolution of 1200 by 1000 pixels, equivalent to 300 dpi. High speed is achieved by using a fast analog to digital signal processor board. The printer is easy to use and paper cost is approximately 25 cents a copy, or about one-half the cost of a film equivalent. A full picture with this high resolution is printed out in 26 seconds; duplicates can be made from the image stored in its memory. Because of its added cost, this printer should be used only when the highest resolution is required and where all the detail obtained from the camera must be recorded on hard copy without any loss in image quality. Table 10-3 compares the characteristics of the various video hard-copy printers.

10.5 SUMMARY

Video security systems rely on hard-copy printout to assist security personnel and law enforcement officials in performing apprehensions of criminals. There is a variety of printers available to capture monochrome or color video images directly from cameras, VCRs or DVRs. These generic printer types include the thermal printer, inkjet or bubble printer, laser or LED printer, and a variety of lesser-used printer types.

In selecting the printer for an application it should first be determined whether a monochrome or color image is required. The resolution required in the printed image and speed of printing the hard copy is also a consideration.

The most commonly used printer is the monochrome thermal printer, which provides low-cost paper and does not need ink cartridges. It produces prints with suitable resolution to match that of most video camera resolutions.

When color is required, the ink jet-bubble jet and laser and LED printers are the most commonly used. If very high resolution is required and speed is not important, the high resolution monochrome laser and color dye-diffusion printers are used.

Chapter 11
Video Switchers

CONTENTS

11.1   Overview
11.2   Background and Evolution
    11.2.1   Small System Switchers
    11.2.2   Midsize Systems
    11.2.3   Analog Matrix Switcher
    11.2.4   Digital Matrix Switcher
    11.2.5   Virtual Matrix Switcher
11.3   Small Analog System Switcher Types
    11.3.1   Manual
    11.3.2   Homing Sequential
    11.3.3   Bridging Sequential
    11.3.4   Looping-Sequential
    11.3.5   Alarming
    11.3.6   Synchronous, Non-Synchronous Video
            Signal
    11.3.7   Switcher Choice
11.4   Matrix Switcher
    11.4.1   Analog Technology
    11.4.2   Matrix Switcher Control Functions
            and Features
    11.4.3   Multiple Locations
    11.4.4   Digital Switcher
11.5   Virtual Matrix Switcher (VMS)
    11.5.1   Evolution
    11.5.2   Technology
    11.5.3   Remote/Multiple Site Monitoring
    11.5.4   Features and Advantages
11.6   Summary

11.1   OVERVIEW

The function of the video switcher, matrix video switcher, and virtual matrix switcher (VMS) in any multiple-camera security system is to connect any camera to any monitor and display the video image in a logical sequence. The switched camera pictures on the monitor can be recorded on a VCR or DVR, printed on a video printer, or transmitted to a remote site. In both small and large installations, the switcher component performs a vital function that simplifies system use and maximizes the information presented to the security operator. In small security systems that have several cameras and one or two monitors, a switcher may not be necessary since all camera scenes can be displayed on several monitors simultaneously. For a medium or large installation (16, 32 cameras, or more), the number of monitors in the control console cannot equal the number of cameras, and a one-to-one, camera-to-monitor correspondence is not practical. Physical space may be limited, and one security guard may not be able to view multiple monitors simultaneously. To view multiple cameras simultaneously on a single monitor, a combiner or splitter, quad or multiplexer is used (Chapters 12, 16).

Analog matrix video switchers cope with the ever-increasing size and complexity of video systems and are used in midsize and large enterprise systems. The essential function of the matrix switcher system is to switch any combination of cameras to any combination of monitors, video recorders, video printers, or transmission channels.

Matrix switchers are based on micro-processor technologies that allow tremendous flexibility in routing and processing the video signals. These switchers come in various forms including compact, self-contained units that control 16 or 32 cameras, and multiple monitors and keyboards. These compact dedicated switchers include such features as text generation and camera identification. Larger enterprise systems having hundreds or thousands of cameras and hundreds of monitors are usually based on a modular construction and rack-mounted equipment. Small and midsize microprocessor controlled switching systems can form the central control center for an integrated security and building management system, combining alarm, access control, fire, and command-and-control functions.

An alternative to the self-contained matrix switcher takes the form of hardware added to a PC system. Some medium-size systems (16–64 cameras) use PC boards installed in a standard PC to effect the video switching. The cables for the cameras, monitors, and any other equipment (multiplexers, quads, etc.) are connected directly to the PC via RS-232 control cables, simplifying installation and reducing system cost. A disadvantage of this configuration is the requirement to purchase and maintain a PC as compared with the dedicated microprocessor-based matrix switcher.

In large systems with hundreds of cameras and monitors or those requiring multiple control consoles at different sites, the approach is to use a PC to control the matrix switcher and other control command functions. The PC is controlled via the microprocessor keyboards connected to the PC using RS-232 or RS-485 protocol. These large systems can connect the images from video cameras to dozens of video monitors, recorders, or printers automatically via the RS-232 communication links. They are software-programmable and can simultaneously switch *multiple* cameras to *multiple* output devices using *salvo* switching techniques. Systems like these are very powerful and have more functions than can be described here.

For these very large systems, the security operator is confronted with the difficulty of remembering the camera number or the site at which it is located, and how to control it. To overcome this problem, a *site plan* monitor is provided having maps of the site programmed into it and overlaid with symbols or icons of the cameras and monitoring locations. With these visual display units (VDU), the operator can select the camera and area of interest on the map. This is accomplished with input from a mouse or with the operator's finger if the monitor has a touch screen. This is the ultimate in system control for analog matrix switcher systems. No knowledge of camera or monitor number is necessary, and operating the system is as simple as touching the site plan touch screen.

In recent years there has been an evolution of the IP-based VMS that can eliminate some of the shortcomings of the large expensive analog matrix switcher. The VMS can digitally multiplex, switch, record, and transmit the camera signals to the control console monitoring equipment and remote locations via LAN, WAN, and wireless LANs (WiFi).

11.2   BACKGROUND AND EVOLUTION

Up until the last few years legacy CCTV surveillance systems have used traditional small switchers, multiplexers, and analog matrix switchers for interconnecting cameras and routing the video signal to monitors, VCRs, video printers, and in large systems to some remote sites via dedicated hardware and cable. These traditional CCTV solutions rely on analog technology and wired cabling to transfer the video images from the analog cameras to the switchers and onto the monitors and video recorders in the console room. These analog systems are characterized by long coaxial video signal and control cable runs, simple analog switchers, or large analog matrix switchers to display and record the camera images. The systems have been acceptable in applications where monitoring and recording was only required at a central location and monitoring console. They prove to be expensive when the requirements are for long distances or when the cameras and console room cross public property or inaccessible locations within a facility.

Large systems with many cameras and monitors have incorporated banks of switchers, multiplexers, and large analog matrix switchers to route the camera signals to the appropriate monitoring equipment. The DVR technology has brought a significant improvement over the analog VCR for recording the video camera images and the ability to distribute them to remote locations, to archive them, and to provide rapid retrieval of video image frames recorded at a particular time.

Within the last few years, traditional video CCTV surveillance technology is converging with PC and networking technology. This convergence has resulted in the evolution of the VMS, using the digital signal from an IP camera and routing the digital signal to the console display or any other remote site via LAN, WAN, and wireless WiFi digital networks. The result is a dramatic improvement in the features and functionality that can be delivered to the security operator and management at an unprecedented price to performance ratio. The digital video cameras, digital video transmission, and computer networking technology is now revolutionizing the analog video security industry. This new digital technology is entirely computer-based and often uses existing IP infrastructure instead of requiring a dedicated video cabling.

11.2.1   Small System Switchers

One-on-one Display.   For a small video surveillance system with perhaps eight cameras, there can be a one-to-one correspondence between camera and monitor. This means that each camera can be displayed on a single individual monitor. In small systems and when the camera-to-monitor distances are short (a few hundred feet), the switcher and the switching controls are one and the same and are located at the console. In installations having larger distances between the cameras and monitor, the switcher has two separate units with the switcher located near the camera sites and the switching controls located near the console monitor.

Increasing the number of cameras makes it difficult for the operator to effectively view all the monitors and take appropriate action when necessary. Increasing the number of cameras requires that the images from more than one camera be displayed on one monitor. Displaying four monitors in a quad configuration or 9, 16, or 32 monitors on a single display reduces the number of monitors required. The sacrifices are that there is a decrease in resolution and the additional requirement that the operator views many camera scenes on a single monitor. See Section 11.3 for small video system switcher types.

11.2.2 Midsize Systems

One-on-one Display vs. Split Screen vs. Sequencing. A midsize system having multiple cameras and monitors offers the designer a choice of displaying all the cameras on the monitor in a one-on-one presentation, or presenting multiple camera images on each monitor. When using one monitor it is impossible for security personnel to observe all camera locations simultaneously. If a camera switcher is sequencing from camera to camera there may be a long time delay before a particular camera is seen again. This can leave a gap in the security function.

11.2.3 Analog Matrix Switcher

Analog matrix switchers route multiple analog video sources to multiple video destinations. They can also route audio signals, controls, and other functions from cameras to monitors and analog and digital recorders. The matrix switcher can route composite video, S-VHS, HDTV, RGB, and other video formats. However, a signal type that is input can only be routed to an output of the same signal type. As an example, a *composite* video input can only go to a *composite* video output. The analog matrix switch is the workhorse of the industry and the most common interconnect device to connect cameras to monitors, etc.

11.2.4 Digital Matrix Switcher

Most cameras, monitors, recorders, and other functional components of analog video systems are now becoming digital in design. The video system designer has been awaiting the arrival of a *digital* solution for the analog matrix switch. The *digital* matrix switch would be a digitized video stream routed to monitors and recorders or other destinations in *digital* form. The truth of the matter is that this scenario of a fully digital matrix switch has not proven effective because the digital matrix switch *just doesn't do enough*. It has also not evolved because of the rapid evolution and acceptance of high-speed digital transmission over LAN and WAN transmission channels, and the rapid use of the Internet.

11.2.5 Virtual Matrix Switcher

Many of the video surveillance components of analog video systems have become digital and the security system designer, integrator, and end user have been awaiting the arrival of a *digital* solution for the analog matrix switch. The digital matrix switch would digitize a video camera stream routed to the monitor, recorder, or other destination in *digital* form. The rapid evolution of high-speed digital transmission over various transmission channels and the rapid use of the Internet have effectively bypassed the necessity for the digital video switch.

The VMS technology has effectively skipped the digital matrix switch and moved directly from the analog matrix switcher to a VMS that is integrated into the overall security system. The VMS provides full analog matrix functionality using a standard matrix keyboard, but takes advantage of the digital video streams and connections available on LAN, WAN, wireless networks (WiFi), and the Internet. Section 11.5 describes the VMS in more detail.

11.3 SMALL ANALOG SYSTEM SWITCHER TYPES

Small to medium video security systems use five basic switcher types: manual, homing, bridging, looping, and alarming. By using one or a combination of these switcher types, cameras at multiple remote sites can be routed to the security console or multiple monitoring locations for direct observation, recording, or printing. Most sequential switchers, whether homing, bridging, looping, or alarming, have a three-position switch for each camera input. When one of these switches is in the up position, it is said to be in the Bypass mode. Any of the camera switches set in this position will cause the switcher to automatically skip the corresponding camera in the sequential switching cycle. The center position of these switches is called Automatic (Auto) mode. Any camera switch in this position will cause the switcher to automatically include the corresponding camera in the normal switching cycle. The down position of these camera switches can have several different functions. Where applicable all camera inputs are automatically electronically terminated in 75 ohms by the switchers. The following sections describe the unique features of each switcher.

11.3.1 Manual

The simplest video switcher is the *manual* switcher, where the console operator manually chooses one camera from a number of cameras and displays the video image on a single video monitor with front panel pushbutton switches, activated manually by the operator to connect the individual camera to the monitor. The manual passive switcher uses a simple switch for contact closure, whereas the manual active switcher uses an electronic switch. Manual switchers are available to switch from 4 to 32 video cameras. Figure 11-1 shows the two types available: manual passive and manual active.

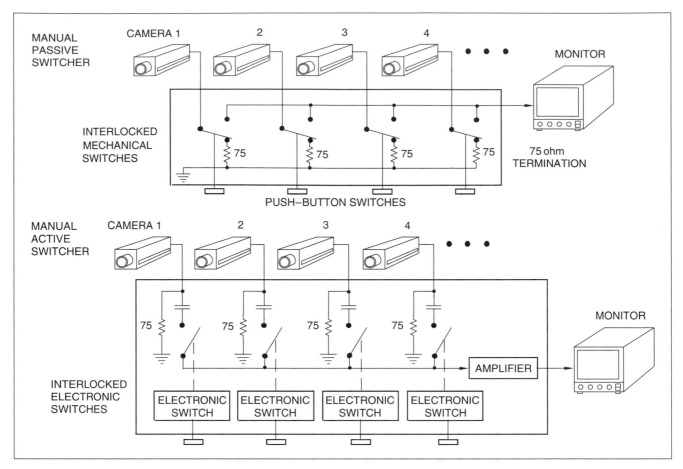

FIGURE 11-1   Manual passive and manual active switchers

11.3.2   Homing Sequential

The homing sequential switcher allows the continuous viewing of any normally sequenced video camera (Figure 11-2). The camera signal is connected to a single monitor. This switcher has a three-position switch for each camera: Automatic, Homing, and Bypass. In the Automatic position, the switcher automatically selects and switches the video signal from one camera after another to the monitor according to the sequence set by the security operator. The length of time each camera picture is presented on the monitor (dwell time) can be changed by the operator. The homing sequential switcher automatically sequences from one camera to the next, assuming the cameras have not been bypassed. When the specific camera control switch is pressed to the Home position, that camera is continuously displayed on the single monitor and the switching sequence stops.

Functionally the three-position front-panel switches on the homing sequential switcher provide three separate camera display functions: automatic sequencing, bypass, and homing (select). When a switch is set to Bypass, that particular camera is not displayed. When the switch is set to Homing, that camera picture is presented continuously on the monitor and in essence overrides the automatic sequencing function. This permits continuous observation of any particular camera at the operator's command. In the Automatic position, all cameras are sequenced onto the monitor, one at a time.

11.3.3   Bridging Sequential

The bridging sequential switcher operates like the homing sequential switcher but has the additional feature that two monitors can display the video cameras. Figure 11-3 shows the block diagram for a bridging sequential switcher. Monitor 1 always displays the cameras selected for sequential viewing. Monitor 2 displays only the camera manually selected for detailed viewing. For instance, pressing the switch for camera 1 to the down position puts the picture on the second or bridged monitor for detailed viewing, while the sequence of all cameras not bypassed continues on the first monitor. Monitor 1 sees the switched sequence of cameras while monitor 2 sees a selected camera continuously.

The first monitor (the sequential monitor) functions as a homing sequential switcher. The bridging monitor displays whatever camera is manually selected. This allows the operator to maintain a system overview while viewing in detail the camera covering a scene of particular interest.

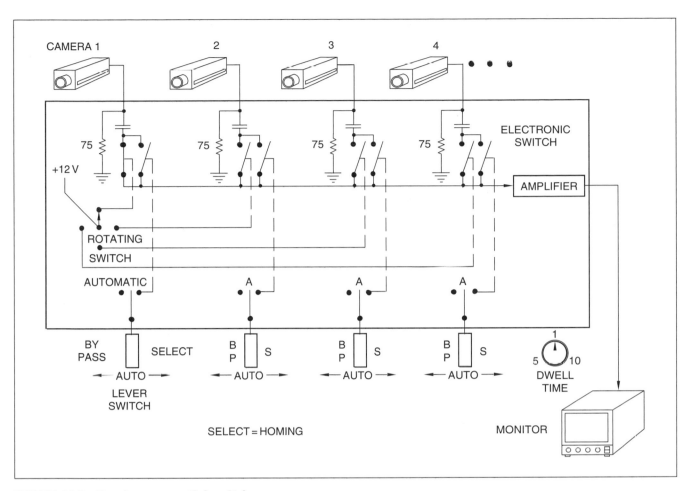

FIGURE 11-2   Homing sequential switcher

11.3.4 Looping-Sequential

Homing Sequential. The looping-homing sequential switcher operates like the homing sequential switcher, with the additional feature that all camera inputs can be brought out to a second switcher or other device at another location (Figure 11-4). The switcher has the ability to drive a second switcher, monitors, recorders, and transmission devices for remote transmission, thereby providing video images at multiple locations for display or recording. Unlike other switchers, the looping-homing sequential switcher camera inputs are not terminated, thereby allowing multiple devices to be connected to the switcher output. For proper operation, one of these devices, generally the last device in the line, is terminated in a 75-ohm impedance.

Bridging Sequential. The looping-bridging sequential switcher operates in the same way as the bridging sequential switcher except that the looping feature is added. As with the looping homing sequential switcher, the camera inputs are not terminated in the switcher. Figure 11-5 shows the block diagram for looping-bridging sequential systems. A looping switcher provides the ability to establish two independently controlled locations. Each station may select any camera for viewing without interfering with the operation of the other station.

Remote Sequential. The use of the manual, homing, bridging, looping, and alarm versions of sequential switchers just described assumes that the distance between the camera location and the monitor (control console) location is relatively short. In many installations this is not the case and the cost becomes prohibitive to provide separate video coaxial cables from each camera to the distant monitor location. Remote sequential switchers overcome this problem. The remote sequential switcher consists of two parts: a control unit and a switching unit. They are available in all of the aforementioned versions to provide complete system design flexibility. Both units are connected by means of multi-conductor cables, fiber-optics, a multiplexed frequency shift key (FSK), or RS-232 communications system (Figure 11-6).

The control unit is located near the monitor, and the switcher unit is located closest to the central location of all the cameras. The physical separation of the switching and control functions avoids the use of individual camera coaxial cables to the control console. Each switcher requires

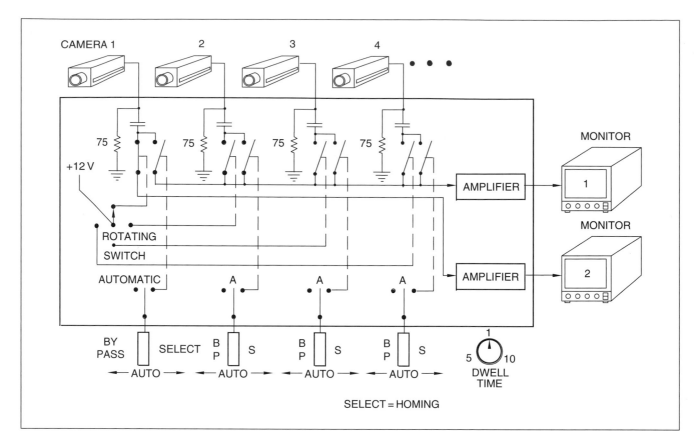

FIGURE 11-3   Bridging sequential switcher

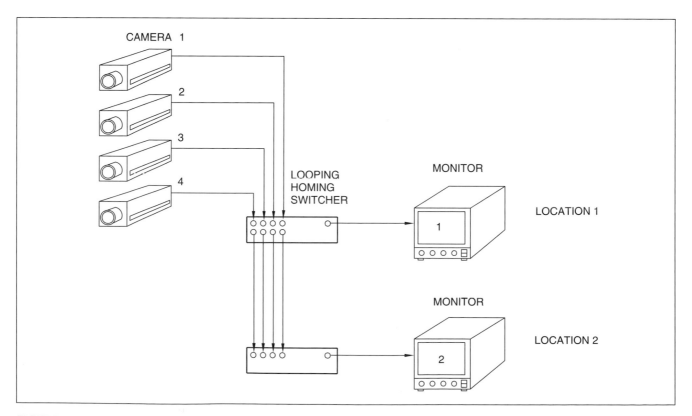

FIGURE 11-4   Looping homing sequential switcher

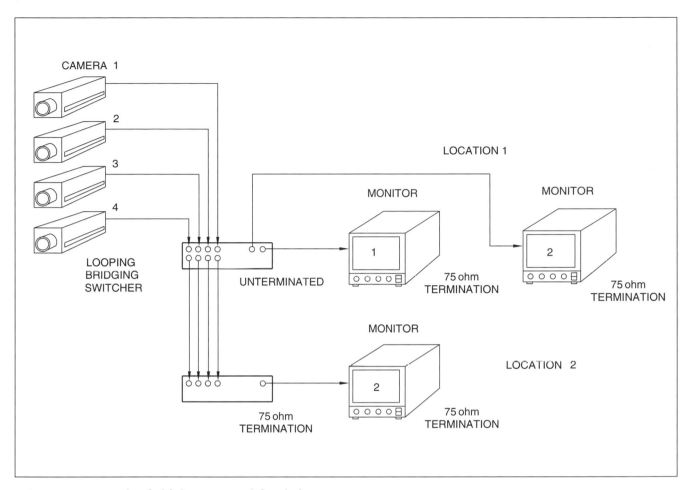

FIGURE 11-5   Looping bridging sequential switcher

only one or two coaxial cables for monitor input. The remote bridging sequential switcher requires two output coaxial cables.

11.3.5 Alarming

An alarming switcher automatically displays a camera image on to a monitor and/or starts a recorder each time it is activated by a camera VMD or other alarm input (Figure 11-7). These switchers are available in homing, bridging, looping-homing, and looping-bridging configurations. When an alarm input signal is received, a corresponding output signal is generated and transmitted to a monitor, recorder, or printer.

The homing, bridging, and remote sequential switchers can be provided with an alarm feature. In the event of an external alarm caused by motion in the video picture and detected by a VMD, an alarm switch closure caused by any type of sensor input, simple switch closure, IR source, or pressure transducer, the alarmed camera will automatically override the pre-selected video on the monitor or be automatically displayed on the sec-

ond monitor. When a bridging type switcher is used, the automatic homing of the alarmed camera overrides any manually bridged display on the second monitor. The sequence of all cameras not bypassed continues on the first monitor.

Simultaneously with this switching, an alarm contact within the switcher closes to operate a recorder, video printer, or any other alarm-indicating equipment. Automatic alarm-programmed switchers are especially suitable for applications where monitors are occasionally unmanned and recorders used to record abnormal events. They are also particularly useful during off hours or over weekends when real-time or TL recorders are used to monitor multiple cameras.

The output monitoring device can be a bell, light, or other signaling unit, which would notify a security guard to dispatch a guard to the scene or alert a guard at the scene. Even if there are multiple monitors affording the opportunity to observe all locations, the use of alarming switchers puts attention in areas where guard action is really required. The activation of the alarm signals a significant occurrence within the field of view covered by a particular camera.

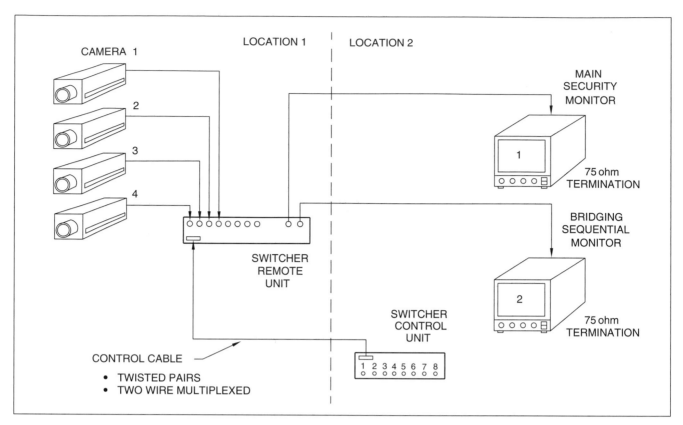

FIGURE 11-6   Remote homing sequential switcher

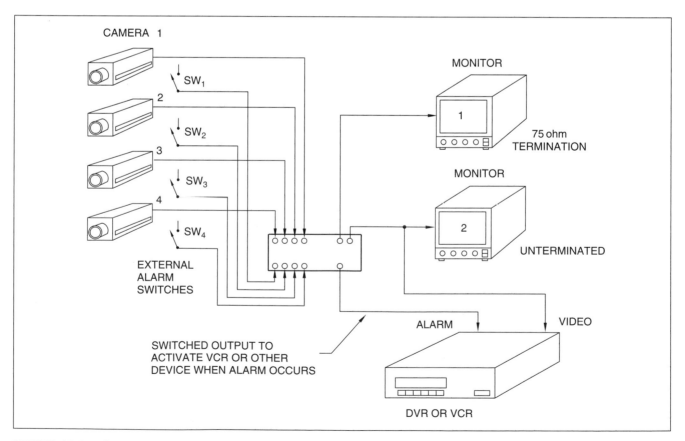

FIGURE 11-7   Alarming bridging sequential switcher

11.3.6 Synchronous, Non-Synchronous Video Signal

There are two types of video signals that are switched: synchronous and non-synchronous. Synchronous signals lend themselves to methods of switching where controlled transition maintains a degree of signal continuity, and provides a clean, noise-free video picture during switching. Non-synchronous signals involve the inherent discontinuity of timing pulses that cannot be corrected by special switching methods, and show up as noise disturbances in the picture. Picture noise in the video signal takes the form of streaks, a momentary black screen, or other picture irregularities. When switching composite video signals, a break may occur during the synchronizing time and the synchronization signal may be completely lost. This results in picture rolling or tearing when the picture from the next camera is displayed on the monitor. The solution to ensure clean video camera switching is vertical-interval switching. With this method, the switching is allowed to occur only during the vertical interval in the video signal between picture frames (Figure 11-8) while no picture

information is being transmitted. Since no visible monitor picture is displayed during the vertical-interval switching time, switching during this period does not cause picture interruption or deterioration. This technique permits switching from one camera to the next with no noise or interruption of intelligence.

To understand vertical-interval switching, refer to Figure 11-9. The camera video signal is generated in the camera sensor. The horizontal camera clocking signal scans from left to right and reads out the video image signal representing the light image on the sensor. When the clocking signal reaches the right side of the sensor, it returns to the left side and begins another scan. During the return time in the analog system, the clocking signal is addressed down to rows of sensor pixels. After it completes $262\frac{1}{2}$ scans (one-half of the full frame), the clocking signal reaches the bottom of the sensor and returns to the top. The clocking signal then scans the alternate pixel rows and after completing the second scan the full sensor has been read out. The return time from the end of the last horizontal scan to the beginning of the first horizontal scan is referred to as the *vertical blanking interval*, since during this

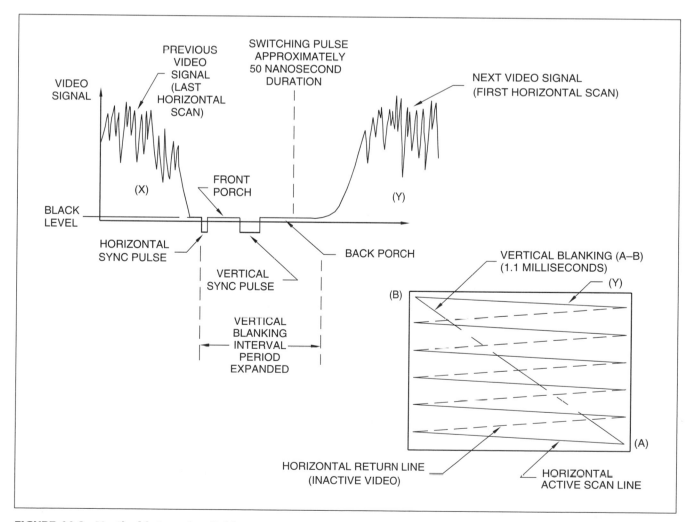

FIGURE 11-8   Vertical interval switching

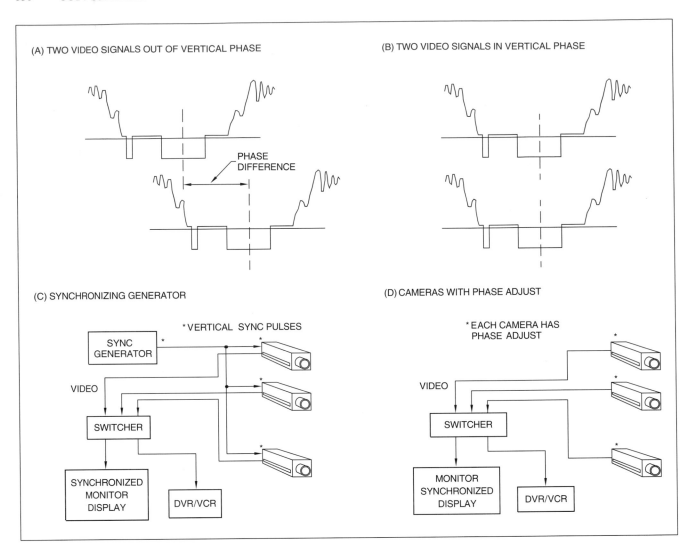

FIGURE 11-9 Sequential switching synchronization

time no video signal is generated. In summary, the picture information occurs during the left-to-right scanning and the vertical blanking in-between scans.

In the typical video surveillance application the cameras will not be synchronized. While they may have waveforms or signals like Figure 11-9a, the time relationship between cameras is not synchronized or in phase.

Since the synchronization pulses from each camera occur at different times, when the switcher switches from one camera signal to the next, a noticeably scrambled or distorted non-synchronized image occurs as the monitor tries to adjust to the synchronization pulses of the new signal. A temporarily distorted picture might be tolerable in some simple direct-viewing applications, but in situations where there are multiple cameras or the information is recorded, the result is unsatisfactory. Since VCR and DVR use the camera synchronizing pulses to synchronize the machines, it takes many frames of video for them to synchronize to the new camera signal. During this interval, noise or other artifacts are generated each time the

switcher is switched. The out-of-phase signals shown in Figure 11-9a are correctable by at least two methods.

One technique for producing in-phase signals is to install a synchronizing generator that provides a synchronizing signal to the cameras and ensures that they are all in the same phase, operating at the same frequency, and synchronized (Figure 11-9b). As an alternative, some cameras can be adjusted so that the phase is the same for each camera. Phasing each camera to be the same does not produce a clean switchover, however. Even though the signals may be in phase, if the switching occurs during the video portion of the signal, there are visible transient effects such as spikes and flashes on the monitor or recorder image. This problem is eliminated by designing the switcher to switch during the vertical interval (Figure 11-8), and hence the name vertical-interval switching.

In operation, the switcher circuitry detects the vertical interval in the signal and delays the actual switchover from one camera to the next, to the time when vertical blanking is occurring. By using this method no transient effects are visible on the monitor or in the recorded image. The vertical-interval switching technique may not be important in simple systems, but is extremely important in medium to large systems, and in any system using a video recorder.

In summary, the quality of switching, or how smoothly (clear, noiseless picture) the monitor picture from a camera 1 can be switched to camera 2, and so on, is influenced by two related factors: (1) the type of signals to be switched—synchronous or non-synchronous; and (2) the switching action itself—the time within the video signal in which the switchover occurs.

11.3.7 Switcher Choice

The following summary suggests which switcher to use in small system video applications:

- **Passive Switcher.** The manual switcher is the simplest and can switch 4, 8, 16, or 32 cameras depending on model, and display any one of them on a single monitor. It is available in either passive or active type. In a simple application, any one of the input cameras can be displayed on a single monitor, one at a time, through manual switching by the security guard.
- **Sequential Switcher.** The sequential switcher is used when it is necessary to switch automatically from camera to camera so that the guard can observe all camera scenes sequentially. As in the manual active switcher, the electronic circuitry provides fast, clean switching with no transients on the screen, and is available with camera dwell times of 1 to 50 or 60 seconds depending on the adjustment made by the operator.
- **Homing Sequential Switcher.** The homing sequential switcher has the additional feature of permitting the operator to stop and look at one particular camera picture continuously or sequentially and display all the camera pictures with a dwell time set by the operator. This system permits the operator to continuously scan through all the cameras and simultaneously pick out one camera and view it continuously. In the sequential mode, the dwell time (length of time any particular camera is viewed) is independently adjustable for each camera. This provides the operator with the flexibility to view different camera scenes for different periods of time. The homing sequential switcher provides the operator with three options and adjustments: (1) automatic switching, (2) timing, and (3) bypass control.
- **Bridging Sequential Switcher.** The bridging sequential switcher has two separate outputs for two monitors. One output is for the programmed sequence of cameras; the second is for the continuous display of a single camera. Unlike the homing sequential switcher, the bridging sequential switcher provides this constant viewing of a selected input without giving up the overview of

all the camera scenes provided by the sequential program. With the bridging sequential switcher, if the operator wants to observe a particular camera continuously, the operator moves the switch to Select, thereby displaying that camera picture on the monitor continuously while simultaneously the other monitor continues to display the sequentially switched camera sequence, including the camera that is displayed on the second monitor continuously.

11.4 MATRIX SWITCHER

11.4.1 Analog Technology

Microprocessors, microcomputers, and massive memory solid-state RAM and magnetic hard drives have revolutionized the video security industry. When a security system has many cameras and monitors and one or more security control consoles in multiple locations, it becomes more efficient to use a configurable microprocessor-controlled video switching and control system called the *matrix switcher* (Figure 11-10).

A matrix switcher is a means for selecting an input source such as video, audio, or control signals and connecting them to one or more outputs. A video matrix switcher is an electronic device that accepts and distributes video signals selected from multiple inputs to multiple outputs.

Many manufacturers produce systems that can switch hundreds (or thousands) of cameras onto hundreds of monitors and recorders. These systems are built in modular form with removable PC boards and rack-mounted modules, permitting the user to begin with a basic system and expand when necessary. The removable modules and plug-in units are divided into several sub-chassis or modules to provide online serviceability and to reduce or eliminate system downtime. A disadvantage of these systems is that expansion is in multiples of 8, 16, and 32, so that if only one or a few new cameras are planned, only the addition of these larger multiple of cameras is possible.

These switchers have:

- Keyboard and joystick desktop console
- Rack-mounted card cage chassis housing the multiple sub-modules for the switching and control functions
- Remote modules located near the cameras for driving the camera, lens, and pan/tilt hardware, as well as for communicating the information to the control unit
- Power supply.

The initial design of any analog matrix video switching system should begin with a detail schematic diagram of the proposed layout showing camera, control locations, and any other accessory equipment. In addition, a site plan diagram should show the distances between equipments and cable routes since many equipments are distance-sensitive.

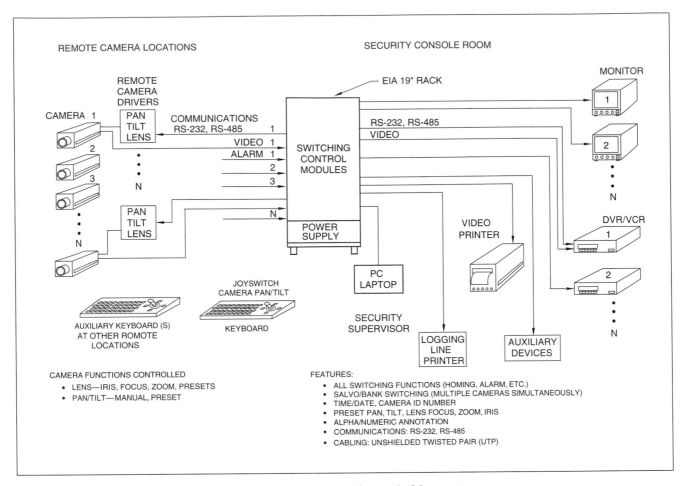

FIGURE 11-10   Configurable microprocessor controlled video switching system

The analog matrix control unit contains the system software and microprocessor hardware. In some systems, customized switching programs are included in the hardware using electrically programmable memories (EPROM). These solid-state memory devices allow storage of switching instructions to be used at a later time when automatic sequencing is desired. Systems have alpha-numeric character generators for camera name and location information or other pertinent data. Matrix switchers have text annotation card providing each video input with time, date, a three-digit camera ID number, and a multiple-line user-programmable alpha-numeric message display.

Medium- to large-size matrix systems use RS-232, RS-422 or RS-485 transmission protocols for controlling camera functions and other output devices. For systems having up to about 200 cameras and 40 monitors, a single microprocessor-controlled keyboard has sufficient processing power to operate the system effectively. One or two slave keyboards may also be added if there is a requirement for more than one person to control the system. Generally, these large video control switching functions are kept separate from any other control functions or other parts of the security systems such as alarm, access control, fire, and safety.

Communication from the console to the remote control camera module is via RS-232 or RS-485 communication protocol. Distances between the control console and remote console can be 1000–5000 feet, with the data signal cable a single twisted-pair, 22-AWG, shielded wire. Most equipment is housed in 5 to 7-inch-high EIA 19-inch rack-mounted modules, thereby removing most of the electronics from the desktop area except for the keyboard. Some systems have the ability to connect several keyboards to the same control system, thereby permitting control of the system from several locations.

All basic microprocessor-controlled systems have the capability for manual, homing, looping, sequential, auto alarming, bridging, and remote switching functions. A unique feature called *salvo* switching allows the operator to switch a selected bank of cameras into a bank of monitors as a synchronized group with all of the monitors switched together in step. The unique salvo switching feature allows the operator to view all scenes in one general area, such as a single floor in a building, before switching to the next floor. This feature can significantly increase the monitoring efficiency of the security guard, since it automatically switches a logical array of cameras.

These systems can provide the same control over alarm functions as over the video network functions. The alarms are constantly monitored by the control console. If one or more of the alarms is activated, the system automatically switches in the camera nearest the alarm and displays its video scene on the appropriate monitor. The types of alarm sensors accommodated include switches, infrared sensors (PIR), and VMDs. Alarm signals can be monitored via an audible tone alert or visual indicator. Real-time images can be recorded automatically by having the recorder switch from TL to real-time recording mode. The operator has the ability to bypass or restore cameras and alarms at will. Individual camera dwell times and sequencing times can be set by the operator on all cameras.

In large systems, the camera, monitor, recorder, and other system functions and hardware are programmed into the PC so that the system can be customized to suit almost any specific security application. System passwords are programmed and lockout tables used to limit access of unauthorized personnel. In addition to the operational switching sequences normally entered from the PC keyboard, complex switching sequences can be programmed off-line using the PC and then downloaded to the microprocessor control system. Examples of such complex switching include pan/tilt presets for camera pointing position, and lens iris, zoom focal length, and focus settings.

These functions are accomplished via receiving modules located at the camera sites and the RS-232 communications. This function is accomplished: (1) by the operator selecting a specific camera and preset number or (2) automatically if the system is preprogrammed, so that when an alarm occurs at a location in the scene, the camera automatically goes to the preset condition. Simultaneously, a recorder is activated into real-time mode and records the activity at the designated preset camera position.

Figure 11-11 illustrates a complete matrix switching system used in a large security application having hundreds of cameras and dozens of monitors, VCRs, DVRs, and printers.

All cameras, lenses, pan/tilt platforms, monitors, recorders, and printers are controlled, monitored, and switched via the central matrix switcher. The switcher communicates control functions to the hardware via RS-232 or RS-485 protocol or time-multiplexed signals. Video signals from the cameras are transmitted from the remote locations via individual coaxial, two-wire, fiber-optic, or wireless channels. The matrix switcher has a separate video input connector for each camera and a separate output connector for each monitor, recorder, or printer device. To bring the matrix switcher and camera and monitoring equipment online, it must first be "configured" or programmed

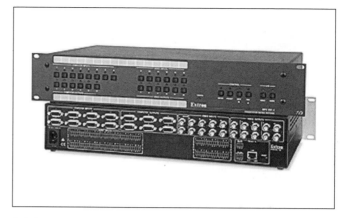

FIGURE 11-11 Microcomputer video switching systems

according to manufacturer instructions, the hardware connected to it, and the required functioning of the system. This can take hours or days to accomplish and requires a detailed plan with methodical procedures. Figure 11-12 shows a block diagram of a typical video matrix switcher used in a large security installation.

11.4.2 Matrix Switcher Control Functions and Features

Matrix switchers are supplied with many different control functions and features. Some of these user-defined and fixed controls and features are listed below:

- On-Screen Display: Monitors can display alpha-numeric characters that can be dynamically changed to show camera information such as video input number and title.
- Auto or Manual Sequencing: Camera tours can be programmed for any video output. The security operator may define a dwell time for any video input to create a custom tour.
- Alarm Switching: Alarm inputs can be routed from any input or group of inputs to any video output from a graphical user interface (GUI) or PC.
- System Priority: Keyboard users can be assigned different levels of security for the control of camera sites. These different levels of access can be granted based on need to know.
- Camera Numbers: Camera IP numbers and names may be assigned to cameras in specific areas around in the facility to better identify camera locations.
- Monitor Numbers: Monitor numbers may be assigned to monitors in different console rooms at a facility or facilities to identify monitor locations.
- Salvo Switching: Banks of cameras may be switched to a bank of monitors with one command.

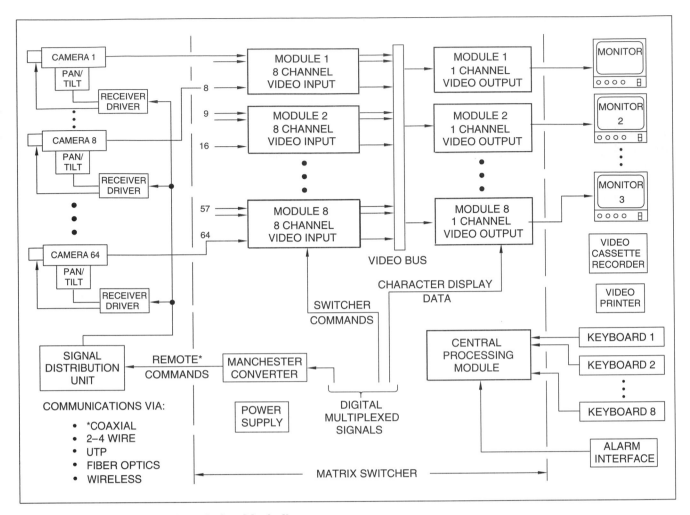

FIGURE 11-12   **Video matrix switcher block diagram**

- Partitioning: Password-protected user accounts can be set up with specific access to cameras, sequence tables, multiplexer tables, and salvo tables.
- Camera and platform pan, tilt, zoom (PTZ) Control
- Hardware support for RS-232, RS-422, and RS-485.

Some important capabilities and restrictions a video matrix switcher system should have are:

- Operator should have passwords that allow access to the system.
- The system should have the capability to limit the number of system controllers (keyboards, etc.) that a given operator can log onto.
- The system should have the capability to limit the number of cameras that can be selected by any given operator.
- The system should have the ability to limit the cameras that can be selected or controlled from any operator control location.
- The system should have the ability to limit the monitors that can be viewed from any operator control location.
- The system should have the ability to limit the cameras that can be shown on any particular monitor.

When given access to the system, the operator should be able to form the following basic functions:

- Switch video signals to the monitors
- Operate the camera functions such as pan, tilt, zoom, and focus
- Activate preprogrammed group presets (set groups of cameras to previously selected positions)
- Activate previously established camera tour sequences
- Acknowledge and reset alarms
- Activate auxiliary contacts
- Access camera-specific features by camera menu.

Selected operators should have the ability to program automated sequences as described below:

- Group presets: Ability to set up camera preset positions, including camera to monitor selections.
- Tour sequences: Preprogrammed camera display sequences in both forward and backward direction. Each step of the sequence consists of the camera number, dwell time, camera position preset, and auxiliary controlled state.

- Group tour sequences: Multiple camera group presets may be linked together with a dwell time.

The matrix switcher can control many other video equipments such as multiplexers, VCRs, DVRs, quads, motion detectors, and video transmission systems using the RS-232 or other control signals. These RS-232 ports connected to the matrix switcher controller generate the commands and appropriate protocols to operate different functions generated from the keys on the keyboard.

11.4.3 Multiple Locations

Video security systems are often required for large buildings with many floors with separate guard consoles located away from the main building site or in widely separated sites.

In large systems with 200 cameras, 40 monitors, or requiring more than two control consoles at different sites, the general approach is to use a PC to control the matrix switcher and other control command functions. The PC is controlled via the microprocessor keyboard connected to the PC using RS-232 or RS-485 protocol. Systems like these are very powerful and have more functions than can be described here. For these large systems, the operator is confronted with the difficulty of remembering the number of the camera, the site at which it is located, and how to control it. To overcome this problem, a site plan monitor is provided that has maps of the site programmed into it and overlaid with symbols or icons of the cameras and monitoring locations. With these VDUs the operator simply selects the area of interest on the map and then selects the camera to be used. This can be accomplished with input from a mouse or with a finger if the monitor has a touch screen. This is the ultimate in system control for analog matrix switcher systems. No knowledge of camera, monitor, or monitor numbers is necessary, and operating the system is as simple as touching the screen.

11.4.4 Digital Switcher

Most of the functional components in legacy analog video systems are now becoming digitally networked. The video security industry has been awaiting the arrival of a digital solution for the analog matrix switch. A digital matrix switch would *digitize* a video signal and route the video stream to the monitor, recorder, or other destination in *digital* form. The truth of the matter is that this scenario of a fully digital matrix switch has not proven effective because it *just doesn't do enough*. It has also not evolved because of the rapid evolution of high-speed digital transmission over various transmission channels and the rapid use of the Internet. The technology is effectively skipping the digital matrix switch. Switching systems are moving

directly from the analog matrix switch to the VMS that is integrated into the overall security system.

11.5 VIRTUAL MATRIX SWITCHER (VMS)

11.5.1 Evolution

The VMS provides full analog matrix functionality using a standard matrix keyboard, but takes advantage of the digital video streams and connections available on LAN, WAN, WiFi, and the Internet. The VMS lays a foundation to integrate and enable the combination of three essential security technologies: the DVR, the multiplexer, and the matrix switch.

Matrix switching has evolved from: (1) first-generation video system using a matrix switch, multiplexer and switches, (2) second-generation matrix switch with DVRs connected to the intranet or Internet network, (3) local matrix switching connected to an Ethernet, LAN/TCP/IP switching network, (4) to a true network-based system using a VMS and all Web-based cameras connected to an Ethernet, LAN/TCP/IP switching network with remote access from any location. These four switching systems are shown in Figure 11-13.

Until recently, traditional analog video matrix systems have been the dominant method for routing video signals (Figure 11-14). At the heart of these systems is an analog cross-point matrix switcher that allows any camera input to be viewed on any monitor output. The switchers are usually connected to text generators used to annotate time, date, camera ID, and name information on the displayed video signal. These digital matrix switchers are used with a keyboard and GUI and other devices to control and provide full-featured surveillance functionality.

Legacy analog video systems have some disadvantages in that the video signals are susceptible to external interference from EMI or RFI noise sources. Coax cables carrying video signals can only be run over distances up to 1000 feet without using optical-fiber or unshielded twisted-pair (UTP) wiring.

Digital networks, on the other hand, deliver significant advantages over analog transmission methods. These include improved signal integrity over long distances and compatibility with off-the-shelf IT hardware. These networks allow video surveillance, access control, alarm, and other functions to be successfully routed through LAN, WAN and Internet networks. The network routing of video over these channels is functionally equivalent to the role of the analog cross-point matrix switcher in the legacy matrix system, but is instead distributed throughout the network structure in digital form. In this digital domain, the network replaces the centralized hardware switcher and coaxial cables in the matrix system. Only the keyboards, controller, and text overlays are left intact to preserve the user experience of the legacy matrix system

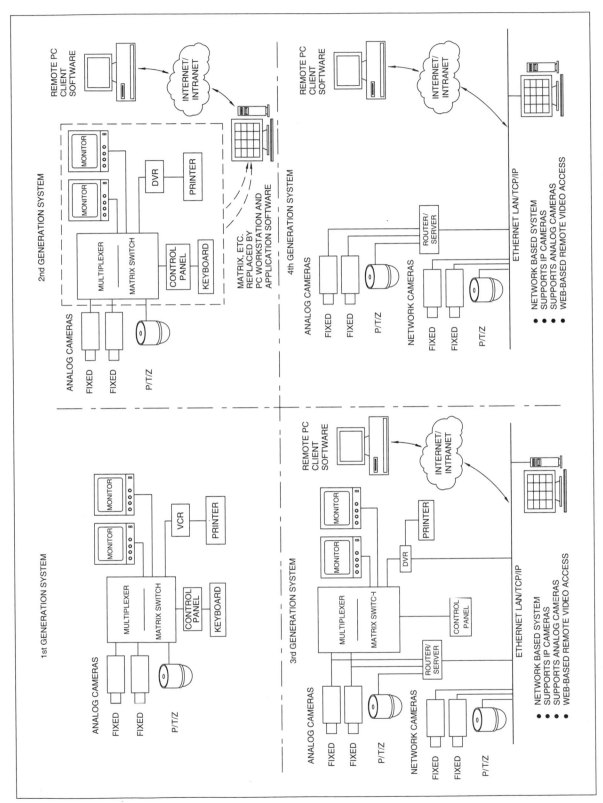

FIGURE 11-13 Evolution of the matrix switcher to the virtual matrix switch

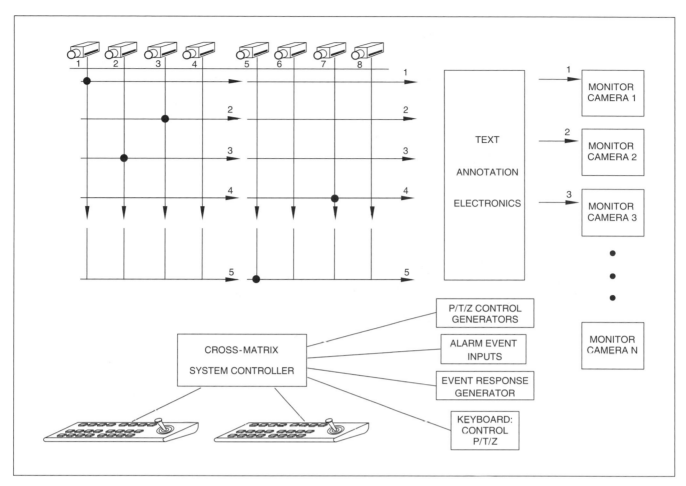

FIGURE 11-14   Traditional analog video cross-matrix switch

while still delivering the powerful functionality of a full-featured matrix switch. For all intents and purposes, the network represents a cross-point matrix and is in fact a VMS—a *virtual* video cross-point matrix.

11.5.2 Technology

The first step in realizing the *virtual video matrix* is to digitize the video signal for transmission over the network using a video IP encoder for each analog camera. Figure 11-15 shows the virtual video matrix in which the video signal has been digitized for transmission over the network using a video encoder for each camera.

Internet Protocol cameras already have these encoders built into them specifically to communicate over these networks. The best encoders are designed to supply high-efficiency digital MPEG video streams. Connections for the video and PTZ control signals from each camera are made to the encoder using standard coaxial serial data wiring. These encoders also have inputs to support alarm sensor contacts and outputs to control relays or other alarm annunciation devices. Two-way audio is also available as an option.

The next step is to connect the encoder to the nearest network via a Cat-5 or Cat-3 cable. Once video signals are present on the network, there are a number of important security applications that are possible.

Several advantages of VMS technology are realized in any midsize or enterprise security system that is already using computer hardware. There is no need to purchase and install the analog matrix switcher. The requirement and expense for installing coaxial cables or other new wiring throughout a facility is eliminated. The VMS system allows the user to leverage the computer, monitor, and network that *already exists* at the facility. Additionally, the hardware is generic so that the end user maintains flexibility and cost control over any new critical hardware decisions.

All analog matrix switch systems have costly and cumbersome scaling limitations. As an example, to add one more monitor to a 32 monitor system requires the addition of shelves of matrix switching equipment, since the systems are based on multiples of 8, 16, and 32 cameras and monitors. This is not true of an integrated software-based VMS system. Only additional user-licenses and encoders or IP cameras in the *exact increment* desired from as small as one to any number of cameras or monitors are needed.

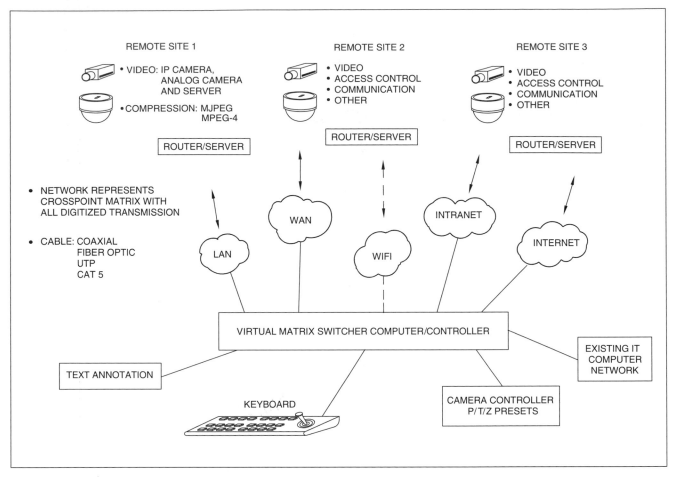

FIGURE 11-15   Virtual video matrix for network transmission and control

11.5.3 Remote/Multiple Site Monitoring

Enterprise-level systems require customized installations of cable and hardware entailing significant costs and wiring needed to bring analog signals back to the control console, not to mention the distance limitations on these cables. VMS technology eliminates these costly and time-consuming demands. If the user needs to move and relocate to a new facility, the cost and miles of wasted coaxial cable represents a major consideration. VMS technology provides the flexibility to meet these demands with minimum cost and time. Upgrading from an analog to VMS does not extend the availability of video information. However, when either the analog or a digital matrix system is integrated into a networked video system, the VMS system provides wide area connectivity, and video data becomes available *anywhere*. The VMS technology allows organizations to fully leverage their security investment. With the level of access and functionality provided by the VMS system: (1) human resources now have a visitor monitoring system, (2) operations have the ability to monitor traffic in the lobby or loading dock areas or elsewhere, (3) retail operations can prevent overloading at cash register lines and can monitor cashiers, and (4) marketing per-

sonnel can remotely monitor the level of interest shown at product displays in stores. Many other applications can be cited.

11.5.4 Features and Advantages

Analog video systems require a dedicated wiring and cabling for each camera. Digital systems using VMS technology require only Cat-3, Cat-5 cables or digital wireless transmission. The VMS with built-in DVR capability can record video images without any degradation loss, support multiple playback, re-recording, and transmission, and can distribute the video images to multiple locations. The VMS represents a centralized control and recording ability allowing local monitoring and remote multiple site viewing. The video camera generates a digital signal using digital signal processing (DSP) in the camera and produces a digital signal at the output. It transmits the digital video signal over the LAN, WAN, or wireless network while retaining complete integrity and image quality. The VMS likewise distributes and records the digital signal so that it remains high quality during switching, reproduction, and transmission.

The digital video system with VMS produces evidence that has high integrity. When producing evidence from a standalone DVR there is no way to verify the actual source of the images as cameras can be switched on the back of the DVR unit. Using IP cameras and the VMS, the images are kept under the MAC address of the specific camera. This is a clear one-to-one identification of the source of images.

Since the VMS uses off-the-shelf servers, workstations, and computers, the system can always be upgraded to the latest hardware for the best price/performance. This is also true of the IP cameras and other software and hardware that support the system. The VMS system can integrate existing analog cameras, infrared (IR) cameras, covert cameras, and of course the IP camera. The digital technology permits object recognition and tracking, face recognition, license plate recognition, direction detection, people/car counting, etc.

11.6 SUMMARY

The heart of a good security system is a highly functional video switching control system. In small systems, the switchers will take the form of simple passive, homing, sequential or alarming switchers. In medium- to large-size systems, the switchers will take the form of an analog cross-point matrix switcher or a VMS. During the design phase of any security system, management and security personnel must decide what information needs to be displayed, acted upon by the security operator, recorded, and printed, and choose the switching system suitable to accomplish the task.

Chapter 12
Quads and Multiplexers

CONTENTS

12.1   Overview
12.2   Background
12.3   Quad Split-Screen Displays
    12.3.1   Quad-4 Image
    12.3.2   Multi-Image 9, 16, 32
12.4   Multiplexer Technology
    12.4.1   Image Rate vs. Number of Cameras
    12.4.2   Encoder/Decoder
12.5   Hardware Implementation
    12.5.1   Simplex
    12.5.2   Duplex/Full Duplex
    12.5.3   Triplex
12.6   Recording and Playback
    12.6.1   Analog and Digital Recording
    12.6.2   Video Playback
12.7   Video Motion Detection
12.8   Alarm Response
12.9   Integrated Multiplexer and DVR
12.10 Remote Distributed Multiplexing
12.11 Summary

12.1   OVERVIEW

Sequential switchers display the images from multiple cameras on one monitor *sequentially*, one at a time, with a dwell time between the display of each camera image. A disadvantage of sequential switching and recording is that when a single video camera is displayed on the monitor *all the other cameras are not being viewed*. This can result in a great loss of intelligence from the cameras not being displayed. Each camera image is displayed for a dwell time set by the operator adjusted from a few seconds to many seconds. With the use of sequential switchers, many activities on many cameras can be missed since not all camera scenes are being displayed simultaneously.

A quad or video multiplexer displays *all* of the images from many cameras onto a single split-screen monitor *simultaneously*. These devices generate a video signal that can record all the images at a much higher refresh rate than is possible with a sequential switcher. The use of video multiplexers eliminates the normal video time gaps created by conventional sequential switchers.

There are basically three generic types of multiplexers: simplex, duplex/full duplex, and triplex. The simplex multiplexer can display multiple images—4, 9, 16, and 32—on the same multi-screen monitor. The duplex multiplexer displays multiple images on a display but can also provide the necessary encoding and decoding signals to *simultaneously* record images on a VCR or a DVR. A triplex multiplexer can *simultaneously* display multiple live images on a display, record camera images on a recorder, and display playback images from a recorder.

Most multiplexers offer some form of basic video motion detection (VMD). This might be listed in a variety of ways in the literature but it essentially amounts to detecting movement in the field of view of the camera by electronically discerning changes in the light level within the image.

In addition to displaying motion, multiplexers can respond to alarm inputs from external sensors (door switch, infrared detectors, glass break, microwave, etc.). Manufacturers are quick to point out, however, that the multiplexer's primary purpose is to furnish efficient video multiplexing and multi-screen display. Alarm handling and motion detection are secondary functions, and the video multiplexer system should not be the only alarm device on site.

12.2   BACKGROUND

Video multiplexing is an example of time division multiplexing. The video multiplexer constructs a sequence of pictures captured from each of a number of cameras, in

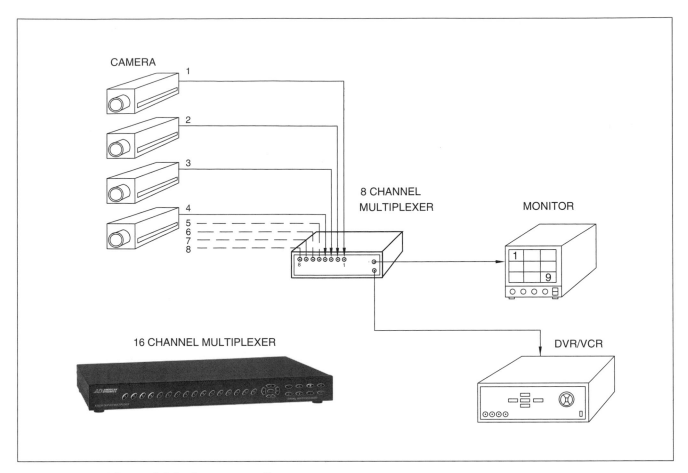

FIGURE 12-1   Video multiplexing system diagram

turn, and displays the video images in a split-screen format on one monitor (Figure 12-1).

The initial electronic image splitters became available in the form of a four-way splitter or quad. Subsequently the 9, 16, and 32 camera image splitters—multiplexers—became available. These larger units had the ability to take synchronized or unsynchronized cameras and display them on a single monitor simultaneously in a synchronized and stable format.

Early multiplexers were basically video switchers that could mark each camera with a unique ID number in the vertical interval. This required the cameras to be gen-locked or v-phased (vertical sync) so the VCR would see a continuously composite sync signal and so that it would not lose servo-lock on the switched incoming video signals. To play-back the camera images, the VCR switched the correct camera onto its output only during its active period on the tape and switched to a gray solid background picture for the rest of the time. This caused severe image flicker but produced a viewable single camera image display and was effective. Later generations of this multiplexer design saved the active camera image until a new picture was displayed eliminating the gray background, providing a better playback result. The primary benefit of this technology was that this device

guaranteed a continuous composite sync to the VCR regardless of the video signal quality. A secondary benefit was that a non-gen-locked or any other camera could be used with this multiplexer. Present-day cameras have quality gen-locking systems, and/or stable line-locked vertical interval sync, and DVRs are used so this is no longer an issue.

The quad or multiplexer can also output these pictures as a single continuous video signal with all the necessary encoding and decoding for recording on a VCR or DVR or network. The multiplexer adds the digital camera ID coding to the signal so that the individual camera fields belonging to each camera can be identified and recovered by the recording equipment on replay. For display monitoring purposes, the same sequential scan process is used and each camera's picture used is electronically reduced in size and displayed in a pre-determined position on the screen. Each camera is assigned a different position so as to produce the familiar *mosaic* or *cameo* of reduced size camera images on a single display monitor.

Most current multiplexers have the ability to display 4, 9, 16, or 32 pictures *simultaneously* on the screen. Usually the image update rate is the same as the output multiplex rate, but some manufacturers have refresh rates up to real-time capability. This feature is useful since the screen is for viewing only the multiplexed output being a full screen high-resolution image. The multi-screen feature to display an alarmed camera in a cameo format is very useful in playback of all recorded images, and later single camera selection when an alarm or some other activity needs to be viewed.

12.3 QUAD SPLIT-SCREEN DISPLAYS

The quad display is the simplest form of this multiplexing technique where the signals from four cameras are processed to appear in four quadrants of a single monitor display.

12.3.1 Quad-4 Image

The quad splitter permits viewing four live video cameras simultaneously or selecting one camera full screen or sequencing through all or selected cameras (Figure 12-2).

The quad splitter can display the images in quad or full screen format while recording to a VCR or DVR in quad format. On playback from the recorder the image from the quad multiplexer can be zoomed up 2X and a freeze frame image can be displayed for detailed analysis. The resolution of the quad ranges from 720×480 pixels up to 1024×512 pixels for high-resolution systems. The units have the ability to annotate the video image with time, date, camera ID, and title in both the live monitor display and recorded image display. The quads provide 30 fields per second, real-time refresh rate.

Figure 12-3 shows diagrammatically the different scene formats that the quad system can display. In the single camera select mode the full screen images from camera 1, camera 2, camera 3, and camera 4 outputs can be selected. In the quad mode, four camera scenes are displayed and each individual picture on the monitor is a full camera scene reduced in size (compressed). Many quad systems can "freeze" a displayed image on the monitor for detailed examination. This permits the security operator to view a single scene in more detail over a period of time until it is released by the operator. In this mode, a recording can be made of the full screen or quad pictures.

Other options include alarm mode, video loss indication, and security lock. In the alarm mode, the system brings the alarmed camera to full screen on the monitor alerting the operator of an alarm activity, all while the recorder records in quad format. Another feature available in some quad multiplexers is called picture in a picture (PIP) in which a reduced image from one camera is embedded into the full screen image of another camera.

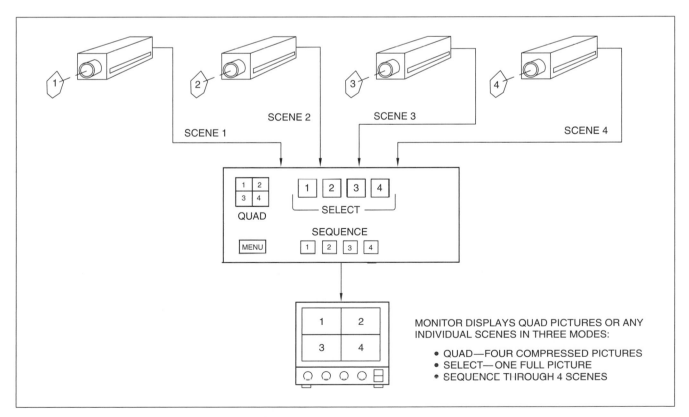

FIGURE 12-2   Quad splitter display block diagram

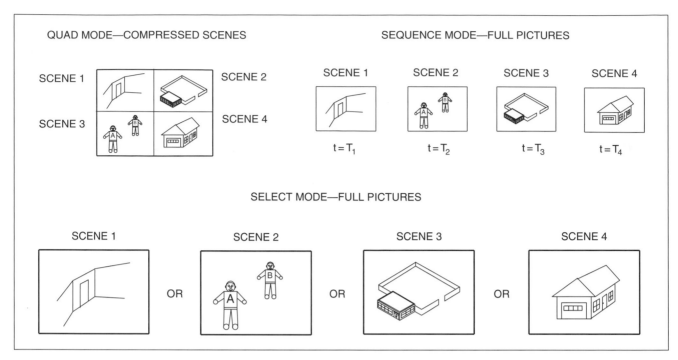

FIGURE 12-3   Quad combiner system

12.3.2   Multi-Image 9, 16, 32

Multiplexers are available to display images from 9 to 32 cameras on the same monitor display and are available with similar features to those found in the quad system. Figure 12-4 shows two 9 and 16 camera examples of these systems and the monitor images. Table 12-1 lists features of some of the quad split-screen equipment available.

12.4   MULTIPLEXER TECHNOLOGY

A quad or multiplexer is an electronic device that time-multiplexes video pictures from many cameras onto one video display or video recorder. This means that the multiplexer displays one field or one frame from one camera, and then immediately following that picture it displays the field or frame from the next camera. It repeats the same procedure for all subsequent cameras, and then starts all over again. These images of multiple cameras are displayed on *one* monitor *simultaneously*. Using this technique the full resolution of each camera is maintained but the dwell time between displayed or recorded image—2–3 second dead time switching time from a sequential switcher—is reduced instead to milliseconds. When recording the camera signal to a VCR or DVR, the multiplexer switches its input circuitry to each of the connected cameras, in turn. To synchronize the cameras during recording, a series of digital codes are embedded into the multiplexer output signal. Part of this code identifies the camera channel number so that the channels may be electronically recognized by the multiplexer during playback. During playback,

another part of the code carries alarm status information so that external alarm events are also recorded on the tape.

Time division multiplexing combines several camera video input signals into one video output signal to display all the camera images on the monitor simultaneously. Single images are digitally captured from each of the video input channels, and then lined up (queued) sequentially to form a continuous video signal of time-sliced camera images. Included with each captured image of video can be status information such as alarms, camera titles, and time/date. Captured images are controlled by an internal library that the multiplexer automatically modifies to respond to alarms, motion detection, or video loss (Figure 12-5).

To generate a multi-picture mosaic display, the multiplexer switches its input circuitry to each of the connected cameras, in turn. The multiplexer has a video frame store (and electronic image memory) used to capture a single picture from each camera. As each image is captured, its size is electronically reduced by a predetermined factor and the resulting *cameo* picture is written into part of the frame store. This results in a small image from the selected camera channel being frozen in one area of the display screen. The same process is provided for each of the cameras to similarly reduce the size and to position the image in a particular location of the monitor display area. As the multiplexer scans repeatedly around the channels, each image is continuously refreshed and updated with new images from the designated camera. This results in the familiar mosaic of small camera images.

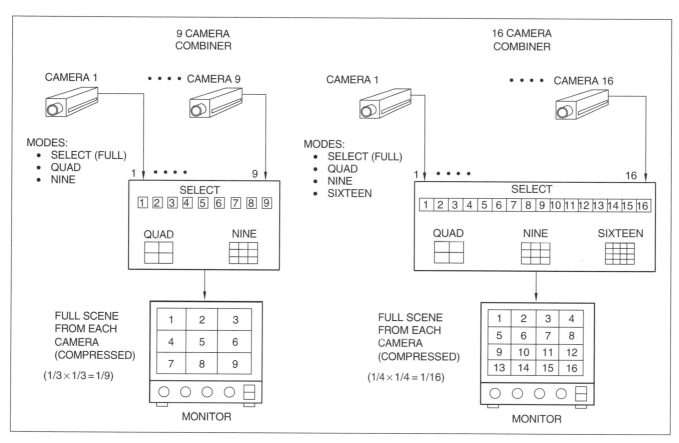

FIGURE 12-4   Multi-image 9, 16, split-screen display

EQUIPMENT TYPE	SCREEN DISPLAY MODE			RESOLUTION–FULL SCREEN ($H \times V$)		GRAY LEVELS	COLORS
	FULL SCREEN	QUAD (4 CAMERA)	SEQUENTIAL	NTSC	CCIR/PAL		
4 CHANNEL—MONOCHROME STANDARD RESOLUTION	√	√	√	512×512	648×512	64	—
4 CHANNEL—MONOCHROME HIGH RESOLUTION	√	√	√	1024×512		256	—
4 CHANNEL—COLOR STANDARD RESOLUTION	√	√	√	720×480	720×576	64	16 M
4 CHANNEL—COLOR HIGH RESOLUTION	√	√	√	1024×512		256	16 M

STANDARD FEATURES ON MOST QUADS:

GRAY SCALE—256   SCREEN FREEZE CAPABILITY
DIGITAL ZOOM—2x   VIDEO LOSS ALARM
ADJUSTABLE SEQUENCE: 1–120 sec   LOOP THROUGH TO DVR/VCR FOR RECORDING AND PLAYBACK
REMOTE CONTROL: RS232, 422, 485   SETUP MENU, ENGLISH, OTHER
ALARM-DRY CONTACTS, RS232, 422, 485   NTSC 525, PAL 625 TV LINES
4-ALARM INPUTS

OPTIONS: TIME/DATE ANNOTATION
           CAMERA ID ANNOTATION

Table 12-1   Quad Split-Screen Equipment Parameters and Features

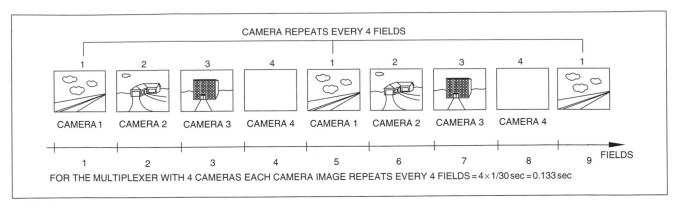

FIGURE 12-5   Multiplexed signal from video stream

Most multiplexers can display the video cameras in four different configurations: (1) quad, 4-way, (2) 9-way, (3) 10-way, and (4) 16-way, and of course full screen for any camera. Many can also display the cameras in different size configurations. Figure 12-6 illustrates some of these split-screen presentations.

In a standard sequential switcher the camera images are displayed at a 30 frame per second rate. They are displayed sequentially on the monitor at a rate determined by the number of cameras in the system and the pre-assigned dwell times for each camera. In the multiplexer switching system the number of images displayed per second is based on the total number of camera inputs.

If there is only one input the multiplexer displays at a 30 fps rate whereas with four camera inputs it display at

a 7.5 images per camera rate. With a larger number of cameras, say 16 camera inputs, the final display rate would only be approximately two images per second per camera, producing a very jerky display (Figure 12-7).

Multiplexers now feature RS-422 and RS-485 and over-the-coax digital PTZ control to eliminate the need to provide additional controlling units for camera platform pointing and lens control. Other features include motion detection, electronic digital zoom, adjustable image sizes, and RS-232 interfaces to other equipments.

The most common type of camera identification is the annotation of digital information into the vertical interval time of the video signal. This is accomplished by dividing a line of video into, say, eight different sections. Each section is defined as a one or zero by either the

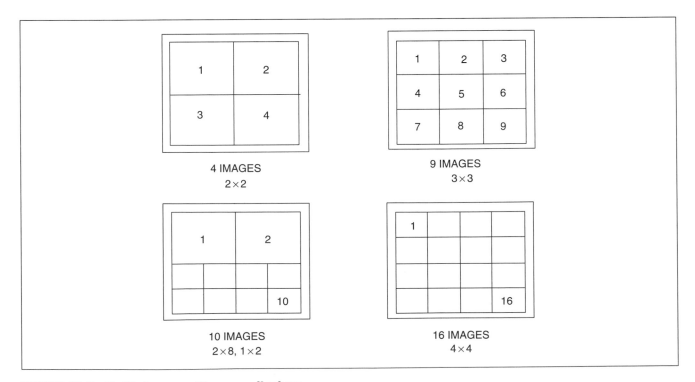

FIGURE 12-6   Multiplexer multi-screen displays

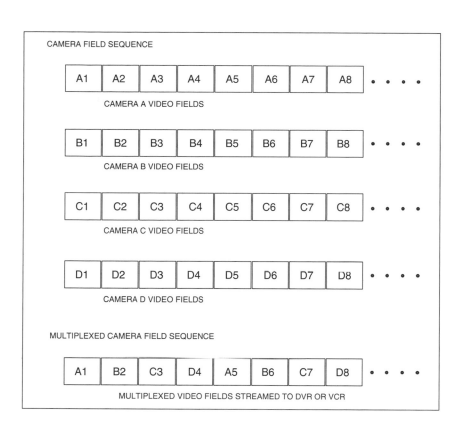

FIGURE 12-7 Multiplex camera sequencing technique

presence or absence of black video or white video. By doing this with eight sections it can be interpreted as one byte of digital data that can be converted to a number from 0 to 255.

12.4.1 Image Rate vs. Number of Cameras

A factor to be considered is that multiplexers are basically fast video switchers. When many cameras are connected and the time lapse (TL) recording is too slow, the time of recording a single image from a particular camera may be too long to catch any event. The multiplexer system basically takes the number of camera inputs and dividing that by the recorded pictures per second. To calculate the refreshed or update rate:

$$\text{Update rate} = \frac{\text{Number of Cameras}}{\text{Recorded Pictures/second}} \quad (12\text{-}1)$$

If there are 16 cameras in the system and the recording time is 168 hours in TL mode, then it will take 17.4 seconds to record a new image from any one camera input. This obviously would have little use in any application since someone could walk by and never be recorded. Reducing the recording time to 24 hours in TL, there would be a new image every 3.2 seconds. This would be more acceptable but not very applicable in high-traffic areas. Going to a 24-hour virtual real-time (pictures per second), there

would be a new image every 0.8 seconds. This would be useful in most applications.

12.4.2 Encoder/Decoder

Multiplexers require encoders and decoders to identify each of the incoming video camera signals for processing. All current encoder/decoder designs use analog to digital (A/D) converters to convert the standard video signal into a digital format for use with common digital logic devices. After the signal is processed, it is later converted from digital to analog (D/A) for output to be displayed back onto the analog video monitor or recorder.

12.5 HARDWARE IMPLEMENTATION

There are basically three different generic types of multiplexers: (1) simplex, (2) duplex/full duplex, and (3) triplex (Figure 12-8).

The simplex multiplexer can display multiple images: 4, 9, 16, and 32—on the same multi-screen monitor. The duplex multiplexer displays multiple images on a display but can also provide the necessary encoding and decoding signals to *simultaneously* record images on a VCR or a DVR. A triplex multiplexer can *simultaneously* display multiple live images on a display, record camera images on a recorder, and display playback images from a recorder.

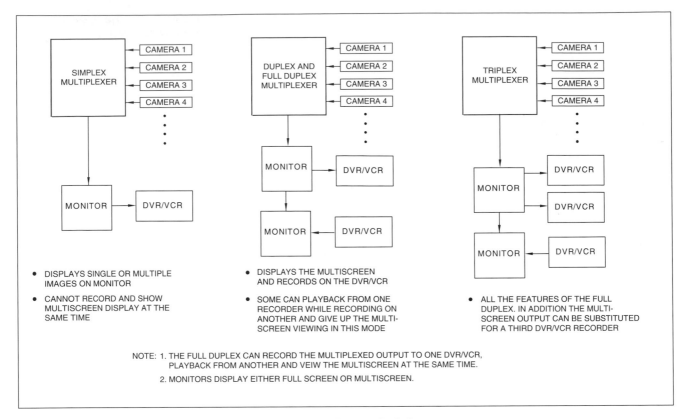

FIGURE 12-8   Generic multiplexer types: simplex, duplex, and triplex

12.5.1   Simplex

The *simplex* multiplexer is the lowest-cost multiplexer type, has the least number of features, and is easy to install and set up. They are generally used in small systems when there is no security operator active at the console. The simplex multiplexer does not have the ability to record and show a multi-screen display and record *simultaneously*. The simplex multiplexer unit can either display or record the video information with the initial setup of the multiplexer determining the choice. They are available for monochrome or color camera systems and with options for VMD and alarm handling.

12.5.2   Duplex/Full Duplex

A *duplex* multiplexer is designed to display either: (1) a live camera view, (2) a live multi-screen display, or (3) previously recorded images. This multiplexer has the ability to *display* the multi-screen camera images and record the multiplexed video and control data to the VCR or DVR. Some duplex multiplexers can playback from one recorder while recording on another but the multi-screen viewing is forfeited.

A *full duplex* multiplexer has the ability to: (1) record the multiplexed output to one recorder, (2) playback

from another, and (3) view the multi-screen at the same time. Duplex and full duplex multiplexers are available for monochrome or color camera systems and with options for VMD and alarm handling.

12.5.3   Triplex

A *triplex* multiplexer allows viewing of *live and recorded* images on one monitor *simultaneously*, eliminating the need for a separate playback monitoring station. The triplex multiplexer has all the features of the full duplex but the multi-screen output can be used for a third recorder, or to display live video which is the more common application (Figure 12-8).

Triplex multiplexers are available with two monitor outputs. Output #1 produces a full screen or multi-screen digital image display that can be frozen on the screen or zoomed in or out. Output #2 displays a full screen, live.

Triplex multiplexers are available for monochrome or color camera systems in 10 and 16 camera models with options for VMD and alarm handling. They have on-screen menu prompts to simplify installation and setup. Table 12-2 lists features of some of the multiplexer equipment available.

EQUIPMENT TYPE NUMBER OF CAMERAS *	MULTISCREEN DISPLAY	RECORD TO DVR/VCR	RECORD TO DVR/VCR, DISPLAY	RESOLUTON	
				NTSC	PAL
SIMPLEX**:					
16 CHANNELS	——	√	√	720×512	720×512
32 CHANNELS	——	√	√		
DUPLEX:					
16 CHANNELS	4, 8, 16	√ †	√	720×480	720×576
32 CHANNELS	4, 8, 16, 32	√ †	√		
FULL DUPLEX:					
16 CHANNELS	4, 8, 16	√	√	720×572	720×572
32 CHANNELS	4, 8, 16, 32	√	√		
TRIPLEX‡:					
16 CHANNELS	4, 8, 16	√	√	720×512	720×512
32 CHANNELS	4, 8, 16, 32	√	√		

* 4 CHANNEL AND 10 CHANNEL ALSO AVAILABLE

** MOST SIMPLEX DO NOT HAVE CAPABILITY TO DISPLAY MULTI-SCREENS

† DUPLEX—SOME CAN PLAYBACK FROM ONE DVR/VCR WHILE RECORDING ON ANOTHER BUT GIVE UP MULTI-SCREEN VIEWING DURING THIS TIME.

‡ TRIPLEX—ALL FEATURES OF DUPLEX BUT MULTI-SCREEN OUTPUTS CAN BE SUBSTITUTED FOR A THIRD DVR/VCR.

FEATURES IN MOST:

    ALARM INPUT: EACH CAMERA
    ALARM OUTPUT ANNUNCIATION
    DIGITAL ZOOM: 2x
    DATE/TIME, CAMERA ID
    VIDEO LOSS INDICATION
    ON-SCREEN MENU

Table 12-2 Multiplexer Equipment Parameters and Features

12.6 RECORDING AND PLAYBACK

12.6.1 Analog and Digital Recording

When recording the camera signal to a VCR or a DVR, the multiplexer switches its input circuitry to each of the connected cameras, in turn. The video frame-store in this mode is used to capture a single full-screen field image from each camera. The separate video fields captured from the cameras are re-synchronized by the frame-store for recording onto the video recorder. Using this method, it is possible to record at an average rate of more than 30 cameras per second. Since the video frame-store inherently time-base corrects the sync and synchronizes the camera signals as part of the camera capture process, the cameras need not be externally synchronized.

To synchronize the camera signals during recording, a series of digital codes are embedded into the multiplexer output signal. Part of this code identifies the camera channel number so that the channels may be electronically recognized by the multiplexer during playback. During playback, another part of the code carries alarm status information so that external alarm events are also recorded.

12.6.2 Video Playback

When the multiplex recording is played back through the multiplexer to the monitor, the multiplexer first extracts the digitally coded data element and uses this to identify the camera ID number information. When a valid channel number is identified, the multiplex captures the associated video images in the frame-store. The simplest playback mode is where a single camera channel is requested for playback. In this mode the multiplexer captures the corresponding video images from this camera and displays them as full screen images, and updates each time it identifies another image with the same camera ID number. The embedded digital data packets are decoded, and all the associated status information, titles, time and date of recording, etc. are re-constructed and displayed with on-screen text during playback.

During playback, the user can select one of several screen formats, the cameras to be displayed, and the camera positions in the multi-screen display on the unit. The playback speed is selected on the recorder, not on the multiplexer unit.

For multi-picture playback mode the frame-store is used in a similar way as that used for live multiplexer viewing. Many channels are reviewed off the recorder alongside one another on the screen. In this mode the same size reduction and image positioning processes go on in the multiplexer as was described for the live multi-picture mode. In this case, however, there is only one input signal, i.e. that coming from the video recorder playback, but there are many camera channels within the signal. The multiplexer recognizes each new camera channel number, it size-reduces the captured image, and places it on the screen in the predetermined location and with a size corresponding to that camera. This results in a multi-picture display very similar to the live one showing recorded information rather than live video. If the operator sees an image in the cameo images of interest, the multiplexer can be switched to the full screen mode for that camera, to examine the scene more closely.

12.7 VIDEO MOTION DETECTION

Most multiplexers offer some form of basic motion sensing or VMD. This might be listed in a variety of ways in the literature but it essentially amounts to detecting movement in the field of view of the camera by electronically discerning changes in the light level within the image.

In operation the multiplexer digital signal processing (DSP) electronics determines if something has changed in the video image of any camera. If nothing has changed the multiplexer records fewer pictures per second from that camera, thereby increasing the images per second recorded for other cameras that have motion or activity and their scenes. One caution regarding VMD: some outdoor environments have complex detection requirements. In those cases, use a non-video motion detector sensor intended specifically for such situations.

Motion sensing can be considered effectively as an alarm that is flagged internally to the multiplexer. This feature is particularly useful in the recording mode since it can

allow the frame/field recording rate of the recorder to be altered such that images showing movement are recorded at a faster rate than the static ones.

The multiplexer can optimize the display and recording by displaying and recording only video camera images in which *activity* is occurring.

12.8 ALARM RESPONSE

Multiplexers offer VMD including built-in zone selection with sensitivity settings and alarm linking per camera. Motion detection is used to adjust the rate at which camera images are recorded and can also act as an intrusion alarm sensor to trigger on alarm input. The VMD can be used to simply optimize recording or as an alarm condition. Motion detection can be used as an alarm condition only if movement is detected where no movement is expected or permitted.

Non-video alarms are signal inputs from external sensors that can be acted upon by alarm monitoring hardware or a security operator at a console (Figure 12-9).

Common alarm sensors take the form of door contacts, PIR, glass break, microwave motion sensors, trip-wire, photo-electric, magnetic, seismic, etc. All are examples of

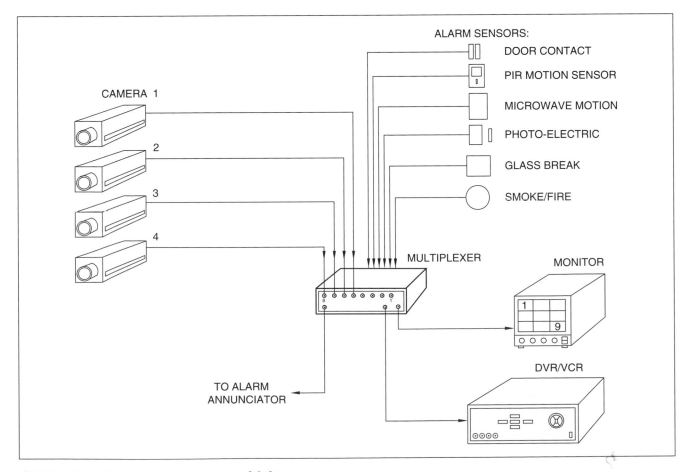

FIGURE 12-9 Alarm signals trigger multiplexer

external devices that can output signals to the multiplexer when an intruder enters a monitored area, and be used for alarm annunciation. All these devices can be used by most multiplexers as an input to bring up the picture of the camera that is located in the alarm sensor area and to annunciate an alarm via sound or light indicator. They are also used to command the VCR or DVR recorder to change from TL to real-time recording mode for that camera, and record at a faster speed. In normal use, the recorder is in TL mode to make economic use of the storage media. When an alarm event occurs, the recorder speed is increased to real-time. State-of-the-art multiplexers can cope with making these changes from TL to real-time and acting on alarm inputs. An input from an external alarm by a contract closure to the recorder or by a serial RS-232 port command will be multiplexed, though, and will cause the recorder to change speed. The multiplexer also makes it possible to select logical groups of cameras and to salvo or bank switching of those cameras. Salvo switching accomplishes the switching of several or many cameras in a related zone *simultaneously* when an alarm input occurs. As an example, in a 20 camera installation the normal recording set up may provide the TL recording for all 20 cameras. There may be PIR, other motion sensors, and/or switch sensors in the area. When an alarm event is triggered via one of these sensors, the multiplexer causes the images from cameras in the area of the sensors to be recorded in real-time. Ideally the video system should take automatic

action as much as possible, and not require the operator to intervene.

12.9 INTEGRATED MULTIPLEXER AND DVR

The VCR has been replaced by the DVR in many video security systems. Consequently, many DVRs are now incorporating the video multiplexer into the DVR unit. The combined video multiplexer–digital recorder simplifies and reduces errors during the hardware setup procedure and simplifies the design, operation, and cost of the system. Figure 12-10 shows a full-featured DVR–multiplexer combination. Table 12-2 lists some of the multiplexer equipment available.

12.10 REMOTE DISTRIBUTED MULTIPLEXING

Digital technology is finding its way into the use of multiplexers in LAN, WAN, etc. as a superior technique for distributing, controlling, and recording video signals especially at remote distances (Figure 12-11).

Some multiplexers designed for larger physical security installations lend themselves to distributed multiplexing. This permits groups of cameras that are located in

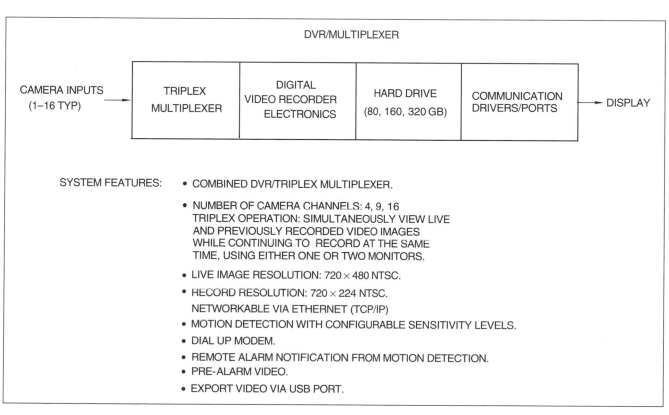

FIGURE 12-10 DVR-multiplexer system

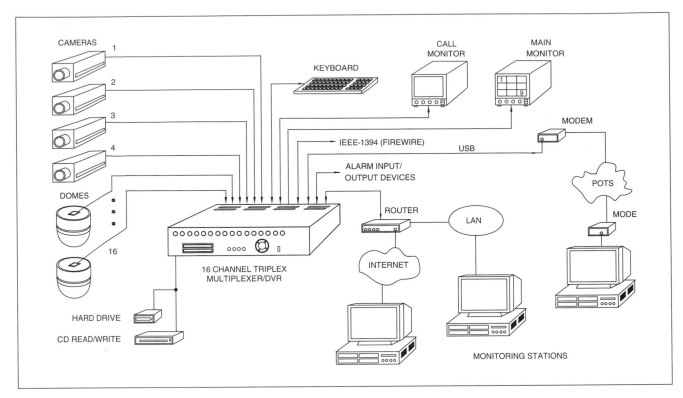

FIGURE 12-11   Remote distributed multiplexing

physically distant locations to be connected to a *slave* multiplexer. Several of these remote multiplexers are controlled from a single master multiplexer at the central location. The master unit communicates over the Internet and provides the video processing, recording, and display process signals. It commands each slave unit to deliver the required camera channels from the slave to the master, where they can be combined by one or several multiplexer recorder systems.

Multiplexing digitally compresses the images of each video frame and transmits them over the digital network to a DVR and onto digital monitors. The video images are compressed before transmission and later decompressed to display them on the monitor.

12.11   SUMMARY

The multiplexer and integrated multiplexer–recorder (DVR) have become an important part of the video surveillance hardware. It is a powerful tool capable of combining many video images onto one multi-screen display, thereby reducing the number of monitors required to view the cameras in the system. It can call up camera images showing motion in the scene. It also provides the capability to prioritize incoming alarm signals from external sensors with the VMD alarms. In an analog network, the multiplexer can send the video images and camera identification signals to a VCR or DVR for proper synchronization on recording and playback to the multiplexer. In a digital network, it can transmit the compressed images over digital networks to monitors and recorders to remote locations for remote site monitoring. The simplex, duplex/full duplex, and triplex types are available to provide a multiplexer solution to most applications.

Chapter 13
Video Motion Detectors

CONTENTS

13.1 Overview
13.2 Background
13.3 Functional Operation
    13.3.1 Surveillance
    13.3.2 Detection Probability
    13.3.3 Motion Assessment
    13.3.4 Scene Lighting
    13.3.5 Training Function
13.4 Analog Video Motion Detector (AVMD)
    13.4.1 Technology
13.5 Digital Video Motion Detector (DVMD)
    13.5.1 Mode of Operation
    13.5.2 Technology
        13.5.2.1 Programming the digital VMD
        13.5.2.2 DVMD Setup Procedures
        13.5.2.3 Sensitivity Settings
        13.5.2.4 Motion Detection Sensitivity
    13.5.3 Hardware
        13.5.3.1 Normal Mode
        13.5.3.2 Trace Mode
        13.5.3.3 DVMD Graphic Site Display
                Maps
    13.5.4 Features
13.6 Guidelines, Pros and Cons
13.7 Summary

13.1 OVERVIEW

The method by which current security systems trigger security alarms can be divided into two classes. At one end of the spectrum there are systems that sense physical movement, such as simple contact switches and PIR sensors. While all these systems can be quite varied in the technology they use, the systems have one thing in common: they can only recognize movement. On the other hand, there are visual detection systems ranging from guards posted at specific locations to camera systems with analog video motion detectors (AVMD) or digital video motion detectors (DVMD). The DVMDs use monitors, real-time and/or TL VCRs or DVRs to discern between *allowable* activities, breach of security or provide identification of individuals, and give instructions to a guard on what a response should be.

Any video security system should include the following four ingredients: (1) surveillance, (2) detection, (3) assessment, and (4) response. The VMD can be a part of the system hardware to provide the surveillance, detection, and assessment, and provide accurate detailed and concise information to the guard force, allowing the force to respond optimally. As a free by-product, the VMD also makes available a training tool to practice and perfect the guard response philosophy. To achieve high detection probabilities in any moderate to large security system, the integrated video system must operate with an automated VMD detection system.

The recent availability of affordable DSP techniques has forever changed the security scenario and eliminated the shortcomings of the simple motion detectors and first generation AVMD detectors. In simple terms, advanced DSP technology has brought *intelligence* into the world of DVMD. DVMD systems combine visual video presentation of the motion detection with recording technology. Intelligent VMD systems go a step further by using sophisticated DSP algorithms so that motion detectors learn or adjust to a changing or new scene, virtually eliminating false alarms that were prevalent in the analog and simple first generation DVMD technologies. Intelligent DVMDs can be programmed to overlook small changes in the scene such as rain, dust, moving tree branches that often render traditional VMDs unusable.

The useful security information displayed on a video monitor often comes from motion within the scene—a moving person, vehicle, object, or some activity involving motion. Irrespective of the number of security monitors, it is important to have an alarming device to alert the guard to motion or activity in a scene. Medium to large video installations generate many camera scenes that must ultimately be displayed on monitors, but it is difficult for a security guard to watch multiple monitors over long periods of time. The video multiplexer goes a long way in reducing the number of monitors the guard must view and at the same time increases the operator's ability to react to real threats, but it is the VMD that electronically analyzes and monitors camera images to detect changes (motion) that are judged to warrant an alarm. The VMD provides an electronic alternative to a guard sitting and staring at the monitors, and can notify the guard immediately of situations requiring attention. VMD systems operate to detect changes in a specified area within the camera FOV. They do this by comparing the light levels of camera pixels from one video frame to the next, looking for changes considered significant. In the simpler, lower-cost AVMD systems, large areas in the incoming frame are compared with those of a previous reference frame. This type of system works reasonably well indoors, where there are few changes in the scene and where lighting is constant. Analog systems are, however, susceptible to false alarms caused by lighting changes, debris passing through the camera FOV, small animals, ripples on bodies of water, or camera vibration. They are therefore *not* recommended for most outdoor applications and instead the DVMD is used. The microprocessor DSP-based DVMD can analyze thousands of picture zones and operate with low false-alarm rates even under severe light-level changes. Most DVMDs, with the exception of those using the latest intelligent image processors and learning algorithms, are not suitable for PTZ applications.

Environment plays a major factor in choosing the DVMD for outdoor applications. The DVMD can tolerate some camera vibration, but the camera should be mounted as securely as possible. The DVMD can also tolerate light-level changes as might occur when a cloud passes in front of the sun, without causing a false alarm. Some DVMD systems can subtract out or ignore inherent scene motions such as waving flags, leaves, or trees, so that they will not be a source of false alarms. Some have the ability to selectively sensitize and desensitize certain portions of the scene in order to prevent false alarms. They desensitize parts of the scene where inherent motion and no real activity is expected, such as leaves rustling on trees. This reduces the chance of false alarms.

After a target has been detected and classified, the DVMD tracks that object within the site as the target moves from camera to camera. Systems are now available that can display images from remote locations showing targets in motion. The system can detect, classify, locate, and track objects within the FOV of the camera. The operator has a mapped display of the site, highlighted with icons of the various types of targets (cars, personnel, gates, etc.), and can see an icon of the moving car or other target on the digitized site map. The path which vehicles take is synthesized in the monitor display of the FOVs of several cameras that the car had passed and traversed. Actual video scenes are available by clicking on the icon. These type systems are finding use in environments such as airports, seaports, and large installations.

13.2 BACKGROUND

In its most general sense, a motion detector is an analog device that responds to movement recognized as a specific type and rate of change within a defined monitored area of coverage. The original motion detectors were designed to detect motion or movement in a stable background by means of PIR technology using pyroelectric detectors. These PIRs sensed gross changes in movement but provided very little intelligence as to the cause of the movement.

A video camera provided with appropriate VMD processing electronics can make the camera operate as an alarm sensor. The VMD processing electronics memorizes the instantaneous video picture, and then if some part of the picture changes by a prescribed amount, the system generates an alarm signal to alert a guard or activate a video recorder. The AVMD or DVMD is connected into the video system as shown in Figure 13-1. The figure shows an individual entering a room and the successive video frames showing the person walking through the facility. The VMD will detect the motion of the person, highlighting the person on the monitor screen, and/or also producing a visual or audible annunciation to the security officer.

Two VMD processing electronic types have been developed: the first-generation analog and the second-generation digital. The DVMD provides significantly more capability and reliability but costs more. Surveillance of any scene is achieved by the use of conventional video cameras and lenses positioned throughout the area of interest at locations that permit recognizing an intruder or movement within the camera FOV. Cameras should be positioned so they can view all activity and targets of interest. Figure 13-2 illustrates the VMD's place in the video surveillance system.

In the 1980s, several DVMD systems became available. These were large, complex, and expensive units with electronic memory and logic that dissected a video image into zones. Each zone represented an area in which motion could be monitored. By dividing the video image into hundreds of zones, the target could be localized in the scene and defined in size and motion, than it could in the original AVMD system. The light level of each zone likewise could be analyzed providing further intelligence about the scene. These systems were only affordable by large commercial institutions and government facilities. It was only

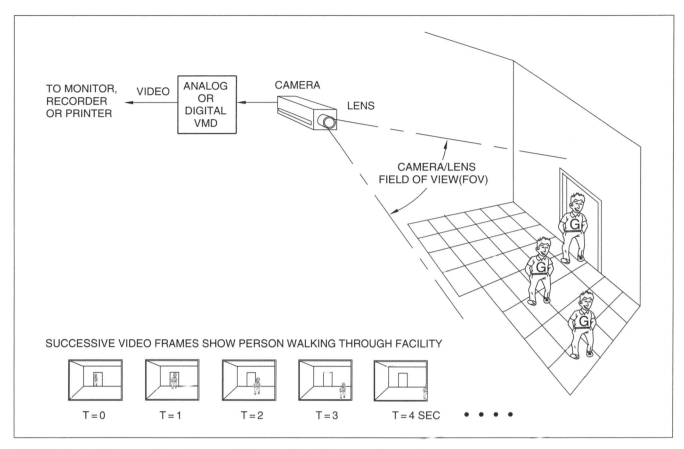

FIGURE 13-1   Video motion detector (VMD) in the video security system

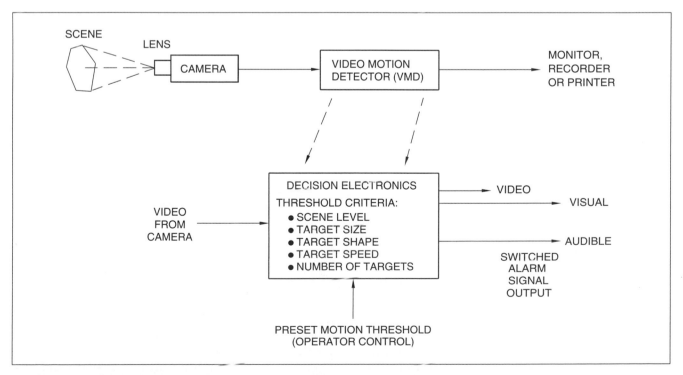

FIGURE 13-2   Video motion detection system and detection parameters

into the mid-1990s that digital electronic costs were sufficiently reduced to make the present DVMD practical in security applications.

The evolution of the AVMD to the DVMD provided a significant step forward in identifying the source of an intrusion or movement in a video scene by providing more intelligence to the security operator. Early analog systems were limited to monochrome video cameras since color cameras were not in widespread use during the 1980s. The modest electronics in the AVMD limited their use to indoor applications as they could not deal with all the uncontrolled lighting, weather, and stray motion interferences in an outside environment. The introduction of the CCD camera in the 1980s and low cost color cameras in the 1990s initiated the advent of a totally new technology in VMD. This, however, was not sufficient to make the AVMD a reliable product for indoor applications and especially not for outdoor applications. In the mid- to late 1990s, however, the introduction of the DVMD in conjunction with the CCD camera with DSP improved motion detection significantly. Digital circuitry and availability of inexpensive solid-state memory brought about the widespread use of DVMD. The DVMD has the ability to dissect the video image and analyze the scene on a pixel-by-pixel basis, thereby allowing sophisticated analysis of the motion in the scene. These new DVMDs have proven to be very reliable for alarm management, and provide automatic intrusion detection and automatic recording of intrusion events. They are used in open areas and relieve console guards of the tedious monitoring of empty hallways, rooms, parking lots, and parking garage levels that have no activity. The improvements in reliability through sensitivity adjustments and digital analysis of movement on a pixel level has given credibility to the idea that video surveillance systems can and should perform automatic motion detection without individual camera scenes requiring active monitoring by a console guard.

Advanced programming for "specific act recognition" is just beginning to emerge from development. This is motion detection that recognizes unique and complicated motions associated with undesirable act phenomena. Recognized acts can be the typical movement of shoplifters, acts of physical violence, or phenomena such as fire. Video smoke detection software programs are currently being marketed. Also emerging is the coupling of motion detection with alpha-numeric character and biometric recognition. This takes the form, for example, of spotting license plates or vehicle signage and processing the numbers or characters remotely. Some facial systems provide recognition of specific faces in a crowd and are finding their way to market.

13.3 FUNCTIONAL OPERATION

Before any AVMD or DVMD can be applied to a particular application, its location—indoor or outdoor—must

be considered. In an indoor application, the light-level changes are usually predictable or at least not very significant. Successful VMD operation depends on recognizing light-level changes in specific parts of the scene (caused by an intrusion or disturbance) in contrast to overall scene light-level changes caused by changing lighting conditions. These two phenomena must be differentiated to avoid undue false alarms. In indoor lighting applications where the light level is controlled by the user, a simpler AVMD system can be used.

13.3.1 Surveillance

Video surveillance is accomplished via the use of cameras and lenses located and positioned for maximum intelligence gathering of a viewing area. The cameras can act synergistically with other alarms as remote eyes to present a visual image of an area as well as the source for an alarm input.

Monitoring a large area such as a parking lot using VMDs presents multiple possibilities including: (1) a wide-angle lens, (2) multiple cameras, and (3) dual-lens, split-screen. When a wide-angle lens is used, the alarm source (intruder) appears small on the monitor screen and a guard does not detect the intruder, especially if the intruder takes cover quickly. The VMD can detect the intruder and register an alarm. With multiple cameras, the parking lot FOV is divided among the cameras, each viewing a section of the overall area. Each camera must use a separate VMD. With the split-screen technique one lens can be wide-angle, the other a medium or narrow-angle lens.

If the system includes pan/tilt equipment the guard must pan, tilt, and zoom the camera/lens to locate the alarm source. This is not a simple task, and in the time required for the guard to perform it, the intruder may be gone. In more sophisticated systems, in order to speed reaction time, the location of the motion in the image is used to point the pan/tilt platform in the direction of the motion.

13.3.2 Detection Probability

The protection of outdoor areas presents the most difficult problem in facility security. All sensing devices are plagued by false alarms due to the unpredictable nature of natural phenomena and intentional artificial alarms. Seismic sensors produce false alarms due to vibrations caused by wind, vehicles, and other objects. Microwave sensors produce false alarms due to moving animals, blowing papers, or leaves. An effective outdoor security system is best augmented using video cameras viewing the actual scenes to filter out and recognize false alarms. Although an alarm denotes that a certain area has been disturbed, without a visual image little information is provided as to the nature of the alarm or the precise location at which it occurred. Without a video image, security personnel must be sent out to investigate and determine the nature of an alarm. Since outdoor monitored areas are often large, in many cases by the time a security guard responds to the alarm, the intruder is gone or the activity has ceased.

A guard monitoring a medium to large video security system must view many monitors that display either: (1) sequenced scenes, (2) several monitors—one for each camera, or (3) monitors with split-screens. To assure a high probability of detection, the camera lens magnification must be such that an intruder is displayed on the monitor magnified enough so that the guard can easily see him and attract his attention. Using multiple cameras is often the best solution to provide the necessary coverage to detect the intruder.

For a guard's response to an intrusion to be effective, the guard must first know that he is responding to a *real* intrusion, its location, and nature. The VMD function is to display only intrusion alarms on the video monitor without any human intervention. The guard then assesses the alarm by viewing the monitor.

The VMD system must give timely information as to the exact location and nature of the activity and must: (1) respond to small changes (motion) in the camera/lens FOV, (2) activate an alarm output on the monitor to alert the guard that an intrusion has occurred, and (3) display the alarmed scene on the monitor. It should also be accompanied by an audible and/or video alarm and activate a VCR or DVR and video printer. For larger digital infrastructures it should be able to provide transmission of the video image over a network. The displayed scene should show the location within the scene that has been activated and give immediate information to security personnel as to the precise location, movement, and nature of the alarm. If an intruder is hiding, a flashing pattern on the monitor should show the path of the intruder from entry of the scene to the point to where he is hiding.

Intrusion detection probability is controlled by the placement of cameras and is a system design parameter. The ideal motion detection system would give a 100% probability of detection of intrusions, zero false-alarm rate, zero nuisance alarms, and zero equipment failure. With proper camera placement and reliable equipment, target-detection probabilities can be 95–99%. Alarm assessment takes place in the time it takes for the operator to view the scene and identify the cause. When a VMD is used, the security operator does not have to identify the camera or locate the movement on the screen, since the cause of the alarm is indicated by the brightened flashing map on the monitor. If it is an intruder, the guard responds accordingly, knowing where the intruder is and who he will be confronting. If it is not an alarm, the guard can press an alarm reset button and go on to the next alarm.

Video motion detectors are valuable not only because they can cue a video response but also because they are an independent source of vital information. There may be particular situations where a specific activity within an area covered by the camera would be difficult to detect with other conventional forms of alarms. It is often important to know not only that an intrusion occurred in a certain space or area but also the path the intruder took. VMDs with enhanced mapping display capability can provide this information.

13.3.3 Motion Assessment

Assessment is the ability of the console operator to identify and evaluate the cause of the alarm. This judgment call is one of the most important decisions for two reasons: (1) if a real intrusion occurs the guard's assessment must be rapid and accurate and depend on a visual judgment, (2) if the alarm is not a valid intrusion, the guard must be able to make that decision rapidly and accurately—which again requires visual observation of the cause of the alarm—and then cancel it.

In some DVMD systems a RAM module stores the alarmed locations in a separate RAM alarm map memory (AMM). Upon alarm, the contents of the AMM are displayed on the alarmed video monitor scene as a flashing, highlighted array of alarm points. This feature is a key to quick, accurate assessment of all alarms. The AMM enables the operator to determine instantly the exact location where the disturbance or intrusion has occurred and provides a quick, precise evaluation of the alarm to provide the appropriate response. To clear the alarm condition after a response has been made, the operator presses an alarm reset switch and the monitor returns to the normal blank condition. This accurate, rapid assessment optimizes the use of the response force. If a second or additional alarm occurs prior to resetting, the alarm scenes are displayed with their alarm maps in sequence on the master monitor, at a selectable rate.

When a large number of cameras are alarmed simultaneously, an assessment problem can occur. By the time the guard views the last camera, the intruder most likely has left the scene and only the map remains. The DVMD effectively controls the situation by providing a video output to record all alarmed camera images. This is done automatically while the guard watches the monitor. The video frames (scenes) are sent to the VCR or DVR at a rate of 30 fps. The pictures are recorded—one from each camera—in sequence and continue until the operator resets the equipment. When a guard realizes a multiple-intrusion attempt is in progress, the guard can playback the recorded video images into the monitor and replay the intrusion with the alarm map to determine the cause of the alarm in the scene. Using this technique the alarm assessment capability is extremely high. The guard need not leave the console during an alarm condition unless it is necessary to initiate a direct response to a real intrusion. The guard can observe the progress of the intruder into the area by observing the monitor as the intrusion map is generated.

13.3.4 Scene Lighting

Since the VMD makes its decision based on the scene the camera is viewing, it is important that lighting at the camera site is adequate. The VMD equipment must be able to compensate for variations in average scene lighting occurring during daylight hours as well as when auxiliary artificial lighting is provided during nighttime operation. VMD systems operate with scenes illuminated by visible or infrared lighting.

In outdoor applications, the environment is not as controllable: significant light-level changes are caused by sunlight, cloud variations, lightning, and many different types of objects passing through the camera/lens FOV. Many DVMD systems operate well under most outdoor conditions but they lose some of their capability under adverse environmental conditions of heavy snow or rain, and alternative systems using other sensors should be relied upon. The DVMD used in an outdoor environment has a significantly higher potential for false alarms due to these unpredictable lighting changes and moving clutter. The DVMD must have outdoor algorithms that correctly account for these rapid changes in overall scene brightness and illumination, as well as area changes in illumination caused by rapidly moving phenomena. If there is movement in the scene it must be detected while the movement is still in the scene. Therefore, if updates of the scene occur at too slow a rate, an object at a distance may elude detection.

To determine whether a target is of interest or a false alarm, the equipment must be able to distinguish its size, speed, and shape. In outdoor applications a DVMD is the only solution.

13.3.5 Training Function

In the intrusion scenario, when an alarm occurs the console operator is called upon for the first time to evaluate the alarm on a previously blank CCTV monitor. The monitor displays the intruder and the exact location within the scene by some flashing indicator superimposed on his exact location.

Management uses AVMD, DVMD, and video recorders to test a security plan and guard response, and evaluate guard and overall system performance. A system using the motion detector permits security personnel to train before an actual event, and when an intrusion does occur, the system can immediately recall the decisions to form an instant plan of action. This directs the efforts of the response force

optimally. This important training improves the plan, the guard response time and method, and overall security.

13.4 ANALOG VIDEO MOTION DETECTOR (AVMD)

For several decades, the AVMD has attempted to identify motion and activity of interest in a video scene. It has enjoyed some degree of success for indoor applications but has not been successful in outdoor environments. With the recent introduction of the DVMD in conjunction with DVRs and digital multiplexers, VMD has now become an important, even essential, tool for video monitoring.

The AVMD system is simple: it monitors any change in the video signal that comes from the camera and produces an output indicating that there was an alarm. Unfortunately, many other changes in light levels are not caused by targets of interest but rather from background changes. The particular causes for these false alarms are:

- An overall change of the scene lighting caused by sudden light changes or fluctuations in overall lighting, and turning lights on and off
- Flashing a light across a scene causing an immediate contrast change
- Open flames, flashing neon signs, cigarette lighters
- The sun passing behind a cloud
- Flying debris: flying paper boxes, etc. through the camera FOV
- Environmental dust, a rainstorm, or snowstorm
- Animals, birds passing through the camera FOV
- Continuous motion from water fountains, revolving doors, escalators, ripples on water, or wave motion.

For all these reasons, the AVMD is not a viable solution for detecting motion, real target, or activity in a video system, and does not find widespread use except in small systems.

13.4.1 Technology

The AVMDs have been available for many years and provide a low-cost video device to detect simple motion in a video scene. They operate reliably only in indoor, well-controlled environmental and lighting conditions and should not be used for outdoor applications. Figure 13-3 shows a block diagram of the AVMD.

The simplest AVMD uses analog subtraction. The reference frame and the frame in which motion has occurred are subtracted and an alarm declared depending on the amount of signal difference between frames. This analog system, while acceptable for most indoor applications, is prone to false alarms and is not suitable for outdoor applications. A digital DVMD should be used in all outdoor applications.

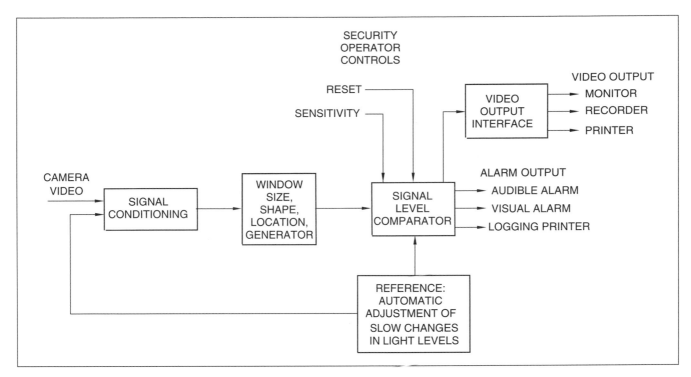

FIGURE 13-3   Analog video motion detector (AVMD) block diagram

Two generic detection options available in many VMDs are: (1) detection of motion or activity, (2) detection of the presence or absence of an object. These systems can be configured so that these two different type windows operate independently and be can be combined within the same camera FOV. Motion windows are designed to detect movement of objects or personnel into and through their detection zones. They also detect anything that moves into the window and stays there even though the object stops moving. They can have a programmable time-out feature so that an object can enter the detection window and stay there for a given length of time without causing an alarm. This ensures that the DVMD does not indefinitely remain in an alarm mode. The motion windows look for significant changes in image contrast or pattern in the detection zone. They detect only significant changes in most objects that are bright or dark but are much smaller then those expected from some debris, and will not trigger a false alarm.

In the object presence or absence mode of operation, the system monitor displays the movement of objects that are expected to remain stationary during the surveillance while ignoring surrounding movement. If particular assets are to be protected and can be defined in space, the VMD defines a tight window around the object to instruct the system to signal an alarm if the object moves while ignoring anyone passing through the FOV. When using either of the two modes the individual windows are augmented by background scene monitoring functions so that the overall scene illumination levels are monitored to detect and compensate for sudden light level changes.

All AVMDs have an adjustable detection-of-motion zone (DMZ), which is a selected portion of the monitor screen. Any movement (change of light level) in the scene within the DMZ automatically triggers any one of four alarms: (1) an internal audible alarm, (2) a front-panel signal light, (3) an AC or DC outlet that can activate an AC- or DC-operated signaling device, or (4) an isolated terminal relay contact to activate a video recorder, printer, bell, or other security device.

On most AVMD equipment, the size, shape, and location of the active area in the entire scene is adjusted with front-panel controls. The DMZ size and configuration chosen depends on the requirements of the surveillance application. Figure 13-4 illustrates some examples of DMZ shapes available, including split-screen, square, rectangle, L-, C-, and U-shaped.

The areas of sensitivity are chosen to surround a location in the scene where motion is expected. The DMZ enables the operator to select (sensitize) specific portions of the camera scene area, while the entire scene is always displayed. An alarm occurs only if there is motion in the DMZ itself. Depending on the equipment, DMZ is represented on the video monitor screen by a brightness-enhanced window (or a brightness-enhanced frame), adjustable via the front-panel controls. After initial setup, the brightened window (or frame) may be switched off so that the scene looks normal to the operator. The active DMZ on the screen can be set up to cover an area anywhere from 5 to 90% of the viewed picture width and height. The AVMD system sensitivity is usually set to respond to a 25% change

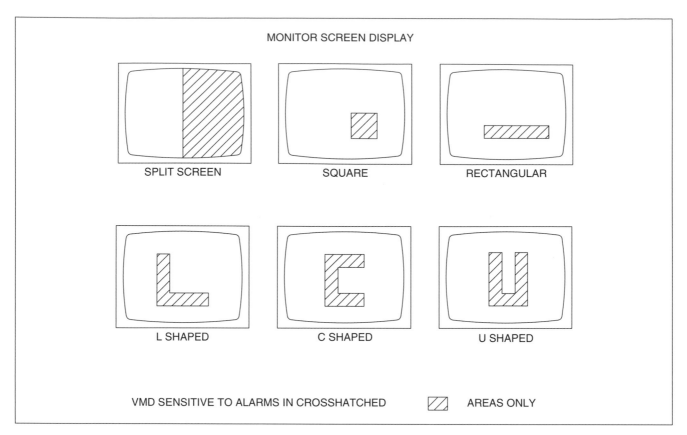

FIGURE 13-4 Detection of motion zones (DMZ) in analog video motion detectors (AVMD)

in video signal level, in 1% of the picture area occurring within a time period of several frames.

The AVMD operates by analyzing the analog video signal from the camera and determining whether the scene has changed. The system "memorizes" the value of a standard reference scene depicted within the DMZ and compares it with a value in the current real-time scene. If the two values are the same within the active DMZ, electronic circuitry declares that there has been no motion and no alarm is declared. On the other hand, if there has been a scene change caused by someone intruding into the scene, an object moving, or some other light-level disturbance, providing the change is larger than a prescribed amount, typically 10–25%, then electronic circuitry decides that a change has occurred, there has been motion in the alarmed area, and an alarm signal is produced. This alarm signal is used to produce an audible or visual alarm, turn on or activate a video printer. The AVMD operates independently of the video monitor or any other recording equipment, and in no way interferes with it.

13.5 DIGITAL VIDEO MOTION DETECTOR (DVMD)

While analog VMDs have been in use for security applications for many years, they have only been moderately successful in *indoor* applications where lighting has been well controlled. In outdoor applications, a far more complex digital electronic system is needed to provide reliable VMD capability. The DVMD must take into account the many variations of lighting, type of target movement, and electrical background disturbances caused by external sources and noise in the system. In the past, these sophisticated expensive systems have been used in large government facilities and nuclear power plants. With lower cost derived from high density memory and more powerful computers, the DVMD is now in more widespread use in commercial installations.

The DVMD allows the user to divide the monitor's video scene into small detection areas called windows, and in some cases even smaller size areas going down to the pixel level. The flexibility of these windows allows the user to specify particular areas or zones of interest. Each window or zone has its own set of programming levels for sensitivity and alarm triggering level. Only the windows are activated or processed for alarm events: all the other parts of the scene which either are not of interest or may contain false alarm producing motion are not. Using this technique, doors to a building may be monitored while headlights from an adjacent car parked or other bright lights in the scene are ignored. Since average light-level changes in the scene occur, the system automatically adjusts to both increasing and decreasing illumination by monitoring and updating reference levels for each video input. The entire scene is also continually monitored for light and illumination changes and full image scene changes such as those caused by a lightning or clouds drifting in front of the sun. The scene changes would not trigger an alarm but rather reset the references for each window, and the VMD would continue monitoring the detection zones for motion or inactivity. The sensitivity of each window is monitored and controlled by the user.

The more sophisticated and expensive DVMD systems use elemental detection zones, in which the scene is divided into a large number of zones (hundreds to thousands) and converted into a digital signal. The processor analyzes these individual zones and makes a decision whether or not an alarm is present. With these microprocessor-based systems, many parameters are analyzed, thereby forming a more reliable basis for an alarm signal decision. Light-level changes in these DVMD systems are compared with the previously stored values ratiometrically—that is, on a percentage basis. Ratio-metric thresholding causes the system to cancel out any gross change in the scene lighting, so that an alarm decision is made strictly on an incremental basis, for a small portion of the total picture area.

The digital electronics in the DVMD subdivides the camera scene into many small elemental zones—as many as 10,000—and makes a zone-by-zone comparison (subtraction) of the non-moving or steady scene with the motion scene. It goes into an alarm mode when a threshold is detected in any one or a multiple of these zones. By converting the signal from analog to digital and dividing it

into many zones, a much more sensitive device results. This technique allows discrimination between real targets and false alarms and other scene lighting variations, and provides a more reliable system for outdoor use.

The user-selected zones are positioned over specific areas where motion is expected. These zones may cover assets to be protected, entry or exit points, parking lot slots, perimeter areas, and perimeter fence lines. Each zone may be set with a different sensitivity appropriate to the percentage change required to trigger the alarm in that zone. The larger the percentage required to cause an alarm, the less sensitive the system is to contrast changes and the less likely it is to produce false alarms. The DVMD is much more sensitive than the large area detection AVMD.

13.5.1 Mode of Operation

The DVMD processing unit converts an analog video signal into a digital code and performs DSP to make it sensitive to specific types of motion in the camera scene (Figure 13-5). For each camera a specific detection pattern or area is selected, or already programmed into the electronics memory. The detection pattern is part or all of the camera image scene within which specific sample points are designated. Depending on the manufacturer, the sample points vary in number and location. At a designated rate, the sample or reference image from a specific camera is converted from the analog to the digital format, and the digital values are stored in temporary memory in the VMD unit. This reference or base image is updated at variable rates

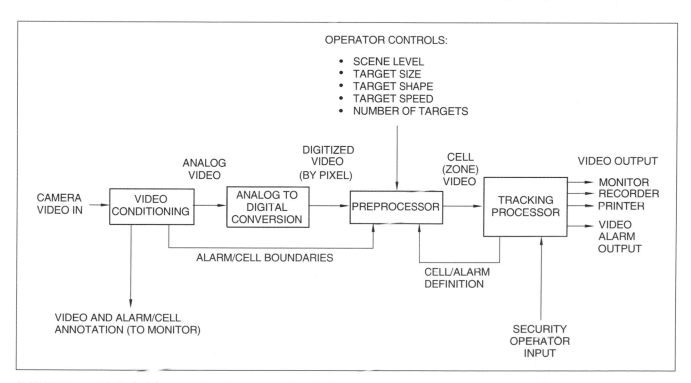

FIGURE 13-5 Digital video motion detector (DVMD) block diagram

to compensate for small changes in the scene that do not constitute alarm events.

At programmable rates at a later time, the camera images are converted into a digital format and electronically compared with the stored reference image. If there has been movement in the scene or any variation in a significant number of sample points over some range, an alarm is triggered. If some harmless objects such as a small animal or bird or debris pass through the scene no alarm will occur. If, however, there is movement within the scene—such as a person entering a window or opening or closing a door—the VMD will be triggered. The number of sample points and the amount of change within the areas to produce an alarm output depend on the particular manufacturer, model, and operator control settings.

Depending on the design, a VMD can process 1, 10, 16, 32, or 64 cameras and sample them serially: that is, camera 1, then camera 2, and so on, and then back to camera 1. Some systems sample and process multiple cameras simultaneously, then analyze and respond to multiple alarms. When a VMD detects an alarm event its output can be used for multiple functions. It can display the alarmed camera on a monitor, alert a guard with a visible or audible signal, record the alarm on a video recorder, send the alarm signal to a remote site, or activate a TL VCR or DVR with an alarm input to change its recording mode from TL to real-time.

In contrast to the AVMD that detects the change in light level in one or a small number of scene locations (zones), the DVMD electronically analyzes hundreds or thousands of zones in the video signal and provides information such as the location in the picture where a motion or intrusion has occurred. Its output drives various audible and visible alarm signals, a graphic monitor map showing the motion path in the image, and a record of the intrusion using a recorder or video printer. In normal operation when there is no motion or change in a scene, the VMD takes the video signal from the camera, stores the video frame (containing no motion), continually updates and memorizes the subsequent frames, and compares them to the previous frame to see if there is a difference in the new frame. If there is no motion there is no alarm. If there is a difference of measurable and defined value, then an alarm is declared and an output produced.

Caution must still be taken for outdoor applications, however, in which there are rapid changes in sunlight, clouds, shadows, distance of objects, rain, snow, movement of trees or shrubbery, camera movement in winds, automobile lights, ripples on the water, and other small moving objects. This can represent a fairly impressive range of problems that must still be considered in outdoor applications. To address some of these problems, DVMD systems have additional automatic adjustments (algorithms) to process the visual signal data to exclude some of these problematic false alarms. One problem, in particular, is to determine the size of a target in the scene. When a

target is viewed from a distance it appears to have a small size on the monitor image. As the target moves closer to the camera it increases its apparent size thereby causing the confusion in target identification. Motion detectors generally have a more positive identification of a target if the target is moving *perpendicularly* or at an angle to the camera, rather than *toward or away* from the camera. If cameras can be mounted to have this relationship to the target, a positive identification can usually be made. The most significant new parameters added to digital VMD processors to improve the capability for outdoor operation have been: (1) improved multi-directional detection, (2) 3-dimensional perspective analysis, and (3) automatic adjustment to changing environmental conditions. Improved multi-directional detection provides the ability to determine whether the object is moving directly toward or away from the camera, especially when the target is at a distance. The ability to automatically adjust to changing environmental conditions removes the technical difficulty to manually readjust the system sensitivity setting to match daily weather variations. Systems not having this ability are difficult to calibrate and require constant recalibration.

13.5.2 Technology

When a video image is converted to data in a digital format, the image information becomes the stored digital value. This digital value changes as the video image (the source of the data) changes. Complex algorithms analyze the changing digital values to recognize patterns. This is considered as video content analysis. These algorithms are a software function and are programmed into electronic chips that can be installed in cameras, standalone modules, DVRs, and dedicated computer processors. DVMD is also available as software for installation in off-the-shelf computers.

Algorithms have been designed to decrease the number of monitors that must be viewed. This is accomplished by scene averaging and filtering techniques to eliminate items that do not fit the model of the motion or activity and do not represent a threat to the site. Once the system detects an object, it applies various tests in an attempt to classify the object, taking into account such characteristics as size, shape, true height to width ratio, and location. If the object or activity fits one of the criteria for a target, it is marked and a more accurate determination is made to identify personnel and activities.

Digital VMD technology has the ability to monitor *every pixel* of every image individually and/or as a group. The light level of each pixel can be memorized in storage and compared to subsequent images to determine if there is a light-level change and how much the change is. By applying this technology over the entire image, the light-level changes in each pixel can be examined and a determination made whether it fits the criterion of an alarm. Algorithms are designed to identify objects of specific size, shape, movement, etc. on a pixel-by-pixel basis. Flying debris and other false alarms can be filtered out by size, object direction and speed, color, and type of motion and pattern.

Determining the size of an object in the FOV is difficult since the object appears as a different size depending on its distance from the camera. If the object is close to the camera it is large and as it moves away from the camera it becomes smaller and smaller. For this reason, parameters such as shape and movement are also required to determine the identity of the object. Object direction can be determined easily since the object activates many pixels and by keeping track of the left-to-right or up-and-down motion it is easily accomplished.

In some cases the color of the object may be useful, and this is easily determined in the color camera by monitoring the color of each pixel in the moving object. This can be important if a person with particular color clothing has been identified as the target. The parameter of color is used to continue tracking that person. Likewise, in outdoor applications if an automobile is identified with a particular color, the color might be the most important criterion for tracking the vehicle. Environmental conditions producing dust, fog, rain, snow, and sleet produce some ambiguity in target detection. These disturbances generally reduce the range over which VMD is effective.

Combining object motion and pattern recognition can provide additional information in determining the identity of a person and the behavior of the target. Algorithms have been devised to identify the movement of a person walking. They have been able to tell the difference between a person walking, a walking dog, a crawling man, and others. There are also various motions that an intruder or criminal makes as compared to our normal movement, and these abnormal motions can be saved and put into storage and can help to identify a person exhibiting such movements in the video image.

An object's speed is used by setting criteria for how fast the object of interest is able to move, and if the object is moving faster or slower than a predetermined speed it is registered as a false alarm. The VMD can have a library that stores information about the unique movement and pattern of particular objects such as paper leaves, ripples on water, birds.

The DVMD has the ability to remove constant motion from the scene which often takes the form of rain storms, snow, sleet, hail, water fountains, waves on water, etc. Algorithms stored in memory are used to filter out these *constant motion* disturbances. If there is an object within such constant motion moving at a different speed the system is able to identify this target.

The DVMD digitizes the frames from each camera into a large number of zones corresponding to exact locations on the monitor screen. The number of digitized zones varies from hundreds to many thousands. The system assigns an absolute gray-scale value (light level) to each zone and stores the digitized gray-scale value and location in RAM. This procedure is carried out for each video camera channel. The DVMD can digitize the picture into 16–256 gray-scale levels, thereby storing (memorizing) the image scene very accurately. After this reference scene has been memorized in RAM, the DVMD digitizes subsequent camera frames and compares them to the stored values, zone by zone. If the stored levels at any location differ by one or two gray scale levels—between the stored frame and the live frame—an alarm condition exists.

Most DVMDs in use today use standard menu screens to monitor and respond to alarms, using either simple keyboards or a mouse device for programming, adjustment, and normal operation. Most current systems do not require a personal computer (PC) for operation, but all provide an RS-232 interface for computer integration or remote programming and reporting. The RS-232 approach and menu-driven screens for operation and control of the digital VMD systems provide a friendly interface to the user.

Self-contained DVMDs are based on proprietary signal processing algorithms and easily integrate into existing multi-camera video systems. Most camera inputs are digitally sampled with a resolution of 768 by 480 pixels and eight bits (256 levels) of grayscale. All images are sampled and displayed at 30 fps (60 fields per second). Each camera is associated with a dedicated event when an alarm output occurs, and can be connected to a video recorder or audible or visual anunciator whenever any window in any camera has been alarmed. Additionally, a video loss output signals an alarm if the camera loses power or no video signal is present, and remains active until the video signal is restored or the time-out feature resets.

Many DVMD systems have two monitor outputs although only one monitor is required for viewing. Many users prefer a dual-monitor approach. One monitor is used to view live sequencing from camera to camera or a specific camera view. The second monitor is used in digital mode to view motion detection windows triggered by an alarm. When alarms occur from multiple cameras, the operator can sequence through the alarming cameras at a user-defined rate or go to the quad or 9 or 16 split image display with the alarming cameras in that mode. In any case, the images from the alarm cameras are highlighted graphically on the display. The minimum hold time for each alarm is user-defined, usually from several seconds to 5–10 minutes. The user can also select freeze times for any of the alarmed images ranging from seconds to minutes. In the freeze frame mode the video display is locked into a full screen. When an event occurs in that camera after the freeze frame time has elapsed, the video continues in full motion allowing the guard to continue monitoring the cameras.

In the playback of recorded images from the VCR or DVR the output can be displayed on either or both monitors. This allows one monitor to be left in the normal display mode monitoring potential alarms while the other plays back the recorded images for review.

13.5.2.1 Programming the digital VMD

The DVMD includes an RS-232 interface to allow the user a choice of using either the front-panel controls or a mouse for system setup. Either way the window placement, size, or sensitivity are simply defined. Each camera can be programmed to include numbers and titles defining the specific camera, which is later displayed whenever that camera is displayed. These titles may be positioned anywhere within the full screen window so as not to obscure any important areas in the image. The system utilizes pull-down programming menus to control split-screen sequence rates, the camera ID information, and any other titles. Menus are available to adjust the sensitivity and scene area balance of the pixel level for alarm functioning.

Some systems can provide not only intruder detection but also lost object detection. Even in the presence of multiple moving objects in the same window, intelligent DVMD systems can accommodate a rapidly changing illumination condition commonly found in outdoor scenes, as well as sudden illumination changes from man-made and natural sources.

13.5.2.2 DVMD Setup Procedures

The DVMD system uses graphic symbols for motion sensitivity settings, simplifying the motion detection setup. In addition to a flashing cursor on screen, text prompts appear as shown in Figure 13-6.

Cameras can have motion detection in particular areas in the scene completely disabled. This should not be confused with enabling or disabling individual zones or pixels in areas of interest. Disabled zones that may contain unimportant or incidental movement include the following:

- Trees that can sway in the wind
- Pedestrians and vehicular motion *that is not important*
- Reflections from glass, bodies of water, or other highly polished surfaces, which can be sources of apparent motion.

The different alarm zones can be designated on the monitor in different colors for identification purposes. Examples are:

Choice	Color of Flashing Cursor
No action	Gray/white
Enable zones	Black/white
Disable zones	Clear/white

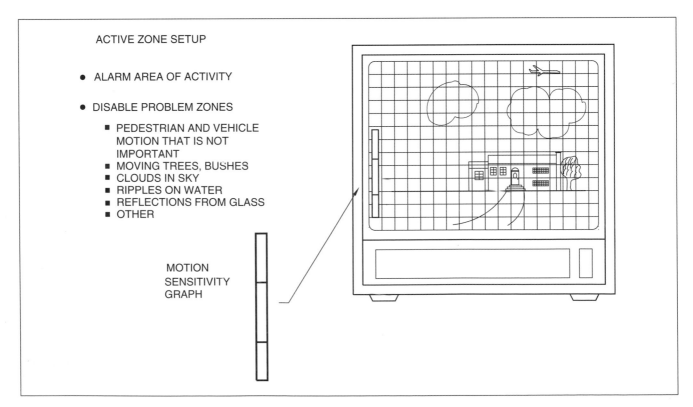

FIGURE 13-6 On-screen digital video motion detector (DVMD) graphic display

13.5.2.3 Sensitivity Settings

A bar graph is often used to illustrate the alarm sensitivity setting for the camera. The bar graph displays the sensitivity setting as a red line. A black line moves from the bottom to the top of the bar to indicate a change in motion or activity in the scene. When the black line reaches the red line above, a motion alarm is activated (Figure 13-7). The user selects a number or sensitivity button between 1 through 10 to change the sensitivity. In practice, *watching the scene* from a camera and *watching the motion* helps to determine the appropriate sensitivity setting for the camera. This procedure is performed for each camera during the initial setup phase of the system.

13.5.2.4 Motion Detection Sensitivity

Motion detection sensitivity for each camera can be set to levels from 1 through 10. The setting is made on a camera-by-camera basis, and applies to all enabled zones in any particular camera scene. Each of the zones distinguishes among 256 grayscale levels averaged over each zone's area. A sensitivity of 1 is the least sensitive to motion and a setting of 10 is the most sensitive to motion. These settings are made using a bar graph similar to that used in the sensitivity settings above. Some recommendations for setup are listed below:

- If motion detection activates without an apparent cause, reduce the sensitivity.

- When setting sensitivity, select the highest setting that does not result in frequent false motion detection.
- The higher the sensitivity, the more likely the incidental movement to be detected as motion.
- When setting high sensitivity, such as 8–10, sources of false motion like reflections and windblown trees should be absent, otherwise alarms will occur.

The DVMD used as a sensor activates alarm inputs, essentially creating a motion-based alarm sensor input. The system in this scenario does not distinguish between an input from an external alarm sensor (switch, PIR, glass break detector, etc.), or when activated internally to the VMD system.

13.5.3 Hardware

Some DVMDs monitor up to 32 separate video cameras by sampling, time-sharing each camera sequentially. Each camera can have a separately adjustable sensitized alarming area, thereby optimizing each camera to the scene it views. Likewise, the number of sensitive zones in each camera is chosen independently to match the scene requirement. If one camera views a large area scene looking for small intrusions, the operator can make the alarming zone small for this first channel. If another camera views a small area scene looking for large intrusions, the operator can make the alarming zone large for this channel, and so on. Equipment setup procedures differ from manufacturer to

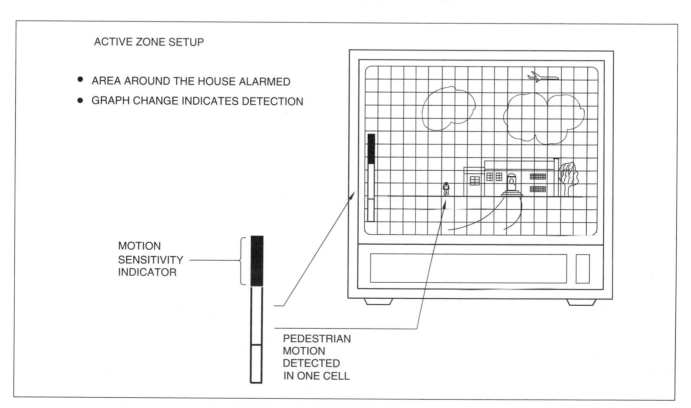

FIGURE 13-7 Bar graph sensitivity display

manufacturer, but there are some common parameters and controls that must be determined and set when initially installing the DVMD system. Typical setup controls include:

- **Channel Mode Control.** A switch selects the mode for each video camera channel. In the down position—INHIBIT—the channel is disabled and no alarms are registered. In the middle position—NORMAL—the cameras are ready for motion detection and alarming. In the up position—SET—the console operator can manually select any camera on the alarm monitor. When released from the SET position the switch returns to the NORMAL mode.
- **Alarm Area Control.** The alarm area control lets the operator manually adjust the position and size of the alarmed area zone. These adjustments can desensitize areas of the camera's FOV where normal movement would cause an unnecessary alarm. For example, in an outdoor scene where a flag is constantly waving, the desensitized area would appear on the monitor but movement within that area would not cause an alarm.
- **Refresh Control.** The refresh rate refers to the time interval during which the reference frame memorized in RAM is stored, before it is again updated. Systems use refresh rates varying from 1/30 second up to several seconds. The operator selects the refresh rate, which is normally a function of the number of cameras and the kinds of alarms expected in the scenes.
- **Ranging Control.** Most systems allow adjustment of the electronic analog dynamic range of the analog-to-digital (A/D) converter. The function of the A/D converter is to change the camera's analog electronic video signal to digital values. To provide the best scene resolution for each camera, the operator adjusts the range of white to black level in the digitized video signal.
- **Masking Control.** The masking control allows the operator to enter scene areas on the monitor screen for which no alarming will occur. It is entered by inserting rectangular, square, or other masked areas. In some systems the operator enters the masking with a light pen. The light pen permits irregular shapes to be desensitized merely by drawing around the object in the CCTV monitor scene.

In many VMD systems the detection zones may be of any shape and be divided into separate areas to accommodate unique detection requirements. Zones can be individually turned on or off to accommodate entrance, hallway, parking area, or other locations. Two examples of zones being turned on or off individually are the following: (1) a zone encompassing a gate or doorway can be turned off during shift changes while other zones in the same scene can remain active to alarm and alert an operator of unauthorized intrusions, (2) a zone encompassing a file cabinet can be left off during normal working hours and turned on overnight. The systems can have independent

16-step zone sensitivity, signal integration (retention), plus multilevel digital filtering to maximize motion alarm detection and minimize false alarms. Periodic automatic rebalancing minimizes the effect of slow light changes, such as those occurring between daylight and nighttime conditions.

In operation, a cell is activated by the changes in the video content of successive picture fields. A higher retention setting delays the automatic rebalancing to optimize detection of slow changes or slow-moving objects. Both the video change (sensitivity) and the rebalancing time (retention) assigned to a zone can be adjusted to optimize detection and minimize false alarms for that zone. Any activated cell in a zone alerts (activates) that zone and channel.

Systems have integral video switchers with dual video outputs and RS-232 port to allow the DVMD to function as a standalone system. An audio output is available to warn the operator of an alert, and a relay closure can start a recorder for recording alerted channels. The RS-232 ports provide both a control input and an alarm output. They permit remote system control via a separate control keyboard, a data terminal, or a computer.

Either of the two on-screen alert presentation modes may be selected to highlight the intruder's path through the facility. They are *normal* or *trace*.

13.5.3.1 Normal Mode

In the normal mode, a bright dot is displayed in the picture on the alarm monitor at the center of each activated cell. With manual reset, this dot remains lighted until the channel is reset. With automatic reset, each dot disappears 16 seconds after the cell was first activated. Thus an intruder moving into a zone will cause a series of dots to appear as he first activates cells and leaves a trail of dots through the zone or to the point in the zone where he stopped or hid.

13.5.3.2 Trace Mode

In the trace mode, a bright dot is displayed in the picture on the alarm monitor at the center of each activated cell as in the normal mode. In addition, each illuminated dot emits a quick burst of flashes 8 seconds after it is activated. With manual reset, this results in a continuous moving trail of flashes at 8-second intervals along the path of intrusion. With automatic reset, a single burst of flashes occurs before each cell is automatically reset. These flashes can assist the operator in determining the size, direction, and location of an intrusion.

Larger monitoring sites require more cameras and monitors and a more comprehensive DVMD digital system. A high-speed microprocessor analyzes detected motion for size, position, and rate of movement to discriminate against undesired targets and to verify a valid intrusion before the system signals an alarm. Verified intrusions initiate audio and visual alarm signals. Video from alarmed cameras are connected to outputs for an alarm monitor, a recorder to monitor and record the track and position of intruders. Independent output relays provide control of external devices. A built-in sequential switcher provides normal system viewing of all cameras by separate video output.

For ease of operation, some systems have user-defined detection of active areas initiated using a light pen. Zones can be individually deactivated while observing the picture to eliminate detection of areas where insignificant or acceptable motion could cause some false alarms. The systems have the ability to perform target discrimination. Each camera module is programmable to optimize target discrimination based on a combination of anticipated characteristics, such as size, rate of movement, and indoor/outdoor scenes. In order to see the intrusion track and position display, zones where motion has been detected are highlighted on the video displays.

The system microprocessor analyzes the cell data and removes background clutter and identifies any changes in the cells as targets to be tracked. The target's motion, speed, direction, and distance traveled are analyzed to see if they match the characteristics of a human intruder. When a human intruder is identified, on-screen graphics highlight his position and an alarm is signaled.

Special setup graphics define the camera zones to be monitored. Target discrimination is based on target size, contrast, speed, and direction. Target tracking is used to verify detection before declaring an alarm, resulting in a low false-alarm rate. The operator sets up sharply defined detection zones configurable for each camera, which may be tailored to reflect the optical differences between near and distant areas and act as distance compensation.

Digital video motion detectors are available in sizes suitable for small to large video surveillance systems (Figure 13-8). A family of products available is suitable for a single channel or four channels all provided with DSP electronics and microprocessors to analyze the entire video scene up to 30 fps for precision video detection of motion. At each update the system measures the precise change in each pixel's gray-scale level, i.e. the change in light intensity. These DVMD units are small in size, easy to install, and have simple pushbutton access for on-screen menu programming. They have access codes and password protection to protect against unwanted changes in programming by unauthorized personnel. The motion detection criteria include duration of motion and sensitivity. There are 99 levels of sensitivity permitting use in a variety of lighting situations. The 4, 9, and 16 channel units have built-in sequential switchers and provide alarm and video output from alarmed cameras. Alarm outputs can trigger TL VCR and DVR recorders, matrix switchers, quads, video printers, or video transmission devices.

One system has the ability to cascade up to 16 of the single channel units via a single host RS-232 serial port (Figure 13-8d). Figure 13-9 shows a block diagram of the multiple camera VMD system. One DVMD digitizes the scene by creating up to 16,000 individual zone locations per scene in up to 16 camera scenes. With this high resolving power, the system can detect an intruder occupying as little as 0.01% of the area. The DVMD system operates normally with a blank monitor. When a camera receives or detects motion, an audible alert is sounded and the disturbed scene appears on the monitor. The DVRs are activated for recording the intrusion scene or for reviewing the alarmed scene at a later time. When the DVMD displays the picture on the monitor, the guard sees the intruder in the scene even though he occupies only a small portion. The guard will also know where the intruder is, even if he is hidden from camera view, since the system displays the intruder's path on the monitor. This display is accomplished by displaying bright flashes on the monitor at all locations the intruder has passed through. The guard now knows not only which scene was intruded upon but also the exact location of the intruder in that scene at that instant. He can therefore concentrate immediately on what decision to make and what action to take.

There is no industry standardization for the design and specifications of AVMD or DVMD systems. The features of some representative VMD systems and specific attributes are described in the following sections and Table 13-1.

13.5.3.3 DVMD Graphic Site Display Maps

An auxiliary display useful with VMD systems is an illuminated graphic display consisting of an overlay that is a plan view diagram of the entire monitored site. The map overlay shows the location of each camera and alarm sensor, and flashes on the display when an intrusion occurs. To ensure that no intrusion is missed, particularly if there are simultaneous intrusions or motions in the scenes, video recorders are used. The recorder records the video scene, the intruder, his track through the scene, as well as a graphic alarm map if available. In the event of multiple video alarms in a single recording system, the recorder is set to record one alarm scene for a predetermined time interval and then switch to the next alarm scene. If a non-video sensor detects an alarm, the system activates the appropriate camera(s) and the recorder. The displayed information enables the console operator to assess the situation rapidly and accurately and report any diversionary tactics. Present DVMD equipments are able to detect 20 times the number of intrusions as those detected by a guard looking at the video monitor without the benefit of the DVMD. This DVMD system is not easily mesmerized!

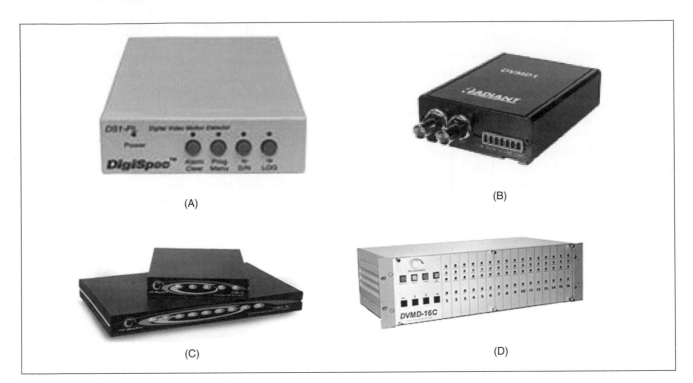

FIGURE 13-8   Single and cascaded-single digital video motion detector (DVMD)

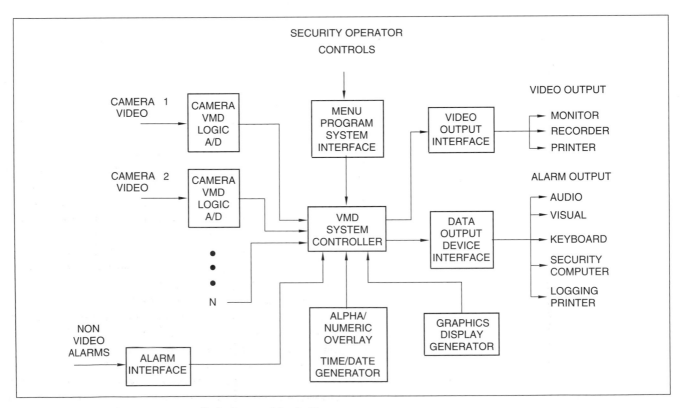

FIGURE 13-9   Multiple camera digital VMD block diagram

The DVMD analyzer detects the alarm condition by storing the scene in solid-state RAM. In one system, the storage process takes approximately 33 milliseconds and consist of sampling the picture scene (up to 16,384 dis-crete locations) that are spaced throughout the scene. At each location the brightness is measured (one of 256 different gray-scale levels). The address (pixel location in the scene and camera) is stored with the brightness number.

DISPLAYED VMD [*] INFORMATION	SETUP PARAMETERS	FEATURES

ACTIVE AREA
MASKED AREA
MOTION ALARM
  LOCATION OF ALARM:
  SIZE OF MOTION AREA
    (H×V) PIXELS)
MOVEMENT OF ALARMED [†]
AREA-TRACKING
	SENSITIVITY [**]
	SIZE OF ACTIVE AREA (ZONES)
	  (NUMBER OF H×V PIXELS)
	NUMBER OF ACTIVE ZONES
	SHAPE OF ACTIVE ZONE(S)
	DISABLED ZONES (ZONE MASK)
	  (SIZE, SHAPE, NUMBER)
	PROBABILITY OF DETECTION [**]
	ALARM LEVEL
	CONTRAST
		ON-SCREEN SETUP MENU
		VIDEO LOSS DETECTION
		NTSC/CCIR/PAL FORMATS
		CONTROL P/T/Z
		ALARM INPUTS
		ALARM OUTPUTS
		PASS THROUGH VIDEO

[*] ON-SCREEN DISPLAY: VARIES WIDELY DEPENDING ON SPECIFIC EQUIPMENT

[**] WHEN SET UP OPTIMALLY: TYPICAL PPROBABILITY OF DETECTION– BETTER THAN 96%
                              TYPICAL NUISANCE ALARM RATE—LESS THAN 2%/DAY
                              TESTS BASED ON INDUSTRY STANDARDS

[†] AVAILABLE ON SOME MODELS

Table 13-1 Digital Video Motion Detector (DVMD) Features

This occurs for all zones in the scene. After the brightness and location information are stored, a comparison process is initiated that compares the present live picture from the camera (which the camera generates 30 times a second) to the stored picture. Whenever there is a brightness discrepancy in any zone, the address of that particular zone location is also stored with its brightness value. Zone locations where these differences are caused by electrical noise or ambient scene motion such as blowing leaves, trees, or flags are processed out and are not considered as alarms. All scene areas where detection is not desired are removed or masked out.

When a sufficient number of zones change, an alarm is processed. The comparison process occurs across the entire scene 30 times a second. The alarm condition is established by counting the number of locations with different values; if a preset threshold count is reached (any number, but generally 1 in 8 counts), the system then alarms. The count is cleared each time a new storage process takes place. The memory is refreshed on a preset basis and ranges from 1/15th of a second to many seconds. Memory refresh prevents normal changes, such as scene lighting, moving clouds, or electronic drifts in the camera from being interpreted as alarm conditions. The camera viewing the intrusion scene is automatically switched to the monitor (any standard video monitor) and the scene displayed. The monitor is usually blank prior to an alarm, since there is no reason to display the scene if no activity is occurring. Table 13-2 summarizes the parameters of several commercially available digital VMD systems.

13.5.4 Features

VMD technology is not standardized, and therefore selecting the appropriate VMD approach requires understanding the VMD features available and requirements of the application. Basic motion detection typically recognizes any type of motion in the camera FOV. A single output then activates automatic call up to the monitor screens for the surveillance personnel and initiates automatic VCR or DVR recording. With the advent of LANs, WANs and the Internet, the video call up is no longer limited to cabled CCTV systems, but can be transmitted over these communications channels, or even wireless. Advanced VMD products enhance the concepts of basic VMD through the use of elaborate algorithms that search out detailed movement patterns, and only activate a system response under very specific conditions. These activity criteria include:

- Intruder Identification: Identifying unauthorized humans in specified areas of the video FOV.
- Environmental Compensation: Recognizing and ignoring wind-blown debris, animals, background traffic, etc.
- Counting: Recognizing a quantity of a particular object or number of persons moving through an area.
- Direction: Ignoring objects moving in one direction, while alarming for objects moving in unauthorized directions (no identification).
- Item Recognition: Activating when specific user-selected items are removed from, placed in, or passed through the FOV.

VMD TYPE	CAMERAS MONITORED	USER SETUP* CONTROLS	TARGET** SENSITIVITY PARAMETERS	RESOLUTION‡ (PIXEL LEVEL)	INPUT/OUTPUT SIGNALS	SIZE (inch)
SINGLE CHANNEL	1	SENSITIVITY OBJECT SIZE OBJECT DIRECTION OBJECT COLOR OBJECT MOTION AND PATTERN OBJECT SPEED	MINIMUM AGE† MINIMUM MOVE (#OF CELLS TO CAUSE ALARM)	720×486 260,000	VIDEO ALARM INPUT/OUTPUT DRY CONTACT	SMALL 1.5×3.5×5
SIXTEEN CHANNEL	16		TARGET SIZE MINIMUM VELOCITY MAXIMUM VELOCITY	720×486 260,000 (PER CHANNEL)	RS232, 422, 485 CONTROL P/T/Z	5 inch RACK MOUNT

*EITHER DONE VIA FRONT PANEL CONTROLS OR THROUGH SOFTWARE AND COMMUNICATION PORT

**TYPICAL PROBABILITY OF DETECTION–BETTER THAN 96%
   TYPICAL NUISANCE ALARM RATE–LESS THAN 2%/DAY
   STANDARD TESTS BASED ON INDUSTRY STANDARDS

†NUMBER OF FRAMES A TARGET MUST BE TRACKED BEFORE IT GENERATES
   AN ALARM. RANGES BETWEEN 1–300 FRAMES

††EACH ZONE IS COMPRISED OF A "BLOCK" OF PIXELS DEFINING THE ACTIVE OR MASKED ZONE

Table 13-2   Digital Video Motion Detector (DVMD) System Parameters

- Subject Tracking: Highlighting and following a specific person or item as it moves about the FOV or from the FOV of one camera to another.
- Multiple Subject Tracking: Highlighting and following multiple persons or items simultaneously as they move about the FOV or from the FOV of one camera to another.

13.6   GUIDELINES, PROS AND CONS

Some basic questions to be answered where VMD is required:

- Detection: Is there anything there?
- Classification: What is it—a car, person, bird, boat, van?
- Location: Where is it?
- Identification: Is it an unauthorized person?
- Is the person in the correct location at the site?

The security director and managers of a facility and the design professional who understand the VMD hardware options should begin a project by asking several important questions:

- What can move in the video image?
- What do we want to know about its movement?

The first objective is to identify what can move. This determines the surveillance areas to be covered by the cameras and begins to define the VMD product required. The answer to what can move includes items of interest and any moving background items that may distract the system. The items of interest can be items that are typically in motion, and therefore either passed through the FOV or stopped in the FOV, these items require identification or must be followed by the surveillance cameras. Some of these moving targets include:

- Vehicles moving through entrances or a prescribed traffic route
- Routine entry and exit by unauthorized personnel
- Baggage left unattended
- Personal property that is carried by the public
- Suspect individuals
- Employee work methods or handling of assets.

Other items or activity that should be of concern include:

- Intruders or unauthorized personnel in an area or perimeter
- Leaks or mechanical failures
- Smoke, fire, or flame
- Violent or erratic behavior
- Counter-flow directional movement.

After the type of movement is understood, the next criteria affecting design and selection should be: What action should be taken when the motion of interest occurs? Does the alarm of interest require immediate response? If the incident requires immediate response, active surveillance personnel must receive the image and understand what they are seeing. They must also have instructions as to what action to take for each type of alarm. If the primary purpose of the video is for documentation or prosecution or litigation, changes in the FOV to accommodate the movement should be minimal, and more cameras should be implemented to confirm the events. In order to minimize controversy and to allow acceptance in court, the graphic enhancement of the VMD, the storage methods for the video, and the signal compression methods must be closely scrutinized.

What should be the response and what action, if any, is warranted on the part of the officer based on the information presented? Video-based motion detection systems are providing many of the answers and solutions to this question.

13.7 SUMMARY

The primary function of the VMD is to allow the security force to make optimum decisions about an intrusion or unlawful activity in a minimum amount of time. Professional intruders and thieves use devious and sophisticated techniques, making the guard's response more complex. The intrusion scenario works to the advantage of criminals because they can spend time planning it, as well as anticipating the guard's action under duress.

The DVMD is a sensitive and valuable video security tool since it provides security personnel the visual information taken at the intrusion location when there is motion in the camera FOV. The intrusion scenario can be displayed on a monitor(s), recorded on a VCR or DVR, printed out on a hard-copy video printer, or transmitted to a remote site over a network.

The use of a DVMD significantly increases the security level and reduces the human error in any security system. The choice of the optimum VMD for a specific application requires that the security designer understands the equipment capabilities and limitations and match them to the problem. Of highest importance is whether the VMD can properly react to the changing lighting conditions in the video scene and generate meaningful alarm information and reject false alarms.

The present state of the art indicates that AVMDs can operate acceptably only in well-controlled indoor environments, while DVMDs can operate in all indoor environments and do well in most outdoor environments. Because of the variety of approaches and differences in DVMD equipment, characteristics of systems manufactured by leaders in the field must be considered on their own merits. Analyzing the systems described exposes the designer to some of the features available and permits asking the manufacturer sensible questions to determine suitability for the problem to be solved. Some helpful comments and hints follow:

- AVMDs or DVMDs are suitable for indoor applications.
- DVMDs should be used for all outdoor applications.
- The VMD should be able to switch video to a VCR or DVR and produce a hard-copy video printout.
- Once the VMD system is set up, most of the decision-making should be automatic.
- Following initial setup, alarm declaration should be automatic, using a menu-driven program.

An important axiom to remember is that the *application should define the system* rather than the system defining the application.

Chapter 14
Dome Cameras

CONTENTS

14.1   Overview
14.2   Speed-Dome Background
14.3   Fixed Dome
    14.3.1   Technology
    14.3.2   Housing
    14.3.3   Hardware
14.4   Speed Dome
    14.4.1   Technology
    14.4.2   Housing
    14.4.3   Hardware
14.5   Dome Mounting Hardware
    14.5.1   Fixed Dome
    14.5.2   Moveable Speed Dome
14.6   Cabling-Video Signal and Controls
14.7   Special Features
14.8   Special Applications
    14.8.1   Outdoor Building Mounts
    14.8.2   Pole Mounts
14.9   Summary

14.1 OVERVIEW

Fixed and Speed-Domes. The fixed dome camera has found widespread use in the video security industry. It has a monochrome or color camera and a fixed focal length lens. The camera is often mounted on a simple manually adjustable pan and tilt mount and the entire assembly mounted on a wall or ceiling.

The pan/tilt speed-dome has become one of the most popular scanning video camera surveillance system in the industry. The primary reason for their popularity is in the large amount of visual intelligence they can provide to the security operator in such a small physical package. The speed dome can be mounted almost anywhere: ceiling, wall, building exterior and pole. High resolution light

sensitive color cameras and compact zoom lenses with auto-focus mounted in ultra-fast pan/tilt module make them very effective in most environments including retail stores, casinos, commercial and government office buildings, warehouses, airports, highways, etc.

One technique used to combine the conventional separate camera, lens, housing, and pan/tilt video surveillance assembly is to integrate them all in a plastic dome. The dome housing is more discrete than most other conventional housings. The dome camera consists of a round or hemispherical clear or tinted dome in which a camera, lens, and a manual or motorized pan/tilt mechanism are housed. The ceiling-mounted, below-the-ceiling, and wall-mounted hemispherical dome looks totally different from the rectangular housing and other shaped housings, and blends in well with many architectural décors. Since the hemispherical dome is circularly symmetrical, it can be in a fixed position and the camera pointed in any direction to view the scene. A pan/tilt module in the dome can rotate and tilt the camera and lens while inside the confines of the dome. This differs from cameras mounted inside rectangular housings where the entire housing assembly and the camera move as one unit, and the pointing direction is known to the observer below. If the dome is tinted then the person down at floor level viewing the dome cannot see the camera and lens, and it is possible to point the camera in any direction without the observer knowing it is there, or seeing it move. This capability can act as an additional security deterrent because the observer does not know when he or she is under surveillance. Domes are less obtrusive and generally accepted in any environment. Bullet cameras (commonly called bullet or lipstick cameras) are smaller and less noticeable, but they are visually directional and the viewing and pointing direction is visible.

The moveable speed-dome camera contains an inverted pan/tilt mechanism suspended inside the dome with an integral zoom lens and video camera module. The dome enclosure containing the camera/lens and pan/tilt mechanism eliminates the precipitation, wind loading, dust, and dirt problem. The dome pan/tilt design is adaptable for use in outdoor applications on poles in parking lots, on building parapets, and under building eaves and passageways.

Indoor and outdoor, fixed and movable camera dome systems are available in many sizes ranging from 5 to 15 inches in diameter depending on the model. Fixed domes with miniature cameras and fixed lenses can be small and discreet and can have a manual pan/tilt adjusted during installation. Speed-dome systems use high-resolution color and monochrome CCD cameras with auto-focus and digital zoom, and zoom lenses.

The dome systems include camera pointing presets for pan, elevation, zoom lens focal length, and other parameters. Another feature some dome systems have is privacy zone blanking that allows specific sections of the camera scene to be masked so that the operator cannot view scenes at pre-programmed camera pointing angles and zoom lens ranges. This prevents viewing the windows of private homes, hotels, or other buildings in the vicinity of the camera, as well as secured and classified areas. The zoom lenses and electronic zoom in the dome cameras can provide powerful zoom capability with magnifications up to 200 times using electronic and optical magnification. The systems have sensitive CCD cameras that provide excellent color viewing during daytime operation and more sensitive monochrome viewing during nighttime operation. Dome cameras can be equipped with VMD and can send an alarm signal to the operator if there is movement in the image when it is viewing a fixed display.

14.2 SPEED-DOME BACKGROUND

There are essentially two types of camera systems that allow the operator to pan, tilt, and zoom the video image onto the monitor. The first type of system has been in use for many years, and uses a fixed camera and zoom lens mounted on a motorized pan/tilt mechanism. The electronics required for communications with the camera and platform motors and switches are installed in a separate enclosure. This type of pan/tilt platform is assembled from separate components and different manufacturers and has several shortcomings:

* The pan/tilt system is bulky and heavy.
* The camera pan/tilt pointing motion is slow—usually less than 10°/sec.
* The camera motion is usually restricted by the interconnected cables, reducing the panning range below 360°.
* The cost for this type system is usually more than the newer speed-dome technology that uses an integrated camera, lens, and pan/tilt all in one dome assembly.

The new high speed dome systems employ newer more sophisticated technology having performance characteristics far superior to the older pan/tilt camera platform system. These speed-dome cameras are small in size: 5–7 inches in diameter and contain all the required control and communication electronics located inside the unit. The dome module weighs far less than the older pan/tilt platforms so that they can be mounted almost anywhere. The panning speed is typically 300–360°/sec and there are no interconnecting cables so that the cameras can be continuously panned without reversing direction. There are various manufacturers that can provide products that have these basic functions.

Prior to the integrated dome with PTZ, pan/tilt platforms were assembled by ordering a housing, a pan/tilt mechanism, a camera, a lens, and wiring them up before installation. In the early 1980s, Sensormatic Inc. made a marketing decision to go into the video speed-dome market. With some of the initial concept coming from a company they had acquired, a large dome system using slip-rings to allow continuous 360° rotation and using a mirror—to reflect the incoming image onto the lens and produce a lower profile dome system—was built. The system also integrated the receiver driver portion of the PTZ control electronics into the dome assembly. To improve accuracy of pan and tilt and increase the speed substantially, stepper motors replaced the AC motors. This also made possible the incorporation of dome pan/tilt pointing presets into the system for defining targets, patterns and boundaries. The entire dome was assembled and tested in 1985, and represented one of the first fully integrated "speed" domes. The first system had a clear viewing bubble 22 inches in diameter and was 8 inches deep. The system used a monochrome vidicon tube camera and weighed approximately 40 lbs. In 1988 a second-generation speed-dome using a color CCD camera imager was produced. The bubble was reduced to 12 inches in diameter and 5 inches deep and weighed 26 lbs. To get the smallest size for the system the CCD sensor and lens were located remotely from the camera body using a high-flex cable. This produced a very short camera-lens assembly. In 1992 the speed-dome received a complete mechanical redesign and used a close-loop DC servo electronic pan/tilt design providing the ability to point to any target in less than one second. The first application for these systems was in casinos and interfaced with American Dynamics matrix switchers.

A second pioneering company in the speed-dome field was Diamond Electronics, producing a high-velocity rate-proportional digital tracking system. It had a slip-ring design to permit continuous 360° rotation at speeds up to 80°/sec and tilt speeds up to 25°/sec. Dynamic braking featured immediate precise stops with ±0.5° accuracy when de-accelerating from any speed. The system had gold and chrome tinted dome capsule enclosures providing one way mirror capsules providing for discrete surveillance. These dome capsules were optically corrected for high-performance monochrome and color camera systems. The drive electronics and camera electronics were all contained within the dome package.

The current and latest generation speed-domes are available in sizes from 4.5 to 10 inches in diameter and have variable high-speed pan/tilt stepper or servo motor drives with continuous 360° rotation obtained with metal or optical slip-rings. Camera-pointing features include Presets, Patterns, and Boundaries. The cameras include high-resolution daytime and nighttime capability using color for daytime and switching to monochrome for higher sensitivity during nighttime operation. Camera features include VMD and alarm activation on motion. These camera-lens modules are equipped with motorized zoom lenses with optical and digital zoom, auto-focus, and iris control. Zoom lenses have 20:1 zoom ratios to obtain telephoto and wide-angle viewing. The camera pan/tilt module is mounted within a rugged, clear, or smoked hemispherical optical grade acrylic plastic dome designed for quick installation, mounting, and servicing in a ceiling, a wall, outdoor on a building parapet, a parking lot pole, or on a highway.

14.3 FIXED DOME

The fixed dome camera assembly has become a very attractive enclosure for providing surveillance in almost any environment. The nature of the round dome with a smoked or tinted dome makes it unobtrusive and does not allow the observer to determine in which direction the camera is viewing. There are many manufacturers producing fixed video domes with fixed camera or manually adjustable pan/tilt mounts. The cameras provided are monochrome or color and the lenses have FOVs from 90° wide-angle to 30° narrow-angle providing an inexpensive, attractive integrated camera for most indoor applications. Some models have variable focal length (vari-focal) lenses to make it easier to obtain just the right camera FOV. For outdoor applications, larger domes with larger and longer focal length lenses are available to provide sufficient magnification for the longer distances. These outdoor domes are available with thermostatically controlled heaters and fans and are sealed against moisture and the environment. All these fixed dome cameras are available with infrared LED to provide operation in nighttime at distance up to 20 feet without any auxiliary lighting.

14.3.1 Technology

The fixed dome cameras use monochrome and color CCD or CMOS cameras with lenses to view narrow-angle, medium- to wide-angle FOVs under most lighting conditions. Typical sensitivities are 1–2 lux for color cameras and 0.1 lux for monochrome. Resolution is typically 480 TV lines for color and 570 TV lines for monochrome. When there is not enough or no lighting an infrared LED camera is used. Many dome manufacturers mount the camera so that it can be manually adjusted in the horizontal and vertical (pan/tilt) directions. These fixed domes are small and lightweight and are easily mounted onto a drop ceiling, hard ceiling, or a wall. Dome cameras are available with standard analog signal outputs for use with coaxial cable, unshielded twisted pair (UTP) or to interface with other transmission means. There are IP network dome cameras that can be connected directly to a LAN, WAN, or the Internet.

14.3.2 Housing

Most indoor fixed dome housings are manufactured using ABS or polycarbonate plastic. The lower dome bubble through which the camera lens views is manufactured from optically clear acrylic plastic. Most systems are provided with a clear, tinted, or smoked plastic bubble. Special variations include bronze, chrome, and gold. The clear bubble essentially transmits all of the light and is used when maximum light throughput is required. The smoked dome loses about 30% of the light (70% transmission), the bronze approximately 50% (50% transmission) of the light, and the gold approximately 75% of the light (25% transmission).

Outdoor housings are available with UV-protected ABS or vinyl, or painted aluminum or steel. For harsh or extreme environments or where corrosive atmospheres or severe vandalism is present, dome housing materials are fabricated from polycarbonate plastic, machined or cast aluminum, or stainless steel.

14.3.3 Hardware

There are many manufacturers of fixed dome camera systems. Figure 14-1 shows examples of indoor and outdoor fixed dome cameras. The size of these domes varies from 4 to 6 inches in diameter and weigh from 1 to 2 lbs. They are available with clear or smoked viewing domes.

14.4 SPEED DOME

The majority of *conventional* camera/lens pan/tilt platforms in housings consist of components obtained from several different manufacturers all assembled by the systems integrator and made to operate as a complete system. This is a practical solution for installations in which the parameters and characteristics of the fixed or movable dome might be unacceptable. The dome camera integrates the camera/lens, pan/tilt, housing, and mounting

FIGURE 14-1 Fixed dome camera systems

(A) FIXED COLOR DAY/NIGHT ANALOG CAMERA

(B) FIXED COLOR INTERNET (IP) MPEG/JPEG CAMERA

system in a single module from a *single* manufacturer. The integral design results in a smaller, lighter weight module having a high scanning speed and wide angular coverage.

Speed-dome systems can scan at a rate of 300°/sec and are capable of panning 360° continuously using slip rings. With 360° continuous horizontal scanning the lens/camera module does not have to come back 360° in order to follow a moving target. All the components can be housed in a 5–7-inch diameter ceiling-mounted dome. Through advanced engineering and compact packaging, these fast scan rates were obtained: the moving parts are small in size, and have low masses and moments of inertia. The obvious advantage of a fast system is that if an incident occurs anywhere within the dynamic FOV of the pan/tilt system, the camera/lens can be pointed in any direction in the shortest possible time while the lens zooms and focuses on the target. Microprocessor-based dome systems with camera-pointing preset capabilities can take advantage of these fast pan/tilt designs.

14.4.1 Technology

The speed-dome assembly contains a high-speed pan/tilt assembly, high resolution day (color) or night (monochrome) CCD camera with a compact 20:1 zoom ratio lens with continuous full-time auto-focus function. One system has a wide dynamic range feature that can provide detailed images when the camera is viewing images that have bright light and low light level image areas.

Camera, Lens. Most speed-dome systems use high sensitivity color cameras that can be: (1) operated in color, (2) operated in monochrome, or (3) switchable from color to monochrome automatically. The CCD cameras have an image format of 1/4 inch, and along with a compact zoom lens, provide a small compact design resulting in high pan-tilt speeds. Overall camera resolution is typically 480 TV lines for color and 570 TV lines for monochrome.

Values of 1 lux sensitivity for color and 0.06 lux or less for monochrome are typical. One system using a patented signal level compression technique can provide images that have over 60 times the dynamic range compared to other cameras. Cameras are also provided with automatic brightness compensation (ABC) so that the camera can view scenes containing both bright and dark areas. This overcomes the problem that if a camera is located in a poorly illuminated room and pointed at a window with a brightly illuminated scene outside, the camera will either set its iris level to optimize the inside or outside scene. This results in one part of display being normal while the other part is either too light or too dark. This also occurs in the evening when viewing oncoming traffic with the headlights turned on. The ABC enables the camera to see both the light and dark areas of the display with reduced flair from the oncoming headlights.

The zoom lenses generally have a 20 to 1 optical zoom (magnification) range that is extended by electronic digital zoom by another factor of 10 providing an overall 200 to 1 zoom range. Sensitivity of the color cameras are down to 1 lux for color and to .05 lux for monochrome. Switchover from color to monochrome is automatic when the light level falls below a predetermined level. To capture image detail in both light and dark regions, Panasonic Inc. uses the Super Dynamic SDII technology which records the scene at two different exposures and then electronically integrates both of them into a single image to preserve the detail throughout the bright and dim areas. This added to additional precise color reproduction creates a dynamic range that is about 64 times greater than that of conventional cameras.

Pan/Tilt Mechanism. The speed dome panning mechanism provides 360° of continuous horizontal panning rotation. To obtain the 360° rotation slip-rings are used. Some systems use a light transmitter and receiver to transmit the signal information rather than a metal slip ring assembly. The tilt mechanism provides for at least a 90° vertical range of travel. In most cases the camera assembly can tilt up above the horizontal a few degrees and down −95° to provide a tilt range beyond looking straight down to looking slightly above the horizon. Precise manual panning and tilting is achieved through a combination of a variable speed control in the form of different speed ranges, with an automatic adjustment of the speed range depending on the zoom position of the lens. For wide-angle zooming the speed is *increased*, whereas for high magnification (telephoto zooming) the panning and tilting speeds are *decreased*. Depending on the manufacturer, the panning and tilting are done using DC servo motors or stepper motors. To provide high torque and precise pointing ability, the DC servo design uses pulse-width modulation and speed feedback to control the acceleration, speed, and de-acceleration of the motors, ensuring a smooth, precise, accurate, and fluid movement. Most manufactures design the drive systems so that there are no belts or pulleys insuring long-term reliable operation.

An example in which panning speed is important follows: A person walks past a dome pan/tilt unit 15 feet away the dome (Figure 14-2). If the person is walking at a normal rate of about 4 feet per second and the dome is panning at a rate of 1 foot per second (12°/sec), the monitor scene at 15 feet is moving at a rate of 3 feet per second. The subject is quickly lost because the pan/tilt cannot pan fast enough to follow the subject. With a high-speed, 60°/sec panning system, a target at 15 feet from the camera produces a picture going by at a rate of 5 feet per second (1 foot per second faster than the target), and the subject is not lost. In this example, the panning speed would be reduced to 4 feet per second to keep the target in the center of the picture.

Slip-Rings.   Most standard pan/tilt platforms use a mechanical stop at each end of the horizontal and vertical panning ranges to prevent the wires connected to the moving

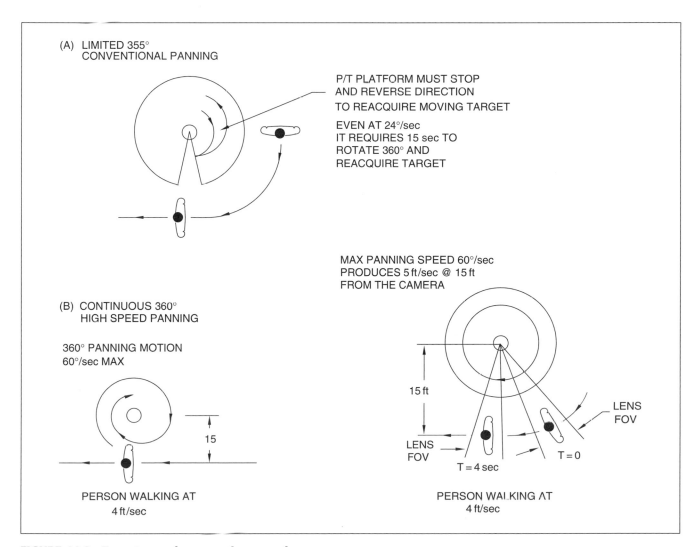

FIGURE 14-2   Target speed vs. panning speed

camera/lens assembly from getting twisted (the wire ends are terminated in the stationary wall mount). This means that the camera cannot scan more than 355° horizontally before it must stop and then pan in the opposite direction. Even at a 24°/sec pan speed, nearly 15 seconds is required to acquire a subject or target that is moving past the end of the panning range. During most of the 15 seconds the target is out of sight of the camera and probably lost. The speed dome camera does not have this limitation as it continues to follow the target. This is one of the salient reasons why speed dome systems are such effective surveillance cameras and have replaced many pan/tilt platforms.

In the panning system using slip-rings, the camera/lens combination rotates continuously and beyond 360° without any concern for twisted wires, since the electrical signals and power pass through the stationary slip-rings. No matter where the target moves in the lens FOV, the panning motion can continue: the subject never leaves the FOV. There are no restricting mechanical stops to limit the pan/tilt unit's rotation.

Most dome manufacturers use gold plated metal slip rings to transfer the video control and power signals from the camera to the dome base and on to the communication channel. Others use optical slip rings for the video. The all-optical connection between the moving camera and the base can provide a higher quality image with less video noise than the metal gold contacts. Transmission of the video signal by a light that requires no physical contacts makes for a better "slip ring." This eliminates the possibility of image noise and enhances the reliability of the dome unit.

14.4.2 Housing

Most indoor speed-dome housings are manufactured from ABS or polycarbonate plastic. The lower dome bubble through which the camera lens views is manufactured from optically clear acrylic plastic. Most systems are provided with a clear or smoked plastic bubble. Other tints available include bronze, chrome, and gold. The clear bubble essentially transmits all of the light and is used for maximum light throughput. The smoked dome loses about 30% of the light, the bronze approximately 50% of the light, and the chrome (aluminum) and gold approximately 75% of the light. Only the clear and smoked versions are generally used for outdoor applications.

If the camera/lens pointing axis is not perpendicular to the dome surface (Figure 14-3) and looks at an oblique angle the images may appear elongated vertically or horizontally. If the dome and camera are in a fixed position with respect to one another, the distortion is generally less noticeable than if the lens is panning or tilting while the dome remains still. Figure 14-4 shows widely used dome housing configurations.

For outdoor applications, the domes are equipped with thermostatically controlled heaters, blowers, and protective sun shrouds. Standard housing colors include gray, white, or black baked on enamel. The lower domes through which the camera views are clear or gray (smoked).

14.4.3 Hardware

There are many manufacturers producing high speed dome camera systems. Table 14-1 shows some of the

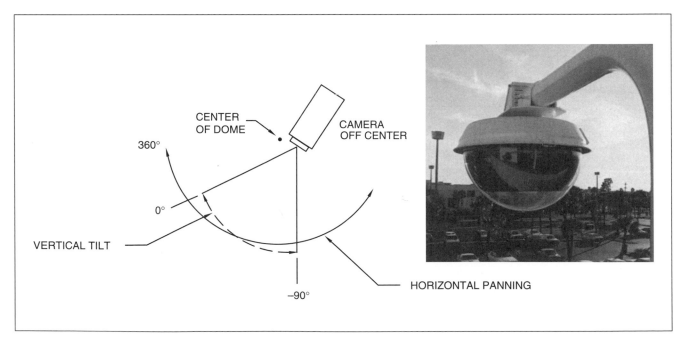

FIGURE 14-3 Camera viewing through dome

(A) 480 TVL COLOR CAMERA
18× OPTICAL MAGNIFICATION
MPEG/JPEG INTERNET (IP)

(B) 510 TVL COLOR CAMERA
22× OPTICAL MAGNIFICATION
ANALOG OUTPUT

FIGURE 14-4 Representative speed-dome systems

- COMPACT SELF CONTAINED CCTV PLATFORM
- INTEGRATED, ENVIRONMENTALLY CLOSED DOME
- HIGH SPEED PANNING—200°/sec
- HIGH POINTING ACCURACY: ±0.1°
- 360° CONTINUOUS PANNING
- COMPACT, UNITIZED CAMERA/LENS/PAN/TILT MODULE
- HIGH ZOOMING (MAGNIFICATION) RANGE:
  - OPTICAL: 10–20×
  - DIGITAL: 10–20×
  - OVERALL: 10–200×
- AUTO-REVERSE FOR DOWNWARD VIEWING
- PRESETS: PAN, TILT, ZOOM, TOUR
- MENU-DRIVEN-REMOTE SETUP

Table 14-1   Key Features of Speed-Dome Systems

features of speed-dome systems available. Section 14.7 describes many extra features not described in Table 14-1.

The two high-end designs by Pelco and Panasonic represent the most complex and full-featured systems. With technology advancing regularly, these systems will continually be updated and supersede the capabilities of those listed in the table. Most of these systems have many features in common but with different specifications (see Section 14.7 for additional features). Table 14-1 briefly outlines the key features of speed domes. Most contain a color camera that is switched electronically, or mechanically moves an optical filter in or out of the image light path to the camera sensor. They contain a high-speed pan/tilt servo or step motor drive system, and a clear, smoked, or other tinted viewing material. The high-quality dome material is of high-quality acrylic and is optically clear with no distortion in any portion of the dome that is viewed through by the camera/lens. These domes are available for indoor wall mounting, ceiling mounting either recessed or as a pendant on a building, or pole

mounted. They are available for outdoor applications for parapet building mounting, on fixed poles in parking lots or highways. The panning speed for most speed domes varies from 0.1 to 360°/sec continuous rotation. The vertical tilt ranges from +2° above the horizon to −92° below the horizon. These systems have manual override for speed control that ranges from 0.1 to 80°/sec in panning to 0.1 to 40°/sec in tilting. In the automatic preset mode, the panning speed can be up to 360°/sec and the tilt speed up to 200°/sec. Most speed domes have capability of programming presets including the ability to select auto-focus modes, iris level, and light compensation. Some systems have the ability to copy a preset command from one camera to another. Programming can be via keyboard through the dome system on-screen menu. Preset accuracy can be as low as ±0.1°. These systems are provided with limit stops that are programmable and used when the operator uses manual panning. Most are provided with an opaque mechanical/optical liner that rotates with the dome to ensure that the camera and pan/tilt assemblies are not visible to the observer. The domes are available with alarm inputs and outputs. Programmable patterns can be user-defined including pan, tilt, and zoom for the preset pointing directions. The security manager can block out specific areas and specific viewing directions to eliminate viewing secured areas and areas requiring privacy. The domes are almost all available with a menu-driven setup and operational modes. The menus can be displayed in different languages for initial installation and operational use. Many have an image flipping feature that inverts the dome image 180° at the bottom of the tilt travel, so that the image is always right-side-up when the camera viewing angle passes through the vertical downward rotation. Depending on the system, communication to and control from the monitoring console is performed through multi-conductor cable, coaxial cable, UTP, fiber-optic, or third-party control systems. Video motion detection is available on most systems when in the preset mode of operation, with alarm outputs activated. Most indoor and outdoor systems are fabricated using painted aluminum construction with outdoor systems available with stainless steel construction; either non-pressurized or pressurized models are available depending on the application.

Figure 14-4 illustrates some of the many standard types of speed-dome systems available. Since most of these domes are mounted at ceiling level, on a parapet atop a building, or on the top of a pole, they must be designed for easy installation and maintenance. Each has a unique quick-disconnect mechanical install and removal interface for mounting the dome section to the permanently mounted base section.

Pelco.   Figure 14-4a shows a speed dome having a variable panning speed from 360°/sec continuous down to 0.1°/sec. The manual control range is from 0.1 to 80°/sec, and pan at 150°/sec in what is called turbo mode. The tilt speed ranges from 0.1 to 40°/sec. When in the automatic preset mode, the panning speed is up to 360°/sec and the tilting speed is up to 200°/sec. The vertical unobstructed tilt is from +2° above the horizon to −92°.

Panasonic.   Figure 14-4b shows a speed dome with a color CCD camera having a 22 times zoom, auto-focus lens, and rotating chassis in a 4.3-inch diameter housing suitable for most indoor locations. It has an additional 10 times electronic digital zoom for a total zoom range of 220. The color camera operates at light levels of 1 lux and produces monochrome images at 0.06 lux. It has full 360° horizontal rotation and 90° vertical panning, and has a speed of 300°/sec. It incorporates digital motion detection for advanced alarm applications. The camera has 510 TV line horizontal resolution.

14.5   DOME MOUNTING HARDWARE

Many manufacturers produce attractive dome housings and mounting configurations for indoor and outdoor fixed and pan/tilt dome systems (Figure 14-5). For indoor applications, the domes are securely attached to a wall or ceiling mounting bracket. The electrical cables connected from the camera and the pan/tilt mechanism are directed into the wall or ceiling.

14.5.1   Fixed Dome

The fixed dome module consists of the camera, lens, and housing with dome and is installed on the surface of a wall, ceiling, building exterior, and pole with appropriate mounting hardware.

14.5.2   Moveable Speed Dome

The speed dome structure consists of two basic parts: (1) the rear box which is installed or mounted on the mounting surface (wall, ceiling, and pole) and (2) the dome with the camera pan/tilt mechanism. Most manufacturers use a quick, positive, mechanical, and electrical disconnect between the rear box and the camera/dome assembly that does not require the use of any tools. This is particularly important in retail stores, warehouses, parking lots, and highway applications since the dome is usually mounted at elevations requiring ladders or other means to reach the dome. This installation and maintenance issue has been addressed by several companies that now produce dome systems that can be installed and maintained at ground level (Section 14.8.2). The domes for these pole-mounted systems are raised and lowered mechanically. The dome is brought down to ground level during installation or servicing and they are raised for operation at the elevated level at the top of the pole. For these video domes the pole is part of the dome system.

In harsh outdoor environments or for chemical protection, type 316 stainless steel enclosures are available with a height of 11 inches including mounting and dome, and a 10 inch diameter. These enclosures require no painting and withstand all outdoor environmental conditions as well as having higher impact ratings that are each important when the systems are located in areas of vandalism or other attacks. Where required, pressurized stainless steel pendants are available with an overall height of 12 inches and an 11 inches diameter. These domes have Schrader type fill and pressure relief valves and operate at 5 lbs/square inch gage (psig) pressure typical and 7 psig pressure relief. These systems usually incorporate internal sensors for pressure, humidity, condensation, and temperature, and are usually equipped with heaters or blowers where the environment requires. These systems are equipped with internal sensors reporting with on-screen displays of sensor indications and sensor out-of-range reporting.

14.6   CABLING-VIDEO SIGNAL AND CONTROLS

The speed-domes communicate to the console and network via built-in multi-protocol receiver/driver assemblies for use with matrix switching systems and other equipments. The types of protocols supported by many manufacturers include: (1) AD Manchester control code using a single 18 AWG shielded twisted pair (STP) to support several daisy chained domes at a maximum of about 5000 feet, (2) 22 AWG UTP to support up to 32 daisy chained domes to a maximum of 3200 feet, (3) AD-UTC and RG-59U video cable to control a dome to a maximum of 1600 feet. These receiver drivers located in the dome provide all the voltage necessary for camera controls, pan and tilt functions, and all motorized lens functions. Most

(A) FLUSH CEILING MOUNT

(B) PENDANT CEILING MOUNT

Panasonic

(C) PENDANT WALL MOUNT

(D) FLUSH WALL/CEILING MOUNT

VICON

FIGURE 14-5   Indoor video dome mounting configurations

dome interfaces support selected third-party protocols for integration into other systems. These can take the form of fiber-optic communications or other types. The dome includes standard support for UTP dome connections that allows the use of CAT cabling for transmission of video or video up the coax dome control signals up to 1000 feet. Communication protocols provided by many manufactures include RS-422, RS-232, and RS-485.

There are several techniques for the console controller to communicate with and control the remote moveable speed-dome camera:

* Direct Wire—video coax with multi-conductor for controls
* UTP—video with multiplexed controls
* Single Coaxial Cable—multiplexed video and controls on coaxial
* Wireless—video and controls transmitted via RF or microwave.

Direct Wire.   The simplest control of the PTZ lens mechanism is via direct wire, using one wire for each control function and a separate video coaxial cable. This straightforward technique is in widespread use for many small or short-run (under a thousand feet) installations. This technique requires no additional driver electronics for transmitting the control signals and no additional receiver electronics at the camera unit. The controller consists of switches that control all functions set manually by the operator or memorized by the system for automatic operation. Wire size must be large enough to minimize voltage drop to the motors and electronics.

Unshielded Twisted Pair (UTP).   For longer distances or when there are many different camera sites, a significant reduction in the number of conductors and wire runs is accomplished by multiplexing (time-sharing) the control signals at the control console onto two UTP wires, sending them to the camera site, and then de-multiplexing them or separating them again to provide the signals necessary to drive the PTZ unit. Since the two wires need to carry only communications information and not current to drive the motors, any long-distance two-wire communication system suffices. Two popular transmission codes (protocols) are the EIA RS-422 and RS-485. The video signal is transmitted on a separate coaxial cable or UTP.

Single Coaxial Cable. Several companies manufacture systems that multiplex or time-share the control signals in video signal on the same video coaxial cable, thereby allowing video to be transmitted from the camera to the monitor console site, and camera control signals to be transmitted from the security console to the camera site, all on one coaxial cable.

For direct wiring, this is an efficient solution since only a single coaxial cable is required. The system requires a simple multiplexer that combines the video and control signals at the camera and the monitor ends. An advantage of multiplexing the control signals onto the video signal is that additional transmission or control signals can be added to the system without adding new cable. These additional functions can include lens controls, alarm functions, or tamper switches.

Wireless. Control signals can be transmitted from the console to the camera location via wireless remote control communication. The control signals are multiplexed onto a single channel and transmitted on RF, microwave, or light-wave (visible or infrared) communication links. In extreme security environments (such as military or nuclear sites), wireless transmission of video, command, and control signals is used as a backup to a hard-wired (copper or fiber-optic) system.

Fiber-optic. The fixed and speed-dome systems have compatibility with fiber-optic transmitters used for long-distance cabling runs. Fiber-optic transmission is an alternative to copper wire, and many manufacturers have equipment that transmits the control signals, alarms, and video signal on a single fiber-optic channel. As mentioned in Chapter 6, the fiber-optic advantages include noise immunity, long transmission distance, absence of ground loops, high security (difficult to tap), and reliable operation from different building sites in harsh environments.

Third-party Communicators. The fixed and speed-dome systems have compatibility with and capability to be connected into optional boards that convert the control signals into a suitable form for the selected third-party controllers.

Digital Network. Fixed and speed-dome camera systems are now available that can be connected directly into analog or digital networks. When the camera is connected to a LAN, WAN, or Ethernet network, the operator can view and operate the system and monitor the images locally or remotely using a PC.

Wiring Access Panel. The installation of the dome base is normally accomplished prior to the purchase or installation of the dome housing itself. The dome base should have an easy access door that allows complete access to the installation wiring, and when closed it should provide complete separation of this wiring from the dome drive.

14.7   SPECIAL FEATURES

Camera Sensitivity. Most dome systems have dual-mode cameras that operate in color mode during daytime and monochrome mode during nighttime. In addition, some cameras have the feature to provide temporary image enhancement under low light level conditions via manual override. This override reduces the shutter speed from the normal 30 fps to 2 fps resulting in a 15 times increase in camera sensitivity.

Memory. Non-volatile memory storage and location-specific dome settings such as presets and patterns are built-in for the camera. If a new dome drive is installed in the system, all the settings are downloaded automatically into the new dome drive.

Motion Detection. Domes support VMD within a preset. The motion detection trigger action includes activating a preset command, activating a pattern, and sending a dome output to the console.

Presets and Patterns. Most domes support camera presets programmed into the dome module so that the dome can point (pan/tilt) to a preset direction. Models with as many as 96 presets and 60 patterns of presets are programmable. Domes are also designed to support a Home Position that automatically returns the dome to a Preset, Pattern, or Preset Sequence after a specified period of inactivity anywhere between 1 minute and 1 hour. Also provided is a freeze frame function that maintains a static image on-screen during dome movement and lens adjustment when presets and patterns are called. This freeze frame function helps preserve hard drive space when a VCR or DVR is used.

The speed-dome parameters that can be preset include: (1) auto-focus mode, (2) iris level, (3) back-light compensation, (4) the ability to command to copy the camera settings from one preset to another to reduce setup time, and (5) to preset programming the control keyboard or the dome system on-screen menu. The preset accuracy can be as high as ±0.1°.

Proportional Pan/Tilt Speed. The system panning and tilting speed can be increased or decreased depending on the instantaneous zoom focal length. To optimize the viewing of the image on the monitor for different zoom positions, when the zoom lens is in wide-angle position the speed is increased, and when it is in the telephoto (high magnification) position it is decreased, and proportionally optimized in between.

Digital Flip.   The speed-dome should have a provision for quick image reversal that automatically pans the camera 180° when the bottom −90° tilt limit is reached to allow for continuous tracking of a target passing directly beneath the dome. This is important when following a person who is passing directly under the camera from one side to the other.

The digital flip feature allows for more convenient monitoring when viewing objects that pass directly below the camera. As the camera pans in the vertical direction to follow the object, DSP automatically flips the image to the bottom as the object passes beneath the camera so that the image remains right-side-up for easier viewing. In addition, the system contains an image-hold feature that prevents blurring when the camera moves and does the 180° flip. It maintains the image prior to flip after the 180° flip.

Privacy Zone-Window Blanking.   Some domes support privacy zones to prevent users from viewing sensitive or secured areas. So as not to interfere with normal surveillance operations, these on-screen shields must block out only the area that has been defined as sensitive. The privacy cell should not cause the screen to blank out.

These privacy windows are available in: (1) four-sided user-defined shapes, (2) opaque gray or translucent smear, (3) blank all video *above* a user-defined tilt angle, and (4) blank all video *below* a user-defined tilt angle.

Zoom-Distance Compensation.   Whether the dome camera is in the privacy zone or the lens is zooming from wide-angle to telephoto the system should compensate for a specific focal length in use at the time. For any specific focal length, the zoom lens should adjust the alarm or privacy zone window to compensate for the changing FOV. This is called zoom-distance compensation.

Monitor Display, Menu.   The speed-dome systems support on-screen programming of the dome parameters including image flip, direction indicators and azimuth, maximum zoom stop, camera line lock or internal crystal synchronization, AGC, white balance, VMD selection, alarm actions and default states, and home position. They also display on-screen programming of: dome names, area names, preset names, pattern names, and alarm names. Most systems provide most of these attributes in English, French, Italian, German, and Spanish, as well as in other languages. The on-screen text characters are available as user-selectable in solid or translucent white, with or without a black outline.

Alarm Inputs.   The dome assemblies have single or multiple alarm inputs as an option and are field programmable to receive normally open or normally close contacts. If the system is operating on an RS-422 network, the domes are capable of receiving the alarm and transmitting it back to the switching system, and/or reacting to the alarm event independent of the switching system. If a Manchester network is used, the dome is capable of processing the alarm

internally in the dome and automatically activating a Preset, Pattern, or Preset Sequence.

Twist Lock Release.   Maintenance is an important factor to consider in ceiling or pole-mounted dome camera systems. To simplify installing and servicing these domes, most systems contain a quick disconnect or twist lock release at the base of the dome. The standard base of the dome is hard mounted to the wall, ceiling, or pole mount and contains a receptacle for direct wiring to the dome assembly. All wiring is done before lifting the camera pan/tilt assembly onto place. The base assembly includes a tamper switch so that if the dome cover is removed, an alarm is sounded. The quick disconnect base allows wiring to be done once directly in place and then installing or servicing the dome assembly without disturbing any of the wires or connections. Normally each base includes diagnostic LEDs to indicate power and proper communications to and from the console or matrix switcher. Some designs require a simple tool to remove the dome assembly; however, others require *no tools* and are simply installed or removed using a twist lock release. It is important that the dome and the base are available separately so that the installation of the base can be accomplished by the installer prior to the purchase of the dome housing/camera assembly.

14.8   SPECIAL APPLICATIONS

The use of fixed and speed domes in elevated locations in buildings, on exterior walls of buildings, and outdoors, in general, has resulted in the design of many different configurations for mounting these domes.

14.8.1   Outdoor Building Mounts

Figure 14-6 illustrates outdoor speed-domes mounted on a building roof edge and capable of scanning 270° and 360° horizontally to view parking garages and lots. With such a large angular FOV to cover (an entire parking lot), this solution should be used where only sporadic activity is monitored, since panning with a standard unit from one end of a building would not keep most of the parking lot under surveillance. Adding additional speed domes would increase coverage.

14.8.2   Pole Mounts

Figure 14-7 shows dome camera pan/tilt assemblies mounted on poles and pedestals to provide wide-angle video surveillance at entry and exit roadways, parking lots, streets, etc. Mounting the camera away from the building on a pole provides good viewing of the entire

**FIGURE 14-6
Standard
outdoor
speed-dome
mounting
configurations**

(A) STANDARD   (B) BUILDING MOUNT

(A) PEDESTAL/WALL MOUNT DOME   (B) CORNER WALL BRACKET   (C) POLE/WALL MOUNT

FIGURE 14-7   Outdoor dome and mounts for buildings, roadways and parking lots

building entry area with a single camera. The presence of the camera system serves as a deterrent to crime while it captures the necessary visual information for possible apprehension and prosecution. The same scanning limitations as described in the previous system apply.

There is one disadvantage of the dome pole camera or any camera mounted on a pole: the difficulty of performing maintenance on it. Several companies have pursued designs that permit easier maintenance. The widespread use of the speed-dome in parking lots, on walkways, and on streets,

highways, etc. has motivated manufacturers to design ingenious means to raise and lower the entire dome assembly *from ground-level* (Figure 14-8). The video dome in Figure 14-8a, b is raised and lowered using an electric drill.

14.9 SUMMARY

There are many varieties of camera housings and integrated camera systems for video surveillance applications. The configuration that has become most popular

(C) HEAVY DUTY

(D) HEAVY DUTY

(A) RAISING AND LOWERING   (B) NORMAL POSITION

FIGURE 14-8   Pole-mounted dome assemblies maintained from ground-level

is the dome housing that is available in a fixed or speed-dome configuration. These dome camera systems are suitable for indoor and outdoor applications available with monochrome cameras, or color cameras that can automatically switch from color for daylight use to monochrome for extended low light level sensitivity and produce optimum performance at most all light levels. The speed dome provides a very powerful video surveillance tool for gathering maximum visual intelligence and is in widespread use in retail establishments, casinos, warehouses, outdoor parking lots, pathways, building exteriors, and streets and highways.

Chapter 15

Integrated Cameras, Camera Housings, and Accessories

CONTENTS

15.1 Overview
15.2 Indoor Housings
    15.2.1 Functional Requirements
    15.2.2 Indoor Types
15.3 Outdoor Housings
    15.3.1 Functional Requirements
    15.3.2 Outdoor Design Materials
    15.3.3 Outdoor Types
15.4 Integrated Cameras
    15.4.1 Indoor
    15.4.2 Outdoor
15.5 Specialty Housings
    15.5.1 High Security
    15.5.2 Elevator
    15.5.3 Dust-Proof and Explosion-Proof
    15.5.4 Pressurized and Air- or Water-Cooled
15.6 NEMA Environmental Ratings
15.7 Housing Accessories
15.8 Housing Guidelines
15.9 Summary

15.1 OVERVIEW

There are many varieties of video camera housings and integrated cameras available for indoor and outdoor security applications. Standard shapes and forms they take include: (1) rectangular—mounted on a wall or ceiling, (2) dome—mounted on a ceiling, wall, pole, and pylon, (3) triangular—mounted in a corner, and (4) wedge—ceiling mounted. The two primary functions for these environmental housing are to protect the camera and lens from vandalism and the environment. To meet these requirements, indoor and outdoor housings and integrated camera modules are fabricated from a variety of materials including aluminum, painted steel, stainless steel, and molded high-impact plastic.

There has been an increasing demand for aesthetically designed housings and cameras to match the decor of a building interior or exterior. While the primary function of the housing is to protect the camera, lens, and electrical wiring, these aesthetic camera housings are especially attractive and unobtrusive as dictated by architectural considerations. To satisfy these requirements, manufacturers have produced attractive designs using injection-molded plastic and other materials and forming techniques.

Housings are used to protect vital electronic video equipment; consequently, the material used for their construction must be chosen carefully. Underwriters Laboratories (UL) has developed guidelines for minimum fire-safety requirements and suggested tests and ratings for fireproof or fire-retardant designs. This is especially important for non-metallic designs. The Electronic Industries Association (EIA) has guidelines for improved interchangeability among manufacturers' products. The National Electrical Manufacturers Association (NEMA) has detailed specifications describing the requirements for indoor and outdoor housing requirements of electrical equipment. These guidelines and ratings relate to materials and finishes, mechanical design parameters such as mounting-hole locations, and electrical-cable entry and fittings.

This chapter describes rectangular, triangular, dome, and all the other special indoor and outdoor housings, including accessories such as heaters, fans, thermostats, and windshield wipers and washers. Most housings have locks or tamperproof hardware to prevent vandalism or theft of the camera and lens.

Camera Housings. The indoor round hemispherical dome-shaped housing has become very popular because it is attractive and has excellent functionality. The dome's symmetrical shape and tinted viewing "window" prevents the observer from seeing the direction in which the camera is pointing. This adds a deterrence factor to the surveillance function. Many security installations require discreet video surveillance equipment that blends in with the surrounding environment, not eye-catching or obtrusive housings. Corner-mounted triangular and wedge-shaped housings are also in widespread use.

Outdoor housings used on facility properties are designed to match landscaping and grounds and/or specific lighting conditions. Outdoor environmental housings that are subject to wind loading or ice buildup should be no larger or heavier than required to house the camera, lens, and associated wiring and accessories. They should be constructed to withstand the harsh outdoor environment and added abuse from vandalism or attack. The camera housing enclosures should have easy access into them via a hinged or sliding interior assembly or removable cover.

The housing, camera, and lens are often within reach of personnel who could damage or remove the equipment. Of particular concern are high-risk locations such as jail cells, building exteriors, and public-access locations that require a more rugged housing fabricated from stainless steel or high-impact polycarbonate plastic. Figure 15-1 shows two examples of standard indoor and outdoor camera housings.

Integrated Cameras. With the increased use of video surveillance cameras, manufacturers, video integrators, and end-users have sought to simplify the purchasing and installation of camera systems. To that end the integrated camera has become very popular and an efficient means to accomplish that function. The integrated camera is a *plug and play* surveillance camera including the camera, lens, and any internal wiring associated with it, and mounted in a small housing that is ready to install at the site in a minimum amount of time. These integrated cameras take on shapes similar to some of the housings described in

the previous section but are smaller and more compact. Very popular types are domes, corner mount, wedge, with environmentally enclosed day/night camera with integral bracket mounting. Figure 15-2 shows examples of these integrated cameras.

15.2 INDOOR HOUSINGS

15.2.1 Functional Requirements

Indoor housings must protect the camera and lens from pollutants such as dust and other particulate matter, a corrosive atmosphere, and tampering or vandalism. Indoor housings are constructed of painted or anodized aluminum, painted steel, stainless steel, and several types of plastic. The material for plastic housings must be flameproof or flame-retardant, as designated by local codes and UL recommendations. The housings must have sufficient strength to protect the lens and camera, and be sturdily mounted onto a fixed wall or ceiling mount, or recessed in a wall or ceiling. The lens should view through a clear window made of safety glass or plastic. Recommended plastic window material is either high impact acrylic or polycarbonate with a mar-resistant finish. The electrical input/output access locations should be designed and positioned for easy maintenance. For easy access and servicing of internal parts, the top half of the housing should be hinged or be able to slide open, or be removable. In some designs, the entire camera/lens assembly is removable for servicing. Figure 15-3 shows the interior of a typical rectangular indoor housing.

The common rectangular housing is available in many sizes and is the least expensive. For vandalism protection, many housings are available with key locks or tamperproof hardware that allows the cover to be removed only with a special tool. In very high risk areas, welded stainless-steel housings with thick polycarbonate windows (3/8 or 1/2 inch) and high-security locks are used. Some housings

(A) INDOOR

(B) OUTDOOR

FIGURE 15-1 Standard indoor and outdoor camera housings

(A) STAINLESS STEEL CORNER MOUNT

(B) CEILING MOUNT-FIXED DOME

(C) SPRINKLER CEILING MOUNT

(D) HARDENED WALL/CEILING

FIGURE 15-2   Popular integrated cameras

are designed to provide concealment and improved aesthetics by recessing them into the wall or ceiling. The five housing types that account for most security installations are: (1) rectangular, (2) dome, (3) wedge, (4) triangular, and (5) wall- and ceiling-recessed and surface-mounted.

15.2.2 Indoor Types

Rectangular. The most popular type of housing is the standard rectangular design since it can be fabricated at low cost, is sturdy, and is available from many manufacturers in many sizes and attractive styles.

Under normal circumstances, indoor housings do not require any special corrosion-resistant finishes. The housings are made from painted or anodized aluminum, painted steel, or high-impact plastic, such as polyvinyl chloride (PVC), acritile buterated styrene (ABS), or polycarbonate (General Electric Lexan, etc.). In high crime areas and jails, stainless steel housings are used.

Accessibility to the camera/lens assembly for installation and servicing is important. Video surveillance cameras are always mounted near or at ceiling height, on a pedestal, or at some elevated location requiring service personnel to be on ladders or power lifts. The housing design must permit

FIGURE 15-3   Indoor housing showing interior

easy access and serviceability under these conditions. Manufacturers provide one of several means to gain access to the housing: (1) removable top cover, (2) hinged top cover, (3) top cover or camera/lens on slide, (4) removable front and/or rear cover, (5) hinged bottom cover (dome), or (6) top cover on slide (Figure 15-4).

Dome. A second category of indoor housing is of a round or hemispherical, clear or tinted dome in which a camera, lens, and an optional pan/tilt mechanism are housed. Chapter 14 described dome cameras in detail. The ceiling-mounted hemispherical dome and the below-the-ceiling and wall-mounted domes on brackets look totally different from the rectangular housing, and often blend in better with architectural decor. Since they look like a lighting fixture, they are less obtrusive than rectangular housings. Since the hemispherical dome is circularly symmetrical, it can be in a fixed position and the CCTV camera pointed in any direction to view the scene. A pan/tilt unit used in a dome can rotate and tilt the camera and lens while still remaining inside the confines of the dome. This is in contrast to cameras inside rectangular and other housings: if the camera moves, the entire housing assembly has to move as a unit.

If the dome is tinted so that the person down at floor level viewing the dome cannot see the camera and lens, it is possible to point the camera in any direction without the observer seeing it move. This capability can act as an additional security deterrent because the observer does not know when he or she is under surveillance.

There are three different types of plastic dome materials through which the lens views the scene: (1) clear, (2) semitransparent aluminum- or chrome-coated, and (3) tinted or smoked plastic. When the dome housing is used for

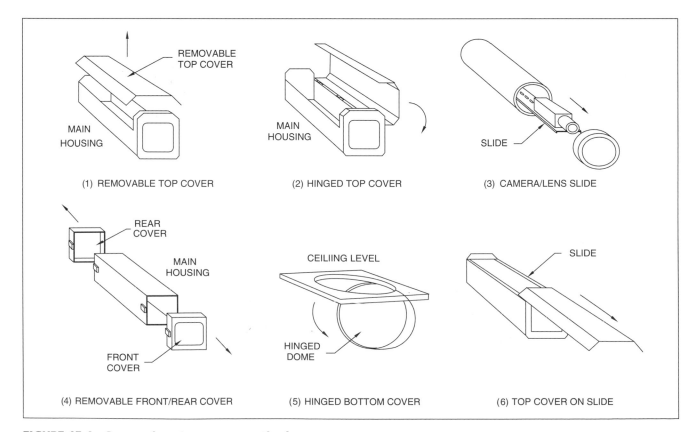

FIGURE 15-4   Camera housing access methods

protection only and its pointing direction need not be concealed, the clear plastic dome is the best choice, since it produces only a small 10 or 15% light loss. If the camera's pointing direction is to be concealed for additional security a coated or tinted dome is required. The aluminized dome is the earliest version of the coated dome and attenuates the light passing through it by approximately two f-stops (equivalent to approximately a 75% light reduction or loss). While this type of dome is still in use, the preferred dome material is a smoked plastic or tinted plastic that attenuates the light approximately one f-stop, or 50%.

In contrast to rectangular housings using flat plastic or glass windows with excellent optical quality and transmission, some dome systems add slight optical distortion to the video picture. In high-quality domes the image distortion is almost negligible, but in some systems the distortion or loss in resolution is noticcable. In any dome-housing application the camera/lens should view through the surface of the dome perpendicularly as shown in Figure 15-5a.

Under this condition, there is at least symmetry of distortion, that is, the primary effect is that of a weak lens producing a small change in the focal length of the total

lensing system and is usually not noticeable. If the camera/lens pointing axis is not perpendicular to the dome surface (Figure 15-5b) and looks at an oblique angle through the dome housing material, noticeable distortion will occur; for example, images may appear elongated vertically or horizontally. If the dome and camera are in a fixed position with respect to one another, the distortion is generally less noticeable than if the lens is scanning or tilting while the dome remains still. Figure 15-6 shows four widely used dome housing configurations.

Wedge Housing.   One version of the wedge housing is designed to replace an existing standard 2 feet × 2 feet drop ceiling tile (Figure 15-7a) and another version (Figure 15-7b) is designed for surface mounting. The wedge housing in Figure 15-7a is a manually rotatable 16-inch high impact white plastic center section with a wedge-shaped camera protruding about 5 inches below the ceiling line. There are no additional accessories required. The design allows for manual pan adjustments of 360° and minor tilt adjustments. After final pointing the center camera/lens section is restricted from rotating by tightening thumbscrews. The camera's wedge shape aims the camera about 15° down from the horizontal. The front of

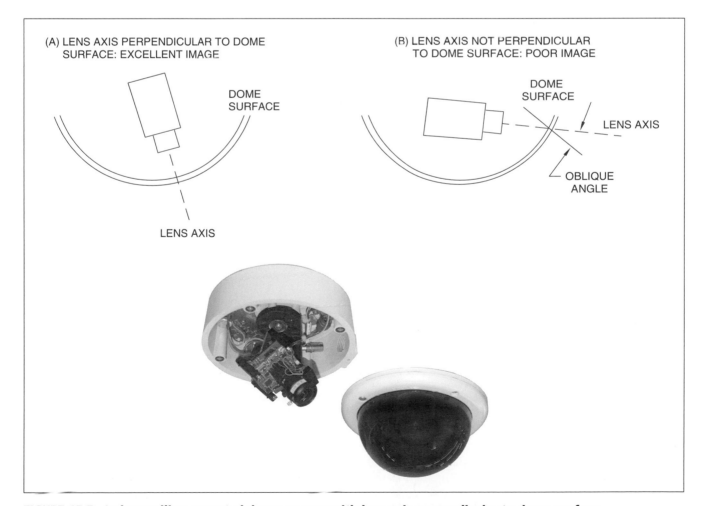

FIGURE 15-5   Indoor ceiling mounted dome camera with lens axis perpendicular to dome surface

(A) INDOOR-N CEILING MOUNT

(B) OUTDOOR-BUILDING/POLE MOUNT

(C) INDOOR-SURFACE MOUNT

(D) OUTDOOR-SURFACE MOUNT

FIGURE 15-6   Dome housing configurations

the protrusion has a viewing window of clear acrylic with no distortion and virtually no light transmission loss.

Another version is a small surface-mounted wedge-shaped housing that can be attached to any ceiling. These are available in either a surface- or recessed-mounting configuration.

Corner Mount. Figure 15-8 illustrates examples of aesthetic and hardened camera/lens housings designed specifically for corner mounting in rooms, elevators, stairwells, jail cells, etc. Figure 15-8a shows a high-security housing of welded stainless steel with a polycarbonate window. The tamperproof corner mount camera housing has a camera bracket assembly permitting the camera to be tilted vertically ±10° for minor adjustments of the vertical pointing angle. The lens viewing window permits viewing a 95° horizontal FOV and 75° vertical FOV. The optimum pointing direction for the lens and camera is 45° with respect to both adjacent walls and 45° down from the ceiling horizontal plane. For an elevator cab application this housing with a wide-angle, 95° horizontal FOV can view entire elevator cab with no hidden areas and provide 100% video coverage of the cab area. The high-security housing has a hinged, lockable cover for easy, controlled access to all internal parts, and a tough mar-resistant poly-

carbonate (Lexan) window. All mounting, video, and electrical power access holes are located on the rear and top surfaces and inaccessible to the public. The installation meets codes that require unbroken firewalls. Three different housing sizes of this design accommodate most CCD solid-state cameras and wide-angle manual- or automatic-iris lenses or variable focus (vari-focal) lenses. Since the housing is exposed to the public, it is securely locked and manufactured using tamperproof materials, such as steel or stainless steel, and a polycarbonate (Lexan) window.

Figure 15-8b shows a housing fabricated from high impact plastic and is a configuration suitable for application requiring moderate security. The plastic housing has a lockable front cover and all mounting and electrical access holes are out of sight, and not accessible to the public. The housing has an adjustable bracket for tilting the camera vertically. There are many manufacturers supplying these types of corner mount housings in materials ranging from stainless steel, steel, and plastic. Finishes include brushed stainless steel and painted aluminum, steel, and plastic.

Figure 15-8c shows a mirror-view corner mount housing that has a tinted or aluminized one-way window. It is a small 7 inch × 7 inch × 7 inch unobtrusive housing that renders the camera and lens covert.

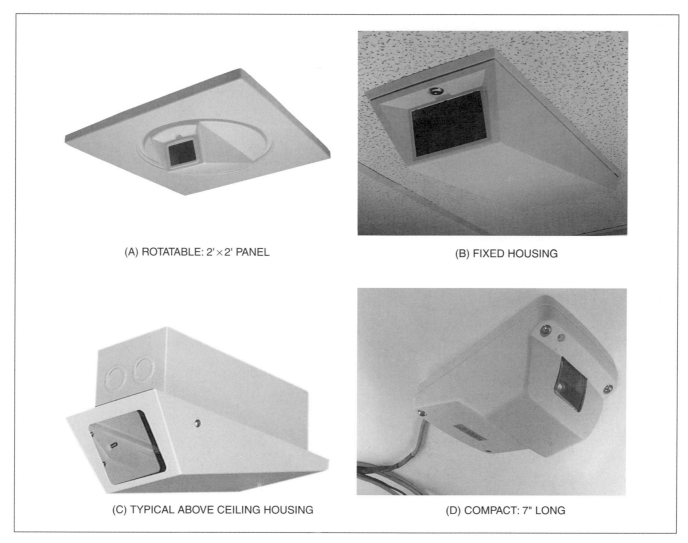

(A) ROTATABLE: 2'×2' PANEL

(B) FIXED HOUSING

(C) TYPICAL ABOVE CEILING HOUSING

(D) COMPACT: 7" LONG

FIGURE 15-7   Wedge camera housings

Ceiling- or Wall-Recessed or Surface Mount.   Recessed or partially concealed housings are often mounted in ceilings and walls. Figure 15-9 shows examples of these housings, including the wedge and dome-shaped types. The round, semicircular, and tapered housings shown offer design flexibility since the camera and lens can be pointed in any horizontal direction while the square or rectangular ceiling tile remains in place. These housings are used where a low-profile (but not covert) type of surveillance camera is required. These cameras are well suited for looking down hallways, at cash registers, etc. In ceiling installations, most of the housing, camera, and lens are mounted *above* the ceiling level. The only portion below ceiling level is a small part of the housing and the window through which the camera lens views. The cameras and lenses are accessible from below ceiling level by unlocking a cover that swings down, or by gaining access from the rear of the housing above the ceiling from an adjacent ceiling tile. It is important that all ceiling tile mount housings be securely attached to a structural member of the building above the ceiling with a chain or cable so that if the hanging ceiling support fails, the housing and contents do not fall to the floor or possibly injure personnel below.

With the increased use of video surveillance in public locations, be they government, industrial, or private, more attention is being given to the decorative and aesthetic features of the housing. These housings often have finishes of brass, gold, or chrome, with satin or polished finishes. They are also available with custom paint colors and textures, and custom-colored plastics. Several manufacturers offer special shapes and custom configurations for matching specific architectural designs.

15.3   OUTDOOR HOUSINGS

Like the indoor housing, the outdoor housing protects the camera and lens from vandalism and adverse outdoor environments. Most outdoor housings are provided

(A) DISCRETE TRIANGULAR ONE-WAY MIRROR

(B) DISCRETE CONVEX TINTED MIRROR

(C) STAINLESS STEEL

(D) HIGH IMPACT PLASTIC

FIGURE 15-8   Corner mount housings

with key locks to prevent unauthorized opening of the housing.

15.3.1   Functional Requirements

Outdoor housings must protect the camera from vandalism as well as adverse environmental conditions. The vandalism encountered can range from rocks or sticks thrown at the housing to bullets and other explosives. These security housings are prime targets since they are mounted on ceilings, walls, building exteriors, and poles and pedestals.

In outdoor installations the camera is mounted in a protective enclosure to protect it against environmental factors such as precipitation: rain, hail, snow, sleet, ice, and condensing humidity. The outdoor housing must also protect against many types of particulate matter including dirt and dust, sand, fly ash, soot, and any other material local to a particular site. Outdoor locations with a corrosive atmosphere can cause rapid deterioration, failure, and premature replacement of the camera and lens if not properly protected. These substances include industrial chemicals, acids, and salt spray. Outdoor housings should have external finishes that withstand the atmosphere in which they are to operate. In hot climates, a sun shield or shroud and a bright aluminum or white finish is desirable to reflect sunlight and eliminate heat buildup in the housing.

Outdoor housings share many of the same requirements as indoor housings. Accessibility to the camera and lens during installation and maintenance are more important in outdoor applications since video equipment is often mounted high above the ground and serviced under adverse conditions.

(A) CONCEALED CEILING

(B) WEDGE

(C) DOME

FIGURE 15-9   Recessed and concealed ceiling, wedge, and dome housings

15.3.2   Outdoor Design Materials

Outdoor housings are manufactured from aluminum, painted steel, stainless steel, and outdoor-rated plastic, including polycarbonate, ABS with a UV protective layer. It is important that plastic outdoor housings be fabricated from UV-inhibiting materials, to prevent the housing from deteriorating due to sunlight. Plastics not treated will crack, and colors will fade. High-quality baked-enamel, painted-steel, and stainless-steel housings will last many years. Where long-lasting, high-security, vandal-proof housings are required, stainless steel is the choice since it does not rust or corrode and is extremely tough.

Aluminum is a good choice for an outdoor housing when anodized and finished in baked polyurethane enamel paint and anodized. Anodized and painted aluminum is the most durable finish. Aluminum and steel housings should not be used when a salt or other corrosive atmosphere is expected. Stainless steel and special plastics are the best choice for a salt spray environment. Consult the housing or materials manufacturer for the proper choice.

15.3.3   Outdoor Types

The outdoor camera housings are similar to the indoor except that they must be furnished with an exterior finish that can resist and withstand the outdoor environment. They should be fitted with a thermostatically controlled heater and fan so that when the temperature extends beyond the range of the camera and lens specifications they can either be heated or cooled.

Rectangular.   For outdoor applications the rectangular plastic, painted aluminum, or stainless steel housings are the most popular choices. These housings are easily mounted from a bracket on a building, wall, or pole, or hung from a building overhang to provide a solid mounting.

Dome.   Dome housings can be mounted on an individual pole or pylon, under the eaves of a building, or on a bracket mounted off the wall of a building. These housings must also use outdoor materials that will withstand the environment.

15.4 INTEGRATED CAMERAS

The integration of the video camera, lens, housing, and mount into one unit has been a natural evolution in the security industry. This evolution has occurred as a result of the availability of small CCD and CMOS cameras and associated small lenses. It has made technologic and economic sense for manufacturers to integrate these components into a single finished product available to the video systems integrator or end-user as a *plug and play* video surveillance module ready for mounting on a wall, a ceiling, outside a building, etc. These integrated cameras have taken the form of domes (see Chapter 14), triangular-corner, wedge, and covert. There are many manufacturers producing hundreds of models for indoor and outdoor applications. They are available in monochrome and color for daylight and nighttime use.

15.4.1 Indoor

Indoor integrated cameras have housings that take the form of those described in Section 15.2. The housing types include the dome, triangular-corner, wedge, and semi-covert models (Figure 15-10).

Dome. The integrated dome camera uses a dome housing with a camera and lens installed. Most dome applications now use the integrated dome camera instead of the component form because of the ease of installing a complete plug and play module and the concomitant lower overall cost. These modules are available for monochrome and color use as well as total darkness using infrared LED illumination. Figure 15-11 illustrates an integrated dome camera and its interior assembly in an electrical duplex outlet box showing the manually adjustable and tilt bracket for the camera lens assembly.

Triangular-Corner. A triangular-shaped integrated camera housing using a one-way mirror installed in the corner of a room at the ceiling level provides an excellent semi-covert surveillance camera. Typical locations are in a small room or lobby, an elevator or a stairwell. Figure 15-12 shows this design using a wide-angle (90° FOV) lens that can view the entire area of a small room or other space.

(A) DAY/NIGHT RUGGEDIZED DOME

(B) SPRINKLER HEAD

(C) CORNER MOUNT MIRROR

(D) RUGGEDIZED WALL MOUNT
WITH LED IR ILLUMINATION

FIGURE 15-10   Indoor integrated cameras

FIGURE 15-11   Integrated dome camera assembly

FIGURE 15-13   Wedge integrated camera

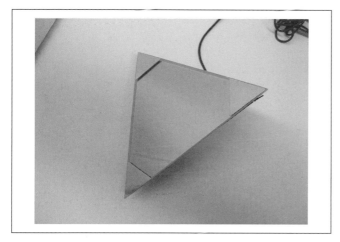

FIGURE 15-12 Discrete triangular corner mount mirror integrated camera

The camera installed in the triangular housing is at a 45° angle pointing down from the ceiling to view the entire area. The triangular housing can be mounted in protected outdoor locations at entrances or exits to buildings, etc. where two walls meet, resulting in a very unobtrusive installation. When mounted in hot or cold environments, the housings must be provided with a thermostatically controlled heater or fan.

Wedge.   The wedge-integrated camera is available as a small, unobtrusive assembly suitable for mounting directly to a hard ceiling or on a ceiling tile. These cameras are lightweight and generally require no additional support structure—they can be mounted directly onto the ceiling tile (Figure 15-13).

Covert.   There are many variations of integrated covert-type video surveillance cameras used to augment overt cameras. These can take the form of a sprinkler head, smoke detector, passive infrared detector, temperature thermostat, etc. (see Chapter 18 for many versions of covert integrated cameras).

15.4.2   Outdoor

Most integrated camera units for outdoor applications take the form of a dome camera assembly in a plug and play form for maximum ease of installation and servicing. Some other forms used include ruggedized camera housings with the camera, lens, heater, and fan, all enclosed in the housing, ready for mounting on an exterior bracket pole or pedestal. Dome assemblies such as those shown in Chapter 14 for outdoor applications are representative of these types.

15.5   SPECIALTY HOUSINGS

There are security applications in which cameras must be located in very hostile environments. To protect the camera and lens from damage and downtime, manufacturers offer housings that can withstand high mechanical impact from hand-thrown or fired projectiles, extreme high temperature, dust, sand, liquid, corrosive chemicals, and explosive gas. The following housings have unique characteristics for solving these extreme security or special environmental applications.

15.5.1   High Security

There are numerous armored camera/lens enclosures for installation in correctional institutions. Figure 15-14 illustrates several high-security housings designed specifically for mounting in jails and detention and holding cells, to provide maximum protection from vandalism. These integrated cameras have no exposed hardware or cabling and all use heavy-duty high security locks with tamper switches. The housings are fabricated from 10-gauge (0.134-inch thick) or heavier welded steel. The window material is 3/8–1/2-inch polycarbonate or cast acrylic plastic having an abrasion-resistant finish. These housings withstand blows and impacts from hammers. Rocks and

FIGURE 15-14 High security integrated cameras

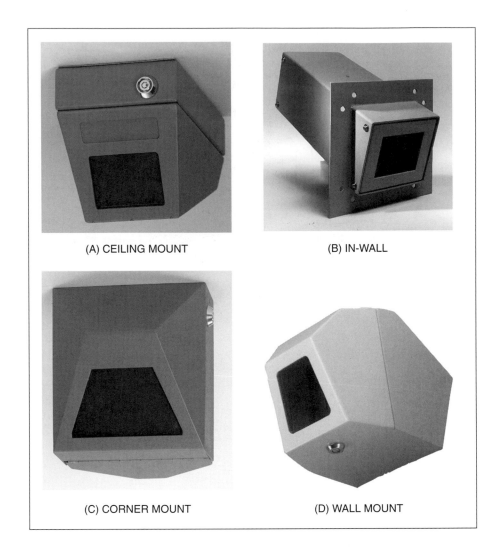

(A) CEILING MOUNT   (B) IN-WALL

(C) CORNER MOUNT   (D) WALL MOUNT

some firearm projectiles cannot penetrate or destroy the integrity of the housing.

15.5.2 Elevator

Figure 15-15 illustrates an example of a hardened camera/lens housing designed specifically for elevator applications. The photograph of the elevator interior illustrates that the full interior of an elevator can be monitored from one wide-angle camera/lens system.

The elevator housing style is available in three sizes: 6, 8, and 12 inches high. These high-security housings are fabricated from welded stainless steel with a 1/4-inch thick polycarbonate window. The tamperproof integrated camera assembly is complete with a monochrome or color CCD camera and a wide-angle, 90° FOV lens in the stainless-steel housing. In this configuration, the camera can be tilted ±10° for minor adjustments of the vertical pointing direction. The high-security housing has a hinged, lockable cover for easy, controlled access to all internal parts, and

a tough mar-resistant polycarbonate (Lexan) viewing window. All mounting and camera power and video electrical cable access holes are located on the rear and top surfaces, and are inaccessible to the public. The installation meets codes that require unbroken firewalls. The three housing sizes accommodate most CCD solid-state cameras using wide-angle manual- or automatic-iris or vari-focal lenses. These integrated cameras can also accommodate cameras with infrared LED lighting to obtain excellent viewing under completely dark, unlighted conditions. The small 6-inch high unit accommodates and protects all small 1/4- and 1/3-inch format cameras and associated wide-angle lenses. Figure 15-16 illustrates the camera viewing and pointing parameters for elevator-cab surveillance.

The optimum pointing direction for the lens and camera is 45° with respect to both adjacent walls and 45° down from the ceiling horizontal plane. With a wide-angle, 90° horizontal FOV the entire elevator cab is viewed with no hidden areas, providing 100% video coverage of the cab area. Since the housing is exposed to the public, it is securely locked and is manufactured using tamperproof steel and stainless steel, and a polycarbonate window.

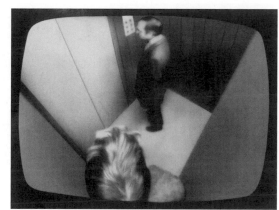
(A) STAINLESS STEEL HOUSING

(B) CAMERA VIEW

FIGURE 15-15   High security corner mount elevator integrated camera

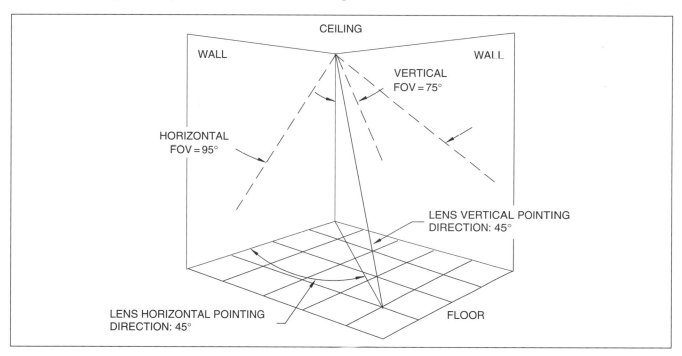

FIGURE 15-16   Elevator cab viewing parameters

15.5.3 Dust-Proof and Explosion-Proof

The dust-proof housing is similar to many other camera housings except that it is totally sealed from the outside atmosphere and therefore can be used in sandy and dusty environments (Figure 15-17). When fabricated from stainless steel, these housings can withstand the effects of corrosive environments. The window material is tempered glass to provide safety and maximum resistance to abrasion and corrosion. To provide some cooling of the camera and lens, a fan is used to circulate the air inside the housing, and an optional sun shield above the camera housing protects it from direct solar heating. The housing is provided with air fittings so that an external, filtered,

compressed-air supply can be used to maintain moderate operating temperatures. These housings are not considered explosion-proof.

Explosion-proof housings are designed to meet the rigorous safety requirements of explosion-proof and dust-ignition-proof electrical equipment, for installation and use in hazardous locations (Figure 15-18). These security housings and cameras meet the requirements of the National Electric Code Class 1, Division 1, and Class 2, Division 1, and are certified as per the requirements of UL 1203 specifications and procedures. These housings are generally of heavy-wall, all-aluminum construction and are available in 6, 8, and 10 inch diameters to accommodate most camera/lens combinations.

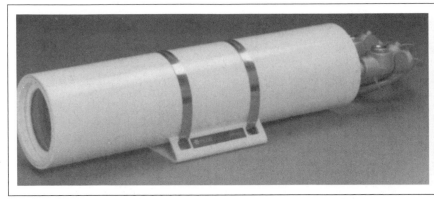

FIGURE 15-17   Dust-proof integrated housing and camera assembly

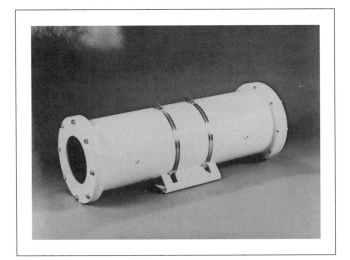

FIGURE 15-18 Explosion-proof integrated housing and camera assembly

They are fitted with explosion-proof, sealable fittings for electrical power/control input and video signal output. Optional sun shrouds are available for operation in hot environments.

15.5.4 Pressurized and Air- or Water-Cooled

Pressurized housings are used in hazardous atmospheres. They meet these requirements by purging (filling) them with an inert gas at a pressure in accordance with National Fire Protection Association specification Number 946 (Figure 15-19).

The housings are fabricated from thick-walled aluminum with corrosion-resistant finishes. The window is 1/2-inch-thick tempered and polished plate glass. These housings can be back-filled (purged) with low-pressure nitrogen gas to a pressure of 15 pounds per square inch gage (psig). Nitrogen is completely inert and prevents an explosion from occurring if there is any spark or electrical malfunction in the housing. The housings have hermetically sealed O-ring seals located between the access cover and the housing. All electrical terminations are made and brought out through hermetic seals. To purge the housing, the access cover is mounted and secured, and the housing is filled with dry nitrogen to a pressure of 15 psig by means of a filling valve and pressure-relief valve. The purge is then closed and the nitrogen filling tube removed. These housings are significantly more expensive than standard housings, since they must be designed to be

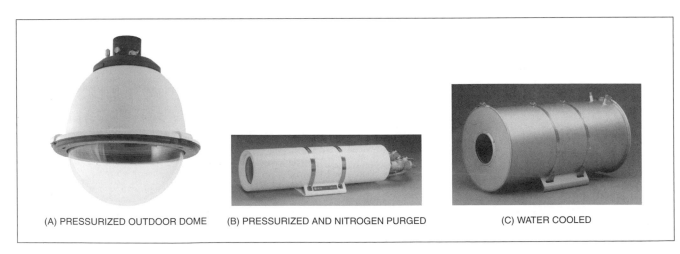

(A) PRESSURIZED OUTDOOR DOME   (B) PRESSURIZED AND NITROGEN PURGED   (C) WATER COOLED

FIGURE 15-19   Pressurized and water cooled environmental housings

hermetically sealed to provide a positive pressure of 15 psig differential pressure, and to withstand an explosion.

Water-cooled housings are designed for use in extremely hot indoor or outdoor locations. They require a constant supply of cooling water for proper operation. A 1-inch-thick water jacket built into the housing effectively shields the camera/lens from the outside environment. Depending on the application, the housings are made from aluminum or stainless steel. An internal fan provides constant air circulation within the housing, aids in efficient heat transfer to the water jacket, and prevents heat buildup. The housing is supplied with a 1/4-inch-thick Pyrex heat-resistant window for operating at temperatures up to 550°F (288°C). Consult the manufacturer to obtain recommendations for the specific operating environment.

15.6 NEMA ENVIRONMENTAL RATINGS

The NEMA has developed a comprehensive set of specifications and ratings for indoor and outdoor electrical housings. Many of the manufacturers of video security housings and integrated camera modules have designed their products to meet some of these housing ratings. Information

on these ratings is included on the manufacturer's literature, and detail information can be obtained from the NEMA organization. Table 15-1 summarizes several NEMA housing ratings for indoor and outdoor designs.

15.7 HOUSING ACCESSORIES

There are numerous accessories available for indoor and outdoor housings. Some of the more common types include thermostatically controlled heaters and fans, window wipers and washers, sun shields and shrouds, and many types of mounts and brackets.

Heater and Fan. In warmer climates where the temperature does not drop below freezing, only a fan and thermostat are required to maintain suitable operating temperatures for the camera and lens. The thermostat is designed to automatically turn on the fan when the temperature in the interior of the housing rises above some value, usually between 90 and 100°F (32–38°C), and turn it off when it falls a few degrees below the set temperature. In cold climates, a heater and thermostat are used to keep the lens and camera above about 45–55°F (7–13°C). The heater prevents condensation on the window and lens and keeps the automatic-iris mechanism and camera operative. In freezing weather, it prevents moisture

PROVIDES PROTECTION AGAINST THE FOLLOWING ENVIRONMENTAL CONDITIONS	NEMA ENCLOSURE TYPE*							
	1	3	4	4X	6	6P	12	13
APPROXIMATE IP EQUIVALENT**	IP30	IP64	IP66	IP66			IP65	IP65
INCIDENTAL CONTACT WITH ENCLOSED EQUIPMENT	√	√	√	√	√	√	√	√
INDOOR	√	√	√	√	√	√	√	√
OUTDOOR		√	√		√	√		
FALLING DIRT	√	√	√	√	√	√	√	√
DRIPPING AND LIGHT SPLASHING LIQUIDS		√	√	√	√	√	√	√
RAIN, SLEET AND SNOW		√	√	√	√	√		
CIRCULATING DUST, LINT, FIBERS, DEBRIS		√	√	√	√	√	√	√
SETTLING DUST, LINT, FIBERS, DEBRIS		√	√	√	√	√	√	√
EXTERNAL ICE		√	√	√	√	√		
HOSEDOWN AND SPLASHING WATER			√	√	√	√		
OIL AND COOLANT SEEPAGE							√	√
OIL AND COOLANT SPRAYING AND SPLASHING								√
CORROSIVE AGENTS				√		√		
OCCASIONAL TEMPORARY SUBMERSION					√	√		
OCCASIONAL PROLONGED SUBMERSION						√		

*NEMA—NATIONAL ELECTRICAL MANUFACTURERS ASSOCIATION

**IP—INGRESS PROTECTION CLASSIFICATION

4 AND 4X ARE THE MOST COMMONLY USED OUTDOOR TYPES

12 AND 13 ARE THE MOST COMMONLY USED INDOOR TYPES

Table 15-1   NEMA Housing Ratings for Non-Hazardous Locations

from freezing on the window and within the environmentally enclosed housing. The thermostat applies power to the heater when the temperature goes down below the dew point. When the camera/lens housing is located in an interior close-to-the-ceiling environment or in an outdoor warm environment, a thermostatically controlled fan is used to cool the camera/lens combination. The fan should contain a removable filter that can be cleaned or replaced periodically.

Heaters require considerable electrical power for their operation. Most heater assemblies supplied by the manufacturer require 24 VAC for their operation. If primary power is supplied from a 117 VAC source then a step-down transformer with a 24 VAC output is required. If 117 VAC power is not locally available at the camera-housing site, the wire supplying the power must be sized correctly. Table 15-2 lists appropriate wire sizes vs. distance between the 117 and 24 VAC sources and the camera.

Window Washer and Wiper. Another accessory is the window washer and wiper. If the housing is rectangular and pointing down at 15° or 20° or more, it is generally unnecessary to provide the housing with a window wiper and washer, as rain will run off the window, along with dirt, and allow proper viewing. If, however, the housing is located in a dusty environment or is in a more horizontal direction, it is advisable to include a window washer/wiper assembly. This assembly is mounted below and in front of the

window and operates like an automobile washer/wiper system. The wiper motor and liquid washing pump can be energized automatically and periodically or remotely from the control console.

Most environmental housings, indoor or outdoor, are supplied with plastic or safety (tempered) glass windows for the lens to view through. These windows may be acrylic, polycarbonate, or glass, depending on the design. The choice of acrylic vs. polycarbonate depends on whether the application is to be maximally tamperproof or only moderately so, and whether the housing is used indoors or outdoors. Acrylic is optically clear and will transmit over 95% of the light. Polycarbonate transmits less—approximately 85%—but has a higher impact resistance than acrylic. Both types are available in a mar-resistant type which is highly recommended, and will remain optically clear under normal cleaning action and withstand outdoor weathering. For maximum resistance to scratching and abrasion, safety glass is used. Window thicknesses range from 1/8 inch for light duty to 1/4 inch for normal service and from 3/8- to 1/2-inch for maximum security housings. For dome systems the portion of the dome that is used for viewing has its surface pointing downward and tends to be self-cleaning; however, they must be cleaned periodically and water droplets on the surface will reduce visibility.

Tamper Switch. In most security applications, it is important that when the camera housing is being opened by authorized or unauthorized personnel, the system or

POWER SOURCE VOLTAGE	CONDUCTOR SIZE AWG*	RESISTANCE ohms/1000 ft†	POWER TO HEATER AND CAMERA OVER TWO CONDUCTOR CABLE MAXIMUM CABLE LENGTH (ft)		
			25 WATT LOAD (0.21 AMP)	50 WATT LOAD (0.42 AMP)	100 WATT LOAD (0.84 AMP)
117 VAC	22	33.0	1656	828	414
	20	20.8	2628	1314	657
	18	13.02	4198	2099	1050
	16	8.18	6683	3341	1671
	14	5.16	10594	5297	2649
	12	3.24	16872	8398	4199
			25 WATT LOAD (1.04 AMP)	50 WATT LOAD (2.08 AMP)	100 WATT LOAD (4.16 AMP)
24 VAC	22	33.0	69	34	17.3
	20	20.8	110	55	27.5
	18	13.02	176	88	44
	16	8.18	281	140.5	70
	14	5.16	445	222.5	111
	12	3.24	709	354.5	177
	10	2.04	1127	563.5	284

*AMERICA WIRE GUAGE
†RESISTANCE REPRESENTS FULL WIRE LENGTH, I.E. 2x CABLE LENGTH
††IF 12 VDC POWER IS USED, USE THE 24 VAC TABLE ABOVE AND DOUBLE THE WIRE LENGTH
Note: BASED ON MAXIMUM VOLTAGE DROP OF 10%

Table 15-2   Wire Size vs. Distance for Housing Heater, Camera, and Other Electronics

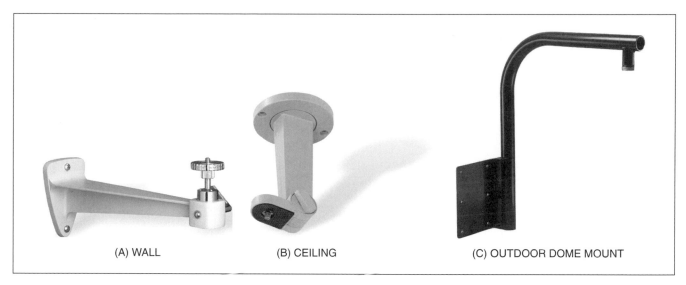

(A) WALL   (B) CEILING   (C) OUTDOOR DOME MOUNT

FIGURE 15-20   Camera housing brackets and mounts

guard be alerted. An electrical switch in the camera housing is used to activate an electrical alarm that can be sent back to the monitoring location when the housing has been opened.

Locks, Security Screws.   There are various levels of security key locks available for indoor and outdoor housings. Most camera housings are supplied with standard locks, but these can be upgraded to high security locks when the application demands it. In place of key locks various types of security screw hardware is available. The manufacturer should be consulted on the different types of key locks and security screws that can be supplied.

Brackets and Mounts.   A large variety of brackets and mounts are available to mount cameras, housings, and pan/tilt platforms safely to walls, ceilings, poles, pedestals, and other structures. Since most mounts are not compatible from manufacturer to manufacturer, the housing and bracket should be purchased from the same manufacturer to avoid extra costs for reworking parts that do not interface properly. Figure 15-20 shows some common camera housing brackets and mounts available.

15.8   HOUSING GUIDELINES

The EIA has written a guideline of recommended design parameters for housing manufacturers for hole configurations on mounting brackets and housing mountings. At present, not all manufacturers use the same mounting-hole configuration. The EIA has recommended guidelines

for the electrical input/output wiring and connector configurations so that there is interchangeability between manufacturers and so that safe procedures are followed by manufacturers and installers. Local building codes and UL codes specify the minimum requirement for electrical enclosure materials. They should be consulted to be sure materials are suitable. The purchaser must be aware of the requirements for each application and look carefully at the manufacturer's specifications to determine the most suitable housing. The NEMA housing recommendations should be consulted to help determine the specific rating for indoor or outdoor housings.

15.9   SUMMARY

The security camera housing plays an important role in protecting the camera and lens from the environment and vandalism, and insuring that they will be in a safe and controlled environment to maximize life and picture quality. Many camera housing designs are available for indoor and outdoor applications.

In an effort to reduce the complexity of choosing a compatible lens, camera, and other accessories at the camera site, the integrated camera design has evolved. This integrated design is lower in cost and requires less installation time resulting in an additional cost savings.

There are many specialty housings to protect the camera and lens in harsh environments and from extreme vandalism. With the large number of housing manufacturers to choose from, there is a housing configuration for almost any application.

Chapter 16

Electronic Video Image Splitting, Reversal, and Annotation

CONTENTS

16.1 Overview
16.2 Electronic Image Splitting—Multiple Image Displays
    16.2.1 Electronic Image-Splitting
    16.2.2 Picture-in-a-Picture
16.3 Video Text, Graphics Annotation
    16.3.1 Time/Date Generator
    16.3.2 Camera ID, Title Inserter
    16.3.3 Message Generator
    16.3.4 Transaction Inserter
16.4 Image Reversal
16.5 Pre- and Post-Alarm Video Recording
16.6 Alarms Over Video Cable
16.7 Multiple Camera Synchronizing Generator
16.8 Summary

16.1 OVERVIEW

There are many video devices and features that can significantly enhance the effectiveness of a video security system. These include: electronic image-splitting and compression, data annotation, picture-in-a-picture, and video scan-reversal.

An electronic image-splitting device is interposed in between the camera and the monitor, VCR, DVR, or video printer. It combines parts of the scenes of two or more cameras and displays them on one monitor. The use of the image splitter increases security in several ways. It: (1) decreases the number of monitors, (2) permits the guard to view a monitor with two or three scenes on it rather than one, and (3) reduces the number of recorders required by combining several scenes onto one video signal. Image splitters *do not* display the entire video scene

from the cameras on the screen. They only display *part* of each camera scene: 1/2 of the scene if it is a 2-way split, 1/3 if 3-way split, and 1/4 if 4-way split.

It is often advantageous to display a *compressed* image of a second scene into another camera scene. The picture-in-a-picture can insert this second image anywhere and in any size into the first camera display.

Video annotation equipment and software can display alphanumeric characters and graphics on a video monitor. Text annotation includes: time, date, camera number, camera scene identifier (hallway, front lobby, etc.), alarm source, and other information for the guard. There is also the ability to display specialized text messages as a requirement occurs. The text and graphics input from access control, emergency, or other systems can be displayed.

The scan-reversal unit reverses the video picture horizontal orientation as required in some mirror optics applications as when a mirror is used with a fixed-focal-length (FFL) lens to redirect the camera viewing angle.

Video signal synchronization generators are used to synchronize the video signal from multiple cameras so that a smooth transition from one camera to another can be made during camera switching.

16.2 ELECTRONIC IMAGE SPLITTING—MULTIPLE IMAGE DISPLAYS

Chapter 4 described several image-splitting optics that image two or three independent scenes from two or three different lenses and superimpose the scenes onto the *same* camera and monitor. When two lenses are used, only *one-half* of each of the original scenes is displayed. For three lenses, only *one-third* of each is displayed. The combined split-image can be viewed on a standard monitor,

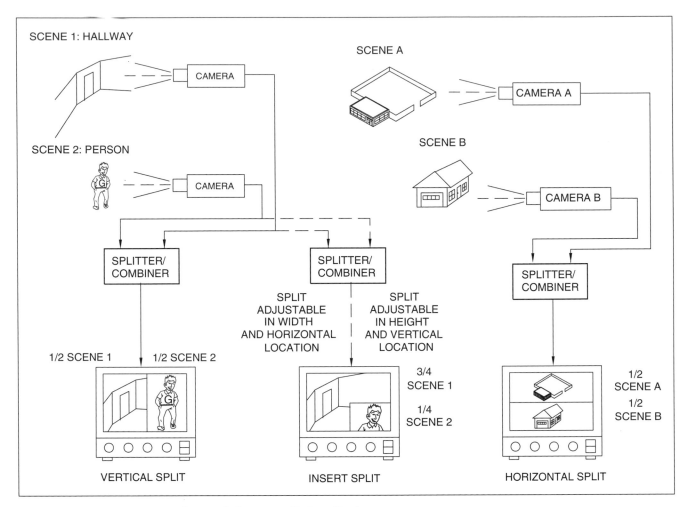

FIGURE 16-1   Two-camera electronic image-splitting displays

recorded on standard VCR or DVR, or printed on a standard video printer. Image-splitting lenses display only a portion or fraction of each individual original scene. Likewise, the electronic splitting devices described below display only a portion or fraction of each scene.

Electronic image-splitting can accomplish the same result using multiple cameras and a video signal combiner-splitter module. Optical and electronic image splitting is different from *image-compression* used in multiplexers that combine the *full* video signals from 4, 9, 16, or 32 individual cameras and display them side by side or one above the other on a single monitor. The multiplexing and compression equipment displays the *full* camera scene from each camera on the monitor but at a *loss in resolution*. The quad (4 scenes) loses half the horizontal resolution and half the vertical resolution from *each* camera. The 9, 16, and 32 cameras lose proportionally more.

16.2.1 Electronic Image-Splitting

Electronic image-splitting (combining) devices take two video monochrome or color camera signals and display a

part of each picture on one monitor (Figure 16-1). The vertical split example shows two camera scenes: 1/2 picture from camera 1 and 1/2 picture from camera 2, each displayed side by side. In the horizontal split case, the same two camera scenes are shown on a single monitor with the image splitter displaying 1/2 of scene A on top and 1/2 of scene B on the bottom. The electronic splitters can locate the split anywhere along the horizontal or vertical axis. They can be adjusted to make a full horizontal or vertical split, make an insert in any corner, or make a "floating" insert anywhere in the image. The split boundary between the individual cameras can be displayed by a gray, black, white, or semi-transparent border.

Some electronic splitting systems require that the two video signals be synchronized while others do not require synchronization. Figure 16-2 shows the connections for synchronizing two cameras and the splitter. One camera can be unsynchronized but should have a vertical and/or horizontal output drive signal to synchronize the second camera. The second camera should be able to be synchronized by an external horizontal or vertical sync signal, or a composite video signal. Alternatively, the two video cameras can be synchronized by some external synchronizing

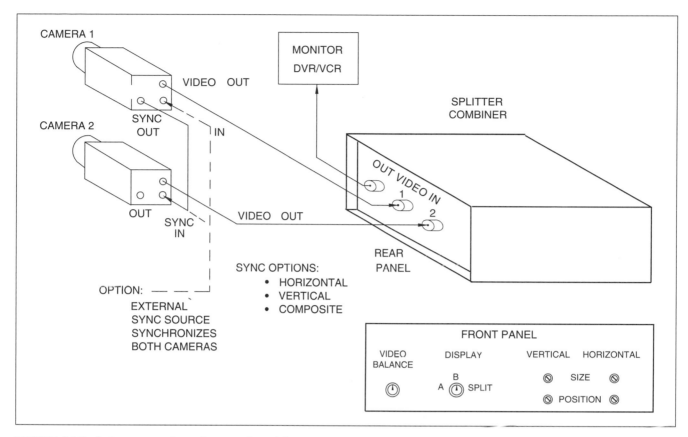

FIGURE 16-2 Interconnections for synchronizing two cameras

source. The best synchronization between the two cameras is obtained when the driving camera has a 2:1 interlace. Normally, any random or 2:1 interlaced camera is used as the master camera and any camera accepting horizontal, vertical, or composite video signal drive is used as a slave camera.

The adjustable front-panel controls on a video splitter include vertical position, vertical size, horizontal position, horizontal size, and video level balance. There is also a three-position switch so that the full camera 1 scene, the full camera 2 scene, or the split-image can be displayed. More than one splitter-inserter may be cascaded in series to display video from more than two cameras on a single monitor. Three cameras require two splitters and four cameras require three splitters. The splitter-inserter selects only a part of each picture: *it does not compress* the picture into a smaller area. When camera scenes must be transmitted to remote monitoring or recording locations, the splitter-inserter technique reduces the number of UTP, coaxial-cable, fiber-optic, microwave, RF, or infrared video links. Eliminating one or more of these links can reduce cost significantly.

A cost-saving retail-store splitter application is shown in Figure 16-3. The monitor displays a quarter-split, three-quarter split picture, where the three-quarter image provides information from a wide-angle lens viewing an entire cash register area and the one-quarter split shows a

close-up of the merchandise on the conveyer. The video output from the screen splitter is standard composite video and is accepted by any standard monitor, VCR, DVR, or video printer, and requires no special processing for transmission, display, recording, or printing.

16.2.2 Picture-in-a-Picture

A very useful application of the image-compression technique is the compressed picture inserter or picture-in-a-picture (Figure 16-4). This insert split shows the compressed scene from camera 2 inserted into the picture of camera 1. The inserted picture is adjustable in size and can be bounded by an adjustable gray, black, white, or semi-transparent border. The inserted picture can be positioned anywhere on the monitor screen.

The picture-in-a-picture unit compresses and inserts the camera picture as part of a full-frame picture. Via a front-panel control the compressed picture can be interchanged with the full picture. Some units have multiple camera inputs to choose from. Most units display monochrome or color pictures on the main image and monochrome on the compressed inserted picture, but some display color on both. Freeze-frame of the compressed picture is available on most units.

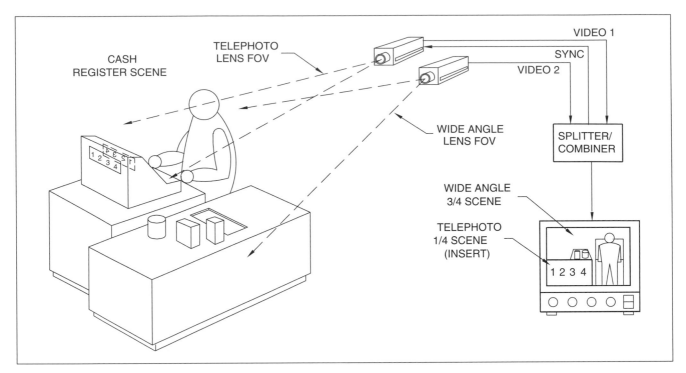

FIGURE 16-3 **Quarter split retail store image-splitting system**

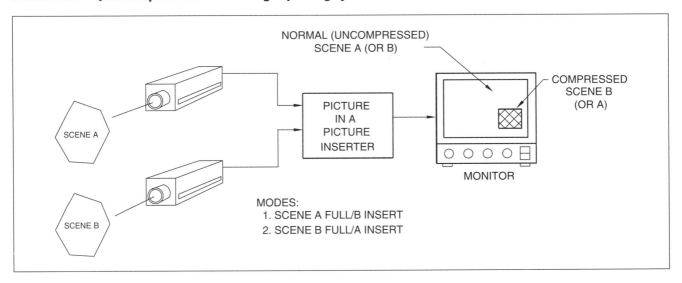

FIGURE 16-4 **Picture-in-a-picture (PIP) technique**

16.3 VIDEO TEXT, GRAPHICS ANNOTATION

It is often necessary to superimpose alphanumeric data and/or graphics on a video display. The information annotated in these displays may include camera ID number, camera scene identifier, time, date, computer terminal transaction number, cash register amount, etc. It can also provide alarm instructions, or other messages that provide the guard with additional useful information, and/or evidence presentable in a courtroom for prosecution. Some units also display graphics, building layouts, and maps. The equipments available to provide these functions vary from very simple time/date generators to comprehensive devices that can store programmed messages and graphics that are displayed on the screen on command or automatically. This section describes various alphanumeric generators used in many video security systems.

16.3.1 Time/Date Generator

The most commonly used video annotation equipment is the time/date generator. Time and date annotation are required when a video recording from a video recorder is used in a courtroom procedure. The time/date unit is connected in series with the camera and monitor, adds time and date to the video signal passing through it, and displays the picture and the time/date on the monitor. Since both the scene and the annotation are on the same composite signal or recorder frame, they are permanently correlated in time. This is important in a security application where prosecution relies on the correlation of two events or connection between an event and an individual. The time and date annotation can be positioned anywhere in the picture area. A backup battery is provided so that if there is a power failure the time/date clock retains correct time and date for many hours. Once the unit has been set up and the time and date adjusted it requires no additional attention. Most units provide year, month, day of month, hours, minutes, and seconds in the annotation. For maximum picture usability and optimum readout of the numeric time/date information on the display, the ability to put a border of black, gray, or white around the time and date, block it, or provide no edges around the time/date digital display is provided. Most units have a 12-hour AM/PM designator mode or a 24-hour mode. Various manufacturers make equipment operating from a 12-volt DC supply for use with portable cameras and recorders. Figure 16-5 illustrates a typical time/date generator system diagram, its screen presentation, and setup controls.

16.3.2 Camera ID, Title Inserter

When multiple cameras are used, it is useful to annotate a video monitor display with a camera ID number and text that describes a particular scene or area in the facility that the camera is viewing. This function is performed by electronics in the camera or by a separate camera ID inserter unit. As with the time/date generator, the camera ID unit when provided separately has the video looped through it so the camera ID number and identifier is superimposed onto the video picture. When the camera supplies the ID number, a slide or "dip" switch or menu program is used to set the camera ID number.

16.3.3 Message Generator

When more comprehensive video display messaging is required, more versatile equipment is needed. A text messaging unit is connected between the video camera and monitor and is programmed via front-panel controls, from a keyboard, or through an RS-232 interface. Most units generate several lines of alphanumeric characters, providing full text and numerals and graphics on the monitor. Figure 16-6 shows examples of video text messaging units.

The systems are menu-driven and all the inputs are via the keyboard and mouse. Once the data have been entered, the keyboard may be removed and the equipment retains the information for call-up via front-panel switches on the unit. The system can display alphanumeric characters and many other standard symbols on the monitor screen. The characters displayed are selected from a built-in programmable read-only memory (PROM) that includes a selection of different characters. The unit also accepts external data, text, and graphics that can be

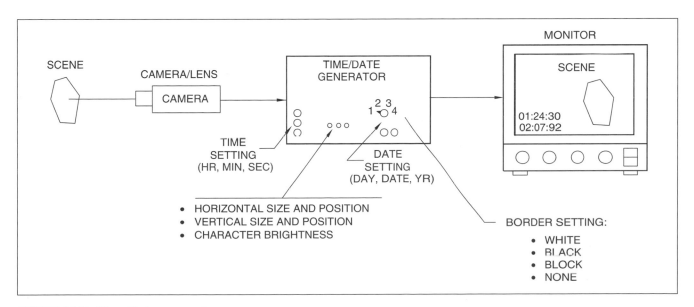

FIGURE 16-5 Time/date generator

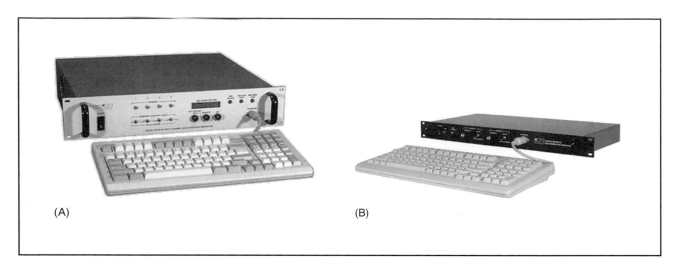

FIGURE 16-6   Video text messaging units

superimposed onto the video picture via an RS-232 input. Built-in digital switches are used to change the character size in both the horizontal and vertical directions. Characters can be positioned anywhere on the display both horizontally and vertically. As with the time/date generator, the displayed characters can be presented in black, white, gray, or semi-transparent color for optimum readability.

A very comprehensive system displays clear legible characters in different sizes from a memory. It can also display many continuous lines of text and is capable of extensive text editing. The system operates with monochrome or color cameras. In color mode, it offers color selections, with a working palette of colors. Some systems provide different speeds for text, scrolling up or down the screen.

16.3.4   Transaction Inserter

Text and graphics generators can be dedicated to specific hardware such as: (1) (ATM), (2) point-of-sale (POS) terminals, (3) cash registers, (4) gas station terminals, (5) credit card verifiers, and (6) electronic scales, etc. These dedicated text inserters combine digital text and graphics with video images for display on a monitor, recording by a VCR or DVR, or printing on a video printer. These message generators and annotators can be programmed to display events such as voids, no sales, cash refunds, and so on.

These systems communicate with peripheral equipment via a standard RS-232 interface or other communication protocol. In the case of cash register, POS, and ATM equipment, the protocol sent by these equipments is interpreted by the message generator, converted into text or graphics, and displayed on the screen. To operate properly with each peripheral device, each unit is programmed

so that it matches the unique protocol of the data terminal. Some equipment is versatile so that it can be set up in the field to match the protocol of the specific terminal.

All the information displayed on the monitor—the video picture and the message and transaction—can be recorded on a recorder to show an audit trail of business transactions, including data on what cash was exchanged, and the time and date. By combining alphanumeric text with a video screen, a concise, easily reviewable record is obtained, offering permanent, positive, and complete identification of activity.

16.4   IMAGE REVERSAL

First-generation monochrome video to cameras could easily be modified to electronically reverse the scan on the tube so that if a mirror was positioned in front of the camera lens—which reverses the picture from right to left—the tube deflection coils could be reversed to produce the correct left-to-right image orientation. This modification was practical for the monochrome tube camera but not for the color tube camera or CCD solid-state-sensor cameras. As a consequence, a device called a scan reversal unit (SRU) was developed for monochrome and color CCD cameras to reinstate the correct left-to-right monitor display (Figure 16-7).

This fix is necessary in some CCD and CMOS camera installations where the camera sees a reversed image because it is viewing via a single mirror in front of the lens. The monochrome SRU stores one line of digitized video signal at a time in a static RAM and reads it out in a reversed sequence during the storage of the next line. By using dual memory chips, each working alternately, the SRU displays the whole picture without any noticeable

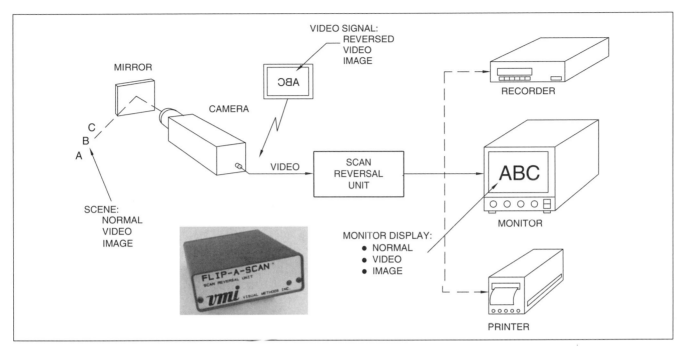

FIGURE 16-7   Scan reversal unit

delay. The units available have approximately 600-line horizontal resolution, which is sufficient for most available CCD cameras. The color SRU uses three of these systems in a single unit.

16.5   PRE- AND POST-ALARM VIDEO RECORDING

The pre- and post-alarm video-capture technique uses a video digitizing board capable of storing multiple video frames. When first switched on, it begins storing the video frames it receives. After a period of time (selectable) it continues recording but begins to discard (write-over) the initial frames recorded. By this technique, when an alarm at the camera location occurs, video frames *prior* to the alarm have been stored in the device. These pre-event scenes and all subsequent ones are available for display and recording. Figure 16-8 illustrate the video capture sequence.

16.6   ALARMS OVER VIDEO CABLE

In most CCTV security applications, alarm information generated by non-video means—that is, not by VMDs but by contact closures or some other means—are transmitted to the console monitor area via separate cable or transmission means. This adds to additional cost to transmit these alarms over the full camera-to-monitor distance. Equipment is available to multiplex the alarm onto a coaxial cable that is also transmitting the video signal, *during the vertical retrace time*, and then demodulate it at the monitor end to extract the alarm information and process it as a normal alarm. This "piggy-back" transmission is accomplished by multiplexing the coded alarm signal onto the video signal during the first 31 lines in the video scan. By encoding this alarm information during a non-picture signal time segment, the alarm information in essence "rides free" on the video signal.

In one configuration, up to 15 alarm points are transmitted on a single coaxial cable by individually coding each alarm point. The alarm inputs are digitally encoded (using a dip switch) and transmitted on the selected line pair of the vertical interval of the video signal, along with a 5-bit dip switch selectable error code to ensure signal integrity. The receiver board at the console decodes the signal information and drives an alarm output signal. The system can encode and decode (selectively) up to 15 alarm points and transmit them down one coaxial cable. The system also works with other devices to transmit pan/tilt and lens control information using the same video lines in the vertical interval time. The encoded vertical interval data line can be set (chosen) from line 1 to line 31 in the video picture or can be put into the active video portion of the picture or visual detection of alarm conditions. The digitally encoded signal can be recorded on a VCR or DVR. When the recorded signal is played back into a receiver unit, the alarm outputs will reflect the recorded alarm data. The addition of alarms to the video signal in no way alters its ability to be transmitted over coaxial-cable, UTP, two-wire, fiber-optic,

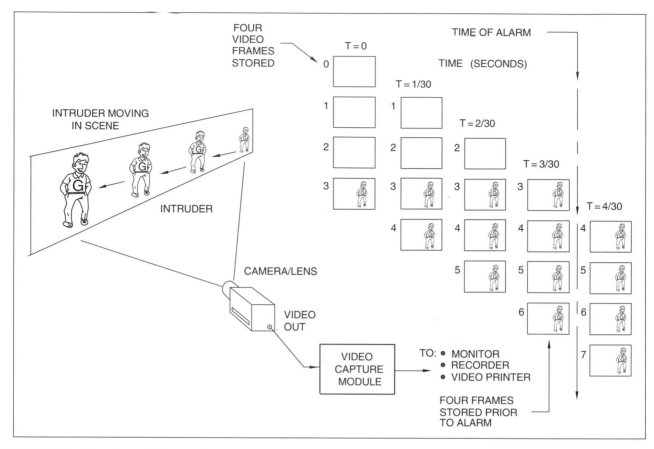

FIGURE 16-8   Pre-alarm video capture

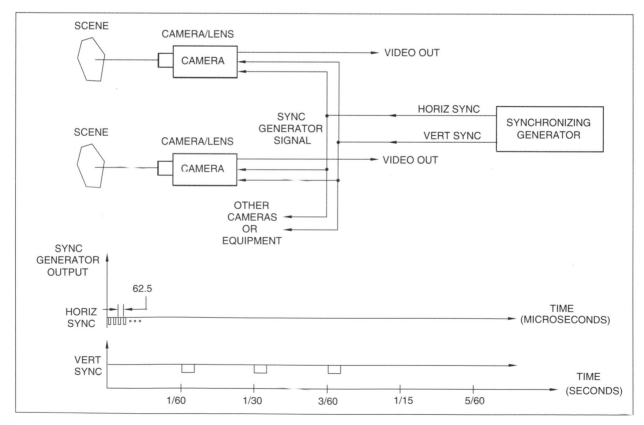

FIGURE 16-9   Multiple camera synchronizing generator

microwave, RF, or IR laser transmission means. Combining the alarm point encoding with the video signal results in increased efficiency and lower cost of data and video transmission.

16.7 MULTIPLE CAMERA SYNCHRONIZING GENERATOR

It is often necessary to synchronize multiple cameras and devices from one timing source to ensure optimum picture quality. This is especially true in systems having multiple cameras and monitors in multiple buildings and locations, including other peripheral equipment such as switchers, recorders, printers, and time/date generators. To accomplish this efficiently, a device called a video synchronizing generator is used. This device produces an accurately clocked set of synchronizing pulses and waveforms including vertical and horizontal sync with suitable signal amplitude and drive power, to synchronize many cameras and devices over long distances. Figure 16-9 shows how the synchronizing generator is connected into the security system.

16.8 SUMMARY

The aforementioned image-splitting, inserting, and annotating devices enhance the intelligence-gathering ability of video systems and help the security guard to be more effective. Video image-splitting devices are used when more camera scenes must be displayed on a monitor permitting security or management personnel to view more camera images even if they are not complete images. The picture-in-a-picture compressing devices allow small complete images to be displayed in a full screen camera display. Video annotation has become important in video monitoring and essential in crime prosecution. Video annotation of time and date are absolutely essential in courtroom prosecution. The video capture technique for viewing alarm scenes *prior* to the alarm illustrates how important video can be for intrusion detection and false-alarm verification. Transmission of video, alarm, and control signals on the same cable can save significant costs in upgrading existing installations and in new installations. The video synchronizing generator insures clean, noise-free synchronization of multiple cameras, monitors, recorders, and printers. There are many special video accessories available from small and large manufacturers to enhance security effectiveness.

Chapter 17
Camera Pan/Tilt Mechanisms

CONTENTS

17.1   Overview
17.2   Scene Coverage Required
    17.2.1   Point Scenes
    17.2.2   Area Scenes
    17.2.3   Volume Scenes
17.3   Panning and Tilting
17.4   Pan/Tilt Mechanism
17.5   Mechanical Configurations
    17.5.1   Above-Mounted
    17.5.2   Side-Mounted
17.6   Indoor
17.7   Outdoor
    17.7.1   Materials and Design
    17.7.2   Wind Loading
    17.7.3   Ice and Snow Loading
    17.7.4   Temperature
    17.7.5   Precipitation Dust, Dirt, and Corrosion
    17.7.6   Outdoor Domes
    17.7.7   Rugged-Precision Platform
17.8   Pan/Tilt—Components vs. Integrated System
17.9   Pan/Tilt/Lens Control Techniques
17.10   Pan/Tilt Mounting
17.11   Slip-Rings and Optical-Couplers
17.12   High-Speed Video-Dome PTZ Systems
    17.12.1   Background
    17.12.2   Technology
        17.12.2.1   Pan/Tilt Mechanism
        17.12.2.2   Camera, Lens
    17.12.3   Hardware: Domes, Pan/Tilt Cameras
        17.12.3.1   American Dynamic
        17.12.3.2   General Electric
        17.12.3.3   Panasonic
        17.12.3.4   Pelco
        17.12.3.5   Sony
17.13   Covert Mirror Pan/Tilt System
17.14   Gimbal Mounting
17.15   Servicing
    17.15.1   Cabling
    17.15.2   Mechanical
    17.15.3   Environmental
17.16   Summary

17.1   OVERVIEW

Pan/tilt mechanisms rotate and tilt the camera to point it in a specified direction. These electro-mechanical platforms are available for lightweight, indoor, small-camera applications as well as for large, outdoor, heavy camera/lens installations. The video lens, camera, and housing are secured to a small platform on the top or side of the pan/tilt mechanism. Pan/tilt mechanisms are designed to operate in manual or automatic mode, using a remote-control joystick mounted on the security control console. Figure 17-1a shows examples of indoor and outdoor pan/tilt units.

At remote distances it is necessary to be able to redirect the pointing direction of the camera/lens combination in order to see a specific person, activity, or scene. The console-mounted pan/tilt controller remotely directs the pan/tilt unit and the camera pointing direction, rotating it in azimuth (panning) and elevation (tilting), like a person moving his head and looking in different directions. Most pan/tilt units provide 355° or continuous azimuth panning and from 0 (horizontal) to 90° (directly downward) tilting. To control the pan/tilt unit, the security operator uses a lever switch, joystick, or thumb trackball at the control console. Units having preset pointing capability will pan/tilt to a preset azimuth and elevation direction automatically. Figure 17-1b shows some typical pan/tilt controllers.

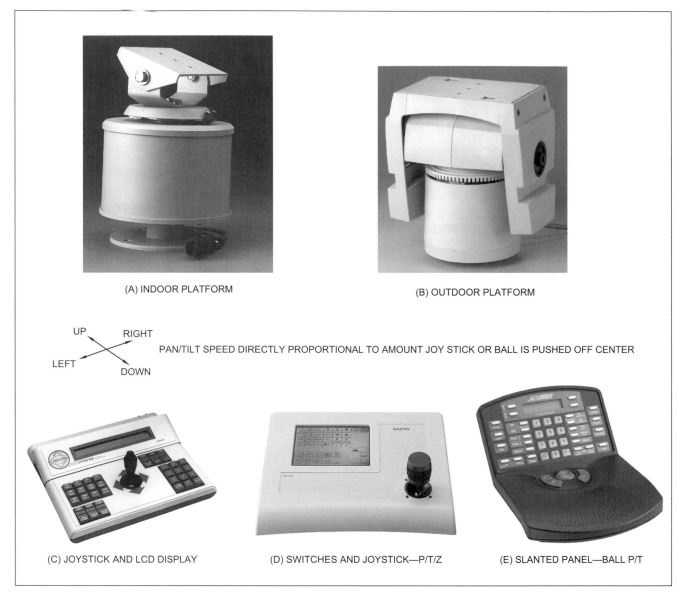

(A) INDOOR PLATFORM

(B) OUTDOOR PLATFORM

UP   RIGHT
LEFT   DOWN

PAN/TILT SPEED DIRECTLY PROPORTIONAL TO AMOUNT JOY STICK OR BALL IS PUSHED OFF CENTER

(C) JOYSTICK AND LCD DISPLAY

(D) SWITCHES AND JOYSTICK—P/T/Z

(E) SLANTED PANEL—BALL P/T

FIGURE 17-1   Indoor and outdoor pan/tilt platform and controllers

The joystick is moved forward or backward, left or right corresponding to the vertical (tilt) and horizontal (pan) movements of the camera/lens unit. Likewise, the thumb trackball is moved using the thumb to initiate pan and tilt. For the disk, touch-pad, and four-button design, left and right initiate panning, and top and bottom initiate tilt. The security officer watches the video monitor and can point the camera to view any area within the pan/tilt rotation range. The platform and camera move in accordance with the control signal sent by the control unit.

Pan/tilt platforms are available in a wide range of sizes from lightweight, pan-only units (scanners) for indoor applications to heavy-duty, environmentally protected pan/tilts for outdoor applications. Rugged outdoor units are environmentally enclosed and intended to withstand severe conditions of temperature, precipitation, dust, humidity, and high winds.

In the late 1990s the requirement for faster, more compact, and discreet PTZ surveillance cameras surfaced from casino, retail store, warehouse, and other applications. This resulted in the development of the *high-speed video-dome* camera system. The technology that made this innovation possible was the availability of small, high resolution, high sensitivity CCD camera sensors and associated DSP electronics. This, in turn, permitted the use of smaller zoom lenses. The Sony and Hitachi companies then developed the core component of the high-speed dome camera: a unitized digital pan/tilt drive package surrounding the miniature camera/lens assembly. Figure 17-2 shows a compact high-speed video-dome pan/tilt system now in widespread use in the security industry.

There are three primary applications for pan/tilt units: (1) monitoring a fixed or point site, (2) monitoring an

FIGURE 17-2 High-speed video dome system

installed in an environmentally enclosed housing or dome. The advantages and disadvantages of these two techniques are discussed.

Complete integrated video camera/lens/pan/tilt/ housing systems have been introduced, in which all these parts are integrated into a custom housing or dome. Typical systems are discussed in the following sections.

In a parking lot or building exterior, pan/tilt lens/ camera systems are mounted on a pedestal or on a wall or ceiling, with mounting brackets (Chapters 14, 15).

For covert applications, all pan/tilt and zoom camera/ lens hardware is hidden behind a wall or ceiling.

The transmission of the video signal and the control of pan/tilt mechanism movement and lens function are accomplished through separate video and control cables or through a multiplexed communication channel where the video signal and the controls are combined on a single coaxial cable or UTP, thereby eliminating additional wiring.

area site, and (3) monitoring a volume site. A point site might correspond to a bank teller, where the area of interest is the teller and customer, and the business transaction. An area site might be a building lobby where the activity in the lobby is of interest. A volume site might be a warehouse where many vertical bays (levels) must be under surveillance at different times. For the fixed or point site, a single fixed camera and lens are suitable to view the entire area. In the area and volume cases, a single fixed camera cannot see the entire area of interest, so a panning and tilting camera and a zoom lens are required.

Applications that use pan/tilt mechanisms can be roughly classified into indoor and outdoor types, mounted in either an overt configuration—without a concealing dome or housing—or a covert application, where the pan/tilt mechanism and lens/camera unit are hidden in a dome, hidden behind some visually opaque window, or camouflaged by some other means. A common type used in indoor applications consists of a panning platform that rotates the camera via direct operator control or automatically pans from side to side to cover the specific area. A second type is the pan/tilt unit in which panning and tilting are done manually (under operator control) or automatically. Both types can be augmented with a remotely controlled zoom lens to change the FOV and therefore the instantaneous camera coverage within the full range of the scanner or pan/tilt unit.

In outdoor applications, the pan/tilt mechanism and the housing containing the camera/lens must be designed to withstand wind loading, precipitation, dust, dirt, and all types of vandalism. In an outdoor application there are two options: (1) the lens and camera can be enclosed in an environmentally shielded housing and mounted on an environmental outdoor pan/tilt mechanism or (2) the lens, camera, and indoor pan/tilt mechanism can be

17.2 SCENE COVERAGE REQUIRED

The intelligence the security guard obtains from the monitor picture is only as good as the information the camera/ lens combination sees. It is therefore important to determine the viewing requirements of each camera/lens and select the optimum combination for transmitting maximum intelligence to the operator. The video system designer must decide whether a camera will be mounted on a fixed mount (pointed in only one direction), or on a pan, tilt, or pan/tilt platform so that the camera can be pointed in any direction (Figure 17-3).

A good analogy is the seeing ability of a human: when we look in a single direction, we see all of the activity in that direction all of the time. When we move our eyes or head in another direction within a large FOV, we cannot see the entire scene at one time, and therefore cannot see all of the activity in the entire FOV that our eyes can see. The video camera in essence time-shares the viewing of the scene, spending a fraction of time looking at any particular portion of the total scene area. In order to analyze this viewing requirement, video applications are divided into three types: point, area, and volume.

17.2.1 Point Scenes

A typical security surveillance *point* scene might be a supermarket checkout line, where the information of interest is the merchandise being rung up, the amount displayed on the cash register, the cashier, and the customer; or the scene might be a bank teller station, where the crucial intelligence is the identity of the customer. In such scenes, all of the activity occurs in a relatively

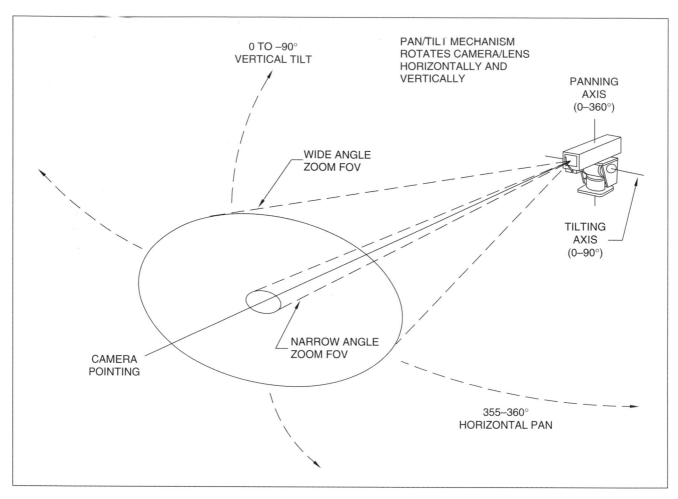

FIGURE 17-3   Spatial coverage using pan/tilt systems

small part of the FOV. Although a single camera with an FFL lens may be satisfactory, a better solution might be a fixed two-lens, one-camera system, with one lens viewing the amount rung up on the cash register and the other viewing the cashier, customer, and merchandise. Another solution is a zoom lens with some panning and tilting motion. This would be necessary in a jewelry or department store where the counter area is viewed with a wide-angle lens and a small piece of jewelry is viewed with a narrow-angle lens. The pan/tilt is necessary with a zoom lens because the high-magnification (telephoto) position results in a very small FOV, so the camera must be pointed at the exact center of the target. Figure 17-4 illustrates the two views of the cashier scene where the zoom lens views the entry area in the wide-field mode and can change to the telephoto position to identify monetary denominations with the pan/tilt mechanism pointing the camera/lens.

In the wide-field scene, the article of interest is not normally centered in the FOV. In this situation, the operator must redirect the camera/lens combination via the pan/tilt control to center the object of interest and make it observable in the high-magnification position.

17.2.2   Area Scenes

A second broad classification of surveillance scenes includes a not-yet-known area of activity within a relatively large location. A typical application might be to observe activity at one or more doors in the front lobby of a building or someone entering a car in a small parking lot. In this situation a camera mounted on a pan/tilt mechanism with zoom lens and located in one corner or on one wall of the lobby can accomplish all necessary surveillance (Figure 17-5).

If only a casual observation of the room is required, a fixed camera and lens may be sufficient; however, any detailed activity will probably be missed. To identify personnel in the lobby or identify a person or some specific activity at one of the distant locations in the lobby, a remote control pan/tilt and zoom lens combination is required. This is called an *area* application, since the camera pointing must be directed to different locations in the room, as selected by the security personnel. To view a specific activity, the operator points the camera to the new location, zooms into the telephoto position, and magnifies the area of activity on the monitor to identify or take further action. While this scenario is similar

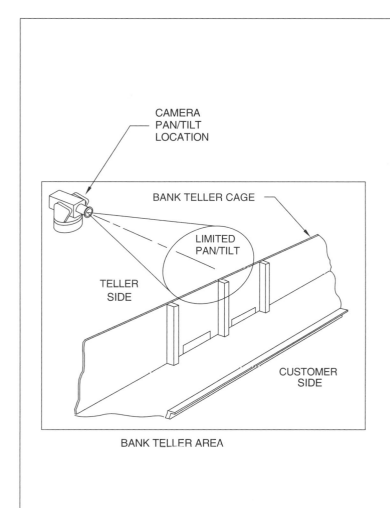

(A) WIDE-FIELD SCENE

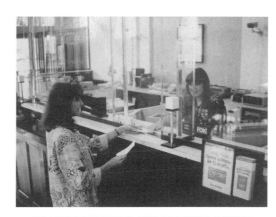

(B) NARROW-FIELD (TELEPHOTO) SCENE

CAMERA
PAN/TILT
LOCATION

BANK TELLER CAGE

LIMITED
PAN/TILT

TELLER
SIDE

CUSTOMER
SIDE

BANK TELLER AREA

FIGURE 17-4   Point scene bank teller cage

to the point scene, this area scene is significantly larger than a point scene and requires a faster pan/tilt to acquire the target quickly.

17.2.3   Volume Scenes

The third category involves very large areas of surveillance, typically a large warehouse area where essentially a *volume* of space must be surveyed. In a warehouse there may be many aisles and high stacks of material to be viewed, ground-level activity of walking or fork lift riding employees, or widely dispersed, elevated areas of interest. For this application the best pan/tilt and zoom lens hardware is required, to provide large ranges of magnification for wide-angle and narrow-angle conditions and to rapidly point the camera in the direction of the activity. Figure 17-6 illustrates the expanded requirements of this volume scene.

Some warehouse and supermarket installations have the camera/lens and pan/tilt mechanism on a roving track-mounted mechanism, so that the combination can move

physically throughout the facility to gain a more advantageous view of the activity. This technique is usually confined to indoor applications since the track mechanism is difficult to protect in an outdoor environment. Since the roving camera cannot be in position to view all areas it does not provide full-time coverage. In a large outdoor parking lot environment where the area to be covered is very large, multiple camera systems on pan/tilt platforms with zoom lenses are used to monitor entering and exiting vehicles and individual parked vehicles.

17.3   PANNING AND TILTING

There are basically two camera-mount configurations to point the camera: (1) panning (or scanning) and (2) panning and tilting. The simplest camera movement consists of horizontal scanning in which the camera is mounted on a rotating platform that moves from left to right and right to left to scan a scene. A motor and gear train provide the panning motion (Figure 17-7).

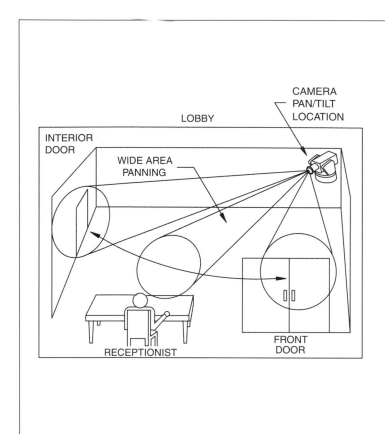

(A) WIDE-FIELD SCENE

(B) NARROW-FIELD (TELEPHOTO) SCENE

FIGURE 17-5   Area scene—front lobby

Most systems can scan through a range of 355° or a full, continuous 360° scanning using slip rings. Panning systems are used in front-lobby applications where all activity of interest occurs in a single horizontal plane: the camera must move only from left to right and stop at some particular location. In the automatic panning mode the camera/lens is rotated automatically through a specified angle at a constant rate, thereby allowing a guard at a monitor to see or a recorder to record the activity occurring in the area. However, when the camera is pointed in a particular direction, say the right-corner door, activity occurring in the center or left part of the scene is not under surveillance. Panning systems can be set to scan a small sector of the entire scanning range and at different speeds from 8 to 80° sec to allow the operator to optimize viewing of the area.

17.4   PAN/TILT MECHANISM

A pan/tilt camera platform is necessary when expected activity is anywhere in a *horizontal and vertical* location. The pan/tilt system moves and points the camera and lens in two different axes of rotation: one around the horizontal

axis to tilt, and the other around the vertical axis to pan (Figure 17-8).

As with panning systems, most platforms using slip-rings available to provide a full 360° continuous panning so that the lens and camera can continue rotating to provide full coverage.

To accomplish vertical movement or pointing to raise or lower the camera/lens angle of view, a second motor and drive-train are required. The angular FOV provided by such a system usually ranges from 0 to −90°, thereby covering activity in most scenes of interest. A joystick, thumb trackball, or four-button setup (Figure 17-1) is used to pan and tilt the camera horizontally and/or vertically. Moving the joystick in between horizontal and vertical, say the 1:30 o'clock position, activates both drives. Most pan/tilt controllers have a proportional joystick control, in which the pan/tilt mechanism speed of movement is proportional to the amount of joystick deflection from its center Off position. This variable speed capability is particularly useful in that it allows the security operator to quickly point the camera in the direction of activity.

When video is integrated with microcomputer-controlled hardware, the security operator can program

(A) WIDE-FIELD SCENE

(B) NARROW-FIELD (TELEPHOTO) SCENE

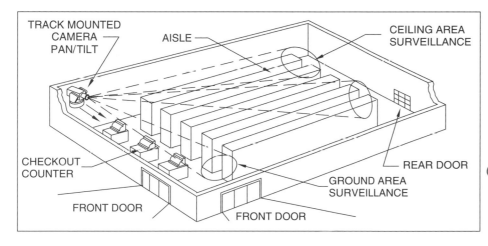

NOTE: CIRCULAR AREA DENOTES PAN/TILT POINTING FIELD OF VIEW (FOV)

(C) VOLUME SCENE STORE/WAREHOUSE

FIGURE 17-6   Volume scene using pan/tilt

various preset lens/camera pointing angles, so that later he has to push only a single switch at the console to automatically direct the pan/tilt platform. This is useful when an alarm sensor activates the camera pointing to the preset direction, pointing the camera at the target in the shortest possible time. Other programmable presets include zoom lens focal length and focus, thereby optimizing the image of the target.

Pan/tilt mechanisms have specific ranges of azimuth and elevation over which they can operate. In the tilt (elevation) axis, electro-mechanical switches sense when the tilt platform and shaft have rotated to the upper or lower extremes (maximum range), and they open to de-energize the tilt drive motor. In the horizontal (azimuth) direction, similar limit switches (or other sensing mechanisms) are incorporated, so that the horizontal travel can be limited to a specific angular sector or go to its extreme horizontal range limits of about 355°. These mechanisms cannot go beyond 355° and must therefore come back around if they are to follow the movement of a person or object

that is moving out of the angular range of the horizontal panning direction (Figure 17-9).

To overcome this limitation and allow continuous rotation (360° and beyond), slip-rings are used. By making all electrical connections from the stationary platform to the moving pan/tilt mechanism and camera lens assembly through slip-rings or optical couplers, the moving platform is able to rotate continuously in any angular direction without having to stop and back up. Limit switches are incorporated if the range of rotation must be reduced, but no mechanical stops are installed if the slip ring mechanism is to provide full travel.

Clutches are used in pan/tilt drives in between the motor and gear-train drives so that if the output shaft encounters resistance, the motor will not stall and burn out—the motor will keep running until the overload is removed. Some pan/tilt mechanisms perform a similar function: when the motor stalls, they sense the overload via the increased electrical current to the motor and then

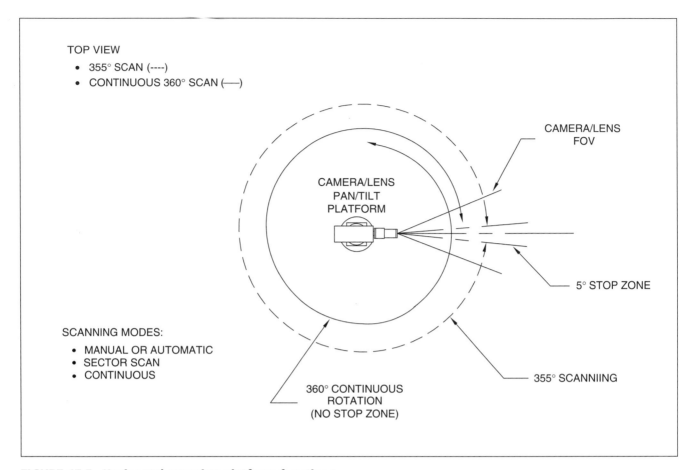

FIGURE 17-7 Horizontal scanning platform functions

reduce the current or turn it off, so that no harm is done to the motor or drive-train.

When the motors are turned off, brakes or anti-drive back-drive gears are used to prevent the platforms from "coasting," so that the platforms come rapidly to a complete stop, and do not continue to move under the load of the camera or other loading factors.

Most systems use micro-switches or other electromagnetic devices to determine when the motor has driven the platform to a particular angular location or to the limit of travel. An installer can move or adjust these switches to change the range of travel. Newer designs use electronic positioning to provide a basis for determining the angular position of the horizontal or vertical platform at any given time. The electronic feedback provides input to the control system to program preset camera/lens parameters. These parameters include horizontal pan angle, vertical tilt angle, zoom lens FL, focus, and iris settings. With modern electronic control systems, the security operator can pan, tilt, and zoom to a particular location, set parameters for the system to memorize as a preset combination, and assign a unique code for that condition. To accomplish this, the system's electronics read and memorize the shaft position on the pan/tilt and camera motors. During operation, if an action occurs at the preset site for that code,

the operator can manually call for that combination; or if an alarm occurs in that area, the system can automatically call up the particular code and view the site. When the code is initiated, the pan/tilt points the camera in the direction of the activity, the zoom lens adjusts to the preset FL and focuses, and the operator sees a scene in the quickest possible way. This operating procedure reduces human stress, effort, and error. This concept has been expanded to multiple cameras and multiple sites, allowing the operator to program different presets and codes so that the system will "tour" the sites. This feature optimizes both human and mechanical efficiency and eliminates the need for the operator to hunt for particular targets or activities.

17.5 MECHANICAL CONFIGURATIONS

There are several different mechanical configurations for pan/tilt platforms, with options for camera/lens location and the rotation axes of the pan/tilt mechanism. A brief analysis of their advantages and disadvantages follows. Figure 17-10 illustrates the two basic configurations.

Historically, the most popular camera/lens location has been above or over-the-center of the pan/tilt mechanism;

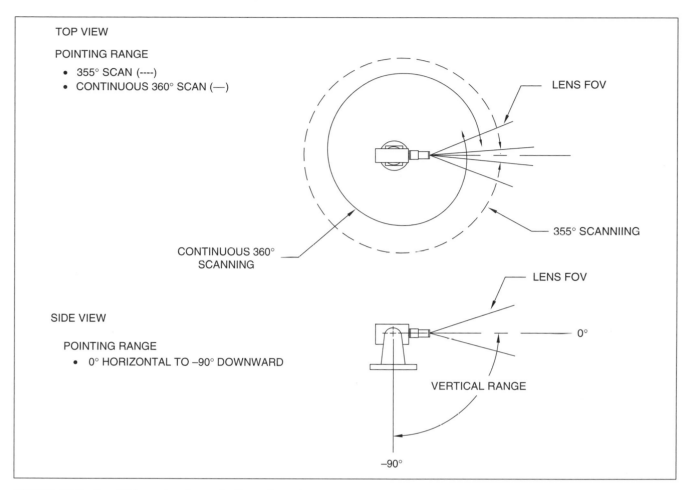

FIGURE 17-8   Pan/tilt mechanism platform functions

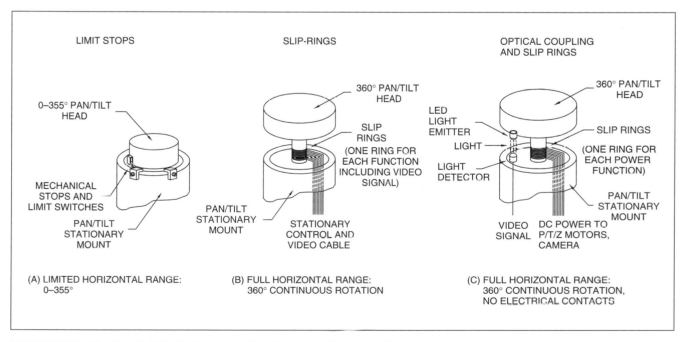

FIGURE 17-9   Horizontal limit stops vs. slip-ring or optical-coupler

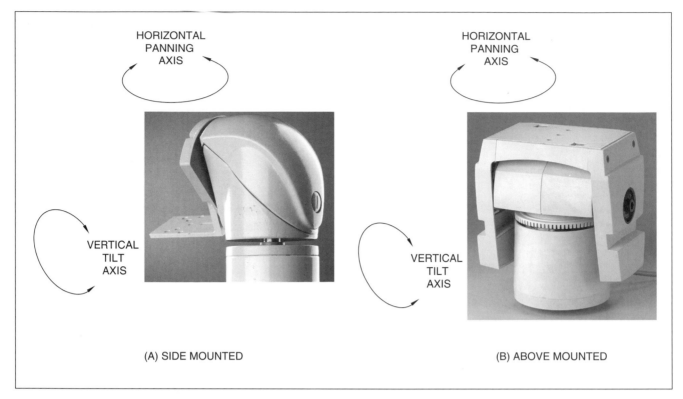

FIGURE 17-10   Above and side-mounted pan/tilt configurations

the majority of manufacturers produced this type. A second configuration, the side-mounted camera/lens places the camera and lens to one side of the vertical planning axis, at the same height as the tilt motor drive and hardware. This side-mounted configuration is designed to reduce the wind and mechanical loading on the vertical drive motor and gear mechanism, thereby improving its performance, life, and reliability.

17.5.1 Above-Mounted

In the over-the-center mounted configuration the system is only balanced horizontally when the camera/lens is horizontal, but when it is rotated up or down the weight of the camera/lens combination becomes unbalanced. To improve balance, additional weights are added to the tilting arm to reduce the stress on the vertical motor, bearings, and gear train. This additional weight must be driven by the vertical tilt motor in addition to the camera/lens/housing load, but as the camera tilts up or down from its normal horizontal position the weights and/or springs counterbalance the load. To invert a top-mounted system, the springs and weights usually have to be removed. Different indoor/outdoor models are available that are capable of carrying loads from 5 to 40 lbs.

17.5.2 Side-Mounted

The side-mounted configuration requires no counterweights or springs if the camera is symmetrically mounted on the tilt arm located to the side of and in line with the horizontal (tilt) rotating axis. While this configuration is not symmetrical in the vertical plane—the camera is off to one side of the vertical (panning) axis—it nevertheless results in a lower imbalance on the horizontal tilting axis, thereby providing less wind loading and less unbalanced forces on the mechanism.

Counterbalancing weights and internal springs are not needed in the side-mounted configuration, and therefore the horizontal axis remains approximately balanced, reducing the power requirement of the tilt motor and gear train assembly. The counterweights and springs are not necessary because the camera, lens, and housing are closer to the center of the axis of rotation. Also, if the side-mounted system must be inverted, when mounted on a ceiling, no changes are required. Different indoor/outdoor models are available that are capable of carrying loads from 5 to 50 lbs.

17.6 INDOOR

Indoor panning or pan/tilt platforms are lightweight and require no environmental protection (Figure 17-1). They can be mounted overtly and directly with wall or ceiling brackets.

In a friendly environment the camera and lens are mounted directly to the pan/tilt platform with no exterior housing, and the cables exposed and suitably dressed to the mount. In a hostile environment the camera and lens are enclosed in an indoor environmental housing to protect them from vandalism, chemicals, etc.

The availability of small solid-state video cameras and small lenses has made it possible to put the lenses and cameras into small dome housings (Chapters 14, 15). Figure 17-11a shows an attractive pan/tilt assembly enclosed in a small hemispherical dome mounted in the ceiling resulting in an architecturally aesthetic installation.

The pan/tilt and camera/lens are all integrated and mounted inside the dome housing with most of the mechanism mounted above the ceiling, providing an attractive, low-profile surveillance pan/tilt camera. Locating the pan/tilt and camera/lens inside a tinted plastic dome provides additional security and deterrence since personnel at floor level cannot determine where the camera is pointing

(A) IN-CEILING

(B) BELOW-CEILING

FIGURE 17-11 In-ceiling and below-ceiling mounted pan/tilt dome cameras

at any particular time. This design deters potential offenders from carrying out harmful overt or covert activities. Figure 17-11b shows a larger integrated pan/tilt camera system suspended in a dome below ceiling level.

17.7 OUTDOOR

The major difference between the indoor and outdoor pan/tilt hardware results from the outdoor environment. Adverse outdoor conditions manifest themselves in wind loading, precipitation, temperature extremes, humidity, dust, dirt, corrosive atmosphere, and higher levels of vandalism. To successfully cope with these additional attacks, the pan/tilt mechanism and housing must be more rugged and have higher environmental resistance.

Consequently, the inherent symmetry in the side-mounted configuration that reduces the turning force required to overcome the unbalanced weight forces when the camera must be tilted, and the wind forces, make the side-mounted design a better choice than the top-mounted configuration.

In the overhead design, the center-of-gravity distance of the camera/lens/housing load is 5–10 inches away from the axis of rotation; in the side-mounted design, the same components are on the horizontal (tilt) rotation axis. While both systems operate satisfactorily in outdoor environments, the motor and gear train size required in the side-mounted design is smaller.

17.7.1 Materials and Design

For long life and reliable service, outdoor pan/tilt units should be completely watertight and dustproof so that rain, snow, dust, dirt, or corrosive materials do not find their way into the bearings, gear train, or motor drive assembly. It is usually necessary to rely on the manufacturer's reputation, as well as information obtained from installers and users, as to the quality and durability of the equipment. There are some guidelines, however:

- Sealed ball bearings are preferred over sleeve bearings.
- All bearing shaft ends should be protected with environmental seals to prevent entry of liquids, dirt, or corrosive materials.
- The pan/tilt mechanism should be constructed of non-corrosive materials, such as die-cast aluminum, magnesium, outdoor plastic, or stainless steel.
- Aluminum and magnesium housing materials should be painted with a durable outdoor enamel or epoxy paint. Any unpainted aluminum surfaces should be anodized.
- Suitable outdoor plastic types include polycarbonate, ABS, and PVC. While many types of plastic can withstand outdoor weathering conditions as well as or better than metal, unsuitable plastic parts may crack or

deteriorate due to: (1) breakdown of the plastic by the sun's rays (ultraviolet radiation), corrosive liquids, or gases; (2) cracking due to large variations in temperature excursions; or (3) cracking caused by ice forming between several parts and then expanding. All plastic outdoor units must have UV inhibiting coatings or finishes, and flame-retardant plastic formulations are absolutely essential.

Additional torques the pan/tilt mechanism must overcome in sub-freezing climatic conditions include those from ice and snow loading. This loading takes two forms: (1) the additional weight of snow or ice that the camera housing must carry, which the motor gear train must try to lift; and (2) freezing ice or snow at the location of the turning shaft (bearing), which must be dislodged. The motor and gear train must overcome this additional force to rotate and point the camera.

17.7.2 Wind Loading

Wind loading must be considered for all outdoor pan/tilt camera systems. It is the force exerted on the camera housing assembly and pan/tilt mechanism that can cause it to move or rotate in an unwanted direction, cause the entire system to vibrate, or prevent proper or any motion of the system. Wind that causes vibration produces a blurred or unfocused image on the monitor. A sufficiently high wind loading on an inadequately designed system will cause mechanical failure of the gear drives or motors. Wind loading is minimized when as small as possible and all components are located as close as possible to the center of rotation of the pan and tilt axes. In Figure 17-12 the wind comes from one direction and produces an unbalanced force on the pan/tilt mechanism and camera housing, causing it to rotate or move in an unwanted direction.

For example, if the camera/lens/housing load is energized to rotate upward (tilt up) and the unbalanced wind force would rotate the camera downward, the motor and gear train must have sufficient torque to overcome the counter-acting wind loading force (torque) and the camera/lens/housing torque. A well-designed system will have sufficient motor/gear torque to overcome the wind and the load, including a safety factor.

The long-term effects of wind, snow, and ice loading on the pan/tilt mechanism are wear and tear and additional maintenance. Even in a well-designed system, the frequent motions and starting and stopping of the motor, gears, and camera assembly require periodic maintenance in the form of lubricating the gear train and/or

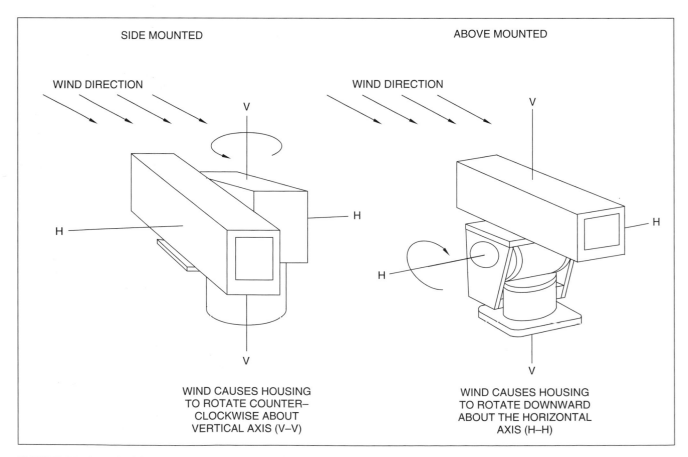

FIGURE 17-12 Wind loading on pan/tilt and camera housing

replacing a motor, clutch, or gear assembly. Careful consideration must be given to choosing the correct pan/tilt design for the application, and recognizing the effects of wind, snow, and ice loading. In most outdoor applications, adding an extra 5 or 10 pounds to the load rating factor of the pan/tilt system is a worthwhile investment.

17.7.3 Ice and Snow Loading

Ice forming between the stationary mount and the panning or tilting mechanism can prevent the motor from "breaking loose" and providing the desired motion. In inclement, freezing weather, it is often advisable to operate pan/tilt mechanisms regularly, to produce heat from the motors and keep ice from forming at these critical locations.

17.7.4 TEMPERATURE

Most pan/tilt mechanisms are designed to operate over temperature ranges found in most parts of the world. However, installations in very severe cold or hot weather require special pan/tilt mechanisms for reliable operation.

In desert and tropical locations, where the temperature may reach 130°F (72°C), special motors with high-temperature insulation on their windings are required. Operating conventional motors under higher temperatures shortens their life or burns out the motor. Likewise, other electrical components must be rated for higher temperatures. The expansion of mechanical parts in a system not designed for higher temperatures could cause binding or jamming and render the system inoperable.

In extremely cold climates with a temperate of −40°F (−10°C) or lower, the grease and lubricants used in the gear train must be chosen so that they do not become too viscous (hard), thereby preventing rotation of the motor and gear train. Most other electrical components in the system should operate without any problem. The pan/tilt mechanism must be properly sealed at the bearing and cable entry/exit locations so that moisture does not enter the mechanism and freeze.

17.7.5 Precipitation Dust, Dirt, and Corrosion

While pan/tilt mechanisms usually operate 10 feet or more above the ground, some locations have sufficient dust, dirt, sand, or corrosive atmosphere to require special attention. A well-designed outdoor pan/tilt mechanism will have seals to prevent these contaminants from entering the bearings and internal parts of the mechanism. Of particular importance is the seal at the electrical cabling entry and exit location.

An installation in a sand-blown environment requires additional protection in the form of more durable finishes to prevent damage from blowing sand or other particulate matter. Fine sand also causes bearing surfaces to wear out sooner.

When an installation is in an area containing a corrosive chemical atmosphere, the pan/tilt platform manufacturer must be provided with the specific names of the chemicals active in the area. Some active chemicals include sulfuric, nitric, and hydrochloric acids, salt spray, and others. While many plastics have excellent corrosive resistance to these chemicals, aluminum and steel that are in widespread use for pan/tilt housings do not have good resistance against most of these hazardous chemicals and salt spray.

17.7.6 Outdoor Domes

One technique used to minimize the entire outdoor pan/tilt mechanism environmental problem is to house the camera, lens, and pan/tilt mechanism in a plastic dome. Figure 17-13 illustrates one such configuration, which is 18 inches in diameter and contains a pan/tilt mechanism inverted and suspended inside the dome, with a zoom lens and CCTV camera.

Enclosing the camera/lens and pan/tilt mechanism in the dome totally eliminates the precipitation, wind loading, dust, and dirt problem for these components. One disadvantage is that the dome can only be cleaned manually whereas an outdoor housing with a flat front window can be cleaned periodically with a window washer and wiper. In any application, the dome's complete protection of the mechanism must be weighed against this disadvantage as compared with the standard outdoor housing

FIGURE 17-13 Outdoor pan/tilt dome configuration

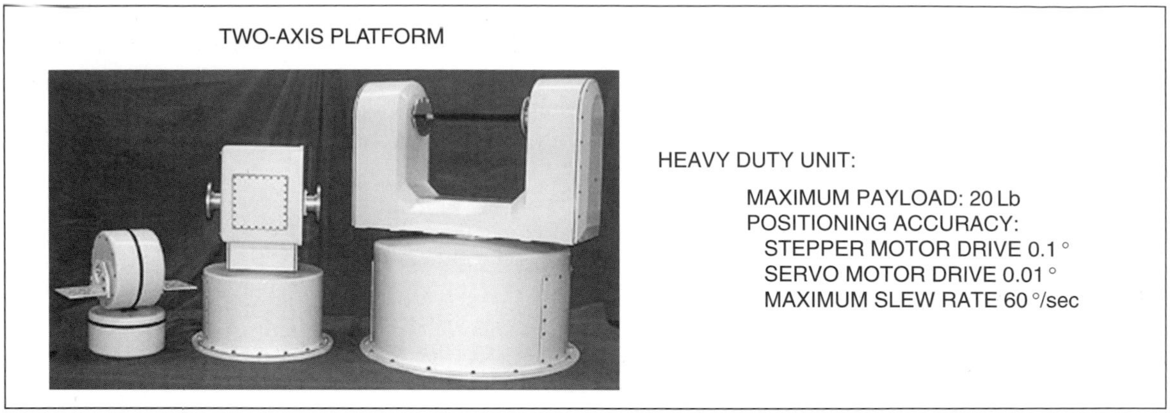

FIGURE 17-14   High precision outdoor pan/tilt platforms

pan/tilt mounting. The small dome pan/tilt design shown in Figure 17-11b is adaptable for use in outdoor applications under building eaves or passageways.

17.7.7   Rugged-Precision Platform

There are some special applications that require rugged, precision panning and tilting platforms. These include:

- Long-range viewing with telephoto lenses
- High wind locations
- Traffic monitoring
- High resolution motion detection surveillance systems
- Government/military.

One pan/tilt system that can satisfy these demands is the outdoor Sagebrush Technology Model 20 having a pointing accuracy of 0.01° and a panning range of 370° (Figure 17-14). This is between 10 and 20 times better than standard video dome systems. The system obtains its zero backlash capability through the use of a patented rotary spring drive. One model can pan and tilt a 20 lb. payload at rates up to 60°/sec. It has provision to mount equipment on a second payload shelf to provide a balanced configuration, keeping the center of gravity of the payload centered on both the pan and tilt axes. The servo motor drives are controlled through a 32-bit microprocessor using RS-232 or RS-485 communication protocol. The unit operates outdoors over a temperature range from −20 to 120°F with no maintenance required. One cable supplies 12 or 24 volts AC or DC for the motors, one cable for RS-232 control and video cable.

17.8   PAN/TILT—COMPONENTS VS. INTEGRATED SYSTEM

Most pan/tilt, camera/lens installations consist of components obtained from several different manufacturers all assembled by the systems integrator and made to operate as a complete system. Considering the wide variety of applications, this is a practical solution for many installations. However, many applications require an integrated camera/lens, pan/tilt, housing, and mounting system from a single manufacturer packaged as a single integrated unit. Special parameters might include higher scanning speed, wider angular coverage, or a dome configuration. Figure 17-15 shows one of the most popular configurations of an integrated camera head system: the high-speed video-dome.

This configuration is available from many manufacturers and is capable of performing surveillance in indoor and outdoor applications in small and large video surveillance systems. Details of the overall system are described in Chapter 14 and only the pan/tilt aspects of the integrated system are described here. Typical speed-dome systems have a maximum scanning rate in the range of 100°/sec and are capable of panning 360° continuously using sliprings or optical-couplers. They are housed in hemispherical or spherical domes 5–12 inches in diameter, flush or ceiling-mounted. With 360° continuous horizontal scanning, the lens/camera does not have to come back 360° in order to follow a moving target. To achieve these results, the moving parts are small and have low mass and moment of inertia. Only through advanced electronic engineering, mechanical packaging, and state-of-the-art optical design are these fast scan rates obtained.

The obvious advantage of the dome camera is that if an incident occurs anywhere within the dynamic FOV of the pan/tilt system the camera can be pointed in any direction in the shortest possible time while the lens zooms and focuses on the target. Computer systems with camera-pointing preset capabilities take advantage of these fast pan/tilt designs. While some traditional pan/tilt mechanisms have relatively high scan rates—up to 80°/sec—when combined with the inertia of the camera and lens, these fast scan rates cannot be maintained and are much slower than the speed-dome designs.

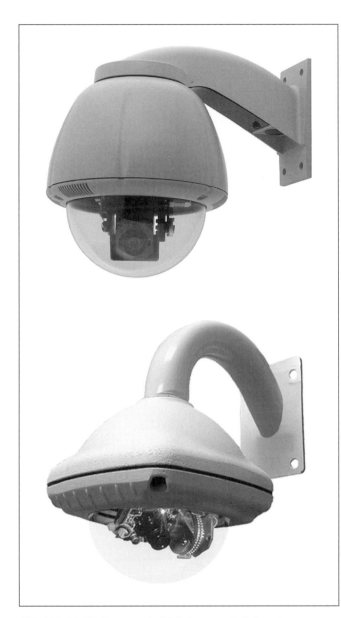

FIGURE 17-15 Integrated high-speed video-dome pan/tilt platform

17.9   PAN/TILT/LENS CONTROL TECHNIQUES

There are several techniques for communicating with and controlling the remote PTZ camera unit from a remote console controller. The techniques range from one-on-one control signal connection to LAN, fiber optics, wireless RF, microwave, or light-wave. The video signal can be transmitted on an individual coaxial cable or multiplexed with the control signal conductors.

- Direct-wire, multi-conductor: controls plus video over coaxial
- Two-wire-multiplexed: controls plus video over coaxial
- Single-cable-multiplexed: controls and video on coaxial
- LAN: controls and video on two conductors

- Fiber optic: controls and video on a single fiber
- Wireless RF, microwave, light-wave: controls and video

Direct-Wire-Multi-Conductor.   The simplest control of the PTZ lens mechanism is via direct wire using one wire for each control function and a separate video coaxial cable (Figure 17-16a). This straightforward system has been in widespread use for many years for small or short-run (under a thousand feet) installations. This technique requires no additional driver electronics for transmitting the control signals and no additional receiver electronics at the camera end. The controller consists of switches that control all functions, set manually by the operator or memorized by the system for automatic operation. Wire size must be large enough to minimize voltage drop to the motors and electronics. The video signal is transmitted over a coaxial cable.

Two- and Four-Wire-Multiplexed.   For longer distances or when there are many different camera sites, a significant reduction in the number of conductors and wire runs is accomplished by multiplexing (time-sharing) the control signals at the control console onto two wires, sending them to the camera site, and then de-multiplexing them or separating them again to provide the signals necessary to drive the PTZ unit (Figure 17-16b).

Since the two wires need carry only communications information and not current to drive the motors, any long-distance two-wire communication system suffices. Two popular transmission protocols are the EIA RS-422 and RS-485. Shorter distances can be accommodated using the RS-232 protocol. The video signal is transmitted on a separate coaxial cable.

Another technique available to control a PTZ camera head system via two wires uses the telephone Touch-Tone communications system. Using this reliable design takes advantage of the world's most advanced large-scale integration technology, developed by AT&T. With this technique, a single twisted cable can route all command tones from the controlling site to a camera site and control the pan, tilt, zoom, iris, focus, and many optional auxiliary functions via a single, simple Touch-Tone keyboard (Figure 17-17).

Touch-Tone remote control allows substantial savings in cable runs and the labor required to install them. Some of the optional auxiliary functions available for the Touch Tone system are camera power on/off, remote switching of AC or DC accessories such as a heater, blower, wiper, or tamper switch, etc. The system can accommodate additional keypads allowing easy expansion to a multi-user system. These products can be interfaced to any telephone network by using an FCC-approved telephone interface unit.

Single-Cable-Multiplexed.   Systems are available that multiplex or time-share the control signals on the *same* video signal cable, thereby allowing video to be transmitted

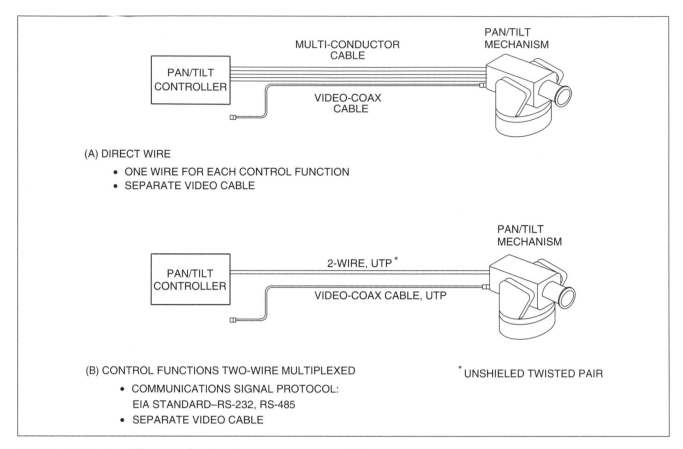

(A) DIRECT WIRE
- ONE WIRE FOR EACH CONTROL FUNCTION
- SEPARATE VIDEO CABLE

(B) CONTROL FUNCTIONS TWO-WIRE MULTIPLEXED
- COMMUNICATIONS SIGNAL PROTOCOL:
  EIA STANDARD–RS-232, RS-485
- SEPARATE VIDEO CABLE

*UNSHIELED TWISTED PAIR

FIGURE 17-16   Pan/tilt control using direct wire and multiplexing

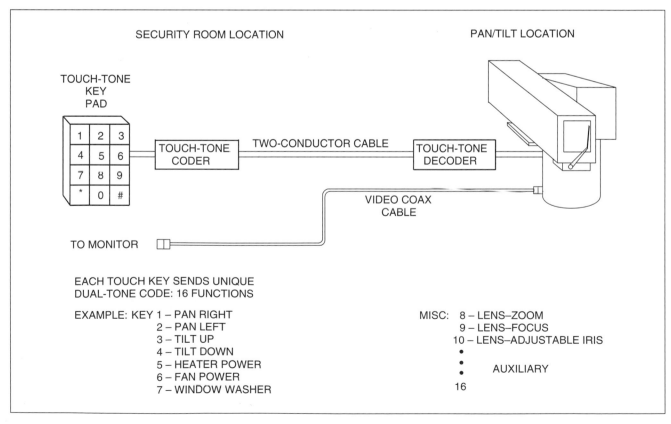

EACH TOUCH KEY SENDS UNIQUE
DUAL-TONE CODE: 16 FUNCTIONS

EXAMPLE: KEY 1 – PAN RIGHT
              2 – PAN LEFT
              3 – TILT UP
              4 – TILT DOWN
              5 – HEATER POWER
              6 – FAN POWER
              7 – WINDOW WASHER

MISC: 8 – LENS–ZOOM
         9 – LENS–FOCUS
        10 – LENS–ADJUSTABLE IRIS
         •
         •   AUXILIARY
         •
        16

FIGURE 17-17   Pan/tilt control using touch-tone communication

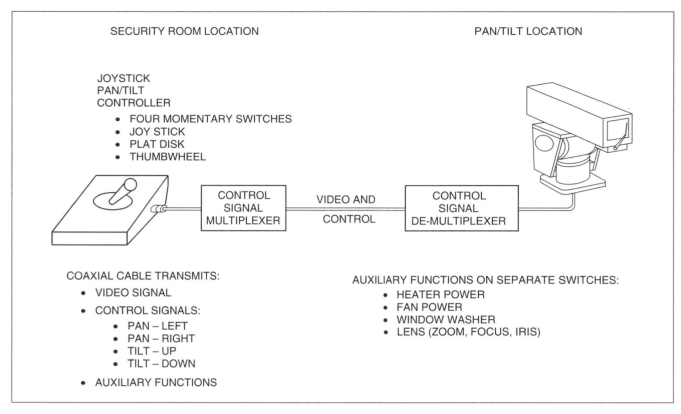

FIGURE 17-18   Multiplexed pan/tilt control signal and video on single cable

from the camera to the monitor console site and camera control signals to be transmitted from the security console to the camera site, all on *one* coaxial cable (Figure 17-18).

For direct wiring, this is the most efficient, minimum-cost technique, since only a single coaxial cable is required. The technique is cost-effective when the distance between camera and monitor is long, and when there are multiple sites. The system requires a special multiplexer that combines and separates the video and control signals at the camera and the monitor ends. An advantage of multiplexing the control signals onto the video signal is that additional transmission or control signals can be added to the system without adding new cable. These additional functions can include lens controls, alarm functions, and tamper switches.

In all three techniques just described, fiber-optic transmission is an alternative to copper wire. Several manufacturers have equipment that transmits the control signals, alarms and other signals, and the video signal on a *single* fiber-optic channel. As described in Chapter 6, the fiber-optic advantages include noise immunity, long distance transmission, and absence of ground loops, high security, and reliable operation from different building sites in harsh environments including lightning storms.

LAN.   The new generation of digital cameras using the IP use a LAN or a WAN to transmit the video and control signals to and from the remotely located camera-monitor locations (Figure 17-19). The video and control signals are digitized and transmitted over the network. Chapter 7 describes the modulation and compression techniques used.

Wireless.   Control signals can be transmitted from the console to the camera location via wireless remote control communication. The control signals are multiplexed onto a single channel and transmitted on RF, microwave, or light-wave (visible or infrared) communication links. For extreme security requirements (military or nuclear sites, etc.), wireless transmission of video, command, and control signals is used as a backup to a hard-wired (copper or fiber-optic) system.

17.10   PAN/TILT MOUNTING

Many manufacturers produce attractive mountings for indoor and outdoor camera/lens and pan/tilt systems. For indoor applications, the pan/tilt unit is securely attached to a wall or ceiling mounting bracket. The electrical cables connected from the camera, housing, and the pan/tilt mechanism are secured to the bracket and directed into the wall or ceiling. The system should be located with enough clearance between the rear of the camera housing (including extended cables) and the wall so that there is no interference when the unit pans over its full range. The unit should be mounted sufficiently below the ceiling so

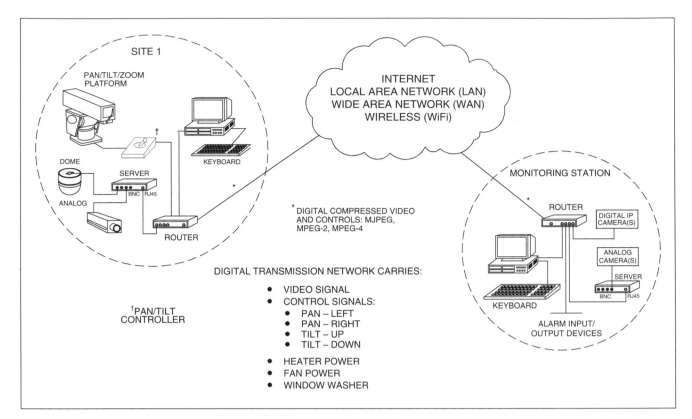

FIGURE 17-19   LAN pan/tilt/zoom and video transmission

that when the camera is pointed straight down the rear of the camera and cable does not collide with the ceiling.

Figure 17-20a illustrates an outdoor pan/tilt unit in standard configuration mounted on a building roof edge and capable of scanning 270° horizontally to view a parking lot. With such a large angular FOV to cover (an entire parking lot), this solution should be used where only sporadic activity is monitored, since panning with a standard unit from one end of a building to the other would typically take 5–10 seconds, which may be unacceptable. If a fast-scan unit is used, the panning time can be reduced to a few seconds, which would be acceptable.

Figure 17-20b shows a camera pan/tilt assembly mounted in a clear plastic dome housing on a pedestal mount, which provides wide-angle surveillance at an entryway and parking lot. Mounting the camera away from the building on a pole provides good viewing of the entire entry area with a single camera. The presence of the camera system serves as a deterrent to crime while it captures the necessary visual information for possible apprehension and prosecution. The same scanning limitations as described in the previous system apply.

17.11   SLIP-RINGS AND OPTICAL-COUPLERS

Pan/tilt platforms use slip-rings or optical-couplers to transfer the electrical signals as the camera/lens combi-

nation rotates continuously—beyond 360°—without any concern for twisted wires. The control signals, video signal, and power pass through stationary slip-ring contacts electrically or the video signal optically through an optical coupler. No matter where the target moves in the lens FOV, the pan motion can continue and the subject never leaves the FOV. There are no restricting mechanical stops to limit the pan/tilt unit's rotation. Since there are no cables and harnesses to flex back and forth as the camera/lens platform pans or tilts, there is a significant improvement in reliability.

Some pan/tilt mechanisms use a mechanical stop at each end of the horizontal and vertical travel to prevent the wires connected to the moving camera/lens assembly and the other end terminated in the stationary wall mount from getting twisted. This limits the camera scan to about 355° horizontally before it must stop and then pan in the opposite direction. Even at a fast scan rate it takes several seconds to rotate back to the 0° position (Figure 17-21a).

An example in which panning speed and continuous motion (more than 360°) is important follows: A person walks past a pan/tilt unit 15 feet away the dome (Figure 17-21b). If the person is walking at a normal rate of about 4 feet per second and the dome is panning at a rate of 1 foot per second (12° sec), the monitor scene at 15 feet is moving at a rate of 3 feet per second. The subject is quickly lost because the pan/tilt cannot pan fast enough

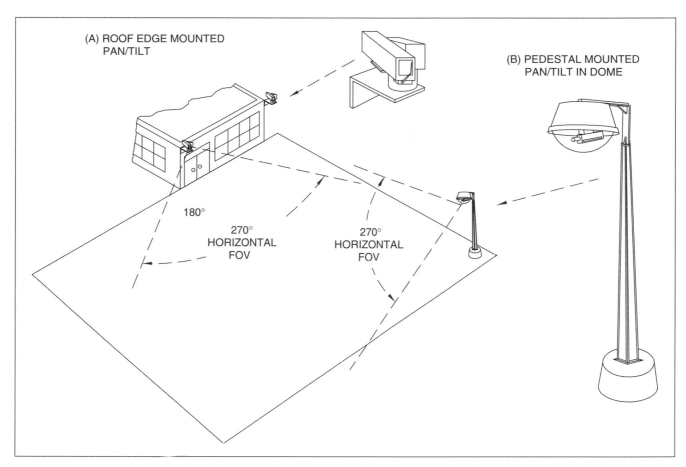

FIGURE 17-20   Building roof pan/tilt surveillance camera

to follow the subject. With a high-speed 60°/sec panning system, a target at 15 feet from the camera produces a picture going by at a rate of 5 feet per second (1 foot per second faster than the target) and the subject is not lost. In this example, the panning speed would be reduced to 4 feet per second to keep the target in the center of the picture.

17.12   HIGH-SPEED VIDEO-DOME PTZ SYSTEMS

The need evolved for a high-speed video-dome camera system for surveillance use in casinos, retail stores, warehouses, and other public, commercial, and government facilities. This resulted in the development of the present generation high-speed video-dome configuration. The miniaturization of camera sensors and electronics, and pan/tilt servo and stepper motor systems permitted the design of a compact module that allowed the rapid movement and pointing of the camera-zoom lens combination. Companies such as Sony and Hitachi were the first to develop these *unitized* PTZ modules that are used in many of the present-day dome systems.

The majority of *conventional* camera/lens pan/tilt platforms in housings consist of components obtained from several different manufacturers all assembled by the systems integrator and made to operate as a complete system. This is a practical solution for installations in which the parameters and characteristics of the fixed or movable dome might be unacceptable. The high-speed video-dome camera is an integrated camera/lens, pan/tilt, dome housing and mounting system in a single unitized module obtained from a *single* manufacturer. The integral design results in a smaller, lighter weight module having a high scanning speed and wide angular coverage.

The high-speed video-dome pan/tilt camera has become one of the most popular scanning video surveillance systems in the industry. The primary reason for the popularity is in the large amount of *visual intelligence* they can provide to the security operator in such a small physical package. The speed dome can be mounted almost anywhere: ceiling, wall, building exterior, and pole. High resolution, sensitive color cameras that switch over to monochrome for higher sensitivity and compact zoom lenses with auto-focus mounted in ultra-fast pan/tilt module make them very effective surveillance camera in most environments including retail stores, casinos, commercial

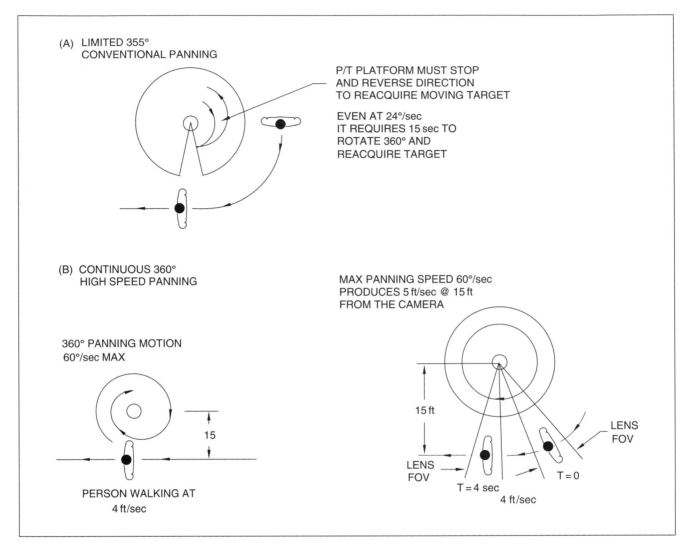

FIGURE 17-21   Relationship between pan/tilt speed and moving target

and government office buildings, warehouses, airports, highways, etc.

17.12.1   BACKGROUND

Prior to the current integrated PTZ high-speed video-dome, pan/tilt platforms were assembled by ordering a housing, a pan/tilt mechanism, a camera, a lens, and mechanically mounting them together and wiring them up for installation. Growing out of a customer need in the early 1980s, Sensormatic Inc. pursued the development of a high-speed video-dome. The entire dome was assembled and tested in 1985 and represented one of the first fully integrated "speed" domes. The first system had a clear viewing inches 22 inches in diameter and was 8 inches deep. The system used a monochrome vidicon tube camera and weighed approximately 40 lbs. In 1988 a second-generation speed-dome using a color

CCD camera imager 12 inches in diameter and 5 inches deep and weighing 26 lbs was produced. In 1992 this dome received a complete mechanical redesign using a close-loop DC servo electronic pan/tilt design to point to any target horizontally or vertically in less than one second. This dome design incorporated pan/tilt pointing presets for defining targets, patterns, and boundaries. The first applications for these systems were in casinos and were interfaced with American Dynamics matrix switchers.

A second pioneering speed-dome company was Diamond Electronics that developed a high-velocity, rate-proportional digital tracking system having slip-rings to permit continuous 360° rotation at speeds up to 80°/sec and tilt speeds up to 25°/sec. Dynamic braking featured immediate, precise stops with ±0.5° accuracy when de-accelerating from any speed. The system had a gold (or chrome) tinted dome capsule enclosure providing one-way mirror capsules for discrete surveillance and were optically corrected for high-performance monochrome and color cameras. All components including pan/tilt mechanism and drive electronics, camera, and lens were contained within the dome package.

These high-speed dome-camera systems employed newer technology having performance characteristics far superior than the older pan/tilt camera platform systems assembled from separate components. The current speed-dome designs are small in size—5–7 inches in diameter—and contain all the required control and communication electronics located inside the unit. They contain the servo or stepper motors and feedback control housed in a unitized module within the dome housing. The video-dome assembly weighs far less than the older pan/tilt platforms so that they can be mounted almost anywhere. Maximum panning speeds are typically 300–360°/sec. They use slip-rings or optical-couplers so that the camera and lens can pan continuously without reversing direction. There are many manufacturers that can provide products having these basic functions.

The current and latest generation high-speed video-domes are available in sizes from 6 to 12 inches in diameter and have high-speed pan/tilt servo or stepper motor drives and use metal slip-rings and optical-couplers to achieve continuous 360° rotation. Camera-pointing features include *presets, patterns,* and *boundaries.* The color cameras have high-resolution and operate in the color mode in daytime and switch-over to monochrome to achieve higher sensitivity for nighttime operation. Camera features include VMD and external alarm activation on motion. These camera-lens modules are equipped with motorized zoom lenses with optical and digital zoom, auto-focus, and iris control. Zoom lenses typically have 20 to 1 zoom ratios to obtain telephoto and wide-angle viewing. The camera pan/tilt module is mounted inside an impact resistant, clear or tinted hemispherical optical grade acrylic plastic dome. The entire dome assembly is designed for quick installation and easy mounting and servicing in a ceiling, a wall, outdoor on a building parapet, a parking lot pole, or on a highway.

17.12.2 Technology

The previous section described the "first generation" pan/tilt platforms designed for the original tube cameras and first-generation solid-state CCD cameras developed in the 1990s that have evolved into the high-speed video-dome systems in widespread use today. These dome designs evolved as a result of the significant size reduction of the CCD camera, zoom lens, and associated pan/tilt mechanism. Through the efforts of the Sony and Hitachi Corporations to integrate them into a unitized module design containing the pan/tilt mechanism, lens/camera assembly have become the *core module* of the present-day

high-speed video-dome (Figure 17-22). The PTZ speed of these platforms is typically 10 times faster than conventional pan/tilt platforms.

The speed-dome assembly contains a high-speed pan/tilt assembly, high resolution day (color) or night (monochrome) CCD camera with a compact zoom lens with continuous full-time auto-focus function. One system has a wide dynamic range feature that can provide detailed images when the camera is viewing images that have bright light and low light level image areas.

Speed-dome systems can scan at a rate of 300°/sec and are capable of panning 360° continuously using slip-rings. With 360° continuous horizontal scanning the lens/camera module does not have to come back 360° in order to follow a moving target. All the components can be housed in a 5–7 inch diameter ceiling-mounted dome. Through advanced engineering and compact packaging, these fast scan rates obtained: the moving parts are small in size and have low masses and moments of inertia. The obvious advantage of a fast system is that if an incident occurs anywhere within the dynamic FOV of the pan/tilt

(A)

(B)

FIGURE 17-22   High-speed video pan/tilt mechanism

system, the camera/lens can be pointed in any direction in the shortest possible time while the lens zooms and focuses on the target. Microprocessor-based dome systems with camera-pointing preset capabilities can take advantage of these fast pan/tilt designs.

17.12.2.1 Pan/Tilt Mechanism

The speed-dome panning mechanism provides 360° of continuous horizontal panning rotation through the use of gold-plated metal slip-rings or LED light couplers. The optical-coupler consists of a light transmitter and light detector-receiver to transmit the signal information rather than a metal slip-ring assembly. The tilt mechanism provides for at least a 90° vertical range of travel. In most cases, the camera assembly can tilt up above the horizontal a few degrees and down −95° to provide a tilt range beyond looking straight down to looking slightly above the horizon. Precise manual panning and tilting is achieved through a combination of a variable speed control in the form of different speed ranges, with an automatic adjustment of the speed range depending on the zoom position of the lens. For wide-angle zooming the speed is *increased*, whereas for high magnification (telephoto zooming) the panning and tilting speeds are *decreased*. Depending on the manufacturer, the panning and tilting are done using DC servo motors or stepper motors. To provide high torque and precise pointing ability, the DC servo design uses pulse-width modulation and speed feedback. This controls the acceleration, speed, and de-acceleration of the motors ensuring a smooth, precise, accurate, and fluid movement. Most manufactures design the drive systems so that there are no belts or pulleys ensuring long-term reliable operation.

17.12.2.2 Camera, Lens

Most video-dome systems use high sensitivity color cameras that can be operated in: (1) color, (2) monochrome, or (3) switch-over from color to monochrome automatically. The CCD cameras have an image format of 1/6 or 1/4 inch. These smaller sensor formats allow for a compact zoom lens and permit the small compact design that results in high pan/tilt speeds. Overall camera resolution is typically 480 TV lines for color and 570 TV lines for monochrome. Values of 1 lux sensitivity for color and 0.06 lux or less for monochrome are typical. Switchover from color to monochrome is automatic when the light level falls below a predetermined level. Cameras are also provided with DSP and automatic brightness control (ABC) so that the camera can view scenes containing both bright and dark areas. To capture image detail in both light and dark regions, Panasonic Inc. uses the Super Dynamic SDII technology, which records the scene at two different exposures and then electronically integrates both of them into a single image to preserve the detail throughout the

bright and dim areas. This added to additional precise color reproduction creates a dynamic range that is about 64 times greater than that of many conventional cameras. This compensation and large dynamic range reduces the problems that occur in a poorly illuminated room and pointed at a window with a brightly illuminated scene outside. Many cameras adjust their iris level to optimize the inside or outside scene resulting in one part of display being light compensated (normal) while the other part is either too light or too dark. This also occurs in the evening when viewing oncoming traffic with vehicle headlights turned on. The ABC and signal compression techniques enable the camera to see both the *light and dark* areas of the scene with reduced flair from the oncoming headlights.

The zoom lenses generally have a 20 to 1 optical zoom (magnification) range that is extended by electronic digital zoom by another factor of 10, providing an overall 200 to 1 zoom range.

17.12.3 Hardware: Domes, Pan/Tilt Cameras

The availability of small cameras and lenses and consequent miniature pan/tilt mechanisms having much lower weight and inertia has resulted in ultra-fast *speed-dome* pan/tilt systems. This reduction in lens/camera pan/tilt mechanism has significantly reduced the overall size of the dome package. Small pan/tilt units are capable of moving at an angular rate of 200°/sec. These systems are suitable for mounting on a wall, in a ceiling, or within a small hemispherical dome. They receive control signals via two-wire cabling that simplifies communications to and from the camera unit.

Another system available is a high-velocity, rate-proportional control, digital-tracking system designed for high-speed positioning of a camera and lens load. The system uses slip-rings to permit 360° continuous rotation, scan speeds from 0 to 80°/sec, and tilt speeds from 0 to 25°/sec. At these high speeds, dynamic braking is used to provide a ±0.5° accuracy of stopping at any speed. Zoom lenses used with this design include the option of a 6:1 or a 10:1 zoom ratio. The system uses a solid-state CCD camera for long life and is often mounted in a hemispherical dome to protect and disguise it.

The system is operated via keypad and joystick control, which is a rate-proportional device: the farther the joystick is moved from the center off position, the faster the speed of the function to be performed. Move the joystick forward or backward and the camera/lens assembly tilts. Moving it to the left or right causes the unit to scan (pan). Move the joystick at an angle between the two and the pan/tilt unit pans and tilts at the same time. Turning the joystick knob clockwise or counterclockwise initiates the lens zoom function. Preset camera and lens parameters are entered into the unit via the keypad. By pressing a two-digit number on the keypad, any one of 99 presets can be executed. The information contained in each camera preset location includes the pan angle, tilt angle, zoom FL, iris opening, focus setting, and camera on/off. This system controls up to 32 cameras, drives two or four output monitors, and is capable of processing alarm inputs to direct the camera at the alarm location.

There are many reputable manufacturers of high-speed video-dome systems for use in video surveillance. Table 17-1 summarizes the specifications and features of a representative sample of this equipment.

Most systems are designed with a tinted dome that conceals the zoom lens, camera, and pan/tilt mechanism from the observer at floor or ground level. A mechanical feature of most systems is the ability to easily remove the functioning part of the system from its base, either from ground level or at a level near the dome, with a simple *twist-lock* disconnect feature. This feature makes servicing and replacement of the dome camera very efficient. The systems are capable of panning 360° continuously through the use of slip-rings, optical-couplers, and tilting over the full vertical range from horizontal pointing to directly below. Many have an auto-flip feature that causes the pan/tilt mechanism to rotate 180° quickly so that the camera and operator can follow a person passing directly beneath the dome. These video dome systems are equipped with full range color/monochrome cameras and operate in color mode during daytime or when there is sufficient illumination, and automatically switch over to a more sensitive monochrome mode under reduced light levels. The systems can also memorize many different preset directions and can memorize patterns and tours around specific boundaries. They also have the ability to lock-out certain views called privacy areas whether for personal or for security purposes. The zoom lenses typically have zoom ranges above 20 to 1 and have additional electronic zoom expansion of 10 times more. Many systems are equipped with auto-focus throughout the operating ranges so that a target of interest will remain in focus throughout the surveillance. All are equipped with variable pan and tilt speeds that are compensated for zoom position.

There are many manufacturers producing these systems. Some of them are described in detail to give an understanding of all of the features that can be available in this popular surveillance camera configuration. The American Dynamics speed-dome contains many of the features available in other systems and is described with three other systems.

17.12.3.1 American Dynamic

The American Dynamic SpeedDome® Ultra VII is a day/night programmable high-speed video-dome system and in many ways represents the current state of the art.

The dome has a diameter of 4.7 inches and a height of 8 inches. It uses a zoom lens with 23 times optical magnification combined with a 10 times digital zoom to provide a total of 230 times magnification. The zoom lens FL range is from 3.6 to 83 mm. The dome electronics incorporates DSP to provide enhanced clarity, color, and detail in well-lighted or low light environment. The dome can clearly distinguish scenes and colors in lighting conditions as low as 0.5 lux in color and 0.01 lux in monochrome mode. The camera horizontal resolution is 470 TV lines and contains continuous auto-focus with manual override. The dome has manual pan/tilt speeds variable from 0.25 to 100°/sec based on the zoom lens position. The preset pan/tilt speed is 220°/sec maximum. Pan travel is 360° continuous and tilt travel is 110°. Pan/tilt accuracy is ±0.5°. The dome system incorporates proportional flip that rotates the camera assembly 180° to permit viewing a person walking directly under the dome and always displaying that person right-side-up on the display monitor. It freezes the previous frame, the image when directed to a new preset pointing direction, so that there is continuous display of video on the monitor. When using the freeze frame feature, before moving to a preset the dome image will freeze the image. This minimizes HD (hard drive) usage when video is digitally recorded. Users can set automatic dome flip on and off, and with this feature turned on, the dome will automatically turn 180° when the camera tilts to its lower limit and stays in that position for a brief, speed-proportional delay. With this feature turned off, users can still manually flip the dome image. The SpeedDome supports up to three patterns, including a preprogrammed "home" default, position and a preprogrammed spiral pan pattern (apple peel) that covers the entire viewing area. The dome supports up to 96 presets when used with suitably equipped controllers. The zoom lens electronics incorporates zoom adjust programming that automatically adjusts the pan/tilt speeds in proportion to the zoom position, even at maximum magnification.

The dome generates on-screen text including dome, area, preset, patterns, and alarm names, as well as direction indicators. These indicators show users the direction the dome is currently pointing, as well as the direction in which it is moving. In addition the direction indicators display the dome's azimuth and elevation. On-screen text also indicates zoom, focus, and iris status. All name information is user-definable and can be turned on or off. When on, it can be set for solid or translucent white, and with or without black outline.

Alarms can be processed internally by the dome, externally by the controller, or by both the dome and the controller. Each of the dome's alarm inputs can automatically call a preset or run a pattern when the alarm is activated.

The dome supports up to 16 viewing areas and users can assign names (up to 19 characters long) and boundaries to these areas: each area can be a different size. Up to eight different-size privacy zones can be programmed to

SPEED DOME SYSTEMS	POINTING SPEED (DEG./sec) AUTOMATIC				POINTING RANGE (DEG.) MANUAL		ZOOM LENS TYPE ZOOM RATIO		SENSOR FORMAT (IN.)	SENSITIVITY (MIN. Lux) DAY (COLOR) / NIGHT (B/W)	RESOLUTION (TV LINES) NTSC	ACCURACY (DEG.)	PRESETS	SIZE DIAMETER / HEIGHT (IN.)	WEIGHT (LBS.)
	PAN	TILT	PAN	TILT	PAN	TILT	OPTICAL	DIGITAL							
INTEGRAL CAMERA/LENS AND HIGH SPEED PAN/TILT INSIDE STATIONARY DOME HOUSING			100	50	360	+5 TO –90	22x	12x	1/4	0.7/0.03	470 COLOR 520 B/W			8/9	
	400	200	TO 120	—	360	0 TO –90	AUTO-FOCUS 22x	12x	1/4	1.0/0.1	470 COLOR	0.375	64	7 BUBBLE	4.3
	300				360		22x	10x	1/4	1.0/0.06	510 COLOR 570 B/W		64	4.3 BUBBLE	
	360	200	0.1 TO 80	0.1 TO 40	360	+2 TO –90	22x	10x	1/4	0.5/0.3	470 COLOR 500 B/W	0.1	80	5.9 BUBBLE × 10.76	
	170	80			360	25 TO –90	AUTO-FOCUS 26x		1/4	1.0/0.15	470			6.5×9.1	5
CAMERA/LENS MOUNTED ON INTEGRAL HIGH SPEED PAN/TILT ASSEMBLY *	170	77			+170 † / –170	+25 TO –90	25x	12x	1/6	2.5	480 COLOR			5/5.8	2.5

* INTERNET PROTOCOL (IP) CAMERA
† TOTAL PAN TRAVEL: 340°
* TOTAL PAN TRAVEL: 340°

STANDARD ON MOST SPEED DOMES:
QUICK DISCONNECT FROM DOME TO PERMANENT MOUNTING
CONTINUOUS ROTATION (OPTICAL SLIP RINGS)
AUTO-FOCUS
DAY/NIGHT OPERATION USING COLOR AND MONOCHROME (B/W) CAMERAS WITH AUTOMATIC SWITCHOVER
AUTOMATIC 180° ROTATION WHEN PASSING THROUGH –90° TO PROVIDE AN UPRIGHT IMAGE

OPTIONS:
CEILING OR WALL MOUNT
DOME TRANSPARANCY/COATING:
    CLEAR, TINTED, CHROME, GOLD

Table 17-1 Comparison of Representative High-Speed Video Domes

prevent users from viewing sensitive areas. These zones automatically change size proportional.

To extend versatility it incorporates an internal multi-protocol receiver to accept different control signals so that it can be connected directly into a host of systems including those from other vendors. The dome can be daisy-chained using RS-422 with up to 10 domes at a maximum distance of 3000 feet using 22 AWG STP conductors. Using Manchester code up to 3 domes at a maximum distance of 5000 feet on one 18 AWG STP is supported.

The features of this system can be extended to outdoor environments using outdoor protective housings. Different indoor and outdoor mounting configurations covering most application requirements are available. There are two mounting base options available with the SpeedDome: the housing dome assembly twist-locks into both mounting bases. The in-out (I/O) electrical board base connects the housing dome assembly in one step. Power, communication, and video cables are connected one time to the I/O PC Board in the mounting base so that the dome assembly simply twist-locks into the base. Service and maintenance are simplified and can be accomplished without a ladder. A dome installation/removal tool provides servicing from ground level.

17.12.3.2 General Electric

The General Electric (GE) CyberDome Day/Nite 25X camera is a PTZ high-speed video-dome with a color camera and removable infrared cut filter for day/night operation. The unit is microprocessor-controlled with keypad and programmable on non-volatile memory. The integral receiver/driver is provided with different switch selectable addressing and has a built in menu system for on-screen setup of camera functions. The CyberDome is capable of 360° continuous pan rotation with vertical tilt of 0 to −90° and uses gold slip-rings for trouble-free performance and high-quality connection for power, video, and data transmission. The unit has proportional speed control and the drive motors have 19,200 micro-steps/revolution to ensure smooth movement at maximum zoom magnification. Pan and tilt accuracy is 0.375° on preset. The system has a speed range from a creep speed up to 120°/sec and a tilt speed of 200°/sec. It has 64 camera preset positions and is capable of individual preset tours consisting of 16 programmed presets each. The tours are linkable and have four programmable speed settings for the tour: (1) slow, (2) medium, (3) fast, and (4) maximum. The system is capable of two learned shadowed tours that each store up to four minutes of manual operation by an operator. The tour is a continuous memorized path, panning, tilting, and zooming at any speed and pausing at selected targets along the way. The CyberDome has a quick-spin feature that automatically pans the camera 180° when the bottom tilt limit is reached to allow for continuous tracking of a target directly below the dome assembly. This feature can be disabled during programming.

The imaging camera is a 1/6 inch CCD image sensor and has a resolution of 470 TV lines (NTSC). The camera has a sensitivity of 2.5 lux for color operation and 0.1 lux for monochrome. The camera mode can be selected manually or automatically with a light level sensor to provide switching between color and monochrome operation. When switching to monochrome low-light nighttime operation the light level sensor automatically removes the IR cut filter to increase sensitivity. Also, in low light conditions, via manual override the shutter speed can be reduced from 30 fps to 4 fps for an increase in camera sensitivity. The camera has a privacy-masking feature and is able to set up 24 privacy masks.

The zoom lens has a 25 times optical zoom ratio and FL range of 2.4–60 mm. Additional magnification is by a 12 times programmable digital zoom for a total of 300 times zoom ratio. The lens can provide a horizontal angular FOV of 45° in wide-angle mode to 2° in telephoto mode and has an auto-focus feature with manual override. Dome signal control and output is via RS-422, RS-232, or RS-485. The entire pan/tilt dome housing assembly features a quick disconnect for ease of servicing and maintenance.

17.12.3.3 Panasonic

The Panasonic WV-CS854B Super Dynamic II color dome camera is a compact PTZ assembly approximately 4.3 inches in diameter. The Super Dynamic II technology delivers over 60 times wider dynamic video range compared to conventional cameras. The camera has a horizontal resolution of 510 TV lines. The camera can operate in day/night applications and can automatically or manually switch from color to monochrome operation. Camera sensitivity is 1.0 lux for color and 0.06 lux for monochrome imaging. The system has a digital flip so that the camera can pan 180° for viewing someone passing directly under the camera. As the camera pans in the vertically downward direction to follow the subject, DSP automatically flips the image top to bottom as the person passes beneath the camera so that the image remains right-side-up on the monitor for easy viewing. It has a built-in DVMD. It has a privacy-zoned masking function and auto-panning function with 64 preset positions. Its maximum panning speed is 360°/sec and 300°/sec preset mode. To provide a usable video image on the monitor and reduce DVR recording time, it has image freeze function during panning. The zoom lens has auto-focus and a zooming ratio of 22 times and a FL range of 3.8–83.4 mm. A 10 times electronic digital zoom results in a total zoom range of 220 times. Communication and control of the dome is accomplished through multiplexed coaxial or RS-485 data communication. There are four alarm inputs and two output terminals for alarm annunciation. The dome is available in an optional smoked or mirrored enclosure for concealing the lens, camera, and pan/tilt mechanism. The camera uses privacy zone masking and patrol learn features. The pan/tilt mechanism uses optical-coupled slip rings for noise free imaging.

17.12.3.4 Pelco

The Pelco Spectrum III SE™ is an indoor/outdoor high-speed video-dome camera system with a variable speed pan/tilt drive having continuous 360° rotation. It uses a 1/4-inch color camera with a horizontal resolution of 470 TV lines and sensitivity in monochrome mode of 0.3 lux. The auto-focus zoom lens provides 23 times optical and the camera provides 10 times digital zoom, providing an overall zoom ratio of 230 times. The system is enclosed and a compact mechanical structure that allows for quick installation and servicing. The pan speed is variable between 360°/sec continuous to 0.1°/sec for precise pointing. Vertical tilt is +2° to −90°. Manual control speed is 0.12°/sec, and pan at 150° sec in *turbo* mode. Tilt operation speed ranges from 0.1 to 40°/sec. Automatic preset speed is 360°/sec for panning and 200°/sec for tilting. The Spectrum III has 80 preset positions with a 20 character label available for each position. Preset accuracy is ±0.1°. The pan/tilt system uses proportional pan speed control so that the speed decreases in proportion to the increasing magnification of the zoom lens setting. The system has capability for eight zones with the ability to blank the video in the zones. The stepper motor can move with a minimum micro-step of 0.015°/step.

The dome system can provide window blanking of different lengths to turn off at user-defined zoom ratios. The window blanking can be set to opaque gray or a translucent smear. It can blank all video *above* a user-defined tilt angle or blank all video *below* a user-defined tilt angle. There are four user-defined programmable patterns including pan, tilt, zoom, and preset functions. These are programmed through the control keyboard or through the dome system on-screen menu. The system has an auto-flip feature to rotate the dome mechanism 180° at the bottom of the tilt travel as a convenience for determining direction of pointing. The system has an on-screen compass display for heading. Transmission options include the ability to plug an optional board into the unit that converts the output to a passive UTP transmission. It also has the ability to plug-in optional third-party boards that convert the video output and control input to fiber-optic transmission and the ability to plug-in an optional board that converts control signals from selected third-party controllers to be compatible with the dome.

17.12.3.5 Sony

The Sony SNC-RZ30N/2 is a high-speed pan/tilt IP camera system providing exceptional versatility for a state-of-the-art surveillance system for monitoring via the LAN, WAN, or Internet network. The system can monitoring high-quality live images from the camera using a Web browser on a computer connected to a 10BASE-T or 100BASE-TX network. Video transmission rate is at a maximum of 30 fps. The video image can be monitored through the Web browser to select a portion and size of the image to be viewed. Up to 50 users can view the image from one camera at the same time.

The camera is provided with a high-speed 340° rotation within two seconds, wide-angle (+170° to −170°) pan mechanism, and a high-speed 150° rotation in 1.5 seconds. The system has a wide-angle (−90 to +25°) tilt mechanism and a high magnification zoom lens with optical zoom of 25 times and electrical zoom of 12 times giving a 250 times overall magnification.

Still images can be recorded and sent from the camera's built-in memory (8 MByte) or a recommended ATA memory card (memory stick inserted into a PC card adapter). Still images from the camera can be sent via an email or FTP server when triggered by an external sensor input, a built-in activity detection function, manual trigger button, day/night function or timer.

The system is capable of saving up to 16 preset positions (PTZ) of the camera and up to 5 tour programs composed from the preset positions. The preset positions can be synchronized with the external sensor input or built-in activity detection function. The cameras are equipped with two sets of alarm outputs.

The system can receive inputs from peripheral devices via the cameras RS-232C or RS-485 interface. The devices can be controlled by the computer over the network and receive data from these devices. For completeness the system has an analog video output that allows connecting to a VCR or DVR or video monitor for local image recording and monitoring.

The camera can be used from ceiling or desktop locations. By default the images from the camera are displayed normal right-side-up when the camera is installed in the ceiling. Using the image-flip function the images from the camera can be flipped vertically so that they are seen in a right-side-up orientation when the camera is placed upright on a desktop.

To set up the SNC-RZ30N/2 for operation the camera must be assigned an IP address. The system is supplied with a CD-ROM with details for the system operation and for assigning the IP address using the setup program. After the system has been set up it can be accessed by a standard Internet Web browser (Microsoft Explorer, Netscape Navigator). The Web browser on the computer is started and the camera IP address is entered in the URL box. The welcome display page for the network camera is seen and is displayed providing instructions on its use.

The system operates using a 32-bit RISC CPU processor having 32 MByte of RAM. The camera image size has 736 by 480 pixel elements. The image from the camera is transmitted in JPEG or MPEG-4 compression format. The camera is a 1/6-inch format CCD having 680,000 picture elements. In color mode operation it has a minimum illumination sensitivity of 2.5 lux which is adequate for most normal illuminated areas. The zoom lens ratio is 25 times, providing a horizontal FOV of between 2° and 45°. The lens focal length is 2.4–16 mm.

The Sony SNC-RZ30N system represents a new generation of high-speed video pan/tilt systems designed for digital networks and remote monitoring from multiple locations. There are many other examples of this new digital security surveillance technology that is finding increased use in the video surveillance industry.

17.13 COVERT MIRROR PAN/TILT SYSTEM

A panning-mirror scanning system having no similarity to those previously discussed is shown in Figure 17-23. It consists of a motorized camera/lens/mirror combination to provide horizontal panning. The only part of the system in view of the observer is the small mirror scanning horizontally to provide viewing in any azimuth direction. The camera, lens, and panning system are mounted above the

ceiling level. Slip-rings provide full 360° continuous rotation with its attendant advantages.

17.14 GIMBAL MOUNTING

A gimbal camera/lens mounting configuration used to point and compensate for motion and to stabilize the camera/lens assembly in the three mutually perpendicular axes of pitch, roll, and yaw is used on moving vehicles, aircraft, ships, and vibrating building mounts as shown in Figure 17-24.

The stabilized gimbal-mounted camera is used extensively in helicopter video surveillance systems used by law-enforcement agencies. Unlike a stabilized lens (Chapter 4) that compensates for unwanted vibration and rotation for a stationary lens, the stabilized gimbaled platform compensates for *vibration and rotation* over its full range of elevation and azimuth travel. The outermost gimbal compensates for front-to-back pitching (tilt) and the inner gimbal for side-to-side rolling. When these two motions are compensated for, the center rotating platform is stable in the horizontal plane. Yaw compensation (horizontal rotation) and azimuth pointing (panning) are accomplished

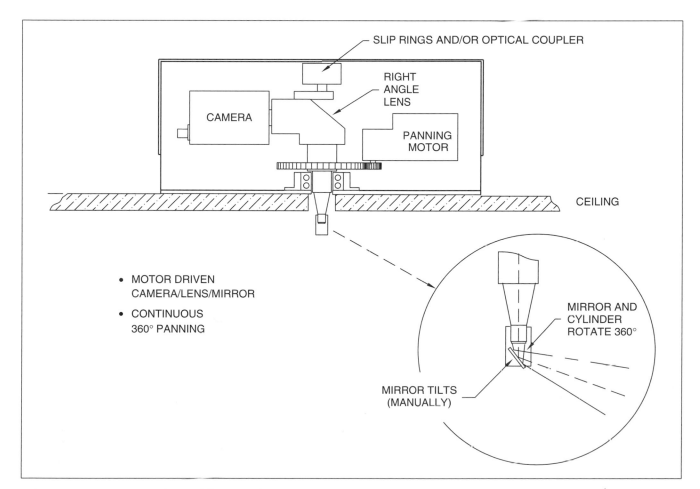

FIGURE 17-23 Covert mirror video panning system

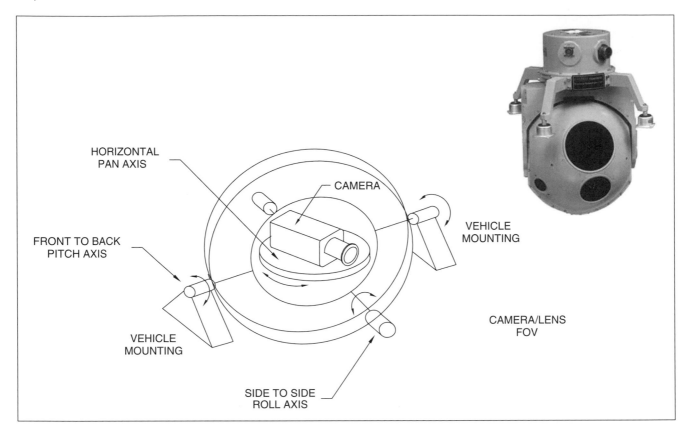

FIGURE 17-24   Gimbal mounted camera/lens assembly

by rotating the camera/lens platform. Since the vehicle is usually pointed in the general direction of the target, the two gimbals and platform angular travel are limited to 90° or less. The two-gimbal camera/lens combination is balanced and centered on all three axes to produce a completely symmetrical loading on the vertical (pitch), horizontal (yaw), and roll axes which aids in stabilization. The gimbaled platform is in limited use because of its high cost but must be used when the video camera package is mounted on an unstable platform.

17.15   SERVICING

Current integrated video security systems are assembled from many different components often from different manufacturers to provide a complete video surveillance system. The component in the system having the lowest reliability and most responsible for downtime is the camera pan/tilt mechanism. Components within this assembly causing problems include: (1) kinked cabling at the pan/tilt mechanism, (2) burned-out motors, (3) failed gear trains, and (4) broken mechanical stops. This section addresses some of these problems, identifies methods to prevent many of them, and outlines procedures for good system design and preventative maintenance.

17.15.1   Cabling

The interface cabling between the pan/tilt moving head and the stationary mount requires occasional servicing. This cable that constantly flexes and moves will eventually break and fail. General-purpose pan/tilt systems contain multiple conductors for control, power, and the video signal, and flex every time the camera points to a new direction or if wind causes the cable to vibrate. To maximize the lifetime of these cables they must be specified and installed correctly. The cables must be dressed (tied or clamped) to the housing and support structure at proper locations, so that over the full motion of the pan/tilt head there is no undue stretching or flexing, or any interference between the cable and any of the moving or stationary parts. Since installations are often in high or difficult-to-reach locations, failure often occurs because the cables have not been installed or dressed properly. To minimize downtime in the event of a cable failure, the flexible cable between the pan/tilt mechanism and the stationary bracket should be installed so that a failed cable can be replaced quickly.

Different grades of wire are suitable for outdoor pan/tilt system use, each with different qualities and lifetimes. The outdoor cable types for pan/tilt mechanisms include coiled cables, in which the coaxial and control cables are enclosed in a single coiled cable that looks like a standard telephone headset cord, protecting them from the environment and overbending.

Many manufacturers use slip-ring (Section 17.11) assemblies that feed the electrical signals through the center shaft of the pan/tilt unit which eliminates the flexing cables. With this design the cable is always protected from damage during installation or due to the environment, and will not deteriorate and cause premature failure. Slip-rings are concentric rings mounted around the shaft with electrical contacts that slide on the rings to provide transmission of the electrical signals and power to and from the stationary mount to the rotating shaft and vice versa. This technique is more expensive than using flexible cables during initial installation, but using slip rings significantly reduces maintenance costs over the life of the equipment and the loss of security when failure occurs. Slip-ring assemblies provide many years of reliable operation in addition to the extra security provided by continuous 360° rotation.

17.15.2 Mechanical

Most pan/tilt systems use motors and gear trains that operate satisfactorily under "normal conditions over long periods of time without servicing. However, there are instances when careless installation, maintenance, or inadvertent abuse causes premature failure. Manufacturers test their designs and equipment thoroughly at the factory but if installers install them improperly under adverse conditions or hazardous circumstances they may fail prematurely. Inadvertent mechanical overload on the pan/tilt axes during installation or maintenance can cause permanent damage to the gear train or motor. The breakaway torque when a unit has been frozen by ice can cause overheating of the motor and eventual damage and failure.

A mechanical stop out of adjustment will cause the motor to drive the unit beyond its end travel and continue driving causing damage to the motor and gear train. A typical failure occurs in a loosened shaft mechanical stop which fails to stop the motor causing damage to the motor and gears. Manufacturers have designed out most of these failure modes using potentiometers, optical, or magnetic encoders to determine the pan/tilt pointing direction (azimuth and elevation) and they use this signal to shut off the motor. Pan/tilt manufacturers all are producing more reliable systems with longer life to ensure lifetime compatibility with the other video components in the system.

17.15.3 Environmental

Water, snow, sleet, or ice precipitation causes deleterious long-term effects on pan/tilt mechanism parts. Mechanical hardware or brackets are not always corrosion-resistant and as they age they corrode and become loose or fail. Water entering between the housing and the shaft and accumulation of dirt with the water or grease can jam the drive causing failure, intermittent, or rough operation of the unit. While close scrutiny of the mechanical design suggests some information on its future performance, feedback from dealers, installers, and end-users provides better information with which to make an intelligent choice of the pan/tilt manufacturer and model.

The best approach to maintain reliable operation is to perform periodic and preventative maintenance and inspection. Manufacturer's lubrication or inspection recommendations should be followed and any questions should be addressed to the manufacturer for additional preventive maintenance.

17.16 SUMMARY

A requirement for any video security surveillance system is its ability to see as large an FOV as possible with as much clarity (resolution) as possible. Since these two parameters work against each other (wide FOV means low resolution and vice versa), a pan/tilt camera/lens platform with a zoom lens solves some of these problems. When a PTZ system is used, dead zones are created, and there is less than 100% viewing of the entire system FOV. New fast-scan systems reduce the dead zones at an increase in cost. To ensure reliable operation of the pan/tilt units, preventive maintenance should be performed at regular intervals.

Chapter 18
Covert Video Surveillance

CONTENTS

18.1 Overview
18.2 Covert Techniques—Background
18.3 Covert Lens/Camera Types
    18.3.1 Pinhole Lenses
    18.3.2 Convertible Pinhole Lens Kit
    18.3.3 Mini-Lenses
        18.3.3.1 Off-Axis Optics
        18.3.3.2 Optical Attenuation Techniques
        18.3.3.3 Mini-Camera/Mini-Lens Combination
    18.3.4 Comparison of Pinhole Lens and Mini-Lens
    18.3.5 Sprinkler-Head Pinhole Lenses
    18.3.6 Mirror-Pinhole Lens
    18.3.7 Fiber-Optic Lenses
        18.3.7.1 Configuration
        18.3.7.2 Rigid Fiber Pinhole Lens
        18.3.7.3 Flexible Fiber
        18.3.7.4 Image Quality
    18.3.8 Bore-Scope Lenses
18.4 Special Covert Cameras
    18.4.1 PC-Board Cameras
    18.4.2 Remote-Head Cameras
18.5 Infrared Covert Lighting
    18.5.1 Concealment Means
    18.5.2 IR Sources
18.6 Low-light-level Cameras
18.7 Imbeded Covert Camera Configurations
18.8 Wireless Transmission
18.9 Covert Checklist
18.10 Summary

18.1 OVERVIEW

Overt video surveillance equipment is installed in full view of the public and is used to observe personnel and activity and letting people know that they are under surveillance. Overt video has had the effect of deterring crime of all types. *Covert* video ideally operates so that the offender is not aware of the surveillance. It can be recorded to produce a permanent video recording for later use in confronting, dismissing, or prosecuting the offender. Overt video security installations are very useful in apprehending offenders; however, in special situations, investigators, police officials, government agencies, retail operations, and security personnel require covert or hidden cameras.

Covert and overt video are often used together to foil professional criminals. The criminal, seeing the overt system, defeats or disables the overt cameras, but the covert cameras can still record the activity. An unrelated reason for using covert video is to avoid changing the architectural aesthetics of a building or surrounding area.

Covert video cameras and lenses have become commonplace, and although these hidden cameras use small optics, they can produce high-quality video images. Covert video cameras are concealed in common objects or located behind a small hole in an opaque barrier (such as a wall or ceiling). Cameras are camouflaged in common objects such as lamps and lamp fixtures, table and wall clocks, radios, or books. A very effective covert system uses a camera and lens camouflaged in a ceiling-mounted sprinkler head.

This chapter will analyze covert video principles, techniques, and unique pinhole lenses and cameras. Lenses are analyzed that have a small front lens diameter thereby permitting the lens and camera to view the scene through a 1/16-inch-diameter hole. Most of these lenses have a medium-to-wide FOV, from 12 to 78°, to cover a large scene area, but still permit identification of persons and the monitoring of activities and actions. Special pinhole lens variations including right-angle, automatic-iris, sprinkler-head, and fiber optic are described, as well as small pinhole cameras combining a mini-lens and sensor into a small camera head and other complete miniature cameras.

In low-light-level (LLL) applications, a CCD camera with a very sensitive sensor and IR light source or an image intensifier is used. Since many covert installations are temporary, wireless transmission systems are used to send the camera signal to the monitor, recorder, or video printer.

18.2   COVERT TECHNIQUES—BACKGROUND

The lens and camera concealment is accomplished by having the lens view through a small hole, a series of small holes, or from behind a semitransparent window. Figure 18-1 shows a typical room in which covert video surveillance is installed.

A number of suitable covert camera locations include the ceiling, a wall, a lamp fixture, a clock, or other articles normally found in the room. Video cameras are installed in one or more locations in the room depending on the activity expected. Covert video systems using small lenses pose unique optical problems compared with overt systems that use standard lenses. Since the diameter of the front lens that views the scene must, by necessity, be small in order to be hidden, the lens is designed to be optically fast, collecting and transmitting as much light as possible from the reflected scene to the camera sensor. As a consequence, small-diameter lenses called pinhole lenses are used. (The term *pinhole* is a misnomer, as these lenses have a front diameter anywhere from 1/16 to 3/8 inch.)

There are several misconceptions regarding the factors determining a good pinhole camera or lens system for covert applications. Figure 18-2 shows the covert security problem. The lens/camera must receive reflected light from an illuminated scene. The lens must collect and transmit the light to the camera sensor and the camera must transmit the video signal to a remote video monitor and/or recorder and video printer. Most covert pinhole lenses are designed for 1/4- and 1/3-inch camera sensor formats. For indoor applications the light sources are typically fluorescent, metal-arc, mercury, or tungsten types. Outdoor light sources include sunlight in the daytime, and mercury, metal-arc, tungsten, sodium, or xenon lighting at night. Figure 18-3 shows two basic configurations for pinhole lenses and cameras located behind a barrier.

The hole in the barrier is usually chosen to be the same diameter (*d*) or smaller than the pinhole lens front lens element. When space permits the straight-type

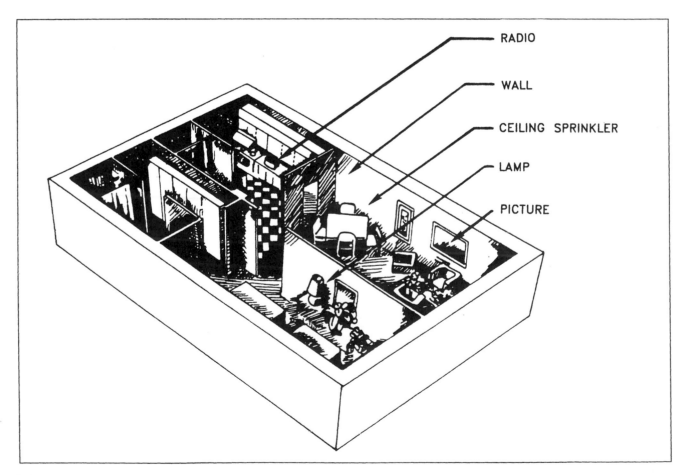

FIGURE 18-1   Covert CCTV lens/camera environment

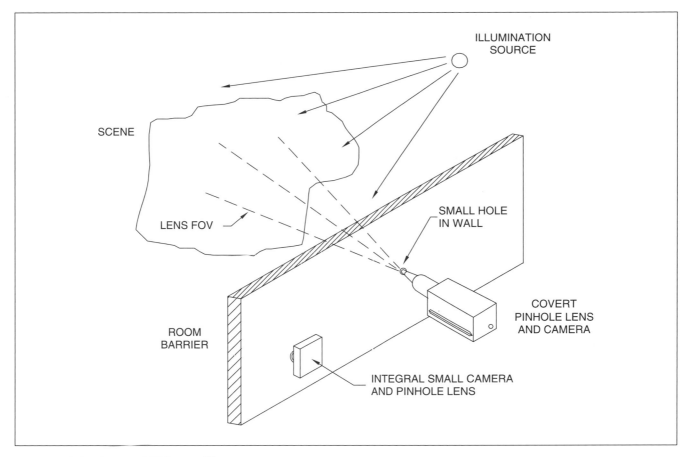

FIGURE 18-2 Covert CCTV surveillance

installation is used. In confined or restricted locations with limited depth behind the barrier, the right-angle pinhole lens/camera is used. In both cases, to obtain the full lens FOV it is imperative that the pinhole lens front lens element be located as close to the front of the barrier as possible to avoid "tunneling" (vignetting). When the pinhole lens front lens element is set back from the barrier surface, the lens is, in effect, viewing through a tunnel, and the image has a narrower FOV than the lens is capable of producing. This appears on the monitor as a porthole-like (vignetted) picture.

An important installation problem often initially overlooked is the lens pointing angle required to see the desired FOV (Figure 18-4). Many applications require that the lens/camera point down at a shallow depression angle (30°) from the ceiling (Figure 18-4a). This is accomplished by using the small-barrel, slow-taper lens. This feature allows pointing the small-barrel lens over a larger part of a room than the wide-barrel lens. Not all lenses can be mounted at a small angle to the ceiling because of the lens barrel shape (Figure 18-4b). Lenses having a large barrel diameter and fast taper at the front cannot be mounted at the shallow angles required. The small-barrel, slow-taper design permits easier installation than the fast-taper since less material must be removed from the barrier, and the

lens has a faster optical speed, since the front lens element is larger and collects more light. Figure 18-4 illustrates this installation problem. It shows a small hole on the scene side of the barrier and some material cut out of the barrier behind it to permit the front lens element to be located close to the front of the barrier surface. A pinhole lens having a small front diameter is simple to install. The smaller tapered barrel can be mounted at a smaller angle to the barrier than the wide-barrel lens. This feature allows pointing the small-barrel lens over a larger part of a room than the wide-barrel lens.

18.3 COVERT LENS/CAMERA TYPES

Pinhole lenses and cameras used for covert security applications include: standard pinhole, compact pinhole lens kit, and mini-lens. There are many single board covert camera designs available using a small lens mounted to a single printed circuit (PC) board housed in a plastic or metal housing (Section 18.4.1). Special covert lens and camera designs include: fiber optic, sprinkler-head, and covert camera/lens combinations uniquely configured in special housings.

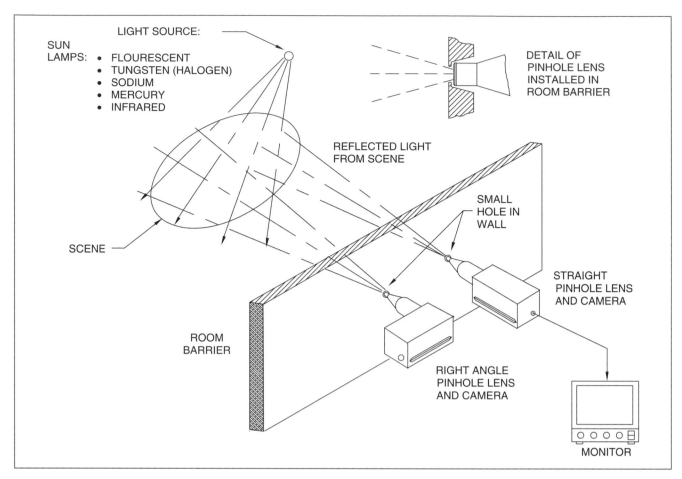

FIGURE 18-3   Straight and right angle pinhole installation

18.3.1   Pinhole Lenses

Figure 18-3 shows how pinhole lenses and cameras are mounted behind a wall, with the lens viewing through a small hole in the wall. Most are designed for 1/4-, and 1/3-inch format cameras and have a manual- or automatic-iris control to adjust the light level reaching the camera. Figure 18-5 shows several samples of the generic pinhole lens types available.

The right-angle version permits locating the camera and lens inside a narrow wall or above a ceiling. The optical speed or f-number (f/#) of the pinhole lens is important for the successful implementation of a covert camera system. The lower the f-number, the more light reaching the camera and the better the video picture. The best theoretical f-number is equal to the lens focal length (FL) divided by its entrance lens diameter (d):

$$f/\# = \mathrm{FL}/d \qquad (18\text{-}1)$$

This theoretical f-number cannot be obtained in practice because of various losses caused by imperfect lens transmission that is caused by reflection, absorption, and other lens-imaging properties. The light getting through the

pinhole lens to the camera sensor is limited primarily by the diameter of the front lens or the mechanical opening through which it views. The larger the lens entrance diameter, the more light getting through to the camera sensor, resulting in better picture quality, all other conditions remaining the same. The light collected and transmitted through a lens system varies *inversely* as the square of the lens f-number. If the lens diameter is increased (or decreased) a small amount, the light passing through the lens increased (or decreases) by a large amount: if the lens diameter is doubled, the light throughput quadruples. An f/2.0 lens transmits *four* times as much light as an f/4.0 lens. The f-number relationship is analogous to water flowing through a pipe: if the pipe diameter is doubled four times as much water flows through it. Likewise if the f-number is halved, four times as much light will be transmitted through the lens.

Many types of covert lenses are commercially available for video surveillance applications. Table 18-1 summarizes the characteristics of most manual- and automatic-iris pinhole lenses.

Most of these lenses are designed for 1/4- and 1/3-inch sensor formats since covert cameras are small. In spite of their small size they have resolutions of 380–420 TV

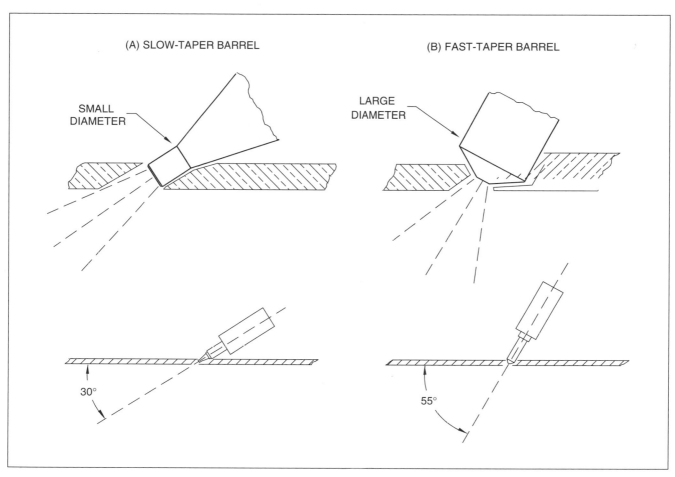

FIGURE 18-4   Pinhole lens pointing angle

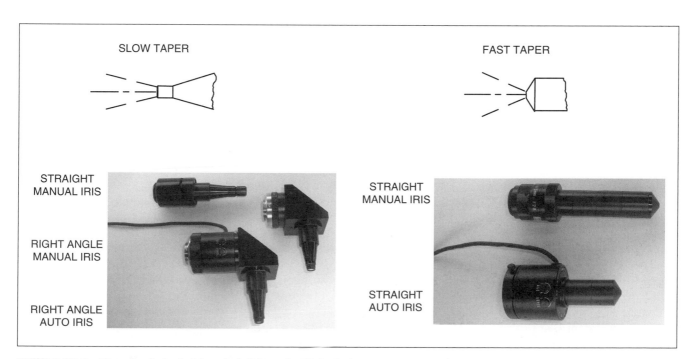

FIGURE 18-5   Standard straight and right-angle Pinhole lenses

FOCAL LENGTH (mm)	f/#	ANGULAR FIELD OF VIEW (FOV) IN DEGREES CAMERA FORMAT (inch)						TYPE	MOUNT
		1/4		1/3		1/2			
		HORIZ	VERT	HORIZ	VERT	HORIZ	VERT		
2.6	2.5	62.4	46.8	83.2	62.4	—	—	STRAIGHT	CS
4.0	2.0	51.2	38.4	68.5	43.1	—	—	STRAIGHT	CS
5.5	3.0	30.2	23.6	38.7	31.0	60.4	47.2	STRAIGHT	C/CS
6.2	2.0	32,4	24.3	42.8	30.1	56.1	42.1	STRAIGHT	CS
8.0	2.0	21.8	16.7	29.4	22.0	43.6	33.4	STRAIGHT	C/CS
8.0	2.2	21.8	16.7	29.4	22.0	43.6	33.4	RIGHT-ANGLE	C/CS
9.0	3.4	22.3	16.8	29.5	22.1	39.1	29.3	STRAIGHT	C/CS
11.0	2.3	16.2	12.3	21.6	16.1	32.4	24.6	STRAIGHT	C/CS
11.0	2.5	16.2	12.3	21.6	16.1	32.4	24.6	RIGHT-ANGLE	C/CS

Table 18-1   Covert Pinhole Lens Parameters

lines for a 1/4- or 1/3-inch color camera and 450–570 TV lines for monochrome cameras. Many pinhole lenses have very small entrance apertures: 0.10 inch (2.5 mm) and are therefore optically slow (f/3.5–f/4.0) by design. From Equation 18-1 a lens with a FL of 9 mm and a 2.5 mm aperture (d) has at best a theoretical f-number of:

$$f/\# = 9\,mm/2.5\,mm = 3.6 \qquad (18\text{-}2)$$

Other lens losses within this type of lens give an overall optical speed of approximately f/4.0.

A covert lens with an 11 mm FL and a 6 mm aperture has a theoretical f-number of:

$$f/\# = 11\,mm/6\,mm = 1.83 \qquad (18\text{-}3)$$

Other lens losses result in an overall optical speed of approximately f/2.0. This means that the 11 mm lens collects *four* times as much light as the 9 mm lens.

The 9 mm lens with the smaller aperture works well if there is sufficient light. An advantage of the 6 mm-aperture (approximately 0.25 inch) lens is that it can be used in applications where a larger hole, that is, 6 mm diameter adequately conceals the lens and there is insufficient light available for the 9 mm FL lens with the 2.5 mm hole. The most important characteristics of a pinhole lens are: (1) how fast is the lens optical speed—that is, how low is the lens f-number (the lower the better) and (2) ease of installation and use. When covert operation is required in locations having widely varying light-level conditions or in a low light level application, a high sensitivity CCD solid-state or other intensified LLL camera used with a pinhole lens with an automatic iris controlling the light reaching the camera sensor is necessary. Shuttered CCD cameras may tolerate the use of manual-iris lenses. Check with the manufacturer for the light range over which the camera will operate. Figure 18-5 shows straight and right-angle pinhole lenses with manual and automatic irises capable of controlling the light level reaching the camera sensor over a 35,000-to-1 light-level range.

A generic characteristic of almost all pinhole-type lenses is that they invert the video picture and therefore the camera must be inverted to get a normal right-side-up picture. Some right-angle pinhole lenses reverse the image right to left and therefore require an electronic scan-reversal unit (Section 16.4) to regain the correct left-to-right orientation. Some pinhole lenses have a focusing ring or the front element of the lens can be adjusted to focus a sharp image on the camera sensor.

18.3.2   Convertible Pinhole Lens Kit

Pinhole lenses have been manufactured for many years in a variety of focal lengths (3.8, 4, 5.5, 6, 8, 9, 11 mm), in straight, right-angle, and manual- and automatic-iris configurations. The FL of most of these lenses can be doubled to obtain one-half the FOV by using a 2X extender. Pinhole lenses with 16 mm and 22 mm FLs are achieved by locating a 2X magnifier in between the 8 and 11 mm lenses and the camera. This automatically doubles the f-number of each lens (only one-fourth of the light transmitted). In many applications, the required FLs and configuration are not known in advance, and the user (or dealer) must have a large assortment of pinhole lenses, or take the risk that he will not have the right lens to do the job. This dilemma was solved with the pinhole lens kit (Figure 18-6).

Eight different FL lenses can be assembled in either a straight or right-angle configuration within minutes with

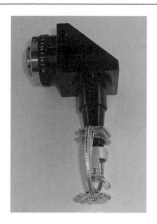

(A) RIGHT-ANGLE SPRINKLER LENS
ASSEMBLED FROM KIT

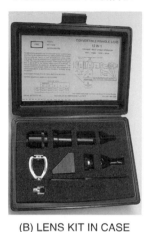

(B) LENS KIT IN CASE

FIGURE 18-6   Pinhole lens kit

Tables 18-3 and 18-4 tabulate the scene areas (width and height) as viewed with the popular pinhole lenses on 1/4- and 1/3-inch sensor format cameras.

Several points should be considered when using standard, fully assembled pinhole lenses or pinhole lenses made from the pinhole lens kit:

• Straight pinhole lenses invert the picture; therefore, the camera should be mounted in an inverted orientation.
• Some right-angle pinhole lenses will show a right-to-left picture orientation instead of left-to-right, as with normal lenses. A camera SRU will correct the problem. Check with the manufacturer.
• The *straight* pinhole lens with the sprinkler-mirror attachment displays a right-to-left picture. Use an electronic SRU to correct the problem. The *right-angle* sprinkler-mirror version displays a correct left-to-right picture.

As an example: choose a pinhole lens and camera to view a scene 6 feet high by 8 feet wide at a distance of 15 feet using a 1/4-inch format camera. Use Table 18-3 and choose an 11 mm FL lens. As another example, the scene area displayed on the monitor with an 8 mm lens on a 1/3-inch format camera in a ceiling at a distance of 20 feet is an area 22 feet wide by 16.4 feet high (Table 18-4).

Note that the FOV when using any of the medium- to long-FL lenses is independent of the hole size through which the lens views, providing the hole produces no tunneling. Viewing through a wall with a wide-angle 4–8 mm FL pinhole lens may require a cone-shaped hole or an array of small holes to prevent tunneling (vignetting) of the scene image.

this kit of pinhole lens parts. An additional four combinations can be assembled in the form of a disguised sprinkler-head covert application (Section 18.3.5). All lenses have a manual iris with automatic iris optional). Table 18-2 lists all the lens combinations for this versatile pinhole lens kit.

18.3.3 Mini-Lenses

Mini-lenses and a mini-lens camera kit consisting of five interchangeable mini-lenses and a very small CCD camera are described in this section. Mini-lenses are small FFL objective lenses used for covert surveillance when space is at a premium (Figure 18.7).

FOCAL LENGTH (mm)	f/#	CONFIGURATION	IMAGE ORIENTATION	COMMENTS
11	2.3	STRAIGHT	NORMAL	PINHOLE LENS
8	2.0	STRAIGHT	NORMAL	PINHOLE LENS
11	2.5	RIGHT ANGLE	REVERSED	PINHOLE LENS
8	2.2	RIGHT ANGLE	REVERSED	PINHOLE LENS
22	4.6	STRAIGHT	NORMAL	PINHOLE LENS
16	4.0	STRAIGHT	NORMAL	PINHOLE LENS
22	5.0	RIGHT ANGLE	REVERSED	PINHOLE LENS
16	4.4	RIGHT ANGLE	REVERSED	PINHOLE LENS
11	2.3	STRAIGHT	NORMAL	SPRINKLER HEAD
22	4.6	STRAIGHT	NORMAL	SPRINKLER HEAD
11	2.5	RIGHT ANGLE	REVERSED	SPRINKLER HEAD
22	5.0	RIGHT ANGLE	REVERSED	SPRINKLER HEAD

Table 18-2   Pinhole Lens Kit Combinations and Parameters

1/4 inch SENSOR FORMAT LENS GUIDE						
PINHOLE LENS FOCAL LENGTH (mm)	CAMERA TO SCENE DISTANCE (D) IN FEET WIDTH AND HEIGHT OF AREA (W×H) IN FEET					
	5	10	15	20	25	30
	W×H	W×H	W×H	W×H	W×H	W×H
2.6	12.3×9.2	24.6×18.5	36.9×27.7	49.2×36.9	61.5×46.1	74.0×55.5
3.7	8.5×6.5	17.3×13.0	30.0×19.5	34.6×26.0	43.3×32.5	60.0×39.0
4.0	8.0×6.0	16.0×12.0	24.0×18.0	32.0×24.0	40.0×30.0	48.0×36.0
6.2	5.2×3.9	10.4×7.8	15.6×11.7	20.8×15.6	26.0×19.5	31.2×23.4
8.0	4.0×3.0	8.0×6.0	12.0×9.0	16.0×12.0	20.0×15.0	24.0×18.0
9.0	3.6×2.7	7.2×5.4	10.8×8.1	14.4×10.8	18.0×13.5	21.6×16.2
11.0	2.9×2.2	5.8×4.4	8.7×6.6	11.6×8.8	14.5×11.0	17.4×13.2
16.0	2.0×1.5	4.0×3.0	6.0×4.5	8.0×6.0	10.0×7.5	12.0×9.0
22.0	1.5×0.8	2.9×2.2	4.4×3.3	5.8×4.4	7.3×5.5	8.7×6.6

Table 18-3   Pinhole Lens Guide for 1/4-Inch Format Camera

1/3-inch SENSOR FORMAT LENS GUIDE						
PINHOLE LENS FOCAL LENGTH (mm)	CAMERA TO SCENE DISTANCE (D) IN FEET WIDTH AND HEIGHT OF AREA (W×H) IN FEET					
	5	10	15	20	25	30
	W×H	W×H	W×H	W×H	W×H	W×H
2.6	8.6×6.5	16.9×12.6	25.8×19.4	33.8×25.2	43.1×32.3	50.8×37.8
3.7	6.1×4.5	11.9×8.7	18.2×13.6	23.8×17.7	30.3×22.7	35.7×26.6
4.0	5.6×4.2	11.2×8.2	16.8×12.6	22.0×16.4	28.0×21.0	33.0×24.6
6.0	3.7×2.8	7.3×5.5	11.2×8.4	14.7×10.9	18.7×14.0	22.0×16.4
8.0	2.8×2.1	5.5×4.1	8.4×6.3	11.0×8.2	14.0×10.5	16.5×12.3
9.0	2.5×1.9	4.9×3.7	7.5×5.7	9.8×7.4	12.5×9.5	14.7×11.1
11.0	2.0×1.5	4.0×3.0	6.0×4.5	8.0×6.0	10.0×7.5	12.0×9.0
16.0	1.4×1.1	2.8×2.1	4.2×3.3	5.6×4.2	7.0×5.5	8.4×6.3
22.0	1.0×.8	2.0×1.5	3.0×2.4	4.0×3.0	5.0×4.0	6.0×4.5

Table 18-4   Pinhole Lens Guide for 1/3-Inch Format Camera

Mini-lenses shown have focal lengths of 3.8, 8, 11 mm, etc. They have front-barrel diameters between 3/8 and 1/2 inch, making them easy to mount behind a barrier or in close quarters. Because these small lenses have no iris, they should be used in applications where the scene light level does not vary widely, or with electronically shuttered cameras. Mini-lenses, like other FFL lenses and unlike pinhole lenses, do not invert the image on the camera. Since the small and short (less than 5/8 inch long) mini-lenses have only three to six optical lens elements, fast optical speeds of f/1.4 to f/1.8 are realized. Pinhole lenses, on the other hand, are 3–5 inches long, and have as many as 10–20 optical elements and optical speeds of f/2.0 to f/4.0. This makes the mini-lens approximately five times faster (able to collect five times more light) than the pinhole lens.

18.3.3.1   Off-Axis Optics

A useful variation of the mini-lens is one that is mounted with its optical axis laterally offset from the camera-sensor axis (Figure 18-8). This offset configuration allows the camera to view a scene at an angle away from the camera-pointing axis. The physical amount the optics must be moved to produce a large offset angle is only a few millimeters, which is easily accomplished with this special mini-lens and its modified mount. The offset angle is chosen so that, with the camera parallel to a mounting surface, the entire lens FOV views the scene of interest without viewing the mounting surface. This angle is 22° for the 8 mm lens and 15° for the 11-mm when using a 1/4-inch format camera. It is 18° and 13°, respectively for the same lenses when using a 1/3-inch camera. This technique has a direct

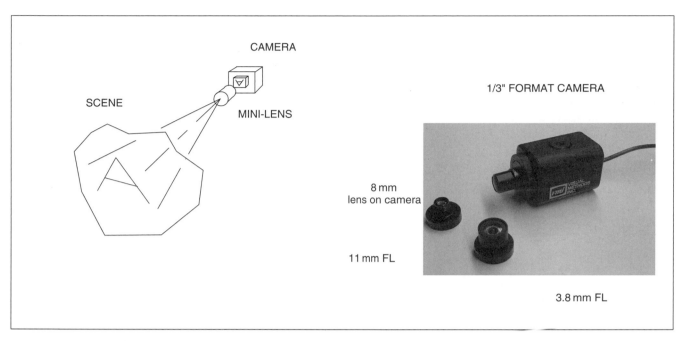

FIGURE 18-7 Mini-lens and optical diagram

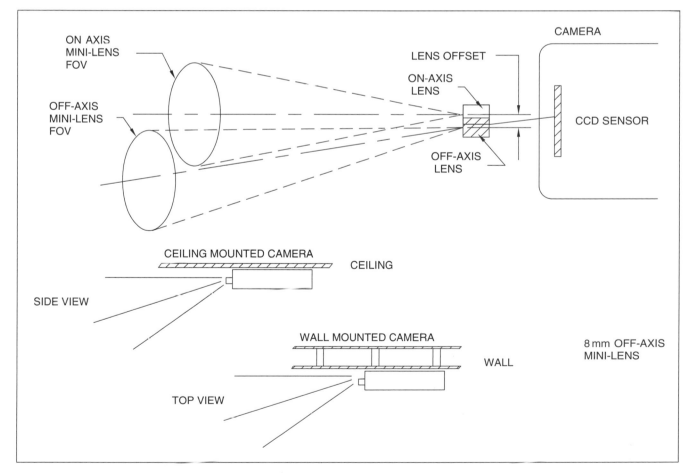

FIGURE 18-8 Off-axis optics configuration

benefit when a camera/lens is mounted flat against a wall or a ceiling or other mounting surface (Figure 18-8).

18.3.3.2 Optical Attenuation Techniques

Since mini-lenses do not have an iris, they should be used when the lighting conditions are fairly constant and do not exceed the dynamic range of the camera. If the scene is very brightly illuminated with an intense artificial light or the sun, several techniques can be used to attenuate the light to the lens/camera (Figure 18-9).

The first technique is to mount the mini-lens behind a light-attenuating filter (Figure 18-9a). This may take the form of a gray neutral-density filter, a partially aluminized film, or a tinted/smoked glass or plastic material. Neutral-density filters are available from photographic supply stores. This technique uniformly attenuates the light across the full aperture of the lens. A second technique shown in Figure 18-9b through 18-9e is to mount the mini-lens behind a small hole, a pattern of small holes, a slit, or other hole(s). This is accomplished by either mounting a small cap with the hole(s) (Figure 18-9b) onto the lens, or mounting the lens behind a hole(s) in the barrier (Figure 18-9c–18-9e). The light level reaching the camera sensor can be set initially by locating the lens behind a hole smaller than the mini-lens diameter. This technique

attenuates the light reaching the lens but does not do it uniformly. For medium-FL lenses (11 mm and above), almost any shape hole results in a satisfactory image on the sensor. When the 11 or 22 mm mini-lens or pinhole lens is mounted behind a viewing barrier, a central hole as small as 1/16th of an inch is suitable for producing a full image of the scene, providing sufficient light available for the camera. When short focal length (2.2, 3, 8 mm, etc.) mini-lens or pinhole lens views through a small hole, an undesirable porthole effect occurs, which is eliminated by having the lens view through a central hole and a series of concentric holes located around the central hole. The hole pattern must extend to the outer limits of the lens so that the full FOV of the lens is maintained. These concentric holes enable the lens to have peripheral vision or wide-angle viewing, and they eliminate vignetting. Figure 18-9(b, d) shows two examples of this extended hole pattern. Either technique can provide attenuations required for sunlit or brightly illuminated scenes.

18.3.3.3 Mini-Camera/Mini-Lens Combination

A high-sensitivity pinhole camera results when a very fast mini-lens—f/1.4 to f/2.0—is coupled directly with the camera sensor. Figure 18-10 illustrates a mini-lens camera kit with three standard on-axis mini-lenses having focal

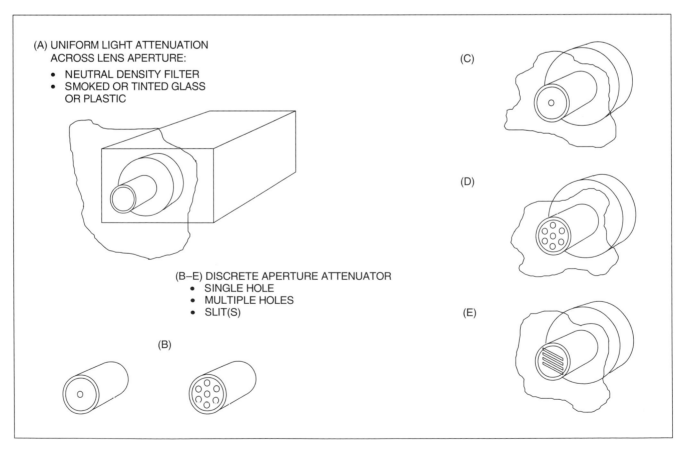

FIGURE 18-9 Lens optical attenuation techniques

(A) MINI-CAMERA
MINI-LENS 3.8 mm FL
ASSEMBLED FROM KIT

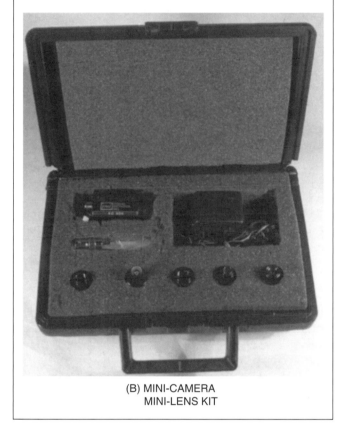

(B) MINI-CAMERA
MINI-LENS KIT

FIGURE 18-10 Mini-camera/mini-lens combination and kit

lengths of 3.8, 8 and 11 mm and two off-axis mounts for the 8 and 11 mm FL lenses, and a very small, sensitive, high-resolution color CCD camera. The complete camera is only $1.25 \times 1.25 \times 1.00$ inches long. The 11-mm FL lens extends 0.3 inch in front of the camera. The camera operates directly from 12 volts DC, requires only 1.5 watts of power, and produces a standard composite video output.

The small lens size and direct coupling to the camera sensor do not leave room for a manual or automatic iris. The camera has excellent electronic light-level compensation, but optimum performance is achieved if the lighting is fairly constant. Under bright light conditions an attenuation technique shown in Figure 18-9 is used.

18.3.4 Comparison of Pinhole Lens and Mini-Lens

To compare different pinhole and mini-lenses with respect to their ability to transmit light to the camera sensor, a light power factor (LPF) is defined, with a slow pinhole lens (f/4.0) as a base reference. Table 18-5 summarizes the optical speed (f-number) and LPF for standard pinhole and mini-lenses.

The f-number is usually critical in nighttime applications with low light levels and where auxiliary lighting cannot be added. Table 18-5 illustrates the significantly higher amount of light passing through the mini-lenses as compared with the pinhole lenses. A camera/lens using an f/1.8 mini-lens transmits almost *five times* as much light to the camera sensor as an f/4 pinhole lens. The f/1.4 mini-lens transmits more than *eight times* as much light as the f/4 pinhole lens.

18.3.5 Sprinkler-Head Pinhole Lenses

A very effective covert system uses a camera and lens camouflaged in a ceiling-mounted sprinkler head. Of the large variety of covert lenses available for the security video industry (pinhole, mini, fiber-optic), this unique, extremely useful product hides the pinhole lens in a ceiling sprinkler fixture, making it very difficult for an observer standing at floor level to detect or identify the lens and camera. Figure 18-11a shows the sprinkler pinhole lens attached to a standard camera mounted on a ceiling.

The covert surveillance sprinkler installed in the ceiling in no way affects the operation of the active fire-suppression sprinkler system; however, it should not be installed in locations that have no sprinkler system, so as not to give a false impression to fire and safety personnel that there is a sprinkler system installed.

The only part of the lens system visible from below is the standard sprinkler head and the small ($3/8 \times 5/8$-inch) mirror assembly. In operation, light from the scene reflecting off the small mirror is directed by the mirror to the front of the pinhole lens. The 11 or 22 mm pinhole lens transmits and focuses the scene onto the camera sensor. In the straight version the image is reversed. In surveillance applications this is often only an annoyance and not really a problem. However, if it needs to be corrected an electronic SRU will correct this condition. The right-angle version (Figure 18-11b) corrects this condition and produces a normal left-to-right image scan. The small mirror can be adjusted in elevation to point at different scene heights. To point in a particular azimuth direction, the entire camera-sprinkler lens assembly is rotated with the mirror pointing in the direction of the target of interest. When installed, most of the pinhole lens and the entire

FOCAL LENGTH (mm)	f/#	LENS TYPE	CONFIGURATION	LIGHT POWER FACTOR (LPF)*	ANGULAR FOV(°)				COMMENTS
					1/4-inch FORMAT		1/3-inch FORMAT		
					HORIZ	VERT	HORIZ	VERT	
2.6	2.0	MINI	STRAIGHT	4.0	62.4	46.8	83.2	62.4	ULTRA WIDE-ANGLE
3.8	1.4	MINI	STRAIGHT	8.16	39.1	31.8	52.1	42.4	ULTRA WIDE-ANGLE
8.0	1.6	MINI	STRAIGHT	6.25	21.8	16.7	29.1	22.3	LONG TAPER
11.0	1.8	MINI	STRAIGHT	4.94	16.2	12.3	21.6	16.4	LONG TAPER
25.0	4.0	MINI	STRAIGHT	1.0	7.0	5.3	9.3	7.1	ULTRA WIDE-ANGLE
3.8	2.0	PINHOLE	STRAIGHT	4.0	39.1	31.8	52.1	42.4	ULTRA WIDE-ANGLE
3.8	2.2	PINHOLE	RIGHT-ANGLE	3.31	39.1	31.8	52.1	42.4	ULTRA WIDE-ANGLE
5.5	3.0	PINHOLE	STRAIGHT	1.78	32.3	25.6	43.1	34.1	WIDE-ANGLE
6.2	2.0	PINHOLE	STRAIGHT	4.00	28.0	21.5	37.3	28.7	WIDE-ANGLE
8.0	2.0	PINHOLE	STRAIGHT	4.00	21.8	17.7	29.1	23.6	SHORT, WIDE-ANGLE
8.0	2.2	PINHOLE	RIGHT-ANGLE	3.31	21.8	17.7	29.1	23.6	LONG TAPER
9.0	3.5	PINHOLE	STRAIGHT	1.31	19.4	15.1	25.9	20.1	LONG TAPER
11.0	2.3	PINHOLE	STRAIGHT	3.02	16.2	12.3	21.6	16.4	SHORT TAPER
11.0	2.5	PINHOLE	RIGHT-ANGLE	2.56	16.2	12.3	21.6	16.4	SHORT TAPER
16.0	4.0	PINHOLE	STRAIGHT	1.00	11.0	8.3	14.7	11.1	NARROW-ANGLE

*INCREASE IN LIGHT LEVEL REACHING SENSOR BASED ON USING VALUE OF 1.00 FOR AN f/4 PINHOLE LENS

Table 18-5   Pinhole Lens and Mini-Lens Light Transmission Comparison

camera is concealed above the ceiling, with only a modified sprinkler head, a small mirror, and small lens in view. For many applications this stationary pinhole lens pointing in one specific direction is adequate. To look in different directions the camera, sprinkler head, and moving mirror assembly are made to pan (scan) via a motor drive. A motor drive sprinkler scanning system can provide remote panning capability. A scanning version of the sprinkler concept has a remote-control 360° continuous panning capability (Figure 18-12).

18.3.6   Mirror-Pinhole Lens

Large plastic domes are often used to conceal a PTZ video surveillance system from the observer (Chapter 14). The purpose for concealing the camera and lens in the dome is so that the observer cannot see the direction in which the camera lens is pointing or whether there is actually a surveillance camera. Using this subterfuge, one camera system can scan and view a large area without the observer knowing at any instant whether he is under observation. Most domes are from 5 to 10 inches in diameter and drop below the ceiling by 5–8 inches. The requirement that the lens view through the dome results in a typical light loss of 50%. A more covert camera/lens assembly takes the form of a camera, pinhole lens, and *small mirror.*

If the right angle lens of the sprinkler-head assembly shown in Figure 18-11 and 18-12 is removed, all that protrudes below the ceiling is a small mirror approximately

3/8 × 5/8 inches. This technique results in a very low profile that is difficult for an observer to detect at ground level. The pinhole/mirror system provides an alternative to some dome applications. The system can be fixed or have a 360° panning range.

Two advantages of the moving mirror system over the dome are: (1) no large protruding dome suspended below the ceiling and (2) easy installation. Installation is easy since only a small hole about 3/4 inch in diameter is required to insert the lens and mirror through the ceiling. The small mirror scanning system has limitations: (1) it cannot view the scene directly below its location and (2) there is no zooming. The dome system has two advantages over the scanning mirror: (1) the dome serves as a deterrent since the observer sees the dome and believes a camera is active in it but does not know at any instant where the camera is looking, and (2) the added capability of full-range zoom optics.

18.3.7   Fiber-Optic Lenses

When the barrier between the scene side and the camera/lens side is a few inches as in Figure 18-3, a pinhole or mini-lens and camera can be mounted directly behind the barrier. For difficult covert video surveillance applications in which small cameras and mini pinhole lenses will not work, coherent fiber-optic-bundle lenses may be the solution.

Fiber optics are used when it is necessary to view a scene on the other side of a thick barrier or inside a confined area. The fiber-optic bundle lens and camera are installed

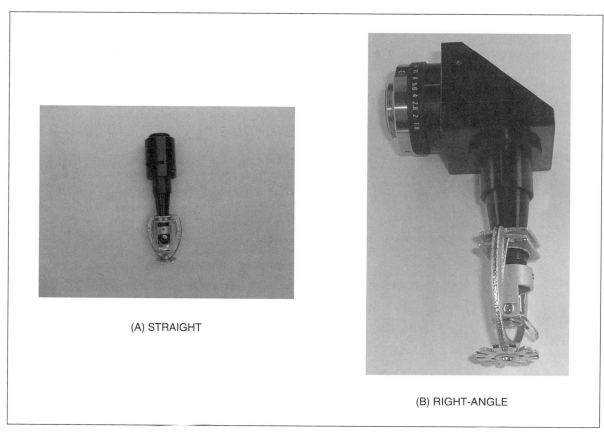

(A) STRAIGHT

(B) RIGHT-ANGLE

FIGURE 18-11   Sprinkler-head pinhole lenses

behind the barrier and the objective lens on the scene side. The lens viewing the scene can be a few inches or a few feet away from the camera. There are three optical techniques to transfer the image, in effect "lengthen" the camera's objective lens: (1) a rigid coherent fiber-optic conduit, (2) a borescope lens, and (3) a flexible fiber-optic bundle. These special lenses can extend the objective lens several inches to several feet in front of the camera sensor. The rigid fiber conduit uses a fused array of fibers and cannot be bent. The flexible fiber lens has hair-like fibers loosely contained in a protective sheath and can be flexed and bent easily. These fiber-optic lenses should not be confused with the single or multiple strands of fiber commonly used to transmit the time-modulated video signal a long distance from a camera to a remote monitoring site (Chapter 6). Coherent fiber-optic lenses typically have 200,000–300,000 individual fibers forming an image-transferring array. Rigid fiber-optic lenses are 1/4–1/2 inch in diameter and from 6 to 12 inches long. Flexible fiber-optic lenses are from 1/8 to 1¼ inch in diameter and up to several feet long. These fiber-optic lenses are available with manual or automatic iris for 1/6-, 1/4-, 1/3-, 1/2-, and 2/3-inch video formats.

By combining lenses with coherent fiber-optic bundles, a long, small-diameter optical lens is produced that requires a small hole for insertion into the barrier. A small aperture hole is drilled completely through at the barrier

surface and connected to the camera on the protected side (Figure 18-13).

This lens/camera system has provided the solution for many banking ATM and correctional-facility security problems. A minor disadvantage of all fiber-optic systems is that the picture obtained is not as "clean" as that obtained with an "all-lens" pinhole lens. These imperfections occur because several hundred thousand individual hair-like fibers make up the fiber-optic bundle some of which are not perfectly transmitting. For most surveillance applications the imperfections do not result in any significant loss of intelligence in the picture. Figure 18-14 shows complete rigid and flexible fiber-optic lenses.

18.3.7.1 Configuration

A fiber-optic lens consists of three parts: (1) an objective lens that focuses the scene onto the front end of the fiber-optic bundle, (2) a rigid conduit or flexible fiber coherent optic bundle that transfers the image a substantial distance (several inches to several feet), and (3) a relay lens at the output end of the fiber bundle that re-images the output image and focuses onto the camera sensor (Figure 18-15).

The objective lens can be like any of the FFL, zoom, pinhole, manual-, or automatic-iris lens. The objective lens

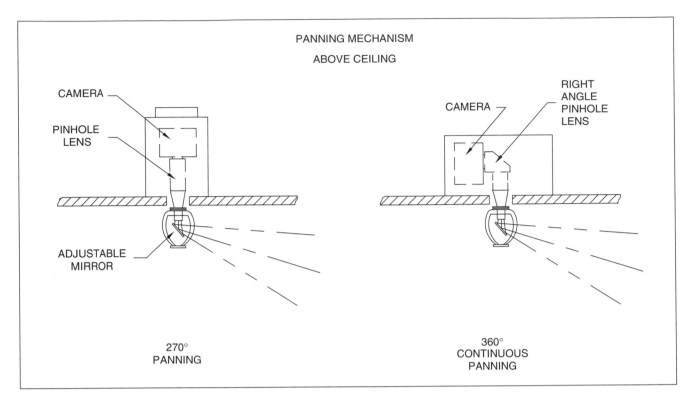

FIGURE 18-12   Panning sprinkler-head pinhole lens system

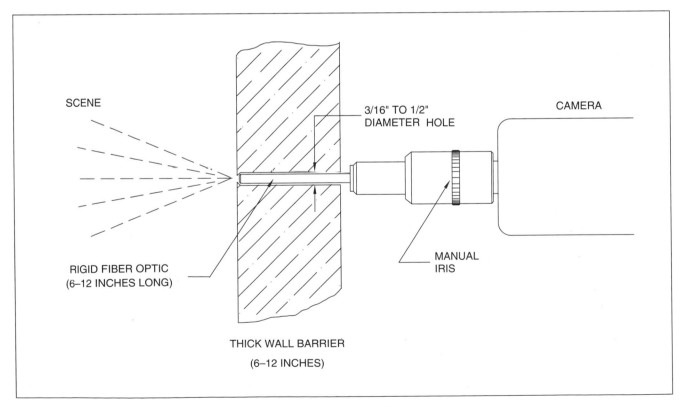

FIGURE 18-13   Fiber-optic pinhole lens installation in thick wall

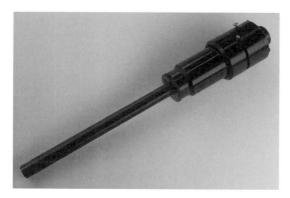

(A) RIGID CONDUIT LENS

OBJECTIVE LENS: 8 mm OR 11 mm FL
FIBER TYPE: RIGID CONDUIT
FIBER LENGTH: 6 inches
RELAY LENS: M = 1:1
IRIS: MANUAL
MOUNT: C OR CS

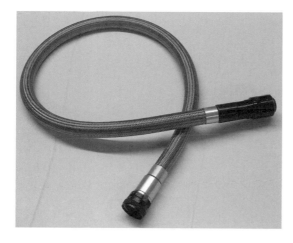

(B) FLEXIBLE BUNDLE LENS

OBJECTIVE LENS: ANY C OR CS MOUNT
FIBER TYPE: FLEXIBLE BUNDLE
FIBER LENGTH: 39 inches
RELAY LENS: M = 1:1
IRIS: MANUAL
MOUNT: C OR CS

FIGURE 18-14 Rigid and flexible fiber-optic lenses

must produce an image large enough to fill the full aperture (cross-sectional area) of the fiber-optic bundle. The coherent fiber-optic bundle consists of several hundred thousand closely packed glass fibers to coherently transfer an image from one end of the fiber to the other, several inches to several feet (Figure 18-16).

Fiber 1 transmits point 1 of the image from the objective lens down the fiber to a corresponding point 1 on the exit end of the fiber bundle. Likewise, all of the remaining points of the entrance image are transferred in an exact one-to-one correspondence to the exit end of the fiber bundle, thereby producing a *coherent* image. Coherent means that each point in the image on the front end of the fiber bundle corresponds to a specific point at the rear end of the fiber bundle.

18.3.7.2 Rigid Fiber Pinhole Lens

The rigid fiber-optic bundle has individual fibers that are fused together to form a rigid glass rod or conduit and is

usually protected from the environment and mechanical damage by a rigid metal tube (Figure 18-14). The fiber-optic bundle is approximately 0.4 inch in diameter for a 2/3-inch format sensor, 0.3 inch for a 1/2 inch, 0.2 inch for a 1/3 inch, and 0.15 inch for a 1/4 inch. For the 2/3 inch format, the outside diameter is about 0.5 inch. It should be noted that the image exiting the fiber-optic lens is *inverted* with respect to the image produced by a standard objective lens. This inversion is corrected by inverting the camera. The fiber-optic lens speed is between f/4 and f/8 depending on the fiber length—slow in comparison with the standard, all-lens type pinhole lens.

18.3.7.3 Flexible Fiber

When the most flexibility between the front objective lens and the camera is required, an alternative to the remote-head CCD camera is a coherent flexible fiber-optic bundle (Figure 18-14). The front of the flexible fiber-optic bundle has a C mount and accepts any pinhole, C, or CS

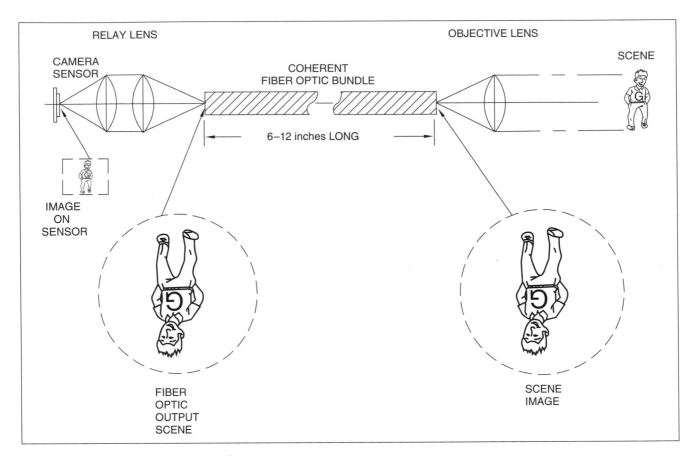

FIGURE 18-15   Fiber-optic lens configuration

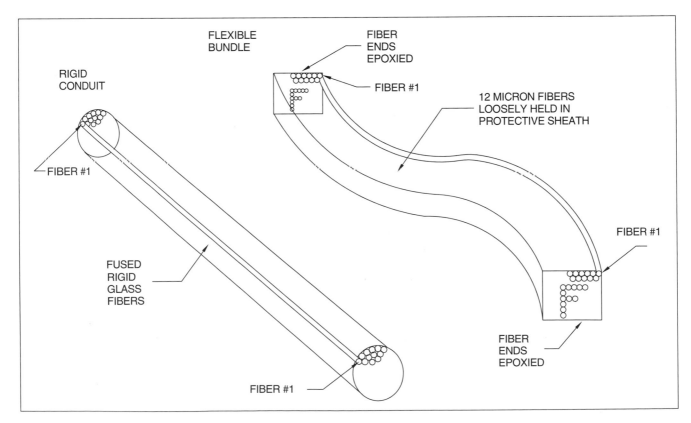

FIGURE 18-16   Fiber bundle construction

mount lens. The rear lens terminates in a male C mount, suitable for any C or CS mount camera. One advantage the fiber-optic lens has over a remote head camera is that there is no electrical connection from the front objective lens to the camera sensor, which may be important in some applications, for example environmental protection (from adverse weather, corrosive environment, or mechanical abuse). It can be twisted through 360° with no image degradation. It, too, has spots like the rigid fiber-optic. The flexible fiber-optic lens has a 180° "twist" built into it and therefore does not invert the picture. The flexible fiber-optic bundle individual fibers are fused together only at the ends, but are free to move in the length between the ends.

18.3.7.4 Image Quality

As shown in Figure 18-16, the fiber-optic bundle is assembled from several hundred thousand individual glass fiber-optic strands. Although high technology and careful assembly techniques are used throughout the fiber bundle manufacturing process to achieve maximum uniform optical transmission, there are small variations in transmission from one fiber to another and some broken fibers. The result is that in almost all fiber-optic systems, the picture obtained is not as "clean" as that obtained with an "all-lens" pinhole lens. There are some cosmetic imperfections that look like dust spots (actually non- or partially transmitting fibers), as well as a geometric pattern caused by packing the fibers during manufacture. These imperfections occur because there are several hundred thousand individual hair-like fibers comprising the fiber-optic bundle, and some of them are not transmitting perfectly. For many

applications these imperfections do not result in any loss of picture intelligence, making the lens system adequate for identification of people, actions, and other information. Some fiber-optic lenses have a resolution of 450–500 TV lines, similar to a high-quality 1/4-, 1/3-, and 1/2-inch camera system. Figure 18-17 shows two examples of images produced from a rigid and flexible fiber-optic lens.

The photographs were taken directly from a 9-inch monochrome monitor using a CCD solid-state camera with resolution of 570 horizontal TV lines. Figure 18-17a shows the typical resolution and image quality obtainable from a 1-meter, flexible fiber-optic lens: approximately 450 TV lines horizontal and 350 vertical. The spots are caused by partially transmitting or non-transmitting fibers. Figure 18-17b shows the same image obtained with an 8-inch rigid fiber-optic lens. The vignetting at the corners of the image was caused by the relay lens, not the fiber bundle. Note the spots and honeycomb pattern in the rigid fiber-optic monitor picture. The honeycomb is caused by the fiber-stacking procedure and consequent heat fusing of the rigid bundle.

18.3.8 Bore-Scope Lenses

The bore-scope lens viewing system is a long thin tube housing with multiple relay lenses used to view inside objects (such as safes) or through barriers. Bore-scope sizes range from 12 to 30 inches long, and from 1/8 to 3/8 inch in diameter (Figure 18-18).

Special mini-bore-scopes are available with 1–2 mm outside diameters, 2–6 inches long. Bore-scopes are constructed from stainless-steel tubing and contain an

(A) FIBER: FLEXIBLE: 39 inches LONG
OBJECTIVE LENS: 25 mm FL, F/1.4
RELAY LENS: M = 1:1
OVERALL F/#: 4.0

(B) FIBER: RIGID: 6 inches LONG
OBJECTIVE LENS: 8 mm FL, F/1.6
RELAY LENS: M = 1:1
OVERALL F/#: 6.0

FIGURE 18-17   Resolution and image quality from fiber-optic lenses

**FIGURE 18-18 Boroscope lens
viewing system**

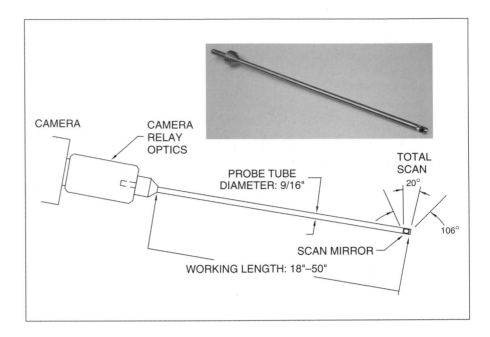

"all-lens" optical system. The long lengths and all-lens design mandate that such lenses have very high f-numbers: they are optically slow. Typical designs have an f-number between f/15 and f/40. By comparison, an f/5 lens transmits 16 times more light than an f/20 lens. The bore-scope must be used with high levels of lighting or an LLL camera (Chapter 19).

18.4 SPECIAL COVERT CAMERAS

18.4.1 PC-Board Cameras

The miniaturization of 1/6-, 1/4-, 1/3-, and 1/2-inch CCD and complimentary metal oxide semiconductor (CMOS) sensors and camera electronics has generated a new family of small single and dual printed-circuit (PC) board surveillance cameras. Three PC-board and housed flat cameras are shown in Figure 18-19.

Figure 18-19a shows a color camera with a CS mount and automatic-iris option. Figure 18-19b shows a 1/3-inch format PC-board CCD camera with an 8 mm FL mini-lens and six IR LEDs for night-time illumination. Other interchangeable lenses—3.8, 5.5, and 11 mm FL—are available. Figure 18-19c shows a compact flat camera sealed in a metal/epoxy case with pin terminals at the rear. The 1/3-inch format camera has 380-TV-line resolution and 0.2-fc sensitivity. All cameras are powered by 12 volts DC.

18.4.2 Remote-Head Cameras

The small size of mini-lenses and CCD and CMOS camera sensors permits the construction of extremely small covert lens-sensor heads by *remoting* the lens and sensor from the camera electronics via a small electrical cable. The cable link between the camera head and the camera electronics can vary from a few inches to 100 feet. Figure 18-20a shows a monochrome 1/3-inch format CCD remote-head camera with an 11-mm FL, f/1.8 lens, and an 18-inch cable connecting the sensor-lens with the camera electronics.

The camera has a resolution of 450 TV lines and a light sensitivity of 0.1 fc. Figure 18-20b shows a small color CCD remote-head camera with a 7.5 mm FL, f/1.6 lens on a 1/2-inch format sensor. The lens-sensor head is 0.69 inch in diameter × 2.25 inches long and weighs only 0.64 ounce. The camera has a resolution of 460 TV lines and a sensitivity of 1.0 fc.

18.5 INFRARED COVERT LIGHTING

Video surveillance augmented with invisible IR covert lighting can significantly increase the usefulness of covert installations. Since the covert camera is intended to be hidden from its target, if the covert video system can operate in near or total darkness the person under surveillance will not be aware that he is under observation. By augmenting the camera system with an IR light, invisible to the human eye but not to the camera, the resulting video image can be as good as that obtained under normal visible daylight conditions. CCD, CMOS, and other LLL cameras are sensitive to this IR radiation and can "see" with this IR lighting. The amount of IR radiation the camera responds to and the resulting quality of the picture depends on the type of IR lamp or LED used, its power level and beam angle (Chapter 3), and the sensitivity of the camera to the IR radiation. This last factor depends on whether an IR cut

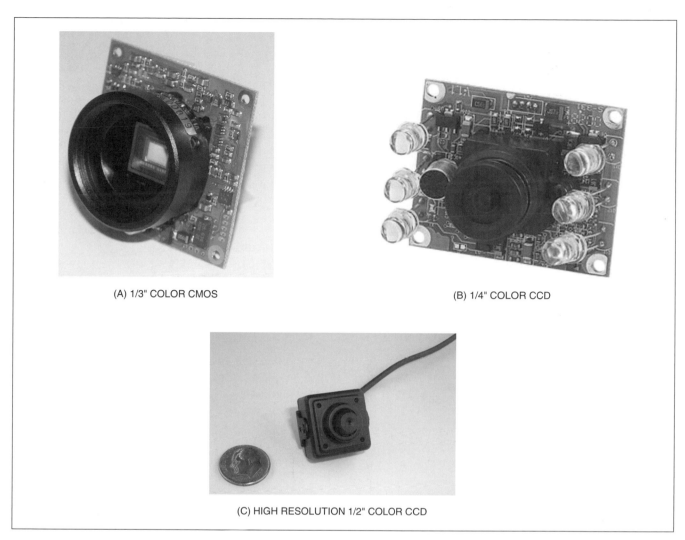

(A) 1/3" COLOR CMOS

(B) 1/4" COLOR CCD

(C) HIGH RESOLUTION 1/2" COLOR CCD

FIGURE 18-19 Flat printed circuit PC-board cameras

filter is in place in the camera and on the CCD sensitivity to the IR energy.

18.5.1 Concealment Means

Light sources that emit both visible and IR light (tungsten, tungsten-halogen, xenon lamps, and others) can be optically filtered so that only the IR radiation leaves the source and irradiates the scene. High-efficiency, low-power LED semiconductors produce sufficient IR energy to illuminate an area suitable for covert operation while being invisible to the eye. Figure 18-22 illustrates the principle and several techniques of producing IR illumination.

The thermal lamp or LED source emits IR radiation that reflects off the scene and off objects in it. The lens and camera collect the reflected IR energy to produce a video image signal. The IR-emitting source is often concealed by installing it behind an opaque (tinted) plastic or one-way (partially aluminized) window. Another technique is to use a spectral beam-splitting window that transmits the invisible IR radiation and blocks the visible radiation. Another technique is to conceal the IR-emitting source just as the pinhole lens is concealed, by locating the source at the focal plane of a pinhole lens and directing the energy at the same target the pinhole lens is viewing. Usually the beam from the pinhole lens IR source is made slightly larger than the FOV of the pinhole lens–camera combination. Alignment is necessary between the camera and IR source since the IR beam must illuminate the same scene the pinhole lens is looking at. When the application is to perform covert surveillance at short distances and in small rooms (10–15 feet), a wide-area IR illuminator is used since the alignment is not critical.

18.5.2 IR Sources

There are numerous commercially available thermal lamp and LED IR sources for covert surveillance applications. They vary from short-range, low-power, wide-angle beams to long-range, high-power, narrow-angle beam

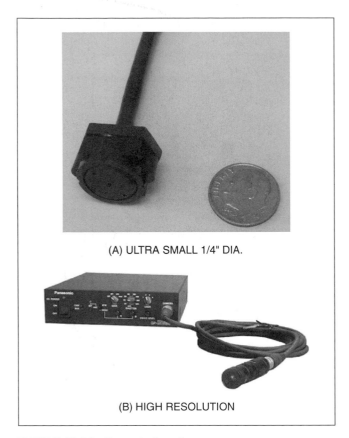

(A) ULTRA SMALL 1/4" DIA.

(B) HIGH RESOLUTION

FIGURE 18-20   Remote head cameras

types. Figure 18-23 illustrates two IR LED and thermal IR source illuminators.

A single IR LED emits enough IR energy to produce a useful picture at ranges up to a few feet with a CCD camera. By stacking many (10 to several 100) LEDs in an array, higher IR power is directed toward the scene, and a larger area at distances up to 50–100 feet may be viewed (Figure 18-23a). Filtered thermal lamp IR sources with power levels up to several hundred watts can illuminate large areas at distances up to several hundred feet (Figure 18-23b). These are usually used in outdoor applications where longer ranges are required and personnel cannot come into close proximity to them. Since the radiation source is not visible to the human eye personnel should not come in close proximity to them.

18.6   LOW-LIGHT-LEVEL CAMERAS

The camera parameter most critical to the successful viewing of a scene under low light level (LLL) conditions with a covert system is the camera sensor sensitivity. Most monochrome CCD cameras have sensitivities of approximately 0.2–1 fc (0.1 lux), which does not result in satisfactory CCTV picture quality under dawn, dusk, nighttime, or poorly lighted indoor conditions. A few special CCD cameras produce sensitivity of 0.003 fc (0.0003 lux) which

substantially increases its usefulness at low light levels. It also boasts a resolution of 570 TV lines.

When CCD camera sensitivity is not sufficient and additional lighting cannot be added, a LLL camera such as an intensified CCD (ICCD) or intensified SIT (ISIT) must be used (Chapter 19). These light-intensified cameras operate at significantly lower light levels than the solid-state cameras. The newer ICCD camera has a sensitivity matching that of the prior generation SIT camera. All this increased sensitivity comes at a cost. Any intensified camera is expensive and should be considered only for critical security applications.

18.7   IMBEDED COVERT CAMERA CONFIGURATIONS

Video cameras and lenses are concealed in many different objects and locations including overhead track lighting fixtures, emergency lighting fixtures, exit signs, tabletop radios, table lamps, wall or desk clocks, shoulder bags, and attaché cases (Figure 18-21).

Figure 18-21a shows a popular emergency light that was modified to house a camera and mini-lens system with the camera viewing from behind the front bezel. The emergency lighting fixture operates normally, can be tested for operation periodically, and its operation is in no way affected by the installation of the camera. The housing has an angled extension that points the housing downward by about 15° so that the lens points downward and optimally views the area. Alternatively an off-axis mini-lens could be used instead of the on-axis mini-lens to make the camera look downward. The lens views through the smoked (tinted) plastic front window and cannot be seen by an observer even at close range.

The exit light fixture is another convenient housing for camouflaging a covert camera system (Figure 18-21b). A wide-angle mini-lens on a small PC-board camera is all that is required for this covert camera installation.

A wall-mounted clock is an ideal location for camouflaging a covert camera/lens combination (Figure 18-21c). The lens views out through one of the black numerals. In this case, the flat camera (approximately 7/8 inch deep) and mini-lens are mounted directly behind the numeral 11 on the clock. The camera uses offset optics (Figure 18-8) so that the camera views downward at approximately a 15° angle even though the clock and camera are mounted vertically on the wall.

Figure 18-23d shows a no smoking sign into which a camera and lens have been installed. The camera views through an imperceptible hole in the sign. Figure 18-24 shows a ceiling-mounted sprinkler-head camera. An option to any of these covert cameras is a wireless RF or microwave transmitter. These covert camera systems can also be designed using a digital IP wireless camera and viewed using an Internet browser. The items into which

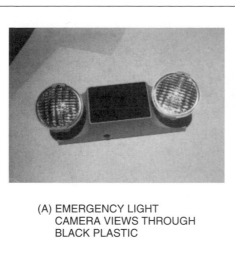

(A) EMERGENCY LIGHT
    CAMERA VIEWS THROUGH
    BLACK PLASTIC

(B) CLOCK
    CAMERA VIEWS THROUGH
    HOLE AT NUMERAL "11"

(C) EXIT SIGN
    CAMERA VIEWS THROUGH
    HOLE IN EITHER ARROW

(D) NO SMOKING SIGN
    B&W CAMERA VIEW THROUGH
    BLACK OPAQUE PLASTIC

FIGURE 18-21   Covert cameras installed in office building fixtures

covert cameras can be installed are limited only by the imagination of the user.

18.8 WIRELESS TRANSMISSION

The video signal from the covert camera is sent to the monitor, VCR, DVR, or over the Internet via RG59/U 75-ohm coaxial cable, UTP, LAN, WAN, or wireless LAN (WiFi). If a dedicated telephone-grade line (two-wire) is available, the UTP using a special line driver and receiver pair provide good transmission of a real-time video signal over several thousand feet of continuous telephone wire (Chapter 6). For digital video transmission CAT-5e cable is used.

Covert video applications often require that the camera/lens system be installed and removed quickly, or that it remain installed on location for only short periods of time. This may mean that a wired transmission link (such as coaxial cable or fiber-optic) cannot be installed and a wireless transmission link from camera to monitor or recorder is required. This takes the form of a low power radio frequency (RF) or microwave video transmitter mounted near the video camera. A description of these transmitters is given in Chapter 6, but those specifically applicable to covert applications are summarized here. The RF transmitters are less than 100 milliwatts output and transmit the video images over ranges from 100 to 2000 feet. In the United States, the FCC restricts the use of the higher-power transmitters to federal or government agencies and allows only low-power units for commercial or industrial use.

Figure 18-25a shows a low power RF, 100-mw transmitter and receiver operating at 920 MHz that can transmit an excellent monochrome or color video picture over a distance of a few hundred feet.

Figure 18-25b shows a 2.4 GHz microwave transmitter that transmits excellent monochrome and color images over distances up to a few hundred feet indoors and 2000 feet outdoors. Using a directional (Yaggi) receiver antenna can increase the range further. While RF and

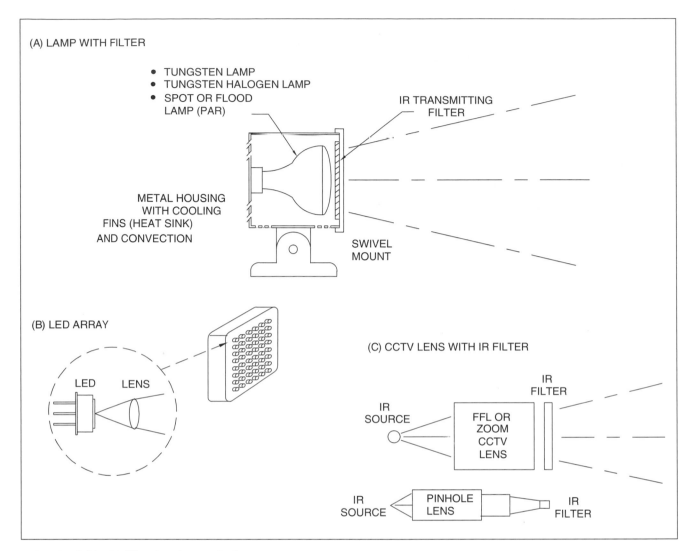

FIGURE 18-22   IR illumination technique

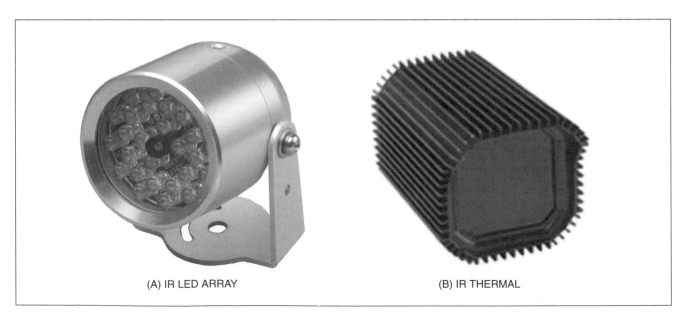

FIGURE 18-23   IR source illuminators: IR LED array, IR thermal lamp

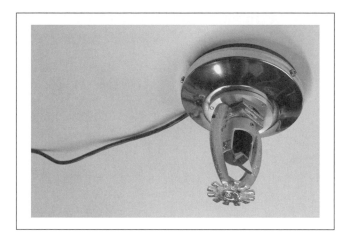

FIGURE 18-24   Sprinkler-head covert camera

microwave transmitters can be used indoors, recognize that these frequencies cannot pass through metal objects and therefore the systems should be tested on site, through a steel building or near other metallic or reinforced concrete structures before an installation is made. While the transmitter may have suitable range under outdoor, unobstructed conditions, when used indoors or between two points with obstructions, the only way to determine the useful range of the link is to put the system into operation. The deleterious effects most readily observed are: (1) reduction in range, (2) ghost images (multiple images produced by reflections of the signal from metallic objects), and (3) unsynchronized pictures (picture breaks up). Repositioning the transmitter or receiver equipment often substantially improves or eliminates such problems. Most microwave systems have a more directional transmitting pattern than RF transmitters. This means the antenna directs the energy toward the receiver, and therefore alignment between transmitter and receiver is more critical. Most microwave installations are line of sight but the microwave energy can be reflected off objects in the path between the transmitter and the receiver to direct the energy to the receiver, at a sacrifice in range. The higher frequency of operation and directionality make microwave installation and alignment more critical than the RF transmitters (Chapter 6).

Commercial microwave transmission systems operate in the 2.4 and 5.8 GHz frequency range and do not require FCC licensing and approval. Other frequencies can only be used by government agencies and some commercial customers if they apply to the FCC for a license. One condition in obtaining approval is to have a frequency search performed to ensure that the system causes no interference to existing equipment in the area.

Another line-of-sight system requiring no FCC approval is a wireless gallium arsenide (GaAs) IR optical transmission system. This light-wave system requires no cable connection between the transmitter and the receiver and achieves ranges of hundreds to several thousands

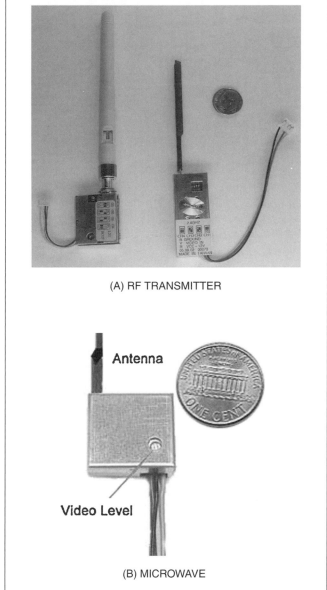

(A) RF TRANSMITTER

FIGURE 18-25 RF and microwave transmitters for covert video transmission

of feet (Chapter 6). Its major limitation is the severe reduction in range under fog or heavy precipitation conditions.

18.9   COVERT CHECKLIST

- Optical speed or f-number is probably the most important reason for choosing one pinhole lens over another. The lower the f-number the better. An f/2 lens transmits four times more light than an f/4. This can mean the difference between using a standard CCD or CMOS camera and using a LLL ICCD.

- Most pinhole lenses have a FL between 3.8 mm and 22 mm and are designed for 1/4- and 1/3-inch format cameras. Tables 18-1, 18-3, 18-4, and 18-5 show the FOVs obtained with these lenses. For example, using these tables or the Lens Finder Kit (Chapter 4), the FOV seen with the 11 mm lens on a 1/3-inch camera format at a distance of 15 feet is an area 6 feet wide by 4.5 feet high displayed on the monitor. Note that the FOV is independent of the hole size through which the lens views, providing a hole produces no tunneling. When viewing through a wall with a wide-angle pinhole lens or mini-lens (3.8, 5.5, or 8 mm), the lens may require a cone-shaped hole or an array of small holes to prevent tunneling (vignetting) of the scene image.
- A short FL lens (3.8 mm) has a wide FOV and low magnification. A long FL lens (25 mm) has a narrow FOV and has high magnification.
- Medium FL lenses produce FOVs wide enough to see much of the action and still have enough resolution to identify the persons or actions in the scene. A short FL lens sees a wide FOV and objects are not well resolved. Long FL lenses see a narrow FOV with objects well resolved (clear).
- Under most conditions, the small-barrel, slow-taper pinhole lens is easier to install and is the preferred type over the wide-barrel, fast-taper shape. The user must weigh the pros and cons of both types.
- The use of a straight or right-angle pinhole lens depends on the space available behind the barrier for mounting the lens and camera, and on the pointing direction of the lens.
- The fastest pinhole video system is a mini-lens coupled to the camera. This is the best choice where the lowest cost and highest light efficiency are desired.
- A manual-iris lens is sufficient in applications where there are no large variations in light level, or where the light level can be controlled. Depending on the camera used, where there is more than a 50:1 change in light level, an automatic-iris pinhole lens or an electronically shuttered camera is needed.
- Most applications are solved using an "all-lens" system. In special cases where a thick barrier exists between a surface and the camera location, a rigid coherent fiber-optic bundle lens or bore-scope is used. If sufficient light is available, an "all-lens" bore-scope type should be used to obtain the cleanest picture. Another alternative is a remote-head camera.
- AC power is preferred for permanent covert camera installations. Either 117 VAC to 12 VDC or 24 VAC wall-mounted converters are used. Using 12 VDC or 24 VAC is preferred over 117 VAC since it eliminates any fire or shock hazard and can be installed by security personnel without outside help. Since most small cameras operate from 12 VDC, a 117 VAC to 12 VDC converter is most popular. For temporary installations, 12 VDC battery operation is used, with rechargeable or non-rechargeable batteries, depending on the application (Chapter 23).

18.10 SUMMARY

Pinhole lenses are used for surveillance problems that cannot be solved adequately using standard FFL or zoom lenses. The fast f-numbers of some of these pinhole lenses make it possible to provide covert surveillance under normal or dimly lighted conditions. The small size of the front lens and barrel permit them to be covertly installed for surveillance applications.

A large variety of mini-lenses and pinhole lenses are available for use in covert security applications. These lenses have FL ranges from 3.8 to 22 mm covering FOVs from 12° to 95°. Variations, including manual- and automatic-iris, standard pinhole, mini- and off-axis-mini, provide the user with a large selection.

Equipment is available to provide covert surveillance under lighted or unlighted conditions. Through the use of IR illumination, scenes can be viewed in total darkness. Compact lenses, small and low-power cameras, wireless RF, microwave, and IR transmission systems make the covert system portable.

The availability of digital IP cameras has now made remote covert video surveillance a reality. The images from these cameras can be viewed using an Internet browser from any Internet access location by anyone having the camera IP address.

Chapter 19

Low-Light-Level Cameras, Thermal Infrared Imagers

CONTENTS

19.1   Overview
19.2   History and Background
19.3   Image-Intensifying Mechanism
19.4   Active vs. Passive
    19.4.1   Active Image Converter
    19.4.2   Passive Image Intensifier
19.5   GEN 1 Image Intensifier
19.6   GEN 2 Micro-Channel Plate Image Intensifier
    19.6.1   Sensitivity
    19.6.2   Resolution
    19.6.3   Light Overload
    19.6.4   Gating MCP Image Intensifier
19.7   GEN 3 Image Intensifier
19.8   Intensified CCD Camera
    19.8.1   GEN 1 Coupled to CCD Camera
    19.8.2   GEN 2 Coupled to CCD Camera
    19.8.3   Comparison of Intensifier Sensitivities
19.9   SIT and Intensified SIT Cameras
    19.9.1   Sensitivity/Gain Mechanism
    19.9.2   Resolution and Image Lag
    19.9.3   Light-Level Overload
19.10 Multi-Sensor Cameras—Image Fusion
    19.10.1 Multi-Sensor
    19.10.2 Sensor Fusion
19.11 Thermal-IR Cameras
    19.11.1 Background
    19.11.2 Micro-Bolometer
    19.11.3 Infrared Optics
19.12 Low-Light-Level Optics
    19.12.1 Comparison of Eye and LLL Camera Optics
    19.12.2 Low Light Level Objective Lenses
19.13 Target Detection and Recognition Parameters
19.14 Summary

19.1 OVERVIEW

Many security surveillance applications require LLL cameras or thermal IR cameras to observe dimly lighted parking lots, warehouses, shopping malls, streets, back alleys, etc. Often the high cost of installing additional lighting to permit use of conventional CCD or CMOS cameras would easily justify the extra cost of LLL cameras. Other applications requiring LLL or IR cameras include areas where it is impossible to install lighting because it is out of the control of the security force. Examples include: (1) looking through darkened windows, (2) reading license plates or identifying vehicles in a darkened building or parking lot, and (3) viewing facial characteristics or witnessing an action in a dark area. In these applications, it is difficult to obtain a satisfactory video image using the highest sensitivity CCD camera; however, it is easily accomplished using an image-intensified camera or thermal imaging system.

In a LLL camera the image viewed by the video image tube or solid-state sensor has been "intensified" or amplified before it reaches the sensor. In contrast to the CCD or CMOS camera, which does not use any image-intensifying mechanism, the image intensifier technique does not add additional illumination to the scene but *amplifies* the reflected scene illumination. After the light image has been amplified, it is processed in the normal way and transmitted to the monitor. The three primary parameters determining the performance of LLL cameras are: (1) the specific spectral content of the light, (2) the level of the scene illumination reaching the intensifier tube faceplate, and (3) the specific type of intensifier camera used.

The thermal IR imager is a camera that makes use of the differences in the thermal heat emitted by warm objects to produce a "visual" image. As the name implies, the IR imager operates in the IR spectrum that is invisible to the human eye but has the ability to detect and image warm objects (human, animal, heated vehicles, etc.) which visible color or monochrome CCD cameras or image-intensified CCD (ICCD) cameras cannot detect.

The thermal IR camera is a night vision device that uses the difference in *temperature* of scene objects with respect to the background to produce a scene-image. These passive devices require no light whatsoever and produce an image based solely on the *thermal temperature difference* of the objects in the scene. Unlike the image intensifier, the thermal viewers can "see" in total darkness by detecting and displaying small temperature differences between objects and their backgrounds. Many objects such as the human body, an automobile, and a motor emit considerable thermal radiation (heat) in the IR wavelength region that easily propagates through the atmosphere in the 3–5-micron and 8–12-micron electromagnetic spectrum. Even objects of relatively low temperature (70°F) are "hot" enough with respect to a background of say 50°F to be detected by these sensitive IR devices. The lower resolution and very high cost of these devices have limited their use to military and other scientific applications. The thermal video viewer uses an IR-transmitting germanium lens to collect and focus far-IR thermal images onto a special thermal detector array or thermal (pyroelectric) television tube.

The name "night vision" is sometimes used to describe LLL cameras and indicates a device that sees in total darkness. By definition, however, it is impossible to see in total darkness with a non-thermal imaging system if the meaning of *seeing* is some sort of information transfer by means of light. Image-intensifying cameras are devices that can extend the threshold of seeing far below normal human limits. Most LLL and the IR cameras described in this chapter are *passive* cameras in that they do not emit any IR or other radiation, and therefore only respond to residual visible and near-IR lighting from such faint objects as stars, moonlight (reflected sunlight), or other artificial lighting. By definition, an image intensifier is any device that *amplifies* and produces an output image that is brighter than its input image. These devices are generically different from video in that all of the points in the image are operated upon simultaneously, rather than sequentially as in CCD video scanning systems that move across the image point by point. The image intensifier operates on all the points in the image *simultaneously* as does the human eye or photographic film. The ICCD and thermal IR cameras help us see at lower illumination levels than conventional cameras.

19.2 HISTORY AND BACKGROUND

Interest in the development of image-intensifier tubes began shortly after the formalization of electron optics in the 1920s. Researchers worked toward improving the sensitivity of television camera tubes and converting IR radiation into visible light in the sensor. Both activities met with some success, resulting in two types of devices: (1) single-stage image intensifiers having a gain of approximately 50 and (2) IR-to-visible-image converters using active IR sources to come illuminate the scene. Following the development of the single-stage devices, various multiple-stage (two- and three-stage) intensifiers were developed, resulting in what is generally referred to as GEN 1 image intensifiers. After early coupling problems associated with two- and three-stage intensifiers were solved by using high-resolution fiber-optic coupling plates, thousands of three-stage image intensifiers were fabricated and used in military applications. These military three-stage intensifiers had gains of approximately 35,000 and a limiting resolution of approximately 30 line pairs per millimeter, or approximately 360-TV-line resolution on a 1-inch (25 mm) tube—considered only fair resolution by normal video standards.

During the 1940s, the need for military LLL imaging devices accelerated the development of compact portable image-intensifying equipment. The silicon-intensified target (SIT) and intensified SIT (ISIT) camera systems were already developed. They had excellent LLL capabilities but they were not rugged or portable and could not be used for military applications. Several generations of image intensifiers have evolved since this period, beginning with generation zero (GEN 0) to present-day generation three (GEN 3). The GEN 0 device uses an IR light source to illuminate the scene. The reflected IR energy is detected by an IR-to-visible light converter tube and the visible scene is relayed to a video camera, thereby producing "night vision." This active system has the disadvantage of being detectable by an adversary with a simple IR viewer. The present state of the art is the GEN 3 micro-channel plate (MCP) image intensifiers. The GEN 3 intensifier has three times the sensitivity of the tube version GEN 2, better resolution, and nearly four times the tube life. This chapter briefly describes GEN 0, GEN 1, and GEN 2, and covers in more detail the more current GEN 2 Plus and GEN 3 devices. The GEN 2 was improved through the use of a GaAs photocathode and was called a GEN 3 intensifier. The combination of an image intensifier with the monochrome CCD camera results in a state-of-the-art LLL camera.

The human eye and many artificial devices such as video cameras and night vision devices operate in different wavelength regions within the visible and IR spectral range called the spectrum of electromagnetic radiation (Figure 19-1).

The human eye and LLL and thermal IR cameras are sensitive to specific wavelength bands within this spectrum. Each is sensitive to only a particular portion of the spectrum. Specifically, the human eye is sensitive to visible light, the spectral band of wavelengths from violet to deep red, covering the wavelength range from 0.4 to 0.7 microns or 400 to 700 nanometers (nm). The image intensifier

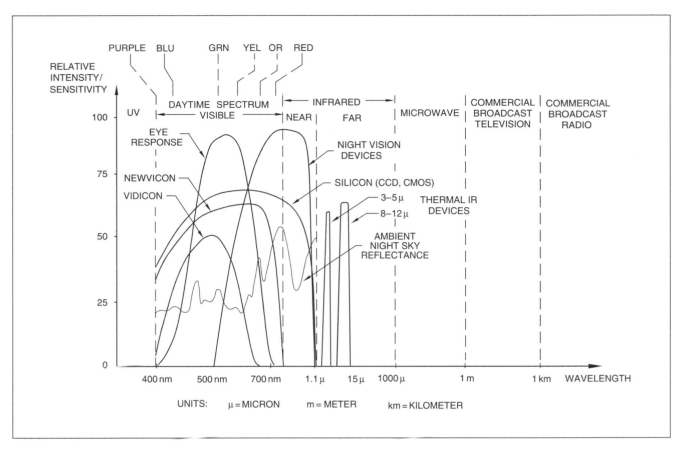

FIGURE 19-1 Optical electromagnetic spectrum

is sensitive to visible spectrum, from 400 to 700 nm and the near-IR range from approximately 700 to 1100 nm, and has a sensitivity below the light threshold level of the human eye. These devices convert the electromagnetic energy into electrical energy that is amplified and converted into visible light via the device's output phosphor screen. This visible light image is then relayed to a camera sensor and processed as in a normal camera.

Thermal IR cameras have been available for use in military and industrial applications for many years but have been too expensive to use in security applications. These first-generation IR cameras used *cooled* detector technology requiring very expensive and difficult-to-operate cryogenic coolers. The newer generation IR cameras developed in the late 1990s use *room temperature* sensors that are orders of magnitude less expensive than their predecessors and put them into a price range acceptable for security applications.

19.3 IMAGE-INTENSIFYING MECHANISM

Image-intensifier tubes extend human visibility beyond that of the unaided eye by using: (1) a photocathode (sensor) that has a higher quantum efficiency than the eye,

(2) a photocathode with a broader spectral response than the human eye, and (3) an objective lens that is larger and can gather more light than the human eye.

Ambient light from sky illumination or residual ground-level illumination is reflected from the scene, collected by the objective lens, transmitted through the fiber-optic faceplate, and focused onto a light-sensitive photocathode. The image-intensifier tube electronically and optically amplifies an image of the scene being viewed and displays it directly on a luminescent (phosphor) screen (Figure 19-2).

The image of the scene produced by the objective lens is focused onto the input faceplate of the intensifier. The basic intensifier consists of a photocathode faceplate, an electron amplifier lens, and an output phosphor screen upon which the final visual image is displayed. Image intensification occurs when the electrons emitted by the photocathode strike the phosphor screen after being accelerated by a high voltage and produce a visual image on the phosphor screen. Each photon from each point in the scene is amplified by the intensifier and produces tens to thousands of photons at the cathode screen. By this method the image is greatly intensified. Luminance gain in single-stage GEN 1 image tube can be on the order of 50–100. By coupling several image tubes, gains

**FIGURE 19-2
Image intensifier
components**

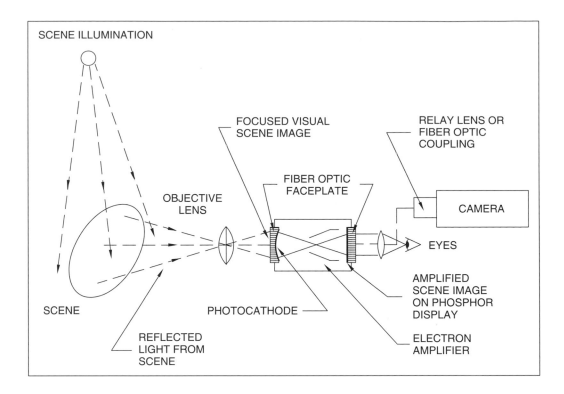

of 100,000–200,000 are achieved. The image intensifier is coupled to a video camera forming a LLL video system. Several different tube types are used and are categorized by the type of electron-optical focusing mechanism used.

19.4 ACTIVE VS. PASSIVE

There are two types of night viewing systems: (1) passive systems that operate by intensifying available light and (2) active systems that require an IR light source to provide illumination. In the GEN 0 active system the ability to see down to light levels below which a standard CCD camera can see is accomplished by illuminating the scene with an artificial IR source. This IR source takes the form of a filtered visible source, an IR LED, or laser diode (LD).

19.4.1 Active Image Converter

To view scenes at practical distances, GEN 0 image converters use an active system that requires the scene to be artificially illuminated by IR radiation to obtain a usable image. The IR light source is either: (1) a thermal lamp with an optical filter that transmits the near-IR light from the light source but blocks or absorbs the visibly emitted light or (2) a semiconductor GaAs IR LED or LD. Since near-IR radiation is easily detected by using IR viewers this technique is not applicable for many security applications. The military and industrial applications for GEN 0 devices represent only a small part of the night vision equipment used. Figure 19-3 shows an active IR source illuminating

the scene to be observed and the LLL device detecting the reflected IR light from the scene.

The lens focuses the IR scene image onto the GEN 0 night vision device converter tube. GEN 0 tubes use a photocathode with an S-1 spectral response to convert IR to visible radiation. In this simple near-IR viewing system, invisible near-IR light reflected from the scene is focused onto a photo-emissive surface (photocathode) sensitive to the 700–1200 nm near-IR radiation. This near-IR energy striking the photocathode surface causes electrons to be emitted from it, which are accelerated by a high voltage until they strike a phosphor screen at the opposite end of the tube, forming an image similar to the display of a miniature television picture tube. An eyepiece fitted with a lens allows this image to be viewed, or a relay lens coupling this phosphor screen to a camera allows viewing the scene on a remote monitor.

19.4.2 Passive Image Intensifier

Passive image intensifiers amplify visible and near-IR radiation and are "passive" in that they operate with available light and require no additional illumination, enabling clear vision in conditions of nearly total darkness. The objective lens collects available light, however faint, and focuses it onto the GEN 1 photocathode sensor that converts the light into electrical energy and directs it toward the phosphor screen at the output end of the tube (Figure 19-4).

In two- or three-stage GEN 1 intensifiers, each stage is coupled to the next via a short fiber-optic faceplate. The

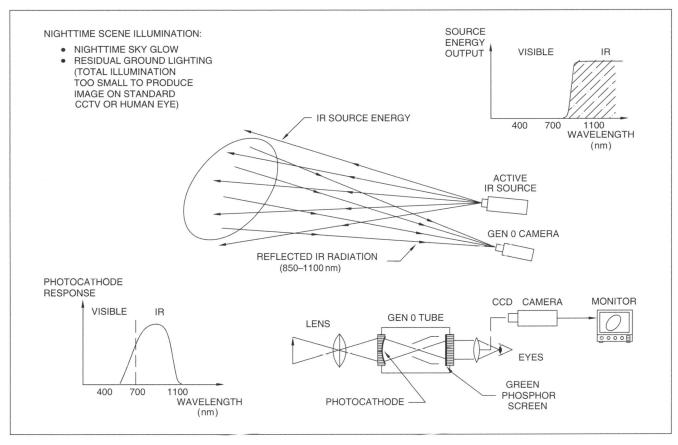

FIGURE 19-3   Active GEN 0 image converter

final, greatly intensified image is formed on the phosphor output screen and viewed through an eyepiece or coupled to a video camera for viewing on a monitor.

19.5   GEN 1 IMAGE INTENSIFIER

The GEN 1 passive intensifier originally developed for military night vision was coupled to an objective lens at the front end and an eyepiece at the rear end. The image intensifier tubes had an S-1 or S-20 spectral response (Figure 19-8) or some other variation of the multi-alkali photocathode. In order to increase amplification (gain), the logical development was to cascade single-stage GEN 1 tubes to form two- and three-stage devices. The result was the GEN 1 system with three stages and a gain of about 30,000. Figure 19-5 shows the internal diagram of a single- and a three-stage GEN 1 image-intensifier tube system.

The GEN 1 intensification system operates by focusing the faint visible and near-IR scene image collected by the objective lens onto the front surface of the first-stage fiber-optic plate. The thin coherent fiber-optic faceplate transfers the scene image onto the light-sensitive photocathode. In the single-stage GEN 1 intensifier the light energy is converted to electrons in the photocathode and

accelerated to a phosphor screen suitable for viewing by the human eye, or coupled to a solid-state monochrome CCD sensor and displayed on a monitor.

The three-stage GEN 1 image intensifier is assembled from *three* single-stage intensifier tubes, fiber-optically coupled into one assembly. Electrons emitted from the input photocathode are accelerated and focused onto the first-stage phosphor screen as in the single-stage tube. These electrons are absorbed by the phosphor and their energy is radiated into a visible (green) image via the phosphor screen. This image is then transmitted via the input fiber optics on the second stage and the process repeated again. Light gains (amplification) of up to 100,000 have been achieved in these three-stage systems; however, a gain of 35,000–40,000 is typical. Expected single-stage gain of $50 \times 50 \times 50 = 125,000$ is not achieved, due to coupling losses. One such loss occurs because the light available for the first and second stages is only green light from the phosphor, which constitutes a narrower spectral range of energy than the broadband scene illumination. Moreover, distortion is multiplied because of the three stages, and resolution reduced from about 50 line pairs per millimeter for a single stage to about 30 line pairs per millimeter for the three stages. Three-stage GEN 1 systems proved to

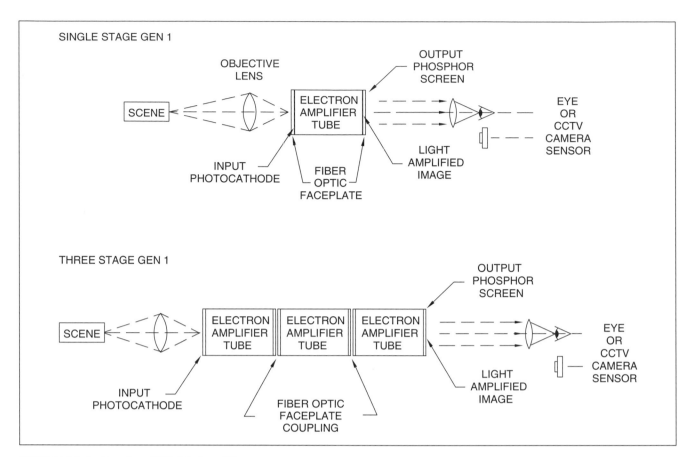

FIGURE 19-4   Passive GEN 1 intensifiers

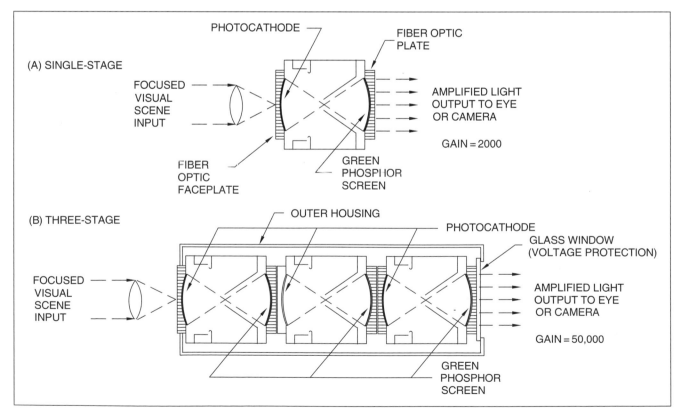

FIGURE 19-5   Diagram of single- and three-stage GEN 1 intensifiers

be useful devices and thousands were manufactured and used by the armed forces and law-enforcement agencies.

The GEN 1 photocathode is sensitive to the 400–850 nm electromagnetic band covering the visible and the near-IR spectrum. Since these tubes can respond to very near-IR radiation, they are able to detect whether someone is using a near-IR illuminator or active LLL system somewhere in the scene they are viewing, while at the same time remaining undetected themselves.

19.6 GEN 2 MICRO-CHANNEL PLATE IMAGE INTENSIFIER

Perhaps the most significant innovation in image intensifiers was made with the invention of the MCP intensifier, originally developed by Bendix Corporation as a single-stage channel multiplier in the 1950s. The GEN 2 MCP image intensifier replaced the GEN 1 electron tube multiplier (Figure 19-6).

The GEN 2 MCP intensifier uses secondary emission of photoelectrons as the gain mechanism and produces electron gains of many tens of thousands, depending on the voltage across the plate. The electrons leaving the MCP are proximity-focused onto the phosphor, but since most of the gain is in the MCP, lower voltages (approximately 5000 volts), compared with the 30,000 volts needed by three-stage GEN 1 intensifiers, are used, thus significantly reducing voltage-breakdown problems. The use of MCPs allowed image tube size and weight to be decreased significantly as compared with GEN 1 three-stage intensifiers. They offer an advantage over the GEN 1 cascaded tubes with respect to overloading by bright lights. This superior MCP system performance is achieved due to the combined effect of inherent MCP saturation and a "smart" power supply. Figure 19-6 illustrates the GEN 2 device showing the input photocathode, amplifying MCP, and output phosphor screen.

The GEN 2 image amplification is achieved through the use of an MCP amplifying device, a wafer-thin slice of hollow glass tubes that have been fused into a mosaic of many hundred thousands of tubes (Figure 19-7a).

Each glass tube has a conductive inside surface with secondary emission characteristics that cause several electrons to be emitted when struck by a single electron, thereby producing gain of the input light signal, to output electron signal. When a dim nighttime scene is focused onto the GEN 2 photocathode, electrons are dislodged and accelerated toward the inside of each glass tube. This effect causes an electron image (considering all the hollow glass tubes together) to pass through the MCP. Each electron striking the MCP inside tube wall causes emission of secondary electrons (gain). Thousands of these secondary electrons impinge on the MCP phosphor output screen,

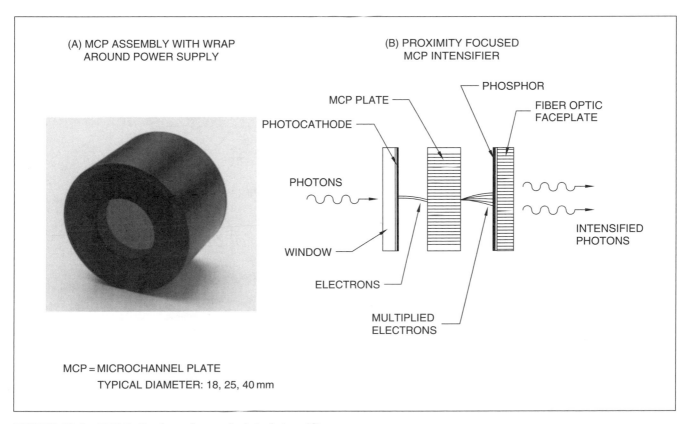

FIGURE 19-6　GEN 2, 3 micro-channel plate intensifier

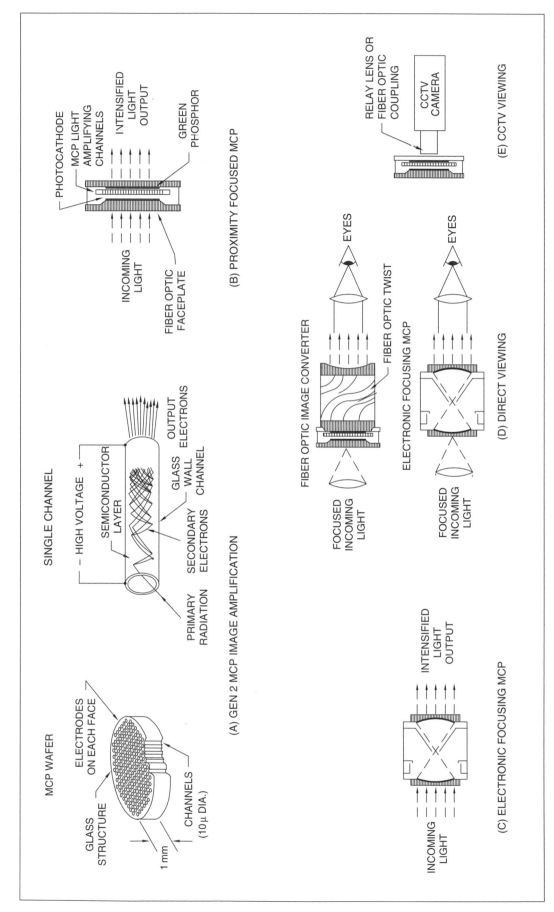

FIGURE 19-7 GEN 2, 3 micro-channel intensifier gain mechanism

converting the electron image into a visible display on the screen. Standard MCP amplification (gain) ranges from 35,000 to 100,000.

The GEN 2 intensifier assembly with power supply and image inverter is much smaller than the GEN 1 (1.5 vs. 6 inches long), since the MCP is only the thickness of a credit card (typically 0.06 inch). It is much lighter in weight than the earlier GEN 1 three-stage tubes (2 ounces vs. 16 ounces). The GEN 2 device overcomes the problems of image flare and light overload caused by bright objects such as headlights, and the image distortion from the GEN 2 device is much lower than that of the GEN 1 device. Resolution for a 25 mm-diameter GEN 2 MCP image intensifier is about 28–35 line pairs per millimeter. The GEN 2 Plus is an improved GEN 2 with a spectral sensitivity extended further into the near-IR region providing higher sensitivity and resolution.

There are two generic types of GEN 2 image intensifiers that are distinguished chiefly by different focusing arrangements between the photocathode and the MCP (Figure 19-7). The two types have many characteristics in common since they both use the MCP to multiply the electron output of the photocathode to produce light gain. The type chosen based on the expected use: for direct viewing by eye or for coupling to a camera. The electron-focusing type inverts the image making it suitable for direct viewing since it compensates for the inverted image produced by the objective lens. Although the proximity-focused type produces an inverted output image directly suitable for video sensors, many systems use the electron-focusing type for video when the camera is inverted. The proximity-focused output type with the addition of a fiber-optic output coupler inverter produces a right-side-up image if direct viewing is necessary. This fiber-optic twist increases the device length to approximately the same size as the electron-focusing version. In the proximity-focused device the screen is placed close to the MCP so that the multiplied electrons travel only a short distance before they impact the screen. This minimizes spreading of the electrons which would otherwise produce a subsequent loss of resolution.

Since most GEN 2 intensifiers have lifetimes of about 2000 hours, tube life is an important consideration. The most significant advantage of the focusing-electron structure over the proximity-wafer structure is its larger volume, which allows residual contaminants in the tube to spread out over a relatively large physical volume, thereby increasing the tube life.

19.6.1 Sensitivity

Image-intensifier photocathode sensitivity is expressed in two ways: (1) luminous sensitivity (sensitivity compared with white light) and (2) radiant sensitivity (sensitivity to near-IR radiation).

The GEN 2 intensifiers use S-25 (S-20ER, extended range) photocathodes, and GEN 3 (Section 19.7) use GaAs photocathodes for increased IR response and higher tube sensitivity. It can be seen that the GaAs photocathode has maximum response (sensitivity) in the red end of the visible and near-IR spectral region (850–920 nm) where the night sky illumination peaks. The higher GaAs efficiency and spectral peaking account for the higher GEN 3 sensitivity. Figure 19-8 shows the spectral sensitivity for the photocathode surfaces available for image intensifiers. Figure 19-8 also shows the spectral output characteristics of the image-intensifier phosphor screen used in GEN 2 and 3 intensifiers.

A typical night sky reflectance is shown, indicating the improved spectral match to the GEN 3 photocathode sensitivity. The P-20 phosphor material chosen for the image-intensifier output phosphor screen optimizes the energy coupling of the light output to the spectral response of the eye or the camera sensor. The yellow–green P-20 phosphor is used primarily for direct viewing applications because the spectral output is highest at the maximum sensitivity of the human eye. P-20 is also used to match the spectral sensitivity of the video sensor. The newer *filmless* GEN 3 has higher sensitivity than the GEN 3.

19.6.2 Resolution

Video system resolution is measured in TV lines. The resolution of photographic film, image intensifiers, and other non-scanning imaging tubes is measured by its modulation transfer function (MTF). An intensified system uses an image intensifier (non-scanned) and a video camera (scanned). Since the intensifier device output is a video signal, the resolution is measured in TV lines. Manufacturers' data sheets may specify MTF and/or TV lines. The limiting resolution value commonly specified in image-intensifier data provides one single point on the MTF characteristic curve. Figure 19-9 gives some typical MTF values for several image-intensifier tube types.

These data are for GEN 1 single-stage, two-stage, and three-stage electrostatically focused image tubes with 18-mm-diameter size, and GEN 2 and GEN 3 MCP. As can be seen, coupling three stages of intensification decreases the MTF and the resolution of the tube approximately to the level of a GEN 2 MCP. Notice that the GEN 2 MCPs have noticeably lower MTF than the GEN 1 single-stage tube. However, the GEN 3 has high MTF, equivalent to 64 lp/mm.

19.6.3 Light Overload

The typical real-world night environment is filled with light sources: flares, flashes, explosions, vehicle headlights,

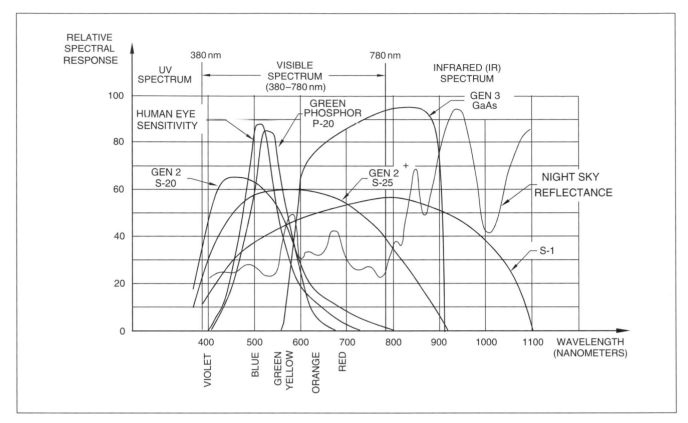

FIGURE 19-8   GEN 2 and GEN 3 MCP intensifier photocathode and phosphor screen spectral sensitivity

**FIGURE 19-9
Intensifier
modulation
transfer function
(MTF)**

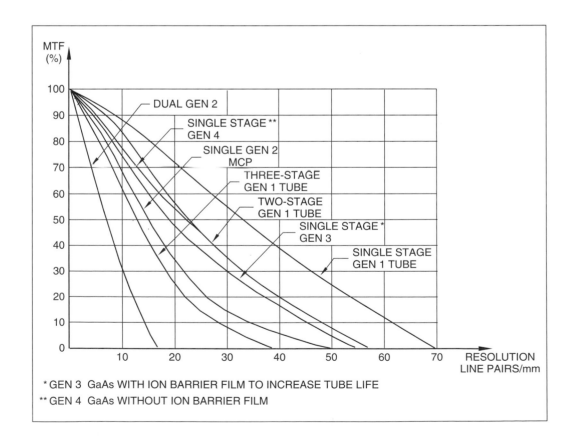

street lights, and others. GEN 1 devices exhibit considerable image persistence that results in image smear and often total obliteration of a scene when there are moving sources of light in the scene. Image blooming from a point source of light is common. The GEN 2 and GEN 3 MCP intensifier has far superior light-overload characteristics and has rapidly replaced the GEN 1 devices in military and commercial applications.

The MCP intensifier improves the scene contrast ratio and suppresses high lights caused by sun-glint or bright lights. The GEN 2 exhibits an inherent high-light saturation effect: high lights are suppressed before they reach the camera sensor. The MCP saturation is a localized effect in that individual micro-channels operate essentially independently of each other. This localized saturation greatly aids in improving "white-out" image blooming that severely affects the three-stage GEN 1 device. The resulting GEN 2 and GEN 3 pictures have a good contrast ratio that enable fine detail to be seen in the shadow areas of a bright source.

The MCP intensifier operates from 10^{-5} fc (10^{-4} lux) up to 0.1 fc (1 lux) with no additional automatic light control system required for the CCD sensor. Figure 19-10 shows the gain saturation curve for the MCP intensifier.

In the range from 10^{-7} fc (10^{-6} lux) to 3×10^{-5} fc (3×10^{-4} lux) faceplate illumination, the device has constant gain, but from 10^{-4} fc (10^{-3} lux) to approximately 10^{-1} fc (1 lux), the tube saturates: the output screen luminance remains constant even though the faceplate illumination increases. This nonlinear gain characteristic from low-light to high-light level accomplishes the highlight suppression resulting in an improved image.

The GEN 2 intensifiers have a remarkable lack of persistence or image smear compared with the three-stage GEN 1 devices. Although the screen phosphors used in both generations of intensifiers have a rapid decay of light output to a low level when light excitation is removed, they have long persistence to final extinction. In GEN 1 intensifiers, this "tail" of the first-stage phosphor is amplified by the second and third stages, with the result that the output image smears or "comet-tails" on moving bright sources. Since GEN 2 tubes require only one phosphor, no persistence is apparent. Filmless GEN 3 exhibits the best overload characteristics.

19.6.4 Gating MCP Image Intensifier

Image intensifiers can be operated under a condition called *gating* for the following reasons: (1) to reduce and control light reaching the passive intensifier system from a

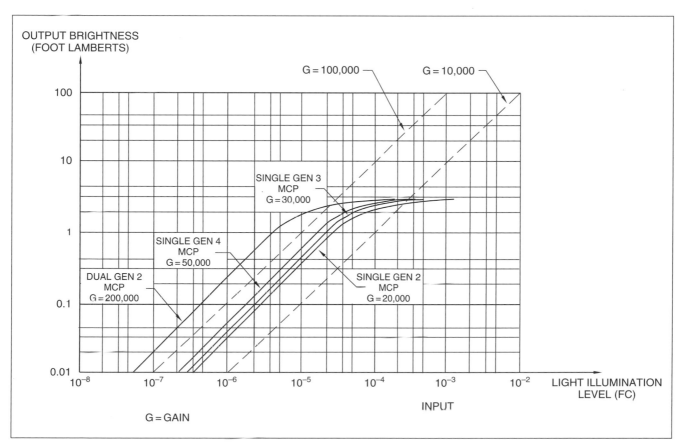

FIGURE 19-10 MCP intensifier gain saturation curve

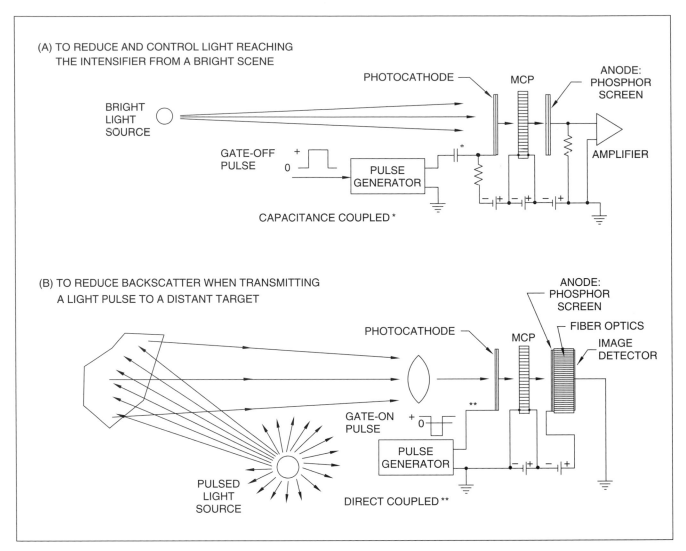

(A) TO REDUCE AND CONTROL LIGHT REACHING
    THE INTENSIFIER FROM A BRIGHT SCENE

(B) TO REDUCE BACKSCATTER WHEN TRANSMITTING
    A LIGHT PULSE TO A DISTANT TARGET

FIGURE 19-11   Range-gated intensifier system

bright scene and (2) to actively transmit a light pulse to a distant target and detect light returned from it (active system) without being overloaded from near-field backscatter that would seriously degrade the picture. Figure 19-11a shows the arrangement to protect the intensifier and improve picture quality.

To control the amount of light (photons) being amplified, the MCP intensifier is electrically gated on and off for short, controlled periods of time. The higher the scene illumination, the shorter the period of time the MCP is amplifying. This time-controlled automatic gain control keeps the brightness of the MCP output phosphor screen relatively constant. It also has the beneficial effects of: (1) protecting the device from high-light-level damage, (2) extending tube life, and (3) improving sensitivity. For shuttering applications the intensifier gain can be turned off by sensing a high-light condition-say daylight condition-to turn off the MCP. This gating technique increases tube

life substantially and most LLL cameras have this protective feature.

Low-light-level cameras can be used in an active gated mode by using a pulsed light source (filtered xenon lamp, LED, or laser) and gating the GEN 2 intensifier (Figure 19-11b). In the application of range-gating with a pulsed laser light source under conditions of fog, if the approximate range of the target is known, the intensifier is gated *off* electrically while the light pulse is being transmitted. The intensifier is turned *on* only when the light pulse reaches the target. The intensifier responds only to the reflected light from the target. This significantly improves the target-return to foreground-clutter ratio as compared with the continuous mode of operation. Range-gating reduces backscatter from near-range reflection caused by fog, precipitation, or other atmospheric aerosols or particles. However, range-gating makes the system active, which is a disadvantage in covert applications.

19.7 GEN 3 IMAGE INTENSIFIER

Military requirements and funding brought about development of the GEN 3 intensifier. The primary improvements sought and achieved were: (1) increased GEN 2 device sensitivity to IR illumination, (2) increased resolution, and (3) increased tube life. Increased sensitivity to IR is important since more IR radiation is available as natural outdoor illumination decreases (Figure 19-1). GEN 3 image intensifiers are structurally similar to GEN 2 except that the photocathode is constructed of high-quantum-efficiency GaAs, a material that is much more sensitive to IR radiation than is the GEN 2 photocathode. Figure 19-8 shows the differences in spectral sensitivity and response of GEN 2 photocathodes constructed from S-20, S-25 (S-20ER), improved GEN 2 Plus multi-alkali, and GEN 3 gallium arsenide–cesium oxide (GaAsCsO) materials. The GEN 3 has a maximum responsivity in the 600–900 nm wave length region, a better match to the night sky reflectance spectrum.

Several manufacturers produce a GEN 3 intensifier with an 18 mm photocathode and a P-20 phosphor screen with non-inverting fiber-optic output window. The intensifier is combined with video cameras either by lens coupling or with a fiber-optic faceplate and fiber-optic image taper, to a fiber-optic faceplate silicon tube or CCD sensor (Section 19.8).

The GEN 3 image intensifier delivers significantly improved performance over GEN 2 by providing greater sensitivity in the near-IR spectrum where night illumination is more abundant. The GEN 3 device triples the photocathode sensitivity compared with GEN 2 and permits it to operate down to starlight illumination levels. The increased IR sensitivity is significant because scene target reflectivity from a variety of materials increases or is higher in the IR region compared with the visible spectrum. The GEN 3 intensifiers more than quadruple tube life compared with GEN 2—from 2000 to approximately 10,000 hours. The GEN 2 and GEN 3 tubes incorporate automatic brightness control to provide constant image brightness under varying light-level conditions and bright source tube protection during exposure to high-light levels.

19.8 INTENSIFIED CCD CAMERA

An LLL system now in use is the intensified CCD (ICCD), a GEN 1, 2, or 3 image intensifier coupled to a CCD or other solid-state sensor. The combination of the GEN 2 or GEN 3 image intensifier with the small solid-state camera provides an extremely small, sensitive, lightweight, low-power LLL device. The ICCD sensor with GEN 2 or GEN 3 compares favorably with the SIT tube in sensitivity. The GEN 2 MCP intensifier coupled with a CCD sensor produces an LLL camera system with a sensitivity comparable to that of the SIT camera. The technologies used to couple the intensifier output to the CCD sensor use lenses or fiber optics in 1:1 magnification or reduced (Figure 19-12). The

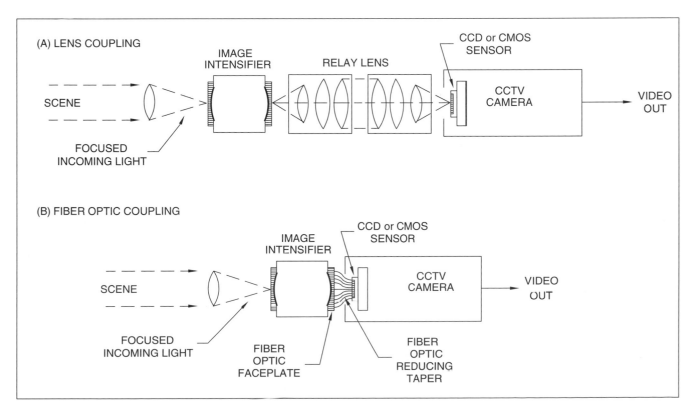

FIGURE 19-12 Methods for coupling intensifiers to CCD and CMOS sensors

following sections describe a GEN 1 intensifier coupled to a CCD sensor, and techniques for coupling the GEN 2 and GEN 3 intensifiers to a CCD sensor.

19.8.1 GEN 1 Coupled to CCD Camera

A single-stage GEN 1 intensifier is used in two ways with video cameras: (1) as a low-gain image intensifier and (2) to demagnify the GEN 2 or GEN 3 output image onto the smaller CCD format without resolution loss. While the GEN 1 is not as sensitive as a GEN 2 or GEN 3 intensifier tube, because of its excellent resolution the GEN 1–coupled, CCD-intensified camera is an excellent replacement for SIT cameras. This combination increases low-light sensitivity by a factor of 10–100 over that of the CCD camera. High resolution is achieved with the use of a high resolution 1/2-inch format CCD sensor. Figure 19-13 shows a diagram of the GEN 1–intensified CCD camera using fiber-optic coupling.

19.8.2 GEN 2 Coupled to CCD Camera

Higher gains and sensitivities can be achieved by substituting a GEN 2 MCP intensifier for the GEN 1 intensifier. With a GEN 2 device having a gain between 20,000 and 30,000 times and using a 4 to 1 tapered fiber-optic bundle reducer, the overall gain over that of a CCD camera is a factor of 5000–7500. Several examples of this new-generation LLL camera are described in this section.

Relay-Lens Coupling.   The simplest technique for coupling the output image from the GEN 1, GEN 2, or GEN 3 image intensifier to the CCD television sensor is to use an optical relay lens having a demagnification of about 0.44 for the 1/2-inch format camera (Figure 19-14).

The amount of demagnification is determined by the image-intensifier output diameter and the CCD sensor size. For a standard 1/2-inch (8 mm diagonal) CCD format (4.8 × 6.4 mm), the size is 0.44. While lens coupling is simple to achieve, relay lenses are large in size and optical coupling is not as efficient as fiber-optic coupling. A typical relay lens system uses an optically fast 25 mm lens in tandem with a 50 or 75 mm lens to demagnify the intensifier phosphor screen and refocus it onto the CCD sensor. An advantage of the lens coupling technique is the ability to replace the intensifier or CCD should it fail.

Fiber-Optic Coupling.   A smaller and more light-efficient technique for coupling a GEN 1, GEN 2, or GEN 3 intensifier output screen to a CCD imager is to use a coherent fiber-optic bundle between the intensifier phosphor screen and the CCD sensor. A coherent fiber-optic bundle is a closely packed (fused) group of several hundred thousand very fine glass fibers (one-tenth the diameter of a human hair) that form an image-carrying conduit. A *tapered* fiber-optic bundle is a conduit in which the entire bundle and fiber diameters change size from one end to the other. The tapered bundle reduces (demagnifies) the 8 mm intensifier image to match the smaller 1/2-inch CCD sensor format (Figure 19-15).

In this design, the coupler input side matches the diameter of the intensifier screen and the output side matches the CCD sensor format size. Tapered fiber optics have the following advantages over lens systems: (1) they are typically five times shorter in length than an equivalent lens system, (2) they result in a sturdy compact construction, and (3) their more efficient coupling permits operating the intensifier at a lower gain and therefore a higher signal-to-noise (S/N) ratio. A disadvantage is that if either the intensifier or the CCD fails, the entire assembly must be replaced.

Although each fiber transmits its portion of the scene from the intensifier phosphor to the CCD array with a loss factor of about 4, this is substantially better than the relay lens coupling technique. Therefore, if a single-stage GEN 1 intensifier produces a gain of 100, the ICCD light output is 25 times the light intensity of the original scene.

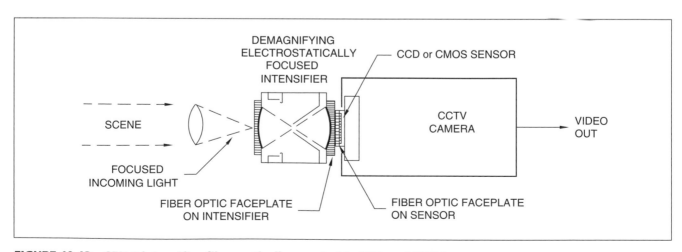

FIGURE 19-13   GEN 1 intensifier fiber optically coupled to CCD and CMOS sensors

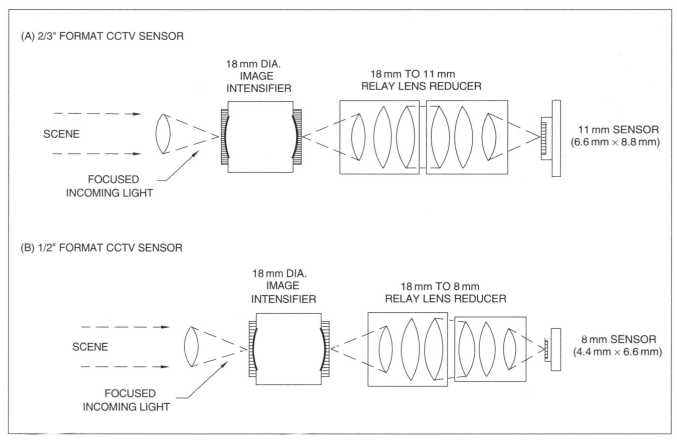

FIGURE 19-14   Relay-lens coupled intensifier

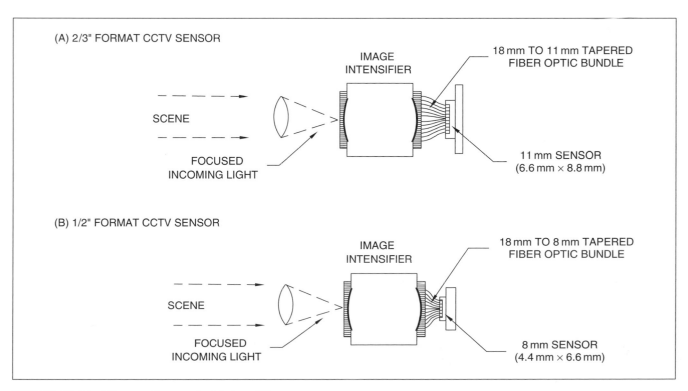

FIGURE 19-15   Fiber-optic coupled intensifier

This is a significant improvement over the standard CCD imager and provides a means for increasing the sensitivity of this device with a lag-free image.

Comparing the GEN 1 and GEN 2 systems, a GEN 2 intensifier fiber-optically coupled to a frame transfer (FT) device CCD has a sensitivity of 3.7×10^{-6} fc (4×10^{-5} lux) for full video output and 1.39×10^{-6} FtCd (1.5×10^{-5} lux) for minimum observable image. The resolution for this configuration is 260 TV lines. With a GEN 2 type and a 16 mm/7 mm fiber-optic reducer, a resolution of 425 TV lines is obtained.

Summarizing the relay-lens and fiber-optic coupling methods, the latter permits a reduced package size because of the short fiber length as compared with the longer lens system. The straight or tapered fiber-optic coupler is approximately 20 mm long compared with a typical relay lens of 70 mm. The advantage of the lens coupling method is the reduced cost and the ability to replace the intensifier or camera in the event of failure.

19.8.3 Comparison of Intensifier Sensitivities

Figure 19-16 shows the available light level under different conditions, from bright sunlight to starlight, and the sensitivities of SIT, ISIT, and ICCD cameras. Across the top of the figure are the types and levels of illumination sources available, ranging from full sunlight to clear starlight conditions.

19.9 SIT AND INTENSIFIED SIT CAMERAS

Since the appearance of the first television camera tube, the trend has been to develop tubes with greater sensitivity to operate at lower and lower levels of faceplate illumination, yet maintain or improve image resolution and quality. From the first image orthocon in 1944 to tubes with built-in image intensifiers in the 1950s, and with fiber-optic coupling in the 1960s, evolved the first generation of practical LLL security cameras in the form of the silicon-diode tube and the SIT, based on the silicon tube in the 1970s. The development of the SIT tube made other devices such as the intensified SIT and intensified CCD possible. The ISIT is still considered the highest-resolution, lowest-light-level imaging device available. The SIT and ISIT cameras offer high static resolution (non-moving targets) under very LLL conditions and presently play a vital role in the US government's ground border interdiction electron-optical surveillance programs, as well

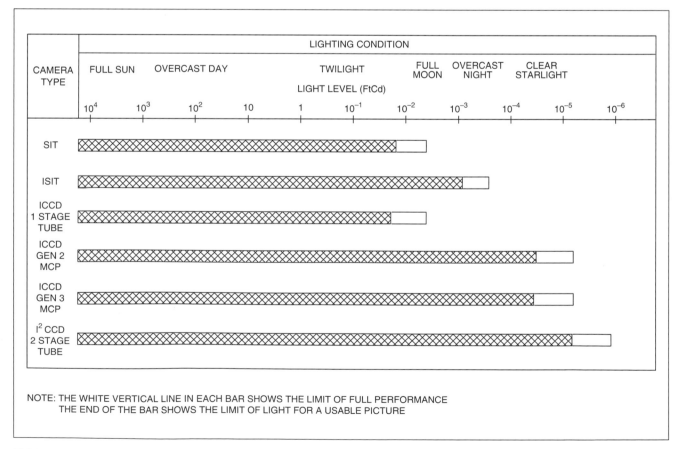

FIGURE 19-16 Illumination levels and intensified camera sensitivities

as in the important function of producing imaging for airport X-ray security equipment to detect contraband and other illegal materials.

The SIT and ISIT cameras offer 100–1000 times improvement over the imaging power of the best CCD and tube cameras. Low-light-level cameras intensify light, while tube and CCDs only detect it. GEN 1, GEN 2, and GEN 3 intensifiers coupled to CCD sensors have replaced the SIT cameras.

19.9.1 Sensitivity/Gain Mechanism

The SIT image-intensifier tube has a photocathode, an electron-optic image-forming system (electrostatic or magnetic), and a phosphor screen that is excited by the photo-electrons. The light output from the image tube is fiber-optically coupled to the fiber-optic faceplate input of the silicon camera tube photocathode (Figure 19-17).

The SIT camera tube uses a photocathode as the prime sensor, and a silicon-diode array target to produce gain by impact of the photo-electrons and a scanning beam to produce an output signal at the target. The most unusual feature of this tube is the silicon target, which produces electron gains of 3000 or more. The target consists of a two-dimensional PN-junction diode array with each diode facing the electron scanning beam of the tube, similar to the vidicon and silicon tubes. The silicon diodes constitute the storage mechanism required for holding the image while the electron beam is scanning the array. The ISIT combination (fiber-optic coupled image intensifier tube as input to the SIT tube) brings the sensitivity very close to the theoretical limit. Table 19-1 summarizes the sensitivity, gain, and resolution characteristics of commercially available tube and MCP intensifier devices.

19.9.2 Resolution and Image Lag

The SIT and ISIT camera resolution is limited by the 1 inch silicon-diode tube, which is about 700 TV lines.

Resolution is only one of the important parameters in an LLL system. The second is image lag, which becomes worse as the signal level decreases. Lag is the residual picture scene or signal measured in the dark and is expressed as the percentage of the original signal present after three television fields ($3 \times 1/60$th second = $1/20$ second) of scanning in the dark. The SIT tubes exhibit significant "third" field lag. The ICCD cameras show little or none of this image lag.

19.9.3 Light-Level Overload

Intensifiers are nighttime surveillance devices designed to work in near-dark conditions and are not intended for use in brightly illuminated park or street scenes at night, but rather poorly illuminated scenes, such as wooded areas, non-illuminated exterior perimeters, dark interior premises, or scenes at long ranges.

The SIT and ISIT intensifiers are subject to the same precautions as other photosensitive tube pickup devices. Prolonged exposure to point sources of bright light results in permanent image retention and/or photocathode surface damage. Optimum intensifier use is obtained when scenes have a reasonably consistent light level throughout the scene. A shoreline under a cloudy, moonlit night or an unlit wooded area are excellent examples of intensified camera applications. A parking lot or loading dock containing bright spotlights in some areas and total darkness in others can result in poor scene images unless the intensified camera views only the dark areas.

As the scene light level is reduced, scene blooming (the expansion of the white overload area due a bright light

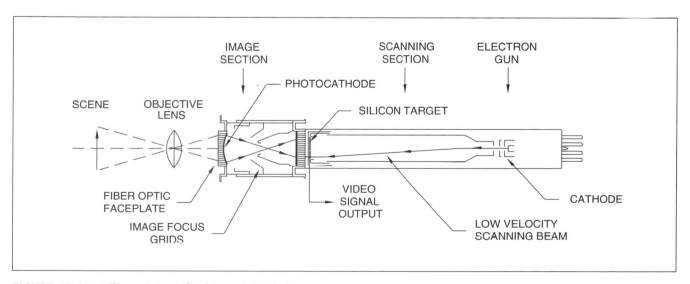

FIGURE 19-17 Silicon intensified target (SIT) diagram

TYPE	AMPLIFYING MECHANISM	TYPICAL[c] GAIN	INTENSIFIER ACTIVE AREA DIAMETER (mm)	PHOTOCATHODE MATERIAL	TUBE LIFE[f] MTBF (HOURS)	RESOLUTION LINE PAIRS/mm (TV LINES)	WAVELENGTH SENSITIVITY (nm)	FACEPLATE SENSITIVITY (FtCd) MINIMUM	FACEPLATE SENSITIVITY (FtCd) FULL VIDEO
GEN 0	NONE (REFERENCE)	CONVERTS IR TO VISIBLE	25	S-1	—	50	700–1200	—	—
GEN 1[a] 1-STAGE	ELECTRON TUBE	75–125	25	S-1, S-20	50,000	50	400–850	—	—
2-STAGE	ELECTRON TUBE	2,500	25	MULTI-ALKALI		40			
3-STAGE	ELECTRON TUBE	65,000	25			30			
GEN 2[a]	MCP[b]	20,000	25	S-25 (S-20ER)[e] TRI-ALKALI	2,000	32–35	350–900	—	—
GEN 3[a]	MCP	25,000	25	GALLIUM ARSENIDE (GaAs)	10,000	64	550–900	1×10^{-4} [g]	—
SIT	SILICON INTENSIFIED TARGET	$1,600^{d}$	16	MULTI-ALKALI	20,000	(700)	350–650	1×10^{-5}	—
ISIT	INTENSIFIED SIT	$90,000^{d}$	16	MULTI-ALKALI		(600)	350–650	1×10^{-6}	—
ICCD	GEN 2 MCP / GEN 3 MCP	3,000–6,000	18	S-25 / GaAs	2,000 / 7,500	(400) (500)	350–900	—	1×10^{-6}
ICCD	GEN 1 TUBE	100	18	S-20, S-25	50,000	50–85 (500)	400–850	1×10^{-5} TO 2.5×10^{-6}	1×10^{-4} TO 2.5×10^{-5}
I²ICCD	GEN 1 TUBE PLUS DEMAGNIFIED GEN 1 TUBE	—	18	S-20, S-25	50,000	(500)	400–850	3×10^{-6}	6×10^{-6}

NOTE: 3 STAGE GEN 1, SIT, AND ISIT CAMERAS PRODUCE MORE PICTURE BLOOMING AND LAG THAN MCP–ICCD COUNTERPARTS
GEN 3 AVAILABLE USING FILM OR FILMLESS TECHNOLOGY
FILMLESS IS REFERRED TO AS GEN 4 TECHNOLOGY
GEN 3 USES AN ION BARRIER FILM WHEREAS GEN 4 DOES NOT

a. DIRECT VIEWING. INTENSIFIER ONLY—NO CAMERA
b. MICROCHANNEL PLATE
c. LIGHT OUTPUT FROM PHOSPHOR SCREEN/LIGHT OUTPUT AT PHOTOCATHODE
d. CURRENT GAIN
e. ER = EXTENDED RANGE
f. MEAN TIME BETWEEN FAILURE
g. REFERENCE 10^{-6} FtCd EQUIVALENT TO STARLIGHT CONDITION

Table 19-1 Low Light Level Intensifier and Intensifier-Camera Characteristics

source at a location in the scene) caused by bright lights becomes a problem and is a phenomenon associated with most camera systems. It is particularly objectionable in LLL applications, where the scene contrast range is very small except for an occasional bright light or flash in the scene. When bright light blooming increases in the display, it obscures the picture information in it, causing a loss of intelligence. When the light intensity exceeds normal operating levels by a factor of approximately 1000 in SIT tubes, blooming becomes a problem. To reduce this objectionable overload, most SIT and ISIT cameras are equipped with automatic-iris lenses to compensate over the full dynamic range over which the cameras will be used. To protect the camera from dangerously bright objects, a shutter mechanism automatically closes the path of light reaching the sensor and protects the tube.

Imaging devices designed to operate under LLL conditions are not usually capable of imaging points of high intensity within the LLL scene without severe spreading of the point source image into adjacent scene areas. Different LLL systems are capable of handling high-light objects in the scenes such as ground fires, flares, vehicle lights, or runway lights with different degrees of success. These bright light sources often contribute light levels much higher than collected from the remainder of the scene, while providing little illumination to the objects under surveillance. The energy emitted by these sources is spread out by the atmosphere and the intensifier optics. The result is a concentration of light spread over an area many times larger than the image of the point source in the

scene, having the effect of obliterating detail over a large portion of the picture area. The GEN 1 tube devices suffer from this phenomenon. The GEN 2 devices have a built-in self-limiting saturation capability and therefore exhibit much less blooming.

The GEN 2 intensifiers provide significantly improved overload immunity to unexpected bright lights from car head-lights, street lights, and so on. The difference between three-stage GEN 1 and GEN 2 and GEN 3 intensifiers is best seen by actual viewing through these devices. The GEN 2 and GEN 3 devices exhibit superior performance over GEN 1 devices with respect to bright lights.

19.10 MULTI-SENSOR CAMERAS—IMAGE FUSION

19.10.1 Multi-Sensor

Multi-sensor camera systems detect radiation in the visible and IR spectrum. The natural and artificial sources of this radiation are shown in Figure 19-18. Multi-sensor cameras are used in applications requiring daytime, dawn/dusk, and nighttime operation (Figure 19-19). During daytime operation, a standard monochrome or color camera is used. During dawn and dusk, a sensitive monochrome CCD camera is used. During nighttime operation, an optically fast lens and LLL image-intensified camera or thermal IR camera with IR transmitting lens is used. The camera most appropriate for the ambient light level is

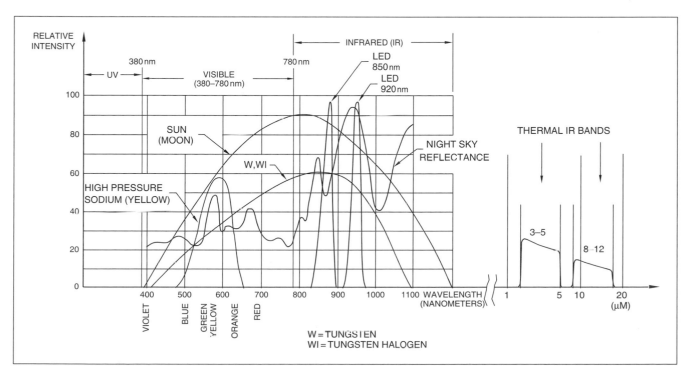

FIGURE 19-18   Visible and infrared radiation from common sources

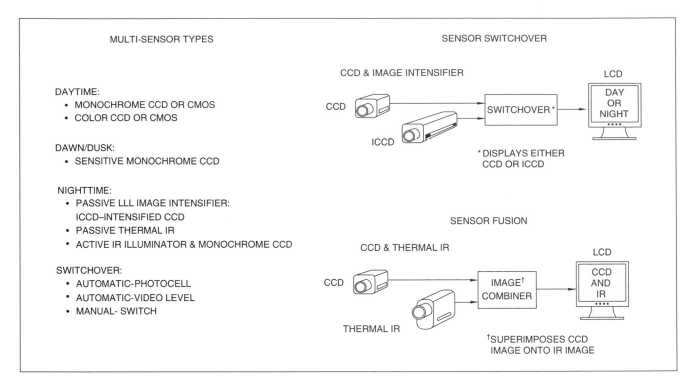

FIGURE 19-19   Multi-sensor video surveillance systems

chosen and switchover accomplished automatically with a photocell or manually by the operator. Above a predetermined light level, the daytime camera operates. When the light level drops below this level, the dawn/dusk camera operates, and at nighttime light level, the intensified camera or IR thermal imager operates. To ensure that damage does not occur to the intensifier photocathode, a neutral-density filter or automatic iris and a shutter mechanism are used. The multi-sensor system is designed to operate under moonlight, dawn/dusk, and bright sunlight conditions. The light level can increase from 10^{-5} to 10^{-1} lux during nighttime, from 0.1 to 100 lux at dawn and dusk, and up to 10^5 lux at midday. This represents a total dynamic light range of 10 orders of magnitude.

19.10.2   Sensor Fusion

The use of sensor fusion technology combines both the thermal IR and the image intensifier technologies and fuses them into a *single video image*. This system exploits the fact that for most objects there exists a contrast between them and their backgrounds that is different in the mid-wave and long-wave IR bands. These sensors are used to differentiate between mid-wave and long-wave IR and provide the contrast to make the targets *stand out* from their background. This characteristic especially helps when searching for camouflaged or partially hidden objects.

19.11   THERMAL-IR CAMERAS

Thermal IR imaging cameras have often been referred to as the camera "of last resort." Until the advent of non-cooled IR cameras the most often cited reason for this was their very high cost ($50K–$100K) compared to visible cameras. Current non-cooled cameras while still relatively expensive ($5K) are within the realm of today's security budgets. In the scene of the past, the most widespread use of these devices were confined to government and military applications. Another reason for their limited use, except in strategic applications, was their poorer image resolution as compared to visible video cameras. This lower image quality occurred due to several reasons: (1) there were fewer pixels in the sensor resulting in lower resolution and (2) the long wavelength IR spectrum correctly portrays the IR image but not a visible image to which the human eye is used to. The high costs for the IR camera comes from the sensor, electronics, and the optics. The optics must be fabricated from expensive and exotic materials such as germanium, calcium fluoride, and zinc selenide that transmit the IR energy (standard video glass optics absorbs the thermal IR radiation). The arrival of non-cooled IR cameras and consequent drop in cost and increase in performance is driving the thermal imaging field.

19.11.1   Background

In the early 1990s, researchers at the Honeywell Corp. developed and demonstrated a completely different type of thermal IR sensor: the micro-bolometer array. Since that time several companies have licensed this technology from Honeywell and have developed commercially viable uncooled thermal camera products and imaging engines. This technology offered a much low-cost alternative to the cooled arrays, thereby expanding the number of potential applications, particularly in the security field.

Although IR radiation includes a significant portion of the electromagnetic spectrum, IR imagers are designed to cover three wavelength ranges. The near-IR also called the short-wavelength IR is between 0.75 and 3 micron. The medium-wavelength IR extends from 3 to 8 microns (only 3–5 microns used). The long-wavelength IR extends to the 8–14 micron region.

Infrared detectors come in two basic varieties: (1) photovoltaic (photon) detectors, which produce electric currents in direct response to photons, and (2) thermal detectors or bolometers which measure the total heat energy absorbed in the sensor, by a change in the temperature of the detector elements (Figure 19-20).

The pyroelectric and bolometric thermal detectors are both sensitive to long-wave IR radiation from 8 to about 12 microns. The detective material physically heats and cools in response to incident radiation. The response time of the normal detector is a function of detector heat capacity. Thermal detectors have historically been characterized by their slow response, but modern techniques allow the fabrication of detector arrays with microscopic elements that offer response times compatible with video timing requirements. Systems that operate at or above standard video rates permit the user to record the imagery with standard video recording devices.

The IR thermal camera measures the change in the temperature of the detector material caused by the absorption of IR energy from the target. This IR energy increases the lattice vibration of the detector material causing an electrical current to flow. If the detector output signal is based on the resulting change in the material's resistance, the device is called a bolometer or *micro-bolometer*. This is now the most popular type of thermal-imaging sensor works since it operates at room temperature.

Until recently only photovoltaic detectors were available and all these thermo electric IR detectors had to be cooled far below room temperature using a mechanical pump. These coolers make the systems very expensive and out of the reach of almost all security applications (excepting military). Cooling to 193 K (−112°F) is required for 3–5 micron detectors and to 77 K (using liquid nitrogen) for 8–14 micron detectors. These cooled detectors, however, can have more than 10 times the sensitivity than room temperature thermal detectors.

The two most popular types are the staring focal plane array (FPA) and the scanning mirror. The FPA uses an IR lens, a cooled linear or area sensor (e.g. a CCD), processing electronics, and a thermal cooler, making for an expensive, complex system. The platinum-silicide area

sensor requires cooling to 77 K for proper operation. The mercury-cadmium-telluride linear sensor requires the scene image to be scanned across it and cooling to 77 K. Both systems are very expensive, used in military and other government projects. The IR vidicon, as its name implies, is an IR-sensitive vidicon. It exhibits low resolution and has found limited use in surveillance.

The room-temperature micro-bolometer uses no cooler and only requires temperature stabilization. This IR camera is a practical solution to many IR video surveillance problems.

There are now many manufacturers supplying these room temperature thermal IR cameras. They are similar in size, have standard video output signals, and consume about the same power as their visible CCD camera counterparts.

19.11.2 Micro-Bolometer

Technology.   A micro-bolometer is a sensor that changes resistance as its temperature changes. This change is sensed electronically to produce an output signal representing the temperature differences in the target scene. The detector is periodically pulsed with a bias current and the resulting voltage is read. The most common detector material used in today's bolometric systems is polycrystalline vanadium oxide.

Micro-bolometer IR camera manufacturers have solved the issue of pixel equilibrium through miniaturization. This only became possible with advances in micro-machining processes based on silicon processing techniques. These advances have made possible a room temperature, non-cooled thermal detector that can operate fast enough for the normal 30 fps video camera scan rate. These techniques have resulted in highly sensitive bolometers that are capable of detecting temperature differences as small as 0.07 K. Figure 19-21 shows the design of a generic thermal detector. The supporting legs must be small enough to achieve an appropriate degree of thermal isolation, yet large enough to conduct any residual heat from the previous measurement to be conducted away from the detector so that it will not interfere with the current measurement.

Micro-bolometer thermal detectors have two significant advantages over photovoltaic types: their response is the same (virtually flat) over a very wide spectral range, and they do not require cryogenic cooling. As mentioned earlier, the current revolution in thermal imaging began with the development of the uncooled micro-bolometer detector array by Honeywell Inc. using silicon device fabrication techniques. These detectors have thicknesses of less than 1.0 micron (0.00004 inch) and consequently bolometers have response times in the tens of milliseconds that enable normal video operation at 30 fps. While they are less sensitive than cooled photovoltaic detectors, a micro-bolometer

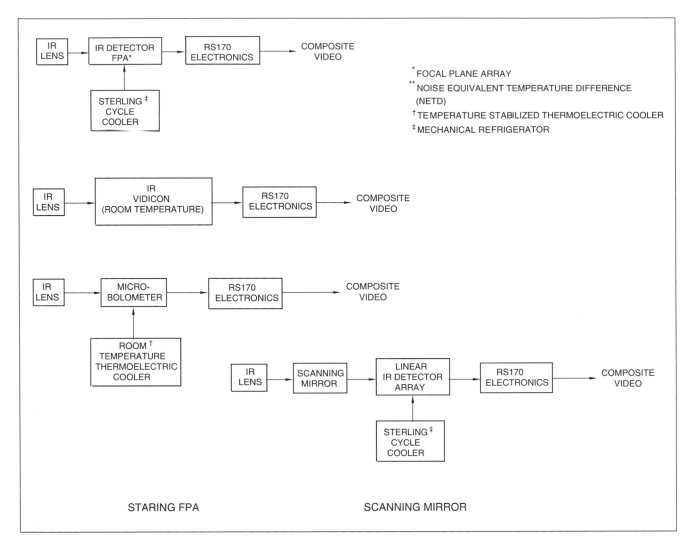

FIGURE 19-20 Cooled and room temperature thermal IR video cameras

pixel readily responds to a temperature change of less than 0.1°C which is detectable in a surveillance scene.

The room temperature IR cameras do not need cooling but many require sensor temperature stabilization which is accomplished using a thermoelectric cooler (TEC) assembly. The sensor and cooler are generally housed in a vacuum package that is thermally isolated from the rest of the camera. The sensor must not view any parts of the camera except the lens optics so that camera temperature and thermal radiation does not affect the sensor and cause a false temperature change. Some camera manufacturers use an elegant electronic stabilization means to compensate for ambient temperature variations without the use of a TEC.

There is a new unique approach to IR sensing that is based on a micro-cantilever technology. This new technology results in an IR detector that approaches the theoretical limits of IR sensitivity and is 10 times more sensitive than the standard micro-bolometer based detectors. Its increased sensitivity lies in the fact that the micro-cantilever technology uses capacitance, rather than

resistance, to measure temperature change. The surface of the detector is coated with an absorbent material, and when the IR radiation converts to heat, the temperature of the cantilever arm rises. When the cantilever is heated, it bends and generates an electrical signal in the detector that is proportional to the intensity of the radiation absorbed by the sensor.

Cooling. Although active cooling is not a requirement for operation, most micro-bolometer based commercial cameras use a thermoelectric cooler to stabilize the temperature of the array and thereby minimize image non-uniformity and artifacts. This additional power drain required by the cooler at the edges of its operating temperature range effectively limits the camera's operating temperature. The alternative is an approach that electronically compensates for temperature changes in the array, eliminating the need for the TEC cooler. This dramatically lowers camera power consumption to close to 1 watt and allows the camera to operate over a wide range of ambient temperatures, from −40 to 55° centigrade.

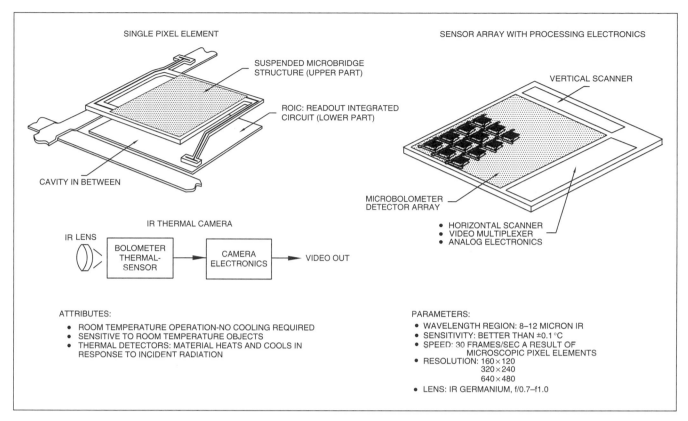

FIGURE 19-21   Generic micro-bolometer sensor structure

The active cooling also eliminates the slow turn-on (settling) time often associated with IR cameras without this active cooling.

Material. Another important consideration in the design of the micro-bolometer is the sensor material. The choice is between vanadium oxide and alpha (amorphous) silicon. The use of vanadium oxide translates directly into better image quality. The key figure a merit for camera sensitivity is its noise equivalent delta temperature (NEDT), the temperature difference that generates a signal equal to the noise of the camera. The best NEDT for commercial cameras based on silicon technology is approximately 0.1 K, when using an f/1.0 lens.

19.11.3 Infrared Optics

An expensive component in the thermal camera (aside from the sensor) is the IR transmitting optics. To achieve adequate sensitivity the optics for the IR detectors must have an f-number (f#) between 0.7 and 1.0. Long wavelength IR energy is not transmitted through ordinary visible glass video optics. Thermal IR imaging systems use germanium (most popular), zinc selenide, and calcium fluoride lens material. The material and fabrication costs of these exotic materials are high. Most IR camera lenses are fixed focal length (FFL) lenses to constrain cost. Short to medium focal length lenses (10–100 mm) use germanium for the lens material. Long focal length, optically fast lenses use reflective front surface aluminized mirrors and refractive germanium (or zinc selenide) materials. It is unlikely that cost for these lenses will be reduced significantly unless high volume production is forthcoming or a new technology evolves a future goal is to eventually produce lighter and less expensive f/1.5 or f/2.0 optics.

Table 19-2 summarizes the parameters and features of some commercially available thermal IR cameras.

19.12 LOW-LIGHT-LEVEL OPTICS

During daytime operation, there is sufficient visible light for color or monochrome video cameras to produce excellent images using standard, small lenses having an aperture (diameter) similar to that of the human eye. When the light level is reduced to that available during dawn or dusk, larger diameter optics are required to obtain a good image. When there is no light and an active IR illuminator is not permissible, large IR transmitting optics is necessary. The use of large optics with LLL and IR cameras partially accounts for the improved capability of these devices over that of the human eye.

CAMERA TYPE	SENSOR PIXELS ($H \times V$)	SENSITIVITY (ΔT K) NETD*	COOLING	POWER WATTS	SIZE (inches)	WEIGHT (lb.)	LENS FOCAL LENGTH (mm) F/#	FOV** (DEGREE)	COMMENTS
ROOM TEMPERATURE MICROBOLOMETER 6–14 MICRONS UNCOOLED	160×240	0.08	NONE	1.5	$1.5 \times 1.5 \times 2$	1.5	25/2.3	35	VERY SMALL
	320×240	0.05		2.5	$2 \times 2.5 \times 2.5$	1.0	13/2.0	57	MEDIUM RESOLUTION
	320×240	0.05		2.0	$2 \times 2 \times 3$	0.5	50/2.3	18	VERY SMALL
	320×240	0.06		5.0	$8 \,\text{Dia} \times 13$	7.9	150/1.0	6.2	FAST LENS LONG RANGE
	320×240	0.1		2.5	$3 \times 3 \times 4$	1.8	50/1.0 25/0.9	18 35	DUAL FOV
	640×480	0.08	NONE	1.5	$1.5 \times 1.5 \times 2.5$	0.5	25/2.3	35	VERY SMALL
COOLED 8–14 MICRONS	512×512	0.10	MECHANICAL STERLING CYCLE—77 K	22	—	10	25/1.2	35	STARING FPA† PLATINUM SILICIDE
	512×512	0.07	MECHANICAL STERLING CYCLE—77 K	18	—	14	50/1.6	18	SCANNING MIRROR LINEAR ARRAY HgCdTE

*NETD—NOISE EQUIVALENT TEMPERATURE DIFFERENCE (ΔT)

**HORIZONTAL FIELD OF VIEW

†FPA—FOCAL PLANE ARRAY

ALL IR CAMERAS USE GERMANIUM OR CATADIOPTRIC LENSES (TABLES 19-3 AND 19-4)

OPTIONS INCLUDE ZOOM LENSES

Table 19-2   Characteristics of Representative Thermal IR Cameras—8 to 14 Micron Region

19.12.1   Comparison of Eye and LLL Camera Optics

The unaided human eye can be compared with video cameras and image-intensified cameras with respect to sensitivity and resolution. As the light level is reduced, seeing is limited by the number of available photons in the visible and near-IR spectral range. The lens of the dark-adapted human eye is approximately 7 mm in diameter and any optical system must concentrate the collected light into this diameter if it is to be useful to the eye. As an example, a standard 7×50 night binocular is a 7-power (magnification) binocular with a 50 mm-diameter objective lens. The diameter of the exiting bundle of light is determined by dividing the objective diameter by the power. The light is thus concentrated into about a 7 mm-diameter bundle, all of which can be collected by the dark-adapted eye. Increasing the size of the light-collecting objective lens for the same magnification results in an exit diameter that is larger than that of the eye, but there is no increase in light to the eye. The LLL camera, however, benefits from the larger diameter objective lens since the intensifier tube can be 18, 25, or 40 mm in diameter or 2.6, 3.6, or 5.7 times larger respectively, than the human eye. Since the light gathered is a function of the area, these are improvement factors of 6.76, 12.96, and 32.49 respectively. A good catadioptric lens used with night vision devices having an effective diameter of 100–200 mm improves sensitivity over the unaided eye by about 500–1000 times. This translates into improvement in resolvable picture elements in a scene by a factor of approximately 1.5 to 3 times when compared with the human eye.

Another factor that improves the image of the LLL camera is the increased quantum efficiency, and extension of the photocathode spectral sensitivity range of the intensifier into the near-IR where the night sky and other artificial light sources provide a greater number of photons and energy mean higher sensitivity over that of the eye.

The human eye cannot "see" thermal IR energy coming from objects or background in a scene and therefore no comparison is made between the two.

19.12.2   Low Light Level Objective Lenses

Low Light Level Lenses.   Objective lenses for LLL video systems vary greatly depending on the application. *Short-range* systems can use fast (low f-number) refractive (all glass) lenses having diameters from 2 to 3 inches and good transmission in visible and near-IR (up to 1000 nm) wavelength range. *Long-range* systems use Cassegrain and catadioptric lenses fabricated from mirror and/or glass/mirror combinations. These 4 to 12 inch diameter lenses weigh less than all-glass lenses and gather maximum visible and near-IR radiation. Figure 19-22 shows two examples of catadioptric lenses used with night vision systems.

Thermal IR Lenses.   Thermal IR imaging cameras require special lenses that can transmit radiation in the 3–12 micron wavelength region. This means that if the lens uses any refractive optics (glass) the material must be able

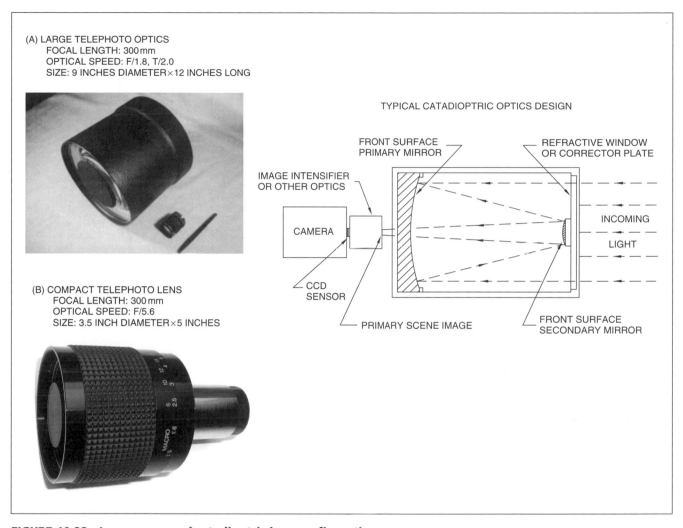

(A) LARGE TELEPHOTO OPTICS
FOCAL LENGTH: 300 mm
OPTICAL SPEED: F/1.8, T/2.0
SIZE: 9 INCHES DIAMETER×12 INCHES LONG

(B) COMPACT TELEPHOTO LENS
FOCAL LENGTH: 300 mm
OPTICAL SPEED: F/5.6
SIZE: 3.5 INCH DIAMETER×5 INCHES

TYPICAL CATADIOPTRIC OPTICS DESIGN

FIGURE 19-22 Long range and catadioptric lens configurations

to transmit well in this wavelength range. The most common material used in refractive IR lenses used in short-range surveillance applications is germanium. For long-range applications, Cassegrain and catadioptric lenses are used. If these lenses use any refractive elements they must transmit the IR energy. Table 19-3 lists some refractive IR transmitting lenses used in short-range applications.

Table 19-4 lists some commercially available Cassegrain and catadioptric lenses used in long-range nighttime surveillance applications.

19.13 TARGET DETECTION AND RECOGNITION PARAMETERS

To illustrate the capability of a LLL system, a typical application might be to view a scene with natural illumination during a clear starlit night, or more difficult yet a cloudy starlit night when the average illumination is down to a level of 10^{-5}–10^{-6} fc.

The probability of detection and recognition of specific objects has been determined experimentally by the Night Vision Laboratory of the US Army Electronics Command. Figure 19-23a shows the probability of detection and recognition as a function of limiting resolution and critical target dimension.

As an example, it can be seen that there is a 60% probability of recognizing a vehicle occupying 3 TV lines or if 3 cycles of spatial information are resolvable (6 picture elements) in the vehicle height. Likewise, there is a 90% probability of recognizing a man with the same number of picture elements resolvable.

How many line pairs of resolution at a target are required to detect, recognize, or identify? Numerous experiments have been performed, which indicate the following (Figure 19-23b):

- 1–2 line pairs across the minimum target dimension are required for target detection (i.e. in order to determine that a discontinuity exists in the field).
- 2–3 line pairs are necessary to determine target orientation.

LENS TYPE	FOCAL LENGTH (mm)	OPTICAL SPEED f/#	IMAGE * FORMAT (mm)	FIELD OF VIEW (FOV) (DEGREES)	SIZE DIAMETER LENGTH (inch)	WEIGHT lb/kg
SHORT RANGE	13	1.0	20	75	0.75	0.25/0.1
	18	1.0	20	58.1	1.00	0.25/0.1
	25	1.0	20	43.6	1.50	0.3/0.14
	50	1.0	20	22.6	2.5	0.5/0.23
	60	1.4	20	18.5	2.75	0.5/0.23
	75	1.0	20	15.2	3.8	0.7/0.3
MEDIUM RANGE	95	1.2	—	13	4.2	4.8/2.2
	100	1.0	20	11.4	5.0	5/2.3
DUAL FOCAL LENGTH LENS	25/50	1.0	20	46/23	1.5/2.5	1.2/0.55
	50/150	1.0	20	23/8	2.5/7.0	2.0/0.9
	75/250	2.0	14	10.7/3.2	2.5/6.5	3.5/1.6

*MAXIMUM IMAGE (SENSOR) SIZE
ALL LENSES REFRACTIVE—GERMANIUM

Table 19-3   Short and Medium Range Thermal IR Lens Parameters

LENS TYPE	FOCAL LENGTH (mm)	OPTICAL SPEED f/#	OPTICAL SPEED T/#**	IMAGE * FORMAT (mm)	FIELD OF VIEW (FOV) (DEGREES)	SIZE DIAMETER (inches)	WEIGHT lb. (kg)
CATADIOPTRIC: (REFRACTIVE AND/OR REFLECTIVE)	150	1.2	—	20	7.6	—	—
	135	1.6	—	25	10.6	3.8	4.4 (2.0)
	155	1.2	—	—	6.6	—	10.8 (4.9)
	170	1.5	—	25	—	4.9	6.6 (3.0)
	200	2.0	—	14	4.5	—	—
	238	1.7	—	—	4.3	—	10.8 (4.9)
	300	1.4	2.0	40	—	9.0	23 (10.5)
	410	1.5	—	—	—	11.25	38 (17.3)
	500	1.6	2.0	16	1.84	13.4	56 (25.5)
	1725	5.6	—	—	0.6	—	59.4 (27)
CATADIOPTRIC: (REFLECTIVE AND/OR REFRACTIVE) MULTI-FOCAL LENGTH	635	3.6				22.5" LONG 11.5" HIGH 10.25" WIDE	—
	1000	5.6	—	—	—		
	1800	10.1					
	2400	13.5					

*MAXIMUM IMAGE (SENSOR) SIZE
**LENS TRANSMITTANCE TAKING INTO ACCOUNT CENTER OBSCURATION OF CATADIOPTRIC LENS

Table 19-4   Long Range Low Light Level or Thermal IR Lens Parameters

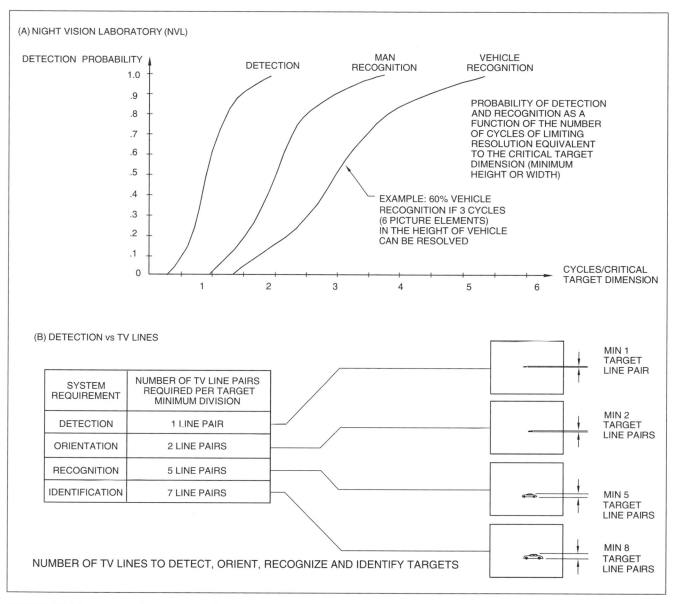

FIGURE 19-23   Target detection and recognition vs. system resolution and target size

- 5–8 line pairs are required for recognition (i.e. to be able to estimate a rough outline and estimate aspect ratio).
- 8–12 line pairs are required for target identification (i.e. to allow the observer to perceive sufficient detail to classify the target as to a particular type).

These rules apply for targets with aspect ratio of about 1:1 to 5:1. Targets with higher aspect ratios are generally easier to detect: a telephone wire or pole is easier to detect than a round object.

19.14 SUMMARY

Devices have been developed for night vision by exploiting four basic imaging techniques: (1) active near-IR image converters (GEN 0) used with searchlights or IR emitters, (2) passive image intensifiers (GEN 1, GEN 2, and GEN 3), and (3) passive mid-IR thermal-imaging devices.

Low light level and IR cameras are used in applications where the available illumination is not adequate for standard CCD and CMOS cameras that cannot produce usable images under nighttime, early dawn, or late dusk illumination conditions. The ICCD image intensifier camera provides the ability to see during periods of low light by *amplifying* the faint off the scene from the moon, stars, or other artificial light. The higher sensitivity of ICCD cameras allow them to function under light levels of a quarter moon (0.001 fc illumination). The ISIT camera can detect images of a scene illuminated with 0.00001 fc (the light available from stars on a moonless night). Unlike near-IR active devices these passive image intensifiers do not require additional light sources other than ambient light or IR radiation reflected from the scene to produce a video output directly displayed on a monitor.

Two disadvantages of the LLL intensifier and thermal IR systems as compared with standard solid-state video cameras are cost and lifetime. They can cost 10–20 times more than a standard video camera. Most GEN 2 or GEN 3 image-intensifier systems have lifetimes of about 2000 and 10,000 hours respectively as compared to standard video cameras that routinely operate continuously for many years as they have no wear-out mechanism.

Chapter 20
Control Room/Console Design

CONTENTS

20.1 Overview
20.2 Human Engineering
    20.2.1 Viewing Angles
    20.2.2 Viewing Distance vs. Monitor Size
    20.2.3 Guard/Monitor Console Configurations
    20.2.4 Split-Screen Monitor Displays
20.3 Security Operator Tasks
20.4 Control Room Layout, Location
20.5 Console Design
    20.5.1 Video Monitors
    20.5.2 Full-Screen, Split-Screen, and Sequencing
          Monitor Presentation
20.6 International Control Room Standard
20.7 Checklist
20.8 Summary

20.1 OVERVIEW

This chapter analyzes the role played by security personnel monitoring video cameras at the security console location and at other fixed or mobile remote locations. Ultimately, the security operator's ability to act as an *alert, motivated* observer determines the effectiveness of the video system. To ensure success, management and the security director should analyze the security guard's duties and the security monitoring hardware. Factors to consider include:

- Number and location of monitors
- Time required to effectively observe each monitor, depending on the activity at each location
- Amount of scene detail needed in each monitor to obtain required intelligence information
- Category of events the guard must monitor
- Actions the guard must take based on the information in each camera scene
- Guard's knowledge of the actual scene: Has the guard visited the actual scene location?

The average adult watches about 4 hours of television a day and can sit through documentaries, comedies, or news programs and remain alert and interested while obtaining the "intelligence" presented on the television screen. On the other hand, the average video security console operator probably sees a boring picture most of the time. The guard may watch a deserted hallway, an empty parking lot, a back door, a front lobby, or an elevator cab, all from his or her own chair for 6–8 hours a day.

The ultimate detector in any video surveillance imaging system is the human eye. While image intensifiers, low-light-level monochrome cameras, and high-resolution cameras may be coupled to a video monitor, the *final image* presented relies on the human eye for interpretation. Security designers and users must keep in mind that the human operator at the security console or remote monitor will make the final analysis on the monitor scene. The video images presented on the monitors must have high enough resolution and quality to permit the security guard to assess the situation at hand. These and other parameters are analyzed in the following sections.

Present security monitoring consoles contain camera switchers, multiplexers, recorders, and a variety of video monitors. The monitors will be either monochrome or color, cathode-ray tube (CRT) or flat screen.

Designing a proprietary security console room can be one of the most important phases of security planning. In many installations the console room is the most visible part of a company's or organization's security program. Since it also represents a very large investment, sufficient time and attention should be focused on its design to ensure that the console operates efficiently, cost-effectively, and that it represents accurately the tremendous protection it provides. The security console design and the location of the security room are the most important contributors to the successful operation of a security system. This chapter covers the security operator's responsibilities and factors affecting the operator's performance, the design of the console with emphasis on the video aspect, and criteria to be considered in locating the security room.

20.2 HUMAN ENGINEERING

Security directors and managers must recognize that a key factor in the successful operation of any video surveillance system is the effectiveness of the security guards that monitor the installation. Progressive security companies have investigated guard performance and implemented fatigue-reducing procedures to alleviate problems associated with monitoring multi-screen video consoles. These problems include backache, stress, headache, and eye strain. The primary cause for guard fatigue and boredom is constant staring at video monitors.

One technique for reducing operator boredom and fatigue is to have someone enter the console area at periodic intervals to speak with the guard, ask of any concerns, praise accomplishments, and break the monotony. Managers have addressed these problems by rotating the guard staff and assigning them shorter on duty times at the console monitors. Security personnel are often required to perform auxiliary duties to relieve boredom and improve performance. These breaks should not detract from the attention needed to respond properly to the many real and false alarms that occur during a security guard shift.

Other technical solutions to improve guard performance include: (1) using sequential video switchers and multiplexers to display multiple camera scenes on a single monitor and reduce the number of monitors (2) using audio and visual alert signals, and (3) creating ergonomic console designs to reduce fatigue, eyestrain, and boredom. Sensor alarms, VMDs, or simple switchers to call up and display a monitor scene that needs attention reduces the burden of the guard and allows him or her to operate more efficiently. An important design criterion in any security system is the optimum design of the security console. If in-house design experience is not available, outside designers should be consulted to accomplish this critical task.

Other factors affecting efficiency and quality of security guard performance include environmental factors such as room temperature, lighting, and noise. Temperatures that are set too high cause fatigue. Background noises should be held to a minimum as they are distracting and lead to lower performance. However, a complete absence of noise will induce sleepiness. Lights mounted overhead or behind the guard can cause glare on monitor screens, as can daylight. To significantly reduce this problem: (1) lights should be mounted judiciously, (2) glare-reducing monitor screen overlays should be used (Section 8.7.2).

For maximum interpretation of the television scene, security console operators should be able to relate to a monitor scene through actual physical objects at the scene location. Operators should be required to visit the physical area and become familiar with it. They should stand at the camera location, observe the scene, and become acquainted with objects in it, note the camera's blind spots, and understand the surveillance requirements. Operators should be tested regularly to determine whether they can recognize individuals, objects, and other events and activities on the monitor screen.

20.2.1 Viewing Angles

The maximum horizontal viewing angle in both directions is approximately 45°. The maximum vertical viewing angle between observer line of sight and the monitor for acceptable monitor image distortion is approximately 30° (Figure 20-1).

20.2.2 Viewing Distance vs. Monitor Size

The optimum distance of the operator from the monitor depends on the monitor size. Table 20-1 summarizes the suggested maximum and minimum viewing distances for different-size monitors.

20.2.3 Guard/Monitor Console Configurations

A semicircular monitor console is optimum for viewing multiple monitors. An observer's station should not consist of more than approximately 15 monitors. Figures 20-2a, b show straight-on and wrap-around configurations for a single-guard operation.

The configurations permit optimum viewing of the monitors with minimum distortion and minimum head rotation to observe all monitors. Figure 20-3 illustrates a fairly complex monitor security consoles in which two guards monitor four to six monitors.

Note that the monitor banks are arranged in a near-semicircular configuration and that the top and lower bank monitors are directed in toward the center. This is so that the guard viewing the monitor bank at central eye level will be looking nearly perpendicularly at each of the monitors, thereby producing minimum distortion.

Some hardware options to make the console monitoring area more efficient and conducive to optimum guard performance include sequential switchers, pan/tilt cameras, motion sensors, and two-way intercom, VCRs, DVRs, and video printers. These components can simplify the

Control Room/Console Design

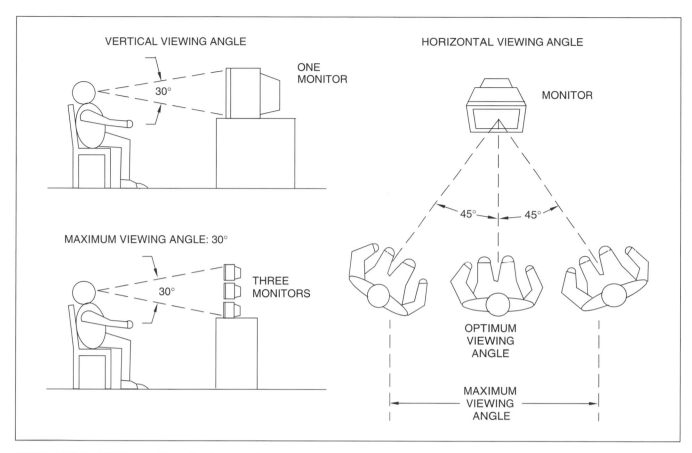

FIGURE 20-1   CCTV monitor viewing angles

monitoring process and reduce the functions that guards might normally have to perform.

An important feature for outdoor monitoring is the sunlight readable display (Section 8.7.3). This display has high brightness and allows viewing the monitor in bright sunlight.

The flat panel digital monitoring equipments used for video monitoring include: LCD and plasma. There are complexities and compromises when connecting analog cameras to digital monitors and when merging past analog techniques with the present digital technology.

The monitor size chosen depends in part on how many security operators will be in the monitoring room. The question of how many cameras to sequence through one monitor is an important one. If each camera is displayed on its own monitor, the guard can view all cameras at any time without switching. However, he cannot realistically view all of the monitors simultaneously. When there are about 10 monitors, the guard can view them all fairly well. In the range of 10 monitors, some of them must be combined (split-screen) and switched through a single monitor to reduce the number of monitors in the console.

The use of sequential switchers to switch many cameras through a single monitor reduces the number of monitors a guard must view. If a sequential switcher is used, it is recommended that a monitor view no more than 12 different cameras to minimize guard fatigue. The maximum number depends on the activity in each scene. For more active applications or many people moving in the scene or some other form of activity, 4 or 8 monitors might be the maximum recommended. Having too many cameras and too many monitors increases stress, with a commensurate decrease in guard effectiveness. Experience has shown that 15 monitors is considered maximum for any operator, with the main viewing screen having a 17–21 inch diagonal and the other monitors a 9 inch diagonal. The use of split-screens with multiple scenes on one

MONITOR SIZE (DIAGONAL–INCHES)	VIEWER TO SCREEN* DISTANCE (inches)
5	12–24
7	16–35
9	20–42
10	22–48
12	24–60
13	26–65
17	30–75
19	35–88
20	36–96

Table 20-1   Viewing Distance vs. Monitor Size

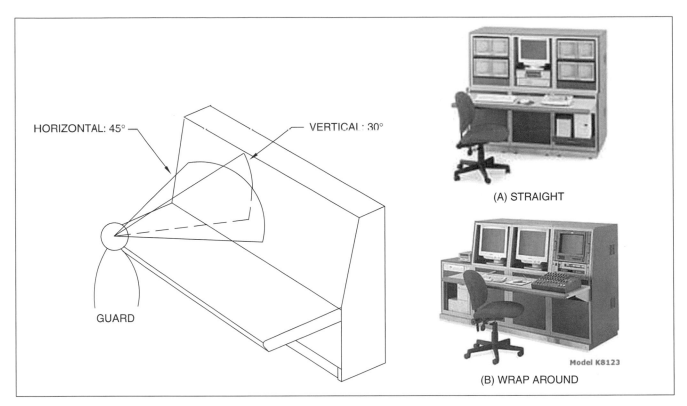

FIGURE 20-2   Single guard security console configuration

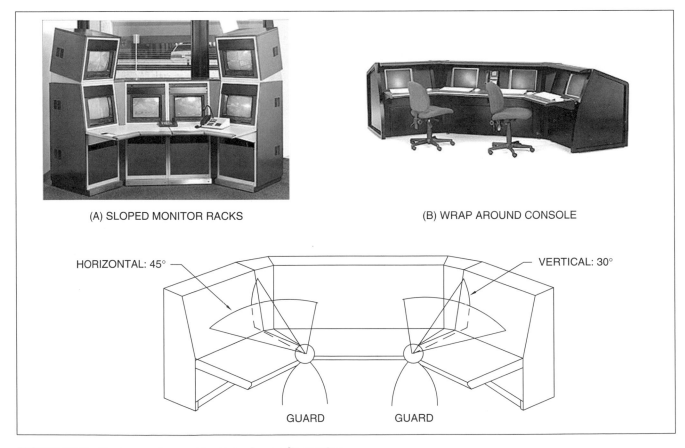

FIGURE 20-3   Two guard security console configuration

monitor also reduce guard fatigue and improves monitoring effectiveness.

Monitors used for security operations have screen size of 5, 7, 9, 14, 17, 19, 21, or 23 inches. In security console environments, the optimum screen size for most applications is a 9 inch diagonal. There are several reasons for this:

- The 9 inch CRT diagonal screen provides the highest resolution from the monitor.
- The optimum viewing distance of the security operator from the 9 inch monitor is approximately 3 feet, a convenient distance in many console rooms.
- Two 9 inch monitors fit side by side in the standard EIA 19 inch rack configuration. This is an important consideration, since space is generally at a premium in the console room and optimum integration and placement of the monitors is important.

The monitor screen size chosen for any particular application depends primarily on the subject-to-monitor distance (Table 20-1). For one-on-one or field-test applications, small screens ranging in size from a few inches up to 9 inches are recommended. Often if the installation is medium to large there are several larger monitors included—17 through 23 inch—since there may be other personnel in the environment who need to view these larger monitors to obtain an overview of the security operation.

Digital LCD monitors have diagonal screen sizes of 5.6, 6.4, 10.4, 13.3, 15.1, 17, 18.1, 22 inches. Larger screens – upto 42 inches using plasma displays are available for use in large rooms and installations.

In applications where more monitors are required and closer viewing and the resolution on some monitors can be sacrificed, a triple-monitor arrangement in a 19 inch rack is used. These monitors are 5 inch diagonal and mounted three across. Figure 20-4 illustrates the dual and triple rack-mounting arrangement. Figure 20-5 shows typical LCD (or other flat panel) displays rack mounted or in tabletop use.

One disadvantage of switching cameras through a monitor is that the guard may miss an event in a single monitor because it was showing the view from another camera. To eliminate this deficiency an alarming device (VMD, switch, and infrared detector) is used to automatically switch the monitor to the camera viewing the area of activity on this monitor. Most systems fall in between the extremes of many monitors, each showing a single camera view and one monitor showing many camera views. When there are several critical scenes to be viewed, each area should be equipped with a dedicated monitor (a camera directly connected to a monitor) without any switching, to ensure that the guard always has 100% viewing of that camera scene.

20.2.4 Split-Screen Monitor Displays

Another technique to view all scenes all the time is to use a split-screen monitor presentation, in which 2, 4, 9, 16, or 32 scenes are simultaneously displayed on a single monitor (Chapter 12). While this technique does provide multiple scenes on a single monitor, it decreases the resolution of each picture proportionally, thereby making identification of action, person, or object more difficult. If a guard needs to see the picture with better resolution, he or she can switch from split-screen presentation to single-screen presentation of the camera of interest.

20.3 SECURITY OPERATOR TASKS

One of the first tasks in designing a security console room is to outline the duties of the security operator. The outline should include daytime operations when most people have access to the site as well as off-hour times, and secured periods (any time the facility is closed). Depending on the size of the installation, security officers on duty in the console room during daytime hours may be responsible not

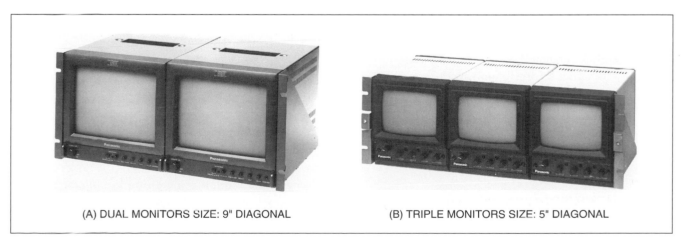

(A) DUAL MONITORS SIZE: 9" DIAGONAL   (B) TRIPLE MONITORS SIZE: 5" DIAGONAL

FIGURE 20-4   Dual and triple rack mounted CRT monitors

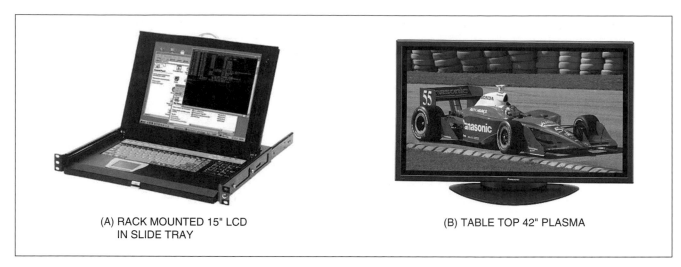

(A) RACK MOUNTED 15" LCD
IN SLIDE TRAY

(B) TABLE TOP 42" PLASMA

FIGURE 20-5   Rack mounted and table top LCD flat panel displays

only for operating the console but also for handling keys, employee badges, access control into restricted areas, parking problems, visitors and visitor badges, contractors and contractor badges, and escort services. In the evening or off-hours, however, the officer's duty might revert only to console room monitoring and an occasional visitor issue.

The director of security and management depend on their security console operators and look toward them as a first line of defense against theft of assets, protection of personnel, and apprehension of criminals. If some unusual activity occurs or there is a sudden system failure, it is the control room operator that is expected to resolve the problem. The task of the designer is to ensure that operators are able to meet the demands imposed on them and operate in an efficient and effective manner. Furthermore, during normal operation a working environment must be created that will provide a continuing challenge to the operators so that they retain motivation and an interest in their work. Boredom and a sloppy approach are just as much a systems failure as is a critical hardware component breakdown.

While appropriately designed and specified electronic video hardware will run consistently, this is not true of the typical security operator. Unfortunately they are prone to suffer from boredom, distraction, and overload. An understanding of these changes in performance is an integral part of the designer's contribution to the overall system design. Ergonomic design is essentially about designing a working environment and using equipment to match personnel capabilities and limitations. The proper application of such techniques reduces errors, improves efficiency, and enhances operator comfort and well-being.

20.4   CONTROL ROOM LAYOUT, LOCATION

The console control room location within the facility is also an important consideration. The console room should be located so that the operator can directly view the facility's main entrance and remotely control all the doors leading out of the lobby. This is especially important if the lobby entrance is the only one accessible to authorized individuals after-hours. Any contractor or visitor has to check in at the console room at the main building before entering any other location. The size of the console room is not necessarily related to the size of the facility. If only one operator is controlling the system it is no value to have a huge console where the guard cannot handle the equipment efficiently. With today's video technology using VMDs to call images on video screens and using split-screens for video image presentation, all the information needed by the operator can be presented on a few monitors. Even in large building facilities, the console design should bring all of the items needed by the operator within an arms reach or as close as possible. Other items that do not need constant attention should be placed away from the operator or in a separate room. Of course for large systems more than one security operator and corresponding keyboard controls are required.

The overall layout of the security monitoring room must take into account the location of the operator(s) in the room. Figures 20-2 and 20-3 show console rooms designed for one or two operators. The location of the operator is obvious since the person must monitor the facility's entrance and lobby and be well positioned so that the guard can have a clear view of the entrance area, the monitors, and other controls necessary for operation. In many cases the operator will face a bullet-resistant window with a deal-tray similar to those used at banking teller windows. The deal-tray maintains the bullet-resistant integrity of the window while giving the operator a convenient way to exchange badges, keys, or identification. Once these windows of viewing panels have been positioned, the rest of the equipment needed in the console room can be located.

Windows pose a particular problem since human factor considerations may conflict with security and safety concerns. There is ample evidence that people do not like working in windowless environments. It is strongly recommended that a window be included in a control room, not for reasons of illumination, but for purely psychological purposes.

Control room lighting is best when there is some daylight available and artificial light is zoned and controllable by dimmers. Ideally, the light controls for the area of the room, including the workstation, monitor bank, and panel equipment, should be on the workstation accessible to the operator.

20.5 CONSOLE DESIGN

It is important to properly design a physical interface between the operator and the equipment. There is a substantial body of knowledge regarding the best ways to arrange equipment around an operator to accomplish this function. Apart from the hard-interface to the hardware (keyboard switches, annunciators), some attention is required for the soft-interfaces. These soft-interfaces include information structuring, relationships between controls and displays—for example, joystick and camera movements—and menu structures. At a more subtle level, the operator must have an understanding of the system being controlled.

The first item in the design is the custom or standard writing counter in front of the guard. This must be suitable for writing reports, answering the telephone and taking telephone messages, exchanging ID badges, and performing other duties that might involve writing. The next equipment group to be positioned in the console room is the main security and fire alarm annunciation controls consisting of a keyboard and monitor screens showing all intrusion and fire alarm information. Also included are means for controlling access from different points of the facility. In addition to electronic access control this might also include video access control monitoring in which a face/badge reader is used. This video monitoring is required when the operator must admit someone without a coded electronic badge and during secured off-hours. The system would include an after-hours entry location equipped with video, intercom, and a card reader so persons without a badge can communicate with the console room operator to establish their identity. Two video monitors are usually used to display the scene at the vehicle or walk-up entrance, and the pedestrian seeking access. The operator views and compares the visitors face with the picture on the ID card or driver's license.

20.5.1 Video Monitors

The major part of the console design is directed toward video surveillance. This involves control of the video cameras throughout the site including the lobby, the building perimeter and parking lots. Depending on the facility, such video coverage may require tens to hundreds of video cameras. Video systems use simple video switchers, quads and multiplexers, matrix switchers, and VMS (Chapter 11). Only active pictures from the cameras are displayed by these devices in the console room when an *abnormal* condition is in view on the camera. As a result, any number of cameras can be installed in the facility, but only 5–10 monitors are likely to be needed in the console room. For this reason the room can remain small even though the site continues to grow. The switchers, multiplexers, matrix switchers, and controls for presenting these cameras on the monitor are included in the main security keyboard in the console room. Every camera in the system can be controlled from the keyboard, and any camera can be called up and displayed on the monitor. The operator can control pan, tilt, and zoom (PTZ) from switches and a joystick on the keyboard.

In operation if an activity occurs that requires the attention of the officer, the appropriate scene from the camera is displayed on the monitor with camera ID number, camera location, and name. The officer then refers to the site map, whether in the form of hard copy or on a video monitor, to determine the exact location of the activity and instructions on the action that should be taken. When the activity occurs, the operator's attention is directed to one or more monitors showing the image of the activity in that zone. In general, security officers are not expected to detect or react to an abnormal condition by watching the video monitors: the security system does the detecting. The video system provides the guard with directions and the opportunity to *follow-up* and determine why the area went into alarm. The system is designed so that all monitors would normally be blank unless some activity requiring the attention of the guard was present. When an alarm occurs the camera scene is automatically displayed on the first monitor. The next alarm goes to the second monitor and so on. In practice the operator can call up the camera on any monitor through the keyboard to check on troublesome spots like a parking lot or shipping dock where an incident might have occurred recently. The guard can glance at these monitors when no other activity is happening to lend that additional level of security. If an alarm occurs while in this mode, the system automatically replaces this casual surveillance image and displays the alarm picture.

While equipment in the real world may perform with 100% reliability, failures on the operator's side can lead to a significant performance degradation of the entire video system. Monitors should be easy to view and control panels simple and straightforward to use. It should be easy to differentiate different types of switches and they should be large enough for easy actuation. Joystick controls should not be unprotected so as to easily disturb domes or pan/tilt platforms inadvertently. Designers of these control panels should also recognize that operators often operate under stressful operational conditions. With this in mind the designer should design control panels with large and easily visible legends, and with keyboard keys laid out for easy and swift execution of functions. The GUI monitor having three help and instruction displays should provide help in a way that an operator can call quickly and efficiently cope with a serious system failure during an incident or activity. In these circumstances simple, easily understood instructions are required to efficiently and effectively resolve the incident.

One advantage of the single keyboard is that the operator requires less movement to control the entire video system. Operator response becomes faster and less confusing, and reduces operator fatigue over a long shift. A second advantage is that the control desk or console itself can be smaller and less cluttered. Only the keyboard and monitors are necessary on the desk itself. All other items can be mounted in a secure rack cabinet or an adjacent equipment room. Training is also simplified since there is only a single keyboard rather than multiple keyboards or control panels.

The layout of the monitors should be such that the operator can see them all clearly. Selecting the right shape and size of a room can go a long way to insure that a workable layout is achieved. Video monitors should be either directly in front of or slightly elevated from the operator but should not be ceiling-mounted. It is well established that raising the eyes over extended periods of time to view the monitors in this way can be very fatiguing. An ergonomically designed workstation layout will insure that equipment that is frequently used is easily at hand, and displays which need to be seen are easily seen and clearly visible from the operator's normal working position.

20.5.2   Full-Screen, Split-Screen, and Sequencing Monitor Presentation

For any security application, the designer must decide how many monitors are necessary for good video security and it requires a decision as to how many camera images will be presented on split-screens, and how many cameras images will be displayed full-screen on individual monitors. The following are guidelines for console monitor displays with images from multiple cameras using full-screen, split-screens, and by time sequencing.

- Operator inattention or fatigue is less likely to occur with a single monitor or only a few monitors with split-screens.
- Camera sequencing (time-sharing) should only be used for non-critical camera views.
- Viewing the scene 100% of the time is especially important in situations involving continuous movement, or when it is important to view and observe activities at several locations simultaneously.

- If a switcher is sequencing from camera to camera, a long time can pass before the scene from that particular camera is seen again. In the case of four cameras, the operator will be viewing each camera only one-fourth of the time. There will be substantial periods of time during which the majority of the facility under CCTV surveillance will not be monitored by the console operator. This may bring into question the cost-effectiveness of cameras whose dwell times (actual time viewing scene) are short and as a result the scene is seen for only a short period of time.
- If there is a failure in a single monitor no pictures will be displayed until it is replaced. Unless a spare monitor can be switched in, there will be some downtime before the new monitor is installed.

20.6   INTERNATIONAL CONTROL ROOM STANDARD

An international standard is currently being drafted for all control room ergonomics called ISO 11064. This is an eight-part standard covering all aspects of control room design including workstation configurations, room layout, the design of displays and controls, and environmental design. Material covered in the eight sections is summarized below.

- Principles for the design of control centers: step-by-step procedure for the ergonomic design and specification of a security control center.
- Control suite layout: architectural considerations including space allocation, functional interrelationships and security.
- Control room layout: covers such aspects as control console arrangement, location of secondary workstations, storage maintenance access, circulation routes, windows, and preferred locations for wall displays.
- Workstation layout dimensions: plan layout principles for single and multiple workstations, vertical dimensions for sit/stand operator positions, secondary workstation layout, maintenance design, panel and equipment layout principles.
- Displays and controls: encompasses such aspects as human–machine interface design, information structuring, input and output devices. Includes overview displays and video monitors.
- Environmental requirements: a distillation of good practices covering artificial lighting, heating, acoustics, interior design, finishes, and the control of natural light.
- Principles of evaluation: presents evaluation techniques and how they can be applied at various stages of the control room design.
- Specific applications: addresses specific types of control room environment for specific applications.

20.7 CHECKLIST

Each application requires individual design and questions that must be answered. Some of the fundamental points that must be considered in designing any effective control console and security room are listed below.

- What are the daytime tasks of the security officer?
- What are the off-hour duties of the security officer?
- What are the security hours and duties of the security officer?
- How many guards will be operating in the console room?
- Are the daytime and nighttime lighting conditions adequate?
- Can the security guard(s) adequately handle all the tasks required?
- Are all the controls within reach of the security guard?
- Are all the cameras' alarm points clearly indicated on the site plan?
- Are the activity and alarm instructions clear for the operator to interpret and act upon?

20.8 SUMMARY

Video surveillance console design requires careful consideration from the human engineering aspect (ergonomics) as well as hardware capability. The number and placement of monitors with respect to the guard(s) must be analyzed carefully in the early stages of design. A list of guard functions and duties should be generated and reviewed with management and security personnel at the facility, and critiqued by a professional consultant. The best system will be ineffective if proper attention is not paid to the human engineering aspects of the console room design.

A trade-off must be made between the number of cameras and monitors used so that the guard can effectively monitor all essential locations. The use of split-screen presentation of camera images should be implemented wherever possible to reduce the number of monitors a guard must monitor.

The security console and control room represent the nerve center of the security system. In any facility or organization, for optimum operation, the security officer must understand the duties required for protecting assets and personnel and have an ergonomic environment to work in that is conducive to efficient and effective operation. For an optimum video-monitoring system there must be a balance between displaying camera images on a single monitor, split-screen monitor, and sequencing camera images through a single monitor. There is a balance between simple systems having a single monitor and those having multiple monitors. Each situation requires analysis to determine the optimum number of monitors and the type of switcher required. The security room layout and console design should lend itself to simple straightforward operation, and have instructions for the security officer to be clear and timely when action and a response is required.

The function of the security console room is to have the security officer respond to and interpret alarms generated from hardware. The alarms are generated through the use of video switching equipment video monitors, keyboards, and other control hardware. The security operator's function is to react to protect facilities, assets, and personnel. The console room environment should be designed with the security operator in mind. All console monitors and controls should have easy access by the operator. Instructions for the operator when action is required should be clear, concise, intuitive, and simple to interpret without ambiguity.

Chapter 21
Rapid Deployment Video Systems

CONTENTS

21.1 Overview
21.2 System Requirements
21.3 Technology
    21.3.1 Hardware
    21.3.2 System Operation
    21.3.3 Remote Monitoring, Command,
        and Control
21.4 Applications and Scenario
    21.4.1 VIP on Travel
    21.4.2 Vehicle, Boat, and Aircraft Protection
    21.4.3 Options and Accessories
21.5 Summary

21.1 OVERVIEW

There is a widespread need for portable personnel and assets protective systems. These equipments are referred to as rapid deployment security (RDS) systems. The RDS system should combine video surveillance cameras, monitors and accessories in a single carrying case that can be transported to a location and set up quickly to become an operational video security system. The RDS should be designed for applications where the required maximum time to become an operational security system, between initial on site arrival of the system and personnel operating it, be as short as *30 to 60 minutes*. The RDS system has optional video recorders and analog or digital video transmission to transmit the information to remote sites for command and control from *anywhere*. Cell phones, PDAs, and laptop computers can be used at local or remote sites to receive the video images to provide worldwide coverage. The video camera images are communicated directly to the portable control unit and/or to remote site(s) using wired or wireless, analog or digital transmission means. Any type of analog or digital camera can be used having daytime and/or nighttime capabilities. For nighttime and long-range outdoor applications, environmentally protected day/night, image intensified (ICCD) and thermal infrared (IR) cameras are used. Likewise for outdoor applications, environmentally protected outdoor day/night cameras are used.

The applications for RDS systems are many:

- Protect VIPs on travel in government, industry, public, and private sector
- Provide a temporary secure area for emergency personnel: first responders, police, fire, and medical
- Protect assets located in a temporary storage facility
- Secure and monitor conference rooms or other temporary facilities against theft or espionage
- Protect parked vehicles, docked boats, and parked or stored aircraft.

21.2 SYSTEM REQUIREMENTS

An RDS system must provide the following basic capabilities: (1) portability, (2) rapid deployment, (3) simple operation, and (4) maximum protection of assets and personnel. With options the RDS system can also provide (1) remote monitoring and (2) remote command and control.

Portability. The system should be housed in a man portable carrying case(s) that can be shipped via conventional carriers without the need for special packing.

Rapid Deployment. The RDS system should be self-contained and have everything needed for installation. It should be designed to be set up quickly to become an operational security system. It should be designed for applications where the required maximum time between initial on site arrival of the system and personnel operating it may be as short as *30 to 60 minutes.*

Simple Operation. An RDS system by definition must be easy to set up and operate. The function of protecting VIP personnel, responding to an emergency, or protecting valuable assets is an important function. The equipment owner, user, or the person chosen to operate the equipment come from varied backgrounds. Some operators will have had no technical background while others might be well versed in operating and understanding video security equipment used in the RDS system. It is therefore important to have the system designed so that it is as easy to operate as possible for any qualified user. The RDS design must have simple procedures for powering up the system, installing the cameras in the environment, and testing the cameras. It must also have simple visual and audible annunciators for the user to act upon when a threat occurs.

Remote Monitoring, Command, and Control. The RDS system should be capable of transmitting analog or digital video from the target location to remote sites for command and control from *anywhere.* The video cameras are either hardwired to the portable control unit or the camera video signals are transmitted *wirelessly* via analog or digital means. PDAs, and laptop computers are used at remote sites to receive video images and location information and be transmitted almost anywhere in the world. When wireless video transmission is used a concern is that unauthorized viewing of the image could take place. An option for the analog video transmission is a sophisticated scrambler, and for the digital video transmission, various levels of digital encryption that prevent unauthorized viewing of the video image.

Maximum Protection of Assets and Personnel. The most important requirement of the RDS system is that it operate reliably and provide maximum security to the personnel and assets it is protecting. This requires that the information obtained from the video cameras be accurately conveyed to and accurately interpreted by the guard so that the necessary response to the threat is taken.

21.3 TECHNOLOGY

The RDS equipment can take many forms having single or multiple cameras used indoors or outside. The cameras can be monochrome or color, low light level or thermal IR. The RDS video system is often integrated with other security personnel. The RDS system operates on 12 volts DC and is provided with an international power supply for compatibility with any type of AC main power and line

frequency (50, 60 Hz) and can be deployed almost anywhere in the world. The system provides monitoring video used for real-time and post deployment video assessment. RDS equipment uses DVRs utilizing either flash memory or compact hard drives to record the video images. Time-lapse or continuous recording can be programmed by the user. Other RDS equipment options include digital video image communication via land lines, email, PDA, or satellite transmission to alert appropriate personnel at remote sites. This is accomplished by using a modem to transmit these video signals anywhere in the world. These RDS systems and all necessary accessories required for set up at the site are housed in a rugged carrying case(s) and ready to be deployed.

21.3.1 Hardware

There are many varieties of RDS systems from the simplest single camera systems to multiple cameras that provide local monitoring or remote monitoring of rooms, vehicles, boats, aircraft, etc. They can be designed to be AC power operated and/or DC battery operated for indoor or outdoor use, daytime or nighttime operation. Figure 21-1 shows a block diagram of the typical multiple camera RDS system.

The RDS system consists of wired or wireless video cameras. The video images are transmitted to the RDS control unit where they are processed. The video images from the cameras are displayed on a single large LCD monitor or on separate smaller LCD monitors depending on the application and requirements of the user. All video cameras and accessories for the basic unit are stored in the case. Figure 21-2 shows some examples of RDS video monitoring systems.

21.3.2 System Operation

An important requirement of any RDS system is that it can be set up quickly and easily by the user and have a simple operating procedure so that the user or security personnel having a varied technical or non-technical background can use the system efficiently. All cables should be color coded and easy to connect, and have a positive locking feature so that there is no possibility of incorrectly connecting the cables to the cameras, sensors, and control unit.

After installing all cameras, the system should be checked out by activating each camera to determine that the proper video is displayed. After installing the wired cameras and cables, the camera images should be viewed on the LCD monitor(s) to determine that the picture quality is satisfactory and that the camera views the required FOV.

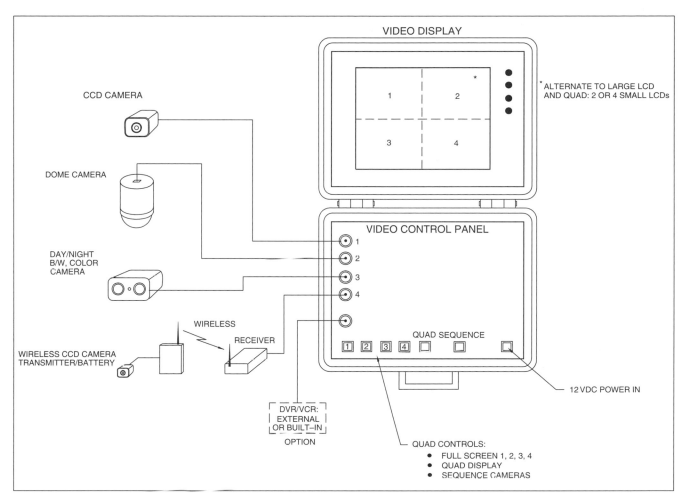

FIGURE 21-1   Block diagram of rapid deployment security (RDS) video system

21.3.3   Remote Monitoring, Command, and Control

If remote monitoring and command and control options are provided with the system, set up and installation will depend on the particular options chosen. For wireless analog transmission of the camera signal, attention will have to be paid to the placement of the video receiver. By trial and error the receiver should be moved and eventually placed in a location that provides for the best image quality and the least interference or picture breakup. Moving the antenna and receiver just a few inches sometimes changes the quality of the video image dramatically.

If digital video transmission and digital alarm data transmission are chosen as an option, specific instructions are provided to make the necessary choices and adjustments on the use of the video applications program used on the laptop computer. The use of digital video monitoring requires user personnel to have a more technical background for its successful operation.

21.4   APPLICATIONS AND SCENARIO

There are many applications for the RDS systems to protect personnel and assets. The scenarios described here are VIPs on travel, protection of vehicles, boats, and aircraft assets. Also described here are additional accessories and options that form part of the RDS system capability.

21.4.1   VIP on Travel

Very Important Persons travel with a guard or companion designated to protect the VIP. The RDS system in the self-contained case (Pelican or other) is hand carried to the hotel or motel room, apartment, conference center, office area, etc. The guard opens the case(s) and connects the system to AC or DC (12 volt battery) power. The video cameras are deployed and mounted at appropriate locations to monitor hallways, entrance doors, windows and are connected to the RDS control unit using the supplied

(A) TWO CAMERA RDS SYSTEM   (B) QUAD RDS SYSTEM

FIGURE 21-2   Typical rapid deployment security (RDS) systems with wired and wireless video monitoring

cables in the case. The system is now tested:, i.e., the video camera monitor images checked to determine that the images are satisfactory.

21.4.2   Vehicle, Boat, and Aircraft Protection

The RDS system in the self-contained case (Pelican or other) accompanies the vehicle (car, van, truck, etc.), boat, or aircraft. At its destination, the security guard (or VIP) deploys the RDS system on and around the vehicle, boat, or aircraft. The system is checked and tested to insure that all cameras are operational and their images properly displayed on the monitor(s).

21.4.3   Options and Accessories

The basic RDS system consists of components necessary to deploy the video assessment system and monitor it *locally*. There are numerous options and accessories that can be added to the basic system to extend its capabilities. Some of these are described below.

Wireless Analog Video Cameras.   The basic RDS system is supplied with hardwired cameras using cables to connect the cameras to the RDS control unit. Optional wireless cameras are available using analog transmission of the video signal and using batteries for the camera and transmitter power. The wireless camera module consists of the camera enclosed in a housing suitable for the environment, with an analog transmitter and rechargeable battery. The RDS system is supplied with a battery charger and a spare battery so that the wireless camera/transmitter module can operate continuously. If AC power is available the wireless camera module can be powered using an AC to 12 volt DC converter. Small, low power analog video transmitters have been available for many years. These transmitters operate at 900 MHz, 1.2 GHz, 2.4 GHz, or 5.8 GHz and can transmit real-time video images over distances of several hundred feet indoors to several thousand feet under outdoor line of sight conditions. By proper choice of these transmitting frequencies usually up to 4–6 different cameras can be operated simultaneously. An additional option to the analog video camera transmission option is a sophisticated scrambler that prevents unauthorized monitoring of the video transmission, thereby providing a secure wireless video link. Another option to the wireless analog video camera is a digital video motion detector (VMD) built into the same module housing.

Remote Digital Video Monitoring Option. An important option to the basic RDS system is ability to transmit the video images from the control unit at the target site to remote locations anywhere, using a LAN, WAN, or wireless LAN (WLAN, WiFi). Figure 21-3 shows the block diagram of a digital RDS system.

The video images can be transmitted to remote locations via 802.11 and received by cell phones, PDAs, and laptops in near real-time to assess the threat. Using the 802.11 digital transmission protocol with compression and encryption, excellent image quality and quality of service (QoS) is obtained under indoor and outdoor transmission conditions. Using the 802.11 protocol offfers the flexibility of using different levels of digital encryption on the video signal, making for a more secure system. Another option to the wireless digital video camera is a digital VMD that can be built into the same camera/transmitter module housing or into the software at the RDS control unit. Figure 21-4 shows a typical digital RDS wireless video monitoring system.

Video Recording Option. Adding an analog or digital video recorder and a VMD to the RDS system allows recording pre-alarm, real-time alarm, and post-alarm images of an incident. These recordings are used to have a permanent record of the incident, identify personnel or assets removed, etc. Digital transmission equipment provides the ability to transmit these recorded video images to a remote site. Again the optimum technique for transmitting these recorded images is the 802.11 protocol or to use local land lines or LAN, satellite or other transmission channels.

Accessories. Standard accessories included in RDS systems are any and all necessary mounting hardware including magnetic bases, flexible goose-neck mounts, mounting clamps, Velcro, removable double coated tape, and putty. These accessories are used to mount the video cameras to walls, doors, ceilings, etc. Also standard are additional lengths of cables for the wired video cameras. If wireless cameras are used, no camera cables are required.

21.5 SUMMARY

There is a widespread need for portable personnel and assets protection systems. These RDS systems protect VIPs on travel, as well as expensive assets: vehicles, boats, aircraft, etc. Typical systems provide video surveillance from a single carrying case that can be transported to a site and set up quickly to become an operational security system.

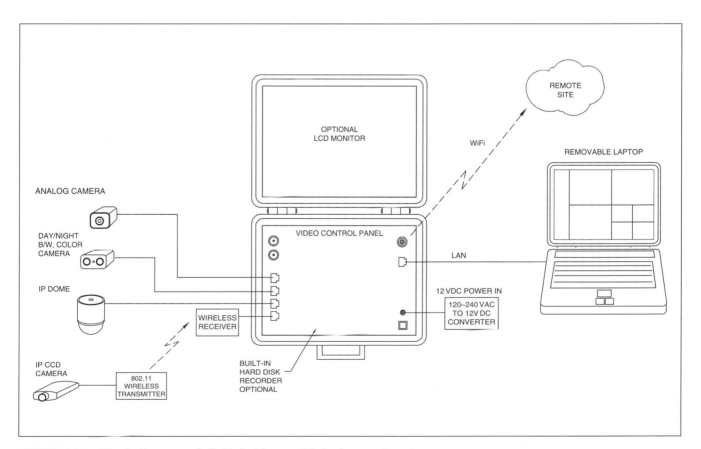

FIGURE 21-3 Block diagram of digital video rapid deployment system

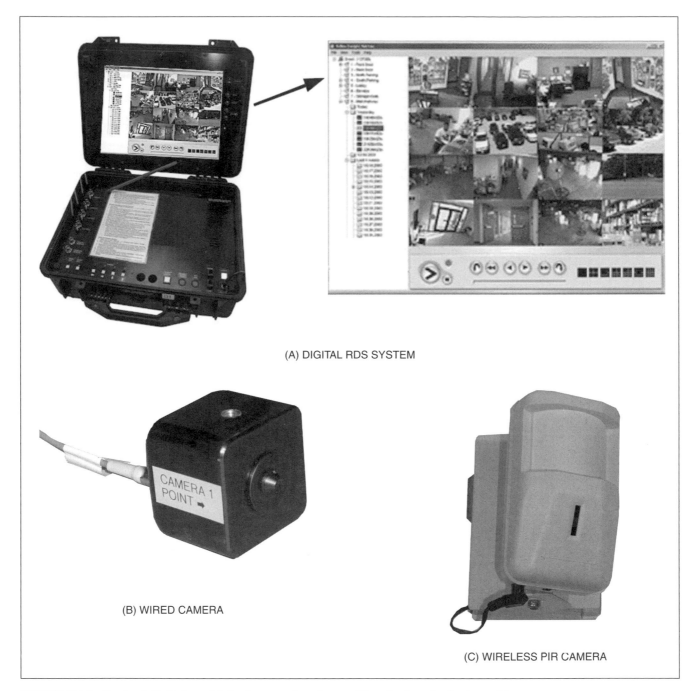

(A) DIGITAL RDS SYSTEM

(B) WIRED CAMERA

(C) WIRELESS PIR CAMERA

FIGURE 21-4   Typical digital rapid deployment system with wired and wireless video

Ideally it should be designed so that the maximum time between initial on-site arrival of the system and personnel operating it may be as short as *30 to 60 minutes.* RDS systems can communicate to cell phones, PDAs, and laptop computers to receive video images and provide worldwide coverage.

Chapter 22

Applications and Solutions—Sample Scenarios

CONTENTS

22.1   Overview

22.2   Lobby Surveillance

     22.2.1   Case: Analog Three-Camera Video Lobby Surveillance System

     22.2.2   Lobby Video Checklist

22.3   Elevator Surveillance

     22.3.1   100% Viewing of Elevator Cab

     22.3.2   Case: Analog Six-Camera Video Elevator Cab and Lobby System

     22.3.3   Elevator Video Checklist

22.4   Office Surveillance

     22.4.1   Case: Analog/Digital Six-Camera Office Video System

     22.4.2   Office Video Checklist

22.5   Retail Store Surveillance

     22.5.1   Small Retail Stores

     22.5.2   Large Retail Stores

         22.5.2.1   Overt Showroom Floor Surveillance

         22.5.2.2   Covert Showroom Floor Surveillance

         22.5.2.3   Case: Analog/Digital Eight-Camera Showroom Floor Video System

         22.5.2.4   Showroom Floor Video Checklist

22.6   Video Rapid Deployment System (RDS)

     22.6.1   Case: Analog Wired/Wireless Rapid Deployment Video System

     22.6.2   RDS System Checklist

22.7   Outdoor Parking Lot and Perimeter Surveillance

     22.7.1   Case: Digital wireless Twelve-Camera Parking Lot and Perimeter Video System

     22.7.2   Parking Lot/Perimeter Video Checklist

22.8   Single Site Digital Video over Wired and Wireless Network

     22.8.1   Case: Digital Video Surveillance at Distribution Warehouse

     22.8.2   Distribution Warehouse Checklist

22.9   Multiple Site Digital Video over Internet

     22.9.1   Case: Digital Video and Control over Internet to Remote Sites

     22.9.2   Internet to Remote Site Checklist

22.10   Correctional Facility Surveillance

     22.10.1   Overt Surveillance

         22.10.1.1   Perimeter

         22.10.1.2   Cell Blocks and Activity Areas

     22.10.2   Covert Surveillance

22.11   Banking and Financial Surveillance

     22.11.1   Public Areas

     22.11.2   Computer, Vault, and Money-Counting Rooms

     22.11.3   Check Identification

     22.11.4   Automatic Teller Machine

     22.11.5   Auto-Teller Drive-In

22.12   Lodging and Casino Surveillance Areas

     22.12.1   Hallway or Corridor

     22.12.2   Casino Floor

22.13   Airport, Seaport, and Highway Surveillance

22.14   Video Access Control

     22.14.1   Video ID System

     22.14.2   Video Storage and Retrieval System

     22.14.3   Video Turnstile

     22.14.4   Video Portal

     22.14.5   Video Vehicle Control

     22.14.6   Video Facial Recognition

     22.14.7   Video Iris and Retina Personnel Identification

22.15 Video to Train Security Personnel
22.16 Choosing a Professional Security Designer and Installer
22.17 Video Applications Checklist
22.18 Summary

22.1 OVERVIEW

Security and safety requirements encompass all the disciplines described in this book. The effectiveness of the video surveillance system compared with its low investment cost attests to its widespread use. This chapter provides design guidelines and hardware information, specific case studies, and a checklist for representative security applications. The institutions, facilities, and surveillance areas cover a wide range: (1) government/industrial/business agencies, (2) small and large retail stores, (3) correctional institutions, (4) banking and financial institutions, (5) lodging and casino establishments, (6) airports, seaports, and highway surveillance, and many others. The applications describe three generic-type systems: (1) legacy analog, (2) combined analog/digital, and (3) all digital systems. It describes a single site and a multiple site digital system, and a portable rapid deployment video system.

All the previous chapters have served as a basis for understanding the design requirements and hardware available to implement a practical video security system. This chapter analyzes specific applications and hardware, specifications, and questions to ask and get answered for several specific scenarios. Each case study states the problem and provides information for choosing hardware. A layout of the security problem identifies equipment locations and system requirements. A detailed block diagram for each case serves to identify the functions, define the hardware, and uncover potential problems. Solution to each case includes a bill of material (BOM) to define and choose the hardware. The BOM also serves as a beginning for a request for quotation from a vendor. The BOM forms the basis for a checklist during the design phase and final system checkout after installation.

Eight Case Studies. Eight case studies are analyzed: two are legacy analog systems, three are a combination of analog/digital, and three are all digital. Within the limited space available in this chapter, these eight specific applications are analyzed to teach the user and practitioner the methodology used in designing a video system. A layout, a block diagram, BOM, and checklist are provided for the following examples.

Analog. Two applications are legacy-based analog video systems. The case studies analyzed are:

- Analog Three-Camera Video Lobby Surveillance System
- Analog Six-Camera Video Elevator Cab and Lobby System.

At present there is a large installed base of video surveillance equipment using legacy cameras, analog transmission means tube monitors and magnetic tape–recording equipment. Much of this equipment will be in continued used for many years but is being augmented and will be replaced by digital equipment in the future. Present legacy systems now interconnected by analog video transmission means will be replaced by wired and wireless digital networks to provide multiple site monitoring.

Analog/Digital. Three applications are based on the combination of analog and digital video systems components. The case studies analyzed are:

- Analog/Digital Six-Camera Office Video System
- Analog/Digital Eight-Camera Showroom Floor Video System
- Analog Wired/Wireless Rapid Deployment Video System.

Integration of legacy analog equipment with digital video makes use of local area networks (LAN) and other networks including intranets and the Internet. Interface equipment is available to integrate the analog cameras and Internet protocol (IP) cameras into the digital system. Installed analog systems, new installations, and new rapid deployment of portable systems provide good scenarios for this type of equipment. Digital, wired and wireless (WiFi) video transmission provides the technical means to transmit the video over long distances and from site to site.

Digital. Three applications are based on the latest digital video hardware techniques. The case studies analyzed are:

- Digital Wireless Twelve-Camera Parking Lot and Perimeter Video System
- Digital Video Surveillance at Distribution Warehouse
- Digital Video and Control over Internet to Remote Sites.

The systems use digital IP cameras and digital transmission for video, communications, control, digital switching, multiplexing, and recording. They provide the most versatile means for intelligent video and automatic video surveillance (AVS). Most systems use wired networks including the Internet and intranet; however many make use of WiFi using the many 802.11x transmission protocols and compression and encryption algorithms to transmit the video images to multiple sites at any location. The video images are monitored on PCs, laptops, and PDAs, and recorded on DVR equipment or via virtual digital recording (VDR).

Video Surveillance Applications. The eight case studies listed above are but a few of the many video security applications encountered. The following are important applications that are not analyzed as case studies but are reviewed to provide insight into their particular requirements. These applications include their use in correctional facilities, banking and financial institutions, lodging and casino surveillance, and in airport, seaport, and highway surveillance. Each has unique requirements, and a brief analysis of each provides insight into optimizing video surveillance solutions for them.

Correctional Facility.   In addition to the standard video surveillance equipment requirements, these institutions require a higher level of physical protection from physical harm for facility guards from incarcerated inmates, and intentional vandalism to equipment. Other unique inmate safety requirements include a means for observing inmates while sleeping and those prone to suicide or other personal physical harm, and a means for observing the inmate and preventing such abuse. For inmate control, video provides the quick response and communications to security guards to thwart an outbreak of violence and subdue or apprehend offenders in *real-time*. Casinos also require specialized smart camera equipment to perform positive identification of customers to prevent unacceptable individuals from gambling.

Banking and Financial Institutions.   These institutions require a special means for protecting documents and money from theft. Other special requirements include monitoring cashiers, money counting rooms, and safes. The systems must provide quick response systems for intercepting holdups and provisions for communicating with internal security and outside law enforcement personnel to assist in apprehending offenders *in real-time*.

Lodging and Casino Establishments.   Hotels and motels require full-time surveillance of many facility locations including outdoor parking areas, indoor lobbies, hallways, reception and cashier areas, elevators, and elevator lobbies. Casinos have special requirements that must satisfy casino security managers, management, and state licensing commissions. Casinos also require specialized smart camera equipment to perform identification of customers to prevent unacceptable individuals from gambling. These video systems are used in: iris scan, retinal scan, and facial recognition.

Airport, Seaport, and Highway Locations and Facilities.   Airport and seaport terminal facilities require large video systems that transmit and operate over long distances and between many buildings. Highway surveillance requires transmission over very long distances. Each application has its unique requirements, some of which are described in this chapter.

Video Access Control and Personnel Identification.   Video systems are used to identify personnel requesting entry to or exit from a facility by having a security person view the face of a person requesting entry (or exit) and comparing it with a stored image of the person. With the use of video digital image analysis algorithms and iris scanning, retina scanning, and facial profiling, the equipment automatically identifies or rejects the person. Other video means for identifying personnel using their biometric descriptors include fingerprint and hand geometry.

Personnel Training Using Video.   Analog and digital video equipment is used extensively to train security personnel in all aspects of security. It is a convenient, cost-effective, and powerful visual tool to acquaint new personnel with the physical facilities, the management, security, and safety procedures. Section 22.15 gives some examples of how video can be used to train security guard personnel, and installing technicians.

Dealers and Installers.   An ingredient in the successful implementation and effective operation of any security system is a professional installer or installing company. Equally important is a professional maintenance program. Section 22.16 outlines criteria to assist in choosing a reliable security system integrator and installer.

Environmental Factors.   In designing the video system, the camera equipment chosen depends on whether it will be used indoors or outdoors. In indoor applications such as lobbies, stairwells, stockrooms, elevators, or computer rooms, minimum environmental protection is required. Outdoor equipment can be subjected to environmental factors including extreme temperature and humidity, high winds, precipitation (rain, sleet, and snow), dirt, dust, chemicals, and sand. The outdoor equipment must be designed to withstand and be serviceable under all these adverse environmental conditions. To maintain proper operation of lenses and cameras in outdoor environments, thermostatically controlled heaters and/or fans must be incorporated to maintain the interior of the housing within the temperature range of the camera and lens equipment. Periodic servicing of pan/tilt mechanisms must be performed, including lubrication of moving parts and checks for wear or deterioration of flexing or exposed wires.

The equipment may be required to operate under wide variations in light level if it is to be used for daytime and nighttime surveillance. Video equipment in outdoor applications operates under extreme variations in light level, ranging from low levels produced by artificial lighting for nighttime use to bright sunlight and sand or snow sun-reflected scenes. This often represents a one-million-to-one change in light level for which the camera system must compensate.

Video cameras and lenses are installed in indoor and outdoor environments using a simple camera bracket, or a camera housing and bracket, or a recessed mounting in the ceiling or wall. Camera brackets serve to fix the camera and lens at a location but do not protect them from vandalism or the environment.

Indoor and outdoor video equipment consists of camera mountings, camera housings, cameras, lenses, pan/tilt mechanisms, domes, visible or IR illuminators, and the cable runs required to transmit the power and control signals to the equipment and to transmit the video signal and any other communication back to the console room. The security room equipment consists of CRT monitors, LCDs, VCRs, DVRs, switchers, multiplexers, time/date, camera ID, message generators, hard-copy video printers, etc.

22.2 LOBBY SURVEILLANCE

A common surveillance area is an entrance lobby to a facility. The lobby has a front entrance door and one or more internal doors and is occupied by a receptionist, possibly a guard, visitors (business or public), and employees of the facility. The security functions to be performed by the video system, receptionist, and security staff include: (1) viewing the lobby area to determine that order prevails, (2) monitoring and controlling entry and exit of personnel through the internal doors, (3) monitoring and controlling material movement into and out of the main entrance, and (4) guarding the receptionist. The following case describes a video lobby surveillance system.

22.2.1 Case: Analog Three-Camera Video Lobby Surveillance System

Figure 22-1 shows a simple but common video security application of monitoring people entering and leaving the front lobby of a building and the surveillance of the reception area.

One camera is located in the lobby close to the ceiling and views the entrance door and lobby with a lens having a wide FOV, wide enough to see at least half of the lobby, the receptionist, and the front door. The second camera on the opposite wall views the other half of the lobby and the internal access door. The third camera is covertly mounted in a wall-mounted clock. Aside from choosing the equipment, choosing the camera locations is most important. The camera/lens should not be pointed in the direction of a bright light or the sun or toward an outside door or window if possible. If sunlight enters the camera lens directly, blooming (white areas in scene) can obliterate a part of the scene. CCD or CMOS cameras use automatic-iris lenses or electronic shuttering to compensate for light-level changes but do not always compensate well for a very bright spot in a scene. A person under surveillance who is back-illuminated by light from an exterior window or door is usually seen on the monitor as a black silhouette and cannot be identified.

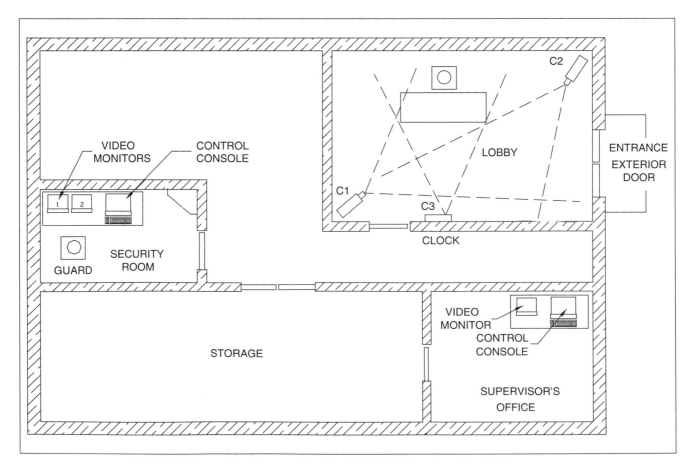

FIGURE 22-1   Analog three-camera lobby surveillance requirements

Some cameras that have automatic back-light compensation improves the image.

The video signals from the two overt video cameras and the covert camera in the lobby with the receptionist are transmitted to one or two monitors located at the remote security guard station. The two overt cameras view people entering and exiting through the front entrance door, most of the lobby, the receptionist, and the internal access door. The third, covert camera provides backup in the event the overt cameras are rendered inoperative. Figure 22-2 shows the block diagram for this system.

Table 22-1 is a BOM for such a three-camera overt/covert video system and lists the hardware necessary to complete such a system.

With each hardware component is a list of parameters that must be specified in order to define it. A logical starting point is the camera type. The cameras can be monochrome or color, 1/4-, 1/3-, or 1/2-inch format, CS mount (CS being most common), 117 or 24 VAC or 12 VDC powered. Choose a color camera, 1/3-inch format, CS mount, 12 VDC or 24 VAC. From Figure 22-1, the lens horizontal FOV for each camera should be 50°. Using Table 4.4 or the Lens Finder Kit, choose a 4.0-mm FL automatic-iris lens capable of covering a 1/3-inch format.

An automatic-iris lens is suggested because there are outside windows and a door. Use a good quality RG59/U coaxial cable or two-wire unshielded twisted pair (UTP) with transmitter and receiver since the distance between camera and security room is less than 600 feet. A multiplexer and four monitors or one monitor and a switcher can be used depending on whether 100% full-time coverage or time-shared (switched) coverage is adequate.

The two overt cameras can be integrated camera-lens-housing assemblies (Chapter 15) mounted directly on brackets, or cameras and lenses installed in housings and then bracket-mounted, depending on the vandalism/environmental factor. For a typical console, the monitor(s) should be of 9 inch diagonal or larger for optimum viewing. The multiplexer is an 8-channel system permitting display of all four cameras in a quad format or each individual camera. The switcher, if used, is a four-position, alarming sequential type. The DVR or VCR is programmed to record the pictures sequentially, in time-lapse mode from all three cameras. In the event the receptionist (or other alarm input) sounds an alarm, the recorder automatically switches to real-time recording. The video printer is available to make hard-copy prints of any video scene from the monitor or recorder.

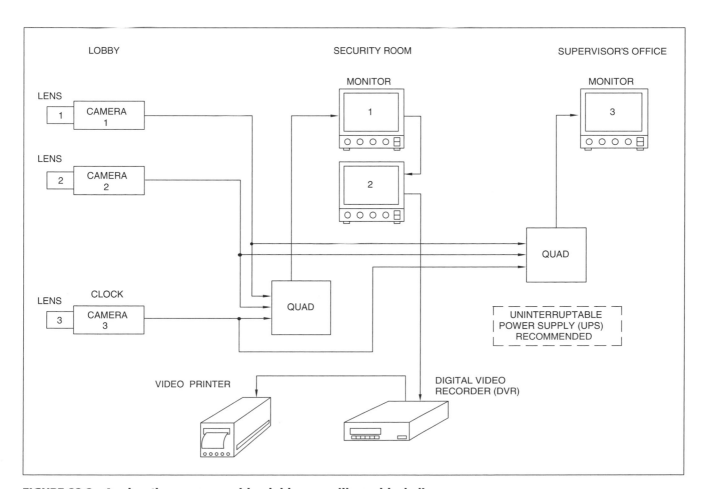

FIGURE 22-2   Analog three-camera video lobby surveillance block diagram

ITEM	QUANTITY	DESCRIPTION	LOCATION	COMMENTS
1	2	INTEGRATED CAMERAS 1, 2	LOBBY	TYPE: COLOR, CCD SENSOR SENSOR FORMAT: 1/4-, 1/3-inch FOCAL LENGTH: 4 mm, F/# 1.4–1.6 LENS MOUNT: CS, AUTOMATIC IRIS SEE TABLES 4-1, 4-2, 4-4, LENS FINDER KIT INPUT VOLTAGE: 24 VAC, OR 12 VDC USING 117 VAC CONVERTER
2	1	CAMERA 3	LOBBY SMALL CAMERA IN WALL CLOCK	TYPE: MONOCHROME OR COLOR, CCD SENSOR SENSOR FORMAT: 1/4- OR 1/3-inch FOCAL LENGTH: 3.6, 8, 11 mm LENS MOUNT: MINI, 12 mm VOLTAGE: 12 VDC USING 117 VAC CONVERTER
3	1	MAIN MONITOR	SECURITY ROOM	TYPE: COLOR, CRT OR LCD SCREEN SIZE: 9-, 13-, 15-, 17-inch MOUNTING: DESKTOP, RACK, BRACKET AUDIO: WITH OR WITHOUT
4	2	AUXILIARY MONITOR 2, 3	SECURITY ROOM SUPERVISORS OFFICE	TYPE: COLOR, CRT OR LCD SCREEN SIZE: 9-, 13-, 15-, 17-inch MOUNTING: DESKTOP, RACK, BRACKET AUDIO: WITH OR WITHOUT
5	1	QUAD	SECURITY ROOM	NUMBER OF CHANNELS: 4 DISPLAY: FULL, QUAD, SEQUENCE
6	1	DIGITAL VIDEO RECORDER (DVR)	SECURITY ROOM, IN LOCKED COMPARTMENT	TYPE: DVR WITH 250 GByte STORAGE, VMD (VIDEO MOTION DETECTOR)
7	1	VIDEO PRINTER	SECURITY ROOM	TYPE: THERMAL, INK-JET, MONOCHROME OR COLOR PRINT SIZE: 3.5×4.0, OR 8½×11 inch
8	—	TRANSMISSION CABLE	CEILING, WALL	TYPE, CAT 5, UTP, COAXIAL CABLE INSTALLATION: FREE AIR, CONDUIT, TRAY, PLENUM
9	1	UNINTERRUPTIBLE POWER SUPPLY (UPS)	SECURITY ROOM	BACKUP POWER DURING POWER OUTAGE INPUT: 120–240 VAC, OUTPUT: 120VAC POWER OUT: 500 WATT

Table 22-1 Three-Camera Analog Lobby Surveillance Bill of Materials

22.2.2 Lobby Video Checklist

- How many cameras are required to cover all pertinent areas?
- Will the light level remain relatively constant or will cameras view direct sunlight?
- Is a manual or automatic-iris lens required?
- Should other covert cameras be installed for backup?
- Should the video recorder be time-lapse or should it record on manual demand or should it be automatic (alarm input)?

22.3 ELEVATOR SURVEILLANCE

Crimes against elevator passengers have increased significantly in recent years; the threat represents a potentially high liability to the building owner. The use of video in elevators reduces the risk and harm being perpetrated on passengers in elevators. From an asset-protection point of view, elevators represent a valuable capital investment. Passengers riding elevators should be under surveillance to deter violators from defacing and vandalizing them. This application describes the equipment to monitor elevator cabs and the lobby.

A passenger entering an elevator with a stranger is temporarily "locked in" with the person until the elevator stops and the door opens on another floor. This serious problem has come about because almost all elevators are automatically controlled and there are no elevator operators. Years ago the elevator operator performed the function (whether consciously or not) of visual surveillance in the "locked" elevator cab. No one was ever alone in the elevator. The operator was a deterrent who could also assist in preventing molestations, robberies, and vandalism. This inherent protection now absent on most elevators is returned via the use of overt video and audio intercom systems.

Repair costs resulting from vandalism in elevators are well known. Building owners expend thousands of dollars to "face-lift" elevator cab interiors that have been defaced and vandalized. Studies and actual practice have shown that the installation of video monitoring systems in public facilities has significantly decreased elevator cab vandalism, as well as crimes against individuals.

22.3.1 100% Viewing of Elevator Cab

The essential requirement of an elevator video surveillance system is to see a picture of the entire elevator interior on a remote video monitor. The picture should maximize the facial view of the occupants of elevator cab and have sufficient image quality and resolution to identify them and their actions.

A wide-FOV lens/camera system in an unobtrusive video housing provides 100% visual coverage of an elevator interior. The video image is displayed remotely in the building lobby and/or manager's office for real-time surveillance. The potential elevator passenger entering the building lobby can view the lobby monitor and determine that the elevator is safe to enter. Likewise the passenger knows that everyone in the elevator is under surveillance by the security guard or other people in the lobby. A study of the elevator cab and camera/lens FOV geometry shows that a wide-FOV camera located in a ceiling corner of the cab optimizes the elevator cab surveillance (Figure 22-3).

The camera system should have a 90° horizontal FOV and about a 70° vertical FOV. The camera/lens optical axis should be directed 45° from each wall and 45° down from the horizontal (ceiling). This viewing geometry results in 100% coverage of the elevator volume and provides excellent probability of occupant and activity identification. Another essential requirement for the cab video camera system is that it be as unobtrusive and as small as possible since the elevator cab is a confined area and space is at a premium.

As with other security-related equipment, it is essential that the camera system in the cab—which is exposed to abuse by potential vandals—be constructed to be vandal-proof, and to adequately protect the lens and camera inside. One durable housing enclosure material is stainless steel (Figure 22-4a).

A brushed, rippled, or textured finish hides the vandal's attempts to deface the surface. A second choice of material is polycarbonate plastic (Figure 22-4b). The mirror corner mount camera uses a one-way acrylic or polycarbonate window to conceal the wide-angle lens and camera (Figure 22-4c). Other desirable features for an elevator video camera system include: (1) a locked, hinged cover, (2) easy access to the lens and camera by maintenance personnel, (3) a removable, unbreakable window part made

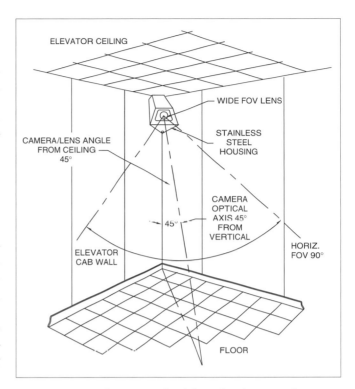

FIGURE 22-3 Elevator cab video viewing requirement

of polycarbonate plastic, and (4) an easily removable camera/lens assembly for servicing. The removable viewing window is usually a 0.25 inch thick mar-resistant polycarbonate material. Tempered glass can be used in place of polycarbonate to provide a scratch- and chemical-resistant window.

Several other camera/lens/housing configurations are available to mount directly into the ceiling corner of the elevator cab. The rear of the camera/lens housing is shaped to fit directly into the ceiling corner of the elevator cab with the front of the housing projecting minimally into the cab interior. Elevator camera systems use wide-angle lenses: 3.5 mm FL for a 1/2-inch camera format, 2.8 mm FL for a 1/3-inch camera, and 2.5 mm or 2.1 mm for a 1/4-inch camera. With either combination, approximately a 90° horizontal by 75° vertical FOV is obtained. Figure 22-5 shows a photograph taken from a video monitor of the camera scene in a 5-foot by 7-foot elevator.

An installation requiring a covert video camera is accomplished by using: (1) a small video camera, (2) a small remote-head camera, or (3) right-angle optics (Figure 22-6).

A small camera (Figure 22-6a) 1 inch × 1 inch × 1/2 inch can be installed inside an elevator cab wall or ceiling with only the front of the lens visible to the passenger. The remote-head camera (Figure 22-6b) is mounted in the elevator cab wall or ceiling with only the wide-FOV 2.8, 2.5, or 2.1 mm lens in view in the cab. The right-angle optical system (Figure 22-6c) redirects the wide-field image by 90° without vignetting (loss of light at the edge of the image) so that a full-size camera can be mounted parallel

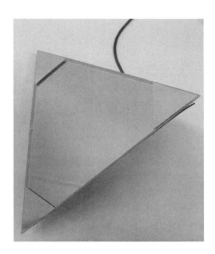

(A) STAINLESS STEEL
PAINTED STEEL
CORNER MOUNT

(B) POLYCARBONATE
CORNER MOUNT

(C) ACRYLIC AND
STEEL CORNER
MIRROR MOUNT

FIGURE 22-4   Wide FOV elevator video systems

MAN TRYING TO HIDE IN CORNER UNDER CAMERA

FIGURE 22-5 Elevator cab with 100% video image coverage

to the cab ceiling. When a high resolution system camera is used, the right-angle lens adapter and wide-FOV lens are completely above the cab ceiling with only the wide-FOV lens visible in the cab. The ceiling camera location is least conspicuous to passengers but has the disadvantage of viewing all occupants from overhead, so that fewer facial views are obtained.

Depending on the elevator cab construction and aesthetics required, the lenses can be hidden behind a semi-transparent window to make them completely covert in all of these installations.

22.3.2   Case: Analog Six-Camera Video Elevator Cab and Lobby System

This case describes a requirement to monitor the elevator cab and lobby. Figure 22-7 shows the six-camera elevator cab and lobby video surveillance system.

The system consists of: (1) one video camera/lens and housing unit installed in each of the elevator cabs (four total), (2) two cameras and lenses in the lobby, (3) four video-transmission cables from the cab cameras to the console room, (4) a video switcher, quad splitter or multiplexer, (5) four monitors: two in the console room and two in the lobby (6) a time-lapse/alarm DVR, and (7) a video hard-copy printer.

Two monitors in the main floor elevator lobby display a quad picture showing the interior of the four elevator cabs. The scenes from the elevator cabs and the two cameras in the lobby are displayed on the two monitors in the security console. A time-lapse recorder in the console room records the elevator or lobby scenes, and a video printer prints out hard copy on demand. Figure 22-8 shows the block diagram for the six-camera elevator cab and lobby surveillance system.

In operation, each video camera in the elevator cab (1, 2, 3, and 4) views the interior of its respective cab and transmits the video picture to the quad splitter/combiner and video switcher, and then on to the monitors, recorder, and video printer. The video output is transmitted via a very flexible cable along the existing traveling cables in the elevator shaft, down to the lobby. The video cable is laced in with the existing cable run, with one end starting at the

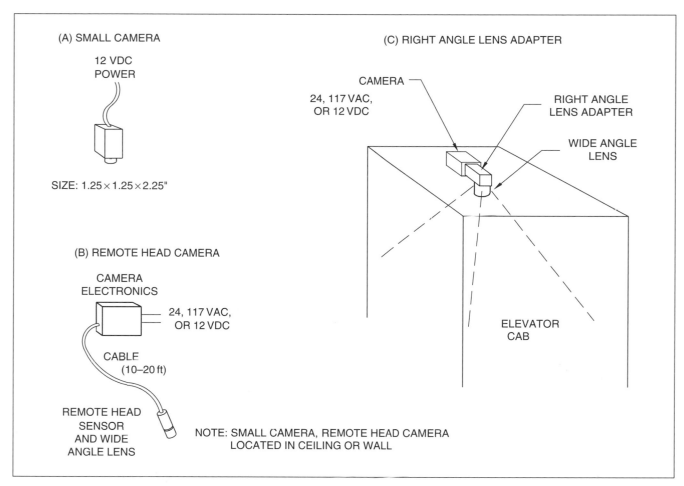

(A) SMALL CAMERA

12 VDC
POWER

SIZE: 1.25 × 1.25 × 2.25"

(B) REMOTE HEAD CAMERA

CAMERA
ELECTRONICS

24, 117 VAC,
OR 12 VDC

CABLE
(10–20 ft)

REMOTE HEAD
SENSOR
AND WIDE
ANGLE LENS

(C) RIGHT ANGLE LENS ADAPTER

CAMERA

24, 117 VAC,
OR 12 VDC

RIGHT ANGLE
LENS ADAPTER

WIDE ANGLE
LENS

ELEVATOR
CAB

NOTE: SMALL CAMERA, REMOTE HEAD CAMERA
LOCATED IN CEILING OR WALL

FIGURE 22-6 Covert elevator cab video systems

elevator cab and ending at a fixed junction terminal box halfway up the elevator shaft. From the junction terminal box, standard coaxial cable, UTP, or fiber-optic cable techniques are used. The length of cable needed is equal to the height of the elevator travel (H). The location of the junction box is usually midway up the elevator shaft ($\frac{1}{2}H$), minimizing the cable length.

The camera power is obtained from an existing 117 VAC power outlet in the cab ceiling on top of the cab. This is not a routine video cable installation, and elevator maintenance personnel should be contacted for information pertinent to the specific installation. Installing the traveling cable uses techniques familiar to experienced elevator installers and maintenance personnel. Since the cable flexes, bends, and twists each time the elevator cab moves, the cable chosen must be flexible to have a long lifetime. Stranded-type RG59/U is the most common coaxial cable used.

Fiber-optic cable offers the advantages of electrical-noise immunity for the transmission of the video signal from the elevator cab to the junction box and on to the monitor. Since the elevator shaft is an electrically "noisy" environment, electronics, relays, motors, solid-state and mechanical switches are in constant use. The use of fiber

optics completely eliminates the possibility of electrical interference (Chapter 6). A recent alternative to coaxial, UTP wired cable, and fiber optics is a digital wireless system using the 802.11 protocol. This system would use the WiFi 802.11 transmission system. Table 22-2 is a BOM for the six-camera elevator cab surveillance system. The system uses analog cameras in the elevator cabs and analog cameras in the lobby.

The elevator camera can be a 1/2-, 1/3-, or 1/4-inch format CCD or CMOS with a CS or minilens (12 mm) mount. Since the lighting from floor to floor varies when this cab stops at floors and the main lobby, an automatic-iris lens, a manual-iris lens, or an electronic shuttered camera is chosen to compensate for the light level changes. From Table 4-4, a 3.5 mm FL will see 104° horizontal on a 1/2-inch format sensor, a 2.8 mm FL lens will see 96° horizontal on a 1/3-inch format and a 2.2 mm a 93° FOV on a 1/4-inch format camera. To obtain the 60° FOV required for the lobby lenses, an 8.0 mm FL lens is used on the 1/2-inch format or a 6 mm FL on a 1/3-inch is used.

The most durable housing for the elevator is the stainless-steel design shown in Figure 22-4. Electrical access holes are drilled in the elevator cab, the housing is mounted, and the camera/lens is installed.

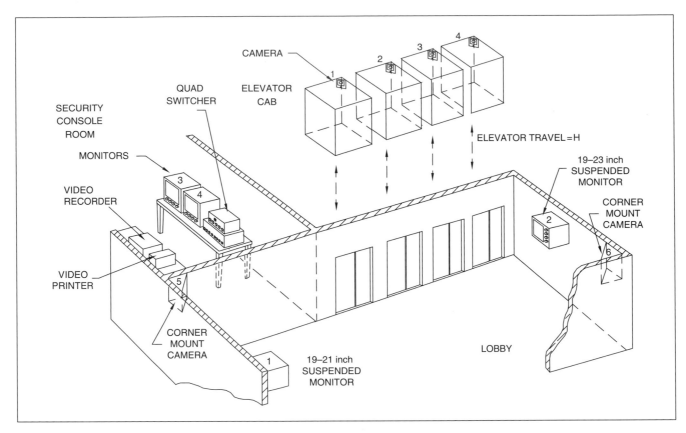

FIGURE 22-7   Analog six-camera elevator cab and lobby requirements

The lobby monitors should be large—17 to 23 inch diagonal—depending on lobby size and viewing distance, and mounted from ceiling or wall brackets. The faces and activities of persons in the elevator cab as seen from these monitors should be visible by anyone in the lobby. The two monitors in the security room are 9-inch CRT or 15-inch LCD, for maximum resolution for the guard. The four channel DVR records the elevator cab images. Alternatively if an analog VCR is chosen for recording, the images are recorded in S-VHS format. The video printer provides a convenient means to issue a hard-copy picture printout to dispatch a guard or for later apprehension or prosecution. For court prosecution, annotated time and date on the video frame is necessary.

22.3.3 Elevator Video Checklist

The following points should be considered for any elevator security requirement to provide maximum deterrence of crime with minimum intimidation of regular passengers.

- Should the cab video cameras be overtly or covertly installed? An overt system with warning labels is the recommended choice and can deter a would-be offender from committing a crime.

- The covert system has the advantage that the offender is not aware that they are being viewed, and immediate apprehension by a guard is more probable.
- Some passengers may be intimidated by overt video; a concealed camera system may be less offensive.
- The elevator cab camera/lens should have a wide FOV. The optimum system has a 90° horizontal FOV (wall to wall) and about a 70° vertical FOV. Pointing should be 45° downward.
- No one should be able to hide anywhere in the elevator.
- The camera housing and window should be vandal-proof and should be constructed to withstand direct impact from destructive blows. It must have a vandal-proof keylock, or tamperproof screws.
- The elevator lighting should be sufficient to use a standard CCD or CMOS camera.
- Does the situation warrant a monitor on each floor for added protection? As a minimum, most installations use a monitor in the lobby and the security room.
- A permanent record of the monitor picture is recommended.

22.4 OFFICE SURVEILLANCE

Numerous government, industrial, and business facilities suffer millions of dollars in lost assets removed from

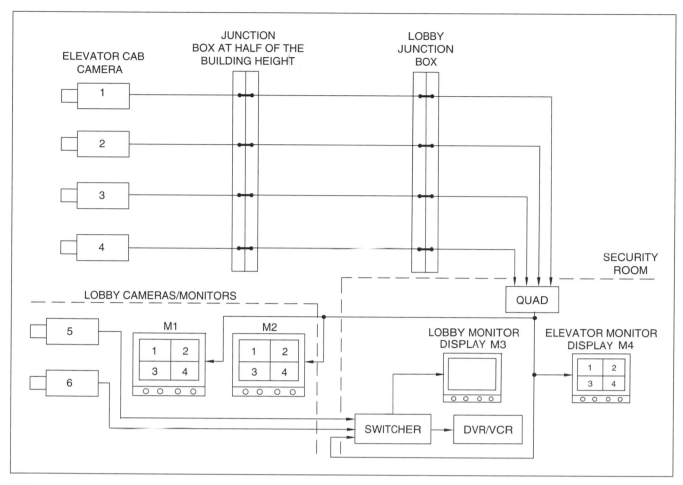

FIGURE 22-8 **Analog six-camera elevator cab and lobby surveillance block diagram**

office facilities by dishonest employees or maintenance contractors. Business hardware such as calculators, telephones, PC and laptop computers, PDAs, and facsimile and copying machines are prime targets and regularly stolen. Company software programs and company data files are physically or electronically copied and removed. The most effective measure an institution can take to reduce or eliminate these losses is the installation of covert video in those affected areas. The following section describes concealed video camera/lens surveillance equipment for an office environment.

22.4.1 Case: Analog/Digital Six-Camera Office Video System

The purpose for covert video surveillance is to observe people carrying out normal behavior as well as those committing unlawful acts. The video system should assist in the apprehension and prosecution of individuals carrying out unlawful acts. The covert system also acts as a backup to an overt video system in the event the overt system is sabotaged or has become inoperative in some way.

Figure 22-9 shows a layout of an office environment and covert cameras concealed judiciously in objects found in a typical office and in the ceiling.

The small cameras and lenses permit the covert video to be easily installed in a ceiling, wall, or other article or fixture in the facility. The cameras can be installed in lamps, pictures, exit signs, emergency lights, radios, file cabinets, computers, etc. If there are analog cameras already installed they can be integrated into a digital system using an analog to IP interface adapter. If the cameras are to replace an old system or a new system is to be added, either analog or digital covert cameras can be used. The covert cameras transmit the video in the image by coax or UTP cable, fiber-optic, wireless analog or wireless digital means. Wireless covert installations are easy to install and require less time for installation. The analog wireless camera uses a 900 MHz or 2.4 GHz analog transmitter/receiver pair. The digital system uses an IP camera and transmits over a LAN and or other digital network. The wireless camera uses the digital 802.11 transmitting protocol.

The covert camera can be disguised as a water sprinkler mounted in the office ceiling to provide an excellent

ITEM	QUANTITY	DESCRIPTION	LOCATION	COMMENTS
1	4	ANALOG CAMERA 1, 2, 3, 4	ONE IN EACH ELEVATOR CAB	TYPE: COLOR, CCD SENSOR SENSOR FORMAT: 1/4, OR 1/3-inch LENS MOUNT: CS OR MINI (12 mm) AUTOMATIC IRIS OR ELECTRONIC SHUTTER INPUT VOLTAGE: 24 VAC, 12 VDC WITH 117 VAC CONVERTER
2	4	LENS	ELEVATOR CAB	IRIS: MANUAL OR AUTOMATIC FOCAL LENGTH: 2.8 mm ON 1/3-inch, 2.5 OR 2.2 mm ON 1/4-inch, F/#: 1.8 MOUNT: CS OR MINI (12 mm) SEE TABLES 4-1, 4-2, 4-4, LENS FINDER KIT
3	2	INTEGRATED ANALOG CAMERA 5, 6	TWO IN LOBBY	TYPE: COLOR, CCD SENSOR SENSOR FORMAT: 1/4, OR 1/3-inch FOCAL LENGTH: 3.8 ON 1/4-inch LENS MOUNT: CS OR MINI (12 mm) AUTOMATIC IRIS OR ELECTRONIC SHUTTER INPUT VOLTAGE: 24 VAC, 12 V DC WITH 117 VAC CONVERTER
4	4	HOUSING	ELEVATOR CAB	TYPE: INDOOR, TRIANGULAR, CORNER, VANDAL PROOF MATERIAL: STAINLESS STEEL, POLYCARBONATE
5	2	HOUSING	LOBBY	TYPE: INDOOR, CEILING MOUNT, VANDAL PROOF MATERIAL: POLYCARBONATE, STAINLESS STEEL
6	2	MONITOR 1, 2	LOBBY	TYPE: COLOR, CRT OR LCD SCREEN SIZE: 19-, 21-, OR 23-inch MOUNTING: HANGING BRACKET AUDIO: WITH OR WITHOUT
7	2	MONITOR 3, 4	SECURITY ROOM	TYPE: COLOR, CRT OR LCD SCREEN SIZE: 9-, 13-, -19, 21-inch MOUNTING: DESKTOP, RACK AUDIO: WITH OR WITHOUT
8	1	QUAD	SECURITY ROOM	DISPLAY 4 ELEVATOR CAB CAMERAS: FULL, QUAD, SEQUENCE
9	1	SWITCHER	SECURITY ROOM	8 CHANNEL, HOMING, SEQUENTIAL
10	1	DIGITAL VIDEO RECORDER (DVR)	SECURITY ROOM, IN LOCKED COMPARTMENT	TYPE: DVR WITH 250 GByte STORAGE, TIME/DATE, CAMERA ID
11	1	VIDEO PRINTER	SECURITY ROOM	½TYPE: THERMAL, INK-JET, MONOCHROME OR COLOR PRINT SIZE: 3.5×4.0 OR 8½×11 inch
12	—	ELEVATOR SHAFT TRANSMISSION CABLE	(A) LACED TO ELEVATOR TRAVELING CABLE (B) JUNCTION BOX TERMINATION IN SHAFT	(A) TYPE: COAXIAL, UTP, FIBER OPTIC (B) INSTALLATION: PLENUM, CONDUIT ON/IN WALL
13	OPTION	WIRELESS TRANSMISSION	VIDEO TRANSMITTED FROM ELEVATOR CAB TO SECURITY ROOM	DIGITAL WIFI USING TRANSMITTER/RECEIVER AND 802.11A, 802.11B, OR 802.11G PROTOCOL
14	OPTION	UNINTERRUPTIBLE POWER SUPPLY(UPS)	SECURITY ROOM	BACKUP POWER DURING POWER OUTAGE INPUT: 120–240 VAC, OUTPUT: 120 VAC POWER OUT: 500 WATT

UTP CABLING FROM THE ELEVATOR CAB TO JUNCTION BOX IN MIDWAY UP ELEVATOR SHAFT. UTP, COAXIAL CABLE OR FIBER-OPTIC CABLE FROM THE JUNCTION BOX TO THE SECURITY ROOM.

Table 22-2   Analog Six-Camera Elevator Cab and Lobby Bill of Materials

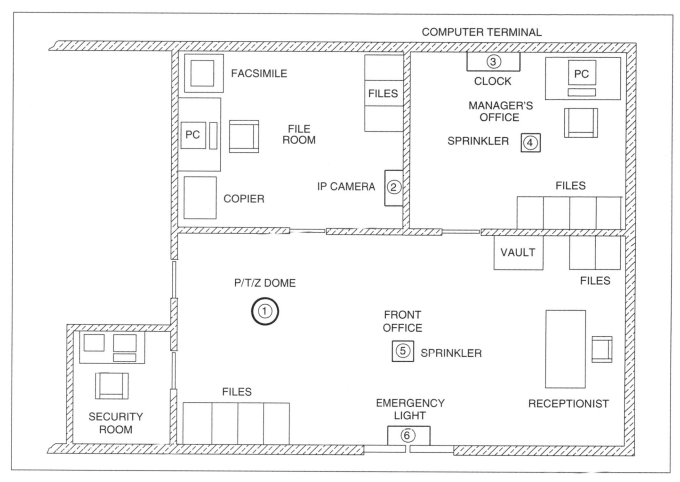

FIGURE 22-9 Six-camera covert office requirements

view of office activities. This unique surveillance system is unobtrusively disguised as a conventional sprinkler head, as used in countless industrial and office premises. In one version a straight or right-angle pinhole lens is mounted on a camera that has a sprinkler-head fixture mounted to the front of the lens with a beam-directing mirror to aim the camera FOV at the desired location. Only the sprinkler head and small mirror assembly protrude below the ceiling. The mirror can be adjusted over a range of angles to provide effective covert surveillance from a horizontal view, down to approximately −60°. One having a straight down view is also available. At normal viewing distances of 10–20 feet, it is unlikely that any observer will recognize or be able to detect the mirror in the sprinkler head. In a second version, an integrated sprinkler-head camera using a single board camera is mounted to the ceiling with a magnetic mount in a drop ceiling application or mechanically attached to the ceiling in a solid ceiling application.

As with any video camera, power is from 117 or 24 VAC, or 12 VDC, and the video is transmitted to the monitor via wired or wireless means. Low-power analog RF, microwave, or IR transmitters can provide analog video transmission from the camera location to the monitor-

ing location if it is impractical to install hard wire cable. Digital WiFi transmitter/receiver pairs can transmit the video image digitally from the camera to the monitoring location.

Areas and objects of particular interest for theft in an office environment include vaults, file cabinets, computers, facsimiles and copiers, software, and company records (Figure 22-9). Figure 22-10 shows suitable covert camera objects. Three cameras and lenses are ceiling-mounted, two disguised as water sprinkler heads, and one dome with a 360° panning capability to increase surveillance coverage and follow a moving person or activity in the scene. The remaining three cameras are hidden in an emergency lighting fixture, a wall clock, and an exit sign. Figure 22-11 is a block diagram of the hardware and electrical interconnections required for the system.

The signals to and from the cameras, lenses, and panning units are transmitted to the security room via hard-wire, fiber optic, or wireless means. The console equipment includes monitors, a recorder, and hard-copy video printer. Table 22-3 is a bill of materials for the six-camera analog/digital covert office surveillance system.

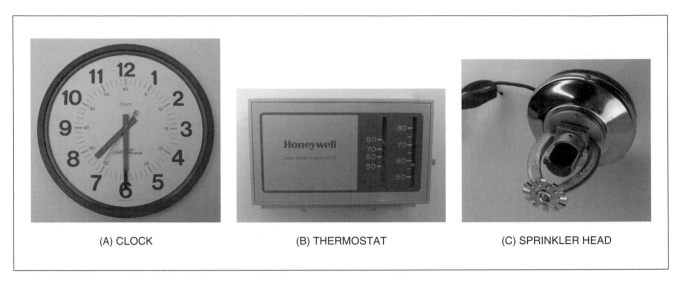

(A) CLOCK   (B) THERMOSTAT   (C) SPRINKLER HEAD

FIGURE 22-10   Typical covert cameras

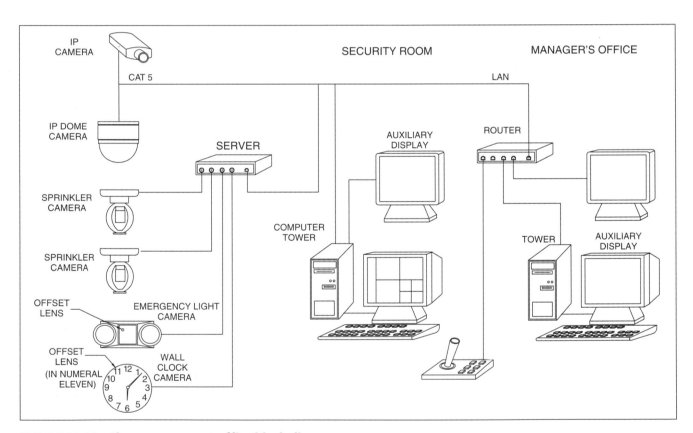

FIGURE 22-11   Six-camera covert office block diagram

The camera/lens in the clock in the manager's office uses a very small CCD or CMOS camera and offset mini-lens optics to view the office door and files (Chapter 4). The fixed ceiling sprinkler monitors the manager's desk and computer terminal. For the file room, an operating wall-mounted emergency lighting fixture monitors the computer, copier, facsimile, and files. The front office personnel, office entrance, vault, and files are monitored with two ceiling-mounted cameras: (1) sprinkler, (2) P/T/Z dome and one wall mounted exit-sign camera. Strictly speaking, the dome camera is not a covert camera but since the observer cannot see whether the camera is pointing in their direction it is considered semi-covert. The dome camera can pan 360°, and uses a zoom lens and 1/4-inch format camera. The exit-sign camera views anyone leaving the manager's office or accessing the vault.

ITEM	QUANTITY	DESCRIPTION	LOCATION	COMMENTS
1	1	DIGITAL IP PAN/TILT DOME CAMERA 1	FRONT OFFICE	CAMERA TYPE: IP COLOR, CCD SENSOR SENSOR FORMAT: 1/4, 1/3-inch LENS TYPE: OPTICAL ZOOM: 20×, DIGITAL ZOOM: 10× HOUSING: TINTED DOME PAN ROTATION: 360° CONTINUOUS TILT: 0 TO −90° VARIABLE SPEED
2	1	DIGITAL IP CAMERA 2	FILE ROOM	CAMERA TYPE: IP COLOR, CCD SENSOR SENSOR FORMAT: 1/4, OR 1/3-inch; LENS MOUNT: CS INPUT VOLTAGE: 117 VAC 24 VAC, 12 VDC USING 117 VAC-TO-12 VDC CONVERTER
3	1	ANALOG CLOCK CAMERA 3	MANAGER'S OFFICE	CAMERA TYPE: ANALOG COLOR, CCD SENSOR SENSOR FORMAT: 1/4-, 1/3-inch; LENS MOUNT: MINI (12 mm) FOCAL LENGTH: 6, 8 mm; F/#: 1.6
4	2	ANALOG SPRINKLER HEAD CAMERA 4, 5	FRONT OFFICE, FILE ROOM	CAMERA TYPE: ANALOG COLOR, CCD SENSOR SENSOR FORMAT: 1/4-, OR 1/3-inch; LENS MOUNT: MINI (12 mm) INTEGRATED SPRINKLER HEAD, CAMERA LENS; FOCAL LENGTH: 8 OR 11 mm F/#: 1.8
5	1	ANALOG EMERGENCY LIGHT CAMERA 6	FRONT OFFICE	CAMERA TYPE: ANALOG COLOR CCD SENSOR SENSOR FORMAT: 1/4-, 1/3-inch LENS MOUNT: MINI (12 mm) FOCAL LENGTH: 6, 8 mm; F/#: 1.6
6	2	MONITORS	SECURITY ROOM, MANAGER'S OFFICE	TYPE: COLOR, CRT OR LCD SCREEN SIZE: 9-, 13-, 15-inch MOUNTING: DESKTOP AUDIO: WITH OR WITHOUT
7	1	ANALOG CAMERA SERVER	SECURITY ROOM	TYPE: 4 CHANNEL
8	1	IP ROUTER	SECURITY ROOM	TYPE: 8 CHANNEL
9	2	DESKTOP/TOWER COMPUTER	SECURITY ROOM, MANAGER'S OFFICE	COMPUTER, DISPLAY, KEYBOARD, 250 GByte STORAGE, VMD
10	1	P/T/Z CONTROLLER	SECURITY ROOM	CONTROLS: PAN/TILT/ZOOM
11	1	VIDEO PRINTER	SECURITY ROOM	TYPE: THERMAL, INK-JET, MONOCHROME OR COLOR PRINT SIZE: 3.5 × 4.0, 8 ½ × 11 inch
12	—	TRANSMISSION CABLE	EACH CAMERA TO SECURITY ROOM	(A) TYPE: CAT-5, UTP, COAXIAL (B) INSTALLATION: PLENUM, CONDUIT ON/IN WALL
13	OPTION	WIRELESS TRANSMISSION	EACH CAMERA TO SECURITY ROOM	DIGITAL WIFI USING TRANSMITTER/RECEIVER AND 802.11A, 802.11B OR 802.11G PROTOCOL
14	OPTION	UNINTERRUPTIBLE POWER SUPPLY (UPS)	SECURITY ROOM	BACKUP POWER DURING POWER OUTAGE INPUT: 120–240 VAC, OUTPUT: 120 VAC POWER OUT: 500 WATT

Table 22-3 Analog/Digital Six-Camera Office Covert Bill of Materials

22.4.2 Office Covert Video Checklist

- Will the covert video installation be temporary or permanent?
- If the installation is temporary, should it be battery or AC-line powered?
- Should the cameras be wired or wireless?
- Should the system be analog or digital? If remote site operation is required it should be digital with some form of security scrambling or encryption.
- Does the security application require immediate guard response and/or video recording for later action or corporate use?
- Will the covert video be installed by management, the security department or by trusted outside security providers?

22.5 RETAIL STORE SURVEILLANCE

The role of video is to provide the "remote eyes" for management and the security department; video is the most effective tool for an overall retail store security system. Security and management personnel should be able to view many locations within the store from the security console and corporate offices. The viewed scenes should be of point-of-sale terminals, cashiers and merchandise, expensive products, and access and exit locations. Cameras can be overt and/or covert and have panning, tilting, and zooming where necessary. Video domes are particularly useful in retail store applications. The video system should also automatically alert the security guard via VMDs, alarm sensors, or signals from security or sales personnel on the floor. DVRs and VCRs should record the viewed camera scenes in real-time or time-lapse. The recorders should automatically change to the real-time mode when activated by these alarms. A video printer can provide hard copy when immediate action is required. Monochrome cameras provide the highest resolution and sensitivity, but the use of color cameras makes identification of persons and objects quicker and more accurate. Video provides a significant cost advantage as compared with the equivalent security personnel required to perform the surveillance function.

22.5.1 Small Retail Stores

The retail industry experts report that inventory shrinkage typically originates at the point of sale. The industry estimates that three times as much shrinkage occurs at the cash register than anywhere else in the store. Inventory shrinkage also occurs through theft out the back door by employees and outside vendors. Shrinkage drops dramatically when point-of-sale data are recorded with a complete video image of exactly what was purchased, by whom, and through which salesperson. For cash register displays, the data include date, time, items purchased with quantities and prices, total cost, the amount tendered, the amount of change, transaction number, register number, and operator name.

At convenience stores, the number one cause of inventory shrinkage is employee theft at the cash register. The use of video surveillance can significantly reduce this loss. When the video image of the cashier, register, customer, and merchandise is combined with the cash register amount, the store manager sees what merchandise was purchased, what items and amounts were entered at the cash register, how payments were made, where they were deposited, and what change was given. Video surveillance in small retail stores is accomplished with equipment similar to the lobby case in Section 22.2.1. To connect the register transaction with the cashier, customer, and merchandise, a cash register interface unit is used which takes the form of an electronic or electro-optical interface.

22.5.2 Large Retail Stores

Successful retail store security systems require the integration of alarm sensors, intrusion detectors, video, and the coordination of personnel to carry out preplanned response procedures. Security personnel and employees need to work as a team. Two-way radio communication between floor security officers, the sales force, and control console personnel provides an effective means for maximizing video capabilities. The security console operator (and management) view the selling floor via the video system and look out for shoplifting, and system and procedural violations. An operator on seeing a violation by an employee or customer on the floor, radios an officer on the floor, who goes to the area in question and assists or apprehends in whatever way necessary. If an officer sees someone coming into the store and thinks that person looks suspicious, the officer will radio the security operator that there is a suspicious person and give a description that allows security personnel at the video console to follow the person and watch his or her actions on the monitor. It is a cooperative effort, with the floor officers directly involved with the console operator and management.

Overt video cameras visible to the customer deter the temptation of the casual shopper, customer, or thief. Professional thieves believe that since the selling floor is too large, and there are too many people, the security personnel can not see everything all the time. They see the overt cameras and know where they are pointing. This suggests the use of optical domes to camouflage the cameras or the use of covert video in the form of disguised sprinkler heads, etc. The plastic domes conceal the panning, tilting, and zooming video system from the observer. The purpose for concealing the system is so that the observer cannot see the direction in which the camera is pointing. By this subterfuge one camera system scans and views a large area without the observers knowing at any instant whether they are under observation. Most new P/T/Z domes in use are from 5 to 7 inches in diameter and drop below the ceiling by 5 to 8 inches. The requirement that the lens view through the dome results in some light loss, typically 50%. Some domes can be "dummy" domes that do not have cameras in them, act as a deterrent and may be wired so that cameras can be installed should the need arise.

22.5.2.1 Overt Showroom Floor Surveillance

The primary objectives for overt video cameras on the sales floor are the deterrence of customer shoplifting and internal theft by employees. Overt cameras located in areas having high visibility to customers and employees can watch areas having expensive merchandise. Color cameras at ceiling level view the main selling floor area. These P/T/Z dome cameras can view large areas and are used effectively by security console operators to identify and watch suspicious actions by customers or potential thieves. The dome camera can track a suspicious person and has an optical and electronic magnification sufficient to identify a person as well as the merchandise. In the case of small jewelry, the use of a color and higher magnification cameras makes it possible to detect a characteristic feature unique to the item that would not be apparent with a monochrome system. Color cameras allow identification of jewelry and other articles, and the identification of an individual through differences in hair and skin color, clothing, etc.

Cameras with digital VMD built into them are useful in pinpointing specific areas on the floor to watch. "windows" can be drawn around specific high volume objects in the video image and an automatic alarm initiated when there is motion within the window. Fixed cameras in small boutique shops in a department store provide good views of the entire area.

To summarize, overt video's first purpose in retail security is deterrence, the second is aiding in the actual identification, apprehension, and prosecution of suspected individuals, and the third is monitoring employee procedures and performance. Cameras function as a deterrent and as a training/tracking system. In the training function, employees on the sales floor are monitored to detect procedural violations, such as leaving a showcase open, leaving a key in a lock, or showing too many pieces at one time.

22.5.2.2 Covert Showroom Floor Surveillance

Covert video in large retail stores is used to spot and apprehend professional thieves and dishonest employees who are able to defeat the use of the overt video system. The thief can not see (and thereby defeat) the covert cameras because they are cleverly concealed within the building structure and its fixtures. The availability of small, wired or wireless covert cameras permits use in internal store investigations, where they can be quickly installed and removed.

Cameras and lenses can be concealed in many locations in a store. A unique combination of a pinhole lens and camera with a ceiling-mounted sprinkler head provides an extremely useful covert surveillance technique. By law, most retail stores are required to have overhead sprinkler fire-suppression water systems. The covert surveillance sprinkler is in addition to and in no way affects the operation of the active fire-suppression sprinkler system. The sprinkler camera is installed in the ceiling at a location to produce the required surveillance scene. At the customers' level on the showroom floor the sprinkler camera goes unnoticed. The entire assembly is rotated to point the camera in the direction of interest and the small mirror adjusted to the desired tilt (elevation) angle. A more sophisticated version of the sprinkler concept has a remote-control 360° panning capability.

22.5.2.3 Case: Analog/Digital Eight-Camera Showroom Floor Video System

This retail store video surveillance system incorporates overt and covert cameras to monitor showroom floor activity. The installation consists of five overt color cameras and three covert monochrome cameras (Figure 22-12).

The one fixed camera uses IP technology. The four speed-dome cameras also use IP video transmission and P/T/Z control. These cameras are fast-scan dome units with a camera and zoom lens module mounted on a high speed pan/tilt platform inside the tinted dome. The CCD camera transmits a digital IP video signal, and pan/tilt platform and zoom lens control signals are transmitted to the lens.

These color cameras with zoom lenses on fast-scan pan/tilt platforms with preset capabilities provide excellent video images of individuals, merchandise, and activities. The combination of fast-scan and preset allows the guard to track and follow a suspicious person or activity, or point and zoom in quickly to a specific predetermined (memorized) location on the floor.

Three covert monochrome cameras hidden as corner mounted cameras view the central areas. One camera views the entrance area; a second the storeroom safe; a third coats and furs. All control (pan, tilt, and lens functions) and video signals are transmitted to and from the camera and security room locations via hard wire or fiber-optic cable. Figure 22-13 shows the eight-camera retail showroom block diagram.

The camera video signals terminate in the security room and manager's office via a router and display on monitors. One monochrome as well as a color monitor displays the

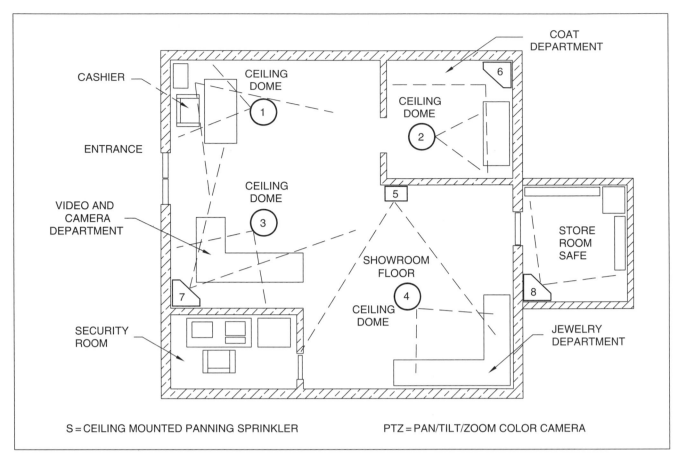

FIGURE 22-12   Analog/digital eight-camera overt/covert retail showroom system requirements

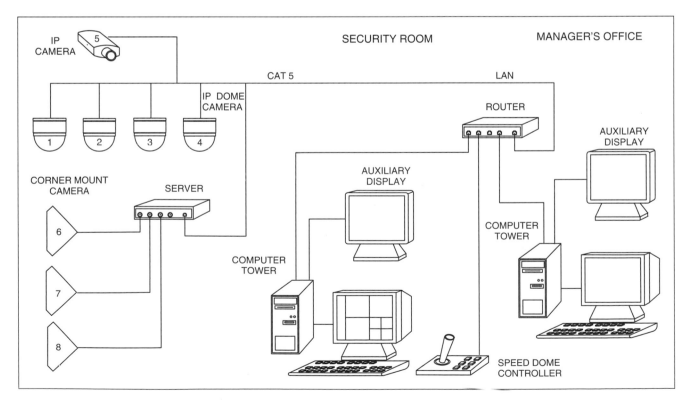

FIGURE 22-13   Analog/digital eight-camera retail showroom block diagram

three covert scenes. Another color monitor displays the four pan/tilt/zoom scenes. All eight camera scenes can be displayed on a color monitor, recorded on a DVR, and printed on a thermal video printer. The four color camera pan/tilt, camera functions, and presets are controlled from the controllers. The zoom lens and controller provide high-speed preset capability for the zoom (focal length), focus, and iris parameters. The pan/tilt platform and controller for the four color cameras provide high-speed camera pointing with presets. Table 22-4 shows the BOM for the eight-camera showroom system.

22.5.2.4 *Showroom Floor Video Checklist*

- What areas must be under surveillance?
- What are the optimum camera locations to view customer and employee activity?
- Should wired or wireless covert transmission be used?
- What areas need high-speed dome?
- What areas require 100% surveillance requiring a fixed camera?
- Should analog or digital IP cameras be used?
- Where should monochrome and color cameras be used?
- Should the cameras be dome-enclosed, P/T/Z, or pan/tilt platforms?
- Is a register/point-of-sale transaction interface required? Electronic or electro-optical?

22.6   VIDEO RAPID DEPLOYMENT SYSTEM (RDS)

The video RDS includes wired or wireless video surveillance cameras and is designed for rapid deployment for the protection of personnel and assets. These systems are self-contained, task-specific security solutions. The equipment is housed in rugged watertight cases for safe transportation. The system provides protection for a temporary location and is either locally or remotely monitored. The video system consists of cameras with convenient mounting options including clamps, magnetic-based tripod accessories (pan/tilt). Options include wireless color cameras having analog or digital transmission over short or long distances. Video motion detection and video encryption are options. Video display is on individual LCD monitors built into the case. One system configuration consists of a single, large, 15 inch LCD monitor and quad processor for displaying a quad video image of the four cameras, or each camera image individually. Figure 22-14 illustrates a hotel RDS application using the system with four video cameras.

Figure 22-15 shows a four-camera, quad RDS application using a four-channel DVR.

22.6.1   Case: Analog/Wired/Wireless Rapid Deployment Video System

This rapid deployment case analyzes a security system for a hotel installation to protect visiting dignitaries. The system is contained in two rugged transportable cases and includes the video cameras, transmission means, and video monitoring display. The system chosen has four cameras: two wired and two wireless, with the video images displayed on a 15-inch-diagonal LCD monitor. The system has analog cameras with options for digital VMD on all cameras, and encryption of the video signals. Table 22-5 lists the RDS components.

22.6.2   RDS System Checklist

- How many cameras are required?
- Camera types: analog, IP, wired, wireless
- What camera to console range is required?

22.7   OUTDOOR PARKING LOT AND PERIMETER SURVEILLANCE

Overall video surveillance of an entire facility including a perimeter fence line, parking lot, building exterior, and loading dock area can range from a modest installation of a few cameras to a large comprehensive system with many cameras and monitors. To provide surveillance to an entire parking lot, the exterior of a building, the driveways leading to the facility, and a perimeter fence line, it is necessary to mount video surveillance cameras on pedestals or poles in the parking lot and/or at roof height on the outside of the building. To eliminate the need and cost for burying cabling under the parking lot, the more cost-effective solution is to use two-way wireless video and camera control transmission from the camera and wireless controls to the pole-mounted domes. Power to the equipment is obtained from the existing power provided for lights on the parking lot poles. In a new system the optimum installation would make use of digital IP color cameras and WiFi digital transmission. Figure 22-16 illustrates the video surveillance scenario encountered in these applications.

Several fencepost or pedestal-mounted cameras are needed along the perimeter to detect intrusion or activity. These cameras, augmented by building-mounted cameras, are used to view parking lots, entrances, and loading dock areas.

Requirements for perimeter parking lot surveillance include viewing a wide FOV (up to 360°) while also having the ability to "home in on" and view a narrow FOV with high resolution. The lens/camera must be able to tilt from 0 to −90° to view an area far away or close in. Some techniques for solving the wide vs. narrow FOV video

ITEM	QUANTITY	DESCRIPTION	LOCATION	COMMENTS
1	4	IP PAN/TILT/ZOOM SPEED DOME 1, 2, 3, 4	SHOWROOM FLOOR, CASHIER AND COAT DEPARTMENT	SPEED-DOME P/T/Z TO VIEW ENTRANCE, FLOOR AREA, SHOWCASES, CUSTOMERS, EMPLOYEES TYPE: INDOOR, HIGH-SPEED CAMERA/LENS PAN/TILT MODULE CAMERA: DIGITAL IP, CCD SENSOR FORMAT: 1/6-, 1/4-, 1/3-inch COLOR/MONOCHROME LENS: OPTICAL ZOOM: 20×, DIGITAL ZOOM: 10× PAN: 360° CONTINUOUS TILT: 0 TO −90° SCAN SPEED: PAN: 200°/sec TILT: 60°/sec. FEATURES: PRESETS, 180° REVERSAL AT −90 TILT, VMD IN SELECTED ZONES, MASKED ZONES
2	1	IP CAMERA, LENS IN INTEGRAL HOUSING, 5	SHOWROOM FLOOR	TYPE: COLOR MONOCHROME, DIGITAL IP SENSOR TYPE: CCD SENSOR FORMAT: 1/3-, OR 1/4-inch LENS: VARI-FOCAL: 3–12 mm, AUTO-IRIS, F/#: 1.2 MOUNT: CS SEE TABLES 4-1, 4-2, LENS FINDER KIT INPUT VOLTAGE: 24 VAC, OR 12 VDC, 117 VAC CONVERTER
3	3	ANALOG CORNER-MOUNT CAMERA 6, 7, 8	COAT DEPARTMENT	TYPE: INTEGRAL CAMERA/HOUSING, COLOR, CCD, ANALOG SENSOR FORMAT: 1/4-, OR 1/3-inch LENS FOCAL LENGTH: 3.8, 6, OR 8 mm OPTICAL SPEED: F/# 1.8 MOUNT: CS OR MINI (12 mm) INPUT VOLTAGE 24 VAC OR 12 VDC, 117 VAC CONVERTER
4	1	SPEED DOME CONTROLLER	SECURITY ROOM	FUNCTIONS: PAN/TILT JOYSTICK, POINTING AND SPEED. ZOOM, PRESETS, VMD ZONES, MASKED ZONES
5	1	ANALOG CAMERA SERVER	SECURITY ROOM	TYPE: 4 CHANNEL
6	1	IP ROUTER	SECURITY ROOM	TYPE: 8 CHANNEL
7	1	DESKTOP/TOWER COMPUTER	SECURITY ROOM	COMPUTER, DISPLAY 15-, 17-inch KEYBOARD, 500 MByte STORAGE, VMD
8	1	AUXILIARY MONITOR	SECURITY ROOM	TYPE: COLOR, CRT OR LCD SCREEN SIZE: 9-, 13-, 15-inch MOUNTING: DESKTOP AUDIO: WITH OR WITHOUT
9	1	VIDEO PRINTER	SECURITY ROOM	TYPE: THERMAL, INK-JET, MONOCHROME OR COLOR PRINT SIZE: 3.5 × 4.0, 8½ × 11 inches
10	OPTION	UNINTERRUPTIBLE POWER SUPPLY (UPS)	SECURITY ROOM	BACKUP POWER DURING POWER OUTAGE INPUT: 120–240 VAC, OUTPUT: 120 VAC POWER OUT: 500 WATT

Table 22-4   Analog/digital Eight-Camera Retail Showroom Bill of Materials

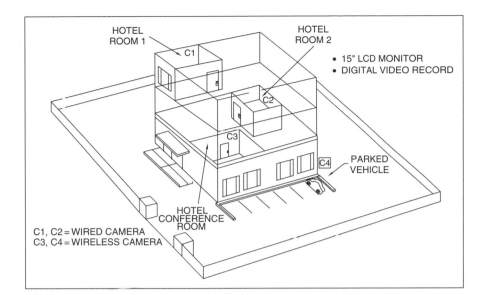

FIGURE 22-14 Four-camera hotel rapid deployment video surveillance system

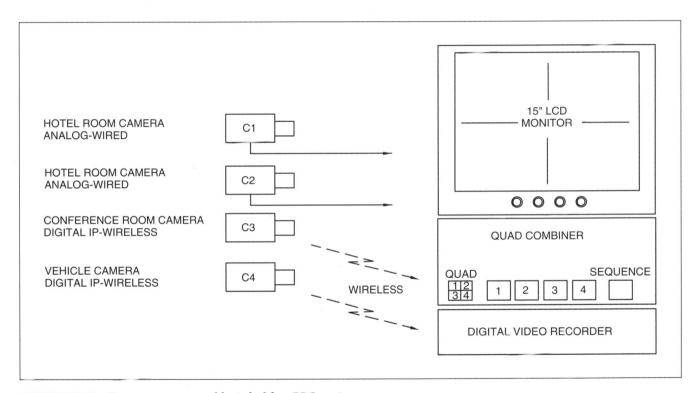

FIGURE 22-15   Four-camera–quad hotel video RDS system

requirements are: (1) using a speed-dome camera or a camera on a pan/tilt platform with a zoom lens, (2) using multiple cameras to split the wide FOV required into narrower FOVs, and (3) using a camera on a pan/tilt with two fixed focal length (FFL) lenses, one having a wide FOV and the other a narrow FOV.

The pan/tilt system (Chapter 17) permits the video camera and lens to rotate horizontally and vertically so that the camera can look at scenes substantially outside the lens FOV. An FFL lens and camera system mounted on a

stationary platform looks at only those parts of the scene as determined by the lens FOV and the camera sensor format (Tables 4-1, 4-2, and 4-4).

A zoom lens in a dome or on a pan/tilt platform has a primary advantage over fixed-position FFL lenses in that it can look at any part of the scene by changing the lens/camera pointing direction via operator control or automatically. The zoom lens with its variable FL and therefore variable FOV provides wide-area coverage in the low-magnification, wide-angle mode and excellent

ITEM	QUANTITY	DESCRIPTION	LOCATION	COMMENTS
1	1	COVERT WIRELESS ANALOG CAMERA: EMERGENCY LIGHT 1	GUEST HOTEL ROOM	TYPE: COLOR, CCD SENSOR FORMAT: 1/3-inch LENS FOCAL LENGTH: 3.8 mm
2	1	INTEGRAL COVERT WIRELESS ANALOG CAMERA 2	GUEST HOTEL ROOM	TYPE: COLOR, CCD SENSOR FORMAT: 1/3-inch LENS FOCAL LENGTH: 3.8 mm
3	1	WIRELESS INDOOR DOME CAMERA 3	CONFERENCE ROOM	TYPE: COLOR DOME, P/T/Z SENSOR TYPE: CCD. SENSOR FORMAT: 1/4-inch
4	1	INTEGRATED WIRELESS, ANALOG, FIXED OUTDOOR DOME CAMERA 4	PARKING LOT	TYPE: DOME, DAY/NIGHT, COLOR/ MONOCHROME, CCD SENSOR FORMAT: -1/4, 1/3-inch LENS FOCAL LENGTH: 3.8 mm
5	2	MICROWAVE TRANSMITTERS CH. 1, 2	GUEST HOTEL ROOM	TRANSMITTER FREQUENCY: 2.4 GHz, CH. 1, 2
6	1	MICROWAVE TRANSMITTER CH. 3	CONFERENCE ROOM	TRANSMITTER FREQUENCY: 2.4 GHz, CH. 3
7	1	MICROWAVE TRANSMITTER CH. 4	PARKING LOT	TRANSMITTER FREQUENCY: 2.4 GHz, CH. 4
8	4	MICROWAVE RECEIVER CH. 1, 2, 3, 4	MONITORING HOTEL ROOM- CONTROL CONSOLE	RECEIVER FREQUENCY: 2.4 GHz, CH. 1, 2, 3, 4
9	1	FOUR CHANNEL QUAD COMBINER	MONITORING HOTEL ROOM- CONTROL CONSOLE	QUAD: DISPLAY (4) CAMERAS IN FULL, QUAD, SEQUENCED MODE VIDEO LOSS DETECTION
10	1	LCD MONITOR	MONITORING HOTEL ROOM- CONTROL CONSOLE	LCD: 15-inch DIAGONAL
11	1	DIGITAL VIDEO RECORDER (DVR)	MONITORING HOTEL ROOM- CONTROL CONSOLE	DVR: 4 CHANNEL, VMD
12	OPTION	UNIVERSAL POWER SUPPLY (UPS)	HOTEL ROOM- MONITORING CONTROL CONSOLE	BACKUP POWER DURING POWER OUTAGE INPUT: 120–240 VAC, 50–60 Hz, OUTPUT: 12 VDC, 100 WATTS
13	OPTION	VIDEO SCRAMBLING MODULES	WIRELESS ANALOG TRANSMITTERS/ RECEIVERS	ANALOG SCRAMBLING CODER/DECODER
14	OPTION	VIDEO MOTION DETECTOR (VMD)	MONITORING ROOM	DIGITAL, 4 CHANNEL

Table 22-5 Four-Camera Analog Hotel Rapid Deployment Video System Components

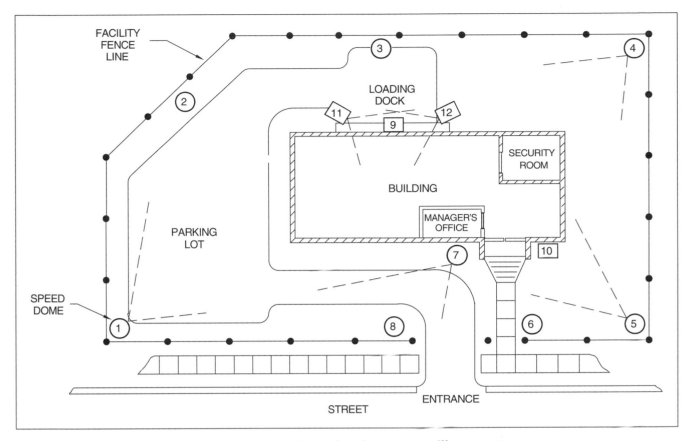

FIGURE 22-16   Twelve camera outdoor parking lot and perimeter surveillance system

resolution in the high-magnification, narrow-angle mode. One disadvantage of the zoom lens installation is the inherent optical viewing dead zone, and operator time and dexterity required to manipulate pan/tilt and zoom functions. The inherent optical dead zone of the speed-dome and pan/tilt system originates because the system cannot be looking at all places at the same time. When it is pointing in a particular direction, the area outside the FOV of the lens is not under surveillance and hence there is effectively no surveillance in those areas for part of the time. Systems with preprogrammed presets eliminate some of this dead time. Figure 22-17 shows the static vs. dynamic FOV of the stationary and pan/tilt systems.

The highlighted lines show the instantaneous FOV of the camera with a zoom lens (narrow- and wide-FOV extremes). The dashed lines show the total pan/tilt dynamic FOV and lens FOV, and represent the total angular coverage that the pan/tilt camera system can view. At any time, most of the area for which surveillance is desired is not being displayed on the television monitor. To partially overcome this shortcoming, when the person hiding from the camera is out of the instantaneous FOV of the video, the camera and pan/tilt mechanism are sometimes hidden, so that the person does not know where the camera is pointing at any particular instant.

The brute force approach to provide video coverage of a perimeter and parking lot is to provide multiple cameras with fixed FOVs. Each camera/lens installation views a part of the entire scene. If the area covered by each camera is small, adequate resolution can be obtained. The primary advantages of the fixed video camera installation over the pan/tilt type are its low initial installation costs, low maintenance costs, and lack of optical dead zones. The primary disadvantage is that only a small FOV can be viewed with good resolution: the wider the FOV, the smaller the amount of detail that can be seen.

The bi-focal optical image splitting lens (Figure 4-36) offers a unique solution to the problem of displaying a wide and narrow FOV (telephoto) scene simultaneously on one monitor with one camera. It is particularly advantageous when expensive LLL ICCD solid-state intensified cameras or IR is used, since only one camera is required. When the system operates with a pan/tilt platform, wide-area coverage is always displayed simultaneously with a close-up of the area of interest. A speed-dome or pan/tilt system, with or without a zoom lens, does not accomplish this. To obtain maximum flexibility and wide-angle coverage, a bi-focal lens with a zoom lens and a narrow-angle (75 or 150 mm FL) lens is an excellent solution. The zoom lens permits a variable FOV coverage from a wide-angle of 40° to a narrow-angle of 4°.

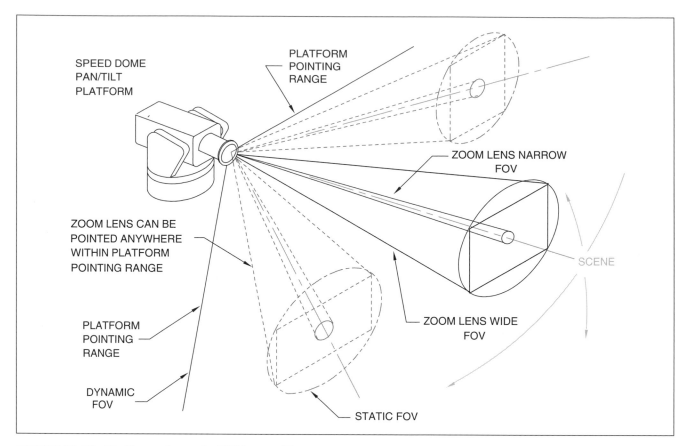

FIGURE 22-17   Static vs. dynamic CCTV surveillance

This combination is particularly good for outdoor parking lot and fence line (perimeter) applications. In the fence line application, if the pan/tilt in its normal condition is left pointing so that the telephoto FOV is looking at a perimeter gate or along the fence line, a video motion sensor programmed to respond only to the narrow-FOV scene could be used to activate an alarm or a VCR or alert a guard. Simultaneously, the wide-FOV zoom lens scene assures no dead zone in the scene.

22.7.1   Case: Digital Wireless Twelve-Camera Parking Lot and Perimeter Video System

Figure 22-18 shows the block diagram for a twelve-camera outdoor parking lot and perimeter system.

Eight pedestal-mounted cameras (1 to 8) use a speed-dome and P/T/Z capability to provide full area coverage of the perimeter, building, and facility grounds. The two covert building cameras (9, 10) provide additional coverage of the facility entrance. Cameras 11 and 12 are on stationary mounts with vari-focal lenses and monitor the loading dock areas.

Video signals from all cameras terminate in the security room. The digital video transmission is via UTP or fiber optic to eliminate any possibility of external electrical interference from machinery, lightning, or other causes. The console room output goes to monitors, a DVR, and a video printer. Table 22-6 is a BOM for the 12-camera surveillance system.

The perimeter speed dome cameras are digital IP, day/night and color/monochrome with automatic switchover and have built-in motion detection. The CCD cameras have 1/3- or 1/4-inch formats with an automatic-iris zoom lens and electronic shuttering capability. The CCD camera operating in monochrome mode can view lower light levels than in the color mode. If no auxiliary lighting is available and viewing at low light levels is required, three choices are available: (1) add auxiliary lighting in the form of pole lighting or add IR illumination to the camera, (2) use a more expensive ICCD camera, and (3) use a thermal IR camera (Chapter 19). The zoom lenses chosen have FLs from 8 to 120 mm on a 1/2-inch sensor or 6 to 90 mm on a 1/3-inch sensor or 5 to 75 mm on a 1/4-inch sensor (sec Table 4-6). Most outdoor housings should have a heater and/or fan, depending on climate. A window washer ensures a better picture in most environments. In cold climates, antifreeze in the washer solution is necessary.

The pan/tilt platform (Chapter 17) should be chosen carefully to be sure its rating exceeds the weight load of the camera, lens, housing, accessories, wind loading and a 10% safety factor. The preferred video transmission

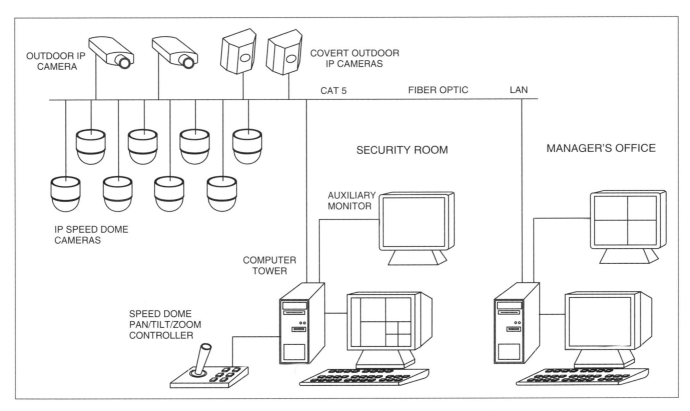

FIGURE 22-18   Twelve-camera outdoor parking lot and perimeter system block diagram

medium is fiber-optic cable, either direct-buried or in a conduit (Chapter 6). Coaxial cable should only be used in geographical locations free of thunder storms.

The building-mounted P/T/Z cameras can be color or monochrome. Color makes identification of cars, equipment, and people easier.

The loading dock cameras are monochrome and use FFL lenses since the area of interest is small and well defined. The combination is chosen so that personnel, actions, and material can be identified on the monitor and recorded image.

If there is insufficient lighting in any of the areas, it should be augmented with auxiliary lighting (Chapter 3), or an LLL camera should be used.

22.7.2   Parking Lot/Perimeter Video Checklist

- Where should FFL, zoom, and bi-focal lenses be used?
- Are "dead zones" in the surveillance areas acceptable?
- Where should monochrome or color cameras be used?
- What type of camera/lens housing (or concealment) should be used?
- What accessories are needed: heater? fan? window washer?
- Is adding auxiliary lighting (visible or IR) more cost-effective than adding LLL cameras?

- What transmission medium should be used: coaxial cable? UTP? fiber optics? Digital wireless? microwave? RF? IR?

22.8   SINGLE SITE DIGITAL VIDEO OVER WIRED AND WIRELESS NETWORK

Most new video surveillance installations are taking advantage of the new digital video technology that has evolved over recent years. The availability of inexpensive PCs, laptop computers and other mobile PDA devices has provided some of the impetus to immediately change from the legacy analog video surveillance hardware to digital hardware and software for new installations. This transition has resulted in the installation of digital IP cameras, multiplexers and DVR equipment. This change to digital equipment has had a corresponding change in the transmission methods from using legacy analog signals over coaxial, UTP, fiber optic and analog wireless transmission paths to digital transmission over LAN, WAN, intranet, and WiFi Internet networks. This case study describes a single site warehouse application in which digital video surveillance technology has been chosen making use of internal intranet and WiFi transmission technology. The software provided permits viewing the scenes from the video cameras and controlling their operation from the control console and having the ability to switch, display and record any and all cameras.

22.8.1 Case: Digital Video Surveillance at Distribution Warehouse

Figure 22-19 shows a single site, twelve camera warehouse digital video surveillance system. The video requirement is to provide surveillance of the facility perimeter, parking lot and outdoor truck loading area on the property. The requirement also includes video surveillance of the office's warehouse entrance, rear dock area and some general surveillance of the warehouse building interior. The

ITEM	QUANTITY	DESCRIPTION	LOCATION	COMMENTS
1	8	OUTDOOR SPEED DOME CAMERAS 1–8	PERIMETER PEDESTAL AND BUILDING MOUNTED	TYPE: DAY/NIGHT COLOR SENSOR TYPE: CCD SENSOR FORMAT: 1/4-, 1/3-, 1/2-inch LENS MOUNT: CS; AUTOMATIC IRIS INPUT VOLTAGE: 117 VAC OR 24 VAC, 12 VDC
2	2	FIXED OUTDOOR IP CAMERA 9, 10	BUILDING MOUNTED LOADING DOCK	TYPE: DAY/NIGHT COLOR SENSOR TYPE: CCD SENSOR FORMAT: 1/4-, 1/3-, 1/2-inch LENS MOUNT: CS; AUTOMATIC IRIS INPUT VOLTAGE: 117 VAC OR 24 VAC, 12 VDC
3	2	LENS	LOADING DOCK CAMERAS	TYPE: VARI-FOCAL FOCAL LENGTH RANGE: 17–90 mm LENS MOUNT: CS LENS CONTROLLER FUNCTIONS: ZOOM, FOCUS, IRIS (MANUAL AND/OR AUTOMATIC) SEE TABLES 4-1, 4-2, LENS FINDER KIT PRESETS: DEPENDS ON APPLICATION
4	2	INTEGRATED COVERT OUTDOOR IP CAMERA 11, 12	BUILDING MOUNTED	TYPE: ZOOM FOCAL LENGTH RANGE: 17–90 mm MOUNT: CS LENS CONTROLLER FUNCTIONS: ZOOM, FOCUS, IRIS (MANUAL AND/OR AUTOMATIC) SEE TABLES 4-1, 4-2, LENS FINDER KIT PRESETS: DEPENDS ON APPLICATION
5	8	PEDESTAL MOUNTING	PERIMETER LINE	SPEED DOME CAMERA MOUNTING: 12–16 ft PEDESTAL SIZED PER LOCAL CODES
6	2	HOUSING LOADING DOCK CAMERAS	BUILDING MOUNTED	TYPE: OUTDOOR, ENVIRONMENTAL (ALUMINUM, PAINTED STEEL, OR PLASTIC) SHAPE: RECTANGULAR SIZE: LARGE ENOUGH TO CONTAIN CAMERA, LENS, AND ACCESSORIES ACCESSORIES: HEATER AND/OR FAN WITH THERMOSTATS, WINDOW WASHER
7	2	SPEED DOME PAN/TILT/ZOOM CONTROLLER	SECURITY ROOM	FUNCTIONS: PAN/TILT SPEED JOYSTICK LENS ZOOMING PRESETS: DEPENDS ON APPLICATION
8	1	COMPUTER 1	SECURITY ROOM	COMPUTER, 500 GHz STORAGE (DVR WITH VMD) SOFTWARE TO MONITOR 8 PERIMETER SPEED DOME CAMERAS DISPLAY: 19-inch LCD, FULL SCREEN, QUAD, OR 9 CAMERAS
9	1	COMPUTER 2	SECURITY ROOM	COMPUTER, 500 GHz STORAGE (DVR WITH VMD) SOFTWARE TO MONITOR 2 DOCK CAMERAS, 2 COVERT CAMERAS DISPLAY: 19-inch LCD, FULL SCREEN OR QUAD

Table 22-6   Twelve-Camera Outdoor Parking Lot and Perimeter Bill of Materials

10	2	AUXILIARY MONITOR	SECURITY ROOM, MANAGER'S OFFICE	TYPE: 23-inch LCD, DISPLAY ALL 12 CAMERAS IN 16 CAMERA FORMAT
11	1	VIDEO PRINTER	SECURITY ROOM	TYPE: THERMAL, INK-JET, MONOCHROME, COLOR PRINT SIZE: 3.5×4.0, 8½×11 inch
12	—	TRANSMISSION OUTDOOR	PERIMETER CAMERAS TO BUILDING	OUTDOOR RATED CAT 5, UTP, FIBER OPTIC IN OUTDOOR CONDUIT
13	—	TRANSMISSION INDOOR	LOADING DOCK CAMERAS TO CONSOLE COVERT CAMERAS TO	INDOOR CAT 5, OR UTP IN CONDUIT OR OVERHEAD TRAY
14	OPTION	UNIVERSAL POWER SUPPLY (UPS)	SECURITY ROOM	BACKUP POWER DURING POWER OUTAGE INPUT: 120–240 VAC, 50–60 Hz, OUTPUT: 12 VDC, 100 WATTS

Table 22-6   Twelve-Camera Outdoor Parking Lot and Perimeter Bill of Materials (*Continued*)

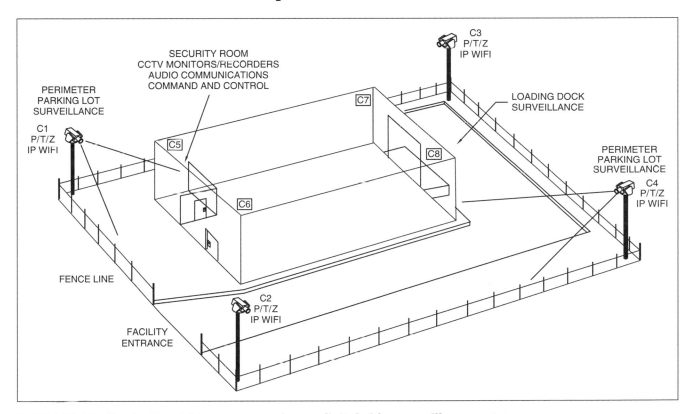

FIGURE 22-19   Single site eight-camera warehouse digital video surveillance system

perimeter of the facility, parking area and loading dock area of the warehouse building is viewed by four, outdoor, speed-dome, P/T/Z cameras mounted along the fence line at the corners looking inward toward the building. These cameras can view vehicles entering and exiting the main gate, the parking lot and chart's loading and unloading in the rear of bay area.

Figure 22-20 shows a block diagram of the equipment required at the camera sites and the security room monitoring site. Four outdoor P/T/Z IP color cameras are mounted on pedestals at the fence line. Two indoor cameras are mounted in the rear of the warehouse, viewing the loading dock area and interior of the trucks. These two cameras are provided with day/night cameras having IR illumination to permit identification of personnel, merchandise and activities at the loading dock area and inside the truck cargo area. Two indoor cameras are located in the warehouse office area and entrance area, to provide general surveillance of personnel and activity in those areas.

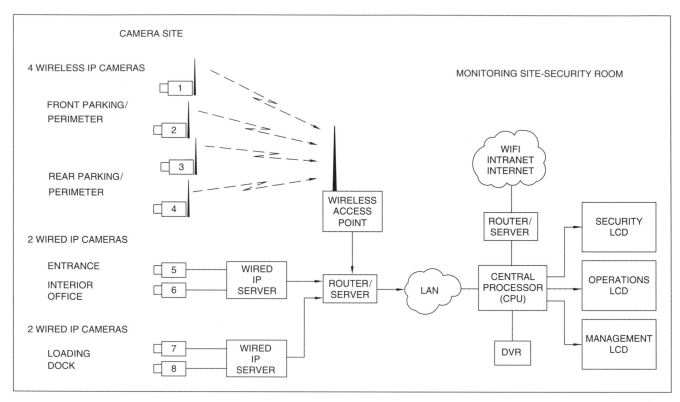

FIGURE 22-20 Single site eight-camera warehouse digital video over wired and wireless network

All indoor cameras use LAN digital networks to transmit the video signal to the monitoring security room multiplexers, switchers, computer, displays and recorders. The digital video signals and P/T/Z control signals for the four outdoor cameras are transmitted to the monitoring security room by wireless digital WiFi means. The security, operations, and management departments are supplied with LCD monitors and keyboards for viewing the images from any of the cameras. Table 22-7 is a BOM for digital video distribution warehouse components.

22.8.2 Distribution Warehouse Checklist

- How many cameras are required for outdoor surveillance of the facility perimeter and parking facilities?
- Is there sufficient outdoor lighting to provide high-quality video images for color cameras?
- How many cameras are required to provide adequate interior warehouse surveillance?
- Are any covert cameras required?

22.9 MULTIPLE SITE DIGITAL VIDEO OVER INTERNET

Section 22.8 described an all-digital single site video surveillance system using IP cameras, wired LAN trans-

mission network, computer, LCD monitors and digital recording. This application requires single site surveillance and monitoring, and multi-site monitoring using LANs and Internet transmission for inter-site video transmission, communications, and control. The video image is available on any device (laptop, PC, PDA) having Internet access.

An alternative (or redundancy) to the digital recording in the control center is the use of a network video recorder (NVR) described in Section 9.3.2.5. The encryption techniques used in WiFi transmission are described in Section 6.8.2 and should be used in wireless transmission to the level required to prevent unauthorized eavesdropping.

22.9.1 Case: Digital Video and Control over Internet to Remote Sites

Figure 22-21 shows the overall multi-site scenario. The block diagram shows the three site enterprise having security control rooms in each site and a remote security control center. The three remote sites are located within one city and the security control center at headquarters in another city. Requirements include real and near real-time and recorded surveillance at each of the remote Sites 1, 2, 3 and remote monitoring at the headquarter site. Access into the surveillance network is also available with other mobile laptops and PDA devices. Each of the three

ITEM	QUANTITY	DESCRIPTION	LOCATION	COMMENTS
1	4	IP SPEED DOME CAMERA 1, 2, 3, 4	OUTDOOR PERIMETER	TYPE: OUTDOOR DOME, PAN/TILT/ZOOM CAMERA: IP CCD DAY/NIGHT, COLOR, MONOCHROME SENSOR FORMAT: 1/4-, 1/3-inch
2	4	PEDESTAL MOUNTING	OUTDOOR PERIMETER	12–16 ft PEDESTAL SIZED PER LOCAL CODES
3	2	IP DOME CAMERA 5, 6	INTERIOR ENTRANCE, OFFICE	TYPE: INDOOR, CCD COLOR, MANUAL PAN/TILT SENSOR FORMAT: 1/4-, 1/3-inch LENS: VARI-FOCAL FOCAL LENGTH: 4–12 mm
4	2	IP CAMERA 7, 8	LOADING DOCK	TYPE: IP CCD COLOR SENSOR FORMAT: 1/4-, 1/3-inch LENS TYPE: VARI-FOCAL, FOCAL LENGTH: 4–12 mm
5	8	WIRELESS ACCESS POINT TRANSMITTER	PERIMETER CAMERAS	TRANSMIT 802.11A, 802.11B, OR 802.11G VIDEO SIGNAL TO SECURITY ROOM
6	8	WIRELESS ACCESS POINT RECEIVER	SECURITY ROOM ACCESS POINT	RECEIVE 802.11A, 802.11B, OR 802.11G VIDEO SIGNAL FROM IP CAMERA ACCESS POINTS
7	1	COMPUTER	SECURITY ROOM	COMPUTER, 500 GHz STORAGE (DVR WITH VMD) SOFTWARE TO MONITOR 8 PERIMETER SPEED DOME CAMERAS DISPLAY: 19-inch LCD, FULL SCREEN, QUAD, OR 9 CAMERAS
8	3	AUXILIARY DISPLAY	SECURITY ROOM MANAGER'S ROOM OPERATIONS ROOM	TYPE: LCD SCREEN SIZE: 21, 23 inch DIAGONAL
9	—	OUTDOOR CABLING	PERIMETER TO WAREHOUSE	TYPE: 24 VAC POWER CABLING FOR (4) IP PAN/TILT/ZOOM DOME CAMERAS PER LOCAL CODES
10	—	INDOOR CABLING	WAREHOUSE	TYPE: 24 VAC POWER CABLING FOR (4) STANDARD AND DOME IP CAMERAS
11	OPTION	UNIVERSAL POWER SUPPLY (UPS)	SECURITY ROOM	BACKUP POWER DURING POWER OUTAGE INPUT: 120–240 VAC, 50–60 Hz, OUTPUT: 12 VDC, 100 WATTS

Table 22-7 Single Site Eight-Camera Digital Video Warehouse Components

remote sites and the headquarters site use digital video equipment similar to that described in the previous single site case study (Section 22.8). In addition the hardware and software must have the ability to transmit and communicate with all of these sites and provide the ability to view the same from each camera and have control over each camera as designed into the system.

Figure 22-22 shows subsystem components for the remote sites and the security control center. Table 22-8 is a partial BOM for the digital video and control over Internet to remote site components.

22.9.2 Internet to Remote Site Checklist

- What type of digital recording suits the application?
- What level of security is required?
- What type of encryption is necessary?

22.10 CORRECTIONAL FACILITY SURVEILLANCE

Large correctional facilities make widespread use of video as primary means for observing and controlling

**FIGURE 22-21
Multi-site video
surveillance scenario**

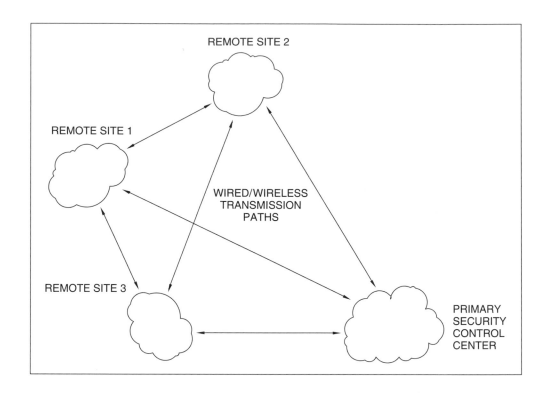

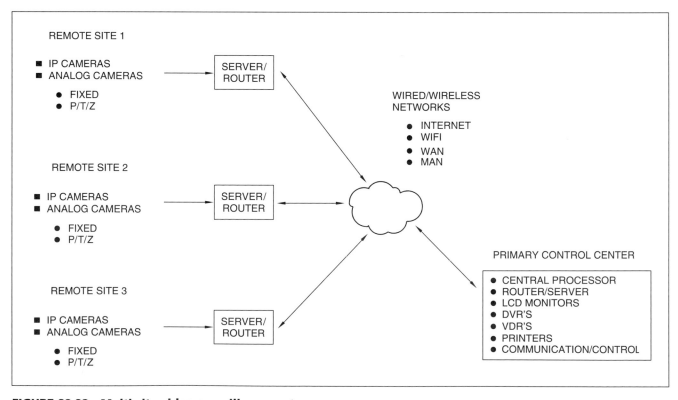

FIGURE 22-22   Multi-site video surveillance system

inmate activities as well as monitoring access and exit of inmates, visitors, vendors, contractors, and employees. Video cameras are used to monitor inmates during initial incarceration, while in cells, and during daily activities. Overt video is particularly important in maintaining secu-

rity along the perimeter of the facility, and in the court-yards through full-time visual monitoring. Some facilities use video at correctional facilities to reduce the need for inmate transportation from the jail to the courtroom and to provide video arraignment of inmates.

ITEM	QUANTITY	DESCRIPTION	LOCATION	COMMENTS
1	—	CAMERAS ANALOG, IP, DAY/NIGHT, INDOOR/OUTDOOR FIXED, PAN/TILT/ZOOM	SITE 1, 2, 3,	ALL CAMERAS, SERVERS AND ROUTERS TO INTERCONNECT AND TRANSMIT THE VIDEO SIGNAL TO LOCAL MONITORS, RECORDERS AND IP GATEWAYS
2	—	ROUTERS, SERVERS	SITE 1, 2, 3,	CONNECT/ROUTE IP AND ANALOG CAMERAS TO GATEWAY
3	—	GATEWAY/ACCESS POINT	SITE 1, 2, 3, PRIMARY CONTROL CENTER	TRANSMIT VIDEO, BETWEEN SITES 1, 2, 3 AND PRIMARY CONTROL CENTER OVER INTERNET, WLAN, WAN, MAN
4	—	COMPUTER	SITE 1, 2, 3, PRIMARY CONTROL CENTER	COMPUTER, 500 GHz STORAGE (DVR WITH VMD) SOFTWARE TO MONITOR ALL CAMERAS DISPLAY: 19-inch LCD, FULL SCREEN
5	—	AUXILIARY LCD MONITOR DISPLAY	PRIMARY CONTROL CENTER	TYPE: LCD SIZE: 15, 17, 19-inch DIAGONAL
6	—	CABLING	SITE 1, 2, 3,	TYPE: CAT-5 OTHER
7	—	UNINTERRUPTIBLE POWER SUPPLY (UPS)	SITE 1, 2, 3, PRIMARY CONTROL CENTER	BACKUP POWER DURING POWER OUTAGE INPUT: 120–240 VAC, OUTPUT: 120 VAC POWER OUT: 500 WATTS
8	OPTION	NETWORK VIDEO RECORDER (NVR)	PRIMARY CONTROL CENTER	

Table 22-8 Components for Digital Video over Internet from Remote Sites to Primary Control Center

To assist safety and security personnel during day-to-day activities and emergency situations, the video systems include comprehensive graphics display capability. These large-screen color monitors integrate and display stored facility maps showing access and exit locations, alarm points, and camera locations. This information, combined with live video information, allows the guard to make on-the-spot decisions to open or close doors, call for reinforcements, and to provide the optimum safety and protection of all personnel.

Since the video system is a vital security component in the overall personnel facility protection plan, it must have an electrical backup power system (Chapter 23). Critical cameras should also have an alternate transmission system and path—preferably wireless—in the event the cabled video transmission path is severed or compromised.

22.10.1 Overt Surveillance

Overt video surveillance is used throughout the correctional facility. It is used both as a deterrent in for monitoring inmates and activities. Video alarm intrusion is used at all perimeter locations to detect entry and exit of personnel and vehicles. Video personnel identification is accomplished using iris-scan, retina-scan, and facial-scan video systems and other identification techniques to ensure identification of anyone entering or leaving the facility.

22.10.1.1 Perimeter

Perimeter surveillance is accomplished by using P/T/Z video equipment similar to that described in Section 22.7.1 including VMD. Video surveillance is also used in conjunction with other intrusion-detection methods such as seismic, E-field, RF, and microwave technologies. Outdoor VMD equipment (Chapter 13) uses digital motion-sensing to achieve the high probability of detection and low false-alarm rates required. Correctional perimeter surveillance requires adequate nighttime lighting to obtain reliable visual identification of persons and activities and effective operation of VMD systems. Camera/lens housings, lighting fixtures, and luminaries should be rugged and capable of surviving attack. When there is insufficient lighting for day/night CCD cameras, ICCD and thermal IR cameras are used.

22.10.1.2 Cell Blocks and Activity Areas

Cells, cell blocks, and activity areas are viewed with low light level (LLL) monochrome or color cameras—color is preferred for more positive, inmate and article identification. Fixed camera/lens positions and high-speed P/T/Z equipment with presets is used depending on the location and requirement. Very wide-angle video systems with 90° horizontal FOV are available to monitor multiple cells with one camera.

Camera/lens housings with IR illuminators are used in holding cells to view inmates 24 hours a day for their protection.

22.10.2 Covert Surveillance

Overt surveillance accomplishes the primary function of video surveillance and in addition acts as a deterrent to unacceptable activities. Covert video surveillance is required to ferret out clandestine activities that otherwise will not be uncovered. Important areas for covert video surveillance include drug-dispensing rooms, disturbed-inmate holding cells, and in locations that assist staff security and law enforcement personnel during inmate uprising and hostage release. There are many suitable locations and video camera equipment available (Chapter 18) to conceal these cameras. Nighttime operation is accomplished using monochrome cameras and IR illuminators.

22.11 BANKING AND FINANCIAL SURVEILLANCE

Video is in widespread use in banking and other financial institutions. More integrated security systems with video as a key element are being implemented as a result of increased governmental regulations. Other reasons are the need for better protection of assets and personnel, and the ability to survive and recover from a disaster. In addition to the assets and personnel protection required, data, telecommunications, and computers must be controlled. Restriction of access to sensitive data processing, money-counting, vault storage, and communications rooms is controlled by video/electronic access-control systems. Automatic teller machines (ATMs), which are in widespread use, require video surveillance cameras to identify customers and tie the transaction with the person using the ATM. This reduces problems associated with money withdrawal and check cashing. Drive-in banking lanes use video surveillance to view customers and general activity.

22.11.1 Public Areas

The bank's main floor and safe deposit rooms require visual surveillance of customers and employees. Video cameras viewing teller/customer areas can record the customer for positive identification during check cashing.

Usually one camera can view two teller stations. A clock and calendar located within the camera FOV documents the transaction time and date.

A high-quality video system must be used for the bank holdup cameras to permit personnel identification. The best solution is digital video using DVRs or virtual digital recording (VDR) to replace the S-VHS VCR recorders (Chapter 9).

22.11.2 Computer, Vault, and Money-Counting Rooms

Sensitive banking areas require video access control and surveillance to maintain security. An integrated electronic and video access control system provides full assets and data security. Electronic access control alone or with a personal identification number (PIN) does not provide full security and should be combined with some form of video identification, preferably a video image storage and retrieval system.

To identify holdup or internal theft suspects, overt video should be augmented with covert video. This may take the form of any of the covert equipments or applications described in Chapters 18 and 22.

22.11.3 Check Identification

An important function that reflects in bank profitability is customer check identification. This can take the form of two different requirements: (1) recording the picture of the customer, check cashed, and time/date, and (2) positively identifying the customer cashing the check. In the first case the system must video record the person's face and the check, annotated with the time/date and transaction number on the same image frame. There are countertop video systems to accomplish these functions. A high-resolution DVR can record the person's face, credential, and other data on the hard disk with sufficient resolution, for use in a prosecution if necessary. The hard-disk video storage system (Section 9.3) accomplishes positive identification of the customer. In operation, the bank officer enrolls the customer into the system by recording the person's face, name, signature, ID number (PIN), and any other personal data onto a digital magnetic or optical storage medium. When the person requests a check to be cashed, the name, ID number, or bank card is entered into the keypad/reader and the image of the customer's face and all personal data are retrieved and displayed on the monitor for the teller's use. The video retrieval system communicates data and video over fiber optic or local area network (LAN) or transmits over long distances via an intranet or Internet transmission to branch offices.

22.11.4   Automatic Teller Machine

Security for the ATMs requires that a video record of the face of the person accessing the machine, the PIN number, the transaction time, date, terminal number, and transaction number be recorded. When a customer disputes a deduction from his or her account for cash dispensed by an ATM, the burden of proof falls on the financial institution. With the message annotator, the recorded video document contains the entire transaction in a single visual record, with all key financial data superimposed on a picture of the person performing the transaction. The ATM video camera also documents any unauthorized withdrawals and holdups.

22.11.5   Auto-Teller Drive-In

Many banks provide drive-in banking for their customers. Some drive-in lanes are situated in such a way that the teller in the bank building can see the customer. In most installations the distance between the customer and the teller precludes direct visual identification. In both cases video cameras, monitors, and recorders are used to record the customer's face, check, etc, and if required, the license plate of the automobile.

22.12   LODGING AND CASINO SURVEILLANCE AREAS

Lodging and casino facilities offer many opportunities for theft, vandalism, and personal injury to their employees, guests, and visitors. For this reason, there is a large variety of video surveillance and access control equipment used at the facilities. Some of the areas requiring surveillance include: (1) lobbies, (2) elevators, (3) hallways, (4) parking lots, (5) building entrances, (6) hotel gaming rooms, and (7) the casino floor. Locations requiring access control include money-counting rooms, sensitive data/equipment operations rooms, and security rooms. Because the casual hotel/motel/casino atmosphere attracts many amateur and professional offenders, the use of overt and covert video security is required.

22.12.1   Hallway or Corridor

Video equipment to monitor hallways and corridors should view as many hallways as possible, showing personnel in the hallway, where they are going, and what they are doing. This can be accomplished using a combination of color and monochrome overt and covert cameras. To reduce the number of cameras at elevator lobby–hallway intersections, dome cameras or a tri-split

lens (Chapter 4) can be used to advantage. This three-lens, one-camera system mounted in a low-profile ceiling housing provides three images from one camera, on one monitor.

22.12.2   Casino Floor

A gambling casino floor requires many different types of video equipment and must satisfy and solve many different types of security requirements for the casino security staff and management, as well as the state and local gaming officials. Video equipments include monochrome and color, overt and covert systems, and fixed-position and P/T/Z systems controlled by large computer-controlled switchers and multiplexers. Fixed-dome and speed-dome cameras are used in large numbers on the casino floor.

Cameras are located to view all gambling tables, all slot machines, bill- and coin-counting rooms, cage and chip rooms, money changing and cashier cages, the main vault, and bars. These cameras are located in the ceiling behind one-way glass or camouflaged in either plastic domes or disguised sprinkler heads. The speed-dome and P/T/Z cameras are located and installed into or below the ceiling to be unobtrusive. All camera installations are aesthetically installed and integrated into the casino decor. These cameras have sufficient resolution to read the cards and count the number of chips in a stack. Many full-size casinos use video matrix switching systems capable of switching many hundreds of cameras, monitors and recorders. This permits switching any camera to many different locations, monitoring, and recording devices. The combination of VMDs and other alarm sensors permits detecting, following, and recording the movements of suspicious persons. Monitors alarmed by these inputs and motion in the alarmed scenes cue the security guard.

22.13   AIRPORT, SEAPORT, AND HIGHWAY SURVEILLANCE

Airport and Seaport.   The threat of terrorism has significantly increased the requirement and use of video surveillance equipment at airport and seaport facilities. The airport cameras installed are both overt and covert, because the crime perpetrator is looking for signs of video surveillance, and if the overt cameras are identified the covert cameras perform the backup. Airport and seaport cameras are usually located remotely from the control security room and at long distances between the camera and security control-center location. As a result of these long distances and the potentially high level of interference from other operating computer and radar equipment at the airport, most airports use hard-wired fiber optic, well-shielded and isolated copper wire, and digital wireless video transmission. Likewise, the seaport terminals cover large expanses of territory and use these same reliable video transmission means.

Highway Surveillance.   The primary functions of highway surveillance are to monitor traffic flow and detect traffic jams and vehicle accidents. The cameras are mounted on the many light poles and traffic signs that are already in the highway/street environment. These pole structure often already have 117 VAC power available on them to power the cameras, lights, and electronic transmission equipment. Using smart cameras with VMD and decision-making algorithms, this equipment provides the transportation and law-enforcement officials the intelligence information needed to make quick assessments of a particular incident and act to solve the problem.

22.14   VIDEO ACCESS CONTROL

Video plays an important role in access control. While most access control applications are solved using electronic access control systems, other means must be used in addition if positive identification of personnel is to be accomplished. An electronic, access control, card reader

system identifies only the card, not the person. The addition of PIN as an identification criterion increases the level of security. Unless the system is augmented with other identifying means such as photo ID or biometric systems (such as fingerprints, voiceprint, hand geometry, or retinal pattern), positive identification does not result. Two forms of video identification are in common use: (1) photo ID badge, and (2) image storage and retrieval.

22.14.1   Video ID System

The simple photo ID badge split-screen system shows the face of the person requesting access on one half of the screen and the person's photo ID card in the other half. This system when used with an electronic, access control system and PIN increases personnel identification significantly. Figure 22-23 shows an example of a video access control photo ID system.

The ID system is mounted immediately adjacent to an access door and contains lights and optics for the camera to view the person's face and the photo ID card presented by the person. A two-way audio intercom and call-button permit a communication between the guard and the person requesting access.

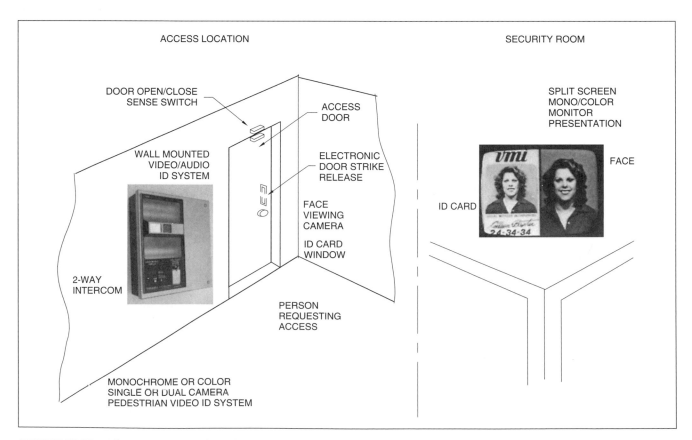

FIGURE 22-23   Photo ID video identification system

22.14.2 Video Storage and Retrieval System

When positive personnel identification from a remote site is required, the video image storage and retrieval method is used (Figure 22-24). With this system, a video image of each person requesting access to a facility is made at the time of enrollment into the system, and is stored in a magnetic or optical storage medium for later retrieval. When a person enrolled in the system requests access, the system retrieves the stored video image of the person, and the guard compares the retrieved picture with the live image of the person obtained with a video camera at the access location. Since the stored and retrieved picture is always under the control of the guard, positive identification results. For the convenience of the person requesting access, systems are offered with the ability of retrieving the image by name, ID number (PIN), or electronic ID card.

22.14.3 Video Turnstile

The video ID units shown in Figure 22-23 can be mounted in a turnstile to eliminate the possibility of "tailgating," that is, an unauthorized person entering the facility immediately behind the person entering. The turnstile is equipped with an overhead video camera that views the confined area. The guard ascertains that only one person is in the controlled/confined area, so that only one person is admitted at a time. The system can be integrated with an electronic access control system and video image storage and retrieval system to obtain positive identification of the person requesting access. Figure 22-25 shows an indoor single-rotor design and Figure 22-26 an outdoor installation using a dual turnstile for entry and exit or dual entry and dual exit. This outdoor installation has an environmental shelter enclosing the turnstile to protect personnel from inclement weather.

22.14.4 Video Portal

A portal (mantrap) is often used when a turnstile is not suitable for the application. The two-door portal provides the same anti-tailgating features as the turnstile, but with an environment more suitable for some security or architectural requirements. The larger space available in this portal allows room for other identification equipment, such as biometric or electronic, and makes for easier use by physically challenged personnel. The portal is often

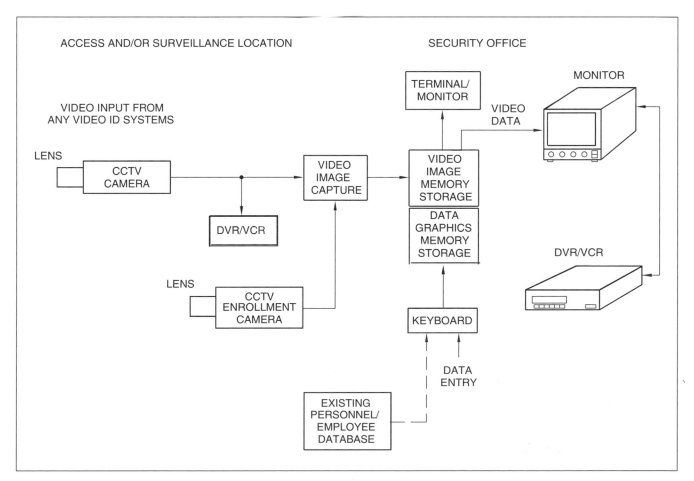

FIGURE 22-24 Video image storage and retrieval system

(A) OVERHEAD VIDEO CAMERA

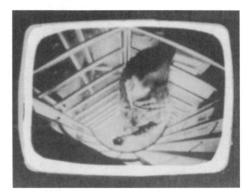

(B) OVERHEAD VIEW

(C) VIDEO/AUDIO ID SYSTEM

(D) SINGLE ROTOR TURNSTILE

FIGURE 22-25   Single rotor video turnstile access control system

used with video storage and retrieval systems and video identification equipment to provide positive personnel identification. Figure 22-27 shows an environmentally controlled outdoor portal enclosing the video ID system and overhead cameras.

22.14.5 Video Vehicle Control

Many personnel and vendors require access to a facility by means of a vehicle. For casual control, an electronic access control system using electronic ID cards or keys can be used. For positively identifying the vehicle driver, a video photo ID system or video image storage and retrieval system must be used. Figure 22-28 shows two video vehicle control systems for identifying: (1) driver in a car, (2) driver in a car, van, or truck, (3) ID credential (photo ID card, etc.). The pedestal-mounted video ID system is for car-height vehicles (Figure 22-28a). The system houses two video cameras to view the vehicle driver's face and a photo ID card or other identification document. The view from the two cameras is displayed on two monitors at the remote guard-room location. The unit has a dual lighting system for daytime and nighttime illumination requirements and a two-way audio intercom

FIGURE 22-26 Dual rotor video turnstile access control system

FIGURE 22-27 Sheltered outdoor portal video ID control system

ENVIRONMENTAL PEDESTAL SIZE:

TRUCK HEIGHT

VAN HEIGHT

CAR HEIGHT

ENVIRONMENTAL KIOSK SIZE:

(A) KIOSK ID UNIT
CAR OCCUPANT
IDENTIFICATION

(B) MOVING CAMERA/LIGHTS ID UNIT
OCCUPANT IDENTIFICATION
CAR, VAN, TRUCK

FIGURE 22-28   Fixed and variable height video vehicle control systems

and call-button annunciator. The housing is environmentally designed with thermostatically controlled heaters and fans. The variable-height system uses multiple color cameras and lights at several different heights to view the occupant in any height vehicle (Figure 22.28b). The system can accommodate a small car or van or a large tractor-trailer.

22.14.6 Video Facial Recognition

The facial recognition system is a non-contact passive digital video means for identifying a person from specific facial features. Facial features act as personal descriptors and are used to identify a person by facial recognition. The person is entered into the system by digitally recording person's face and extracting and recording in a data file the specific characteristics and features in the person's face. This file is assigned an address that is later accessed and digitally compared to corresponding facial features of the person requesting access to the facility. Manufacturers claim positive ID accuracy of 90% and false acceptance of 1%.

22.14.7 Video Iris and Retina Personnel Identification

Video iris-and-retina personal identification systems look at a person's eye, specifically the iris or retina. Since the iris

or retina of every person is uniquely different, a positive identification of the person is obtained.

For the iris system, sections of the iris are chosen that will not be obscured by the person's eyelids.

For the retina system, a low power eye-safe beam of light illuminates the eye and is reflected back from the retina into the video camera and forms a retinal image that is unique to each person.

22.15 VIDEO TO TRAIN SECURITY PERSONNEL

A video security system can be used for on-the-job and new employee training. All new employees can visit the console room, where they witness the use of the television security installation and are shown its capabilities and its purposes. Employees can view previously recorded surveillance recordings that constitute valuable training tools for management and security personnel. In a retail store, the employees are trained by showing them instances recorded on camera where a salesperson has left the merchandise vulnerable to theft, and are instructed on how the salesperson should have watched a customer's actions. This is shown to new and existing employees to illustrate what happened, why it is wrong, and what was (or could be) lost as a result of faulty procedures, and the proper action described. New employees can also see positive actions where someone has tried to operate against a salesperson.

Incidents where the salesperson was alert and protected the merchandise are pointed out to new employees. Examples such as these teach a new trainee what to look for, and how people operate.

22.16 CHOOSING A PROFESSIONAL SECURITY DESIGNER AND INSTALLER

To assemble an effective and successful security operation, management and the security director must know what needs to be protected, and what cost expenditure is justified to protect it. The security director must choose and collaborate with a reputable consultant, architect and engineer, and a security systems supplier to design an effective system together. High-quality equipment that will provide reliable service over many years must be chosen. The plan for response to a threat must be well organized, documented, explained, and agreed upon.

A successful security installation must include the use of a knowledgeable security dealer who understands the customer's security problems and the current technology available. The system requirements, design, and installation should be a joint effort between the requirements of the management/security staff and the capabilities of the security company. Video equipment is complex and requires the use of quality hardware and professional service and maintenance to produce continuous, 24-hours-a-day, 365-days-a-year operation. It must be installed reliably and the dealer must provide prompt response time to an emergency requirement. The real key is knowing that the vendors used stand behind their products and that the dealer/installer is reputable and has a high commitment to service. The bottom line in any sales and service industry is that the service sells the product.

22.17 VIDEO APPLICATIONS CHECKLIST

The following list enumerates some questions that should be asked when designing a CCTV surveillance system.

- What is to be protected: Assets? Personnel?
- What is the value of the protected asset or personnel, and what is the cost of the system needed to protect it?
- Are goods and/or personnel to be under surveillance?
- Is the application daytime only? Daytime and nighttime?
- What type of and how many cameras are required to view the personnel and articles to be protected?
- Where should cameras be for the best view?
- What should be the FOV of each camera?
- Are fixed-cameras or P/T/Z cameras required?
- Which cameras should be overt?
- Which cameras should be covert?
- What monitoring equipment is needed at the console?
- What is the number of monitors?

- Should the monitors be CRT, or LCD or plasma?
- Should the display be multi-scene (split or combined screen) monitors? How many splits?
- Color or monochrome or day/night cameras?
- Number and type of video recorders? DVR or NVR?
- What type of digital recording?
- Video switcher: manual, alarming, alarming with preset, Salvo (gang) switching, matrix?
- Video quad or Multiplexer?
- Video printer: Monochrome or color? Thermal, ink-jet, laser?
- Is there sufficient lighting or must additional lighting be added? Visible, IR?
- Are intensified or thermal IR cameras required?
- Should video be interfaced with door, window, or perimeter sensors?
- Where should digital VMDs be used?
- Should analog or digital IP cameras be used?
- What type of analog transmission: Coaxial cable, UTP, fiber optic, RF, microwave?
- What type of digital transmission: LAN, intranet, Internet, WiFi? Which 802.11 protocol?
- What type of compression: MPEG-4? H.264? Is recording to be used internally or for prosecution?
- Is video scrambling or encryption required? If yes, At what level?

22.18 SUMMARY

Applications covered in this chapter apply to facilities occupied by governmental agencies, manufacturers, industrial companies, and retail and commercial business services, etc. The video surveillance applications include lobbies, elevators, offices, rear doors, shipping areas, hallways, cashier checkout areas, and warehouses. Temporary and permanent covert video systems are used in installations for viewing the general public entering a facility as well as for monitoring employees. Wide FOV optics and zoom lenses are used for parking lots and perimeter-fenceline environments. The video systems described are indoor and outdoor, analog or digital, and single site, multiple site, and remote site. The rapid deployment application includes a wireless alarm-intrusion system.

The video surveillance industry has gone through a rapid evolution since the latter half of 1990s. Prior to the widespread use of digital equipment, IP cameras, computer, and digital networks including the Internet, all video surveillance for security applications were performed using legacy analog video. In view of this large installed base of analog equipment, many new installations will still be performed using new analog equipment. New facilities that do not yet have video equipment will install digital video equipment. Upgrades of existing video surveillance systems will use analog or digital video equipment depending on each individual circumstance.

Successful video surveillance systems are the result of a careful plan and a professional installation. Manufacturers have a wealth of information. Ask them for it. Attend educational seminars and exhibitor training courses to obtain first hand professional information. Attend manufacturers' exhibits and see *real, functioning hardware.* Write a system specification or have a consultant prepare one and send it out to several vendors for a quotation. Choose a well-established dealer/installer that you think will be in business to service the installation five to ten years hence. Choose one system integrator to make sure all system components and software are compatible. Include a training course for management and personnel who will operate the system.

Chapter 23
System Power Sources

CONTENTS

23.1   Overview
23.2   AC Power
23.3   DC Power
    23.3.1   DC Power Supply
    23.3.2   Batteries
        23.3.2.1   Lead-Acid
        23.3.2.2   Carbon–Zinc
        23.3.2.3   Nickel Cadmium
        23.3.2.4   Nickel Metal Hydride
                (NiMH)
        23.3.2.5   Lithium
        23.3.2.6   Alkaline
        23.3.2.7   Mercury
23.4   Power-Line Disturbances
    23.4.1   Voltage Surges
    23.4.2   Voltage Spikes
    23.4.3   Voltage Dips
    23.4.4   Brownouts
    23.4.5   Blackouts
    23.4.6   Electrical Noise
23.5   Equipment Requiring Backup Power
23.6   Uninterrupted Power Supply (UPS)
    Systems
    23.6.1   On-Line UPS System
    23.6.2   Line-Conditioner UPS
    23.6.3   Line-Interactive UPS
23.7   Solar Power
    23.7.1   Silicon Solar Cells
    23.7.2   Flexible Solar Panel Array
    23.7.3   Solar Powered Wireless Video
23.8   Power/Signal Distribution System
    23.8.1   Parallel Network
    23.8.2   Radial Network
23.9   Ground Loops
23.10   Summary

23.1 OVERVIEW

Video security equipment operates from either alternating current (AC) or direct current (DC) type power sources. The type (AC or DC) and voltage level used depend on the equipment chosen and the application intended. Most CCTV security systems use the AC power available from utility companies in standard 117 volt AC (VAC) 60 Hz outlets or at 24 VAC provided by step-down transformers (Europe: 240 VAC, 50 Hz). By far the most convenient power available for most security equipment is 117 VAC power. When it is necessary to locate the equipment remotely from the power source it is convenient to use 24 VAC equipment and reduce the voltage to 24 VAC via a transformer, or 12 volt DC (VDC) using an AC to DC step-down converter. If the security equipment is installed for temporary surveillance, 12 VDC power obtained from batteries is a convenient solution. Another power source available in remote areas or for portable applications is solar power, either as the prime power source or as a battery charger, usually providing 12 VDC.

An important factor to consider in powering any video equipment is the backup equipment immediately available in the event the primary AC or DC source fails or is degraded. This backup power usually takes the form of an uninterruptible power supply (UPS). To protect the video equipment from external, deleterious electrical noise (from electrical storms, etc.), surge protectors or power conditioning equipment is used.

While the subject of security system power sources, backup power, and power-conditioning equipment may not seem exciting or important, it is absolutely *crucial* in the event the power source for some or all of the video equipment fails. If this happens the result is equivalent to having *no security* at all. Therefore, it is absolutely necessary when installing is any system to decide whether part or all of the video equipment is critical to the security operation, and how to implement the backup power in the event of primary power failure.

23.2 AC POWER

Most security equipment for including video surveillance equipment is powered from an AC power source conveniently provided from outlets in the facility. In the United States, the standard power is single-phase 117 VAC, 60 Hz. Table 23-1 summarizes the utility power sources available in countries around the world indicating the differences in voltages available, from 100 VAC in Japan to 240 VAC in many European countries.

The alternating frequency is either 50 or 60 Hz, depending on the country. Most video suppliers provide equipment suitable for operation for almost any of the combinations of voltages available around the world. The rated voltage listed is the nominal or ideal voltage; utility

companies usually supply this voltage within a tolerance of ±10% of the voltage, and a frequency plus or minus 1 or 2 Hz. These numbers vary depending on the particular utility and the country.

For safety reasons, many video installations use equipment operating from 24 VAC rather than 117 VAC. The 117 VAC power can give an electrical shock if the wires are exposed and a person touches the live wire (117 VAC) and the ground wire or grounded equipment. When the voltage is reduced to 24 VAC using a transformer, the voltage is too low to give a person an electrical shock and the equipment is therefore safer to install. A second attribute is that Class II rated transformers are available that provide a 24 VAC output or lower (18, 16, and 10 VAC are also common). The designation Class II indicates that if the output terminals or wires are inadvertently shorted (touch each other) continuously, the transformer will not overheat or start a fire. For this reason, a Class II transformer can be installed by anyone, not just a professional

COUNTRY	AC VOLTAGE (RMS)	FREQUENCY (HERTZ)	STANDARD	COLOR SYSTEM	NUMBER OF TV LINES	CHANNEL BANDWIDTH (MHz)	VIDEO BANDWIDTH (MHz)
ARGENTINA	220	50	N	PAL	625	6	4.2
AUSTRALIA	240	50	B	PAL	625	7	5
AUSTRIA	220	50	B, G	PAL	625	7, 8	5
BELGIUM	220	50	B, G	PAL	625	7, 8	5
BERMUDA	120	60	M	NTSC	525	6	4.2
CANADA	120	60	M	NTSC	525	6	4.2
CHINA	220	50	D	PAL	625	8	6
COLOMBIA	110	60	M	NTSC	525	6	4.2
DENMARK	220	50	B, G	PAL	625	7, 8	5, 8
EGYPT	220	50	B	SECAM (V)	625	7	5
FINLAND	220	50	B, G	PAL	625	7, 8	5
FRANCE	220	50	E, L	SECAM (V)	625	14, 8	10, 6
GERMANY	220	50	B, G	PAL	625	7, 8	5
(FORMER EAST)	220	50	B, G	SECAM (V)	625	7, 8	5
GREECE	220	50	B	SECAM (H)	625	7	5
INDIA	230	50	B	PAL	625	7	5
ISRAEL	230	50	B, G	PAL	625	7, 8	5
ITALY	220	50	B, G	PAL	625	7, 8	5
JAPAN	100	60	M	NTSC	525	6	4.2
KOREA	100	60	M	NTSC	525	6	4.2
NETHERLANDS	220	50	B, G	PAL	625	7, 8	5
NEW ZEALAND	230	50	B	PAL	625	7	5
NORWAY	230	50	B	PAL	625	7	5
POLAND	220	50	D, K	SECAM (V)	625	8	8
PORTUGAL	220	50	B, G	PAL	625	7, 8	M
PUERTO RICO	120	60	M	NTSC	525	6	5
SAUDI ARABIA	220	50	B, G	SECAM (H)	625	7, 8	5
SOUTH AFRICA	220	50	I	PAL	625	8	5.5
SPAIN	220	50	B, G	PAL	625	7, 8	5
SWEDEN	220	50	B, G	PAL	625	7, 8	5
SWITZERLAND	220	50	B, G	PAL	625	7, 8	5
TURKEY	220	50	B, G	PAL	625	7, 8	5
UAE	220	50	B, G	PAL	625	7, 8	5
UK	240	50	A, I	PAL	625	5, 8	5, 5.5
USA	120	60	M	NTSC	525	6	4.2
RUSSIA	220	50	D, K	SECAM (V)	625	8	8
VENEZUELA	120	60	M	NTSC	525	6	6

THE FIELD FREQUENCY IS 50 Hz EXCEPT FOR SYSTEM M WHICH USES 60 Hz.
THE FM SOUND DEVIATION IS ±50 KHz EXCEPT FOR SYSTEM M WHICH USES ±25 KHz.
SYSTEMS C,E,F AND H ARE BECOMING OBSOLETE AND ARE BEING REPLACED BY B, G OR L.

Table 23-1   International TV Standards in Selected Countries

electrician. When a 117 or 24 VAC system is installed, the voltage drop occurring along the cable from the power source to the equipment location must be considered. Table 23-2 summarizes the voltage drop occurring in different diameter (size) electrical conductors used to power equipment (check with local electrical codes)

Table 23-2 gives an indication of the wire size required to power equipments of various power consumptions. For example, if a camera requires 25 watts to operate and is located at a distance of 400 feet from the 24 VAC source and requires a minimum of 22.5 volts to operate normally, what wire size is required? From the fundamental electrical relationship between power (P), voltage (V), and current (I):

$$\text{Power} = \text{voltage} \times \text{current} \qquad (23\text{-}1)$$
$$P = VI$$

Power is measured in watts (or volt-amperes), voltage in volts, and current in amperes. The current drawn by the equipment is as follows:

$$I = P/V = 25 \text{ watts}/24 \text{ volts} \approx 1 \text{ ampere} \qquad (23\text{-}2)$$

The maximum voltage drop is 24–22.5 volts or 1.5 volts.

From Ohm's Law, the voltage drop in a wire is equal to the current in the wire times the resistance (measured in ohms) of the wire.

$$\text{Voltage} = \text{current} \times \text{resistance} \qquad (23\text{-}3)$$
$$V = IR$$

For a 1.5 volt drop and a 1 ampere current,

$$R = V/I = 1.5 \text{ volts}/1 \text{ ampere} = 1.5 \text{ ohms} \qquad (23\text{-}4)$$

From Table 23-2, the 18 AWG size would match the requirements. If there is a question of which wire size to choose, always choose the next larger wire size to provide an extra safety factor.

There are many manufacturers of 117 to 24 VAC plug-in wall-mounted transformers with Class II specification for powering video equipment. Figure 23-1 shows several Class II transformers used for security systems.

To choose the correct Class II transformer size, it is necessary to know the video equipment power consumption. The manufacturer specifies this in terms of watts or volt-amperes (VA) consumed by the equipment. Transformers are also rated in watts or volt-amps. For example, if a system requires two cameras at a location, each requiring 24 VAC and consuming 8 watts each (16 watts total), use a Class II transformer with a 20 watt capacity.

CONDUCTOR SIZE AWG[*]	SOLID WIRE DIAMETER (inches)	WIRE CMA[**]	CURRENT CARRYING CAPACITY[†]	RESISTANCE (Ohms/1000 ft)	TWO CONDUCTOR CABLE LENGTH VS. CURRENT DRAW[‡]							
					(mA)					(amps)		
					100	300	500	700	900	1.1	1.3	1.5
28	0.013	159	0.16	66.20								
26	0.016	253	0.254	41.60								
24	0.020	404	0.404	26.20	467	156	93	67	52	42	36	31
22	0.025	640	0.642	16.50	745	248	149	106	83	68	57	50
20	0.032	1020	1.02	10.40	1,200	400	240	171	133	109	92	80
19	0.036	1290	1.29	8.21								
18	0.040	1620	1.62	6.51	1,875	625	375	268	208	170	144	125
16	0.051	2580	2.58	4.09	3,000	1,000	600	429	333	273	231	200
14	0.064	4110	4.11	2.58	4,800	1,600	960	686	533	436	369	320
12	0.08	6530	6.53	1.62	7,500	2,500	1,500	1,071	833	682	571	500
10					12,000	4,000	2,400	1,715	1,333	1,090	923	800

[*] AMERICAN WIRE GAUGE
[**] CIRCULAR MIL AREA.
FOR STRANDED WIRE, MEASURE DIAMETER OF ONE STRAND IN MILS (0.001 in).
SQUARE THE DIAMETER, AND MULTIPLY BY THE TOTAL NUMBER OF STRANDS TO CALCULATE CMA.
[‡] CABLE LENGTHS (ft) FOR A 10% VOLTAGE DROP
[†] BASED ON 1000 CIRCULAR MILS PER AMP

Table 23-2   Wire Size vs. Current Capacity and Voltage Drop

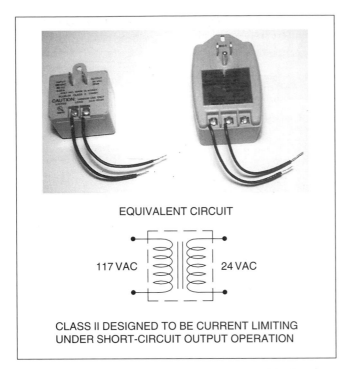

EQUIVALENT CIRCUIT

117 VAC   24 VAC

CLASS II DESIGNED TO BE CURRENT LIMITING
UNDER SHORT-CIRCUIT OUTPUT OPERATION

FIGURE 23-1 Class II AC transformers suitable for security equipment

Most cameras operate from 117 VAC or 24 VAC. If a 117 VAC outlet is available at the camera location, use it. If power is to be run from a remote location to the camera, use a 117 to 24 VAC Class II step-down transformer.

Step-down transformers with a 10, 20, or 50 VA power rating are readily available and adequate to power the camera.

23.3 DC POWER

Many video devices operate from DC power. This can be derived from an AC source using an AC to DC converter, a metal chassis power supply or a battery. Common DC voltages used are 6, 9, 12, 24, and 28 VDC; 12 VDC is the most common.

23.3.1 DC Power Supply

Many small CCD and CMOS video cameras and other components operate from 12 VDC power (normally 12–13.5) supplied by wall-mounted 117 VAC to 12 VDC, AC to DC converters. When more current or better voltage regulation is required, small power supplies housed in metal electronic enclosures that have a standard 117 VAC power cord and 12 VDC output terminals are used. These supplies should be fused or have a thermal circuit breaker for safety and to protect the equipment in case of electrical failure. Figure 23-2 shows examples of a wall-outlet-mounted unit and the chassis-mounted power supply.

As in the case of the AC-powered transformers, it is necessary to determine the equipment current requirements and to size the DC power supply accordingly. As

FIGURE 23-2 DC wall and chassis-mounted power converters

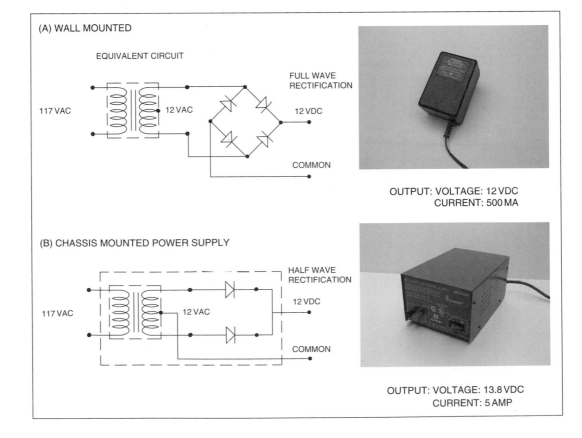

(A) WALL MOUNTED

EQUIVALENT CIRCUIT

FULL WAVE RECTIFICATION

117 VAC   12 VAC   12 VDC

COMMON

OUTPUT: VOLTAGE: 12 VDC
CURRENT: 500 MA

(B) CHASSIS MOUNTED POWER SUPPLY

HALF WAVE RECTIFICATION

117 VAC   12 VAC   12 VDC

COMMON

OUTPUT: VOLTAGE: 13.8 VDC
CURRENT: 5 AMP

an example, if there are three cameras and an infrared illuminator operating at 12 VDC and requiring 4 watts for each camera (333 milliamperes) and 24 watts (2 amperes) for the illuminator (2.333 amperes total), choose a 117 VAC to 12 VDC power supply or AC to DC converter with a minimum capacity of 2.5 amperes. If the next higher value power or current rating of power supply is also a choice, choose it.

23.3.2 Batteries

A very convenient source of DC power is a battery. Batteries come in many shapes, sizes, and types, suitable for portable, temporary, or permanent applications. The endurance or power-delivering capability of a battery is measured in *ampere-hours* and is the product of its current capacity (amperes) and operation time (hours). As an example, a 5-ampere-hour (5-AH) battery is one that is capable of supplying 5 amperes of current for 1 hour. This current and time for a particular battery is an example; the battery does not have to deliver that current for that period of time. It can also deliver 1 ampere for 5 hours or some other combination of current and time (10 amperes for 30 minutes, 1/2 ampere for 10 hours, and so on) within its ampere-hour range of operation. As the battery runs down, its voltage generally does not remain exactly constant but also decreases. The same battery can last longer if it is used intermittently rather than continuously, and as batteries get older, their ampere-hour rating decreases. Trying to extend a battery's life by using it as seldom as possible is not the answer either, since most batteries have a rated shelf life.

23.3.2.1 Lead-Acid

A common battery used for portable video security applications is the gel-cell lead-acid automobile battery. It is probably the most frequently used battery for security systems in portable applications or for backup operation because it is readily available, provides reliable operation, and has the lowest initial cost. The lead-acid battery takes the form of a car or motorcycle battery or a smaller, more portable version having less ampere-hour capacity and packaged in a safer sealed gel-cell configuration. This gel-cell lead-acid battery has its lead-acid solution contained in a "gel" that prevents spilling of the lead-acid solution in the event the battery case ruptures. This permits using the battery in any orientation.

The lead-acid battery cell has a voltage (potential) of approximately 2.15 VDC per cell. For the so-called "12-volt battery," 6 cells are connected in series to produce a total terminal voltage of almost 13 VDC. The gel-cell battery charging rate is categorized as rapid, quick, standard, or trickle. The lead-acid battery is a *secondary* type battery and can therefore be recharged. Table 23-3 gives typical values for lead-acid battery sizes, weights, and ampere-hour capacity.

23.3.2.2 Carbon–Zinc

The carbon–zinc battery is the most popular type used in small, low-power-drain, portable electronic equipment. All such batteries provide the standard voltage of 1.50 VDC and are available in the common sizes AAA, AA, C, and D. The carbon–zinc battery is a primary battery and cannot be recharged. Its popularity derives from its low cost, standardization, and availability. Table 23-4 summarizes the ampere-hour capacity, sizes, and weights.

23.3.2.3 Nickel Cadmium

The nickel cadmium battery, popularly referred to as the NiCd, is available as a packaged assembly designed to power

NOMINAL VOLTAGE (VDC)	NORMAL CAPACITY (AH)*			WEIGHT lb. (kg)	DIMENSIONS $L \times W \times H$ (inches)
	5 hr	10 hr	20 hr		
6	0.85	0.91	1	0.61 (.275)	2×1.65×2
6	4.2	4.6	5	2.2 (.98)	2.63×2.63×3.78
6	10	10.9	12	4.4 (2)	6×2×3.7
12	1.7	1.8	2	1.8 (.83)	1.34×2.36×2.6
12	3.4	3.7	4	3.4 (1.53)	3.54×2.75×4
12	6.0	6.4	7	5.4 (2.45)	6×2.56×3.7
12	20.4	22	24	19.1 (8.7)	6.9×6.9×4.92
12	80	91	100	70.4 (32)	6.85×8.42×9.41
12	160	182	200	118.8 (54)	20.1×10.6×9.2

*AMPERE HOURS
ATTRIBUTES:
   SEALED, MAINTENANCE FREE, LOW COST
   6–12 MONTH SHELF LIFE
   SECONDARY BATTERY—RECHARGEABLE

Table 23-3 Lead-Acid and Gel-Cell Battery Characteristics

BATTERY DESIGNATION	SIZE DIA×H (inches)	NOMINAL VOLTAGE	AMP-HOUR CAPACITY (mAH)		WEIGHT (oz)	
			C-ZINC	ALKALINE	C-ZINC	ALKALINE
AAA	0.413×1.75	1.5	N/A	1100	0.34	0.34
AA	0.57×1.99	1.5	N/A	2850	0.67	0.84
C	1.03×1.97	1.5	N/A	7800	1.80	2.47
D	1.34×2.42	1.5	N/A	17000	3.52	4.97
	L×W×H					
9V	1.9×1.04×0.69	9.0	N/A	570	1.34	1.65

N/A—NOT AVAILABLE
ATTRIBUTES:
  LOW COST, MOST EASILY OBTAINABLE
  1–2 YEAR SHELF LIFE
  PRIMARY BATTERY—NON RECHARGEABLE

Table 23-4   Carbon–Zinc and Alkaline Battery Characteristics

many electronic security devices. The NiCd battery ranges in size from the AAA, AA, C, and D sizes up to sizes providing several ampere-hours in many standard and custom configurations. The output voltage of the NiCd is slightly lower than the carbon–zinc, between 1.25 and 1.4 VDC. The letter-size designations are slightly shorter than their carbon–zinc counterparts and are often interchangeable with them. NiCd batteries are *secondary* cells, are rechargeable, and in this respect are more closely related to lead-acid storage cells. A NiCd battery is about one-third lighter than a common lead-acid battery of equal power rating and smaller as well. Table 23-5 shows sizes, ampere-hour capacity and the charging rates for typical NiCd batteries.

The discharge voltage curve for a NiCd battery is quite flat (voltage remains constant) for about the first 3 or 4 hours, after which the voltage drops faster. Although NiCd batteries are initially more expensive than their equivalent non-rechargeable type, they are more economical in the long run since they can be recharged many hundreds of times before having to be replaced. One disadvantage of the NiCd battery is that it has a "memory": when it is recharged, it may not recharge to its previous maximum charge. If this occurs, the battery will not work at its full capacity. To prevent this condition, the NiCd battery should be allowed to discharge almost completely prior to recharging, and it should be recharged to its full condition, not partially recharged.

As a precaution, a NiCd or any battery should never be discharged by shorting the two output (plus and minus) terminals or leads. This dangerous procedure produces excess heat and will damage or destroy the battery and possibly cause a fire.

BATTERY DESIGNATION	SIZE DIA×H	NOMINAL VOLTAGE (VDC)	AMP HOUR CAPACITY (mAH) C/5 *	WEIGHT (oz)
1/3 AA	0.55×0.65	1.2	120	0.23
AAA	0.39×1.75	1.2	280	0.35
AA	0.55×1.95	1.2	600	0.78
2/3 C	1.0×1.2	1.2	1000	1.59
C	1.0×1.94	1.2	2500	2.65
D	1.27×2.36	1.2	4500	4.80

* NiCd MUST BE FULLY DISCHARGED BEFORE RECHARGING TO AVIOID "MEMORY" EFFECT AND
   TO PREVENT LOWERING VOLTAGE AND AMPERE-HOUR CAPACITY
ATTRIBUTES:
  MAINTENANCE FREE, 3–6 MONTHS SHELF LIFE
  EXCELLENT LOW TEMPERATURE PERFORMANCE
  SECONDARY BATTERY—RECHARGEABLE

Table 23-5   Nickel Cadmium (NiCd) Battery Characteristics

23.3.2.4 Nickel Metal Hydride (NiMH)

The NiMH battery is used extensively in the video surveillance industry to power portable equipment, and as a standby backup battery power source. The NiMH technology is used extensively in power and consumer-products and the security industry has benefited as a result (low price and a diversity of configurations). The NiMH battery is a *secondary* battery and can be recharged hundreds of times. A significant advantage of the NiMH over the NiCd battery is that it does not suffer from "memory." It can be charged at any part of the discharge cycle without having

to first discharge the battery as is required of the NiCd. Table 23-6 summarizes the ampere-power capacity, sizes, weights, and charging rates for typical NiMH batteries.

23.3.2.5 Lithium

The lithium (Li) battery is used when the smallest and lightest-weight battery is required, recharging is not required, and cost is not a primary concern. The standard Li battery is a *primary* battery and cannot be recharged; however, a special version is rechargeable. The Li battery

BATTERY DESIGNATION	SIZE DIA×H (inches)	NOMINAL VOLTAGE	AMPERE-HOUR CAPACITY (AH)	WEIGHT oz. (g)
AAA	0.41×1.75	1.2	600	0.46
AA	0.57×1.97	1.2	1500	0.92
A	0.67×1.97	1.2	2200	1.34
C	0.91×1.7	1.2	3000	6.0
D	1.3×2.4	1.2	6500	2.0
—	0.63×2.5	1.2	3500	2.0

ATTRIBUTES:
  NO "MEMORY" EFFECT
  1–2 YEAR SHELF LIFE
  SECONDARY BATTERY—RECHARGEABLE

Table 23-6   Nickel Metal Hydride (NiMH) Battery Characteristics

TYPE *	BATTERY DESIGNATION	SIZE DIA×H (inches)	NOMINAL VOLTAGE	AMPERE-HOUR CAPACITY (mAH)	RATED LOAD (mA)	WEIGHT (oz)
LITHIUM	AA	0.56×1.98	2.8	1.1	46	0.49
LITHIUM	C	1.0×1.56	2.8	3.4	125	1.55
LITHIUM	D	1.31×3.19	2.8	8.3	175	2.82
LITHIUM-ION	AA	0.67×1.95	3.6	800	250	0.90
LITHIUM-ION	A	0.73×2.56	3.6	1800	600	1.5
LITHIUM	CR2	0.6×1.06	3.0	750	20	0.38
LITHIUM	CR123A	0.67×1.35	3.0	1400	20	0.60
LITHIUM	CR-V3p	1.1×2.04	3.0	3000	200	1.36
LITHIUM-ION	—	1.34×1.97×0.41 **	3.0	1800	500	1.4

*LITHIUM: PRIMARY BATTERY—NON RECHARGEABLE
LITHIUM-ION: RECHARGEABLE

** $L×W×H$

ATTRIBUTES:
  SEALED, HIGH ENERGY DENSITY
  EXCELLENT HIGH-LOW TEMPERATURE PERFORMANCE
  EXCELLENT SHELF LIFE: 5–10 YEARS
  FLAT VOLTAGE DISCHARGE
  NO "MEMORY" EFFECT

Table 23-7   Lithium (Li) and Lithium-Ion Battery Characteristics

weighs approximately half as much as the NiCd battery and approximately one-third as much as the lead-acid battery. The Li battery is available in sizes AAA, AA, C, D, and larger (Table 23-7).

A recent innovation has produced a rechargeable Li battery based on a variation of the Li technology. One convenient feature of the rechargeable Li battery is that it does not exhibit any "memory" effect and retains its charge for over five years. Its output voltage is a direct indication of the charge in the battery: as the battery discharges, its output voltage slowly decreases. Monitoring this voltage provides an accurate measure of the available capacity remaining in the battery. This change is accurate over the entire battery life cycle irrespective of the voltage range chosen.

23.3.2.6 Alkaline

Alkaline batteries are often used in place of carbon–zinc to provide longer operation on the same battery. The alkaline battery is a *primary* battery and cannot be re-charged.

23.3.2.7 Mercury

Mercury batteries are used in applications where long shelf life is required. The open-circuit voltage remains relatively constant over the useful life of the battery. The mercury battery is a *primary* battery and cannot be re-charged.

23.4 POWER-LINE DISTURBANCES

Power problems are defined as any irregularity, disturbance, or interruption induced upon or occurring along a power line. These problems range from common electrical noise and line-frequency harmonics, microsecond faults, voltage dips and surges, line spikes, and brownouts.

Although everyone refers to power outlets as having a single voltage (such as 117 VAC in the United States), actually the instantaneous voltage at the outlet is constantly changing 60 times a second (in the United States), and increases to approximately +170 volts and then plunges to approximately −170 volts. The effect of this rapid variation of voltage is to produce a similar pulsation of electrical current (the flow of electrons) following at exactly the same rate in the wire. Since the term "power" is the combination (product) of voltage and current, it too is alternating or pulsing. The effect of this varying voltage at 60 Hz is to produce an "effective" or average 117 VAC. This is referred to as the root mean square (RMS) voltage. This assumes that there are no external influences to change the ideal power, current, and voltage being supplied. Add onto the standard power the line-voltage variations described previously (line dip, surges, spikes, brownouts, and so on) and the voltage, current, and power being delivered to a system looks like that shown in Figure 23-3.

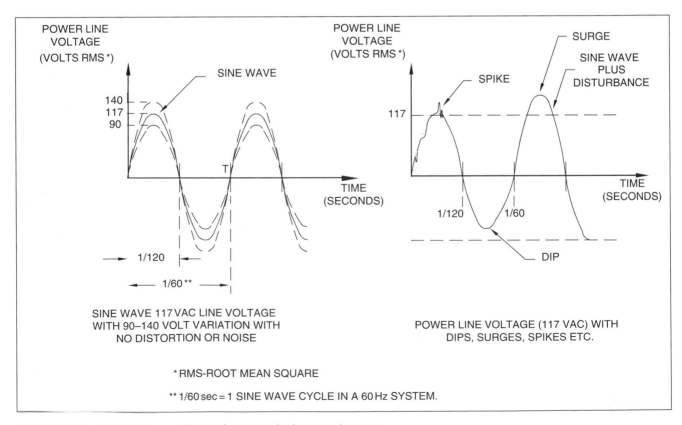

FIGURE 23-3 Typical power line voltage variations and surges

The shape of the waveform delivered by a utility company is a sine wave. When the utility company is doing its job correctly and there are no other external causes of electrical disturbances in the power line, the waveform at the output of every power outlet should be a perfect sine wave. In the real world, this situation does not occur. Power utility standards vary around the world and within any country. In countries supplying nominal 117 volts RMS, the voltage varies from 90 to 130 volts (depending on the country), and the frequency is nominally 60 Hz plus or minus 1 Hz. In countries supplying 220 VAC, 50 Hz power, the voltage may vary from 200 to 250 VAC and 50 plus or minus 1 Hz. Most electronic systems are designed to operate from "clean" sine waves. The power generated by most utility companies is closely regulated in both amplitude and frequency so that it meets the requirements of the millions of devices and equipments connected to the system. Unfortunately, there is little anyone can do to stop the voltage distortions caused by storms, heavy machinery, and other disturbances from entering the power-line grid and creating problems. The following paragraphs describe six different deleterious conditions that alter and degrade equipment power.

23.4.1 Voltage Surges

A voltage surge is a temporary rise in voltage amplitude on a power-line. Unlike short voltage spikes, a voltage surge is defined as lasting at least one-half cycle (1/120 second). In many cases, this type of disturbance is caused by switching off high-powered electric motors or other electrical equipment (causing a reduced current load and corresponding increase in voltage). Even something as commonplace as an air-conditioning system can momentarily boost the line voltage thousands of volts. Almost everyone has witnessed the short change in brightness of lights coinciding with the activity of nearby electrical motors (such as air conditioners, refrigerators, tools). This is caused by an uncontrolled voltage and current surge and matching increase in power dissipation in the light resulting in a momentary brighter light. Figure 23-4 illustrates the waveform of a typical voltage surge.

23.4.2 Voltage Spikes

When lightning strikes a power line or the ground nearby, a large, damaging voltage pulse can enter electronic equipment and destroy everything in its path. While the spike may last only a few milliseconds (a few thousandths of a second) it may reach thousands of volts in magnitude. Storm-induced voltage spikes are responsible for huge equipment losses every year. If it were an option, the best course of action during a storm would be to keep the equipment unplugged and thereby totally removed from the source of spikes. Unfortunately, this is not possible in security applications. Security cannot shut down because of a storm and this critical system must remain in operation. The only practical answer is to have a high-quality power-line protection system.

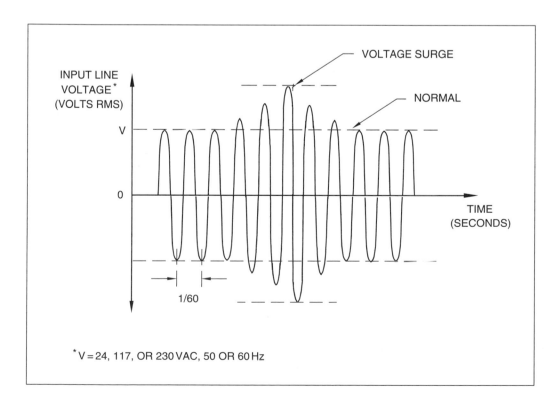

**FIGURE 23-4
Voltage surge characteristics**

23.4.3 Voltage Dips

A voltage dip is the opposite of a voltage surge. During a voltage dip, the line voltage decreases for a short period lasting at least one-half cycle (1/120 second) (Figure 23-5).

Dips are usually caused by a nearby sudden increase in the electrical load or power dissipated such as turning on a high-powered electrical motor, air conditioner, refrigerator etc. Depending on the time required by the motor to come up to speed, the accompanying voltage dip can last for several seconds. During this time, all other electric equipment is forced to make due with reduced voltage, current, and power. The longer the situation continues the more likely it is to cause problems in the video system.

23.4.4 Brownouts

During periods of unusually high power demand (during hot summer days with many air conditioners operating), the power utility may not have enough generating capacity and might intentionally reduce the line voltage by up to 15%. Brownouts can last from several hours to several days, depending on the condition. The brownout has the same effect on equipment as a prolonged voltage dip. Since most electronic equipment is designed to operate with its normal level of electrical power, brownouts can create many forms of abnormal behavior and failure. The only way to safeguard the operation of critical video equipment is to use auxiliary equipment to bring back the voltage to normal level.

23.4.5 Blackouts

The ultimate power problem is a blackout when the power goes off and the devices that rely on it cease to operate. The seriousness associated with blackouts is a result of their unpredictability. One minute a computer or video system is humming along, the next minute it is suddenly down and video images in the data are lost (or erroneous data are produced). The only way to keep critical electrical security equipment running during a blackout is to bring a new supply of power online either from batteries to generate the AC voltage or from a mechanical generator (run on gasoline, diesel, or other fuel) to replace the original electrical power source.

23.4.6 Electrical Noise

Noise is often defined as any unwanted electrical signal. One type of undesirable noise in an electrical system is power-line noise. Lightning, radio transmitters, welding equipment, electrical switching equipment, poor brush contacts on DC motors, and many other electronic devices having switching power supplies are all sources of unwanted electrical noise. When these noise producers are operating they disrupt the smooth sinusoidal power-line voltage and add many sharp-edged, high-frequency voltage changes. The noise may be repetitive or transient (i.e. occurring intermittently or only once) but the effect on the equipment is the same (Figure 23-6).

Noise entering the equipment may be able to get past various safeguards against noise suppression (filters, surge

FIGURE 23-5 Voltage dip characteristics

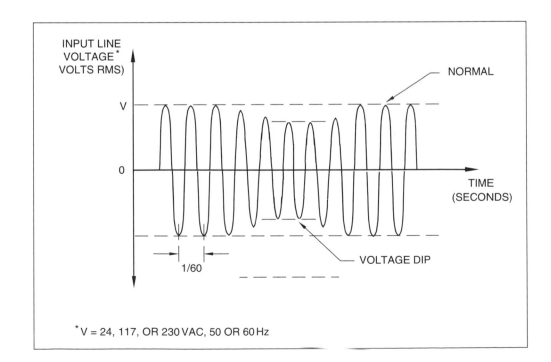

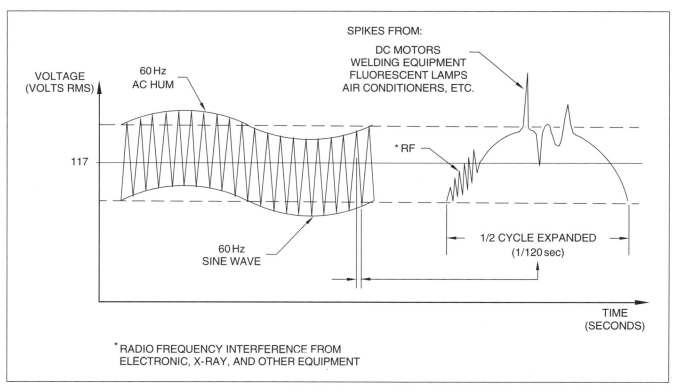

FIGURE 23-6 Electrical noise disturbances

protectors) and into the internal electronics. Since all electronic circuits are not designed to operate with small high-frequency voltage variations, the noise has a tendency to randomly disrupt the normal operation and create havoc. Computer "bugs," "glitches," and errors are often the only outward symptoms that noise is causing a problem. The only real solution is to prevent noise from entering the equipment by filtering the power-line input.

23.5 EQUIPMENT REQUIRING BACKUP POWER

Computers, telecommunications equipment, video equipment, and other sensitive electronic devices should not be connected directly to raw line power because of all of the potential problems just mentioned. This equipment requires line conditioning and filtering to provide a source of *continuous uninterrupted* power at all times, including complete blackouts.

To gain independence from the less-than-perfect AC power services available, a UPS is used. Numerous manufacturers have UPS designs that satisfactorily eliminate most of the problems mentioned. Most UPS systems operate over a maximum period of several minutes to several hours to maintain uninterrupted power. Some UPS designed for the needs of large systems have power capacities from a few kilowatts to hundreds of kilowatts. The majority of UPS systems in use have an output power range of 1 kilowatt.

Uninterruptible power supply sources are categorized by output power capacity and are generally configured for continuous duty or standby operation. In the first type, also called online, power is supplied continuously to the load by a device called static converter that gets its own power from a storage battery. The battery is charged continuously through the incoming 117 VAC power line. The following sections describe the traditional UPS vs. the line conditioner UPS.

23.6 UNINTERRUPTED POWER SUPPLY (UPS) SYSTEMS

The UPS system was first introduced in the 1950s when the silicon-controlled rectifier (SCR) was invented. The SCR is an electronic switch that either conducts or blocks electrical power and can continuously vary the amount of power reaching a load, in this case the security equipment. There are several UPS technologies used to provide backup power. They involve the use of AC/DC converters, rectifiers, DC/AC converters, ferro-resonant circuits, and batteries. The following sections summarize these systems.

23.6.1 On-Line UPS System

The first type of UPS technology to evolve, and one that is still commonly used uses a large rectifier and charger system (Figure 23-7).

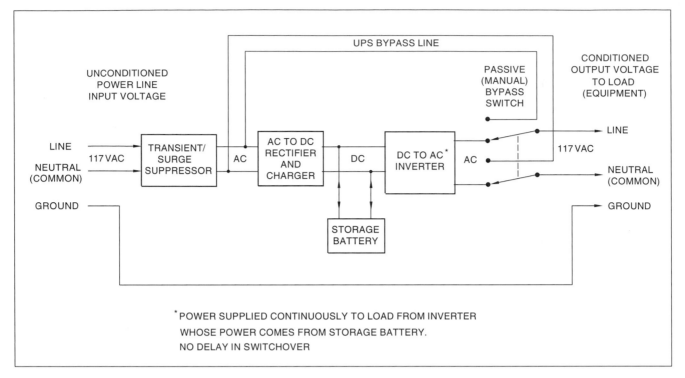

FIGURE 23-7   On-line UPS system block diagram

This type of system converts AC utility power into DC power and then back into AC power. This "double-conversion" process ensures consistent power quality that is completely isolated from any utility power disturbances offering complete protection for attached equipment. The direct current generated is used to charge a battery bank and provide power to a DC-to-AC inverter. The inverter changes the DC back into AC that is then used by the security equipment. In all these systems, there is a static or manual bypass switch to allow the incoming power to be passed directly to the load if the UPS fails.

While this device provides good protection against almost all power variations and particularly against outages and deep brownouts, it does have one major drawback: its vulnerability to failure. That is the reason for inclusion of the bypass switch. The probability of failure exists because all components are constantly in use and under electrical and thermal stress. A second weakness is its low efficiency; in some cases only 60% of the original power input is delivered to the electrical equipment being powered. The remaining power is converted to heat and that often calls for additional air conditioning. Larger rated units are noisy and are rarely placed in the working environment. Remoting this equipment incurs additional expense in wiring cable between the UPS and the security equipment location.

23.6.2   Line-Conditioner UPS

In 1983 a major breakthrough in the UPS design occurred with the introduction of the ferro-resonant UPS system.

This innovation solves many problems at once by conditioning the power line at all times whether the load is being powered by the line or by the UPS internal batteries. The previously described double-conversion technology was superseded in effect by a technology incorporating a constant-voltage, ferro-resonant transformer, and sophisticated line-sensing circuitry (Figure 23-8).

This type of system provides surge and spike protection as well as battery backup when utility power fails. Voltage regulation is handled using internal batteries. This is a standby UPS system. When the unit is operating in a normal mode, that is when the incoming power line is stable, the UPS transformer *cleans up* the raw line power eliminating spikes, dips, surges, noise, and minor brownouts or drops in voltage.

In the event of power-line failure the ferro-resonant transformer continues to provide energy from its magnetic field and capacitor circuits up to 23 milliseconds before a significant drop in output voltage occurs. This is often called the transformer's *flywheel* effect. During the 23 milliseconds the electronic line-loss circuits detect the power-line problem and energize its battery-operated DC-to-AC inverter section *before* the transformer output voltage drops noticeably. The security equipment being powered is unaware that the power being supplied is now coming from batteries rather than the electric line. Thus uninterruptible power is being delivered to the load because there is no break in the voltage or current supplied to the equipment.

There are additional benefits in the use of ferro-resonant transformer technology in the UPS including

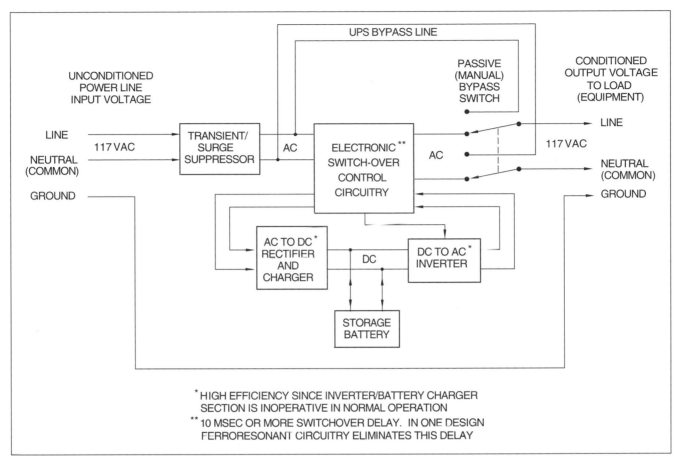

UPS BYPASS LINE

UNCONDITIONED
POWER LINE
INPUT VOLTAGE

PASSIVE
(MANUAL)
BYPASS
SWITCH

CONDITIONED
OUTPUT VOLTAGE
TO LOAD
(EQUIPMENT)

LINE

117 VAC

NEUTRAL
(COMMON)

TRANSIENT/
SURGE
SUPPRESSOR

AC

ELECTRONIC**
SWITCH-OVER
CONTROL
CIRCUITRY

AC

LINE

117 VAC

NEUTRAL
(COMMON)

GROUND

GROUND

AC TO DC*
RECTIFIER
AND
CHARGER

DC

DC TO AC*
INVERTER

STORAGE
BATTERY

*HIGH EFFICIENCY SINCE INVERTER/BATTERY CHARGER
SECTION IS INOPERATIVE IN NORMAL OPERATION
**10 MSEC OR MORE SWITCHOVER DELAY. IN ONE DESIGN
FERRORESONANT CIRCUITRY ELIMINATES THIS DELAY

FIGURE 23-8 Standby UPS system block diagram

90% power efficiency since double conversion has been eliminated. There is also higher reliability since the double-conversion rectifier is eliminated entirely and the inverter is on only when the batteries are supplying power rather than all the time. The UPS provides continuous power conditioning with the ferro-resonant transformer eliminating the need for separate line filters and conditioners. This second-generation ferro-resonant transformer UPS costs less, since the older-technology hardware is eliminated and the design is simpler, more reliable, smaller, requires no air conditioning, and is quieter.

23.6.3 Line-Interactive UPS

The line-interactive UPS system provides full protection from voltage surges and sags without switching to batteries thereby increasing battery life for blackout conditions. The unit interacts with the utility line to regulate small changes in voltage. Minor voltage fluctuations are raised or lowered by the automatic voltage regulator (AVR) function of the UPS.

While UPS systems might seem like an extra cost burden on the video and security system budget, they actually save money and provide a cost-effective solution to

computer and video security system power backup problem. Studies by Bell Laboratories, IBM, and the Institute of Electrical and Electronic Engineers (IEEE) over the years have revealed that 87% of power problems affecting computers and video equipment are caused by power sags or outages, and 13% are caused by surges and spikes. With 95% of computer failures caused by the AC power, it makes sense to protect security computers from such disturbances. Likewise, with 48% of software problems caused by the AC power source, it is prudent to install these protective systems for most security systems.

In a small security system, the entire video system and computer equipment can have backup power provided at reasonable cost. In medium-to-large systems, it is often difficult to justify 100% backup power for all video and security equipment. A judgment must be made regarding which equipment will have backup power, as determined by its strategic value in the overall installation and security plan. Any security system has certain essential camera, monitor, and recording equipment that *must* continue operating in the event of a power disturbance or blackout. There are other categories of equipment that, while useful in normal security functions, can afford to be inoperative without jeopardizing the primary assets or safety of the facility. Essential items might include access control and identification equipment at critical points around the facility, internal video surveillance cameras in areas critical to the operation of the facility or protection of valuable assets, and any monitoring and recording equipment for these scenes.

Once the equipment that must have backup power has been identified, the location and power consumption of this equipment must be determined and calculated. The next step is to outline the procedure by which this equipment will be transferred from the primary AC power source to the short-term UPS backup power source. The most practical device for the temporary transfer and temporary backup is the UPS. Figure 23-9 shows a block diagram of an integrated analog/IP, ten-camera system with the equipment to be backed up, and how the UPS equipment fits into the scenario.

The following example illustrates how to determine the size and type of UPS system to choose for an installation having ten video cameras, two monitors, auxiliary console equipment, video recorder, and video printer. The total backup power required is 715 VA (watts). Since UPS systems are usually available in 250, 500, and 1000 VA ratings, choose the 1000 VA unit. This will provide a good margin of safety (Table 23-8).

23.7 SOLAR POWER

Solar photovoltaic (PV) power generators produce electricity directly from sunlight or overcast sky. If sunlight is not available for long periods of time, the system includes rechargeable batteries so that the solar panels charge the batteries during sunlight and the batteries provide the power to the video equipment on a continuous basis—day and night. In this latter case, the solar panels are used to charge the batteries that then act as the source of power to the equipment around the clock. The PV generator is used when an independent source of electrical power is required.

A wide range of PV modules are available from small panels delivering 1 watt of power to large ones producing up to 60 watts of power. They are used alone or in multiple arrays when many kilowatts of power are required. These panels use third-generation PV technology and are constructed from thin-film amorphous silicon modules capable of long life (up to ten years). They are available with standard output voltages ranging from 6 to 30 VDC, capable of providing power for most security equipment operating between 6 and 28 VDC. The panels are rugged, easy to use, and weatherproof for continuous outdoor use. In

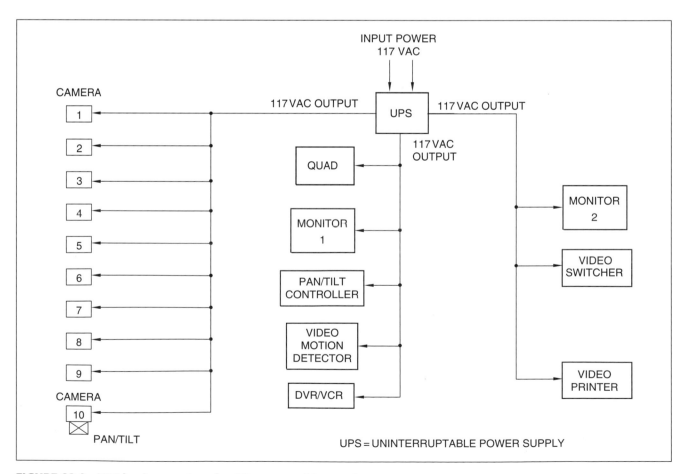

FIGURE 23-9   UPS backup system for 10 camera video system

EQUIPMENT	QUANTITY	POWER (WATTS)	TOTAL VA * (VOLT-AMPERE)
IP/ANALOG CAMERAS	10	10	100
QUAD/MULTIPLEXER	1	30	30
20" CRT MONITOR	1	100	100
17" LCD	1	50	50
DESKTOP COMPUTER	1	300	300
DVR/VCR	1	60	60
PAN/TILT	1	10	10
PRINTER	1	30	30
SWITCHER	1	10	10
MISC.	—	25	25
	TOTAL		715

*ASSUMING RESISTANCE LOAD (POWER FACTOR=1)
VA=WATTS

Table 23-8   Backup Power Requirements for Ten-Camera Video System

some designs, the solar cells are laminated between sheets of ethylene vinyl acetate and protected with either tempered glass or a polycarbonate plastic. Depending on the material, the panels are extremely resistant to mechanical stress, including impact of hail, and special types are available for protection against projectiles. Modules subject to rigorous environmental testing meet or exceed repetitive cycling between −40 and 90 °C at 85% relative humidity with no performance degradation. Some are also capable of withstanding high winds up to 125 miles per hour.

23.7.1 Silicon Solar Cells

Figure 23-10 shows a 11.5 watt solar panel module de-signed to power 6 or 12 VDC loads or rechargeable batteries.

The panel consists of forty 2.5 × 10 cm semi-crystalline silicon solar cells. The dual voltage capability is enabled by movable jumper leads in the module's junction box. By connecting the 40 cells in a series string, 12 VDC power is achieved. When connected as two 20-cell series strings, with outputs in parallel, 6 VDC power is achieved.

The electrical output characteristics of these two configurations are shown in Figure 23-10. The output voltage available to a load at various load currents is a function of the load current. Some form of voltage regulation is required at the input of the electronic equipment being powered from them. As shown in Figure 23-10, the panel generates a minimum of 10 watts power at 6 or 12 VDC. The current at rated load is approximately 680 mA (0.68 amperes) at 12 VDC and 1360 mA (1.36 amperes) at 6 VDC.

The solar panel current and power output are proportional to the illumination intensity (from the sun or other source). At a given light intensity, a module's output current is determined by the operating voltage: as voltage decreases, current decreases in conformance with the curve (Figure 23-10). Temperature also affects the performance as shown by the electrical performance data in the figure and the table.

23.7.2 Flexible Solar Panel Array

A flexible, amorphous solar panel array is available for use in applications where a rigid structure is not suitable. These panels are used as primary DC power sources for equipment or for recharging batteries that are then used as the power source. These flexible panels convert daylight, sunlight, into electricity and provide power from 3 to 280 watts, with charging levels of 1 to 80 ampere-hours per day. They are capable of charging NiMH, NiCd, gel-cell, and heavy-duty vehicular batteries. They are available in compact, lightweight, stowable packages that can be deployed rapidly for temporary or permanent use. The panels are completely weatherproof and are designed to operate under water if necessary. The units are rugged, shatterproof, and are designed to resist damage. In most cases, they can continue to operate even after being pierced by a hail of bullets. Many different sizes are available. A portable compact unit that provides from 3 to 10 watts is designed to charge batteries for portable video cameras, transmitters, and recorders (Figure 23-11a).

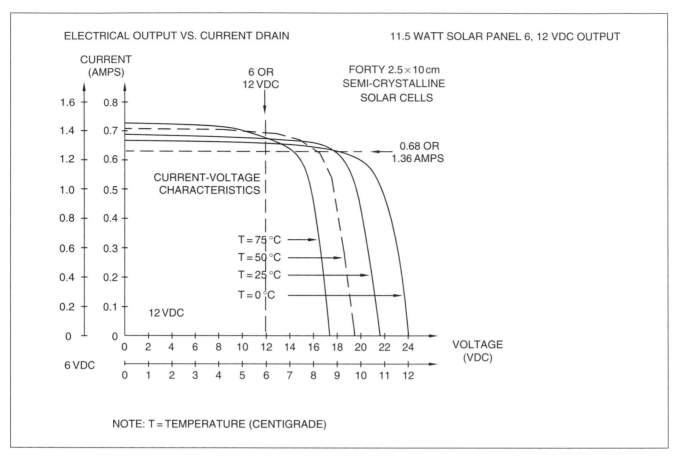

FIGURE 23-10   Solar panel module

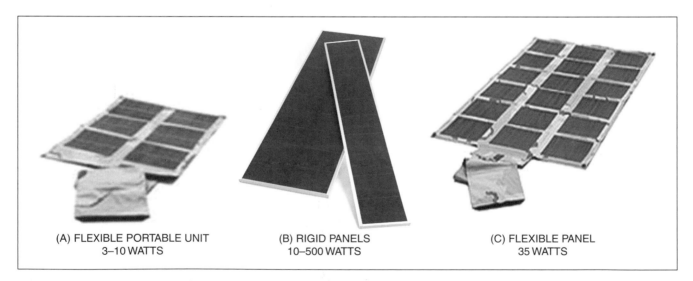

FIGURE 23-11   Portable and flexible solar panel arrays

An intermediate-size module powers from 15 to 100 watts. A 100-watt unit can power multiple cameras and transmitters and a low-power IR source at a remote location. A vehicular battery-charging unit can maintain a full charge on two 100-ampere-hour 12-volt batteries connected in series by supplying over 300 mA at 28.5 VDC Figure 23-11b shows several rigid panels. Figure 23-11c is

a photograph of one of the flexible panels, which can be formed around a circular or other uneven shape without any harm caused to the solar panel.

Figure 23-12 shows a portable solar electric generator/ battery charger designed primarily for military application.

It is flexible, stowable for outdoor use, and can eliminate the need for rechargeable batteries in the field and

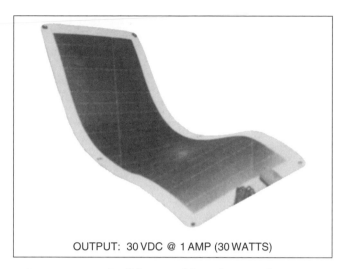

OUTPUT: 30 VDC @ 1 AMP (30 WATTS)

FIGURE 23-12   Flexible portable solar panel

non-breakable, and easily transported and deployed when needed. The units are easily camouflaged when deployed and since they emit no noise, heat, or other characteristic signature, they are self-camouflaged. The panel front surface is a dark color with a non-reflective finish. The outer covering is a weather-resistant nylon fabric. Table 23-9 summarizes representative solar panel load characteristics.

23.7.3   Solar Powered Wireless Video

Unattended portable video systems operating from battery power require solar panel backup power for continuous wireless video transmission operation. These portable systems can be assembled from components including: (1) video camera, (2) auxiliary nighttime lighting, (3) video transmitter, and (4) solar panel for charging the battery. Figure 23-13 shows a pole-mounted camera with solar panel, transmitter and antenna, and battery box.

eliminate the need for a spare primary battery or other power source. It provides 30 VDC with up to 1 ampere current and is designed to charge batteries used in military operations for remote video surveillance. This module takes advantage of the amorphous silicon-alloy technology in which the cell material is deposited in thin film layers onto a flexible substrate. The unit is lightweight, tough,

23.8   POWER/SIGNAL DISTRIBUTION SYSTEM

Selecting the best power supply for video security applications is only half the battle. There is still the problem of getting the power to the active electronic components—camera, pan/tilt, switcher, etc. A large percentage of

TYPE	POWER (WATTS)	VOLTAGE (DC) NOMINAL/ PEAK POWER*	CURRENT (A)	SIZE (inches) $H \times W \times D$	WEIGHT (lb.)	COMMENTS
POLY-CRYSTALLINE CRYSTALLINE SILICON GLASS BASED	5	12	0.26	13.5×10.25×0.8	4	RIGID PANEL
	18.5	12	1.2	16.6×18.4×2.1	6.5	↑
	20	12/15.4	1.7	12×48×0.5	12	
	30	12	2.2	23.3×19.8×2.1	8.5	
	40	12/15.4	2.6	25×48×0.5	25	
	60	12	3.4	43.7×19.8×2.1	1.6	↓
	80	12/15.4	5.1	51×40×0.5	50	RIGID PANEL
POLY-CRYSTALLINE SILICON, STAINLESS STEEL BASED	110	12/17	6.5	63×26×1.4	28	MODERATE FLEXING
	64	12/16.5	3.9	53.8×29.2×0.75	20.2	MODERATE FLEXING
PLASTIC BASE FLEXIBLE	8.5	24–28	0.250	17.5×12.4×0.13	2	FLEXIBLE FIELD USE
	28	24–28	0.80	12.4×10.1×3**	8	FLEXIBLE FIELD USE
	120	24–28	7.0	44.4×39.0×2.0	30	FLEXIBLE FIELD USE

* MAXIMUM POWER TO LOAD. PEAK DROPS TO 12 VDC DURING BATTERY CHARGING
** PANEL FOLDED IN HALF
POLY-CRYSTALLINE SILICON—EFFICIENCY 6-8%, LOWEST COST
MONO-CRYSTALLINE SILICON—EFFICIENCE 15%, HIGH COST
THIN FILM ORGANIC—LOWEST EFFICIENCY, FLEXIBLE

Table 23-9   Solar Panel Load Characteristics

FIGURE 23-13   Solar powered wireless video system

security system equipment degradation can be traced to improper power distribution and/or ground loops. The symptoms of these inadequate designs are excessive noise in the picture or recorded image caused by: (1) voltage spikes or other radiated noise into the system, (2) crosstalk between different signals, (3) AC power-line noise pickup (such as hum) or (4) poor load voltage regulation that causes erratic or unpredictable picture image degradation or equipment malfunctioning.

The primary function of any power distribution system is to provide a path for utility power (or other power) to reach the video equipment. Aside from meeting the electrical requirements of the security equipment, any wires or cables must meet the fire and safety codes of the locality in which they are used. Wire and cable must have insulation, voltage breakdown, and physical characteristics suitable for the voltage, current, power, and environment in which they will be used.

When a device is connected to the utility or power supply output, the conductor size (wire diameter) must be sufficiently large so that there are no significant voltage drops on the conductors between the power supply and the equipment locations that would result in too low a voltage for the equipment. By specifying the proper conductor size based on the distance of the power source to the equipment and the amount of current the equipment requires, the voltage drop will be minimized. When there are multiple loads connected to the same power source and the loads are at various distances from it, the calculations are more complex.

There are two basic network types for delivering power to the video surveillance equipments, parallel and radial. As a rule of thumb, low-power devices are powered using a parallel network and high-power devices using a radial network. In practice, most systems use a combination of both networks.

23.8.1 Parallel Network

In most security installations, the low-power video equipment is connected in *parallel* across the power source as shown in Figure 23-14.

Depending on the location at which each equipment is connected to the power conductors along the power line, each will receive a slightly different (lower) voltage, with the lowest voltage occurring at the last equipment on the line. For reliable operation, all equipments including the

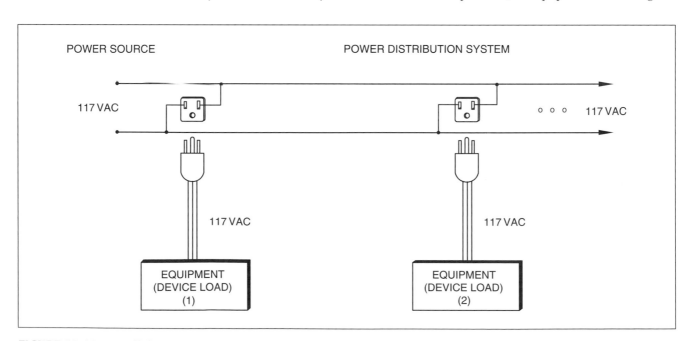

FIGURE 23-14   Parallel power source distribution system

one at the end of the line must receive the minimum-rated voltage for that equipment, usually 105 VAC in a 117-volt US system. It is important that this voltage be available even during the normal-line voltage variations provided by the utility company. As described previously, all equipments should receive their rated voltage during brownouts or other unusual circumstances, with a UPS used for this purpose.

Most electronic equipment functions with two generic cable types, low voltage signal and control, and power. For safety purposes and to keep extraneous noise from contaminating signals, these two cable types are not routed in close proximity to each other. For safety reasons, most local electrical codes require that the electrical power cables be run in a separate conduit from the signal cables. The reason for this is that the power cables are manufactured with insulation sufficient to withstand the higher voltages used in powering systems (120, 240 volt), whereas the signal cables generally have insulation sufficient for voltages up to perhaps only 50 or 100 volts. To prevent accidental shorting and sparks and perhaps fire due to a voltage breakdown between the higher-voltage power cable and the low-voltage signal cable, these two cables must be routed in separate conduits.

With respect to contamination of the signal cable by power-line voltage transient surges, the signal and power cables use separate shielded cables or conduits to avoid this problem. A general practice is to shield the signal cables with solid foil or stranded shielding to prevent external electrical noise from reaching the signal cable conductors. The UTP has no shield.

In larger video security installations, the security equipment is powered with a parallel network. In more complex installations where several parallel power-line paths are used or where equipment is located in different buildings or receiving power from different parts of the electric utility grid, the voltages may vary appreciably between different power distribution lines (Figure 23-15). The use of fiber-optic cable for signal transmission eliminates these problems.

In these installations, several factors must be checked: (1) Are all voltages within the range required by the equipment? and (2) Are there significant potential differences (more than a few volts) between the ground levels of each of the distribution lines? More often than not, there may be several volts—up to 25 volts—between what should be ground points on the ground line of each distribution line. If this condition exists, when the video equipment grounds are connected, the result will be damage to the equipment and/or degradation of the equipment's performance. As described in Chapter 6, hum bars appearing on the video image are a very apparent effect of a difference in ground voltage when multiple distribution lines are used. In more serious cases equipment damage or

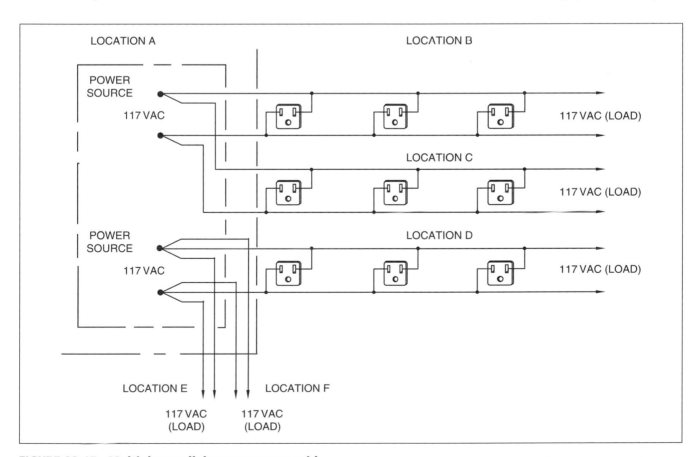

FIGURE 23-15   Multiple parallel power source grid

personnel injury can occur when equipments at different ground levels are connected together. These problems (see Chapter 6) are eliminated when fiber-optic data and video links are used between the equipment and/or electrical isolation transformers or optical couplers.

23.8.2 Radial Network

A second technique for connecting security equipment to power lines is called the *radial* system in which each equipment is connected to the power supply terminals by a separate line (Figure 23-16).

Although there will still be different voltages at each equipment caused by unequal conductor lengths, these differences can be minimized by careful selection of conductor size. This technique eliminates some of the electrical noise that may be induced on the power lines of sensitive equipment caused by heavy equipment on the line. Although the advantages of radial distribution over the parallel feed are evident on paper, they may be difficult to obtain in practice because of the many extra conductors required in the radial distribution system. In practice, a practical technique is a compromise in which some equipments requiring only small amounts of current are combined in a parallel grid structure and the radial elements are used to power equipments with high current requirements. Figure 23-17 illustrates the combined use of the parallel and radial distribution system combining these two techniques. In this example, light loads are powered by parallel distribution lines and heavy loads are powered radially.

23.9 GROUND LOOPS

An important aspect of the electrical distribution system is the use of good grounding practices and the elimination or avoidance of ground loops in the system. Ground loops are undesirable current paths coupling earthed points, equipment-ground points, or signal-return connections. The optimum configuration can be determined only after a thorough analysis of the distribution system as well as chassis and power-line grounding configuration. Most electronic equipment is designed such that electronic circuitry is grounded at one or multiple points on the equipment chassis. The system should be designed so that these ground points are connected electrically with a good conductive path from each equipment to the next, and to the chassis or earth ground (green wire) of the power distribution grid. In the case of battery or solar systems, one point in the system is chosen and all equipment grounds are brought back to this one point. In the installation of a UPS into the system, an appropriate chassis ground from the backup UPS or other voltage-transient suppression equipment must go back to the chassis ground. For safety purposes, all equipment chassis grounds should be connected with an electrical wire to the mechanical frame housing the equipment, and eventually the conductor going from this housing to earth ground through the third wire (green wire) in the system (Figure 23-18).

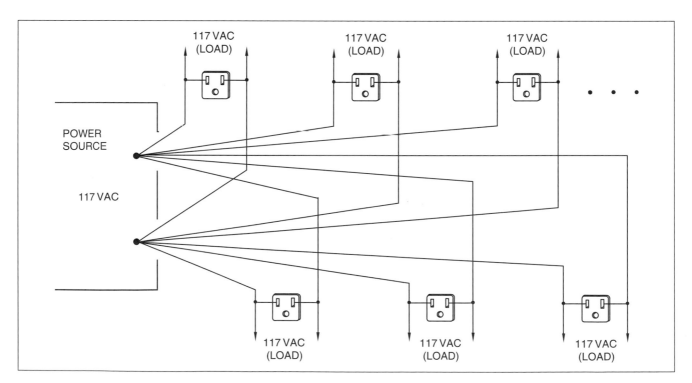

FIGURE 23-16   Radial power distribution system

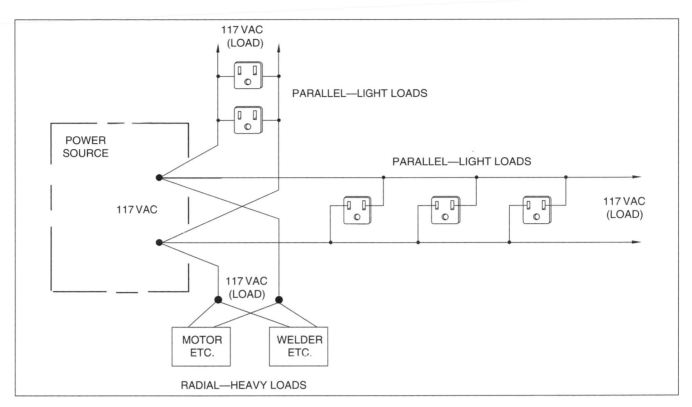

FIGURE 23-17   Parallel and radial combined power grid

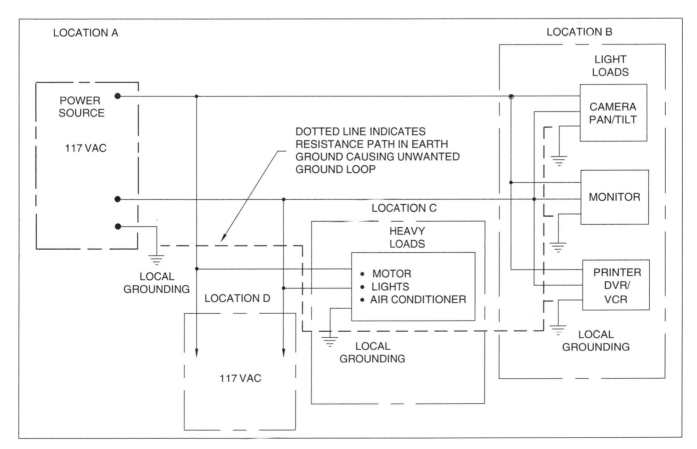

FIGURE 23-18   Potential ground loop sources

The finite resistance, inductance, and capacitance of conductors that carry these ground-loop currents provide a common cross-coupling impedance to inject unwanted signals, noise, and crosstalk into sensitive input signal circuits. The resistance and inductance can be minimized with heavy cable and short lengths. Also, when connecting several facility equipments to earth, approximately equal cable lengths and sizes should be used. To reduce or eliminate electrical interference from heavy machinery (motors, lights, air conditioner), use a radial power distribution system (Figure 23-19).

Equal impedances to a single earthed point help equalize potentials between different units and reduce both the inter-coupling of interference and shock hazards. Independent cables to a single earthed point eliminate common impedance paths among different equipment units. A single earthed point avoids the ground-current circulation that can occur when several earthed points are used. Signals from different locations should be isolated using fiber optics or isolation transformers.

Shielded signal cables are needed for interference-free signal handling. Cables carrying substantial power that can induce interference into signal cables should also be shielded—especially when both signals and power must flow in close proximity. Available types of shielded cable include single-wire, multi-wire, twisted-pair, coaxial, and multiple-shield. UTP cable is not shielded.

Shields for all these types are made of braided metal, solid conduit, or metal foil. Braided shielding is light and easy to handle. The shielding effectiveness decreases with increasing frequency because of discontinuities and openings inherent in the weave. Shielding effectiveness, of course, depends on the type and thickness of the material used for the braid and the tightness of the weave. Both solid and foil shields are very effective, especially at high frequencies; the solid material has no discontinuities or openings.

The following guideline lists recommended practices to achieve noise-free video image performance; proper equipment grounding is a start.

- Coaxial cables should be terminated at both ends.
- Equipment chassis and cable shields should never be used for signal-return paths (with the exception of coaxial cable).
- Signal circuits should use balanced cable, such as unshielded twisted-pair (UTP), or shielded or balanced coaxial lines.
- Individual shields of balanced coaxial cables when contained by a common shield should be insulated from one another and from the common shield.
- Cables that carry high-level signals should not be bundled with cables carrying low-level signals whether shielded or not.
- Each signal line should have its own independent return line running as close as possible to the signal line. In

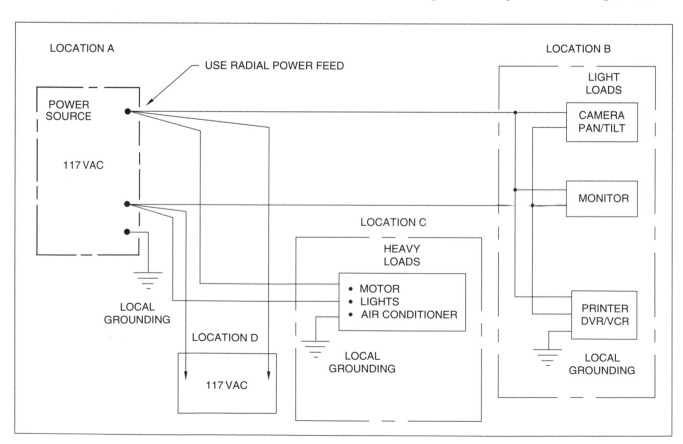

FIGURE 23-19   Practices for eliminating ground loops

this way, the loop area is reduced and coupling with other signals avoided.

- Use twisted-pair cable UTP (signal and return lines together) to ensure a minimum pickup-loop area. The voltage induced in one twist tends to cancel an oppositely induced voltage in the adjacent twist.

23.10 SUMMARY

Backup electrical power and power-line conditions are an essential consideration in any video security system. UPS equipment is available and should be used for all strategic video security and safety equipment. The proper power line filtering and conditioning saves time and money, and increases security.

There is a choice of AC or DC power in the form of power line, power converters, batteries, and solar panels for powering all equipment necessary for any video security application.

Distribution and ground loop problems should not be attacked with "black magic" fixes because these solutions tend to be temporary and often create other chronic problems. A thoughtful examination of each current-demanding element in the system and its effect on the overall distribution network is far more valuable than a dozen quick fixes.

Improper grounding and shielding of power and signal lines are major causes of noise interference in sensitive electronic equipment. Improper grounding occurs primarily because equipment designers often forget that every conductor to ground has resistance, inductance, and shunt capacitance. Moreover, when the ground conductors form ground loops, they can inject, radiate, or pick up both low- and high-frequency interference.

Chapter 24
Video-Security Systems Integration

CONTENTS

24.1   Overview
24.2   Integration Evolution
24.3   Integration Function
    24.3.1   Security System Integration
    24.3.2   Overall Facility Control
24.4   Technology and Equipment
24.5   Potential Problems-Solutions
24.6   Summary

24.1   OVERVIEW

There are many layers in *security system* integration and *security system with building system* integration. The overall integrated *security system* includes the following subsystems:

- Alarms and alarm monitoring
- Legacy analog CCTV or digital video
- Access control
- ID badging
- Perimeter intrusion detection
- Intercom communications.

Security integration projects often involve single or multiple sites. Security dealers, integrators, consultants, architect, and engineers, etc. must understand the technology required to effectively integrate these subsystems.

The role of an integrated security system is well known. An alarm and perimeter system is used to detect movement approaching and within the perimeter of a facility, the video system provides the eyes of the security system, access control regulates who enters and exits the facility at gates and other portals, and audio communications provide security, safety, and intelligence transmission.

The highest level of integration combines the *security system with building control*: the fire, heating, ventilation, air-conditioning (HVAC), lighting, and *all* facility communication functions. This all-encompassing integration now represents only a small part of the overall security market because of the disparate types of systems involved in the complex integration and to functions required of the overall system.

Integration of security technology is a worldwide trend providing increased security benefits at a lower cost. It is important to understand the technological evolution of integrated security systems and the many *layers* of understanding that are needed for proper implementation.

Although security systems integration can be viewed in many ways, there are two basic functions: (1) systems integration that involves the integration of the various subsystems of a security system at *one site* and (2) integration that involves the use of communications technology to integrate the security system at *multiple sites*.

The functions of centralized security monitoring stations vary among organizations. They can be classified into several categories to describe the security function: (1) active hours, (2) after hours, (3) simultaneous, and (4) remote.

24.2   INTEGRATION EVOLUTION

There has been an evolution of security integration from guard, to guard and security system. This evolution has changed from a "hands on" security system using the guard as the primary source for security to one with a complex and sophisticated electronic system that removes much of the decision-making from the guard. Much of the human decision-making has been transferred to and is accomplished by the security subsystems.

First Generation.   There have been several generations of security system integration over the years. First-generation systems in the late 1970s and 1980s were a new concept and used limited integration of electronic security equipment. Initially the guard provided limited security tasks for a site. With the introduction of electronic systems the role of the guard changed. The guard began controlling the entire site and responding to the alarm, CCTV, access control, and other electronic systems.

As these guard control and monitoring functions escalated, the guard could no longer function efficiently. Controlling all these subsystems having their own unique user interfaces and control protocols that did not communicate with each other resulted in some confusion and inefficiencies.

Second Generation. Second-generation integrated systems were designed to overcome some of these problems and make the entire system more user-friendly and more effective by interfacing and integrating the subsystems. These integrated systems electronically responded to activity detected by another subsystem and did not require much human intervention or judgment. This worked to some extent, however there were some difficulties in that some manufacturers continued to use their own proprietary operating protocols. The systems often did not "speak" the same language and stop-gap solutions had to be designed by writing interface software to accomplish communication among the subsystems.

Current Generation. The current generation of integrated security equipment is still in evolution and is being developed into a multi-media mode so that different security functions are smoothly integrated with each other to provide maximum security and operator efficiency. This has occurred as a result of the evolution of electronic equipment design from analog to digital technology. The multimedia digital systems can handle video, data, and audio by using the appropriate computer hardware and software. One commonality between all of the different security subsystem is that they are all *computer based*: digital information and protocols can be transmitted from one subsystem or computer to another with full recognition. Present integrated systems can accept and process the data produced by alarm and access control subsystems, video generated by CCTV systems and audio produced by intercom communications systems. Once the information is transmitted to the computer, software can manipulate that data and display it for the operator in a coherent and usable form to perform monitoring, control, and response.

24.3 INTEGRATION FUNCTION

There are essentially two levels of integration function: (1) security system and (2) security system plus building control system (fire, HVAC, etc.). In the previous section, the integration function described was for *security* only. This section describes the security function and the *security plus building control* function.

24.3.1 Security System Integration

The security system integration consists of *layers* of integration. If the security system is all at one site, it is easy to connect the various security subsystems via cable to the control console. This transmission can be accomplished using copper wire (coaxial, twisted-pair, multi-conductor), fiber optic or in special cases wireless transmission.

If a site is remote or there are multi-sites, the communication link is very important. If the transmission occurs outside the boundaries of the organization, it is important that the network outside the facility is secure and that proper protection is provided so that no outsiders can tap into the communications. To obtain this, protection usually takes some form of signal scrambling or encryption.

The functions of centralized monitoring stations may vary among organizations but in general they can be classified into four main categories:

Active Hours Monitoring. During the main work shift or open hours of an organization, the guard/security operator monitors and controls security functions. A guard monitoring station at each site monitors its own operation during normal office hours (Figure 24-1).

After Hours Monitoring. After normal office hours the monitoring and control passes to a central monitoring station. The central station monitors alarms and accesses each site periodically via a LAN and reviews alarm status and views surveillance cameras routinely. This is like a guard tour, with the benefits of the system being that this remote monitoring is laborsaving and provides continuous monitoring.

Simultaneous Monitoring. Monitoring of both the local site and the central monitoring station functions simultaneously. The central station monitors alarms and accesses any site surveillance cameras via a WAN, intranet or the Internet and operates the security system through its own networked keyboard. The fixed cameras can be controlled by operators at two locations at the same time. If these are pan-tilt cameras, a priority system is set up with one site overriding the other. In an alarm situation, both the local and the remote systems are activated and the operator of each system handles the control and switching network independently (Figure 24-2).

Remote Monitoring. The remote monitoring integrated system is particularly beneficial for small and large sites where it may not be economical to have local monitoring. Laborsavings in security is the major advantage here. In large site applications, the advantage is that the system allows a single or multiple sites to be monitored or controlled from any of the sites in the organization, wherever they may be (Figure 24-3).

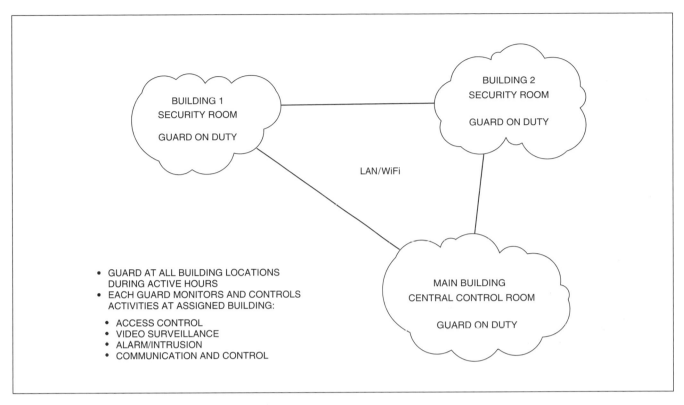

FIGURE 24-1   Active hours monitoring configuration

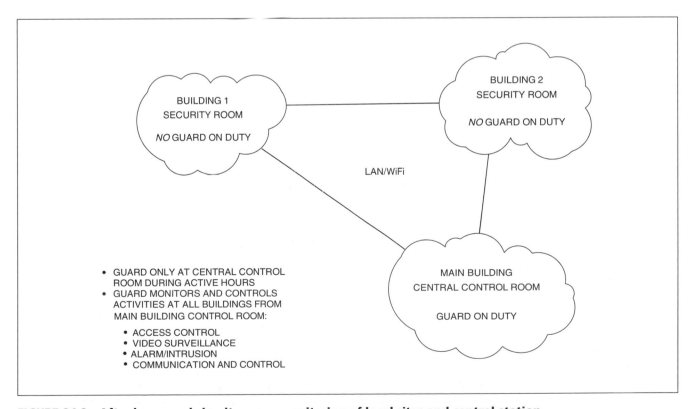

FIGURE 24-2   After hours and simultaneous monitoring of local sites and central station

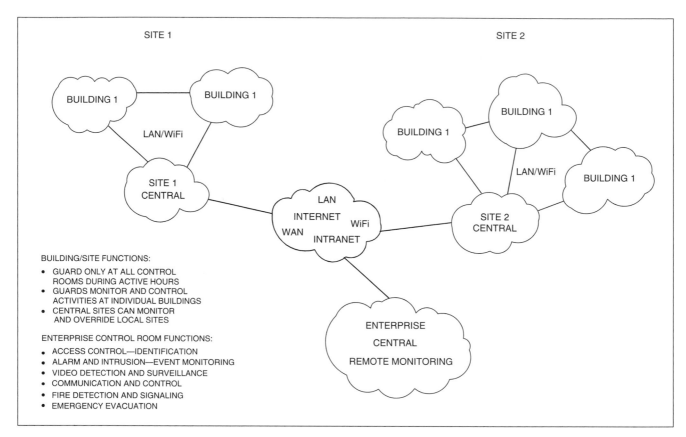

SITE 1

SITE 2

BUILDING 1

BUILDING 1

LAN/WiFi

SITE 1
CENTRAL

LAN
INTERNET
WAN   WiFi
INTRANET

BUILDING 1

BUILDING 1

BUILDING 1

LAN/WiFi

SITE 2
CENTRAL

BUILDING/SITE FUNCTIONS:
- GUARD ONLY AT ALL CONTROL
  ROOMS DURING ACTIVE HOURS
- GUARDS MONITOR AND CONTROL
  ACTIVITIES AT INDIVIDUAL BUILDINGS
- CENTRAL SITES CAN MONITOR
  AND OVERRIDE LOCAL SITES

ENTERPRISE CONTROL ROOM FUNCTIONS:
- ACCESS CONTROL—IDENTIFICATION
- ALARM AND INTRUSION—EVENT MONITORING
- VIDEO DETECTION AND SURVEILLANCE
- COMMUNICATION AND CONTROL
- FIRE DETECTION AND SIGNALING
- EMERGENCY EVACUATION

ENTERPRISE
CENTRAL
REMOTE MONITORING

FIGURE 24-3   Multiple site integrated system monitoring configuration

24.3.2   Overall Facility Control

The highest level of integration combines the security system *with* the fire, HVAC, lighting, and overall personnel communication functions. This all-encompassing total site integration now represents a small part of the overall security market because of the disparate types of systems involved in the integration and the complex functions required of the overall system. Unlike the integration of security subsystems with IT systems and functions that are occurring rapidly throughout the industry, it still remains to be seen when and to what extent integration of security of multiple building systems and security into a single control unit will become an industry norm. Such efforts are occurring primarily in settings such as government buildings, high-rise, data centers, museums, or other new construction of office complexes, etc. The slow adoption of this seemingly desirable model is management and technology related, however some level of integration is occurring and will grow in the coming years.

Building system integration is desirable and has been used in many "smart" buildings. There are many benefits in "building automation" (another term for integrated multiple building systems) that bring different functions together under one operational umbrella. Combining the fire system with access control has the advantage of being

able to automatically deactivate the alarm on doors when a fire alarm sounds. The integration of fire detection with HVAC can help control smoke by using advanced systems to contain it to a particular floor. Integrating the CCTV surveillance system with fire systems allows end users to view footage and discover the cause of a blaze as well as monitoring and view the fire as it is occurring.

In 1999 a study conducted by the US National Institute of Standards and Technology estimated that building automation could reduce the annual operating costs of buildings significantly. Building Automation and Control Networks (BACnet) and Local Operating Network (LonWorks) use different approaches to system integration. BACnet developed in the mid-1990s is a communications-only standard developed for the building's mechanical and electrical systems, particularly heating, ventilation, and air-conditioning. LonWorks, on the other hand, combines a communications standard with a *neuron* chip. This custom-integrated circuit was developed in the early 1990s and is used extensively in the transportation and utilities industries and has been adapted for buildings. At the time of this writing, it is unclear how widely used these communications standards will become in the future but they, along with advancements in control panels and other technologies, are offering a chance to turn the tide on the slow growth of building system integration. LonWorks developed by Echelon Inc. offers an alternative to the vendor-specific software and communications protocol that can make linking systems from multiple suppliers a difficult task.

There are many companies active in the field of security systems integration with other building functions for the purpose of controlling all functions from one console display screen. An example of such a system is the UniNet 2000 system by Notifier Inc. that integrates fire, security, access control, and CCTV on a single network. The UniNet 2000 is UL listed for fire, security, and access control and offers facility managers and building owners integrated networking, with a comprehensive interface for diverse systems. Its client–server technology allows easy upward migration as new features become available, can monitor non-Notifier fire alarm panels, and seamlessly integrate diverse fire and security building systems into a customized, graphics-oriented platform, creating a unified command center for monitoring and controlling building safety systems.

24.4 TECHNOLOGY AND EQUIPMENT

Security systems are assembled from separate disparate equipments and unique functions. In general, these systems do not communicate easily with each other. The integrated security platform integrates the CCTV, access control, alarm, perimeter intrusion detection, fire, and communications into *one* operating system. The benefits of this synergistic system are that the overall monitoring and control of a facility can be conducted from a single display monitor at one site or individual monitors at multiple sites. This results in a more efficient and higher level of security as well as cost savings.

Signal Transmission to Multiple Sites. There are several techniques to transmit the video, alarm, access control, and communications data over outside networks to remote sites. The PSTN telephone transmission network has been available for many years and uses a modem having a maximum speed of transmission of 56.6 kilobits per second (kbps). While this transmission speed may have been adequate for alarm and access control systems in the past, it is too slow for real-time or near real-time video images, even using digital picture compression. Using a compression of 20 kilobytes (KB) per frame, two or three frames per second can be transmitted. This is usually not sufficient for video monitoring. The integrated services digital network (ISDN) telephone line has a bandwidth of 128 kbps and using a compressed video picture of 20 KByte can send images a rate of 6 fps. Compressed to 5 KByte, video images could be transmitted at 24 fps which is essentially real-time. While ISDN has capabilities suitable for video and security surveillance, the technology has never become main stream because special equipment is required at the site

and many local telephone exchanges are not compatible with this mode of transmission.

Asymmetrical digital subscriber line (ADSL) is a communications technology that is now being used with the Internet and has applications for video. ADSL uses high-speed modulation techniques whereby it can send 1500 kbps from the camera or other device to the control room, and transmit 640 kbps in the opposite direction (for control or audio) from the control room to the device location. This technology is standard in many upscale computers and applications, and with this technology it is possible to send real-time video pictures using standard copper wires.

Graphical User Interface. A graphical user interface (GUI) is designed into the monitor and used to display the integrated data. Many manufacturers are designing hardware and software using these GUIs so that the entire security system including the video function can be controlled from a single monitor with a touchscreen and/or keyboard or mouse. When an alarm or other input requiring action is displayed, a full facility layout or map can be displayed to pinpoint the exact location of the alarm or incident with annunciation using flashing lights and sounds. A camera image of the alarmed area can be displayed in a window on the same computer screen. All the security functions can be controlled from the same terminal. The use of the GUI, mouse, and keyboard make the system very user-friendly. Using standard networking techniques such as LAN, WAN, intranet, or Internet the security system can be controlled by any terminal on the network at the local site or remote site locations.

24.5 POTENTIAL PROBLEMS-SOLUTIONS

Potential Problems. There are some problems and potential solutions with building automation and the integrated facility. While the advantages are impressive, some have found the road to multi-system integration a bit bumpy. The first and most obvious problem has been the complexity of linking together disparate systems with disparate functions, from different manufacturers. Many manufacturers still use proprietary hardware and communication protocols specific to their product and each is essentially designed to work on its own.

A second major problem with successful building systems integration implementation is finding one vendor with the expertise in all disciplines needed to make the integrated system work. Most vendors have a general understanding of various building applications but they lack *detailed* knowledge of the design and application of systems not in their area of expertise. One commonality in all these different systems, however, is that they are *computer-driven*. Although this means they speak a similar language, it does not diminish the need for specialized knowledge for implementing each system. To provide a solution to this problem, some large security equipment suppliers have created partnerships with various systems experts in order to offer customers a one-stop building integration package. This technique brings together the expertise of the security integrators, HVAC specialists, mechanical engineers and others, all under one umbrella. One downside of such efforts is that these integration packages are often proprietary making the future prospect of integrating products from other brands difficult.

Another issue is: what if the HVAC, fire, burglar, alarm, video, and access control systems fail *simultaneously* because they are being controlled through a centralized system? *Systems must be designed so this never occurs.* Any system combining fire with security and other functions *must* be UL listed if it plans to host the fire system. National and local fire codes must be considered.

Design Considerations, Solutions.   There are numerous factors that are helping the integration effort and making it a reality. Advancements in computer technology with the all-important ability to back-up data and create redundant systems has helped ease some of the concerns over losing data and having all-building systems shut down simultaneously.

Technological advances in commercial control panels for security systems have also played a role. The panels now allow several systems to operate from the same control panel, such as access control and CCTV paired with HVAC or access control and CCTV paired with lighting and temperature controls. There are various control panels providing different combinations of the building components available.

Two open communications standards for building automation are making their way to the market. As mentioned earlier, the BACnet standard is being developed to help the building integration movement. LonWorks was developed by Echelon Inc. and offers an alternative to the vendor specific software and communications protocols that can make linking systems from multiple suppliers a difficult task.

24.6 SUMMARY

Integration of security technology is a worldwide trend providing increased security benefits at a lower cost. Security integration projects often involve single or multiple sites. Security dealers, integrators, consultants, architect, and engineers, etc. must understand the technology required to effectively integrate security subsystems. There are essentially two levels of integration function: (1) security system and (2) security system plus building control system (fire, HVAC, etc.). The highest level of integration combines the *security system with building control:* the fire, heating, ventilation, air-conditioning (HVAC), lighting, and *all* facility communication functions.

Chapter 25
Video System Test Equipment

CONTENTS

25.1 Overview
25.2 Video Signal Test Equipment
    25.2.1   Waveform Monitor
    25.2.2   Vectorscope
    25.2.3   Hand-Held Meters
25.3 Digital Signal Test Equipment
25.4 Wireless RF and Microwave Meters
25.5 Visible Light Illumination and IR Power
    Level Meters
25.6 Optical Design and Test Devices
    25.6.1   Lens Field of View (FOV) Calculator
    25.6.2   Fiber-Optic Transmission Meters
    25.6.3   Hidden Camera Detector
25.7 Summary

25.1 OVERVIEW

Video surveillance systems use electrical, mechanical, and optical components and as such require the use of test and alignment equipment for their installation and maintenance. Specific electrical test equipments include video waveform generators, vector oscilloscopes, timing generators, digital diagnostic equipment, and other meters. These devices measure and adjust camera parameters, transmitter signal levels, and measure the performance of other components such as multiplexers, switchers, digital networks, analog and digital recorders, etc. These instruments are used in the initial design and final testing to determine that the video components and system are operating within specifications. Test equipment is used to measure signal level, signal strength, signal distortion, signal-to-noise ratio, frequency and phase response, and video waveform integrity over wired and wireless video transmission paths.

Lens field of view (FOV) calculators are used to determine the optimum lens focal length (FL) during the initial design and for checkout during the installation phase. Light meters are used to measure the ambient illumination reaching the camera lens during daytime and nighttime conditions from natural or artificial lighting sources. Optical power meters are used to measure the visible or near infrared (IR) radiation emitted from natural or artificial sources (lamps). Light power meters are used to measure optical signal strength in line of sight optical transmission systems. Optical test equipment is used to test the functionality of fiber-optic transmission systems and to measure cable continuity and attenuation, and fiber-optic connector and splice coupling efficiencies.

In addition to the above test equipment, there are many common tools and other devices required during the initial design, installation, operation, and maintenance of the analog or digital video equipment.

25.2 VIDEO SIGNAL TEST EQUIPMENT

There are many manufacturers supplying test equipment for analyzing video waveforms and video system components. Some of these include Tektronix, Leader, DK-Technologies, Protek, and Astro. There is a very comprehensive set of application notes available from Leader Inc. including a primer on video test signals, and the use of waveform monitors and vectorscopes for obtaining an in-depth treatise on the subject.

25.2.1 Waveform Monitor

The most common tests performed on cameras are to determine the output characteristics and levels of the

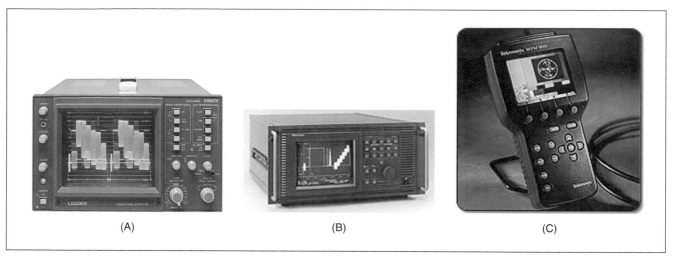

(A)   (B)   (C)

FIGURE 25-1   Video waveform generator and monitor

video and sync signals. Comprehensive testing and alignment of the camera video output signal is accomplished using a video waveform monitor (WFM). The WFM is basically an oscilloscope that has been tailored specifically to monitor composite analog video and sync signals. Most waveform monitors are used in the laboratory, however there are portable hand held units for using in the field. Some examples are shown in Figure 25-1.

The video waveform monitoring oscilloscope has provision for making measurements on vertical interval test signals (VITS) and provides filtering to allow separate examination of the luminance and chrominance components of color video signals.

The WFM draws a graph of voltage (vertically) vs. time (from left to right). The composite video amplitude has been standardized at 1 volt peak to peak (p-p) across a cable that has been terminated in 75 ohms. This standard video signal is routed at this standardized level from the source, such as the camera, to the various components in the video system: switchers, distribution amplifiers, video recorders, multiplexers, monitors, etc. The vertical sensitivity of the WFM is calibrated for full-scale deflection when a 1 volt p-p signal is applied. Full scale on the WFM screen is measured in terms of IRE units at the left of the graticule (Figure 25-2).

In the IRE scale, the video signal display ranges from black to peak white and is assigned a value of 100 units. This makes it very convenient to express intermediate values as simple percentages. A reference point at zero IRE forms the dividing line between the active video picture that grows upward from the blanking level of the signal and sync-pulse amplitude that extends downward from the blanking level to a value of −40 IRE. The full swing from −40 to +100 or 140 IR units equals 1 volt p-p.

Most WFMs set the horizontal sweep to display two full horizontal lines (2H display) representing a full frame. This means that two horizontal TV lines (2 fields) are displayed in a total of 127 microseconds. Since the display is repetitive, two lines followed by the next two followed by the next two are superimposed one over the other. It is often easier to measure vertical blanking width in raster lines rather than in time units. The FCC specifies a maximum of 21 lines for the blanking width. The RS-170A specifies 20 lines for blanking.

The period from the start of the *front porch* to the end of the *back porch* is the duration of horizontal blanking during which the picture monitor screen is blanked to allow the sweep signal to retrace back to the left edge of the screen to start a new horizontal scan. Horizontal sync is inside the blanking as is the *color burst,* a sample of the sub-carrier frequency used for color synchronization that sits on the back porch. Note that during the active portion between blanking pulses, the black floor (dark scene level) of the signal rises above blanking to 7.5 IRE units. This is the *setup* or *pedestal level.* It is good practice to set this at 7.5 units in the camera to keep the video monitors from losing detail in the dark parts of the picture.

In Figure 25-3a the camera lens is capped so there is no picture information. However, the sync amplitude is unaffected by lens opening and the sync signal extends the standard −40 IR units downwards from the blanking level. The vertical blanking level has been set to the zero IRE graticule line. In Figure 25-2 the blanking signal level with the front porch and back porch of the sync composite video signal is evident. This is illustrated in detail in Figure 25-2.

In Figure 25-2b, the camera lens is *uncapped* and the iris is opened partially. Note that the video picture signal grows vertically with the brightest (white) part of the image forming the high peaks. However, the monitor's image generally looks dark and low in contrast. In Figure 25-2c, the iris has been opened fully so that the video signal makes use of the full dynamic range of the system. That is, white peaks extend to 100 IRE and the full amplitude of the signal is 1 volt p-p. Normally the camera lens opening is set to put the white peaks at 100 IRE and the camera auto-iris systems operate to maintain that peak level.

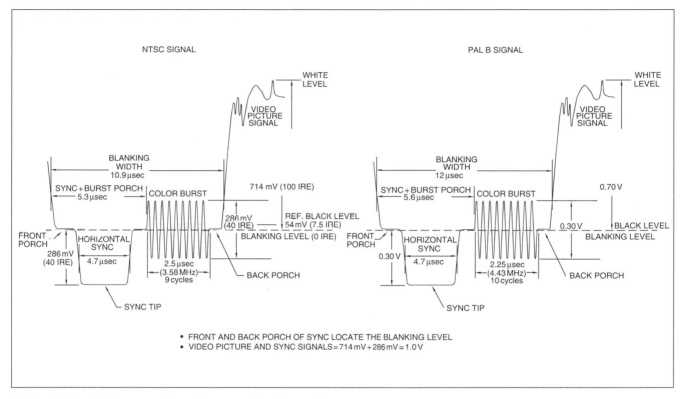

FIGURE 25-2   Video sync signal front and back porch

When the brightest part of the picture is white, such as a performer's shirt, it is easy to set lens opening or signal amplitude to 100%. However, if the brightest part of the picture is highly saturated and is *not white*, as an example a yellow flower, it is difficult to judge the correct brightness level setting. The solution is to simply strip out most of the color sub-carrier so the brightest part of the signal can be viewed alone. This is what the *IRE filter* does.

Automatic iris systems work from the luminance or brightness (Y) signal and ignore the chrominance (C) signal. They also partially average the signal to ignore small specular highlights and also ignore the top third or quarter of the picture so that accidental inclusion of a bright light will not affect the picture.

It is standard practice to gauge video levels in terms of IRE units. However, the use of conventional oscilloscopes without an IRE scale requires a conversion from IRE units to volts, actually millivolts since all values are typically 1 volt or less. Since 140 IRE translates into 1 volt p-p, a simple proportion may be set up to solve for intermediate levels. For example, to translate the 140 IRE level for sync into millivolts use the equation (25-1):

$$\text{Video Signal Voltage } V \text{ (in millivolts)}$$
$$= \frac{1000 \times \text{IRE value}}{140} \qquad (25\text{-}1)$$
$$V = \frac{1000 \times 40}{140} = 286 \, \text{mV}$$

Or more easily, to change IRE units to mV, divide IRE units by 0.14. To change mV to IRE units, multiply mV by 0.14.

The DC restorer is a signal clamp that pins down the blanking level. It is actually that part of blanking that occupies the horizontal back porch to the correct average scene level even when the average picture level of the signal changes radically. Without DC restoration the waveform drifts up and down depending on the average picture level. The reasons for this is that AC coupling, a single coupling capacitor anywhere in the signal train, removes the DC component of the original signal. It then tends to move and settle itself above or below an average value where the total signal area is equal above or below the average. The clamp in affect "restores" the DC component lost through AC coupling.

After the waveform monitor has been calibrated using the manufacturer's instructions, the cameras composite monochrome or color video signal is connected to the waveform monitor input. Using the calibrated screen reference graticule the signal amplitude is measured. It should be 1 volt p-p from sync tip to peak white. The video signal level should be between the +100 IRE and −40 IRE limits on the graticule. If the amplitude is less than or greater than this level, there is a possibility that some video equipment (switchers, multiplexers, recorders) will either overload or not give the best or acceptable performance.

All video signals are designed to drive a 75 ohm load. When cable runs loop through one or more pieces of

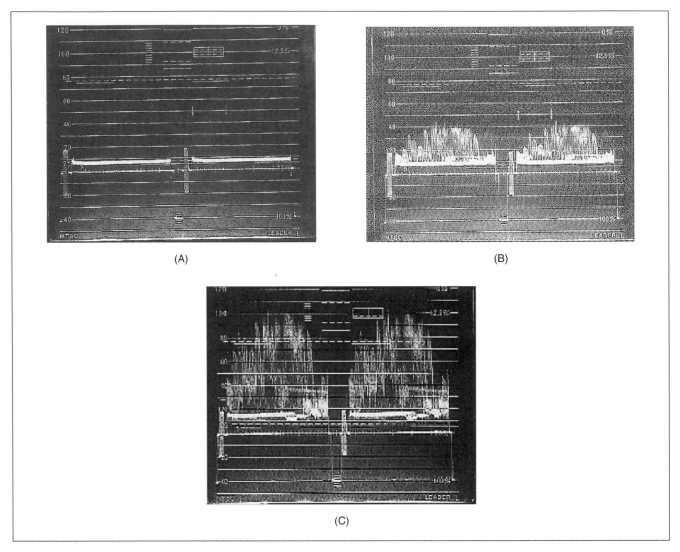

(A)

(B)

(C)

FIGURE 25-3 Waveform monitor (WFM) display

equipment in daisy chain fashion, the 75 ohm terminating resistance must be placed at the very end of the run, the last piece in the chain. Failure to terminate properly causes an open line and reflections from the end wreak havoc on frequency response and can cause "ghosts" on long cable runs. The most obvious result of a missing termination is a doubling of signal amplitude. The reason is that video sources operate as 2 volt p-p generators with an internal source impedance of 75 ohm. When a proper 75 ohm load is in place, the signal divides equally between source and load resulting in 1 volt p-p across the load. If the load is eliminated by removing the termination, a full 2 volt p-p signal will appear across the cable. Waveforms that look too "hot" with burst and sync amplitudes twice as big as they should are sure signs of a missing termination. Figure 25-4 shows the NTSC monochrome video waveform.

Figure 25-5 shows the color video waveform.

25.2.2 Vectorscope

In addition to the video signal waveform monitor (WFM) described in the previous section, a video vectorscope is used to make comprehensive measurements of color television equipment, and to deal with the *color* aspects of the composite video signal only, and ignore the luminance (black and white, sync). Figure 25-6a, b show vectorscopes used to monitor and calibrate color video equipment.

The vectorscope is designed to evaluate color parameters using the standard color bar signal with 75% amplitude and fully saturated colors as per EIA RS-189A or SMPTE ECR1-1978 standards. Color bars form the basic color test signal are shown in Figure 25-7.

After the vectorscope has been calibrated using the manufacturer's instructions, a composite color video signal is connected to the vectorscope input. A detailed description of the test procedure is beyond the scope of this book; however, some insight into the measurements follows.

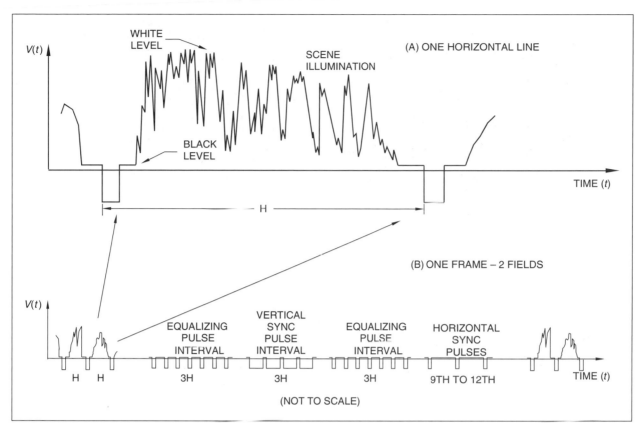

FIGURE 25-4   Composite NTSC monochrome video waveform

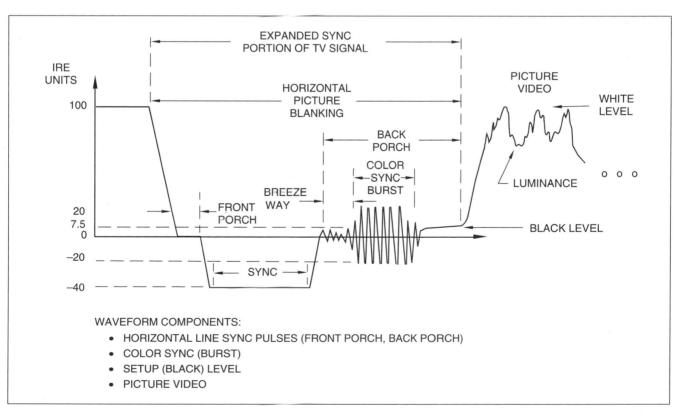

FIGURE 25-5   Composite NTSC color video waveform

(A)   (B)

FIGURE 25-6   Vectorscope for calibrating color video equipment

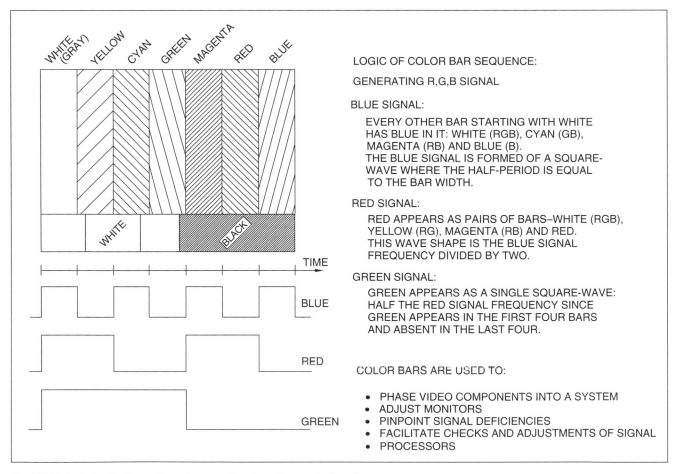

FIGURE 25-7   Color bars forming the basic color test signal

The previous section described the WFM which is basically an oscilloscope. It draws a graph of voltage (up and down) vs. time (left to right). The vector-scope is quite different. It also draws a graph but this time the amplitude of the 3.58 MHz chroma signal is plotted as a *radius* whose amplitude is plotted outward from the center of the screen and whose *phase angle* is measured around the circle much as time is marked off on a clock face, with 0° in the direction of the positive axis and rotating in a counterclockwise (CCW) direction. Engineers call this graph a *polar plot*. Since this form of plotting a signal may be unfamiliar, a short example is given to explain the concept of vectors and vector addition (Figure 25-8).

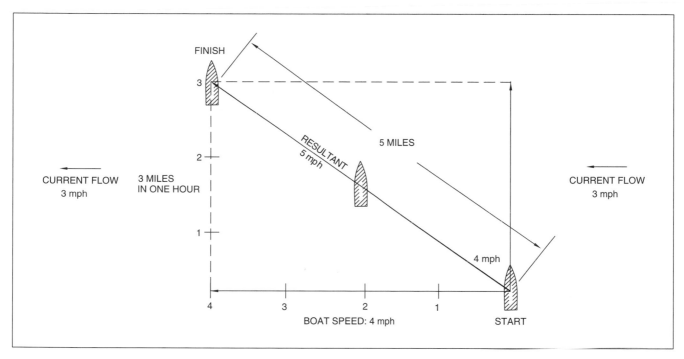

FIGURE 25-8   Example describing polar plotting using a vectorscope

If a boat leaves one side of a stream and crosses the stream at 4 mph and the stream has a current flow of 3 mph, the boat will not reach the exact opposite bank of the stream from where it started but rather somewhere downstream. As shown in Figure 25-8, after one hour the boat has crossed the stream and simultaneously moved down the stream 3 mi. The total distance traveled by the boat is 5 mi. at a speed over the river bed at 5 mph and it reaches the opposite bank 3 mi. down stream. In a likewise fashion, vectors are used to solve problems of AC voltages that have the same frequency but differ in *phase*. In the NTSC system, two-phase modulation is used to carry two color signals on the same 3.58 MHz sub carrier signal. Two modulators operating with sub carrier signals that are 90° apart in phase are fed with the color difference signals red minus yellow (R−Y) and blue minus yellow (B−Y). The outputs of the two modulators are simply added together using vector addition to find the resultant and the vector plot is made. Figure 25-9 shows the basic vector diagram for these signals, in this case red, and represents a typical vectorscope display for all the other color signal measurements. The specific plot shown in Figure 25-9 is for the red signal plotted as a vector using values for the R−Y and B−Y signals.

The *burst* signal also shows up as a vector (dot) on the vectorscope display. It is the phase reference and sub carrier sample of the color decoder in the receiver or monitor and is used to regenerate the carrier needed for the demodulation process. By convention the burst phase is at 180°, that is on the—(B−Y) axis at the 9 o'clock position. Figure 25-10 shows the burst vector at the indicated position. When viewing any NTSC signal the front panel phase

control is adjusted to put the burst vector at the 9 o'clock position as in Figure 25-10.

Only one color, red, has been shown so far on the vectorscope. The standard color bar signal provides eight colors if white and black are included as "colors." These bars are in order from left to right: white, yellow, cyan, green, magenta, red, blue, and black. White and black are balanced colors. That is, the color difference signals go to zero for neutral white, gray, or black. There is no output from the encoder modulators in these cases and the 3.58 MHz sub carrier also goes to 0. Thus any neutral gray, white, or black has no effect on the vectorscope display. The remaining colors, the primaries red, green, and blue and the complements cyan, magenta, and yellow, all produce vectors that can be plotted as was shown for the red color example. The vectorscope plots these vectors and is basically a very simple device. It simply decodes the input composite signal into R−Y and B−Y components and applies them to an X, Y display so that R−Y deflects the electron beam up and down and the B−Y left and right. It is doing this job accurately and that causes vectorscopes to be somewhat expensive ($1-2K).

To summarize the basics of the vectorscope:

- The vectorscope is an excellent tool for evaluating the chrominance signals for video equipment.
- The vectorscope makes a polar plot of the 3.58 MHz chroma signal.
- Phase angle and the hue of reproduced color are plotted CCW from the 3 o'clock position.
- Amplitude and saturation are plotted outward from the origin.

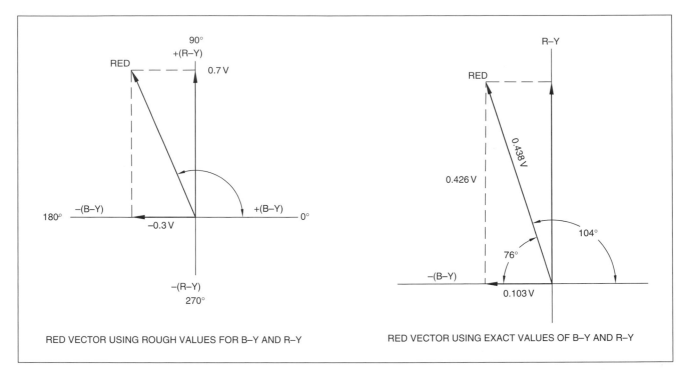

FIGURE 25-9 Red chroma signal plotted as a vector using values for R–Y and B–Y

• The vectorscope graticule is calibrated to locate the precise phase angle and amplitude locations of the primary and complimentary colors of the standard color bar signal specified in standard RS-189A.

Figure 25-11 shows the vectorscope display of the primary and complimentary colors of a standard color bar signal.

Table 25-1 summarizes most of the NTSC parameters as applied to color video signals. The table includes timing and voltage information as defined by IRE units vs. volts.

Figure 25-12 illustrates in detail the waveform monitor display IRE units vs. the oscilloscope display voltage units. The figure illustrates all the voltages pertaining to the horizontal blanking portion of the color video signal.

Sync Amplitude.   The sync amplitude is measured from the sync tip to blanking. However, the ratio of the sync to the carrier is more important: 40/140 of a composite video signal should be sync. On a 1 volt signal, the sync amplitude should be 286 millivolts.

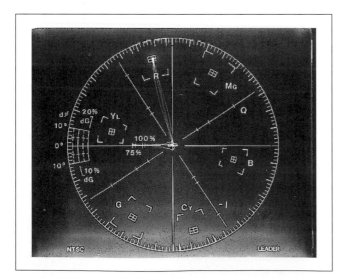

FIGURE 25-10 Red chroma signal and burst signal as displayed on the vectorscope

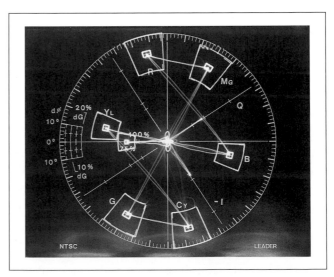

FIGURE 25-11 Vectorscope display of primary and complimentary colors of standard color bar signal

KEY FREQUENCIES/PERIODS

HORIZONTAL LINE FREQUENCY: 15.73426 KHz

HORIZONTAL LINE PERIOD: 63.556 µs
VERTICAL FIELD RATE: 59.94 Hz
VERTICAL FRAME RATE: 27.97 Hz
SUBCARRIER FREQUENCY: 3.579545 MHz
SUBCARRIER PERIOD: 279.4 ns

PULSE DURATIONS (RS-170A)

HORIZONTAL SYNC: 4.7 µs (MEASURED AT –20 IRE)
HORIZONTAL BLANKING: 10.9 µs (MEASURED AT +20 IRE)
FRONT PORCH: 1.5 µs (MEASURED FROM +4 TO –20 IRE)
LEADING EDGE OF HORIZONTAL SYNC TO BURST: 5.3 µs
   (19 SUB-CARRIER CYCLES)
VERTICAL BLANKING: 20H (LINES) +1, –0

IRE UNITS vs. VOLTS

FULL SWING FROM BLACK TO PEAK WHITE SPANS
   100% (100 IRE UNITS)
SYNC EXTENDS TO –40 IRE UNITS
FULL VIDEO+SYNC SPANS 140 IRE UNITS p-p
TO CONNVERT IRE UNITS TO MILLIVOLTS (mv)
   MULTIPLY IRE UNITS BY 0.14

KEY SIGNAL LEVELS

	IRE UNITS	TOLERANCE (IRE UNITS) (RS-170A)	mV
SYNC	–40	+2	286
BURST (p-p)	40	±2	286
SETUP	7.5	±2	54
100% WHITE	100		714
75% WHITE	77		550
(7.5% SETUP)			

CABLE DATA PERTAINING TO NTSC COLOR

TYPE: RG-59 (SOLID CONDUCTOR/DIELECTRIC)

CHARACTERISTIC IMPEDANCE: 75 ohm

ATTENUATION: 0.7 dB/100 ft@5 MHz
   3.4 dB/100 ft@100 MHz

PROPOGATION DELAY OF SUBCARRIER:
   360°/180 ft
   180°/90 ft
   1°/0.5 ft

VIDEO LEVEL vs. TRANSMITTER % MODULATION

IRE	% MODULATION
–40 (SYNC TIP)	100
0 (BLANKING	75
100 (PEAK WHITE)	12.5
120	0

Table 25-1   Color Video Signal NTSC Parameters

Burst Amplitude. The color burst from EIA standards should be equal in amplitude to the synchronizing signal, and centered on the blanking level. To measure the burst amplitude, the signal can be measured directly on the IRE scale of a waveform monitor and should be 40 units p-p. Whenever possible the burst amplitude signal should be compared to the sync signal to see if it is within specifications.

Vertical Blanking. The vertical blanking is the time between the last picture information at the bottom of one field and the first picture information at the top of the following field. Vertical blanking is measured from the leading-edge of the first equalizing pulse. Measured in terms of time, the vertical blanking must be greater than 1.17 milliseconds and less than 1.33 milliseconds. In terms of scanning lines, the maximum vertical blanking is 21 lines.

The waveform monitor permits measuring all of the video waveforms including vertical sync pulse, horizontal blanking pulse, and front porch. The amplitudes, pulse widths, and rise times of all these signals can be measured.

Subcarrier Frequency. The frequency of the color subcarrier or burst signal must be held within 10 Hz of 3.579545 MHz. The short time duration of the burst signal makes direct frequency counting accurate. The burst frequency can be measured or verified in several ways depending on the equipment available: (1) using the vector scope with known reference sub-carrier frequency, (2) using a vectorscope, variable oscillator, and frequency counter. The signal generator is set near 3.58 MHz and slowly adjusted until the vector-scope display rotates very slowly or not all. The oscillator frequency is measured with the counter and should provide a very close measurement of the actual sub-carrier frequency.

Linear and Non-linear Distortion. There are two broad classifications of signal distortion in video systems: linear and nonlinear. Nonlinear distortion varies with the average or instantaneous amplitude of the picture signal, whereas linear distortions manifest themselves independent of the signal level. Linear distortions usually occur in a system as a result of incorrect frequency response.

Video Signal-to-Noise Ratio. Noise components on a video signal that are sufficiently large will degrade the video monitor image. One objective in designing and implementing the video system is to keep these noise components to an absolute minimum. Each video component that the signal passes through adds its own noise to the video signal. Video signal noise is measured and expressed as a ratio between the normal picture signal level, 714 millivolts, and the RMS amplitude of the noise components contained on the signal. This ratio is expressed in decibels.

Differential Phase. If the phase of the color sub-carrier changes as a result of changes in the amplitude of the luminance signal, this distortion is known as differential phase. Differential phase is measured by using a stair-step

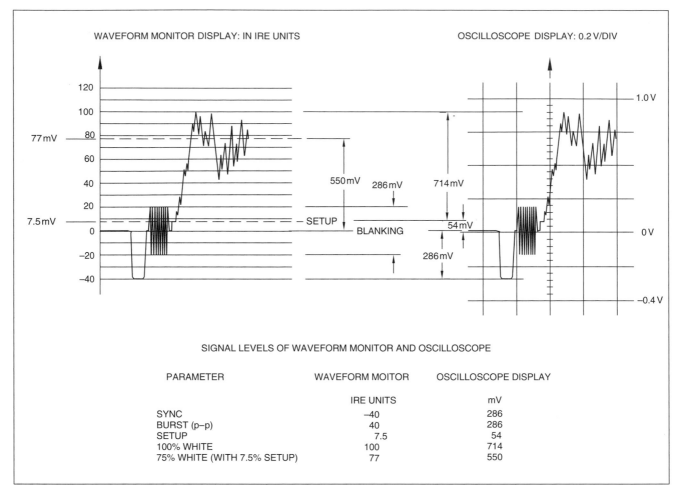

WAVEFORM MONITOR DISPLAY: IN IRE UNITS   OSCILLOSCOPE DISPLAY: 0.2 V/DIV

SIGNAL LEVELS OF WAVEFORM MONITOR AND OSCILLOSCOPE

PARAMETER	WAVEFORM MOITOR	OSCILLOSCOPE DISPLAY
	IRE UNITS	mV
SYNC	−40	286
BURST (p–p)	40	286
SETUP	7.5	54
100% WHITE	100	714
75% WHITE (WITH 7.5% SETUP)	77	550

FIGURE 25-12   Voltages pertaining to the horizontal blanking portion of the color video signal

signal with constant amplitude chrominance added to the stair-step risers. When the sub-carrier signal is viewed on a vector-scope, any phase difference between the chrominance on the steps indicates differential phase. The difference in degrees between the two steps that are farthest apart is a measure of the differential phase.

25.2.3 Hand-Held Meters

When installing or testing video equipment it is generally not practical to bring the waveform monitor or vectorscope test equipment into the field. To accomplish video signal measurements or alignment and repairs in the field, it is more practical to use small hand-held signal strength and frequency meters (Figure 25-13).

Video Timing Meter (VTM).   The VTM is a digital, handheld, battery-operated meter that measures the degree of synchronization between any two cameras that are synchronized from the line power in terms of the difference in the number of horizontal lines between them. This enables rapid synchronization between the two cameras

and adjustment to zero error with the VTM. This can be done right on the camera that needs adjustment at the camera location. The VTM is used with the VTG (below) to synchronize all cameras to one master.

Video Timing Generator (VTG).   The VTG sends master synchronizing signals to ten cameras at a time. The sync signal can go to each camera via the coaxial cable where the VTM is used, to synchronize that camera. Using this set up one person can synchronize all cameras without the need for a radio link to a second technician. Both monochrome and color cameras can be synchronized using this technique.

Camera Monitor (CM 1).   The FM systems CM-1 is a digital, handheld, battery-operated meter that measures five different camera characteristics:

- SYNC: measures sync level
- LUMINANCE: measures IRIS setting
- COMPOSITE: measures overall video level
- COLOR BURST: measures the 3.58 MHz level. Used to adjust coaxial cable equalizers for color cameras
- FOCUS: used to accurately adjust camera focus.

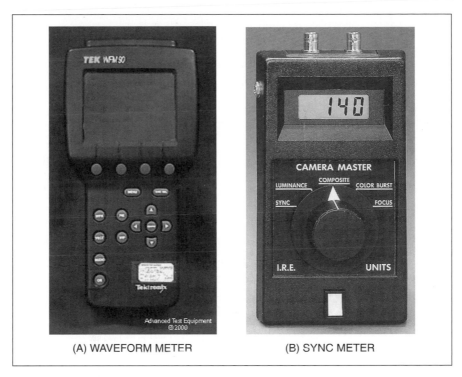

(A) WAVEFORM METER   (B) SYNC METER

FIGURE 25-13   Hand held video signal waveform and sync signal meters

25.3 DIGITAL SIGNAL TEST EQUIPMENT

Digital signal test equipment suitable for video systems includes frequency and digital pulse generators, high-speed oscilloscopes, and logic analyzers. These are used to check transmission protocols in digital networks, including LANs, WANs, etc. Some of the manufactures that produces this equipment include Tektronix, Hewlett-Packard, Leader, and others.

25.4 WIRELESS RF AND MICROWAVE METERS

Wireless analog and digital video transmission uses radio frequency (RF) and microwave frequencies as a transmission means. Installing these wireless systems requires knowledge of the RF or microwave transmitter signal strength and frequency. At the receiver end, it is important to know signal level, signal/noise ratio, and the transmission frequency. Most analog wireless devices are used in the 900 MHz, 1.2 GHz, 2.4 GHz, and 5.8 GHz bands. Most digital wireless transmission devices use the 802.11 protocol in the 2.4 GHz and 5.8 GHz bands. Most meters and spectrums analyzers measure the 2.4 and 5.8 GHz bands. Some can measure any frequency from a few MHz to 6-10 GHz. Figure 25-14 shows two portable devices for measuring the RF and microwave signal parameters.

These are RF and microwave meters similar to wideband radio receivers but having signal strength electronics built into them. They feature very high sensitivity and broadband in that they span high-frequency (HF), shortwave (SW), very high frequency (VHF), ultra high frequency (UHF), and microwave frequencies. These equipments have high sensitivity and wide bandwidths as a result of new telecommunications integrated circuits developed for use in cell phones and other wireless devices. They are hundreds of times more sensitive than previous generation field strength meters and permit the detection of the very weakest signals down to baseline ambient levels. These devices display those signals in a linear (standard) or logarithmic (compressed) form. The meters can determine signal characteristics whether analog, digital, pulse, frequency hopping, or spread spectrum. Each meter has an analog scale and LED display that is visible from a distance at nighttime. Options available include audio output to hear signal strength levels and identify sources by their characteristics sounds. Some have a switch enabled silent vibrator to alert the user. Some have a high frequency band that filters out noise and interfering signals to allow for high sensitivity and detection of microwave signals above 1.5 GHz. Some units have a USB output connection for distant monitoring, remote powering, and accessory switching. These hand-held meters are used in the field by personnel installing wireless surveillance and security products, and other communications equipment.

The meters can also be useful for detecting RF signals in applications of eavesdropping detection and countersurveillance (Section 25.6.3). The meters allow the measurement of RF signal strength to determine antenna radiation and transmitter radiation patterns for personnel involved in securing and maintaining good RF communication links. The meters are used by networking personnel

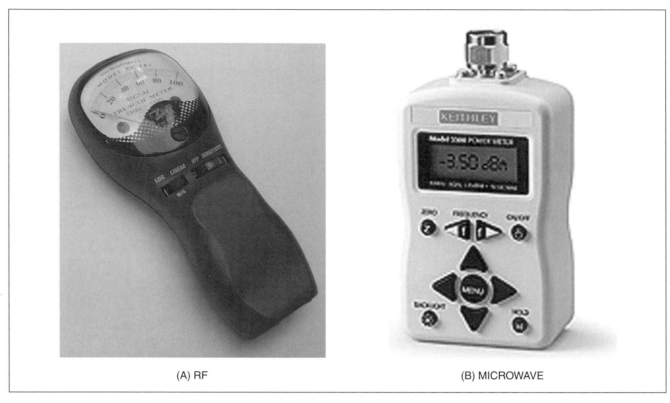

(A) RF   (B) MICROWAVE

FIGURE 25-14   Radio frequency (RF) and microwave meters

to optimize hub and satellite sites, confirm transmissions, detect hot and cold spots, measure baseline signal levels, detect and locate RFI, plot radiating patterns, and aim wireless communication antennas.

For video transmission, these hand-held meters can be used to perform quick tests to determine:

- What is the ambient level of RF and microwave radiation?
- What is the level of radio frequency interference (RFI) at the site?
- Where are all the hot and cold spots?
- Where are the optimal sites for transmitter/receiver placement?

For counter-surveillance scenarios, these meters have the capability for measuring RF and microwave radiation and have the following attributes:

- High sensitivity: sense covert devices from a distance.
- Broad receiving bandwidth: measures the frequency of the covert transmitter.
- Different modes of detection: enables initial detection of a very small signal from a distant transmitter and then homes in to pinpoint its location.
- Display modalities: detects RF and microwave signals and allows their display in an unobserved manner even at nighttime.
- Reasonable cost: practical instrumentation to detect radiation at an affordable price—hundreds of dollars.

25.5   VISIBLE LIGHT ILLUMINATION AND IR POWER LEVEL METERS

When designing, testing, and installing video surveillance systems, there are several optical measurements that must be made. One important measurement is the illumination level for a monochrome or color camera. Chapter 3 described the light levels (FtCd, lux) present in typical indoor and outdoor environments produced by natural and artificial illuminating sources.

Chapters 5 and 19 gave the sensitivities of typical monochrome and color cameras, image intensified CCD cameras (ICCD) and thermal IR cameras. When designing a video surveillance system using visible daylight or nighttime cameras, the illumination reaching the camera should be measured using a light meter (Figure 25-15). Thermal IR cameras respond to temperature differences and do not require a "thermal meter."

The hand-held light meters measure either the radiation from a light source or light reflected from a surface. The standard units of measure are the FtCd and lux, where 1 FtCd equals approximately 10 lux (0.093 FtCd = 1 lux). The light meters have multiple scales covering the light range from 0 to 2000 FtCd (0–20,000 lux). The two types of measurements are shown in Figure 25-16.

It should be noted that light meters utilize a photopic light filter that matches the sensitivity of the human eye so that these meters are not useful for measuring the "light" level from IR LED illuminators. These light meters do not

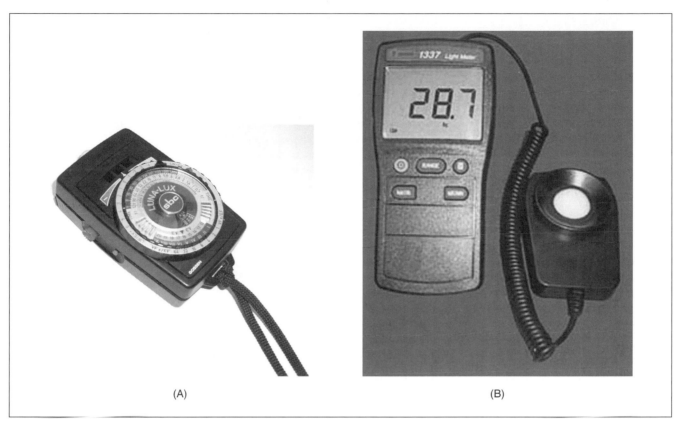

FIGURE 25-15   Visible light meters

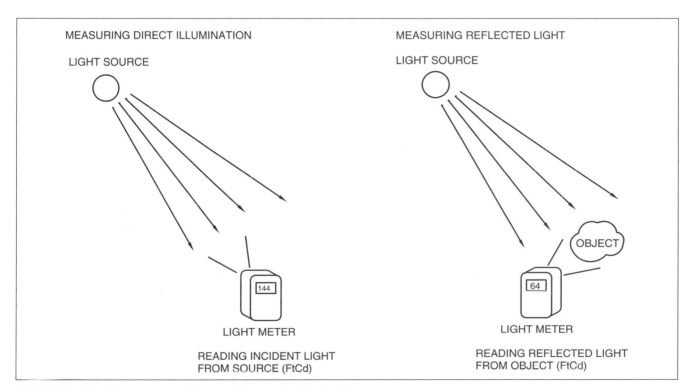

FIGURE 25-16   Direct source illumination and reflected light

FACILITY TYPE	LOCATION	MEASURED IN	
		FtCd	lux
FACTORY	EMERGENCY STAIRS, WAREHOUSE EXIT/ENTRANCE PASSAGES PACKING/SHIPPING AREA VISUAL WORK: PRODUCTION LINE TYPSETTING, INSPECTION WORK	2–7 7–15 15–30 30–75 75–150	20–70 70–150 15–300 300–750 750–1500
OFFICE	INDOOR EMERGENCY STAIRS CORRIDOR STAIRS CONFERENCE, RECEPTION ROOM CLERICAL WORK TYPING, DRAFTING	7–10 10–20 20–75 75–150 150–200	70–100 100–200 200–750 750–1500 1500–2000
RETAIL STORE	INDOOR SELLING FLOOR CORRIDOR/STAIR RECEPTION ELEVATOR	7–25 15–20 20–30 50–75	70–250 15–200 200–300 500–750
SUPERMARKET	INDOOR SELLING FLOOR CASH REGISTERS	10–25 15–30	100–250 150–300
HOSPITAL	EMERGENCY STAIRS STAIRS SICK ROOM, WAREHOUSE WAITING ROOM OPERATING/EMERGENCY ROOM	3–10 7–10 10–15 15–20 75–150	30–100 70–100 100–150 150–200 750–1500
LIBRARY	PUBLIC CIRCULATION AREA BOOK AISLES	30–40 40–50	300–400 400–500

Table 25-2   Typical Light Levels in Indoor Locations

respond to the IR radiation from these sources. The light level present in indoor environments varies greatly from one location to another, and even greater from indoor to outdoor environments. Table 25-2 represents typical light levels in various indoor locations.

The radiation levels from near-IR sources whether thermal or LED IR sources are measured using an optical power meter. These meters are portable and available for measuring power up to several hundred watts in the near-IR range from 700 nm and beyond. The power meters are available as a single self-contained meter and IR sensor or commonly as a separate meter and power-head (Figure 25-17).

25.6   OPTICAL DESIGN AND TEST DEVICES

When designing, testing, and installing video surveillance systems, there are several optical measurements that must be made. These may involve calculating the FOV of a camera lens, the transmission and attenuation in a fiber-optic transmission link, or the detection and location of a covert camera. The following sections describe the equipments used for these tests.

FIGURE 25-17   Infrared (IR) optical power meter

25.6.1   Lens Field of View (FOV) Calculator

There are many devices for measuring the FOV as seen by the video lens–camera combination. Tables and slide rules for finding lens angular FOVs abound. These devices include linear and circular slide rules scales to simplify the task of choosing the best lens for a particular security application. One very convenient circular scale described in Chapter 4 is the Lens Finder Kit (copyright H. Kruegle). The kit consists of transparent circular plastic disks that contain most of the standard fixed focal length lenses and corresponding horizontal and vertical angles (FOVs) that they generate on the CCD, CMOS or other sensors. The

most common sensor sizes in use are 1/4-, 1/3-, or 1/2-inch, and Figure 25-18 shows these three disks.

Figure 25-19 shows how to use the Lens Finder Kit to quickly determine the correct lens for an application.

There is a separate scale on each of the disks for each of the three camera-sensor sizes: 1/4-, 1/3-, 1/2-inch. The scale for each camera format shows the FL of standard lenses and the corresponding horizontal and vertical FOVs

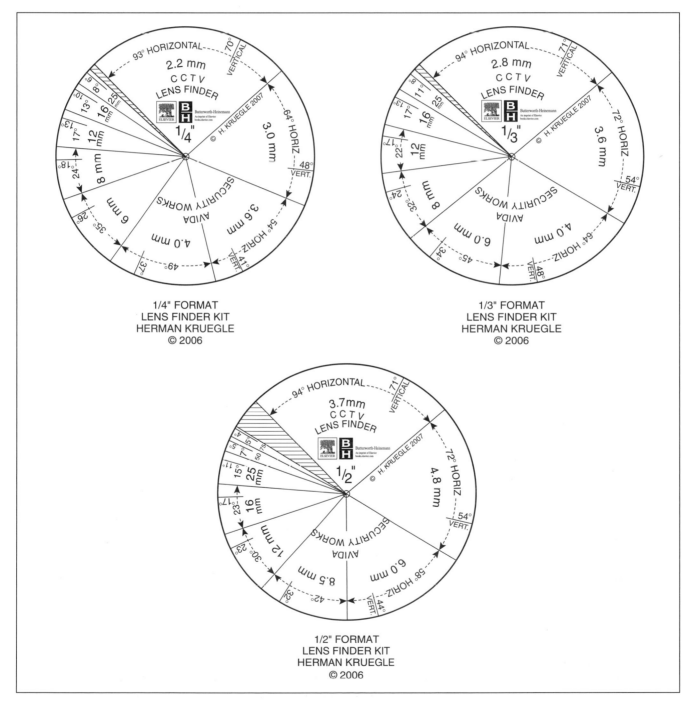

FIGURE 25-18   Lens Finder Kit disks for 1/4-, 1/3-, and 1/2-inch sensor formats

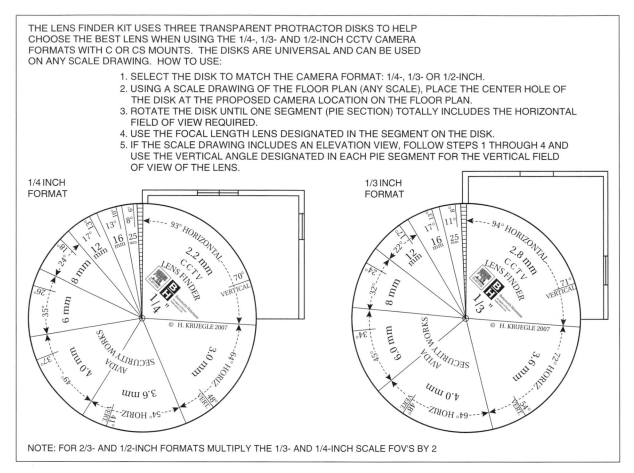

THE LENS FINDER KIT USES THREE TRANSPARENT PROTRACTOR DISKS TO HELP
CHOOSE THE BEST LENS WHEN USING THE 1/4-, 1/3- AND 1/2-INCH CCTV CAMERA
FORMATS WITH C OR CS MOUNTS. THE DISKS ARE UNIVERSAL AND CAN BE USED
ON ANY SCALE DRAWING. HOW TO USE:

1. SELECT THE DISK TO MATCH THE CAMERA FORMAT: 1/4-, 1/3- OR 1/2-INCH.
2. USING A SCALE DRAWING OF THE FLOOR PLAN (ANY SCALE), PLACE THE CENTER HOLE OF
   THE DISK AT THE PROPOSED CAMERA LOCATION ON THE FLOOR PLAN.
3. ROTATE THE DISK UNTIL ONE SEGMENT (PIE SECTION) TOTALLY INCLUDES THE HORIZONTAL
   FIELD OF VIEW REQUIRED.
4. USE THE FOCAL LENGTH LENS DESIGNATED IN THE SEGMENT ON THE DISK.
5. IF THE SCALE DRAWING INCLUDES AN ELEVATION VIEW, FOLLOW STEPS 1 THROUGH 4 AND
   USE THE VERTICAL ANGLE DESIGNATED IN EACH PIE SEGMENT FOR THE VERTICAL FIELD
   OF VIEW OF THE LENS.

NOTE: FOR 2/3- AND 1/2-INCH FORMATS MULTIPLY THE 1/3- AND 1/4-INCH SCALE FOV'S BY 2

FIGURE 25-19   Choosing a lens with the Lens Finder Kit

that the camera will see with the corresponding lens. To use the disk, place it on the facility plan drawing and choose the lens FL that gives the desired camera FOV coverage. For example, a 1/3-inch format camera is to view a horizontal FOV (64°) in a front lobby 30 feet wide at a distance of 30 feet from the camera (Figure 25-20). What FL lens should be used?

To find the horizontal angular FOV, draw the following lines to scale on the plan: (1) a line to a distance of 30 feet from the camera to the center of the scene to be viewed, (2) a line 30 feet long and perpendicular to the first line and (3) two lines from the camera location to the endpoints of the second 30 foot line. Place the 1/3 inch Lens Finder disk on the plan drawing (top view) with the center at the camera location and choose the FL closest to the horizontal angle required. A 4.8 mm FL lens is closest. This lens will see a horizontal scene width of 30 feet. Likewise for scene height, using the elevation drawing (side-view), the horizontal scene height is 22.5 feet.

25.6.2   Fiber-Optic Transmission Meters

Fiber-optic transmission systems require specialized electro-optical test equipment for testing the light transmission from a LED or laser transmitter to the photodiode receiver. Light parameters that need to be measured include: (1) signal level, (2) signal distortion, (3) signal attenuation, (4) pulse rise-time, and (5) pulse width. There are many manufacturers of electron-optic and specifically fiber-optic transmission test equipment for measuring fiber and connector attenuation as well as signal level from the transmitter and receiver units. The measurements are made using equipment such as that shown in Figure 25-21.

25.6.3   Hidden Camera Detector

Section 25.4 described electronic meters for detecting RF and microwave radiation for the purposes of countering (locating) hidden transmitters for security countermeasure applications. There are hidden camera detector devices that can locate a hidden camera by detecting the *radiation* being emitted from the camera electronics or by detecting the *optical lens and sensor* used by the camera. This permits quick, efficient, and discrete sweeps of the home, office, hotel, or conference room.

Figure 25-22a shows a small hand-held device that detects transmit frequencies between 50 MHz and 3 GHz,

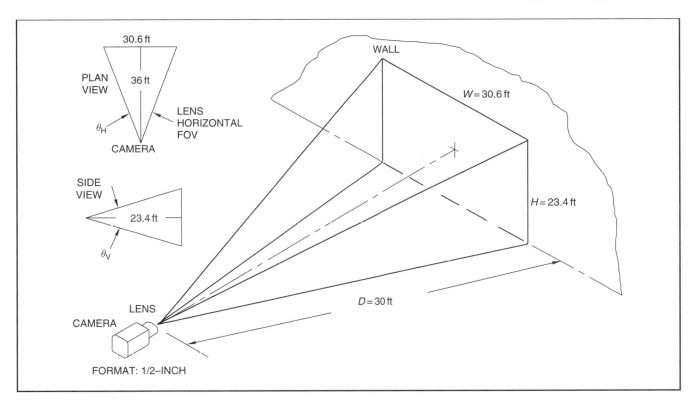

FIGURE 25-20   Determining lobby lens horizontal and vertical field of view (FOV)

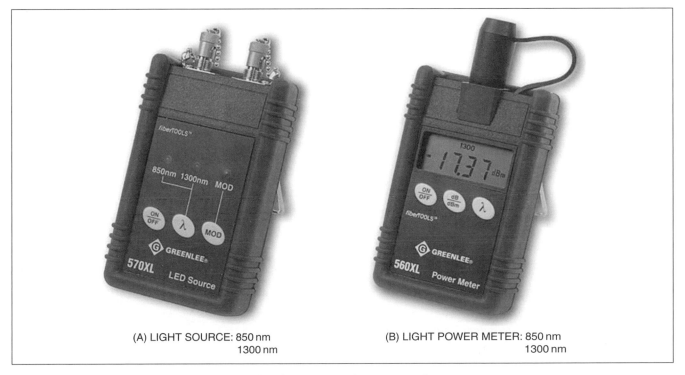

(A) LIGHT SOURCE: 850 nm
1300 nm

(B) LIGHT POWER METER: 850 nm
1300 nm

FIGURE 25-21   Fiber-optic light source and light transmission test equipment

and sounds an audible alarm or illuminates an LED to alert the user of the presence of a transmitting device being used with the camera.

Figure 25-22b shows an easy-to-use hand-held device that *optically* locates hidden (covert) cameras whether they have their power turned *on* or *off*.

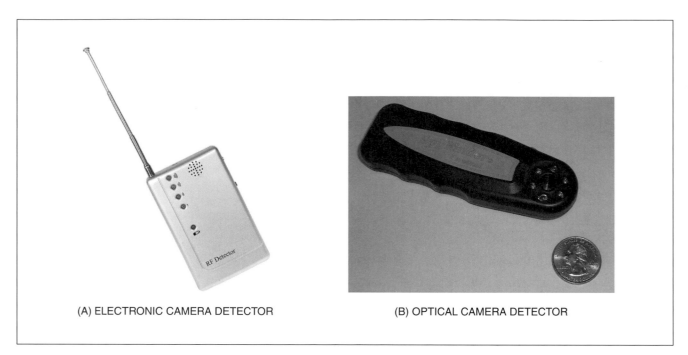

(A) ELECTRONIC CAMERA DETECTOR   (B) OPTICAL CAMERA DETECTOR

FIGURE 25-22   Hidden camera detectors using emitted transmitter signal or optical interrogation

The device uses an array of pulsating, ultra bright LEDs to illuminate the hidden camera to detect and locate it. When a camera is found it is seen as a bright spot in the user's FOV, where it appears as a flickering bright spot of light. The unit can only detect optical devices when the camera detector and user are within the FOV of the camera or other optical device. The unit can locate standard analog video cameras, digital cameras, auto-focus cameras, camcorders, pinhole cameras, and other optical devices including the human eye. The unit is intended primarily for indoor use at distances from 3 to 30 feet. It operates best in a darkened environment (indoors or outdoors) which produces the brightest spot visible in the user's FOV. Some objects within an area being scanned will generate false-positive signals. These are caused by items that will reflect the LED light from the unit back to the users' eyes. Curved surfaces that are reflective are the most common source of false-positives, like doorknobs or other rounded reflective surfaces.

25.7 SUMMARY

The professional design, implementation, and maintenance of CCTV and networked analog or digital video systems require a large variety of test equipment. The electrical test equipment takes the form of analog waveform monitors, vectorscopes, digital timing and frequency meters as well as many other specialized types of equipment for analyzing digital signals. When a wireless transmission system is part of the video surveillance network, specialized RF and microwave test equipment are required to determine the suitability and functionality of the analog and digital transmission equipment. At the front end of the video system, light measuring equipment to determine illumination levels from visible and near-IR natural and artificial lighting are required. In analyzing the environment for a covert video application, or for a rapid deployment video equipment for personnel (VIP) protection and assessment scenarios, electronic and optical interrogation equipment are required to measure signal strength and to locate covert cameras or other clandestine imaging devices. Specialized electronic and optical equipment—both analog and digital—are required for testing analog or digital electrically wired networks or fiber-optic transmission networks. Prior to the video equipment purchase or installation all possible electronic and optical tests should be made by the designer, consultant, and systems integrator.

Chapter 26
Video Check List

CONTENTS

26.1   Overview
26.2   Checklist
    26.2.1   General
    26.2.2   Electrical
        26.2.2.1   Power
        26.2.2.2   Control
    26.2.3   Mechanical
    26.2.4   Lighting
    26.2.5   Cameras
    26.2.6   Video Motion Detector
    26.2.7   Optical
    26.2.8   Transmission
    26.2.9   Security/Encryption
    26.2.10   Recording, Printing
    26.2.11   Console
    26.2.12   Integration
26.3   Video Project Checklist Form
26.4   Summary

26.1 OVERVIEW

The previous chapters have analyzed video technology and the essential components of video surveillance security systems. Chapter 22 analyzed eight different video applications. This chapter is a checklist that summarizes some of salient points for the overall video surveillance system. These basic questions must be answered at the outset of any system design. The checklist concludes with a table that can be used as a startup questionnaire/form for the video project.

26.2 CHECKLIST

The following list enumerates questions that should be asked when designing a video surveillance security system. The checklist has been divided to cover the general requirements and specific video equipment categories: electrical, mechanical, optical, cameras, monitors, etc. The checklist contains questions that should be answered by the user, consultant, and equipment providers.

26.2.1 General

- What is the purpose of the video system: crime deterrence, vandalism, detection, offender identification? What is to be protected? What is the *value* of what is to be protected? And what is the *cost* of the system needed to protect it?
- Are assets and/or personnel to be under surveillance?
- Should the video system be overt, covert, or both? Which cameras should be overt? Which cameras should be covert?
- Where should cameras be positioned for the best view?
- Is the surveillance indoor, outdoor, or both?
- Is the system based on analog or digital technology, or a combination of both?
- Is a switcher needed? Switcher type: sequential, homing, looping, alarming, matrix
- How many cameras/monitors/recorders must be switched?
- Should a multiplexer be used?
- Is video access control a part of the security system?
- Must any or all equipment meet Underwriters Laboratory (UL), Canadian Safety Association (CSA), or other federal, state, or local codes?

- What local codes apply?
- Are all system components compatible?

26.2.2 Electrical

26.2.2.1 Power

- Is backup power required to ensure 100% operation, zero down-time? If not 100%, what cameras, monitors, and other equipment must operate as a minimum to maintain adequate security and recovery?
- What power conditioning and UPS equipment should be used?
- Should the system be powered from 117 or 24 VAC, or 12 VDC, or a combination? Will solar power and batteries be required for outdoor applications?
- Will batteries be used as a backup?
- What national and local electrical codes apply?

26.2.2.2 Control

- Will separate conductors be used for each command?
- Will RS232C, RS422, or RS485 control protocol be used?
- Will a LAN, WAN, other networks, or 802.11× wireless protocol be used?

26.2.3 Mechanical

- What type of indoor camera housing is needed: conventional rectangular, dome, other?
- What cameras require a pan/tilt mechanism?
- What panning range should the pan/tilt/zoom cameras have? 255° limited or 360° continuous rotation?
- Installation environment: Building structure material? Single or multiple floors? Single or multiple buildings? Outdoor pedestal or fence line?
- Are heaters, fans required for outdoor cameras? Any special heating or cooling in extreme environments?
- Are a window washer and wiper required?

26.2.4 Lighting

- Is there sufficient lighting for daytime/nighttime operation?
- Is the lighting natural or artificial?
- Is additional lighting required?
- What kind: halogen flourescent, etc?

26.2.5 Cameras

- Should the cameras be monochrome or color?
- Will the cameras be analog or digital, or a combination?

- How many cameras are required to view the personnel, activity, or articles to be protected?
- Is a Low Light Level (ICCD) or thermal IR camera required?
- Are video dome cameras required?

26.2.6 Video Motion Detector

- Will DVMD be used to activate monitor displays and video recorders?
- Will the system be interfaced with other alarms?

26.2.7 Optical

- Will the lenses be fixed focal length (FFL), zoom, or varifocal?
- Will manual or automatic iris be required? With or without presets?
- Do any lenses require auto-focus?
- What should be the field of view (FOV) of each camera?
- Will special pinhole or other lenses be used?

26.2.8 Transmission

- Type: analog, digital, or a combination?
- Wired or wireless?
- Analog transmission cabling type: coaxial, CAT-5, unshielded twisted-pair (UTP), fiber optic?
- Wired digital transmission type: LAN, WAN, intranet, Internet?
- Wireless: WiFi?
- What wireless 802.11× protocol will be used?
- What digital compression standard will be used: MJPEG, MPEG-4, H.264, other?

26.2.9 Security/Encryption

- Does the video signal require scrambling or encryption?
- What encryption standard will be used: WEP, AES, DES, GIPS, other?

26.2.10 Recording, Printing

- Is video recording required? What type of video recording equipment should be used: DVR, other?
- Number of video recorders? Real or non-real-time (TL)?
- Is a hard-copy video printer necessary? If so, monochrome or color?
- Printer type: thermal, ink jet, laser?
- Will non-video alarms be used to alert guards and activate recorders and printers?

26.2.11 Console

- What monitoring equipment is needed at the console?
- How many console monitoring locations?
- How many cameras/monitors/recorders must be switched?
- Number of monitors? Should they be multi-scene (split-screen)? Should a quad, multiplexer, or screen combiner be used?
- Security console: What is the level of the personnel monitoring the system? How many are there? What are the duties of monitoring personnel?

26.2.12 Integration

- Will the video system be integrated with video or electronic access control?
- Is the system interfaced and with other security functions: audio, alarm inputs, paging, and law-enforcement or fire systems?

26.3 VIDEO PROJECT CHECKLIST FORM

The Video Project Checklist Form can be used as a starting point for any video surveillance application (Table 26-1). It is divided into subsections covering the main categories of the project.

26.4 SUMMARY

The video surveillance function requires a comprehensive analysis and site survey of the property and buildings to be protected. Prior to the start of any design, a detailed checklist should be generated and completed with the help of in-house security and management personnel, and with outside consultants and any equipment integrators and installers that have been identified.

GENERAL

What is to be protected? Assets? Personnel?
What is the value of the assets to be protected?
What is the system costs needed to protect the assets?
What level of security is needed to protect personnel and or assets? Low? Medium? High? Strategic?
Will all surveillance be done at one location, multiple sites or at remote locations?
Where should the cameras be located for best view?
Will the video be interfaced with other perimeter sensors?
Is the video surveillance to be overt? Covert? Both?
Is the application daytime? Nighttime? Both?
At what locations are pan/tilt/zoom platforms required?
Is there sufficient lighting or must additional lighting be added for nighttime use?
If nighttime operation with insufficient lighting, wll active LED IR illuminators or passive image intensifiers or thermal IR cameras be used?
Will analog or digital transmission be used?
What type of analog transmission: coaxial cable, UTP, fiber optic, RF, microwave?
What type of digital transmission: LAN, Internet, intranet, WiFi?
What type of digital compression: M-PEG, M-JPEG, and H.264?
Is video scrambling or encryption required? At what encryption level?
Will security system be installed by single or multiple contractors?

EQUIPMENT

Will the hardware be analog based? Digital? Both (hybrid)?
What type and how many cameras are required to view the personnel and assets to be protected?
Will the cameras be analog, IP, or a combination? Color or monochrome cameras?
What should be the field of view ((FOV) of each camera? What focal length?
What type lens should be used on each camera: Fixed focus? Vari-focal? zoom?
Will simple switchers, quads or multiplexers be used?
How will the cameras be switched? Simplex, duplex, or triplex multiplexers?
Will video motion detectors be used indoor and or outdoor?
What monitoring equipment is needed at the console?
What type of monitors: CRT, LCD or plasma? How many monitors are required at each site?
Should it be displays be multi-scene? How many images on a single screen?
What type digital video recorder (DVR) will be used?
How many channels of video will be recorded on each DVR? How many DVRs are required?
Will video images be recorded on local DVRs or a networked DVR?
Will color or monochrome video printers be required for hardcopy printout of video images?

OPERATION

Will the video system be integrated with other functions: access control, alarm, fire, communications?
How many security operators will there be at each monitoring site?
How many monitoring sites will there be sites will there be?
How will alarm inputs at the monitoring site interface with specific video display call-ups?

POWER AND BACKUP POWER

What backup power is required to ensure 100% operation, zero downtime?
If not 100%, backup, what cameras, monitors, and other equipment must remain operating?
What power conditioning and UPS equipment is required?

SECURITY

Does the video signal require encryption? What level of encryption is required: WEP, AES, DES?
What firewalls are necessary?
What type of network security: VPN, other?

MAINTENANCE

Will maintenance be done in-house?
Outside maintenance vendor? What vendor?
What level of maintenance? Yearly contract or multiple year contract?
Repair turnaround time in case of equipment failure: 24 hours, other?

Table 26-1 Video Project Checklist Form

Chapter 27
Education, Standards, Certification

CONTENTS

27.1 Overview
27.2 Educational Seminars, Exhibitions
27.3 Industry Associations
27.4 Standards—Laboratory Testing
27.5 Certification
27.6 Summary

27.1 OVERVIEW

The successful implementation of a video surveillance system integrated into an overall security plan requires a thorough understanding of the technology, and its interoperability with the overall security system. The designer/installer must attend professional seminars and see manufacturer's demonstrations to remain informed of the latest techniques and technologies in the industry. The end user must likewise attend security personnel and assets protection seminars, and manufacturer's exhibits and demonstrations to remain informed of the latest techniques and technologies in the industry.

Crucial to the implementation of any successful video system is the assemblage of a detailed, well-conceived, professional specification/bid package. Writing this package forces management, security personnel, consultants, and architect/engineers (A&E) to itemize what functions the system should perform and how it should function with the other parts of the security system. The written plan should be detailed and include suggested manufacturers, dealers, and installers. To design for maximum reliability, compatibility, and safety, all system hardware and installation techniques should conform to the Institute of Electronic and Electrical Engineers (IEEE), Security Industry Association (SIA), and Underwriters Laboratory (UL) safety recommendations. All electrical equipment must meet applicable local electrical and fire codes.

27.2 EDUCATIONAL SEMINARS, EXHIBITIONS

Numerous organizations conduct educational seminars in the United States, Europe, Asia, and elsewhere and exhibit manufacturer's products and services. All these venues educate security system designers, consultants, systems integrators, and end users. Attending these educational seminars periodically is essential to the successful implementation of a video surveillance system. The use of video surveillance in the overall security plan has taken on a more important role since the devastating attack on the Twin Towers in New York on September 11, 2001. Another reason for attending seminars periodically is to stay abreast of the rapid advancements being made in video technology and security methods. The rapid deployment of new solid-state technology from the computer industry, the application of digital technology to cameras, transmission, and digital recording in the security industry requires regular attendance at these seminars and expositions. Seminar attendance and fulfillment of course requirements from these organizations and earning continuing education units (CEU) can lead to professional certification.

Numerous organizations conduct local, national, and international manufacturer's exhibitions. Hundreds of manufacturers and service providers have booths at these shows and exhibit their latest security equipment and present their services. It is important that security system designers, consultants, systems integrators, and end users attend these exhibitions on a regular basis to become familiar with the actual hardware and software available for video security and to recognize how they fit into the overall security plan. It is important for all concerned to have first-hand, hands-on familiarity with as much of the video hardware and services specified for the application. The availability of new digital solid-state technology from the computer and consumer industries has accelerated the application of digital technology into the security industry, particularly digital video. Areas where significant advances have been made include: cameras using DSP resulting in "smart" cameras, video transmission using compression and encryption providing secure video communications to remote sites, and digital recorders that record days and weeks of high-resolution digital video images that can be recorded or transmitted anywhere without loss of quality. Attending and educational seminar at least once every two years (preferably one) is essential for having the latest information about these new advances.

American Society for Industrial Security.   The American Society for Industrial Security (ASIS) is a leading organization providing comprehensive educational seminars and technical papers primarily directed toward security directors, corporate management, and government officials covering all aspects of assets protection. It conducts an annual national convention with multi-track seminars conducted by professionals in the security industry. ASIS issue's continuing education units (CEU) to participants successfully completing its courses. Accumulating these CEU credits eventually leads to certification. ASIS conducts these seminars in conjunction with a large exhibit by security manufacturers and security service providers. In between attending the seminars, participants can walk the exhibit floor and visit hundreds of exhibitors over a period of three days, to see and have a "hands-on" experience with the hardware and technology and talking with company representatives. ASIS publishes a monthly periodical journal providing many case histories and testimonials on new security guidelines for all aspects of security including video surveillance.

International Security Conference.   International Security Conference (ISC) is a trade organization that holds a manufacturers and service providers exhibition twice a year, and conducts comprehensive multi-track classroom seminars that teach the latest in video technology. ISC issue's CEU to participants successfully completing its courses. Accumulating these CEU credits eventually leads to certification. Hundreds of security manufacturer display their products and have representatives available to discuss the technology and to answer questions. The exhibition is designed primarily to attract dealers, systems integrators consultants, architects and engineers (A&Es), but it also attracts many end users.

LTC Training Center, Other.   The LTC Training Center provides comprehensive seminars for many video applications and offers several CCTV certification programs via printed manuals, VHS tape, and DVDs. Its mission is to provide professional up-to-date, plain language training for the applications/design and/or installation/field service personnel in the field of CCTV systems. The series covers CCTV from video through site assessment and design. The courses are designed for all persons involved in design, sales, or management of CCTV systems. LTC issue's CEU to participants successfully completing its courses. Accumulating the CEU credits eventually leads to certification.

STAM MultiMedia Training.   The SIA in cooperation with STAM MultiMedia has created an interactive, self-directed based training course that gives a complete overview of CCTV, its technology and applications. The online course covers the principles, types, features, installation, and troubleshooting techniques for each CCTV component.

27.3 INDUSTRY ASSOCIATIONS

Institute of Electronic and Electrical Engineers.   The Institute of Electronic and Electrical Engineers (IEEE) and its predecessors, the American Institute of Electrical Engineers (AIEE), and the Institute of Radio Engineers (IRE) date back to 1884. In 1963 the IRE and the AIEE realized an overlap of technologies and merged to become the IEEE. The IEEE is a nonprofit, technical professional association of more than 360,000 individual members in approximately 175 countries. The IEEE has advanced the theory and application of electronics and provides a national forum to establish technical standards and educate practitioners. The IEEE analog television standards RS-170, RS-330, etc., form the basis of all US video standards. The IEEE RS-232, RS-422, and RS-485 serve as the communications protocol for almost all security and other electronic applications.

Electronic Industries Association.   The Electronic Industries Association (EIA) is the national trade organization representing hundreds of US electronics manufacturers. EIA represents the entire spectrum of companies involved in the design and manufacture of electronic components systems and equipment for communications. EIA generates standards and specifications that facilitate the design and manufacture of electronic components and systems, and provides an optimum route for their procurement and support. EIA standards cover a broad range of consumer, industrial, and manufacturing electronics including audio and video hardware, LAN, etc.

Security Industry Association.   The Security Industry Association (SIA) was formed in 1969 and provides its members with a full-service international trade association promoting growth, expansion and professionalism within the security industry. It does this by providing education, research, technical standards, and representation in defense of member's interests. The SIA has over 300 member companies representing manufacturers, distributors, service providers, integrators, and others. SIA members are involved in market segments such as CCTV, access control, biometrics, computer security, fire, burglar alarm, and home automation.

The SIA has working groups that write guidelines and specifications so that manufacturers designing video equipment provide maximum compatibility and interchangeability among manufacturers. This commitment is manifest in many areas of equipment design, including: (1) common video input and output signal parameters for cameras, monitors, switchers, recorders, printers, etc.; (2) common pin and terminal connections and mechanical configurations for power, video, automatic-iris lens, pan/tilt and lens controls, switcher functions, and others; and (3) common mechanical mounting configurations, hole pattern, location, and fastening hardware for camera mounts, pan/tilt mechanisms, monitor mounts, etc.

National Institute for Certification in Engineering Technologies. SIA and SecurityLearningNetwork.com (SLN) are working with the National Institute for Certification in Engineering Technologies (NICET), a nonprofit division of the National Society of Professional Engineers (NSPE), to develop a CCTV certification course.

The SecurityLearningNetwork.com is an online security industry education and training resource. Available are computer-based programs, classroom-based courses, and instructor-led education and training programs. Technical as well as workplace performance courses are offered through this site.

Since NICET was founded in 1961, more than 113,000 technicians and technologists have met NICETs certification criteria. The number is growing rapidly as more employers in local and state governments rely on NICET certification to measure the qualifications of their workforce. NICET defines *engineering technicians* as "hands-on" members of the engineering team who work under the direction of engineers, scientists, and technologists. It defines *engineering technologists* as members of the engineering team who worked closely with engineers, scientists, and technicians. Technologists have a firm knowledge of the equipment, applications, and established state-of-the-art design and implementation methods in a particular engineering area.

The certification recognizes CCTV professionals who have achieved a higher knowledge in CCTV installation and planning competency. NICET regularly brings together industry leaders to identify industry needs in design and maintain technician certification programs that promote technical knowledge and skills. The institute promotes the continuing professional development of its certified technicians and technologists through a re-certification process that emphasizes updated skills and state-of-the-art knowledge. NICET certification *does not* entitle the certificate holder to practice engineering. The practice of engineering is defined and regulated by state engineering licensing boards.

27.4 STANDARDS—LABORATORY TESTING

The Underwriters Laboratory (UL) Corp. is a testing laboratory that tests and certifies electrical equipment submitted by manufacturers, and issues a UL seal of approval if the equipment meets its standards. The UL standards have resulted from industry requests to satisfy their needs for reliable and safe equipment. The criteria for approval are listed in various standards written by UL, and designers of video security systems should be knowledgeable of the documents applicable to the industry. Equipments using voltages below 24 VAC do not need this approval. Many state and local governments require that electronic equipment used for video and other security applications use equipment having this UL seal of approval.

The demand for UL certification of CCTV equipment is generated primarily by corporate industrial end users who need to meet insurance requirements. In an attempt to establish a separate standard for industrial video equipment the CCTV Manufacturers Association (CCTMA) collaborated with UL in the mid-1990s. CCTMA was the CCTV division of EIA but is no longer active. To create a separate standard for its products, the CCTMA and UL wanted to differentiate CCTV security products from commercial video equipment and residential cameras and VCRs. UL worked with CCTMA and insurance companies to develop a set of guidelines UL 2044, to cover the potential electric shock and fire hazards associated with CCTV equipment. The standard was published in June 1993. The second phase of the video standards developed includes performance guidelines that can be used to verify manufacturer's claims. Test patterns are used to determine the camera TV lines of resolution, and to match those results with the manufactures claims. This performance standard has been designated UL 3044. A manufacture can have a product checked for electric shock and fire and listed on UL 2044, or UL 3044 if they want to verify the performance aspect of the product. The third UL 4044 standard developed a set of installation guidelines. The basic philosophy regarding this standard considers both the equipment and how it is installed. Video equipments might be manufactured to the highest standards, but if a dealer does not install them correctly they are not likely to work. Other security areas such as burglar and fire alarm already have standards that cover installation and it makes sense to have these for CCTV.

A by-product of CCTV UL standards is increased costs. The typical cost of having a brand-new product UL listed ranges between $10,000 and $15,000 and these costs are certainly passed on to dealers and end users. None of the UL's CCTV standards are mandatory.

27.5 CERTIFICATION

Seminar attendance and fulfillment of course requirements for organizations described in Section 27.4 and others can lead to professional certification. Personnel attending seminar and courses at recognized organizations receive CEU credits. Some of the many organizations conducting seminars and courses on video security (and other security fields) that issue CEUs have been described in Sections 27.2 and 27.3. These organizations include they as ASIS, ISC, NICET, SLN, LTC, and STAM.

27.6 SUMMARY

There are many excellent human resources for obtaining all the information necessary to make an informed decision on the requirements for a video surveillance system and proper techniques for implementing the design and installation. These include experienced in-house security personnel, outside consultants, A&Es, manufacturers representatives, and system integrators. There are many seminars, educational courses, and books and articles in the literature teaching video technology. There are many organizations teaching video technology and issuing CEU credits leading to certification. Many of these organizations have been cited in Chapter 27, in this book and in the References and Glossary.

Chapter 28
New Video Technology

CONTENTS

28.1 Overview
28.2 Camera Technology
    28.2.1 Smart Cameras
    28.2.2 Infrared Cameras
    28.2.3 Millimeter Wave Technology
    28.2.4 Two Camera Three Dimensions (3D)
    28.2.5 Multi-Camera Three Dimensions (3D)
    28.2.6 Hybrid Eye Camera
28.3 Monitor Display Technology
    28.3.1 Organic LED
    28.3.2 Three Dimensional Monitor
28.4 Video Recording
28.5 Integrated Systems
28.6 Remote Surveillance
28.7 Transmission
28.8 Summary

28.1 OVERVIEW

The video industry has witnessed unprecedented growth and advancements in technology in the last decade. This has included the refinement of components and increased capability of legacy analog cameras, multiplexers, and introduction of large switching systems and of *digital* video equipment into the security market. The initial indications are that digital video technology will cause an explosion in the use of video for local and remote surveillance for security, safety, and other business functions. Digital technology provides new important functions including: (1) high-resolution color images integrated with graphics or digital data and (2) true remote video transmission, viewing, and recording anywhere on the globe. Digital technology will rapidly replace analog for all video security requirements. Transmission of the information will take form of two-way high speed LAN, WAN, MAN, and WLAN (WiFi) networks with encryption to provide high-level security. One factor responsible for this rapid growth has been the miniaturization and increased density of electronic circuits that have resulted in smaller equipment with more capabilities. Specific product areas benefiting from this technology advancement include solid-state cameras, DVR, digital signal processing (DSP) computers, solid-state and very small magnetic hard drive memories for viewing, transmitting, displaying, and storing digital video images. In the coming decade these and other technological advances will continue, further enhance the capability of existing products, and generate new ones. This chapter describes some of the advances that will come to fruition and find applications in the security field.

28.2 CAMERA TECHNOLOGY

Conventional lens technology has matured to meet the requirements of most visible video camera applications. There are some new possibilities, however, for extracting more information from a target scene. These include three-dimensional displays (3D), and "human eye" type optics-sensor combinations.

Technology will continue to improve in solid-state sensors used in visual and thermal IR video cameras. Color cameras whose development is driven by the consumer market will benefit from increased sensitivity and resolution. Improvements in camera-sensor dynamic range should all but eliminate the need for automatic-iris lenses. The greatest camera advances will come with thermal IR cameras having increased resolution and sensitivity. A breakthrough in manufacturing technology will result in competitively priced monochrome IR cameras operating at room temperature that can "see" through fog.

28.2.1 Smart Cameras

Smart cameras will get smarter. They will provide intelligent "human making decisions" and be able to "learn" and react to a changing situation, activity, or environment. They will use pattern recognition and sophisticated software algorithms to perform automatic decision-making based on a stored library of information.

28.2.2 Infrared Cameras

Legacy IR imaging cameras using mechanically cooled IR sensors and are prohibitively expensive (50–100K dollars). These high resolution, high sensitivity cameras are relegated to military applications. The latest generation IR cameras use room temperature IR sensors and provide medium to good resolution and sensitivity at affordable prices (5–10K dollars). In the coming years, there will be a refinement and evolution of the room temperature thermal IR camera from its present form to an IP camera that will be a combined (fusion) visual/infrared camera.

A new technology that radically reduces the cost of thermal imaging cameras is emerging that will reduce the price to a $1000 level. The technology called thermal light valve (TLV) translates the difficult-to-image thermal IR radiation into light radiation that can be imaged by a standard CMOS camera. The conversion chip in the camera is based on technology already developed for major communications networks. Figure 28-1 shows the tuned imager construction and the IR camera block diagram. In operation, the 8-14 micron image is focused onto the temperature tunable filter (TTF) stack along with an 850 nm reference light beam. The output from the TTF is an 850 nm image of the IR image. The CCD or CMOS sensor detects the 850 nm image, and the result is a camera output representing the IR image.

28.2.3 Millimeter Wave Technology

A detection technology that looks beyond infrared imaging and metal detection is needed for screening personnel and equipment entering and exiting a facility. The combination of video and passive millimeter wave technology that can scan individuals and crowds from close-up to standoff distances of 30 to 40 feet is needed. The millimeter wave camera will include graphical on-screen windows superimposed on the area of the person's clothing concealing the item, or inside an enclosed container. This will permit detection of a gun, knife, or other suspicious items. The millimeter sensor will not have the ability to create recognizable image of people or objects but will be able to distinguish (detect) foreign objects within the scene. The millimeter wave sensor operates in a similar way to the infrared sensor, but in a longer wavelength region.

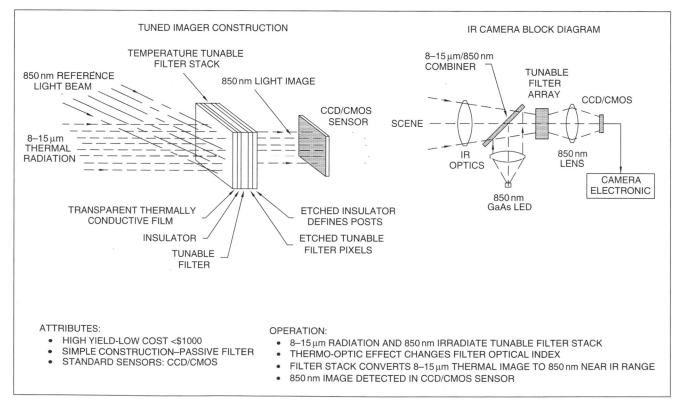

FIGURE 28-1   Thin film room temperature tuned thermal imager

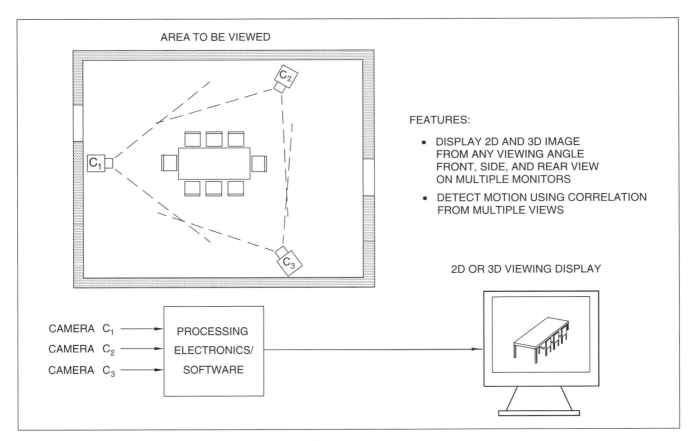

FIGURE 28-2   Multiple camera 3D volumetric imaging

Each object gives off a different radiation signature and the millimeter sensor detects this difference.

28.2.4 Two Camera Three Dimensions (3D)

There are several 3D video system techniques in use. 3D can significantly increase the intelligence in a video image and can increase a guard's ability to make a better judgment call if he/she were viewing a 3D image rather than the information from a 2D, flat-screen monitor. The 3D systems use two cameras and two video channels and some optical means to display the two images as one 3D image for the viewer. Using a bi-split lens or a dual-lens/camera combination, a 3D image of the scene would be displayed on a 3D monitor. Future security systems will use some form of 3D for special surveillance functions.

28.2.5 Multi-Camera Three Dimensions (3D)

Another form of 3D volumetric imaging technology collects the images from multiple cameras viewing the same area in a room and digitizes and stores them, and with the known location and viewing angle of each camera, re-creates a 3D image from *any* vantage point and any

zooming distance in the room (Figure 28-2). This technology requires the high computing power of presently available computers.

28.2.6 Hybrid Eye Camera

The hybrid eye camera would have a high-resolution central segment and a low-resolution outside segment (Figure 28-3). As in the human eye central field would be and sharp focus, and the pherprial not in sharp focus. The peripheral would detect the motion of a moving target, and a pan/tilt mechanism would point the camera to the target and center the target in the central high-resolution segment of the sensor.

28.3 MONITOR DISPLAY TECHNOLOGY

28.3.1 Organic LED

A new organic LED (OLED) technology is evolving and will bring significant cost reductions and improved performance to the video displays. The OLED display has lower power requirements for an equivalent screen brightness because the light is *emitted* from the display directly rather

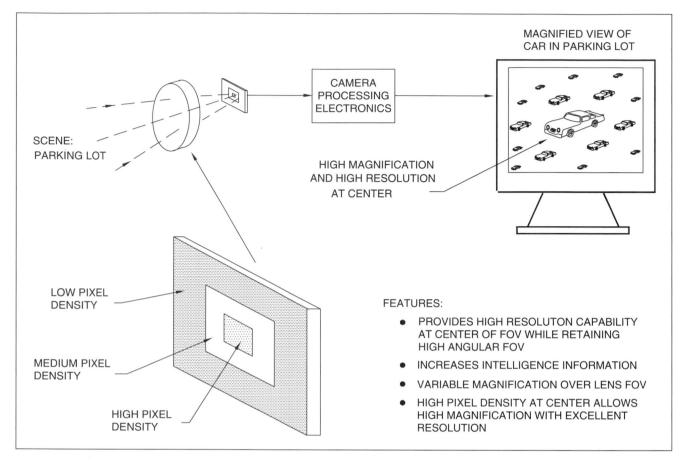

FIGURE 28-3   Hybrid eye video camera

than back illuminated and transmitted through a transmission LCD matrix panel. The OLED technology permits displays that are flexible and more durable than other flat-panel displays.

28.3.2   Three-Dimensional Monitor

The 3D LCD technology uses a secondary LCD as a parallax barrier (Figure 28-4). This LCD is switchable and when Off, the display acts the same as a normal LCD monitor. When the barrier display is switched On, the light passing through the primary TFT LCD is directed, such that odd pixel columns are focused toward the left eye and even pixel columns are focus toward the right eye. In this way, when the software displays a 3D image, the two different perspective views are shown to each eye and the brain fuses these into a realistic 3D view.

28.4   VIDEO RECORDING

Video recording has evolved from an analog to a digital technology; however, the DVR is evolving into a *virtual* video image storage database located in a local or remote computer(s). This allows video recording and storage that is limited only by the size of the network computer memory capacity. This image database can be accessed using LAN, WAN, wireless WiFi, and Internet from anywhere with proper password, etc.

28.5   INTEGRATED SYSTEMS

Video surveillance is being integrated with other security components: alarms, fire, etc. Evolution from analog to digital video system permits integration of all of the security functions into one system. Maturation of the software, the increase in digital transmission speed, and data encryption permits to a fully integrated security systems and encompassing video surveillance, fire, alarm, access control and two-way communication systems via LAN, WAN, WiFi, etc. The key words are "integrated security systems" and system "interoperability." The availability of powerful computers and integrated multi-tasking software provides the platform for an integrated remote site operation and will add significantly to the security function. The availability of real-time video over fiber-optic networks over long distances increases security capabilities significantly. Combining Internet and satellite transmission and global

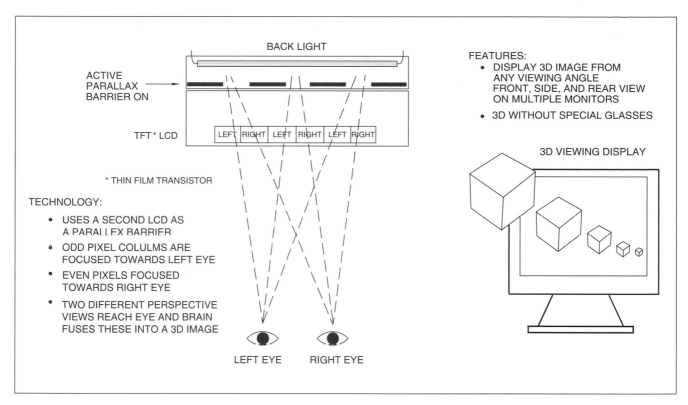

ACTIVE PARALLAX BARRIER ON

BACK LIGHT

TFT * LCD

| LEFT | RIGHT | LEFT | RIGHT | LEFT | RIGHT |

* THIN FILM TRANSISTOR

TECHNOLOGY:

- USES A SECOND LCD AS A PARALLEX BARRIER
- ODD PIXEL COLULMS ARE FOCUSED TOWARDS LEFT EYE
- EVEN PIXELS FOCUSED TOWARDS RIGHT EYE
- TWO DIFFERENT PERSPECTIVE VIEWS REACH EYE AND BRAIN FUSES THESE INTO A 3D IMAGE

LEFT EYE   RIGHT EYE

FEATURES:

- DISPLAY 3D IMAGE FROM ANY VIEWING ANGLE FRONT, SIDE, AND REAR VIEW ON MULTIPLE MONITORS
- 3D WITHOUT SPECIAL GLASSES

3D VIEWING DISPLAY

FIGURE 28-4   3D LCD monitor schematic

security from one security console location will become commonplace.

28.6   REMOTE SURVEILLANCE

The video surveillance industry has benefited from consumer- and business-related technologies. These include all the digital networks, Internet, cell phone, and versions of WiFi protocol 802.11×. As these technologies continue to mature the security industry is upgrading the capabilities of the transmission options and reaping the benefits they offer. Appropriately connected they offer a remote video system with control and video surveillance from anywhere in which there is a digital wired or wireless connection available.

28.7   TRANSMISSION

The wireless video transmission function (WLAN, WiFi) has provided the greatest challenge to the security industry. The aspects most challenging are (1) range, (2) quality of service (QoS), and (3) security. The use of wireless digital transmission can provide a significant cost reduction and increased video coverage as compared with wired networks. Reliable wireless transmission with high QoS and secure transmission over practical ranges are challenges to be met in this decade.

Range.   The IEEE 802.11× protocols are in a state of evolution with emphasis on improving the QoS over a given range. The goal is to maximize range and preserve QoS. As the range is increased, QoS is reduced. Using multiple-in, multiple-out (MIMO) transmission technology, range can be doubled over standard single or diversity antenna systems.

Quality of Service.   Quality of service pertains to how well the wireless video signal is received when transmitted over the wireless transmission network. Loss of signal or an intermittent signal can be caused by low signal strength, fading, interference from other electronic signals, or "collisions" with other 802.11× video transmitting devices. One technique to improve QoS is through the use of a *mesh* transmission network that provides multiple, overlapping transmission paths (links) so that at least one multi-link path always provides a high-quality service. The MIMO technique is available but in a state of evolution and improvement. Advances are being made in the use of multiple signals (direct and multi-path) between the transmitter and receiver to *improve* the QoS. This methodology is in contrast to most the existing multiple antenna (diversity) wireless 802.11× systems that use two or more receiver antennas to *eliminate* the multi-path signals. The MIMO concept takes advantage of the multiple path signals.

Security.   A primary concern when using WiFi video transmission is security of the video images, i.e. no one outside of the network should be able to view the video images. Advances in video encryption are being made to that end. Encryption protocols to improve security include FIPS, AES, DES, and others.

28.8 SUMMARY

Each decade brings new and innovative products that improve the quality of video surveillance. Some come from new ideas, some from refinements of existing technology. Others originate from adaptations of ideas and equipments already in use in the consumer, business, and industrial markets. Communication between the manufacturer, systems integrator, and user can be a catalyst to bring a new concept to fruition.

The ultimate goal of course is to assemble an automatic video surveillance (AVS) system that maximizes intelligence to the security officer and manager. Only the real activities and threats should be presented for action, with the necessary instructions for optimized response. Any new technology that moves in that direction improves the video surveillance function.

Glossary

Many terms and definitions used in the security industry are unique to CCTV surveillance; others derive from the electro-optical and information-computer industries. This comprehensive glossary will help the reader better understand the literature, interpret manufacturers' specifications, and write bid specifications and requests for quotation. These terms encompass the CCTV, physical computer and communications industries, basic physics, electricity, mechanics, and optics.

Aberration   Failure of an optical lens to produce exact point-to-point correspondence between an object and its image.

ABC Automatic brightness control   In display devices, the self-acting mechanism that controls brightness as a function of ambient light.

Access point   An electronic device for connecting wireless PC cameras directly to the Internet.

Achromatic lens   A lens consisting of two or more elements, usually of crown and flint glass, that has been corrected for chromatic aberration with respect to two selected colors or light wavelengths.

Active Video Lines   The video lines producing the picture. All video lines not occurring in the horizontal and vertical blanking intervals.

ADSL Asymmetric DSL   A DSL technology providing asymmetrical bandwidth over a single wire pair. The downstream bandwidth going from the network to the subscriber is typically greater than the upstream bandwidth going from the subscriber to the network. see **Direct Subscriber Line**.

AF Auto-focus   A system by which the camera lens automatically focuses on a selected part of the video scene.

AFC Automatic frequency control   A feature whereby the frequency of an oscillator is automatically maintained within specified limits.

AGC Automatic gain control   A process by which gain is automatically adjusted as a function of input or other specified parameter to maintain the output nearly constant.

Alarming switcher   see **Switcher, Alarming**.

Ambient temperature   The temperature of the environment. The temperature of the surrounding medium, such as air, gas or liquid that comes into contact with the apparatus.

Amplifier   A device whose output is essentially an enlarged reproduction of the input and that which does not draw power from the input source.

Amplifier, distribution   A device that provides several isolated outputs from one looping or bridging input. The amplifier has sufficiently high input impedance and input-to-output isolation to prevent loading of the input source.

Analog Signal   The representation of data by continuously variable quantities in digital format as opposed to a finite number of discrete quantities. An electrical signal that varies continuously, not having discrete values.

Analog Television   The "standard" television broadcast. Analog signals varying continuously representing fluctuations in color and brightness of a visual scene.

Angle of view   The maximum scene angle that can be seen through a lens or optical-sensor assembly. Usually described in degrees, for horizontal, vertical, or circular dimension.

Antenna   An electrical signal gathering or transmitting device used with electrical receivers and transmitters for collecting or propagating an electrical signal through the airwaves. The primary antenna specifications are vertical and horizontal directivity and gain, input impedance and bandwidth, and power handling capacity.

Aperture   An opening that will pass light, electrons, or other forms of radiation. In an electron gun, the aperture determines the size of, and has an effect on, the shape of the electron beam. In television optics, the aperture is the effective diameter of the lens that controls the amount of light reaching the image sensor.

Aperture, clear   see **Clear aperture**.

Aperture, numerical   see **Numerical aperture**.

Aperture stop   An optical opening or hole that defines or limits the amount of light passing through a lens system. The aperture stop takes the form of the front lens diameter in a pinhole lens, an iris diaphragm, a neutral density or spot filter.

Arc lamp   An electric-discharge lamp with an electric arc between two electrodes to produce illumination. The illumination results from the incandescence of the positive electrode and from the heated, luminous, ionized gases that surround the arc.

ASIS   American Society for Industrial Security.

Aspect ratio   The ratio of width to height for the frame of the video picture in CCTV or broadcast television. The NTSC and PAL standard is 4:3. The aspect ratio for high-definition television HDTV is 16:9.

Aspheric   An optical element having one or more surfaces that are not spherical. The spherical surface of the lens is slightly altered to reduce spherical aberration thereby improving image quality.

Astigmatism   A lens aberration that causes an object point to be imaged as a pair of short lines at right angles to each other.

ATM Asynchronous Transfer Mode   The communications standard that allows multiple traffic types (voice, video, or data) to be conveyed in fixed-length cells rather than the random length "packets" as used in Ethernet and Fiber Distributed Data Interface (FDDI). This enables very high speeds, making ATMs popular for demanding network backbones. Newer ATMs also support WAN transmissions.

ATSC Advanced Television Systems Committee   An international organization with a committee responsible for digital television standards and development.

Attenuation   A reduction in light or electrical signal or energy strength. In electrical systems attenuation is often measured in decibels or decibel per unit distance. In optical systems the units of measure are f-number or optical density. see also **Decibel**.

Audio frequency   Any frequency corresponding to a normally audible sound wave—roughly from 15 to 15,000 Hz.

Auto balance   A system for detecting errors in color balance in the white and black areas of the picture and automatically adjusting the white and black levels of both the red and blue signals as needed.

Auto light range   The range of light—such as sunlight to moonlight or starlight—over which a TV camera is capable of automatically operating at specified output and within its dynamic range.

Automatic iris   A mechanical diaphragm device in the lens that self-adjusts optically to light level changes via the video signal from the television camera. The iris diaphragm opens or closes the aperture to control the light transmitted through the lens. Typical compensation ranges are 10,000–300,000 to 1. Automatic iris lenses are used on solid-state CCD, ICCD and CMOS cameras and SIT, ISIT tube cameras.

Automatic iris control   An electro-optic accessory to a lens that measures the video level of the camera and opens and closes the iris diaphragm to compensate for light changes.

Automatic light compensation   The degree to which a CCTV camera can adapt to varying lighting conditions.

Automatic light control   The process by which the illumination incident upon the face of a pickup device is automatically adjusted as a function of scene brightness.

Automatic sensitivity control   The self-acting mechanism that varies system sensitivity as a function of specified control parameters. This may include automatic target control, automatic light control, etc. or any combination thereof.

Axis, optical   see **Optical axis**.

Backbone   The part of a network that acts as the primary network path for traffic moving between, rather than within networks.

Back focus   The distance from the last glass surface of a lens to the focused image on the sensor.

Back porch   That part of a composite video signal that lies between the trailing edge of a horizontal sync pulse and the trailing edge of the corresponding blanking pulse. The color burst, if present, is not considered part of the back porch.

Band pass   A specific range of frequencies that will be passed through an optical or electronic device or system.

Bandwidth   The data carrying capacity of a device or network connection. The number of hertz (Hz, cycles per second) expressing the difference between the lower and upper limiting frequencies of a frequency band. Also, the width of a band of frequencies.

Bandwidth limited gain control   A control that adjusts the gain of an amplifier while varying the bandwidth. An increase in gain reduces the bandwidth.

Barrel distortion An electronic or optical distortion in television systems that makes the video image appear to bulge outward on all sides like a barrel.

Beam A concentrated, unidirectional flow of electrons, photons, or other energy: 1) A shaft or column of light; a bundle of rays consisting of parallel, converging, or diverging rays. 2) A concentrated stream of particles that is unidirectional. 3) A unidirectional concentrated flow of electromagnetic waves.

Beam splitter An optical device for dividing a light beam into two or more separate beams. The splitting can be done in the parallel (collimated) beam or in the focused image plane.

Beam width, angular beam width The angular beam width of a conical beam of light. The vertex angle of the cone, which determines the rate at which a beam of energy diverges or converges. Lasers produce very narrow angle or very nearly parallel beams. Thermal light sources (filament, fluorescent, etc.) produce wide-angle beams.

Beta format An original 1/2-inch Sony video cassette recorder format not compatible with the VHS format.

Bifocal lens A lens system having two different focal length lenses that image two identical or different scenes onto a single camera sensor. The two scenes appear as a split image on the monitor.

Bit Binary digit The smallest unit of computer memory. A bit is a binary digit representing two different states (1, 0), either on or off. A method of storing information that maps an image bit by bit.

Bitmap A bitmap defines a display space and the color for each pixel or "bit" in the display space. GIF and JPEG are examples of graphic image file types that contain bitmaps.

Bit rate The bit rate is the number of bits transmitted per second (bps).

Blackbody A thermally heated body that radiates energy at all wavelengths according to specific physical laws.

Black clamp An electronic circuit that automatically maintains the black video level (no light) at a constant voltage.

Black level The picture signal level corresponding to a specified maximum limit for black peaks.

Black negative The television picture signal in which the polarity of the voltage corresponding to black is negative with respect to that which corresponds to the white area of the picture signal.

Blanking The process whereby the beam in an image pickup or cathode ray display tube is cut off during the retrace period so that it won't create any visible information on the screen.

Blanking level The level of a composite picture signal that separates the range containing picture information from the range containing synchronizing information; also called pedestal, or blacker-than-black.

Blooming In a camera, the visual effects caused by over exposing a CCD or other sensor. In CRT monitors, the condition that occurs when the phosphors on the screen are driven harder than they should be. This causes defocusing of regions of the picture where the brightness is at an excessive level, due to enlargement of spot size and halation of the screen of the CRT tube.

BNC Bayonet-Neil-Concelman A connector named after its designers and widely used in the video and RF transmission industry for terminating and coupling coaxial cables. The BNC connector is easy to install, reliable and with little video signal loss. Used with 75 ohm cable for video applications cable and 50 ohm cable for RF.

Borescope An optical device used for the internal inspection of mechanical and other parts. The long tube contains a multiple lens telescope system that usually has a high f-number (low amount of light transmitted).

Boresight An optical instrument used to check alignment or pointing direction. A small telescope mounted on a weapon or video camera so that the optical axis of the telescope and the mechanical axis of the device coincide. The term also applies to the process of aligning other optical equipment.

Bounce Sudden variation in picture presentation (brightness, size, and so on) independent of scene illumination.

Breezeway In NTSC color, that portion of the back porch between the trailing edge of the sync pulse and the start of the color burst.

Bridge A digital electronic device that passes data packets between multiple network segments using the same communication protocol. If a packet is destined for use within the sender's own network segment, the bridge keeps the packet local. If the packet is bound for another segment, the bridge passes the packet onto the network backbone.

Bridging Connecting two electrical circuits in parallel. Usually the input impedances are large enough so as not to affect the signal level.

Bridging amplifier An amplifier for bridging an electrical circuit without introducing an apparent change in the performance of that circuit.

Brightness The attribute of visual perception whereby an area appears to emit more or less light. Luminance is the recommended name for this photometric quantity, which has also been called brightness.

Brightness control   The manual bias control on a cathode ray tube or other display device that determines both the average brightness and the contrast of a picture.

Browser   An application program that provides a way to look at and interact with all the information on the World Wide Web. The two most popular Web browsers are Netscape and Microsoft Internet Explorer.

Buffer   A temporary computer storage area usually held in RAM and used as a temporary holding area for data.

Burn-in   Also called burn. An image that persists in a fixed position in the output signal of a camera tube after the camera has been pointed toward a different scene. An image that persists on the face of a CRT monitor with no input video signal present.

Byte   A group of 8 bits or 256 discrete items of information, such as color, brightness, etc. The basic unit of information for the computer.

C-mount   An industry standard for lens mounting. The C-mount has a thread with a 1-inch diameter and 32 threads per inch. The distance from the lens mounting surface to the sensor surface is 0.69 inches (17.526 mm).

Cable   A number of electrical conductors (wires) bound in a common sheath. These may be video, data, control or voice cables. They may also take the form of coaxial or fiber-optic cables.

Cable Modem   A class of modem that is used for connecting to a cable TV network, which in turn can connect directly to the Internet. Cable based connections to the Internet are typically much faster than dial-up modems.

Camera control unit CCU   Remote module that provides control of camera electronic circuitry such as camera shutter speed, video amplification and lens parameters.

Camera format   Video cameras have 1/6, 1/4, 1/3, 1/2, and 2/3-inch sensor image formats. The actual scanned areas used on the sensors are 3.2 mm horizontal × 2.4 mm vertical for the 1/4-inch, 4.8 mm horizontal × 3.6 mm vertical for the 1/3-inch, 6.4 mm horizontal × 4.8 mm vertical for the 1/2-inch and 8.8 mm horizontal × 6.6 mm vertical for the 2/3-inch.

Camera housing   An enclosure designed to protect the video camera from tampering or theft when indoors or outdoors or from undue environmental exposure when placed outdoors.

Camera, television   An electronic device containing a solid state sensor or an electronic image tube and processing electronics. The image formed by a lens ahead of the sensor is clocked out for a solid state sensor, or rapidly scanned by a moving electron beam in a tube camera. The sensor signal output varies with the local brightness of the image on the sensor. These variations are transmitted to a CRT, LCD or other display device, where the brightness of the scanning spot is controlled. The scanned location (pixel) at the camera and the scanned spot at the display are accurately synchronized.

Camera tube   An electron tube that converts an optical image into an electrical current by a scanning process. Also called a pickup tube or television camera tube.

Candela cd   Unit of measurement of luminous intensity. The candela is the international unit that replaces the candle.

Candle power, cp   Light intensity expressed in candles. One foot-candle (fc) is the amount of light emitted by a standard candle at 1-foot distance.

Catadioptric system   A telephoto optical system embodying both lenses and image-forming mirrors. Examples are the Cassegrain, Schmidt and Maksutov, telescope. Mirrors are used to reduce the size and weight of these long focal length lenses.

CAT Cable   A class of cables using unshielded twisted pairs (UTP) for transmitting video, audio, data and controls. The differences are base mainly on bandwidth, copper size and electrical performance. The most common are CAT 3, 4, 5, 5e and 6, as defined by the EIA and TIA (Telecommunications Industry Association).

Cathode ray tube CRT   A vacuum tube in which electrons emitted by a heated cathode are focused into a beam and directed toward a phosphor-coated surface, which then becomes luminescent at the point where the electron beam strikes. Prior to striking the phosphor, the focused electron beam is deflected by electromagnets or two pairs of electrostatically charged plates located between the electron "gun" and the screen.

CATV Cable television, Community antenna television   A cable television distribution system primarily used for consumer TV broadcast programming to a building or small community.

CCD Charge coupled device   A solid-state semiconductor imaging device used in most current security cameras. This sensor has hundreds of thousands of photo-sites (pixels) that convert light energy into electronic signals and with the camera electronics eventually into the video signal. The CCD sensor sizes is used in security systems are: 1/6, 1/4, 1/3, and 1/2 inch (measured diagonally).

CCIR International Radio Consultative Committee   A global organization responsible for establishing television standards. The CCIR format uses 625 lines per picture frame, with a 50 Hz power line frequency.

CCTMA Closed Circuit Television Manufacturers Association   A former division of the EIA, a full-service national trade organization promoting the CCTV industry and the interests of its members.

CCTV camera   The part of a CCTV system that captures a scene image and converts the light image into an electrical representation for transmission to a display or recording device.

CCTV Closed-circuit television A closed television system used within a building or complex to visually monitor a location or activity for security or industrial purposes. CCTV does not broadcast consumer TV signals but transmits in analog or digital form over a closed circuit via an electrically conducting cable, fiber-optic cable or wireless transmission.

CCTV monitor That part of the CCTV system which receives the picture from the CCTV camera and displays it.

Character generator The equipment used to create titles or other text in a video image. The device is used to generate words and numbers in a video format.

Chroma The characteristics of color information, independent of luminance intensity. Hue and saturation are qualities of chroma. Black, gray, and white objects do not have chroma characteristics.

Chromatic aberration A design flaw in a lens or lens system that causes the lens to have different focal lengths for radiation of different wavelengths. The dispersive power of a simple positive lens focuses light from the blue end of the spectrum at a shorter distance than light from the red end. This deficiency produces an image that is not sharp.

Chrominance signal The portion of a video signal that carries hue and saturation color information.

CIF Common Image Format A standard defining a digital pixel resolution. In the HDTV format the CIF resolution is $1,920 \times 1,080$ pixels, not to be confused with common Intermediate Format.

CIF Common Intermediate Format A commonly used television standard for measuring resolution. One CIF equals 352×240 pixels for NTSC and 352×288 for PAL. Full resolution is considered to be 4CIF, which is 704×480 pixels for NTSC and 704×576 pixels for PAL. Quarter resolution or 1/4CIF equals 176×120 for NTSC and 176×144 for PAL.

Clamping The process and circuitry that establishes a fixed level for the television picture level at the beginning of each scanning line.

Clear aperture The physical opening in a lens, or optical system that restricts the extent of the bundle of rays incident on the given surface. It is usually circular and specified by its diameter.

Client A networked PC or terminal that shares "services" with other PCs. These services are stored on or administered by a server.

Client/Server Client/Server describes the relationship between two computer programs in which one program, the client, makes a service request from another program, the server, which fulfills the request. The client server

model is one of the founding concepts of network computing. Most business applications written today use the client/server model-as does the Internet's main program, TCP/IP.

Clipping The shearing off of the peaks of a signal. For a picture signal, clipping may affect either the positive (white) or negative (black) peaks. For a composite video signal, the sync signal may be affected.

Close-up lens A low-magnification (low power) accessory lens that permits focusing on objects closer to the lens than it has been designed for.

CMYK The primary *colors* of light are red, green, and blue. The primary colors of *pigments* such as ink or paint are cyan, magenta, and yellow. Adding all three pigments together should produce black but often produce a poor black. Therefore black is obtained from sources such as carbon and called the fourth "primary" in the printing process. The letter K is used for black. The grouping of the letters CMYK is usually associated with the color print industry.

Coaxial cable A cable capable of carrying a wide range of frequencies with low signal loss. In its simplest form it consists of a stranded metallic shield with a single wire accurately placed along the center of the shield and isolated from the shield by an insulator.

Codec EnCOder/DECcoder A process or device by which or in which a signal is encoded for transmission or storage, then decoded for play back. An algorithm that handles the compression and decompression of video files. As a device, a box or computer card that accomplishes the encode/decode process.

Collimated A parallel beam of light or electrons.

Color bar test pattern A special test pattern for adjusting color TV receivers or color encoders. The upper portion consists of vertical bars of saturated colors and white. The lower horizontal bars have black-and-white areas and I and Q signals.

Color saturation The degree of mixture of a color and white. When a color is mixed with little or no white, it is said to have a high saturation. Low saturation denotes the addition of a great amount of white, as in pastel colors.

Color temperature The term used to denote the temperature of a blackbody light source that produces the same color as the light under consideration. Stated in degrees Kelvin.

Component video The uncoded output of a video camera, recorder etc., whereby the red, green, blue, chrominance and luminance signals are kept separate. Not to be confused with composite video.

COM port A serial communication port that supports the RS-232 standard of communication.

Composite video   An analog, encoded signal used in television transmission, including the picture signal (intensity and color), a blanking signal, and vertical and horizontal synchronizing signals. All components of the composite video signal are transmitted down a single cable simultaneously.

Compression, Analog   The reduction in gain at one level of a analog signal with respect to the gain at another level of the same signal.

Compression, Digital   The removal of redundant information from a signal to decrease the digital transmission or storage requirements. The use of mathematical algorithms to remove redundant data (bits) at the sending end without changing its essential content (encoding). The two generic types are *lossy* and *lossless*. There are many compression algorithms with the most common being MPEG, M-JPEG, H.264 and wavelet.

Concave   A term describing a hollow curved surface of a lens or mirror; curved inward.

Contrast   The range of difference between light and dark values in a picture, usually expressed as contrast ratio (the ratio between the maximum and minimum brightness values).

Control panel   A rack at the monitor location containing a number of controls governing camera selection, pan and tilt controls, focus and lens controls, etc.

Convergence   The crossover of the three electron beams of a three-gun tri-color picture tube. This normally occurs at the plane of the aperture mask.

Convex   A term denoting a spherically shaped optical surface of a lens or mirror; curved outward.

Corner reflector, corner cube prism   A corner reflector having three mutually perpendicular surfaces and a hypotenuse face. Light entering through the hypotenuse is totally internally reflected by each of the three surfaces in turn, and emerges through the hypotenuse face parallel to the entering beam and returns entering beams to the source. It may be constructed from a prism or three mutually perpendicular front surface mirrors.

Covert surveillance   In television security, the use of camouflaged (hidden) lenses and cameras for the purpose of viewing a scene without being seen.

Cross-talk   Interference between adjacent video, audio, or optical channels.

CS-mount   An industry standard for lens mounting. The CS-mount has a thread with a 1-inch diameter and 32 threads per inch. The distance from the lens mounting surface to the sensor surface is 0.492 inches (12.497 mm).

Cutoff frequency   That frequency beyond which no appreciable energy is transmitted. It may refer to either an upper or lower limit of a frequency band.

Dark current   The charge accumulated by pixels while not exposed to light. The current that flows in a photoconductor when it is placed in total darkness.

Dark current compensation   A circuit that compensates for the dark current level change with temperature.

DC restoration   The re-establishment by a sampling process of the DC and low-frequency components of a video signal that has been suppressed by AC transmission.

DC transmission   A form of transmission in which the DC component of the video signal is transmitted.

Decibel dB   A measure of the voltage or power ratio of two signals. In system use, a measure of the voltage or power ratio of two signals provided they are measured across the same value of impedance. Decibel gain or loss is 20 times log base 10 of the voltage or current ratio (Voutput/Vinput), and 10 times log base 10 of the power ratio (Poutput/Pinput).

Decoder   The circuitry in a receiver that transforms the detected signal into a form suitable to extract the original modulation or intelligence.

De-Compression   The process of taking a compressed video signal and returning it to its original (or near original) form it had before compression.

Definition   The fidelity of a television system with respect to the original scene.

Delay distortion   Distortion resulting from the non-uniform speed of transmission of the various frequency components of a signal, caused when various frequency components of the signal have different times of travel (delay) between the input and the output of a circuit.

Delay line   A continuous or periodic structure designed to delay the arrival of an electrical or acoustical signal by a predetermined amount.

Density   A measure of the light-transmitting or reflecting properties of an optical material. It is expressed by the common logarithm of the ratio of incident to transmitted light flux. A material having a density of 1 transmits 10% of the light, of 2 transmits 1%, of 3 transmits 0.1%, etc. see **Neutral density filter**.

Depth of field   The area between the nearest and the farthest objects in focus. For a lens, the area along the line of sight in which objects are in reasonable focus. It is the measured from the distance behind an object to the distance in front of the object when the viewing lens shows the object to be in focus. Depth of field increases with smaller lens aperture (higher f-numbers), shorter focal lengths, and greater distances from the lens.

Depth of focus   The range of detector-to-lens distance for which the image formed by the lens is clearly focused.

Detail contrast   The ratio of the amplitude of video signal representing high-frequency components with the amplitude representing the reference low-frequency component, usually expressed as a percentage at a particular line number.

Detail enhancement   Also called image enhancement. A system in which each element of a picture is analyzed in relation to adjacent horizontal and vertical elements. When differences are detected, a detail signal is generated and added to the luminance signal to enhance it.

Detection, image   In video, the criterion used to determine whether an object or person is observed (detected) in the scene. Detection requires the activation of only 1 TV line pair.

DHCP Dynamic Host Configuration Protocol   A protocol that lets network administrators automate and centrally manage the assignment of dynamic IP addresses to devices or a network. These are temporary addresses that are created anew for each transmission. The DHCP keeps track of both dynamic and static IP addresses, saving network administrator the additional task of manually assigning them each time a new device is added to the network.

Diaphragm   see **Iris diaphragm**.

Differential gain   The amplitude change, usually of the 3.58-MHz color subcarrier, introduced by the overall video circuit, measured in dB or percent, as the picture signal on which it rides is varied from blanking to white level.

Differential phase   The phase change of the 3.58-MHz color sub carrier introduced by the overall circuit, measured in degrees, as the picture signal on which it rides is varied from blanking to white level.

Digital 8   A Sony format that uses Hi8 or 8mm tapes to store digital video.

Digital signal   A video signal that is comprised from bits of binary data, otherwise known as ones and zeros (1, 0). The video signal travels from the point of its inception to the place where it is stored, and then on to the place where it is displayed either as an analog or digital presentation.

Digital Zoom   The process by which a camera takes a small geometrical part of the original captured frame and zooms it digitally with interpolation. Generally causes image degradation above 2X to 3X zoom ratios.

Diopter   A term describing the optical power of long focal length lenses. It is the reciprocal of the focal length in meters. For example, a lens with a focal length of 25 cm (0.25 m) has a power of 4 diopters.

Dipole antenna   The most common antenna used in video for wireless transmission of the analog or digital video signal consists of a 50 ohm coaxial with a length of exposed center conductor equal to a quarter wavelength of the transmission frequency. see also **Yaggi antenna**.

Direct-Sequence Spread Spectrum DSSS   see **Spread Spectrum**.

Distortion, electrical   An undesired change in the waveform from that of the original signal.

Distortion, optical   A general term referring to the situation in which an image is not a true reproduction of an object. There are many types of distortion.

Distribution amplifier   see **Amplifier, distribution**.

Dot bar generator   A device that generates a specified output pattern of dots and bars. It is used to measure scan linearity and geometric distortion in video cameras and monitors. Also used for converging cathode ray tubes.

DRAM Dynamic random access memory   A type of computer memory that is lost when the power is turned off.

Drive pulses   Synchronizing and blanking pulses.

DSL Direct Subscriber Line   A digital phone service that provides full voice, video and digital data over existing phone systems at higher speeds than are available in typical dial-up Internet sessions. There are four types: ADSL, HDSL, SDSL, and VDSL. All operate via modem pairs: one modem located at a central office and the other at the customer site. Asymmetric DSL technology provides asymmetrical bandwidth over a single wire pair. The downstream bandwidth from network to the subscriber is typically greater than the upstream bandwidth from the subscriber to the network.

DSL Modem   A modem that connects a PC to a network, which in turn connects to the Internet.

DTV Digital Television   Refers to all formats of digital video, including SDTV and HDTV.

DVD   Originally called Digital video disks, now called digital versatile disk. These high-capacity optical disks now store everything from massive computer applications to full-length movies. Although similar in physical size and appearance to a CD or a CD-ROM the DVD significantly improves on its predecessors 650 MB of storage. A standard single layer single-sided DVD can store 4.7 GB of data. The two layer, single-sided version boosts the capacity to 8.5 GB. The double-sided version stores 17 GB but requires a different disk drive for the PC.

DVR Digital video recorder   Records video pictures digitally.

Dynamic range   In television, the useful camera operating light range from highlight to shadow, in which detail can be observed in a static scene when both highlights and shadows are present. In electronics, the voltage or power difference between the maximum allowable signal level and the minimum acceptable signal level.

Echo   A signal that has been reflected at one or more points during transmission with sufficient magnitude and time difference as to be detected as a signal distinct from that of the primary signal. Echoes can be either leading or lagging the primary signal and appear on displays as reflections or "ghosts".

EDTV Extended definition television A marketing term for a standard definition television set that displays a progressive scan (non-interlaced) picture and usually has a horizontal resolution near the high end of SDTV (over 600 pixels).

EIA Electronics Industry Association EIA is a trade alliance for its members engaged in or associated with the manufacture, sale or distribution of many categories of electronic equipment.

EIA interface A standardized set of signal characteristics (time duration, waveform, delay, voltage, current) specified by the Electronic Industries Association.

EIA sync signal The signal used for the synchronizing of scanning specified in the Electrical Industry Association standards RS-170 (for monochrome), RS-170A (for color), RS-312, RS-330, RS-420, or subsequent specifications.

Electromagnetic focusing A method of focusing a cathode ray beam to a fine spot by application of electromagnetic fields to one or more deflection coils of an electron lens system.

Electronic viewfinder   see **Viewfinder, electronic**.

Electron Beam A stream of electrons emitted from the cathode of a cathode ray tube.

Electrostatic focusing A method of focusing a cathode ray beam to a fine spot by application of electrostatic potentials to one or more elements of an electron lens system.

Endoscope An optical instrument resembling a long, thin periscope used to examine the inside of objects by inserting one end of the instrument into an opening in the object. Endoscopes comprise a coherent fiber-optic bundle with a small objective lens to form an image of the object onto one end of the bundle, and a relay magnifier lens at the sensor end to focus the fiber bundle image onto the sensor. In an illuminated version, light from an external lamp is piped down to the object by a second set of thicker fibers surrounding the image-forming bundle. see also **Fiberscope**.

Equalizer An electronic circuit that introduces compensation for frequency discrimination effects of elements within the television system.

Ethernet The most widely installed local area network technology that uses collision detection to move data packets between workstations. Originally developed by Zerox and then developed further by Digital Equipment Corp. (DEC) and Intel. An Ethernet local area network (LAN) typically uses coaxial or fiber optic cable, or twisted pair wires. The most common Ethernet is called 10BASE-T

and provides transmission speeds up to 10 Mbps. see **Fast Ethernet**, **GIGABIT ETHERNET**.

Extranet A network that provides external users (suppliers, independent sales agents, dealers) access to company documents such as price lists, inventory reports, shipping schedules, and more.

Fader A control and associated circuitry for effecting fade-in and fade-out of video or audio signals.

Fast Ethernet The 100BASE-T10 Ether net provides transmission speeds up to 100 Mbps, 10 times faster than 10BASE-T.

FCC Federal Communications Commission The FCC is an independent federal regulatory agency charged with establishing policies to cover interstate and international communications via radio, television, wire, satellite and cable.

FDDI Fiber Distributed Data Interface A LAN technology based on a 100 Mbps token passing networking over fiber-optic cable. FDDI is usually reserved for network backbones in larger organizations.

Fiber-optic bundle, coherent An optical component consisting of many thousands of hair-like fibers coherently assembled so that an image is transferred from one end of the bundle to the other. The length of each fiber is much greater than its diameter. The fiber bundle transmits a picture from one end of the bundle to the other, around curves and into otherwise inaccessible places by a process of total internal reflection. The positions of all fibers at both ends are located in an exact one-to-one relationship with each other.

Fiber-optic transmission The process whereby light is transmitted through a long, transparent, flexible fiber, such as glass or plastic, by a series of internal reflections. For video, audio, or data transmission over long distances (thousands of feet, many miles) the light is modulated and transmitted over a single fiber in a protective insulating jacket. For light *image* transmission closely packed bundles of fibers can transmit an entire coherent image where each single fiber transmits but one component of the whole image.

Fiberscope A bundle of systematically arranged fibers that transmits a monochrome or full-color image which remains undisturbed when the bundle is bent. By mounting an objective lens on one end of the bundle and a relay or magnifying lens on the other, the system images remote objects onto a sensor. see **Endoscope**.

Field One of the two equal parts into which a television frame is divided in an interlaced system of scanning. There are 60 fields per second in the NTSC system and 50 in the CCIR and PAL systems. The NTSC field contains 262 1/2 horizontal TV lines and the CCIR, PAL 312.5 TV lines.

Field frequency   The number of fields transmitted per second in a television system. Also called field repetition rate. The U.S. standard is 60 fields per second (60-Hz power source). The European standard is 50 fields per second (50-Hz power source).

Field lens   A lens used to affect the transfer of the image formed by an optical system to a following lens system with minimum vignetting (loss of light).

Filter   An optically transparent material characterized by selective absorption of light with respect to wavelength (color). Electrical network of components to limit the transmission of frequencies to a special range (bandwidth).

FireWire   Also known as IEEE 1394 or i.LINK, FireWire is a two-way digital connection between computers and peripherals like digital camcorders and cameras. Most equipment uses 4-pin ports and connectors, but some use the 6-pin version.

FFL Fixed focal length lens   A lens having one or more elements producing a singular focal length. The focal length is measured in: millimeters or inches.

FHSS Frequency Hopping Spread Spectrum   see **Spread Spectrum Modulation**.

Firewall   A set of programs that protects the resources of a private network from outside users.

Flatness of field   Appearance of the image to be flat and focused. The object is imaged as a plane.

Fluorescent lamp   A high-efficiency, low-wattage arc lamp used in general lighting. A tube containing mercury vapor and lined with a phosphor. When current is passed through the vapor, the strong ultraviolet emission excites the phosphor, which emits visible light. The ultraviolet energy cannot emerge from the lamp as it is absorbed by the glass.

FM Frequency modulation   A process of translating baseband information to a higher frequency. The process: the two input signals that are inputs to an FM modulator are the baseband signal (video) and the carrier frequency (a constant amplitude and constant frequency signal.). The frequency of the carrier is modulated i.e. changed and increased and decreased about its center frequency by the amplitude of the baseband signal.

f-number   The optical speed or ability of a lens to pass light. The f-number (f/#) denotes the ratio of the equivalent focal length (FL) of an objective lens to the diameter (D) of its entrance pupil (f/# = FL/D). The f-number is directly proportional to the focal length and inversely proportional to the lens diameter. A smaller f-number indicates a faster lens.

Focal length, FL   The distance from the lens center, or second principal plane to a location (plane) in space where the image of a distant scene or object is focused. FL is expressed in millimeters or inches.

Focal length, back   The distance from the rear vertex of the lens to the lens focal plane.

Focal plane   A plane (through the focal point) at right angles to the principal axis of a lens or mirror. That surface on which the best image is formed.

Focal point   The point at which a lens or mirror will focus parallel incident radiation from a distant point source of light.

Focus   (1) The focal point. (2) The adjustment of the eyepiece or objective of a visual optical device so that the image is clearly seen by the observer. (3) The adjustment of a camera lens, image sensor, plate, or film holder so that the image is sharp. (4) The point at which light rays or an electron beam form a minimum-size spot. Also the action of bringing light or electron beams to a fine spot.

Focus control, electronic   A manual electric adjustment for bringing the electron beam of an image sensor tube or picture tube to a minimum size spot, producing the sharpest image.

Focus control, mechanical   A manual mechanical adjustment for moving the television sensor toward or away from the focal point of the objective lens to produce the sharpest image.

Foot-candle fc   A unit of illuminance on a surface 1 square foot in area on which there is incident light of 1 lumen. The illuminance of a surface placed 1 foot from a light source that has a luminous intensity of 1 candle.

Foot-lambert   A measure of reflected light in a 1 ft. area. A unit of luminance equal to 1 candela per square foot or to the uniform luminance at a perfectly diffusing surface emitting or reflecting light at the rate of 1 lumen per square foot.

FOV Field of view   The width, height, or diameter of a scene to be monitored, determined by the lens focal length, the sensor size, and the lens-to-subject distance. The maximum angle of view that can be seen through a lens or optical assembly. Usually described in degrees, for a horizontal, vertical, or circular dimension.

Frame   A frame is a complete video picture made up of two separate fields of 262.5 lines (NTSC) and 312.5 lines in (CCIR). In the standard U.S. NTSC 525-line system, the frame time is 1/30 second. In the European 625-line system, the frame time is 1/25 second. In a camera with progressive scan, each frame is scanned line-by-line and not interlaced.

Frame frequency   The number of times per second that the frame is scanned. The U.S. NTSC standard is 30 times per second. The European standard is 25 times per second.

Frequency interlace The method by which color and black-and-white sideband signals are interwoven within the same channel bandwidth.

Frequency response The range or band of frequencies to which a unit of electronic equipment will offer essentially the same characteristics.

Front (First) surface mirror An optical mirror with the reflecting surface applied to the front surface of the glass instead of to the back. The first surface mirror is used to avoid ghost images. In the more common rear surface mirror the light has to first pass through the mirror glass, strike the rear surface and then exit back out through the front of the mirror. This causes a secondary image or ghost image. The reflecting material on first surface mirrors is usually aluminum with a silicon monoxide protective overcoat.

Front porch That portion of a composite picture signal which lies between the leading edge of the horizontal blanking pulse and the leading edge of the corresponding sync pulse.

f-stop see **f-number**.

FTP File Transfer Protocol A part of the primary Internet protocol group TCP/IP is the simplest way to transfer files between computers from the Internet servers to the client computer. Like HTTP which transfers displayable web pages and related files, and which transfers e-mail, FTP is an application protocol that uses the Internet's TCP/IP protocols.

Gain An increase in voltage, current, power, or light usually expressed as a positive number or in decibels.

GaAs Gallium arsenide diode A light-emitting diode (LED) semiconductor device that emits low-power infrared radiation. Used in television systems for covert area illumination or with fiber optics for signal transmission. The radiation is incoherent and has a typical beam spread of 10 to 50 degrees and radiates at 850 or 960 nanometers in the IR spectrum.

Gallium arsenide laser A narrow-band, narrow-beam IR radiation device. The radiation is coherent and has a very narrow beam pattern, typically less than $1/2$ to 2 degrees, and radiates in the IR spectrum.

Galvanometer A device that converts an electrical signal into mechanical movement without the complexity of a DC motor. Used to control the iris vanes in the camera lens.

Gamma A numerical value of the degree of contrast in a television picture that is used to approximate the curve of output magnitude versus input magnitude over the region of interest. Gamma values range from 0.6 to 1.0.

Gamma correction To provide for a linear transfer characteristic from input to output device by adjusting the gamma.

Genlock An electronic device used to lock the frequency of an internal sync generator to an external source.

Geometric distortion Any aberration that causes the reproduced picture to be geometrically dissimilar to the original scene.

Ghost A spurious image resulting from an echo (electrical) or a second or multiple reflection (optical). A front surface mirror produces no ghost, while a rear surface mirror produces a ghost. Airwave RF and microwave signals reaching a receiver after reflecting from multiple paths produce ghosts.

GIF Graphics Interchange Format One of the two most common file formats for graphic images on the World Wide Web. The other is JPEG.

Gigabit Ethernet The latest version of Ethernet offering 1000 Mbps or 1 gigabit per second (Gbps) bandwidth that is 100 times faster than the original Ethernet. It is compatible with existing Ethernets since it uses the same CSMA/CD and MAC protocols.

Gray scale Variations in value from white, through shades of gray, to black, on a television screen. The gradations approximate the tonal values of the original image picked up by the TV camera. Most analog video cameras produce at least 10 shades of gray. Digital cameras typically produce 256 levels of gray.

GUI Graphic User Interface A digital user control and processing for the user of that system. The Macintosh or Microsoft Windows operating systems are examples of GUI systems.

H.264 A powerful MPEG compression algorithm standard developed through the combined effort of the ITU and MPEG organizations providing excellent compression efficiency and motion detection attributes. see **MPEG**.

Halo A glow or diffusion that surrounds a bright spot on a television picture tube screen or image intensifier tube.

Hertz (Hz) The frequency of an alternating signal formerly called cycles per second. The U.S. in Japan power-line frequency is 60 Hz. Most European countries use a 50 Hz power line frequency.

High-contrast image A picture in which strong contrast between light and dark areas is visible and where intermediate values however, may be missing.

High Definition Television HDTV A television standard using digital signals. HDTV signals contain over 720 TV lines of resolution compared with 525 TV line (NTSC) and 625 TV line (PAL) in legacy analog standards. HDTV video formats generally use a 1080i or 720p image format and have a 16:9 aspect ratio.

High-frequency distortion Distortion effects that occur at high frequency. In television, generally considered as any frequency above 15.75 KHz.

Highlights The maximum brightness of the TV picture occurring in regions of highest illumination.

Horizontal blanking Blanking of the picture during the period of horizontal retrace.

Horizontal hum bars Relatively broad horizontal bars, alternately black and white, that extend over the entire picture. They may be stationary or may move up or down. Sometimes referred to as a "venetian-blind" effect. In 60-Hz systems, hum bars are caused by approximate 60-Hz interfering frequency or one of its harmonic frequencies (such as 120 Hz).

Horizontal retrace The return of the electron beam from the right to the left side of the raster after scanning one horizontal line.

Horizontal, vertical resolution see **Resolution**.

HTM Hypertext Markup Language A simple document formatting language used for preparing documents to be viewed by a tool such as a WWW browser. A set of markup symbols or codes inserted in a file posted on the WWW browser. HTML instructs the web browser how to display web pages and images.

HTTP Hypertext Transfer Protocol A set of rules for exchanging files that governs transmission of formatted documents (text, graphic images, sound, video and other files) for viewing over the WWW and Internet. HTTP is an application protocol relative to the TCP/IP suite of protocols, which are the basis for information exchange on the Internet.

Hub A networking device that enables attached devices to receive data streams that are transmitted over a network and interconnects clients and servers. This device makes it possible for devices to share the network bandwidth available on a network. In data communications a hub is a place of convergence where data arrives from one or more locations and is forwarded to one or more other locations. The hub acts as a wiring concentrator in networks based on *star* topologies, rather than bus topologies in which computers are *daisy-chained* together. A hub usually includes a switch, which is also sometimes considered a hub. With respect to its switching capability, a hub can also be considered a router.

Hue Corresponds to colors such as red, blue, and so on. Black, gray, and white do not have hue.

Hum Electrical disturbance at the power supply frequency or harmonics thereof.

Hum modulation Modulation of a radio frequency, video or detected signal, by hum.

ICCD Intensified CCD A charge coupled device sensor camera, fiber optically coupled to an image intensifier. The intensifier is a tube or microchannel plate.

IEC International Telecommunications Union An international organization that sets standards for the goods and services in electrical and electronic engineering, see **ISO**.

IDE Integrated Drive Electronics A hard disk drive with built-in electronics necessary for use with a computer. A popular interface to attach hard drives to PC's where the electronics of the controller are integrated with the drive instead of on a separate PC card.

Identification, image In television, the criterion used to determine whether an object or person can be identified in the scene. It requires approximately 7 TV-line pairs to identify an object or person.

IEEE Institute of Electronic and Electrical Engineers A technical organization writing standards and publishing technical articles for the electronic and electrical industry.

Illuminance Luminous flux incident per unit area of a surface; luminous incidence.

Illumination, direct The lighting produced by visible radiation that travels from the light source to the object without reflection.

Illumination, indirect The light formed by visible radiation that, in traveling from the light source to the object, undergoes one or more reflections.

Image A reproduction of an object produced by light rays. An image-forming optical system collects light diverging from an object point and transforms it into a beam that converges toward another point. Transforming all the points produces an image.

Image distance The axial distance measured from the image to the second principal point of a lens.

Image format In television, the size of the area of the image at the focal plane of a lens, which is scanned by the video sensor.

Image intensifier A class of electronic imaging tubes equipped with a light-sensitive photocathode—electron emitter at one end, and a phosphor screen at the other end for visual viewing. An electron tube or microchannel plate (MCP) amplifying (intensifying) mechanism produces an image at its output brighter than the input. The intensifier can be coupled by fiber optics or lenses to a CCD or CMOS sensor. The intensifier can be single stage or multistage, tube or MCP.

Image pickup tube An electron tube that reproduces an image on its fluorescent screen of an irradiation pattern incident on its input photosensitive surface.

Image plane The plane at right angles to the optical axis at the image point.

Impedance The input or output characteristic of an electrical system or component. For maximum power and signal transfer, a cable used to connect two systems or components must have the same characteristic impedance as the system or component. Impedance is expressed in ohms. Video distribution systems have standardized on 75-ohm unbalanced and 124-ohm balanced coaxial cable. UPT uses a 100 ohm impedance. RF and microwave systems use 50 Ohm impedance coax.

Incident light   The light that falls directly onto an object.

Infrared radiation   The invisible portion of the electromagnetic spectrum that lies beyond about 750 nanometers (red end of the visible spectrum) and extends out to the microwave spectrum.

Interference   Extraneous energy that interferes and degrades the desired signal.

Interlace, 2 to 1   A scanning format used in video systems in which the two fields comprising the frame are synchronized precisely in a 2 to 1 ratio, and where the time or phase relationship between adjacent lines in successive fields is *fixed*.

Interlace, random   A scanning technique used in some systems in which the two fields making up the frame are not synchronized, and where there is **no** fixed time or phase relationship between adjacent lines in successive fields.

Interlaced scanning   A scanning process used to reduce image flicker and electrical bandwidth. The interlace is 2:1 in the NTSC system.

Internet   A massive global network that interconnects tens of thousands of computers and networks worldwide and is accessible from any computer with a modem or router connection and the appropriate software.

Intranet   A network internal to an organization that takes advantage of some of the same tools popularized on the Internet. These include browsers for viewing material, HTML for preparing company directories or announcements etc.

IP Address   On the Internet each computer and connected appliance, (camera switcher, router, etc.) must have a unique address. This series of numbers functions similarly to a street address, identifying the location of both sender and recipient for information dispatched over the computer network. The IP address has 32 bits in an 8 bit quad format. The four groups in decimal format are separated by a period (.). Two quad groups represent the network and two the machine or host address. An example of an IP address is 124.55.19.64 see **Subnet, Subnet mask**.

IP Internet Protocol   The method by which data is sent from one computer to another over the Internet. Each computer, known as a host on the Internet has one address that uniquely identifies it from all other computers on the Internet. A Web page or an e-mail is sent or received by dividing it into blocks called packets. Each packet contains both the sender's Internet address and the receiver's address. Each of these packets can arrive in an order different from the order from which they were sent in. The IP just delivers them and the Transmission Control Protocol TCP puts them in the correct order. The most widely used version of the IP is IP Version 4 (IPv4).

Iris   An adjustable optical-mechanical aperture built into a camera lens to permit control of the amount of light passing through the lens.

Iris diaphragm   A mechanical device within a lens used to control the size of the aperture through which light passes. A device for opening and closing the lens aperture to adjust the f-stop of a lens.

ISC International Security Conference   A trade organization to provide a forum for manufactures to display their products. ISC provides accredited security seminars for attendees.

ISDN Integrated Services Digital Network   is a communication protocol offered by telephone companies that permits high-speed connections between computers and networks in remote locations.

ISIT Intensified silicon intensified target   A SIT tube with an additional intensifier, fiber-optically coupled to provide increased sensitivity.

ISO   A worldwide federation of national standards bodies from over 130 countries to promote the worldwide standardization of goods and services. ISO's work results in international agreements that are published as international standards. The scope of ISO covers all technical fields except electrical and electronic engineering, which is the responsibility of IEC. Among well-known ISO standards are the ISO 9000 business standard that provides a framework for quality management and quality assurance.

Isolation amplifier   An amplifier with input and output circuitry designed to eliminate the effects of changes made by either upon the other.

ISP   Internet Service Provider   A company or organization that provides Internet access for companies, organizations or individuals.

ITU International Telecommunications Union   An international organization within which governments in the private sector coordinate global telecom networks and services.

Jitter   Instability of a signal in either its amplitude, phase, delay, or pulse width due to environmental disturbances or to changes in supply voltage, temperature, component characteristics, etc.

JPEG Joint Photographic Experts Group   A standards group that defined a compression algorithm commonly called JPEG that is used to compress the data in portrait or still video images. The JPEG file format is the ISO standard 10918 that includes 29 distinct coding processes. Not all must be used by the implementer. The JPEG file type used with the GIF format is supported by the WWW protocol, usually with the file suffix "jpg".

Kell factor The ratio of the vertical resolution to the number of scanning lines. The empirical number that reduces the vertical resolution of television images from the actual number of lines to 0.7 of that number. For the NTSC system the maximum resolution is reduced to approximately 350 lines.

Lag The persistence of the electrical charge image for two or more frames after excitation is removed and found in an intensifier tube or monitor display.

LAN Local Area Network A digital network or group of network segments confined to one building or campus. The LAN consists of a series of PCs that have been joined together via cabling so that resources can be shared, including file and print services.

LASER Light Amplification by Stimulated Emission of Radiation A LASER is an optical cavity, with plane or spherical mirrors at the ends, that is filled with a light-amplifying material, and an electrical or optical means of stimulating (energizing) the material. The light produced by the atoms of the material generates a brilliant beam of light that is emitted through one of the semi-transparent mirrors. The output beam is highly monochromatic (pure color), coherent and has a narrow beam (small fraction of a degree).

Laser diode see **Gallium arsenide laser**.

LCD Liquid Crystal Display A solid-state video display created by sandwiching an electrically reactive substance between two electrodes. LCDs can be darkened or lightened by applying and removing power. Large numbers of LCD pixels group closely together act as pixels in a flat-panel display.

Leading edge The major portion of the rise of a pulse, waveform taken from the 10 to 90% level of total amplitude.

Lens A transparent optical component consisting of one or more optical glass elements with surfaces so curved (usually spherical) that they serve to converge or diverge the transmitted rays of an object, thus forming a real or virtual image of that object.

Lens, fresnel Figuratively a lens that is cut into narrow rings and flattened out. In practice a thin plastic lens that has narrow concentric rings or steps, each acting to focus radiation into an image.

Lens speed Refers to the ability of a lens to transmit light. Represented as the ratio of the focal length to the diameter of the lens. A fast lens would be rated f/1.4. A much slower lens might be designated as f/8. The larger the f-number, the slower the lens. see **f-number**.

Lens system Two or more lenses so arranged as to act in conjunction with one another.

Light Electromagnetic radiation detectable by the eye, ranging in wavelength from about 400 nm (blue) to 750 nm (red).

Limiting resolution A measure of resolution usually expressed in terms of the maximum number of TV lines per TV picture height discernible on a test chart.

Line amplifier An amplifier for audio or video signals that drive a transmission line. An amplifier, generally broadband, installed at an intermediate location in a main cable run, to compensate for signal loss.

Linearity The state of an output that incrementally changes directly or proportionally as the input changes.

Line pairs The term used in defining television resolution. One TV line pair constitutes one black line and one white line. The 525 NTSC system has 485 line pairs displayed.

LLL Low light level Camera and video systems capable of operating below normal visual response. An intensified video camera such as an ICCD capable of operating in extremely poorly lighted areas.

Load That component which receives the output energy of an electrical device.

Loss A reduction in signal level or strength, usually expressed in dB. A power dissipation serving no useful purpose.

Lossless Compression A form of video compression that does not degrade the quality of the image.

Lossy Compression A form of compression in which image quality is degraded during compression.

Low-frequency distortion Distortion effects that occur at low frequency. In video, generally considered as any frequency below 15.75 kHz.

Lumen (lm) The unit of luminous flux, equal to the flux through a unit solid angle (steradian) from a uniform point source of 1 candela or to the flux on a unit surface of which all points are at a unit distance from a uniform point source of 1 candela.

Luminance A parameter that represents brightness in the video picture. Luminous intensity (photometric brightness) of any surface in a given direction per unit of projected area of the surface as viewed from that direction, measured in foot-lamberts. Abbreviated as Y.

Luminance signal The part of the NTSC composite color signal that contains the scene brightness or black and white information.

Luminous flux The time rate of flow of light.

Lux International system unit of illumination in which the meter is the unit of length. One Lux equals 1 lumen per square meter.

MAC Media Access Control Protocol   The MAC is the physical address for any device used in a network: a computer, router, IP camera, etc. The address consists of two parts and is 6 bytes long. The first 3 bytes identify the company and the last 3 bytes are the device serial number.

Magnetic focusing   A method of focusing an electron beam by the action of a magnetic field.

Magnification   A number expressing the change in object to image size. Usually expressed with a 1-inch focal length lens and a 1-inch format sensor as a reference (magnification $= M = 1$). A lens with a 2-inch focal length is said to have a magnification of $M = 2$.

MAN Metropolitan Area Network   A large network usually connected via fiber optics to obtain the Gbit speeds and huge volumes of digital transmission over long distances.

Matching   The obtaining of like electrical impedances to provide a reflection-free transfer of signal.

Matrix switcher   A combination or array of electromechanical or electronic switches that route a number of signal sources to one or more designations. In video, cameras are switched to monitors, recorders and networks.

Maximum aperture   The largest size the iris diaphragm of the lens can be opened resulting in the lowest lens f-number.

Megabits per second Mbps   Defines the speed at which data is traveling and is measured in millions of bits per second. This is a measure of the performance of a device.

Mercury arc lamp   An intense electric arc lamp that generates blue-white light when electric current flows through mercury vapor in the lamp.

Metal arc lamp   An intense arc lamp that generates a white light when an electric current flows through the multimetal vapor in the lamp.

MHz Megahertz   Unit of frequency equal to 1 million Hz.

Microcomputer   A tabletop or portable digital computer composed of a microprocessor, active memory storage, and permanent memory storage (disk) and which computes and controls functions via a software operating system and applications program.

Micron   Unit of length: one millionth of a meter.

Microphonics   Audio-frequency noise caused by the mechanical vibration of elements within a system or component.

Microprocessor   The brain of the microcomputer. A very large scale integrated circuit comprising the computing engine of a microcomputer. The electronic chip (circuit) that does all the calculations and control of data. In larger machines it is called the central processing unit (CPU).

Microwave transmission   In television, a transmission means that converts the camera video signal to a modulated (AM or FM) microwave signal via a transmitter, and a receiver that demodulates the received microwave signal to the baseband CCTV signal for display on a monitor.

Mirror, first or front surface   An optical component on which the reflecting surface is applied to the *front* of the glass instead of the back, the front being the first surface of incidence and reflectance. It produces a single image with no ghost. see **First Surface Mirror**.

Mirror, rear surface   The common mirror in which the reflecting surface is applied to the *rear* of the glass. It produces a secondary or ghost image.

M-JPEG   A digital video compression format developed from JPEG, a compression standard for still images. When JPEG is extended to a sequence of pictures in the video stream it becomes M-JPEG or motion-JPEG.

Modem   Derived from its function: **modulator-demodulator**. A device that enables a computer to connect to other computers and networks using ordinary phone lines. Modems modulate the digital signals of the computer into analog signals for transmission and then demodulate those analog signals back into digital language that the computer on the other end can recognize. see **CODEC**.

Modulation   The process, or results of the process, whereby some characteristic of one signal is varied in accordance with another signal. The modulated signal is called the carrier. The carrier may be modulated in several fundamental ways including: by varying the amplitude, called amplitude modulation (AM); by varying the frequency, called frequency modulation (FM); or by varying the phase, called phase modulation (PM).

Moire pattern   The spurious pattern in the reproduced picture resulting from interference beats between two sets of periodic structures in the image. Usually caused by tweed or checkerboard patterns in the scene.

Monitor   A CRT based monochrome or color display for viewing a television picture from a camera output. The monitor does not incorporate a VHF or UHF tuner and channel selector and displays the composite video signal directly from the camera, DVR, VCR or any special-effects generator. Monitors take the form of a CRT, LCD, plasma and other.

Monochrome signal   A black and white video signal with all shades of gray. In monochrome television, a signal for controlling the brightness values in the picture. In color television, that part of the signal which has major control of the brightness values of the picture, whether displayed in color or in monochrome. The minimum number of shades of gray for good image rendition is 10.

Monochrome transmission   The transmission of a signal wave that represents the brightness values in the picture, not the color (chrominance) values.

Motion detector   A device used in security systems that reacts to any movement in a CCTV camera image by automatically setting off an alarm and/or indicating the motion on the monitor.

Motorized lens   A camera lens fitted with small electric motors that can focus the lens, open or close the iris diaphragm, or in the case of the zoom lens, change the focal length by remote control.

MPEG-4   A compression standard formulated by the Moving Pictures Experts Group. The MPEG-4 standard for digital video and audio compression is optimized for moving images in which the compression is based on the similarity of successive pictures. MPEG-4 files carry an .mpg suffix. see also **H.264**.

Multicasting   Refers to the propagation from one source to a subset of potential destinations. A technique for simultaneously sending multiple digital video streams on a single channel.

Multiplexer   High speed electronic switch that combines two or more video signals into a single channel to provide full-screen images up to 16 or 32 displayed simultaneously in split image format. Multiplexers can play back everything that happened on any one camera without interference from the other cameras on the system.

NAB National Association of Broadcasters

Nanometer (nm)   Unit of length: one billionth of a meter.

NA Numerical aperture   The sine of the half-angle of the widest bundle of rays capable of entering a lens, multiplied by the refractive index of the medium containing that bundle. In air, the refractive index $n = 1$.

ND Spot Filter   A graduated filter at the center of a lens that has minimal effect when the iris is wide open but increases its effect as the iris closes. The filter has a varying density as a function of the distance from the center of the lens with maximum density at the center of the filter.

ND Neutral density filter   An optical attenuating device or light filter that reduces the intensity of light without changing the spectral distribution of the light. Can be attached to the lens of the camera to assist in preventing over exposure of an image. see **Density**.

Negative image   A picture signal having a polarity that is opposite to normal polarity and that results in a picture in which the roles of white and black areas are reversed.

Network   A collection of devices that include computers, printers, and storage devices that are connected together for the purpose of sharing information and resources.

Newvicon   A former television pickup tube with a cadmium and zinc telluride target with sensitivity about 20 times that of a vidicon target. It had a spectral response of 470 to 850 nm, good resolution and was relatively free from burn-in.

NIC Network Interface Card   A device that provides for connecting a PC to a network. NIC cards are also called network adapters and provide an essential link between a device and the network.

Noise   The word noise originated in audio practice and refers to random spurts of acoustical or electrical energy, or interference. In television, it produces a "salt-and-pepper" pattern over the televised picture. Heavy noise is sometimes referred to as "snow."

Non-browning   A term used in connection with lens glass, faceplate glass, fiber optics, used in radiation-tolerant television cameras. Non-browning glass does not discolor (turn brown) when irradiated with atomic particles and waves.

Non-composite video   A video signal containing all information except synchronization pulses.

Notch filter   A special filter designed to reject a very narrow band of electrical frequencies or optical wavelengths.

NTSC National Television Systems Committee.   The committee that worked with the FCC in formulating standards for the original monochrome and present-day U.S. color television system. NTSC has 525 horizontal scan lines, 30 frames per second, and a bandwidth of 4.2 MHz. NTSC uses a 3.579545 MHz color sub-carrier. It employs 525 lines per frame, 29.97 frames/sec and 59.94 fields/sec. The NTSC standard is used in the United States and Japan.

NVR Network Video Recorder   A software or computer that records video on a hard disk. Like a DVR, it records digitally so the user can instantly search by time, date and camera. It collects video from network cameras, network video servers or a DVR, over the network.

Object distance   The distance between the object and the cornea of the eye, or the first principal point of the objective in an optical device.

Objective lens   The optical element that receives light from an object scene and forms the first or primary image. In cameras, the image produced by the objective is the final image. In telescopes and microscopes, when used visually, the image formed by the objective is magnified by an eyepiece.

Optical axis   The line passing through the centers of curvatures of the optical surfaces of a lens or the geometric center of a mirror or window; the optical centerline.

Optical splitter   An optical lens-prism and/or mirror system that combines two or more scenes and images them onto one video camera. Only optical components are used to combine the scene.

Optical Zoom   Optical zoom is produced by the lens itself by moving sets of lenses in the zoom lens to provide a continuous, smooth change in focal length from wide-angle to narrow-angle (telephoto).

Orientation, image   In television, the criterion used to determine the angular orientation of a target (object, person) in an image. At least 2 TV-line pairs are required.

Overshoot   The initial transient response to a unidirectional change in input, which exceeds the steady-state response.

Overt surveillance   In television, the use of any openly displayed television lenses or cameras to view a scene.

Packet   A block of data with a "header" attached that can indicate what the packet contains and where it is headed. A packet is a "data envelope" with the header acting as an address.

PAL Phase Alternating Line   A European color television system using a 625 lines per frame 25 frames/second composite analog color video system at 5.5 MHz bandwidth. In this system the sub-carrier derived from the color burst is inverted in phase from one line to the next in order to minimize errors in hue that may occur in color transmission. The PAL format is used in Western Europe, Australia, parts of Africa, and the Middle East.

Pan and tilt   Camera-mounting platform that allows movement in both the azimuth (pan) and the elevation (tilt) planes.

Pan, panning   Rotating or scanning a camera around a vertical axis to view an area in a horizontal direction.

Pan/tilt/zoom   Three terms associated with television cameras, lenses and mounting platforms to indicate the horizontal (pan), vertical (tilt), and magnification (zoom) they are capable of producing.

Passive   In video, cameras using ambient visible or IR, contrasted to using an active IR illuminator. In electronics, a non-powered device that generally presents some loss to a system and is incapable of generating power or amplification.

Peak-to-peak   The amplitude (voltage) difference between the most positive and the most negative excursions (peaks) of an electrical signal.

Pedestal level   see **Blanking level**.

Persistence   In a cathode ray tube, the period of time a phosphor continues to glow after excitation is removed.

Phased array antenna   A transmit or receive antenna comprised of multiple identical radiating elements in a regular arrangement and fed or connected to obtain a prescribed radiation pattern.

Phosphor   A substance capable of luminescence used in fluorescent lamps, television monitors, viewfinders, and image intensifier screens.

Phosphor-dot faceplate   A glass plate in a tri-color picture tube. May be the front face of the tube or a sep-

arate internal plate. Its rear surface is covered with an orderly array of tri-color lines or phosphor dots. When excited by electron beams in proper sequence, the phosphors glow in red, green, and blue to produce a full-color picture.

Photocathode   An electrode used for obtaining photoelectric emission.

Photoconductivity   The changes in the electrical conductivity (reciprocal of resistance) of a material as a result of absorption of photons (light).

Photoconductor   A material whose electrical resistance varies in relationship with exposure to light.

Photoelectric emission   The phenomenon of emission of electrons by certain materials upon exposure to radiation in and near the visible region of the spectrum.

Photon-limited sensitivity   When the quantity of available light is the limiting factor in the sensitivity of a device.

Photopic vision   Vision that occurs at moderate and high levels of luminance and permits distinction of colors. This light-adapted vision is attributed to the retinal cones in the eye. In contrast, twilight or scotopic vision uses primarily the rods responding to overall light level.

Pickup tube   A television camera image pickup tube. see **Image pickup tube**.

Picture size   The useful area of an image sensor or display. In the standard NTSC format, the horizontal to vertical ratio is 4:3. The diagonal is 5 units. The HDTV ratio is 16:9.

Picture tube   see **Cathode ray tube**.

Pin-cushion distortion   Distortion in a television picture that makes all sides appear to bulge inward.

Pinhole lens   A lens designed to have a relatively small (0.06 inch to 0.375 inch) front lens diameter to permit its use in covert (hidden) camera applications.

PIP Picture in a picture   A video display mode which puts several complete video images on the screen at the same time. Most common is one small image into a large image.

Pixel   Short for Picture element. Any segment of a scanning line, the dimension of which along the line is exactly equal to the nominal line width. A single imaging unit that can be identified by a computer.

Pixelization   An effect seen when an image is enlarged (electronically zoomed) too much and the pixels become visible to the eye.

POTS Plain Old Telephone Service   The original and slowest telephone system.

Preamplifier   An amplifier used to increase the output of a low-level source so that the signal can be further processed without additional deterioration of the signal-to-noise ratio.

Preset A term used in television pointing systems (pan/tilt/zoom). A computer stores pre-entered azimuth, elevation, zoom (magnification), focus, and iris combinations, which are later accessed when commanded by an operator or automatically on alarm.

Primary colors Three colors wherein no mixture of any two can produce the third. In color television these are the additive primary colors red, green, and blue (R,G,B).

Progressive or sequential scan A method of image scanning that processes image data one line of pixels at a time. Each frame is composed of a single field. Contrasted to interlace scanning having two fields per frame.

PSTN Public Switched Telephone Network The traditional, wired telephone network.

Pulse A variation of a quantity whose value is normally constant. This variation is characterized by a rise and decay, and has finite amplitude and duration.

Pulse rise-time Time interval between upper and lower limits of instantaneous signal amplitude; specifically, 10 and 90% of the peak-pulse amplitude, unless otherwise stated.

Quad An electronic device having four camera inputs that can display the four cameras simultaneously in a quad format, singly full screen, or full screen sequentially. Alarm input contacts are provided so that the unit switches from a quad display to a full screen image of the alarmed camera.

Radiation Pattern A graphical representation in either polar or rectangular coordinates of the spatial energy distributions of an antenna.

RAID Redundant Array of Independent Disks A system in which a number of hard drives are connected into one large segmented mass storage device. There are RAID-0 to RAID 6 systems.

RAM Random Access Memory The location in the computer, where the operating system, application programs, and data in current use are temporarily kept so that they can be quickly reached by the computers processor. RAM is volatile memory, meaning that when the computer is turned off, crashes, or loses power, the contents of the memory are lost.

Random interlace see **Interlace, random**.

Raster The blank white screen that results from the scanning action of the electron beam in a CRT with no video picture information applied. A predetermined pattern of scanning lines that provides substantially uniform coverage of an area. The area of a camera or CRT tube scanned by the electron beam.

Raster burn see **Burn-in**.

Recognition, image In television, the criterion used to determine whether an object or person can be recognized in a television scene. A minimum of 5 TV-line pairs are required to recognize a person or object.

Reference black level The picture signal level corresponding to a specified maximum limit for black peaks.

Reference white level The picture signal level corresponding to a specified maximum limit for white peaks.

Resolution A measure of how clear and sharp a video image is displayed on a monitor. The more pixels, the higher the resolution. It measures picture details that can be distinguished on the television screen. Vertical resolution refers to the number of *horizontal* black-and-white or color lines that can be resolved in the picture height. Horizontal resolution refers to the number of *vertical* black-and-white or color lines that can be resolved in a picture width equal to the picture height.

Resolution, horizontal The amount of resolvable detail in the horizontal direction in a picture; the maximum number of individual picture elements that can be distinguished. It is usually expressed as a number of distinct vertical lines, alternately black and white, that can be seen in a distance equal to picture height. 500 to 600 TV lines are typical with the standard 4.2-MHz CCTV bandwidth. In analog video systems the horizontal resolution is dependent on the system bandwidth.

Resolution, vertical The amount of resolvable detail in the vertical direction in a picture. It is usually expressed as the number of distinct horizontal lines, alternately black and white, which can be seen in a picture. 350 TV lines are typical in the 525 NTSC system.

Retained image Also called image burn. A change produced in or on the sensor target that remains on the output device (such as a CRT) for a large number of frames after the removal of a previously stationary light image.

RF Radio frequency A frequency at which coherent electromagnetic radiation of energy is useful for communication purposes. The entire range of such frequencies, including the AM and FM radio spectrum and the VHF and UHF television spectrum.

RGB Red, Green, and Blue Abbreviations for the three primary colors captured by a CCD or CMOS imager and displayed in analog and digital video systems. Specifically, the CCD or CMOS camera sensors and CRT, LCD and plasma displays use RGB resolution elements or pixels. The color signals are mixed electronically to create all the other colors in the spectrum.

Right-angle lens A multi-element optical component that causes the optical axis of the incoming radiation (from a scene or image focal plane) to be redirected by

90 degrees. It is used when a wide-angle lens is necessary to view a scene at right angles to the camera.

Ringing   In electronic circuits, an oscillatory transient occurring in the output of a system as a result of a sudden change in input.

Ripple   Amplitude variations in the output voltage of a power supply caused by insufficient filtering.

Roll   A loss of vertical synchronization that causes the displayed video image to move (roll) up or down on a television receiver or video monitor.

Roll off   A gradual decrease or attenuation of a signal voltage as a function of frequency.

Router   A device that moves data between different network segments and can look into a packet header to determine the best path for the packet to travel. On the Internet, a device or in some cases software in a computer that determines the next network point to which a data packet should be forwarded towards its final destination. The router analyzes the network status and chooses the optimum path to send each information packet. The router can be located at any juncture of a network or gateway including any Internet access point. The router creates and maintains a table of available network routes and their status. Using distance and cost algorithms it determines the best route for any given packet. Routers allow all users in a network to share a single connection to the Internet or a WAN.

RS170   The original EIA broadcast studio standard issue in November, 1953 for the NTSC black-and-white video format. It described a 2:1 interlaced, 525 line TV standard with the total number of lines occurring in 1/30 second. The vertical frequency was 60 hertz, signal amplitude 1.4 volts peak to peak including sync signal, and bandwidth from 30 Hz to 4.2 MHz.

RS170A   The proposed standard for the NTSC composite color video system. Its contents were used in the television industry as a reference, but the document was never adopted. The current color standard is SMPTE 170-1999.

RS232, RS232C   A low speed protocol established by the EIA. The standard describes the physical interface and protocol between computers and related devices (printers, modems, etc.). The PC contains a universal asynchronous receiver-transmitter (UART) chip that converts the parallel computer data into serial data for RS232 transmission. The standard recommends a maximum range of 50 feet (15.2 meters) and maximum baud rate of 20 Kbps. There is a standard pinout and the connectors used are D-9 and D-25.

RS422   is a protocol established by the EIA consisting of a differential pair of conductors and specified pinout or connectors. The differential pair is one signal transmitted across two separate wires in opposite states: one is inverted and the other is non-inverted. In this differential signal transmission when both lines are exposed to external noise, both lines are affected equally and cancel out. RS422 is usually used in full duplex, four wire mode for point-to-point communication but one transmitter can drive up to 10 receivers. Maximum recommended range and baud rate are 4000 feet and 10Mbps respectively.

RS485   This protocol is an upgraded version of the RS422 and can handle up to 32 transmitters and receivers by using tri-state drivers. Maximum recommended range and baud rate are 4000 feet and 10 Mbps respectively.

Server   A computer or software program that provides services to other computer programs in the same computer or other computers. When a computer runs a server program, the computer is called a server. When the server is connected to the Web the server program serves the requested HTML pages or files to the client. Web browsers are clients that request HTML files from Web servers. A server provides services to clients such as: files storage (file server), programs (application server), printer sharing (printer's server), fax or modem sharing.

Saturation   In color, the degree to which a color is undiluted with white light, or is pure. The vividness of a color, described by such terms as bright, deep, pastel, pale, and so on. Saturation is directly related to the amplitude of the television chrominance signal.

SCADA Supervisory Control and Data Acquisition   An industrial measurement and control system consisting of a central host or master terminal unit (MTU), one or more field data gathering and control units or remotes, and a collection of standard and/or custom software used to monitor and control remotely located field data elements.

Scanning   Moving the electron beam of an image pickup or a CRT picture tube horizontally across and slowly down the target or screen area respectively. Moving the charge packets out of a CCD, CMOS or IR sensor.

Scotopic vision   Vision that occurs in faint light, or in dark adaptation. It is attributed to the operation of the retinal rods in the eye and contrasted with daylight or photopic vision, using primarily the cones.

SCSI Small Computer System Interface   A high speed input/output bus that is faster than serial and parallel ports, but slower and harder to configure than USB and FireWire ports. SCSI enables a computer to interact with external peripheral hardware, such as CD-ROM drives, printers, and scanners. SCSI is being supplanted by the newer USB standard.

SDTV Standard Definition Television   Used to describe our 525 line and 625 line interlaced television systems as they are used in the context of DTV.

SECAM Sequential Couleur A'Memorie   A color television system developed in France and used in some countries that do not use either the NTSC or PAL systems. Like PAL, SECAM has 625 horizontal scan lines and 25 frames per second but differs significantly in the method of producing color signals.

Sensitivity   In television, a factor expressing the incident illumination upon a specified scene to produce a specified picture signal at the video camera output.

Set Top Box   A unit similar to a cable box capable of receiving and decoding DTV broadcasts.

Sharpness   Refers to the ability to see the greatest detail in video monitor picture. Color sets marketed before the mid 1980s had sharpness controls to optimize the fine detail in the picture. The use of comb filters in present monitors eliminate the need for the sharpness control. see **Resolution**.

Shutter   In an optical system, an opaque material placed in front of a lens, optical system, or sensor for the purpose of protecting the sensor from bright light sources, or for timing the length of time the light source reaches the sensor or film.

Shuttering   An electronic technique used in solid-state cameras to reduce the charge accumulation from scene illumination for the purpose of increasing the dynamic range of the camera sensor. Analogous to the electronic shutter in a film camera.

Signal strength   The intensity of the video signal measured in volts, millivolts, microvolts, or decibels. Using 0 dB as the standard reference is equal to 1000 microvolts (1 millivolt) in RF systems, and 1 volt in video systems.

Signal-to-noise ratio S:R, S/N   The ratio of the peak value of the video signal to the value of the noise. Usually expressed in decibels. The ratio between a useful television signal and disturbing, unwanted image noise or "snow".

Silicon monoxide   A thin-film dielectric (insulator) used as a protective layer on aluminized mirrors. It is evaporated onto the mirror as a thin layer, and after exposure to the air the monoxide tends to become silicon dioxide or quartz, which is very hard and completely transparent.

Silicon target tube   The successor to the vidicon. A high-sensitivity television image pickup tube of the direct-readout type using a silicon diode target made up of a mosaic of light-sensitive silicon material. It has a sensitivity between 10 and 100 times more than a sulfide vidicon and has high resistance to image burn-in.

SIT Silicon intensified target   A predecessor to the ICCD. An image intensifier fiber-optically coupled to a silicon faceplate resulting in a sensitivity 500 times that of a standard vidicon.

Slow-scan   A first generation video transmission system consisting of a transmitter and receiver to transmit single frame video images at rates slower than the normal NTSC frame rate of 30 per second. The CCTV frames were modulated and transmitted over the phone lines to a distant receiver-demodulator and displayed on a CCTV monitor. The slow-scan process periodically sends "snapshots" of the scene with typical sending rates of 1 to 5 frames per second.

Sodium lamp   A low or high-pressure discharge metal vapor arc lamp using sodium as the luminous radiation source. The lamp produces a yellow light and has the highest electrical-to-light output efficiency (efficacy) of any lamp. Because of their poor color balance neither is recommended for color CCTV systems, but can be used for monochrome systems.

SMPTE Society of Motion Picture and Television Engineers   A global organization based in the U.S. that sets standards for baseband visual communications.

SMTP Simple Mail Transfer Protocol   A TCP/IP that is used for sending and receiving e-mail. To improve its usefulness it is used with the POP3 or IMAP protocols, allowing the user to save messages in a server mailbox and download them periodically from the server. Users use the SMTP to send messages and POP3 or IMAP to receive messages from the local server.

Snow   Heavy random noise manifest on a phosphor screen as a changing black and white or colored "peppered" random noise. see **Noise**.

Speckle   Noise manifest in image intensifiers in the form of small, localized bright light spots or flashes seen in the device monitor.

Spike   A transient of short duration, comprising part of a pulse, during which the amplitude considerably exceeds the average amplitude of the pulse.

Spread Spectrum Modulation SSM   A communication technique that spreads a signal bandwidth over a wide range of frequencies for transmission and then de-spreads it to the original data bandwidth at the receiver. see **Frequency Hopping**.

Subnet   A uniquely identifiable part of a network. The subnet may represent a particular department at a location or a particular geographical location of the subnet in a building on the local area network (LAN). Dividing the network into sub-networks allows it to be connected to the Internet with a single shared network address. see **IP address**.

Subnet mask   This set of numbers tells a signal router which numbers are relevant under the IP address mask. In the binary mask system a "1" over a number indicates that the number under the 1 is relevant, and a "0" over a number says ignore the number under it. Using the mask means the router does not have to look at all 32-bits in the IP address. see **IP address**.

Super VGA   A video format providing high-quality analog video by separating the video signal into three color signals, R, G, B, allowing for exceptionally clear and bright images.

S-VHS Super VHS   A video tape format in which the chrominance and luminance signals are recorded and played back separately providing for better picture quality.

S-Video   An encoded video signal that separates the luminance (brightness) part of the signal from the chrominance (color) to provide better picture quality.

Switch   A network device that improves network performance by segmenting the network and reducing competition for bandwidth. The switch selects a path or circuit for sending a packet of data to its next destination. When a switch port receives data packets, it forwards those packets only to the appropriate port for the intended recipient. A switch can also provide the function of routing the data packet to the next point in the network. The switcher is faster than the router and can more effectively determine the route the data takes.

Switcher   A video electronic device that connects one of many input cameras to one or several output monitors, recorders, etc., by means of a panel switch or electronic input signal.

Switcher, alarming   An automatic switcher that is activated by a variety of sensing devices. Once activated, the switcher connects the camera to the output device (monitor, recorder, etc.).

Switcher, bridging   A sequential switcher with separate outputs for two monitors, one for a programmed sequence and the second for extended display of a single camera scene.

Switcher, homing   A switcher in which: 1) the outputs of multiple cameras can be switched sequentially to a monitor, 2) one or more cameras can be bypassed (not displayed), or 3) any one of the cameras can be selected for continuous display on the monitor (homing). The switcher has three front-panel controllable modes: 1) Skip, 2) Automatic (sequential) and 3) Select (display one camera continuously). The lengths of time each camera output is displayed are independently selectable by the operator.

Switcher, manual   A switcher in which the individual cameras are chosen by the operator manually by pushing the switch for the camera output signal chosen to be displayed, recorded, or printed.

Switcher, sequential   A generic switcher type that allows the video signals from multiple cameras to be displayed, recorded, or printed one at a time in sequence.

Sync   A contraction of synchronous or synchronization.

Sync generator   A device for generating a synchronizing signal.

Synchronizing   Maintaining two or more scanning processes or signals in phase.

Sync level   The level of the peaks of the synchronizing signal.

Sync signal   The signal employed for the synchronizing of scanning.

Talk-back   A voice inter-communicator; an intercom.

Target   In solid-state sensors, a semiconductor structure using picture elements to accumulate the picture charge, and a scanning readout mechanism to generate the video signal. In surveillance, an object (person, vehicle, etc.) or activity of interest present in an image of the scene under observation. In image pickup tubes, a structure using a storage surface that is scanned by an electron beam to generate a signal output current corresponding to a charge-density pattern stored on it.

TCP Transmission control protocol   A protocol used along with the IP to send data in the form of message units between computers, over the Internet. While IP takes care of handling the actual delivery of the data, TCP takes care of keeping track of the individual units of data (called packets) that a message is divided into, for efficient routing over the Internet.

TCP/IP Transmission control protocol/Internet protocol   The basic communication language (or protocol) of the Internet. It is also used as a communications protocol in private networks called intranets, and extranets. TCP/IP communication is primarily point-to-point in which each communication is from one point (or host computer) to another. The TCP of TCP/IP handles the tracking of the data packets.

TDMA Time Division Multiple Access   A digital multiplexing (channel sharing) technique whereby each signal is sent at a repeating time slot in a frequency channel. Because the data from each user always appears in the same time slot, the receiver can separate the signals.

Telephoto lens   A long focal length lens, producing a narrow field of view. Telephoto lenses are used to magnifier objects within their field of view.

Test pattern   A chart especially prepared for checking overall performance of a television system. It contains combinations of lines and geometric shapes of specific sizes and spacings. In use, the camera is focused on the chart, and the pattern is viewed at the monitor for image fidelity (resolution). The chart most commonly used is the EIA resolution chart.

TFT LCD Thin film transistor LCD   A type of LCD flat-panel display screen. The TFT technology provides the best resolution of all the flat-panel techniques and is also the most expensive. TFT screens are sometimes called active-matrix LCDs.

Tilt A low frequency signal distortion. A deviation from the ideal low-frequency response. Example: Instead of a square wave having a constant amplitude, has a tilt.

Time lapse Capturing a series of images at preset intervals.

Time Lapse Recorder The video cassette recorder extends the elapsed time over which it records by recording user selected samples of the video fields or frames instead of recording in real-time. For example, recording every other field produces a 15 field/sec recording and doubles the elapsed time recorded on the tape. Recording every 30th field produces a 1 ficld/sec recording and providcs 30 times the elapsed recording time.

Token Ring LAN technology in which packets are conveyed between network end stations by a "token" moving continuously around a closed ring between all the stations. Operates at 4 or 16 Mbps.

Transient An unwanted signal existing for a brief period of time that is superimposed on a signal or power line voltage.

Triaxial Cable A double shielded cable construction having a conductor and two isolated braid shields both insulated from each other. The second braid is applied over an inner jacket, and an outer jacket applied over the outer braid.

Tri-split lens A multi-element optical assembly that combines one-third of each of three scenes and brings them to focus (adjacent to one another) at the focal plane of a video camera sensor. Three separate objective lenses are used to focus the scenes onto the splitter assembly.

T-stop A measurement system used primarily for rating the light throughput of a catadioptric lens having a central obscuration. It provides an equivalent aperture of a lens having 100% transmission efficiency. This system is based on actual light transmission and is considered a more realistic test than the f-stop system.

Tungsten-halogen lamp An improved tungsten lamp once called quartz-iodine having a tungsten filament and halogen gas in a fused quartz enclosure. The iodine or bromine added to the fill produces a tungsten-halogen cycle that provides self-cleaning and an extended lifetime. The higher filament temperature produces more light and a "whiter" light (higher color temperature).

Tungsten lamp A light source using a tungsten filament surrounded by an inert gas (nitrogen, xenon) enclosed in a glass or quartz envelope. An AC or DC electric current passing though the filament causes it to heat to incandescence, producing visible and infrared radiation.

TV Lines A convention used in the video industry to specify the resolution of a video image. Horizontal resolution is measured in TV lines across a width equal to the height of the display. Typical horizontal resolutions in the security industry are 480 TV lines for color and 570 TV lines for monochrome. Vertical resolution is the number of horizontal lines multiplied by the Kell factor.

Twin-lead A transmission line having two parallel conductors separated by insulating material. Line impedance is determined by the diameter and spacing of the conductors and the insulating material, and is usually 300 ohms for television receiving antennas.

Twin-split lens A multi-element optical assembly that combines one half of each of two scenes and brings them to focus (adjacent to one another) at the focal plane of a video camera sensor. Two separate objective lenses are used to focus the scenes onto the splitter assembly.

UHF Ultra-high frequency In television, a term used to designate the part of the RF spectrum in which channels 14 through 83 are transmitted. The UHF signals are in the 300 to 3000 MHz frequency range.

UL certified A certification given by Underwriters Laboratory to certain items that are impractical to UL list and which the manufacturer can use to identify the item.

UL listed A label that signifies that a product meets the safety requirements as set forth by UL safety testing standards.

UL Underwriters Laboratory A testing laboratory that writes safety standards used by manufacturers when designing products. UL tests and approves manufactured items for certification or listing providing they meet required safety standards.

UNIX A computer operating system like DOS or MacOS. UNIX is designed to be used by many people at the same time and has TCP/IP built-in. The UNIX operating system was developed by AT&T Bell Labs and was used to develop the Internet.

URL Uniform resource locator The address of a web site.

USB Universal serial bus A high-speed port found on most computers that allows a much faster transfer speed than a serial or parallel-port.

UTP Unshielded twisted pair Two insulated conductors in an insulating jacket in which the two conductors are twisted along the length of the cable. When provided with appropriate transmitter and receiver, UTP provides an alternative to the RG59 coaxial cable.

UV Ultraviolet An invisible region of the optical spectrum located immediately beyond the violet end of the visible spectrum, and between the wavelengths of approximately 100 and 380 nanometers. Radiation just beyond the visible spectrum (at the blue end of the visible spectrum) ordinarily filtered or blocked to prevent eye damage.

Varifocal Lens A lens having a manually adjustable focal length providing a range of field of view.

VCR Video cassette recorder A device that accepts signals from a video camera and a microphone and records images and sound on 1/2" or 1/4" magnetic tape in a cassette. The VCR can play back the recorded images and sound for viewing on a television receiver or CCTV monitor or printing out single frames on a video printer.

Vectorscope A special oscilloscope used for color camera and color video system calibration. The vectorscope decodes the color information into R-Y and B-Y signals which are used to drive the x and y axis of the scope. The absence of color in the video signal is displayed as a dot at the center of the display. The angle-distance around the circle, and magnitude-distance away from the sensor, indicate the phase and amplitude of the color signal. The vectorscope graphically indicates on a CRT the absolute phase angle between the different color signals with respect to a reference signal, and to each other. These angles represent the phase differences between the signals.

Vertical blanking, Retrace The process of bringing the scanning electron beam in a CRT from the bottom of the picture back to the top. Vertical retrace occurs between writing each field of a picture. The beam is shut off and blanked during the retrace.

Vertical resolution The number of horizontal lines that can be seen in the reproduced image of a television pattern. The 525 TV line NTSC system and Kell effect limits the vertical resolution to appproximately 350 TV lines maximum.

Vertical retrace The return of the electron beam to the top of the picture tube screen or the pickup tube target, at the completion of the field scan. The retrace is not displayed on the monitor.

VGA A standard display format having an image resolution of 640 × 480 pixels.

VHF Very High Frequency In television, a term used to designate the part of the RF spectrum in which channels 2 through 13 are transmitted. A signal in the frequency range of from 30 to 300 MHz.

VHS Victor home system The 1/2" video tape cassette recording format in most widespread use.

Video A term pertaining to the bandwidth and spectrum position of the signal resulting from television scanning. In current CCTV usage video means a bandwidth between 30 Hz and 6 and MHz.

Video amplifier A wideband amplifier used for amplifying video picture signals.

Video band The frequency band used to transmit a composite video signal.

Video signal, non-composite The picture signal. A signal containing visual information without the horizontal and vertical synchronization and blanking pulses. see **Composite video**.

Vidicon tube An early imaging tube used to convert a visible image into an electrical signal. The spectral response covers most of the visible spectrum and most closely approximates the human eye response (400–700 nm).

Viewfinder A small electronic or optical viewing device attached to a video camera so that the operator at the camera location, can view the scene that the camera sees.

Vignetting The loss of light through a lens or optical system at the edges of the field due to using an undersized lens or inadequate lens design. Most well-designed lenses minimize vignetting.

Visible spectrum That portion of the electromagnetic spectrum to which the human eye is sensitive. The range covers from 400 to 700 nanometers.

VPN Virtual Private Network A private data network that makes use of the public telecommunications infrastructure. The VPN enables IP traffic to travel securely over a public TCP/IP network by encrypting all traffic from one network to another. The VPN maintains privacy through the use of a "tunneling" protocol and security procedures. It does this at a much lower cost than privately owned or leased lines. Many companies use a VPN for both Extranets and wide-area networks (WAN).

WAN Wide Area Network A public or private network that provides coverage over a broad geographic area. WANs are typically used for connecting several metropolitan areas as part of a larger network. Universities and large corporations use WANs to connect geographically remote locations.

Waveform monitor A specialized oscilloscope with controls that allow the display and analysis of analog and digital video waveforms. Parameters analyzed include frequency, waveform shape, presence or absence of synchronizing pulses, etc.

Wavelength The length of an electromagnetic energy wave measured from any point on one wave to the corresponding point on the next wave, usually measured from crest to crest. Wavelength defines the nature of the various forms of radiant energy that compose the electromagnetic spectrum and determines the color of light. Common units for measurement are the nanometer (1/10,000 micron), micron, millimicron, and the Angstrom.

Wavelet A unique mathematical function used in signal processing and video image compression. The process is similar to Fourier analysis.

Web browser A web program that allows Web browsers to retrieve files from computers connected to the Internet. Its main function is to serve pages to other remote computers.

Web server A program that allows web browsers to retrieve files from computers connected to the Internet. The web server listens for requests from web browsers and upon receiving a request for a file sends it back to the browser.

White clipper A nonlinear electronic circuit providing linear amplification up to a predetermined voltage and then unity amplification for signals above the predetermined voltage.

White compression Amplitude compression of the signals corresponding to the white regions of the picture.

White level The top end of the gray scale. The picture signal level corresponding to a specified maximum limit for white peaks.

White peak The maximum excursion of the picture signal in the white direction.

White peak clipping Limiting the amplitude of the picture signal to a pre-selected maximum white level.

Wi-Fi Wireless Fidelity The Institute of Electrical and Electronic Engineers (IEEE) 802.11 wireless standard for transmitting video images and other data over the airwaves between computers, access points, routers or other digital video devices.

WLAN Wireless Local Area Network or Wireless LAN A wireless computer-to-computer data communications network having a nominal range of 1000 ft.

Working distance The distance between the front surface of an objective lens and the object being viewed.

WWW World Wide Web The name of the total space for highly graphical and multimedia applications on the Internet.

Xenon arc lamp An arc lamp containing the rare gas xenon, that is excited electrically to emit a brilliant white light. The lamps are available in short-arc (high-pressure) and long-arc (low-pressure).

Yagi Antenna A multiple element parasitic antenna originated by Yagi-Uda in Japan. A common means of achieving high antenna gain in a compact physical size in the VHF and UHF frequency range. The Yagi antenna consists of a driven element, a reflector element, and one or more director elements.

Y/C The term used to describe the separate luminance (Y) and chrominance (C) signals. Separating the signals improves the final video image.

Zoom Optical zooming using a lens to enlarge or reduce the size of the scene image on the video sensor on a continuously variable basis. The wide-angle setting provides low magnification. Narrow-angle (telephoto) setting provides high magnification. Electronic zooming magnifies or de-magnifies the image size of a video scene electronically. All magnification is referenced to the human eye with a magnification of 1.

Zoom lens A lens capable of providing variable focal lengths. An optical lens system of continuously variable focal length with the focal plane remaining in a fixed position at the camera sensor. Groups of lens components are moved to change their relative physical positions, thereby varying the focal length and angle of view through a specified range of magnifications.

Zoom range The degree to which the focal length of a camera lens can be adjusted from wide-angle to telephoto. Usually defined with a numerical ratio like 10:1 (telephoto: wide-angle).

Bibliography

Chapter 1
Walsh, Timothy J. *Protection of Assets.* The Merritt Co., 1985.

Chapter 2
Sampat, Nitin. The RS-170 Video Standard and Scientific Imaging: The Problems. *Advanced Imaging*, February 1991.

Chapter 3
Dubois, Paul A. The Design and Application of Security Lighting. *Security Management*, September 1985.
Jefferson, Robert. Shedding Light on Security Problems, *Security Management*, December 1992.
Lighting Design. *American Electric Co.* Pub. No. LSBC, 1991, 168–84.
McHale, John J. Tungsten Transport in Quartz-Iodine Lamps. *Illuminating Engineering*, April 1971.
North American Philips. Security Lighting. Publication P-3368, 1992.

Chapter 5
Abram, Frank. Super Dynamic Camera Technology Arrives, Sanyo Security Products, *Security Technology and Design*, June 1998, 79–81.
Nilsson, Fredrick. What is a Network Camera-White Paper, *Axis Communications*, 2002, 1–9.
Wimmer, Robert. Networked Camera Technology, *Video Security Consultants, Security Technology & Design*, March 2002, 44–47.
Zarnowski, Terry. The Active Column Sensor CMOS Imager, *Sensors*, April 2000, 81–82.
Zarnowski, Terry. CMOS and CCD Sensors Contend for Imaging Use, *Vision Systems Design*, February 2001, 29–35.

Chapter 6
Anderson, John Eric. Fiber Optics: Multi-Mode Transmissions. Technical Memorandum. *Galileo Electro-Optics*, 1990.
Berman, Bruce. Digitally-Encoded Video in Fiber-optic Networks, *International Fiber Systems*.
Colombo, Allan. How to Install Fiber Optic Connectors, *Security Distributing Marketing*, November 1997.
Cook, Jack. Making Low-Loss Single-Mode Connectors, Dorran Photonics, *Laser Focus*, 1983.
The Fiber Optics Association. Wavelength Division Multiplexing (WDM), April 2006.
Extron Electronics, UTP Technology-White Paper, 2006, 1–7.
Galileo Electro-Optics. Fiber Optics: Theory and Applications-Technical Memorandum, 1990.
Herman, Jeffrey. Simplifying CATV Cabling with UTP, *Cabling Business Magazine*, March 1999, 48–59.
Herman, Jeffrey. Streamlining Surveillance, *Cabling Business Magazine*.
Lampen, Stephen. Video and UTP, *Belden Electronics Division*, April 2006.
Schumacher, William. Test Conditions for Fiber Optic Connectors and Splices. *AMP Inc.* 1982.
Technician's Guide to Fiber Optics, 2nd ed. *AMP Inc.* 1993.
Wong, Michael. Transmitting Video Over CAT-5 Cable, *Imaging/Video/Imaging*.

Chapter 7
Array Microsystems. The Video Compression for the Digital Video Surveillance Market: A Comparison of MPEG, Wavelet and JPEG Formats-White Paper, July 2001, 1–11.

Autosophy. Image and Video Compression Techniques-White Paper, 1–17.

Brown, William. Spread Spectrum Technology, *Metric Systems*, 2001.

DSPR Research. Video Technology, H.264.

Engebretson, David. How to Manage IP Addressing, *Security Distributing and Marketing*, April 2005, 74–75.

Farpoint Group. Advanced Wireless Technologies: MIMO Comes of Age-White Paper, 1–9.

Firetide, A Guide to Video Mesh Networking-White Paper, 2005, 1–12.

Ford, Merilee, et al. Internet Protocols, Internetworking Technologies Overview, *Cisco*, June 2005, Chapter 30, 1–23.

Ford, Merilee, et al. Virtual Private Networks (VPNs), Internetworking Technologies Overview, *Cisco*, June 2005, Chapter 19, 1–8.

Golston, Jeremiah, et al. Video Compression: System Trade-Offs with H.264, VC-1 and Other Advanced CODECs-White Paper, *Texas Instruments*, 2006, 1–15.

Hopwood, Keith. Power over Ethernet (PoE)-White Paper, *Phihong*.

Huotari, Allen. A Comparison of 802.11a, and 802.11b Wireless LAN Standards, *Linksys*, May 2002.

Kamaci, Nejat, et al. Performance Comparison of the Merging H.264 Video Coding Standard with the Existing Standards, *Georgia Institute of Technology*.

Lee, Kenneth, et al. Wavelet-based Image and Video Compression. *www.seas.upenn.edu*, 1–11.

Levine, D.E. Network Firewalls, *Security Technology and Design*, June 2002.

Nilsson, Fredrick. What is a Video Server?-White Paper, *Axis Communications*, 2002, 1–8.

PixelTools. H.264 Advanced Video Coding: A Whirlwind Tour-White Paper, 2006, 1–8.

Scibor-Marchocki. A tribute to Hedy Lamarr (Spread Spectrum).

Slack, David. What is Spread Spectrum Technology and Where did it Come From? *Security Technology and Design*, March 1994, 36–39.

Telexis. Introduction to Video Compression Standards, 1–6.

3com, In-Stat/MDR Group. Deploying 802.11 Wireless LANs, 2002.

3e Technologies International, Cresting the Wireless Wave with Security Solutions, 2003, 1–8, *www.3eti.com*.

Wikipedia. Common Intermediate Format (CIF).

Wikipedia. H.264/MPEG-4 AVC.

Wikipedia. Transmission Control Protocol.

Wimmer, Robert. Essentials of Digital Video Compression Part 1, A1-A7, Video Security Consultants. *Security Sales*.

Wimmer, Robert. Essentials of Network Design and Function (IP Address), Part 3, A1-A7, Video Security Consultants. *Security Sales*.

Chapter 8

Cambridge Display Technology. Active and Passive Matrix (OLED), April 2006.

Rayel, Eric. Merging Television with PCs-Which Display is in the Picture? Brooktree Division, Rockwell Semiconductor Systems, *Electronic Design*, April 1997, 141–146.

Rogowitz, Bernice E. Displays: The Human Factor. *Byte*, July 1992, 195–200.

Chapter 9

Advanced Technology Video. Record Speed Samples.

Gilge, Michael. Beyond DVRs-Networked Digital Video Storage, *Video Communication Systems, Security Products*, April 2003, 28–24.

Chapter 10

Reis, Charles. Your Range of Choices in Color Hard Copy Devices, *Advanced Imaging*, September 1990, 54–59.

Chapter 19

Kreider, Jim, et al. Uncooled Infrared Arrays Sense Image Scenes, Boeing North American, *Laser Focus World*, August 1997, 139–150.

National Institute of Law Enforcement and Criminal Justice. Active Night Vision Devices, Standard NILECJ, June 1975.

O'Brien, James T. Intensified Cameras for Low Light Situations, *Advanced Imaging*, June 1989.

Oda, Naoki, et al. Performance of 320x240 Bolometer-Type Uncooled Infrared Detector, *NEC Electronics*, April 2003.

Richmond, Joseph C. Test Procedures for Night Vision Devices Report. *National Institute of Law Enforcement and Criminal Justice*.

Rintz, Carlton L., George A. Robinson. A High-Resolution Intensified CCD Imager, *Burle*.

Senesac, L.R. et al. IR Imaging Using Uncooled Microcantilever Detectors, Oak Ridge National Laboratory, *Elsevier*, 2003.

Chapter 23

Goldstein, Herbert. Consider the Options When Choosing Your Uninterruptible Power Supply, *Security Technology and Design*, March/April 1993.

Martzloff, Francois. Protecting Computer Systems Against Power Transients, *IEEE Spectrum*, April 1990, 37–40.

Chapter 24

Echelon. Open Systems Overview (Lonworks), 2004.

Chapter 18

Cole, Wayne. Video and the Law, *Government Video*, September 2000, 22.

Emigh, Jacqueline. Secret Codes, *Government Security*, April 2005, 32, 34, 36.

Wimmer, Robert. Modern Video Covert Surveillance Options, *Video Security Consultants, Security Technology and Design*, October 2003, 46-48.

Gutierrez, Jocelyn. Limiting Liability in the Video Age, *Security Sales*, November 2003, 46–50.

Chapter 23

Ultralife Batteries, Transportation Regulations for Lithium, Lithium Ion and Polymer Cells and Batteries, April 2003, 1–7.

Chapter 24

Thompson, Steve. Harvesting Advantages of Security Integration Technologies, *Johnson Controls, Security World Magazine*, July 2004.

Savage, Bill. Building System Integration Faces Challenges, *Security Technology and Design*, April 2005, 42–46.

Security Director News, Security Systems News. Building Tomorrow's Security Solutions Today, September 2004, 1–15.

Chapter 25

ePanorama.net. RS-170 Video Signal, 1–5.

Granite Island Group. The Video Signal Eavesdropping Threat Tutorial, 1–12. *www.tscm.com*.

Hiebert, Robert. Take a Peak Inside Today's Spectrum Analyzers, *Electronic Design*, September 2005, 75–82.

Leader Instruments. Technical Primer Series, Waveform Monitors-Vectorscopes.

Chapter 27

IEEE. IEEE History. *www.ieee.org*.

NICET. About NICET: Vision and Mission. *www.nicet.org*.

Chapter 28

Allan, Roger. Uncooled Thermal Imaging Has Mass-Market Appeal, *Electronic Design*, July 2005, 43–44.

Other Video References

BroadWare, Understanding Video Formats-White Paper, 2003, 1–10. *www.broadware.com*.

Cieszynski, Joe. Closed Circuit Television, 2nd ed. *Elsevier*, 2005.

Damjanovski, Vlado. CCTV Networking and Digital Technology, 2nd ed. Elsevier, 2005.

Fennelly, Lawrence J. Handbook of Loss Prevention and Crime Prevention, 3rd ed. Chapter 16, CCTV Surveillance, Herman Kruegle, *Butterworth-Heinemann*, 1996, 281-295.

Fennelly, Lawrence J. Handbook of Loss Prevention and Crime Prevention, 4th ed. Closed Circuit Television, Herman Kruegle, *Elsevier*, 2004.

Horak, Ray. Communications Systems and Networks, 3rd ed. *Wiley*, 2002.

Inglis, Andrew F. *Video Engineering*. New York: McGraw-Hill, 1993.

Laurin, Teddi. Photonics Design and Applications Handbook, 49th ed. *Laurin Publishing*, 2003.

Laurin, Teddi. Photonics Dictionary, 49th ed. *Laurin Publishing*, 2003.

Luther, Arch C. Digital Video in the PC Environment, 2nd ed. *McGraw-Hill*, 1991.

McPartland, Joseph F. National Electrical Code Handbook, 18th ed. *McGraw-Hill*, 1984.

Nilsson, Fredrick. The Top 10 Myths About Network Video-White Paper, *Axis Communications*, 2002, 1–10.

Nilsson, Fredrick. Converting an Analog CCTV System to IP-Surveillance-White Paper, *Axis Communications*, 2002, 1–9.

Smith, Cecil. The Resolution Solution. *AV Video Journal*, November 1991.

Smith, Cecil. Mastering Television Technology, *Newman Smith*, 1991.

Smith, Warren J. Modern Optical Engineering, 2nd ed. *McGraw-Hill*, 1990.

Index

100BASE-T, 203, 204, 227

Above-mounted pan/tilt
   configuration, 424
AC power, 554–55
Access control, 1, 35, 39, 42, 44, 45
Active column sensors (ACS),
   129–30
Active hours monitoring, 578
Active infrared (IR)
   auto-focusing, 38
Active pixel sensors (APS), 130
Addresses, network, A, B, C, 243
Advanced encryption standard
   (AES), 236–37
After hours monitoring, 578
Airports, 515, 545
Alarm map memory (AMM), 357
Alarm-programmed sequential
   switcher, 327
Alarming switchers, 327
Alarms over video cable, 411–12
Aliasing, 124, 136
Alkaline batteries, 560
Aluminum cable, 156
American Society for Industrial
   Security (ASIS), 608
Analog cameras, 33, 111, 112,
   117–20
   color–monochrome
      switchover, 119
   color–single sensor, 118
   color–three sensor, 119–20
   monochrome, 117
Analog monitors, 252–59
   cathode ray tubes, 252–55
   color, 257–58
   monochrome, 255–57
Analog to digital, migration from,
   200–01

Analog video recorders, 276, 278–85
   options, 283–84
   time-lapse VCR, 281–83
   VCR formats, 278–81
   video cassette recorders, 278
Analog video surveillance system,
   16, 23, 27
Analog VMDs, 132, 360
Angular field of view, 76–77
Annotator, 16
Antennas
   dipole, 189
   directional, 183, 184
   omnidirectional, 184, 189
   satellite transmission, 508, 612
   stub (whip), 189
   Yaggi, 188, 189, 465, 621
Anti-glare screens, 271–72
Aperture, numerical. *See* Numerical
   aperture
Apparent color temperature, 64
Applications, 513–51
Arc lamps, 12
Area applications, 418
Area scenes, 418–19
Artificial light, 23–24, 53–64
   compact short-arc lamps, 60–62
   flourescent, 68
   high-intensity-discharge lamps,
      24, 56–58
   infrared lighting, 4, 19, 62–69
   low-pressure arc lamps, 59–60
   tungsten-halogen lamps, 23,
      55–56
   tungsten lamps, 23, 53–55
Asset protection, 1–3
   role of video in, 3–8
Asynchronous transfer mode,
   234–35

Atmospheric windows, 191
Attenuation techniques
   coaxial cable, 150
   optical techniques, 119
Attenuation, coaxial cable,
   148–52
Audio/video signal, 194
Authentication, 299–300
Auto-focus lenses, 85–86
Auto-teller drive-in, 545
Automated teller machines, 544
Automated video surveillance
   (AVS), 200
Automatic iris lens, 12, 84,
   85, 616
Average/peak response
   weighting, 85
Axis point, 206. *See also* Router

Back porch, 588, 589
Backup power supplies, 567
Balanced two-conductor coaxial
   cable transmission, 153–57
   aluminum cable, 156
   electrical interference, 155
   grounding problems, 155–56
   indoor cable, 154
   outdoor cable, 154–55
Bandwidth, 299
Banking and financial institutions,
   515, 544–45
   auto-teller drive-in, 545
   automated teller machines, 545
   check identification, 544
   computer, vault and
      money-counting rooms, 544
Base-band signal analysis, 148
Batteries, 557–60
   alkaline, 560
   carbon–zinc, 557

Batteries (*Continued*)
lead-acid, 557
lithium–ion, 559
mercury, 560
nickel metal hydride, 559
nickel–cadmium, 557–58
Bayonet mounts, 139
Beam angle, 50–51
Beam deflection, 254
Beam pattern, 51
Beam-splitting prism, 119
Beta format, 617
Bids, 605, 615
Bifocal/trifocal image splitting
lenses, 101–04
Bill of materials (BOM)
elevator surveillance, 518
lobby surveillance, 517
multi-site surveillance, 200,
540, 578
office surveillance, 523–28
parking lot and perimeter
surveillance, 531–37
rapid deployment hotel
surveillance, 533
showroom surveillance, 529
warehouse surveillance, 540
Bitmap image, 259
Black level, 115
Blackbody radiation, 64
Blackouts, 562
Blanking interval, horizontal, 113
Blanking, vertical, 269, 329
Blooming
Image, 479
Scene, 485
BNC connectors, 149, 152, 189, 256
Bore-scope lenses, 101–02, 104,
461–62
Boredom, guard, 498
Brackets
Camera, 515
camera housings, 31–33
Brakes in pan/tilt systems, 26,
436, 441
Bridge, digital, 156
Bridging sequential switchers, 324
Broadband microwave, 215–16
Brownouts, 562
Browser, WWW, 625
Bubble jet printers, 306, 310
Bucket brigade device, 126
Burst amplitude, 590
Burst signal color, 115, 588, 589
Byte, 148

Cable, 209–10
aluminum, 156–57
fiber-optic. *See* Fiber-optic cable
indoor, 154
outdoor, 154–55
Cable television (CATV), 195–96
Cable(s)
Coaxial, 148
tri-axial, 155
unshielded twisted pair
(UTP), 25
Camera housings, 15–16, 42–44, 388
accessories
brackets and mounts, 403
heater and fan, 401–03
locks and security screws, 403
tamper switch, 403
window washer and wiper, 403
air and water cooled, 400–01
dome, 16, 44, 375. *See also* Dome
cameras
guidelines, 403–04
indoor, 388–89
outdoor, 394–96
plug and play, 44
rectangular, 44
specialty, 44, 397–400
dust/explosion proof, 400
elevator, 398–99
high security, 398
pressurized, 400
triangular, 396
Camera ID, 45
Camera module, 96–97, 139–41
Camera monitor, 592
Camera switcher. *See* Switchers,
video
Camera switching/selecting, 15,
283–84
Camera video annotation, 45
Cameras, 14, 19, 30–31, 109–43. *See
also* Video security systems
analog, 33, 111, 112, 117–20
block diagram, 111
charged coupled device
(CCD), 37
color, 8, 38, 118, 119
complimentary metal oxide
semiconductor (CMOS),
7, 462
covert, 87, 97
digital, 33, 111, 112, 120–23
function, 111–17
horizontal, 27
hybrid eye, 613
ID number, 124

image format sizes, 137
infrared, 17, 612
intensified CCD (ICCD), 125
Internet, 33, 123–25
ISIT (intensified SIT), 20, 125
lens mounts, 139
low-light-level intensified, 34, 125
monochrome, 11, 12
new technology, 3, 43, 123
new technology, 611–13
panoramic, 34, 141–42
plug and play, 16
printed circuit board, 30
remote-head, 462
resolution and sensitivity, 133–37
resolution of, 133–36
scanning. *See* Scanning
sensitivity, 119
sensors. *See* Sensors
smart, 612
solid-state, 32–33
spectral characteristics, 53
static vs. dynamic, 535
thermal infrared imaging, 17,
34, 125
universal system bus (USB), 125
versus human eye, 19
vertical, 27
Candela, 49
Carbon–zinc batteries, 557
Cassegrain lens, 89, 492, 493
CAT-3, 5, 5e cable, 157–159
Catadioptric lens, 8, 89
Cathode ray tubes (CRT), 20, 40,
252–55
audio/visual, 255
beam deflection, 253–54
brightness, 255
interlacing and flicker, 254–55
phosphors, 254
spot size and resolution, 254
Cell phones, 248
Certification, 610
Character generators, 3, 34,
285, 332
Charge coupled devices (CCD), 3,
18, 126–28
Charge-injection devices (CID), 111
Charge-priming devices (CPD), 111
Charge-transfer devices (CTD), 111
Check identification, 544
Check sum, 299
Checklist, CCTV, 601
Chips, 229
Class II transformer, 554, 555

Cliff effect, 122
Clock, covert CCTV, 41
Closed circuit television
    (CCTV), 146
Closed Circuit Television
    Manufacturers Association
    (CCTMA), 607
Clutches in pan/tilt
    drives, 89
Complimentary metal oxide
    semiconductor (CMOS), 3,
    18, 111, 129–30
CS mount camera, lens, 461
C-mount camera, lens,
    461, 617
Coaxial cable, 15, 35, 148–53,
    196–97
    alarms over, 411
    aluminum, 156–57
    amplifiers, 152–53
    checklist, 196–97
    connectors, 151–52
    construction, 149
    indoor, 424
    outdoor, 425
    plenum, 157
    run capabilities, 150
    signal attenuation vs.
        frequency, 151
    signal attenuation vs.
        length, 151
    unbalanced single-conductor
        cable, 150
Coherent fiber-optic bundle, 100,
    456, 457, 459, 482
Color
    additive in cameras, 115
    subtractive in printers, 113
Color bars, 588, 590
Color camera
    color signal, 115
    light requirements, 50
    sensitivity, 8
    single vs. three-sensor, 118
Color-dye diffusion
    printers, 309
Color hue, 116
Color monitors, 40, 257–58
Color saturation, 116
Color synchronization, 115
Color systems, 4
Color temperature, 64, 133
Color thermal printers, 305
Combiner, 16
Common Intermediate Format
    (CIF), 217, 218

Communication channels, 202–16
    wired, 202–11. See also Wired
        video transmission; Wireless
        transmission
    fiber optic. See Fiber-optic
        transmission
    Internet, 3, 36, 201, 206–09
    LAN, 3, 36, 201, 203
    leased land lines, DSL and
        cable, 209
    power over Ethernet (PoE),
        203–06
    wide area network (WAN), 14,
        35, 201, 206
    wireless, 210–16. See also Wireless
        transmission
    broadband microwave, 215–16
    indoor–outdoor, 215
    infrared, 147, 189–92,
        198, 216
    mesh network, 212–13
    multiple input/multiple
        output, 213–15
    wireless fidelity (WiFi), 211
Communications
    control signal, 381
    voice, 201
Compact short-arc lamps, 60–62
Complimentary MOS. See CMOS
Compressed image format, 299
Compression, 124–25
    digital, 296–98
Compressors, screen, 223
Conditioners. See Backup power-line
        conditioners, UPS
Cone angle, light source, 175
Cone ferrule connector, 171, 172
Connector, types
    balanced unshielded twisted pair
        (UTP), 25
    BNC, 149
    cone ferrule, 171, 172
    cylindrical ferrule, 172, 173
    fiber-optic, 173
    unbalanced single-conductor
        coaxial, 154
Consoles, 606
    configurations, 498–501
        one guard, 500
        two guards, 500
    design, 497–505
        full-screen, split-screen and
            sequencing monitors, 504
        video monitors, 503–04
Control console,
    microcomputer, 420

Control data signals, 148
Control room/console design,
    497–505
    console design, 503–04
        full-screen, split-screen and
            sequencing monitors, 504
        video monitors, 503–04
    control room layout and location,
        502–03
    human engineering, 498–501
        guard/monitor console
            configurations, 498–501
        split-screen displays, 501
        viewing angles, 498
        viewing distance vs. monitor
            size, 498
    international control room
        standard, 504–05
    security operator tasks, 501–02
Control signal, 192–94
Control signal communication
    direct-wire, 429
    local area network (LAN), 37
    multiplexed, 226
    wireless, 192
Controllers, pan/tilt, 415
Convertible pinhole lens kit,
    450–51
Correctional facilities, 515,
    541–44
    covert surveillance, 544
    overt surveillance, 543–44
Corrosion, 427
Corrosion effects on pan/tilt
    mechanisms, 443
Cost(s)
    Lighting, 64
    low light level cameras, 464
    monochrome monitors, 29
Coupling efficiency, 171–72
Covert mirror pan/tilt
    system, 440
Covert pinhole lenses, 29
Covert video surveillance, 10,
    445–68
    background, 446–47
    checklist, 467–68
    correctional facilities, 541–44
    imbedded covert camera
        configurations, 464
    infrared covert lighting,
        462–64
        concealment, 463
    installation techniques, 462
    IR sources, 463–64

Covert video surveillance
(*Continued*)
  lens/camera types, 447
    bore scope lenses, 100–01, 104, 461
    convertible pinhole lens kit, 450–51
    fiber-optic lenses, 456–61
    mini-lenses, 451–55
    mirror-pinhole lenses, 456
    optical attenuation techniques,
    pinhole lenses, 97–98, 448–51, 455–56
    sprinkler-head pinhole lenses, 455–56
  low-light-level cameras, 464
  PC-board cameras, 462
  remote-head cameras, 462
  wireless transmission, 465–67
Critical angle, 164, 165
CTD, Charge Transfer Device, 111, 126
Cut filter, infrared, 439
Cylindrical ferrule
  connector, 172

Date/time generator, 408–09
Daytime illumination, 48–49
DC power, 556–60
  batteries, 557–60
    alkaline, 560
    carbon–zinc, 557
    lead-acid, 557
    lithium–ion, 559–60
    mercury, 560
    nickel metal hydride, 559
    nickel–cadmium, 557–58
  DC power supply, 556–57
Dead zone viewing areas, 95
Decibel (dB), 616
Defense Advanced Research
  Projects Agency
  (DARPA), 3
Delta-delta system, 257
Demodulation, 148, 177
Depth of field, 84
DES, Digital encryption standard, 202, 236
Detection-of-motion zone
  (DMZ), 359
Detection probability, 356–57
Differential phase, 591–92
Digital audio tape, 289
Digital cameras, 32, 111, 112, 120–23
  digital signal processing, 121–22

legal considerations, 123
  smart camera, 122–23
Digital CCTV, 2
Digital encryption standard, 236–37
Digital image, 259
Digital image processing, 218
Digital scanning, 32
Digital signal processing, 16, 121–22
Digital signal test equipment, 593
Digital subscriber line (DSL), 209, 291, 299
Digital video motion detectors
  (VMDs)
  block diagram, 201, 353
  image capture, 294
  mode of operation, 286–88
  multiple-channel, 292–94
  setup, 364
  single-channel, 146
  storing process, 289
  system parameters, 370
Digital video recorders, 41–42, 201–02, 276–77, 285–302
  basic, 277
  digital compression and
    encryption, 296–97
  display format, 299
  DVR in a box, 277, 292
  hardware/software protection, 302
  hybrid DVR/NVR system, 295
  image quality, 298–99
  mobile, 297
  multi-channel, 278, 293–94
  multiplex, 277–78, 293
  network/DVR security, 299–300
  network video recorder (NVR), 278, 294–95
  operating systems, 295–96
  pros and cons, 302–03
  technology, 286–92
    communication control, 292
    digital audio tape, 289
    digital storage software, 290
    erasable optical disk, 289
    hard disk drive storage, 287
    optical disk image storage, 288
    transmission, 291–92
    video motion detection, 287–88
    WORM optical disk, 288–89
Digital video storage, 287
Digital video system, 16
Diodes, light-emitting
  Infrared, 176
  visible (dark red), 12

Dips, voltage, 562
Direct cosine transform, 220
Direct spread spectrum modulation
  (DSSM), 228–35
Directional antennas, 183, 184
Dirt, 427
Discrete wavelet transform, 221
Dither , 309, 315
Dome cameras, 373–86
  alarm inputs, 383
  cabling video signal and controls, 380–82
  camera sensitivity, 382
  digital flip, 383
  fixed dome, 375, 376
  indoor, 33
  memory, 383
  monitor display and menu, 383
  motion detection, 382
  mounting, 380
  outdoor, 427–28
  outdoor building mounts, 383
  pole mounts, 383–85
  pole mounted, 380
  presets and patterns, 382
  privacy zone-window
    blanking, 383
  proportional pan/tilt
    speed, 382
  speed dome, 374–80
    background, 374–75
    camera and lens, 376
    hardware, 378–80
    housing, 378
    pan/tilt mechanism, 376–77
    slip-rings, 377–78
  twist lock release, 383
  zoom-distance compensation, 383
Dome housings, 16, 44, 375
Dropout, 217
Dual-split-image lens, 19
Dust
  atmospheric attenuation, 6
  dust-proof camera housing, 399–400
  effects on pan/tilt mechanisms, 4, 31, 43, 415–44
DVR. *See* Digital video recorders
Dwell time, 324
Dye-diffusion printers, 309, 315
Dynamic host configuration
  protocol, 244

Education. *See* Training and
  education
Efficacy, lighting, 66

Efficiency, optical coupling, 482
EIA target, resolution chart, 634
Electrical interference, 155
Electrical noise, 562–63
Electrically programmable
    memories (EPROM), 332
Electromagnetic radiation,
    spectrum, 470, 627, 631
Electronic image splitting, 405–08
Electronic Industries Association
    (EIA), 624
Electronic shuttering, 133
Electronic zoom, 132–33
Elemental detection
    zones, 361
Elevator surveillance, 518–19
    100 percent viewing of elevator
        cab, 519–20
    analog six-camera elevator
        cab/lobby system, 520–22
    checklist, 522
Emergency and disaster planning,
    5–7
    documenting emergency, 6
    emergency shutdown and
        restoration, 6
    optimizing loss control, 6
    protecting life and minimizing
        injury, 6
    reducing exposure of physical
        assets, 6
    restoration of normal
        operations, 6
    standby power and
        communications, 6–7
    testing the plan, 7
Emergency light, covert, 97
Emergency shutdown and
    restoration, 6
EMI. See Electrical interference
Employees
    dealers, 515
    end user, 396
    installers, 515
    integrator, 396
Encryption, 195
    digital, 296–98
Environmental factors,
    215, 515
Erasable optical disk, 289
Ethernet, 203–06
Exhibitions, 607–08
Exit sign, covert camera, 97,
    465, 526
Explosion-proof camera housing,
    31–34, 388, 618

Eye, human
    camera sensor comparison,
        130, 492
    flicker threshold, 255
    lens compared to, 8
    lens iris compared to, 84,
        333, 626

F-number (f/#), 82–84, 89
Facial recognition, 549
Facility control, 580–81
Fast hopper SSM (FHSSM), 230–31
Fatigue, guard, 27, 498–501
Feed horn, 186–87
Ferro-resonant UPS system, 564
Ferrule connectors, 171–73
Fiber-optic cable, 10, 15, 36, 196
    construction and sizes, 169–70
Fiber-optic coupling, 470, 482–84
Fiber-optic lenses, 100–01, 104,
    456–61
    configuration, 457
    flexible fiber, 459
    image quality, 461
    rigid fiber pinhole lens, 459
Fiber-optic transmission,
    161–82, 210
    advantages and disadvantages,
        178–79
    background, 161–64
    cable types, 166–71
    checklist, 181
    connectors and fiber termination,
        171–74
    construction, 169
    multi-signal, single-fiber
        transmission, 177–78
    multimode graded-index fiber,
        168–69
    multimode step-index fiber, 166
    receivers, 176–77
    simplified theory, 164–65
    sizes, 169
    splicing fibers, 174
    transmitters, 174–76
Fiber-optic transmission meters, 597
Field of view (FOV), 18, 74–78
    angular, 81
    calculations, 75–78
Field of view calculator lens finder
    disks, 597
Field synchronization pulse, 116
Fields, 112
Film printers, 317
Filtered lamp infrared source, 62–63
Filters, infrared cut, 439

Firewalls, 237
Fixed dome cameras, 375, 376
Fixed-focal-length lenses, 18, 27,
    87–89
    automatic-iris, 7, 12, 84–85, 133
    mini-lens, 98, 139, 451–55
    narrow-angle telephoto viewing,
        89
    off-axis configuration, 100, 452,
        455, 464, 468
    optical attenuation techniques,
        454
    wide-angle viewing, 88–89
Flat-screen digital monitors, 259–60
    digital technology, 259
    interfacing analog signal to,
        267–68
    liquid crystal display, 261–63
    organic LED, 264–65
    plasma, 263
Flexible fiber lenses, 459
Flicker, 254–55
Fluorescent lighting, 23
Focal length, 74–78
Focal plane array (FPA), 489
Fog, signal loss from, 131, 191
Foot candles (FC), 22, 625
Frame rate, 217, 298–99
Frame transfer (FT) CCD imager,
    128
Frequency hopping SSM (FHSSM),
    230
Fresnel reflections, 171

Gallium arsenide (GaAs) IR
    transmission system, 467, 624
Gel-cell batteries, 557
GEN 0 image converter, 472
GEN 1 image intensifier, 473–75
GEN 2 micro-channel plate (MCP)
    image intensifier, 475–80
    gating MCP image intensifier,
        479–80
    light overload, 477–79
    resolution, 477
    sensitivity, 477
GEN 3 MCP image intensifier, 481
GEN 4 MCP image intensifier, 479
Genlock, 177, 624
Geometric accuracy, 133
Gimbal mounted pan/tilt
    mechanism, 441–42
Graded-index fiber, multimode,
    168–69
Graphics annotation. See Video text
Ground loops, 572–75

Grounding, 302
Guard(s)
  environmental factors affecting
    performance, 515–16
  fatigue or boredom, 27, 498–501
  response to VMD, alarms, 42, 352
  role of, 41–42, 578

H.263 standard, 225
H.264 compression standard, 223
Hackers, 202, 237
Halogen lamp regenerative cycle,
    55–56, 63, 635
Hand-held meters, 592
Hard-copy printers, 15, 42, 305–19
  bubble jet, 305, 309–10
  dye-diffusion, 315–16
  film, 315–17
  hardware and ink cartridges, 317
  ink jet, 305, 309–10
  laser, 306, 310–15
  LED, 306, 310–15
  paper types, 317
  resolution and speed, 317
  thermal, 305, 306–09
  wax-transfer, 315
Hard disk drives, 4, 287
Hard-wired transmission, 35–36
  coaxial cable, 15, 36
  LAN, WAN, intranet and
    Internet, 36
  unshielded twisted-pair (UTP)
    cable, 10, 15, 36
Heaters, 33, 375, 378, 401
Hi-8 Sony format, 30, 621
Hidden camera detector, 597–601
High definition television (HDTV),
    142, 266, 618
High-intensity-discharge lamps, 24,
    56–58
  spectral output, 56–58
High pressure sodium lighting, 23
High-security lighting, 67–68
High-speed video-dome, 416, 417,
    434–40
  hardware, 436–40
    American Dynamic, 438
    General Electric, 438–39
    Panasonic, 439–40
    Pelco, 439–40
    Sony, 440
  technology, 435–36
    camera and lens, 436
    pan/tilt mechanism, 436–38
Highways, 515, 545–46

Homing sequential switchers,
    324, 325
Horizontal blanking interval, 113
Horizontal line synchronization
    pulses, 115
Hotels and casinos, 515, 545
  casino floor, 545
  hallway or corridor, 545
Housing, camera
  access methods, 390
  dome, 5, 33
  dust-proof and
    explosion-proof, 399
  high-security, 392, 397–98
  indoor, 5, 388–93
  indoor/outdoor accessories,
    49, 440
  mounts and brackets, 401
  outdoor, 5, 31, 393–95
  over pan/tilt mechanisms, 4, 31,
    43, 415–44
  pressurized, 400
  recessed in ceiling or wall,
    393, 515
  rectangular, 373, 388, 390–91
  specialty, 397–401
  triangular, 397
  water-cooled, 401
HTTP, Hypertext Transfer Protocol,
    206, 624–25
Hue, 115–17, 124, 625
Hum bars, 151, 153, 156, 571, 625
Hum voltage, 153
Human engineering, 498–501, 505
Hybrid eye cameras, 613

ICCD sensors, 130
Ice and snow loading, 426
ID numbers, camera, 124, 332, 349,
    408–09
ID video access control system,
    45, 544
IEEE standard 802.11a, b, g,
    i, n, 233
Illumination. See Lighting; Scene
    illumination
Image blooming, 479
Image capture, 3, 123, 201
Image compression, 221, 225, 286,
    290, 298
Image enhancement, 382, 621
Image intensifiers, 138, 472–73
  active, 472
  passive, 472–73
Image lag, 143, 485
Image reversal, 45, 411

Image smear, 479
Image splitting, 405–13
  electronic, 405–06
  lenses, 101, 102, 104
  picture-in-a-picture, 407
Image splitting lens, bi-focal
    optics, 535
Image transformation-doughnut to
    rectangular, 23
Incandescent lamp rated life, 53, 66
Index of refraction (n), 166, 168
Indoor cables, 154, 170
Indoor housings, 388–94
  ceiling/wall recessed or surface
    mount, 393–94
  corner mount, 392–93
  dome, 396
  functional requirements, 388–89
  rectangular, 389
  wedge housing, 391–93
Indoor illumination, 49
Indoor pan/tilt systems, 424–25
Infrared auto-focusing, active, 85
Infrared cameras, 17, 612
Infrared covert lighting, 462–64
  concealment, 463
  IR sources, 463–64
Infrared cut filter, 439
Infrared-emitting diodes, 63
Infrared lighting, 7, 19, 62–64
  filtered lamp infrared source,
    62–63
  infrared-emitting diodes, 63
  thermal infrared sources, 63–64
Infrared radiation from common
    sources, 487
Infrared transmission, 147, 189–92,
    198, 216
  attenuation, 150
  transmission path considerations,
    182–83, 188, 191
Infrared transmission link, 198, 216
Ink cartridges, 317
Ink jet printers, 305, 309–10
Inserter, 16
Insertion loss, 178
Institute of Electronic and Electrical
    Engineers (IEEE), 608
Integrated cameras, 388, 389,
    396–97
  indoor, 396
    covert, 396
    dome, 396
    triangular-corner, 396
    wedge, 396
  outdoor, 396–97

Integrated systems, 8, 606
  new technology, 612
Intensified CCD camera (ICCD),
    481–84
  comparison of intensifier
      sensitivities, 484
  GEN 1 coupled to CCD camera,
      484
  GEN 2 coupled to CCD camera,
      482–83
  GEN 3 coupled to CCD camera,
      481
  GEN 4 coupled to CCD camera,
      479
Intensified SIT. *See* ISIT
Intensifier coupling
  fiber-optic, 470, 482, 484
  relay lens, 472, 482
Interactive touch-screen monitors,
    269–71
  capacitive, 271
  infrared, 270–71
  projected capacitance technology,
      271
  resistive, 271
Interference(s)
  electrical (EMI), 155–56, 163,
      178–79, 302
  lens/mount, 139
  RF and microwave transmission,
      182–88, 198, 215, 628
Interlace scanning, 112, 254–55
Interline transfer (ILT), 127–28
International Security Conference
    (ISC), 608
Internet, 3, 36, 201, 207–09
  checklist, 248
  cons, 249
  features, 248
  network configurations,
      225–28
    multi-point to point, 226
    point to multi-point, 226
    point to point, 226
    video unicast/multicast, 226–28
  pros, 249
  security. *See* Network security
Internet cameras, 31, 123–25
  compression for transmission,
      124–25
  IP camera ID, 124
  remote viewing, 124
Internet Corporation for Assigned
    Names and Numbers
    (ICANN), 239

Internet Protocol. *See* IP addressable
    cameras
Intranet, 36, 203
Inventory shrinkage, 528
Inverse square law, 49
IP addressable cameras, 3, 237–45
  IP camera address, 237–45
  IP camera protocols, 238–39
  IP protocol network cameras, 238
IP camera, 540, 551, 610, 628
IRE units, 584–85, 590
Iris
  automatic, 84–85
  manual, 84
Iris diaphragm, 7, 72, 84, 201,
    616, 626
Iris/retina personnel
    identification, 549
ISIT sensors, 130

Joystick, 141, 331, 415–16, 420
JPEG, 221, 298
JPEG 2000, 224
JVC Company, 278

Kell factor, 134, 627, 635
Kevlar reinforcement, 169–70

Laboratory testing, 609–10
Lag, 26
Lamp life, 54, 56–57, 66–67
Lamp spectral characteristics, 56.
    See also Lighting
LANs. *See* Local area networks
Laptops, 247
Laser printers, 306, 310–15, 316
  page description languages, 313
LCD technology
  reflective twisted nematic, 261
  thin-film transistor (TFT), 263
Lead-acid batteries, 557
Leased land lines, 209–10
LED printers, 306, 310–15
Lens finder kit disks, 75, 81–82
Lens formats, 78
Lens iris
  human eye compared, 8
  manual and automatic, 84–85
Lens mount interferences, 139
Lens mount types, 79
Lens mounts, 139
  bayonet, 139
  C and CS, 139
  mini-lens, 139
Lens–camera sensor
    magnification, 78

Lenses, 18, 19, 27, 611
  angular field of view, 81
  auto-focus, 85–86
  bifocal/trifocal imaging splitting,
      101–04
  bore scope, 100–01, 103
  Cassegrain, 89, 492
  catadioptric, 89, 492
  covert pinhole, 29
  depth of field, 84
  fiber-optic, 100–01, 104
  field of view, 18, 74–78
  fixed-focal-length, 18, 27,
      87–90
  focal length, 74–78
  lens finder kit, 75, 81–82
  magnification, 78–80
  mini, 20
  motorized zoom, 20
  optical speed (f-number),
      82–84, 89
  panoramic, 27–29, 101, 102
  pinhole, 97–98
  relay, 104, 106
  right-angle, 104
  special, 29–30, 98–100. *See also*
      individual types
  stabilized, 86–87
  straight pinhole, 20
  telephoto, 18, 20
  vari-focal, 19, 27, 90
  versus human eye, 73
  wide angle, 88
  zoom, 19, 27, 90–97
Lens–mount interferences, 139
Light emitting diode (LED)
  infrared, 375, 396, 398
  visible, 132
Light levels, 22
Light output, 49
Light overload, 477–79
Light power factor, LPF, 455
Lighting, 17–18, 605. *See also* Scene
    illumination
  artificial light, 23–24, 53–64
  natural light, 22–23, 51–53
Lighting design, 64–69
  costs, 64–67
  high-security lighting, 67–69
  lamp life, 66–67
  security lighting levels, 67
Lighting, artificial, characteristics
  beam angle, 50–51
  design considerations, 64–69
  high-security lighting, 67–68
  light output, 48, 53–57

Lighting, artificial, characteristics (*Continued*)
lighting costs, 64–66
security lighting level, 67
Lighting, natural
outdoor illumination, 11, 12
spectral output, 50, 58–61
Lightning, fiber-optic cable immunity from, 24–25, 164, 170–71
Limit switches, 421
Line-conditioner, UPS system, 564–65
Linear distortion, 591
Liquid crystal displays (LCD), 40, 261–63
brightness, 261–62
operating modes, 262–63
Lithium–ion batteries, 559–60
LNA (low-noise amplifier), 187
Lobby surveillance, 516
analog six-camera elevator cab/lobby system, 520–22
analog three-camera system, 516–18
checklist, 518
Local area networks (LAN), 3, 36, 201, 203–06
Long-arc lamps, 53
Long-tapered pinhole lens, 99
Looping bridging sequential switchers, 325
Looping homing sequential switchers, 325
Looping-sequential switchers, 325–27
Loops, ground, 155–58, 572–74
Loose-tube cabling, 169
Lossless compression, 219–20
Lossy compression, 220–21
direct cosine transform, 220
discrete wavelet transform, 221
Low-light-level cameras
GEN 4 coupled to CCD camera, 481
Low-light-level cameras, 464, 469–96
active vs. passive, 472–73
GEN 1 image intensifier, 473–75
GEN 2 micro-channel plate image intensifier, 475–80
gating MCP image intensifier, 479–80
light overload, 477–79
resolution, 477
sensitivity, 477
GEN 3 image intensifier, 481

history and background, 470–71
image-intensifying mechanism, 471–72
intensified CCD camera, 481–84
comparison of intensifier sensitivities, 484
GEN 1 coupled to CCD camera, 482
GEN 2 coupled to CCD camera, 482–84
low-light-level optics, 491–93
eye versus camera, 492
objective lenses, 492–93
multi-sensor cameras, 487–88
sensor fusion, 488
SIT and intensified SIT cameras, 484–87
light-level overload, 485–87
resolution and image lag, 485
sensitivity/gain, 485
target detection and recognition parameters, 493–95
thermal-IR cameras, 488–91
background, 488–89
infrared optics, 491
micro-bolometer, 489–91
Low-light-level conditions, 4, 19
Low-light-level intensified cameras, 34, 125
Low-noise amplifier (LNA), 187
Low-pressure arc lamps, 59–60
light output, 60
LPF, light power factor, 455
LTC Training Center, 608
Luminance, 115
Lux, unit of illumination, 627

MAC, Media Access Control protocol, 628
Magnetic hard disk, 287–89
Magnetic tape, 4
Magnification, 78–80
MAN, Metropolitan Area Network, 628
Mantrap (portal), video, 547
Manual switchers, 323
Masking control, 366
Matrix switchers, 331–35
analog, 323, 331–33
control functions and features, 333–35
digital, 323, 335
multiple locations, 335
Memory, alarm map (AMM), 357
Mercury batteries, 560
Mercury lamp, 12, 53, 58, 62

Mercury-xenon lamp, 60–61
Mesh network, 212–13
Message generator, 409–10
Metal-arc lamp, 12, 64
Metal-halide HID lamp, 56, 58
Metal oxide semiconductor (MOS), 3
Micro-bolometer, 489–91
Microprocessor-controlled switchers, 37
Microwave meters, 593–94
Microwave transmission, 183–88, 198
interference sources, 188
satellite equipment, 186
terrestrial equipment, 183–86
Millimeter wave technology, 612–13
MIMO, multiple in-multiple out, 213–15
Mini-camera, 454
Mini-lens mounts, 139
Mini-lenses, 20, 451–54
mini-camera/mini-lens combination, 455
off-axis optics, 452–54
optical attenuation, 454
Mini-pinhole, 98
Mirror-pinhole lenses, 456
Mirror, scanning, 489, 490
M-JPEG, 220
Mobile displays, 273
Modem, 203, 209, 618, 628
Modulation, 148
Monitor display formats, 265–67
high definition 16:9, 266
multistandard, multi-sync, 267
screen size and resolution, 267
split-screen presentation, 266–67
standard 4:3, 266
Monitor magnification, 78, 80
Monitors, 14, 20–22, 38–40, 251–74
analog, 252–59
anti-glare screens, 271–72
audio/video, 41
color, 40, 255
CRT, LCD and plasma displays, 40
flat-screen digital, 259–65
interactive touch-screen, 269–71
monochrome, 40, 255–57
multistandard, 267
multi-sync, 267
new technology, 611–16
optimum viewing distance, 29
organic LED, 613
resolution, 14, 27

size, 498
split-screen, 501
sunlight-readable, 272–73
three-dimensional, 614
viewing angle, 499
Monochrome monitors, 40,
    255–57
Monochrome thermal printers, 31,
    305–07, 317–19
Monochrome video signal, 116, 124
Moonlight, 53
Motion assessment, 357–58
Motion detectors. *See* Video motion
    detectors (VMDs)
Motion effects, 26–27
Motorized zoom lenses, 20
MPEG, 298
MPEG 4-AVC (H.264), 125, 223–24
MPEG-2 standard, 221
MPEG-4
    advanced video coding, 223–24
    standard, 222
    visual standard, 222–23
MTF, modulation transfer function,
    135, 478
Multi-camera three dimensions, 613
Multi-channel DVR, 278
Multi-point to point network, 226
Multi-sensor cameras, 487–88
Multi-sensor low-light-level (LLL)
    camera, 23, 464
Multi-sync monitors, 267
Multimode graded-index
    fiber, 168
Multimode step-index fiber, 166–68
Multiple camera synchronization
    generator, 412
Multiple-channel digital VMD, 179,
    183, 195–96
Multiple image displays. *See* Image
    splitting
Multiple input/multiple output
    (MIMO)networks, 213–15
Multiple site systems, 5
    digital video over internet,
        540–42, 582
Multiplex DVR, 277–78
Multiplexers, 14, 38, 341–52
    alarm response, 350–51
    hardware implementation, 347–48
        duplex/full duplex, 348
        simplex, 348
        triplex, 348
    integrated multiplexer and
        DVR, 351
    quad split-screen displays, 343–44

recording and playback, 349–50
    analog and digital
        recording, 349
    video playback, 349–50
    remote distributed multiplexing,
        351–52
    technology, 344–47
        encoder/decoder, 347
        image rate vs. number of
            cameras, 347
    video motion detection, 350
Multiplexing, audio and control
    signal, 159, 182, 194

Narrow-angle (telephoto) lens, 89
National Electrical Manufacturers
    Association, NEMA, 387
National Institute for Certification
    in Engineering Technologies
    (NICET), 609
National Television System
    Committee, NTSC, 15, 21
Natural light, 22–23, 51–53
    moonlight and starlight, 53
    sunlight, 52–53
NEMA environmental rating, 401
Network DVRs, 201–02
Network security, 202, 235–37
    advanced encryption standard
        (AES), 236–37
    digital encryption standard
        (DES), 236–37
    firewalls, viruses and
        hackers, 237
    virtual private network
        (VPN), 236
    WiFi protected access, 236
    wired equivalent privacy
        (WEP), 235
Network video recorder, 278
New technology, 611–16
    cameras, 611–13
        hybrid eye camera, 613
        infrared cameras, 612
        millimeter wave technology,
            612–13
        multi-camera three dimensions,
            613
        smart cameras, 612
        two camera three dimensions,
            613
    high-definition television
        (HDTV), 618
    integrated systems, 614
    monitors, 613–14
        organic LED, 613–14

three-dimensional monitor, 614
    remote surveillance, 615
    transmission, 615–16
    video recording, 614
Nickel metal hydride
    batteries, 559
Nickel–cadmium batteries, 557–58
Night vision. *See* Low-light-level
    cameras
Nighttime conditions, 4
Nighttime illumination, 48–49
Noise, electrical, 562–63
Non-linear distortion, 591
NTSC television scan rate, 25
Numerical aperture, NA, 165, 629

Off-axis optics, 452–54
Office surveillance, 522–28
    analog/digital six-camera office
        covert system, 523–28
    checklist, 528
Okidata Company, 306
On-screen annotating/editing, 285
One-on-one display, 322–23
Open circuit television (OCT), 146,
    200
Optical attenuation techniques, 454
Optical design and test devices,
    595–600
    fiber-optic transmission meters,
        597
    hidden camera detector, 597–600
    lens field of view calculator, 597
Optical disks, 42, 288
Optical speed (f-number), 82–84, 89
    fixed focal length lenses, 16, 87
    pinhole lenses, 98, 448–50,
        455–56
    vari-focal lenses, 27, 90–91
    zoom lenses, 90
Organic LED (OLED) displays,
    264–65
Organizational unique
    identifier, 240
Outdoor cables, 155, 170
Outdoor housings, 394–96
    design materials, 395–96
    dome, 396
    functional requirements, 395
    rectangular, 396
Outdoor illumination, 49
Outdoor pan/tilt mechanisms, 425
    domes, 427
    ice and snow loading, 426
    materials and design, 425

Outdoor pan/tilt mechanisms (*Continued*)
  precipitation, dust, dirt and corrosion, 427
  rugged-precision platform, 427–28
  temperature, 427
  wind loading, 426
Outdoor parking lot and perimeter surveillance, 531–37
  checklist, 541
  digital wireless twelve-camera system, 536–37
Overt video, 10

Pan/tilt mechanisms, 15, 415–43
  clutches, 421
  components vs. integrated system, 428–29
  control techniques, 429–32
    direct-wire-multi-conductor, 429
    LAN, 430–32
    single-cable-multiplexed, 430
    two- and four-wire-multiplexed, 429–31
    wireless, 432
  covert mirror system, 440
  gimbal mounting, 440
  high-speed video-dome, 416, 434–40
  indoor, 424–25
  mechanical configurations, 422–24
    above-mounted, 422–24
    side-mounted, 424
  micro-switches, 421
  mounting, 432–33
  optical couplers, 433
  outdoor, 427–28
    domes, 427–28
    ice and snow loading, 426
    materials and design, 425
    precipitation, dust, dirt and corrosion, 427
    rugged-precision platform, 427
    temperature, 427–28
    wind loading, 427
  panning and tilting, 419–20
  platforms, 424
  scene coverage, 417–19
    area scenes, 418
    point scenes, 417–18
    volume scenes, 418–19
  servicing, 441–43
    cabling, 441–42

    environmental, 443
    mechanical, 442–43
  slip-rings, 423, 433
  zoom lenses, 93
Pan/tilt mounts, 42, 44–45
Panoramic 360° cameras, 34–35, 141–42
Panoramic 360° lenses, 27–29, 100, 141
Parking lot surveillance, 531
PC-board cameras, 464
Perimeter protection, 3
Personal computers, 246–48
  merging video with, 268
Personal digital assistants (PDA), 247–48
Personnel identification, 515, 549
Personnel training using video, 515, 549
Phase alternating line (PAL), 116
Phosphors, 254
Photo ID video identification system, 546
Picture-in-a-picture, 407
Picture integrity, 217
PIL (precision in-line) tube, 257
Pinhole lenses, 98, 448–50, 455–56. *See also* Covert video surveillance
  generic pinhole types, 97, 448
  mini-pinhole, 98
  mirror, 456
  pointing angle, 447
  rigid fiber, 459
  short vs. long tapered, 99
  sprinkler-head, 97–98, 455–56
  straight vs. right-angle, 9, 29, 97, 98, 449, 450, 525
  zoom, 96
Pixels, 259, 260
Plans
  Disaster, 39–41
  Emergency, 39–45
  security, 32–43
Plasma displays, 40–41, 263
Platforms, 424
  rugged-precision, 427–28, 430
Plenum cables, 157–58
Plug and play cameras, 16
Plug and play housings, 43
PoE. *See* Power over Ethernet
Point scenes, 417–18
Point to multi-point network, 226
Point to point network, 226

Pole mounted dome, ground accessible, 383, 531
Portal, video mantrap, 547–48
PostScript, 313
Power level meters, 595
Power-line conditioners. *See* Backup power-line conditioners, UPS
Power-line disturbances, 560–63
  blackouts, 563
  brownouts, 562
  electrical noise, 562–63
  voltage dips, 562
  voltage spikes, 561
  voltage surges, 565
Power over Ethernet, 203–06
Power over LAN, 203
Power sources, 553–75
  AC power, 554–56
  backup power, 569
  DC power, 556–59
    batteries, 557–59
    DC power supply, 556
  ground loops, 572–75
  power-line disturbances, 560–63
  power/signal distribution system, 569–72
  solar power, 566–69
  uninterrupted power supplies (UPS), 563–65
Power/signal distribution systems, 569–72
  parallel network, 570–72
  radial network, 572
Pre- and post-alarm video recording, 411
Precipitation, 427
Pressurized camera housing, 400
Printed circuit board cameras, 30
Printer Control Language, 313
Printer paper, 319
Printers. *See* Hard-copy printers
Processing gain, 232
Progressive scanning, 31
Projected capacitance technology, 271
Projection display, 274
PSTN-ISDN link, 209
Public switched telephone network (PSTN), 203
Pulsed light, 480

QoS, Quality of Service, 216–17
Quad split-screen displays, 343–44. *See also* Multiplexers
Quartz-halogen lamp, 66

RS-232 communications, 284
Radial power distribution
        systems, 574
Radio frequency meters, 593, 594
Radio frequency transmission,
        188–89, 198
    equipment, 188–89
    transmission path, 188
RAID system, 294
Random access memory
        (RAM), 2
Random-interlace cameras, 21
Range-gated intensifier
        system, 480
Rapid deployment video systems,
        507–12, 531
    analog/digital wired/wireless
        system, 531
    applications, 509–11
        options and accessories, 510–11
        vehicle, boat and aircraft
            protection, 510
        VIP on travel, 509
    checklist, 537
    components, 540
    hardware, 508
    remote monitoring, command
        and control, 509
    system operation, 509–10
    system requirements, 507–08
Raster graphics image, 259
Raster scanning, 32
Reaction time, 11
Receiver/monitors, 273
Recording, 14, 22, 41–42
    digital video recorders, 41–42
    new technology, 616
    optical disk, 41
    video cassette recorders, 41
Redundant array of independent
        disks. See RAID system
Reflection, 17–18
Reflectivity, 25–26
Refractive index (n), 164
Relay lenses, 104
Reliability, 202
Remote alarm
        monitoring, 514
Remote-head cameras, 462
Remote monitoring, 578
    internet cameras, 121
    new technology, 612
    rapid deployment systems, 512
    switchers, 335–39
Remote viewing, 124

Resolution, 133–37, 217, 252, 254,
        259–60
    EIA target, 134, 135
    horizontal, 134
    static vs. dynamic, 136
    vertical, 134–36
Retail store surveillance, 528–31
    large retail stores, 528–31
        analog/digital eight-camera
            showroom floor system, 529
        checklist, 531
        covert showroom floor
            surveillance, 529
        overt showroom floor
            surveillance, 529
    small retail stores, 528
RFI noise, 335
RG11/U coaxial cable, 151
RG58/U coaxial cable, 149
RG59/U coaxial cable, 149, 163, 517
RG6/U coaxial cable, 150
RGB, red, green, blue, 115–19, 253
Right-angle lenses, 104
Rigid fiber optics lens, 19
Router, 245–47
Rugged-precision platform, 427

Safety applications, 10
Safety glass windows, 388, 402
Salvo switching, 332–33
Satellite equipment, 186–88
Scan reversal unit (SRU), 410–11
Scanning, 31–32, 112–14
    digital and progressive scan, 32
    raster, 31
Scanning mirror, 456, 489
Scene blooming, 485
Scene characteristics, 25–27
    motion effects, 26–27
    reflectivity, 25–26
    target size, 25
    temperature, 27
Scene coverage, 417–19
    area scenes, 418
    point scenes, 417–18
    volume scenes, 418–19
Scene illumination, 22–24, 48–49,
        359
    artificial light, 23–24
    daytime/nighttime, 48–49
    indoor/outdoor, 49
    natural light, 22–23
Scene size calculations, 80–81
Scene size tables, 75
Scrambling, 194–95
Screen splitters, 45

Seaports, 515
SECAM, 116
Secure video transmission, 194–95
    encryption, 195
    scrambling, 194–95
Security, 609
Security designers/installers, 550
Security guards, 7
    role in video security, 8
    training using video, 515–16,
        549–50
Security Industry Association
        (SIA), 608
Security investigations, 7
Security lighting levels, 67
Security operator tasks, 501–02
Security plan, 1–11
Security surveillance, 10
Security system integration,
        577–82
    evolution of, 577–78
    integration function, 578–81
    problems and solutions, 581–82
    technology and equipment, 581
Seminars, 607–08
Sensitivity, 137
Sensor fusion, 132, 488
Sensors, 78, 110, 111, 125, 126
    active column, 129–30
    active pixel, 130
    formats, 78, 137
    image intensifier, 138
    solid-state, 137–38
    solid state-visible, 126–29
    thermal infrared, 130–32, 139
    visible/infrared, 132
    visible/near IR, 130
September 11, 1
Sequencing, 506–07
Server, 201, 245, 632
Setup, 115
Seven layer OSI model, 242
Shutters
    electronic, 133
    mechanical, 98
Side-mounted pan/tilt
        configuration, 424
Signal bandwidth, 148
Signal multiplexing/
        de-multiplexing, 194
Signal to noise ratio, 591–92
Silicon-intensified target. See SIT
        and intensified SIT cameras
Silicon solar cells, 567
Simultaneous monitoring, 578
Single camera systems, 14

Single-channel digital VMD, 146
Single site systems, 3
    digital video over wired/wireless
        network, 537–40
    distribution warehouse, 538–40
SIT and intensified SIT cameras,
        484–87
    light-level overload, 485–87
    resolution and image lag, 485
    sensitivity/gain, 485
SIT sensors, 130
Slip rings, 377
Slow hopper SSM, 230
Slow-scan transmission, 147, 159–61
Small-fiber resilient (SFR) bonded
        connector, 173
Smart cameras, 122, 612
SMA-style connector, 174
Smear, 26
SMICT standard, 225, 298
Sodium lamp, 58–60, 633
Solar power, 569–72
    flexible solar panel arrays, 567–69
    silicon solar cells, 567
    solar powered wireless video, 569
Solid state, 4
Solid-state cameras, 32–34
Solid-state sensors, 136, 137
Spatial redundancy, 219
Spectral output, 50
Speed dome cameras, 374,
        378, 381
    background, 374–75
    camera and lens, 373
    fixed, 380
    hardware, 380
    housing, 378
    moveable, 380–81
    pan/tilt mechanism, 376–78
    slip-rings, 377–78
Spikes, voltage, 561
Splicing fiber optic cable, 171, 174
Split-image optics, 104
Split-screen displays, 266,
        343–44, 504
Splitter/combiner, 5
Spread spectrum modulation
        (SSM), 201, 228–35
    direct, 231–32
    fast hoppers, 230–31
    frequency hopping, 230
    slow hoppers, 230
Sprinkler head pinhole lenses,
        97–98, 455–56
SRU (scan-reversal unit), 405, 450

SSM. *See* Spread spectrum
        modulation
Stabilized lenses, 86–87
STAM MultiMedia Training, 608
Standby power and
        communications, 7
Starlight, 53
Stub antennas (whip), 189
Subcarrier frequency, 591
Subnet mask, 243
Sunlight, 52–53
Sunlight-readable displays, 269, 274
Surges, voltage, 561
Surveillance, 10, 358
    analog systems, 14, 20, 31
    automated, 200
    covert. *See* Covert video
        surveillance
    elevators, 518–22
    lobbies, 516–18
    offices, 528
    overt, 544
    perimeter, 531–37
    remote, 615
    retail stores, 528–29
Switch, video, digital, 335
Switchers, 37, 321–39
    background and evolution,
        322–23
    matrix, 331–39
        analog, 323, 331–35
        control functions and features,
            333–34
        digital, 323, 335
        multiple locations, 335
    microprocessor-controlled, 37
    midsize systems, 323
    small system, 322–23, 331
        alarming, 327
        bridging sequential, 324
        choice of, 331
        homing sequential, 324, 325
        looping-sequential,
            325–27
        manual, 323
        synchronous/non-synchronous
            video signal, 329–31
    standard, 37
    virtual matrix, 323, 335–38
        evolution, 335–37
        features and advantages, 338
        remote/multiple site
            monitoring, 338
        technology, 337–39
Switches, limit, 96, 421
Sync amplitude, 590

Synergy, 8–9
System hardware, 8–9

Tapes, VCR, 276
Target detection criteria, 493–95
Target size, 24
Telephoto lens, 18, 27
Television standards, international
Temperature, 27, 427, 472
    color, 64, 133
Tempered glass windows, 402
Temporal redundancy, 219
Termination kit, fiber-optic, 175
Termination, fiber-optic, 174
Terrorism, 1
Test equipment, 583–601
    digital signal test equipment, 593
    optical design and test devices,
        595–601
        fiber-optic transmission meters,
            597
        hidden camera detector,
            597–98
        lens field of view calculator, 597
    video signal test equipment,
        583–92
        hand-held meters, 592
        vectorscope, 586–92
        waveform monitor, 583–86
    visible light illumination and
        power level meters, 595
    wireless radio frequency and
        microwave meters, 593–94
Theft, 1, 2
Thermal infrared sensors, 131
Thermal infrared sources,
        63–63
Thermal IR cameras, 18, 34, 131,
        488–91
    background, 488–89
    infrared optics, 491
    micro-bolometer, 489–91
Thermal printers, 306
    color-dye diffusion, 309
    monochrome, 306–07
    wax transfer, 307
Thermal sublimation printers, 306,
        309, 315
Thermal temperature difference,
        470
Three-dimensional monitors, 614
Three-sensor color camera, 119
Thumb trackball, 415–16
Tight buffer jacket, 169
Time-lapse VCRs, recording time vs.
        playback speed, 30, 283

Time/date generator, 408–09
Title inserter, 409
Touch-screen monitors, 269–71
Touch-Tone system, 192
Training and education, 7–8, 609
    certification, 610
    industry associations, 608–09
    seminars and exhibitions, 610
    use of video, 518, 541, 545
Transaction inserter, 410
Transformer, class II, 554
Transmission, 35–36, 291–92, 605
    fiber-optic. *See* Fiber-optic
        transmission
    hard-wired, 35–36
    new technology, 615–16
    wireless. *See* Wireless transmission
Transmission link, 15, 19–20
Transmission security, fiber-optic
    cable, 178–79
Tri-axial cable, 155
Tri-split lens, 104, 635
Triangular camera housing, 396
Trinitron, 254, 257, 260
Tungsten-halogen lamps, 23,
    55–56
Tungsten lamps, 23, 53–55
Turnstiles, 547
Two camera three dimensions, 613
Two-wire cable UTP transmission,
    157–61, 196
    balanced 2-wire attributes, 158
    slow-scan transmission, 159–61
    UTT technology, 158
    UTP implementation, 159

Ultra high frequency, UHF, 593, 635
Underwriters Laboratories, UL, 387
Uninterrupted power supplies
    (UPS), 302, 563–66
    line-conditioner, 564–65
    line-interactive, 565–66
    on-line system, 569–70
Universal system bus cameras, 125
UNIX, 296
Unshielded-twisted-pair (UTP)
    cable, 10, 14, 35, 36
UPS systems
    voltage dips, 562
    voltage spikes, 561
    voltage surges, 561
User datagram protocol, 242
UTP. *See* Unshielded-twisted-pair
    (UTP) cable

Vandalism, 5, 31, 67, 69, 375, 380,
    387–88
Vari-focal lenses, 27, 90–91
Vector graphics, 259
Vectorscope, 592
Vehicle control, 548–49, 550–52
Vertical blanking, 113, 329, 591
Vertical interval test signals, 584
Vertical retrace time, 411
Very high frequency, VHF, 146,
    593, 636
VHS format, 286
Victor Home System, VHS
    videocassette, 30, 278, 636
Video access control, 10–11, 515,
    546–49
    facial recognition, 549
    ID system, 546
    iris and retina personnel
        identification, 549
    portal, 547
    storage and retrieval system,
        547–48
    turnstile, 547
    vehicle control, 548–49
Video bright light compression, 133
Video cassette recorders (VCR),
    41, 278
    formats, 278–81
        8 mm, Hi-8 Sony, 279
        magnetic tape types, 228
        VHS, VHS-C, S-VHS, 279
    hardware/software protection,
        302
    options, 283–85
        camera switching/selecting,
            283–84
        on-screen annotating/editing,
            285
        RS-232 communications, 284
        scrambling, 284–85
    pros and cons, 302–03
    time-lapse, 281–83
Video checklist, 606
Video compression algorithms,
    221–25
    JPEG, 221
    JPEG 2000, 224–25
    M-JPEG, 221
    MPEG-2 standard, 221
    MPEG-4 advanced video coding
        (AVC, H.264), 223–24
    MPEG-4 standard, 222
    MPEG-4 visual standard, 222–23
    wavelet, 224–25
Video encryption, 195, 531, 614

Video frames, 112
Video ID system, 546
Video image quality, 216–17
    picture integrity and dropout, 217
    quality of service, 216–17
    resolution vs. frame rate, 217
Video motion detectors, 8, 45,
    353–71, 605
    analog, 358–60
    background, 354–56
    detection probability, 356–57
    digital, 360–70
        mode of operation, 361–62
    guidelines, pros and cons, 370
    motion assessment, 357–58
    features, 369–70
    hardware, 365–69
    technology, 362–65
    scene lighting, 358
    surveillance, 358
    training function, 358
Video picture signal, 148
Video portal, mantrap, 547
Video router/access point, 246, 247
Video security systems, 3, 116.
    See also Cameras
    emergency and disaster
        planning, 5–6
    employee training and
        education, 7
    guard's role, 9
    multiple site, 3
    overt vs. covert, 9–10
    role and applications, 9–11
    safety, 7
    security investigations, 7
    single site, 4
Video server, 245
Video signal, 114–17
    color, 114, 115
    monochrome, 114
Video signal compression, 217–25
    lossless compression, 219
    lossy compression, 219–20
    video compression algorithms,
        221–25
Video signal test equipment, 583–92
    hand-held meters, 592
    vectorscope, 586–92
    waveform monitor, 583–86
Video signal transmission
    audio and control signal
        multiplexing, 192, 194
    balanced two-conductor, 153–57
    cable TV, CATV, 238, 618

Video signal transmission
        (*Continued*)
    coaxial cable, 25, 148,
        196–97, 619
    encryption, 195
    fiber-optic cable, 25, 146,
        163–64, 197
    infrared atmospheric, 189–91
    microwave, 190, 198, 216
    radio frequency, RF, 188–89,
        198, 631
    scrambling, 194–95
    signal attenuation vs.
        frequency, 151
    signal attenuation vs. length, 151
    transmission checklist, 181–82
    transmitter, 24
    unbalanced single-conductor,
        150–51
    unshielded twisted pair, UTP, 25,
        381, 574
    wireless, analog, digital, 507
Video switch, 246
Video switchers. *See* Switchers
Video synchronization signal, 148
Video system, 17–22
    analog, 14, 19, 21
    camera function, 19
    digital, 14
    lens function, 18
    light and reflection, 17–18
    monitor, 14, 20
    recording, 14, 22
    transmission link, 15, 19–20
Video text, 408–10
    camera ID and title inserter, 409
    message generator, 409–10
    time/date generator, 409
    transaction inserter, 410
Video timing generator, 592
Video timing meter, 592
Video transmission, 2
Video turnstile, 547
Video unicast/multicast, 226
Vidicon tube sensor, 3
Viewfinders, 273
Viewing angles, 498
Viewing distance, 498
Virtual matrix switchers, 322, 323,
        335–39

evolution, 335–37
features and advantages, 338
remote/multiple site
        monitoring, 338
technology, 336–37
Virtual private networks (VPN),
        236, 301
    hybrid, 301
    secure, 300
    trusted, 300
Viruses, 202, 237
Visible/infrared sensors, 132
Visitor badge, 502
VMD. *See* Video motion detectors
        (VMDs)
Voice signal, 148
Voltage dips, 562
Voltage spikes, 561
Voltage surges, 561
Volume scenes, 418–19

WANs. *See* Wide area networks
Water-cooled camera housing,
        400–01
Watermark, 301
Waveform monitor, 591
Wavelet compression, 224–25, 298
Wax transfer printers, 306, 307, 315
White balance, 133
Wide-angle lens, 104, 398
Wide area networks (WAN), 14, 32,
        201, 206–07
Wideband video signal, 194
WiFi protected access, 236
Wind loading, 426
Window washer and wiper, 192, 402
Windows (Microsoft), 295–96, 624
Windows operating systems,
        296, 301
Wire size, 381, 429
Wired control signal
        transmission, 182
Wired equivalent privacy, 235–36
Wired video transmission, 148–82,
        196. *See also* Communication
        channels;
Wireless transmission
    balanced two-conductor coaxial
        cable transmission, 153
    coaxial cable, 148–53

fiber-optic transmission, 161–82
two-wire cable UTP transmission,
        157–61
Wired transmission, 36, 146,
        182–92, 197–98. *See also*
        Communication channels;
Wired video transmission
    covert video surveillance, 465
    frequency and transmission path,
        182–83
    infrared atmospheric
        transmission, 189–92
    microwave transmission, 183–88
    radio frequency transmission,
        188–89
    solar powered, 569
    types of, 178
Wireless 802.11, 201
Wireless control signal transmission,
        192–94
Wireless fidelity (WiFi), 14, 36, 201,
        211–12
    802.11a standard, 233
    802.11b standard, 233
    802.11g standard, 234
    802.11i standard, 235
    802.11n standard, 234
Wireless LAN. *See* WiFi
World Wide Web (WWW), 3, 14,
        206–09
WORM optical disks, 288

Xenon lamp, 12, 53, 61–62
Xerox printers, 306

Zero visibility, 17
Zoom lenses, 16, 27, 90–97
    camera module, 96–97, 139–41
    checklist, 97
    configurations, 92
    electrical connections, 95
    electronic, 132–33
    initial lens focusing, 95–96
    manual versus motorized, 92–93
    operation, 91–92
    optical speed, 92
    pan/tilt, 93
    pinhole, 97–98
    preset zoom and focus, 95
    zooming, 90–91

Time/date generator, 408–09
Title inserter, 409
Touch-screen monitors, 269–71
Touch-Tone system, 192
Training and education, 7–8, 609
   certification, 610
   industry associations, 608–09
   seminars and exhibitions, 610
   use of video, 518, 541, 545
Transaction inserter, 410
Transformer, class II, 554
Transmission, 35–36, 291–92, 605
   fiber-optic. See Fiber-optic
      transmission
   hard-wired, 35–36
   new technology, 615–16
   wireless. See Wireless transmission
Transmission link, 15, 19–20
Transmission security, fiber-optic
      cable, 178–79
Tri-axial cable, 155
Tri-split lens, 104, 635
Triangular camera housing, 396
Trinitron, 254, 257, 260
Tungsten-halogen lamps, 23,
      55–56
Tungsten lamps, 23, 53–55
Turnstiles, 547
Two camera three dimensions, 613
Two-wire cable UTP transmission,
      157–61, 196
   balanced 2-wire attributes, 158
   slow-scan transmission, 159–61
   UTT technology, 158
   UTP implementation, 159

Ultra high frequency, UHF, 593, 635
Underwriters Laboratories, UL, 387
Uninterrupted power supplies
      (UPS), 302, 563–66
   linc-conditioner, 564–65
   line-interactive, 565–66
   on-line system, 569–70
Universal system bus cameras, 125
UNIX, 296
Unshielded-twisted-pair (UTP)
      cable, 10, 14, 35, 36
UPS systems
   voltage dips, 562
   voltage spikes, 561
   voltage surges, 561
User datagram protocol, 242
UTP. See Unshielded-twisted-pair
      (UTP) cable

Vandalism, 5, 31, 67, 69, 375, 380,
      387–88
Vari-focal lenses, 27, 90–91
Vector graphics, 259
Vectorscope, 592
Vehicle control, 548–49, 550–52
Vertical blanking, 113, 329, 591
Vertical interval test signals, 584
Vertical retrace time, 411
Very high frequency, VHF, 146,
      593, 636
VHS format, 286
Victor Home System, VHS
      videocassette, 30, 278, 636
Video access control, 10–11, 515,
      546–49
   facial recognition, 549
   ID system, 546
   iris and retina personnel
      identification, 549
   portal, 547
   storage and retrieval system,
      547–48
   turnstile, 547
   vehicle control, 548–49
Video bright light compression, 133
Video cassette recorders (VCR),
      41, 278
   formats, 278–81
      8 mm, Hi-8 Sony, 279
      magnetic tape types, 228
      VHS, VHS-C, S-VHS, 279
   hardware/software protection,
      302
   options, 283–85
      camera switching/selecting,
         283–84
      on-screen annotating/editing,
         285
      RS-232 communications, 284
      scrambling, 284–85
   pros and cons, 302–03
   time-lapse, 281–83
Video checklist, 606
Video compression algorithms,
      221–25
   JPEG, 221
   JPEG 2000, 224–25
   M-JPEG, 221
   MPEG-2 standard, 221
   MPEG-4 advanced video coding
      (AVC, H.264), 223–24
   MPEG-4 standard, 222
   MPEG-4 visual standard, 222–23
   wavelet, 224–25
Video encryption, 195, 531, 614

Video frames, 112
Video ID system, 546
Video image quality, 216–17
   picture integrity and dropout, 217
   quality of service, 216–17
   resolution vs. frame rate, 217
Video motion detectors, 8, 45,
      353–71, 605
   analog, 358–60
   background, 354–56
   detection probability, 356–57
   digital, 360–70
      mode of operation, 361–62
   guidelines, pros and cons, 370
   motion assessment, 357–58
      features, 369–70
      hardware, 365–69
      technology, 362–65
   scene lighting, 358
   surveillance, 358
   training function, 358
Video picture signal, 148
Video portal, mantrap, 547
Video router/access point, 246, 247
Video security systems, 3, 116.
      See also Cameras
   emergency and disaster
      planning, 5–6
   employee training and
      education, 7
   guard's role, 9
   multiple site, 3
   overt vs. covert, 9–10
   role and applications, 9–11
   safety, 7
   security investigations, 7
   single site, 4
Video server, 245
Video signal, 114–17
   color, 114, 115
   monochrome, 114
Video signal compression, 217–25
   lossless compression, 219
   lossy compression, 219–20
   video compression algorithms,
      221–25
Video signal test equipment, 583–92
   hand-held meters, 592
   vectorscope, 586–92
   waveform monitor, 583–86
Video signal transmission
   audio and control signal
      multiplexing, 192, 194
   balanced two-conductor, 153–57
   cable TV, CATV, 238, 618